The DIGITAL MILLENNIUM COPYRIGHT ACT

Text, History, and Caselaw

with an Overview by

Christopher Wolf

Proskauer Rose LLP
Washington, D.C.

Pike & Fischer, Inc.
A subsidiary of The Bureau of National Affairs, Inc.

The Digital Millennium Copyright Act: Text, History, and Caselaw

ISBN 0-937275-11-5

This publication is designed to provide accurate and authoritative information in regard to the subject matter covered. It is sold with the understanding that the publisher is not engaged in rendering legal, accounting, or other professional service.

Zachary J. Wheat, *Group Publisher*
Mark E. Smith, *Managing Editor*
Christopher J. Oberst, *Legal Editor*
Daniel J. Gobble, *Copy Editor*
Michael M. Eisenstadt, *Operations Manager*

Pike & Fischer, Inc.
A subsidiary of The Bureau of National Affairs, Inc.
1010 Wayne Avenue, Suite 1400 • Silver Spring, MD 20910 • 301-562-1530
< www.pf.com >

Pike & Fischer INTERNET Law & Regulation is available at < www.ilrweb.com >

The Digital Millennium Copyright Act
Text, History, and Caselaw

TABLE OF CONTENTS

Overview of the Digital Millennium Copyright Act

Christopher Wolf[1]

PROSKAUER ROSE LLP
WASHINGTON, D.C.

In 1998, Congress engaged in a significant revision of the Copyright Act with the enactment of the Digital Millennium Copyright Act ("DMCA").[2] While heralded by some as the single most important piece of legislation in the history of the Internet,[3] the DMCA is more accurately described as an amalgamation of specific legislative objectives bound together by a common theme. The DMCA carries forth several distinct legislative objectives, including: (1) the implementation of certain U.S. World Intellectual Property Organization ("WIPO") treaty obligations by, most notably, creating new liabilities concerning the circumvention of access or copying restrictions and the integrity of authorship information embedded in a copyrighted work; (2) the further refinement of performance rights in sound recordings first enacted into law for online media in 1995;[4] (3) the provision of a highly detailed set of guidelines for the infringement liability of ISPs; (4) conforming the pre-existing ephemeral recording provisions to the realities of the Internet; and (5) changing the permitted library and archival copying practices to accommodate and account for digital delivery systems.

The two most important areas of the DMCA to Internet-related copyright law are online service provider liability and the anti-circumvention protections.

Online Service Provider Liability

The DMCA grants online service providers several "safe harbors," which will, in certain circumstances, afford the compliant service provider immunity from liability for damages flowing from the infringing activities of its end-users. Preliminarily, this immunity is predicated upon the provider's adoption and implementation of reasonable policies providing for the termination of users who repeatedly infringe upon the rights of others; and accommodating and not interfering with standard technical measures used by copyright owners to protect and manage rights in electronic versions of their copyrighted works. The provider is not required, under the DMCA, to monitor its service or seek information regarding potential infringement to qualify for the safe harbors, nor does the provider have to access, remove or block material in order to qualify. However, providers must comply with the DMCA "notice and takedown" procedures which require service providers to adopt and reasonably implement a policy of removing or disabling access to alleged infringing material upon notice from the aggrieved party until the dispute is resolved.[5] Qualified service providers[6] operating in compliance with this system are entitled to a complete bar to liability for copyright damages. Among the protections granted are safe harbors for:

System Storage and Information Location Tools. These safe harbors apply to storing of material (such as bulletin boards or web pages) on the service providers' servers at the request of a user, and the referring of users to material at other online sites by means of a search engine or hypertext link. So long as the provider has no actual knowledge of any incidences of infringement, no reason to know of any infringement, does not receive a direct financial benefit from the infringement and complies with the notice and take down procedures established by the DMCA to resolve any dispute regarding infringement, the provider will be entitled to the protection of these safe harbors.[7]

System Caching. Service providers are granted an additional safe harbor with respect to temporary copies of infringing material residing on their servers, but only to the extent that such material (1) was originally placed online by someone other than the provider; (2) is transmitted by the provider to a third party at the request of the originating party; (3) is not modified in any way by the provider; and (4) the cached copy is made by automatic process in compliance with the originator's guidelines. Service providers seeking the protection of this safe harbor also must comply with the DMCA notice and take down provisions.[8]

Transmission and Routing. A further safe harbor is granted to service providers to shield them from liability stemming from the transient storage of information routed through the service provider system at the request of another party. To qualify for protection, the information must be transferred without modification and the provider can make no copies of the information.

The courts have had occasion to interpret the scope of both the §512(a) (transmission and routing) and §512(d) (information location tools) safe harbor provisions in *A&M Records, Inc. v. Napster*, a case involving Internet users' transfer of digitally compressed "MP3" music files[9] over the defendant's file-sharing service. First, the Northern District of California held that, although Napster's indexing system provided the addresses which made the transfer of MP3 files between end-users possible, the files themselves did not pass *through* the Napster system. However, because Napster was not a mere passive conduit for the transmission of communications by end-users, but an active participant, the court held that the safe-harbor provision of §512(a) did not apply.[10]

In later proceedings, the court rejected Napster's §512(d) defense, as well. In affirming the district court's finding that Napster likely did not qualify for the Information Locator Tool safe harbor, the Ninth Circuit found that "Plaintiffs have raised and continue to raise significant questions under this statute, including: (1) whether Napster is an Internet service provider as defined by 17 USC §512(d); (2) whether copyright owners must give a service provider "official" notice of infringing activity in order for it to have knowledge or awareness of infringing activity on its system; and (3) whether Napster complies with §512(i), which requires a service provider to timely establish a detailed copyright compliance policy."[11]

A more recent case involved the obligation of an ISP to comply with a DMCA subpoena and reveal the identity of an otherwise anonymous user who downloaded music files through a peer-to-peer system, but who only used the ISP for transmission, not storage of the music files.[12] In that case, a district court judge ordered Verizon Internet Services to divulge the name of a Verizon subscriber to the Recording Industry Association of America (RIAA) because the subscriber allegedly used KaZaA peer-to-peer software to download and share music online.

The RIAA sought the information from Verizon using the subpoena provision provided in Section 512(h) of the DMCA. The DMCA subpoena provision mandates that ISPs provide copyright owners with information about alleged infringers. Verizon refused to divulge the subscriber's identity, claiming that the provision didn't cover alleged copyright-infringing material that resides on individuals' *own* computers. Verizon argued that the subpoena provision only covers material that resides on an *ISP's own* servers. The case is on appeal as of this writing.

The Fourth Circuit interpreted the §512(c) safe harbor (system storage) in *ALS Scan, Inc. v. RemarQ Communities, Inc.*[13] The court held that the holder of a copyright in adult photographs substantially complied with the infringement notice requirement of the Act such that the defendant online service provider was not afforded the protection of the Act's safe harbor provision simply because the plaintiff's notice of infringing activities was allegedly imperfect. The court found that once a service provider has substantial notice that identifies infringing material, it must comply with the DMCA notice and takedown provisions to maintain immunity under the statute.

Anti-Circumvention Provisions

The DMCA also added a new chapter to federal copyright law, creating civil and criminal liabilities for (1) the importation, making or selling of devices designed to be used to circumvent technical measures preventing the unauthorized access to or copying of a copyrighted work;[14] (2) the actual circumvention of technical access restrictions;[15] and (3) the knowing alteration, removal, or provision of false copyright management information.[16]

The first wave of decisions interpreting these provisions has happened. The leading case in this area is *Universal City Studios, Inc. v. Reimerdes*,[17] Plaintiff motion picture studios filed claims under the anti-circumvention provisions of the DMCA to enjoin certain Internet web site owners from disseminating a computer software program known as "DeCSS" that decrypted digitally encrypted movies on digital versatile disks (DVDs) (via a program known as "CSS"), and from including hyperlinks to other web sites that similarly made DeCSS available. In entering the injunction in favor of the plaintiffs, the lower court rejected each defense proffered by defendants.

Defendants argued that the DMCA should not be construed to reach their conduct because, as applied, the law could prevent those who sought access to encrypted or scrambled digital copyrighted works in order to make fair—that is, non-infringing—uses of them from doing so.[18] In rejecting that defense, the district court took a practical view toward protection. It found restrictions on circumvention of access control measures essential to incentivize copyright holders to make their works available in digital form, in light of the fact that digital works otherwise could be pirated too easily.[19] The court held that defendants' derivative argument under the "substantial noninfringing use" doctrine, set forth in *Sony Corp. v. Universal City Studios Inc.*, has no application to an anti-circumvention violation. In *Sony*, the Supreme Court refused to enjoin the manufacture and distribution of the VCR, even though it could be used to make infringing, archival copies of copyrighted movies and television programs, because it had a "substantial non-infringing use," *i.e.*, it could be used to "time shift" programs offered on free television for later viewing (which, presumably, would subsequently be taped over and not "archived" or "libraried"). The court in *Universal City Studios* found the *Sony* doctrine overridden by the DMCA: "[a] given device or piece of technology might have 'a substantial noninfringing use, and hence be immune from attack under Sony's construction of the Copyright Act—but nonetheless still be subject to suppression under Section 1201.' "[20]

The court also dismissed defendants' several arguments that their conduct fell under DMCA's statutory defenses.[21] For example, the court noted that even if, as defendants claimed, DeCSS was created for the purpose of enabling the development of a DVD player that would run under a non-Windows operating system, the motivation of the creators of DeCSS was immaterial to whether the defendants violated the DMCA's anti-trafficking provisions by creating a program that decrypted the plaintiff studios' DVD encoding generally.

Discrediting defendants' argument that an injunction would be "futile" and "comparable to locking the barn door after the horse is gone," since DeCSS already was widely available on the Internet, the court concluded that allowing defendants to continue violating the DMCA simply because others, many at defendants' urging, were also doing so would "create all the wrong incentives," and would encourage other defendants to ensure that others engage in the same unlawful conduct so as to set up the defense.[22]

Finally, the district court found the defendants' constitutional arguments—that computer source code is "speech," and thus exempt from regulation by government—baseless. The court reasoned that, because source code causes computers to perform desired functions, its expressive elements could not immunize its functional aspects from regulation, and that Congress must be able to regulate the use and dissemination of computer code in appropriate circumstances.[23] The constitutional argument was a major premise of the appeal in this case, which the Second Circuit similarly rejected.[24]

Likewise, in *Sony Computer Entertainment America, Inc. v. Gamemasters*,[25] the Northern District of California granted a preliminary injunction under the anti-circumvention provisions of the DMCA where the plaintiff claimed that defendant's game enhancer product circumvented the mechanism on the plaintiff's game console that ensured that the console operated only when encrypted data was read from an authorized CD-ROM. And in *RealNetworks, Inc. v. Streambox, Inc.*,[26] the Western District of Washington held that the DMCA prohibits developers from distributing products that circumvent technological measures employed to prevent consumers from obtaining unauthorized access to or making copies of copyrighted works. Nevertheless, the court denied plaintiff's motion enjoining the defendant's sale or dissemination of software, which allowed conversion of files from the plaintiff's format to other formats because the product had legitimate and commercially significant uses other than the circumvention of access and copying control technologies. However, the court entered injunctive relief as to part of a second device, finding that the device's ability to enable users to modify the plaintiff's product jeopardized the plaintiff's exclusive relationship with a third party, tipping the balance of hardships in plaintiff's favor.[27]

However, Title 12 DMCA actions are not always successful. In *Kelly v. Arriba Soft Corp.*, the Central District of California granted defendant's motion for summary judgment over plaintiff's allegation that the defendant had violated the DMCA by indexing copyrighted "thumbnail" pictures without displaying the corresponding copyright management information.[28] In so doing, the court held that the DMCA only prohibits the removal of copyright management information from a plaintiff's work as a whole.[29] The defendant therefore did not violate the DMCA because the copyright notices and other "management information" associated with the pictures were not originally overwritten on the pictures themselves, but rather were presented in the surrounding text on the pages they were posted. By simply copying the photos *without* the surrounding text, defendant did not remove the copyright management information and thus did not violate the DMCA.[30]

Critics of the DMCA, and cases under it, have complained that it chills free speech, jeopardizes fair use, and impedes competition and innovation. *See, e.g., Electronic Frontier Foundation, Unintended Consequences: Three Years Under the DMCA (2002)*[31] Proponents say the Act has worked exactly as Congress intended, that the law and case decisions have created a legal framework that will help spur creativity by content providers without stifling the growth of new technology. The debate is far from over, as new technologies bump up against the barriers of the DMCA and as online theft of intellectual property proliferates. There will be many caselaw refinements of the Act in the months and years ahead.

----

[1] Mr. Wolf is a partner in the Washington office of Proskauer Rose LLP, and co-chairs the Firm's iPractice Group. He regularly represents content owners, including recording companies, software companies and publishers, with respect to Internet intellectual property. Mr. Wolf's e-mail address is *cwolf@proskauer.com*.

Mr. Wolf gratefully acknowledges the substantial assistance of his colleagues Jennifer deWolf Paine, Carla Miller, and Gregg Goldman in preparing this material.

[2] Pub. L. 105-304, 112 Stat. 2860 (Oct. 28, 1998). Note that the Constitutional validity of the DMCA itself has been adjudicated. The court in *Universal City Studios, Inc. v. Reimerdes*, 6 ILR (P&F) 1, 111 F Supp 2d 294 (SD NY 2000), *judgment entered*, 6 ILR (P&F) 794, 111 F Supp 2d 346 (SD NY 2000), rejected the defendants' argument that the DMCA violated the First Amendment, holding that (1) the value of the free expression of decryption ideas was outweighed by the government's interest in preventing infringement and promoting the availability of content in a digital form; (2) an imminent threat of danger flowing from the dissemination of the software existed that far outweighed the need for the unfettered communication of that software; (3) the DMCA was not unconstitutionally vague; and (4) the DMCA did not constitute an unlawful prior restraint.

[3] Joel Deane, *New Law Limits ISPs' Copyright Infringement Liability*, ZDNet News from ZDWire, 1998 WL 28813487 (Nov. 4, 1998) (quoting Association of Online Professionals Executive Director David McClure, who refers to the DMCA as "probably the single most important piece of legislation in the history of the internet").

[4] *See* Digital Performance Right in Sound Recordings Act of 1995, Pub. L. 104-39, 109 Stat. 336, 17 USC §115 (c)(2), (3), (d) (Nov. 1, 1995). The DMCA creates a statutory licensing scheme for qualifying "webcasters" (essentially, Internet radio stations). A Copyright Royalty Arbitration Panel has been convened to determine the statutory rate. *See, e.g.,* <http://www.loc.gov/copyright/carp/114schedule.html>. Both the webcasting community and the record companies have submitted competing proposals for the panel's consideration. Webcasters have proposed a rate of $0.0015 cents per music webcast listener hour. *See* <http://www.digmedia.org/webcasting/CARP.html>. The record companies have proposed a rate of $0.004 per streamed performance. *Id.*

[5]   17 USC §512(c).

[6]   *Id.* at §512(k)(1)(A), (B). The DMCA additionally requires ISPs to designate an agent to receive notice of any claimed infringements. The Copyright Office web site has a suggested form, available at <http://www.loc.gov/copyright/onlinesp/>. A list of designated agents is available at <http://www.loc.gov/copyright/onlinesp/list/>.

[7]   17 USC §512(c), (d).

[8]   *Id.* at §512(b).

[9]   5 ILR (P&F) 418, 54 USPQ2d 1746; 2000 WL 573136 (ND Cal May 12, 2000), *aff'd,* 7 ILR (P&F) 1, 239 F3d 1004 (9th Cir 2001); MP3 is a compression technology that "permits rapid and efficient conversion of compact disc recordings ('CDs') to computer files easily accessed over the Internet." *See UMG Recordings, Inc. v. MP3.com,* 5 ILR (P&F) 415, 92 F Supp 2d 349 (SD NY 2000).

[10]   *Napster, Inc., id.*

[11]   *Napster, Inc.,* 239 F3d 1004, 1025 (9th Cir 2001).

[12]   *In re Verizon Internet Services, Inc. Subpoena Enforcement Matter,* 12 ILR (P&F) 640 (D DC, 2003).

[13]   7 ILR (P&F) 69, 239 F3d 619, 625-26 (4th Cir 2001).

[14]   17 USC §1201(a)(2).

[15]   *Id.* at §1201(a). Significantly, these new provisions do not prohibit the actual circumvention of copying control measures, such as the unauthorized duplication, distribution, and performance of a copyrighted work.

[16]   *Id.* at §1202.

[17]   6 ILR (P&F) 1, 111 F Supp 2d 294 (SD NY 2000), *aff'd,* 9 ILR (P&F) 330, 273 F3d 429 (2d Cir 2001).

[18]   The Supreme Court has described fair use as a way to "permit[ ] courts to avoid rigid application of the [copyright statute] when, on occasion, [it] would stifle the very creativity which that law is designed to foster." *Campbell v. Acuff-Rose Music, Inc.,* 510 US 569 (1994) (citing *Stewart v. Abend,* 495 US 207 (1990)). Fair use began as a judicially-created doctrine more than a century and a half ago, in *Folsom v. Marsh,* 9 F Cas 342, 348 (No. 4,901) (CCD Mass 1841). The doctrine was codified in the 1976 Copyright Act at 17 USC §107. It provides that, notwithstanding general protection granted to rightsholders, copying and reproduction of protected material is permissible in various media if used for purposes such as criticism, comment, news reporting, teaching (including multiple copies for classroom use), scholarship, or research. In determining whether the use made of a work in any particular case is "fair," and thus non-infringing, courts consider: (1) the purpose and character of the use, including whether such use is of a commercial nature or is for nonprofit educational purposes; (2) the nature of the copyrighted work; (3) the amount and substantiality of the portion used in relation to the copyrighted work as a whole; and (4) the effect of the use upon the potential market for or value of the copyrighted work.

[19]   *Id.* 111 F Supp 2d at 321-23.

[20]   *Id.* at 323, citing *Sony Corp.,* 464 US 417 (1984) (and noting that, to the extent there were inconsistencies between *Sony* and the DMCA, the statute effectively overruled the case).

[21]   *See* 17 USC §1201(f)-(h); *Universal City Studios,* 111 F Supp 2d at 319-322. The court earlier rejected defendants' argument that DeCSS was not covered by the DMCA because its 40-bit encryption key is a weak cipher that does not "effectively control" access to plaintiffs works, noting that such a construction of the statute would provide protection when none is needed, (*i.e.,* when an access control measure successfully thwarts circumvention), while withholding protection when it is most essential, (*i.e.,* where the measure *can* be circumvented), *id.* at 317.

[22]   *Universal City Studios,* 111 F Supp 2d at 344.

[23]   *Id.* at 325-342.

[24]   *See* note 16, *supra.*

[25]   1999 ILRWeb (P&F) 3001, 87 F Supp 2d 976 (ND Cal 1999).

[26]   5 ILR (P&F) 251, 2000 WL 127311 (WD Wash Jan. 18, 2000).

[27]   *Id.*

[28]   4 ILR (P&F) 306, 77 F Supp 2d 1116, 1121-22 (CD Cal 1999).

[29]   *Id.*

[30]   *Id.*

[31]   <http://www.eff.org/IP/DMCA/20020503_dmca_consequences.pdf>.

The Digital Millennium Copyright Act
Text, History, and Caselaw

II. STATUTORY TEXT

PUBLIC LAW 105–304—OCT. 28, 1998

DIGITAL MILLENNIUM COPYRIGHT ACT

112 STAT. 2860   PUBLIC LAW 105–304—OCT. 28, 1998

Public Law 105–304
105th Congress

An Act

Oct. 28, 1998
[H.R. 2281]

To amend title 17, United States Code, to implement the World Intellectual Property
  Organization Copyright Treaty and Performances and Phonograms Treaty, and
  for other purposes.

*Be it enacted by the Senate and House of Representatives of
the United States of America in Congress assembled,*

Digital
Millennium
Copyright Act.
17 USC 101 note.

SECTION 1. SHORT TITLE.

This Act may be cited as the "Digital Millennium Copyright
Act".

SEC. 2. TABLE OF CONTENTS.

PUBLIC LAW 105–304—OCT. 28, 1998   112 STAT. 2861

TITLE I—WIPO TREATIES IMPLEMENTATION

WIPO Copyright and Performances and Phonograms Treaties Implementation Act of 1998. 17 USC 101 note.

SEC. 101. SHORT TITLE.

This title may be cited as the "WIPO Copyright and Performances and Phonograms Treaties Implementation Act of 1998".

SEC. 102. TECHNICAL AMENDMENTS.

(a) DEFINITIONS.—Section 101 of title 17, United States Code, is amended—

(1) by striking the definition of "Berne Convention work";

(2) in the definition of "The 'country of origin' of a Berne Convention work"—

(A) by striking "The 'country of origin' of a Berne Convention work, for purposes of section 411, is the United States if" and inserting "For purposes of section 411, a work is a 'United States work' only if";

(B) in paragraph (1)—

(i) in subparagraph (B) by striking "nation or nations adhering to the Berne Convention" and inserting "treaty party or parties";

(ii) in subparagraph (C) by striking "does not adhere to the Berne Convention" and inserting "is not a treaty party"; and

(iii) in subparagraph (D) by striking "does not adhere to the Berne Convention" and inserting "is not a treaty party"; and

(C) in the matter following paragraph (3) by striking "For the purposes of section 411, the 'country of origin' of any other Berne Convention work is not the United States.";

(3) by inserting after the definition of "fixed" the following:

"The 'Geneva Phonograms Convention' is the Convention for the Protection of Producers of Phonograms Against Unauthorized Duplication of Their Phonograms, concluded at Geneva, Switzerland, on October 29, 1971.";

(4) by inserting after the definition of "including" the following:

"An 'international agreement' is—

"(1) the Universal Copyright Convention;

"(2) the Geneva Phonograms Convention;

"(3) the Berne Convention;

"(4) the WTO Agreement;

"(5) the WIPO Copyright Treaty;

"(6) the WIPO Performances and Phonograms Treaty; and

"(7) any other copyright treaty to which the United States is a party.";

(5) by inserting after the definition of "transmit" the following:

"A 'treaty party' is a country or intergovernmental organization other than the United States that is a party to an international agreement.";

(6) by inserting after the definition of "widow" the following:

112 STAT. 2862   PUBLIC LAW 105–304—OCT. 28, 1998

"The 'WIPO Copyright Treaty' is the WIPO Copyright Treaty concluded at Geneva, Switzerland, on December 20, 1996.";

(7) by inserting after the definition of "The 'WIPO Copyright Treaty'" the following:

"The 'WIPO Performances and Phonograms Treaty' is the WIPO Performances and Phonograms Treaty concluded at Geneva, Switzerland, on December 20, 1996."; and

(8) by inserting after the definition of "work made for hire" the following:

"The terms 'WTO Agreement' and 'WTO member country' have the meanings given those terms in paragraphs (9) and (10), respectively, of section 2 of the Uruguay Round Agreements Act.".

(b) SUBJECT MATTER OF COPYRIGHT; NATIONAL ORIGIN.—Section 104 of title 17, United States Code, is amended—

(1) in subsection (b)—

(A) in paragraph (1) by striking "foreign nation that is a party to a copyright treaty to which the United States is also a party" and inserting "treaty party";

(B) in paragraph (2) by striking "party to the Universal Copyright Convention" and inserting "treaty party";

(C) by redesignating paragraph (5) as paragraph (6);

(D) by redesignating paragraph (3) as paragraph (5) and inserting it after paragraph (4);

(E) by inserting after paragraph (2) the following:

"(3) the work is a sound recording that was first fixed in a treaty party; or";

(F) in paragraph (4) by striking "Berne Convention work" and inserting "pictorial, graphic, or sculptural work that is incorporated in a building or other structure, or an architectural work that is embodied in a building and the building or structure is located in the United States or a treaty party"; and

(G) by inserting after paragraph (6), as so redesignated, the following:

"For purposes of paragraph (2), a work that is published in the United States or a treaty party within 30 days after publication in a foreign nation that is not a treaty party shall be considered to be first published in the United States or such treaty party, as the case may be."; and

(2) by adding at the end the following new subsection:

"(d) EFFECT OF PHONOGRAMS TREATIES.—Notwithstanding the provisions of subsection (b), no works other than sound recordings shall be eligible for protection under this title solely by virtue of the adherence of the United States to the Geneva Phonograms Convention or the WIPO Performances and Phonograms Treaty.".

(c) COPYRIGHT IN RESTORED WORKS.—Section 104A(h) of title 17, United States Code, is amended—

(1) in paragraph (1), by striking subparagraphs (A) and (B) and inserting the following:

"(A) a nation adhering to the Berne Convention;

"(B) a WTO member country;

"(C) a nation adhering to the WIPO Copyright Treaty;

"(D) a nation adhering to the WIPO Performances and Phonograms Treaty; or

"(E) subject to a Presidential proclamation under subsection (g).";

(2) by amending paragraph (3) to read as follows:

"(3) The term 'eligible country' means a nation, other than the United States, that—

"(A) becomes a WTO member country after the date of the enactment of the Uruguay Round Agreements Act;

"(B) on such date of enactment is, or after such date of enactment becomes, a nation adhering to the Berne Convention;

"(C) adheres to the WIPO Copyright Treaty;

"(D) adheres to the WIPO Performances and Phonograms Treaty; or

"(E) after such date of enactment becomes subject to a proclamation under subsection (g).";

(3) in paragraph (6)—

(A) in subparagraph (C)(iii) by striking "and" after the semicolon;

(B) at the end of subparagraph (D) by striking the period and inserting "; and"; and

(C) by adding after subparagraph (D) the following:

"(E) if the source country for the work is an eligible country solely by virtue of its adherence to the WIPO Performances and Phonograms Treaty, is a sound recording.";

(4) in paragraph (8)(B)(i)—

(A) by inserting "of which" before "the majority"; and

(B) by striking "of eligible countries"; and

(5) by striking paragraph (9).

(d) REGISTRATION AND INFRINGEMENT ACTIONS.—Section 411(a) of title 17, United States Code, is amended in the first sentence—

(1) by striking "actions for infringement of copyright in Berne Convention works whose country of origin is not the United States and"; and

(2) by inserting "United States" after "no action for infringement of the copyright in any".

(e) STATUTE OF LIMITATIONS.—Section 507(a) of title 17, United State Code, is amended by striking "No" and inserting "Except as expressly provided otherwise in this title, no".

SEC. 103. COPYRIGHT PROTECTION SYSTEMS AND COPYRIGHT MANAGEMENT INFORMATION.

(a) IN GENERAL.—Title 17, United States Code, is amended by adding at the end the following new chapter:

"CHAPTER 12—COPYRIGHT PROTECTION AND MANAGEMENT SYSTEMS

"Sec.
"1201. Circumvention of copyright protection systems.
"1202. Integrity of copyright management information.
"1203. Civil remedies.
"1204. Criminal offenses and penalties.
"1205. Savings clause.

"§ 1201. Circumvention of copyright protection systems

"(a) VIOLATIONS REGARDING CIRCUMVENTION OF TECHNOLOGICAL MEASURES.—(1)(A) No person shall circumvent a technological measure that effectively controls access to a work protected

112 STAT. 2864   PUBLIC LAW 105–304—OCT. 28, 1998

Effective date.

under this title. The prohibition contained in the preceding sentence shall take effect at the end of the 2-year period beginning on the date of the enactment of this chapter.

"(B) The prohibition contained in subparagraph (A) shall not apply to persons who are users of a copyrighted work which is in a particular class of works, if such persons are, or are likely to be in the succeeding 3-year period, adversely affected by virtue of such prohibition in their ability to make noninfringing uses of that particular class of works under this title, as determined under subparagraph (C).

Reports.
Regulations.

"(C) During the 2-year period described in subparagraph (A), and during each succeeding 3-year period, the Librarian of Congress, upon the recommendation of the Register of Copyrights, who shall consult with the Assistant Secretary for Communications and Information of the Department of Commerce and report and comment on his or her views in making such recommendation, shall make the determination in a rulemaking proceeding on the record for purposes of subparagraph (B) of whether persons who are users of a copyrighted work are, or are likely to be in the succeeding 3-year period, adversely affected by the prohibition under subparagraph (A) in their ability to make noninfringing uses under this title of a particular class of copyrighted works. In conducting such rulemaking, the Librarian shall examine—

"(i) the availability for use of copyrighted works;

"(ii) the availability for use of works for nonprofit archival, preservation, and educational purposes;

"(iii) the impact that the prohibition on the circumvention of technological measures applied to copyrighted works has on criticism, comment, news reporting, teaching, scholarship, or research;

"(iv) the effect of circumvention of technological measures on the market for or value of copyrighted works; and

"(v) such other factors as the Librarian considers appropriate.

Publication.

"(D) The Librarian shall publish any class of copyrighted works for which the Librarian has determined, pursuant to the rulemaking conducted under subparagraph (C), that noninfringing uses by persons who are users of a copyrighted work are, or are likely to be, adversely affected, and the prohibition contained in subparagraph (A) shall not apply to such users with respect to such class of works for the ensuing 3-year period.

"(E) Neither the exception under subparagraph (B) from the applicability of the prohibition contained in subparagraph (A), nor any determination made in a rulemaking conducted under subparagraph (C), may be used as a defense in any action to enforce any provision of this title other than this paragraph.

"(2) No person shall manufacture, import, offer to the public, provide, or otherwise traffic in any technology, product, service, device, component, or part thereof, that—

"(A) is primarily designed or produced for the purpose of circumventing a technological measure that effectively controls access to a work protected under this title;

"(B) has only limited commercially significant purpose or use other than to circumvent a technological measure that effectively controls access to a work protected under this title; or

PUBLIC LAW 105–304—OCT. 28, 1998   112 STAT. 2865

"(C) is marketed by that person or another acting in concert with that person with that person's knowledge for use in circumventing a technological measure that effectively controls access to a work protected under this title.

"(3) As used in this subsection—

"(A) to 'circumvent a technological measure' means to descramble a scrambled work, to decrypt an encrypted work, or otherwise to avoid, bypass, remove, deactivate, or impair a technological measure, without the authority of the copyright owner; and

"(B) a technological measure 'effectively controls access to a work' if the measure, in the ordinary course of its operation, requires the application of information, or a process or a treatment, with the authority of the copyright owner, to gain access to the work.

"(b) ADDITIONAL VIOLATIONS.—(1) No person shall manufacture, import, offer to the public, provide, or otherwise traffic in any technology, product, service, device, component, or part thereof, that—

"(A) is primarily designed or produced for the purpose of circumventing protection afforded by a technological measure that effectively protects a right of a copyright owner under this title in a work or a portion thereof;

"(B) has only limited commercially significant purpose or use other than to circumvent protection afforded by a technological measure that effectively protects a right of a copyright owner under this title in a work or a portion thereof; or

"(C) is marketed by that person or another acting in concert with that person with that person's knowledge for use in circumventing protection afforded by a technological measure that effectively protects a right of a copyright owner under this title in a work or a portion thereof.

"(2) As used in this subsection—

"(A) to 'circumvent protection afforded by a technological measure' means avoiding, bypassing, removing, deactivating, or otherwise impairing a technological measure; and

"(B) a technological measure 'effectively protects a right of a copyright owner under this title' if the measure, in the ordinary course of its operation, prevents, restricts, or otherwise limits the exercise of a right of a copyright owner under this title.

"(c) OTHER RIGHTS, ETC., NOT AFFECTED.—(1) Nothing in this section shall affect rights, remedies, limitations, or defenses to copyright infringement, including fair use, under this title.

"(2) Nothing in this section shall enlarge or diminish vicarious or contributory liability for copyright infringement in connection with any technology, product, service, device, component, or part thereof.

"(3) Nothing in this section shall require that the design of, or design and selection of parts and components for, a consumer electronics, telecommunications, or computing product provide for a response to any particular technological measure, so long as such part or component, or the product in which such part or component is integrated, does not otherwise fall within the prohibitions of subsection (a)(2) or (b)(1).

"(4) Nothing in this section shall enlarge or diminish any rights of free speech or the press for activities using consumer electronics, telecommunications, or computing products.

"(d) EXEMPTION FOR NONPROFIT LIBRARIES, ARCHIVES, AND EDUCATIONAL INSTITUTIONS.—(1) A nonprofit library, archives, or educational institution which gains access to a commercially exploited copyrighted work solely in order to make a good faith determination of whether to acquire a copy of that work for the sole purpose of engaging in conduct permitted under this title shall not be in violation of subsection (a)(1)(A). A copy of a work to which access has been gained under this paragraph—

"(A) may not be retained longer than necessary to make such good faith determination; and

"(B) may not be used for any other purpose.

"(2) The exemption made available under paragraph (1) shall only apply with respect to a work when an identical copy of that work is not reasonably available in another form.

"(3) A nonprofit library, archives, or educational institution that willfully for the purpose of commercial advantage or financial gain violates paragraph (1)—

"(A) shall, for the first offense, be subject to the civil remedies under section 1203; and

"(B) shall, for repeated or subsequent offenses, in addition to the civil remedies under section 1203, forfeit the exemption provided under paragraph (1).

"(4) This subsection may not be used as a defense to a claim under subsection (a)(2) or (b), nor may this subsection permit a nonprofit library, archives, or educational institution to manufacture, import, offer to the public, provide, or otherwise traffic in any technology, product, service, component, or part thereof, which circumvents a technological measure.

"(5) In order for a library or archives to qualify for the exemption under this subsection, the collections of that library or archives shall be—

"(A) open to the public; or

"(B) available not only to researchers affiliated with the library or archives or with the institution of which it is a part, but also to other persons doing research in a specialized field.

"(e) LAW ENFORCEMENT, INTELLIGENCE, AND OTHER GOVERNMENT ACTIVITIES.—This section does not prohibit any lawfully authorized investigative, protective, information security, or intelligence activity of an officer, agent, or employee of the United States, a State, or a political subdivision of a State, or a person acting pursuant to a contract with the United States, a State, or a political subdivision of a State. For purposes of this subsection, the term 'information security' means activities carried out in order to identify and address the vulnerabilities of a government computer, computer system, or computer network.

"(f) REVERSE ENGINEERING.—(1) Notwithstanding the provisions of subsection (a)(1)(A), a person who has lawfully obtained the right to use a copy of a computer program may circumvent a technological measure that effectively controls access to a particular portion of that program for the sole purpose of identifying and analyzing those elements of the program that are necessary to achieve interoperability of an independently created computer program with other programs, and that have not previously been readily available to the person engaging in the circumvention, to the extent any such acts of identification and analysis do not constitute infringement under this title.

"(2) Notwithstanding the provisions of subsections (a)(2) and (b), a person may develop and employ technological means to circumvent a technological measure, or to circumvent protection afforded by a technological measure, in order to enable the identification and analysis under paragraph (1), or for the purpose of enabling interoperability of an independently created computer program with other programs, if such means are necessary to achieve such interoperability, to the extent that doing so does not constitute infringement under this title.

"(3) The information acquired through the acts permitted under paragraph (1), and the means permitted under paragraph (2), may be made available to others if the person referred to in paragraph (1) or (2), as the case may be, provides such information or means solely for the purpose of enabling interoperability of an independently created computer program with other programs, and to the extent that doing so does not constitute infringement under this title or violate applicable law other than this section.

"(4) For purposes of this subsection, the term 'interoperability' means the ability of computer programs to exchange information, and of such programs mutually to use the information which has been exchanged.

"(g) ENCRYPTION RESEARCH.—

"(1) DEFINITIONS.—For purposes of this subsection—

"(A) the term 'encryption research' means activities necessary to identify and analyze flaws and vulnerabilities of encryption technologies applied to copyrighted works, if these activities are conducted to advance the state of knowledge in the field of encryption technology or to assist in the development of encryption products; and

"(B) the term 'encryption technology' means the scrambling and descrambling of information using mathematical formulas or algorithms.

"(2) PERMISSIBLE ACTS OF ENCRYPTION RESEARCH.—Notwithstanding the provisions of subsection (a)(1)(A), it is not a violation of that subsection for a person to circumvent a technological measure as applied to a copy, phonorecord, performance, or display of a published work in the course of an act of good faith encryption research if—

"(A) the person lawfully obtained the encrypted copy, phonorecord, performance, or display of the published work;

"(B) such act is necessary to conduct such encryption research;

"(C) the person made a good faith effort to obtain authorization before the circumvention; and

"(D) such act does not constitute infringement under this title or a violation of applicable law other than this section, including section 1030 of title 18 and those provisions of title 18 amended by the Computer Fraud and Abuse Act of 1986.

"(3) FACTORS IN DETERMINING EXEMPTION.—In determining whether a person qualifies for the exemption under paragraph (2), the factors to be considered shall include—

"(A) whether the information derived from the encryption research was disseminated, and if so, whether

17

it was disseminated in a manner reasonably calculated to advance the state of knowledge or development of encryption technology, versus whether it was disseminated in a manner that facilitates infringement under this title or a violation of applicable law other than this section, including a violation of privacy or breach of security;

"(B) whether the person is engaged in a legitimate course of study, is employed, or is appropriately trained or experienced, in the field of encryption technology; and

"(C) whether the person provides the copyright owner of the work to which the technological measure is applied with notice of the findings and documentation of the research, and the time when such notice is provided.

"(4) USE OF TECHNOLOGICAL MEANS FOR RESEARCH ACTIVITIES.—Notwithstanding the provisions of subsection (a)(2), it is not a violation of that subsection for a person to—

"(A) develop and employ technological means to circumvent a technological measure for the sole purpose of that person performing the acts of good faith encryption research described in paragraph (2); and

"(B) provide the technological means to another person with whom he or she is working collaboratively for the purpose of conducting the acts of good faith encryption research described in paragraph (2) or for the purpose of having that other person verify his or her acts of good faith encryption research described in paragraph (2).

Deadline.

"(5) REPORT TO CONGRESS.—Not later than 1 year after the date of the enactment of this chapter, the Register of Copyrights and the Assistant Secretary for Communications and Information of the Department of Commerce shall jointly report to the Congress on the effect this subsection has had on—

"(A) encryption research and the development of encryption technology;

"(B) the adequacy and effectiveness of technological measures designed to protect copyrighted works; and

"(C) protection of copyright owners against the unauthorized access to their encrypted copyrighted works.

The report shall include legislative recommendations, if any.

"(h) EXCEPTIONS REGARDING MINORS.—In applying subsection (a) to a component or part, the court may consider the necessity for its intended and actual incorporation in a technology, product, service, or device, which—

"(1) does not itself violate the provisions of this title; and

"(2) has the sole purpose to prevent the access of minors to material on the Internet.

"(i) PROTECTION OF PERSONALLY IDENTIFYING INFORMATION.—

"(1) CIRCUMVENTION PERMITTED.—Notwithstanding the provisions of subsection (a)(1)(A), it is not a violation of that subsection for a person to circumvent a technological measure that effectively controls access to a work protected under this title, if—

"(A) the technological measure, or the work it protects, contains the capability of collecting or disseminating personally identifying information reflecting the online activities of a natural person who seeks to gain access to the work protected;

PUBLIC LAW 105–304—OCT. 28, 1998   112 STAT. 2869

"(B) in the normal course of its operation, the technological measure, or the work it protects, collects or disseminates personally identifying information about the person who seeks to gain access to the work protected, without providing conspicuous notice of such collection or dissemination to such person, and without providing such person with the capability to prevent or restrict such collection or dissemination;

"(C) the act of circumvention has the sole effect of identifying and disabling the capability described in subparagraph (A), and has no other effect on the ability of any person to gain access to any work; and

"(D) the act of circumvention is carried out solely for the purpose of preventing the collection or dissemination of personally identifying information about a natural person who seeks to gain access to the work protected, and is not in violation of any other law.

"(2) INAPPLICABILITY TO CERTAIN TECHNOLOGICAL MEASURES.—This subsection does not apply to a technological measure, or a work it protects, that does not collect or disseminate personally identifying information and that is disclosed to a user as not having or using such capability.

"(j) SECURITY TESTING.—

"(1) DEFINITION.—For purposes of this subsection, the term 'security testing' means accessing a computer, computer system, or computer network, solely for the purpose of good faith testing, investigating, or correcting, a security flaw or vulnerability, with the authorization of the owner or operator of such computer, computer system, or computer network.

"(2) PERMISSIBLE ACTS OF SECURITY TESTING.—Notwithstanding the provisions of subsection (a)(1)(A), it is not a violation of that subsection for a person to engage in an act of security testing, if such act does not constitute infringement under this title or a violation of applicable law other than this section, including section 1030 of title 18 and those provisions of title 18 amended by the Computer Fraud and Abuse Act of 1986.

"(3) FACTORS IN DETERMINING EXEMPTION.—In determining whether a person qualifies for the exemption under paragraph (2), the factors to be considered shall include—

"(A) whether the information derived from the security testing was used solely to promote the security of the owner or operator of such computer, computer system or computer network, or shared directly with the developer of such computer, computer system, or computer network; and

"(B) whether the information derived from the security testing was used or maintained in a manner that does not facilitate infringement under this title or a violation of applicable law other than this section, including a violation of privacy or breach of security.

"(4) USE OF TECHNOLOGICAL MEANS FOR SECURITY TESTING.—Notwithstanding the provisions of subsection (a)(2), it is not a violation of that subsection for a person to develop, produce, distribute or employ technological means for the sole purpose of performing the acts of security testing described

112 STAT. 2870   PUBLIC LAW 105–304—OCT. 28, 1998

in subsection (2), provided such technological means does not otherwise violate section (a)(2).

"(k) CERTAIN ANALOG DEVICES AND CERTAIN TECHNOLOGICAL MEASURES.—

"(1) CERTAIN ANALOG DEVICES.—

Effective date.

"(A) Effective 18 months after the date of the enactment of this chapter, no person shall manufacture, import, offer to the public, provide or otherwise traffic in any—

"(i) VHS format analog video cassette recorder unless such recorder conforms to the automatic gain control copy control technology;

"(ii) 8mm format analog video cassette camcorder unless such camcorder conforms to the automatic gain control technology;

"(iii) Beta format analog video cassette recorder, unless such recorder conforms to the automatic gain control copy control technology, except that this requirement shall not apply until there are 1,000 Beta format analog video cassette recorders sold in the United States in any one calendar year after the date of the enactment of this chapter;

"(iv) 8mm format analog video cassette recorder that is not an analog video cassette camcorder, unless such recorder conforms to the automatic gain control copy control technology, except that this requirement shall not apply until there are 20,000 such recorders sold in the United States in any one calendar year after the date of the enactment of this chapter; or

"(v) analog video cassette recorder that records using an NTSC format video input and that is not otherwise covered under clauses (i) through (iv), unless such device conforms to the automatic gain control copy control technology.

Effective date.

"(B) Effective on the date of the enactment of this chapter, no person shall manufacture, import, offer to the public, provide or otherwise traffic in—

"(i) any VHS format analog video cassette recorder or any 8mm format analog video cassette recorder if the design of the model of such recorder has been modified after such date of enactment so that a model of recorder that previously conformed to the automatic gain control copy control technology no longer conforms to such technology; or

"(ii) any VHS format analog video cassette recorder, or any 8mm format analog video cassette recorder that is not an 8mm analog video cassette camcorder, if the design of the model of such recorder has been modified after such date of enactment so that a model of recorder that previously conformed to the four-line colorstripe copy control technology no longer conforms to such technology.

Manufacturers that have not previously manufactured or sold a VHS format analog video cassette recorder, or an 8mm format analog cassette recorder, shall be required to conform to the four-line colorstripe copy control technology in the initial model of any such recorder manufactured after the date of the enactment of this chapter, and thereafter to continue conforming to the four-line colorstripe copy control technology. For purposes of this subparagraph, an analog video cassette recorder 'conforms to' the four-line colorstripe copy control technology if it records a signal that, when played back by the playback function of that recorder in the normal viewing mode, exhibits, on a reference display device, a display containing distracting visible lines through portions of the viewable picture.

"(2) CERTAIN ENCODING RESTRICTIONS.—No person shall apply the automatic gain control copy control technology or colorstripe copy control technology to prevent or limit consumer copying except such copying—

"(A) of a single transmission, or specified group of transmissions, of live events or of audiovisual works for which a member of the public has exercised choice in selecting the transmissions, including the content of the transmissions or the time of receipt of such transmissions, or both, and as to which such member is charged a separate fee for each such transmission or specified group of transmissions;

"(B) from a copy of a transmission of a live event or an audiovisual work if such transmission is provided by a channel or service where payment is made by a member of the public for such channel or service in the form of a subscription fee that entitles the member of the public to receive all of the programming contained in such channel or service;

"(C) from a physical medium containing one or more prerecorded audiovisual works; or

"(D) from a copy of a transmission described in subparagraph (A) or from a copy made from a physical medium described in subparagraph (C).

In the event that a transmission meets both the conditions set forth in subparagraph (A) and those set forth in subparagraph (B), the transmission shall be treated as a transmission described in subparagraph (A).

"(3) INAPPLICABILITY.—This subsection shall not—

"(A) require any analog video cassette camcorder to conform to the automatic gain control copy control technology with respect to any video signal received through a camera lens;

"(B) apply to the manufacture, importation, offer for sale, provision of, or other trafficking in, any professional analog video cassette recorder; or

"(C) apply to the offer for sale or provision of, or other trafficking in, any previously owned analog video cassette recorder, if such recorder was legally manufactured and sold when new and not subsequently modified in violation of paragraph (1)(B).

"(4) DEFINITIONS.—For purposes of this subsection:

"(A) An 'analog video cassette recorder' means a device that records, or a device that includes a function that records, on electromagnetic tape in an analog format the electronic impulses produced by the video and audio portions of a television program, motion picture, or other form of audiovisual work.

"(B) An 'analog video cassette camcorder' means an analog video cassette recorder that contains a recording function that operates through a camera lens and through a video input that may be connected with a television or other video playback device.

"(C) An analog video cassette recorder 'conforms' to the automatic gain control copy control technology if it—

"(i) detects one or more of the elements of such technology and does not record the motion picture or transmission protected by such technology; or

"(ii) records a signal that, when played back, exhibits a meaningfully distorted or degraded display.

"(D) The term 'professional analog video cassette recorder' means an analog video cassette recorder that is designed, manufactured, marketed, and intended for use by a person who regularly employs such a device for a lawful business or industrial use, including making, performing, displaying, distributing, or transmitting copies of motion pictures on a commercial scale.

"(E) The terms 'VHS format', '8mm format', 'Beta format', 'automatic gain control copy control technology', 'colorstripe copy control technology', 'four-line version of the colorstripe copy control technology', and 'NTSC' have the meanings that are commonly understood in the consumer electronics and motion picture industries as of the date of the enactment of this chapter.

"(5) VIOLATIONS.—Any violation of paragraph (1) of this subsection shall be treated as a violation of subsection (b)(1) of this section. Any violation of paragraph (2) of this subsection shall be deemed an 'act of circumvention' for the purposes of section 1203(c)(3)(A) of this chapter.

"§ 1202. Integrity of copyright management information

"(a) FALSE COPYRIGHT MANAGEMENT INFORMATION.—No person shall knowingly and with the intent to induce, enable, facilitate, or conceal infringement—

"(1) provide copyright management information that is false, or

"(2) distribute or import for distribution copyright management information that is false.

"(b) REMOVAL OR ALTERATION OF COPYRIGHT MANAGEMENT INFORMATION.—No person shall, without the authority of the copyright owner or the law—

"(1) intentionally remove or alter any copyright management information,

"(2) distribute or import for distribution copyright management information knowing that the copyright management information has been removed or altered without authority of the copyright owner or the law, or

"(3) distribute, import for distribution, or publicly perform works, copies of works, or phonorecords, knowing that copyright management information has been removed or altered without authority of the copyright owner or the law,

knowing, or, with respect to civil remedies under section 1203, having reasonable grounds to know, that it will induce, enable, facilitate, or conceal an infringement of any right under this title.

"(c) Dᴇғɪɴɪᴛɪᴏɴ.—As used in this section, the term 'copyright management information' means any of the following information conveyed in connection with copies or phonorecords of a work or performances or displays of a work, including in digital form, except that such term does not include any personally identifying information about a user of a work or of a copy, phonorecord, performance, or display of a work:

"(1) The title and other information identifying the work, including the information set forth on a notice of copyright.

"(2) The name of, and other identifying information about, the author of a work.

"(3) The name of, and other identifying information about, the copyright owner of the work, including the information set forth in a notice of copyright.

"(4) With the exception of public performances of works by radio and television broadcast stations, the name of, and other identifying information about, a performer whose performance is fixed in a work other than an audiovisual work.

"(5) With the exception of public performances of works by radio and television broadcast stations, in the case of an audiovisual work, the name of, and other identifying information about, a writer, performer, or director who is credited in the audiovisual work.

"(6) Terms and conditions for use of the work.

"(7) Identifying numbers or symbols referring to such information or links to such information.

"(8) Such other information as the Register of Copyrights may prescribe by regulation, except that the Register of Copyrights may not require the provision of any information concerning the user of a copyrighted work.

"(d) Lᴀᴡ Eɴғᴏʀᴄᴇᴍᴇɴᴛ, Iɴᴛᴇʟʟɪɢᴇɴᴄᴇ, ᴀɴᴅ Oᴛʜᴇʀ Gᴏᴠᴇʀɴᴍᴇɴᴛ Aᴄᴛɪᴠɪᴛɪᴇs.—This section does not prohibit any lawfully authorized investigative, protective, information security, or intelligence activity of an officer, agent, or employee of the United States, a State, or a political subdivision of a State, or a person acting pursuant to a contract with the United States, a State, or a political subdivision of a State. For purposes of this subsection, the term 'information security' means activities carried out in order to identify and address the vulnerabilities of a government computer, computer system, or computer network.

"(e) Lɪᴍɪᴛᴀᴛɪᴏɴs ᴏɴ Lɪᴀʙɪʟɪᴛʏ.—

"(1) Aɴᴀʟᴏɢ ᴛʀᴀɴsᴍɪssɪᴏɴs.—In the case of an analog transmission, a person who is making transmissions in its capacity as a broadcast station, or as a cable system, or someone who provides programming to such station or system, shall not be liable for a violation of subsection (b) if—

"(A) avoiding the activity that constitutes such violation is not technically feasible or would create an undue financial hardship on such person; and

"(B) such person did not intend, by engaging in such activity, to induce, enable, facilitate, or conceal infringement of a right under this title.

"(2) Dɪɢɪᴛᴀʟ ᴛʀᴀɴsᴍɪssɪᴏɴs.—

"(A) If a digital transmission standard for the placement of copyright management information for a category of works is set in a voluntary, consensus standard-setting process involving a representative cross-section of broadcast stations or cable systems and copyright owners of a category of works that are intended for public performance by such stations or systems, a person identified in paragraph (1) shall not be liable for a violation of subsection (b) with respect to the particular copyright management information addressed by such standard if—

"(i) the placement of such information by someone other than such person is not in accordance with such standard; and

"(ii) the activity that constitutes such violation is not intended to induce, enable, facilitate, or conceal infringement of a right under this title.

"(B) Until a digital transmission standard has been set pursuant to subparagraph (A) with respect to the placement of copyright management information for a category or works, a person identified in paragraph (1) shall not be liable for a violation of subsection (b) with respect to such copyright management information, if the activity that constitutes such violation is not intended to induce, enable, facilitate, or conceal infringement of a right under this title, and if—

"(i) the transmission of such information by such person would result in a perceptible visual or aural degradation of the digital signal; or

"(ii) the transmission of such information by such person would conflict with—

"(I) an applicable government regulation relating to transmission of information in a digital signal;

"(II) an applicable industry-wide standard relating to the transmission of information in a digital signal that was adopted by a voluntary consensus standards body prior to the effective date of this chapter; or

"(III) an applicable industry-wide standard relating to the transmission of information in a digital signal that was adopted in a voluntary, consensus standards-setting process open to participation by a representative cross-section of broadcast stations or cable systems and copyright owners of a category of works that are intended for public performance by such stations or systems.

"(3) DEFINITIONS.—As used in this subsection—

"(A) the term 'broadcast station' has the meaning given that term in section 3 of the Communications Act of 1934 (47 U.S.C. 153); and

"(B) the term 'cable system' has the meaning given that term in section 602 of the Communications Act of 1934 (47 U.S.C. 522).

"§ 1203. Civil remedies

"(a) CIVIL ACTIONS.—Any person injured by a violation of section 1201 or 1202 may bring a civil action in an appropriate United States district court for such violation.

"(b) POWERS OF THE COURT.—In an action brought under subsection (a), the court—

"(1) may grant temporary and permanent injunctions on such terms as it deems reasonable to prevent or restrain a violation, but in no event shall impose a prior restraint on free speech or the press protected under the 1st amendment to the Constitution;

"(2) at any time while an action is pending, may order the impounding, on such terms as it deems reasonable, of any device or product that is in the custody or control of the alleged violator and that the court has reasonable cause to believe was involved in a violation;

"(3) may award damages under subsection (c);

"(4) in its discretion may allow the recovery of costs by or against any party other than the United States or an officer thereof;

"(5) in its discretion may award reasonable attorney's fees to the prevailing party; and

"(6) may, as part of a final judgment or decree finding a violation, order the remedial modification or the destruction of any device or product involved in the violation that is in the custody or control of the violator or has been impounded under paragraph (2).

"(c) AWARD OF DAMAGES.—

"(1) IN GENERAL.—Except as otherwise provided in this title, a person committing a violation of section 1201 or 1202 is liable for either—

"(A) the actual damages and any additional profits of the violator, as provided in paragraph (2), or

"(B) statutory damages, as provided in paragraph (3).

"(2) ACTUAL DAMAGES.—The court shall award to the complaining party the actual damages suffered by the party as a result of the violation, and any profits of the violator that are attributable to the violation and are not taken into account in computing the actual damages, if the complaining party elects such damages at any time before final judgment is entered.

"(3) STATUTORY DAMAGES.—(A) At any time before final judgment is entered, a complaining party may elect to recover an award of statutory damages for each violation of section 1201 in the sum of not less than $200 or more than $2,500 per act of circumvention, device, product, component, offer, or performance of service, as the court considers just.

"(B) At any time before final judgment is entered, a complaining party may elect to recover an award of statutory damages for each violation of section 1202 in the sum of not less than $2,500 or more than $25,000.

"(4) REPEATED VIOLATIONS.—In any case in which the injured party sustains the burden of proving, and the court finds, that a person has violated section 1201 or 1202 within 3 years after a final judgment was entered against the person for another such violation, the court may increase the award of damages up to triple the amount that would otherwise be awarded, as the court considers just.

"(5) INNOCENT VIOLATIONS.—

"(A) IN GENERAL.—The court in its discretion may reduce or remit the total award of damages in any case in which the violator sustains the burden of proving, and

PUBLIC LAW 105–304—OCT. 28, 1998

the court finds, that the violator was not aware and had no reason to believe that its acts constituted a violation.

"(B) NONPROFIT LIBRARY, ARCHIVES, OR EDUCATIONAL INSTITUTIONS.—In the case of a nonprofit library, archives, or educational institution, the court shall remit damages in any case in which the library, archives, or educational institution sustains the burden of proving, and the court finds, that the library, archives, or educational institution was not aware and had no reason to believe that its acts constituted a violation.

"§ 1204. Criminal offenses and penalties

"(a) IN GENERAL.—Any person who violates section 1201 or 1202 willfully and for purposes of commercial advantage or private financial gain—

"(1) shall be fined not more than $500,000 or imprisoned for not more than 5 years, or both, for the first offense; and

"(2) shall be fined not more than $1,000,000 or imprisoned for not more than 10 years, or both, for any subsequent offense.

"(b) LIMITATION FOR NONPROFIT LIBRARY, ARCHIVES, OR EDUCATIONAL INSTITUTION.—Subsection (a) shall not apply to a nonprofit library, archives, or educational institution.

"(c) STATUTE OF LIMITATIONS.—No criminal proceeding shall be brought under this section unless such proceeding is commenced within 5 years after the cause of action arose.

"§ 1205. Savings clause

"Nothing in this chapter abrogates, diminishes, or weakens the provisions of, nor provides any defense or element of mitigation in a criminal prosecution or civil action under, any Federal or State law that prevents the violation of the privacy of an individual in connection with the individual's use of the Internet.".

(b) CONFORMING AMENDMENT.—The table of chapters for title 17, United States Code, is amended by adding after the item relating to chapter 11 the following:

"12. Copyright Protection and Management Systems .... **1201".**

17 USC 109 note.   **SEC. 104. EVALUATION OF IMPACT OF COPYRIGHT LAW AND AMENDMENTS ON ELECTRONIC COMMERCE AND TECHNOLOGICAL DEVELOPMENT.**

(a) EVALUATION BY THE REGISTER OF COPYRIGHTS AND THE ASSISTANT SECRETARY FOR COMMUNICATIONS AND INFORMATION.—The Register of Copyrights and the Assistant Secretary for Communications and Information of the Department of Commerce shall jointly evaluate—

(1) the effects of the amendments made by this title and the development of electronic commerce and associated technology on the operation of sections 109 and 117 of title 17, United States Code; and

(2) the relationship between existing and emergent technology and the operation of sections 109 and 117 of title 17, United States Code.

Deadline.   (b) REPORT TO CONGRESS.—The Register of Copyrights and the Assistant Secretary for Communications and Information of the Department of Commerce shall, not later than 24 months after the date of the enactment of this Act, submit to the Congress a joint report on the evaluation conducted under subsection (a),

PUBLIC LAW 105–304—OCT. 28, 1998   112 STAT. 2877

including any legislative recommendations the Register and the Assistant Secretary may have.

SEC. 105. EFFECTIVE DATE.

17 USC 101 note.

(a) IN GENERAL.—Except as otherwise provided in this title, this title and the amendments made by this title shall take effect on the date of the enactment of this Act.

(b) AMENDMENTS RELATING TO CERTAIN INTERNATIONAL AGREEMENTS.—(1) The following shall take effect upon the entry into force of the WIPO Copyright Treaty with respect to the United States:

(A) Paragraph (5) of the definition of "international agreement" contained in section 101 of title 17, United States Code, as amended by section 102(a)(4) of this Act.

(B) The amendment made by section 102(a)(6) of this Act.

(C) Subparagraph (C) of section 104A(h)(1) of title 17, United States Code, as amended by section 102(c)(1) of this Act.

(D) Subparagraph (C) of section 104A(h)(3) of title 17, United States Code, as amended by section 102(c)(2) of this Act.

(2) The following shall take effect upon the entry into force of the WIPO Performances and Phonograms Treaty with respect to the United States:

(A) Paragraph (6) of the definition of "international agreement" contained in section 101 of title 17, United States Code, as amended by section 102(a)(4) of this Act.

(B) The amendment made by section 102(a)(7) of this Act.

(C) The amendment made by section 102(b)(2) of this Act.

(D) Subparagraph (D) of section 104A(h)(1) of title 17, United States Code, as amended by section 102(c)(1) of this Act.

(E) Subparagraph (D) of section 104A(h)(3) of title 17, United States Code, as amended by section 102(c)(2) of this Act.

(F) The amendments made by section 102(c)(3) of this Act.

TITLE II—ONLINE COPYRIGHT INFRINGEMENT LIABILITY LIMITATION

Online Copyright Infringement Liability Limitation Act.

SEC. 201. SHORT TITLE.

17 USC 101 note.

This title may be cited as the "Online Copyright Infringement Liability Limitation Act".

SEC. 202. LIMITATIONS ON LIABILITY FOR COPYRIGHT INFRINGEMENT.

(a) IN GENERAL.—Chapter 5 of title 17, United States Code, is amended by adding after section 511 the following new section:

"§ 512. Limitations on liability relating to material online

"(a) TRANSITORY DIGITAL NETWORK COMMUNICATIONS.—A service provider shall not be liable for monetary relief, or, except as provided in subsection (j), for injunctive or other equitable relief, for infringement of copyright by reason of the provider's transmitting, routing, or providing connections for, material through a system or network controlled or operated by or for the service provider, or by reason of the intermediate and transient storage of that material in the course of such transmitting, routing, or providing connections, if—

"(1) the transmission of the material was initiated by or at the direction of a person other than the service provider;

"(2) the transmission, routing, provision of connections, or storage is carried out through an automatic technical process without selection of the material by the service provider;

"(3) the service provider does not select the recipients of the material except as an automatic response to the request of another person;

"(4) no copy of the material made by the service provider in the course of such intermediate or transient storage is maintained on the system or network in a manner ordinarily accessible to anyone other than anticipated recipients, and no such copy is maintained on the system or network in a manner ordinarily accessible to such anticipated recipients for a longer period than is reasonably necessary for the transmission, routing, or provision of connections; and

"(5) the material is transmitted through the system or network without modification of its content.

"(b) SYSTEM CACHING.—

"(1) LIMITATION ON LIABILITY.—A service provider shall not be liable for monetary relief, or, except as provided in subsection (j), for injunctive or other equitable relief, for infringement of copyright by reason of the intermediate and temporary storage of material on a system or network controlled or operated by or for the service provider in a case in which—

"(A) the material is made available online by a person other than the service provider;

"(B) the material is transmitted from the person described in subparagraph (A) through the system or network to a person other than the person described in subparagraph (A) at the direction of that other person; and

"(C) the storage is carried out through an automatic technical process for the purpose of making the material available to users of the system or network who, after the material is transmitted as described in subparagraph (B), request access to the material from the person described in subparagraph (A),

if the conditions set forth in paragraph (2) are met.

"(2) CONDITIONS.—The conditions referred to in paragraph (1) are that—

"(A) the material described in paragraph (1) is transmitted to the subsequent users described in paragraph (1)(C) without modification to its content from the manner in which the material was transmitted from the person described in paragraph (1)(A);

"(B) the service provider described in paragraph (1) complies with rules concerning the refreshing, reloading, or other updating of the material when specified by the person making the material available online in accordance with a generally accepted industry standard data communications protocol for the system or network through which that person makes the material available, except that this subparagraph applies only if those rules are not used by the person described in paragraph (1)(A) to prevent or unreasonably impair the intermediate storage to which this subsection applies;

"(C) the service provider does not interfere with the ability of technology associated with the material to return to the person described in paragraph (1)(A) the information that would have been available to that person if the material had been obtained by the subsequent users described in paragraph (1)(C) directly from that person, except that this subparagraph applies only if that technology—

"(i) does not significantly interfere with the performance of the provider's system or network or with the intermediate storage of the material;

"(ii) is consistent with generally accepted industry standard communications protocols; and

"(iii) does not extract information from the provider's system or network other than the information that would have been available to the person described in paragraph (1)(A) if the subsequent users had gained access to the material directly from that person;

"(D) if the person described in paragraph (1)(A) has in effect a condition that a person must meet prior to having access to the material, such as a condition based on payment of a fee or provision of a password or other information, the service provider permits access to the stored material in significant part only to users of its system or network that have met those conditions and only in accordance with those conditions; and

"(E) if the person described in paragraph (1)(A) makes that material available online without the authorization of the copyright owner of the material, the service provider responds expeditiously to remove, or disable access to, the material that is claimed to be infringing upon notification of claimed infringement as described in subsection (c)(3), except that this subparagraph applies only if—

"(i) the material has previously been removed from the originating site or access to it has been disabled, or a court has ordered that the material be removed from the originating site or that access to the material on the originating site be disabled; and

"(ii) the party giving the notification includes in the notification a statement confirming that the material has been removed from the originating site or access to it has been disabled or that a court has ordered that the material be removed from the originating site or that access to the material on the originating site be disabled.

"(c) INFORMATION RESIDING ON SYSTEMS OR NETWORKS AT DIRECTION OF USERS.—

"(1) IN GENERAL.—A service provider shall not be liable for monetary relief, or, except as provided in subsection (j), for injunctive or other equitable relief, for infringement of copyright by reason of the storage at the direction of a user of

112 STAT. 2880   PUBLIC LAW 105–304—OCT. 28, 1998

material that resides on a system or network controlled or operated by or for the service provider, if the service provider—

"(A)(i) does not have actual knowledge that the material or an activity using the material on the system or network is infringing;

"(ii) in the absence of such actual knowledge, is not aware of facts or circumstances from which infringing activity is apparent; or

"(iii) upon obtaining such knowledge or awareness, acts expeditiously to remove, or disable access to, the material;

"(B) does not receive a financial benefit directly attributable to the infringing activity, in a case in which the service provider has the right and ability to control such activity; and

"(C) upon notification of claimed infringement as described in paragraph (3), responds expeditiously to remove, or disable access to, the material that is claimed to be infringing or to be the subject of infringing activity.

"(2) DESIGNATED AGENT.—The limitations on liability established in this subsection apply to a service provider only if the service provider has designated an agent to receive notifications of claimed infringement described in paragraph (3), by making available through its service, including on its website in a location accessible to the public, and by providing to the Copyright Office, substantially the following information:

"(A) the name, address, phone number, and electronic mail address of the agent.

"(B) other contact information which the Register of Copyrights may deem appropriate.

Records.
Public
information.

The Register of Copyrights shall maintain a current directory of agents available to the public for inspection, including through the Internet, in both electronic and hard copy formats, and may require payment of a fee by service providers to cover the costs of maintaining the directory.

"(3) ELEMENTS OF NOTIFICATION.—

"(A) To be effective under this subsection, a notification of claimed infringement must be a written communication provided to the designated agent of a service provider that includes substantially the following:

"(i) A physical or electronic signature of a person authorized to act on behalf of the owner of an exclusive right that is allegedly infringed.

"(ii) Identification of the copyrighted work claimed to have been infringed, or, if multiple copyrighted works at a single online site are covered by a single notification, a representative list of such works at that site.

"(iii) Identification of the material that is claimed to be infringing or to be the subject of infringing activity and that is to be removed or access to which is to be disabled, and information reasonably sufficient to permit the service provider to locate the material.

"(iv) Information reasonably sufficient to permit the service provider to contact the complaining party, such as an address, telephone number, and, if available, an electronic mail address at which the complaining party may be contacted.

"(v) A statement that the complaining party has a good faith belief that use of the material in the manner complained of is not authorized by the copyright owner, its agent, or the law.

"(vi) A statement that the information in the notification is accurate, and under penalty of perjury, that the complaining party is authorized to act on behalf of the owner of an exclusive right that is allegedly infringed.

"(B)(i) Subject to clause (ii), a notification from a copyright owner or from a person authorized to act on behalf of the copyright owner that fails to comply substantially with the provisions of subparagraph (A) shall not be considered under paragraph (1)(A) in determining whether a service provider has actual knowledge or is aware of facts or circumstances from which infringing activity is apparent.

"(ii) In a case in which the notification that is provided to the service provider's designated agent fails to comply substantially with all the provisions of subparagraph (A) but substantially complies with clauses (ii), (iii), and (iv) of subparagraph (A), clause (i) of this subparagraph applies only if the service provider promptly attempts to contact the person making the notification or takes other reasonable steps to assist in the receipt of notification that substantially complies with all the provisions of subparagraph (A).

"(d) INFORMATION LOCATION TOOLS.—A service provider shall not be liable for monetary relief, or, except as provided in subsection (j), for injunctive or other equitable relief, for infringement of copyright by reason of the provider referring or linking users to an online location containing infringing material or infringing activity, by using information location tools, including a directory, index, reference, pointer, or hypertext link, if the service provider—

"(1)(A) does not have actual knowledge that the material or activity is infringing;

"(B) in the absence of such actual knowledge, is not aware of facts or circumstances from which infringing activity is apparent; or

"(C) upon obtaining such knowledge or awareness, acts expeditiously to remove, or disable access to, the material;

"(2) does not receive a financial benefit directly attributable to the infringing activity, in a case in which the service provider has the right and ability to control such activity; and

"(3) upon notification of claimed infringement as described in subsection (c)(3), responds expeditiously to remove, or disable access to, the material that is claimed to be infringing or to be the subject of infringing activity, except that, for purposes of this paragraph, the information described in subsection (c)(3)(A)(iii) shall be identification of the reference or link, to material or activity claimed to be infringing, that is to be removed or access to which is to be disabled, and information reasonably sufficient to permit the service provider to locate that reference or link.

"(e) LIMITATION ON LIABILITY OF NONPROFIT EDUCATIONAL INSTITUTIONS.—(1) When a public or other nonprofit institution of higher education is a service provider, and when a faculty member or graduate student who is an employee of such institution is performing a teaching or research function, for the purposes of subsections (a) and (b) such faculty member or graduate student shall be considered to be a person other than the institution, and for the purposes of subsections (c) and (d) such faculty member's or graduate student's knowledge or awareness of his or her infringing activities shall not be attributed to the institution, if—

"(A) such faculty member's or graduate student's infringing activities do not involve the provision of online access to instructional materials that are or were required or recommended, within the preceding 3-year period, for a course taught at the institution by such faculty member or graduate student;

"(B) the institution has not, within the preceding 3-year period, received more than two notifications described in subsection (c)(3) of claimed infringement by such faculty member or graduate student, and such notifications of claimed infringement were not actionable under subsection (f); and

"(C) the institution provides to all users of its system or network informational materials that accurately describe, and promote compliance with, the laws of the United States relating to copyright.

Applicability.

"(2) INJUNCTIONS.—For the purposes of this subsection, the limitations on injunctive relief contained in subsections (j)(2) and (j)(3), but not those in (j)(1), shall apply.

"(f) MISREPRESENTATIONS.—Any person who knowingly materially misrepresents under this section—

"(1) that material or activity is infringing, or

"(2) that material or activity was removed or disabled by mistake or misidentification,

shall be liable for any damages, including costs and attorneys' fees, incurred by the alleged infringer, by any copyright owner or copyright owner's authorized licensee, or by a service provider, who is injured by such misrepresentation, as the result of the service provider relying upon such misrepresentation in removing or disabling access to the material or activity claimed to be infringing, or in replacing the removed material or ceasing to disable access to it.

"(g) REPLACEMENT OF REMOVED OR DISABLED MATERIAL AND LIMITATION ON OTHER LIABILITY.—

"(1) NO LIABILITY FOR TAKING DOWN GENERALLY.—Subject to paragraph (2), a service provider shall not be liable to any person for any claim based on the service provider's good faith disabling of access to, or removal of, material or activity claimed to be infringing or based on facts or circumstances from which infringing activity is apparent, regardless of whether the material or activity is ultimately determined to be infringing.

"(2) EXCEPTION.—Paragraph (1) shall not apply with respect to material residing at the direction of a subscriber of the service provider on a system or network controlled or operated by or for the service provider that is removed, or to which access is disabled by the service provider, pursuant to a notice provided under subsection (c)(1)(C), unless the service provider—

"(A) takes reasonable steps promptly to notify the subscriber that it has removed or disabled access to the material;

PUBLIC LAW 105–304—OCT. 28, 1998   112 STAT. 2883

"(B) upon receipt of a counter notification described in paragraph (3), promptly provides the person who provided the notification under subsection (c)(1)(C) with a copy of the counter notification, and informs that person that it will replace the removed material or cease disabling access to it in 10 business days; and

"(C) replaces the removed material and ceases disabling access to it not less than 10, nor more than 14, business days following receipt of the counter notice, unless its designated agent first receives notice from the person who submitted the notification under subsection (c)(1)(C) that such person has filed an action seeking a court order to restrain the subscriber from engaging in infringing activity relating to the material on the service provider's system or network.

"(3) CONTENTS OF COUNTER NOTIFICATION.—To be effective under this subsection, a counter notification must be a written communication provided to the service provider's designated agent that includes substantially the following:

"(A) A physical or electronic signature of the subscriber.

"(B) Identification of the material that has been removed or to which access has been disabled and the location at which the material appeared before it was removed or access to it was disabled.

"(C) A statement under penalty of perjury that the subscriber has a good faith belief that the material was removed or disabled as a result of mistake or misidentification of the material to be removed or disabled.

"(D) The subscriber's name, address, and telephone number, and a statement that the subscriber consents to the jurisdiction of Federal District Court for the judicial district in which the address is located, or if the subscriber's address is outside of the United States, for any judicial district in which the service provider may be found, and that the subscriber will accept service of process from the person who provided notification under subsection (c)(1)(C) or an agent of such person.

"(4) LIMITATION ON OTHER LIABILITY.—A service provider's compliance with paragraph (2) shall not subject the service provider to liability for copyright infringement with respect to the material identified in the notice provided under subsection (c)(1)(C).

"(h) SUBPOENA TO IDENTIFY INFRINGER.—

"(1) REQUEST.—A copyright owner or a person authorized to act on the owner's behalf may request the clerk of any United States district court to issue a subpoena to a service provider for identification of an alleged infringer in accordance with this subsection.

"(2) CONTENTS OF REQUEST.—The request may be made by filing with the clerk—

"(A) a copy of a notification described in subsection (c)(3)(A);

"(B) a proposed subpoena; and

"(C) a sworn declaration to the effect that the purpose for which the subpoena is sought is to obtain the identity of an alleged infringer and that such information will only be used for the purpose of protecting rights under this title.

"(3) CONTENTS OF SUBPOENA.—The subpoena shall authorize and order the service provider receiving the notification and the subpoena to expeditiously disclose to the copyright owner or person authorized by the copyright owner information sufficient to identify the alleged infringer of the material described in the notification to the extent such information is available to the service provider.

"(4) BASIS FOR GRANTING SUBPOENA.—If the notification filed satisfies the provisions of subsection (c)(3)(A), the proposed subpoena is in proper form, and the accompanying declaration is properly executed, the clerk shall expeditiously issue and sign the proposed subpoena and return it to the requester for delivery to the service provider.

"(5) ACTIONS OF SERVICE PROVIDER RECEIVING SUBPOENA.— Upon receipt of the issued subpoena, either accompanying or subsequent to the receipt of a notification described in subsection (c)(3)(A), the service provider shall expeditiously disclose to the copyright owner or person authorized by the copyright owner the information required by the subpoena, notwithstanding any other provision of law and regardless of whether the service provider responds to the notification.

"(6) RULES APPLICABLE TO SUBPOENA.—Unless otherwise provided by this section or by applicable rules of the court, the procedure for issuance and delivery of the subpoena, and the remedies for noncompliance with the subpoena, shall be governed to the greatest extent practicable by those provisions of the Federal Rules of Civil Procedure governing the issuance, service, and enforcement of a subpoena duces tecum.

"(i) CONDITIONS FOR ELIGIBILITY.—

"(1) ACCOMMODATION OF TECHNOLOGY.—The limitations on liability established by this section shall apply to a service provider only if the service provider—

"(A) has adopted and reasonably implemented, and informs subscribers and account holders of the service provider's system or network of, a policy that provides for the termination in appropriate circumstances of subscribers and account holders of the service provider's system or network who are repeat infringers; and

"(B) accommodates and does not interfere with standard technical measures.

"(2) DEFINITION.—As used in this subsection, the term 'standard technical measures' means technical measures that are used by copyright owners to identify or protect copyrighted works and—

"(A) have been developed pursuant to a broad consensus of copyright owners and service providers in an open, fair, voluntary, multi-industry standards process;

"(B) are available to any person on reasonable and nondiscriminatory terms; and

"(C) do not impose substantial costs on service providers or substantial burdens on their systems or networks.

Applicability.   "(j) INJUNCTIONS.—The following rules shall apply in the case of any application for an injunction under section 502 against a service provider that is not subject to monetary remedies under this section:

PUBLIC LAW 105–304—OCT. 28, 1998   112 STAT. 2885

"(1) SCOPE OF RELIEF.—(A) With respect to conduct other than that which qualifies for the limitation on remedies set forth in subsection (a), the court may grant injunctive relief with respect to a service provider only in one or more of the following forms:

"(i) An order restraining the service provider from providing access to infringing material or activity residing at a particular online site on the provider's system or network.

"(ii) An order restraining the service provider from providing access to a subscriber or account holder of the service provider's system or network who is engaging in infringing activity and is identified in the order, by terminating the accounts of the subscriber or account holder that are specified in the order.

"(iii) Such other injunctive relief as the court may consider necessary to prevent or restrain infringement of copyrighted material specified in the order of the court at a particular online location, if such relief is the least burdensome to the service provider among the forms of relief comparably effective for that purpose.

"(B) If the service provider qualifies for the limitation on remedies described in subsection (a), the court may only grant injunctive relief in one or both of the following forms:

"(i) An order restraining the service provider from providing access to a subscriber or account holder of the service provider's system or network who is using the provider's service to engage in infringing activity and is identified in the order, by terminating the accounts of the subscriber or account holder that are specified in the order.

"(ii) An order restraining the service provider from providing access, by taking reasonable steps specified in the order to block access, to a specific, identified, online location outside the United States.

"(2) CONSIDERATIONS.—The court, in considering the relevant criteria for injunctive relief under applicable law, shall consider—

"(A) whether such an injunction, either alone or in combination with other such injunctions issued against the same service provider under this subsection, would significantly burden either the provider or the operation of the provider's system or network;

"(B) the magnitude of the harm likely to be suffered by the copyright owner in the digital network environment if steps are not taken to prevent or restrain the infringement;

"(C) whether implementation of such an injunction would be technically feasible and effective, and would not interfere with access to noninfringing material at other online locations; and

"(D) whether other less burdensome and comparably effective means of preventing or restraining access to the infringing material are available.

"(3) NOTICE AND EX PARTE ORDERS.—Injunctive relief under this subsection shall be available only after notice to the service provider and an opportunity for the service provider

Courts.

35

112 STAT. 2886   PUBLIC LAW 105–304—OCT. 28, 1998

to appear are provided, except for orders ensuring the preservation of evidence or other orders having no material adverse effect on the operation of the service provider's communications network.

"(k) DEFINITIONS.—

"(1) SERVICE PROVIDER.—(A) As used in subsection (a), the term 'service provider' means an entity offering the transmission, routing, or providing of connections for digital online communications, between or among points specified by a user, of material of the user's choosing, without modification to the content of the material as sent or received.

"(B) As used in this section, other than subsection (a), the term 'service provider' means a provider of online services or network access, or the operator of facilities therefor, and includes an entity described in subparagraph (A).

"(2) MONETARY RELIEF.—As used in this section, the term 'monetary relief' means damages, costs, attorneys' fees, and any other form of monetary payment.

"(l) OTHER DEFENSES NOT AFFECTED.—The failure of a service provider's conduct to qualify for limitation of liability under this section shall not bear adversely upon the consideration of a defense by the service provider that the service provider's conduct is not infringing under this title or any other defense.

"(m) PROTECTION OF PRIVACY.—Nothing in this section shall be construed to condition the applicability of subsections (a) through (d) on—

"(1) a service provider monitoring its service or affirmatively seeking facts indicating infringing activity, except to the extent consistent with a standard technical measure complying with the provisions of subsection (i); or

"(2) a service provider gaining access to, removing, or disabling access to material in cases in which such conduct is prohibited by law.

"(n) CONSTRUCTION.—Subsections (a), (b), (c), and (d) describe separate and distinct functions for purposes of applying this section. Whether a service provider qualifies for the limitation on liability in any one of those subsections shall be based solely on the criteria in that subsection, and shall not affect a determination of whether that service provider qualifies for the limitations on liability under any other such subsection.".

(b) CONFORMING AMENDMENT.—The table of sections for chapter 5 of title 17, United States Code, is amended by adding at the end the following:

"512. Limitations on liability relating to material online.".

17 USC 512 note.   **SEC. 203. EFFECTIVE DATE.**

This title and the amendments made by this title shall take effect on the date of the enactment of this Act.

Computer Maintenance Competition Assurance Act.

TITLE III—COMPUTER MAINTENANCE OR REPAIR COPYRIGHT EXEMPTION

17 USC 101 note.   **SEC. 301. SHORT TITLE.**

This title may be cited as the "Computer Maintenance Competition Assurance Act".

SEC. 302. LIMITATIONS ON EXCLUSIVE RIGHTS; COMPUTER PROGRAMS.

Section 117 of title 17, United States Code, is amended—

(1) by striking "Notwithstanding" and inserting the following:

"(a) MAKING OF ADDITIONAL COPY OR ADAPTATION BY OWNER OF COPY.—Notwithstanding";

(2) by striking "Any exact" and inserting the following:

"(b) LEASE, SALE, OR OTHER TRANSFER OF ADDITIONAL COPY OR ADAPTATION.—Any exact"; and

(3) by adding at the end the following:

"(c) MACHINE MAINTENANCE OR REPAIR.—Notwithstanding the provisions of section 106, it is not an infringement for the owner or lessee of a machine to make or authorize the making of a copy of a computer program if such copy is made solely by virtue of the activation of a machine that lawfully contains an authorized copy of the computer program, for purposes only of maintenance or repair of that machine, if—

"(1) such new copy is used in no other manner and is destroyed immediately after the maintenance or repair is completed; and

"(2) with respect to any computer program or part thereof that is not necessary for that machine to be activated, such program or part thereof is not accessed or used other than to make such new copy by virtue of the activation of the machine.

"(d) DEFINITIONS.—For purposes of this section—

"(1) the 'maintenance' of a machine is the servicing of the machine in order to make it work in accordance with its original specifications and any changes to those specifications authorized for that machine; and

"(2) the 'repair' of a machine is the restoring of the machine to the state of working in accordance with its original specifications and any changes to those specifications authorized for that machine.".

TITLE IV—MISCELLANEOUS PROVISIONS

SEC. 401. PROVISIONS RELATING TO THE COMMISSIONER OF PATENTS AND TRADEMARKS AND THE REGISTER OF COPYRIGHTS

(a) COMPENSATION.—(1) Section 3(d) of title 35, United States Code, is amended by striking "prescribed by law for Assistant Secretaries of Commerce" and inserting "in effect for level III of the Executive Schedule under section 5314 of title 5, United States Code".

(2) Section 701(e) of title 17, United States Code, is amended—

(A) by striking "IV" and inserting "III"; and

(B) by striking "5315" and inserting "5314".

(3) Section 5314 of title 5, United States Code, is amended by adding at the end the following:

"Assistant Secretary of Commerce and Commissioner of Patents and Trademarks.

"Register of Copyrights.".

(b) CLARIFICATION OF AUTHORITY OF THE COPYRIGHT OFFICE.— Section 701 of title 17, United States Code, is amended—

(1) by redesignating subsections (b) through (e) as subsections (c) through (f), respectively; and

(2) by inserting after subsection (a) the following:

"(b) In addition to the functions and duties set out elsewhere in this chapter, the Register of Copyrights shall perform the following functions:

"(1) Advise Congress on national and international issues relating to copyright, other matters arising under this title, and related matters.

"(2) Provide information and assistance to Federal departments and agencies and the Judiciary on national and international issues relating to copyright, other matters arising under this title, and related matters.

"(3) Participate in meetings of international intergovernmental organizations and meetings with foreign government officials relating to copyright, other matters arising under this title, and related matters, including as a member of United States delegations as authorized by the appropriate Executive branch authority.

"(4) Conduct studies and programs regarding copyright, other matters arising under this title, and related matters, the administration of the Copyright Office, or any function vested in the Copyright Office by law, including educational programs conducted cooperatively with foreign intellectual property offices and international intergovernmental organizations.

"(5) Perform such other functions as Congress may direct, or as may be appropriate in furtherance of the functions and duties specifically set forth in this title.".

SEC. 402. EPHEMERAL RECORDINGS.

Section 112(a) of title 17, United States Code, is amended—

(1) by redesignating paragraphs (1), (2), and (3) as subparagraphs (A), (B), and (C), respectively;

(2) by inserting "(1)" after "(a)";

(3) by inserting after "under a license" the following: ", including a statutory license under section 114(f),";

(4) by inserting after "114(a)," the following: "or for a transmitting organization that is a broadcast radio or television station licensed as such by the Federal Communications Commission and that makes a broadcast transmission of a performance of a sound recording in a digital format on a nonsubscription basis,"; and

(5) by adding at the end the following:

"(2) In a case in which a transmitting organization entitled to make a copy or phonorecord under paragraph (1) in connection with the transmission to the public of a performance or display of a work is prevented from making such copy or phonorecord by reason of the application by the copyright owner of technical measures that prevent the reproduction of the work, the copyright owner shall make available to the transmitting organization the necessary means for permitting the making of such copy or phonorecord as permitted under that paragraph, if it is technologically feasible and economically reasonable for the copyright owner to do so. If the copyright owner fails to do so in a timely manner in light of the transmitting organization's reasonable business requirements, the transmitting organization shall not be liable for

PUBLIC LAW 105–304—OCT. 28, 1998   112 STAT. 2889

a violation of section 1201(a)(1) of this title for engaging in such activities as are necessary to make such copies or phonorecords as permitted under paragraph (1) of this subsection.".

SEC. 403. LIMITATIONS ON EXCLUSIVE RIGHTS; DISTANCE EDUCATION.

(a) RECOMMENDATIONS BY REGISTER OF COPYRIGHTS.—Not later than 6 months after the date of the enactment of this Act, the Register of Copyrights, after consultation with representatives of copyright owners, nonprofit educational institutions, and nonprofit libraries and archives, shall submit to the Congress recommendations on how to promote distance education through digital technologies, including interactive digital networks, while maintaining an appropriate balance between the rights of copyright owners and the needs of users of copyrighted works. Such recommendations shall include any legislation the Register of Copyrights considers appropriate to achieve the objective described in the preceding sentence. *Deadline.*

(b) FACTORS.—In formulating recommendations under subsection (a), the Register of Copyrights shall consider—

(1) the need for an exemption from exclusive rights of copyright owners for distance education through digital networks;

(2) the categories of works to be included under any distance education exemption;

(3) the extent of appropriate quantitative limitations on the portions of works that may be used under any distance education exemption;

(4) the parties who should be entitled to the benefits of any distance education exemption;

(5) the parties who should be designated as eligible recipients of distance education materials under any distance education exemption;

(6) whether and what types of technological measures can or should be employed to safeguard against unauthorized access to, and use or retention of, copyrighted materials as a condition of eligibility for any distance education exemption, including, in light of developing technological capabilities, the exemption set out in section 110(2) of title 17, United States Code;

(7) the extent to which the availability of licenses for the use of copyrighted works in distance education through interactive digital networks should be considered in assessing eligibility for any distance education exemption; and

(8) such other issues relating to distance education through interactive digital networks that the Register considers appropriate.

SEC. 404. EXEMPTION FOR LIBRARIES AND ARCHIVES.

Section 108 of title 17, United States Code, is amended—

(1) in subsection (a)—

(A) by striking "Notwithstanding" and inserting "Except as otherwise provided in this title and notwithstanding";

(B) by inserting after "no more than one copy or phonorecord of a work" the following: ", except as provided in subsections (b) and (c)"; and

(C) in paragraph (3) by inserting after "copyright" the following: "that appears on the copy or phonorecord that is reproduced under the provisions of this section, or includes a legend stating that the work may be protected by copyright if no such notice can be found on the copy or phonorecord that is reproduced under the provisions of this section";

(2) in subsection (b)—

(A) by striking "a copy or phonorecord" and inserting "three copies or phonorecords";

(B) by striking "in facsimile form"; and

(C) by striking "if the copy or phonorecord reproduced is currently in the collections of the library or archives." and inserting "if—

"(1) the copy or phonorecord reproduced is currently in the collections of the library or archives; and

"(2) any such copy or phonorecord that is reproduced in digital format is not otherwise distributed in that format and is not made available to the public in that format outside the premises of the library or archives."; and

(3) in subsection (c)—

(A) by striking "a copy or phonorecord" and inserting "three copies or phonorecords";

(B) by striking "in facsimile form";

(C) by inserting "or if the existing format in which the work is stored has become obsolete," after "stolen,";

(D) by striking "if the library or archives has, after a reasonable effort, determined that an unused replacement cannot be obtained at a fair price." and inserting "if—

"(1) the library or archives has, after a reasonable effort, determined that an unused replacement cannot be obtained at a fair price; and

"(2) any such copy or phonorecord that is reproduced in digital format is not made available to the public in that format outside the premises of the library or archives in lawful possession of such copy."; and

(E) by adding at the end the following:

"For purposes of this subsection, a format shall be considered obsolete if the machine or device necessary to render perceptible a work stored in that format is no longer manufactured or is no longer reasonably available in the commercial marketplace.".

SEC. 405. SCOPE OF EXCLUSIVE RIGHTS IN SOUND RECORDINGS; EPHEMERAL RECORDINGS.

(a) Scope of Exclusive Rights in Sound Recordings.—Section 114 of title 17, United States Code, is amended as follows:

(1) Subsection (d) is amended—

(A) in paragraph (1) by striking subparagraph (A) and inserting the following:

"(A) a nonsubscription broadcast transmission;"; and

(B) by amending paragraph (2) to read as follows:

"(2) Statutory licensing of certain transmissions.—The performance of a sound recording publicly by means of a subscription digital audio transmission not exempt under paragraph (1), an eligible nonsubscription transmission, or a transmission not exempt under paragraph (1) that is made by a preexisting satellite digital audio radio service shall be subject to statutory licensing, in accordance with subsection (f) if—

"(A)(i) the transmission is not part of an interactive service;

"(ii) except in the case of a transmission to a business establishment, the transmitting entity does not automatically and intentionally cause any device receiving the transmission to switch from one program channel to another; and

"(iii) except as provided in section 1002(e), the transmission of the sound recording is accompanied, if technically feasible, by the information encoded in that sound recording, if any, by or under the authority of the copyright owner of that sound recording, that identifies the title of the sound recording, the featured recording artist who performs on the sound recording, and related information, including information concerning the underlying musical work and its writer;

"(B) in the case of a subscription transmission not exempt under paragraph (1) that is made by a preexisting subscription service in the same transmission medium used by such service on July 31, 1998, or in the case of a transmission not exempt under paragraph (1) that is made by a preexisting satellite digital audio radio service—

"(i) the transmission does not exceed the sound recording performance complement; and

"(ii) the transmitting entity does not cause to be published by means of an advance program schedule or prior announcement the titles of the specific sound recordings or phonorecords embodying such sound recordings to be transmitted; and

"(C) in the case of an eligible nonsubscription transmission or a subscription transmission not exempt under paragraph (1) that is made by a new subscription service or by a preexisting subscription service other than in the same transmission medium used by such service on July 31, 1998—

"(i) the transmission does not exceed the sound recording performance complement, except that this requirement shall not apply in the case of a retransmission of a broadcast transmission if the retransmission is made by a transmitting entity that does not have the right or ability to control the programming of the broadcast station making the broadcast transmission, unless—

"(I) the broadcast station makes broadcast transmissions—

"(aa) in digital format that regularly exceed the sound recording performance complement; or

"(bb) in analog format, a substantial portion of which, on a weekly basis, exceed the sound recording performance complement; and

"(II) the sound recording copyright owner or its representative has notified the transmitting entity in writing that broadcast transmissions of the copyright owner's sound recordings exceed the sound recording performance complement as provided in this clause;

"(ii) the transmitting entity does not cause to be published, or induce or facilitate the publication, by means of an advance program schedule or prior announcement, the titles of the specific sound recordings to be transmitted, the phonorecords embodying such sound recordings, or, other than for illustrative purposes, the names of the featured recording artists, except that this clause does not disqualify a transmitting entity that makes a prior announcement that a particular artist will be featured within an unspecified future time period, and in the case of a retransmission of a broadcast transmission by a transmitting entity that does not have the right or ability to control the programming of the broadcast transmission, the requirement of this clause shall not apply to a prior oral announcement by the broadcast station, or to an advance program schedule published, induced, or facilitated by the broadcast station, if the transmitting entity does not have actual knowledge and has not received written notice from the copyright owner or its representative that the broadcast station publishes or induces or facilitates the publication of such advance program schedule, or if such advance program schedule is a schedule of classical music programming published by the broadcast station in the same manner as published by that broadcast station on or before September 30, 1998;

"(iii) the transmission—

"(I) is not part of an archived program of less than 5 hours duration;

"(II) is not part of an archived program of 5 hours or greater in duration that is made available for a period exceeding 2 weeks;

"(III) is not part of a continuous program which is of less than 3 hours duration; or

"(IV) is not part of an identifiable program in which performances of sound recordings are rendered in a predetermined order, other than an archived or continuous program, that is transmitted at—

"(aa) more than 3 times in any 2-week period that have been publicly announced in advance, in the case of a program of less than 1 hour in duration, or

"(bb) more than 4 times in any 2-week period that have been publicly announced in advance, in the case of a program of 1 hour or more in duration,

except that the requirement of this subclause shall not apply in the case of a retransmission of a broadcast transmission by a transmitting entity that does not have the right or ability to control the programming of the broadcast transmission, unless the transmitting entity is given notice in writing by the copyright owner of the sound recording that the broadcast station makes broadcast

transmissions that regularly violate such requirement;

"(iv) the transmitting entity does not knowingly
perform the sound recording, as part of a service that
offers transmissions of visual images contemporaneously with transmissions of sound recordings, in a
manner that is likely to cause confusion, to cause mistake, or to deceive, as to the affiliation, connection,
or association of the copyright owner or featured
recording artist with the transmitting entity or a
particular product or service advertised by the
transmitting entity, or as to the origin, sponsorship,
or approval by the copyright owner or featured recording artist of the activities of the transmitting entity
other than the performance of the sound recording
itself;

"(v) the transmitting entity cooperates to prevent,
to the extent feasible without imposing substantial
costs or burdens, a transmission recipient or any other
person or entity from automatically scanning the
transmitting entity's transmissions alone or together
with transmissions by other transmitting entities in
order to select a particular sound recording to be
transmitted to the transmission recipient, except that
the requirement of this clause shall not apply to a
satellite digital audio service that is in operation, or
that is licensed by the Federal Communications
Commission, on or before July 31, 1998;

"(vi) the transmitting entity takes no affirmative
steps to cause or induce the making of a phonorecord
by the transmission recipient, and if the technology
used by the transmitting entity enables the transmitting entity to limit the making by the transmission
recipient of phonorecords of the transmission directly
in a digital format, the transmitting entity sets such
technology to limit such making of phonorecords to
the extent permitted by such technology;

"(vii) phonorecords of the sound recording have
been distributed to the public under the authority of
the copyright owner or the copyright owner authorizes
the transmitting entity to transmit the sound recording, and the transmitting entity makes the transmission from a phonorecord lawfully made under the
authority of the copyright owner, except that the
requirement of this clause shall not apply to a retransmission of a broadcast transmission by a transmitting
entity that does not have the right or ability to control
the programming of the broadcast transmission, unless
the transmitting entity is given notice in writing by
the copyright owner of the sound recording that the
broadcast station makes broadcast transmissions that
regularly violate such requirement;

"(viii) the transmitting entity accommodates and
does not interfere with the transmission of technical
measures that are widely used by sound recording
copyright owners to identify or protect copyrighted
works, and that are technically feasible of being

transmitted by the transmitting entity without imposing substantial costs on the transmitting entity or resulting in perceptible aural or visual degradation of the digital signal, except that the requirement of this clause shall not apply to a satellite digital audio service that is in operation, or that is licensed under the authority of the Federal Communications Commission, on or before July 31, 1998, to the extent that such service has designed, developed, or made commitments to procure equipment or technology that is not compatible with such technical measures before such technical measures are widely adopted by sound recording copyright owners; and

"(ix) the transmitting entity identifies in textual data the sound recording during, but not before, the time it is performed, including the title of the sound recording, the title of the phonorecord embodying such sound recording, if any, and the featured recording artist, in a manner to permit it to be displayed to the transmission recipient by the device or technology intended for receiving the service provided by the transmitting entity, except that the obligation in this clause shall not take effect until 1 year after the date of the enactment of the Digital Millennium Copyright Act and shall not apply in the case of a retransmission of a broadcast transmission by a transmitting entity that does not have the right or ability to control the programming of the broadcast transmission, or in the case in which devices or technology intended for receiving the service provided by the transmitting entity that have the capability to display such textual data are not common in the marketplace.".

(2) Subsection (f) is amended—

(A) in the subsection heading by striking "NONEXEMPT SUBSCRIPTION" and inserting "CERTAIN NONEXEMPT";

(B) in paragraph (1)—

(i) in the first sentence—

(I) by striking "(1) No" and inserting "(1)(A) No";

(II) by striking "the activities" and inserting "subscription transmissions by preexisting subscription services and transmissions by preexisting satellite digital audio radio services"; and

(III) by striking "2000" and inserting "2001"; and

(ii) by amending the third sentence to read as follows: "Any copyright owners of sound recordings, preexisting subscription services, or preexisting satellite digital audio radio services may submit to the Librarian of Congress licenses covering such subscription transmissions with respect to such sound recordings."; and

(C) by striking paragraphs (2), (3), (4), and (5) and inserting the following:

Federal Register, publication.

"(B) In the absence of license agreements negotiated under subparagraph (A), during the 60-day period commencing 6 months after publication of the notice specified in subparagraph (A), and upon the filing of a petition in accordance with section 803(a)(1), the Librarian of Congress shall, pursuant to chapter 8, convene a copyright arbitration royalty panel to determine and publish in the Federal Register a schedule of rates and terms which, subject to paragraph (3), shall be binding on all copyright owners of sound recordings and entities performing sound recordings affected by this paragraph. In establishing rates and terms for preexisting subscription services and preexisting satellite digital audio radio services, in addition to the objectives set forth in section 801(b)(1), the copyright arbitration royalty panel may consider the rates and terms for comparable types of subscription digital audio transmission services and comparable circumstances under voluntary license agreements negotiated as provided in subparagraph (A).

"(C)(i) Publication of a notice of the initiation of voluntary negotiation proceedings as specified in subparagraph (A) shall be repeated, in accordance with regulations that the Librarian of Congress shall prescribe— *Regulations.*

"(I) no later than 30 days after a petition is filed by any copyright owners of sound recordings, any preexisting subscription services, or any preexisting satellite digital audio radio services indicating that a new type of subscription digital audio transmission service on which sound recordings are performed is or is about to become operational; and

"(II) in the first week of January 2001, and at 5-year intervals thereafter.

"(ii) The procedures specified in subparagraph (B) shall be repeated, in accordance with regulations that the Librarian of Congress shall prescribe, upon filing of a petition in accordance with section 803(a)(1) during a 60-day period commencing—

"(I) 6 months after publication of a notice of the initiation of voluntary negotiation proceedings under subparagraph (A) pursuant to a petition under clause (i)(I) of this subparagraph; or

"(II) on July 1, 2001, and at 5-year intervals thereafter.

"(iii) The procedures specified in subparagraph (B) shall be concluded in accordance with section 802.

"(2)(A) No later than 30 days after the date of the enactment of the Digital Millennium Copyright Act, the Librarian of Congress shall cause notice to be published in the Federal Register of the initiation of voluntary negotiation proceedings for the purpose of determining reasonable terms and rates of royalty payments for public performances of sound recordings by means of eligible nonsubscription transmissions and transmissions by new subscription services specified by subsection (d)(2) during the period beginning on the date of the enactment of such Act and ending on December 31, 2000, or such other date as the parties may agree. Such rates and terms shall distinguish among the different types of eligible nonsubscription transmission services and new subscription services then in operation and shall include a minimum fee for each such type of service. Any copyright owners of sound recordings or any entities performing sound recordings affected by this paragraph may submit to the Librarian of Congress licenses covering *Deadline. Federal Register, publication. Notice.*

such eligible nonsubscription transmissions and new subscription services with respect to such sound recordings. The parties to each negotiation proceeding shall bear their own costs.

Federal Register, publication.

"(B) In the absence of license agreements negotiated under subparagraph (A), during the 60-day period commencing 6 months after publication of the notice specified in subparagraph (A), and upon the filing of a petition in accordance with section 803(a)(1), the Librarian of Congress shall, pursuant to chapter 8, convene a copyright arbitration royalty panel to determine and publish in the Federal Register a schedule of rates and terms which, subject to paragraph (3), shall be binding on all copyright owners of sound recordings and entities performing sound recordings affected by this paragraph during the period beginning on the date of the enactment of the Digital Millennium Copyright Act and ending on December 31, 2000, or such other date as the parties may agree. Such rates and terms shall distinguish among the different types of eligible nonsubscription transmission services then in operation and shall include a minimum fee for each such type of service, such differences to be based on criteria including, but not limited to, the quantity and nature of the use of sound recordings and the degree to which use of the service may substitute for or may promote the purchase of phonorecords by consumers. In establishing rates and terms for transmissions by eligible nonsubscription services and new subscription services, the copyright arbitration royalty panel shall establish rates and terms that most clearly represent the rates and terms that would have been negotiated in the marketplace between a willing buyer and a willing seller. In determining such rates and terms, the copyright arbitration royalty panel shall base its decision on economic, competitive and programming information presented by the parties, including—

"(i) whether use of the service may substitute for or may promote the sales of phonorecords or otherwise may interfere with or may enhance the sound recording copyright owner's other streams of revenue from its sound recordings; and

"(ii) the relative roles of the copyright owner and the transmitting entity in the copyrighted work and the service made available to the public with respect to relative creative contribution, technological contribution, capital investment, cost, and risk.

In establishing such rates and terms, the copyright arbitration royalty panel may consider the rates and terms for comparable types of digital audio transmission services and comparable circumstances under voluntary license agreements negotiated under subparagraph (A).

Regulations.

"(C)(i) Publication of a notice of the initiation of voluntary negotiation proceedings as specified in subparagraph (A) shall be repeated in accordance with regulations that the Librarian of Congress shall prescribe—

"(I) no later than 30 days after a petition is filed by any copyright owners of sound recordings or any eligible nonsubscription service or new subscription service indicating that a new type of eligible nonsubscription service or new subscription service on which sound recordings are performed is or is about to become operational; and

"(II) in the first week of January 2000, and at 2-year intervals thereafter, except to the extent that different years for the repeating of such proceedings may be determined in accordance with subparagraph (A).

"(ii) The procedures specified in subparagraph (B) shall be repeated, in accordance with regulations that the Librarian of Congress shall prescribe, upon filing of a petition in accordance with section 803(a)(1) during a 60-day period commencing—

"(I) 6 months after publication of a notice of the initiation of voluntary negotiation proceedings under subparagraph (A) pursuant to a petition under clause (i)(I); or

"(II) on July 1, 2000, and at 2-year intervals thereafter, except to the extent that different years for the repeating of such proceedings may be determined in accordance with subparagraph (A).

"(iii) The procedures specified in subparagraph (B) shall be concluded in accordance with section 802.

"(3) License agreements voluntarily negotiated at any time between 1 or more copyright owners of sound recordings and 1 or more entities performing sound recordings shall be given effect in lieu of any determination by a copyright arbitration royalty panel or decision by the Librarian of Congress.

"(4)(A) The Librarian of Congress shall also establish requirements by which copyright owners may receive reasonable notice of the use of their sound recordings under this section, and under which records of such use shall be kept and made available by entities performing sound recordings.

"(B) Any person who wishes to perform a sound recording publicly by means of a transmission eligible for statutory licensing under this subsection may do so without infringing the exclusive right of the copyright owner of the sound recording—

"(i) by complying with such notice requirements as the Librarian of Congress shall prescribe by regulation and by paying royalty fees in accordance with this subsection; or

Regulations.

"(ii) if such royalty fees have not been set, by agreeing to pay such royalty fees as shall be determined in accordance with this subsection.

"(C) Any royalty payments in arrears shall be made on or before the twentieth day of the month next succeeding the month in which the royalty fees are set.".

(3) Subsection (g) is amended—

(A) in the subsection heading by striking "SUBSCRIPTION";

(B) in paragraph (1) in the matter preceding subparagraph (A), by striking "subscription transmission licensed" and inserting "transmission licensed under a statutory license";

(C) in subparagraphs (A) and (B) by striking "subscription"; and

(D) in paragraph (2) by striking "subscription".

(4) Subsection (j) is amended—

(A) by striking paragraphs (4) and (9) and redesignating paragraphs (2), (3), (5), (6), (7), and (8) as paragraphs (3), (5), (9), (12), (13), and (14), respectively;

(B) by inserting after paragraph (1) the following:

"(2) An 'archived program' is a predetermined program that is available repeatedly on the demand of the transmission recipient and that is performed in the same order from the beginning, except that an archived program shall not include a recorded event or broadcast transmission that makes no more than an incidental use of sound recordings, as long as such recorded event or broadcast transmission does not contain an entire sound recording or feature a particular sound recording.";

(C) by inserting after paragraph (3), as so redesignated, the following:

"(4) A 'continuous program' is a predetermined program that is continuously performed in the same order and that is accessed at a point in the program that is beyond the control of the transmission recipient.";

(D) by inserting after paragraph (5), as so redesignated, the following:

"(6) An 'eligible nonsubscription transmission' is a noninteractive nonsubscription digital audio transmission not exempt under subsection (d)(1) that is made as part of a service that provides audio programming consisting, in whole or in part, of performances of sound recordings, including retransmissions of broadcast transmissions, if the primary purpose of the service is to provide to the public such audio or other entertainment programming, and the primary purpose of the service is not to sell, advertise, or promote particular products or services other than sound recordings, live concerts, or other music-related events.

"(7) An 'interactive service' is one that enables a member of the public to receive a transmission of a program specially created for the recipient, or on request, a transmission of a particular sound recording, whether or not as part of a program, which is selected by or on behalf of the recipient. The ability of individuals to request that particular sound recordings be performed for reception by the public at large, or in the case of a subscription service, by all subscribers of the service, does not make a service interactive, if the programming on each channel of the service does not substantially consist of sound recordings that are performed within 1 hour of the request or at a time designated by either the transmitting entity or the individual making such request. If an entity offers both interactive and noninteractive services (either concurrently or at different times), the noninteractive component shall not be treated as part of an interactive service.

"(8) A 'new subscription service' is a service that performs sound recordings by means of noninteractive subscription digital audio transmissions and that is not a preexisting subscription service or a preexisting satellite digital audio radio service.";

(E) by inserting after paragraph (9), as so redesignated, the following:

"(10) A 'preexisting satellite digital audio radio service' is a subscription satellite digital audio radio service provided pursuant to a satellite digital audio radio service license issued by the Federal Communications Commission on or before July 31, 1998, and any renewal of such license to the extent of

PUBLIC LAW 105–304—OCT. 28, 1998   112 STAT. 2899

the scope of the original license, and may include a limited number of sample channels representative of the subscription service that are made available on a nonsubscription basis in order to promote the subscription service.

"(11) A 'preexisting subscription service' is a service that performs sound recordings by means of noninteractive audio-only subscription digital audio transmissions, which was in existence and was making such transmissions to the public for a fee on or before July 31, 1998, and may include a limited number of sample channels representative of the subscription service that are made available on a nonsubscription basis in order to promote the subscription service."; and

(F) by adding at the end the following:

"(15) A 'transmission' is either an initial transmission or a retransmission.".

(5) The amendment made by paragraph (2)(B)(i)(III) of this subsection shall be deemed to have been enacted as part of the Digital Performance Right in Sound Recordings Act of 1995, and the publication of notice of proceedings under section 114(f)(1) of title 17, United States Code, as in effect upon the effective date of that Act, for the determination of royalty payments shall be deemed to have been made for the period beginning on the effective date of that Act and ending on December 1, 2001. *17 USC 114 note.*

(6) The amendments made by this subsection do not annul, limit, or otherwise impair the rights that are preserved by section 114 of title 17, United States Code, including the rights preserved by subsections (c), (d)(4), and (i) of such section. *17 USC 114 note.*

(b) EPHEMERAL RECORDINGS.—Section 112 of title 17, United States Code, is amended—

(1) by redesignating subsection (e) as subsection (f); and

(2) by inserting after subsection (d) the following:

"(e) STATUTORY LICENSE.—(1) A transmitting organization entitled to transmit to the public a performance of a sound recording under the limitation on exclusive rights specified by section 114(d)(1)(C)(iv) or under a statutory license in accordance with section 114(f) is entitled to a statutory license, under the conditions specified by this subsection, to make no more than 1 phonorecord of the sound recording (unless the terms and conditions of the statutory license allow for more), if the following conditions are satisfied:

"(A) The phonorecord is retained and used solely by the transmitting organization that made it, and no further phonorecords are reproduced from it.

"(B) The phonorecord is used solely for the transmitting organization's own transmissions originating in the United States under a statutory license in accordance with section 114(f) or the limitation on exclusive rights specified by section 114(d)(1)(C)(iv).

"(C) Unless preserved exclusively for purposes of archival preservation, the phonorecord is destroyed within 6 months from the date the sound recording was first transmitted to the public using the phonorecord.

"(D) Phonorecords of the sound recording have been distributed to the public under the authority of the copyright owner or the copyright owner authorizes the transmitting entity to transmit the sound recording, and the transmitting entity

112 STAT. 2900   PUBLIC LAW 105–304—OCT. 28, 1998

makes the phonorecord under this subsection from a phono-record lawfully made and acquired under the authority of the copyright owner.

"(3) Notwithstanding any provision of the antitrust laws, any copyright owners of sound recordings and any transmitting organizations entitled to a statutory license under this subsection may negotiate and agree upon royalty rates and license terms and conditions for making phonorecords of such sound recordings under this section and the proportionate division of fees paid among copyright owners, and may designate common agents to negotiate, agree to, pay, or receive such royalty payments.

Deadline.
Federal Register, publication.
Notice.

"(4) No later than 30 days after the date of the enactment of the Digital Millennium Copyright Act, the Librarian of Congress shall cause notice to be published in the Federal Register of the initiation of voluntary negotiation proceedings for the purpose of determining reasonable terms and rates of royalty payments for the activities specified by paragraph (2) of this subsection during the period beginning on the date of the enactment of such Act and ending on December 31, 2000, or such other date as the parties may agree. Such rates shall include a minimum fee for each type of service offered by transmitting organizations. Any copyright owners of sound recordings or any transmitting organizations entitled to a statutory license under this subsection may submit to the Librarian of Congress licenses covering such activities with respect to such sound recordings. The parties to each negotiation proceeding shall bear their own costs.

Federal Register, publication.

"(5) In the absence of license agreements negotiated under paragraph (3), during the 60-day period commencing 6 months after publication of the notice specified in paragraph (4), and upon the filing of a petition in accordance with section 803(a)(1), the Librarian of Congress shall, pursuant to chapter 8, convene a copyright arbitration royalty panel to determine and publish in the Federal Register a schedule of reasonable rates and terms which, subject to paragraph (6), shall be binding on all copyright owners of sound recordings and transmitting organizations entitled to a statutory license under this subsection during the period beginning on the date of the enactment of the Digital Millennium Copyright Act and ending on December 31, 2000, or such other date as the parties may agree. Such rates shall include a minimum fee for each type of service offered by transmitting organizations. The copyright arbitration royalty panel shall establish rates that most clearly represent the fees that would have been negotiated in the marketplace between a willing buyer and a willing seller. In determining such rates and terms, the copyright arbitration royalty panel shall base its decision on economic, competitive, and programming information presented by the parties, including—

"(A) whether use of the service may substitute for or may promote the sales of phonorecords or otherwise interferes with or enhances the copyright owner's traditional streams of revenue; and

"(B) the relative roles of the copyright owner and the transmitting organization in the copyrighted work and the service made available to the public with respect to relative creative contribution, technological contribution, capital investment, cost, and risk.

In establishing such rates and terms, the copyright arbitration royalty panel may consider the rates and terms under voluntary license agreements negotiated as provided in paragraphs (3) and (4). The Librarian of Congress shall also establish requirements by which copyright owners may receive reasonable notice of the use of their sound recordings under this section, and under which records of such use shall be kept and made available by transmitting organizations entitled to obtain a statutory license under this subsection.

"(6) License agreements voluntarily negotiated at any time between 1 or more copyright owners of sound recordings and 1 or more transmitting organizations entitled to obtain a statutory license under this subsection shall be given effect in lieu of any determination by a copyright arbitration royalty panel or decision by the Librarian of Congress.

"(7) Publication of a notice of the initiation of voluntary negotia- Regulations. tion proceedings as specified in paragraph (4) shall be repeated, in accordance with regulations that the Librarian of Congress shall prescribe, in the first week of January 2000, and at 2-year intervals thereafter, except to the extent that different years for the repeating of such proceedings may be determined in accordance with paragraph (4). The procedures specified in paragraph (5) shall be repeated, in accordance with regulations that the Librarian of Congress shall prescribe, upon filing of a petition in accordance with section 803(a)(1), during a 60-day period commencing on July 1, 2000, and at 2-year intervals thereafter, except to the extent that different years for the repeating of such proceedings may be determined in accordance with paragraph (4). The procedures specified in paragraph (5) shall be concluded in accordance with section 802.

"(8)(A) Any person who wishes to make a phonorecord of a sound recording under a statutory license in accordance with this subsection may do so without infringing the exclusive right of the copyright owner of the sound recording under section 106(1)—

"(i) by complying with such notice requirements as the Librarian of Congress shall prescribe by regulation and by paying royalty fees in accordance with this subsection; or

"(ii) if such royalty fees have not been set, by agreeing to pay such royalty fees as shall be determined in accordance with this subsection.

"(B) Any royalty payments in arrears shall be made on or before the 20th day of the month next succeeding the month in which the royalty fees are set.

"(9) If a transmitting organization entitled to make a phonorecord under this subsection is prevented from making such phonorecord by reason of the application by the copyright owner of technical measures that prevent the reproduction of the sound recording, the copyright owner shall make available to the transmitting organization the necessary means for permitting the making of such phonorecord as permitted under this subsection, if it is technologically feasible and economically reasonable for the copyright owner to do so. If the copyright owner fails to do so in a timely manner in light of the transmitting organization's reasonable business requirements, the transmitting organization shall not be liable for a violation of section 1201(a)(1) of this title for engaging in such activities as are necessary to make such phonorecords as permitted under this subsection.

"(10) Nothing in this subsection annuls, limits, impairs, or otherwise affects in any way the existence or value of any of the exclusive rights of the copyright owners in a sound recording, except as otherwise provided in this subsection, or in a musical work, including the exclusive rights to reproduce and distribute a sound recording or musical work, including by means of a digital phonorecord delivery, under sections 106(1), 106(3), and 115, and the right to perform publicly a sound recording or musical work, including by means of a digital audio transmission, under sections 106(4) and 106(6).".

17 USC 112 note.

(c) SCOPE OF SECTION 112(a) OF TITLE 17 NOT AFFECTED.—Nothing in this section or the amendments made by this section shall affect the scope of section 112(a) of title 17, United States Code, or the entitlement of any person to an exemption thereunder.

(d) PROCEDURAL AMENDMENTS TO CHAPTER 8.—Section 802 of title 17, United States Code, is amended—

(1) in subsection (f)—

(A) in the first sentence by striking "60" and inserting "90"; and

(B) in the third sentence by striking "that 60-day period" and inserting "an additional 30-day period"; and

(2) in subsection (g) by inserting after the second sentence the following: "When this title provides that the royalty rates or terms that were previously in effect are to expire on a specified date, any adjustment by the Librarian of those rates or terms shall be effective as of the day following the date of expiration of the rates or terms that were previously in effect, even if the Librarian's decision is rendered on a later date.".

(e) CONFORMING AMENDMENTS.—(1) Section 801(b)(1) of title 17, United States Code, is amended in the second sentence by striking "sections 114, 115, and 116" and inserting "sections 114(f)(1)(B), 115, and 116".

(2) Section 802(c) of title 17, United States Code, is amended by striking "section 111, 114, 116, or 119, any person entitled to a compulsory license" and inserting "section 111, 112, 114, 116, or 119, any transmitting organization entitled to a statutory license under section 112(f), any person entitled to a statutory license".

(3) Section 802(g) of title 17, United States Code, is amended by striking "sections 111, 114" and inserting "sections 111, 112, 114".

(4) Section 802(h)(2) of title 17, United States Code, is amended by striking "section 111, 114" and inserting "section 111, 112, 114".

(5) Section 803(a)(1) of title 17, United States Code, is amended by striking "sections 114, 115" and inserting "sections 112, 114, 115".

(6) Section 803(a)(5) of title 17, United States Code, is amended—

(A) by striking "section 114" and inserting "section 112 or 114"; and

(B) by striking "that section" and inserting "those sections".

SEC. 406. ASSUMPTION OF CONTRACTUAL OBLIGATIONS RELATED TO TRANSFERS OF RIGHTS IN MOTION PICTURES.

(a) IN GENERAL.—Part VI of title 28, United States Code, is amended by adding at the end the following new chapter:

"CHAPTER 180—ASSUMPTION OF CERTAIN CONTRACTUAL OBLIGATIONS

"Sec. 4001. Assumption of contractual obligations related to transfers of rights in motion pictures.

"§ 4001. Assumption of contractual obligations related to transfers of rights in motion pictures

"(a) ASSUMPTION OF OBLIGATIONS.—(1) In the case of a transfer of copyright ownership under United States law in a motion picture (as the terms 'transfer of copyright ownership' and 'motion picture' are defined in section 101 of title 17) that is produced subject to 1 or more collective bargaining agreements negotiated under the laws of the United States, if the transfer is executed on or after the effective date of this chapter and is not limited to public performance rights, the transfer instrument shall be deemed to incorporate the assumption agreements applicable to the copyright ownership being transferred that are required by the applicable collective bargaining agreement, and the transferee shall be subject to the obligations under each such assumption agreement to make residual payments and provide related notices, accruing after the effective date of the transfer and applicable to the exploitation of the rights transferred, and any remedies under each such assumption agreement for breach of those obligations, as those obligations and remedies are set forth in the applicable collective bargaining agreement, if—

"(A) the transferee knows or has reason to know at the time of the transfer that such collective bargaining agreement was or will be applicable to the motion picture; or

"(B) in the event of a court order confirming an arbitration award against the transferor under the collective bargaining agreement, the transferor does not have the financial ability to satisfy the award within 90 days after the order is issued.

"(2) For purposes of paragraph (1)(A), 'knows or has reason to know' means any of the following:

"(A) Actual knowledge that the collective bargaining agreement was or will be applicable to the motion picture.

"(B)(i) Constructive knowledge that the collective bargaining agreement was or will be applicable to the motion picture, arising from recordation of a document pertaining to copyright in the motion picture under section 205 of title 17 or from publication, at a site available to the public on-line that is operated by the relevant union, of information that identifies the motion picture as subject to a collective bargaining agreement with that union, if the site permits commercially reasonable verification of the date on which the information was available for access.

"(ii) Clause (i) applies only if the transfer referred to in subsection (a)(1) occurs— *Applicability.*

"(I) after the motion picture is completed, or

"(II) before the motion picture is completed and—

"(aa) within 18 months before the filing of an application for copyright registration for the motion picture under section 408 of title 17, or

"(bb) if no such application is filed, within 18 months before the first publication of the motion picture in the United States.

"(C) Awareness of other facts and circumstances pertaining to a particular transfer from which it is apparent that the collective bargaining agreement was or will be applicable to the motion picture.

"(b) SCOPE OF EXCLUSION OF TRANSFERS OF PUBLIC PERFORMANCE RIGHTS.—For purposes of this section, the exclusion under subsection (a) of transfers of copyright ownership in a motion picture that are limited to public performance rights includes transfers to a terrestrial broadcast station, cable system, or programmer to the extent that the station, system, or programmer is functioning as an exhibitor of the motion picture, either by exhibiting the motion picture on its own network, system, service, or station, or by initiating the transmission of an exhibition that is carried on another network, system, service, or station. When a terrestrial broadcast station, cable system, or programmer, or other transferee, is also functioning otherwise as a distributor or as a producer of the motion picture, the public performance exclusion does not affect any obligations imposed on the transferee to the extent that it is engaging in such functions.

"(c) EXCLUSION FOR GRANTS OF SECURITY INTERESTS.—Subsection (a) shall not apply to—

"(1) a transfer of copyright ownership consisting solely of a mortgage, hypothecation, or other security interest; or

"(2) a subsequent transfer of the copyright ownership secured by the security interest described in paragraph (1) by or under the authority of the secured party, including a transfer through the exercise of the secured party's rights or remedies as a secured party, or by a subsequent transferee.

The exclusion under this subsection shall not affect any rights or remedies under law or contract.

"(d) DEFERRAL PENDING RESOLUTION OF BONA FIDE DISPUTE.— A transferee on which obligations are imposed under subsection (a) by virtue of paragraph (1) of that subsection may elect to defer performance of such obligations that are subject to a bona fide dispute between a union and a prior transferor until that dispute is resolved, except that such deferral shall not stay accrual of any union claims due under an applicable collective bargaining agreement.

"(e) SCOPE OF OBLIGATIONS DETERMINED BY PRIVATE AGREEMENT.—Nothing in this section shall expand or diminish the rights, obligations, or remedies of any person under the collective bargaining agreements or assumption agreements referred to in this section.

"(f) FAILURE TO NOTIFY.—If the transferor under subsection (a) fails to notify the transferee under subsection (a) of applicable collective bargaining obligations before the execution of the transfer instrument, and subsection (a) is made applicable to the transferee solely by virtue of subsection (a)(1)(B), the transferor shall be liable to the transferee for any damages suffered by the transferee as a result of the failure to notify.

"(g) DETERMINATION OF DISPUTES AND CLAIMS.—Any dispute concerning the application of subsections (a) through (f) shall be determined by an action in United States district court, and the court in its discretion may allow the recovery of full costs by or against any party and may also award a reasonable attorney's fee to the prevailing party as part of the costs.

PUBLIC LAW 105–304—OCT. 28, 1998   112 STAT. 2905

"(h) STUDY.—The Comptroller General, in consultation with the Register of Copyrights, shall conduct a study of the conditions in the motion picture industry that gave rise to this section, and the impact of this section on the motion picture industry. The Comptroller General shall report the findings of the study to the Congress within 2 years after the effective date of this chapter.".

Reports.

(b) CONFORMING AMENDMENT.—The table of chapters for part VI of title 28, United States Code, is amended by adding at the end the following:

"180. **Assumption of Certain Contractual Obligations** .... 4001".

SEC. 407. EFFECTIVE DATE.

17 USC 108 note.

Except as otherwise provided in this title, this title and the amendments made by this title shall take effect on the date of the enactment of this Act.

TITLE V—PROTECTION OF CERTAIN ORIGINAL DESIGNS

Vessel Hull Design Protection Act.

SEC. 501. SHORT TITLE.

17 USC 101 note.

This Act may be referred to as the "Vessel Hull Design Protection Act".

SEC. 502. PROTECTION OF CERTAIN ORIGINAL DESIGNS.

Title 17, United States Code, is amended by adding at the end the following new chapter:

"CHAPTER 13—PROTECTION OF ORIGINAL DESIGNS

"§ 1301. Designs protected

"(a) DESIGNS PROTECTED.—

"(1) IN GENERAL.—The designer or other owner of an original design of a useful article which makes the article attractive or distinctive in appearance to the purchasing or using public may secure the protection provided by this chapter upon complying with and subject to this chapter.

"(2) VESSEL HULLS.—The design of a vessel hull, including a plug or mold, is subject to protection under this chapter, notwithstanding section 1302(4).

"(b) DEFINITIONS.—For the purpose of this chapter, the following terms have the following meanings:

"(1) A design is 'original' if it is the result of the designer's creative endeavor that provides a distinguishable variation over prior work pertaining to similar articles which is more than merely trivial and has not been copied from another source.

"(2) A 'useful article' is a vessel hull, including a plug or mold, which in normal use has an intrinsic utilitarian function that is not merely to portray the appearance of the article or to convey information. An article which normally is part of a useful article shall be deemed to be a useful article.

"(3) A 'vessel' is a craft, especially one larger than a rowboat, designed to navigate on water, but does not include any such craft that exceeds 200 feet in length.

"(4) A 'hull' is the frame or body of a vessel, including the deck of a vessel, exclusive of masts, sails, yards, and rigging.

"(5) A 'plug' means a device or model used to make a mold for the purpose of exact duplication, regardless of whether the device or model has an intrinsic utilitarian function that is not only to portray the appearance of the product or to convey information.

"(6) A 'mold' means a matrix or form in which a substance for material is used, regardless of whether the matrix or form has an intrinsic utilitarian function that is not only to portray the appearance of the product or to convey information.

"§ 1302. Designs not subject to protection

"Protection under this chapter shall not be available for a design that is—

"(1) not original;

"(2) staple or commonplace, such as a standard geometric figure, a familiar symbol, an emblem, or a motif, or another shape, pattern, or configuration which has become standard, common, prevalent, or ordinary;

"(3) different from a design excluded by paragraph (2) only in insignificant details or in elements which are variants commonly used in the relevant trades;

"(4) dictated solely by a utilitarian function of the article that embodies it; or

"(5) embodied in a useful article that was made public by the designer or owner in the United States or a foreign country more than 1 year before the date of the application for registration under this chapter.

"§ 1303. Revisions, adaptations, and rearrangements

"Protection for a design under this chapter shall be available notwithstanding the employment in the design of subject matter excluded from protection under section 1302 if the design is a substantial revision, adaptation, or rearrangement of such subject matter. Such protection shall be independent of any subsisting protection in subject matter employed in the design, and shall not be construed as securing any right to subject matter excluded from protection under this chapter or as extending any subsisting protection under this chapter.

"§ 1304. Commencement of protection

"The protection provided for a design under this chapter shall commence upon the earlier of the date of publication of the registration under section 1313(a) or the date the design is first made public as defined by section 1310(b).

"§ 1305. Term of protection

"(a) IN GENERAL.—Subject to subsection (b), the protection provided under this chapter for a design shall continue for a term of 10 years beginning on the date of the commencement of protection under section 1304.

"(b) EXPIRATION.—All terms of protection provided in this section shall run to the end of the calendar year in which they would otherwise expire.

"(c) TERMINATION OF RIGHTS.—Upon expiration or termination of protection in a particular design under this chapter, all rights under this chapter in the design shall terminate, regardless of the number of different articles in which the design may have been used during the term of its protection.

"§ 1306. Design notice

"(a) CONTENTS OF DESIGN NOTICE.—(1) Whenever any design for which protection is sought under this chapter is made public under section 1310(b), the owner of the design shall, subject to the provisions of section 1307, mark it or have it marked legibly with a design notice consisting of—

"(A) the words 'Protected Design', the abbreviation 'Prot'd Des.', or the letter 'D' with a circle, or the symbol '*D*';

"(B) the year of the date on which protection for the design commenced; and

"(C) the name of the owner, an abbreviation by which the name can be recognized, or a generally accepted alternative designation of the owner.

Any distinctive identification of the owner may be used for purposes of subparagraph (C) if it has been recorded by the Administrator before the design marked with such identification is registered.

"(2) After registration, the registration number may be used instead of the elements specified in subparagraphs (B) and (C) of paragraph (1).

"(b) LOCATION OF NOTICE.—The design notice shall be so located and applied as to give reasonable notice of design protection while the useful article embodying the design is passing through its normal channels of commerce.

"(c) SUBSEQUENT REMOVAL OF NOTICE.—When the owner of a design has complied with the provisions of this section, protection under this chapter shall not be affected by the removal, destruction, or obliteration by others of the design notice on an article.

"§ 1307. Effect of omission of notice

"(a) ACTIONS WITH NOTICE.—Except as provided in subsection (b), the omission of the notice prescribed in section 1306 shall not cause loss of the protection under this chapter or prevent recovery for infringement under this chapter against any person who, after receiving written notice of the design protection, begins an undertaking leading to infringement under this chapter.

"(b) ACTIONS WITHOUT NOTICE.—The omission of the notice prescribed in section 1306 shall prevent any recovery under section 1323 against a person who began an undertaking leading to infringement under this chapter before receiving written notice of the design protection. No injunction shall be issued under this chapter with respect to such undertaking unless the owner of the design reimburses that person for any reasonable expenditure or contractual obligation in connection with such undertaking that was incurred before receiving written notice of the design protection, as the court in its discretion directs. The burden of providing written notice of design protection shall be on the owner of the design.

"§ 1308. Exclusive rights

"The owner of a design protected under this chapter has the exclusive right to—

"(1) make, have made, or import, for sale or for use in trade, any useful article embodying that design; and

"(2) sell or distribute for sale or for use in trade any useful article embodying that design.

"§ 1309. Infringement

"(a) ACTS OF INFRINGEMENT.—Except as provided in subsection (b), it shall be infringement of the exclusive rights in a design protected under this chapter for any person, without the consent of the owner of the design, within the United States and during the term of such protection, to—

"(1) make, have made, or import, for sale or for use in trade, any infringing article as defined in subsection (e); or

"(2) sell or distribute for sale or for use in trade any such infringing article.

"(b) ACTS OF SELLERS AND DISTRIBUTORS.—A seller or distributor of an infringing article who did not make or import the article shall be deemed to have infringed on a design protected under this chapter only if that person—

"(1) induced or acted in collusion with a manufacturer to make, or an importer to import such article, except that merely purchasing or giving an order to purchase such article in the ordinary course of business shall not of itself constitute such inducement or collusion; or

"(2) refused or failed, upon the request of the owner of the design, to make a prompt and full disclosure of that person's source of such article, and that person orders or reorders such article after receiving notice by registered or certified mail of the protection subsisting in the design.

"(c) ACTS WITHOUT KNOWLEDGE.—It shall not be infringement under this section to make, have made, import, sell, or distribute, any article embodying a design which was created without knowledge that a design was protected under this chapter and was copied from such protected design.

"(d) ACTS IN ORDINARY COURSE OF BUSINESS.—A person who incorporates into that person's product of manufacture an infringing article acquired from others in the ordinary course of business,

PUBLIC LAW 105–304—OCT. 28, 1998   112 STAT. 2909

or who, without knowledge of the protected design embodied in an infringing article, makes or processes the infringing article for the account of another person in the ordinary course of business, shall not be deemed to have infringed the rights in that design under this chapter except under a condition contained in paragraph (1) or (2) of subsection (b). Accepting an order or reorder from the source of the infringing article shall be deemed ordering or reordering within the meaning of subsection (b)(2).

"(e) Infringing Article Defined.—As used in this section, an 'infringing article' is any article the design of which has been copied from a design protected under this chapter, without the consent of the owner of the protected design. An infringing article is not an illustration or picture of a protected design in an advertisement, book, periodical, newspaper, photograph, broadcast, motion picture, or similar medium. A design shall not be deemed to have been copied from a protected design if it is original and not substantially similar in appearance to a protected design.

"(f) Establishing Originality.—The party to any action or proceeding under this chapter who alleges rights under this chapter in a design shall have the burden of establishing the design's originality whenever the opposing party introduces an earlier work which is identical to such design, or so similar as to make prima facie showing that such design was copied from such work.

"(g) Reproduction for Teaching or Analysis.—It is not an infringement of the exclusive rights of a design owner for a person to reproduce the design in a useful article or in any other form solely for the purpose of teaching, analyzing, or evaluating the appearance, concepts, or techniques embodied in the design, or the function of the useful article embodying the design.

"§ 1310. Application for registration

"(a) Time Limit for Application for Registration.—Protection under this chapter shall be lost if application for registration of the design is not made within 2 years after the date on which the design is first made public.

"(b) When Design Is Made Public.—A design is made public when an existing useful article embodying the design is anywhere publicly exhibited, publicly distributed, or offered for sale or sold to the public by the owner of the design or with the owner's consent.

"(c) Application by Owner of Design.—Application for registration may be made by the owner of the design.

"(d) Contents of Application.—The application for registration shall be made to the Administrator and shall state—

"(1) the name and address of the designer or designers of the design;

"(2) the name and address of the owner if different from the designer;

"(3) the specific name of the useful article embodying the design;

"(4) the date, if any, that the design was first made public, if such date was earlier than the date of the application;

"(5) affirmation that the design has been fixed in a useful article; and

"(6) such other information as may be required by the Administrator.

112 STAT. 2910   PUBLIC LAW 105–304—OCT. 28, 1998

The application for registration may include a description setting forth the salient features of the design, but the absence of such a description shall not prevent registration under this chapter.

"(e) SWORN STATEMENT.—The application for registration shall be accompanied by a statement under oath by the applicant or the applicant's duly authorized agent or representative, setting forth, to the best of the applicant's knowledge and belief—

"(1) that the design is original and was created by the designer or designers named in the application;

"(2) that the design has not previously been registered on behalf of the applicant or the applicant's predecessor in title; and

"(3) that the applicant is the person entitled to protection and to registration under this chapter.

If the design has been made public with the design notice prescribed in section 1306, the statement shall also describe the exact form and position of the design notice.

"(f) EFFECT OF ERRORS.—(1) Error in any statement or assertion as to the utility of the useful article named in the application under this section, the design of which is sought to be registered, shall not affect the protection secured under this chapter.

"(2) Errors in omitting a joint designer or in naming an alleged joint designer shall not affect the validity of the registration, or the actual ownership or the protection of the design, unless it is shown that the error occurred with deceptive intent.

"(g) DESIGN MADE IN SCOPE OF EMPLOYMENT.—In a case in which the design was made within the regular scope of the designer's employment and individual authorship of the design is difficult or impossible to ascribe and the application so states, the name and address of the employer for whom the design was made may be stated instead of that of the individual designer.

"(h) PICTORIAL REPRESENTATION OF DESIGN.—The application for registration shall be accompanied by two copies of a drawing or other pictorial representation of the useful article embodying the design, having one or more views, adequate to show the design, in a form and style suitable for reproduction, which shall be deemed a part of the application.

"(i) DESIGN IN MORE THAN ONE USEFUL ARTICLE.—If the distinguishing elements of a design are in substantially the same form in different useful articles, the design shall be protected as to all such useful articles when protected as to one of them, but not more than one registration shall be required for the design.

"(j) APPLICATION FOR MORE THAN ONE DESIGN.—More than one design may be included in the same application under such conditions as may be prescribed by the Administrator. For each design included in an application the fee prescribed for a single design shall be paid.

"§ 1311. Benefit of earlier filing date in foreign country

"An application for registration of a design filed in the United States by any person who has, or whose legal representative or predecessor or successor in title has, previously filed an application for registration of the same design in a foreign country which extends to designs of owners who are citizens of the United States, or to applications filed under this chapter, similar protection to that provided under this chapter shall have that same effect as if filed in the United States on the date on which the application was first filed in such foreign country, if the application in the United States is filed within 6 months after the earliest date on which any such foreign application was filed.

"§ 1312. Oaths and acknowledgments

"(a) In General.—Oaths and acknowledgments required by this chapter—

"(1) may be made—

"(A) before any person in the United States authorized by law to administer oaths; or

"(B) when made in a foreign country, before any diplomatic or consular officer of the United States authorized to administer oaths, or before any official authorized to administer oaths in the foreign country concerned, whose authority shall be proved by a certificate of a diplomatic or consular officer of the United States; and

"(2) shall be valid if they comply with the laws of the State or country where made.

"(b) Written Declaration in Lieu of Oath.—(1) The Administrator may by rule prescribe that any document which is to be filed under this chapter in the Office of the Administrator and which is required by any law, rule, or other regulation to be under oath, may be subscribed to by a written declaration in such form as the Administrator may prescribe, and such declaration shall be in lieu of the oath otherwise required.

"(2) Whenever a written declaration under paragraph (1) is used, the document containing the declaration shall state that willful false statements are punishable by fine or imprisonment, or both, pursuant to section 1001 of title 18, and may jeopardize the validity of the application or document or a registration resulting therefrom.

"§ 1313. Examination of application and issue or refusal of registration

"(a) Determination of Registrability of Design; Registration.—Upon the filing of an application for registration in proper form under section 1310, and upon payment of the fee prescribed under section 1316, the Administrator shall determine whether or not the application relates to a design which on its face appears to be subject to protection under this chapter, and, if so, the Register shall register the design. Registration under this subsection shall be announced by publication. The date of registration shall be the date of publication.

Publication.

"(b) Refusal To Register; Reconsideration.—If, in the judgment of the Administrator, the application for registration relates to a design which on its face is not subject to protection under this chapter, the Administrator shall send to the applicant a notice of refusal to register and the grounds for the refusal. Within 3 months after the date on which the notice of refusal is sent, the applicant may, by written request, seek reconsideration of the application. After consideration of such a request, the Administrator shall either register the design or send to the applicant a notice of final refusal to register.

"(c) Application To Cancel Registration.—Any person who believes he or she is or will be damaged by a registration under this chapter may, upon payment of the prescribed fee, apply to the Administrator at any time to cancel the registration on the ground that the design is not subject to protection under this chapter, stating the reasons for the request. Upon receipt of an application for cancellation, the Administrator shall send to the owner of the design, as shown in the records of the Office of the Administrator, a notice of the application, and the owner shall have a period of 3 months after the date on which such notice is mailed in which to present arguments to the Administrator for support of the validity of the registration. The Administrator shall also have the authority to establish, by regulation, conditions under which the opposing parties may appear and be heard in support of their arguments. If, after the periods provided for the presentation of arguments have expired, the Administrator determines that the applicant for cancellation has established that the design is not subject to protection under this chapter, the Administrator shall order the registration stricken from the record. Cancellation under this subsection shall be announced by publication, and notice of the Administrator's final determination with respect to any application for cancellation shall be sent to the applicant and to the owner of record.

Regulations.

Publication.

"§ 1314. Certification of registration

"Certificates of registration shall be issued in the name of the United States under the seal of the Office of the Administrator and shall be recorded in the official records of the Office. The certificate shall state the name of the useful article, the date of filing of the application, the date of registration, and the date the design was made public, if earlier than the date of filing of the application, and shall contain a reproduction of the drawing or other pictorial representation of the design. If a description of the salient features of the design appears in the application, the description shall also appear in the certificate. A certificate of registration shall be admitted in any court as prima facie evidence of the facts stated in the certificate.

"§ 1315. Publication of announcements and indexes

"(a) PUBLICATIONS OF THE ADMINISTRATOR.—The Administrator shall publish lists and indexes of registered designs and cancellations of designs and may also publish the drawings or other pictorial representations of registered designs for sale or other distribution.

"(b) FILE OF REPRESENTATIVES OF REGISTERED DESIGNS.—The Administrator shall establish and maintain a file of the drawings or other pictorial representations of registered designs. The file shall be available for use by the public under such conditions as the Administrator may prescribe.

"§ 1316. Fees

"The Administrator shall by regulation set reasonable fees for the filing of applications to register designs under this chapter and for other services relating to the administration of this chapter, taking into consideration the cost of providing these services and the benefit of a public record.

"§ 1317. Regulations

"The Administrator may establish regulations for the administration of this chapter.

"§ 1318. Copies of records

"Upon payment of the prescribed fee, any person may obtain a certified copy of any official record of the Office of the Administrator that relates to this chapter. That copy shall be admissible in evidence with the same effect as the original.

"§ 1319. Correction of errors in certificates

"The Administrator may, by a certificate of correction under seal, correct any error in a registration incurred through the fault of the Office, or, upon payment of the required fee, any error of a clerical or typographical nature occurring in good faith but not through the fault of the Office. Such registration, together with the certificate, shall thereafter have the same effect as if it had been originally issued in such corrected form.

"§ 1320. Ownership and transfer

"(a) PROPERTY RIGHT IN DESIGN.—The property right in a design subject to protection under this chapter shall vest in the designer, the legal representatives of a deceased designer or of one under legal incapacity, the employer for whom the designer created the design in the case of a design made within the regular scope of the designer's employment, or a person to whom the rights of the designer or of such employer have been transferred. The person in whom the property right is vested shall be considered the owner of the design.

"(b) TRANSFER OF PROPERTY RIGHT.—The property right in a registered design, or a design for which an application for registration has been or may be filed, may be assigned, granted, conveyed, or mortgaged by an instrument in writing, signed by the owner, or may be bequeathed by will.

"(c) OATH OR ACKNOWLEDGEMENT OF TRANSFER.—An oath or acknowledgment under section 1312 shall be prima facie evidence of the execution of an assignment, grant, conveyance, or mortgage under subsection (b).

"(d) RECORDATION OF TRANSFER.—An assignment, grant, conveyance, or mortgage under subsection (b) shall be void as against any subsequent purchaser or mortgagee for a valuable consideration, unless it is recorded in the Office of the Administrator within 3 months after its date of execution or before the date of such subsequent purchase or mortgage.

"§ 1321. Remedy for infringement

"(a) IN GENERAL.—The owner of a design is entitled, after issuance of a certificate of registration of the design under this chapter, to institute an action for any infringement of the design.

"(b) REVIEW OF REFUSAL TO REGISTER.—(1) Subject to paragraph (2), the owner of a design may seek judicial review of a final refusal of the Administrator to register the design under this chapter by bringing a civil action, and may in the same action, if the court adjudges the design subject to protection under this chapter, enforce the rights in that design under this chapter.

"(2) The owner of a design may seek judicial review under this section if—

"(A) the owner has previously duly filed and prosecuted to final refusal an application in proper form for registration of the design;

"(B) the owner causes a copy of the complaint in the action to be delivered to the Administrator within 10 days after the commencement of the action; and

"(C) the defendant has committed acts in respect to the design which would constitute infringement with respect to a design protected under this chapter.

"(c) Administrator as Party to Action.—The Administrator may, at the Administrator's option, become a party to the action with respect to the issue of registrability of the design claim by entering an appearance within 60 days after being served with the complaint, but the failure of the Administrator to become a party shall not deprive the court of jurisdiction to determine that issue.

"(d) Use of Arbitration To Resolve Dispute.—The parties to an infringement dispute under this chapter, within such time as may be specified by the Administrator by regulation, may determine the dispute, or any aspect of the dispute, by arbitration. Arbitration shall be governed by title 9. The parties shall give notice of any arbitration award to the Administrator, and such award shall, as between the parties to the arbitration, be dispositive of the issues to which it relates. The arbitration award shall be unenforceable until such notice is given. Nothing in this subsection shall preclude the Administrator from determining whether a design is subject to registration in a cancellation proceeding under section 1313(c).

§ 1322. Injunctions

"(a) In General.—A court having jurisdiction over actions under this chapter may grant injunctions in accordance with the principles of equity to prevent infringement of a design under this chapter, including, in its discretion, prompt relief by temporary restraining orders and preliminary injunctions.

"(b) Damages for Injunctive Relief Wrongfully Obtained.—A seller or distributor who suffers damage by reason of injunctive relief wrongfully obtained under this section has a cause of action against the applicant for such injunctive relief and may recover such relief as may be appropriate, including damages for lost profits, cost of materials, loss of good will, and punitive damages in instances where the injunctive relief was sought in bad faith, and, unless the court finds extenuating circumstances, reasonable attorney's fees.

"§ 1323. Recovery for infringement

"(a) Damages.—Upon a finding for the claimant in an action for infringement under this chapter, the court shall award the claimant damages adequate to compensate for the infringement. In addition, the court may increase the damages to such amount, not exceeding $50,000 or $1 per copy, whichever is greater, as the court determines to be just. The damages awarded shall constitute compensation and not a penalty. The court may receive expert testimony as an aid to the determination of damages.

"(b) Infringer's Profits.—As an alternative to the remedies provided in subsection (a), the court may award the claimant the infringer's profits resulting from the sale of the copies if the court finds that the infringer's sales are reasonably related to the use of the claimant's design. In such a case, the claimant shall be required to prove only the amount of the infringer's sales and

PUBLIC LAW 105–304—OCT. 28, 1998   112 STAT. 2915

the infringer shall be required to prove its expenses against such sales.

"(c) STATUTE OF LIMITATIONS.—No recovery under subsection (a) or (b) shall be had for any infringement committed more than 3 years before the date on which the complaint is filed.

"(d) ATTORNEY'S FEES.—In an action for infringement under this chapter, the court may award reasonable attorney's fees to the prevailing party.

"(e) DISPOSITION OF INFRINGING AND OTHER ARTICLES.—The court may order that all infringing articles, and any plates, molds, patterns, models, or other means specifically adapted for making the articles, be delivered up for destruction or other disposition as the court may direct.

"§ 1324. Power of court over registration

"In any action involving the protection of a design under this chapter, the court, when appropriate, may order registration of a design under this chapter or the cancellation of such a registration. Any such order shall be certified by the court to the Administrator, who shall make an appropriate entry upon the record.

"§ 1325. Liability for action on registration fraudulently obtained

"Any person who brings an action for infringement knowing that registration of the design was obtained by a false or fraudulent representation materially affecting the rights under this chapter, shall be liable in the sum of $10,000, or such part of that amount as the court may determine. That amount shall be to compensate the defendant and shall be charged against the plaintiff and paid to the defendant, in addition to such costs and attorney's fees of the defendant as may be assessed by the court.

"§ 1326. Penalty for false marking

"(a) IN GENERAL.—Whoever, for the purpose of deceiving the public, marks upon, applies to, or uses in advertising in connection with an article made, used, distributed, or sold, a design which is not protected under this chapter, a design notice specified in section 1306, or any other words or symbols importing that the design is protected under this chapter, knowing that the design is not so protected, shall pay a civil fine of not more than $500 for each such offense.

"(b) SUIT BY PRIVATE PERSONS.—Any person may sue for the penalty established by subsection (a), in which event one-half of the penalty shall be awarded to the person suing and the remainder shall be awarded to the United States.

"§ 1327. Penalty for false representation

"Whoever knowingly makes a false representation materially affecting the rights obtainable under this chapter for the purpose of obtaining registration of a design under this chapter shall pay a penalty of not less than $500 and not more than $1,000, and any rights or privileges that individual may have in the design under this chapter shall be forfeited.

112 STAT. 2916   PUBLIC LAW 105–304—OCT. 28, 1998

"§ 1328. Enforcement by Treasury and Postal Service

"(a) REGULATIONS.—The Secretary of the Treasury and the United States Postal Service shall separately or jointly issue regulations for the enforcement of the rights set forth in section 1308 with respect to importation. Such regulations may require, as a condition for the exclusion of articles from the United States, that the person seeking exclusion take any one or more of the following actions:

"(1) Obtain a court order enjoining, or an order of the International Trade Commission under section 337 of the Tariff Act of 1930 excluding, importation of the articles.

"(2) Furnish proof that the design involved is protected under this chapter and that the importation of the articles would infringe the rights in the design under this chapter.

"(3) Post a surety bond for any injury that may result if the detention or exclusion of the articles proves to be unjustified.

"(b) SEIZURE AND FORFEITURE.—Articles imported in violation of the rights set forth in section 1308 are subject to seizure and forfeiture in the same manner as property imported in violation of the customs laws. Any such forfeited articles shall be destroyed as directed by the Secretary of the Treasury or the court, as the case may be, except that the articles may be returned to the country of export whenever it is shown to the satisfaction of the Secretary of the Treasury that the importer had no reasonable grounds for believing that his or her acts constituted a violation of the law.

"§ 1329. Relation to design patent law

"The issuance of a design patent under title 35, United States Code, for an original design for an article of manufacture shall terminate any protection of the original design under this chapter.

"§ 1330. Common law and other rights unaffected

"Nothing in this chapter shall annul or limit—

"(1) common law or other rights or remedies, if any, available to or held by any person with respect to a design which has not been registered under this chapter; or

"(2) any right under the trademark laws or any right protected against unfair competition.

"§ 1331. Administrator; Office of the Administrator

"In this chapter, the 'Administrator' is the Register of Copyrights, and the 'Office of the Administrator' and the 'Office' refer to the Copyright Office of the Library of Congress.

"§ 1332. No retroactive effect

"Protection under this chapter shall not be available for any design that has been made public under section 1310(b) before the effective date of this chapter.".

SEC. 503. CONFORMING AMENDMENTS.

(a) TABLE OF CHAPTERS.—The table of chapters for title 17, United States Code, is amended by adding at the end the following:

"13. Protection of Original Designs .... 1301".

PUBLIC LAW 105–304—OCT. 28, 1998   112 STAT. 2917

(b) Jᴜʀɪsᴅɪᴄᴛɪᴏɴ ᴏғ Dɪsᴛʀɪᴄᴛ Cᴏᴜʀᴛs Oᴠᴇʀ Dᴇsɪɢɴ Aᴄᴛɪᴏɴs.—
(1) Section 1338(c) of title 28, United States Code, is amended by inserting ", and to exclusive rights in designs under chapter 13 of title 17," after "title 17".

(2)(A) The section heading for section 1338 of title 28, United States Code, is amended by inserting "**designs,**" after "**mask works,**".

(B) The item relating to section 1338 in the table of sections at the beginning of chapter 85 of title 28, United States Code, is amended by inserting "designs," after "mask works,".

(c) Pʟᴀᴄᴇ ғᴏʀ Bʀɪɴɢɪɴɢ Dᴇsɪɢɴ Aᴄᴛɪᴏɴs.—(1) Section 1400(a) of title 28, United States Code, is amended by inserting "or designs" after "mask works".

(2) The section heading for section 1400 of title 28, United States Code, is amended to read as follows:

"Patents and copyrights, mask works, and designs".

(3) The item relating to section 1400 in the table of sections at the beginning of chapter 87 of title 28, United States Code, is amended to read as follows:

"1400. Patents and copyrights, mask works, and designs.".

(d) Aᴄᴛɪᴏɴs Aɢᴀɪɴsᴛ ᴛʜᴇ Uɴɪᴛᴇᴅ Sᴛᴀᴛᴇs.—Section 1498(e) of title 28, United States Code, is amended by inserting ", and to exclusive rights in designs under chapter 13 of title 17," after "title 17".

SEC. 504. JOINT STUDY OF THE EFFECT OF THIS TITLE.

17 USC 1301 note.
Deadlines.
Reports.

(a) Iɴ Gᴇɴᴇʀᴀʟ.—Not later than 1 year after the date of the enactment of this Act, and not later than 2 years after such date of enactment, the Register of Copyrights and the Commissioner of Patents and Trademarks shall submit to the Committees on the Judiciary of the Senate and the House of Representatives a joint report evaluating the effect of the amendments made by this title.

(b) Eʟᴇᴍᴇɴᴛs ғᴏʀ Cᴏɴsɪᴅᴇʀᴀᴛɪᴏɴ.—In carrying out subsection (a), the Register of Copyrights and the Commissioner of Patents and Trademarks shall consider—

(1) the extent to which the amendments made by this title has been effective in suppressing infringement of the design of vessel hulls;

(2) the extent to which the registration provided for in chapter 13 of title 17, United States Code, as added by this title, has been utilized;

(3) the extent to which the creation of new designs of vessel hulls have been encouraged by the amendments made by this title;

(4) the effect, if any, of the amendments made by this title on the price of vessels with hulls protected under such amendments; and

(5) such other considerations as the Register and the Commissioner may deem relevant to accomplish the purposes of the evaluation conducted under subsection (a).

112 STAT. 2918   PUBLIC LAW 105–304—OCT. 28, 1998

17 USC 1301
note.

SEC. 505. EFFECTIVE DATE.

The amendments made by sections 502 and 503 shall take effect on the date of the enactment of this Act and shall remain in effect until the end of the 2-year period beginning on such date of enactment. No cause of action based on chapter 13 of title 17, United States Code, as added by this title, may be filed after the end of that 2-year period.

Approved October 28, 1998.

LEGISLATIVE HISTORY—H.R. 2281 (S. 2037):

HOUSE REPORTS: Nos. 105–551, Pt. 1 (Comm. on the Judiciary) and Pt. 2 (Comm. on Commerce) and 105–796 (Comm. of Commerce).
SENATE REPORTS: No. 105–190 accompanying S. 2037 (Comm. on the Judiciary).
CONGRESSIONAL RECORD, Vol. 144 (1998):
    Aug. 4, considered and passed House.
    Sept. 17, considered and passed Senate, amended, in lieu of S. 2037.
    Oct. 8, Senate agreed to conference report.
    Oct. 12, House agreed to conference report.
WEEKLY COMPILATION OF PRESIDENTIAL DOCUMENTS, Vol. 34 (1998):
    Oct. 28, Presidential statement.

○

The Digital Millennium Copyright Act
Text, History, and Caselaw

III. LEGISLATIVE HISTORY

Calendar No. 358

105TH CONGRESS 2d Session	SENATE	REPORT 105–190

THE DIGITAL MILLENNIUM COPYRIGHT ACT OF 1998

MAY 11, 1998.—Ordered to be printed

Mr. HATCH, from the Committee on the Judiciary,
submitted the following

REPORT

together with

ADDITIONAL VIEWS

[To accompany S. 2037]

The Committee on the Judiciary reported an original bill (S. 2037), to amend title 17, United States Code, to implement the WIPO Copyright Treaty and the WIPO Performances and Phonograms Treaty, to provide limitations on copyright liability relating to material online, and for other purposes, having considered the same, reports favorably thereon and recommends that the bill do pass.

CONTENTS

I. PURPOSE

The "Digital Millennium Copyright Act of 1998" is designed to facilitate the robust development and world-wide expansion of electronic commerce, communications, research, development, and edu-

59–010

2

cation in the digital age. Title I will implement the new World Intellectual Property Organization (WIPO) Copyright Treaty and the WIPO Performances and Phonograms Treaty, thereby bringing U.S. copyright law squarely into the digital age and setting a marker for other nations who must also implement these treaties. Title II will provide certainty for copyright owners and Internet service providers with respect to copyright infringement liability online. Title III will provide a clarifying exemption in the Copyright Act to ensure that the lawful owner or lessee of a computer machine May authorize an independent service technician to activate the computer in order to service its hardware components. Finally, Title IV will begin to update our nation's copyright laws with respect to library, archive, and educational uses of copyrighted works in the digital age.

II. LEGISLATIVE HISTORY

Copyright laws have struggled through the years to keep pace with emerging technology from the struggle over music played on a player piano roll in the 1900's[1] to the introduction of the VCR in the 1980's.[2] With this constant evolution in technology, the law must adapt in order to make digital networks safe places to disseminate and exploit copyrighted materials. The legislation implementing the treaties, Title I of this bill, provides this protection and creates the legal platform for launching the global digital online marketplace for copyrighted works. It will also make available via the Internet the movies, music, software, and literary works that are the fruit of American creative genius. Title II clarifies the liability faced by service providers who transmit potentially infringing material over their networks. In short, Title II ensures that the efficiency of the Internet will continue to improve and that the variety and quality of services on the Internet will expand.

The process to update U.S. copyright law with respect to digital transmissions began in February, 1993, with the formation of the Information Infrastructure Task Force (IITF) to implement the Administration's vision for the National Information Infrastructure (NII).[3] The IITF then established the Working Group on Intellectual Property Rights to investigate the effects of emerging digital technology on intellectual property rights and make recommendations on any appropriate changes to U.S. intellectual property law and policy. This task force issued a report in 1995 known as the White Paper, which discussed the application of existing copyright law to the NII and recommended changes to keep copyright law current with new technology.[4]

To prepare the report, the Working Group held a public hearing in November 1993, at which 30 witnesses testified reflecting the views of copyright industries, libraries, educators, and beneficiaries of the public domain. The Working Group also solicited written comments and received some 70 statements during a public com-

[1] *White-Smith Music Publishing Co.* v. *Apollo Co.*, 209 U.S. 1 (1908).
[2] *Sony Corporation of America* v. *Universal City Studios, Inc.*, 464 U.S. 417 (1984).
[3] Information Infrastructure Task Force, Intellectual Property and the National Information Infrastructure: The Report of the Working Group on Intellectual Property Rights 1 (1995). The "National Information Infrastructure" encompasses digital, interactive services now available, such as the Internet, as well as those contemplated for the future.
[4] Id. at 2.

3

ment period.[5] Following the Working Group's review of the public comments and analysis of the issues, it released a "Green Paper" on July 7, 1994.[6] Following the release of the Green Paper, the Working Group again heard testimony from the public in four days of hearings in Chicago, Los Angeles, and Washington, D.C., in September 1994. More than 1,500 pages of written comments were filed during the four-month comment period by more than 150 individuals and organizations.[7]

The Working Group also convened a Conference on Fair Use (CONFU) to explore the particularly complex issue of fair use in a digital environment and to develop guidelines for uses of copyrighted works by librarians and educators.[8] CONFU issued an Interim Report in December, 1996, and a report in September, 1997, that concluded the first phase of CONFU.[9] The 1997 report addressed the issues of digital images, distance learning, educational multimedia, electronic reserve systems, and use of computer software in libraries.

Interested parties had numerous opportunities to submit their views on the intellectual property implications of the development and use of the NII and on the Working Group's Green Paper. This open process resulted in a voluminous record indicating the views of a wide variety of interested parties including service providers, libraries, copyright owners, and the entertainment industries.[10]

On September 28, 1995, Chairman Hatch, with Senator Leahy, introduced the National Information Infrastructure (NII) Copyright Protection Act of 1995 (S. 1284), which embodied the legislative recommendations of the White Paper. Congressman Moorhead introduced identical legislation (H.R. 2441) in the House on September 29, 1995, with Congresswoman Schroeder as an original cosponsor.[11] The Senate Judiciary Committee and the Subcommittee on Courts and Intellectual Property of the House Judiciary Committee held a joint hearing on November 15, 1995, to consider the NII legislation. Dr. Mihaly Ficsor, Assistant Director General, World Intellectual Property Organization; Bruce A. Lehman, Assistant Secretary of Commerce and Commissioner of Patents and Trademarks; and Marybeth Peters, Register of Copyrights and Associate Librarian for Copyright Services testified at the hearing.

The House Subcommittee on Courts and Intellectual Property held a second set of hearings to consider H.R. 2441 on February 7 and 8, 1996. On February 7, the Subcommittee heard testimony from Jack Valenti, Chairman and CEO, Motion Picture Association of America; Frances W. Preston, President and CEO, Broadcast

---

[5] See Request for Comments on Intellectual Property Issues Involved in the National Information Infrastructure Initiative, 58 Fed. Reg. 53,917 (Oct. 19, 1993).

[6] See Information Infrastructure Task Force, Working Group on Intellectual Property Rights, Intellectual Property and the National Information Infrastructure: A Preliminary Draft of the Report of the Working Group on Intellectual Property Rights (July 1994).

[7] See Notice of Hearings and Request for Comments on Preliminary Draft of the Report of the Working Group on Intellectual Property Rights, 59 Fed. Reg. 42,819 (Aug. 19, 1994); Extension of Deadline for Comments on Preliminary Draft of the Report of the Working Group on Intellectual Property Rights, 59 Fed. Reg. 50,222 (Oct. 3, 1994).

[8] See, supra note 3, at 4 (1995).

[9] See The Conference on Fair Use; An Interim Report to the Commissioner (December 1996); Report to the Commissioner on the Conclusion of the First Phase of the Conference on Fair Use (September 1997).

[10] See, supra note 3, at 5 (1995).

[11] Representatives Coble, Bono, Burr, Minge, Luther, and Jacobs cosponsored H.R. 2241.

4

Music, Inc. (BMI); Edward P. Murphy, President and CEO, National Music Publishers Association; Robert Holleyman, II, President, Business Software Alliance; Edward J. Black, Computer & Communications Industry Association; Barbara A. Munder, Senior Vice President, Corporate Affairs, McGraw Hill Co. and on behalf of the Information Industry Association; Gary L. Shapiro, Chairman, Home Recording Rights Coalition and President, Consumer Electronics Manufacturers Association; Garry L. McDaniels, President, Skills Bank Corporation; and David M. Ostfeld, Vice Chairman, U.S. Activities Board Institute for Electrical and Electronics Engineers, and Vice Chairman, United States Intellectual Property Committee.

On February 8, the Subcommittee heard testimony from Jeanne Hurley Simon, Chair, U.S. National Commission on Libraries and Information Science; Dr. Tuck Tinsley III, President, American Printing House for the Blind, Inc.; Richard Robinson, Chair, President & CEO, Scholastic Corp., for the Association of American Publishers; Cornelius Pings, President, Association of American Universities; Stephen M. Heaton, Secretary and General Counsel, CompuServe, Inc.; Scott Purcell, President, HLC-Internet, Inc.; William J. Cook, Partner, William, Brinks, Hofer, Gilson & Lione; Catherine Simmons-Gill, President, International Trademark Association.

On May 7, 1996, the Senate Judiciary Committee also an additional hearing to consider S. 1284. The Committee heard testimony from John Bettis of the American Society of Composers, Authors, and Publishers (ASCAP); William W. Burrington, Assistant General Counsel and Director of Public Policy, America Online, Inc.; Robert L. Oakley, Professor of Law and Director of the Law Library, Georgetown University Law Center, on behalf of the Digital Future Coalition; and Daniel Burton, Vice President of Government Relations, Novell, Inc.

These hearings were supplemented by a series of negotiations overseen by Congressman Goodlatte of the House Subcommittee on Courts and Intellectual Property in which representatives of copyright owners and Internet and online service providers sought to resolve the contentious issue of the scope of liability of service providers for the infringing acts of their users. Agreement was reached on some issues, but many of the core issues remained unresolved. Negotiations resumed under the auspices of the Patent and Trademark Office in the summer of 1996, but produced no resolution of those issues. Ultimately, the NII Copyright Protection Act stalled in the 104th Congress due largely to the unsettled nature of these and other issues.

Meanwhile, parallel efforts to ensure protection of copyrighted works in the digital age proceeded on the international front. These efforts originated shortly after the United States ratified the Berne Convention in 1989, when the governing body of the Berne Union called upon WIPO to form a Committee of Experts concerning a possible supplementary agreement to the Berne Convention to clarify the existing provisions and explore the scope of the treaty.[12] The

---

[12] Basic Proposal for the Substantive Provisions of the Treaty on Certain Questions Concerning the Protection of Literary and Artistic Works to Be Considered by the Diplomatic Conference

5

result was the introduction of formal proposals to update the Berne Convention to reflect the challenges of the digital age ("Protocol") and to supplement that instrument with enhanced protections for performers and producers of phonograms ("New Instrument"). In December, 1996, the World Intellectual Property Organization held a diplomatic conference in Geneva, Switzerland, which culminated with the adoption of two treaties, the "WIPO Copyright Treaty" and the "WIPO Performances and Phonograms Treaty," which were agreed to by consensus of 160 countries.

The WIPO Copyright Treaty originally contained a provision, article 7, which would have defined the term "reproduction" of a copyrighted work to include any direct or indirect reproduction whether permanent or temporary, in any manner or form.[13] This article proved to be too controversial and was deleted from the treaty prior to its adoption. Instead, the treaty was accompanied by an agreed upon statement that simply confirmed that the reproduction right in Article 9 of the Berne Convention applies fully in the digital environment. The treaty also originally contained language that banned circumvention devices. Again, controversy resulted in a milder declaration that member countries "shall provide adequate legal protection and effective legal remedies against the circumvention of effective technological measures that are used by authors in connection with the exercise of their rights under this Treaty." [14] The end result is that the treaty shifted the debate over technological circumvention measures and on-line service provider liability back to the national level, where each nation will determine how to best conform with the treaty.

The President submitted the WIPO treaties to the U.S. Senate on July 29, 1997, where they were referred to the Foreign Relations Committee. The Administration also submitted draft implementing legislation, which Chairman Hatch introduced by request as S. 1121 on July 31, 1997. Senators Leahy, Thompson, and Kohl joined as original cosponsors. Congressman Coble introduced identical legislation in the House as H.R. 2281 on July 29, 1997.[15] S. 1121 later became the basis for Title I of the Digital Millennium Copyright Act in the Senate Judiciary Committee.

With respect to the issue of service provider liability, two bills were introduced in the first session of the 105th Congress. Congressman Coble introduced H.R. 2180 on July 17, 1997, with Congressman Hyde as a cosponsor. Senator Ashcroft introduced S. 1146 on September 3, 1997, which proposed limitations on copyright liability relating to material on-line for service providers as well as amendments to the Copyright Act to implement the WIPO Treaties and make certain changes to accommodate libraries and educators in the digital environment.

The Senate Judiciary Committee conducted hearings on September 4, 1997, to consider the issues surrounding service provider li-

---

on Certain Copyright and Neighboring Rights Questions, WIPO Document AB/XX/2, Annex A, item PRG.02(2), paragraph 1 (Aug. 30, 1996).
[13] World Intellectual Property Organization, Basic Proposal for the Substantive Provisions of the Treaty on Certain Questions Concerning the Protection of Literary and Artistic Works to Be Considered by the Diplomatic Conference, art. 7(1) (Aug. 30, 1996).
[14] Diplomatic Conference on Certain Copyright and Neighboring Rights Questions, WIPO Copyright Treaty, art. 11, WIPO Document CRNR/DC/94 (December 20, 1996).
[15] Representatives Hyde, Conyers, Frank, Bono, McCullum, and Berman cosponsored the bill.

6

ability. Testimony was heard from Fritz Attaway, Senior Vice President, Government Relations and Washington General Counsel, Motion Picture Association of America; Cary Sherman, General Counsel, Recording Industry Association of America; Daniel F. Burton, Vice President, Government Relations, Novell; George Vradenburg, Senior Vice President and General Counsel, America Online, Inc.; Roy Neel, President and C.E.O., U.S. Telephone Association; and Professor Robert L. Oakley, Director of Law Library and Professor Law, Georgetown University Law Center. At this hearing, parties on all sides were urged by Chairman Hatch and the Ranking Member, Senator Leahy, to resolve the remaining issues prior to the end of the year.

Shortly thereafter, a series of hearings were held in the House on these issues as well as on the issue of WIPO implementation. The Subcommittee on Courts and Intellectual Property of the House Judiciary Committee held two days of hearings on H.R. 2281, the WIPO Copyright Treaties Implementation Act, and H.R. 2180, the Online Copyright Liability Limitation Act, on September 16 and 17, 1997. Bruce Lehman, Assistant Secretary of Commerce and Commissioner of Patents and Trademarks, Patent and Trademark Office, and Marybeth Peters, Register of Copyrights, Copyright Office of the United States, Library of Congress testified on behalf of the Administration. The Subcommittee also heard testimony from Roy Neel, President and Chief Executive Officer, United States Telephone Association; Jack Valenti, President and Chief Executive Officer, Motion Picture Association of America; Robert Holleyman, II, President, Business Software Alliance; M.R.C. Greenwood, Chancellor, University of California, Santa Cruz, on behalf of the Association of American Universities and the National Association of State Universities and Land Grant Colleges; Tushar Patel, Vice President and Managing Director, USWeb, Lawrence Kenswil, Executive Vice President, Business and Legal Affairs, Universal Music Group; Marc Jacobson, General Counsel, Prodigy Services, Inc.; Ken Wasch, President, Software Publishers Association; Ronald G. Dunn, President, Information Industry Association; John Bettis, Songwriter, on behalf of the American Society of Composers, Authors, and Publishers; Allee Willis, Songwriter, on behalf of Broadcast Music, Inc. (BMI); Robert L. Oakley, Professor of Law, Georgetown University Law Center and Director, Georgetown Law Library, on behalf of a Coalition of Library and Educational Organizations; Johnny Cash, Vocal Artist, with Hilary Rosen, President and Chief Executive Officer, Recording Industry Association of America; Allan Adler, Vice President, Legal and Governmental Affairs, Association of American Publishers; Gail Markels, General Counsel and Senior Vice President, Interactive Digital Software Association; Mike Kirk, Executive Director, American Intellectual Property Law Association; Thomas Ryan, President, SciTech Software, Inc.; Mark Belinsky, Vice President Copy Protection Group, Macrovision, Inc.; Douglas Bennett, President, Earlham College, Vice President, American Council of Learned Societies, on behalf of the Digital Futures Coalition; Edward J. Black, President, Computer and Communications Industry Association; Christopher Byrne, Director of Intellectual Property, Silicon Graphics, Inc., on behalf of the Information Technology Industry Council; and Gary

7

Shapiro, President, Consumer Electronics Manufacturer's Association, and Chairman, Home Recording Rights Coalition.

In January, 1998, Chairman Hatch initiated comprehensive negotiations within the Judiciary Committee among copyright owners and Internet and online service providers to resolve the issue of service provider liability. These negotiations centered around a draft proposal put forth by Chairman Hatch, which built upon the efforts over the previous two years. These negotiations continued under the supervision of the Chairman for three months, from January to April, 1998.

On February 26, 1998, the House Subcommittee on Courts and Intellectual Property conducted a markup of H.R. 2281, the WIPO Copyright Treaties Implementation Act, and of H.R. 3209, the On-Line Copyright Infringement Liability Limitation Act. H.R. 2281 and H.R. 3209 were reported favorably by voice vote to the House Judiciary Committee. On April 1, 1998, the full Committee adopted a substitute amendment to H.R. 2281, offered by Congressmen Coble, Hyde, Conyers, and Goodlatte, which incorporated both the provisions of H.R. 2281 and provisions regarding service provider liability in anticipation of a resolution of this issue that appeared to be close in the Senate Judiciary Committee. H.R. 2281 was then favorably reported to the House of Representatives.

On April 2, 1998, Chairman Hatch offered the "Digital Millennium Copyright Act of 1998" at an executive business meeting of the Committee. This bill incorporated the text of S. 1121, a proposal for resolving the issue of service provider liability for copyright infringement, and a provision that had been agreed to by the House Judiciary Committee with respect to computer maintenance and repair.

On April 23, 1998, the Committee met again in executive session to consider the bill. At that meeting, the Committee considered and accepted two amendments offered by Chairman Hatch, with Senators Leahy and Ashcroft, and one amendment offered by Senator Ashcroft, with Senators Leahy and Hatch, en bloc, by unanimous consent. These amendments dealt with reverse engineering of computer programs for interoperability purposes, ephemeral recordings, and an exemption for libraries and archives from copyright infringement liability.

On April 30, 1998, the Judiciary Committee resumed consideration of the bill and accepted the following ten amendments en bloc, by unanimous consent: an amendment by the Chairman (for himself, Mr. Leahy and Mr. Ashcroft), with respect to ephemeral recordings; an amendment by the Chairman (for himself, Mr. Leahy and Mr. Ashcroft), with respect to the use of copyright management information in the course of certain analog and digital transmissions; an amendment by the Chairman (for himself and Mr. Leahy), to make certain clarifying amendments; an amendment by Mr. Ashcroft (for himself, Mr. Leahy and Mr. Hatch), with respect to protection of subscribers of online and Internet service providers; an amendment by Mr. Ashcroft (for himself, Mr. Hatch and Mr. Leahy), with respect to the accommodation of particular technological protection measures; an amendment by Mr. Ashcroft (for himself, Mr. Hatch and Mr. Leahy), with respect to protection of personal privacy interests; an amendment by Mr. Ashcroft (for

8

himself, Mr. Hatch and Mr. Leahy), with respect to the preservation of the ability to control minors' access to material on the Internet; an amendment by Mr. Ashcroft (for himself, Mr. Leahy and Mr. Hatch), with respect to distance education through digital technologies; an amendment by Mr. Grassley (for himself and Mr. Kyl), with respect to law enforcement and intelligence activities; and an amendment by Mrs. Feinstein, with respect to the liability of nonprofit educational institutions for copyright infringement online. The Committee then unanimously ordered the Digital Millennium Copyright Act of 1998 reported favorably, as amended.

III. DISCUSSION

The Digital Millennium Copyright Act (DMCA) in Title I implements the World Intellectual Property (WIPO) treaties on copyright and on performers and phonograms, and in Title II limits the copyright infringement liability of on-line and Internet service providers (OSPs and ISPs) under certain circumstances. The DMCA also provides in Title III a minor but important clarification of copyright law that the lawful owner or lessee of a computer may authorize someone to turn on their computer for the purposes of maintenance or repair. Title IV addresses the issues of ephemeral recordings, distance education, and digital preservation for libraries and archives.

Due to the ease with which digital works can be copied and distributed worldwide virtually instantaneously, copyright owners will hesitate to make their works readily available on the Internet without reasonable assurance that they will be protected against massive piracy. Legislation implementing the treaties provides this protection and creates the legal platform for launching the global digital on-line marketplace for copyrighted works. It will facilitate making available quickly and conveniently via the Internet the movies, music, software, and literary works that are the fruit of American creative genius. It will also encourage the continued growth of the existing off-line global marketplace for copyrighted works in digital format by setting strong international copyright standards.

At the same time, without clarification of their liability, service providers may hesitate to make the necessary investment in the expansion of the speed and capacity of the Internet. In the ordinary course of their operations service providers must engage in all kinds of acts that expose them to potential copyright infringement liability. For example, service providers must make innumerable electronic copies by simply transmitting information over the Internet. Certain electronic copies are made to speed up the delivery of information to users. Other electronic copies are made in order to host World Wide Web sites. Many service providers engage in directing users to sites in response to inquiries by users or they volunteer sites that users may find attractive. Some of these sites might contain infringing material. In short, by limiting the liability of service providers, the DMCA ensures that the efficiency of the Internet will continue to improve and that the variety and quality of services on the Internet will continue to expand.

Besides the major copyright owners and the major OSP's and ISP's (e.g., the local telephone companies, the long distance car-

9

riers, America OnLine, etc.), the Committee heard from representatives of individual copyright owners and small ISP's, from representatives of libraries, archives and educational institutions, from representatives of broadcasters, computer hardware manufacturers, and consumers. Title II, for example, reflects 3 months of negotiations supervised by Chairman Hatch and assisted by Senator Ashcroft among the major copyright owners and the major OSP's and ISP's. Intense discussions took place on distance education too, with the participation of representatives of libraries, teachers, and educational institutions, under the supervision of Chairman Hatch, Senator Leahy, Senator Ashcroft, and the Copyright Office.

As a result, the Committee took substantial steps to refine the discussion draft that Chairman Hatch laid down before the Committee through a series of amendments, each of which was adopted unanimously. For example, the current legislation contains: (1) a provision to ensure that parents will be able to protect their children from pornography and other inappropriate material on the Internet; (2) provisions to provide for the updating of the copyright laws so that educators, libraries, and archives will be able to take advantage of the promise of digital technology; (3) important procedural protections for individual Internet users to ensure that they will not be mistakenly denied access to the World Wide Web; (4) provisions to ensure that the current practice of legitimate reverse engineering for software interoperability may continue; and (5) provisions to accommodate the needs of broadcasters for ephemeral recordings and regarding copyright management information. These provisions are in addition to provisions Chairman Hatch had already incorporated into the discussion draft, such as provisions on library browsing, provisions addressing the special needs of individual creators regarding copyright management information, and provisions exempting nonprofit archives, nonprofit educational institutions, and nonprofit libraries from criminal penalties and, in the case of civil penalties, remitting damages entirely when such an institution was not aware and had no reason to believe that its acts constituted a violation.

Consequently, the DMCA enjoys widespread support from the motion picture, recording, software, and publishing industries, as well as the telephone companies, long distance carriers, and other OSP's and ISP's. It is also supported by the Information Technology Industry Council, which includes the leading computer hardware manufacturers, and by representatives of individual creators, such as the Writers Guild, the Directors Guild, the Screen Actors Guild, and the American Federation of Television and Radio Artists. The breadth of support for this bill is reflected in the unanimous roll call vote (18–0) by which the DMCA was reported out of Committee.

TITLE I

Title I implements the WIPO Copyright Treaty and the WIPO Performances and Phonograms Treaty. These treaties were concluded by the Clinton administration in December 1996. The treaties are best understood as supplements to the Berne Convention for the Protection of Literary and Artistic Works. The Berne Convention is the leading multilateral treaty on copyright and related

10

rights, with 130 countries adhering to it. The United States ratified the Berne Convention in 1989. The two new WIPO treaties were adopted at a diplomatic conference by a consensus of over 150 countries. In general, the Copyright Treaty updates the Berne Convention for digital works and the growth of the Internet and other digital communications networks, and the Performances and Phonograms Treaty supplements the Berne Convention with comprehensive copyright protection for performances and sound recordings (called "phonograms" in international parlance).

The importance of the treaties to the protection of American copyrighted works abroad cannot be overestimated. The treaties, as well as the Berne Convention, are based on the principle of national treatment; that is, that adhering countries are obliged to grant the same protection to foreign works that they grant to domestic works. Even more importantly, the Berne Convention and the treaties set minimum standards of protection. Thus, the promise of the treaties is that, in an increasing global digital marketplace, U.S. copyright owners will be able to rely upon strong, nondiscriminatory copyright protection in most of the countries of the world.

The copyright industries are one of America's largest and fastest growing economic assets. According to International Intellectual Property Alliance statistics, in 1996 (when the last full set of figures was available), the U.S. creative industries accounted for 3.65 percent of the U.S. gross domestic product (GDP)—$278.4 billion. In the last 20 years (1977–1996), the U.S. copyright industries' share of GDP grew more than twice as fast as the remainder of the economy—5.5 percent vs. 2.6 percent. Between 1977 and 1996, employment in the U.S. copyright industries more than doubled to 3.5 million workers—2.8 percent of total U.S. employment. Between 1977 and 1996 U.S. copyright industry employment grew nearly three times as fast as the annual rate of the economy as a whole—4.6 percent vs. 1.6 percent. In fact, the copyright industries contribute more to the U.S. economy and employ more workers than any single manufacturing sector, including chemicals, industrial equipment, electronics, food processing, textiles and apparel, and aircraft. More significantly for the WIPO treaties, in 1996 U.S. copyright industries achieved foreign sales and exports of $60.18 billion, for the first time leading all major industry sectors, including agriculture, automobiles and auto parts, and the aircraft industry.

The WIPO treaties contain many important provisions. For example, the Copyright Treaty contains significant provisions such as: (1) explicit recognition that computer programs are covered by the Berne Convention; (2) recognition of a broad right of public distribution; (3) recognition of a broad right of communication to the public that includes the Internet; (4) an official statement that interprets the existing reproduction right of the Berne Convention to "fully apply in the digital environment";[16] (5) an obligation to provide "legal protection and effective legal remedies" against circumventing technological measures, e.g. encryption and password protection, that are used by copyright owners to protect their works

[16] Concerning Art. 1(4).

11

from piracy; [17] and (6) an obligation to provide "adequate and effective legal remedies" to preserve the integrity of "rights management information." [18] The Performances and Phonograms Treaty recognizes certain rights of performers over their performances and basically gives the copyright owners of sound recordings the same protection for their works as exist in the Berne Convention for other works.

The Committee believes that in order to adhere to the WIPO treaties, legislation is necessary in two primary areas—anticircumvention of technological protection measures and protection of the integrity of rights management information, or "copyright management information" (CMI), as it is referred to in the bill. This view is shared by the Clinton administration. In drafting implementing legislation for the WIPO treaties, the Committee has sought to address those two areas, as well as avoid government regulation of the Internet and encourage technological solutions. The Committee is keenly aware that other countries will use U.S. legislation as a model.

A. ANTICIRCUMVENTION

Title I encourages technological solutions, in general, by enforcing private parties' use of technological protection measures with legal sanctions for circumvention and for producing and distributing products or providing services that are aimed at circumventing technological protection measures that effectively protect copyrighted works. For example, if unauthorized access to a copyrighted work is effectively prevented through use of a password, it would be a violation of this section to defeat or bypass the password and to make the means to do so, as long as the primary purpose of the means was to perform this kind of act. [19] This is roughly analogous to making it illegal to break into a house using a tool, the primary purpose of which is to break into houses.

Legislation prohibiting circumvention devices is not unprecedented. The Copyright Act in section 1002(c) already protects sound recordings and musical works by prohibiting devices which circumvent any program or circuit that implements a serial copy management system or similar system included in digital audio recording devices and digital audio interface devices. The Communications Act in section 605(e)(4) prohibits devices that are "primarily of assistance in the unauthorized decryption of satellite cable programming." In addition to the WIPO Copyright Treaty, the NAFTA in article 1707(b) requires each party to make it a criminal offense to make available a device or system that is "primarily of assistance in decoding an encrypted program-carrying

---

[17] Art. 11.

[18] Rights management information is "information which identifies the work, the author of the work, the owner of any right in the work, or information about the terms and conditions of use of the work . . . which is attached to a copy of a work or appears in connection with communication of the work to the public." Art. 12. Rights management information is more commonly referred to in the U.S. as copyright management information (CMI). The purpose of CMI is to facilitate licensing of copyright for use on the Internet and to discourage piracy.

[19] Note that even if a device does not have circumvention as its primary purpose or design, that is, that it does not fall within the prohibition of section 1201(a)(2)(A), the device would still be illegal if it fell within the prohibitions of *either* 1201 (a)(2)(B) and (C).

12

satellite signal without the authorization of the lawful distributor of such signal.'

Although sections 1201(a)(2) and 1201(b) of the bill are worded similarly and employ similar tests, they are designed to protect two distinct rights and to target two distinct classes of devices. Subsection 1201(a)(2) is designed to protect access to a copyrighted work. Section 1201(b) is designed to protect the traditional copyright rights of the copyright owner. As a consequence, subsection 1201(a)(2) prohibits devices primarily designed to circumvent effective technological measures that limit access to a work. Subsection 1201(b), on the other hand, prohibits devices primarily designed to circumvent effective technological protection measures that limit the ability of the copyrighted work to be copied, or otherwise protect the copyright rights of the owner of the copyrighted work. The two sections are not interchangeable, and many devices will be subject to challenge only under one of the subsections. For example, if an effective technological protection measure does nothing to prevent access to the plain text of the work, but is designed to prevent that work from being copied, then a potential cause of action against the manufacturer of a device designed to circumvent the measure lies under subsection 1201(b), but not under subsection 1201(a)(2). Conversely, if an effective technological protection measure limits access to the plain text of a work only to those with authorized access, but provides no additional protection against copying, displaying, performing or distributing the work, then a potential cause of action against the manufacturer of a device designed to circumvent the measure lies under subsection 1201(a)(2), but not under subsection 1201(b).

This, in turn, is the reason there is no prohibition on conduct in 1201(b) akin to the prohibition on circumvention conduct in 1201(a)(1). The prohibition in 1201(a)(1) is necessary because prior to this Act, the conduct of circumvention was never before made unlawful. The device limitation in 1201(a)(2) enforces this new prohibition on conduct. The copyright law has long forbidden copyright infringements, so no new prohibition was necessary. The device limitation in 1201(b) enforces the longstanding prohibitions on infringements.

Accommodation of particular technological protection measures

The Committee was concerned that the provisions of subsections 1201(a)(2) and (b) might be read to mandate that manufacturers of consumer electronics, telecommunications, and computing products design their products and components to respond to particular technological protection measures employed to protect copyrighted works. Subsection 1201(d)(3) addresses this concern and clarifies that section 1201 does not impose any affirmative design mandates on manufacturers of consumer electronics, telecommunications, and computing products. The fact that a product or component does not respond to any particular technological protection measure, standing alone, neither creates liability under section 1201 nor immunizes those trafficking in the product, part or component from liability. This provision recognizes that there may be legitimate reasons for a product or component's failure to respond to a particular technological measure—such as design efficiency or ensuring high

13

quality output from the product—as well as illegitimate reasons—such as an unlawful intent to circumvent the protection measure.

That a component or part's failure to respond to a technological measure does not immunize the product or component from further review under section 1201 is made clear by the following example. Suppose a device expressly intended to circumvent an effective technological protection measure commonly employed to protect copyrighted works contained a component that was critical to the effectiveness of the device in achieving its stated purpose. Suppose further that the product was marketed as a circumvention device and had no commercially significant purposes or use other than to circumvent. That component would not provide the desired response to the effective technological protection measure, but the product would still clearly run afoul of section 1201 in light of the device manufacturer's unlawful intent, the marketing strategy and the lack of other commercially significant uses for the product.

On the other hand, suppose a manufacturer of a state-of-the-art consumer electronics device, which did not circumvent any technological protection measure when it was introduced into the market and which was designed and marketed for a purpose other than circumventing any technological protection measures, was sued for violating section 1201 because the device did not accommodate a particular technological protection measure developed after the device was designed and sold. In such a case, section 1201(d)(3) would make it clear that the device's failure to accommodate this new protection measure does not render the device unlawful, and in light of the nature of the product, the manner in which it functions, the way it had been marketed and its obvious legitimate uses (assuming the device continues to be marketed and produced for the same legitimate uses), there would clearly be no basis for arguing that the device was unlawful under section 1201.

Library browsing

Section 1201(e) allows nonprofit libraries, archives, and educational institutions to gain access to a commercially exploited copyrighted work solely to make the determination of whether to acquire a copy of the work.

Reverse engineering

Sections 1201(g)–(j) are intended to allow legitimate software developers to continue engaging in certain activities for the purpose of achieving interoperability to the extent permitted by law prior to the enactment of this chapter. The objective is to ensure that the effect of current case law interpreting the Copyright Act is not changed by enactment of this legislation for certain acts of identification and analysis done in respect of computer programs. *See, Sega Enterprises Ltd.* v *Accolade, Inc.*, 977 F.2d 1510, 24 U.S.P.Q.2d 1561 (9th Cir. 1992.). The purpose of this section is to foster competition and innovation in the computer and software industry.

Controlling the access of minors to material on the Internet

The Committee supports the voluntary efforts underway by a broad group of Internet users, library groups, publishers and other

14

copyright industry groups, family-focused organizations, on-line service providers, and civil liberties groups to empower parents to supervise and control the material their children access from the Internet. Nothing in this bill is intended to undercut these efforts.

To emphasize this point, an amendment (section 1201(k)) sponsored by Senator Ashcroft, Chairman Hatch and Senator Leahy was adopted unanimously by the Committee to ensure that the prohibitions in section 1201(a) did not inadvertently make it unlawful for parents to protect their children from pornography and other inappropriate material available on the Internet, or have unintended legal consequences for manufacturers of products designed solely to enable parents to protect their children in this fashion. Section 1201(k) makes clear that in a suit brought under section 1201(a), a court may consider the necessity for a challenged component or part's intended and actual incorporation into a technology, product, service or device, which does not itself violate the provisions of new chapter 12 on Copyright Protection and Management Systems, and which has the sole purpose of preventing the access of minors to pornography or other inappropriate material on the Internet. This provision applies to subsection 1201(a) in its entirety (as opposed to subsection 1201(a)(2) alone) in order to clarify that the bill protects the actions of parents in ensuring that their children do not have access to inappropriate material on-line.

A variety of tools available now allow parents to exercise control in a manner consistent with their own family values, of their children's access to online materials. In the event that, in the future, any of these tools incorporates a part or component which circumvents a technological protection measure effectively controlling access to a copyrighted work solely in order to provide a parent with the information necessary to ascertain whether that material is appropriate for his or her child, this provision authorizes a court to take into consideration the necessity for incorporating such part or component in a suit alleging a violation of section 1201(a).

This provision is limited to the application of subsection (a) because the Committee does not anticipate that it would be necessary for parental empowerment tools to make copies of questionable material, or to distribute or perform it, in order to carry out their important function of assisting parents in guiding their children on the Internet. Accordingly, circumvention of copy controls, or of similar measures, should never be a necessary capability of a parental empowerment tool. By the same token, if a technology, product, service or device which (1) has the sole purpose of preventing the access of minors to certain materials on the Internet, and (2) that technology, product, service or device circumvents a technological protection measure that effectively controls access to a work as defined in subsection 1201(a)(3) only for the purpose of gaining access to the work to ascertain whether it is suitable for a minor, but does not otherwise defeat any copy protection for that work, then that technology, product, service or device is only subject to challenge under subsection 1201(a)(2) and not subsection 1201(b). In such circumstances, no cause of action would lie under section 1201(b) and therefore limiting language would be unnecessary.

This provision is not to be interpreted to allow the wholesale access to copyrighted works in their entirety, but merely to allow par-

15

ents to have an ability to determine whether a work is inappropriate for that parent's child.

Encryption research

The purpose of the Committee in proposing enactment of section 1201 is to improve the ability of copyright owners to prevent the theft of their works, including by applying technological protection measures. The effectiveness of such measures depends in large part on the rapid and dynamic development of better technologies, including encryption-based technological protection measures. The development of encryption sciences requires, in part, ongoing research and testing activities by scientists of existing encryption methods, in order to build on those advances, thus promoting and advancing encryption technology generally.

The goals of section 1201 would be poorly served if these provisions had the undesirable and unintended consequence of chilling legitimate research activities in the area of encryption. It is the view of the Committee, after having conducted extensive consultations, and having examined a number of hypothetical situations, that Section 1201 should not have such an unintended negative effect.

It is the view of the Committee that generally available encryption testing tools would not be made illegal by this Act. Each of those tools has a legitimate and substantial commercial purpose—testing security and effectiveness—and are not prohibited by Section 1201. In addition, the testing of specific encryption algorithms would not fall within the scope of 1201, since mathematical formulas as such are not protected by copyright. Thus, testing of an encryption algorithm or program that has multiple uses, including a use as a technical protection measure for copyrighted works, would not fall within the prohibition of section 1201(a) when that testing is performed on the encryption when it is in a form not implemented as a technical protection measure. Similarly, the testing of encryption technologies developed by or on behalf of the government of the United States, would not violate section 1201 since copyright does not subsist in such subject matter. Finally, there are many situations in which encryption research will be undertaken with the consent or at the direction of the copyright owner and therefore will not give rise to any action under section 1201.

For these reasons, it is the view of the Committee that the following types of encryption testing are not generally prohibited by section 1201.

If a cryptographer uses various cryptanalytic research techniques to discover a flaw in, for example, the U.S. government's Escrowed Encryption Standard (EES) used in the Clipper Chip and Fortezza cards. The flaw allows users to circumvent essential features of the algorithm. Since these encryption products are not covered by copyright, because they are merely mathematical algorithms in addition to being owned by the U.S. government, these acts do not violate 1201, and the results may be made available to the public.

If a company, in the course of developing a new cryptographic product, sponsors a crypto-cracking contest with cash prizes, contestants would not violate section 1201 since the research acts are specifically authorized.

16

Significantly, section 1201 does not make illegal cryptographic devices that have substantial legitimate purposes other than to circumvent technological protection measures as applied to a work. For example, many popular word processing and other computer programs include a security feature allowing users to password-protect documents (employing a low-grade form of encryption.) It is not uncommon for users of such products to forget or lose their passwords for such documents, making their own protected works unrecoverable. As a result, many independent programmers have created utilities designed to assist in the recovery of passwords or password-protected works. Several of these utilities are distributed over the Internet as freeware or shareware. Because these utilities have a substantial legitimate use, and because they would be used by persons to gain access to their own works, these devices do not violate section 1201.

The law would also not prohibit certain kinds of commercial "key-cracker" products, e.g., a computer program optimized to crack certain 40-bit encryption keys. Such machines are often rented to commercial customers for the purpose of quick data recovery of encrypted data. So long as these devices would have a substantial legitimate use, and they do not become principally used to facilitate infringement, they would not be prohibited by section 1201.

Today, network and web site management and security tools increasingly contain components that automatically test systems security and identify common vulnerabilities. These programs are valuable tools for systems administrators and web site operators, to use in the course of their regular testing of their systems' security. Again, because these devices do not meet the test of section 1201, because they are good products put to a good use, the devices do not fall within the scope of this statute.

B. COPYRIGHT MANAGEMENT INFORMATION

Copyright Management Information (CMI) is an important element in establishing an efficient Internet marketplace in copyrighted works free from governmental regulation. Such information will assist in tracking and monitoring uses of copyrighted works, as well as licensing of rights and indicating attribution, creation and ownership.

Under the bill, CMI includes such items as the title of the work, the author, the copyright owner, and in some instances, the writer, performer, and director. CMI need not be in digital form, but CMI in digital form is expressly included. It is important to note that the DMCA does not *require* CMI, but if CMI is provided, the bill protects it from falsification, removal or alteration. Information that is not defined as CMI under the bill would not be protected by these provisions, although its removal or falsification might be protected under other laws, such as unfair trade. The definition of CMI may be expanded by regulation prescribed by the Register of Copyrights.

Section 1202(a) prohibits knowingly providing CMI that is false or knowingly distributing CMI that is false with the intent to induce, enable, facilitate or conceal infringement. Section 1202(b) prohibits (1) the intentional removal or alteration of CMI, (2) the distribution of CMI knowing that the information has been re-

17

moved or altered, and (3) the distribution or public performance of works knowing or having reason to know that CMI has been removed or altered, so long as, regarding the prohibited acts described in section 1202(b), there is knowledge or reasonable grounds to know that these acts will induce, enable, facilitate or conceal an infringement.

Section 1202(e) recognizes special problems that certain broadcasting entities may have with the transmission of copyright management information. Under this subsection, radio and television broadcasters, cable systems, and persons who provide programming to such broadcasters or systems, who do not intend to induce, enable, facilitate or conceal infringement (eligible persons) may be eligible for a limitation on liability for violation of the copyright management information provisions of section 1202(b) in certain, limited circumstances.

C. CIVIL REMEDIES AND CRIMINAL PENALTIES

Section 1203 gives civil remedies and section 1204 imposes criminal penalties for violations of sections 1201 and 1202.

In addition to an award of damages, section 1203(b) provides for various kinds of affirmative relief in civil actions such as temporary and permanent injunctions, impoundment, and, as part of a final judgment or decree finding a violation, the court may order remedial modification or destruction of the offending device or product. Such affirmative relief is currently found in the Copyright Act for copyright infringements.

Regarding monetary relief, section 1203 provides for actual damages, profits derived from the unlawful activity, statutory damages, and treble damages for repeat offenders. Such monetary relief is available under the current Copyright Act.

An important feature of section 1203 is the remittitur for innocent violators and for nonprofit libraries, archives, and educational institutions. In the case of a violator who was not aware and had no reason to believe that the acts at issue constituted a violation, the court may reduce or remit the total award of damages. In the cases of nonprofit libraries, archives, and educational institutions the court must remit damages if the institution was not aware and had no reason to believe that its acts constituted a violation.

The current Copyright Act provides for criminal penalties for copyright infringement. Section 1204 of the bill also provides criminal penalties for violations of section 1201(a) and (b). Specifically, willful violations of sections 1201 or 1202 for purposes of commercial advantage or private financial gain are punished by up to $500,000 in fines or imprisonment for up to 5 years. Repeat offenses are punishable by up to $1,000,000 in fines or imprisonment for up to 10 years. The bill requires that criminal proceedings be commenced within 5 years after the cause of action arose. Criminal penalties do not apply to nonprofit libraries, archives, and educational institutions.

D. PROTECTING PERSONAL PRIVACY INTERESTS

Section 1205 responds to concerns expressed by some that certain technologies used to gather personally identifiable information

18

from Internet users could be characterized as technological protection measures for copyrighted materials, and that therefore efforts by Internet users to protect their privacy by disabling or bypassing such technologies could be prohibited by section 1201. The Committee does not believe that enactment of this legislation will have this effect. No specific example of such a privacy-invasive technology in use today that would be affected in this way has been called to the Committee's attention. For example, even if "cookie" files—which are automatically deposited on the hard drives of computers of users who visit World Wide Web sites—are considered to be invasive of personal privacy (and are deemed to be copyrighted works), all commercially significant browser programs can be readily configured to reject "cookies," and such a configuration raises no issue of any violation of section 1201.

In fact, enactment of section 1201 should have a positive impact on the protection of personal privacy on the Internet. The same technologies that copyright owners use to control access to and use of their works can and will be used to protect the personal privacy of Internet users by, for example, encrypting e-mail communications, or requiring a password for access to personal copyrighted information on an individual's web site. By outlawing the activities of those who make it their business to provide the tools for circumventing these protective technologies, this legislation will substantially enhance the degree to which individuals may protect their privacy as they work, play and communicate on the Internet.

However, because of the privacy concerns expressed that existing or future technologies may evolve in such a way that an individual would have to circumvent a technological protection measure to protect his or her privacy, the committee concluded that it was prudent to rule out any scenario in which section 1201 might be relied upon to make it harder, rather than easier, to protect personal privacy on the Internet. Accordingly, Senator Ashcroft, Chairman Hatch and Senator Leahy proposed a savings clause to clarify that nothing in the new chapter 12 will abrogate, diminish or weaken the provisions of any Federal or State law that prevents the violation of an individual's privacy in connection with the individual's use of the Internet. The savings clause also specifies that section 1201 cannot be used to provide a defense, or an element of mitigation, in any civil or criminal action to enforce such a law. For example, if a valid Federal or State law regulates, on personal privacy grounds, the use of "cookie" files, which are automatically placed on the computer hard drives of users as they visit Internet web sites, and a party with standing sues to enforce the limitations contained in that law, the defendant may not excuse his actions in violation of those limitations by pointing to anything in chapter 12 of title 17.

Law enforcement

Sections 1201(f) and 1202(d) create exceptions for the lawfully authorized investigative, protective, or intelligence activities of an officer, agent, or employee of, the United States, a State, or a political subdivision of a State, or of persons acting pursuant to a contract with such an entity. These exceptions will protect officers, agents, employees, or contractors of, or other persons acting at the

19

direction of, a law enforcement or intelligence agency of the United States, a State, or a political subdivision of a State, who are performing lawfully authorized investigative, protective, or intelligence activities. These exceptions will also protect officers, agents, employees, or contractors of, or other persons acting at the direction of, elements or divisions of an agency or department of the United States, a State, or a political subdivision of a State, which does not have law enforcement or intelligence as its primary function, but who may nevertheless, in the course of lawfully authorized protective, intelligence, or criminal investigative activities, engage in actions otherwise prohibited by this bill. These exceptions only apply to individuals covered under this section when they are performing investigative, protective, or intelligence activities, within the scope of their duties and in furtherance of lawfully authorized activities.

The Committee is concerned that these sections should not be misinterpreted as an opportunity to circumvent the WIPO Copyright Treaty. It should be clear that this is a routine law enforcement and intelligence exception. As such, the exceptions under sections 1201(f) and 1202(d) are to be narrowly construed. In addition, these exceptions are to be construed in a manner consistent with similar law enforcement and intelligence exceptions found elsewhere in U.S. law, such as 18 U.S.C. 1029(f), 1030(f), or 2512(2)(b).

TITLE II

Although the copyright infringement liability of on-line and Internet service providers (OSPs and ISPs) is not expressly addressed in the actual provisions of the WIPO treaties, the Committee is sympathetic to the desire of such service providers to see the law clarified in this area. There have been several cases relevant to service provider liability for copyright infringement.[20] Most have approached the issue from the standpoint of contributory and vicarious liability. Rather than embarking upon a wholesale clarification of these doctrines, the Committee decided to leave current law in its evolving state and, instead, to create a series of "safe harbors," for certain common activities of service providers. A service provider which qualifies for a safe harbor, receives the benefit of limited liability.

In the beginning, the Committee identified the following activities: (1) digital network communications, (2) system caching, (3) information stored on service providers, and (4) information location tools. In the end, Title II contains five general categories of activities, which are addressed in a newly created section 512 in Chapter 5 of the Copyright Act. This new section contains limitations on service providers' liability for five general categories of activity set forth in subsections (a) through (d) and subsection (f). As provided in subsection (k), Section 512 is not intended to imply that a service provider is or is not liable as an infringer either for conduct that qualifies for a limitation of liability or for conduct that fails to so qualify. Rather, the limitations of liability apply if the provider is found to be liable under existing principles of law.

---

[20] For example, *Religious Technology Center* v. *Netcom On-line Communications Services*, 907 F. Supp. 1361 (N.D. Cal. 1995); *Playboy Enterprises* v. *Frena*, 839 F. Supp. 1552 (M.D. Fla. 1993); and *Marobie-FL* v. *Nat. Assn. Of Fire Equipment Distributors*, 983 F. Supp. 1167 (N.D. Ill. 1997).

20

The limitations in subsections (a) through (d) protect qualifying service providers from liability for all monetary relief for direct, vicarious and contributory infringement. Monetary relief is defined in subsection (j)(2) as encompassing damages, costs, attorneys' fees, and any other form of monetary payment. These subsections also limit injunctive relief against qualifying service providers to the extent specified in subsection (I). To qualify for these protections, service providers must meet the conditions set forth in subsection (h), and service providers' activities at issue must involve a function described in subsection (a), (b), (c), (d) or (f), respectively. The liability limitations apply to networks "operated by or for the service provider," thereby protecting both service providers who offer a service and subcontractors who may operate parts of, or an entire, system or network for another service provider.

Title II preserves strong incentives for service providers and copyright owners to cooperate to detect and deal with copyright infringements that take place in the digital networked environment. At the same time, it provides greater certainty to service providers concerning their legal exposure for infringements that may occur in the course of their activities.

Particular concerns of educational institutions

At least two concerns have been raised concerning the applicability of section 512 to educational institutions, such as universities and libraries, when they act as on-line service providers. The first concerns the extent to which the knowledge of faculty members using the Internet will be imputed to a college or university as a whole or the specific department within the college or university responsible for providing Internet service. To the extent such knowledge is imputed, the on-line service provider might fail to qualify for certain of the exceptions to liability included in this section. This is one of the specific questions upon which the Copyright Office study authorized in section 204 of this Act will focus. Without prejudging any issues to be considered in that study, it seems that the extent to which knowledge is imputed to the service provider in the case of colleges and universities, and in other settings in which the service provider and end-user share an employee-employer or other relationship, is a matter of the relevant State law of respondeat superior, rather than a matter of Federal copyright law. As a consequence, there may be much that a non-profit educational institution can do to structure the internal relationships between its faculty and its online service provider functions. What is more, nothing in this Act should be read to preclude a Federal court from taking into account the special circumstances of a non-profit educational institution in applying agency law to determine whether knowledge should be imputed to such an institution in its capacity as an online service provider.

The second concern raised about the applicability of section 512 to public universities and libraries, and indeed other public entities which operate as online service providers, is that by complying with the notice and take-down provisions of section 512, the public entities might violate the due process rights of their users. Any such due process objection suffers at least two flaws. In the first place, a prerequisite to any due process claim is a state law prop-

21

erty interest. In the case of the relatively new concept of Internet access, the service provider contract, rather than any common law property interest, would appear to be the yardstick of the Internet user's property interest in continued access. The contract for Internet service, therefore, can limit any property interest that would form the basis for a procedural due process claim. Second, and even more important, the procedural protections afforded by the notification requirements of subsection 512(c)(3) and the provisions for the replacement of removed or disabled materials in subsection 512(f) provide all the process that is due. The Committee was acutely concerned that it provide all end-users—whether contracting with private or public sector online service providers—with appropriate procedural protections to ensure that material is not disabled without proper justification. The provisions in the bill balance the need for rapid response to potential infringement with the end-users legitimate interests in not having material removed without recourse.

In order to explore these and other issues more fully, the Committee provides in section 204 for a study to be conducted by the Register of Copyrights.

TITLE III

Computer maintenance or repair

Title III of the bill amends section 117 of the Copyright Act (17 U.S.C. 117) to ensure that independent service organizations do not inadvertently become liable for copyright infringement merely because they have turned on a machine in order to service its hardware components.

When a computer is activated, that is when it is turned on, certain software or parts thereof (generally the machine's operating system software) is automatically copied into the machine's random access memory, or "RAM". During the course of activating the computer, different parts of the operating system may reside in the RAM at different times because the operating system is sometimes larger than the capacity of the RAM. Because such copying has been held to constitute a "reproduction" under section 106 of the Copyright Act (17 U.S.C. 106),[21] a person who activated the machine without the authorization of the copyright owner of that software could be liable for copyright infringement. This legislation has the narrow and specific intent of relieving independent service providers, persons unaffiliated with either the owner or lessee of the machine, from liability under the Copyright Act when, solely by virtue of activating the machine in which a computer program resides, they inadvertently cause an unauthorized copy of that program to be made.

This title is narrowly crafted to achieve the foregoing objective without prejudicing the rights of copyright owners of computer software. Thus, for example, 1201(k) does not relieve from liability persons who make unauthorized adaptations, modifications, or other changes to the software. This title also does not relieve from liabil-

---

[21] *See MAI Sys. Corp.* v. *Peak Computer,* 991 F.2d 511 (9th Cir. 1993), *cert. denied,* 114 S.Ct. 671 (1994).

22

ity persons who make any unauthorized copies of software other than those caused solely by activation of the machine.

TITLE IV

A. Ephemeral Recordings

Section 401 of the bill amends section 112 of the Copyright Act to address two issues concerning the application of the ephemeral recording exemption in the digital age.

The first of these issues is the relationship between the ephemeral recording exemption and the Digital Performance Right in Sound Recordings Act of 1995 ("DPRA"). The DPRA granted sound recording copyright owners the exclusive right to perform their works publicly by means of digital audio transmission, subject to certain limitations, particularly those set forth in section 114(d). Among those limitations is an exemption for nonsubscription broadcast transmissions, which are defined as those made by terrestrial broadcast stations licensed as such by the FCC. 17 U.S.C. 114(d)(1)(A)(iii) and (j)(2). The ephemeral recording exemption presently privileges certain activities of a transmitting organization when it is entitled to transmit a performance or display under a license or transfer of copyright ownership or under the limitations on exclusive rights in sound recordings specified by section 114(a). The Committee believes that the ephemeral recording exemption should apply to broadcast radio and television stations when they make nonsubscription digital broadcasts permitted by the DPRA. The Committee has therefore changed the existing language of the ephemeral recording exemption (redesignated as 112(a)(1)) to extend explicitly to broadcasters the same privilege they already enjoy with respect to analog broadcasts.

The second of these issues is the relationship between the ephemeral recording exemption and the anticircumvention provisions that the bill adds as section 1201 of the Copyright Act. Concerns were expressed that if use of copy protection technologies became widespread, a transmitting organization might be prevented from engaging in its traditional activities of assembling transmission programs and making ephemeral recordings permitted by section 112 for purposes of its own transmissions within its local service area and of archival preservation and security. To address this concern, the Committee has added to section 112 a new paragraph that permits transmitting organizations to engage in activities that otherwise would violate section 1201(a)(1) in certain limited circumstances when necessary for the exercise of the transmitting organization's privilege to make ephemeral recordings under redesignated section 112(a)(1). By way of example, if a radio station could not make a permitted ephemeral recording from a commercially available phonorecord without violating section 1201(a)(1), then the radio station could request from the copyright owner the necessary means of making a permitted ephemeral recording. If the copyright owner did not then either provide a phonorecord that could be reproduced or otherwise provide the necessary means of making a permitted ephemeral recording from the phonorecord already in the possession of the radio station, the radio station would not be liable for violating section 1201(a)(1) for taking the steps

23

necessary for engaging in activities permitted under section 112(a)(1). The radio station would, of course, be liable for violating section 1201(a)(1) if it engaged in activities prohibited by that section in other than the limited circumstances permitted by section 112(a)(1).

B. DISTANCE EDUCATION

New technology, especially digital technology, is increasingly being used by educational institutions in their distance learning programs. In the past, distance learning programs were developed primarily for students who, because of their special circumstances, could not be taught in a traditional classroom. Section 110(2) of the copyright law contains an exemption that accommodates this type of activity. The current exemption is designed to cover instructional broadcasting, and allows the use of only certain categories of works. Future distance education, however, may involve a wider range of activities, including the use of interactive digital transmissions, and be designed for a broader audience of students working from personal computers in their own homes.

The Committee believes that the scope of the distance education exemption should be re-examined in light of the range of educational activities made possible by digital technologies. The Committee therefore initiated discussions on distance learning with representatives of libraries, educational institutions and copyright owners, and asked the Register of Copyrights to recommend any appropriate legislative language for an updated distance education exemption. In response to this request by Chairman Hatch, Senator Leahy and Senator Ashcroft, the Register reported the conclusion that digital distance education is an evolving field, and the range of activities contemplated is diverse and potentially far-reaching in impact and scope.

In light of the complexity, importance and potential scope of the issues implicated by distance education, the Committee has determined that further study of the issues would be useful. The Committee therefore has directed the Copyright Office to provide Congress with a report recommending ways to promote distance learning through digital technologies no later than six months after enactment of this legislation. In conducting this study, the Copyright Office is required to consult with representatives of copyright owners, nonprofit educational institutions, libraries and archives. The Committee anticipates that the Copyright Office will also consult with others with relevant expertise, where appropriate, such as the Department of Education.

The Committee underscores the importance to the public of a speedy resolution of any copyright issues associated with distance learning and commits itself to developing a fair and effective distance learning regime promptly after receipt of the Register's Report.

Fair use

The bill does not amend section 107 of the Copyright Act, the fair use provision. The Committee determined that no change to section 107 was required because section 107, as written, is technologically

24

neutral, and therefore, the fair use doctrine is fully applicable in the digital world as in the analog world.

C. Exemption for Libraries and Archives

Section 108 of title 17 permits libraries and archives of the type described in that section to make and, in some cases, distribute a limited number of copies of certain types of copyrighted works, without the permission of the copyright holder, for specified purposes relating to these entities' functions as repositories of such works for public reference. Section 403 of the bill updates section 108 to allow these entities to take advantage of digital technologies when engaging in specified preservation activities.

IV. VOTE OF THE COMMITTEE

Pursuant to paragraph 7 of rule XXVI of the Standing Rules of the Senate, each Committee is to announce the results of rollcall votes taken in any meeting of the Committee on any measure or amendment. The Senate Committee on the Judiciary, with a quorum present, met on Thursday, April 23, 1998, at 10 a.m., to consider the Digital Millennium Copyright Act of 1998. The Committee considered and accepted the following three amendments en bloc, by unanimous consent: an amendment by the Chairman (for himself, Mr. Leahy, and Mr. Ashcroft), with respect to reverse engineering of computer programs for interoperability purposes; an amendment by the Chairman (for himself, Mr. Leahy and Mr. Ashcroft), with respect to ephemeral recordings; and, an amendment by Mr. Ashcroft (for himself, Mr. Leahy, and Mr. Hatch), with respect to the exemption from copyright infringement liability for libraries and archives.

The Committee, with a quorum present, met to resume consideration of the Digital Millennium Copyright Act on Thursday, April 30, 1998, at 10 a.m. The Committee considered and accepted the following amendments en bloc, by unanimous consent: an amendment by the Chairman (for himself, Mr. Leahy, and Mr. Ashcroft), with respect to ephemeral recordings; an amendment by the Chairman (for himself, Mr. Leahy, and Mr. Ashcroft), with respect to the use of copyright management information in the course of certain analog and digital transmissions; an amendment by the Chairman (for himself and Mr. Leahy), to make certain clarifying amendments; an amendment by Mr. Ashcroft (for himself, Mr. Leahy, and Mr. Hatch), with respect to protection of subscribers of online and Internet service providers; an amendment by Mr. Ashcroft (for himself, Mr. Hatch, and Mr. Leahy), with respect to the accommodation of particular technological protection measures; an amendment by Mr. Ashcroft (for himself, Mr. Hatch, and Mr. Leahy), with respect to protection of personal privacy interests; an amendment by Mr. Ashcroft (for himself, Mr. Hatch, and Mr. Leahy), with respect to the preservation of the ability to control minors" access to material on the Internet; an amendment by Mr. Ashcroft (for himself, Mr. Leahy, and Mr. Hatch), with respect to distance education through digital technologies; an amendment by Mr. Grassley (for himself and Mr. Kyl), with respect to law enforcement and intelligence activities; and an amendment by Mrs. Feinstein, with re-

25

spect to the liability of nonprofit educational institutions for copyright infringement online. The Committee then ordered the Digital Millennium Copyright Act of 1998 reported favorably, as amended, with a recommendation that the bill do pass, by a rollcall vote of 18 yeas to 0 nays.

YEAS	NAYS
Thurmond (by proxy)	
Grassley (by proxy)	
Specter (by proxy)	
Thompson	
Kyl	
DeWine	
Ashcroft	
Abraham (by proxy)	
Sessions	
Leahy	
Kennedy	
Biden (by proxy)	
Kohl (by proxy)	
Feinstein	
Feingold	
Durbin (by proxy)	
Torricelli (by proxy)	
Hatch	

V. SECTION-BY-SECTION ANALYSIS

Section 1. Short title

This Act may be cited as the "Digital Millennium Copyright Act of 1998.'

Section 2. Table of contents

TITLE I—WIPO TREATIES IMPLEMENTATION

Section 101. Short title

This Title may be cited as the "WIPO Copyright and Performances and Phonograms Treaties Implementation Act of 1998."

Section 102. Technical amendments

To comply with the obligations of the WIPO Treaties, several technical amendments to the U.S. Copyright Act are necessary. These amendments are needed to ensure that works from countries that join the two new WIPO Treaties, including works in existence on the date each treaty becomes effective for the United States, will be protected in the United States on a formality-free basis, as required by the provisions of each treaty. Three sections of the Copyright Act require amendment: (1) section 104, which specifies the conditions on which works from other countries are protected in the United States; (2) section 104A, which restores protection to certain preexisting works from other countries that have fallen into the public domain in the United States; and (3) section 411(a), which makes copyright registration a precondition to bringing suit for infringement for some works. In addition, the amendments made to

26

these sections require some additions to, and changes in, the definition section of the Copyright Act, section 101.

Subsection (a)—Amendments to Section 101: Definitions.—The bill amends section 101 of the Copyright Act (17 U.S.C. 101) to define "treaty party" as "any country or intergovernmental organization that is a party to an international agreement" and to define "international agreement" to include, *inter alia,* the two new WIPO Treaties. Definitions of the two new WIPO Treaties are also provided. In addition, a definition of "United States work" was added for purposes of section 411 of the Copyright Act (17 U.S.C. 411), as amended by the bill.

Subsection (b)—Amendments to Section 104: Subject Matter of Copyright: National Origin.—Section 104 of the Copyright Act (17 U.S.C. 104) identifies the criteria that must be met for a work to qualify for protection under the U.S. copyright law (i.e., "points of attachment"). Among those protected under section 104 are nationals or domiciliaries of those countries with which we have an appropriate treaty relationship. Section 104, as it is presently written, explicitly identifies those treaty relationships, but does not refer to the two new WIPO Treaties. Therefore, section 104 needs to be amended to provide for points of attachment for the two new WIPO Treaties.

Subsection (b) amends section 104 so that all countries that have copyright relations with the United States would be referred to collectively by the term "treaty parties." This change, in conjunction with the amendments to section 101, which define "treaty party" and "international agreement," serves to ensure that the two new WIPO Treaties are covered by section 104. This subsection also amends section 104 to extend protection to foreign works from any treaty party based on four points of attachment: nationality of the author, place of first publication of the work, place of fixation of the sounds embodied in a sound recording, and the situs of a constructed architectural work.

The way section 104 is presently written requires that it be amended each time U.S. treaty membership changes. By defining "treaty party" in section 101 and amending section 104 to refer to "treaty party," future changes in the treaties to which the U.S. is a party would not require changes to section 104. It is much clearer and less unwieldy to have a single set of criteria for eligibility in section 104 as proposed by this bill, rather than multiple, overlapping criteria in a long list of complex definitions in section 101. If the U.S. joins any future treaties, those treaties can simply be added to the list of "international agreements" without any detailed amendments repeating the criteria for eligibility. The amendment to section 104 also makes clear that membership in the Geneva Phonograms Convention and the WIPO Performances and Phonograms Treaty provides national eligibility for sound recordings only, not other types of works.

Subsection (c)—Amendments to Section 104A: Copyright in Restored Works.—Subsection (c) amends section 104A(h) of the Copyright Act (17 U.S.C. 104A(h)) by adding the two new WIPO Treaties to the definitions of "date of adherence or proclamation" and "eligible country." It would also add a paragraph to the definition of "restored work" to ensure that copyrighted works other than

27

sound recordings do not qualify as restored works where the sole basis for protection in the United States is adherence to the WIPO Performances and Phonograms Treaty.

Subsection (d)—Amendments to Section 411(a): Registration and Infringement Actions.—In its current form, section 411(a) of the Copyright Act (17 U.S.C. 411(a)) requires works to be registered with the Copyright Office before suit can be brought for their infringement, but exempts Berne Convention works whose country of origin is not the United States. Subsection (d) amends section 411(a) of the Copyright Act to include works from members of the two new WIPO Treaties within the exemption.

The amendments made by subsection (d) reframe the registration requirement in the affirmative—essentially the converse of the current section 411(a). In other words, the provision would state affirmatively that "United States works" must be registered before suit. Rather than frame an exemption from that requirement for certain works whose origin *is not* the United States, section 411(a) would, as amended by this subsection, merely limit the requirement of registration as a precondition to suit to those works whose country of origin *is* the United States. "United States works" are defined in section 101 of the Copyright Act (17 U.S.C. 101), as amended by this Title. As discussed with respect to the amendments in subsection (b) to section 104 of the Copyright Act, section 411(a), as amended by this subsection, may be easily updated each time the United States joins another treaty, without the need to change several interrelated provisions of the Act.

Subsection (e)—Amendment to section 507(a).—Section 507(a) of the Copyright Act (17 U.S.C. 507(a)) provides for a 3-year statute of limitations period for all criminal copyright actions. Subsection (e) amends section 507(a) to recognize exceptions to the 3-year limitations period if expressly provided elsewhere in title 17. This amendment is necessary in light of the 5-year criminal limitation period contained in the new chapter 12 of title 17, which is created by this title.

Section 103. Copyright protection systems and copyright management information

The two new WIPO Treaties include substantively identical provisions on technological measures of protection (also commonly referred to as the "black box" or "anticircumvention" provisions). These provisions require contracting parties to provide "adequate legal protection and effective legal remedies against the circumvention of effective technological measures that are used by authors in connection with the exercise of their rights under this Treaty or the Berne Convention and that restrict acts, in respect of their works, which are not authorized by the authors concerned or permitted by law."

Both of the new WIPO treaties also include substantively identical provisions requiring contracting parties to protect the integrity of copyright management information. The treaties define copyright management information as "information which identifies the work, the author of the work, the owner of any right in the work, or information about the terms and conditions of use of the work, and any numbers or codes that represent such information,

28

when any of these items of information is attached to a copy of a work or appears in connection with the communication of a work to the public.'

Legislation is required to comply with both of these provisions. To accomplish this, the bill adds a new chapter (chapter twelve) to title 17 of the United States Code. This new chapter twelve includes five sections—(1) section 1201, which prohibits the circumvention of technological copyright protection measures; (2) section 1202, which protects the integrity of copyright management information; (3) section 1203, which provides for civil remedies for violations of sections 1201 and 1202; (4) section 1204, which provides for criminal penalties for violations of sections 1201 and 1202; and (5) section 1205, which provides a savings clause to preserve the effectiveness of federal and state laws in protecting individual privacy on the Internet.

Section 1201. Circumvention of copyright protection systems

Subsection (a)—Violations regarding circumvention of technological protection measures.—Subsection (a) applies when a person has not obtained authorized access to a copy or a phonorecord of a work that is protected under the Copyright Act and for which the copyright owner has put in place a technological measure that effectively controls access to his or her work. The relevant terminology is defined in paragraph (a)(3), as described below.

Paragraph (a)(1) establishes a general prohibition against gaining unauthorized access to a work by circumventing a technological protection measure put in place by the copyright owner where such protection measure otherwise effectively controls access to a work protected under title 17 of the U.S. Code. This paragraph does not apply to the subsequent actions of a person once he or she has obtained authorized access to a copy of a work protected under title 17, even if such actions involve circumvention of other types of technological protection measures.

In order to provide meaningful protection and enforcement of the copyright owner's right to control access to his or her copyrighted work, paragraph (a)(2) supplements the prohibition against the act of circumvention in paragraph (a)(1) with prohibitions on creating and making available certain technologies, products and services used, developed or advertised to defeat technological protections against unauthorized access to a work. Similar laws have been enacted in related contexts. See, *e.g.*, 17 U.S.C. 1002(a) (prohibiting the import, manufacture, or distribution of digital audio recording equipment lacking specified characteristics and prohibiting the import, manufacture, or distribution of any device, or the offer to perform any service, the primary purpose or effect of which is to circumvent the serial copy management system required for digital audio equipment); 47 U.S.C. 553(a)(2) (prohibiting the manufacture or distribution of equipment intended for the unauthorized reception of cable television service); 47 U.S.C. 605(e)(4) (prohibiting the manufacture, assembly, import, and sale of equipment used in the unauthorized decryption of satellite cable programming.)

Specifically, paragraph (a)(2) prohibits manufacturing, importing, offering to the public, providing, or otherwise trafficking in certain technologies, products, services, devices, components, or parts that

29

can be used to circumvent a technological protection measure that otherwise effectively controls access to a work protected under title 17. It is drafted carefully to target "black boxes," and to ensure that legitimate multipurpose devices can continue to be made and sold. For a technology, product, service, device, component, or part thereof to be prohibited under this subsection, one of three conditions must be met. It must: (1) be primarily designed or produced for the purpose of circumventing; (2) have only a limited commercially significant purpose or use other than to circumvent; or (3) be marketed by the person who manufactures it, imports it, offers it to the public, provides it or otherwise traffics in it, or by another person acting in concert with that person with that person's knowledge, for use in circumventing a technological protection measure that effectively controls access to a work protected under title 17. This provision is designed to protect copyright owners, and simultaneously allow the development of technology.

Paragraph (a)(3) defines certain terms used throughout paragraph (a). Subparagraph (1) defines the term "circumvent a technological protection measure" as meaning "to descramble a scrambled work, to decrypt an encrypted work, or otherwise to avoid, bypass, remove, deactivate, or impair a technological protection measure, without the authority of the copyright owner." This definition applies to paragraph (a) only, which covers protections against unauthorized initial access to a copyrighted work. Subparagraph (2) states that a technological protection measure "effectively controls access to a work" if the measure, in the ordinary course of its operation, requires the application of information, or a process or a treatment, with the authority of the copyright owner, to gain access to the work.

Subsection (b)—Additional violations.—Subsection (b) applies to those technological measures employed by a copyright owner that effectively protect his or her copyright rights in a work, as opposed to those technological protection measures covered by subsection (a), which prevent unauthorized access to a copyrighted work. Unlike subsection (a), which prohibits the circumvention of access control technologies, subsection (b) does not, by itself, prohibit the circumvention of effective technological copyright protection measures. It is anticipated that most acts of circumventing a technological copyright protection measure will occur in the course of conduct which itself implicates the copyright owners rights under title 17. This subsection is not intended in any way to enlarge or diminish those rights. Thus, for example, where a copy control technology is employed to prevent the unauthorized reproduction of a work, the circumvention of that technology would not itself be actionable under section 1201, but any reproduction of the work that is thereby facilitated would remain subject to the protections embodied in title 17.

Paralleling paragraph (a)(2), above, paragraph (b)(1) seeks to provide meaningful protection and enforcement of copyright owners' use of technological protection measures to protect their rights under title 17 by prohibiting the act of making or selling the technological means to overcome these protections and thereby facilitate copyright infringement. Paragraph (b)(1) prohibits manufacturing, importing, offering to the public, providing, or otherwise

30

trafficking in certain technologies, products, services, devices, components, or parts thereof that can be used to circumvent a technological protection measure that effectively protects a right of a copyright owner under title 17 in a work or portion thereof. Again, for a technology, product, service, device, component, or part thereof to be prohibited under this subsection, one of three conditions must be met. It must: (1) be primarily designed or produced for the purpose of circumventing; (2) have only limited commercially significant purpose or use other than to circumvent; or (3) be marketed by the person who manufactures it, imports it, offers it to the public, provides it, or otherwise traffics in it, or by another person acting in concert with that person with that person's knowledge, for use in circumventing a technological protection measure that effectively protects the right of a copyright owner under title 17 in a work or a portion thereof. Like paragraph (a)(2), this provision is designed to protect copyright owners, and simultaneously allow the development of technology.

Paragraph (b)(2) defines certain terms used in subsection (b). Subparagraph (b)(2)(A) defines the term "circumvent protection afforded by a technological protection measure" as "avoiding, bypassing, removing, deactivating, or otherwise impairing a technological protection measure." Subparagraph (b)(2)(B) provides that a technological protection measure "effectively protects a right of a copyright owner under title 17" if the measure, in the ordinary course of its operation, prevents, restricts, or otherwise limits the exercise of a right under Title 17 of a copyright owner.

Subsection (c)—Importation.—Subsection (c) prohibits the importation, sale for importation, or sale within the United States after importation by the owner, importer or consignee of any technology, product, service, device, component, or part thereof covered by subsections (a) or (b). This paragraph further provides that violations of this provision are actionable under section 337 of the Tariff Act (19 U.S.C. 1337), which authorizes actions by the International Trade Commission against unfair import practices.

Subsection (d)—Other rights, etc., not affected.—Subsection (d) sets forth several provisions clarifying the scope of section 1201. Paragraph (d)(1) provides that section 1201 shall not have any effect on rights, remedies, limitations, or defenses to copyright infringement, including fair use, under title 17. Paragraph (d)(2) provides that section 1201 shall not alter the existing doctrines of contributory or vicarious liability for copyright infringement in connection with any technology, product, service, device, component or part thereof. Together, these provisions are intended to ensure that none of the provisions in section 1201 affect the existing legal regime established in the Copyright Act and case law interpreting that statute.

Paragraph (d)(3) clarifies that nothing in section 1201 creates a mandate requiring manufacturers of consumer electronics, telecommunications, and computing products to design their products or their parts and components to respond to any particular technological measure employed to protect a copyrighted work. The provision also makes clear, however, that while the failure of a product to respond to a particular technological measure does not in and of itself create liability, neither does the failure of the product to re-

31

spond to a particular technological protection measure immunize those trafficking in the product from liability under section 1201(a)(2) or (b), if the tests of liability in those provisions are met.

Subsection (e)—Exemption for nonprofit libraries, archives, and educational institutions.—Subsection (e) provides a limited exemption from the prohibition on circumvention of technological protection measures contained in section 1201(a)(1) for qualified nonprofit libraries, archives, and educational institutions.

Paragraph (1) of this subsection allows a nonprofit library, nonprofit archives or nonprofit educational institution to obtain access to a copyrighted work for the sole purpose of making a good faith determination as to whether it wishes to acquire a copy, or portion of a copy, of that work in order to engage in conduct permitted under the Copyright Act, such as a fair use under section 107. A qualifying institution may not gain access for a period of time longer than necessary to determine whether it wishes to obtain a copy, or portion of a copy, for such purposes, and the right to gain access shall not apply for any other purpose.

Paragraph (2) provides that the right to obtain access under this paragraph only applies when the nonprofit library, nonprofit archives, or nonprofit educational institution cannot obtain a copy of an identical work by other means, and such an entity may not use the exemption in this paragraph for commercial advantage or financial gain without penalty.

Paragraph (3) seeks to protect the legitimate interests of copyright owners by providing a civil remedy against a library, archive, or educational institution that violates section 1201(a) by gaining access to a commercially exploited copyrighted work and willfully and for the purpose of commercial advantage or financial gain failing to comply with the provisions of paragraph (1)(A) (requiring that a qualifying library, archive, or educational institution not retain the work for longer than necessary to make a good faith determination as to whether to acquire a copy or portion of the work) or paragraph (1)(B) (requiring that a qualifying library, archive, or educational institution not use the work to which it has gained access for any purpose other than to make a good faith determination as to whether to acquire a copy or portion of the work). Under this paragraph, a violator shall be subject to civil remedies under section 1203 for the first time it gains access in violation of section 1201(a) without complying with the requirements of paragraph (1). For subsequent offenses, the violator shall not only be subject to civil remedies under section 1203, but also lose the benefit of the exemption provided by this subsection.

Paragraph (4) provides that this subsection may not be used as a defense to the prohibitions on manufacturing or selling devices contained in sections 1201(a)(2) or 1202(b).

Finally, paragraph (5) provides that a library or archive, to be eligible for the exemption in paragraph (1), must maintain its collections open to the public and available, not only to researchers affiliated with the library or archives or with the institution of which it is a part, but also to other persons doing research in a specialized field.

Subsection (f)—Law enforcement and intelligence activities.—Subsection (f) creates an exception for the lawfully authorized inves-

32

tigative, protective, or intelligence activities of an officer, agent, or employee of, the United States, a State, or a political subdivision of a State, or of persons acting pursuant to a contract with such an entity. This exception will protect officers, agents, employees, or contractors of, or other persons acting at the direction of, a law enforcement or intelligence agency of the United States, a State, or a political subdivision of a State, who are performing lawfully authorized investigative, protective, or intelligence activities. This exception will also protect officers, agents, employees, or contractors of, or other persons acting at the direction of, elements or divisions of an agency or department of the United States, a State, or a political subdivision of a State, which does not have law enforcement or intelligence as its primary function, but who may nevertheless, in the course of lawfully authorized protective, intelligence, or criminal investigative activities, engage in actions otherwise prohibited by this bill. This exception only applies to individuals covered under this section when they are performing investigative, protective, or intelligence activities, within the scope of their duties and in furtherance of lawfully authorized activities.

Subsections (g)–(j)—Interoperability of computer programs.—Subsections (g) through (j) are intended to allow legitimate software developers to continue engaging in certain activities for the purpose of achieving interoperability to the extent permitted by law prior to the enactment of this chapter. The objective is to ensure that the effect of current case law interpreting the Copyright Act is not changed by enactment of this legislation for certain acts of identification and analysis done in respect of computer programs. See, *Sega Enterprises Ltd.* v. *Accolade, Inc.*, 977 F.2d 1510, 24 U.S.P.Q.2d 1561 (9th Cir. 1992.). The purpose of this section is to foster competition and innovation in the computer and software industry.

Subsection (g) permits the circumvention of access control technologies for the sole purpose of achieving software interoperability. For example, this subsection permits a software developer to circumvent an access control technology applied to a portion or portions of a program in order to perform the necessary steps to identify and analyze the information necessary to achieve interoperability. Subsection (g) permits the act of circumvention in only certain instances. First, the copy of the computer program which is the subject of the analysis must be lawfully acquired. That is the computer program must be acquired from a legitimate source, along with any necessary serial codes, passwords, or other such means as may be necessary to be able to use the program as it was designed to be used by a consumer of the product. The permitted acts must be limited to those elements of the program which must be analyzed to achieve the sole permitted purpose, which is interoperability of an independently created program with other programs. Interoperability is defined in subsection (j) as the ability of computer programs to exchange information, and for such programs mutually to use the information which has been exchanged. The resulting product must be a new and original work, in that it may not infringe the original computer program. In addition, the objective of the analysis must be to identify and extract such elements as are necessary to achieve interoperability which are not

33

otherwise available to the person. Finally, the goal of this section is to ensure that current law is not changed, and not to encourage or permit infringement. Thus, each of the acts undertaken must avoid infringing the copyright of the author of the underlying computer program.

Subsection (h) recognizes that to accomplish the acts permitted under subsection (g) a person may, in some instances, have to make and use certain tools. In most instances these will be generally available tools that programmers use in developing computer programs, such as compilers, trace analyzers and disassemblers, which are not prohibited by this section. In certain instances, it is possible that a person may have to develop special tools to achieve the permitted purpose of interoperability. Thus, this provision creates an exception to the prohibition on making circumvention tools contained in subsections 1201(a)(2) and (b). These tools can be either software or hardware. Again, this provision is limited by a general admonition not to act in a way that constitutes infringing activity.

Subsection (i) recognizes that developing complex computer programs often involves the efforts of many persons. For example, some of these persons may be hired to develop a specific portion of the final product. For that person to perform these tasks, some of the information acquired through the permitted analysis, and the tools to accomplish it, may have to be made available to that person. This subsection allows developers of independently created software to rely on third parties either to develop the necessary circumvention tools or to identify the necessary information to achieve interoperability. The ability to rely on third parties is particularly important for small software developers who do not have the capability of performing these functions in-house. This provision permits such sharing of information and tools. Recognizing, however, that making such circumvention information or tools generally available would undermine the objectives of this Act, this section imposes strict limitations. Such acts of sharing information and tools is permitted solely for the purpose of achieving interoperability of an independently created computer program with other programs. If a person makes this information available for a purpose other than to achieve interoperability of an independently created computer program with other programs, that action is a violation of this Act. In addition, these acts are permitted only to the extent that doing so does not constitute infringement under this title, or violate applicable law other than this title.

Subsection (j) defines "interoperability" as the ability of computer programs to exchange information, and for such programs mutually to use the information which has been exchanged. The seamless exchange of information is an key element of creating such an interoperable independently created program. This provision applies to computer programs as such, regardless of their medium of fixation and not to works generally, such as music or audiovisual works, which may be fixed and distributed in digital form. Accordingly, since the goal of interoperability is the touchstone of the exceptions contained in subsections 1201(g) through (j), nothing in those subsections can be read to authorize the circumvention of any technological protection measure that controls access to any work other

34

than a computer program, or the trafficking in products or services for that purpose.

Subsection (k).—The Committee was concerned that section 1201(a) might inadvertently make it unlawful for parents to protect their children from pornography and other harmful material available on the Internet, or have unintended legal consequences for manufacturers of products designed solely to enable parents to protect their children in this fashion. Subsection (k) addresses these concerns.

Section 1202: Integrity of copyright management information

Section 1202 implements the obligation contained in Article 12 of the WIPO Copyright Treaty and Article 19 of the WIPO Performances and Phonograms Treaty that Contracting Parties "provide adequate and effective legal remedies" against any person who knowingly and without authority removes or alters copyright management information (CMI), or who distributes, imports, broadcasts, or communicates to the public, works or copies of works knowing that such information has been removed or altered without authority.[22] This section does not mandate the use of CMI, nor does it prescribe the choice of any particular type of CMI for those who do use it. It merely protects the integrity of CMI if a party chooses to use it in connection with a copyrighted work by prohibiting its deliberate deletion or alteration. Furthermore, this section imposes liability for specified acts. It does not address the question of liability for persons who manufacture devices or provide services.

Subsection (a)—False copyright management information.—Subsection (a) establishes a general prohibition against intentionally providing false copyright management information, as defined in subsection (c), and against distributing or importing for distribution false copyright management information. There are two prerequisites that must be met for these prohibitions to be violated:

---

[22] Article 12 of the WIPO Copyright Treaty provides:

(1) Contracting Parties shall provide adequate and effective legal remedies against any person knowingly performing any of the following acts knowing, or with respect to civil remedies having reasonable grounds to know, that it will induce, enable, facilitate or conceal an infringement of any right covered by this Treaty or the Berne Convention:

(i) to remove or alter any electronic rights management information without authority;

(ii) to distribute, import for distribution, broadcast or communicate to the public, without authority, works or copies of works knowing that electronic rights management information has been removed or altered without authority.

(2) As used in this Article, "rights management information" means information which identifies the work, the author of the work, the owner of any right in the work, or information about the terms and conditions of use of the work, and any numbers or codes that represent such information, when any of these items of information is attached to a copy of a work or appears in connection with the communication of the work to the public.

Article 19 of the WIPO Performances and Phonograms Treaty provides:

(1) Contracting Parties shall provide adequate and effective legal remedies against any person knowingly performing any of the following acts knowing, or with respect to civil remedies having reasonable grounds to know, that it will induce, enable, facilitate or conceal an infringement of any right covered by this Treaty:

(i) to remove or alter any electronic rights management information without authority;

(ii) to distribute, import for distribution, broadcast, communicate or make available to the public, without authority, performances, copies of fixed performances or phonograms knowing that electronic rights management information has been removed or altered without authority.

(2) As used in this Article, "rights management information" means information which identifies the performer, the performance of the performer, the producer of the phonogram, the phonogram, the owner of any right in the performance or phonogram, or information about the terms and conditions of use of the performance or phonogram, and any numbers or codes that represent such information, when any of these items of information is attached to a copy of a fixed performance or a phonogram or appears in connection with the communication or making available of a fixed performance or a phonogram to the public.

35

(1) the person providing, distributing or importing the false CMI must know the CMI is false, and (2) the person providing, distributing, or importing the false CMI must do so with the intent to induce, enable, facilitate or conceal an infringement of any right under title 17.

Subsection (b)—Removal or alteration of copyright management information.—Subsection (b) establishes general prohibitions against removing or altering CMI, against distributing or importing for distribution altered CMI, and against distributing, importing for distribution or publicly performing works in which CMI has been removed. There are three specific acts prohibited if they are committed without the authority of the copyright owner or the law, and if they are done knowing, or with respect to civil remedies under section 1203, having reasonable grounds to know, that they will induce, enable, facilitate or conceal a copyright infringement: (1) intentionally removing or altering CMI; (2) distributing or importing for distribution CMI knowing that it has been altered without the authority of the copyright owner or the law; or (3) distributing, importing for distribution, or publicly performing works, copies of works, or phonorecords knowing that CMI has been removed or altered without the authority of the copyright owner or the law.

Subsection (c)—Definition.—Subsection (c) defines "copyright management information." To fall within the definition, there is a threshold requirement that the information be conveyed in connection with copies or phonorecords, performances or displays of the copyrighted work. The term "conveyed" is used in its broadest sense and is not meant to require any type of transfer, physical or otherwise, of the information. It merely requires that the information be accessible in conjunction with, or appear with, the work being accessed. Such information is "copyright management information" as defined in this subsection if it falls within the categories enumerated in paragraphs (1) through (6).

Paragraph (1) describes information that identifies the copyrighted work, including the title of a work. This paragraph makes clear that the information set forth on a notice of copyright is included within the definition of copyright management information.

Paragraph (2) describes information that identifies the author of the work.

Paragraph (3) describes information that identifies the copyright owner.

Paragraph (4) describes information that identifies a performer whose performance is fixed in a work, other than an audiovisual work. Information that identifies such a performer is excluded from the definition of CMI, however, when such information is conveyed by a radio or television broadcast station in connection with the public performance of a work.

Paragraph (5) describes, in the case of an audiovisual work, information that identifies the writer, performer, or director who is credited in the work. Paralleling paragraph (4), information that identifies such a writer, performer, or director is excluded from the definition of CMI when such information is conveyed by a radio or television broadcast station in connection with the public performance of a work.

36

Paragraph (6) describes numbers and symbols which refer to or represent the above information. As noted above, both the WIPO Copyright Treaty and the WIPO Performances and Phonograms Treaty require that numbers and symbols be included within the definition of CMI. Links, such as embedded pointers and hypertext links, to the above information are also included. The phrase "links to such information" was included because removing or altering a link to the information will have the same adverse effect as removing or altering the information itself.

Finally, paragraph (7) permits the Register of Copyrights to prescribe by regulation other information that, if conveyed in connection with a work, is to be protected as copyright management information. To protect the privacy of users of copyrighted works, however, the Register of Copyrights may not include within the definition of CMI any information concerning users of copyrighted works.

Consistent with the proviso contained in paragraph (7), it should be noted that the definition of "copyright management information" does not encompass, nor is it intended to encompass, tracking or usage information relating to the identity of users of the works. The definition of CMI is limited by this subsection to the types of information listed, and it would be inconsistent with the purpose and construction of this bill, and contrary to the protection of privacy to include, tracking and usage information within the definition of CMI.

Subsection (d)—Law enforcement and intelligence activities.—Section 1202(d) creates an exception for the lawfully authorized investigative, protective, or intelligence activities of an officer, agent, or employee of, the United States, a State, or a political subdivision of a State, or of persons acting pursuant to a contract with such an entity. This exception will protect officers, agents, employees, or contractors of, or other persons acting at the direction of, a law enforcement or intelligence agency of the United States, a State, or a political subdivision of a State, who are performing lawfully authorized investigative, protective, or intelligence activities. This exception will also protect officers, agents, employees, or contractors of, or other persons acting at the direction of, elements or divisions of an agency or department of the United States, a State, or a political subdivision of a State, which does not have law enforcement or intelligence as its primary function, but who may nevertheless, in the course of lawfully authorized protective, intelligence, or criminal investigative activities, engage in actions otherwise prohibited by this section. This exception only applies to individuals covered under this subsection when they are performing investigative, protective, or intelligence activities, within the scope of their duties and in furtherance of lawfully authorized activities.

Subsection (e)—Limitations on Liability.—Subsection (e) recognizes special problems that certain broadcasting entities may have with the transmission of copyright management information. Under this subsection, radio and television broadcasters, cable systems, and persons who provide programming to such broadcasters or systems, who do not intend to induce, enable, facilitate or conceal infringement (eligible persons) may be eligible for a limitation on liability for violation of the copyright management information provisions of subsection (b) in certain, limited circumstances.

37

In the case of an analog transmission, paragraph (1) provides that an eligible person will not be held liable for violating provisions of subsection (b) if it is not "technically feasible" for that person to avoid the violation or if avoiding the violation would "create an undue financial hardship." Avoiding a violation of subsection (b) with respect to the transmission of credits that are of an excessive duration in relation to standard practice in the relevant industries (for instance, the motion picture and television broadcast industries) is one example of an activity that may "create an undue financial hardship" under paragraph (1). As indicated above, this limitation on liability applies only if such person did not intend, by engaging in such activity, to induce, enable, facilitate or conceal infringement.

Paragraph (2) provides a limitation on liability in the case of a digital transmission, and contemplates voluntary digital transmission standards for the placement of copyright management information. Separate standards are likely to be set for the location of copyright management information in different categories of works. For instance, the standard(s) for the location of the name of the copyright owner in a sound recording or musical work to be broadcast by radio stations may differ—and be set in a separate standard-setting process(es)—from the standard for the location of such information in a motion picture to be broadcast by television stations.

Paragraph (2)(A) provides that if a digital transmission standard for the placement of copyright management information for a category of works is set in a voluntary, consensus standard-setting process involving a representative cross-section of the relevant copyright owners and relevant transmitting industry, including but not limited to representatives of radio or television broadcast stations, cable systems, and copyright owners of a category of works that are intended for public performance by such stations or systems, an eligible person will not be liable for a violation of subsection (b) if the copyright management information involved in the violation was not placed in a location specified by the standard for that information. The eligible person, however, cannot qualify for this limitation on liability if that person was responsible for the nonconforming placement.

Paragraph (2)(B)(i) provides that until such a standard is set for a category of works, an eligible person will not be liable for a violation of subsection (b) if the transmission of the copyright management information would cause a perceptible visual or aural degradation of the digital signal. Paragraph (2)(B)(ii) provides that during this time period before a standard is set, an eligible person also will not be liable if the digital transmission of the information would conflict with an applicable government regulation or industry standard relating to transmission of information in a digital signal, such as the regulation requiring the placement of closed captioning in line 21 of the vertical blanking interval (47 C.F.R. 79.1, implementing 47 U.S.C. 613). For purposes of this paragraph, however, the applicable industry-wide standard must be of a type specified in paragraphs (2)(B)(ii)(II) or (III). The first type, defined in paragraph (2)(B)(ii)(II), includes only those standards that were adopted by a voluntary, consensus standards body, such as the Ad-

38

vanced Television Systems Committee, before the effective date of section 1202. The other type, defined in paragraph (2)(B)(ii)(III), includes only those standards adopted in a voluntary, consensus standards-setting process open to participation by groups, including but not limited to a representative cross-section of radio or television broadcast stations, cable systems, and copyright owners of a category of works that are intended for public performance by such stations or systems.

Section 1203—Civil remedies

Subsection (a)—Civil actions.—Subsection (a) sets forth the general proposition that civil remedies are available for violations of sections 1201 and 1202. This paragraph establishes the jurisdiction for such civil actions as the "appropriate U.S. district court" and limits standing to bring a civil action to those persons injured by a violation of section 1201 or 1202.

Subsection (b)—Powers of the court.—Subsection (b) sets out the powers of the court that hears the case. Paragraph (1) authorizes the court to grant temporary and permanent injunctions on such terms as it deems reasonable to prevent or restrain a violation of section 1201 or 1202. Paragraph (2) authorizes the court to order the impounding of any device or product that is in the custody or control of the alleged violator and that the court has reasonable cause to believe was involved in a violation. Under paragraph (3), the court may award damages as provided in subsection (c). Paragraph (4) authorizes the court to allow the recovery of costs by or against any party other than the United States or an officer thereof. Under paragraph (5), the court may award reasonable attorneys' fees to the prevailing party. Finally, paragraph (6) authorizes the court to order the remedial modification or the destruction of any device or product involved in a violation of section 1201 or 1202 that is in the custody or control of the violator or has been impounded under paragraph (2).

Subsection (c)—Award of damages.—Subsection (c) is divided into five paragraphs, each of which addresses the awarding of damages to the prevailing party.

Paragraph (1) establishes the general proposition that a person who violates section 1201 or 1202 is liable for either actual damages and any additional profits of the violator, or statutory damages.

Paragraphs (2) and (3) specify that the complaining party may finalize a choice between the two types of damage awards at any time until the final judgment is entered.

Paragraph (2) provides that, when the prevailing party opts for actual damages, the court shall award to that party the actual damages suffered by the party as a result of the violations, as well as any profits of the violator that are attributable to the violation and are not taken into account in computing the actual damages.

Paragraph (3) provides different statutory award amounts depending upon whether the civil action involves a section 1201 or 1202 violation. When the violation is a section 1201 violation and the prevailing party opts to recover an award of statutory damages, the prevailing party will be awarded statutory damages of not less than $200 or more than $2,500 per act of circumvention, device, product, component, offer, or performance of service. When the violation is a section 1202 violation and the prevailing party opts to recover an award of statutory damages, the prevailing party will be awarded statutory damages of not less than $2,500 or more than $25,000 for each violation.

Paragraphs (4) and (5) set forth circumstances in which it would be appropriate to increase or decrease a damage award.

Paragraph (4) provides for an increased damage award when the violator is a repeat offender. Specifically, when the prevailing party establishes that a person violated section 1201 or 1202 within three years after a final judgment was entered against that person for another such violation, the award of damages may be increased to a sum of up to triple the amount that would otherwise be awarded.

Paragraph (5)(A) provides that, when a violator of section 1201 or 1202 was not aware and had no reason to believe that its acts constituted a violation, the damage award *may* be reduced or remitted. Paragraph (5)(B) requires the reduction or remission of damages in certain circumstances by providing that, when a nonprofit library, nonprofit archives, or nonprofit educational institution violator of section 1201 or 1202 was not aware and had no reason to believe that its acts constituted a violation, the damage award *shall* be remitted entirely.

Section 1204—Criminal offenses and penalties

Subsection (a)—In general.—Subsection (a) provides for the availability of criminal penalties for violations of sections 1201 and 1202. The standard applicable under this subsection is identical to the standard used in section 506 of the Copyright Act to establish criminal violations. Subsection (a)(1) sets forth the penalties available for a criminal violation of sections 1201 and 1202 as "not more than $500,000 or imprisonment for not more than five years, or both" for the first offense. If the person who is found guilty of criminal violation of sections 1201 or 1202 is a repeat offender, subsection (a)(2) provides that penalties may be increased to "not more than $1,000,000 or imprisonment for not more than ten years, or both."

Subsection (b)—Limitation for nonprofit library, archives, or educational institution.—Subsection (b) exempts completely any nonprofit library, nonprofit archives or nonprofit educational institution from the criminal penalties contained in subsection (a).

Subsection (c)—Statute of limitations.—Subsection (c) provides for a 5-year statute of limitations for criminal offenses under chapter 12.

Section 104. Conforming amendment

This section amends the table of chapters for title 17 to reflect the addition of new chapter 12.

Section 105. Effective date

Subsection (a)—In general.—Subsection (a) establishes the effective date of the proposed amendments in this bill as the date the bill is enacted into law, subject to the exceptions enumerated in subsection (b).

40

Subsection (b)—Amendments relating to certain international agreements.—Subsection (b) sets forth several exceptions to the effective date established by subsection (a). These exceptions only apply to the technical amendments that are proposed in section 102 of the bill. Section 105 of the bill changes the effective date of any provision in section 102 of the bill that specifically refers to the WIPO Copyright Treaty or the WIPO Performances and Phonograms Treaty from the date the bill is enacted into law to the date the Treaty enters into force.

These exceptions are necessary because, as of the drafting of this bill, the two treaties have not entered into force and will not do so until three months after 30 States deposit their instruments of ratification or accession with the Director General of WIPO. The exceptions ensure that the amendments that refer specifically to the two treaties do not become effective until the treaties themselves become effective. In addition, it was necessary to refer to each treaty separately in this section, because it is possible that the two treaties may enter into force at different times and the amendments particular to each treaty had to be grouped together to ensure that the provisions relating specifically to one treaty do not become effective once the other treaty enters into force. Finally, it was necessary to add the phrase "with respect to the United States" in paragraphs (1) and (2) to ensure that, if the Treaties enter into force before the United States deposits its instrument of accession, the United States does not extend benefits to Member States of these Treaties until the United States becomes party to the Treaties.

TITLE II—INTERNET COPYRIGHT INFRINGEMENT LIABILITY

The liability of online service providers and Internet access providers for copyright infringements that take place in the online environment has been a controversial issue. Title II of the Digital Millennium Copyright Act, the Internet Copyright Infringement Liability Clarification Act, addresses this complex issue. Title II preserves strong incentives for service providers and copyright owners to cooperate to detect and deal with copyright infringements that take place in the digital networked environment. At the same time, it provides greater certainty to service providers concerning their legal exposure for infringements that may occur in the course of their activities.

New section 512 contains limitations on service providers' liability for five general categories of activity set forth in subsections (a) through (d) and subsection (f). As provided in subsection (k), section 512 is not intended to imply that a service provider is or is not liable as an infringer either for conduct that qualifies for a limitation of liability or for conduct that fails to so qualify. Rather, the limitations of liability apply if the provider is found to be liable under existing principles of law.

The limitations in subsections (a) through (d) protect qualifying service providers from liability for all monetary relief for direct, vicarious and contributory infringement. Monetary relief is defined in subsection (j)(2) as encompassing damages, costs, attorneys' fees, and any other form of monetary payment. These subsections also limit injunctive relief against qualifying service providers to the ex-

41

tent specified in subsection (i). To qualify for these protections, service providers must meet the conditions set forth in subsection (h), and service providers' activities at issue must involve a function described in subsection (a), (b), (c), (d) or (f), respectively. The liability limitations apply to networks "operated by or for the service provider," thereby protecting both service providers who offer a service and subcontractors who may operate parts of, or an entire, system or network for another service provider.

Section 201. Short title

This title may be cited as the "Internet Copyright Infringement Liability Clarification Act of 1998."

Section 202. Limitations on liability for Internet copyright infringement

This section amends chapter 5 of the Copyright Act (17 U.S.C. 501, *et. seq.*) to create a new section 512, titled "Liability of service providers for online infringement of copyright."

Subsection (a)—Digital network communications.—Subsection (a) applies to communications functions associated with sending digital communications of others across digital networks, such as the Internet and other online networks. It establishes a limitation on liability for infringements that may occur in the provision of services falling within the definition of subsection (j)(1)(A). The limitations on injunctive relief set forth in subsection (i)(1)(B) are applicable when the functions at issue fall within the provisions of subsection (a), and the service provider meets the threshold criteria of subsection (h).[23]

Subsection (a) applies to service providers transmitting, routing, or providing connections for material, and some forms of intermediate and transient storage of material in the course of performing these functions. For example, in the course of moving packets of information across digital online networks, many intermediate and transient copies of the information may be made in routers and servers along the way. Such copies are created as an automatic consequence of the transmission process. In this context, "intermediate and transient" refers to such a copy made and/or stored in the course of a transmission, not a copy made or stored at the points where the transmission is initiated or received.

The use of the term "transmitting" throughout section 512 is not intended to be limited to transmissions of "a performance or display" of "images or sounds" within the meaning of section 101 of the Copyright Act.

Subsections (a)(1) through (5) limit the range of activities that qualify under this subsection to ones in which a service provider plays the role of a "conduit" for the communications of others. This limitation on liability applies if: (1) the communication was initiated by or at the direction of a person other than the service provider; (2) it is carried out through an automatic technical process without selection of the material by the service provider; (3) the service provider does not select the recipients of the material except as an automatic response to the request of another; (4) no copy

---

[23] These threshold criteria apply to all of the liability limitations contained in section 512.

42

of the material made in the course of intermediate or transient storage is maintained on the system or network so that it is ordinarily accessible to other than the anticipated recipients, and no copy is maintained on the system or network in a manner ordinarily accessible to the anticipated recipients for a longer period than is reasonably necessary for the communication; and (5) the content (but not necessarily the form) of the material is not modified in the course of transmission. Thus, for example, an e-mail transmission may appear to the recipient without bolding or italics resulting from format codes contained in the sender's message.

The Committee intends the term "selection of the material" in subsection (a)(2) to reflect an editorial function of determining what material to send, or the specific sources of material to place online (*e.g.,* a radio station), rather than "an automatic technical process" of responding to a command or request, such as one from a user, an Internet location tool, or another network. The term "automatic response to the request of another" is intended to encompass a service provider's actions in responding to requests by a user or other networks, such as requests to forward e-mail traffic or to route messages to a mailing list agent (such as a Listserv) or other discussion group. The Committee intends subsection (a)(4) to cover copies made of material while it is *en route* to its destination, such as copies made on a router or mail server, storage of a web page in the course of transmission to a specific user, store and forward functions, and other transient copies that occur en route. The term "ordinarily accessible" is intended to encompass stored material that is routinely accessible to third parties. For example, the fact that an illegal intruder might be able to obtain access to the material would not make it ordinarily accessible to third parties. Neither, for example, would occasional access in the course of maintenance by service provider personnel, nor access by law enforcement officials pursuant to subpoena make the material "ordinarily accessible." However, the term does not include copies made by a service provider for the purpose of making the material available to other users. Such copying is addressed in subsection (b).

Subsection (b)—System caching.—Subsection (b) applies to a different form of intermediate and temporary storage than is addressed in subsection (a). In terminology describing current technology, this storage is a form of "caching," which is used on some networks to increase network performance and to reduce network congestion generally, as well as to reduce congestion and delays to popular sites. This storage is intermediate in the sense that the service provider serves as an intermediary between the originating site and ultimate user. The material in question is stored on the service provider's system or network for some period of time to facilitate access by users subsequent to the one who previously sought access to it.

For subsection (b) to apply, the material must be made available on an originating site, transmitted at the direction of another person through the system or network operated by or for the service provider to a different person, and stored through an automatic technical process so that users of the system or network who subsequently request access to the material from the originating site may obtain access to the material from the system or network.

43

Subsections (b)(1) through (b)(5) further refine the circumstances under which subsection (b) applies. Subsection (b)(1) provides that the material must be transmitted to subsequent users without modification to its content in comparison to the way it was originally transmitted from the originating site. The Committee intends that this restriction apply, for example, so that a service provider who caches material from another site does not change the advertising associated with the cached material on the originating site without authorization from the originating site.

Subsection (b)(2) limits the applicability of the subsection to circumstances where the service provider complies with certain updating commands.

Subsection (b)(3) provides that the service provider shall not interfere with the ability of certain technology that is associated with the work by the operator of the originating site to return to the originating site information, such as user "hit" counts, that would have been available to the site had it not been cached. The technology must: (i) not significantly interfere with the performance of the storing provider's system or network or with intermediate storage of the material; (ii) be consistent with generally accepted industry standard communications protocols applicable to Internet and online communications, such as those approved by the Internet Engineering Task Force and the World Wide Web Consortium; and (iii) not extract information beyond that which would have been obtained had the subsequent users obtained access to the material directly on the originating site.

Subsection (b)(4) applies to circumstances in which the originating site imposes a prior condition on access.

Subsection (b)(5) establishes a notification and take down procedure for cached material modeled on the procedure under subsection (c). However, this take down obligation does not apply unless the material has previously been removed from the originating site, or the party submitting the notification has obtained a court order for it to be removed from the originating site and notifies the service provider's designated agent of that order. This proviso has been added to subsection (b)(5) because storage under subsection (b) occurs automatically and unless infringing material has been removed from the originating site, the infringing material would ordinarily simply be re-cached.

Subsection (c)—Information stored on service providers.—Subsection (c) limits the liability of qualifying service providers for claims of direct, vicarious and contributory infringement for storage at the direction of a user of material that resides on a system or network controlled or operated by or for the service provider. Examples of such storage include providing server space for a user's web site, for a chatroom, or other forum in which material may be posted at the direction of users. Subsection (c) defines the scope of this limitation on liability. It also sets forth procedural requirements that copyright owners or their agents and service providers must follow with respect to notifications of claimed infringement under subsection (c)(3). Information that resides on the system or network operated by or for the service provider through its own acts or decisions and not at the direction of a user does not fall within the liability limitation of subsection (c).

44

Subsection (c)(1)—In general.—Subsection (c)(1)(A) sets forth the applicable knowledge standard. This standard is met either by actual knowledge of infringement or in the absence of such knowledge by awareness of facts or circumstances from which infringing activity is apparent. The term "activity" is intended to mean activity using the material on the system or network. The Committee intends such activity to refer to wrongful activity that is occurring at the site on the provider's system or network at which the material resides, regardless of whether copyright infringement is technically deemed to occur at that site or at the location where the material is received. For example, the activity at an online site offering audio or video may be unauthorized public performance of a musical composition, a sound recording, or an audio-visual work, rather than (or in addition to) the creation of an unauthorized copy of any of these works.

Subsection (c)(1)(A)(ii) can best be described as a "red flag" test. As stated in subsection (l), a service provider need not monitor its service or affirmatively seek facts indicating infringing activity (except to the extent consistent with a standard technical measure complying with subsection (h)), in order to claim this limitation on liability (or, indeed any other limitation provided by the legislation). However, if the service provider becomes aware of a "red flag" from which infringing activity is apparent, it will lose the limitation of liability if it takes no action. The "red flag" test has both a subjective and an objective element. In determining whether the service provider was aware of a "red flag," the subjective awareness of the service provider of the facts or circumstances in question must be determined. However, in deciding whether those facts or circumstances constitute a "red flag"—in other words, whether infringing activity would have been apparent to a reasonable person operating under the same or similar circumstances—an objective standard should be used.

Subsection (c)(1)(A)(iii) provides that once a service provider obtains actual knowledge or awareness of facts or circumstances from which infringing material or activity on the service provider's system or network is apparent, the service provider does not lose the limitation of liability set forth in subsection (c) if it acts expeditiously to remove or disable access to the infringing material. Because the factual circumstances and technical parameters may vary from case to case, it is not possible to identify a uniform time limit for expeditious action.

Subsection (c)(1)(B) sets forth the circumstances under which a service provider would lose the protection of subsection (c) by virtue of its benefit from and control over infringing activity. In determining whether the financial benefit criterion is satisfied, courts should take a common-sense, fact-based approach, not a formalistic one. In general, a service provider conducting a legitimate business would not be considered to receive a "financial benefit directly attributable to the infringing activity" where the infringer makes the same kind of payment as non-infringing users of the provider's service. Thus, receiving a one-time set-up fee and flat periodic payments for service from a person engaging in infringing activities would not constitute receiving a "financial benefit directly attributable to the infringing activity." Nor is subparagraph (B) intended

45

to cover fees based on the length of the message (per number of bytes, for example) or by connect time. It would however, include any such fees where the value of the service lies in providing access to infringing material.

Subsection (c)(1)(C) establishes that in cases where a service provider is notified of infringing activity by a copyright owner or its authorized agent, in accordance with the notification procedures of subsection (c)(3), the limitation on the service provider's liability shall be maintained only if the service provider acts expeditiously either to remove the infringing material from its system or to prevent further access to the infringing material on the system or network. This "notice and takedown" procedure is a formalization and refinement of a cooperative process that has been employed to deal efficiently with network-based copyright infringement.

Section 512 does not require use of the notice and take-down procedure. A service provider wishing to benefit from the limitation on liability under subsection (c) must "take down" or disable access to infringing material residing on its system or network of which it has actual knowledge or that meets the "red flag" test, even if the copyright owner or its agent does not notify it of a claimed infringement. On the other hand, the service provider is free to refuse to "take down" the material or site, even after receiving a notification of claimed infringement from the copyright owner; in such a situation, the service provider's liability, if any, will be decided without reference to section 512(c). For their part, copyright owners are not obligated to give notification of claimed infringement in order to enforce their rights. However, neither actual knowledge nor awareness of a red flag may be imputed to a service provider based on information from a copyright owner or its agent that does not comply with the notification provisions of subsection (c)(3), and the limitation of liability set forth in subsection (c) may apply.

Subsection (c)(2)—Designated agent.—Subsection (c)(2) provides that to qualify for the liability limitation of subsection (c), the service provider must designate an agent to receive notifications under subsection (c)(1)(C). The designation, provided to the Register of Copyrights, and made available on the service provider's web site is to contain certain information necessary to communicate with the service provider concerning allegedly infringing material or activity. The Register of Copyrights is directed to maintain a directory of designated agents available for inspection by the public, both on the web site of the Library of Congress, and in hard copy format on file at the Copyright Office. The Committee does not intend or anticipate that the Register will publish hard copies of the directory. The directory shall have entries for the name, address, telephone number and electronic mail address of an agent designated by service providers. The service provider's designation shall substantially comply with these elements.

Subsection (c)(3)—Elements of notification.—Subsection (c)(3) sets forth the procedures under which copyright owners and their agents may provide effective notification to a service provider of allegations of infringement on the provider's system or network. Subsection (c)(3)(A) requires that to count as an effective notification, the notification must be in writing and submitted to the service provider's designated agent.

46

Subsections (c)(3)(A)(i)–(vi) then set forth the information to be included in an effective notification. The standard against which a notification is to be judged is one of substantial compliance. Subsection (c)(3)(A)(i) provides that the notification must be signed by the copyright owner or its authorized agent to be effective. The requirement for signature, either physical or electronic, relates to the verification requirements of subsections (c)(3)(A)(v) and (vi). Subsection (c)(3)(A)(ii) requires that the copyright owner identify the copyrighted work alleged to be infringed. Where multiple works at a single online site are covered by a single notification, a representative list of such works at that site is sufficient. Thus, where a party is operating an unauthorized Internet jukebox from a particular site, it is not necessary for a compliant notification to list every musical composition or sound recording that has been or could be infringed at that site, so long as a representative list of those compositions or recordings is provided so that the service provider can understand the nature and scope of the infringement being claimed.

Subsection (c)(3)(A)(iii) requires that the copyright owner or its authorized agent provide the service provider with information reasonably sufficient to permit the service provider to identify and locate the allegedly infringing material. An example of such sufficient information would be a copy or description of the allegedly infringing material and the URL address of the location (web page) which is alleged to contain the infringing material. The goal of this provision is to provide the service provider with adequate information to find and address the allegedly infringing material expeditiously.

Subsection (c)(3)(A)(iv) requires that the copyright owner or its authorized agent provide reasonably sufficient identifying information concerning the owner or its agent who submits the notification, such as an address, telephone number, and if available an electronic mail address so that the service provider may contact the complaining party.

Subsection (c)(3)(A)(v) makes clear that the notification from complaining parties must contain a statement that the complaining party has a good faith belief that the use of the material in the manner complained of is not authorized by the copyright owner, or its agent, or the law.

Subsection (c)(3)(A)(vi) specifies that the notification must contain a statement that the information contained therein is accurate. The complaining party—whether the copyright owner, or an authorized representative—also must confirm under penalty of perjury, that it has authority to act on behalf of the owner of the exclusive right that is alleged to be infringed. The term "perjury" is used in the sense found elsewhere in the United States Code. See 28 U.S.C. 1746; 18 U.S.C. 1621.

Subsection (c)(3)(B) addresses the effect of notifications that do not substantially comply with the requirements of subsection (c)(3). Under this subsection, the court shall not consider such notifications as evidence of whether the service provider has actual knowledge, is aware of facts or circumstances, or has received a notification for purposes of subsection (c)(1)(A). However, a defective notice provided to the designated agent may be considered in evaluating the service provider's knowledge or awareness of facts and circumstances, if (i) the complaining party has provided the requisite information concerning the identification of the copyrighted work, identification of the allegedly infringing material, and information sufficient for the service provider to contact the complaining party, and (ii) the service provider does not promptly attempt to contact the person making the notification or take other reasonable steps to assist in the receipt of notification that substantially complies with paragraph (3)(A). If the service provider subsequently receives a substantially compliant notice, the provisions of paragraph (1)(C) would then apply upon receipt of the notice.

The Committee intends that the substantial compliance standard in subsections (c)(2) and (c)(3) be applied so that technical errors (such as misspelling a name, supplying an outdated area code if the phone number is accompanied by an accurate address, or supplying an outdated name if accompanied by an e-mail address that remains valid for the successor of the prior designated agent or agent of a copyright owner) do not disqualify service providers and copyright owners from the protections afforded under subsection (c). The Committee expects that the parties will comply with the functional requirements of the notification provisions—such as providing sufficient information so that a designated agent or the complaining party submitting a notification may be contacted efficiently—in order to ensure that the notification and take down procedures set forth in this subsection operate smoothly.

Subsection (d)—Information location tools.—Subsection (d) applies to referring or linking users to an online location containing infringing material or infringing activity using information location tools. The reference to "infringing activity" is intended to refer to wrongful activity that is occurring at the location to which the link or reference refers, without regard to whether copyright infringement is technically deemed to occur at that location or at the location where the material is received. The term information location tools includes, for example: a directory or index of online sites or material such as a search engine that identifies pages by specified criteria, a reference to other online material such as a list of recommended sites, a pointer that stands for an Internet location or address, or a hypertext link which allows users to access material without entering its address.

Subsection (d) incorporates the notification and take down structure of subsection (c) and applies it to the provision of references and links to infringing sites. A service provider is entitled to the liability limitations of subsection (d) if it: (1) lacks actual knowledge of infringement on the other site, and is not aware of facts or circumstances from which infringing activity in that location is apparent; (2) does not receive a financial benefit directly attributable to the infringing activity on the site, where the service provider has the right and ability to control the infringing activity; and (3) responds expeditiously to remove or disable the reference or link upon receiving a notification of claimed infringement as described in subsection (c)(3). The notification procedures under subsection (d) follow those set forth in subsection (c). However, the information submitted by the complaining party under subsection (c)(3)(A)(iii) is identification of the reference or link to infringing

48

material or activity, and information reasonably sufficient to permit the service provider to locate that reference or link.

Section 512(d) provides a safe harbor that would limit the liability of a service provider that refers or links users to an online location containing infringing material or activity by using "information location tools," such as hyperlink directories and indexes. A question has been raised as to whether a service provider would be disqualified from the safe harbor based solely on evidence that it had viewed the infringing Internet site. If so, there is concern that online directories prepared by human editors and reviewers, who view and classify various Internet sites, would be denied eligibility to the information location tools safe harbor, in an unintended number of cases and circumstances. This is an important concern because such online directories play a valuable role in assisting Internet users to identify and locate the information they seek on the decentralized and dynamic networks of the Internet.

Like the information storage safe harbor in section 512(c), a service provider would qualify for this safe harbor if, among other requirements, it "does not have actual knowledge that the material or activity is infringing" or, in the absence of such actual knowledge, it is "not aware of facts or circumstances from which infringing activity is apparent." Under this standard, a service provider would have no obligation to seek out copyright infringement, but it would not qualify for the safe harbor if it had turned a blind eye to "red flags" of obvious infringement.

For instance, the copyright owner could show that the provider was aware of facts from which infringing activity was apparent if the copyright owner could prove that the location was clearly, at the time the directory provider viewed it, a "pirate" site of the type described below, where sound recordings, software, movies or books were available for unauthorized downloading, public performance or public display. Absent such "red flags" or actual knowledge, a directory provider would not be similarly aware merely because it saw one or more well known photographs of a celebrity at a site devoted to that person. The provider could not be expected, during the course of its brief cataloguing visit, to determine whether the photograph was still protected by copyright or was in the public domain; if the photograph was still protected by copyright, whether the use was licensed; and if the use was not licensed, whether it was permitted under the fair use doctrine.

The important intended objective of this standard is to exclude sophisticated "pirate" directories—which refer Internet users to other selected Internet sites where pirate software, books, movies, and music can be downloaded or transmitted—from the safe harbor. Such pirate directories refer Internet users to sites that are obviously infringing because they typically use words such as "pirate," "bootleg," or slang terms in their uniform resource locator (URL) and header information to make their illegal purpose obvious to the pirate directories and other Internet users. Because the infringing nature of such sites would be apparent from even a brief and casual viewing, safe harbor status for a provider that views such a site and then establishes a link to it would not be appropriate. Pirate directories do not follow the routine business practices of legitimate service providers preparing directories, and thus

49

evidence that they have viewed the infringing site may be all that is available for copyright owners to rebut their claim to a safe harbor.

In this way, the "red flag" test in section 512(d) strikes the right balance. The common-sense result of this "red flag" test is that online editors and catalogers would not be required to make discriminating judgments about potential copyright infringement. If, however, an Internet site is obviously pirate, then seeing it may be all that is needed for the service provider to encounter a "red flag." A provider proceeding in the face of such a red flag must do so without the benefit of a safe harbor.

Information location tools are essential to the operation of the Internet; without them, users would not be able to find the information they need. Directories are particularly helpful in conducting effective searches by filtering out irrelevant and offensive material. The Yahoo! directory, for example, currently categorizes over 800,000 online locations and serves as a "card catalogue" to the World Wide Web, which over 35,000,000 different users visit each month. Directories such as Yahoo!'s usually are created by people visiting sites to categorize them. It is precisely the human judgment and editorial discretion exercised by these cataloguers which makes directories valuable.

This provision is intended to promote the development of information location tools generally, and Internet directories such as Yahoo!'s in particular, by establishing a safe-harbor from copyright infringement liability for information location tool providers if they comply with the notice and takedown procedures and other requirements of subsection (d). The knowledge or awareness standard should not be applied in a manner which would create a disincentive to the development of directories which involve human intervention. Absent actual knowledge, awareness of infringement as provided in subsection (d) should typically be imputed to a directory provider only with respect to pirate sites or in similarly obvious and conspicuous circumstances, and not simply because the provider viewed an infringing site during the course of assembling the directory.

Subsection (e)—Misrepresentations.—Subsection (e) establishes a right of action against any person who knowingly misrepresents that material or activity online is infringing, or that material or activity was removed or disabled by mistake or misidentification under the "put back" procedure set forth in subsection (f). Actions may be brought under subsection (e) by any copyright owner, copyright owner's licensee, or by a service provider, who is injured by such misrepresentation, as a result of the service provider relying upon the misrepresentation in either taking down material or putting material back online. Defendants who make such a knowing misrepresentation are liable for any damages, including costs and attorneys" fees, incurred by any of these parties as a result of the service provider's reliance upon the misrepresentation. This subsection is intended to deter knowingly false allegations to service providers in recognition that such misrepresentations are detrimental to rights holders, service providers, and Internet users.

Subsection (f)—Immunity for take downs and user put back procedure.—Subsection (f) provides immunity to service providers for

50

taking down infringing material, and establishes a "put back" procedure under which subscribers may contest a complaining party's notification of infringement provided under subsection (c)(3). The put back procedures were added as an amendment to this title in order to address the concerns of several members of the Committee that other provisions of this title established strong incentives for service providers to take down material, but insufficient protections for third parties whose material would be taken down.

Subsection (f)(1) immunizes service providers from any claim based on the service provider's good faith disabling of access to, or removal of, material or activity claimed to be infringing. The immunity also applies to material or activity that a service provider disables access to or removes based on facts or circumstances from which infringing activity is apparent. This immunity applies even if the material or activity is ultimately determined not to be infringing. The purpose of this subsection is to protect service providers from liability to third parties whose material service providers take down in a good faith effort to comply with the requirements of subsection (c)(1).

Subsection (f)(2) establishes a "put back" procedure through an exception to the immunity set forth in subsection (f)(1). The exception applies in a case in which the service provider, pursuant to a notification provided under subsection (c)(1)(C) in accordance with subsection (c)(3), takes down material that a subscriber has posted to the system or network. In such instances, to retain the immunity set forth in subsection (f)(1) with respect to the subscriber whose content is taken down, the service provider is to follow up to three steps.

Under subsection (f)(2)(A), the service provider is to take reasonable steps to notify the subscriber promptly of the removal or disabling of access to the subscriber's material. The Committee intends that "reasonable steps" include, for example, sending an e-mail notice to an e-mail address associated with a posting, or if only the subscriber's name is identified in the posting, sending an e-mail to an e-mail address that the subscriber submitted with its subscription. The Committee does not intend that this subsection impose any obligation on service providers to search beyond the four corners of a subscriber's posting or their own records for that subscriber in order to obtain contact information. Nor does the Committee intend to create any right on the part of subscribers who submit falsified information in their postings or subscriptions to complain if a service provider relies upon the information submitted by the subscriber.

The subscriber may then file a counter notification, in accordance with the requirements of subsection (f)(3), contesting the original take down on grounds of mistake or misidentification of the material and requesting "put back" of the material that the service provider has taken down. If a subscriber files a counter notification with the service provider's designated agent, subparagraph (f)(2) calls for the service provider to promptly forward a copy to the complaining party who submitted the take down request. Finally, under subsection (f)(2)(C), the service provider is to place the subscriber's material back online or cease disabling access to it between 10 and 14 business days after receiving the counter notifica-

51

tion unless the designated agent receives a further notice from the complaining party that the complaining party has filed an action seeking a court order to restrain the subscriber from engaging in infringing activity on the service provider's system or network with regard to the material in question.

Subscriber counter notifications must substantially comply with defined requirements set forth in subsection (f)(3). Notifications shall be signed by the subscriber physically or by electronic signature; identify the material taken down and the location from which it was taken down; include a statement under penalty of perjury that the subscriber has a good faith belief that the material was taken down as a result of mistake or misidentification of the material; and include the subscriber's contact information, as well as a statement consenting to the jurisdiction of a Federal district court and to accept service of process from the complaining party or the complaining party's agent. The substantial compliance standard is the same as that set forth in subsections (c)(2) and (3).

Subsection (f)(4) is included to make clear the obvious proposition that a service provider's compliance with the put back procedure does not subject it to liability for copyright infringement or cause it to lose its liability limitation with respect to the replaced material.

Subsection (g)—Identification of direct infringer.—Subsection (g) creates a procedure by which copyright owners or their authorized agents who have submitted or will submit a request for notification satisfying the requirements of subsection (c)(3)(A) may obtain an order for identification of alleged infringers who are users of a service provider's system or network. Under this procedure, the copyright owner or agent files three documents with the clerk of any U.S. District Court: a copy of the notification, a proposed order, and a sworn declaration that the purpose of the order is to obtain the identity of an alleged infringer and that the information obtained will only be used to protect the owner's rights under this Title.

Orders issued under subsection (g) shall authorize and order the service provider expeditiously to disclose to the person seeking the order information sufficient to identify the alleged infringer to the extent such information is available to the service provider. The Committee intends that an order for disclosure be interpreted as requiring disclosure of information in the possession of the service provider, rather than obliging the service provider to conduct searches for information that is available from other systems or networks. The Committee intends that such orders be expeditiously issued if the notification meets the provisions of subsection (c)(3)(A) and the declaration is properly executed. The issuing of the order should be a ministerial function performed quickly for this provision to have its intended effect. After receiving the order, the service provider shall expeditiously disclose to the copyright owner or its agent the information required by the order to the extent that the information is available to the service provider, regardless of whether the service provider responds to the notification of claimed infringement.

Subsection (h)—Conditions for eligibility.—Subsection (h) sets forth two conditions that a service provider must satisfy to be eligi-

52

ble for the limitations of liability provided in subsections (a) through (d).

First, the service provider is expected to adopt and reasonably implement a policy for the termination in appropriate circumstances of the accounts of subscribers [24] of the provider's service who are repeat online infringers of copyright. The Committee recognizes that there are different degrees of online copyright infringement, from the inadvertent to the noncommercial, to the willful and commercial. In addition, the Committee does not intend this provision to undermine the principles of subsection (l) or the knowledge standard of subsection (c) by suggesting that a provider must investigate possible infringements, monitor its service, or make difficult judgments as to whether conduct is or is not infringing. However, those who repeatedly or flagrantly abuse their access to the Internet through disrespect for the intellectual property rights of others should know that there is a realistic threat of losing that access.

Second, a provider's system must accommodate, and not interfere with, standard technical measures used to identify or protect copyrighted works. The Committee believes that technology is likely to be the solution to many of the issues facing copyright owners and service providers in this digital age. For that reason, we have included subsection (h)(1)(B), which is intended to encourage appropriate technological solutions to protect copyrighted works. The Committee strongly urges all of the affected parties expeditiously to commence voluntary, interindustry discussions to agree upon and implement the best technological solutions available to achieve these goals.

Subsection (h)(1)(B) is explicitly limited to "standard technical measures" that have been developed pursuant to a broad consensus of both copyright owners and service providers in an open, fair, voluntary, multi-industry standards process. The Committee anticipates that these provisions could be developed both in recognized open standards bodies or in ad hoc groups, as long as the process used is open, fair, voluntary, and multi-industry and the measures developed otherwise conform to the requirements of the definition of standard technical measures set forth in paragraph (h)(2). A number of recognized open standards bodies have substantial experience with Internet issues. The Committee also notes that an ad-hoc approach has been successful in developing standards in other contexts, such as the process that has developed copy protection technology for use in connection with DVD.

Subsection (i)—Injunctions.—Subsection (i) defines the terms and conditions under which an injunction may be issued against a service provider that qualifies for the limitations of liability set forth in subsections (a) through (d), but is otherwise subject to an injunction under existing principles of law. Subsection (i)(1) limits the scope of injunctive relief that may be ordered against a qualifying

---

[24] By "subscribers,"the Committee intends to include account holders who are parties with a business relationship to the service provider that justifies treating them as subscribers, for the purposes of section 512, even if no formal subscription agreement exists. Examples include students who are granted access to a university's system or network for digital online communications; employees who have access to their employer's system or network; or household members with access to a consumer online service by virtue of a subscription agreement between the service provider and another member of that household.

53

provider. Subsection (i)(2) identifies factors a court must consider in deciding whether to grant injunctive relief and in determining the appropriate scope of injunctive relief.

Subsection (i)(1)—Scope of relief.—Subsection (i)(1) is divided into two subparagraphs. Subparagraph (A) defines the scope of injunctive relief available against service providers who qualify for the limitations of liability set forth in subsections (b), (c) or (d). Only three forms of injunctive relief may be granted. First, the court may provide for the removal or blocking of infringing material or activity that is residing at a specific location on the provider's system or network. This is essentially an order to take the actions identified in subsection (c)(1)(C) to "remove, or disable access" to the material that is claimed to be infringing or to be the subject of infringing activity.

Second, the court may order the provider to terminate the accounts of a subscriber [25] of the provider's service who is engaging in infringing activity.

Subsection (i)(1)(A) permits the court, under appropriate circumstances, to enter a different form of injunction if the court considers it necessary to prevent or restrain infringement of specific copyrighted material that resides at an identified online location. If a court enters an injunction other than that contemplated in the first two clauses of subparagraph (A), the court must determine that the injunctive relief is the least burdensome to the service provider among those forms of relief that are comparably effective.

Subsection (i)(1)(B) sets forth a different set of remedies available for injunctions against service providers qualifying for the limitation on remedies set forth in subsection (a). In such cases, if a court determines that injunctive relief is appropriate, it may only grant injunctive relief in one or both of two specified forms. The first is an order to the service provider to terminate subscriber accounts that are specified in the order. The second form of relief, available in cases in which a provider is engaging in infringing activity relating to a foreign online location, is an order to take reasonable steps to block access to a specific, identified foreign online location. Such blocking orders are not available against a service provider qualifying under subsection (a) in the case of infringing activity on a site within the United States or its territories.

Subsection (i)(2)—Considerations.—Subsection (i)(2) sets forth mandatory considerations for the court beyond those that exist under current law. These additional considerations require the court to consider factors of particular significance in the digital online environment.

Subsection (i)(3)—Notice and ex parte orders.—Subsection (i)(3) prohibits most forms of ex parte injunctive relief (including temporary and preliminary relief) against a service provider qualifying for a liability limitation under section 512. A court may issue an order to ensure the preservation of evidence or where the order will have no material adverse effect on the operation of the provider's network.

Subsection (j)—Definitions.—Subsection (j) sets forth two definitions of the term "service provider" as used in this title, as well as

---

[25] See footnote 24.

54

a definition of the term "monetary relief." Only an entity that is performing the functions of a "service provider" is eligible for the limitations on liability set forth in section 512 with respect to those functions.

The first definition of a service provider, set forth in subsection (j)(1)(A), defines a narrower range of functions and applies to use of the term in subsection (a). As used in that subsection the term "service provider" means any entity offering the transmission, routing or providing of connections for digital online communications, between or among points specified by a user, of material of a user's choosing without modification to the content of the material as sent or received. This freestanding definition is derived from the definition of "telecommunications" found in 47 U.S.C. 153(48) in recognition of the fact that the functions covered by this definition are conduit activities, but the Committee has reworked the definition and written subsection (j)(1)(A) to make it appropriate for the Internet and online media. Thus, the subsection (j)(1)(A) definition includes the offering of transmission, routing or providing of connections. Although the transmission, routing or providing of connections may occur over digital or analog networks, the service provider must be providing such services for communications that are both digital and online. By online communications, the Committee intends to refer to communications over an interactive computer network, such as the Internet. Thus, over-the-air broadcasting, whether in analog or digital form, or a cable television system, or a satellite television service would not qualify, except to the extent it provides users with online access to a digital network such as the Internet, or it provides transmission, routing or connections to connect material to such a network, and then only with respect to those functions. An entity is not disqualified from being a "service provider" because it alters the form of the material, so long as it does not alter the content of the material. As a threshold matter, a service provider's performance of a particular function with respect to allegedly infringing activity falls within the (j)(1)(A) definition of service provider if and only if such function is within the range of functions set forth in subsection (j)(1)(A). For example, hosting a World Wide Web site does not fall within the subsection (j)(1)(A) definition; providing connectivity for a world wide web site does fall within that definition. The subparagraph (A) definition of service provider is not intended to exclude providers that perform other functions in addition to those set forth in subparagraph (A), including the functions identified in subsection (j)(1)(B). Conversely, the fact that a provider performs some functions that fall within the definition of subparagraph (A) does not imply that its other functions that do not fall within the definition of subparagraph (A) qualify for the limitation of liability under subsection (a).

The second definition of "service provider," set forth in subsection (j)(1)(B), applies to the term as used in any other subsection of section 512. This definition is broader than the first, covering providers of online services or network access, or the operator of facilities therefor. This definition includes, for example, services such as providing Internet access, e-mail, chat room and web page hosting services. The (j)(1)(B) definition of service provider, for example, includes universities and schools to the extent they perform the func-

55

tions identified in subsection (j)(1)(B). The definition also specifically includes any entity that falls within the first definition of service provider. A broadcaster or cable television system or satellite television service would not qualify, except to the extent it performs functions covered by (j)(1)(B).

Finally, subsection (j)(2) defines the term "monetary relief" broadly for purposes of this section as encompassing damages, costs, attorneys' fees and any other form of monetary payment.

Subsection (k)—Other defenses not affected.—Subsection (k) clarifies that other defenses under copyright law are not affected and codifies several important principles.

New section 512 does not define what is actionable copyright infringement in the online environment, and does not create any new exceptions to the exclusive rights under copyright law. The rest of the Copyright Act sets those rules. Similarly, new section 512 does not create any new liabilities for service providers or affect any defense available to a service provider. Enactment of section 512 does not bear upon whether a service provider is or is not an infringer when its conduct falls within the scope of section 512. Even if a service provider's activities fall outside the limitations on liability specified in the bill, the service provider is not necessarily an infringer; liability in these circumstances would be adjudicated based on the doctrines of direct, vicarious or contributory liability for infringement as they are articulated in the Copyright Act and in the court decisions interpreting and applying that statute, which are unchanged by section 512. In the event that a service provider does not qualify for the limitation on liability, it still may claim all of the defenses available to it under current law. New section 512 simply defines the circumstances under which a service provider, as defined in this Section, may enjoy a limitation on liability for copyright infringement.

Subsection (l)—Protection of privacy.—Subsection (l) is designed to protect the privacy of Internet users. This subsection makes clear that the applicability of subsections (a) through (d) is no way conditioned on a service provider: (1) monitoring its service or affirmatively seeking facts indicating infringing activity except to the extent consistent with implementing a standard technical measure under subsection (h); or (2) accessing, removing or disabling access to material if such conduct is prohibited by law, such as the Electronic Communications Privacy Act.

Subsection (m)—Rule of construction.—Subsection (m) establishes a rule of construction applicable to subsections (a) through (d). Section 512's limitations on liability are based on functions, and each limitation is intended to describe a separate and distinct function. Consider, for example, a service provider that provides a hyperlink to a site containing infringing material which it then caches on its system in order to facilitate access to it by its users. This service provider is engaging in at least three functions that may be subject to the limitation on liability: transitory digital network communications under subsection (a), system caching under subsection (b), and information location tools under subsection (d). If this service provider (as defined in subsection (j)(1)(A) in the case of transitory digital communications, or as defined in subsection (j)(1)(B) in the case of system caching or information location tools) meets the

56

threshold criteria spelled out in subsection (h)(1), then for its acts of system caching defined in subsection (b), it may avail itself of the liability limitations stated in subsection (b), which incorporate the limitations on injunctive relief described in subsection (i)(1)(B) and (i)(3). If it is claimed that the same company is committing an infringement by using information location tools to link its users to infringing material, as defined in subsection (d), then its fulfillment of the requirements to claim the system caching liability limitation does not affect whether it qualifies for the liability limitation for information location tools; the criteria in subsection (d), rather than those in subsection (b), are applicable. Section 512(m) codifies this principle by providing that the determination of whether a service provider qualifies for one liability limitation has no effect on the determination of whether it qualifies for a separate and distinct liability limitation under another subsection of section 512.

Section 203. Conforming amendment

This section amends the table of sections for chapter 5 of the Copyright Act (17 U.S.C. 501 et. seq.) to reflect the new section 512, as created by this title.

Section 204. Liability of educational institutions for online infringement of copyright

Subsection 204(a) directs the Register of Copyrights to consult with representatives of copyright owners and nonprofit educational institutions and to submit to the Congress within 6 months after enactment of the bill recommendations regarding the liability of nonprofit educational institutions for copyright infringements that take place through the use of the institution's computer system or network, where the institution qualifies as a "service provider" under the provisions of this Title. Included in the Register's report are to be any recommendations for legislation that the Register considers appropriate.

Subsection 204(b) sets forth specific considerations that the Register shall take into account, where relevant, in formulating her recommendations to the Congress.

TITLE III—COMPUTER MAINTENANCE OR REPAIR

Section 301. Limitation on exclusive rights; computer programs

This section effects a minor, yet important clarification in section 117 of the Copyright Act (17 U.S.C. 117) to ensure that the lawful owner or lessee of a computer machine may authorize an independent service provider—a person unaffiliated with either the owner or lessee of the machine—to activate the machine for the sole purpose of servicing its hardware components. When a computer is activated, certain software or parts thereof is automatically copied into the machine's random access memory, or "RAM". A clarification in the Copyright Act is necessary in light of judicial decisions holding that such copying is a "reproduction" under section 106 of the Copyright Act (17 U.S.C. 106),[26] thereby calling into question the right of an independent service provider who is not the licensee of

---

[26] See MAI Sys. Corp. v. Peak Computer, 991 F.2d 511 (9th Cir. 1993), cert. denied, 114 S.Ct. 671 (1994).

57

the computer program resident on the client's machine to even activate that machine for the purpose of servicing the hardware components. This section does not in any way alter the law with respect to the scope of the term "reproduction" as it is used in the Copyright Act. Rather, this section it is narrowly crafted to achieve the objectives just described—namely, ensuring that an independent service provider may turn on a client's computer machine in order to service its hardware components, provided that such service provider complies with the provisions of this section designed to protect the rights of copyright owners of computer software.

Paragraphs (1) and (2) make technical changes to the structure of section 117, dividing the existing provisions between two subsections, the first entitled "(a) Making of Additional Copy or Adaptation by Owner of Copy" and the second entitled "(b) Lease, Sale, or Other Transfer of Additional Copy or Adaptation." The operative provisions, and limitations, are in paragraph (3), which creates two new subsections in section 117, subsections (c) and (d).

Subsection (c)—Machine maintenance or repair.—The bill creates a new subsection (c) in section 117 of the Copyright Act (17 U.S.C. 117), which delineates the specific circumstances under which a reproduction of a computer program would not constitute infringement of copyright. The goal is to maintain undiminished copyright protection afforded under the Copyright Act to authors of computer programs, while making it possible for third parties to perform servicing of the hardware. This new subsection states that it is not an infringement of copyright for the owner or lessee of a machine to make or authorize the making of a copy of a computer program provided that the following conditions are met:

First, subsection (c) itself makes clear that the copy of the computer program must have been made solely and automatically by virtue of turning on the machine in order to perform repairs or maintenance on the hardware components of the machine. Moreover, the copy of the computer program which is reproduced as a direct and sole consequence of activation must be an authorized copy that has lawfully been installed in the machine. Authorized copies of computer programs are only those copies that have been made available with the consent of the copyright owner. Also, the acts performed by the service provider must be authorized by the owner or lessee of the machine.

Second, in accordance with paragraph (c)(1), the resulting copy may not be used by the person performing repairs or maintenance of the hardware components of the machine in any manner other than to effectuate the repair or maintenance of the machine. Once these tasks are completed, the copy of the program must be destroyed, which generally will happen automatically once the machine is turned off.

Third, as is made clear in paragraph (c)(2), the amendment is not intended to diminish the rights of copyright owners of those computer programs, or parts thereof, that also may be loaded into RAM when the computer is turned on, but which did not need to be so loaded in order for the machine to be turned on. A hardware manufacturer or

58

software developer might, for example, provide diagnostic and utility programs that load into RAM along with or as part of the operating system, even though they market those programs as separate products—either as freestanding programs, or pursuant to separate licensing agreements. Indeed, a password or other technical access device is sometimes required for the owner of the machine to be able to gain access to such programs. In other cases, it is not the hardware or software developer that has arranged for certain programs automatically to be reproduced when the machine is turned on; rather, the owner of the machine may have configured its computer to load certain applications programs into RAM as part of the boot-up process (such as a word processing program on a personal computer). This subsection is not intended to derogate from the rights of the copyright owners of such programs. In order to avoid inadvertent copyright infringement, these programs need to be covered by subsection (c), but only to the extent that they are automatically reproduced when the machine is turned on. This subsection is not intended to legitimize unauthorized access to and use of such programs just because they happen to be resident in the machine itself and are reproduced with or as a part of the operating system when the machine is turned on. According to paragraph (c)(2), if such a program is accessed or used without the authorization of the copyright owner, the initial reproduction of the program shall not be deemed exempt from infringement by this subsection.

Subsection (d)—Definitions.—Subsection (d) defines two terms not previously defined by the Copyright Act. Paragraph (1) defines the term "maintenance" as the servicing of the machine in order to make it work in accordance with its original specifications and any changes to those specifications authorized for that machine. These acts can include, but are not limited to, cleaning the machine, tightening connections, installing new components such as memory chips, circuit boards and hard disks, checking the proper functioning of these components, and other similar acts.

Paragraph (2) defines the term "repair" as the restoring of the machine to the state of working in accordance with its original specifications and any changes to those specifications authorized for that machine. These acts of repairing the hardware include, but are not limited to, replacing worn or defective components such as memory chips, circuit boards and hard disks, correcting the improper installation of new components, and other similar acts.

Both paragraphs (1) and (2) of this subsection are subject to the same limitations, which are intended to clarify that activating a machine in order to perform maintenance or repair does not constitute infringement as provided in subsection (c) if the maintenance or repair is undertaken to make the machine work in accordance with the parameters specified for such a machine and its component parts. Because technological improvements may lead customers to upgrade their machines, the language of both definitions authorizes service providers to maintain those components of the hardware that have been installed since the time the machine was originally acquired, or to install new components. But their acts shall be noninfringing under subsection (c) only if the components being serviced have been lawfully acquired and installed. Finally, the terms "maintenance" and "repair" do not include unauthorized adaptations, modifications, error corrections or any other changes to any software which may be in the machine being serviced.

TITLE IV—EPHEMERAL RECORDINGS; DISTANCE EDUCATION;
EXEMPTION FOR LIBRARIES AND ARCHIVES

Section 401. Ephemeral recordings

Section 401 amends section 112 of the Copyright Act (17 U.S.C. 112) to address two issues concerning the application of the ephemeral recording exemption in the digital age.

The first of these issues is the relationship between the ephemeral recording exemption and the Digital Performance Right in Sound Recordings Act of 1995 ("DPRA"). The DPRA granted sound recording copyright owners the exclusive right to perform their works publicly by means of digital audio transmission, subject to certain limitations, particularly those set forth in section 114(d). Among those limitations is an exemption for nonsubscription broadcast transmissions, which are defined as those made by terrestrial broadcast stations licensed as such by the FCC. 17 U.S.C. 114(d)(1)(A)(iii) and (j)(2). The ephemeral recording exemption presently privileges certain activities of a transmitting organization when it is entitled to transmit a performance or display under a license or transfer of copyright ownership or under the limitations on exclusive rights in sound recordings specified by section 114(a). The Committee believes that the ephemeral recording exemption should apply to broadcast radio and television stations when they make nonsubscription digital broadcasts permitted by the DPRA. The Committee has therefore changed the existing language of the ephemeral recording exemption (redesignated as 112(a)(1)) to extend explicitly to broadcasters the same privilege they already enjoy with respect to analog broadcasts.

The second of these issues is the relationship between the ephemeral recording exemption and the anticircumvention provisions that the bill adds as section 1201 of the Copyright Act. Concerns were expressed that if use of copy protection technologies became widespread, a transmitting organization might be prevented from engaging in its traditional activities of assembling transmission programs and making ephemeral recordings permitted by section 112 for purposes of its own transmissions within its local service area and of archival preservation and security. To address this concern, the Committee has added to section 112 a new paragraph that permits transmitting organizations to engage in activities that otherwise would violate section 1201(a)(1) in certain limited circumstances when necessary for the exercise of the transmitting organization's privilege to make ephemeral recordings under redesignated section 112(a)(1). By way of example, if a radio station could not make a permitted ephemeral recording from a commercially available phonorecord without violating section 1201(a)(1), then the radio station could request from the copyright owner the necessary means of making a permitted ephemeral recording. If the

60

copyright owner did not then either provide a phonorecord that could be reproduced or otherwise provide the necessary means of making a permitted ephemeral recording from the phonorecord already in the possession of the radio station, the radio station would not be liable for violating section 1201(a)(1) for taking the steps necessary for engaging in activities permitted under section 112(a)(1). The radio station would, of course, be liable for violating section 1201(a)(1) if it engaged in activities prohibited by that section in other than the limited circumstances permitted by section 112(a)(1).

Section 402. Limitation on exclusive rights; distance education

Section 402(a) directs the Register of Copyrights to consult with representatives of copyright owners, nonprofit educational institutions, and nonprofit libraries and archives and to submit recommendations to the Congress no later than 6 months after the date of enactment of the bill on how to promote distance education through digital technologies, including interactive digital networks, while maintaining an appropriate balance between the rights of copyright owners and the needs of users. Where appropriate, the Register shall include legislative recommendations to achieve those objectives.

Section 402(b) specifies considerations which the Register shall take into account in formulating such recommendations.

Section 403. Exemption for libraries and archives

Section 108 of the Copyright Act (17 U.S.C. 108) permits libraries and archives of the type described in that section to make and, in some cases, distribute a limited number of copies of certain types of copyrighted works, without the permission of the copyright holder, for specified purposes relating to these entities' functions as repositories of such works for public reference. Section 403 of the bill updates section 108 to allow these entities to take advantage of digital technologies when engaging in specified preservation activities.

Except for the amendment to paragraph (a)(3), which deals with the inclusion of copyright notice on all copies or phonorecords of works made or distributed pursuant to section 108, the amendments revise either subsection (b), which addresses the reproduction and distribution of a copy or phonorecord of an unpublished work for purposes of preservation and security or for deposit for research use in another library or archive of the type described; or subsection (c), which addresses the reproduction of a copy or phonorecord of a published work for the purpose of replacement of a copy of that work that is damaged, deteriorating, lost, or stolen, if an unused replacement copy cannot be obtained at a fair price.

The amendment to paragraph (a)(3) of section 108 is intended to ease the burden on libraries and archives of the current law's requirement that a notice of copyright be included on copies that are reproduced under section 108. Under this amendment, such notice would be required only where the particular copy that is reproduced by the library or archives itself bears a notice. In other words, a notice appearing on the material copied would still need to be maintained, and could not be deleted. On the other hand, if

61

the copy being reproduced does not bear a copyright notice, the library or archives would fully satisfy its obligation under this section by simply placing on the reproduction a legend that states "This work may be protected by copyright," or words to that effect. This minimal obligation is similar to those found in subsections (e) and (f) of existing section 108, which condition the exemption in those subsections on the display of a general notice or warning of potential copyright protection.

Subsection (b) currently permits a library or archive under this section to make and distribute one copy or phonorecord of an unpublished work solely for purposes of preservation and security or for deposit for research use in another library or archives, provided that the duplication of the work occurs "in facsimile form." The legislative history to that section makes clear that, when this language was enacted more than twenty years ago, Congress intended to permit the copy to be made by microfilm or electrostatic photocopying process, but not in a computerized form i.e., "in machine readable language for storage in an information system." [27]

The amendment to subsection (b) permits a library or archive to make (for itself or another library or archive of the type described by clause (2) of subsection (a)) up to 3 copies or phonorecords for these purposes, rather than just one, and permits such copies or phonorecords to be made in digital as well as analog formats. In recognition of the risk that uncontrolled public access to the copies or phonorecords in digital formats could substantially harm the interests of the copyright owner by facilitating immediate, flawless and widespread reproduction and distribution of additional copies or phonorecords of the work, the amendment provides that any copy of a work that the library or archive makes in a digital format must not be otherwise distributed in that format and must not be made available in that format to the public outside the premises of the library or archives. In this way, the amendment permits the utilization of digital technologies solely for the purposes of this subsection.

Similarly, subsection (c) currently permits a library or archives under this section to make one copy or phonorecord of any published work solely for purposes of replacement of a copy or phonorecord that is damaged, deteriorating, lost or stolen, provided that the library or archive has determined after a reasonable effort that an unused replacement cannot be obtained at a fair price, and provided that the duplication of the work occurs "in facsimile form."

As in subsection (b), the amendment to subsection (c) permits a library or archive to make and use three copies or phonorecords for these purposes, rather than just one, and permits such copies or phonorecords to be made in digital as well as analog formats, with the proviso that any copy of a work that the library or archive makes in a digital format must not be made available to the public in that format except for use on the premises of a library or archives in lawful possession of such copy. In the view of the Committee, this proviso is necessary to ensure that the amendment strikes the appropriate balance, permitting the use of digital technology by libraries and archives while guarding against the poten-

---

[27] *See* H.R. Rep. No. 1476, 94th Cong., 2d Sess. (1976).

62

tial harm to the copyright owner's market from patrons obtaining unlimited access to digital copies from any location.

The amendment to subsection (c) also broadens its coverage to allow the updating of obsolete formats. It permits the making of such copies or phonorecords of a work "if the existing format in which the work is stored has become obsolete." This provision is intended to permit libraries and archives to ensure that copies of works in their collections continue to be accessible and useful to their patrons. In order to ensure that the provision does not inadvertently result in the suppression of ongoing commercial offerings of works in still-usable formats, the amendment explicitly provides that, for purposes of this subsection, a format will be considered obsolete only if the machine or device necessary to render perceptible a work stored in that format is no longer manufactured or reasonably available in a commercial marketplace. Under this language, if the needed machine or device can only be purchased in second-hand stores, it should not be considered "reasonably available."

Finally, the Committee wants to make clear that, just as when section 108 of the Copyright Act was first enacted, the term "libraries" and "archives" as used and described in this provision still refer to such institutions only in the conventional sense of entities that are established as, and conduct their operations through, physical premises in which collections of information may be used by researchers and other members of the public. Although online interactive digital networks have since given birth to online digital "libraries" and "archives" that exist only in the virtual (rather than physical) sense on websites, bulletin boards and homepages across the Internet, it is not the Committee's intent that section 108 as revised apply to such collections of information. The ease with which such sites are established online literally allows anyone to create his or her own digital "library" or "archives." The extension of the application of section 108 to all such sites would be tantamount to creating an exception to the exclusive rights of copyright holders that would permit any person who has an online website, bulletin board or a homepage to freely reproduce and distribute copyrighted works. Such an exemption would swallow the general rule and severely impair the copyright owners' right and ability to commercially exploit their copyrighted works. Consequently, the Committee intends that references to "the premises of the library or archives" in amended sections 108 (b)(2) and (c)(2) mean only physical premises.

VI. COST ESTIMATE

U.S. CONGRESS,
CONGRESSIONAL BUDGET OFFICE,
Washington, DC, May 11, 1998.

Hon. ORRIN G. HATCH,
Chairman, Committee on the Judiciary, U.S. Senate, Washington, DC.

DEAR MR. CHAIRMAN: The Congressional Budget Office has prepared the enclosed cost estimate for S. 2037, the Digital Millennium Copyright Act of 1998.

63

If you wish further details on this estimate, we will be pleased to provide them. The CBO staff contacts are Kim Cawley (for federal costs), Pepper Santalucia (for the state and local impact), and Matthew Eyles (for the private-sector impact).

Sincerely,

JAMES L. BLUM
(For June E. O'Neill, Director).

Enclosure.

CONGRESSIONAL BUDGET OFFICE COST ESTIMATE

S. 2037—DIGITAL MILLENNIUM COPYRIGHT ACT OF 1998

CBO estimates that enacting S. 2037 would have no significant impact on the federal budget. Enacting the bill would establish new criminal penalties and thus could affect both receipts and direct spending. hence, pay-as-you-go procedures would apply, but we expect that any changes in receipts and direct spending would be insignificant. S. 2037 contains an intergovernmental and a private-sector mandate as defined in the Unfunded Mandates Reform Act of 1995 (UMRA), but the costs of the mandates would not exceed the thresholds in the law.

Title I of S. 2037 would amend U.S. copyright law to comply with two treaties produced by the December 1996 conference of the World Intellectual Property Organization—one regarding the use of copyrighted material in digital environments, and the other dealing with international copyright protection of performers and producers of phonograms. Section 103 would establish criminal fines of up to $1 million for anyone attempting to circumvent copyright protection systems or falsifying or altering copyright management information. Enacting this provision could increase governmental receipts from the collection of fines, but we estimate that any such increase would be less than $500,000 annually. Criminal fines are deposited in the Crime Victims Fund and are spent in the following year. Thus any change in direct spending from the fund would also amount to less than $500,000 annually.

Title II would limit the liability for copyright infringement of persons who are providers of on-line services or network access. Title III would amend copyright law to allow copies of computer programs to be made for the purpose of repairing or maintaining a computer. Title IV would require copyright owners that protect their audio recordings with technical measures to prevent the reproduction of such work, to make available to transmitting organizations entitled to make a copy of such work the necessary means of making a copy, provided that it is technologically and economically feasible for the copyright owner to do so. The bill would direct the Copyright Office to make recommendations to the Congress concerning the liability for copyright infringement of nonprofit educational institutions when they are providers of Internet services. The bill also would seek recommendations from the Copyright Office in using digital technologies to promote distance learning while protecting the rights of copyright owners. Based on information from the Copyright Office, CBO estimates that preparing these provisions would cost less than $300,000.

64

Section 4 of UMRA excludes from the application of that act any legislative provisions that are necessary for the ratification or implementation of international treaty obligations. CBO has determined that Title I of the bill fits within that exclusion, because it is necessary for the implementation of the WIPO Copyright Treaty and the WIPO Performances and Phonograms Treaty.

Title IV of S. 2037 would impose a mandate on certain owners of copyrights who apply technical protections to works that prevent their reproduction. Title IV would require copyright owners who employ mechanisms that prevent the reproduction of copyrighted works to make available to federally licensed broadcasters the necessary means to copy such works. Under current law, federally licensed broadcasters are authorized to reproduce copyright-protected material under specific conditions. Since this mandate would apply to both public and private entities that own copyrights, it would be considered both a private-sector and an intergovernmental mandate.

The use of reproduction protections envisioned in the bill is not yet widespread. Furthermore, copyright owners may claim economic hardship or technical infeasibility to avoid the new requirement and the costs of providing federally licensed broadcasters with the means to copy technically protected works would likely be modest. Therefore, CBO estimates that the direct cost of the new mandates would be well below the statutory thresholds in UMRA.

The CBO staff contacts for this estimate are Kim Cawley (for Federal costs); Pepper Santalucia (for the State and local impact); and Matthew Eyles (for the private-sector impact). This estimate was approved by Paul N. Van de Water, Assistant Director for Budget Analysis.

VII. REGULATORY IMPACT STATEMENT

In compliance with paragraph 11(b)(1), rule XXVI of the Standing Rules of the Senate, the Committee, after due consideration, concludes that S. 2037 will not have significant regulatory impact.

VIII. ADDITIONAL VIEWS OF MR. LEAHY

The successful adoption by the World Intellectual Property Organization (WIPO) in December 1996 of two new copyright treaties—one on written material and one on sound recordings—was appropriately lauded in the United States. The WIPO Copyright Treaty and the WIPO Performances and Phonograms Treaty will give a significant boost to the protection of intellectual property rights around the world, and stand to benefit important American creative industries—from movies, recordings, computer software and many other copyrighted materials that are subject to piracy online.

According to Secretary Daley of the Department of Commerce, for the most part, "the treaties largely incorporate intellectual property norms that are already part of U.S. law." What the treaties will do is give American owners of copyrighted material an important tool to protect their intellectual property in those countries that become a party to the treaties. With an ever-expanding global marketplace, such international protection is critical to protect American companies and, ultimately, American jobs and the U.S. economy.

The President submitted the two WIPO treaties to the U.S. Senate on July 29, 1997, as well as draft legislation to implement the two treaties. I was proud to introduce this draft implementing legislation, S. 1121, with Senators Hatch, Thompson, and Kohl on July 29, 1997.

This legislation is the culmination of an effort to ensure that the appropriate copyright protections are in place around the world to foster the enormous growth of the Internet and other digital computer networks. Our dependence on interconnected computers only grows as a means to communicate, manage our personal and business affairs and obtain the goods and services we want. Indeed, computer networks will increasingly become the means of transmitting copyrighted works in the years ahead. This presents great opportunities but also poses significant risks to authors and our copyright industries.

We must make sure that our copyright laws protect the intellectual property rights of creative works available online in ways that promote the use of the Internet, both by content providers and users. The future growth of computer networks like the Internet and of digital, electronic communications requires it. Otherwise, owners of intellectual property will be unwilling to put their material online. If there is no content worth reading online, the growth of this medium will be stifled, and public accessibility will be retarded.

The Clinton administration showed great foresight when it formed, in 1993, the Information Infrastructure Task Force (IITF), which in turn established the Working Group on Intellectual Property Rights to examine and recommend changes to keep copyright

(65)

66

law current with new technology. In 1995, the Administration's Working Group on Intellectual Property Rights released its report, "Intellectual Property and the National Information Infrastructure," in which it explained the importance of adequate copyright protection for the future of the Internet:

> The full potential of the NII will not be realized if the education, information and entertainment products protected by intellectual property laws are not protected effectively when disseminated via the NII. Creators and other owners of intellectual property will not be willing to put their interests at risk if appropriate systems—both in the U.S. and internationally—are not in place to permit them to set and enforce the terms and conditions under which their works are made available in the NII environment. Likewise, the public will not use the services available on the NII and generate the market necessary for its success unless a wide variety of works are available under equitable and reasonable terms and conditions, and the integrity of those works is assured. All the computers, telephones, fax machines, scanners, cameras, keyboards, televisions, monitors, printers, switches, routers, wires, cables, networks, and satellites in the world will not create a successful NII, if there is no content. What will drive the NII is the content moving through it.

The same year that report was issued, Senator Hatch and I joined together to introduce "The NII Copyright Protection Act of 1995", S. 1284, which incorporated the recommendations of the Administration. That legislative proposal confronted fundamental questions about the role of copyright in the next century—many of which are echoed by the Digital Millennium Copyright Act (DMCA), which was reported by the Senate Judiciary Committee.

I note that the Report of the Administration's Working Group on Intellectual Property also generally supported "the amendments to the copyright law and the criminal law (which sets out sanctions for criminal copyright violations) set forth in S. 1122, introduced in the 104th Congress by Senators Leahy and Feingold following consultations with the Justice Department." While the 104th Congress did not act on this legislation, I revised and reintroduced this bill as S. 1044 in 1997. This important legislation, the No Electronic Theft Act, to adapt to the emerging digital environment was finally enacted in this Congress.

Title I of the DMCA is based on the administration's recommendations for legislation to implement the two WIPO treaties, as reflected in S. 1121. In sum, Title I makes certain technical changes to conform our copyright laws to the treaties and substantive amendments to comply with two new treaty obligations. Specifically, the treaties oblige the signatories to provide legal protections against circumvention of technological measures used by copyright owners to protect their works, and against violations of the integrity of copyright management information (CMI), which identifies a work, its author, the copyright owner and any information about the terms and conditions of use of the work. The bill adds a new chapter to U.S. copyright law to implement the

67

anticircumvention and CMI provisions, along with corresponding civil and criminal penalties. Title II of the DMCA provides limitations, under certain conditions, on copyright infringement liability for Internet service providers (ISP's) and online service providers (OSP's). Title III provides a statutory exemption in the Copyright Act to ensure that the lawful owner or lessee of a computer machine may authorize an independent service technician to activate the computer in order to service its hardware components. Title IV begins the process of updating our Nation's copyright laws with respect to library, archives, and educational uses of copyrighted works in the digital age.

Following intensive discussions with a number of interested parties, including libraries, universities, small businesses, ISP's and OSP's, telephone companies, computer users, broadcasters, content providers and device manufacturers, the Senate Judiciary Committee was able to reach unanimous agreement on certain modifications and additions incorporated into the DMCA.

For example, significant provisions were added to the bill in Title II to clarify the liability for copyright infringement of online and Internet service providers. These provisions set forth "safe harbors" from liability for ISP's and OSP's under clearly defined circumstances, which both encourage responsible behavior and protect important intellectual property rights. In addition, during the Committee's consideration of this bill, an Ashcroft-Leahy-Hatch amendment was adopted to ensure that computer users are given reasonable notice of when their Web sites are the subject of infringement complaints, and to provide procedures for computer users to have material that is mistakenly taken down put back online.

This bill contains a number of provisions designed to help libraries and archives. First, libraries expressed concerns about the possibility of criminal sanctions or potentially ruinous monetary liability for actions taken in good faith. This bill makes sure that libraries acting in good faith can never be subject to fines or civil damages. Specifically, a library is exempt from monetary liability in a civil suit if it was not aware and had no reason to believe that its acts constituted a violation. In addition, libraries are completely exempt from the criminal provisions.

Second, the bill contains a "browsing" exception for libraries. Libraries have indicated that in an online environment dominated by encrypted works it may be impossible for them to gain access to works to decide whether or not to acquire them. The current version of the bill permits libraries to disregard access prevention technologies in order to make a good faith determination of whether or not it would like to buy a copy of a work. If the library decides that it wishes to acquire the work it must negotiate with the copyright owner just as libraries do today.

Third, Senator Hatch, Senator Ashcroft, and I crafted an amendment to provide for the preservation of digital works by qualified libraries and archives. The ability of libraries to preserve legible copies of works in digital form is one I consider critical. Under present law, libraries are permitted to make a single facsimile copy of works in their collections for preservation purposes, or to replace lost, damaged or stolen copies of works that have become commercially unavailable. This law, however, has become outmoded by

68

changing technology and preservation practices. The bill ensures that libraries' collections will continue to be available to future generations by permitting libraries to make up to three copies in any format—including in digital form. This was one of the proposals in The National Information Infrastructure (NII) Copyright Protection Act of 1995, which I sponsored in the last Congress. The Register of Copyrights, among others, has supported that proposal.

In addition, the bill would permit a library to transfer a work from one digital format to another if the equipment needed to read the earlier format becomes unavailable commercially. This change addresses a problem that should be familiar to anyone whose office has boxes of eight-inch floppy disks tucked away somewhere.

These provisions go a long way toward meeting the concerns that libraries have expressed about the original bill, S. 1121.

Another issue that the bill addresses is distance learning. When Congress enacted the present copyright law it recognized the potential of broadcast and cable technology to supplement classroom teaching, and to bring the classroom to those who, because of their disabilities or other special circumstances, are unable to attend classes. At the same time, Congress also recognized the potential for unauthorized transmissions of works to harm the markets for educational uses of copyrighted materials. In the present Copyright Act, we struck a careful balance and crafted a narrow exemption. But as with so many areas of copyright law, the advent of digital technology requires us to take another look at the issue.

I recognize that the issue of distance learning has been under consideration for the past several years by the Conference on Fair Use (CONFU) that was established by the administration to consider issues relating to fair use in the digital environment. In spite of the hard work of the participants, CONFU has so far been unable to forge a comprehensive agreement on guidelines for the application of fair use to digital distance learning.

We made tremendous strides in the Committee to chart the appropriate course for updating the Copyright Act to permit the use of copyrighted works in valid distance learning activities. Senator Hatch, Senator Ashcroft, and I joined together to ask the Copyright Office to facilitate discussions among interested library and educational groups and content providers with a view toward making recommendations that could be incorporated into the DMCA at the April 30 markup.

Based on the Copyright Office's recommendations, we incorporated into the DMCA a new section 122 requiring the Copyright Office to make broader recommendations to Congress on digital distance education within six months. Upon receiving the Copyright Office's recommendations, it is my hope that the Senate Judiciary Committee will promptly commence hearings on the issue and move expeditiously to enact further legislation on the matter. I know that all members on this Committee are as anxious as I am to complete the process that we started in Committee of updating the Copyright Act to permit the appropriate use of copyrighted works in valid distance learning activities. This step should be viewed as a beginning—not an end, and we are committed to reaching that end point as quickly as possible.

69

Senator Feinstein had sought to clarify when a university would be held responsible for the actions of its employees in connection with its eligibility for the safe harbors spelled out in title II of the bill. I and others on the Committee agreed with Senator Feinstein that, because of the importance, complexity, and implications for other online service providers, including libraries and archives of this issue, we should have the Copyright Office examine the issue in a comprehensive fashion as well.

Amendments sponsored by Senator Ashcroft, Senator Hatch, and I were also crafted to address the issues of reverse engineering, ephemeral recordings and to clarify the use of copyright management information in the course of certain analog and digital transmissions in broadcasting. Additional legislative language was incorporated into the bill to clarify that the law enforcement exemptions apply to all government agencies which conduct law enforcement and intelligence work, as well as to government contractors engaging in intelligence, investigative, or protective work.

Finally, to assuage the concerns of the consumer electronics manufacturers and others that the bill might require them to design their products to respond to any particular technological protection measure, Senator Hatch, Senator Ashcroft, and I crafted an amendment that clarified the bill on this issue. We also agreed to incorporate provisions into the bill clarifying that nothing in the bill will prevent parents form controlling their children's access to the Internet or individuals from protecting personal identifying information.

The DMCA is a product of the Senate Judiciary Committee's recognition that ours is a time of unprecedented challenge to copyright protection. Copyright has been the engine that has traditionally converted the energy of artistic creativity into publicly available arts and entertainment. Historically, the Government's role has been to encourage creativity and innovation by protecting copyrights that create incentives for the dissemination to the public of new works and forms of expression. That is the tradition which I have sought to honor and which I intend to continue to promote.

Now, with the DMCA, the Senate Judiciary Committee takes another important step toward protecting American ingenuity and creative expression. This bill is a well-balanced package of proposals that address the needs of creators, consumers and commerce in the digital age and well into the next century.

PATRICK LEAHY.

IX. CHANGES IN EXISTING LAW

In compliance with paragraph 12 of rule XXVI of the Standing Rules of the Senate, changes in existing law made by S. 2037, as reported, are shown as follows (existing law proposed to be omitted is enclosed in black brackets, new matter is printed in italic, and existing law in which no change is proposed is shown in roman):

UNITED STATES CODE

* * * * * * *

TITLE 17—COPYRIGHTS

CHAPTER 1—SUBJECT MATTER AND SCOPE OF COPYRIGHT

* * * * * * *

§ 101. Definitions

Except as otherwise provided in this title, as used in this title, the following terms and their variant forms mean the following:

* * * * * * *

[A work is a "Berne Convention work" if—

[(1) in the case of an unpublished work, one or more of the authors is a national of a nation adhering to the Berne Convention, or in the case of a published work, one of more of the authors is a national of a nation adhering to the Berne Convention on the date of first publication;

[(2) the work was first published in a nation adhering to the Berne Convention, or was simultaneously first published in a nation adhering to the Berne Convention and in a foreign nation that does not adhere to the Berne Convention;

[(3) in the case of an audiovisual work—

[(A) if one or more of the authors is a legal entity, that author has its headquarters in a nation adhering to the Berne Convention; or

[(B) if one or more of the authors is an individual, that author is domiciled, or has his or her habitual residence in a nation adhering to the Berne Convention;

(70)

71

⟦(4) in the case of a pictorial, graphic, or sculptural work that is incorporated in a building or other structure, the building or structure is located in a nation adhering to the Berne Convention; or

⟦(5) in the case of an architectural work embodied in a building, such building is erected in a country adhering to the Berne Convention.

⟦For purposes of paragraph (1), an author who is domiciled in or has his or her habitual residence in, a nation adhering to the Berne Convention is considered to be a national of that nation. For purposes of paragraph (2), a work is considered to have been simultaneously published in two or more nations if its dates of publication are within 30 days of one another.⟧

*   *   *   *   *   *   *

⟦The "country of origin" of a Berne Convention work, for⟧ *For* purposes of section 411, ⟦is the United States⟧ *a work is a "United States work" only* if—

(1) in the case of a published work, the work is first published—

(A) in the United States;

(B) simultaneously in the United States and another ⟦nation or nations adhering to the Berne Convention⟧ *treaty party or parties*, whose law grants a term of copyright protection that is the same as or longer than the term provided in the United States;

(C) simultaneously in the United States and a foreign nation that ⟦does not adhere to the Berne Convention⟧ *is not a treaty party*; or

(D) in a foreign nation that ⟦does not adhere to the Berne Convention⟧ *is not a treaty party*, and all of the authors of the work are nationals, domiciliaries, or habitual residents of, or in the case of an audiovisual work legal entities with headquarters in, the United States;

(2) in the case of an unpublished work, all the authors of the work are nationals, domiciliaries, or habitual residents of the United States, or, in the case of an unpublished audiovisual work, all the authors are legal entities with headquarters in the United States; or

(3) in the case of a pictorial, graphic, or sculptural work incorporated in a building or structure, the building or structure is located in the United States.

⟦For the purposes of section 411, the "country of origin" of any other Berne Convention work is not the United States.⟧

*   *   *   *   *   *   *

A work is "fixed" in a tangible medium of expression when its embodiment in a copy or phonorecord, by or under the authority of the author, is sufficiently permanent or stable to permit it to be perceived, reproduced, or otherwise communicated for a period of more than transitory duration. A work consisting of sounds, images, or both, that are being transmitted, is "fixed" for purposes of this title if a fixation of the work is being made simultaneously with its transmission.

72

The "Geneva Phonograms Convention" is the Convention for the Protection of Producers of Phonograms Against Unauthorized Duplication of Their Phonograms, concluded at Geneva, Switzerland on October 29, 1971.

The terms "including" and "such as" are illustrative and not limitative.

An "international agreement" is—
    (1) the Universal Copyright Convention;
    (2) the Geneva Phonograms Convention;
    (3) the Berne Convention;
    (4) the WTO Agreement;
    (5) the WIPO Copyright Treaty;
    (6) the WIPO Performances and Phonograms Treaty; and
    (7) any other copyright treaty to which the United States is a party.

*   *   *   *   *   *   *

To "transmit" a performance or display is to communicate it by any device or process whereby images or sounds are received beyond the place from which they are sent.

A "treaty party" is a country or intergovernmental organization other than the United States that is a party to an international agreement.

*   *   *   *   *   *   *   *

The author's "widow" or "widower" is the author's surviving spouse under the law of the author's domicile at the time of his or her death, whether or not the spouse has later re-married.

The "WIPO Copyright Treaty" is the WIPO Copyright Treaty concluded at Geneva, Switzerland, on December 20, 1996.

The "WIPO Performances and Phonograms Treaty" is the WIPO Performances and Phonograms Treaty concluded at Geneva, Switzerland on December 20, 1996.

*   *   *   *   *   *   *   *

A "work made for hire" is—
    (1) a work prepared by an employee within the scope of his or her employment; or

*   *   *   *   *   *   *

The "WTO Agreement" is the Agreement Establishing the World Trade Organization entered into on April 15, 1994. The terms "WTO Agreement" and "WTO member country" have the meanings given those terms in paragraphs (9) and (10) respectively of section 2 of the Uruguay Round Agreements Act.

*   *   *   *   *   *   *

§ 104. Subject matter of copyright: National origin

(a) UNPUBLISHED WORKS.—The works specified by sections 102 and 103, while unpublished, are subject to protection under this title without regard to the nationality or domicile of the author.

(b) PUBLISHED WORKS.—The works specified by sections 102 and 103, when published, are subject to protection under this title if—
    (1) on the date of first publication, one or more of the authors is a national or domiciliary of the United States, or is a

73

national domiciliary, or sovereign authority of a [foreign nation that is a party to a copyright treaty to which the United States is also a party] *treaty party*, or is a stateless person, wherever that person may be domiciled; or

(2) the work is first published in the United States or in a foreign nation that, on the date of first publication, is a [party to the Universal Copyright Convention] *treaty party*; or

(3) the work is a sound recording that was first fixed in a treaty party; or

(4) the work is a [Berne Convention work] *pictorial, graphic or sculptural work that is incorporated in a building or other structure, or an architectural work that is embodied in a building and the building or structure is located in the United States or a treaty party;* or

[(3)] *(5)* the work is first published by the United Nations or any of its specialized agencies, or by the Organization of American States; or

[(5)] *(6)* the work comes within the scope of a Presidential proclamation. Whenever the President finds that a particular foreign nation extends, to works by authors who are nationals or domiciliaries of the United States or to works that are first published in the United States, copyright protection on substantially the same basis as that on which the foreign nation extends protection to works of its own nationals and domiciliaries and works first published in that nation, the President may by proclamation extend protection under this title to works of which one or more of the authors is, on the date of first publication, a national, domiciliary, or sovereign authority of that nation, or which was first published in that nation. The President may revise, suspend, or revoke any such proclamation or impose any conditions or limitations on protection under a proclamation.

(7) For purposes of paragraph (2), a work that is published in the United States or a treaty party within thirty days of publication in a foreign nation that is not a treaty party shall be considered first published in the United States or such treaty party as the case may be.

*   *   *   *   *   *   *

(d) EFFECT OF PHONOGRAMS TREATIES.—Notwithstanding the provisions of subsection (b), no works other than sound recordings shall be eligible for protection under this title solely by virtue of the adherence of the United States to the Geneva Phonograms Convention or the WIPO Performances and Phonograms Treaty.

§ 104A. Copyright in restored works

(a) AUTOMATIC PROTECTION AND TERM.—

(1) TERM.—

(A) Copyright subsists, in accordance with this section, in restored works, and vests automatically on the date of restoration.

*   *   *   *   *   *   *

(h) DEFINITIONS.—For purposes of this section and section 109(a):

74

(1) The term "date of adherence or proclamation" means the earlier of the date on which a foreign nation which, as of the date the WTO Agreement enters into force with respect to the United States, is not a nation adhering to the Berne Convention or a WTO member country, becomes—

[(A) a nation adhering to the Berne Convention or a WTO member country; or]

[(B) subject to a Presidential proclamation under subsection (g).]

(A) a nation adhering to the Berne Convention;

(B) a WTO member country;

(C) a nation adhering to the WIPO Copyright Treaty;

(D) a nation adhering to the WIPO Performances and Phonograms Treaty; or

(E) subject to a Presidential proclamation under subsection (g).

*　　*　　*　　*　　*　　*　　*

[(3) The term "eligible country" means a nation, other than the United States, that is a WTO member country, adheres to the Berne Convention, or is subject to a proclamation under section 104A(g).]

(3) the term "eligible country" means a nation, other than the United States that—

(A) becomes a WTO member country after the date of enactment of the Uruguay Round Agreements Act;

(B) on the date of enactment is, or after the date of enactment becomes, a nation adhering to the Berne Convention;

(C) adheres to the WIPO Copyright Treaty;

(D) adheres to the WIPO Performances and Phonograms Treaty; or

(E) after such date of enactment becomes subject to a proclamation under subsection (g).

*　　*　　*　　*　　*　　*　　*

(6) The term "restored work" means an original work of authorship that—

(A) is protected under subsection (a);

(B) is not in the public domain in its source country through expiration of term of protection;

(C) is in the public domain in the United States due to—

*　　*　　*　　*　　*　　*　　*

(iii) lack of national eligibility; [and]

(D) has at least one author or rightholder who was, at the time the work was created, a national or domiciliary of an eligible country, and if published, was first published in an eligible country and not published in the United States during the 30-day period following publication in such eligible country[.]*; and*

(E) if the source country for the work is an eligible country solely by virtue of its adherence to the WIPO Performances and Phonograms Treaty, is a sound recording.

*　　*　　*　　*　　*　　*　　*

(8) The "source country" of a restored work is—

75

(A) a nation other than the United States;
(B) in the case of an unpublished work—
(i) the eligible country in which the author or rightholder is a national or domiciliary, or, if a restored work has more than 1 author or rightholder, *of which* the majority of foreign authors or rightholders are nationals or domiciliaries [of eligible countries]; or

* * * * * * *

[(9) The terms "WTO Agreement" and "WTO member country" have the meanings given those terms in paragraphs (9) and (10), respectively, of section 2 of the Uruguay Round Agreements Act.]

* * * * * * *

§ 108. Limitations on exclusive rights: Reproduction by libraries and archives

(a) [Notwithstanding] *Except as otherwise provided and notwithstanding* the provisions of section 106, it is not an infringement of copyright for a library or archives, or any of its employees acting within the scope of their employment, to reproduce no more than one copy or phonorecord of a work *except as provided in subsections (b) and (c),* or to distribute such copy or phonorecord, under the conditions specified by this section, if—

* * * * * * *

(3) the reproduction or distribution of the work includes a notice of copyright *if such notice appears on the copy of phonorecord that is reproduced under the provisions of this section, or a legend stating that the work may be protected by copyright if no such notice can be found on the copy or phonorecord that is reproduced under the provisions of this section.*

(b) The rights of reproduction and distribution under this section apply to [a copy or phonorecord] *three copies or phonorecords* of an unpublished work duplicated [in facsimile form] solely for purposes of preservation and security or for deposit for research use in another library or archives of the type described by clause (2) of subsection (a), [if the copy or phonorecord reproduced is currently in the collections of the library or archives.] *if*—
(1) *the copy or phonorecord reproduced is currently in the collections of the library or archives; and*
(2) *any such copy or phonorecord that is reproduced in digital format is not otherwise distributed in that format and is not made available to the public outside the premises of the library or archives in that format.*

(c) The right of reproduction under this section applies to [a copy or phonorecord] *three copies or phonorecords* of a published work duplicated [in facsimile form] solely for the purpose of replacement of a copy or phonorecord that is damaged, deteriorating, lost, or stolen, *or if the existing format in which the work is stored has become obsolete,* [if the library or archives has, after a reasonable effort, determined that an unused replacement cannot be obtained at a fair price.] *if*—

76

(1) the library or archives has, after a reasonable effort, determined that an unused replacement cannot be obtained at a fair price; and

(2) any such copy or phonorecord that is reproduced in digital format is not made available to the public in that format except for use on the premises of the library or archives in lawful possession of such copy.

For purposes of this subsection, a format shall be considered obsolete if the machine or device necessary to render perceptible a work stored in that format is no longer manufactured or is no longer reasonably available in the commercial marketplace.

*   *   *   *   *   *   *

§ 112. Limitations on exclusive rights: Ephemeral recordings

〖(a)〗 *(a)(1)* Notwithstanding the provisions of section 106, and except in the case of a motion picture or other audiovisual work, it is not an infringement of copyright for a transmitting organization entitled to transmit to the public a performance or display of a work, under a license or transfer of the copyright or under the limitations on exclusive rights in sound recordings specified by section, 114(a), *or for a transmitting organization that is broadcast radio or television station licensed as such by the Federal Communications Commission that broadcasts a performance of a sound recording in a digital format on a nonsubscription basis.* to make no more than one copy or phonorecord of a particular transmission program embodying the performance or display, if—

〖(1)〗 *(A)* the copy of phonorecord is retained and used solely by the transmitting organization that made it, and no further copies or phonorecords are reproduced from it; and

〖(2)〗 *(B)* the copy or phonorecord is used solely for the transmitting organization's own transmissions within its local service area, or for purposes of archival preservation or security; and

〖(3)〗 *(C)* unless preserved exclusively for archival purposes, the copy or phonorecord is destroyed within six months from the date the transmission program was first transmitted to the public.

(2) Where a transmitting organization entitled to make a copy or phonorecord under section 112(a)(1) in connection with the transmission to the public of a performance or display or a work pursuant to that section is prevented from making such copy or phonorecord by reason of the application by the copyright owner or technical measures that prevent the reproduction of the work, such copyright owner shall make available to the transmitting organization the necessary means for permitting the making of such copy of phonorecord within the meaning of that section, provided that it is technologically feasible and economically reasonable for the copyright owner to do so, and provided further that, if such copyright owner fails to do so in a timely manner in light of the transmitting organizations' reasonable business requirements, the transmitting organization shall not be liable for a violation of section 1201(a)(1) of this

77

title for engaging in such activities as are necessary to make such copies or phonorecords as permitted under section 112(a)(1).

* * * * * * *

§ 117. Limitations on exclusive rights: Computer programs

[Notwithstanding] *(a) MAKING OF ADDITIONAL COPY OR ADAPTATION BY OWNER OF COPY.—Notwithstanding* the provisions of section 106, it is not an infringement for the owner of a copy of a computer program to make or authorize the making of another copy or adaption of that computer program provided:

* * * * * * *

[Any exact] *(b) LEASE, SALE, OR OTHER TRANSFER OF ADDITIONAL COPY OR ADAPTATION.—Any exact* copies prepared in accordance with the provisions of this section may be leased, sold, or otherwise transferred, along with the copy from which such copies were prepared, only as part of the lease, sale, or other transfer of all rights in the program. Adaptations so prepared may be transferred only with the authorization of the copyright owner.

(c) MACHINE MAINTENANCE OR REPAIR.—Notwithstanding the provisions of section 106, it is not an infringement for an owner or lessee of a machine to make or authorize the making of a copy of a computer program if such copy is made solely by virtue of the activation of a machine that lawfully contains an authorized copy of the computer program, for purposes only of maintenance or repair of that machine, if—

(1) such new copy is used in no other manner and is destroyed immediately after the maintenance or repair is completed; and

(2) with respect to any computer program or part thereof that is not necessary for that machine to be activated, such program or part thereof is not accessed or used other than to make such new copy by virtue of the activation of the machine.

(d) DEFINITIONS.—For purposes of this section—

(1) the "maintenance" of a machine is the servicing of the machine in order to make it work in accordance with its original specifications and any changes to those specifications authorized for that machine; and

(2) the "repair" of a machine is the restoring of the machine to the state of working in accordance with its original specifications and any changes to those specifications authorized for that machine.

* * * * * * *

CHAPTER 4—COPYRIGHT NOTICE, DEPOSIT, AND REGISTRATION

* * * * * * *

§ 411. Registration and infringement actions

(a) Except for [actions for infringement of copyright in Berne Convention works whose country of origin is not the United States and] an action brought for a violation of the rights of the author under section 106A(a), and subject to the provisions of subsection

78

(b), no action for infringement of the copyright in any *United States* work shall be instituted until registration of the copyright claim has been made in accordance with this title. In any case, however, where the deposit, application, and fee required for registration have been delivered to the Copyright Office in proper form and registration has been refused, the applicant is entitled to institute an action for infringement if notice thereof, with a copy of the complaint, is served on the Register of Copyrights. The Register may, at his or her option, become a party to the action with respect to the issue of registrability of the copyright claim by entering an appearance within sixty days after such service, but the Register's failure to become a party shall not deprive the court of jurisdiction to determine that issue.

* * * * * * *

CHAPTER 5—COPYRIGHT INFRINGEMENT AND REMEDIES

Sec.
501. Infringement of copyright.

* * * * * * *

511. Liability of States, instrumentalities of States, and State officials for infringement of copyright.
512. Liability of service providers for online infringement of copyright.

* * * * * * *

§ 507. Limitations on actions

(a) CRIMINAL PROCEEDINGS.—*Except as expressly provided elsewhere in this title,* [No] *no* criminal proceeding shall be maintained under the provisions of this title unless it is commenced within three years after the cause of action arose.

* * * * * * *

§ 512. Liability of service providers for online infringement of copyright

(a) DIGITAL NETWORK COMMUNICATIONS.—*A service provider shall not be liable for monetary relief, or except as provided in subsection (i) for injunctive or other equitable relief, for infringement for the provider's transmitting, routing, or providing connections for, material through a system or network controlled or operated by or for the service provider, or the intermediate and transient storage of such material in the course of such transmitting, routing or providing connections, if—*

(1) it was initiated by or at the direction of a person other than the service provider;

(2) it is carried out through an automatic technical process without selection of such material by the service provider;

(3) the service provider does not select the recipients of such material except as an automatic response to the request of another;

(4) no such copy of such material made by the service provider is maintained on the system or network in a manner ordinarily accessible to anyone other than anticipated recipients, and no such copy is maintained on the system or network in a

79

manner ordinarily accessible to the anticipated recipients for a longer period than is reasonably necessary for the communication; and

(5) the material is transmitted without modification to its content.

(b) System Caching.—A service provider shall not be liable for monetary relief, or except as provided in subsection (i) for injunctive or other equitable relief, for infringement for the intermediate and temporary storage of material on the system or network controlled or operated by or for the service provider, where (i) such material is made available online by a person other than such service provider, (ii) such material is transmitted from the person described in clause (i) through such system or network to someone other than that person at the direction of such other person, and (iii) the storage is carried out through an automatic technical process for the purpose of making such material available to users of such system or network who subsequently request access to that material from the person described in clause (i), provided that:

(1) such material is transmitted to such subsequent users without modification to its content from the manner in which the material otherwise was transmitted from the person described in clause (i);

(2) such service provider complies with rules concerning the refreshing, reloading or other updating of such material when specified by the person making that material available online in accordance with an accepted industry standard data communications protocol for the system or network through which that person makes the material available; provided that the rules are not used by the person described in clause (i) to prevent or unreasonably impair such intermediate storage;

(3) such service provider does not interfere with the ability of technology associated with such material that returns to the person described in clause (i) the information that would have been available to such person if such material had been obtained by such subsequent users directly from such person, provided that such technology—

(A) does not significantly interfere with the performance of the provider's system or network or with the intermediate storage of the material;

(B) is consistent with accepted industry standard communications protocols; and

(C) does not extract information from the provider's system or network other than the information that would have been available to such person if such material had been accessed by such users directly from such person;

(4) either—

(A) the person described in clause (i) does not currently condition access to such material; or

(B) if access to such material is so conditioned by such person, by a current individual pre-condition, such as a pre-condition based on payment of a fee, or provision of a password or other information, the service provider permits access to the stored material in significant part only to

80

users of its system or network that have been so authorized and only in accordance with those conditions; and

(5) if the person described in clause (i) makes that material available online without the authorization of the copyright owner, then the service provider responds expeditiously to remove, or disable access to, the material that is claimed to be infringing upon notification of claimed infringements described in subsection (c)(3); provided that the material has previously been removed from the originating site, and the party giving the notification includes in the notification a statement confirming that such material has been removed or access to it has been disabled or ordered to be removed or have access disabled.

(c) INFORMATION STORED ON SERVICE PROVIDERS.—

(1) IN GENERAL.—A service provider shall not be liable for monetary relief, or except as provided in subsection (i) for injunctive or other equitable relief, for infringement for the storage at the direction of a user of material that resides on a system or network controlled or operated by or for the service provider, if the service provider—

(A)(i) does not have actual knowledge that the material or activity is infringing,

(ii) in the absence of such actual knowledge, is not aware of facts or circumstances from which infringing activity is apparent, or

(iii) if upon obtaining such knowledge or awareness, the service provider acts expeditiously to remove or disable access to, the material;

(B) does not receive a financial benefit directly attributable to the infringing activity, where the service provider has the right and ability to control such activity; and

(C) in the instance of a notification of claimed infringement as described in paragraph (3), responds expeditiously to remove, or disable access to, the material that is claimed to be infringing or to be the subject of infringing activity.

(2) DESIGNATED AGENT.—The limitations on liability established in this subsection apply only if the service provider has designated an agent to receive notifications of claimed infringement described in paragraph (3), by substantially making the name, address, phone number, electronic mail address of such agent, and other contact information deemed appropriate by the Register of Copyrights, available through its service, including on its website, and by providing such information to the Copyright Office. The Register of Copyrights shall maintain a current directory of agents available to the public for inspection, including through the Internet, in both electronic and hard copy formats.

(3) ELEMENTS OF NOTIFICATION.—

(A) To be effective under this subsection, a notification of claimed infringement means any written communication provided to the service provider's designated agent that includes substantially the following:

(i) a physical or electronic signature of a person authorized to act on behalf of the owner of an exclusive right that is allegedly infringed;

81

(ii) identification of the copyrighted work claimed to have been infringed, or, if multiple such works at a single online site are covered by a single notification, a representative list of such works at that site;

(iii) identification of the material that is claimed to be infringing or to be the subject of infringing activity that is to be removed or access to which is to be disabled, and information reasonably sufficient to permit the service provider to locate the material;

(iv) information reasonably sufficient to permit the service provider to contact the complaining party, such as an address, telephone number, and, if available an electronic mail address at which the complaining party may be contacted;

(v) a statement that the complaining party has a good faith belief that use of the material in the manner complained of is not authorized by the copyright owner, or its agent, or the law; and

(vi) a statement that the information in the notification is accurate, and under penalty of perjury, that the complaining party has the authority to enforce the owner's rights that are claimed to be infringed.

(B) A notification from the copyright owner or from a person authorized to act on behalf of the copyright owner that fails substantially to conform to the provisions of paragraph (3)(A) shall not be considered under paragraph (1)(A) in determining whether a service provider has actual knowledge or is aware of facts or circumstances from which infringing activity is apparent, provided that the provider promptly attempts to contact the complaining party or takes other reasonable steps to assist in the receipt of notice under paragraph (3)(A) when the notice is provided to the service provider's designated agent and substantially satisfies the provisions of subparagraphs (3)(A)(ii), (iii), and (iv).

(d) INFORMATION LOCATION TOOLS.—A service provider shall not be liable for monetary relief, or except as provided in subsection (i) for injunctive or other equitable relief, for infringement for the provider referring or linking users to an online location containing infringing material or activity by using information location tools, including a directory, index, reference, pointer or hypertext link, if the provider—

(1) does not have actual knowledge that the material or activity is infringing or, in the absence of such actual knowledge, is not aware of facts or circumstances from which infringing activity is apparent;

(2) does not receive a financial benefit directly attributable to the infringing activity, where the service provider has the right and ability to control such activity; and

(3) responds expeditiously to remove or disable the reference or link upon notification of claimed infringement as described in subsection (c)(3); provided that for the purposes of this paragraph, the element in subsection (c)(3)(A)(iii) shall be identification of the reference or link, to material or activity claimed to

82

be infringing, that is to be removed or access to which is to be disabled, and information reasonably sufficient to permit the service provider to locate such reference or link.

(e) MISREPRESENTATIONS.—Any person who knowingly materially misrepresents under this section (1) that material or activity is infringing, or (2) that material or activity was removed or disabled by mistake or misidentification, shall be liable for any damages, including costs and attorneys' fees, incurred by the alleged infringer, by any copyright owner or copyright owner's authorized licensee, or by the service provider, who is injured by such misrepresentation, as the result of the service provider relying upon such misrepresentation in removing or disabling access to the material or activity claimed to be infringing, or in replacing the removed material or ceasing to disable access to it.

(f) REPLACEMENT OF REMOVED OR DISABLED MATERIAL AND LIMITATION ON OTHER LIABILITY.—

(1) Subject to paragraph (2) of this subsection, a service provider shall not be liable to any person for any claim based on the service provider's good faith disabling of access to, or removal of, material or activity claimed to be infringing or based on facts or circumstances from which infringing activity is apparent, regardless or whether the material or activity is ultimately determined to be infringing.

(2) Paragraph (1) of this subsection shall not apply with respect to material residing at the direction of a subscriber of the service provider on a system or network controlled or operated by or for the service provider that is removed, or provided under subsection (c)(1)(C), unless the service provider:—

(A) takes reasonable steps promptly to notify the subscriber that it has removed or disabled access to the material;

(B) upon receipt of a counter notice as described in paragraph (3), promptly provides the person who provided the notice under subsection (c)(1)(C) with a copy of the counter notice, and informs such person that it will replace the removed material or cease disabling access to it in ten business days; and

(C) replaces the removed material and ceases disabling access to it not less than ten, nor more than fourteen, business days following receipt of the counter notice, unless its designated agent first receives notice from the person who submitted the notification under subsection (c)(1)(C) that such person has filed an action seeking a court order to restrain the subscriber from engaging in infringing activity relating to the material on the service provider's system or network.

(3) To be effective under this subsection, a counter notification means any written communication provided to the service provider's designated agent that includes substantially the following:

(A) a physical or electronic signature of the subscriber;

(B) identification of the material that has been removed or to which access has been disabled and the location at

which such material appeared before it was removed or access was disabled;

(C) a statement under penalty of perjury that the subscriber has a good faith belief that the material was removed or disabled as a result of mistake or misidentification of the material to be removed or disabled;

(D) the subscriber's name, address and telephone number, and a statement that the subscriber consents to the jurisdiction of Federal Court for the judicial district in which the address is located, or if the subscriber's address is outside of the United States, for any judicial district in which the service provider may be found, and that the subscriber will accept service of process from the person who provided notice under subsection (c)(1)(C) or agent of such person.

(4) A service provider's compliance with paragraph (2) shall not subject the service provider to liability for copyright infringement with respect to the material identified in the notice provided under subsection (c)(1)(C).

(g) IDENTIFICATION OF DIRECT INFRINGER.—The copyright owner or a person authorized to act on the owner's behalf may request an order for release of identification of an alleged infringer by filing (i) a copy of a notification described in subsection (c)(3)(A), including a proposed order, and (ii) a sworn declaration that the purpose of the order is to obtain the identity of an alleged infringer and that such information will only be used for the purpose of this title, with the clerk of any United States district court. The order shall authorize and order the service provider receiving the notification to disclose expeditiously to the copyright owner or person authorized by the copyright owner information sufficient to identify the alleged direct infringer of the material described in the notification to the extent such information is available to the service provider. The order shall be expeditiously issued if the accompanying notification satisfies the provisions of subsection (c)(3)(A) and the accompanying declaration is properly executed. Upon receipt of the order, either accompanying or subsequent to the receipt of a notification described in subsection (c)(3)(A), a service provider shall expeditiously give to the copyright owner or person authorized by the copyright owner the information required by the order, notwithstanding any other provision of law and regardless of whether the service provider responds to the notification.

(h) CONDITIONS FOR ELIGIBILITY.—

(1) ACCOMMODATION OF TECHNOLOGY.—The limitations on liability established by this section shall apply only if the service provider—

(A) has adopted and reasonably implemented, and informs subscribers of the service of, a policy for the termination of subscribers of the service who are repeat infringers; and

(B) accommodates and does not interfere with standard technical measures as defined in this subsection.

(2) DEFINITION.—As used in this section, "standard technical measures" are technical measures, used by copyright owners to identify or protect copyrighted works, that—

84

(A) *have been developed pursuant to a broad consensus of copyright owners and service providers in an open, fair, voluntary, multi-industry standards process;*

(B) *are available to any person on reasonable and non-discriminatory terms; and*

(C) *do not impose substantial costs on service providers or substantial burdens on their systems or networks.*

(i) INJUNCTIONS.—*The following rules shall apply in the case of any application for an injunction under section 502 against a service provider that is not subject to monetary remedies by operation of this section:*

(1) SCOPE OF RELIEF.—

(A) *With respect to conduct other than that which qualifies for the limitation on remedies as set forth in subsection (a), the court may only grant injunctive relief with respect to a service provider in one or more of the following forms:*

(i) *an order restraining it from providing access to infringing material or activity residing at a particular online site on the provider's system or network;*

(ii) *an order restraining it from providing access to an identified subscriber of the service provider's system or network who is engaging in infringing activity by terminating the specified accounts of such subscriber; or*

(iii) *such other injunctive remedies as the court may consider necessary to prevent or restrain infringement of specified copyrighted material at a particular online location, provided that such remedies are the least burdensome to the service provider that are comparably effective for that purpose.*

(B) *If the service provider qualifies for the limitation on remedies described in subsection (a), the court may only grant injunctive relief in one or both of the following forms:*

(i) *an order restraining it from providing access to an identified subscriber of the service provider's system or network who is using the provider's service to engage in infringing activity by terminating the specified accounts of such subscriber; or*

(ii) *an order restraining it from providing access, by taking specified reasonable steps to block access, to a specific, identified, foreign online location.*

(2) CONSIDERATIONS.—*The court, in considering the relevant criteria for injunctive relief under applicable law, shall consider:*

(A) *whether such an injunction, either alone or in combination with other such injunctions issued against the same service provider under this subsection, would significantly burden either the provider or the operation of the provider's system or network;*

(B) *the magnitude of the harm likely to be suffered by the copyright owner in the digital network environment if steps are not taken to prevent or restrain the infringement;*

(C) *whether implementation of such an injunction would be technically feasible and effective, and would not interfere*

85

*with access to noninfringing material at other online loca-
tions; and*

*(D) whether other less burdensome and comparably effec-
tive means of preventing or restraining access to the infringing material are available.*

*(3) NOTICE AND EX PARTE ORDERS.—Injunctive relief under
this subsection shall not be available without notice to the service provider and an opportunity for such provider to appear, except for orders ensuring the preservation of evidence or other orders having no material adverse effect on the operation of the
service provider's communications network.*

(j) DEFINITIONS.—

*(1)(A) As used in subsection (a), the term "service provider"
means an entity offering the transmission, routing or providing
of connections for digital online communications, between or
among points specified by a user, of material of the user's choosing, without modification to the content of the material as sent
or received.*

*(B) As used in any other subsection of this section, the term
"service provider" means a provider of online services or network access, or the operator of facilities therefor, and includes
an entity described in the preceding paragraph of this subsection.*

*(2) As used in this section, the term "monetary relief" means
damages, costs, attorneys' fees, and any other form of monetary
payment.*

*(k) OTHER DEFENSES NOT AFFECTED.—The failure of a service
provider's conduct to qualify for limitation of liability under this
section shall not bear adversely upon the consideration of a defense
by the service provider that the service provider's conduct is not infringing under this title or any other defense.*

*(l) PROTECTION OF PRIVACY.—Nothing in this section shall be con-
strued to condition the applicability of subsections (a) through (d)
on—*

*(1) a service provider monitoring its service or affirmatively
seeking facts indicating infringing activity except to the extent
consistent with a standard technical measure complying with
the provisions of subsection (h); or*

*(2) a service provider accessing, removing, or disabling access
to material where such conduct is prohibited by law.*

*(m) RULE OF CONSTRUCTION.—Subsections (a), (b), (c), and (d)
are intended to describe separate and distinct functions for purposes
of analysis under this section. Whether a service provider qualifies
for the limitation on liability in any one such subsection and shall
be based solely on the criteria in each such subsection and shall not
affect a determination of whether such service provider qualifies for
the limitations on liability under any other such subsection.*

*   *   *   *   *   *   *

CHAPTER 12—COPYRIGHT PROTECTION AND MANAGEMENT SYSTEMS

86

§ 1201. *Circumvention of copyright protection systems*

(a) VIOLATIONS REGARDING CIRCUMVENTION OF TECHNOLOGICAL PROTECTION MEASURES.—(1) *No person shall circumvent a technological protection measure that effectively controls access to a work protected under this title.*

(2) *No person shall manufacture, import, offer to the public, provide or otherwise traffic in any technology, product, service, device, component, or part thereof that—*

> (A) *is primarily designed or produced for the purpose of circumventing a technological protection measure that effectively controls access to a work protected under this title;*

> (B) *has only limited commercially significant purpose or use other than to circumvent a technological protection measure that effectively controls access to a work protected under this title; or*

> (C) *is marketed by that person or another acting in concert with that person with that person's knowledge for use in circumventing a technological protection measure that effectively controls access to a work protected under this title.*

(3) *As used in this subsection—*

> (A) *to "circumvent a technological protection measure" means to descramble a work, to decrypt an encrypted work, or otherwise to avoid, bypass, remove, deactivate, or impair a technological protection measure, without the authority of the copyright owner; and*

> (B) *a technological protection measure "effectively controls access to a work" if the measure, in the ordinary course of its operation, requires the application of information, or a process or a treatment, with the authority of the copyright owner, to gain access to the work.*

(b) ADDITIONAL VIOLATIONS.—(1) *No person shall manufacture, import, offer to the public, provide, or otherwise traffic in any technology, product, service, device, component, or part thereof that—*

> (A) *is primarily designed or produced for the purpose of circumventing protection afforded by a technological protection measure that effectively protects a right of a copyright owner under this title in a work or a portion thereof;*

> (B) *has only limited commercially significant purpose or use other than to circumvent protection afforded by a technological protection measure that effectively protects a right of a copyright owner under this title in a work or a portion thereof; or*

> (C) *is marketed by that person or another acting in concert with that person with that person's knowledge for use in circumventing protection afforded by a technological protection measure that effectively protects a right of a copyright owner under this title in a work or a portion thereof.*

(2) *As used in this subsection—*

> (A) *to "circumvent protection afforded by a technological protection measure" means avoiding, bypassing, removing, deacti-*

87

vating, or otherwise impairing a technological protection measure; and

(B) a technological protection measure "effectively protects a right of a copyright owner under this title" if the measure, in the ordinary course of its operation, prevents, restricts, or otherwise limits the exercise of a right of a copyright owner under this title.

(c) IMPORTATION.—The importation into the United States, the sale for importation, or the sale within the United States after importation by the owner, importer, or consignee of any technology, product, service, device, component, or part thereof as described in subsection (a) or (b) shall be actionable under section 337 of the Tariff Act of 1930 (19 U.S.C. 1337).

(d) OTHER RIGHTS, ETC., NOT AFFECTED.—(1) Nothing in this section shall affect rights, remedies, limitations, or defenses to copyright infringement, including fair use, under this title.

(2) Nothing in this section shall enlarge or diminish vicarious or contributory liability for copyright infringement in connection with any technology, product, service, device, component or part thereof.

(3) Nothing in this section shall require that the design of, or design and selection of parts and components for, a consumer electronics, telecommunications, or computing product provide for a response to any particular technological protection measure, so long as such part or component or the product, in which such part or component is integrated, does not otherwise fall within the prohibitions of subsections (a)(2) or (b)(1).

(e) EXEMPTION FOR NONPROFIT LIBRARIES, ARCHIVES, AND EDUCATIONAL INSTITUTIONS.—(1) A nonprofit library, archives, or educational institution which gains access to a commercially exploited copyrighted work solely in order to make a good faith determination of whether to acquire a copy of that work for the sole purpose of engaging in conduct permitted under this title shall not be in violation of subsection (a)(1). A copy of a work to which access has been gained under this paragraph—

(A) may not be retained longer than necessary to make such good faith determination; and

(B) may not be used for any other purpose.

(2) The exemption made available under paragraph (1) shall only apply with respect to a work when an identical copy of that work is not reasonably available in another form.

(3) A nonprofit library, archives, or educational institution that willfully for the purpose of commercial advantage or financial gain violates paragraph (1)—

(A) shall, for the first offense, be subject to the civil remedies under section 1203; and

(B) shall, for repeated or subsequent offenses, in addition to the civil remedies under section 1203, forfeit the exemption provided under paragraph (1).

(4) This subsection may not be used as a defense to a claim under subsection (a)(2) or (b), nor may this subsection permit a nonprofit library, archives, or educational institution to manufacture, import, offer to the public, provide or otherwise traffic in any technology which circumvents a technological protection measure.

88

(5) *In order for a library or archives to qualify for the exemption under this subsection, the collections of that library or archives shall be—*

    (A) *open to the public;*

    (B) *available not only to researchers affiliated with the library or archives or with the institution of which it is a part, but also to other persons doing research in a specialized field.*

(f) LAW ENFORCEMENT AND INTELLIGENCE ACTIVITIES.—*This section does not prohibit any lawfully authorized investigative, protective, or intelligence activity of an officer, agent or employee of the United States, a State, or a political subdivision of a State, or a person acting pursuant to a contract with such entities.*

(g) *Notwithstanding the provisions of subsection 1201(a)(1), a person who has lawfully obtained the right to use a copy of a computer program may circumvent a technological protection measure that effectively controls access to a particular portion of that program for the sole purpose of identifying and analyzing those elements of the program that are necessary to achieve interoperability of an independently created computer program with other programs, and that have not previously been readily available to the person engaging in the circumvention, to the extent any such acts of identification and analysis do not constitute infringement under this title.*

(h) *Notwithstanding the provisions of subsections 1201(a)(2) and (b), a person may develop and employ technological means to circumvent for the identification and analysis described in subsection (g), or for the limited purpose of achieving interoperability of an independently created computer program with other programs, where such means are necessary to achieve such interoperability, to the extent that doing so does not constitute infringement under this title.*

(i) *The information acquired through the acts permitted under subsection (g), and the means permitted under subsection (h), may be made available to others if the person referred to in subsections (g) or (h) provides such information or means solely for the purpose of achieving interoperability of an independently created computer program with other programs, and to the extent that doing so does not constitute infringement under this title, or violate applicable law other than this title.*

(j) *For purposes of subsections (g), (h) and (i), the term "interoperability" means the ability of computer programs to exchange information, and for such programs mutually to use the information which has been exchanged.*

(k) *In applying subsection (a) to a component or part, the court may consider the necessity for its intended and actual incorporation in a technology, product, service or device, which (i) does not itself violate the provisions of this chapter and (ii) has the sole purpose to prevent the access of minors to material on the Internet.*

§ 1202. Integrity of copyright management information

(a) FALSE COPYRIGHT MANAGEMENT INFORMATION.—*No person shall knowingly—*

    (1) *provide copyright management information that is false, or*

89

(2) *distribute or import for distribution copyright management information that is false, with the intent to induce, enable, facilitate or conceal infringement.*

(b) REMOVAL OR ALTERATION OF COPYRIGHT MANAGEMENT INFORMATION.—*No person shall, without the authority of the copyright owner or the law—*

(1) *intentionally remove or alter any copyright management information,*

(2) *distribute or import for distribution copyright management information knowing that the copyright management information has been removed or altered without authority of the copyright owner or the law, or*

(3) *distribute, import for distribution, or publicly perform works, copies of works, or phonorecords, knowing that copyright management information has been removed or altered without authority of the copyright owner or the law, knowing, or, with respect to civil remedies under section 1203, having reasonable grounds to know, that it will induce, enable, facilitate or conceal an infringement of any right under this title.*

(c) DEFINITION.—*As used in this chapter, copyright management information means the following information conveyed in connection with copies or phonorecords of a work or performances or displays of a work, including in digital form—*

(1) *the title and other information identifying the work, including the information set forth on a notice of copyright;*

(2) *the name of, and other identifying information about, the author of a work;*

(3) *the name of, and other identifying information about, the copyright owner of the work, including the information set forth in a notice of copyright;*

(4) *with the exception of public performances of works by radio and television broadcast stations the name of, and other identifying information about, a performer whose performance is fixed in a work other than an audiovisual work;*

(5) *with the exception of public performances of works by radio and television broadcast stations, in the case of an audiovisual work, the name of, and other identifying information about, a writer, performer, or director who is credited in the audiovisual work;*

(6) *identifying numbers of symbols referring to such information or links to such information; or*

(7) *such other information as the Register of Copyrights may prescribe by regulation, except that the Register of Copyrights may not require the provision of any information concerning the user of a copyrighted work.*

(d) LAW ENFORCEMENT AND INTELLIGENCE ACTIVITIES.—*This section does not prohibit any lawfully authorized investigative, protective, or intelligence activity of an officer, agent, or employee of the United States, a State, or a political subdivision of a State, or a person acting pursuant to a contract with such entities.*

(e) LIMITATIONS ON LIABILITY.—

(1) ANALOG TRANSMISSIONS.—*In the case of an analog transmission, a person who is making transmissions in its capacity as a radio or television broadcast station, or as a cable system,*

90

or someone who provides programming to such station or system, shall not be liable for a violation of subsection (b) if—

(A) avoiding the activity that constitutes such violation is not technically feasible or would create an undue financial hardship on such person; and

(B) such person did not intend, by engaging in such activity, to induce, enable, facilitate or conceal infringement.

(2) DIGITAL TRANSMISSIONS.—

(A) If a digital transmission standard for the placement of copyright management information for a category of works is set in a voluntary, consensus standard-setting process involving a representative cross-section or radio or television broadcast stations or cable systems and copyright owners of a category of works that are intended for public performance by such stations or systems, a person identified in subsection (e)(1) shall not be liable for a violation of subsection (b) with respect to the particular copyright management information addressed by such standard if—

(i) the placement of such information by someone other than such person is not in accordance with such standard; and

(ii) the activity that constitutes such violation is not intended to induce, enable, facilitate or conceal infringement.

(B) Until a digital transmission standard has been set pursuant to subparagraph (A) with respect to the placement of copyright management information for a category or works, a person identified in subsection (e)(1) shall not be liable for a violation of subsection (b) with respect to such copyright management information, where the activity that constitutes such violation is not intended to induce, enable, facilitate or conceal infringement, if—

(i) the transmission of such information by such person would result in a perceptible visual or aural degradation of the digital signal; or

(ii) the transmission of such information by such person would conflict with

(I) an applicable government regulation relating to transmission of information in a digital signal;

(II) an applicable industry-wide standard relating to the transmission of information in a digital signal that was adopted by a voluntary consensus standards body prior to the effective date of this section; or

(III) an applicable industry-wide standard relating to the transmission of information in a digital signal that was adopted in a voluntary, consensus standards-setting process open to participation by a representative cross-section of radio or television broadcast stations or cable systems and copyright owners of a category of works that are intended for public performance by such stations or systems.

91

§ 1203. Civil remedies

(a) CIVIL ACTIONS.—Any person injured by a violation of section 1201 or 1202 may bring a civil action in an appropriate United States district court for such violation.

(b) POWERS OF THE COURT.—In an action brought under subsection (a), the court—

(1) may grant temporary and permanent injunctions on such terms as it deems reasonable to prevent or restrain a violation;

(2) at any time while an action is pending, may order the impounding, on such terms as it deems reasonable, or any device or product that is in the custody or control of the alleged violator and that the court has reasonable cause to believe was involved in a violation;

(3) may award damages under subsection(c);

(4) in its discretion may allow the recovery of costs by or against any party other than the United States or an officer thereof;

(5) in its discretion may award reasonable attorney's fees to the prevailing party; and

(6) may, as part of a final judgment or decree finding a violation, order the remedial modification or the destruction of any device or product involved in the violation that is in the custody or control of the violator or has been impounded under paragraph (2).

(c) AWARD OF DAMAGES.—

(1) IN GENERAL.—Except as otherwise provided in this chapter, a person committing a violation of section 1201 or 1202 is liable for either—

(A) the actual damages and any additional profits of the violator, as provided in paragraph (2), or

(B) statutory damages, as provided in paragraph (3).

(2) ACTUAL DAMAGES.—The court shall award to the complaining party the actual damages suffered by the party as a result of the violation, and any profits of the violator that are attributable to the violation and are not taken into account in computing the actual damages, if the complaining party elects such damages at any time before final judgment is entered.

(3) STATUTORY DAMAGES.—

(A) At any time before final judgment is entered, a complaining party may elect to recover an award of statutory damages for each violation of section 1201 in the sum of not less than $200 or more than $2,500 per act of circumvention, device, product, component, offer, or performance of service, as the court considers just.

(B) At any time before final judgment is entered, a complaining party may elect to recover an award of statutory damages for each violation of section 1202 in the sum of not less than $2,500 or more than $25,000.

(4) REPEATED VIOLATIONS.—In any case in which the injured party sustains the burden of proving, and the court finds, that a person has violated section 1201 or 1202 within three years after a final judgment was entered against the person for another such violation, the court may increase the award of dam-

92

ages up to triple the amount that would otherwise be awarded, as the court considers just.

   (5) INNOCENT VIOLATIONS.—

     (A) IN GENERAL.—The court in its discretion may reduce or remit the total award of damages in any case in which the violator sustains the burden of proving, and the court finds, that the violator was not aware and had no reason to believe that its acts constituted a violation.

     (B) NONPROFIT LIBRARY, ARCHIVES, OR EDUCATIONAL INSTITUTIONS.—In the case of a nonprofit library, archives, or educational institution, the court shall remit damages in any case in which the library archives, or educational institution sustains the burden of proving, and the court finds, that the library, archives, or educational institution was not aware and had no reason to believe that its acts constituted a violation.

§ 1204. Criminal offenses and penalties

   (a) IN GENERAL.—Any person who violates section 1201 or 1202 willfully and for purposes of commercial advantage or private financial gain—

     (1) shall be fined not more than $500,000 or imprisoned for not more than 5 years, or both for the first offense; and

     (2) shall be fined not more than $1,000,000 or imprisoned for not more than 10 years, or both for any or subsequent offense.

   (b) LIMITATION FOR NONPROFIT LIBRARY, ARCHIVES, OR EDUCATIONAL INSTITUTION.—Subsection (a) shall not apply to a nonprofit library, archives, or educational institution.

   (c) STATUTE OF LIMITATIONS.—Notwithstanding section 507(a) of this title, no criminal proceeding shall be brought under this section unless such proceeding is commenced within five years after the cause of action arose.

§ 1205. Savings Clause

   Nothing in this chapter abrogates, diminishes or weakens the provisions of, nor provides any defense or element or mitigation in a criminal prosecution or civil action under, any federal or state law that prevents the violation of the privacy of an individual in connection with the individual's use of the Internet.

○

105TH CONGRESS }
2d Session } HOUSE OF REPRESENTATIVES { REPT. 105–551
Part 2

DIGITAL MILLENNIUM COPYRIGHT ACT OF 1998

JULY 22, 1998.—Committed to the Committee of the Whole House on the State of the Union and ordered to be printed

Mr. BLILEY, from the Committee on Commerce,
submitted the following

REPORT

together with

ADDITIONAL VIEWS

[To accompany H.R. 2281]

[Including cost estimate of the Congressional Budget Office]

The Committee on Commerce, to whom was referred the bill (H.R. 2281) to amend title 17, United States Code, to implement the World Intellectual Property Organization Copyright Treaty and Performances and Phonograms Treaty, having considered the same, report favorably thereon with an amendment and recommend that the bill as amended do pass.

CONTENTS

49–910

2

The amendment is as follows:

Strike out all after the enacting clause and insert in lieu thereof the following:

SECTION 1. SHORT TITLE.

This Act may be cited as the "Digital Millennium Copyright Act of 1998".

SEC. 2. TABLE OF CONTENTS.

TITLE I—WIPO TREATIES IMPLEMENTATION

SEC. 101. SHORT TITLE.

This title may be cited as the "WIPO Copyright Treaties Implementation Act".

SEC. 102. CIRCUMVENTION OF COPYRIGHT PROTECTION SYSTEMS.

(a) VIOLATIONS REGARDING CIRCUMVENTION OF TECHNOLOGICAL PROTECTION MEASURES.—(1)(A) The Secretary of Commerce shall issue regulations prohibiting any person from circumventing a technological protection measure that effectively controls access to a work protected under title 17, United States Code, to the extent provided in this subsection, effective at the end of the 2-year period beginning on the date of the enactment of this Act.

(B) During the 2-year period described in subparagraph (A), and in each succeeding 2-year period, the Secretary of Commerce, in consultation with the Assistant Secretary of Commerce for Communications and Information, the Commissioner of Patents and Trademarks, and the Register of Copyrights, shall conduct a rule-making on the record to determine whether users of copyrighted works have been, or are likely to be in the succeeding 2-year period, adversely affected by the implementation of technological protection measures that effectively control access to works protected under title 17, United States Code, in their ability to make lawful uses under title 17, United States Code, of copyrighted works. In conducting such rulemaking, the Secretary shall examine—

(i) the availability for use of copyrighted works;

(ii) the availability for use of works for archival, preservation, and educational purposes;

(iii) the impact of the application of technological protection measures to copyrighted works on criticism, comment, news reporting, teaching, scholarship, or research;

(iv) the effect of circumvention of technological protection measures on the market for or value of copyrighted works; and

3

(v) such other factors as the Secretary, in consultation with the Assistant Secretary of Commerce for Communications and Information, the Commissioner of Patents and Trademarks, and the Register of Copyrights, considers appropriate.

(C) The Secretary, with respect to each particular class of copyrighted works for which the Secretary has determined, pursuant to the rulemaking conducted under subparagraph (B), that lawful uses have been, or are likely to be, adversely affected, shall waive the applicability of the regulations issued under subparagraph (A) for the ensuing 2-year period. The determinations made in the rulemaking shall not be admissible in any action to enforce any provision of this Act other than this paragraph.

(2) No person shall manufacture, import, offer to the public, provide, or otherwise traffic in any technology, product, service, device, component, or part thereof, that—

(A) is primarily designed or produced for the purpose of circumventing a technological protection measure that effectively controls access to a work protected under title 17, United States Code;

(B) has only limited commercially significant purpose or use other than to circumvent a technological protection measure that effectively controls access to a work protected under title 17, United States Code; or

(C) is marketed by that person or another acting in concert with that person with that person's knowledge for use in circumventing a technological protection measure that effectively controls access to a work protected under title 17, United States Code.

(3) As used in this subsection—

(A) to "circumvent a technological protection measure" means to descramble a scrambled work, to decrypt an encrypted work, or otherwise to avoid, bypass, remove, deactivate, or impair a technological protection measure, without the authority of the copyright owner; and

(B) a technological protection measure "effectively controls access to a work" if the measure, in the ordinary course of its operation, requires the application of information, or a process or a treatment, with the authority of the copyright owner, to gain access to the work.

(b) ADDITIONAL VIOLATIONS.—(1) No person shall manufacture, import, offer to the public, provide, or otherwise traffic in any technology, product, service, device, component, or part thereof, that—

(A) is primarily designed or produced for the purpose of circumventing protection afforded by a technological protection measure that effectively protects a right of a copyright owner under title 17, United States Code, in a work or a portion thereof;

(B) has only limited commercially significant purpose or use other than to circumvent protection afforded by a technological protection measure that effectively protects a right of a copyright owner under title 17, United States Code, in a work or a portion thereof; or

(C) is marketed by that person or another acting in concert with that person with that person's knowledge for use in circumventing protection afforded by a technological protection measure that effectively protects a right of a copyright owner under title 17, United States Code, in a work or a portion thereof.

(2) As used in this subsection—

(A) to "circumvent protection afforded by a technological protection measure" means avoiding, bypassing, removing, deactivating, or otherwise impairing a technological protection measure; and

(B) a technological protection measure "effectively protects a right of a copyright owner under title 17, United States Code" if the measure, in the ordinary course of its operation, prevents, restricts, or otherwise limits the exercise of a right of a copyright owner under title 17, United States Code.

(c) OTHER RIGHTS, ETC., NOT AFFECTED.—(1) Nothing in this section shall affect rights, remedies, limitations, or defenses to copyright infringement, including fair use, under title 17, United States Code.

(2) Nothing in this section shall enlarge or diminish vicarious or contributory liability for copyright infringement in connection with any technology, product, service, device, component, or part thereof.

(3) Nothing in this section shall require that the design of, or design and selection of parts and components for, a consumer electronics, telecommunications, or computing product provide for a response to any particular technological protection measure.

(4) Nothing in this section shall enlarge or diminish any rights of free speech or the press for activities using consumer electronics, telecommunications, or computing products.

4

(d) Exemption for Nonprofit Libraries, Archives, and Educational Institutions.—(1) A nonprofit library, archives, or educational institution which gains access to a commercially exploited copyrighted work solely in order to make a good faith determination of whether to acquire a copy of that work for the sole purpose of engaging in conduct permitted under title 17, United States Code, shall not be in violation of the regulations issued under subsection (a)(1)(A). A copy of a work to which access has been gained under this paragraph—

(A) may not be retained longer than necessary to make such good faith determination; and

(B) may not be used for any other purpose.

(2) The exemption made available under paragraph (1) shall only apply with respect to a work when an identical copy of that work is not reasonably available in another form.

(3) A nonprofit library, archives, or educational institution that willfully for the purpose of commercial advantage or financial gain violates paragraph (1)—

(A) shall, for the first offense, be subject to the civil remedies under section 104; and

(B) shall, for repeated or subsequent offenses, in addition to the civil remedies under section 104, forfeit the exemption provided under paragraph (1).

(4) This subsection may not be used as a defense to a claim under subsection (a)(2) or (b), nor may this subsection permit a nonprofit library, archives, or educational institution to manufacture, import, offer to the public, provide, or otherwise traffic in any technology, product, service, component, or part thereof, which circumvents a technological protection measure.

(5) In order for a library or archives to qualify for the exemption under this subsection, the collections of that library or archives shall be—

(A) open to the public; or

(B) available not only to researchers affiliated with the library or archives or with the institution of which it is a part, but also to other persons doing research in a specialized field.

(e) Law Enforcement and Intelligence Activities.—This section does not prohibit any lawfully authorized investigative, protective, or intelligence activity of an officer, agent, or employee of the United States, a State, or a political subdivision of a State, or a person acting pursuant to a contract with the United States, a State, or a political subdivision of a State.

(f) Reverse Engineering.—(1) Notwithstanding the regulations issued under subsection (a)(1)(A), a person who has lawfully obtained the right to use a copy of a computer program may circumvent a technological protection measure that effectively controls access to a particular portion of that program for the sole purpose of identifying and analyzing those elements of the program that are necessary to achieve interoperability of an independently created computer program with other programs, and that have not previously been readily available to the person engaging in the circumvention, to the extent any such acts of identification and analysis do not constitute infringement under title 17, United States Code.

(2) Notwithstanding the provisions of subsections (a)(2) and (b), a person may develop and employ technological means to circumvent a technological protection measure, or to circumvent protection afforded by a technological protection measure, in order to make the identification and analysis permitted under paragraph (1), or for the limited purpose of achieving interoperability of an independently created computer program with other programs, if such means are necessary to achieve such interoperability, to the extent that doing so does not constitute infringement under title 17, United States Code.

(3) The information acquired through the acts permitted under paragraph (1), and the means permitted under paragraph (2), may be made available to others if the person referred to in paragraph (1) or (2), as the case may be, provides such information or means solely for the purpose of achieving interoperability of an independently created computer program with other programs, and to the extent that doing so does not constitute infringement under title 17, United States Code, or violate other applicable law.

(4) For purposes of this subsection, the term "interoperability" means the ability of computer programs to exchange information, and of such programs mutually to use the information which has been exchanged.

(g) Encryption Research.—

(1) Definitions.—For purposes of this subsection—

(A) the term "encryption research" means activities necessary to identify and analyze flaws and vulnerabilities of encryption technologies applied to copyrighted works, if these activities are conducted to advance the state of

5

knowledge in the field of encryption technology or to assist in the development of encryption products; and

    (B) the term "encryption technology" means the scrambling and descrambling of information using mathematical formulas or algorithms.

(2) PERMISSIBLE ACTS OF ENCRYPTION RESEARCH.—Notwithstanding the provisions of subsection (a)(1)(A), it is not a violation of the regulations issued under that subsection for a person to circumvent a technological protection measure as applied to a copy, phonorecord, performance, or display of a published work in the course of an act of good faith encryption research if—

    (A) the person lawfully obtained the encrypted copy, phonorecord, performance, or display of the published work;

    (B) such act is necessary to conduct such encryption research;

    (C) the person made a good faith effort to obtain authorization before the circumvention; and

    (D) such act does not constitute infringement under title 17, United States Code, or a violation of applicable law other than this section, including section 1030 of title 18, United States Code, and those provisions of title 18, United States Code, amended by the Computer Fraud and Abuse Act of 1986.

(3) FACTORS IN DETERMINING EXEMPTION.—In determining whether a person qualifies for the exemption under paragraph (2), the factors to be considered shall include—

    (A) whether the information derived from the encryption research was disseminated, and if so, whether it was disseminated in a manner reasonably calculated to advance the state of knowledge or development of encryption technology, versus whether it was disseminated in a manner that facilitates infringement under title 17, United States Code, or a violation of applicable law other than this section, including a violation of privacy or breach of security;

    (B) whether the person is engaged in a legitimate course of study, is employed, or is appropriately trained or experienced, in the field of encryption technology; and

    (C) whether the person provides the copyright owner of the work to which the technological protection measure is applied with notice of the findings and documentation of the research, and the time when such notice is provided.

(4) USE OF TECHNOLOGICAL MEANS FOR RESEARCH ACTIVITIES.—Notwithstanding the provisions of subsection (a)(2), it is not a violation of that subsection for a person to—

    (A) develop and employ technological means to circumvent a technological protection measure for the sole purpose of performing the acts of good faith encryption research described in paragraph (2); and

    (B) provide the technological means to another person with whom he or she is working collaboratively for the purpose of conducting the acts of good faith encryption research described in paragraph (2) or for the purpose of having that other person verify his or her acts of good faith encryption research described in paragraph (2).

(5) REPORT TO CONGRESS.—Not later than 1 year after the date of the enactment of this Act, the Assistant Secretary of Commerce for Communications and Information shall report to the Congress on the effect this subsection has had on—

    (A) encryption research and the development of encryption technology;

    (B) the adequacy and effectiveness of technological protection for copyrighted works; and

    (C) protection of copyright owners against the unauthorized access to their encrypted copyrighted works.

The Assistant Secretary shall include in such report recommendations, if any, on proposed amendments to this Act.

(h) COMPONENTS OR PARTS TO PREVENT ACCESS OF MINORS TO THE INTERNET.—In applying subsection (a) and the regulations issued under subsection (a)(1)(A) to a component or part, the court may consider the necessity for its intended and actual incorporation in a technology, product, service, or device, which—

    (1) does not itself violate the provisions of title 17, United States Code; and

    (2) has the sole purpose to prevent the access of minors to material on the Internet.

(i) PROTECTION OF PERSONALLY IDENTIFYING INFORMATION.—

    (1) CIRCUMVENTION PERMITTED.—Notwithstanding the provisions of subsection (a)(1)(A), it is not a violation of the regulations issued under that sub-

6

section for a person to circumvent a technological protection measure that effectively controls access to a work protected under title 17, United States Code, if—

(A) the technological protection measure, or the work it protects, contains the capability of collecting or disseminating personally identifying information reflecting the online activities of a natural person who seeks to gain access to the work protected;

(B) in the normal course of its operation, the technological protection measure, or the work it protects, collects or disseminates personally identifying information about the person who seeks to gain access to the work protected, without providing conspicuous notice of such collection or dissemination to such person, and without providing such person with the capability to prevent or restrict such collection or dissemination;

(C) the act of circumvention has the sole effect of identifying and disabling the capability described in subparagraph (A), and has no other effect on the ability of any person to gain access to any work; and

(D) the act of circumvention is carried out solely for the purpose of preventing the collection or dissemination of personally identifying information about a natural person who seeks to gain access to the work protected, and is not in violation of any other law.

(2) INAPPLICABILITY TO CERTAIN TECHNOLOGICAL PROTECTION MEASURES.— This subsection does not apply to a technological protection measure, or a work it protects, that does not collect or disseminate personally identifying information and that is disclosed to a user as not having or using such capability.

SEC. 103. INTEGRITY OF COPYRIGHT MANAGEMENT INFORMATION.

(a) FALSE COPYRIGHT MANAGEMENT INFORMATION.—No person shall knowingly and with the intent to induce, enable, facilitate, or conceal infringement—

(1) provide copyright management information that is false, or

(2) distribute or import for distribution copyright management information that is false.

(b) REMOVAL OR ALTERATION OF COPYRIGHT MANAGEMENT INFORMATION.—No person shall, without the authority of the copyright owner or the law—

(1) intentionally remove or alter any copyright management information,

(2) distribute or import for distribution copyright management information knowing that the copyright management information has been removed or altered without authority of the copyright owner or the law, or

(3) distribute, import for distribution, or publicly perform works, copies of works, or phonorecords, knowing that copyright management information has been removed or altered without authority of the copyright owner or the law, knowing, or, with respect to civil remedies under section 104, having reasonable grounds to know, that it will induce, enable, facilitate, or conceal an infringement of any right under title 17, United States Code.

(c) DEFINITIONS.—As used in this section—

(1) the terms "distribute", "publicly perform", "copies", and "phonorecords" have the meanings given those terms in title 17, United States Code; and

(2) the term "copyright management information" means any of the following information conveyed in connection with copies or phonorecords of a work or performances or displays of a work, including in digital form, except that such term does not include any personally identifying information about a user of a work or of a copy, phonorecord, performance, or display of a work:

(A) The title and other information identifying the work, including the information set forth on a notice of copyright.

(B) The name of, and other identifying information about, the author of a work.

(C) The name of, and other identifying information about, the copyright owner of the work, including the information set forth in a notice of copyright.

(D) With the exception of public performances of works by radio and television broadcast stations, the name of, and other identifying information about, a performer whose performance is fixed in a work other than an audiovisual work.

(E) With the exception of public performances of works by radio and television broadcast stations, in the case of an audiovisual work, the name of, and other identifying information about, a writer, performer, or director who is credited in the audiovisual work.

(F) Terms and conditions for use of the work.

(G) Identifying numbers or symbols referring to such information or links to such information.

(H) Such other information as the Register of Copyrights may prescribe by regulation, except that the Register of Copyrights may not require the provision of any information concerning the user of a copyrighted work.

(d) LAW ENFORCEMENT AND INTELLIGENCE ACTIVITIES.—This section does not prohibit any lawfully authorized investigative, protective, or intelligence activity of an officer, agent, or employee of the United States, a State, or a political subdivision of a State, or a person acting pursuant to a contract with the United States, a State, or a political subdivision of a State.

(e) LIMITATIONS ON LIABILITY.—

(1) ANALOG TRANSMISSIONS.—In the case of an analog transmission, a person who is making transmissions in its capacity as a broadcast station, or as a cable system (as defined in section 602 of the Communications Act of 1934), or someone who provides programming to such station or system, shall not be liable for a violation of subsection (b) if—

(A) avoiding the activity that constitutes such violation is not technically feasible or would create an undue financial hardship on such person; and

(B) such person did not intend, by engaging in such activity, to induce, enable, facilitate, or conceal infringement of a right under title 17, United States Code.

(2) DIGITAL TRANSMISSIONS.—

(A) If a digital transmission standard for the placement of copyright management information for a category of works is set in a voluntary, consensus standard-setting process involving a representative cross-section of broadcast stations or cable systems and copyright owners of a category of works that are intended for public performance by such stations or systems, a person identified in paragraph (1) shall not be liable for a violation of subsection (b) with respect to the particular copyright management information addressed by such standard if—

(i) the placement of such information by someone other than such person is not in accordance with such standard; and

(ii) the activity that constitutes such violation is not intended to induce, enable, facilitate, or conceal infringement of a right under title 17, United States Code.

(B) Until a digital transmission standard has been set pursuant to subparagraph (A) with respect to the placement of copyright management information for a category or works, a person identified in paragraph (1) shall not be liable for a violation of subsection (b) with respect to such copyright management information, if the activity that constitutes such violation is not intended to induce, enable, facilitate, or conceal infringement of a right under title 17, United States Code, and if—

(i) the transmission of such information by such person would result in a perceptible visual or aural degradation of the digital signal; or

(ii) the transmission of such information by such person would conflict with—

(I) an applicable government regulation relating to transmission of information in a digital signal;

(II) an applicable industry-wide standard relating to the transmission of information in a digital signal that was adopted by a voluntary consensus standards body prior to the effective date of this title; or

(III) an applicable industry-wide standard relating to the transmission of information in a digital signal that was adopted in a voluntary, consensus standards-setting process open to participation by a representative cross-section of broadcast stations or cable systems and copyright owners of a category of works that are intended for public performance by such stations or systems.

(3) DEFINITIONS.—As used in this subsection—

(A) the term "broadcast station" has the meaning given that term in section 3 of the Communications Act of 1934 (47 U.S.C. 153)); and

(B) the term "cable system" has the meaning given that term in section 602 of the Communications Act of 1934 (47 U.S.C. 522)).

SEC. 104. CIVIL REMEDIES.

(a) CIVIL ACTIONS.—Any person injured by a violation of section 102 or 103, or of any regulation issued under section 102(a)(1), may bring a civil action in an appropriate United States district court for such violation.

8

(b) POWERS OF THE COURT.—In an action brought under subsection (a), the court—

(1) may grant temporary and permanent injunctions on such terms as it deems reasonable to prevent or restrain a violation, but in no event shall impose a prior restraint on free speech or the press protected under the 1st amendment to the Constitution;

(2) at any time while an action is pending, may order the impounding, on such terms as it deems reasonable, of any device or product that is in the custody or control of the alleged violator and that the court has reasonable cause to believe was involved in a violation;

(3) may award damages under subsection (c);

(4) in its discretion may allow the recovery of costs by or against any party other than the United States or an officer thereof;

(5) in its discretion may award reasonable attorney's fees to the prevailing party; and

(6) may, as part of a final judgment or decree finding a violation, order the remedial modification or the destruction of any device or product involved in the violation that is in the custody or control of the violator or has been impounded under paragraph (2).

(c) AWARD OF DAMAGES.—

(1) IN GENERAL.—Except as otherwise provided in this title, a person committing a violation of section 102 or 103, or of any regulation issued under section 102(a)(1), is liable for either—

(A) the actual damages and any additional profits of the violator, as provided in paragraph (2), or

(B) statutory damages, as provided in paragraph (3).

(2) ACTUAL DAMAGES.—The court shall award to the complaining party the actual damages suffered by the party as a result of the violation, and any profits of the violator that are attributable to the violation and are not taken into account in computing the actual damages, if the complaining party elects such damages at any time before final judgment is entered.

(3) STATUTORY DAMAGES.—

(A) At any time before final judgment is entered, a complaining party may elect to recover an award of statutory damages for each violation of section 102, or of a regulation issued under section 102(a)(1), in the sum of not less than $200 or more than $2,500 per act of circumvention, device, product, component, offer, or performance of service, as the court considers just.

(B) At any time before final judgment is entered, a complaining party may elect to recover an award of statutory damages for each violation of section 103 in the sum of not less than $2,500 or more than $25,000.

(4) REPEATED VIOLATIONS.—In any case in which the injured party sustains the burden of proving, and the court finds, that a person has violated section 102 or 103, or any regulation issued under section 102(a)(1), within three years after a final judgment was entered against the person for another such violation, the court may increase the award of damages up to triple the amount that would otherwise be awarded, as the court considers just.

(5) INNOCENT VIOLATIONS.—

(A) IN GENERAL.—The court in its discretion may reduce or remit the total award of damages in any case in which the violator sustains the burden of proving, and the court finds, that the violator was not aware and had no reason to believe that its acts constituted a violation.

(B) NONPROFIT LIBRARY, ARCHIVES, OR EDUCATIONAL INSTITUTIONS.—In the case of a nonprofit library, archives, or educational institution, the court shall remit damages in any case in which the library, archives, or educational institution sustains the burden of proving, and the court finds, that the library, archives, or educational institution was not aware and had no reason to believe that its acts constituted a violation.

SEC. 105. CRIMINAL OFFENSES AND PENALTIES.

(a) IN GENERAL.—Any person who violates section 102 or 103, or any regulation issued under section 102(a)(1), willfully and for purposes of commercial advantage or private financial gain—

(1) shall be fined not more than $500,000 or imprisoned for not more than 5 years, or both, for the first offense; and

(2) shall be fined not more than $1,000,000 or imprisoned for not more than 10 years, or both, for any subsequent offense.

9

(b) LIMITATION FOR NONPROFIT LIBRARY, ARCHIVES, OR EDUCATIONAL INSTITUTION.—Subsection (a) shall not apply to a nonprofit library, archives, or educational institution.

(c) STATUTE OF LIMITATIONS.—No criminal proceeding shall be brought under this section unless such proceeding is commenced within five years after the cause of action arose.

SEC. 106. SAVINGS CLAUSE.

Nothing in this title abrogates, diminishes, or weakens the provisions of, nor provides any defense or element of mitigation in a criminal prosecution or civil action under, any Federal or State law that prevents the violation of the privacy of an individual in connection with the individual's use of the Internet.

SEC. 107. DEVELOPMENT AND IMPLEMENTATION OF TECHNOLOGICAL PROTECTION MEASURES.

(a) STATEMENT OF CONGRESSIONAL POLICY AND OBJECTIVE.—It is the sense of the Congress that technological protection measures play a crucial role in safeguarding the interests of both copyright owners and lawful users of copyrighted works in digital formats, by facilitating lawful uses of such works while protecting the private property interests of holders of rights under title 17, United States Code. Accordingly, the expeditious implementation of such measures, developed by the private sector through voluntary industry-led processes, is a key factor in realizing the full benefits of making available copyrighted works through digital networks, including the benefits set forth in this section.

(b) TECHNOLOGICAL PROTECTION MEASURES.—The technological protection measures referred to in subsection (a) shall include, but not be limited to, those which—

(1) enable nonprofit libraries, for nonprofit purposes, to continue to lend to library users copies or phonorecords that such libraries have lawfully acquired, including the lending of such copies or phonorecords in digital formats in a manner that prevents infringement;

(2) effectively protect against the infringement of exclusive rights under title 17, United States Code, and facilitate the exercise of those exclusive rights; and

(3) promote the development and implementation of diverse methods, mechanisms, and arrangements in the marketplace for making available copyrighted works in digital formats which provide opportunities for individual members of the public to make lawful uses of copyrighted works in digital formats.

(c) PROCEDURES FOR DEVELOPING AND IMPLEMENTING TECHNOLOGICAL PROTECTION MEASURES.—The technological protection measures whose development and implementation the Congress anticipates are those which—

(1) are developed pursuant to a broad consensus in an open, fair, voluntary, and multi-industry process;

(2) are made available on reasonable and nondiscriminatory terms; and

(3) do not impose substantial costs or burdens on copyright owners or on manufacturers of hardware or software used in conjunction with copyrighted works in digital formats.

(d) OVERSIGHT AND REPORTING.—(1) The Secretary of Commerce, in consultation with the Assistant Secretary of Commerce for Communications and Information and the Register of Copyrights, shall review the impact of the enactment of section 102 of this Act on the access of individual users to copyrighted works in digital formats and shall report annually thereon to the Committees on Commerce and on the Judiciary of the House of Representatives and the Committees on Commerce, Science, and Transportation and on the Judiciary of the Senate.

(2) Each report under paragraph (1) shall address the following issues:

(A) The status of the development and implementation of technological protection measures, including measures that advance the objectives of this section, and the effectiveness of technological protection measures in protecting the private property interests of copyright owners under title 17, United States Code.

(B) The degree to which individual lawful users of copyrighted works—

(i) have access to the Internet and digital networks generally;

(ii) are dependent upon such access for their use of copyrighted works;

(iii) have available to them other channels for obtaining and using copyrighted works, other than the Internet and digital networks generally;

(iv) are required to pay copyright owners or intermediaries for each lawful use of copyrighted works in digital formats to which they have access; and

(v) are able to utilize nonprofit libraries to obtain access, through borrowing without payment by the user, to copyrighted works in digital formats.

(C) The degree to which infringement of copyrighted works in digital formats is occurring.

10

(D) Whether and the extent to which section 102, and the regulations issued under section 102(a)(1), are asserted as a basis for liability in claims brought against persons conducting research and development, including reverse engineering of copyrighted works, and the extent to which such claims constitute a serious impediment to the development and production of competitive goods and services.

(E) The degree to which individual users of copyrighted materials in digital formats are able effectively to protect themselves against the use of technological protection measures to carry out or facilitate the undisclosed collection and dissemination of personally identifying information concerning the access to and use of such materials by such users.

(F) Such other issues as the Secretary of Commerce, in consultation with the Assistant Secretary of Commerce for Communications and Information and the Register of Copyrights, identifies as relevant to the impact of the enactment of section 102 on the access of individual users to copyrighted works in digital formats.

(3) The first report under this subsection shall be submitted not later than one year after the date of the enactment of this Act, and the last such report shall be submitted not later than three years after the date of the enactment of this Act.

(4) The reports under this subsection may include such recommendations for additional legislative action as the Secretary of Commerce and the Register of Copyrights consider advisable in order to further the objectives of this section.

SEC. 108. TECHNICAL AMENDMENTS.

(a) DEFINITIONS.—Section 101 of title 17, United States Code, is amended—

(1) by striking the definition of "Berne Convention work";

(2) in the definition of "The 'country of origin' of a Berne Convention work"—

(A) by striking "The 'country of origin' of a Berne Convention work, for purposes of section 411, is the United States if" and inserting "For purposes of section 411, a work is a 'United States work' only if";

(B) in paragraph (1)—

(i) in subparagraph (B) by striking "nation or nations adhering to the Berne Convention" and inserting "treaty party or parties";

(ii) in subparagraph (C) by striking "does not adhere to the Berne Convention" and inserting "is not a treaty party"; and

(iii) in subparagraph (D) by striking "does not adhere to the Berne Convention" and inserting "is not a treaty party"; and

(C) in the matter following paragraph (3) by striking "For the purposes of section 411, the 'country of origin' of any other Berne Convention work is not the United States.";

(3) by inserting after the definition of "fixed" the following:

"The 'Geneva Phonograms Convention' is the Convention for the Protection of Producers of Phonograms Against Unauthorized Duplication of Their Phonograms, concluded at Geneva, Switzerland, on October 29, 1971.";

(4) by inserting after the definition of "including" the following:

"An 'international agreement' is—

"(1) the Universal Copyright Convention;

"(2) the Geneva Phonograms Convention;

"(3) the Berne Convention;

"(4) the WTO Agreement;

"(5) the WIPO Copyright Treaty;

"(6) the WIPO Performances and Phonograms Treaty; and

"(7) any other copyright treaty to which the United States is a party.";

(5) by inserting after the definition of "transmit" the following:

"A 'treaty party' is a country or intergovernmental organization other than the United States that is a party to an international agreement.";

(6) by inserting after the definition of "widow" the following:

"The 'WIPO Copyright Treaty' is the WIPO Copyright Treaty concluded at Geneva, Switzerland, on December 20, 1996.";

(7) by inserting after the definition of "The 'WIPO Copyright Treaty'" the following:

"The 'WIPO Performances and Phonograms Treaty' is the WIPO Performances and Phonograms Treaty concluded at Geneva, Switzerland, on December 20, 1996."; and

(8) by inserting after the definition of "work made for hire" the following:

"The terms 'WTO Agreement' and 'WTO member country' have the meanings given those terms in paragraphs (9) and (10), respectively, of section 2 of the Uruguay Round Agreements Act.".

11

(b) SUBJECT MATTER OF COPYRIGHT; NATIONAL ORIGIN.—Section 104 of title 17, United States Code, is amended—
    (1) in subsection (b)—
        (A) in paragraph (1) by striking "foreign nation that is a party to a copyright treaty to which the United States is also a party" and inserting "treaty party";
        (B) in paragraph (2) by striking "party to the Universal Copyright Convention" and inserting "treaty party";
        (C) by redesignating paragraph (5) as paragraph (6);
        (D) by redesignating paragraph (3) as paragraph (5) and inserting it after paragraph (4);
        (E) by inserting after paragraph (2) the following:
    "(3) the work is a sound recording that was first fixed in a treaty party; or";
        (F) in paragraph (4) by striking "Berne Convention work" and inserting "pictorial, graphic, or sculptural work that is incorporated in a building or other structure, or an architectural work that is embodied in a building and the building or structure is located in the United States or a treaty party"; and
        (G) by inserting after paragraph (6), as so redesignated, the following:
"For purposes of paragraph (2), a work that is published in the United States or a treaty party within 30 days after publication in a foreign nation that is not a treaty party shall be considered to be first published in the United States or such treaty party, as the case may be."; and
    (2) by adding at the end the following new subsection:
"(d) EFFECT OF PHONOGRAMS TREATIES.—Notwithstanding the provisions of subsection (b), no works other than sound recordings shall be eligible for protection under this title solely by virtue of the adherence of the United States to the Geneva Phonograms Convention or the WIPO Performances and Phonograms Treaty.".
    (c) COPYRIGHT IN RESTORED WORKS.—Section 104A(h) of title 17, United States Code, is amended—
    (1) in paragraph (1), by striking subparagraphs (A) and (B) and inserting the following:
        "(A) a nation adhering to the Berne Convention;
        "(B) a WTO member country;
        "(C) a nation adhering to the WIPO Copyright Treaty;
        "(D) a nation adhering to the WIPO Performances and Phonograms Treaty; or
        "(E) subject to a Presidential proclamation under subsection (g).";
    (2) by amending paragraph (3) to read as follows:
    "(3) The term 'eligible country' means a nation, other than the United States, that—
        "(A) becomes a WTO member country after the date of the enactment of the Uruguay Round Agreements Act;
        "(B) on such date of enactment is, or after such date of enactment becomes, a nation adhering to the Berne Convention;
        "(C) adheres to the WIPO Copyright Treaty;
        "(D) adheres to the WIPO Performances and Phonograms Treaty; or
        "(E) after such date of enactment becomes subject to a proclamation under subsection (g).";
    (3) in paragraph (6)—
        (A) in subparagraph (C)(iii) by striking "and" after the semicolon;
        (B) at the end of subparagraph (D) by striking the period and inserting "; and"; and
        (C) by adding after subparagraph (D) the following:
        "(E) if the source country for the work is an eligible country solely by virtue of its adherence to the WIPO Performances and Phonograms Treaty, is a sound recording.";
    (4) in paragraph (8)(B)(i)—
        (A) by inserting "of which" before "the majority"; and
        (B) by striking "of eligible countries"; and
    (5) by striking paragraph (9).
    (d) REGISTRATION AND INFRINGEMENT ACTIONS.—Section 411(a) of title 17, United States Code, is amended in the first sentence—
    (1) by striking "actions for infringement of copyright in Berne Convention works whose country of origin is not the United States and"; and
    (2) by inserting "United States" after "no action for infringement of the copyright in any".

12

(e) STATUTE OF LIMITATIONS.—Section 507(a) of title 17, United State Code, is amended by striking "No" and inserting "Except as expressly provided otherwise in this title, no".

SEC. 109. EFFECTIVE DATE.

(a) IN GENERAL.—Subject to subsection (b), the amendments made by this title shall take effect on the date of the enactment of this Act.

(b) AMENDMENTS RELATING TO CERTAIN INTERNATIONAL AGREEMENTS.—(1) The following shall take effect upon the entry into force of the WIPO Copyright Treaty with respect to the United States:

(A) Paragraph (5) of the definition of "international agreement" contained in section 101 of title 17, United States Code, as amended by section 108(a)(4) of this Act.

(B) The amendment made by section 108(a)(6) of this Act.

(C) Subparagraph (C) of section 104A(h)(1) of title 17, United States Code, as amended by section 108(c)(1) of this Act.

(D) Subparagraph (C) of section 104A(h)(3) of title 17, United States Code, as amended by section 108(c)(2) of this Act.

(2) The following shall take effect upon the entry into force of the WIPO Performances and Phonograms Treaty with respect to the United States:

(A) Paragraph (6) of the definition of "international agreement" contained in section 101 of title 17, United States Code, as amended by section 108(a)(4) of this Act.

(B) The amendment made by section 108(a)(7) of this Act.

(C) The amendment made by section 108(b)(2) of this Act.

(D) Subparagraph (D) of section 104A(h)(1) of title 17, United States Code, as amended by section 108(c)(1) of this Act.

(E) Subparagraph (D) of section 104A(h)(3) of title 17, United States Code, as amended by section 108(c)(2) of this Act.

(F) The amendments made by section 108(c)(3) of this Act.

TITLE II—INTERNET COPYRIGHT INFRINGEMENT LIABILITY

SEC. 201. SHORT TITLE.

This title may be cited as the "Internet Copyright Infringement Liability Clarification Act of 1998".

SEC. 202. LIMITATIONS ON LIABILITY FOR INTERNET COPYRIGHT INFRINGEMENT.

(a) IN GENERAL.—Chapter 5 of title 17, United States Code, is amended by adding after section 511 the following new section:

"§ 512. Liability of service providers for online infringement of copyright

"(a) DIGITAL NETWORK COMMUNICATIONS.—A service provider shall not be liable for monetary relief, or except as provided in subsection (i) for injunctive or other equitable relief, for infringement for the provider's transmitting, routing, or providing connections for, material through a system or network controlled or operated by or for the service provider, or the intermediate and transient storage of such material in the course of such transmitting, routing or providing connections, if—

"(1) it was initiated by or at the direction of a person other than the service provider;

"(2) it is carried out through an automatic technical process without selection of such material by the service provider;

"(3) the service provider does not select the recipients of such material except as an automatic response to the request of another;

"(4) no such copy of such material made by the service provider is maintained on the system or network in a manner ordinarily accessible to anyone other than anticipated recipients, and no such copy is maintained on the system or network in a manner ordinarily accessible to the anticipated recipients for a longer period than is reasonably necessary for the communication; and

"(5) the material is transmitted without modification to its content.

"(b) SYSTEM CACHING.—A service provider shall not be liable for monetary relief, or except as provided in subsection (i) for injunctive or other equitable relief, for infringement for the intermediate and temporary storage of material on the system or network controlled or operated by or for the service provider: *Provided,* That—

"(1) such material is made available online by a person other than such service provider,

13

"(2) such material is transmitted from the person described in paragraph (1) through such system or network to someone other than that person at the direction of such other person,

"(3) the storage is carried out through an automatic technical process for the purpose of making such material available to users of such system or network who subsequently request access to that material from the person described in paragraph (1):

Provided further, That—

"(4) such material is transmitted to such subsequent users without modification to its content from the manner in which the material otherwise was transmitted from the person described in paragraph (1);

"(5) such service provider complies with rules concerning the refreshing, reloading or other updating of such material when specified by the person making that material available online in accordance with an accepted industry standard data communications protocol for the system or network through which that person makes the material available: *Provided further,* That the rules are not used by the person described in paragraph (1) to prevent or unreasonably impair such intermediate storage;

"(6) such service provider does not interfere with the ability of technology associated with such material that returns to the person described in paragraph (1) the information that would have been available to such person if such material had been obtained by such subsequent users directly from such person: *Provided further,* That such technology—

"(A) does not significantly interfere with the performance of the provider's system or network or with the intermediate storage of the material;

"(B) is consistent with accepted industry standard communications protocols; and

"(C) does not extract information from the provider's system or network other than the information that would have been available to such person if such material had been accessed by such users directly from such person;

"(7) either—

"(A) the person described in paragraph (1) does not currently condition access to such material; or

"(B) if access to such material is so conditioned by such person, by a current individual pre-condition, such as a pre-condition based on payment of a fee, or provision of a password or other information, the service provider permits access to the stored material in significant part only to users of its system or network that have been so authorized and only in accordance with those conditions; and

"(8) if the person described in paragraph (1) makes that material available online without the authorization of the copyright owner, then the service provider responds expeditiously to remove, or disable access to, the material that is claimed to be infringing upon notification of claimed infringements described in subsection (c)(3): *Provided further,* That the material has previously been removed from the originating site, and the party giving the notification includes in the notification a statement confirming that such material has been removed or access to it has been disabled or ordered to be removed or have access disabled.

"(c) INFORMATION STORED ON SERVICE PROVIDERS.—

"(1) IN GENERAL.—A service provider shall not be liable for monetary relief, or except as provided in subsection (i) for injunctive or other equitable relief, for infringement for the storage at the direction of a user of material that resides on a system or network controlled or operated by or for the service provider, if the service provider—

"(A)(i) does not have actual knowledge that the material or activity is infringing,

"(ii) in the absence of such actual knowledge, is not aware of facts or circumstances from which infringing activity is apparent, or

"(iii) if upon obtaining such knowledge or awareness, the service provider acts expeditiously to remove or disable access to, the material;

"(B) does not receive a financial benefit directly attributable to the infringing activity, where the service provider has the right and ability to control such activity; and

"(C) in the instance of a notification of claimed infringement as described in paragraph (3), responds expeditiously to remove, or disable access to, the material that is claimed to be infringing or to be the subject of infringing activity.

14

"(2) DESIGNATED AGENT.—The limitations on liability established in this sub-section apply only if the service provider has designated an agent to receive no-tifications of claimed infringement described in paragraph (3), by substantially making the name, address, phone number, electronic mail address of such agent, and other contact information deemed appropriate by the Register of Copyrights, available through its service, including on its website, and by pro-viding such information to the Copyright Office. The Register of Copyrights shall maintain a current directory of agents available to the public for inspec-tion, including through the Internet, in both electronic and hard copy formats.

"(3) ELEMENTS OF NOTIFICATION.—

"(A) To be effective under this subsection, a notification of claimed in-fringement means any written communication provided to the service pro-vider's designated agent that includes substantially the following—

"(i) a physical or electronic signature of a person authorized to act on behalf of the owner of an exclusive right that is allegedly infringed;

"(ii) identification of the copyrighted work claimed to have been in-fringed, or, if multiple such works at a single online site are covered by a single notification, a representative list of such works at that site;

"(iii) identification of the material that is claimed to be infringing or to be the subject of infringing activity that is to be removed or access to which is to be disabled, and information reasonably sufficient to per-mit the service provider to locate the material;

"(iv) information reasonably sufficient to permit the service provider to contact the complaining party, such as an address, telephone num-ber, and, if available an electronic mail address at which the complain-ing party may be contacted;

"(v) a statement that the complaining party has a good faith belief that use of the material in the manner complained of is not authorized by the copyright owner, or its agent, or the law; and

"(vi) a statement that the information in the notification is accurate, and under penalty of perjury, that the complaining party has the au-thority to enforce the owner's rights that are claimed to be infringed.

"(B) A notification from the copyright owner or from a person authorized to act on behalf of the copyright owner that fails substantially to conform to the provisions of paragraph (3)(A) shall not be considered under para-graph (1)(A) in determining whether a service provider has actual knowl-edge or is aware of facts or circumstances from which infringing activity is apparent: *Provided,* That the provider promptly attempts to contact the complaining party or takes other reasonable steps to assist in the receipt of notice under paragraph (3)(A) when the notice is provided to the service provider's designated agent and substantially satisfies the provisions of paragraphs (3)(A) (ii), (iii), and (iv).

"(d) INFORMATION LOCATION TOOLS.—A service provider shall not be liable for monetary relief, or except as provided in subsection (i) for injunctive or other equi-table relief, for infringement for the provider referring or linking users to an online location containing infringing material or activity by using information location tools, including a directory, index, reference, pointer or hypertext link, if the pro-vider—

"(1) does not have actual knowledge that the material or activity is infringing or, in the absence of such actual knowledge, is not aware of facts or cir-cumstances from which infringing activity is apparent;

"(2) does not receive a financial benefit directly attributable to the infringing activity, where the service provider has the right and ability to control such ac-tivity; and

"(3) responds expeditiously to remove or disable the reference or link upon no-tification of claimed infringement as described in subsection (c)(3): *Provided,* That for the purposes of this paragraph, the element in subsection (c)(3)(A)(iii) shall be identification of the reference or link, to material or activity claimed to be infringing, that is to be removed or access to which is to be disabled, and information reasonably sufficient to permit the service provider to locate such reference or link.

"(e) MISREPRESENTATIONS.—Any person who knowingly materially misrepresents under this section—

"(1) that material or activity is infringing, or

"(2) that material or activity was removed or disabled by mistake or misidentification,

shall be liable for any damages, including costs and attorneys' fees, incurred by the alleged infringer, by any copyright owner or copyright owner's authorized licensee, or by the service provider, who is injured by such misrepresentation, as the result of the service provider relying upon such misrepresentation in removing or disabling access to the material or activity claimed to be infringing, or in replacing the removed material or ceasing to disable access to it.

"(f) REPLACEMENT OF REMOVED OR DISABLED MATERIAL AND LIMITATION ON OTHER LIABILITY.—

"(1) Subject to paragraph (2) of this subsection, a service provider shall not be liable to any person for any claim based on the service provider's good faith disabling of access to, or removal of, material or activity claimed to be infringing or based on facts or circumstances from which infringing activity is apparent, regardless of whether the material or activity is ultimately determined to be infringing.

"(2) Paragraph (1) of this subsection shall not apply with respect to material residing at the direction of a subscriber of the service provider on a system or network controlled or operated by or for the service provider that is removed, or to which access is disabled by the service provider pursuant to a notice provided under subsection (c)(1)(C), unless the service provider—

"(A) takes reasonable steps promptly to notify the subscriber that it has removed or disabled access to the material;

"(B) upon receipt of a counter notice as described in paragraph (3), promptly provides the person who provided the notice under subsection (c)(1)(C) with a copy of the counter notice, and informs such person that it will replace the removed material or cease disabling access to it in ten business days; and

"(C) replaces the removed material and ceases disabling access to it not less than 10, nor more than 14, business days following receipt of the counter notice, unless its designated agent first receives notice from the person who submitted the notification under subsection (c)(1)(C) that such person has filed an action seeking a court order to restrain the subscriber from engaging in infringing activity relating to the material on the service provider's system or network.

"(3) To be effective under this subsection, a counter notification means any written communication provided to the service provider's designated agent that includes substantially the following:

"(A) A physical or electronic signature of the subscriber.

"(B) Identification of the material that has been removed or to which access has been disabled and the location at which such material appeared before it was removed or access was disabled.

"(C) A statement under penalty of perjury that the subscriber has a good faith belief that the material was removed or disabled as a result of mistake or misidentification of the material to be removed or disabled.

"(D) The subscriber's name, address and telephone number, and a statement that the subscriber consents to the jurisdiction of Federal Court for the judicial district in which the address is located, or if the subscriber's address is outside of the United States, for any judicial district in which the service provider may be found, and that the subscriber will accept service of process from the person who provided notice under subsection (c)(1)(C) or agent of such person.

"(4) A service provider's compliance with paragraph (2) shall not subject the service provider to liability for copyright infringement with respect to the material identified in the notice provided under subsection (c)(1)(C).

"(g) IDENTIFICATION OF DIRECT INFRINGER.—The copyright owner or a person authorized to act on the owner's behalf may request an order for release of identification of an alleged infringer by filing—

"(1) a copy of a notification described in subsection (c)(3)(A), including a proposed order, and

"(2) a sworn declaration that the purpose of the order is to obtain the identity of an alleged infringer and that such information will only be used for the purpose of this title, with the clerk of any United States district court.

The order shall authorize and order the service provider receiving the notification to disclose expeditiously to the copyright owner or person authorized by the copyright owner information sufficient to identify the alleged direct infringer of the material described in the notification to the extent such information is available to the service provider. The order shall be expeditiously issued if the accompanying notification satisfies the provisions of subsection (c)(3)(A) and the accompanying declaration is properly executed. Upon receipt of the order, either accompanying or subsequent to the receipt of a notification described in subsection (c)(3)(A), a service provider shall expeditiously give to the copyright owner or person authorized by the

16

copyright owner the information required by the order, notwithstanding any other provision of law and regardless of whether the service provider responds to the notification.

"(h) CONDITIONS FOR ELIGIBILITY.—

"(1) ACCOMMODATION OF TECHNOLOGY.—The limitations on liability established by this section shall apply only if the service provider—

"(A) has adopted and reasonably implemented, and informs subscribers of the service of, a policy for the termination of subscribers of the service who are repeat infringers; and

"(B) accommodates and does not interfere with standard technical measures as defined in this subsection.

"(2) DEFINITION.—As used in this section, 'standard technical measures' are technical measures, used by copyright owners to identify or protect copyrighted works, that—

"(A) have been developed pursuant to a broad consensus of copyright owners and service providers in an open, fair, voluntary, multi-industry standards process;

"(B) are available to any person on reasonable and nondiscriminatory terms; and

"(C) do not impose substantial costs on service providers or substantial burdens on their systems or networks.

"(i) INJUNCTIONS.—The following rules shall apply in the case of any application for an injunction under section 502 against a service provider that is not subject to monetary remedies by operation of this section.

"(1) SCOPE OF RELIEF.—

"(A) With respect to conduct other than that which qualifies for the limitation on remedies as set forth in subsection (a), the court may only grant injunctive relief with respect to a service provider in one or more of the following forms—

"(i) an order restraining it from providing access to infringing material or activity residing at a particular online site on the provider's system or network;

"(ii) an order restraining it from providing access to an identified subscriber of the service provider's system or network who is engaging in infringing activity by terminating the specified accounts of such subscriber; or

"(iii) such other injunctive remedies as the court may consider necessary to prevent or restrain infringement of specified copyrighted material at a particular online location: *Provided,* That such remedies are the least burdensome to the service provider that are comparably effective for that purpose.

"(B) If the service provider qualifies for the limitation on remedies described in subsection (a), the court may only grant injunctive relief in one or both of the following forms—

"(i) an order restraining it from providing access to an identified subscriber of the service provider's system or network who is using the provider's service to engage in infringing activity by terminating the specified accounts of such subscriber; or

"(ii) an order restraining it from providing access, by taking specified reasonable steps to block access, to a specific, identified, foreign online location.

"(2) CONSIDERATIONS.—The court, in considering the relevant criteria for injunctive relief under applicable law, shall consider—

"(A) whether such an injunction, either alone or in combination with other such injunctions issued against the same service provider under this subsection, would significantly burden either the provider or the operation of the provider's system or network;

"(B) the magnitude of the harm likely to be suffered by the copyright owner in the digital network environment if steps are not taken to prevent or restrain the infringement;

"(C) whether implementation of such an injunction would be technically feasible and effective, and would not interfere with access to noninfringing material at other online locations; and

"(D) whether other less burdensome and comparably effective means of preventing or restraining access to the infringing material are available.

"(3) NOTICE AND EX PARTE ORDERS.—Injunctive relief under this subsection shall not be available without notice to the service provider and an opportunity for such provider to appear, except for orders ensuring the preservation of evi-

17

dence or other orders having no material adverse effect on the operation of the service provider's communications network.

"(j) DEFINITIONS.—

"(1)(A) As used in subsection (a), the term 'service provider' means an entity offering the transmission, routing or providing of connections for digital online communications, between or among points specified by a user, of material of the user's choosing, without modification to the content of the material as sent or received.

"(B) As used in any other subsection of this section, the term 'service provider' means a provider of online services or network access, or the operator of facilities therefor, and includes an entity described in the preceding paragraph of this subsection.

"(2) As used in this section, the term 'monetary relief' means damages, costs, attorneys' fees, and any other form of monetary payment.

"(k) OTHER DEFENSES NOT AFFECTED.—The failure of a service provider's conduct to qualify for limitation of liability under this section shall not bear adversely upon the consideration of a defense by the service provider that the service provider's conduct is not infringing under this title or any other defense.

"(l) PROTECTION OF PRIVACY.—Nothing in this section shall be construed to condition the applicability of subsections (a) through (d) on—

"(1) a service provider monitoring its service or affirmatively seeking facts indicating infringing activity except to the extent consistent with a standard technical measure complying with the provisions of subsection (h); or

"(2) a service provider accessing, removing, or disabling access to material where such conduct is prohibited by law.

"(m) RULE OF CONSTRUCTION.—Subsections (a), (b), (c), and (d) are intended to describe separate and distinct functions for purposes of analysis under this section. Whether a service provider qualifies for the limitation on liability in any one such subsection shall be based solely on the criteria in each such subsection and shall not affect a determination of whether such service provider qualifies for the limitations on liability under any other such subsection.".

(b) CONFORMING AMENDMENT.—The table of sections for chapter 5 of title 17, United States Code, is amended by adding at the end the following:

"512. Liability of service providers for online infringement of copyright.".

SEC. 203. LIMITATIONS ON EXCLUSIVE RIGHTS; COMPUTER PROGRAMS.

Section 117 of title 17, United States Code, is amended—

(1) by striking "Notwithstanding" and inserting the following:

"(a) MAKING OF ADDITIONAL COPY OR ADAPTATION BY OWNER OF COPY.—Notwithstanding";

(2) by striking "Any exact" and inserting the following:

"(b) LEASE, SALE, OR OTHER TRANSFER OF ADDITIONAL COPY OR ADAPTATION.—Any exact"; and

(3) by adding at the end the following:

"(c) MACHINE MAINTENANCE OR REPAIR.—Notwithstanding the provisions of section 106, it is not an infringement for the owner or lessee of a machine to make or authorize the making of a copy of a computer program if such copy is made solely by virtue of the activation of a machine that lawfully contains an authorized copy of the computer program, for purposes only of maintenance or repair of that machine, if—

"(1) such new copy is used in no other manner and is destroyed immediately after the maintenance or repair is completed; and

"(2) with respect to any computer program or part thereof that is not necessary for that machine to be activated, such program or part thereof is not accessed or used other than to make such new copy by virtue of the activation of the machine.

"(d) DEFINITIONS.—For purposes of this section—

"(1) the 'maintenance' of a machine is the servicing of the machine in order to make it work in accordance with its original specifications and any changes to those specifications authorized for that machine; and

"(2) the 'repair' of a machine is the restoring of the machine to the state of working in accordance with its original specifications and any changes to those specifications authorized for that machine.".

SEC. 204. LIABILITY OF EDUCATIONAL INSTITUTIONS FOR ONLINE INFRINGEMENT OF COPYRIGHT.

(a) RECOMMENDATIONS BY REGISTER OF COPYRIGHTS.—Not later than six months after the date of the enactment of this Act, the Register of Copyrights, after con-

18

sultation with representatives of copyright owners and nonprofit educational institutions, shall submit to the Congress recommendations regarding the liability of nonprofit educational institutions for copyright infringement committed with the use of computer systems for which such an institution is a service provider, as that term is defined in section 512 of title 17, United States Code (as added by section 202 of this Act), including recommendations for legislation that the Register of Copyrights considers appropriate regarding such liability, if any.

(b) FACTORS.—In formulating recommendations under subsection (a), the Register of Copyrights shall consider, where relevant—

(1) current law regarding the direct, vicarious, and contributory liability of nonprofit educational institutions for infringement by faculty, administrative employees, students, graduate students, and students who are employees of such nonprofit educational institutions;

(2) other users of their computer systems for whom nonprofit educational institutions may be responsible;

(3) the unique nature of the relationship between nonprofit educational institutions and faculty;

(4) what policies nonprofit educational institutions should adopt regarding copyright infringement by users of their computer systems;

(5) what technological measures are available to monitor infringing uses;

(6) what monitoring of their computer systems by nonprofit educational institutions is appropriate;

(7) what due process nonprofit educational institutions should afford in disabling access by users of their computer systems who are alleged to have committed copyright infringement;

(8) what distinctions, if any, should be drawn between computer systems which may be accessed from outside the nonprofit educational systems, those which may not, and combinations thereof;

(9) the tradition of academic freedom; and

(10) such other issues relating to the liability of nonprofit educational institutions for copyright infringement committed with the use of computer systems for which such an institution is a service provider that the Register considers appropriate.

SEC. 205. EVALUATION OF IMPACT OF COPYRIGHT LAW AND AMENDMENTS ON ELECTRONIC COMMERCE AND TECHNOLOGICAL DEVELOPMENT.

(a) FINDINGS.—In order to maintain strong protection for intellectual property and promote the development of electronic commerce and the technologies to support that commerce, the Congress must have accurate and current information on the effects of intellectual property protection on electronic commerce and technology. The emergence of digital technology and the proliferation of copyrighted works in digital media, along with the amendments to copyright law contained in this Act, make it appropriate for the Congress to review these issues to ensure that neither copyright law nor electronic commerce inhibits the development of the other.

(b) EVALUATION BY SECRETARY OF COMMERCE.—The Secretary of Commerce, in consultation with the Assistant Secretary of Commerce for Communications and Information and the Register of Copyrights, shall evaluate—

(1) the effects of this Act and the amendments made by this Act on the development of electronic commerce and associated technology; and

(2) the relationship between existing and emergent technology and existing copyright law.

(c) REPORT TO CONGRESS.—The Secretary of Commerce shall, not later than 1 year after the date of the enactment of this Act, submit to the Congress a report on the evaluation conducted under subsection (b), including any legislative recommendations the Secretary may have.

SEC. 206. EFFECTIVE DATE.

This title and the amendments made by this title shall take effect on the date of the enactment of this Act.

TITLE III—EPHEMERAL RECORDINGS; DISTANCE EDUCATION; EXEMPTION FOR LIBRARIES AND ARCHIVES

SEC. 301. EPHEMERAL RECORDINGS.

Section 112(a) of title 17, United States Code, is amended—

19

(1) by redesignating paragraphs (1), (2), and (3) as subparagraphs (A), (B), and (C), respectively;

(2) by inserting "(1)" after "(a)"; and

(3) by inserting after "114(a)," the following: "or for a transmitting organization that is a broadcast radio or television station licensed as such by the Federal Communications Commission that broadcasts a performance of a sound recording in a digital format on a nonsubscription basis,"; and

(4) by adding at the end the following:

"(2) In a case in which a transmitting organization entitled to make a copy or phonorecord under paragraph (1) in connection with the transmission to the public of a performance or display of a work described in that paragraph is prevented from making such copy or phonorecord by reason of the application by the copyright owner of technical measures that prevent the reproduction of the work, the copyright owner shall make available to the transmitting organization the necessary means for permitting the making of such copy or phonorecord within the meaning of that paragraph, if it is technologically feasible and economically reasonable for the copyright owner to do so. If the copyright owner fails to do so in a timely manner in light of the transmitting organization's reasonable business requirements, the transmitting organization shall not be liable for a violation of the regulations issued under section 102(a)(1)(A) of the WIPO Copyright Treaties Implementation Act for engaging in such activities as are necessary to make such copies or phonorecords as permitted under paragraph (1) of this subsection.".

SEC. 302. LIMITATIONS ON EXCLUSIVE RIGHTS; DISTANCE EDUCATION.

(a) RECOMMENDATIONS BY NATIONAL TELECOMMUNICATIONS AND INFORMATION ADMINISTRATION.—Not later than 6 months after the date of the enactment of this Act, the Assistant Secretary of Commerce for Communications and Information, after consultation with representatives of copyright owners, nonprofit educational institutions, and nonprofit libraries and archives, shall submit to the Congress recommendations on how to promote distance education through digital technologies, including interactive digital networks, while maintaining an appropriate balance between the rights of copyright owners and the needs of users of copyrighted works. Such recommendations shall include any legislation the Assistant Secretary considers appropriate to achieve the foregoing objective.

(b) FACTORS.—In formulating recommendations under subsection (a), the Assistant Secretary of Commerce for Communications and Information shall consider—

(1) the need for an exemption from exclusive rights of copyright owners for distance education through digital networks;

(2) the categories of works to be included under any distance education exemption;

(3) the extent of appropriate quantitative limitations on the portions of works that may be used under any distance education exemption;

(4) the parties who should be entitled to the benefits of any distance education exemption;

(5) the parties who should be designated as eligible recipients of distance education materials under any distance education exemption;

(6) whether and what types of technological measures can or should be employed to safeguard against unauthorized access to, and use or retention of, copyrighted materials as a condition to eligibility for any distance education exemption, including, in light of developing technological capabilities, the exemption set out in section 110(2) of title 17, United States Code;

(7) the extent to which the availability of licenses for the use of copyrighted works in distance education through interactive digital networks should be considered in assessing eligibility for any distance education exemption; and

(8) such other issues relating to distance education through interactive digital networks that the Assistant Secretary considers appropriate.

SEC. 303. EXEMPTION FOR LIBRARIES AND ARCHIVES.

Section 108 of title 17, United States Code, is amended—

(1) in subsection (a)—

(A) by striking "Notwithstanding" and inserting "Except as otherwise provided in this title and notwithstanding";

(B) by inserting after "no more than one copy or phonorecord of a work" the following: ", except as provided in subsections (b) and (c)"; and

(C) in paragraph (3) by inserting after "copyright" the following: "that appears on the copy or phonorecord that is reproduced under the provisions of this section, or includes a legend stating that the work may be protected by copyright if no such notice can be found on the copy or phonorecord that is reproduced under the provisions of this section";

20

(2) in subsection (b)—

(A) by striking "a copy or phonorecord" and inserting "three copies or phonorecords";

(B) by striking "in facsimile form"; and

(C) by striking "if the copy or phonorecord reproduced is currently in the collections of the library or archives." and inserting "if—

"(1) the copy or phonorecord reproduced is currently in the collections of the library or archives; and

"(2) any such copy or phonorecord that is reproduced in digital format is not otherwise distributed in that format and is not made available to the public in that format outside the premises of the library or archives."; and

(3) in subsection (c)—

(A) by striking "a copy or phonorecord" and inserting "three copies or phonorecords";

(B) by striking "in facsimile form";

(C) by inserting "or if the existing format in which the work is stored has become obsolete," after "stolen,"; and

(D) by striking "if the library or archives has, after a reasonable effort, determined that an unused replacement cannot be obtained at a fair price." and inserting "if—

"(1) the library or archives has, after a reasonable effort, determined that an unused replacement cannot be obtained at a fair price; and

"(2) any such copy or phonorecord that is reproduced in digital format is not made available to the public in that format except for use on the premises of the library or archives in lawful possession of such copy."; and

(E) by adding at the end the following:

"For purposes of this subsection, a format shall be considered obsolete if the machine or device necessary to render perceptible a work stored in that format is no longer manufactured or is no longer reasonably available in the commercial marketplace.".

TITLE IV—RELATED PROVISIONS

SEC. 401. REPORT BY NATIONAL TELECOMMUNICATIONS AND INFORMATION ADMINISTRATION.

Not later than 6 months after the date of the enactment of this Act, the Assistant Secretary of Commerce for Communications and Information shall report to the Congress on appropriate mechanisms to encourage the development of access protocols, encryption testing methods, and security testing methods which would allow lawful access to, with appropriate safeguards to prevent the unlawful copying of, encrypted works. The Assistant Secretary shall include in such report recommendations on proposed amendments to this Act, if any, for achieving such result and for mechanisms to ensure that such safeguards—

(1) would be developed pursuant to a broad consensus of copyright owners and cryptographic researchers and security administrators in an open, fair, voluntary standards-setting process;

(2) to the extent feasible, would protect copyright owners against the unauthorized distribution or reproduction of their encrypted works; and

(3) would not limit encryption research, to the extent such research is permitted by law as of the enactment of this Act.

PURPOSE AND SUMMARY

The purpose of H.R. 2281, the Digital Millennium Copyright Act of 1998, is to implement two international treaties (i.e., the "Copyright Treaty," and the "Performances and Phonograms Treaty") signed by the United States and more than 125 other countries before the World Intellectual Property Organization (WIPO). The Clinton Administration's WIPO Treaties implementing legislation would have amended Title 17 of the United States Code to grant copyright owners a new right against "circumvention" of "technological protection measures," and to establish new provisions dealing with the integrity of "copyright management information." As reported by the Committee on the Judiciary, H.R. 2281 included

21

two titles: Title I would implement the two WIPO treaties; and Title II would provide for limitations on copyright infringement liability for on-line and other service providers.

Title I of H.R. 2281, as reported by the Committee on Commerce, also would implement the WIPO treaties, but through free-standing provisions of law rather than as amendments to Title 17. Title II, as amended by the Committee on Commerce, includes comprehensive provisions addressing copyright infringement liability for on-line and other service providers. Title III, as added by the Committee on Commerce, would address ephemeral recordings, the use of computer and other networks to foster distance learning, and exemptions for libraries and archives to permit them to use the latest technology to preserve deteriorating manuscripts and other works. With these proposed revisions, the Committee believes it has appropriately balanced the interests of content owners, on-line and other service providers, and information users in a way that will foster the continued development of electronic commerce and the growth of the Internet.

BACKGROUND AND NEED FOR LEGISLATION

LEGISLATIVE HISTORY

Much like the agricultural and industrial revolutions that preceded it, the digital revolution has unleashed a wave of economic prosperity and job growth. Today, the information technology industry is developing versatile and robust products to enhance the lives of individuals throughout the world, and our telecommunications industry is developing new means of distributing information to these consumers in every part of the globe. In this environment, the development of new laws and regulations will have a profound impact on the growth of electronic commerce and the Internet.

In recognition of these developments, and as part of the effort to begin updating national laws for the digital era, delegates from over 150 countries (including the United States) convened in December 1996 to negotiate the Copyright Treaty and the Performances and Phonograms Treaty under the auspices of the World Intellectual Property Organization (WIPO). In July 1997, the Clinton Administration submitted the treaties to the Senate for ratification and submitted proposed implementing legislation to both the House and the Senate.

On May 22, 1998, the Committee on the Judiciary reported H.R. 2281, the "WIPO Copyright Treaties Implementation Act" to the House. H.R. 2281 was sequentially referred to the Committee on Commerce for its consideration, initially for a period not to extend beyond June 19, 1998. Meanwhile, on May 14, 1998, the Senate adopted S. 2037, the "Digital Millennium Copyright Act." The Senate included provisions to explicitly authorize reverse engineering for purposes of achieving interoperability between computer products. The Senate also added a provision to ensure that librarians and archivists could use the latest technology to preserve deteriorating manuscripts and other works. It also added a so-called "no mandate" provision with respect to the design of consumer electronics, telecommunications, and computer products.

22

On June 5, 1998, the Subcommittee on Telecommunications, Trade, and Consumer Protection held a legislative hearing on H.R. 2281. The Committee had been advised that both H.R. 2281, as reported by the Committee on the Judiciary, and S. 2037, as passed by the Senate, were "compromises" that enjoyed "broad support." But it became apparent at the hearing that both bills faced significant opposition from many private and public sector interests, including libraries, institutions of higher learning, consumer electronics and computer product manufacturers, and others with a vital stake in the growth of electronic commerce and the Internet. In light of the serious concerns raised at the hearing, and in recognition of the complexity of the issues posed by the legislation, Chairman Bliley requested that the Committee's referral be further extended. The Committee's referral was subsequently extended, for a period not to extend beyond July 22, 1998.

PROMOTING ELECTRONIC COMMERCE

The Committee on Commerce is in the midst of a wide-ranging review of all issues relating to electronic commerce, including the issues raised by this legislation. The growth of electronic commerce is having a profound impact on the nation's economy. Over the past decade, the information technology sector of our economy has grown rapidly and is seen by many as playing a leading role in the current economic expansion. According to The Emerging Digital Economy, a recent Department of Commerce report on electronic commerce, the information technology sector now constitutes 8.2 percent of the Nation's gross domestic product, up from 4.5 percent in 1985. At the end of 1997, approximately 7.4 million Americans were employed in this field. It is expected that estimates of the total value of economic activity conducted electronically in 2002 will range from $200 billion to more than $500 billion, compared to just $2.6 billion in 1996.

H.R. 2281 is one of the most important pieces of legislation affecting electronic commerce that the 105th Congress will consider. It establishes a wide range of rules that will govern not only copyright owners in the marketplace for electronic commerce, but also consumers, manufacturers, distributors, libraries, educators, and on-line service providers. H.R. 2281, in other words, is about much more than intellectual property. It defines whether consumers and businesses may engage in certain conduct, or use certain devices, in the course of transacting electronic commerce. Indeed, many of these rules may determine the extent to which electronic commerce realizes its potential.

The Committee on Commerce's role in considering this legislation is therefore critical. The Committee has a long-standing interest in addressing all issues relating to interstate and foreign commerce, including commerce transacted over all electronic mediums, such as the Internet, and regulation of interstate and foreign communications. This legislation implicates each of those interests in numerous ways.

23

UNDERSTANDING THE NEXUS BETWEEN ELECTRONIC COMMERCE AND INTELLECTUAL PROPERTY

The debate on this legislation highlighted two important priorities: promoting the continued growth and development of electronic commerce; and protecting intellectual property rights. These goals are mutually supportive. A thriving electronic marketplace provides new and powerful ways for the creators of intellectual property to make their works available to legitimate consumers in the digital environment. And a plentiful supply of intellectual property—whether in the form of software, music, movies, literature, or other works—drives the demand for a more flexible and efficient electronic marketplace.

As electronic commerce and the laws governing intellectual property (especially copyright laws) change, the relationship between them may change as well. To ensure that Congress continues to enact policies that promote both of the above goals, it is important to have current information about the effects of these changes. For example, many new technologies for distributing real-time audio and video through the Internet function by storing small parts of copyrighted works in the memory of the recipient's computer. This technology is increasingly commonplace, but some providers of the technology are concerned that the making of these transient copies may subject them or their customers to liability under current copyright law. In another example, an increasing number of intellectual property works are being distributed using a "client-server" model, where the work is effectively "borrowed" by the user (e.g., infrequent users of expensive software purchase a certain number of uses, or viewers watch a movie on a pay-per-view basis). To operate in this environment, content providers will need both the technology to make new uses possible and the legal framework to ensure they can protect their work from piracy.

The Committee on Commerce believes it is important to more precisely define the relationship between intellectual property and electronic commerce, and to understand the practical implications of this relationship on the development of technology to be used in promoting electronic commerce. To that end, the Committee adopted an amendment that directs the Secretary of Commerce (the Secretary) to report on the effects of this legislation on the development of electronic commerce and the relationship between technology and copyright law. In the course of preparing the report, the Secretary is directed to consult with both the Assistant Secretary of Commerce for Communications and Information (given the Assistant Secretary's expertise in the area of telecommunications and information services and technologies) and the Register of Copyrights (given the Register's expertise in the field of copyright).

PROHIBITING CERTAIN DEVICES

H.R. 2281, as reported by the Committee on the Judiciary, would regulate—in the name of copyright law—the manufacture and sale of devices that can be used to improperly circumvent technological protection measures. The Committee on Commerce adopted an amendment that moves the anti-circumvention provisions out of Title 17 and establishes them as free-standing provisions of law.

24

The Committee believes that this is the most appropriate way to implement the treaties, in large part because these regulatory provisions have little, if anything, to do with copyright law. The anti-circumvention provisions (and the accompanying penalty provisions for violations of them) would be separate from, and cumulative to, the existing claims available to copyright owners. In the Committee's judgment, it therefore is more appropriate to implement the treaties through free-standing provisions of law rather than codifying them in Title 17.

Article 1, Section 8, Clause 8 of the United States Constitution authorizes the Congress to promulgate laws governing the scope of proprietary rights in, and use privileges with respect to, intangible "works of authorship." As set forth in the Constitution, the fundamental goal is "[t]o promote the Progress of Science and useful Arts. * * *." In the more than 200 years since enactment of the first Federal copyright law in 1790, the maintenance of this balance has contributed significantly to the growth of markets for works of the imagination as well as the industries that use such works.

Congress has historically advanced this constitutional objective by regulating the use of information—not the devices or means by which the information is delivered or used by information consumers—and by ensuring an appropriate balance between the interests of copyright owners and information users. For example, Section 106 of the Copyright Act (17 U.S.C. § 106) establishes certain rights copyright owners have in their works, including limitations on the use of these works without their authorization. Likewise, Sections 107 through 121 of the Copyright Act (17 U.S.C. §§ 107–121) set forth the circumstances in which such uses will be deemed permissible, or otherwise lawful even though unauthorized. And Sections 501 through 511, as well as Section 602 of the Copyright Act (17 U.S.C. §§ 501–511, 602) specify rights of action for copyright infringement, and prescribe penalties in connection with those actions.

In general, all of these provisions are technology neutral. They do not regulate commerce in information technology, i.e., products and devices for transmitting, storing, and using information. Instead, they prohibit certain actions and create exceptions to permit certain conduct deemed to be in the greater public interest, all in a way that balances the interests of copyright owners and users of copyrighted works. In a September 16, 1997, letter to Congress, 62 copyright law professors expressed their concern about the implications of regulating devices in the name of copyright law. They said in relevant part:

> Although [they] would be codified in Title 17, [the anti-circumvention provisions] would not be an ordinary copyright provision; liability under the section would result from conduct separate and independent from any act of copyright infringement or any intent to promote infringement. Thus, enactment of [the anti-circumvention provisions] would represent an unprecedented departure into the zone of what might be called paracopyright—an uncharted new domain of legislative provisions designed to strengthen copyright protection by regulating conduct

25

which traditionally has fallen outside the regulatory sphere of intellectual property law.

While the Committee on Commerce agrees with these distinguished professors, the Committee also recognizes that the digital environment poses a unique threat to the rights of copyright owners, and as such, necessitates protection against devices that undermine copyright interests. In contrast to the analog experience, digital technology enables pirates to reproduce and distribute perfect copies of works—at virtually no cost at all to the pirate. As technology advances, so must our laws. The Committee thus seeks to protect the interests of copyright owners in the digital environment, while ensuring that copyright law remain technology neutral. Hence, the Committee has removed the anti-circumvention provisions from Title 17, and established them as free-standing provisions of law.

FAIR USE IN THE DIGITAL ENVIRONMENT

H.R. 2281, as reported by the Committee on the Judiciary, provided that "[n]o person shall circumvent a technological protection measure that effectively controls access to a work protected under Title 17, United States Code." The Committee on Commerce devoted substantial time and resources to analyzing the implications of this broad prohibition on the traditional principle of "fair use." A recent editorial by the Richmond Times-Dispatch succinctly states the Committee's dilemma:

> Copyrights traditionally have permitted public access while protecting intellectual property. The U.S. approach—known as "fair use"—benefits consumers and creators. A computer revolution that has increased access to information also creates opportunities for the holders of copyrights to impose fees for, among other things, research and the use of excerpts from published works. And digital technology—whatever that means—could be exploited to erode fair use.[1]

The principle of fair use involves a balancing process, whereby the exclusive interests of copyright owners are balanced against the competing needs of users of information. This balance is deeply embedded in the long history of copyright law. On the one hand, copyright law for centuries has sought to ensure that authors reap the rewards of their efforts and, at the same time, advance human knowledge through education and access to society's storehouse of knowledge on the other. This critical balance is now embodied in Section 106 of the Copyright Act (17 U.S.C. § 106), which grants copyright holders a "bundle" of enumerated rights, and in Section 107, which codifies the "fair use" doctrine. Under the Copyright Act, "fair use" may be made of a copyrighted work "for purposes such as criticism, comment, news reporting, teaching * * * scholarship or research" under certain circumstances without the permission of the author.

Fair use, thus, provides the basis for many of the most important day-to-day activities in libraries, as well as in scholarship and edu-

---

[1] Fair Use, Richmond Times-Dispatch, July 13, 1998, at A–6.

26

cation. It also is critical to advancing the personal interests of consumers. Moreover, as many testified before the Committee, it is no less vital to American industries, which lead the world in technological innovation. As more and more industries migrate to electronic commerce, fair use becomes critical to promoting a robust electronic marketplace. The Committee on Commerce is in the midst of a wide-ranging review of all issues relating to electronic commerce, including the issues raised by this legislation. The digital environment forces this Committee to understand and, where necessary, modernize the rules of commerce as they apply to a digital environment—including the rules that ensure that consumers have a stake in the growth in electronic commerce.

The Committee was therefore concerned to hear from many private and public interests that H.R. 2281, as reported by the Committee on the Judiciary, would undermine Congress' long-standing commitment to the concept of fair use. A June 4, 1998, letter to the Committee from the Consumers' Union is representative of the concerns raised by the fair use community in reaction to H.R. 2281, as reported by the Committee on the Judiciary. The letter states in part:

> These newly-created rights will dramatically diminish public access to information, reducing the ability of researchers, authors, critics, scholars, teachers, students, and consumers to find, to quote for publication and otherwise make fair use of them. It would be ironic if the great popularization of access to information, which is the promise of the electronic age, will be short-changed by legislation that purports to promote this promise, but in reality puts a monopoly stranglehold on information.

The Committee on Commerce felt compelled to address these risks, including the risk that enactment of the bill could establish the legal framework that would inexorably create a "pay-per-use" society. At the same time, however, the Committee was mindful of the need to honor the United States' commitment to effectively implement the two WIPO treaties, as well as the fact that fair use principles certainly should not be extended beyond their current formulation. The Committee has struck a balance that is now embodied in Section 102(a)(1) of the bill, as reported by the Committee on Commerce. The Committee has endeavored to specify, with as much clarity as possible, how the right against anti-circumvention would be qualified to maintain balance between the interests of content creators and information users. The Committee considers it particularly important to ensure that the concept of fair use remains firmly established in the law. Consistent with the United States" commitment to implement the two WIPO treaties, H.R. 2281, as reported by the Committee on Commerce, fully respects and extends into the digital environment the bedrock principle of "balance" in American intellectual property law for the benefit of both copyright owners and users.

PROMOTING ENCRYPTION RESEARCH

H.R. 2281, as reported by the Committee on the Judiciary, provided no exception for the field of encryption research to the bill's

27

broad prohibition against the circumvention of technological protection measures. Recognizing the importance of the field of encryption research to electronic commerce, the Committee on Commerce crafted a provision that provides for an exception to the bill's anti-circumvention provisions.

The effectiveness of technological protection measures to prevent theft of works depends, in large part, on the rapid and dynamic development of better technologies, including encryption-based technological protection measures. The development of encryption sciences requires, in part, ongoing research and testing activities by scientists of existing encryption methods, in order to build on those advances, thus promoting and advancing encryption technology generally. This testing could involve attempts to circumvent or defeat encryption systems for the purpose of detecting flaws and learning how to develop more impregnable systems. The goals of this legislation would be poorly served if these provisions had the undesirable and unintended consequence of chilling legitimate research activities in the area of encryption.

In many cases, flaws in cryptography occur when an encryption system is actually applied. Research of such programs as applied is important both for the advancement of the field of encryption and for consumer protection. Electronic commerce will flourish only if legitimate encryption researchers discover, and correct, the flaws in encryption systems before illegitimate hackers discover and exploit these flaws. Accordingly, the Committee has fashioned an affirmative defense to permit legitimate encryption research.

PROTECTING PERSONAL PRIVACY IN THE DIGITAL ENVIRONMENT

H.R. 2281, as reported by the Committee on the Judiciary, contains numerous protections to protect the rights of copyright owners to ensure that they feel secure in releasing their works in a digital, on-line environment. The Committee on Commerce, however, believes that in reaching to protect the rights of copyright owners, Congress need not encroach upon the privacy interests of consumers.

Digital technology is robust and versatile enough that it can surreptitiously gather consumers' personal information, and do so through the use of software that is protected, or "cloaked," by a technological protection measure. And to the extent a consumer seeks to disable the gathering of such information, he or she may unwittingly violate the provisions of this bill. The Committee regards this as an extreme result, and believes that consumers must be accorded certain rights to protect their personal privacy.

The Committee on Commerce adopted an amendment to strike a balance between the interests of copyright owners and the personal privacy of consumers. The amendment deals with the critical issue of privacy by creating a marketplace incentive for copyright owners to deal "above board" with consumers on personal data gathering practices. Indeed, the copyright community itself has expressed a strong desire to give consumers comfort in knowing that their personal privacy is being protected. The Committee views consumer confidence as critical to promoting a robust and reliable marketplace for electronic commerce. Once consumers are confident that their personal privacy is protected, this should all but eliminate the

28

need for consumers to circumvent technological protection measures for the purpose of protecting their privacy. Copyright owners
can help consumers to realize confidence in the digital environment
by disclosing personal data gathering practices.

HEARINGS

The Subcommittee on Telecommunications, Trade, and Consumer
Protection held a hearing on H.R. 2281 on June 5, 1998. The Sub-
committee received testimony from: Mr. Marc Rotenberg, Director,
Electronic Privacy Information Center; Mr. Gary Shapiro, Presi-
dent, Consumer Electronics Manufacturers Association; Mr. Jona-
than Callas, Chief Technology Officer, Network Associates, Inc.;
Mr. Chris Bryne, Director of Intellectual Property, Silicon Graph-
ics, Inc., representing Information Technology Industry Council;
Mr. Robert Holleyman, CEO, Business Software Alliance; Ms.
Hilary Rosen, President and CEO, Recording Industry Association
of America; Mr. Walter H. Hinton, Vice President, Strategy and
Marketing, Storage Technology Corp.; Mr. George Vradenburg, III,
Senior Vice President and General Counsel, America OnLine, Inc.;
Mr. Steve Metalitz, Vice President, International Intellectual Property Alliance, representing the Motion Picture Association of Amer-
ica; Mr. Seth Greenstein, representing Digital Media Association
[listed on witness list]; Mr. Robert Oakley, Director of the Law Library, Georgetown University Law Center; and Mr. Charles E.
Phelps, Provost, University of Rochester.

COMMITTEE CONSIDERATION

The Subcommittee on Telecommunications, Trade, and Consumer
Protection met in open markup session on June 17, 1998, and June
18, 1998, to consider H.R. 2281, a bill to amend Title 17, United
States Code, to implement the World Intellectual Property Organization Copyright Treaty and Performances and Phonograms Treaty. On June 18, 1998, the Subcommittee approved H.R. 2281, the
Digital Millennium Copyright Act of 1998, for Full Committee consideration, amended, by a voice vote. On July 17, 1998, the Committee on Commerce met in open markup session and ordered H.R.
2281 reported to the House, amended, by a roll call vote of 41 yeas
to 0 nays.

ROLL CALL VOTES

Clause 2(l)(2)(B) of Rule XI of the Rules of the House requires
the Committee to list the recorded votes on the motion to report
legislation and amendments thereto. A motion by Mr. Bliley to
order H.R. 2281 reported to the House, amended, was agreed to by
a roll call vote of 41 yeas to 0 nays. The following are the recorded
vote on motion to report H.R. 2281, including the names of those
Members voting for and against, and the voice votes taken on
amendments offered to H.R. 2281.

29

COMMITTEE ON COMMERCE — 105TH CONGRESS
ROLL CALL VOTE #56

BILL: H.R. 2281, Digital Millennium Copyright Act of 1998

MOTION: Motion by Mr. Bliley to order H.R. 2281 reported to the House, amended.

DISPOSITION: AGREED TO, by a roll call vote of 41 yeas to 0 nays.

REPRESENTATIVE	YEAS	NAYS	PRESENT	REPRESENTATIVE	YEAS	NAYS	PRESENT
Mr. Bliley	X			Mr. Dingell			
Mr. Tauzin	X			Mr. Waxman	X		
Mr. Oxley	X			Mr. Markey	X		
Mr. Bilirakis				Mr. Hall	X		
Mr. Schaefer	X			Mr. Boucher	X		
Mr. Barton				Mr. Manton	X		
Mr. Hastert				Mr. Towns	X		
Mr. Upton	X			Mr. Pallone			
Mr. Stearns	X			Mr. Brown	X		
Mr. Paxon				Mr. Gordon	X		
Mr. Gillmor	X			Ms. Furse	X		
Mr. Klug	X			Mr. Deutsch	X		
Mr. Greenwood				Mr. Rush	X		
Mr. Crapo	X			Ms. Eshoo	X		
Mr. Cox	X			Mr. Klink	X		
Mr. Deal	X			Mr. Stupak	X		
Mr. Largent	X			Mr. Engel	X		
Mr. Burr	X			Mr. Sawyer	X		
Mr. Bilbray	X			Mr. Wynn	X		
Mr. Whitfield	X			Mr. Green			
Mr. Ganske	X			Ms. McCarthy	X		
Mr. Norwood	X			Mr. Strickland	X		
Mr. White	X			Ms. DeGette	X		
Mr. Coburn							
Mr. Lazio							
Mrs. Cubin	X						
Mr. Rogan	X						
Mr. Shimkus	X						

7/17/98

30

COMMITTEE ON COMMERCE -- 105TH CONGRESS
VOICE VOTES
7/17/98

BILL: H.R. 2281, Digital Millennium Copyright Act of 1998

AMENDMENT: Amendment by Mr. Tauzin, #1, to provide an exception to the anti-circumvention provisions of the bill for legitimate encryption research purposes.

DISPOSITION: AGREED TO by a voice vote.

AMENDMENT: Amendment by Mr. Markey, #2, to clarify the privacy provisions in the bill to ensure that consumers are capable of protecting their personal information while at the same time still protecting copyrighted works.

DISPOSITION: AGREED TO by a voice vote.

AMENDMENT: Amendment by Mr. Stearns, #3, to provide for a process to define the term technological protection measure.

DISPOSITION: WITHDRAWN by unanimous consent.

AMENDMENT: Amendment by Mr. Dingell, #4, to extend the existing National Telecommunications Information Administration (NTIA) study to cover a determination of the impact of the anti-circumvention provisions on research and development, including reverse engineering.

DISPOSITION: AGREED TO by a voice vote.

AMENDMENT: Amendment by Mr. Klug, #5, to provide a process for the Secretary of Commerce to waive the implementation of rules preventing circumvention of a technological protection measure in certain circumstances for classes of copyrighted works.

DISPOSITION: AGREED TO by a voice vote.

AMENDMENT: Amendment by Mr. White, #6, to clarify that the anti-circumvention provisions of the bill and the corresponding civil remedies do not infringe on the rights of users to exercise their First Amendment rights.

DISPOSITION: AGREED TO by a voice vote.

AMENDMENT: Amendment by Mr. White, #7, to require the Secretary of Commerce to conduct a study on the relationship between the development of electronic commerce and copyright law and report to Congress within one year after enactment.

DISPOSITION: AGREED TO by a voice vote.

31

AMENDMENT: Amendment by Mr. White, #5, to provide a framework that allows for negotiations between Internet broadcasters and content providers on royalty payments and for temporary storage of copyrighted content in computer servers.

DISPOSITION: WITHDRAWN by unanimous consent.

32

COMMITTEE OVERSIGHT FINDINGS

Pursuant to clause 2(l)(3)(A) of Rule XI of the Rules of the House of Representatives, the Committee held a legislative hearing and made findings that are reflected in this report.

COMMITTEE ON GOVERNMENT REFORM AND OVERSIGHT

Pursuant to clause 2(l)(3)(D) of Rule XI of the Rules of the House of Representatives, no oversight findings have been submitted to the Committee by the Committee on Government Reform and Oversight.

NEW BUDGET AUTHORITY, ENTITLEMENT AUTHORITY, AND TAX EXPENDITURES

In compliance with clause 2(l)(3)(B) of Rule XI of the Rules of the House of Representatives, the Committee finds that H.R 2281, the Digital Millennium Copyright Act of 1998, would result in no new or increased budget authority, entitlement authority, or tax expenditures or revenues.

COMMITTEE COST ESTIMATE

The Committee adopts as its own the cost estimate prepared by the Director of the Congressional Budget Office pursuant to section 402 of the Congressional Budget Act of 1974.

CONGRESSIONAL BUDGET OFFICE ESTIMATE

Pursuant to clause 2(l)(3)(C) of Rule XI of the Rules of the House of Representatives, the following is the cost estimate provided by the Congressional Budget Office pursuant to section 402 of the Congressional Budget Act of 1974:

U.S. CONGRESS,
CONGRESSIONAL BUDGET OFFICE,
Washington, DC, July 22, 1998.

Hon. TOM BLILEY,
Chairman, Committee on Commerce,
House of Representatives, Washington, DC.

DEAR MR. CHAIRMAN: The Congressional Budget Office has prepared the enclosed cost estimate for H.R. 2281, Digital Millennium Copyright Act of 1998.

If you wish further details on this estimate, we will be pleased to provide them. The CBO staff contact is Mark Hadley (for federal costs), Pepper Santalucia (for the state and local impact), and Matt Eyles (for the private-sector impact).

Sincerely,

JUNE E. O'NEILL, *Director.*

Enclosure.

H.R. 2281—Digital Millennium Copyright Act of 1998

Summary: H.R. 2281 would amend existing copyright laws to implement two World Intellectual Property Organization (WIPO) treaties, limit the liability of Internet providers for copyright infringe-

33

ment by their customers, clarify the treatment of ephemeral recordings, and require the study of various issues related to copyrights and emerging technologies.

Assuming the appropriation of the necessary funds, CBO estimates that implementing H.R. 2281 would result in new federal spending of about $2 million in fiscal year 1999 and less than $250,000 a year over the 2000–2003 period. Enacting the bill would establish new criminal penalties and thus could affect both receipts and direct spending. Hence, pay-as-you-go procedures would apply, but CBO expects that any changes in receipts and direct spending would not be significant.

H.R. 2281 contains an intergovernmental and a private-sector mandate as defined in the Unfunded Mandates Reform Act (UMRA), but the costs of the mandates would not exceed the thresholds in the law. (The thresholds are $50 million and $100 million in 1996, respectively, indexed annually for inflation.)

Estimated cost to the Federal Government: For the purpose of this estimate, CBO assumes that H.R. 2281 will be enacted by the end of fiscal year 1998, and that the estimated amounts will be appropriated by the start of each fiscal year. The costs of this legislation fall within budget function 370 (commerce and housing credit).

Title I of H.R. 2281 would amend U.S. copyright law to comply with two treaties produced by the December 1996 conference of the WIPO—one regarding the use of copyrighted material in digital environments and the other dealing with international copyright protection of performers and producers of phonograms. Title II would limit the liability for copyright infringement of persons who are providers of on-line services or network access. Title III would clarify the treatment of ephemeral recordings and exempt libraries and archives from some provisions of this bill. Title IV would require the National Telecommunications and Information Administration (NTIA) to submit a report on encryption testing methods and mechanisms to encourage access protocols.

H.R. 2281 would require the Register of Copyrights, the Secretary of Commerce, the Assistant Secretary of Commerce for Communications and Information, and the NTIA to submit six reports on issues related to copyrights in the digital age, including encryption, distance learning, liability of educational institutions, personal identifying information, and electronic commerce. In addition, title I would require the Secretary of Commerce to issue regulations prohibiting any person from circumventing technological protection measures on copyrighted works. Assuming the appropriation of the necessary amounts, producing reports and promulgating regulations required by H.R. 2281 would increase federal spending by about $2 million in fiscal year 1999 and less than $250,000 a year over the 2000–2003 period.

The bill would establish new criminal penalties and thus could affect both receipts and direct spending; therefore, pay-as-you-go procedures would apply. Section 105 would establish criminal fines of up to $1 million for anyone attempting to circumvent copyright protection systems, or falsifying or altering copyright management information. Enacting this provision could increase governmental receipts from the collection of fines, but we estimate that any such increase would be less than $500,000 annually. Criminal fines are

34

deposited in the Crime Victims Fund and are spent in the following year. Thus any change in direct spending from the fund would also amount to less than $500,000 annually.

Pay-as-you-go considerations: The Balanced Budget and Emergency Deficit Control Act specifies pay-as-you-go procedures for legislation affecting direct spending and receipts. Enacting H.R. 2281 could affect both direct spending and receipts, but CBO estimates that any such changes would be insignificant.

Intergovernmental and private-sector impact: Section 4 of UMRA excludes from the application of that act any legislative provisions that are necessary for the ratification or implementation of international treaty obligations. CBO has determined that title I of the bill fits within that exclusion because it is necessary for the implementation of the WIPO Copyright Treaty and the WIPO Performances and Phonograms Treaty.

Title III of H.R. 2281, however, would impose a mandate on certain owners of copyrights who apply technical protections to works that prevent their reproduction. Title III would require copyright owners who employ mechanisms that prevent the reproduction of copyrighted works to make available to federally licensed broadcasters the necessary means to copy such works. Under current law, federally licensed broadcasters are authorized to reproduce copyright-protected material under specific conditions. Since this mandate would apply to both public and private entities that own copyrights, it would be considered both a private-sector and an intergovernmental mandate.

However, the use of reproduction protections envisioned in the bill is not yet widespread. Furthermore, copyright owners may claim economic hardship or technological infeasibility to avoid the new requirement, and the costs of providing federally licensed broadcasters with the means to copy technically protected works would likely be modest. Therefore, CBO estimates that the direct cost of the new mandates would be well below the statutory thresholds in UMRA.

Previous CBO estimate: On May 12, 1998, CBO transmitted an estimate of H.R. 2281 as ordered reported by the House Committee on the Judiciary on April 1, 1998. The Judiciary Committee's version of the bill included the first two titles, but did not require any of the reports required by the Commerce Committee's version. CBO estimated that enactment of the Judiciary Committee's version of H.R. 2281 would have no significant impact on the federal budget.

Estimate prepared by: Federal Costs: Mark Hadley. Impact on State, Local, and Tribal Governments: Pepper Santalucia. Impact on the Private Sector: Matt Eyles.

Estimate approved by: Paul N. Van de Water, Assistant Director for Budget Analysis.

Federal Mandates Statement

The Committee adopts as its own the estimate of Federal mandates prepared by the Director of the Congressional Budget Office pursuant to section 423 of the Unfunded Mandates Reform Act.

35

ADVISORY COMMITTEE STATEMENT

No advisory committees within the meaning of section 5(b) of the Federal Advisory Committee Act were created by this legislation.

CONSTITUTIONAL AUTHORITY STATEMENT

Pursuant to clause 2(l)(4) of Rule XI of the Rules of the House of Representatives, the Committee finds that the Constitutional authority for this legislation is provided in Article I, section 8, clause 3, which grants Congress the power to regulate commerce with foreign nations, among the several States, and with the Indian tribes.

APPLICABILITY TO LEGISLATIVE BRANCH

The Committee finds that the legislation does not relate to the terms and conditions of employment or access to public services or accommodations within the meaning of section 102(b)(3) of the Congressional Accountability Act.

SECTION-BY-SECTION ANALYSIS OF THE LEGISLATION

Section 1. Short title

Section 1 establishes that this Act may be cited as the "Digital Millennium Copyright Act of 1998."

Section 2. Table of contents

Section 2 sets out the table of contents.

TITLE I—WIPO TREATIES IMPLEMENTATION

Section 101. Short title

Section 101 establishes that the short title of Title I is the "WIPO Copyright Treaties Implementation Act."

Section 102. Circumvention of copyright protection systems

As previously discussed in the background section to this report, the Committee was concerned that H.R. 2281, as reported by the Committee on the Judiciary, would undermine Congress' longstanding commitment to the principle of fair use. Throughout our history, the ability of individual members of the public to access and to use copyrighted materials has been a vital factor in the advancement of America's economic dynamism, social development, and educational achievement. In its consideration of H.R. 2281, the Committee on Commerce paid particular attention to how changing technologies may affect users' access in the future. Section 102(a)(1) of the bill responds to this concern.

The growth and development of the Internet has already had a significant positive impact on the access of American students, researchers, consumers, and the public at large to informational resources that help them in their efforts to learn, acquire new skills, broaden their perspectives, entertain themselves, and become more active and informed citizens. A plethora of information, most of it embodied in materials subject to copyright protection, is available to individuals, often for free, that just a few years ago could have been located and acquired only through the expenditure of consid-

36

erable time, resources, and money. New examples of this greatly expanded availability of copyrighted materials occur every day.

Still, the Committee is concerned that marketplace realities may someday dictate a different outcome, resulting in less access, rather than more, to copyrighted materials that are important to education, scholarship, and other socially vital endeavors. This result could flow from a confluence of factors, including the elimination of print or other hard-copy versions, the permanent encryption of all electronic copies, and the adoption of business models that depend upon restricting distribution and availability, rather than upon maximizing it. In this scenario, it could be appropriate to modify the flat prohibition against the circumvention of effective technological measures that control access to copyrighted materials, in order to ensure that access for lawful purposes is not unjustifiably diminished.

Given the threat of a diminution of otherwise lawful access to works and information, the Committee on Commerce believes that a "fail-safe" mechanism is required. This mechanism would monitor developments in the marketplace for copyrighted materials, and allow the enforceability of the prohibition against the act of circumvention to be selectively waived, for limited time periods, if necessary to prevent a diminution in the availability to individual users of a particular category of copyrighted materials.

Section 102(a)(1) of the bill creates such a mechanism. It converts the statutory prohibition against the act of circumvention into a regulation, and creates a rulemaking proceeding in which the issue of whether enforcement of the regulation should be temporarily waived with regard to particular categories of works can be fully considered and fairly decided on the basis of real marketplace developments that may diminish otherwise lawful access to works.

(a) Violations regarding circumvention of technological protection measures

Section 102(a)(1) gives two responsibilities to the Secretary of Commerce. The first is to issue regulations against the circumvention of technological protection measures that effectively control access to a copyrighted work. The second is to convene a rulemaking proceeding and, in conjunction with other specified officials, to determine whether to waive the applicability of the regulations for the next two years with respect to any particular category of copyrighted materials.

The Secretary's responsibility under subparagraph (A) is essentially ministerial. He or she is to simply recast, in the form of a regulation, the statutory prohibition against the act of circumvention of technological protection measures that effectively control access to copyrighted materials that was set forth in Section 102(a)(1) prior to its amendment.

The Committee has chosen a regulatory, rather than a statutory, route for establishing this prohibition for only one reason: to provide greater flexibility in enforcement, through the rulemaking proceeding set forth in the subsequent subparagraphs of this subsection 102(a)(1). It does not intend to make any substantive change in the scope or meaning of the prohibition as it appeared in the bill prior its amendment, and it is not empowering the Sec-

37

retary of Commerce to do so either. The regulation should conform in every particular to the provisions of the statute, which addresses all other relevant aspects of the regulatory prohibition, including exceptions (such as for privacy or for encryption research) as well as civil and criminal enforcement mechanisms and penalties. No additional definitions, limitations, defenses or other provisions may be added. The regulation is to take effect two years after the enactment of the statute.

Subparagraph (B) sets forth the parameters of the Secretary's second responsibility: the convening of a rulemaking proceeding, consistent with the requirements of the Administrative Procedures Act. The goal of the proceeding is to assess whether the implementation of technological protection measures that effectively control access to copyrighted works is adversely affecting the ability of individual users to make lawful uses of copyrighted works. Many such technological protection measures are in effect today: these include the use of "password codes" to control authorized access to computer programs, for example, or encryption or scrambling of cable programming, videocassettes, and CD–ROMs. More such measures can be expected to be introduced in the near future. The primary goal of the rulemaking proceeding is to assess whether the prevalence of these technological protections, with respect to particular categories of copyrighted materials, is diminishing the ability of individuals to use these works in ways that are otherwise lawful.

The main purpose for delaying for two years the effective date of the prohibition against circumvention of access control technologies is to allow the development of a sufficient record as to how the implementation of these technologies is affecting availability of works in the marketplace for lawful uses. The Committee also intends that the rulemaking proceeding should focus on distinct, verifiable and measurable impacts; should not be based upon *de minimis* impacts; and will solicit input to consider a broad range of evidence of past or likely adverse impacts.

The criteria listed in subparagraph (B) are illustrative of the questions that the rulemaking proceeding should ask. In each case, the focus must remain on whether the implementation of technological protection measures (such as encryption or scrambling) has caused adverse impact on the ability of users to make lawful uses. Adverse impacts that flow from other sources, or that are not clearly attributable to implementation of a technological protection measure, are outside the scope of the rulemaking. The rulemaking will be repeated on a biennial basis, and on each occasion, the assessment of adverse impacts on particular categories of works is to be determined de novo. The regulatory prohibition is presumed to apply to any and all kinds of works, including those as to which a waiver of applicability was previously in effect, unless, and until, the Secretary makes a new determination that the adverse impact criteria have been met with respect to a particular class and therefore issues a new waiver. In conducting the rulemaking proceeding, the Secretary must consult closely with the National Telecommunications and Information Administration, as well as with the Patent and Trademark Office and the Register of Copyrights.

38

Subparagraph (C) spells out the determination that the Secretary must make at the conclusion of the rulemaking proceeding. If the rulemaking has produced insufficient evidence to determine whether there have been adverse impacts with respect to particular classes of copyrighted materials, the circumvention prohibition should go into effect with respect to those classes. Only in categories as to which the Secretary finds that adverse impacts have occurred, or that such impacts are likely to occur within the next two years, should he or she waive the applicability of the regulations for the next two years.

The issue of defining the scope or boundaries of a "particular class" of copyrighted works as to which the implementation of technological protection measures has been shown to have had an adverse impact is an important one to be determined during the rulemaking proceedings. In assessing whether users of copyrighted works have been, or are likely to be adversely affected, the Secretary shall assess users' ability to make lawful uses of works "within each particular class of copyrighted works specified in the rulemaking." The Committee intends that the "particular class of copyrighted works" be a narrow and focused subset of the broad categories of works of authorship than is identified in Section 102 of the Copyright Act (17 U.S.C. § 102). The Secretary's determination is inapplicable in any case seeking to enforce any other provision of this legislation, including the manufacture or trafficking in circumvention devices that are prohibited by Section 102(a)(2) or 102(b)(1).

To provide meaningful protection and enforcement of the copyright owner's right to control access to his or her copyrighted work (as defined under Section 102(a)(1)), Section 102(a)(2) supplements Section 102(a)(1) with prohibitions on creating and making available certain technologies, products and services used, developed or advertised to defeat technological protection measures that protect against unauthorized access.[2]

Specifically, Section 102(a)(2) prohibits any person from manufacturing, importing, offering to the public, providing, or otherwise trafficking in certain technologies, products, services, devices, components, or parts that can be used to circumvent a technological protection measure that otherwise effectively controls access to a copyrighted work. The Committee believes it is very important to emphasize that Section 102(a)(2) is aimed fundamentally at outlawing so-called "black boxes" that are expressly intended to facilitate circumvention of technological protection measures for purposes of gaining access to a work. This provision is not aimed at products that are capable of commercially significant noninfringing uses, such as consumer electronics, telecommunications, and computer products—including videocassette recorders, telecommunications switches, personal computers, and servers—used by businesses and consumers for perfectly legitimate purposes.

---

[2] The Committee has previously reported laws that similarly protect against unauthorized access to works. See, e.g., 47 U.S.C. § 553(a)(2) (prohibiting the manufacture or distribution of equipment intended for the unauthorized reception of cable television service); 47 U.S.C. § 605(e)(4) (prohibiting the manufacture, assembly, import, and sale of equipment used in the unauthorized decryption of satellite cable programming); see also H. Rep. No. 780, 102d Cong., 2d Sess. (1992) (report accompanying H.R. 4567, which would have established the Audio Home Recording Act's anti-circumvention provisions as free-standing provisions of law).

39

Thus, for a technology, product, service, device, component, or part thereof to be prohibited under this subsection, one of three conditions must be met. It must: (1) be primarily designed or produced for the purpose of circumventing; (2) have only a limited commercially significant purpose or use other than to circumvent; or (3) be marketed by the person who manufactures it, imports it, offers it to the public, provides it or otherwise traffics in it, or by another person acting in concert with that person with that person's knowledge, for use in circumventing a technological protection measure that effectively controls access to a copyrighted work. This provision is designed to protect copyright owners, and simultaneously allow the development of technology.

Section 102(a)(3) defines certain terms used throughout Section 102(a). Subparagraph (A) defines the term "circumvent a technological protection measure" as meaning "to descramble a scrambled work, to decrypt an encrypted work, or otherwise to avoid, bypass, remove, deactivate, or impair a technological protection measure, without the authority of the copyright owner." This definition applies to subsection (a) only, which covers protections against unauthorized initial access to a copyrighted work. Subparagraph (B) states that a technological protection measure "effectively controls access to a work" if the measure, in the ordinary course of its operation, requires the application of information, or a process or a treatment, with the authority of the copyright owner, to gain access to the work. In the Committee's view, measures that can be deemed to "effectively control access to a work" would be those based on encryption, scrambling, authentication, or some other measure which requires the use of a "key" provided by a copyright owner to gain access to a work.

(b) Additional violations

Section 102(b) applies to those technological protection measures employed by copyright owners that effectively protect their copyrights, as opposed to those technological protection measures covered by Section 102(a), which prevent unauthorized access to a copyrighted work. Unlike subsection (a), which prohibits the circumvention of access control technologies, subsection (b) does not, by itself, prohibit the circumvention of effective technological copyright protection measures.

Paralleling Section 102(a)(2), Section 102(b)(1) seeks to provide meaningful protection and enforcement of copyright owners' use of technological protection measures to protect their rights by prohibiting the act of making or selling the technological means to overcome these protections and thereby facilitate copyright infringement. Subsection (b)(1) prohibits manufacturing, importing, offering to the public, providing, or otherwise trafficking in certain technologies, products, services, devices, components, or parts thereof that can be used to circumvent a technological protection measure that effectively protects a right of a copyright owner. As previously stated in the discussion of Section 102(a)(2), the Committee believes it is very important to emphasize that Section 102(b)(1) is aimed fundamentally at outlawing so-called "black boxes" that are expressly intended to facilitate circumvention of technological protection measures for purposes of gaining access to a work. This pro-

40

vision is not aimed at products that are capable of commercially significant noninfringing uses, such as consumer electronics, telecommunications, and computer products—including videocassette recorders, telecommunications switches, personal computers, and servers—used by businesses and consumers for perfectly legitimate purposes.

Thus, once again, for a technology, product, service, device, component, or part thereof to be prohibited under this subsection, one of three conditions must be met. It must: (1) be primarily designed or produced for the purpose of circumventing; (2) have only limited commercially significant purpose or use other than to circumvent; or (3) be marketed by the person who manufactures it, imports it, offers it to the public, provides it, or otherwise traffics in it, or by another person acting in concert with that person with that person's knowledge, for use in circumventing a technological protection measure that effectively protects the right of a copyright owner. Like Section 102(a)(2), this provision is designed to protect copyright owners, and simultaneously allow the development of technology.

Section 102(b)(2) defines certain terms used solely within subsection (b). In particular, subparagraph (A) defines the term "circumvent protection afforded by a technological protection measure" as "avoiding, bypassing, removing, deactivating, or otherwise impairing a technological protection measure." Subparagraph (B) provides that a technological protection measure "effectively protects a right of a copyright owner" if the measure, in the ordinary course of its operation, prevents, restricts, or otherwise limits the exercise of a copyright owner's rights. In the Committee's view, measures that can be deemed to "effectively control access to a work" would be those based on encryption, scrambling, authentication, or some other measure which requires the use of a "key" provided by a copyright owner to gain access to a work.

With respect to the effectiveness of technological protection measures, the Committee believes it is important to stress as well that those measures that cause noticeable and recurring adverse effects on the authorized display or performance of works should not be deemed to be effective. Unless product designers are adequately consulted about the design and implementation of technological protection measures (and the means of preserving copyright management information), such measures may cause severe "playability" problems. The Committee on Commerce is particularly concerned that the introduction of such measures not impede the introduction of digital television monitors or new digital audio playback devices. The Committee has a strong, long-standing interest in encouraging the introduction in the market of exciting new products. Recently, for example, the Committee learned that, as initially proposed, a proprietary copy protection scheme that is today widely used to protect analog motion pictures could have caused significant viewability problems, including noticeable artifacts, with certain television sets until it was modified with the cooperation of the consumer electronics industry.

Under the bill as reported, nothing would make it illegal for a manufacturer of a product or device (to which Section 102 would otherwise apply) to design or modify the product or device solely to

41

the extent necessary to mitigate a frequently occurring and noticeable adverse effect on the authorized performance or display of a work that is caused by a technological protection measure in the ordinary course of its design and operation. Similarly, recognizing that a technological protection measure may cause a problem with a particular device, or combination of devices, used by a consumer, it is the Committee's view that nothing in the bill should be interpreted to make it illegal for a retailer or individual consumer to modify a product or device solely to the extent necessary to mitigate a noticeable adverse effect on the authorized performance or display of a work that is communicated to or received by that particular product or device if that adverse effect is caused by a technological protection measure in the ordinary course of its design and operation.

The Committee believes that the affected industries should be able to work together to avoid such problems. The Committee is aware that multi-industry efforts to develop copy control technologies that are both effective and avoid such noticeable and recurring adverse effects have been underway over the past two years. The Committee strongly encourages the continuation of those efforts, which it views as offering substantial benefits to copyright owners in whose interest it is to achieve the introduction of effective technological protection (and copyright management information) measures that do not interfere with the normal operations of affected products.

(c) Other rights, etc., not affected

Subsection (c) sets forth several provisions clarifying the scope of Section 102. Section 102(c)(1) provides that Section 102 shall not have any effect on rights, remedies, limitations, or defenses to copyright infringement, including fair use, under Title 17. Section 102(c)(2) provides that Section 102 shall not alter the existing doctrines of contributory or vicarious liability for copyright infringement in connection with any technology, product, service, device, component or part thereof. Section 102(c)(3) clarifies that nothing in Section 102 creates an affirmative mandate requiring manufacturers of consumer electronics, telecommunications, and computing products to design their products or their parts and components to affirmatively respond to any particular technological protection measure employed to protect a copyrighted work. Lastly, Section 102(c)(4) makes clear that nothing in Section 102 enlarges or diminishes any rights of free speech or the press for activities using consumer electronics, telecommunications, or computing products.

(d) Exemption for nonprofit libraries, archives, and educational institutions

Section 102(d) provides a limited exemption from the regulations issued pursuant to Section 102(a)(1)(A) to qualified nonprofit libraries, archives, and educational institutions. In particular, Section 102(d)(1) allows a nonprofit library, nonprofit archives or nonprofit educational institution to obtain access to a copyrighted work for the sole purpose of making a good faith determination as to whether it wishes to acquire a copy, or portion of a copy, of that work in order to engage in permitted conduct. A qualifying institution

42

may not gain access for a period of time longer than necessary to determine whether it wishes to obtain a copy, or portion of a copy, for such purposes, and the right to gain access shall not apply for any other purpose. Section 102(d)(2) provides that the right to obtain access under this paragraph only applies when the nonprofit library, nonprofit archives, or nonprofit educational institution cannot obtain a copy of an identical work by other means, and such an entity may not use the exemption in this paragraph for commercial advantage or financial gain without penalty.

Section 102(d)(3) seeks to protect the legitimate interests of copyright owners by providing a civil remedy against a library, archive, or educational institution that violates Section 102(d)(1). Section 102(d)(4) provides that this subsection may not be used as a defense to the prohibitions on manufacturing or selling devices contained in Sections 102(a)(2) or 102(b). Finally, Section 102(d)(5) provides that a library or archive, to be eligible for the exemption in paragraph (1), must maintain its collections open to the public and available, not only to researchers affiliated with the library or archives or with the institution of which it is a part, but also to other persons doing research in a specialized field.

(e) Law enforcement and intelligence activities

Section 102(e) creates an exception for the lawfully authorized investigative, protective, or intelligence activities of an officer, agent, or employee of, the United States, a State, or a political subdivision of a State, or of persons acting pursuant to a contract with such an entity.

(f) Reverse engineering

Section 102(f) is intended to promote reverse engineering by permitting the circumvention of access control technologies for the sole purpose of achieving software interoperability. Section 102(f)(1) permits the act of circumvention in only certain instances. To begin with, the copy of the computer program which is the subject of the analysis must be lawfully acquired (i.e., the computer program must be acquired from a legitimate source, along with any necessary serial codes, passwords, or other such means as may be necessary to be able to use the program as it was designed to be used by a consumer of the product). In addition, the acts must be limited to those elements of the program which must be analyzed to achieve interoperability of an independently created program with other programs. The resulting product must also be a new and original work, in that it may not infringe the original computer program. Moreover, the objective of the analysis must be to identify and extract such elements as are necessary to achieve interoperability which are not otherwise available to the person. Finally, the goal of this section is to ensure that current law is not changed, and not to encourage or permit infringement. Thus, each of the acts undertaken must avoid infringing the copyright of the author of the underlying computer program.

Section 102(f)(2) recognizes that, to accomplish the acts permitted under Section 102(f)(1), a person may need to make and use certain tools. The Committee believes that such tools are generally available and used by programmers today in developing computer

43

programs (e.g., compilers, trace analyzers, and disassemblers). Such tools are not prohibited by this Section. But the Committee also recognizes that, in certain instances, it is possible that a person may need to develop special tools to achieve the permitted purpose of interoperability. Thus, Section 102(f)(2) creates an exception to the prohibition on making circumvention tools contained in Sections 102(a)(2) and 102(b)(1). These excepted tools can be either software or hardware. Once again, though, Section 102(f)(2) limits any person from acting in a way that constitutes infringing activity.

Similarly, Section 102(f)(3) recognizes that developing complex computer programs often involves the efforts of many persons. For example, some of these persons may be hired to develop a specific portion of the final product. For that person to perform these tasks, some of the information acquired through the permitted analysis, and the tools to accomplish it, may have to be made available to that person. Section 102(f)(3) allows developers of independently created software to rely on third parties either to develop the necessary circumvention tools, or to identify the necessary information to achieve interoperability. The ability to rely on third parties is particularly important for small software developers who do not have the capability of performing these functions in-house. This provision permits such sharing of information and tools.

The Committee, however, recognizes that making such information or tools generally available could undermine the objectives of Section 102. Section 102(f)(3) therefore imposes strict limitations on the exceptions created in Section 102(f). Acts of sharing information and tools is permitted solely for the purpose of achieving interoperability of an independently created computer program with other programs. If a person makes this information available for a purpose other than to achieve interoperability of an independently created computer program with other programs, then such action is a violation of this Act. In addition, these acts are permitted only to the extent that doing so does not constitute infringement, or violate other applicable law.

Section 102(f)(4) defines "interoperability" as the ability of computer programs to exchange information, and for such programs mutually to use the information which has been exchanged. The seamless exchange of information is a key element of software interoperability. Hence, Section 102(f) applies to computer programs as such, regardless of their medium of fixation and not to works generally, such as music or audiovisual works, which may be fixed and distributed in digital form. Because the goal of interoperability is the touchstone of the exceptions contained in Section 102(f), the Committee emphasizes that nothing in those subsections can be read to authorize the circumvention of any technological protection measure that controls access to any work other than a computer program, or the trafficking in products or services for that purpose.

(g) Encryption research

As previously discussed in the background section to this report, the Committee views encryption research as critical to the growth and vibrancy of electronic commerce. Section 102(g) therefore pro-

44

vides statutory clarification for the field of encryption research, in light of the prohibitions otherwise contained in Section 102. Section 102(g)(1) defines "encryption research" and "encryption technology." Section 102(g)(2) identifies permissible encryption research activities, notwithstanding the provisions of Section 102(a)(1)(A), including: whether the person lawfully obtained the encrypted copy; the necessity of the research; whether the person made a good faith effort to obtain authorization before circumventing; and whether the research constitutes infringement or a violation of other applicable law.

The Committee recognizes that courts may be unfamiliar with encryption research and technology, and may have difficulty distinguishing between a legitimate encryption research and a so-called "hacker" who seeks to cloak his activities with this defense. Section 102(g)(3) therefore contains a non-exhaustive list of factors a court shall consider in determining whether a person properly qualifies for the encryption research defense.

Section 102(g)(4) is concerned with the development and distribution of tools—typically software—which are needed to conduct permissible encryption research. In particular, subparagraph (A) provides that it is not a violation of Section 102(a)(2) to develop and employ technological means to circumvent for the sole purpose of performing acts of good faith encryption research permitted under Section 102(g)(2). Subparagraph (B) permits a person to provide such technological means to another person with whom the first person is collaborating in good faith encryption research permitted under Section 102(g)(2). Additionally, a person may provide the technological means to another person for the purpose of having the second person verify the results of the first person's good faith encryption research.

The Committee is aware of additional concerns that Section 102 might inadvertently restrict a systems operator's ability to perform certain functions critical to the management of sophisticated computer networks. For example, many independent programmers have created utilities designed to assist in the recovery of passwords or password-protected works when system users have forgotten their passwords. Because Section 102 prohibits circumvention without the authorization of the copyright owner, circumvention to gain access to one's own work, as a matter of logic, does not violate Section 102.

The law would also not prohibit certain kinds of commercial "key-cracker" products, e.g., a computer program optimized to crack certain "40-bit" encryption keys. Such machines are often rented to commercial customers for the purpose of quick data recovery of encrypted data. Again, if these products do not meet any of the three criteria under Section 102(a)(2) because these products facilitate a person's access to his or her own works, they would not be prohibited by Section 102.

In addition, network and web site management programs increasingly contain components that test systems security and identify common vulnerabilities. These programs are valuable tools for systems administrators and web site operators to use in the course of their regular testing of their systems' security. The testing of such "firewalls" does not violate Section 102 because in most cases

45

the firewalls are protecting computer and communications systems and not necessarily the specific works stored therein. Accordingly, it is the view of the Committee that no special exception is needed for these types of legitimate products.

Finally, Section 102(g)(5) requires the Assistant Secretary of Commerce for Communications and Information to report to Congress, within one year of enactment, on the effect Section 102(g) has had on the field of encryption research, the adequacy of technological protection for copyrighted works, and protection of copyright owners against unauthorized access.

(h) Components or parts to prevent access of minors to the Internet

The Committee is concerned that Section 102(a) might inadvertently make it unlawful for parents to protect their children from pornography and other harmful material available on the Internet, or have unintended legal consequences for manufacturers of products designed solely to enable parents to protect their children in this fashion. Section 102(h) addresses these concerns.

(i) Protection of personally identifying information

As previously stated in the background section to this report, Section 102(i)(1) is designed to ensure that if a copyright owner conspicuously discloses that the technological protection measure, or any work it protects, contains any personal data gathering capability, and the consumer is given the capability to curtail or prohibit effectively any such gathering or dissemination of personal information, then the consumer could not legally circumvent the technological protection measure. In addition, under Section 102(i)(2), if the copyright holder conspicuously discloses that the technological protection measure, or any work it protects, does not contain the capability of collecting or disseminating personally identifying information reflecting the on-line activities of a person who seeks to gain access to the work protected, then (once again) the consumer could not legally circumvent the technological protection measure.

In both such circumstances, there would be no need for consumers to circumvent technological protection measures because conspicuous disclosures indicate whether data gathering is being conducted and if so, the capability for thwarting such privacy invasions is extended to consumers. Only if there is no disclosure of privacy-related practices, or instances where consumers are left without the capability to disable the gathering of personal information, could a consumer circumvent a technological protection measure to protect his or her own privacy.

Section 103. Integrity of copyright management information

Section 103 implements the obligation contained in Article 12 of the Copyright Treaty and Article 19 of the Performances and Phonograms Treaty that contracting parties "provide adequate and effective legal remedies" against any person who knowingly and without authority removes or alters copyright management information (CMI), or who distributes, imports, broadcasts, or commu-

46

nicates to the public, works or copies of works knowing that such information has been removed or altered without authority.

(a) False copyright management information

Section 103(a) establishes a general prohibition against intentionally providing false copyright management information, as defined in subsection (c), and against distributing, or importing for distribution, false copyright management information.

(b) Removal or alteration of copyright management information

Section 103(b) establishes general prohibitions against removing or altering CMI, against distributing or importing for distribution altered CMI, and against distributing, importing for distribution or publicly performing works in which CMI has been removed.

(c) Definitions

Section 103(c) defines "copyright management information." To fall within the definition, the information must be conveyed in connection with copies or phonorecords, performances or displays of the copyrighted work.

(d) Law enforcement and intelligence activities

Section 103(d) creates an exception for the lawfully authorized investigative, protective, or intelligence activities of an officer, agent, or employee of, the United States, a State, or a political subdivision of a State, or of persons acting pursuant to a contract with such an entity.

(e) Limitations on liability

Section 103(e) recognizes special problems that certain broadcasting or cable entities may have with the transmission of copyright management information. Under Section 103(e), radio and television broadcasters, cable systems, and persons who provide programming to such broadcasters or systems, who do not intend to induce, enable, facilitate or conceal infringement may be eligible for a limitation on liability for violation of the copyright management information provisions of Section 103(b) in certain, limited situations.

In the case of an analog transmission, Section 103(e)(1) provides that an eligible person will not be held liable for violating provisions of subsection (b) if it is not "technically feasible" for that person to avoid the violation or if avoiding the violation would "create an undue financial hardship." Avoiding a violation of subsection (b) with respect to the transmission of credits that are of an excessive duration in relation to standard practice in the relevant industries (for instance, the motion picture and television broadcast industries) is one example of an activity that may "create an undue financial hardship" under Section 103(e)(1). As indicated above, this limitation on liability applies only if such person did not intend, by engaging in such activity, to induce, enable, facilitate, or conceal infringement.

Section 103(e)(2) provides a limitation on liability in the case of a digital transmission, and contemplates voluntary digital trans-

47

mission standards for the placement of copyright management information. Separate standards are likely to be set for the location of copyright management information in different categories of works. For instance, the standard(s) for the location of the name of the copyright owner in a sound recording or musical work to be broadcast by radio stations may differ—and be set in a separate standard-setting process—from the standard for the location of such information in a motion picture to be broadcast by television stations.

Paragraph (2)(A) provides that if a digital transmission standard for the placement of copyright management information for a category of works is set in a voluntary, consensus standard-setting process involving a representative cross-section of the relevant copyright owners and relevant transmitting industry, including, but not limited to, representatives of radio or television broadcast stations, cable systems, and copyright owners of a category of works that are intended for public performance by such stations or systems, an eligible person will not be liable for a violation of subsection (b) if the copyright management information involved in the violation was not placed in a location specified by the standard for that information. The eligible person, however, cannot qualify for this limitation on liability if that person was responsible for the nonconforming placement.

Section 103(e)(2)(B)(i) provides that until such a standard is set for a category of works, an eligible person will not be liable for a violation of subsection (b) if the transmission of the copyright management information would cause a perceptible visual or aural degradation of the digital signal. Section 103(e)(2)(B)(ii) provides that during this time period before a standard is set, an eligible person also will not be liable if the digital transmission of the information would conflict with an applicable government regulation or industry standard relating to transmission of information in a digital signal, such as the regulation requiring the placement of closed captioning in line 21 of the vertical blanking interval (47 U.S.C. § 613; 47 C.F.R. § 79.1). For purposes of this paragraph, however, the applicable industry-wide standard must be of a type specified in subparagraphs (2)(B)(ii) (II) or (III). The first type, defined in paragraph (2)(B)(ii)(II), includes only those standards that were adopted by a voluntary, consensus standards body, such as the Advanced Television Systems Committee, before the effective date of Section 103. The other type, defined in subparagraph (2)(B)(ii)(III), includes only those standards adopted in a voluntary, consensus standards-setting process open to participation by groups, including but not limited to a representative cross-section of radio or television broadcast stations, cable systems, and copyright owners of a category of works that are intended for public performance by such stations or systems.

Section 104. Civil remedies

(a) Civil actions

Section 104(a) sets forth the general proposition that civil remedies are available for violations of Sections 102 and 103. This provision also establishes the jurisdiction for such civil actions as the

48

"appropriate U.S. district court" and limits standing to those persons injured by a violation of Sections 102 or 103.

(b) Powers of the court

Section 104(b) defines the powers of the court hearing a case brought under Section 104(a).

(c) Award of damages

Section 104(c) is divided into five paragraphs, each of which addresses the awarding of damages to a prevailing party in an action brought under Section 104(a).

Section 105. Criminal offenses and penalties

(a) In general

Section 105(a) provides for criminal penalties for violations of Sections 102 and 103.

(b) Limitation for nonprofit library, archives, or educational institution

Section 105(b) exempts completely any nonprofit library, nonprofit archives, or nonprofit educational institution from the criminal penalties contained in subsection (a).

(c) Statute of limitations

Section 105(c) provides for a 5-year statute of limitations for criminal offenses.

Section 106. Savings clause

Section 106 establishes that nothing in Title I in any way limits the applicability of Federal or State privacy laws relating to the use of the Internet.

Section 107. Development and implementation of technological protection measures

Section 107 establishes a mechanism for monitoring, evaluating, and informing the Congress of the impact of this legislation, especially on the key issue of the role of technological protection measures.

(a) Statement of congressional policy and objective

Section 107(a) expresses the sense of Congress that technological protection measures, developed by the private sector through voluntary, industry-led processes, will play a crucial role in the healthy development of the Internet and other new paths for dissemination of copyrighted materials. Such measures can facilitate lawful uses of such materials, while safeguarding the private property interests that are recognized by the copyright law. Section 107(a) thus identifies an open, voluntary, multi-industry process for expeditious implementation of these technological protection measures.

49

(b) Technological protection measures

Section 107(b) mandates at least three technological protection measures for implementation pursuant to Section 107(a) that are especially important in achieving the full potential of the Internet and other digital media: (1) those that enable nonprofit libraries to continue in their critical role of lending copyrighted materials to individual patrons; (2) those that effectively protect against infringement of copyrighted materials; and (3) those that facilitate a diversity of legitimate uses, by individual members of the public, of copyrighted works in digital formats.

(c) Procedures for developing and implementing technological protection measures

Section 107(c) makes clear that Congress anticipates that the technological protection measures whose development and implementation are mandated pursuant to Section 107(a) will: be developed pursuant to a broad, private sector consensus; be made available on reasonable and non-discriminatory terms; and not impose substantial costs or burdens on copyright owners or on manufacturers of hardware and software used in conjunction with copyrighted works in digital formats.

(d) Oversight and reporting

Section 107(d) establishes an oversight process for monitoring the impact of this legislation, and specifically its anti-circumvention provisions, on the access of individuals to copyrighted materials in digital formats. For example, the Secretary would have to evaluate the extent to which Section 102 and the regulations issued thereunder pose a serious impediment to the development and production of competitive goods and services. It specifically directs the Secretary of Commerce, in consultation with the Register of Copyrights and the Assistant Secretary of Commerce for Communications and Information, to report, over the course of the next three years, annually to the House Committees on Commerce and on the Judiciary, and the Senate Committees on Commerce, Science, and Transportation and on the Judiciary on the extent of that impact.

Section 108. Technical amendments

Section 108 incorporates numerous technical amendments.
Section 109. Effective date.
Section 109 makes the effective date the date of enactment.

TITLE II—INTERNET COPYRIGHT INFRINGEMENT LIABILITY

The liability of on-line service providers and Internet access providers for copyright infringements that take place in the on-line environment has been a controversial issue. Title II of the Digital Millennium Copyright Act addresses this complex issue. Title II preserves strong incentives for service providers and copyright owners to cooperate to detect and deal with copyright infringements that take place in the digital networked environment. At the same time, it provides greater certainty to service providers con-

50

cerning their legal exposure for infringements that may occur in the course of their activities.

New Section 512 contains limitations on service providers' liability for five general categories of activity set forth in subsections (a) through (d) and subsection (f). As provided in subsection (k), new Section 512 is not intended to imply that a service provider is or is not liable as an infringer either for conduct that qualifies for a limitation of liability or for conduct that fails to so qualify. Rather, the limitations of liability apply if the provider is found to be liable under existing principles of law.

The limitations in subsections (a) through (d) protect qualifying service providers from liability for all monetary relief for direct, vicarious and contributory infringement. Monetary relief is defined in subsection (j)(2) as encompassing damages, costs, attorneys' fees, and any other form of monetary payment. These subsections also limit injunctive relief against qualifying service providers to the extent specified in subsection (i). To qualify for these protections, service providers must meet the conditions set forth in subsection (h), and service providers' activities at issue must involve a function described in subsection (a), (b), (c), (d) or (f), respectively. The liability limitations apply to networks "operated by or for the service provider," thereby protecting both service providers who offer a service and subcontractors who may operate parts of, or an entire, system or network for another service provider.

Section 201. Short title

Section 201 establishes the short title for Title II as the "Internet Copyright Infringement Liability Clarification Act of 1998."

Section 202. Limitations on liability for Internet copyright infringement

(a) In general

Section 202(a) amends chapter 5 of the Copyright Act (17 U.S.C. § 501, et seq.) to create a new Section 512, titled "Liability of service providers for on-line infringement of copyright." New Section 512(a) applies to communications functions associated with sending digital communications of others across digital networks, such as the Internet and other on-line networks. It establishes a limitation on liability for infringements that may occur in the provision of services falling within the definition of subsection (j)(1)(A). The limitations on injunctive relief set forth in subsection (i)(1)(B) are applicable when the functions at issue fall within the provisions of subsection (a), and the service provider meets the threshold criteria of subsection (h). These threshold criteria apply to all of the liability limitations contained in new Section 512.

Subsection (a) applies to service providers transmitting, routing, or providing connections for material, and some forms of intermediate and transient storage of material in the course of performing these functions. For example, in the course of moving packets of information across digital on-line networks, many intermediate and transient copies of the information may be made in routers and servers along the way. Such copies are created as an automatic consequence of the transmission process. In this context, "inter-

51

mediate and transient" refers to such a copy made and/or stored in the course of a transmission, not a copy made or stored at the points where the transmission is initiated or received. The use of the term "transmitting" throughout new Section 512 is not intended to be limited to transmissions of "a performance or display" of "images or sounds" within the meaning of Section 101 of the Copyright Act.

Subsections (a)(1) through (5) limit the range of activities that qualify under this subsection to ones in which a service provider plays the role of a "conduit" for the communications of others. This limitation on liability applies if: (1) the communication was initiated by or at the direction of a person other than the service provider; (2) it is carried out through an automatic technical process without selection of the material by the service provider; (3) the service provider does not select the recipients of the material except as an automatic response to the request of another; (4) no copy of the material made in the course of intermediate or transient storage is maintained on the system or network so that it is ordinarily accessible to anyone other than the anticipated recipients, and no copy is maintained on the system or network in a manner ordinarily accessible to the anticipated recipients for a longer period than is reasonably necessary for the communication; and (5) the content (but not necessarily the form) of the material is not modified in the course of transmission. Thus, for example, an e-mail transmission may appear to the recipient without bolding or italics resulting from format codes contained in the sender's message.

The term "selection of the material" in subsection (a)(2) means the editorial function of determining what material to send, or the specific sources of material to place on-line (e.g., a radio station), rather than "an automatic technical process" of responding to a command or request, such as one from a user, an Internet location tool, or another network. The term "automatic response to the request of another" is intended to encompass a service provider's actions in responding to requests by a user or other networks, such as requests to forward e-mail traffic or to route messages to a mailing list agent (such as a "Listserv") or other discussion group. The Committee intends subsection (a)(4) to cover copies made of material while it is en route to its destination, such as copies made on a router or mail server, storage of a web page in the course of transmission to a specific user, store and forward functions, and other transient copies that occur en route. The term "ordinarily accessible" is intended to encompass stored material that is routinely accessible to third parties. For example, the fact that an illegal intruder might be able to obtain access to the material would not make it ordinarily accessible to third parties. Neither, for example, would occasional access in the course of maintenance by service provider personnel, nor access by law enforcement officials pursuant to subpoena make the material "ordinarily accessible." However, the term does not include copies made by a service provider for the purpose of making the material available to other users. Such copying is addressed in subsection (b).

New Section 512(b) applies to a different form of intermediate and temporary storage than is addressed in subsection (a). In ter-

52

minology describing current technology, this storage is a form of "caching," which is used on some networks to increase network performance and to reduce network congestion generally, as well as to reduce congestion and delays to popular sites. This storage is intermediate in the sense that the service provider serves as an intermediary between the originating site and the ultimate user. The material in question is stored on the service provider's system or network for some period of time to facilitate access by users subsequent to the one who previously sought access to it. For subsection (b) to apply, the material must be made available on an originating site, transmitted at the direction of another person through the system or network operated by or for the service provider to a different person, and stored through an automatic technical process so that users of the system or network who subsequently request access to the material from the originating site may obtain access to the material from the system or network.

Subsections (b)(1) through (b)(5) clarify the circumstances under which subsection (b) applies. Subsection (b)(1) provides that the material must be transmitted to subsequent users without modification to its content in comparison to the way it was originally transmitted from the originating site. The Committee intends that this restriction apply, for example, so that a service provider who caches material from another site does not change the advertising associated with the cached material on the originating site without authorization from the originating site.

Subsection (b)(2) limits the applicability of the subsection to circumstances where the service provider complies with certain updating commands.

Subsection (b)(3) provides that the service provider shall not interfere with the ability of certain technology that is associated with the work by the operator of the originating site to return to the originating site information, such as user "hit" counts, that would have been available to the site had it not been cached. The technology, however, must: (i) not significantly interfere with the performance of the storing provider's system or network or with intermediate storage of the material; (ii) be consistent with generally accepted industry standard communications protocols applicable to Internet and on-line communications, such as those approved by the Internet Engineering Task Force and the World Wide Web Consortium; and (iii) not extract information beyond that which would have been obtained had the subsequent users obtained access to the material directly on the originating site.

Subsection (b)(4) applies to circumstances in which the originating site imposes a prior condition on access.

Subsection (b)(5) establishes a notification and take-down procedure for cached material modeled on the procedure under new Section 512(c). However, this take-down obligation does not apply unless the material has previously been removed from the originating site, or the party submitting the notification has obtained a court order for it to be removed from the originating site and notifies the service provider's designated agent of that order. This proviso has been added to subsection (b)(5) because storage under subsection (b) occurs automatically, and unless infringing material has been

53

removed from the originating site, the infringing material would ordinarily simply be re-cached.

New Section 512(c) limits the liability of qualifying service providers for claims of direct, vicarious and contributory infringement for storage at the direction of a user of material that resides on a system or network controlled or operated by or for the service provider. Examples of such storage include providing server space for a user's web site, for a chatroom, or other forum in which material may be posted at the direction of users. Subsection (c) defines the scope of this limitation on liability. It also sets forth procedural requirements that copyright owners or their agents and service providers must follow with respect to notifications of claimed infringement under subsection (c)(3). Information that resides on the system or network operated by or for the service provider through its own acts or decisions and not at the direction of a user does not fall within the liability limitation of subsection (c).

New subsection (c)(1)(A) sets forth the applicable knowledge standard. This standard is met either by actual knowledge of infringement or, in the absence of such knowledge, by awareness of facts or circumstances from which infringing activity is apparent. The term "activity" is intended to mean activity using the material on the system or network. The Committee intends such activity to refer to wrongful activity that is occurring at the site on the provider's system or network at which the material resides, regardless of whether copyright infringement is technically deemed to occur at that site or at the location where the material is received. For example, the activity at an on-line site offering audio or video may be unauthorized public performance of a musical composition, a sound recording, or an audio-visual work, rather than (or in addition to) the creation of an unauthorized copy of any of these works.

New subsection (c)(1)(A)(ii) can best be described as a "red flag" test. As stated in new subsection (c)(l), a service provider need not monitor its service or affirmatively seek facts indicating infringing activity (except to the extent consistent with a standard technical measure complying with new subsection (h)), in order to claim this limitation on liability (or, indeed any other limitation provided by the legislation). However, if the service provider becomes aware of a "red flag" from which infringing activity is apparent, it will lose the limitation of liability if it takes no action. The "red flag" test has both a subjective and an objective element. In determining whether the service provider was aware of a "red flag," the subjective awareness of the service provider of the facts or circumstances in question must be determined. However, in deciding whether those facts or circumstances constitute a "red flag"—in other words, whether infringing activity would have been apparent to a reasonable person operating under the same or similar circumstances—an objective standard should be used.

New subsection (c)(1)(A)(iii) provides that once a service provider obtains actual knowledge or awareness of facts or circumstances from which infringing material or activity on the service provider's system or network is apparent, the service provider does not lose the limitation of liability set forth in subsection (c) if it acts expeditiously to remove or disable access to the infringing material. Because the factual circumstances and technical parameters may vary

54

from case to case, it is not possible to identify a uniform time limit for expeditious action.

New subsection (c)(1)(B) sets forth the circumstances under which a service provider would lose the protection of subsection (c) by virtue of its benefit from and control over infringing activity. In determining whether the financial benefit criterion is satisfied, courts should take a common-sense, fact-based approach, not a formalistic one. In general, a service provider conducting a legitimate business would not be considered to receive a "financial benefit directly attributable to the infringing activity" where the infringer makes the same kind of payment as non-infringing users of the provider's service. Thus, receiving a one-time set-up fee and flat, periodic payments for service from a person engaging in infringing activities would not constitute receiving a "financial benefit directly attributable to the infringing activity." Nor is subsection (c)(1)(B) intended to cover fees based on the length of the message (e.g., per number of bytes) or by connect time. It would however, include any such fees where the value of the service lies in providing access to infringing material.

New subsection (c)(1)(C) establishes that in cases where a service provider is notified of infringing activity by a copyright owner or its authorized agent, in accordance with the notification procedures of new subsection (c)(3), the limitation on the service provider's liability shall be maintained only if the service provider acts expeditiously either to remove the infringing material from its system or to prevent further access to the infringing material on the system or network. This "notice and take-down" procedure is a formalization and refinement of a cooperative process that has been employed to deal efficiently with network-based copyright infringement.

The Committee emphasizes that new Section 512 does not specifically mandate use of a notice and take-down procedure. Instead, a service provider wishing to benefit from the limitation on liability under new subsection (c) must "take down" or disable access to infringing material residing on its system or network in cases where it has actual knowledge or that the criteria for the "red flag" test are met—even if the copyright owner or its agent does not notify it of a claimed infringement. On the other hand, the service provider is free to refuse to "take down" the material or site—even after receiving a notification of claimed infringement from the copyright owner. In such a situation, the service provider's liability, if any, will be decided without reference to new Section 512(c).

At the same time, copyright owners are not obligated to give notification of claimed infringement in order to enforce their rights. However, neither actual knowledge nor awareness of a "red flag" may be imputed to a service provider based on information from a copyright owner or its agent that does not comply with the notification provisions of new subsection (c)(3), in which case the limitation on liability set forth in new subsection (c) may still apply.

New Section 512(c)(2) provides that to qualify for the limitation on liability in new subsection (c), the service provider must designate an agent to receive notifications under new subsection (c)(1)(C). The designation, provided to the Register of Copyrights, and made available on the service provider's web site, is to contain

55

certain information necessary to communicate with the service provider concerning allegedly infringing material or activity. The Register of Copyrights is directed to maintain a directory of designated agents available for inspection by the public, both on the web site of the Library of Congress, and in hard copy format on file at the Copyright Office. The Committee does not intend or anticipate that the Register will publish hard copies of the directory. The directory shall have entries for the name, address, telephone number, and electronic mail address of an agent designated by service providers. The service provider's designation shall substantially comply with these elements.

New Section 512(c)(3) sets forth the procedures under which copyright owners and their agents may provide effective notification to a service provider of allegations of infringement on the provider's system or network. New subsection (c)(3)(A) requires that to count as an effective notification, the notification must be in writing and submitted to the service provider's designated agent. New subsections (c)(3)(A)(i)–(vi) then set forth the information to be included in an effective notification. The standard against which a notification is to be judged is one of substantial compliance. New subsection (c)(3)(A)(i) provides that the notification must be signed by the copyright owner, or its authorized agent, to be effective. The requirement for signature, either physical or electronic, relates to the verification requirements of new subsections (c)(3)(A)(v) and (vi). New subsection (c)(3)(A)(ii) requires that the copyright owner identify the copyrighted work alleged to have been infringed. Where multiple works at a single on-line site are covered by a single notification, a representative list of such works at that site is sufficient. Thus, for example, where a party is operating an unauthorized Internet jukebox from a particular site, it is not necessary that the notification list every musical composition or sound recording that has been, may have been, or could be infringed at that site. Instead, it is sufficient for the copyright owner to provide the service provider with a representative list of those compositions or recordings in order that the service provider can understand the nature and scope of the infringement being claimed.

New subsection (c)(3)(A)(iii) requires that the copyright owner or its authorized agent provide the service provider with information reasonably sufficient to permit the service provider to identify and locate the allegedly infringing material. An example of such sufficient information would be a copy or description of the allegedly infringing material and the so-called "uniform resource locator" (URL) (i.e., web site address) which allegedly contains the infringing material. The goal of this provision is to provide the service provider with adequate information to find and examine the allegedly infringing material expeditiously.

New subsection (c)(3)(A)(iv) requires that the copyright owner or its authorized agent provide reasonably sufficient identifying information concerning the owner or its agent who submits the notification, such as an address, telephone number, and (if available) an electronic mail address so that the service provider may contact the complaining party. New subsection (c)(3)(A)(v) makes clear that the notification from complaining parties must contain a statement that the complaining party has a good faith belief that the alleg-

56

edly infringing use is not authorized by the copyright owner, or its agent, or the law.

New subsection (c)(3)(A)(vi) specifies that the notification must contain a statement that the information contained therein is accurate. The complaining party—be it the copyright owner, or an authorized representative—also must confirm under penalty of perjury, that it has authority to act on behalf of the owner of the exclusive right that is allegedly being infringed. The term "perjury" is used in the sense found elsewhere in the United States Code. See, e.g., 28 U.S.C. § 1746; 18 U.S.C. § 1621.

New subsection (c)(3)(B) addresses the effect of notifications that do not substantially comply with the requirements of new subsection (c)(3). Under new subsection (c)(3)(B), the court shall not consider such notifications as evidence of whether the service provider has actual knowledge, is aware of facts or circumstances, or has received a notification for purposes of new subsection (c)(1)(A). However, a defective notice provided to the designated agent may be considered in evaluating the service provider's knowledge or awareness of facts and circumstances, if: (i) the complaining party has provided the requisite information concerning the identification of the copyrighted work, identification of the allegedly infringing material, and information sufficient for the service provider to contact the complaining party; and (ii) the service provider does not promptly attempt to contact the person making the notification or take other reasonable steps to assist in the receipt of notification that substantially complies with new subsection (c)(3)(A). If the service provider subsequently receives a substantially compliant notice, the provisions of new subsection (c)(1)(C) would then apply upon receipt of such notice.

The Committee intends that the substantial compliance standard in new subsections (c)(2) and (c)(3) be applied so that technical errors (e.g., misspelling a name, supplying an outdated area code if the phone number is accompanied by an accurate address, supplying an outdated name if accompanied by an e-mail address that remains valid for the successor of the prior designated agent or agent of a copyright owner) do not disqualify service providers and copyright owners from the protections afforded under subsection (c). The Committee expects that the parties will comply with the functional requirements of the notification provisions—such as providing sufficient information so that a designated agent or the complaining party submitting a notification may be contacted efficiently—in order to ensure that the notification and take-down procedures set forth in this subsection operate efficiently.

New Section 512(d) addresses instances where information location tools refer or link users to an on-line location containing infringing material or infringing activity. The term "infringing activity" means the wrongful activity that is occurring at the location to which the user is linked or referred by the information location tool, without regard to whether copyright infringement is technically deemed to have occurred at that location or at the location where the material is received. The term "information location tools" includes: a directory or index of on-line sites or material, such as a search engine that identifies pages by specified criteria; a reference to other on-line material, such as a list of recommended

57

sites; a pointer that stands for an Internet location or address; and a hypertext link which allows users to access material without entering its address.

New subsection (d) incorporates the notification and take-down procedures of new subsection (c), and applies them to the provision of references and links to infringing sites. A service provider is entitled to the liability limitations of new subsection (d) if it: (1) lacks actual knowledge of infringement on the other site, and is not aware of facts or circumstances from which infringing activity in that location is apparent; (2) does not receive a financial benefit directly attributable to the infringing activity on the site, where the service provider has the right and ability to control the infringing activity; and (3) responds expeditiously to remove or disable the reference or link upon receiving a notification of claimed infringement as described in new subsection (c)(3). The notification procedures under new subsection (d) follow those set forth in new subsection (c). However, the information submitted by the complaining party under new subsection (c)(3)(A)(iii) is the identification of the reference or link to infringing material or activity, and the information reasonably sufficient to permit the service provider to locate that reference or link.

New Section 512(d) provides a safe harbor that would limit the liability of a service provider that refers or links users to an on-line location containing infringing material or activity by using "information location tools," such as hyperlink directories and indexes. A question has been raised as to whether a service provider would be disqualified from the safe harbor based solely on evidence that it had viewed the infringing Internet site. If so, there is concern that on-line directories prepared by human editors and reviewers, who view and classify various Internet sites, would be denied eligibility to the information location tools safe harbor, in an unintended number of cases and circumstances. This is an important concern because such on-line directories play a valuable role in assisting Internet users to identify and locate the information they seek on the decentralized and dynamic networks of the Internet.

Like the information storage safe harbor in Section 512(c), a service provider would qualify for this safe harbor if, among other requirements, it "does not have actual knowledge that the material or activity is infringing" or, in the absence of such actual knowledge, it is "not aware of facts or circumstances from which infringing activity is apparent." Under this standard, a service provider would have no obligation to seek out copyright infringement, but it would not qualify for the safe harbor if it had turned a blind eye to "red flags" of obvious infringement.

For instance, the copyright owner could show that the provider was aware of facts from which infringing activity was apparent if the copyright owner could prove that the location was clearly, at the time the directory provider viewed it, a "pirate" site of the type described below, where sound recordings, software, movies, or books were available for unauthorized downloading, public performance, or public display. Absent such "red flags" or actual knowledge, a directory provider would not be similarly aware merely because it saw one or more well known photographs of a celebrity at a site devoted to that person. The provider could not be ex-

58

pected, during the course of its brief cataloguing visit, to determine whether the photograph was still protected by copyright or was in the public domain; if the photograph was still protected by copyright, whether the use was licensed; and if the use was not licensed, whether it was permitted under the fair use doctrine.

The intended objective of this standard is to exclude from the safe harbor sophisticated "pirate" directories—which refer Internet users to other selected Internet sites where pirate software, books, movies, and music can be downloaded or transmitted. Such pirate directories refer Internet users to sites that are obviously infringing because they typically use words such as "pirate," "bootleg," or slang terms in their URL and header information to make their illegal purpose obvious, in the first place, to the pirate directories as well as other Internet users. Because the infringing nature of such sites would be apparent from even a brief and casual viewing, safe harbor status for a provider that views such a site and then establishes a link to it would not be appropriate. Pirate directories do not follow the routine business practices of legitimate service providers preparing directories, and thus evidence that they have viewed the infringing site may be all that is available for copyright owners to rebut their claim to a safe harbor.

In this way, the "red flag" test in new Section 512(d) strikes the right balance. The common-sense result of this "red flag" test is that on-line editors and catalogers would not be required to make discriminating judgments about potential copyright infringement. If, however, an Internet site is obviously pirate, then seeing it may be all that is needed for the service provider to encounter a "red flag." A provider proceeding in the face of such a "red flag" must do so without the benefit of a safe harbor.

Information location tools are essential to the operation of the Internet; without them, users would not be able to find the information they need. Directories are particularly helpful in conducting effective searches by filtering out irrelevant and offensive material. The Yahoo! directory, for example, currently categorizes over 800,000 on-line locations and serves as a "card catalogue" to the World Wide Web, which over 35,000,000 different users visit each month. Directories such as Yahoo!'s usually are created by people visiting sites to categorize them. It is precisely the human judgment and editorial discretion exercised by these cataloguers which makes directories valuable.

This provision is intended to promote the development of information location tools generally, and Internet directories such as Yahoo!'s in particular, by establishing a safe harbor from copyright infringement liability for information location tool providers if they comply with the notice and take-down procedures and other requirements of new subsection (d). The knowledge or awareness standard should not be applied in a manner which would create a disincentive to the development of directories which involve human intervention. Absent actual knowledge, awareness of infringement as provided in new subsection (d) should typically be imputed to a directory provider only with respect to pirate sites or in similarly obvious and conspicuous circumstances, and not simply because the provider viewed an infringing site during the course of assembling the directory.

59

New Section 512(e) establishes a right of action against any person who knowingly misrepresents that material or activity on-line is infringing, or that material or activity was removed or disabled by mistake or misidentification under the "put-back" procedure set forth in new subsection (f). Actions may be brought under new subsection (e) by any copyright owner, a copyright owner's licensee, or by a service provider, who is injured by such misrepresentation, as a result of the service provider relying upon the misrepresentation in either taking down material or putting material back on-line. Defendants who make such a knowing misrepresentation are liable for any damages, including costs and attorneys" fees, incurred by any of these parties as a result of the service provider's reliance upon the misrepresentation. This subsection is intended to deter knowingly false allegations to service providers in recognition that such misrepresentations are detrimental to rights holders, service providers, and Internet users.

New Section 512(f) provides immunity to service providers for taking down infringing material, and establishes a "put back" procedure under which subscribers may contest a complaining party's notification of infringement provided under new subsection (c)(3). The put-back procedures were added to balance the incentives created in new Section 512 for service providers to take down material against third parties' interests in ensuring that material not be taken down. In particular, new subsection (f)(1) immunizes service providers from any claim based on the service provider's good-faith disabling of access to, or removal of, material or activity claimed to be infringing. The immunity also applies where the service provider disables access to, or removes, material or activity based on facts or circumstances from which infringing activity is apparent. This immunity is available even if the material or activity is ultimately determined not to be infringing. The purpose of this subsection is to protect service providers from liability to third parties whose material service providers take down in a good faith effort to comply with the requirements of new subsection (c)(1).

New subsection (f)(2) establishes a "put back" procedure through an exception to the immunity set forth in new subsection (f)(1). The exception applies in a case in which the service provider, pursuant to a notification provided under new subsection (c)(1)(C) in accordance with new subsection (c)(3), takes down material that a subscriber has posted to the system or network. In such instances, to retain the immunity set forth in new subsection (f)(1) with respect to the subscriber whose content is taken down, the service provider must take three steps.

First, under new subsection (f)(2)(A), the service provider is to take reasonable steps to notify the subscriber promptly of the removal or disabling of access to the subscriber's material. The Committee intends that "reasonable steps" include, for example, sending an e-mail notice to an e-mail address associated with a posting, or if only the subscriber's name is identified in the posting, sending an e-mail to an e-mail address that the subscriber submitted with its subscription. The Committee does not intend that this subsection impose any obligation on service providers to search beyond the four corners of a subscriber's posting or their own records for that subscriber in order to obtain contact information. Nor does the

60

Committee intend to create any right on the part of subscribers who submit falsified information in their postings or subscriptions to complain if a service provider relies upon the information submitted by the subscriber.

Second, pursuant to new subsection (f)(2)(B), the subscriber may then file a counter notification, in accordance with the requirements of new subsection (f)(3), contesting the original take down on grounds of mistake or misidentification of the material and requesting "put back" of the material that the service provider has taken down. If a subscriber files a counter notification with the service provider's designated agent, new subsection (f)(2)(B) calls for the service provider to promptly forward a copy to the complaining party who submitted the take down request.

And third, under new subsection (f)(2)(C), the service provider is to place the subscriber's material back on-line, or cease disabling access to it, between 10 and 14 business days after receiving the counter notification, unless the designated agent receives a further notice from the complaining party that the complaining party has filed an action seeking a court order to restrain the subscriber from engaging in the infringing activity on the service provider's system or network with regard to the material in question.

Subscriber counter notifications must substantially comply with defined requirements set forth in new subsection (f)(3). Notifications shall be signed by the subscriber physically or by electronic signature; identify the material taken down and the location from which it was taken down; include a statement under penalty of perjury that the subscriber has a good faith belief that the material was taken down as a result of mistake or misidentification of the material; and include the subscriber's contact information, as well as a statement consenting to the jurisdiction of a Federal district court and to accept service of process from the complaining party or the complaining party's agent. The substantial compliance standard is the same as that set forth in new subsections (c) (2) and (3).

New subsection (f)(4) is included to make clear the obvious proposition that a service provider's compliance with the put-back procedure does not subject it to liability for copyright infringement or cause it to lose its liability limitation with respect to the replaced material.

New Section 512(g) creates a procedure by which copyright owners or their authorized agents who have submitted or will submit a request for notification satisfying the requirements of new subsection (c)(3)(A) may obtain an order for identification of alleged infringers who are users of a service provider's system or network. Under this procedure, the copyright owner or agent files three documents with the clerk of any Federal district court: a copy of the notification; a proposed order; and a sworn declaration that the purpose of the order is to obtain the identity of an alleged infringer, and that the information obtained will only be used to protect the owner's rights under this Title.

Orders issued under new subsection (g) shall authorize and order the service provider expeditiously to disclose to the person seeking the order information sufficient to identify the alleged infringer to the extent such information is available to the service provider.

61

The Committee intends that an order for disclosure be interpreted as requiring disclosure of information in the possession of the service provider, rather than obliging the service provider to conduct searches for information that is available from other systems or networks. The Committee intends that such orders be expeditiously issued if the notification meets the provisions of new subsection (c)(3)(A) and the declaration is properly executed. The issuing of the order should be a ministerial function performed quickly for this provision to have its intended effect. After receiving the order, the service provider shall expeditiously disclose to the copyright owner or its agent the information required by the order to the extent that the information is available to the service provider, regardless of whether the service provider responds to the notification of claimed infringement.

New Section 512(h) sets forth two conditions that a service provider must satisfy to be eligible for the limitations on liability provided in new subsections (a) through (d). First, the service provider is expected to adopt and reasonably implement a policy for the termination in appropriate circumstances of the accounts of subscribers[3] of the provider's service who are repeat on-line infringers of copyright. The Committee recognizes that there are different degrees of on-line copyright infringement, from the inadvertent and noncommercial, to the willful and commercial. In addition, the Committee does not intend this provision to undermine the principles of new subsection (l) or the knowledge standard of new subsection (c) by suggesting that a provider must investigate possible infringements, monitor its service, or make difficult judgments as to whether conduct is or is not infringing. However, those who repeatedly or flagrantly abuse their access to the Internet through disrespect for the intellectual property rights of others should know that there is a realistic threat of losing that access.

Second, a provider's system must accommodate, and not interfere with, standard technical measures used to identify or protect copyrighted works. The Committee believes that technology is likely to be the solution to many of the issues facing copyright owners and service providers in this digital age. For that reason, the Committee has included new subsection (h)(1)(B), which is intended to encourage appropriate technological solutions to protect copyrighted works. The Committee strongly urges all of the affected parties expeditiously to commence voluntary, inter-industry discussions to agree upon and implement the best technological solutions available to achieve these goals.

New subsection (h)(1)(B) is explicitly limited to "standard technical measures" that have been developed pursuant to a broad consensus of both copyright owners and service providers in an open, fair, voluntary, multi-industry standards process. The Committee anticipates that these provisions could be developed both in recognized open standards bodies or in ad hoc groups, as long as the

---

[3] In using the term "subscribers," the Committee intends to include account holders that have a business relationship with the service provider that justifies treating them as subscribers, for the purposes of new Section 512, even if no formal subscription agreement exists. For example, "subscribers" would include students who are granted access to a university's system or network for digital on-line communications; employees who have access to their employer's system or network; or household members with access to a consumer on-line service by virtue of a subscription agreement between the service provider and another member of that household.

62

process used is open, fair, voluntary, and multi-industry and the measures developed otherwise conform to the requirements of the definition of standard technical measures set forth in new subsection (h)(2). A number of recognized open standards bodies have substantial experience with Internet issues. The Committee also notes that an ad hoc approach has been successful in developing standards in other contexts, such as the process that has developed copy protection technology for use in connection with digital video disk players.

New Section 512(i) defines the terms and conditions under which an injunction may be issued against a service provider that qualifies for the limitations on liability set forth in new subsections (a) through (d), but is otherwise subject to an injunction under existing principles of law. New subsection (i)(1) limits the scope of injunctive relief that may be ordered against a qualifying provider. New subsection (i)(2) identifies factors a court must consider in deciding whether to grant injunctive relief and in determining the appropriate scope of injunctive relief.

New subsection (i)(1) is divided into two subparagraphs. New subparagraph (A) defines the scope of injunctive relief available against service providers who qualify for the limitations of liability set forth in new subsections (b), (c) or (d). Only three forms of injunctive relief may be granted. First, pursuant to new subsection (i)(1)(A)(i), the court may provide for the removal or blocking of infringing material or activity that is residing at a specific location on the provider's system or network. This is essentially an order to take the actions identified in new subsection (c)(1)(C) to "remove, or disable access" to the material that is claimed to be infringing or to be the subject of infringing activity.

Second, under new subsection (i)(1)(A)(ii), the court may order the provider to terminate the accounts of a subscriber[4] of the provider's service who is engaging in infringing activity. And third, pursuant to new subsection (i)(1)(A)(iii), the court may, under appropriate circumstances, enter a different form of injunction if the court considers it necessary to prevent or restrain infringement of specific copyrighted material that resides at an identified on-line location. If a court enters an injunction other than that contemplated in new subparagraphs (A) (i) or (ii), the court must determine that the injunctive relief is the least burdensome relief to the service provider among those forms of relief that are comparably effective.

New subsection (i)(1)(B) sets forth a different set of remedies available for injunctions against service providers qualifying for the limitation on remedies set forth in new subsection (a). In such cases, if a court determines that injunctive relief is appropriate, it may only grant injunctive relief in one or both of two specified forms. The first, pursuant to new subparagraph (B)(i), is an order to the service provider to terminate subscriber accounts that are specified in the order. The second form of relief, pursuant to new subparagraph (B)(ii) and available in cases in which a provider is engaging in infringing activity relating to a foreign on-line location, is an order to take reasonable steps to block access to a specific,

---

[4] See supra note 3.

63

identified foreign on-line location. Such blocking orders are not available against a service provider qualifying under new subsection (a) in the case of infringing activity on a site within the United States or its territories.

New subsection (i)(2) sets forth mandatory considerations for the court beyond those that exist under current law. These additional considerations require the court to consider factors of particular significance in the digital on-line environment. New subsection (i)(3) prohibits most forms of *ex parte* injunctive relief (including temporary and preliminary relief) against a service provider qualifying for a liability limitation under new Section 512. A court may issue an order to ensure the preservation of evidence or where the order will have no material adverse effect on the operation of the provider's network.

New Section 512(j) provides definitions of the term "service provider" as used in this Title, as well as a definition of the term "monetary relief." Only an entity that is performing the functions of a "service provider" is eligible for the limitations on liability set forth in new Section 512 with respect to those functions.

The first definition of a "service provider," set forth in new subsection (j)(1)(A), narrowly defines a range of functions and applies only to use of the term in new subsection (a). As used in new subsection (a), the term "service provider" means any entity offering the transmission, routing or providing of connections for digital on-line communications, between or among points specified by a user, of material of a user's choosing without modification to the content of the material as sent or received. This free-standing definition is derived from the definition of "telecommunications" found in the Communications Act of 1934 (47 U.S.C. § 153(48)) in recognition of the fact that the functions covered by new subsection (a) are essentially conduit-only functions. The Committee, however, has tweaked the definition for purposes of new subsection (j)(1)(A) to ensure that it captures offerings over the Internet and other on-line media. Thus, the definition in new subsection (j)(1)(A) not only includes "the offering of transmission, routing or providing of connections," but also requires that the service provider be providing such services for communications that are both "digital" and "on-line." By "on-line" communications, the Committee means communications over interactive computer networks, such as the Internet. Thus, over-the-air broadcasting, whether in analog or digital form, or a cable television system, or a satellite television service, would not qualify, except to the extent it provides users with on-line access to a digital network such as the Internet, or it provides transmission, routing, or connections to connect material to such a network, and then only with respect to those functions. An entity is not disqualified from being a "service provider" because it alters the form of the material, so long as it does not alter the content of the material. As a threshold matter, a service provider's performance of a particular function with respect to allegedly infringing activity falls within the "service provider" definition in new subsection (j)(1)(A) if and only if such function is within the range of functions defined in new subsection (j)(1)(A). For example, hosting a web site does not fall within the new subsection (j)(1)(A) definition, whereas the mere provision of connectivity to a web site does

64

fall within that definition. The new subsection (j)(1)(A) definition is not intended to exclude providers that perform additional functions, including the functions identified in new subsection (j)(1)(B). Conversely, the fact that a provider performs some functions that fall within the definition of new subparagraph (A) does not imply that its other functions that do not fall within the definition of new subparagraph (A) qualify for the limitation of liability under new subsection (a).

The second definition of "service provider," set forth in new subsection (j)(1)(B), applies to the term as used in any other new subsection of new Section 512. This definition is broader than the first, covering providers of on-line services or network access, or the operator of facilities therefor. This definition includes, for example, services such as providing Internet access, e-mail, chat room and web page hosting services. The new subsection (j)(1)(B) definition of service provider, for example, includes universities and schools to the extent they perform the functions identified in new subsection (j)(1)(B). The definition also specifically includes any entity that falls within the first definition of service provider. A broadcaster or cable television system or satellite television service would not qualify, except to the extent it performs functions covered by (j)(1)(B).

Finally, new subsection (j)(2) defines the term "monetary relief" broadly for purposes of this Section as encompassing damages, costs, attorneys' fees and any other form of monetary payment.

New Section 512(k) clarifies that other defenses under copyright law are not affected and codifies several important principles. In particular, new Section 512 does not define what is actionable copyright infringement in the on-line environment, and does not create any new exceptions to the exclusive rights under copyright law. The rest of the Copyright Act sets those rules. Similarly, new Section 512 does not create any new liabilities for service providers or affect any defense available to a service provider. Enactment of new Section 512 does not bear upon whether a service provider is or is not an infringer when its conduct falls within the scope of new Section 512. Even if a service provider's activities fall outside the limitations on liability specified in the bill, the service provider is not necessarily an infringer; liability in these circumstances would be adjudicated based on the doctrines of direct, vicarious or contributory liability for infringement as they are articulated in the Copyright Act and in the court decisions interpreting and applying that statute, which are unchanged by new Section 512. In the event that a service provider does not qualify for the limitation on liability, it still may claim all of the defenses available to it under current law. New section 512 simply defines the circumstances under which a service provider, as defined in this new Section, may enjoy a limitation on liability for copyright infringement.

New Section 512(l) is designed to protect the privacy of Internet users. This new subsection makes clear that the applicability of new subsections (a) through (d) is in no way conditioned on a service provider: (1) monitoring its service or affirmatively seeking facts indicating infringing activity except to the extent consistent with implementing a standard technical measure under new subsection (h); or (2) accessing, removing or disabling access to, material if

65

such conduct is prohibited by law, such as the Electronic Communications Privacy Act.

New Section 512(m) establishes a rule of construction applicable to new subsections (a) through (d). New Section 512's limitations on liability are based on functions, and each limitation is intended to describe a separate and distinct function. Consider, for example, a service provider that provides a hyperlink to a site containing infringing material which it then caches on its system in order to facilitate access to it by its users. This service provider is engaging in at least three functions that may be subject to the limitation on liability: transitory digital network communications under new subsection (a); system caching under new subsection (b); and information location tools under new subsection (d). If this service provider (as defined in new subsection (j)(1)(A) in the case of transitory digital communications, or as defined in new subsection (j)(1)(B) in the case of system caching or information location tools) meets the threshold criteria spelled out in new subsection (h)(1), then for its acts of system caching defined in new subsection (b), it may avail itself of the liability limitations stated in new subsection (b), which incorporate the limitations on injunctive relief described in new subsection (i)(1)(B) and (i)(3). If it is claimed that the same company is committing an infringement by using information location tools to link its users to infringing material, as defined in new subsection (d), then its fulfillment of the requirements to claim the system caching liability limitation does not affect whether it qualifies for the liability limitation for information location tools; the criteria in new subsection (d), rather than those in new subsection (b), are applicable. New Section 512(m) codifies this principle by providing that the determination of whether a service provider qualifies for one liability limitation has no effect on the determination of whether it qualifies for a separate and distinct liability limitation under another new subsection of new Section 512.

(a) Conforming amendment

Section 202(b) amends the table of sections for chapter 5 of the Copyright Act (17 U.S.C. § 501 et seq.) to reflect the new Section 512, as created by this title.

Section 203. Limitation on exclusive rights; computer programs

Section 203 effects a minor, yet important, clarification in Section 117 of the Copyright Act (17 U.S.C. § 117) to ensure that the lawful owner or lessee of a computer machine may authorize an independent service provider—a person unaffiliated with either the owner or lessee of the machine—to activate the machine for the sole purpose of servicing its hardware components.

Section 204. Liability of educational institutions for online infringement of copyright

(a) Recommendations by Register of Copyrights

Section 204(a) directs the Register of Copyrights to consult with representatives of copyright owners and nonprofit educational institutions and to submit to the Congress within 6 months after enactment of the bill recommendations regarding the liability of non-

66

profit educational institutions for copyright infringements that take place through the use of the institution's computer system or network, where the institution qualifies as a "service provider" under the provisions of this Title. Included in the Register's report are to be any recommendations for legislation that the Register considers appropriate.

(b) Factors

Section 204(b) sets forth specific considerations that the Register shall take into account, where relevant, in formulating recommendations to the Congress.

Section 205. Evaluation of impact of copyright law and amendments on electronic commerce and technological development

As previously stated in the background section to this report, the Committee believes it is important to more precisely evaluate the relationship between intellectual property and electronic commerce, and to understand the practical implications of this relationship on the development of technology to be used in promoting electronic commerce. Section 205 enables Congress to make that evaluation.

(a) Findings

Section 205(a) finds that Congress must have accurate and current information on the effects of intellectual property protection on electronic commerce and technology.

(b) Evaluation by Secretary of Commerce

Section 205(b) directs the Secretary of Commerce, in consultation with the Assistant Secretary of Commerce for Communications and Information and the Register of Copyrights, to evaluate the effects of this legislation on the development of electronic commerce and associated technology, as well as the relationship between existing and emergent technology, on the one hand, and existing copyright law, on the other.

(c) Report to Congress

Section 205(c) directs the Secretary of Commerce to submit a report to Congress, within one year of enactment, on the evaluation required pursuant to Section 205(b).

Section 206. Effective date

Section 206 establishes the effective date for Title II as the date of enactment.

TITLE III—EPHEMERAL RECORDINGS; DISTANCE EDUCATION; EXEMPTION FOR LIBRARIES AND ARCHIVES

Section 301. Ephemeral recordings

Section 301 amends Section 112 of the Copyright Act (17 U.S.C. § 112) to address two issues concerning the application of the ephemeral recording exemption in the digital age. The first of these issues is the relationship between the ephemeral recording exemption and the Digital Performance Right in Sound Recordings Act of 1995 (DPRA). DPRA granted sound recording copyright owners the

67

exclusive right to perform their works publicly by means of digital audio transmission, subject to certain limitations, particularly those set forth in Section 114(d). Among those limitations is an exemption for non-subscription broadcast transmissions, which are defined as those made by terrestrial broadcast stations licensed as such by the Federal Communications Commission. (17 U.S.C. § 114(d)(1)(A)(iii), (j)(2)). The ephemeral recording exemption presently privileges certain activities of a transmitting organization when it is entitled to transmit a performance or display under a license or transfer of copyright ownership or under the limitations on exclusive rights in sound recordings specified by Section 114(a). The Committee believes that the ephemeral recording exemption should apply to broadcast radio and television stations when they make non-subscription digital broadcasts permitted by DPRA. The Committee has therefore changed the existing language of the ephemeral recording exemption (redesignated as Section 112(a)(1)) to extend explicitly to broadcasters the same privilege they already enjoy with respect to analog broadcasts.

The second of these issues is the relationship between the ephemeral recording exemption and the anti-circumvention provisions that the bill adds as Section 102 of this legislation. Concerns were expressed that if use of copy protection technologies became widespread, a transmitting organization might be prevented from engaging in its traditional activities of assembling transmission programs and making ephemeral recordings permitted by Section 112 for purposes of its own transmissions within its local service area and of archival preservation and security. To address this concern, the Committee has added to Section 112 a new paragraph that permits transmitting organizations to engage in activities that otherwise would violate the regulations to be issued under Section 102(a)(1) in certain limited circumstances when necessary for the exercise of the transmitting organization's privilege to make ephemeral recordings under redesignated Section 112(a)(1). By way of example, if a radio station could not make a permitted ephemeral recording from a commercially available phonorecord without violating the regulations to be issued under Section 102(a)(1), then the radio station could request from the copyright owner the necessary means of making a permitted ephemeral recording. If the copyright owner did not then either provide a phonorecord that could be reproduced or otherwise provide the necessary means of making a permitted ephemeral recording from the phonorecord already in the possession of the radio station, the radio station would not be liable for violating the regulations to be issued under Section 102(a)(1) for taking the steps necessary for engaging in activities permitted under Section 112(a)(1). The radio station would, of course, be liable for violating the regulations to be issued under Section 102(a)(1) if it engaged in activities prohibited by that Section in other than the limited circumstances permitted by Section 112(a)(1).

68

Section 302. Limitation on exclusive rights; distance education

(a) Recommendations by National Telecommunications and Information Administration

Section 302(a) directs the Assistant Secretary of Commerce for Communications and Information to consult with representatives of copyright owners, non-profit educational institutions, and nonprofit libraries and archives and to submit recommendations to the Congress no later than 6 months after the date of enactment of the bill on how to promote distance education through digital technologies, including interactive digital networks, while maintaining an appropriate balance between the rights of copyright owners and the needs of users. Where appropriate, the Assistant Secretary shall include legislative recommendations to achieve those objectives.

(b) Factors

Section 302(b) specifies considerations which the Assistant Secretary of Commerce for Communications and Information shall take into account in formulating such recommendations.

Section 303. Exemption for libraries and archives

Section 303 allows libraries and archives to take advantage of digital technologies when engaging in specified preservation activities.

TITLE IV—RELATED PROVISIONS

Section 401. Report by the National Telecommunications and Information Administration

Section 401 requires the Assistant Secretary of Commerce for Communications and Information to submit a report to Congress, within six months on enactment, on appropriate mechanisms to encourage the development of access protocols, encryption testing methods, and security testing methods which would allow lawful access to, with appropriate safeguards to prevent the unlawful copying of, encrypted works.

CHANGES IN EXISTING LAW MADE BY THE BILL, AS REPORTED

In compliance with clause 3 of rule XIII of the Rules of the House of Representatives, changes in existing law made by the bill, as reported, are shown as follows (existing law proposed to be omitted is enclosed in black brackets, new matter is printed in italic, existing law in which no change is proposed is shown in roman):

TITLE 17, UNITED STATES CODE

*   *   *   *   *   *   *

CHAPTER 1—SUBJECT MATTER AND SCOPE OF COPYRIGHT

*   *   *   *   *   *   *

69

§ 101. Definitions

Except as otherwise provided in this title, as used in this title, the following terms and their variant forms mean the following:

An "anonymous work" is a work on the copies or phonorecords of which no natural person is identified as author.

* * * * * * *

[A work is a "Berne Convention work" if—

[(1) in the case of an unpublished work, one or more of the authors is a national of a nation adhering to the Berne Convention, or in the case of a published work, one or more of the authors is a national of a nation adhering to the Berne Convention on the date of first publication;

[(2) the work was first published in a nation adhering to the Berne Convention, or was simultaneously first published in a nation adhering to the Berne Convention and in a foreign nation that does not adhere to the Berne Convention;

[(3) in the case of an audiovisual work—

[(A) if one or more of the authors is a legal entity, that author has its headquarters in a nation adhering to the Berne Convention; or

[(B) if one or more of the authors is an individual, that author is domiciled, or has his or her habitual residence in, a nation adhering to the Berne Convention;

[(4) in the case of a pictorial, graphic, or sculptural work that is incorporated in a building or other structure, the building or structure is located in a nation adhering to the Berne Convention; or

[(5) in the case of an architectural work embodied in a building, such building is erected in a country adhering to the Berne Convention.

For purposes of paragraph (1), an author who is domiciled in or has his or her habitual residence in, a nation adhering to the Berne Convention is considered to be a national of that nation. For purposes of paragraph (2), a work is considered to have been simultaneously published in two or more nations if its dates of publication are within 30 days of one another.]

* * * * * * *

[The "country of origin" of a Berne Convention work, for purposes of section 411, is the United States if] *For purposes of section 411, a work is a "United States work" only if—*

(1) in the case of a published work, the work is first published—

(A) in the United States;

(B) simultaneously in the United States and another [nation or nations adhering to the Berne Convention] *treaty party or parties,* whose law grants a term of copyright protection that is the same as or longer than the term provided in the United States;

70

(C) simultaneously in the United States and a foreign nation that [does not adhere to the Berne Convention] *is not a treaty party*; or

(D) in a foreign nation that [does not adhere to the Berne Convention] *is not a treaty party*, and all of the authors of the work are nationals, domiciliaries, or habitual residents of, or in the case of an audiovisual work legal entities with headquarters in, the United States;

* * * * * * *

(3) in the case of a pictorial, graphic, or sculptural work incorporated in a building or structure, the building or structure is located in the United States.

[For the purposes of section 411, the "country of origin" of any other Berne Convention work is not the United States.]

* * * * * * *

A work is "fixed" in a tangible medium of expression when its embodiment in a copy or phonorecord, by or under the authority of the author, is sufficiently permanent or stable to permit it to be perceived, reproduced, or otherwise communicated for a period of more than transitory duration. A work consisting of sounds, images, or both, that are being transmitted, is "fixed" for purposes of this title if a fixation of the work is being made simultaneously with its transmission.

The "Geneva Phonograms Convention" is the Convention for the Protection of Producers of Phonograms Against Unauthorized Duplication of Their Phonograms, concluded at Geneva, Switzerland, on October 29, 1971.

The terms "including" and "such as" are illustrative and not limitative.

An "international agreement" is—

(1) the Universal Copyright Convention;
(2) the Geneva Phonograms Convention;
(3) the Berne Convention;
(4) the WTO Agreement;
(5) the WIPO Copyright Treaty;
(6) the WIPO Performances and Phonograms Treaty; and
(7) any other copyright treaty to which the United States is a party.

* * * * * * *

To "transmit" a performance or display is to communicate it by any device or process whereby images or sounds are received beyond the place from which they are sent.

A "treaty party" is a country or intergovernmental organization other than the United States that is a party to an international agreement.

* * * * * * *

The author's "widow" or "widower" is the author's surviving spouse under the law of the author's domicile at the time of his or her death, whether or not the spouse has later remarried.

The "WIPO Copyright Treaty" is the WIPO Copyright Treaty concluded at Geneva, Switzerland, on December 20, 1996.

71

The "WIPO Performances and Phonograms Treaty" is the WIPO Performances and Phonograms Treaty concluded at Geneva, Switzerland, on December 20, 1996.

*   *   *   *   *   *   *

A "work made for hire" is—
      (1) * * *

*   *   *   *   *   *   *

The terms "WTO Agreement" and "WTO member country" have the meanings given those terms in paragraphs (9) and (10), respectively, of section 2 of the Uruguay Round Agreements Act.

*   *   *   *   *   *   *

§ 104. Subject matter of copyright: National origin

(a) UNPUBLISHED WORKS.—The works specified by sections 102 and 103, while unpublished, are subject to protection under this title without regard to the nationality or domicile of the author.

(b) PUBLISHED WORKS.—The works specified by sections 102 and 103, when published, are subject to protection under this title if—

      (1) on the date of first publication, one or more of the authors is a national or domiciliary of the United States, or is a national, domiciliary, or sovereign authority of a [foreign nation that is a party to a copyright treaty to which the United States is also a party] *treaty party*, or is a stateless person, wherever that person may be domiciled; or

      (2) the work is first published in the United States or in a foreign nation that, on the date of first publication, is a [party to the Universal Copyright Convention] *treaty party*; or

      (3) the work is a sound recording that was first fixed in a treaty party; or

      (4) the work is a [Berne Convention work] *pictorial, graphic, or sculptural work that is incorporated in a building or other structure, or an architectural work that is embodied in a building and the building or structure is located in the United States or a treaty party*; or

      [(3)] *(5)* the work is first published by the United Nations or any of its specialized agencies, or by the Organization of American States; or

      [(5)] *(6)* the work comes within the scope of a Presidential proclamation. Whenever the President finds that a particular foreign nation extends, to works by authors who are nationals or domiciliaries of the United States or to works that are first published in the United States, copyright protection on substantially the same basis as that on which the foreign nation extends protection to works of its own nationals and domiciliaries and works first published in that nation, the President may by proclamation extend protection under this title to works of which one or more of the authors is, on the date of first publication, a national, domiciliary, or sovereign authority of that nation, or which was first published in that nation. The President may revise, suspend, or revoke any such proclama-

72

tion or impose any conditions or limitations on protection under a proclamation.

For purposes of paragraph (2), a work that is published in the United States or a treaty party within 30 days after publication in a foreign nation that is not a treaty party shall be considered to be first published in the United States or such treaty party, as the case may be.

* * * * * * *

(d) EFFECT OF PHONOGRAMS TREATIES.—Notwithstanding the provisions of subsection (b), no works other than sound recordings shall be eligible for protection under this title solely by virtue of the adherence of the United States to the Geneva Phonograms Convention or the WIPO Performances and Phonograms Treaty.

§ 104A. Copyright in restored works

(a) * * *

* * * * * * *

(h) DEFINITIONS.—For purposes of this section and section 109(a):
(1) The term "date of adherence or proclamation" means the earlier of the date on which a foreign nation which, as of the date the WTO Agreement enters into force with respect to the United States, is not a nation adhering to the Berne Convention or a WTO member country, becomes—

[(A) a nation adhering to the Berne Convention or a WTO member country; or

[(B) subject to a Presidential proclamation under subsection (g).]

(A) a nation adhering to the Berne Convention;

(B) a WTO member country;

(C) a nation adhering to the WIPO Copyright Treaty;

(D) a nation adhering to the WIPO Performances and Phonograms Treaty; or

(E) subject to a Presidential proclamation under subsection (g).

* * * * * * *

[(3) The term "eligible country" means a nation, other than the United States, that—

[(A) becomes a WTO member country after the date of the enactment of the Uruguay Round Agreements Act;

[(B) on such date of enactment is, or after such date of enactment becomes, a member of the Berne Convention; or

[(C) after such date of enactment becomes subject to a proclamation under subsection (g).

For purposes of this section, a nation that is a member of the Berne Convention on the date of the enactment of the Uruguay Round Agreements Act shall be construed to become an eligible country on such date of enactment.]

(3) The term "eligible country" means a nation, other than the United States, that—

(A) becomes a WTO member country after the date of the enactment of the Uruguay Round Agreements Act;

73

(B) on such date of enactment is, or after such date of enactment becomes, a nation adhering to the Berne Convention;
(C) adheres to the WIPO Copyright Treaty;
(D) adheres to the WIPO Performances and Phonograms Treaty; or
(E) after such date of enactment becomes subject to a proclamation under subsection (g).

*   *   *   *   *   *   *

(6) The term "restored work" means an original work of authorship that—
(A) * * *

*   *   *   *   *   *   *

(C) is in the public domain in the United States due to—
(i) * * *

*   *   *   *   *   *   *

(iii) lack of national eligibility; [and]
(D) has at least one author or rightholder who was, at the time the work was created, a national or domiciliary of an eligible country, and if published, was first published in an eligible country and not published in the United States during the 30-day period following publication in such eligible country[.]*; and*
(E) if the source country for the work is an eligible country solely by virtue of its adherence to the WIPO Performances and Phonograms Treaty, is a sound recording.

*   *   *   *   *   *   *

(8) The "source country" of a restored work is—
(A) a nation other than the United States;
(B) in the case of an unpublished work—
(i) the eligible country in which the author or rightholder is a national or domiciliary, or, if a restored work has more than 1 author or rightholder, *of which* the majority of foreign authors or rightholders are nationals or domiciliaries [of eligible countries]; or

*   *   *   *   *   *   *

[(9) The terms "WTO Agreement" and "WTO member country" have the meanings given those terms in paragraphs (9) and (10), respectively, of section 2 of the Uruguay Round Agreements Act.]

*   *   *   *   *   *   *

§ 108. Limitations on exclusive rights: Reproduction by libraries and archives

(a) [Notwithstanding] *Except as otherwise provided in this title and notwithstanding* the provisions of section 106, it is not an infringement of copyright for a library or archives, or any of its employees acting within the scope of their employment, to reproduce no more than one copy or phonorecord of a work, *except as provided in subsections (b) and (c),* or to distribute such copy or phonorecord, under the conditions specified by this section, if—

74

(1) * * *

   *   *   *   *   *   *   *

(3) the reproduction or distribution of the work includes a notice of copyright *that appears on the copy or phonorecord that is reproduced under the provisions of this section, or includes a legend stating that the work may be protected by copyright if no such notice can be found on the copy or phonorecord that is reproduced under the provisions of this section.*

(b) The rights of reproduction and distribution under this section apply to [a copy or phonorecord] *three copies or phonorecords* of an unpublished work duplicated [in facsimile form] solely for purposes of preservation and security or for deposit for research use in another library or archives of the type described by clause (2) of subsection (a), [if the copy or phonorecord reproduced is currently in the collections of the library or archives.] *if—*

    (1) the copy or phonorecord reproduced is currently in the collections of the library or archives; and

    (2) any such copy or phonorecord that is reproduced in digital format is not otherwise distributed in that format and is not made available to the public in that format outside the premises of the library or archives.

(c) The right of reproduction under this section applies to [a copy or phonorecord] *three copies or phonorecords* of a published work duplicated [in facsimile form] solely for the purpose of replacement of a copy or phonorecord that is damaged, deteriorating, lost, or stolen, *or if the existing format in which the work is stored has become obsolete,* [if the library or archives has, after a reasonable effort, determined that an unused replacement cannot be obtained at a fair price.] *if—*

    (1) the library or archives has, after a reasonable effort, determined that an unused replacement cannot be obtained at a fair price; and

    (2) any such copy or phonorecord that is reproduced in digital format is not made available to the public in that format except for use on the premises of the library or archives in lawful possession of such copy.

For purposes of this subsection, a format shall be considered obsolete if the machine or device necessary to render perceptible a work stored in that format is no longer manufactured or is no longer reasonably available in the commercial marketplace.

    *   *   *   *   *   *   *

§ 112. Limitations on exclusive rights: Ephemeral recordings

(a)*(1)* Notwithstanding the provisions of section 106, and except in the case of a motion picture or other audiovisual work, it is not an infringement of copyright for a transmitting organization entitled to transmit to the public a performance or display of a work, under a license or transfer of the copyright or under the limitations on exclusive rights in sound recordings specified by section 114(a), *or for a transmitting organization that is a broadcast radio or television station licensed as such by the Federal Communications Commission that broadcasts a performance of a sound recording in a digital format on a nonsubscription basis,* to make no more than one copy or phonorecord of a particular transmission program embodying the performance or display, if—

[(1)] *(A)* the copy or phonorecord is retained and used solely by the transmitting organization that made it, and no further copies or phonorecords are reproduced from it; and

[(2)] *(B)* the copy or phonorecord is used solely for the transmitting organization's own transmissions within its local service area, or for purposes of archival preservation or security; and

[(3)] *(C)* unless preserved exclusively for archival purposes, the copy or phonorecord is destroyed within six months from the date the transmission program was first transmitted to the public.

(2) In a case in which a transmitting organization entitled to make a copy or phonorecord under paragraph (1) in connection with the transmission to the public of a performance or display of a work described in that paragraph is prevented from making such copy or phonorecord by reason of the application by the copyright owner of technical measures that prevent the reproduction of the work, the copyright owner shall make available to the transmitting organization the necessary means for permitting the making of such copy or phonorecord within the meaning of that paragraph, if it is technologically feasible and economically reasonable for the copyright owner to do so. If the copyright owner fails to do so in a timely manner in light of the transmitting organization's reasonable business requirements, the transmitting organization shall not be liable for a violation of section 102(a)(1) of the WIPO Copyright Treaties Implementation Act for engaging in such activities as are necessary to make such copies or phonorecords as permitted under paragraph (1) of this subsection.

*　　*　　*　　*　　*　　*　　*

§ 117. Limitations on exclusive rights: Computer programs

[Notwithstanding] *(a) MAKING OF ADDITIONAL COPY OR ADAPTATION BY OWNER OF COPY.—Notwithstanding* the provisions of section 106, it is not an infringement for the owner of a copy of a computer program to make or authorize the making of another copy or adaptation of that computer program provided:

(1) * * *

*　　*　　*　　*　　*　　*　　*

[Any exact] *(b) LEASE, SALE, OR OTHER TRANSFER OF ADDITIONAL COPY OR ADAPTATION.—Any exact* copies prepared in accordance with the provisions of this section may be leased, sold, or otherwise transferred, along with the copy from which such copies were prepared, only as part of the lease, sale, or other transfer of all rights in the program. Adaptations so prepared may be transferred only with the authorization of the copyright owner.

(c) MACHINE MAINTENANCE OR REPAIR.—Notwithstanding the provisions of section 106, it is not an infringement for the owner or lessee of a machine to make or authorize the making of a copy of a computer program if such copy is made solely by virtue of the activation of a machine that lawfully contains an authorized copy of the

76

computer program, for purposes only of maintenance or repair of that machine, if—

(1) such new copy is used in no other manner and is destroyed immediately after the maintenance or repair is completed; and

(2) with respect to any computer program or part thereof that is not necessary for that machine to be activated, such program or part thereof is not accessed or used other than to make such new copy by virtue of the activation of the machine.

(d) Definitions.—For purposes of this section—

(1) the "maintenance" of a machine is the servicing of the machine in order to make it work in accordance with its original specifications and any changes to those specifications authorized for that machine; and

(2) the "repair" of a machine is the restoring of the machine to the state of working in accordance with its original specifications and any changes to those specifications authorized for that machine.

*   *   *   *   *   *   *

CHAPTER 4—COPYRIGHT NOTICE, DEPOSIT, AND REGISTRATION

*   *   *   *   *   *   *

§ 411. Registration and infringement actions

(a) Except for [actions for infringement of copyright in Berne Convention works whose country of origin is not the United States and] an action brought for a violation of the rights of the author under section 106A(a), and subject to the provisions of subsection (b), no action for infringement of the copyright in any *United States* work shall be instituted until registration of the copyright claim has been made in accordance with this title. In any case, however, where the deposit, application, and fee required for registration have been delivered to the Copyright Office in proper form and registration has been refused, the applicant is entitled to institute an action for infringement if notice thereof, with a copy of the complaint, is served on the Register of Copyrights. The Register may, at his or her option, become a party to the action with respect to the issue of registrability of the copyright claim by entering an appearance within sixty days after such service, but the Register's failure to become a party shall not deprive the court of jurisdiction to determine that issue.

*   *   *   *   *   *   *

CHAPTER 5—COPYRIGHT INFRINGEMENT AND REMEDIES

Sec.
501. Infringement of copyright.

*   *   *   *   *   *   *

512. *Liability of service providers for online infringement of copyright.*

*   *   *   *   *   *   *

77

§ 507. Limitations on actions

(a) CRIMINAL PROCEEDINGS.—[No] *Except as expressly provided otherwise in this title, no* criminal proceeding shall be maintained under the provisions of this title unless it is commenced within 5 years after the cause of action arose.

*   *   *   *   *   *   *

§512. *Liability of service providers for online infringement of copyright*

(a) DIGITAL NETWORK COMMUNICATIONS.—*A service provider shall not be liable for monetary relief, or except as provided in subsection (i) for injunctive or other equitable relief, for infringement for the provider's transmitting, routing, or providing connections for, material through a system or network controlled or operated by or for the service provider, or the intermediate and transient storage of such material in the course of such transmitting, routing or providing connections, if—*

> *(1) it was initiated by or at the direction of a person other than the service provider;*
>
> *(2) it is carried out through an automatic technical process without selection of such material by the service provider;*
>
> *(3) the service provider does not select the recipients of such material except as an automatic response to the request of another;*
>
> *(4) no such copy of such material made by the service provider is maintained on the system or network in a manner ordinarily accessible to anyone other than anticipated recipients, and no such copy is maintained on the system or network in a manner ordinarily accessible to the anticipated recipients for a longer period than is reasonably necessary for the communication; and*
>
> *(5) the material is transmitted without modification to its content.*

(b) SYSTEM CACHING.—*A service provider shall not be liable for monetary relief, or except as provided in subsection (i) for injunctive or other equitable relief, for infringement for the intermediate and temporary storage of material on the system or network controlled or operated by or for the service provider: Provided, That—*

> *(1) such material is made available online by a person other than such service provider,*
>
> *(2) such material is transmitted from the person described in paragraph (1) through such system or network to someone other than that person at the direction of such other person,*
>
> *(3) the storage is carried out through an automatic technical process for the purpose of making such material available to users of such system or network who subsequently request access to that material from the person described in paragraph (1):*

Provided further, That—

> *(4) such material is transmitted to such subsequent users without modification to its content from the manner in which the material otherwise was transmitted from the person described in paragraph (1);*

78

(5) such service provider complies with rules concerning the refreshing, reloading or other updating of such material when specified by the person making that material available online in accordance with an accepted industry standard data communications protocol for the system or network through which that person makes the material available: Provided further, That the rules are not used by the person described in paragraph (1) to prevent or unreasonably impair such intermediate storage;

(6) such service provider does not interfere with the ability of technology associated with such material that returns to the person described in paragraph (1) the information that would have been available to such person if such material had been obtained by such subsequent users directly from such person: Provided further, That such technology—

(A) does not significantly interfere with the performance of the provider's system or network or with the intermediate storage of the material;

(B) is consistent with accepted industry standard communications protocols; and

(C) does not extract information from the provider's system or network other than the information that would have been available to such person if such material had been accessed by such users directly from such person;

(7) either—

(A) the person described in paragraph (1) does not currently condition access to such material; or

(B) if access to such material is so conditioned by such person, by a current individual pre-condition, such as a pre-condition based on payment of a fee, or provision of a password or other information, the service provider permits access to the stored material in significant part only to users of its system or network that have been so authorized and only in accordance with those conditions; and

(8) if the person described in paragraph (1) makes that material available online without the authorization of the copyright owner, then the service provider responds expeditiously to remove, or disable access to, the material that is claimed to be infringing upon notification of claimed infringements described in subsection (c)(3): Provided further, That the material has previously been removed from the originating site, and the party giving the notification includes in the notification a statement confirming that such material has been removed or access to it has been disabled or ordered to be removed or have access disabled.

(c) Information Stored on Service Providers.—

(1) In general.—A service provider shall not be liable for monetary relief, or except as provided in subsection (i) for injunctive or other equitable relief, for infringement for the storage at the direction of a user of material that resides on a system or network controlled or operated by or for the service provider, if the service provider—

(A)(i) does not have actual knowledge that the material or activity is infringing,

79

(ii) in the absence of such actual knowledge, is not aware of facts or circumstances from which infringing activity is apparent, or

(iii) if upon obtaining such knowledge or awareness, the service provider acts expeditiously to remove or disable access to, the material;

(B) does not receive a financial benefit directly attributable to the infringing activity, where the service provider has the right and ability to control such activity; and

(C) in the instance of a notification of claimed infringement as described in paragraph (3), responds expeditiously to remove, or disable access to, the material that is claimed to be infringing or to be the subject of infringing activity.

(2) DESIGNATED AGENT.—The limitations on liability established in this subsection apply only if the service provider has designated an agent to receive notifications of claimed infringement described in paragraph (3), by substantially making the name, address, phone number, electronic mail address of such agent, and other contact information deemed appropriate by the Register of Copyrights, available through its service, including on its website, and by providing such information to the Copyright Office. The Register of Copyrights shall maintain a current directory of agents available to the public for inspection, including through the Internet, in both electronic and hard copy formats.

(3) ELEMENTS OF NOTIFICATION.—

(A) To be effective under this subsection, a notification of claimed infringement means any written communication provided to the service provider's designated agent that includes substantially the following—

(i) a physical or electronic signature of a person authorized to act on behalf of the owner of an exclusive right that is allegedly infringed;

(ii) identification of the copyrighted work claimed to have been infringed, or, if multiple such works at a single online site are covered by a single notification, a representative list of such works at that site;

(iii) identification of the material that is claimed to be infringing or to be the subject of infringing activity that is to be removed or access to which is to be disabled, and information reasonably sufficient to permit the service provider to locate the material;

(iv) information reasonably sufficient to permit the service provider to contact the complaining party, such as an address, telephone number, and, if available an electronic mail address at which the complaining party may be contacted;

(v) a statement that the complaining party has a good faith belief that use of the material in the manner complained of is not authorized by the copyright owner, or its agent, or the law; and

(vi) a statement that the information in the notification is accurate, and under penalty of perjury, that the

80

complaining party has the authority to enforce the owner's rights that are claimed to be infringed.

(B) A notification from the copyright owner or from a person authorized to act on behalf of the copyright owner that fails substantially to conform to the provisions of paragraph (3)(A) shall not be considered under paragraph (1)(A) in determining whether a service provider has actual knowledge or is aware of facts or circumstances from which infringing activity is apparent: Provided, That the provider promptly attempts to contact the complaining party or takes other reasonable steps to assist in the receipt of notice under paragraph (3)(A) when the notice is provided to the service provider's designated agent and substantially satisfies the provisions of paragraphs (3)(A) (ii), (iii), and (iv).

(d) INFORMATION LOCATION TOOLS.—A service provider shall not be liable for monetary relief, or except as provided in subsection (i) for injunctive or other equitable relief, for infringement for the provider referring or linking users to an online location containing infringing material or activity by using information location tools, including a directory, index, reference, pointer or hypertext link, if the provider—

(1) does not have actual knowledge that the material or activity is infringing or, in the absence of such actual knowledge, is not aware of facts or circumstances from which infringing activity is apparent;

(2) does not receive a financial benefit directly attributable to the infringing activity, where the service provider has the right and ability to control such activity; and

(3) responds expeditiously to remove or disable the reference or link upon notification of claimed infringement as described in subsection (c)(3): Provided, That for the purposes of this paragraph, the element in subsection (c)(3)(A)(iii) shall be identification of the reference or link, to material or activity claimed to be infringing, that is to be removed or access to which is to be disabled, and information reasonably sufficient to permit the service provider to locate such reference or link.

(e) MISREPRESENTATIONS.—Any person who knowingly materially misrepresents under this section—

(1) that material or activity is infringing, or

(2) that material or activity was removed or disabled by mistake or misidentification,

shall be liable for any damages, including costs and attorneys' fees, incurred by the alleged infringer, by any copyright owner or copyright owner's authorized licensee, or by the service provider, who is injured by such misrepresentation, as the result of the service provider relying upon such misrepresentation in removing or disabling access to the material or activity claimed to be infringing, or in replacing the removed material or ceasing to disable access to it.

(f) REPLACEMENT OF REMOVED OR DISABLED MATERIAL AND LIMITATION ON OTHER LIABILITY.—

(1) Subject to paragraph (2) of this subsection, a service provider shall not be liable to any person for any claim based on the service provider's good faith disabling of access to, or removal of, material or activity claimed to be infringing or based

on facts or circumstances from which infringing activity is apparent, regardless of whether the material or activity is ultimately determined to be infringing.

(2) Paragraph (1) of this subsection shall not apply with respect to material residing at the direction of a subscriber of the service provider on a system or network controlled or operated by or for the service provider that is removed, or to which access is disabled by the service provider pursuant to a notice provided under subsection (c)(1)(C), unless the service provider—

(A) takes reasonable steps promptly to notify the subscriber that it has removed or disabled access to the material;

(B) upon receipt of a counter notice as described in paragraph (3), promptly provides the person who provided the notice under subsection (c)(1)(C) with a copy of the counter notice, and informs such person that it will replace the removed material or cease disabling access to it in ten business days; and

(C) replaces the removed material and ceases disabling access to it not less than 10, nor more than 14, business days following receipt of the counter notice, unless its designated agent first receives notice from the person who submitted the notification under subsection (c)(1)(C) that such person has filed an action seeking a court order to restrain the subscriber from engaging in infringing activity relating to the material on the service provider's system or network.

(3) To be effective under this subsection, a counter notification means any written communication provided to the service provider's designated agent that includes substantially the following:

(A) A physical or electronic signature of the subscriber.

(B) Identification of the material that has been removed or to which access has been disabled and the location at which such material appeared before it was removed or access was disabled.

(C) A statement under penalty of perjury that the subscriber has a good faith belief that the material was removed or disabled as a result of mistake or misidentification of the material to be removed or disabled.

(D) The subscriber's name, address and telephone number, and a statement that the subscriber consents to the jurisdiction of Federal Court for the judicial district in which the address is located, or if the subscriber's address is outside of the United States, for any judicial district in which the service provider may be found, and that the subscriber will accept service of process from the person who provided notice under subsection (c)(1)(C) or agent of such person.

(4) A service provider's compliance with paragraph (2) shall not subject the service provider to liability for copyright infringement with respect to the material identified in the notice provided under subsection (c)(1)(C).

(g) IDENTIFICATION OF DIRECT INFRINGER.—The copyright owner or a person authorized to act on the owner's behalf may request an order for release of identification of an alleged infringer by filing—

82

(1) a copy of a notification described in subsection (c)(3)(A), including a proposed order, and

(2) a sworn declaration that the purpose of the order is to obtain the identity of an alleged infringer and that such information will only be used for the purpose of this title, with the clerk of any United States district court.

The order shall authorize and order the service provider receiving the notification to disclose expeditiously to the copyright owner or person authorized by the copyright owner information sufficient to identify the alleged direct infringer of the material described in the notification to the extent such information is available to the service provider. The order shall be expeditiously issued if the accompanying notification satisfies the provisions of subsection (c)(3)(A) and the accompanying declaration is properly executed. Upon receipt of the order, either accompanying or subsequent to the receipt of a notification described in subsection (c)(3)(A), a service provider shall expeditiously give to the copyright owner or person authorized by the copyright owner the information required by the order, notwithstanding any other provision of law and regardless of whether the service provider responds to the notification.

(h) CONDITIONS FOR ELIGIBILITY.—

(1) ACCOMMODATION OF TECHNOLOGY.—The limitations on liability established by this section shall apply only if the service provider—

(A) has adopted and reasonably implemented, and informs subscribers of the service of, a policy for the termination of subscribers of the service who are repeat infringers; and

(B) accommodates and does not interfere with standard technical measures as defined in this subsection.

(2) DEFINITION.—As used in this section, "standard technical measures" are technical measures, used by copyright owners to identify or protect copyrighted works, that—

(A) have been developed pursuant to a broad consensus of copyright owners and service providers in an open, fair, voluntary, multi-industry standards process;

(B) are available to any person on reasonable and non-discriminatory terms; and

(C) do not impose substantial costs on service providers or substantial burdens on their systems or networks.

(i) INJUNCTIONS.—The following rules shall apply in the case of any application for an injunction under section 502 against a service provider that is not subject to monetary remedies by operation of this section.

(1) SCOPE OF RELIEF.—

(A) With respect to conduct other than that which qualifies for the limitation on remedies as set forth in subsection (a), the court may only grant injunctive relief with respect to a service provider in one or more of the following forms—

(i) an order restraining it from providing access to infringing material or activity residing at a particular online site on the provider's system or network;

83

(ii) an order restraining it from providing access to an identified subscriber of the service provider's system or network who is engaging in infringing activity by terminating the specified accounts of such subscriber; or

(iii) such other injunctive remedies as the court may consider necessary to prevent or restrain infringement of specified copyrighted material at a particular online location: Provided, That such remedies are the least burdensome to the service provider that are comparably effective for that purpose.

(B) If the service provider qualifies for the limitation on remedies described in subsection (a), the court may only grant injunctive relief in one or both of the following forms—

(i) an order restraining it from providing access to an identified subscriber of the service provider's system or network who is using the provider's service to engage in infringing activity by terminating the specified accounts of such subscriber; or

(ii) an order restraining it from providing access, by taking specified reasonable steps to block access, to a specific, identified, foreign online location.

(2) CONSIDERATIONS.—The court, in considering the relevant criteria for injunctive relief under applicable law, shall consider—

(A) whether such an injunction, either alone or in combination with other such injunctions issued against the same service provider under this subsection, would significantly burden either the provider or the operation of the provider's system or network;

(B) the magnitude of the harm likely to be suffered by the copyright owner in the digital network environment if steps are not taken to prevent or restrain the infringement;

(C) whether implementation of such an injunction would be technically feasible and effective, and would not interfere with access to noninfringing material at other online locations; and

(D) whether other less burdensome and comparably effective means of preventing or restraining access to the infringing material are available.

(3) NOTICE AND EX PARTE ORDERS.—Injunctive relief under this subsection shall not be available without notice to the service provider and an opportunity for such provider to appear, except for orders ensuring the preservation of evidence or other orders having no material adverse effect on the operation of the service provider's communications network.

(j) DEFINITIONS.—

(1)(A) As used in subsection (a), the term "service provider" means an entity offering the transmission, routing or providing of connections for digital online communications, between or among points specified by a user, of material of the user's choosing, without modification to the content of the material as sent or received.

84

(B) As used in any other subsection of this section, the term "service provider" means a provider of online services or network access, or the operator of facilities therefor, and includes an entity described in the preceding paragraph of this subsection.

(2) As used in this section, the term "monetary relief" means damages, costs, attorneys' fees, and any other form of monetary payment.

(k) OTHER DEFENSES NOT AFFECTED.—The failure of a service provider's conduct to qualify for limitation of liability under this section shall not bear adversely upon the consideration of a defense by the service provider that the service provider's conduct is not infringing under this title or any other defense.

(l) PROTECTION OF PRIVACY.—Nothing in this section shall be construed to condition the applicability of subsections (a) through (d) on—

(1) a service provider monitoring its service or affirmatively seeking facts indicating infringing activity except to the extent consistent with a standard technical measure complying with the provisions of subsection (h); or

(2) a service provider accessing, removing, or disabling access to material where such conduct is prohibited by law.

(m) RULE OF CONSTRUCTION.—Subsections (a), (b), (c), and (d) are intended to describe separate and distinct functions for purposes of analysis under this section. Whether a service provider qualifies for the limitation on liability in any one such subsection shall be based solely on the criteria in each such subsection and shall not affect a determination of whether such service provider qualifies for the limitations on liability under any other such subsection.

*   *   *   *   *   *   *

ADDITIONAL VIEWS OF SCOTT KLUG AND RICK BOUCHER

Although we support the House Commerce Committee's changes and improvements to H.R. 2281, the Digital Millennium Copyright Act of 1998, we remain troubled by the implications of this legislation.

In its original version, H.R. 2281 contained a provision that would have made it unlawful to circumvent technological protection measures that effectively control access to a work, for any reason. In other words, the bill, if passed unchanged, would have given copyright owners the legislative muscle to "lock up" their works in perpetuity—unless each and every one of us separately negotiated for access. In short, this provision converted an unobstructed marketplace that tolerates "free" access in some circumstances to a "pay-per-access" system, no exceptions permitted.

In our opinion, this not only stands copyright law on its head, it makes a mockery of our Constitution. Article I, Section 8, Clause 8 is very clear in its directive: "The Congress shall have Power * * * To Promote the Progress of Science and useful Arts, by securing for *limited* Times to Authors and Inventors the exclusive Right to their respective Writing and Discoveries." (emphasis added). Congress has limited these rights both in terms of scope and duration. In interpreting the Copyright Clause, the Supreme Court has said:

> The monopoly privileges that Congress may authorize are neither unlimited nor primarily designed to provide special private benefit. Rather, the limited grant is a means by which an important public purpose may be achieved. It is intended to motivate the creative activity of authors and inventors by the provision of a special reward, and *to allow the public access to the products of their genius after the limited period of exclusive control has expired.* The copyright law, like the patent statutes, makes reward to the owner a secondary consideration. *Sony Corporation* v. *Universal City Studios, Inc.,* 464 U.S. 417, 429 (1984) (emphasis added).

The anti-circumvention language of H.R. 2281, even as amended, bootstraps the limited monopoly into a perpetual right. It also fundamentally alters the balance that has been carefully struck in 200 years of copyright case law, by making the private incentive of content owners the paramount consideration—at the expense of research, scholarship, education, literary or political commentary, indeed, the future viability of information in the public domain. In so doing, this legislation goes well beyond the rights contemplated for copyright owners in the Constitution.

The Klug amendment, representing a compromise between those on the content side and "fair use" proponents, simply delays this

(85)

86

constitutional problem for a period of two years. Delegating authority to develop anti-circumvention regulations to the Secretary of Commerce was a means to eliminate the stalemate that existed, but it is not, by itself a comment on the need for limitations on this anti-circumvention rights. It also strikes us that Congress is not acting prudently by passing a law guaranteed to create lifetime employment for attorneys and copyright specialists, given the constitutional and definitional problems already identified.

What we set out to do was to restore some balance in the discussion and to place private incentive in its proper context. We had proposed to do this by legislating an equivalent fair use defense for the new right to control access. For reasons not clear to us, and despite the WIPO Treaty language "recognizing the need to maintain a balance between the rights of authors and the larger public interest, particularly education, research and access to information * * *," our proposal was met with strenuous objection. It continued to be criticized even after it had been redrafted, and extensively tailored, in response to the myriad of piracy concerns that were raised.

The compromise amendment that Representative Klug ultimately offered at full committee is silent on the applicability of traditional copyright limitations and defenses, though it does give "information users" the ability to argue that the application of technological protection measures adversely impacts their ability to access information. This diminution in availability includes both access under license terms and traditional free access to information. Our expectation is that the rulemaking will also focus on the extent to which exceptions and limitations to this prohibition are appropriate and necessary to maintain balance in our copyright laws.

In view of this legislation's overwhelming attention to the regulation of devices in other contexts, it should be clearly understood that the Section 102(a)(1) amendment addresses conduct only and does not delegate to the Secretary of Commerce the power to regulate the design of devices.

Moreover, the bill, by its terms (like the WIPO treaties), covers only those measures that are "effective." Pursuant to this limitation, an amendment we offered which was adopted at subcommittee clarified that device and component designers and manufacturers are not under any legal obligation to respond to or to accommodate any particular technological protection measure. Without such clarification, the bill could have been construed as governing not only those technological protection measures that are already "effective", such as those based on encryption, but also those that might conceivably be made "effective" through enactment of the legislation. This result would be a far cry from governing "circumvention." For similar reasons, it was clearly understood in the full committee consideration that a measure is not "effective", and consequently not covered by this bill, to the extent that protecting the measure against circumvention would cause degradation of the otherwise lawful performance of a device or authorized display of a work.

In the end, this legislation purports to protect creators. It may well be that additional protections are necessary, though we think the 1976 Copyright Act is sufficiently flexible to deal with changing

87

technology. Whatever protections Congress grants should not be wielded as a club to thwart consumer demand for innovative products, consumer demand for access to information, consumer demand for tools to exercise their lawful rights, and consumer expectations that the people and expertise will exist to service these products.

SCOTT KLUG.
RICK BOUCHER.

○

DIGITAL MILLENNIUM COPYRIGHT ACT

OCTOBER 8, 1998.—Ordered to be printed

Mr. COBLE, from the committee of conference,
submitted the following

CONFERENCE REPORT

[To accompany H.R. 2281]

The committee of conference on the disagreeing votes of the two Houses on the amendment of the Senate to the bill (H.R. 2281), to amend title 17, United States Code, to implement the World Intellectual Property Organization Copyright Treaty and Performances and Phonograms Treaty, and for other purposes, having met, after full and free conference, have agreed to recommend and do recommend to their respective Houses as follows:

That the House recede from its disagreement to the amendment of the Senate and agree to the same with an amendment as follows:

In lieu of the matter proposed to be inserted by the Senate amendment, insert the following:

SECTION 1. SHORT TITLE.

This Act may be cited as the "Digital Millennium Copyright Act".

SEC. 2. TABLE OF CONTENTS.

69–006

2

TITLE I—WIPO TREATIES IMPLEMENTATION

SEC. 101. SHORT TITLE.

This title may be cited as the "WIPO Copyright and Performances and Phonograms Treaties Implementation Act of 1998".

SEC. 102. TECHNICAL AMENDMENTS.

(a) DEFINITIONS.—Section 101 of title 17, United States Code, is amended—

(1) by striking the definition of "Berne Convention work";

(2) in the definition of "The 'country of origin' of a Berne Convention work"—

(A) by striking "The 'country of origin' of a Berne Convention work, for purposes of section 411, is the United States if" and inserting "For purposes of section 411, a work is a 'United States work' only if";

(B) in paragraph (1)—

(i) in subparagraph (B) by striking "nation or nations adhering to the Berne Convention" and inserting "treaty party or parties";

(ii) in subparagraph (C) by striking "does not adhere to the Berne Convention" and inserting "is not a treaty party"; and

(iii) in subparagraph (D) by striking "does not adhere to the Berne Convention" and inserting "is not a treaty party"; and

(C) in the matter following paragraph (3) by striking "For the purposes of section 411, the 'country of origin' of any other Berne Convention work is not the United States.";

(3) by inserting after the definition of "fixed" the following:

"The 'Geneva Phonograms Convention' is the Convention for the Protection of Producers of Phonograms Against Unauthorized Duplication of Their Phonograms, concluded at Geneva, Switzerland, on October 29, 1971.";

(4) by inserting after the definition of "including" the following:

"An 'international agreement' is—

3

"(1) the Universal Copyright Convention;
"(2) the Geneva Phonograms Convention;
"(3) the Berne Convention;
"(4) the WTO Agreement;
"(5) the WIPO Copyright Treaty;
"(6) the WIPO Performances and Phonograms Treaty; and
"(7) any other copyright treaty to which the United States is a party.";

(5) by inserting after the definition of "transmit" the following:

"A 'treaty party' is a country or intergovernmental organization other than the United States that is a party to an international agreement.";

(6) by inserting after the definition of "widow" the following:

"The 'WIPO Copyright Treaty' is the WIPO Copyright Treaty concluded at Geneva, Switzerland, on December 20, 1996.";

(7) by inserting after the definition of "The 'WIPO Copyright Treaty'" the following:

"The 'WIPO Performances and Phonograms Treaty' is the WIPO Performances and Phonograms Treaty concluded at Geneva, Switzerland, on December 20, 1996."; and

(8) by inserting after the definition of "work made for hire" the following:

"The terms 'WTO Agreement' and 'WTO member country' have the meanings given those terms in paragraphs (9) and (10), respectively, of section 2 of the Uruguay Round Agreements Act.".

(b) SUBJECT MATTER OF COPYRIGHT; NATIONAL ORIGIN.—Section 104 of title 17, United States Code, is amended—

(1) in subsection (b)—

(A) in paragraph (1) by striking "foreign nation that is a party to a copyright treaty to which the United States is also a party" and inserting "treaty party";

(B) in paragraph (2) by striking "party to the Universal Copyright Convention" and inserting "treaty party";

(C) by redesignating paragraph (5) as paragraph (6);

(D) by redesignating paragraph (3) as paragraph (5) and inserting it after paragraph (4);

(E) by inserting after paragraph (2) the following:

"(3) the work is a sound recording that was first fixed in a treaty party; or";

(F) in paragraph (4) by striking "Berne Convention work" and inserting "pictorial, graphic, or sculptural work that is incorporated in a building or other structure, or an architectural work that is embodied in a building and the building or structure is located in the United States or a treaty party"; and

(G) by inserting after paragraph (6), as so redesignated, the following:

"For purposes of paragraph (2), a work that is published in the United States or a treaty party within 30 days after publication in a foreign nation that is not a treaty party shall be considered to be

4

first published in the United States or such treaty party, as the case may be."*; and*

    (2) by adding at the end the following new subsection:

"*(d)* EFFECT OF PHONOGRAMS TREATIES.—*Notwithstanding the provisions of subsection (b), no works other than sound recordings shall be eligible for protection under this title solely by virtue of the adherence of the United States to the Geneva Phonograms Convention or the WIPO Performances and Phonograms Treaty.*".

    (c) COPYRIGHT IN RESTORED WORKS.—*Section 104A(h) of title 17, United States Code, is amended—*

    (1) in paragraph (1), by striking subparagraphs (A) and (B) and inserting the following:

        "*(A) a nation adhering to the Berne Convention;*

        "*(B) a WTO member country;*

        "*(C) a nation adhering to the WIPO Copyright Treaty;*

        "*(D) a nation adhering to the WIPO Performances and Phonograms Treaty; or*

        "*(E) subject to a Presidential proclamation under subsection (g).*";

    (2) by amending paragraph (3) to read as follows:

    "*(3) The term 'eligible country' means a nation, other than the United States, that—*

        "*(A) becomes a WTO member country after the date of the enactment of the Uruguay Round Agreements Act;*

        "*(B) on such date of enactment is, or after such date of enactment becomes, a nation adhering to the Berne Convention;*

        "*(C) adheres to the WIPO Copyright Treaty;*

        "*(D) adheres to the WIPO Performances and Phonograms Treaty; or*

        "*(E) after such date of enactment becomes subject to a proclamation under subsection (g).*";

    (3) in paragraph (6)—

        (A) in subparagraph (C)(iii) by striking "and" after the semicolon;

        (B) at the end of subparagraph (D) by striking the period and inserting "; and"; and

        (C) by adding after subparagraph (D) the following:

        "*(E) if the source country for the work is an eligible country solely by virtue of its adherence to the WIPO Performances and Phonograms Treaty, is a sound recording.*";

    (4) in paragraph (8)(B)(i)—

        (A) by inserting "of which" before "the majority"; and

        (B) by striking "of eligible countries"; and

    (5) by striking paragraph (9).

    (d) REGISTRATION AND INFRINGEMENT ACTIONS.—*Section 411(a) of title 17, United States Code, is amended in the first sentence—*

    (1) by striking "actions for infringement of copyright in Berne Convention works whose country of origin is not the United States and"; and

    (2) by inserting "United States" after "no action for infringement of the copyright in any".

5

(e) STATUTE OF LIMITATIONS.—Section 507(a) of title 17, United State Code, is amended by striking "No" and inserting "Except as expressly provided otherwise in this title, no".

SEC. 103. COPYRIGHT PROTECTION SYSTEMS AND COPYRIGHT MANAGEMENT INFORMATION.

(a) IN GENERAL.—Title 17, United States Code is amended by adding at the end the following new chapter:

"CHAPTER 12—COPYRIGHT PROTECTION AND MANAGEMENT SYSTEMS

"Sec.
"1201. Circumvention of copyright protection systems.
"1202. Integrity of copyright management information.
"1203. Civil remedies.
"1204. Criminal offenses and penalties.
"1205. Savings clause.

"§ 1201. Circumvention of copyright protection systems

"(a) VIOLATIONS REGARDING CIRCUMVENTION OF TECHNOLOGICAL MEASURES.—(1)(A) No person shall circumvent a technological measure that effectively controls access to a work protected under this title. The prohibition contained in the preceding sentence shall take effect at the end of the 2-year period beginning on the date of the enactment of this chapter.

"(B) The prohibition contained in subparagraph (A) shall not apply to persons who are users of a copyrighted work which is in a particular class of works, if such persons are, or are likely to be in the succeeding 3-year period, adversely affected by virtue of such prohibition in their ability to make noninfringing uses of that particular class of works under this title, as determined under subparagraph (C).

"(C) During the 2-year period described in subparagraph (A), and during each succeeding 3-year period, the Librarian of Congress, upon the recommendation of the Register of Copyrights, who shall consult with the Assistant Secretary for Communications and Information of the Department of Commerce and report and comment on his or her views in making such recommendation, shall make the determination in a rulemaking proceeding on the record for purposes of subparagraph (B) of whether persons who are users of a copyrighted work are, or are likely to be in the succeeding 3-year period, adversely affected by the prohibition under subparagraph (A) in their ability to make noninfringing uses under this title of a particular class of copyrighted works. In conducting such rulemaking, the Librarian shall examine—

"(i) the availability for use of copyrighted works;

"(ii) the availability for use of works for nonprofit archival, preservation, and educational purposes;

"(iii) the impact that the prohibition on the circumvention of technological measures applied to copyrighted works has on criticism, comment, news reporting, teaching, scholarship, or research;

"(iv) the effect of circumvention of technological measures on the market for or value of copyrighted works; and

6

"(v) such other factors as the Librarian considers appropriate.

"(D) The Librarian shall publish any class of copyrighted works for which the Librarian has determined, pursuant to the rulemaking conducted under subparagraph (C), that noninfringing uses by persons who are users of a copyrighted work are, or are likely to be, adversely affected, and the prohibition contained in subparagraph (A) shall not apply to such users with respect to such class of works for the ensuing 3-year period.

"(E) Neither the exception under subparagraph (B) from the applicability of the prohibition contained in subparagraph (A), nor any determination made in a rulemaking conducted under subparagraph (C), may be used as a defense in any action to enforce any provision of this title other than this paragraph.

"(2) No person shall manufacture, import, offer to the public, provide, or otherwise traffic in any technology, product, service, device, component, or part thereof, that—

"(A) is primarily designed or produced for the purpose of circumventing a technological measure that effectively controls access to a work protected under this title;

"(B) has only limited commercially significant purpose or use other than to circumvent a technological measure that effectively controls access to a work protected under this title; or

"(C) is marketed by that person or another acting in concert with that person with that person's knowledge for use in circumventing a technological measure that effectively controls access to a work protected under this title.

"(3) As used in this subsection—

"(A) to 'circumvent a technological measure' means to descramble a scrambled work, to decrypt an encrypted work, or otherwise to avoid, bypass, remove, deactivate, or impair a technological measure, without the authority of the copyright owner; and

"(B) a technological measure 'effectively controls access to a work' if the measure, in the ordinary course of its operation, requires the application of information, or a process or a treatment, with the authority of the copyright owner, to gain access to the work.

"(b) ADDITIONAL VIOLATIONS.—(1) No person shall manufacture, import, offer to the public, provide, or otherwise traffic in any technology, product, service, device, component, or part thereof, that—

"(A) is primarily designed or produced for the purpose of circumventing protection afforded by a technological measure that effectively protects a right of a copyright owner under this title in a work or a portion thereof;

"(B) has only limited commercially significant purpose or use other than to circumvent protection afforded by a technological measure that effectively protects a right of a copyright owner under this title in a work or a portion thereof; or

"(C) is marketed by that person or another acting in concert with that person with that person's knowledge for use in circumventing protection afforded by a technological measure that

7

effectively protects a right of a copyright owner under this title in a work or a portion thereof.

"(2) As used in this subsection—

"(A) to 'circumvent protection afforded by a technological measure' means avoiding, bypassing, removing, deactivating, or otherwise impairing a technological measure; and

"(B) a technological measure 'effectively protects a right of a copyright owner under this title' if the measure, in the ordinary course of its operation, prevents, restricts, or otherwise limits the exercise of a right of a copyright owner under this title.

"(c) OTHER RIGHTS, ETC., NOT AFFECTED.—(1) Nothing in this section shall affect rights, remedies, limitations, or defenses to copyright infringement, including fair use, under this title.

"(2) Nothing in this section shall enlarge or diminish vicarious or contributory liability for copyright infringement in connection with any technology, product, service, device, component, or part thereof.

"(3) Nothing in this section shall require that the design of, or design and selection of parts and components for, a consumer electronics, telecommunications, or computing product provide for a response to any particular technological measure, so long as such part or component, or the product in which such part or component is integrated, does not otherwise fall within the prohibitions of subsection (a)(2) or (b)(1).

"(4) Nothing in this section shall enlarge or diminish any rights of free speech or the press for activities using consumer electronics, telecommunications, or computing products.

"(d) EXEMPTION FOR NONPROFIT LIBRARIES, ARCHIVES, AND EDUCATIONAL INSTITUTIONS.—(1) A nonprofit library, archives, or educational institution which gains access to a commercially exploited copyrighted work solely in order to make a good faith determination of whether to acquire a copy of that work for the sole purpose of engaging in conduct permitted under this title shall not be in violation of subsection (a)(1)(A). A copy of a work to which access has been gained under this paragraph—

"(A) may not be retained longer than necessary to make such good faith determination; and

"(B) may not be used for any other purpose.

"(2) The exemption made available under paragraph (1) shall only apply with respect to a work when an identical copy of that work is not reasonably available in another form.

"(3) A nonprofit library, archives, or educational institution that willfully for the purpose of commercial advantage or financial gain violates paragraph (1)—

"(A) shall, for the first offense, be subject to the civil remedies under section 1203; and

"(B) shall, for repeated or subsequent offenses, in addition to the civil remedies under section 1203, forfeit the exemption provided under paragraph (1).

"(4) This subsection may not be used as a defense to a claim under subsection (a)(2) or (b), nor may this subsection permit a nonprofit library, archives, or educational institution to manufacture, import, offer to the public, provide, or otherwise traffic in any tech-

8

nology, product, service, component, or part thereof, which circumvents a technological measure.

"(5) In order for a library or archives to qualify for the exemption under this subsection, the collections of that library or archives shall be—

"(A) open to the public; or

"(B) available not only to researchers affiliated with the library or archives or with the institution of which it is a part, but also to other persons doing research in a specialized field.

"(e) LAW ENFORCEMENT, INTELLIGENCE, AND OTHER GOVERNMENT ACTIVITIES.—This section does not prohibit any lawfully authorized investigative, protective, information security, or intelligence activity of an officer, agent, or employee of the United States, a State, or a political subdivision of a State, or a person acting pursuant to a contract with the United States, a State, or a political subdivision of a State. For purposes of this subsection, the term 'information security' means activities carried out in order to identify and address the vulnerabilities of a government computer, computer system, or computer network.

"(f) REVERSE ENGINEERING.—(1) Notwithstanding the provisions of subsection (a)(1)(A), a person who has lawfully obtained the right to use a copy of a computer program may circumvent a technological measure that effectively controls access to a particular portion of that program for the sole purpose of identifying and analyzing those elements of the program that are necessary to achieve interoperability of an independently created computer program with other programs, and that have not previously been readily available to the person engaging in the circumvention, to the extent any such acts of identification and analysis do not constitute infringement under this title.

"(2) Notwithstanding the provisions of subsections (a)(2) and (b), a person may develop and employ technological means to circumvent a technological measure, or to circumvent protection afforded by a technological measure, in order to enable the identification and analysis under paragraph (1), or for the purpose of enabling interoperability of an independently created computer program with other programs, if such means are necessary to achieve such interoperability, to the extent that doing so does not constitute infringement under this title.

"(3) The information acquired through the acts permitted under paragraph (1), and the means permitted under paragraph (2), may be made available to others if the person referred to in paragraph (1) or (2), as the case may be, provides such information or means solely for the purpose of enabling interoperability of an independently created computer program with other programs, and to the extent that doing so does not constitute infringement under this title or violate applicable law other than this section.

"(4) For purposes of this subsection, the term 'interoperability' means the ability of computer programs to exchange information, and of such programs mutually to use the information which has been exchanged.

"(g) ENCRYPTION RESEARCH.—

"(1) DEFINITIONS.—For purposes of this subsection—

9

"(A) the term 'encryption research' means activities necessary to identify and analyze flaws and vulnerabilities of
encryption technologies applied to copyrighted works, if
these activities are conducted to advance the state of knowledge in the field of encryption technology or to assist in the
development of encryption products; and
"(B) the term 'encryption technology' means the scrambling and descrambling of information using mathematical
formulas or algorithms.
"(2) PERMISSIBLE ACTS OF ENCRYPTION RESEARCH.—Notwithstanding the provisions of subsection (a)(1)(A), it is not a
violation of that subsection for a person to circumvent a technological measure as applied to a copy, phonorecord, performance,
or display of a published work in the course of an act of good
faith encryption research if—
"(A) the person lawfully obtained the encrypted copy,
phonorecord, performance, or display of the published
work;
"(B) such act is necessary to conduct such encryption
research;
"(C) the person made a good faith effort to obtain authorization before the circumvention; and
"(D) such act does not constitute infringement under
this title or a violation of applicable law other than this
section, including section 1030 of title 18 and those provisions of title 18 amended by the Computer Fraud and
Abuse Act of 1986.
"(3) FACTORS IN DETERMINING EXEMPTION.—In determining
whether a person qualifies for the exemption under paragraph
(2), the factors to be considered shall include—
"(A) whether the information derived from the
encryption research was disseminated, and if so, whether it
was disseminated in a manner reasonably calculated to advance the state of knowledge or development of encryption
technology, versus whether it was disseminated in a manner that facilitates infringement under this title or a violation of applicable law other than this section, including a
violation of privacy or breach of security;
"(B) whether the person is engaged in a legitimate
course of study, is employed, or is appropriately trained or
experienced, in the field of encryption technology; and
"(C) whether the person provides the copyright owner of
the work to which the technological measure is applied
with notice of the findings and documentation of the research, and the time when such notice is provided.
"(4) USE OF TECHNOLOGICAL MEANS FOR RESEARCH ACTIVI-
TIES.—Notwithstanding the provisions of subsection (a)(2), it is
not a violation of that subsection for a person to—
"(A) develop and employ technological means to circumvent a technological measure for the sole purpose of
that person performing the acts of good faith encryption research described in paragraph (2); and
"(B) provide the technological means to another person
with whom he or she is working collaboratively for the pur-

10

pose of conducting the acts of good faith encryption research described in paragraph (2) or for the purpose of having that other person verify his or her acts of good faith encryption research described in paragraph (2).

"(5) REPORT TO CONGRESS.—Not later than 1 year after the date of the enactment of this chapter, the Register of Copyrights and the Assistant Secretary for Communications and Information of the Department of Commerce shall jointly report to the Congress on the effect this subsection has had on—

(A) encryption research and the development of encryption technology;

"(B) the adequacy and effectiveness of technological measures designed to protect copyrighted works; and

"(C) protection of copyright owners against the unauthorized access to their encrypted copyrighted works.

The report shall include legislative recommendations, if any.

"(h) EXCEPTIONS REGARDING MINORS.—In applying subsection (a) to a component or part, the court may consider the necessity for its intended and actual incorporation in a technology, product, service, or device, which—

"(1) does not itself violate the provisions of this title; and

"(2) has the sole purpose to prevent the access of minors to material on the Internet.

"(i) PROTECTION OF PERSONALLY IDENTIFYING INFORMATION.—

(1) CIRCUMVENTION PERMITTED.—Notwithstanding the provisions of subsection (a)(1)(A), it is not a violation of that subsection for a person to circumvent a technological measure that effectively controls access to a work protected under this title, if—

"(A) the technological measure, or the work it protects, contains the capability of collecting or disseminating personally identifying information reflecting the online activities of a natural person who seeks to gain access to the work protected;

"(B) in the normal course of its operation, the technological measure, or the work it protects, collects or disseminates personally identifying information about the person who seeks to gain access to the work protected, without providing conspicuous notice of such collection or dissemination to such person, and without providing such person with the capability to prevent or restrict such collection or dissemination;

"(C) the act of circumvention has the sole effect of identifying and disabling the capability described in subparagraph (A), and has no other effect on the ability of any person to gain access to any work; and

"(D) the act of circumvention is carried out solely for the purpose of preventing the collection or dissemination of personally identifying information about a natural person who seeks to gain access to the work protected, and is not in violation of any other law.

"(2) INAPPLICABILITY TO CERTAIN TECHNOLOGICAL MEASURES.—This subsection does not apply to a technological measure, or a work it protects, that does not collect or disseminate

11

personally identifying information and that is disclosed to a user as not having or using such capability.

"(j) SECURITY TESTING.—

"(1) DEFINITION.—For purposes of this subsection, the term 'security testing' means accessing a computer, computer system, or computer network, solely for the purpose of good faith testing, investigating, or correcting, a security flaw or vulnerability, with the authorization of the owner or operator of such computer, computer system, or computer network.

"(2) PERMISSIBLE ACTS OF SECURITY TESTING.—Notwithstanding the provisions of subsection (a)(1)(A), it is not a violation of that subsection for a person to engage in an act of security testing, if such act does not constitute infringement under this title or a violation of applicable law other than this section, including section 1030 of title 18 and those provisions of title 18 amended by the Computer Fraud and Abuse Act of 1986.

"(3) FACTORS IN DETERMINING EXEMPTION.—In determining whether a person qualifies for the exemption under paragraph (2), the factors to be considered shall include—

"(A) whether the information derived from the security testing was used solely to promote the security of the owner or operator of such computer, computer system or computer network, or shared directly with the developer of such computer, computer system, or computer network; and

"(B) whether the information derived from the security testing was used or maintained in a manner that does not facilitate infringement under this title or a violation of applicable law other than this section, including a violation of privacy or breach of security.

"(4) USE OF TECHNOLOGICAL MEANS FOR SECURITY TESTING.—Notwithstanding the provisions of subsection (a)(2), it is not a violation of that subsection for a person to develop, produce, distribute or employ technological means for the sole purpose of performing the acts of security testing described in subsection (2), provided such technological means does not otherwise violate section (a)(2).

"(k) CERTAIN ANALOG DEVICES AND CERTAIN TECHNOLOGICAL MEASURES.—

"(1) CERTAIN ANALOG DEVICES.—

"(A) Effective 18 months after the date of the enactment of this chapter, no person shall manufacture, import, offer to the public, provide or otherwise traffic in any—

"(i) VHS format analog video cassette recorder unless such recorder conforms to the automatic gain control copy control technology;

"(ii) 8mm format analog video cassette camcorder unless such camcorder conforms to the automatic gain control technology;

"(iii) Beta format analog video cassette recorder, unless such recorder conforms to the automatic gain control copy control technology, except that this requirement shall not apply until there are 1,000 Beta format analog video cassette recorders sold in the United

12

States in any one calendar year after the date of the enactment of this chapter;

"(iv) 8mm format analog video cassette recorder that is not an analog video cassette camcorder, unless such recorder conforms to the automatic gain control copy control technology, except that this requirement shall not apply until there are 20,000 such recorders sold in the United States in any one calendar year after the date of the enactment of this chapter; or

"(v) analog video cassette recorder that records using an NTSC format video input and that is not otherwise covered under clauses (i) through (iv), unless such device conforms to the automatic gain control copy control technology.

"(B) Effective on the date of the enactment of this chapter, no person shall manufacture, import, offer to the public, provide or otherwise traffic in—

"(i) any VHS format analog video cassette recorder or any 8mm format analog video cassette recorder if the design of the model of such recorder has been modified after such date of enactment so that a model of recorder that previously conformed to the automatic gain control copy control technology no longer conforms to such technology; or

"(ii) any VHS format analog video cassette recorder, or any 8mm format analog video cassette recorder that is not an 8mm analog video cassette camcorder, if the design of the model of such recorder has been modified after such date of enactment so that a model of recorder that previously conformed to the four-line colorstripe copy control technology no longer conforms to such technology.

Manufacturers that have not previously manufactured or sold a VHS format analog video cassette recorder, or an 8mm format analog cassette recorder, shall be required to conform to the four-line colorstripe copy control technology in the initial model of any such recorder manufactured after the date of the enactment of this chapter, and thereafter to continue conforming to the four-line colorstripe copy control technology. For purposes of this subparagraph, an analog video cassette recorder 'conforms to' the four-line colorstripe copy control technology if it records a signal that, when played back by the playback function of that recorder in the normal viewing mode, exhibits, on a reference display device, a display containing distracting visible lines through portions of the viewable picture.

"(2) CERTAIN ENCODING RESTRICTIONS.—No person shall apply the automatic gain control copy control technology or colorstripe copy control technology to prevent or limit consumer copying except such copying—

"(A) of a single transmission, or specified group of transmissions, of live events or of audiovisual works for which a member of the public has exercised choice in selecting the transmissions, including the content of the trans-

13

missions or the time of receipt of such transmissions, or both, and as to which such member is charged a separate fee for each such transmission or specified group of transmissions;

"(B) from a copy of a transmission of a live event or an audiovisual work if such transmission is provided by a channel or service where payment is made by a member of the public for such channel or service in the form of a subscription fee that entitles the member of the public to receive all of the programming contained in such channel or service;

"(C) from a physical medium containing one or more prerecorded audiovisual works; or

"(D) from a copy of a transmission described in subparagraph (A) or from a copy made from a physical medium described in subparagraph (C).

In the event that a transmission meets both the conditions set forth in subparagraph (A) and those set forth in subparagraph (B), the transmission shall be treated as a transmission described in subparagraph (A).

"(3) INAPPLICABILITY.—This subsection shall not—

"(A) require any analog video cassette camcorder to conform to the automatic gain control copy control technology with respect to any video signal received through a camera lens;

"(B) apply to the manufacture, importation, offer for sale, provision of, or other trafficking in, any professional analog video cassette recorder; or

"(C) apply to the offer for sale or provision of, or other trafficking in, any previously owned analog video cassette recorder, if such recorder was legally manufactured and sold when new and not subsequently modified in violation of paragraph (1)(B).

"(4) DEFINITIONS.—For purposes of this subsection:

"(A) An 'analog video cassette recorder' means a device that records, or a device that includes a function that records, on electromagnetic tape in an analog format the electronic impulses produced by the video and audio portions of a television program, motion picture, or other form of audiovisual work.

"(B) An 'analog video cassette camcorder' means an analog video cassette recorder that contains a recording function that operates through a camera lens and through a video input that may be connected with a television or other video playback device.

"(C) An analog video cassette recorder 'conforms' to the automatic gain control copy control technology if it—

"(i) detects one or more of the elements of such technology and does not record the motion picture or transmission protected by such technology; or

"(ii) records a signal that, when played back, exhibits a meaningfully distorted or degraded display.

"(D) The term 'professional analog video cassette recorder' means an analog video cassette recorder that is de-

14

signed, manufactured, marketed, and intended for use by a person who regularly employs such a device for a lawful business or industrial use, including making, performing, displaying, distributing, or transmitting copies of motion pictures on a commercial scale.

"(E) The terms 'VHS format,' '8mm format,' 'Beta format,' 'automatic gain control copy control technology,' 'colorstripe copy control technology,' 'four-line version of the colorstripe copy control technology,' and 'NTSC' have the meanings that are commonly understood in the consumer electronics and motion picture industries as of the date of the enactment of this chapter.

"(5) VIOLATIONS.—Any violation of paragraph (1) of this subsection shall be treated as a violation of subsection (b)(1) of this section. Any violation of paragraph (2) of this subsection shall be deemed an 'act of circumvention' for the purposes of section 1203(c)(3)(A) of this chapter.

"§ 1202. Integrity of copyright management information

"(a) FALSE COPYRIGHT MANAGEMENT INFORMATION.—No person shall knowingly and with the intent to induce, enable, facilitate, or conceal infringement—

"(1) provide copyright management information that is false, or

"(2) distribute or import for distribution copyright management information that is false.

"(b) REMOVAL OR ALTERATION OF COPYRIGHT MANAGEMENT INFORMATION.—No person shall, without the authority of the copyright owner or the law—

"(1) intentionally remove or alter any copyright management information,

"(2) distribute or import for distribution copyright management information knowing that the copyright management information has been removed or altered without authority of the copyright owner or the law, or

"(3) distribute, import for distribution, or publicly perform works, copies of works, or phonorecords, knowing that copyright management information has been removed or altered without authority of the copyright owner or the law,

knowing, or, with respect to civil remedies under section 1203, having reasonable grounds to know, that it will induce, enable, facilitate, or conceal an infringement of any right under this title.

"(c) DEFINITION.—As used in this section, the term 'copyright management information' means any of the following information conveyed in connection with copies or phonorecords of a work or performances or displays of a work, including in digital form, except that such term does not include any personally identifying information about a user of a work or of a copy, phonorecord, performance, or display of a work:

"(1) The title and other information identifying the work, including the information set forth on a notice of copyright.

"(2) The name of, and other identifying information about, the author of a work.

15

"(3) The name of, and other identifying information about, the copyright owner of the work, including the information set forth in a notice of copyright.

"(4) With the exception of public performances of works by radio and television broadcast stations, the name of, and other identifying information about, a performer whose performance is fixed in a work other than an audiovisual work.

"(5) With the exception of public performances of works by radio and television broadcast stations, in the case of an audiovisual work, the name of, and other identifying information about, a writer, performer, or director who is credited in the audiovisual work.

"(6) Terms and conditions for use of the work.

"(7) Identifying numbers or symbols referring to such information or links to such information.

"(8) Such other information as the Register of Copyrights may prescribe by regulation, except that the Register of Copyrights may not require the provision of any information concerning the user of a copyrighted work.

"(d) LAW ENFORCEMENT, INTELLIGENCE, AND OTHER GOVERNMENT ACTIVITIES.—This section does not prohibit any lawfully authorized investigative, protective, information security, or intelligence activity of an officer, agent, or employee of the United States, a State, or a political subdivision of a State, or a person acting pursuant to a contract with the United States, a State, or a political subdivision of a State. For purposes of this subsection, the term 'information security' means activities carried out in order to identify and address the vulnerabilities of a government computer, computer system, or computer network.

"(e) LIMITATIONS ON LIABILITY.—

"(1) ANALOG TRANSMISSIONS.—In the case of an analog transmission, a person who is making transmissions in its capacity as a broadcast station, or as a cable system, or someone who provides programming to such station or system, shall not be liable for a violation of subsection (b) if—

"(A) avoiding the activity that constitutes such violation is not technically feasible or would create an undue financial hardship on such person; and

"(B) such person did not intend, by engaging in such activity, to induce, enable, facilitate, or conceal infringement of a right under this title.

"(2) DIGITAL TRANSMISSIONS.—

"(A) If a digital transmission standard for the placement of copyright management information for a category of works is set in a voluntary, consensus standard-setting process involving a representative cross-section of broadcast stations or cable systems and copyright owners of a category of works that are intended for public performance by such stations or systems, a person identified in paragraph (1) shall not be liable for a violation of subsection (b) with respect to the particular copyright management information addressed by such standard if—

16

"*(i) the placement of such information by someone other than such person is not in accordance with such standard; and*

"*(ii) the activity that constitutes such violation is not intended to induce, enable, facilitate, or conceal infringement of a right under this title.*

"*(B) Until a digital transmission standard has been set pursuant to subparagraph (A) with respect to the placement of copyright management information for a category or works, a person identified in paragraph (1) shall not be liable for a violation of subsection (b) with respect to such copyright management information, if the activity that constitutes such violation is not intended to induce, enable, facilitate, or conceal infringement of a right under this title, and if—*

"*(i) the transmission of such information by such person would result in a perceptible visual or aural degradation of the digital signal; or*

"*(ii) the transmission of such information by such person would conflict with—*

"*(I) an applicable government regulation relating to transmission of information in a digital signal;*

"*(II) an applicable industry-wide standard relating to the transmission of information in a digital signal that was adopted by a voluntary consensus standards body prior to the effective date of this chapter; or*

"*(III) an applicable industry-wide standard relating to the transmission of information in a digital signal that was adopted in a voluntary, consensus standards-setting process open to participation by a representative cross-section of broadcast stations or cable systems and copyright owners of a category of works that are intended for public performance by such stations or systems.*

"*(3) DEFINITIONS.—As used in this subsection—*

"*(A) the term 'broadcast station' has the meaning given that term in section 3 of the Communications Act of 1934 (47 U.S.C. 153)); and*

"*(B) the term 'cable system' has the meaning given that term in section 602 of the Communications Act of 1934 (47 U.S.C. 522)).*

"*§ 1203. Civil remedies*

"*(a) CIVIL ACTIONS.—Any person injured by a violation of section 1201 or 1202 may bring a civil action in an appropriate United States district court for such violation.*

"*(b) POWERS OF THE COURT.—In an action brought under subsection (a), the court—*

"*(1) may grant temporary and permanent injunctions on such terms as it deems reasonable to prevent or restrain a violation, but in no event shall impose a prior restraint on free*

17

speech or the press protected under the 1st amendment to the Constitution;

"(2) at any time while an action is pending, may order the impounding, on such terms as it deems reasonable, of any device or product that is in the custody or control of the alleged violator and that the court has reasonable cause to believe was involved in a violation;

"(3) may award damages under subsection (c);

"(4) in its discretion may allow the recovery of costs by or against any party other than the United States or an officer thereof;

"(5) in its discretion may award reasonable attorney's fees to the prevailing party; and

"(6) may, as part of a final judgment or decree finding a violation, order the remedial modification or the destruction of any device or product involved in the violation that is in the custody or control of the violator or has been impounded under paragraph (2).

"(c) AWARD OF DAMAGES.—

"(1) IN GENERAL.—Except as otherwise provided in this title, a person committing a violation of section 1201 or 1202 is liable for either—

"(A) the actual damages and any additional profits of the violator, as provided in paragraph (2), or

"(B) statutory damages, as provided in paragraph (3).

"(2) ACTUAL DAMAGES.—The court shall award to the complaining party the actual damages suffered by the party as a result of the violation, and any profits of the violator that are attributable to the violation and are not taken into account in computing the actual damages, if the complaining party elects such damages at any time before final judgment is entered.

"(3) STATUTORY DAMAGES.—(A) At any time before final judgment is entered, a complaining party may elect to recover an award of statutory damages for each violation of section 1201 in the sum of not less than $200 or more than $2,500 per act of circumvention, device, product, component, offer, or performance of service, as the court considers just.

"(B) At any time before final judgment is entered, a complaining party may elect to recover an award of statutory damages for each violation of section 1202 in the sum of not less than $2,500 or more than $25,000.

"(4) REPEATED VIOLATIONS.—In any case in which the injured party sustains the burden of proving, and the court finds, that a person has violated section 1201 or 1202 within three years after a final judgment was entered against the person for another such violation, the court may increase the award of damages up to triple the amount that would otherwise be awarded, as the court considers just.

"(5) INNOCENT VIOLATIONS.—

"(A) IN GENERAL.—The court in its discretion may reduce or remit the total award of damages in any case in which the violator sustains the burden of proving, and the court finds, that the violator was not aware and had no reason to believe that its acts constituted a violation.

18

"(B) NONPROFIT LIBRARY, ARCHIVES, OR EDUCATIONAL INSTITUTIONS.—In the case of a nonprofit library, archives, or educational institution, the court shall remit damages in any case in which the library, archives, or educational institution sustains the burden of proving, and the court finds, that the library, archives, or educational institution was not aware and had no reason to believe that its acts constituted a violation.

"§ 1204. Criminal offenses and penalties

"(a) IN GENERAL.—Any person who violates section 1201 or 1202 willfully and for purposes of commercial advantage or private financial gain—

"(1) shall be fined not more than $500,000 or imprisoned for not more than 5 years, or both, for the first offense; and

"(2) shall be fined not more than $1,000,000 or imprisoned for not more than 10 years, or both, for any subsequent offense.

"(b) LIMITATION FOR NONPROFIT LIBRARY, ARCHIVES, OR EDUCATIONAL INSTITUTION.—Subsection (a) shall not apply to a nonprofit library, archives, or educational institution.

"(c) STATUTE OF LIMITATIONS.—No criminal proceeding shall be brought under this section unless such proceeding is commenced within five years after the cause of action arose.

"§ 1205. Savings clause

"Nothing in this chapter abrogates, diminishes, or weakens the provisions of, nor provides any defense or element of mitigation in a criminal prosecution or civil action under, any Federal or State law that prevents the violation of the privacy of an individual in connection with the individual's use of the Internet.".

(b) CONFORMING AMENDMENT.—The table of chapters for title 17, United States Code, is amended by adding after the item relating to chapter 11 the following:

"**12. Copyright Protection and Management Systems** .... **1201**".

SEC. 104. EVALUATION OF IMPACT OF COPYRIGHT LAW AND AMENDMENTS ON ELECTRONIC COMMERCE AND TECHNOLOGICAL DEVELOPMENT.

(a) EVALUATION BY THE REGISTER OF COPYRIGHTS AND THE ASSISTANT SECRETARY FOR COMMUNICATIONS AND INFORMATION.—The Register of Copyrights and the Assistant Secretary for Communications and Information of the Department of Commerce shall jointly evaluate—

(1) the effects of the amendments made by this title and the development of electronic commerce and associated technology on the operation of sections 109 and 117 of title 17, United States Code; and

(2) the relationship between existing and emergent technology and the operation of sections 109 and 117 of title 17, United States Code.

(b) REPORT TO CONGRESS.—The Register of Copyrights and the Assistant Secretary for Communications and Information of the Department of Commerce shall, not later than 24 months after the date of the enactment of this Act, submit to the Congress a joint report on the evaluation conducted under subsection (a), including

19

any legislative recommendations the Register and the Assistant Sec-retary may have.

SEC. 105. EFFECTIVE DATE.

(a) IN GENERAL.—*Except as otherwise provided in this title, this title and the amendments made by this title shall take effect on the date of the enactment of this Act.*

(b) AMENDMENTS RELATING TO CERTAIN INTERNATIONAL AGREEMENTS.—*(1) The following shall take effect upon the entry into force of the WIPO Copyright Treaty with respect to the United States:*

(A) *Paragraph (5) of the definition of "international agree-ment" contained in section 101 of title 17, United States Code, as amended by section 102(a)(4) of this Act.*

(B) *The amendment made by section 102(a)(6) of this Act.*

(C) *Subparagraph (C) of section 104A(h)(1) of title 17, United States Code, as amended by section 102(c)(1) of this Act.*

(D) *Subparagraph (C) of section 104A(h)(3) of title 17, United States Code, as amended by section 102(c)(2) of this Act.*

(2) The following shall take effect upon the entry into force of the WIPO Performances and Phonograms Treaty with respect to the United States:

(A) *Paragraph (6) of the definition of "international agree-ment" contained in section 101 of title 17, United States Code, as amended by section 102(a)(4) of this Act.*

(B) *The amendment made by section 102(a)(7) of this Act.*

(C) *The amendment made by section 102(b)(2) of this Act.*

(D) *Subparagraph (D) of section 104A(h)(1) of title 17, United States Code, as amended by section 102(c)(1) of this Act.*

(E) *Subparagraph (D) of section 104A(h)(3) of title 17, United States Code, as amended by section 102(c)(2) of this Act.*

(F) *The amendments made by section 102(c)(3) of this Act.*

TITLE II—ONLINE COPYRIGHT INFRINGEMENT LIABILITY LIMITATION

SEC. 201. SHORT TITLE.

This title may be cited as the "Online Copyright Infringement Liability Limitation Act".

SEC. 202. LIMITATIONS ON LIABILITY FOR COPYRIGHT INFRINGE-MENT.

(a) IN GENERAL.—*Chapter 5 of title 17, United States Code, is amended by adding after section 511 the following new section:*

"§ 512. Limitations on liability relating to material online

"(a) TRANSITORY DIGITAL NETWORK COMMUNICATIONS.—*A serv-ice provider shall not be liable for monetary relief, or, except as pro-vided in subsection (j), for injunctive or other equitable relief, for in-fringement of copyright by reason of the provider's transmitting, routing, or providing connections for, material through a system or network controlled or operated by or for the service provider, or by reason of the intermediate and transient storage of that material in the course of such transmitting, routing, or providing connections, if—*

20

"(1) the transmission of the material was initiated by or at the direction of a person other than the service provider;

"(2) the transmission, routing, provision of connections, or storage is carried out through an automatic technical process without selection of the material by the service provider;

"(3) the service provider does not select the recipients of the material except as an automatic response to the request of another person;

"(4) no copy of the material made by the service provider in the course of such intermediate or transient storage is maintained on the system or network in a manner ordinarily accessible to anyone other than anticipated recipients, and no such copy is maintained on the system or network in a manner ordinarily accessible to such anticipated recipients for a longer period than is reasonably necessary for the transmission, routing, or provision of connections; and

"(5) the material is transmitted through the system or network without modification of its content.

"(b) SYSTEM CACHING.—

"(1) LIMITATION ON LIABILITY.—*A service provider shall not be liable for monetary relief, or, except as provided in subsection (j), for injunctive or other equitable relief, for infringement of copyright by reason of the intermediate and temporary storage of material on a system or network controlled or operated by or for the service provider in a case in which—*

"(A) the material is made available online by a person other than the service provider,

"(B) the material is transmitted from the person described in subparagraph (A) through the system or network to a person other than the person described in subparagraph (A) at the direction of that other person, and

"(C) the storage is carried out through an automatic technical process for the purpose of making the material available to users of the system or network who, after the material is transmitted as described in subparagraph (B), request access to the material from the person described in subparagraph (A),

if the conditions set forth in paragraph (2) are met.

(2) CONDITIONS.—*The conditions referred to in paragraph (1) are that—*

"(A) the material described in paragraph (1) is transmitted to the subsequent users described in paragraph (1)(C) without modification to its content from the manner in which the material was transmitted from the person described in paragraph (1)(A);

"(B) the service provider described in paragraph (1) complies with rules concerning the refreshing, reloading, or other updating of the material when specified by the person making the material available online in accordance with a generally accepted industry standard data communications protocol for the system or network through which that person makes the material available, except that this subparagraph applies only if those rules are not used by the person described in paragraph (1)(A) to prevent or unreasonably

21

impair the intermediate storage to which this subsection applies;

"(C) the service provider does not interfere with the ability of technology associated with the material to return to the person described in paragraph (1)(A) the information that would have been available to that person if the material had been obtained by the subsequent users described in paragraph (1)(C) directly from that person, except that this subparagraph applies only if that technology—

"(i) does not significantly interfere with the performance of the provider's system or network or with the intermediate storage of the material;

"(ii) is consistent with generally accepted industry standard communications protocols; and

"(iii) does not extract information from the provider's system or network other than the information that would have been available to the person described in paragraph (1)(A) if the subsequent users had gained access to the material directly from that person;

"(D) if the person described in paragraph (1)(A) has in effect a condition that a person must meet prior to having access to the material, such as a condition based on payment of a fee or provision of a password or other information, the service provider permits access to the stored material in significant part only to users of its system or network that have met those conditions and only in accordance with those conditions; and

"(E) if the person described in paragraph (1)(A) makes that material available online without the authorization of the copyright owner of the material, the service provider responds expeditiously to remove, or disable access to, the material that is claimed to be infringing upon notification of claimed infringement as described in subsection (c)(3), except that this subparagraph applies only if—

"(i) the material has previously been removed from the originating site or access to it has been disabled, or a court has ordered that the material be removed from the originating site or that access to the material on the originating site be disabled; and

"(ii) the party giving the notification includes in the notification a statement confirming that the material has been removed from the originating site or access to it has been disabled or that a court has ordered that the material be removed from the originating site or that access to the material on the originating site be disabled.

"(c) INFORMATION RESIDING ON SYSTEMS OR NETWORKS AT DIRECTION OF USERS.—

"(1) IN GENERAL.—A service provider shall not be liable for monetary relief, or, except as provided in subsection (j), for injunctive or other equitable relief, for infringement of copyright by reason of the storage at the direction of a user of material that resides on a system or network controlled or operated by or for the service provider, if the service provider—

22

"(A)(i) does not have actual knowledge that the material or an activity using the material on the system or network is infringing;

"(ii) in the absence of such actual knowledge, is not aware of facts or circumstances from which infringing activity is apparent; or

"(iii) upon obtaining such knowledge or awareness, acts expeditiously to remove, or disable access to, the material;

"(B) does not receive a financial benefit directly attributable to the infringing activity, in a case in which the service provider has the right and ability to control such activity; and

"(C) upon notification of claimed infringement as described in paragraph (3), responds expeditiously to remove, or disable access to, the material that is claimed to be infringing or to be the subject of infringing activity.

"(2) DESIGNATED AGENT.—The limitations on liability established in this subsection apply to a service provider only if the service provider has designated an agent to receive notifications of claimed infringement described in paragraph (3), by making available through its service, including on its website in a location accessible to the public, and by providing to the Copyright Office, substantially the following information:

"(A) the name, address, phone number, and electronic mail address of the agent.

"(B) other contact information which the Register of Copyrights may deem appropriate.

The Register of Copyrights shall maintain a current directory of agents available to the public for inspection, including through the Internet, in both electronic and hard copy formats, and may require payment of a fee by service providers to cover the costs of maintaining the directory.

"(3) ELEMENTS OF NOTIFICATION.—

"(A) To be effective under this subsection, a notification of claimed infringement must be a written communication provided to the designated agent of a service provider that includes substantially the following:

"(i) A physical or electronic signature of a person authorized to act on behalf of the owner of an exclusive right that is allegedly infringed.

"(ii) Identification of the copyrighted work claimed to have been infringed, or, if multiple copyrighted works at a single online site are covered by a single notification, a representative list of such works at that site.

"(iii) Identification of the material that is claimed to be infringing or to be the subject of infringing activity and that is to be removed or access to which is to be disabled, and information reasonably sufficient to permit the service provider to locate the material.

"(iv) Information reasonably sufficient to permit the service provider to contact the complaining party, such as an address, telephone number, and, if available, an electronic mail address at which the complaining party may be contacted.

"(v) A statement that the complaining party has a good faith belief that use of the material in the manner complained of is not authorized by the copyright owner, its agent, or the law.

"(vi) A statement that the information in the notification is accurate, and under penalty of perjury, that the complaining party is authorized to act on behalf of the owner of an exclusive right that is allegedly infringed.

"(B)(i) Subject to clause (ii), a notification from a copyright owner or from a person authorized to act on behalf of the copyright owner that fails to comply substantially with the provisions of subparagraph (A) shall not be considered under paragraph (1)(A) in determining whether a service provider has actual knowledge or is aware of facts or circumstances from which infringing activity is apparent.

"(ii) In a case in which the notification that is provided to the service provider's designated agent fails to comply substantially with all the provisions of subparagraph (A) but substantially complies with clauses (ii), (iii), and (iv) of subparagraph (A), clause (i) of this subparagraph applies only if the service provider promptly attempts to contact the person making the notification or takes other reasonable steps to assist in the receipt of notification that substantially complies with all the provisions of subparagraph (A).

"(d) INFORMATION LOCATION TOOLS.—A service provider shall not be liable for monetary relief, or, except as provided in subsection (j), for injunctive or other equitable relief, for infringement of copyright by reason of the provider referring or linking users to an online location containing infringing material or infringing activity, by using information location tools, including a directory, index, reference, pointer, or hypertext link, if the service provider—

"(1)(A) does not have actual knowledge that the material or activity is infringing;

"(B) in the absence of such actual knowledge, is not aware of facts or circumstances from which infringing activity is apparent; or

"(C) upon obtaining such knowledge or awareness, acts expeditiously to remove, or disable access to, the material;

"(2) does not receive a financial benefit directly attributable to the infringing activity, in a case in which the service provider has the right and ability to control such activity; and

"(3) upon notification of claimed infringement as described in subsection (c)(3), responds expeditiously to remove, or disable access to, the material that is claimed to be infringing or to be the subject of infringing activity, except that, for purposes of this paragraph, the information described in subsection (c)(3)(A)(iii) shall be identification of the reference or link, to material or activity claimed to be infringing, that is to be removed or access to which is to be disabled, and information

24

reasonably sufficient to permit the service provider to locate that reference or link.

"(e) LIMITATION ON LIABILITY OF NONPROFIT EDUCATIONAL IN-STITUTIONS.—(1) When a public or other nonprofit institution of higher education is a service provider, and when a faculty member or graduate student who is an employee of such institution is performing a teaching or research function, for the purposes of subsections (a) and (b) such faculty member or graduate student shall be considered to be a person other than the institution, and for the purposes of subsections (c) and (d) such faculty member's or graduate student's knowledge or awareness of his or her infringing activities shall not be attributed to the institution, if—

"(A) such faculty member's or graduate student's infringing activities do not involve the provision of online access to instructional materials that are or were required or recommended, within the preceding 3-year period, for a course taught at the institution by such faculty member or graduate student;

"(B) the institution has not, within the preceding 3-year period, received more than 2 notifications described in subsection (c)(3) of claimed infringement by such faculty member or graduate student, and such notifications of claimed infringement were not actionable under subsection (f); and

"(C) the institution provides to all users of its system or network informational materials that accurately describe, and promote compliance with, the laws of the United States relating to copyright.

"(2) INJUNCTIONS.—For the purposes of this subsection, the limitations on injunctive relief contained in subsections (j)(2) and (j)(3), but not those in (j)(1), shall apply.

"(f) MISREPRESENTATIONS.—Any person who knowingly materially misrepresents under this section—

"(1) that material or activity is infringing, or

"(2) that material or activity was removed or disabled by mistake or misidentification,

shall be liable for any damages, including costs and attorneys' fees, incurred by the alleged infringer, by any copyright owner or copyright owner's authorized licensee, or by a service provider, who is injured by such misrepresentation, as the result of the service provider relying upon such misrepresentation in removing or disabling access to the material or activity claimed to be infringing, or in replacing the removed material or ceasing to disable access to it.

"(g) REPLACEMENT OF REMOVED OR DISABLED MATERIAL AND LIMITATION ON OTHER LIABILITY.—

"(1) NO LIABILITY FOR TAKING DOWN GENERALLY.—Subject to paragraph (2), a service provider shall not be liable to any person for any claim based on the service provider's good faith disabling of access to, or removal of, material or activity claimed to be infringing or based on facts or circumstances from which infringing activity is apparent, regardless of whether the material or activity is ultimately determined to be infringing.

"(2) EXCEPTION.—Paragraph (1) shall not apply with respect to material residing at the direction of a subscriber of the

25

service provider on a system or network controlled or operated by or for the service provider that is removed, or to which access is disabled by the service provider, pursuant to a notice provided under subsection (c)(1)(C), unless the service provider—

"(A) takes reasonable steps promptly to notify the subscriber that it has removed or disabled access to the material;

"(B) upon receipt of a counter notification described in paragraph (3), promptly provides the person who provided the notification under subsection (c)(1)(C) with a copy of the counter notification, and informs that person that it will replace the removed material or cease disabling access to it in 10 business days; and

"(C) replaces the removed material and ceases disabling access to it not less than 10, nor more than 14, business days following receipt of the counter notice, unless its designated agent first receives notice from the person who submitted the notification under subsection (c)(1)(C) that such person has filed an action seeking a court order to restrain the subscriber from engaging in infringing activity relating to the material on the service provider's system or network.

"(3) CONTENTS OF COUNTER NOTIFICATION.—To be effective under this subsection, a counter notification must be a written communication provided to the service provider's designated agent that includes substantially the following:

"(A) A physical or electronic signature of the subscriber.

"(B) Identification of the material that has been removed or to which access has been disabled and the location at which the material appeared before it was removed or access to it was disabled.

"(C) A statement under penalty of perjury that the subscriber has a good faith belief that the material was removed or disabled as a result of mistake or misidentification of the material to be removed or disabled.

"(D) The subscriber's name, address, and telephone number, and a statement that the subscriber consents to the jurisdiction of Federal District Court for the judicial district in which the address is located, or if the subscriber's address is outside of the United States, for any judicial district in which the service provider may be found, and that the subscriber will accept service of process from the person who provided notification under subsection (c)(1)(C) or an agent of such person.

"(4) LIMITATION ON OTHER LIABILITY.—A service provider's compliance with paragraph (2) shall not subject the service provider to liability for copyright infringement with respect to the material identified in the notice provided under subsection (c)(1)(C).

"(h) SUBPOENA TO IDENTIFY INFRINGER.—

"(1) REQUEST.—A copyright owner or a person authorized to act on the owner's behalf may request the clerk of any United States district court to issue a subpoena to a service provider

26

for identification of an alleged infringer in accordance with this subsection.

"(2) CONTENTS OF REQUEST.—The request may be made by filing with the clerk—

"(A) a copy of a notification described in subsection (c)(3)(A);

"(B) a proposed subpoena; and

"(C) a sworn declaration to the effect that the purpose for which the subpoena is sought is to obtain the identity of an alleged infringer and that such information will only be used for the purpose of protecting rights under this title.

"(3) CONTENTS OF SUBPOENA.—The subpoena shall authorize and order the service provider receiving the notification and the subpoena to expeditiously disclose to the copyright owner or person authorized by the copyright owner information sufficient to identify the alleged infringer of the material described in the notification to the extent such information is available to the service provider.

"(4) BASIS FOR GRANTING SUBPOENA.—If the notification filed satisfies the provisions of subsection (c)(3)(A), the proposed subpoena is in proper form, and the accompanying declaration is properly executed, the clerk shall expeditiously issue and sign the proposed subpoena and return it to the requester for delivery to the service provider.

"(5) ACTIONS OF SERVICE PROVIDER RECEIVING SUBPOENA.— Upon receipt of the issued subpoena, either accompanying or subsequent to the receipt of a notification described in subsection (c)(3)(A), the service provider shall expeditiously disclose to the copyright owner or person authorized by the copyright owner the information required by the subpoena, notwithstanding any other provision of law and regardless of whether the service provider responds to the notification.

"(6) RULES APPLICABLE TO SUBPOENA.—Unless otherwise provided by this section or by applicable rules of the court, the procedure for issuance and delivery of the subpoena, and the remedies for noncompliance with the subpoena, shall be governed to the greatest extent practicable by those provisions of the Federal Rules of Civil Procedure governing the issuance, service, and enforcement of a subpoena duces tecum.

"(i) CONDITIONS FOR ELIGIBILITY.—

"(1) ACCOMMODATION OF TECHNOLOGY.—The limitations on liability established by this section shall apply to a service provider only if the service provider—

"(A) has adopted and reasonably implemented, and informs subscribers and account holders of the service provider's system or network of, a policy that provides for the termination in appropriate circumstances of subscribers and account holders of the service provider's system or network who are repeat infringers; and

"(B) accommodates and does not interfere with standard technical measures.

"(2) DEFINITION.—As used in this subsection, the term 'standard technical measures' means technical measures that

27

are used by copyright owners to identify or protect copyrighted works and—
"(A) have been developed pursuant to a broad consensus of copyright owners and service providers in an open, fair, voluntary, multi-industry standards process;
"(B) are available to any person on reasonable and nondiscriminatory terms; and
"(C) do not impose substantial costs on service providers or substantial burdens on their systems or networks.
"(j) INJUNCTIONS.—The following rules shall apply in the case of any application for an injunction under section 502 against a service provider that is not subject to monetary remedies under this section:
"(1) SCOPE OF RELIEF.—(A) With respect to conduct other than that which qualifies for the limitation on remedies set forth in subsection (a), the court may grant injunctive relief with respect to a service provider only in one or more of the following forms:
"(i) An order restraining the service provider from providing access to infringing material or activity residing at a particular online site on the provider's system or network.
"(ii) An order restraining the service provider from providing access to a subscriber or account holder of the service provider's system or network who is engaging in infringing activity and is identified in the order, by terminating the accounts of the subscriber or account holder that are specified in the order.
"(iii) Such other injunctive relief as the court may consider necessary to prevent or restrain infringement of copyrighted material specified in the order of the court at a particular online location, if such relief is the least burdensome to the service provider among the forms of relief comparably effective for that purpose.
"(B) If the service provider qualifies for the limitation on remedies described in subsection (a), the court may only grant injunctive relief in one or both of the following forms:
"(i) An order restraining the service provider from providing access to a subscriber or account holder of the service provider's system or network who is using the provider's service to engage in infringing activity and is identified in the order, by terminating the accounts of the subscriber or account holder that are specified in the order.
"(ii) An order restraining the service provider from providing access, by taking reasonable steps specified in the order to block access, to a specific, identified, online location outside the United States.
"(2) CONSIDERATIONS.—The court, in considering the relevant criteria for injunctive relief under applicable law, shall consider—
"(A) whether such an injunction, either alone or in combination with other such injunctions issued against the same service provider under this subsection, would significantly burden either the provider or the operation of the provider's system or network;

28

"(B) the magnitude of the harm likely to be suffered by the copyright owner in the digital network environment if steps are not taken to prevent or restrain the infringement;

"(C) whether implementation of such an injunction would be technically feasible and effective, and would not interfere with access to noninfringing material at other online locations; and

"(D) whether other less burdensome and comparably effective means of preventing or restraining access to the infringing material are available.

"(3) NOTICE AND EX PARTE ORDERS.—Injunctive relief under this subsection shall be available only after notice to the service provider and an opportunity for the service provider to appear are provided, except for orders ensuring the preservation of evidence or other orders having no material adverse effect on the operation of the service provider's communications network.

"(k) DEFINITIONS.—

"(1) SERVICE PROVIDER.—(A) As used in subsection (a), the term 'service provider' means an entity offering the transmission, routing, or providing of connections for digital online communications, between or among points specified by a user, of material of the user's choosing, without modification to the content of the material as sent or received.

"(B) As used in this section, other than subsection (a), the term 'service provider' means a provider of online services or network access, or the operator of facilities therefor, and includes an entity described in subparagraph (A).

"(2) MONETARY RELIEF.—As used in this section, the term 'monetary relief' means damages, costs, attorneys' fees, and any other form of monetary payment.

"(l) OTHER DEFENSES NOT AFFECTED.—The failure of a service provider's conduct to qualify for limitation of liability under this section shall not bear adversely upon the consideration of a defense by the service provider that the service provider's conduct is not infringing under this title or any other defense.

"(m) PROTECTION OF PRIVACY.—Nothing in this section shall be construed to condition the applicability of subsections (a) through (d) on—

"(1) a service provider monitoring its service or affirmatively seeking facts indicating infringing activity, except to the extent consistent with a standard technical measure complying with the provisions of subsection (i); or

"(2) a service provider gaining access to, removing, or disabling access to material in cases in which such conduct is prohibited by law.

"(n) CONSTRUCTION.—Subsections (a), (b), (c), and (d) describe separate and distinct functions for purposes of applying this section. Whether a service provider qualifies for the limitation on liability in any one of those subsections shall be based solely on the criteria in that subsection, and shall not affect a determination of whether that service provider qualifies for the limitations on liability under any other such subsection.".

29

(b) CONFORMING AMENDMENT.—The table of sections for chapter 5 of title 17, United States Code, is amended by adding at the end the following:

"512. Limitations on liability relating to material online.".

SEC. 203. EFFECTIVE DATE.

This title and the amendments made by this title shall take effect on the date of the enactment of this Act.

TITLE III—COMPUTER MAINTENANCE OR REPAIR COPYRIGHT EXEMPTION

SEC. 301. SHORT TITLE.

This title may be cited as the "Computer Maintenance Competition Assurance Act".

SEC. 302. LIMITATIONS ON EXCLUSIVE RIGHTS; COMPUTER PROGRAMS.

Section 117 of title 17, United States Code, is amended—

(1) by striking "Notwithstanding" and inserting the following:

"(a) MAKING OF ADDITIONAL COPY OR ADAPTATION BY OWNER OF COPY.—Notwithstanding";

(2) by striking "Any exact" and inserting the following:

"(b) LEASE, SALE, OR OTHER TRANSFER OF ADDITIONAL COPY OR ADAPTATION.—Any exact"; and

(3) by adding at the end the following:

"(c) MACHINE MAINTENANCE OR REPAIR.—Notwithstanding the provisions of section 106, it is not an infringement for the owner or lessee of a machine to make or authorize the making of a copy of a computer program if such copy is made solely by virtue of the activation of a machine that lawfully contains an authorized copy of the computer program, for purposes only of maintenance or repair of that machine, if—

"(1) such new copy is used in no other manner and is destroyed immediately after the maintenance or repair is completed; and

"(2) with respect to any computer program or part thereof that is not necessary for that machine to be activated, such program or part thereof is not accessed or used other than to make such new copy by virtue of the activation of the machine.

"(d) DEFINITIONS.—For purposes of this section—

"(1) the 'maintenance' of a machine is the servicing of the machine in order to make it work in accordance with its original specifications and any changes to those specifications authorized for that machine; and

"(2) the 'repair' of a machine is the restoring of the machine to the state of working in accordance with its original specifications and any changes to those specifications authorized for that machine.".

TITLE IV—MISCELLANEOUS PROVISIONS

SEC. 401. PROVISIONS RELATING TO THE COMMISSIONER OF PATENTS AND TRADEMARKS AND THE REGISTER OF COPYRIGHTS

(a) COMPENSATION.—(1) Section 3(d) of title 35, United States Code, is amended by striking "prescribed by law for Assistant Sec-

30

retaries of Commerce" and inserting "in effect for level III of the Executive Schedule under section 5314 of title 5, United States Code".

(2) Section 701(e) of title 17, United States Code, is amended—

(A) by striking "IV" and inserting "III"; and

(B) by striking "5315" and inserting "5314".

(3) Section 5314 of title 5, United States Code, is amended by adding at the end the following:

"Assistant Secretary of Commerce and Commissioner of Patents and Trademarks.

"Register of Copyrights.".

(b) CLARIFICATION OF AUTHORITY OF THE COPYRIGHT OFFICE.— Section 701 of title 17, United States Code, is amended—

(1) by redesignating subsections (b) through (e) as subsections (c) through (f), respectively; and

(2) by inserting after subsection (a) the following:

"(b) In addition to the functions and duties set out elsewhere in this chapter, the Register of Copyrights shall perform the following functions:

"(1) Advise Congress on national and international issues relating to copyright, other matters arising under this title, and related matters.

"(2) Provide information and assistance to Federal departments and agencies and the Judiciary on national and international issues relating to copyright, other matters arising under this title, and related matters.

"(3) Participate in meetings of international intergovernmental organizations and meetings with foreign government officials relating to copyright, other matters arising under this title, and related matters, including as a member of United States delegations as authorized by the appropriate Executive branch authority.

"(4) Conduct studies and programs regarding copyright, other matters arising under this title, and related matters, the administration of the Copyright Office, or any function vested in the Copyright Office by law, including educational programs conducted cooperatively with foreign intellectual property offices and international intergovernmental organizations.

"(5) Perform such other functions as Congress may direct, or as may be appropriate in furtherance of the functions and duties specifically set forth in this title."

SEC. 402. EPHEMERAL RECORDINGS.

Section 112(a) of title 17, United States Code, is amended—

(1) by redesignating paragraphs (1), (2), and (3) as subparagraphs (A), (B), and (C), respectively;

(2) by inserting "(1)" after "(a)";

(3) by inserting after "under a license" the following: ", including a statutory license under section 114(f),";

(4) by inserting after "114(a)," the following: "or for a transmitting organization that is a broadcast radio or television station licensed as such by the Federal Communications Commission and that makes a broadcast transmission of a performance of a sound recording in a digital format on a nonsubscription basis,"; and

(5) by adding at the end the following:

31

"(2) In a case in which a transmitting organization entitled to make a copy or phonorecord under paragraph (1) in connection with the transmission to the public of a performance or display of a work is prevented from making such copy or phonorecord by reason of the application by the copyright owner of technical measures that prevent the reproduction of the work, the copyright owner shall make available to the transmitting organization the necessary means for permitting the making of such copy or phonorecord as permitted under that paragraph, if it is technologically feasible and economically reasonable for the copyright owner to do so. If the copyright owner fails to do so in a timely manner in light of the transmitting organization's reasonable business requirements, the transmitting organization shall not be liable for a violation of section 1201(a)(1) of this title for engaging in such activities as are necessary to make such copies or phonorecords as permitted under paragraph (1) of this subsection.".

SEC. 403. LIMITATIONS ON EXCLUSIVE RIGHTS; DISTANCE EDUCATION.

(a) RECOMMENDATIONS BY REGISTER OF COPYRIGHTS.—Not later than 6 months after the date of the enactment of this Act, the Register of Copyrights, after consultation with representatives of copyright owners, nonprofit educational institutions, and nonprofit libraries and archives, shall submit to the Congress recommendations on how to promote distance education through digital technologies, including interactive digital networks, while maintaining an appropriate balance between the rights of copyright owners and the needs of users of copyrighted works. Such recommendations shall include any legislation the Register of Copyrights considers appropriate to achieve the objective described in the preceding sentence.

(b) FACTORS.—In formulating recommendations under subsection (a), the Register of Copyrights shall consider—

(1) the need for an exemption from exclusive rights of copyright owners for distance education through digital networks;

(2) the categories of works to be included under any distance education exemption;

(3) the extent of appropriate quantitative limitations on the portions of works that may be used under any distance education exemption;

(4) the parties who should be entitled to the benefits of any distance education exemption;

(5) the parties who should be designated as eligible recipients of distance education materials under any distance education exemption;

(6) whether and what types of technological measures can or should be employed to safeguard against unauthorized access to, and use or retention of, copyrighted materials as a condition of eligibility for any distance education exemption, including, in light of developing technological capabilities, the exemption set out in section 110(2) of title 17, United States Code;

(7) the extent to which the availability of licenses for the use of copyrighted works in distance education through interactive digital networks should be considered in assessing eligibility for any distance education exemption; and

32

(8) *such other issues relating to distance education through interactive digital networks that the Register considers appropriate.*

SEC. 404. EXEMPTION FOR LIBRARIES AND ARCHIVES.

Section 108 of title 17, United States Code, is amended—

(1) in subsection (a)—

(A) by striking "Notwithstanding" and inserting "Except as otherwise provided in this title and notwithstanding";

(B) by inserting after "no more than one copy or phonorecord of a work" the following: ", except as provided in subsections (b) and (c)"; and

(C) in paragraph (3) by inserting after "copyright" the following: "that appears on the copy or phonorecord that is reproduced under the provisions of this section, or includes a legend stating that the work may be protected by copyright if no such notice can be found on the copy or phonorecord that is reproduced under the provisions of this section";

(2) in subsection (b)—

(A) by striking "a copy or phonorecord" and inserting "three copies or phonorecords";

(B) by striking "in facsimile form"; and

(C) by striking "if the copy or phonorecord reproduced is currently in the collections of the library or archives." and inserting "if—

"(1) the copy or phonorecord reproduced is currently in the collections of the library or archives; and

"(2) any such copy or phonorecord that is reproduced in digital format is not otherwise distributed in that format and is not made available to the public in that format outside the premises of the library or archives."; and

(3) in subsection (c)—

(A) by striking "a copy or phonorecord" and inserting "three copies or phonorecords";

(B) by striking "in facsimile form";

(C) by inserting "or if the existing format in which the work is stored has become obsolete," after "stolen,"; and

(D) by striking "if the library or archives has, after a reasonable effort, determined that an unused replacement cannot be obtained at a fair price." and inserting "if—

"(1) the library or archives has, after a reasonable effort, determined that an unused replacement cannot be obtained at a fair price; and

"(2) any such copy or phonorecord that is reproduced in digital format is not made available to the public in that format outside the premises of the library or archives in lawful possession of such copy."; and

(E) by adding at the end the following:

"For purposes of this subsection, a format shall be considered obsolete if the machine or device necessary to render perceptible a work stored in that format is no longer manufactured or is no longer reasonably available in the commercial marketplace.".

33

SEC. 405. SCOPE OF EXCLUSIVE RIGHTS IN SOUND RECORDINGS; EPHEMERAL RECORDINGS.

(a) SCOPE OF EXCLUSIVE RIGHTS IN SOUND RECORDINGS.—Section 114 of title 17, United States Code, is amended as follows:

(1) Subsection (d) is amended—

(A) in paragraph (1) by striking subparagraph (A) and inserting the following:

"(A) a nonsubscription broadcast transmission;"; and

(B) by amending paragraph (2) to read as follows:

"(2) STATUTORY LICENSING OF CERTAIN TRANSMISSIONS.—The performance of a sound recording publicly by means of a subscription digital audio transmission not exempt under paragraph (1), an eligible nonsubscription transmission, or a transmission not exempt under paragraph (1) that is made by a preexisting satellite digital audio radio service shall be subject to statutory licensing, in accordance with subsection (f) if—

"(A)(i) the transmission is not part of an interactive service;

"(ii) except in the case of a transmission to a business establishment, the transmitting entity does not automatically and intentionally cause any device receiving the transmission to switch from one program channel to another; and

"(iii) except as provided in section 1002(e), the transmission of the sound recording is accompanied, if technically feasible, by the information encoded in that sound recording, if any, by or under the authority of the copyright owner of that sound recording, that identifies the title of the sound recording, the featured recording artist who performs on the sound recording, and related information, including information concerning the underlying musical work and its writer;

"(B) in the case of a subscription transmission not exempt under paragraph (1) that is made by a preexisting subscription service in the same transmission medium used by such service on July 31, 1998, or in the case of a transmission not exempt under paragraph (1) that is made by a preexisting satellite digital audio radio service—

"(i) the transmission does not exceed the sound recording performance complement; and

"(ii) the transmitting entity does not cause to be published by means of an advance program schedule or prior announcement the titles of the specific sound recordings or phonorecords embodying such sound recordings to be transmitted; and

"(C) in the case of an eligible nonsubscription transmission or a subscription transmission not exempt under paragraph (1) that is made by a new subscription service or by a preexisting subscription service other than in the same transmission medium used by such service on July 31, 1998—

"(i) the transmission does not exceed the sound recording performance complement, except that this requirement shall not apply in the case of a retrans-

34

mission of a broadcast transmission if the retransmission is made by a transmitting entity that does not have the right or ability to control the programming of the broadcast station making the broadcast transmission, unless—

"(I) the broadcast station makes broadcast transmissions—

"(aa) in digital format that regularly exceed the sound recording performance complement; or

"(bb) in analog format, a substantial portion of which, on a weekly basis, exceed the sound recording performance complement; and

"(II) the sound recording copyright owner or its representative has notified the transmitting entity in writing that broadcast transmissions of the copyright owner's sound recordings exceed the sound recording performance complement as provided in this clause;

"(ii) the transmitting entity does not cause to be published, or induce or facilitate the publication, by means of an advance program schedule or prior announcement, the titles of the specific sound recordings to be transmitted, the phonorecords embodying such sound recordings, or, other than for illustrative purposes, the names of the featured recording artists, except that this clause does not disqualify a transmitting entity that makes a prior announcement that a particular artist will be featured within an unspecified future time period, and in the case of a retransmission of a broadcast transmission by a transmitting entity that does not have the right or ability to control the programming of the broadcast transmission, the requirement of this clause shall not apply to a prior oral announcement by the broadcast station, or to an advance program schedule published, induced, or facilitated by the broadcast station, if the transmitting entity does not have actual knowledge and has not received written notice from the copyright owner or its representative that the broadcast station publishes or induces or facilitates the publication of such advance program schedule, or if such advance program schedule is a schedule of classical music programming published by the broadcast station in the same manner as published by that broadcast station on or before September 30, 1998;

"(iii) the transmission—

"(I) is not part of an archived program of less than 5 hours duration;

"(II) is not part of an archived program of 5 hours or greater in duration that is made available for a period exceeding 2 weeks;

"(III) is not part of a continuous program which is of less than 3 hours duration; or

35

"*(IV) is not part of an identifiable program in which performances of sound recordings are rendered in a predetermined order, other than an archived or continuous program, that is transmitted at—*

"*(aa) more than 3 times in any 2-week period that have been publicly announced in advance, in the case of a program of less than 1 hour in duration, or*

"*(bb) more than 4 times in any 2-week period that have been publicly announced in advance, in the case of a program of 1 hour or more in duration,*

except that the requirement of this subclause shall not apply in the case of a retransmission of a broadcast transmission by a transmitting entity that does not have the right or ability to control the programming of the broadcast transmission, unless the transmitting entity is given notice in writing by the copyright owner of the sound recording that the broadcast station makes broadcast transmissions that regularly violate such requirement;

"*(iv) the transmitting entity does not knowingly perform the sound recording, as part of a service that offers transmissions of visual images contemporaneously with transmissions of sound recordings, in a manner that is likely to cause confusion, to cause mistake, or to deceive, as to the affiliation, connection, or association of the copyright owner or featured recording artist with the transmitting entity or a particular product or service advertised by the transmitting entity, or as to the origin, sponsorship, or approval by the copyright owner or featured recording artist of the activities of the transmitting entity other than the performance of the sound recording itself;*

"*(v) the transmitting entity cooperates to prevent, to the extent feasible without imposing substantial costs or burdens, a transmission recipient or any other person or entity from automatically scanning the transmitting entity's transmissions alone or together with transmissions by other transmitting entities in order to select a particular sound recording to be transmitted to the transmission recipient, except that the requirement of this clause shall not apply to a satellite digital audio service that is in operation, or that is licensed by the Federal Communications Commission, on or before July 31, 1998;*

"*(vi) the transmitting entity takes no affirmative steps to cause or induce the making of a phonorecord by the transmission recipient, and if the technology used by the transmitting entity enables the transmitting entity to limit the making by the transmission recipient of phonorecords of the transmission directly in*

36

a digital format, the transmitting entity sets such technology to limit such making of phonorecords to the extent permitted by such technology;

"(vii) phonorecords of the sound recording have been distributed to the public under the authority of the copyright owner or the copyright owner authorizes the transmitting entity to transmit the sound recording, and the transmitting entity makes the transmission from a phonorecord lawfully made under the authority of the copyright owner, except that the requirement of this clause shall not apply to a retransmission of a broadcast transmission by a transmitting entity that does not have the right or ability to control the programming of the broadcast transmission, unless the transmitting entity is given notice in writing by the copyright owner of the sound recording that the broadcast station makes broadcast transmissions that regularly violate such requirement;

"(viii) the transmitting entity accommodates and does not interfere with the transmission of technical measures that are widely used by sound recording copyright owners to identify or protect copyrighted works, and that are technically feasible of being transmitted by the transmitting entity without imposing substantial costs on the transmitting entity or resulting in perceptible aural or visual degradation of the digital signal, except that the requirement of this clause shall not apply to a satellite digital audio service that is in operation, or that is licensed under the authority of the Federal Communications Commission, on or before July 31, 1998, to the extent that such service has designed, developed, or made commitments to procure equipment or technology that is not compatible with such technical measures before such technical measures are widely adopted by sound recording copyright owners; and

"(ix) the transmitting entity identifies in textual data the sound recording during, but not before, the time it is performed, including the title of the sound recording, the title of the phonorecord embodying such sound recording, if any, and the featured recording artist, in a manner to permit it to be displayed to the transmission recipient by the device or technology intended for receiving the service provided by the transmitting entity, except that the obligation in this clause shall not take effect until 1 year after the date of the enactment of the Digital Millennium Copyright Act and shall not apply in the case of a retransmission of a broadcast transmission by a transmitting entity that does not have the right or ability to control the programming of the broadcast transmission, or in the case in which devices or technology intended for receiving the service provided by the transmitting entity that

37

have the capability to display such textual data are not common in the marketplace.".

(2) Subsection (f) is amended—

(A) in the subsection heading by striking "NONEXEMPT SUBSCRIPTION" and inserting "CERTAIN NONEXEMPT";

(B) in paragraph (1)—

(i) in the first sentence—

(I) by striking "(1) No" and inserting "(1)(A) No";

(II) by striking "the activities" and inserting "subscription transmissions by preexisting subscription services and transmissions by preexisting satellite digital audio radio services"; and

(III) by striking "2000" and inserting "2001"; and

(ii) by amending the third sentence to read as follows: "Any copyright owners of sound recordings, preexisting subscription services, or preexisting satellite digital audio radio services may submit to the Librarian of Congress licenses covering such subscription transmissions with respect to such sound recordings."; and

(C) by striking paragraphs (2), (3), (4), and (5) and inserting the following:

"(B) In the absence of license agreements negotiated under subparagraph (A), during the 60-day period commencing 6 months after publication of the notice specified in subparagraph (A), and upon the filing of a petition in accordance with section 803(a)(1), the Librarian of Congress shall, pursuant to chapter 8, convene a copyright arbitration royalty panel to determine and publish in the Federal Register a schedule of rates and terms which, subject to paragraph (3), shall be binding on all copyright owners of sound recordings and entities performing sound recordings affected by this paragraph. In establishing rates and terms for preexisting subscription services and preexisting satellite digital audio radio services, in addition to the objectives set forth in section 801(b)(1), the copyright arbitration royalty panel may consider the rates and terms for comparable types of subscription digital audio transmission services and comparable circumstances under voluntary license agreements negotiated as provided in subparagraph (A).

"(C)(i) Publication of a notice of the initiation of voluntary negotiation proceedings as specified in subparagraph (A) shall be repeated, in accordance with regulations that the Librarian of Congress shall prescribe—

"(I) no later than 30 days after a petition is filed by any copyright owners of sound recordings, any preexisting subscription services, or any preexisting satellite digital audio radio services indicating that a new type of subscription digital audio transmission service on which sound recordings are performed is or is about to become operational; and

"(II) in the first week of January, 2001, and at 5-year intervals thereafter.

38

"(ii) The procedures specified in subparagraph (B) shall be repeated, in accordance with regulations that the Librarian of Congress shall prescribe, upon filing of a petition in accordance with section 803(a)(1) during a 60-day period commencing—

"(I) 6 months after publication of a notice of the initiation of voluntary negotiation proceedings under subparagraph (A) pursuant to a petition under clause (i)(I) of this subparagraph; or

"(II) on July 1, 2001, and at 5-year intervals thereafter.

"(iii) The procedures specified in subparagraph (B) shall be concluded in accordance with section 802.

"(2)(A) No later than 30 days after the date of the enactment of the Digital Millennium Copyright Act, the Librarian of Congress shall cause notice to be published in the Federal Register of the initiation of voluntary negotiation proceedings for the purpose of determining reasonable terms and rates of royalty payments for public performances of sound recordings by means of eligible nonsubscription transmissions and transmissions by new subscription services specified by subsection (d)(2) during the period beginning on the date of the enactment of such Act and ending on December 31, 2000, or such other date as the parties may agree. Such rates and terms shall distinguish among the different types of eligible nonsubscription transmission services and new subscription services then in operation and shall include a minimum fee for each such type of service. Any copyright owners of sound recordings or any entities performing sound recordings affected by this paragraph may submit to the Librarian of Congress licenses covering such eligible nonsubscription transmissions and new subscription services with respect to such sound recordings. The parties to each negotiation proceeding shall bear their own costs.

"(B) In the absence of license agreements negotiated under subparagraph (A), during the 60-day period commencing 6 months after publication of the notice specified in subparagraph (A), and upon the filing of a petition in accordance with section 803(a)(1), the Librarian of Congress shall, pursuant to chapter 8, convene a copyright arbitration royalty panel to determine and publish in the Federal Register a schedule of rates and terms which, subject to paragraph (3), shall be binding on all copyright owners of sound recordings and entities performing sound recordings affected by this paragraph during the period beginning on the date of the enactment of the Digital Millennium Copyright Act and ending on December 31, 2000, or such other date as the parties may agree. Such rates and terms shall distinguish among the different types of eligible nonsubscription transmission services then in operation and shall include a minimum fee for each such type of service, such differences to be based on criteria including, but not limited to, the quantity and nature of the use of sound recordings and the degree to which use of the service may substitute for or may promote the purchase of phonorecords by consumers. In establishing rates and terms for transmissions by eligible nonsubscription services and new subscription services, the copyright arbitration royalty panel shall establish rates and terms that most clearly rep-

39

resent the rates and terms that would have been negotiated in the marketplace between a willing buyer and a willing seller. In determining such rates and terms, the copyright arbitration royalty panel shall base its decision on economic, competitive and programming information presented by the parties, including—

"(i) whether use of the service may substitute for or may promote the sales of phonorecords or otherwise may interfere with or may enhance the sound recording copyright owner's other streams of revenue from its sound recordings; and

"(ii) the relative roles of the copyright owner and the transmitting entity in the copyrighted work and the service made available to the public with respect to relative creative contribution, technological contribution, capital investment, cost, and risk.

In establishing such rates and terms, the copyright arbitration royalty panel may consider the rates and terms for comparable types of digital audio transmission services and comparable circumstances under voluntary license agreements negotiated under subparagraph (A).

"(C)(i) Publication of a notice of the initiation of voluntary negotiation proceedings as specified in subparagraph (A) shall be repeated in accordance with regulations that the Librarian of Congress shall prescribe—

"(I) no later than 30 days after a petition is filed by any copyright owners of sound recordings or any eligible nonsubscription service or new subscription service indicating that a new type of eligible nonsubscription service or new subscription service on which sound recordings are performed is or is about to become operational; and

"(II) in the first week of January 2000, and at 2-year intervals thereafter, except to the extent that different years for the repeating of such proceedings may be determined in accordance with subparagraph (A).

"(ii) The procedures specified in subparagraph (B) shall be repeated, in accordance with regulations that the Librarian of Congress shall prescribe, upon filing of a petition in accordance with section 803(a)(1) during a 60-day period commencing—

"(I) 6 months after publication of a notice of the initiation of voluntary negotiation proceedings under subparagraph (A) pursuant to a petition under clause (i)(I); or

"(II) on July 1, 2000, and at 2-year intervals thereafter, except to the extent that different years for the repeating of such proceedings may be determined in accordance with subparagraph (A).

"(iii) The procedures specified in subparagraph (B) shall be concluded in accordance with section 802.

"(3) License agreements voluntarily negotiated at any time between 1 or more copyright owners of sound recordings and 1 or more entities performing sound recordings shall be given effect in lieu of any determination by a copyright arbitration royalty panel or decision by the Librarian of Congress.

40

"(4)(A) The Librarian of Congress shall also establish requirements by which copyright owners may receive reasonable notice of the use of their sound recordings under this section, and under which records of such use shall be kept and made available by entities performing sound recordings.

"(B) Any person who wishes to perform a sound recording publicly by means of a transmission eligible for statutory licensing under this subsection may do so without infringing the exclusive right of the copyright owner of the sound recording—

"(i) by complying with such notice requirements as the Librarian of Congress shall prescribe by regulation and by paying royalty fees in accordance with this subsection; or

"(ii) if such royalty fees have not been set, by agreeing to pay such royalty fees as shall be determined in accordance with this subsection.

"(C) Any royalty payments in arrears shall be made on or before the twentieth day of the month next succeeding the month in which the royalty fees are set.".

(3) Subsection (g) is amended—

(A) in the subsection heading by striking "SUBSCRIPTION";

(B) in paragraph (1) in the matter preceding subparagraph (A), by striking "subscription transmission licensed" and inserting "transmission licensed under a statutory license";

(C) in subparagraphs (A) and (B) by striking "subscription"; and

(D) in paragraph (2) by striking "subscription".

(4) Subsection (j) is amended—

(A) by striking paragraphs (4) and (9) and redesignating paragraphs (2), (3), (5), (6), (7), and (8) as paragraphs (3), (5), (9), (12), (13), and (14), respectively;

(B) by inserting after paragraph (1) the following:

"(2) An 'archived program' is a predetermined program that is available repeatedly on the demand of the transmission recipient and that is performed in the same order from the beginning, except that an archived program shall not include a recorded event or broadcast transmission that makes no more than an incidental use of sound recordings, as long as such recorded event or broadcast transmission does not contain an entire sound recording or feature a particular sound recording.";

(C) by inserting after paragraph (3), as so redesignated, the following:

"(4) A 'continuous program' is a predetermined program that is continuously performed in the same order and that is accessed at a point in the program that is beyond the control of the transmission recipient.";

(D) by inserting after paragraph (5), as so redesignated, the following:

"(6) An 'eligible nonsubscription transmission' is a noninteractive nonsubscription digital audio transmission not exempt under subsection (d)(1) that is made as part of a service that provides audio programming consisting, in whole or in part, of performances of sound recordings, including retrans-

41

missions of broadcast transmissions, if the primary purpose of the service is to provide to the public such audio or other entertainment programming, and the primary purpose of the service is not to sell, advertise, or promote particular products or services other than sound recordings, live concerts, or other music-related events.

"(7) An 'interactive service' is one that enables a member of the public to receive a transmission of a program specially created for the recipient, or on request, a transmission of a particular sound recording, whether or not as part of a program, which is selected by or on behalf of the recipient. The ability of individuals to request that particular sound recordings be performed for reception by the public at large, or in the case of a subscription service, by all subscribers of the service, does not make a service interactive, if the programming on each channel of the service does not substantially consist of sound recordings that are performed within 1 hour of the request or at a time designated by either the transmitting entity or the individual making such request. If an entity offers both interactive and noninteractive services (either concurrently or at different times), the noninteractive component shall not be treated as part of an interactive service.

"(8) A 'new subscription service' is a service that performs sound recordings by means of noninteractive subscription digital audio transmissions and that is not a preexisting subscription service or a preexisting satellite digital audio radio service.";

(E) by inserting after paragraph (9), as so redesignated, the following:

"(10) A 'preexisting satellite digital audio radio service' is a subscription satellite digital audio radio service provided pursuant to a satellite digital audio radio service license issued by the Federal Communications Commission on or before July 31, 1998, and any renewal of such license to the extent of the scope of the original license, and may include a limited number of sample channels representative of the subscription service that are made available on a nonsubscription basis in order to promote the subscription service.

"(11) A 'preexisting subscription service' is a service that performs sound recordings by means of noninteractive audio-only subscription digital audio transmissions, which was in existence and was making such transmissions to the public for a fee on or before July 31, 1998, and may include a limited number of sample channels representative of the subscription service that are made available on a nonsubscription basis in order to promote the subscription service."; and

(F) by adding at the end the following:

"(15) A 'transmission' is either an initial transmission or a retransmission.".

(5) The amendment made by paragraph (2)(B)(i)(III) of this subsection shall be deemed to have been enacted as part of the Digital Performance Right in Sound Recordings Act of 1995, and the publication of notice of proceedings under section 114(f)(1) of title 17, United States Code, as in effect upon the

42

effective date of that Act, for the determination of royalty payments shall be deemed to have been made for the period beginning on the effective date of that Act and ending on December 1, 2001.

(6) The amendments made by this subsection do not annul, limit, or otherwise impair the rights that are preserved by section 114 of title 17, United States Code, including the rights preserved by subsections (c), (d)(4), and (i) of such section.

(b) EPHEMERAL RECORDINGS.—Section 112 of title 17, United States Code, is amended—

(1) by redesignating subsection (e) as subsection (f); and

(2) by inserting after subsection (d) the following:

"(e) STATUTORY LICENSE.—(1) A transmitting organization entitled to transmit to the public a performance of a sound recording under the limitation on exclusive rights specified by section 114(d)(1)(C)(iv) or under a statutory license in accordance with section 114(f) is entitled to a statutory license, under the conditions specified by this subsection, to make no more than 1 phonorecord of the sound recording (unless the terms and conditions of the statutory license allow for more), if the following conditions are satisfied:

"(A) The phonorecord is retained and used solely by the transmitting organization that made it, and no further phonorecords are reproduced from it.

"(B) The phonorecord is used solely for the transmitting organization's own transmissions originating in the United States under a statutory license in accordance with section 114(f) or the limitation on exclusive rights specified by section 114(d)(1)(C)(iv).

"(C) Unless preserved exclusively for purposes of archival preservation, the phonorecord is destroyed within 6 months from the date the sound recording was first transmitted to the public using the phonorecord.

"(D) Phonorecords of the sound recording have been distributed to the public under the authority of the copyright owner or the copyright owner authorizes the transmitting entity to transmit the sound recording, and the transmitting entity makes the phonorecord under this subsection from a phonorecord lawfully made and acquired under the authority of the copyright owner.

"(3) Notwithstanding any provision of the antitrust laws, any copyright owners of sound recordings and any transmitting organizations entitled to a statutory license under this subsection may negotiate and agree upon royalty rates and license terms and conditions for making phonorecords of such sound recordings under this section and the proportionate division of fees paid among copyright owners, and may designate common agents to negotiate, agree to, pay, or receive such royalty payments.

"(4) No later than 30 days after the date of the enactment of the Digital Millennium Copyright Act, the Librarian of Congress shall cause notice to be published in the Federal Register of the initiation of voluntary negotiation proceedings for the purpose of determining reasonable terms and rates of royalty payments for the activities specified by paragraph (2) of this subsection during the period beginning on the date of the enactment of such Act and ending on December 31, 2000, or such other date as the parties may agree. Such

43

rates shall include a minimum fee for each type of service offered by transmitting organizations. Any copyright owners of sound recordings or any transmitting organizations entitled to a statutory license under this subsection may submit to the Librarian of Congress licenses covering such activities with respect to such sound recordings. The parties to each negotiation proceeding shall bear their own costs.

"(5) In the absence of license agreements negotiated under paragraph (3), during the 60-day period commencing 6 months after publication of the notice specified in paragraph (4), and upon the filing of a petition in accordance with section 803(a)(1), the Librarian of Congress shall, pursuant to chapter 8, convene a copyright arbitration royalty panel to determine and publish in the Federal Register a schedule of reasonable rates and terms which, subject to paragraph (6), shall be binding on all copyright owners of sound recordings and transmitting organizations entitled to a statutory license under this subsection during the period beginning on the date of the enactment of the Digital Millennium Copyright Act and ending on December 31, 2000, or such other date as the parties may agree. Such rates shall include a minimum fee for each type of service offered by transmitting organizations. The copyright arbitration royalty panel shall establish rates that most clearly represent the fees that would have been negotiated in the marketplace between a willing buyer and a willing seller. In determining such rates and terms, the copyright arbitration royalty panel shall base its decision on economic, competitive, and programming information presented by the parties, including—

"(A) whether use of the service may substitute for or may promote the sales of phonorecords or otherwise interferes with or enhances the copyright owner's traditional streams of revenue; and

"(B) the relative roles of the copyright owner and the transmitting organization in the copyrighted work and the service made available to the public with respect to relative creative contribution, technological contribution, capital investment, cost, and risk.

In establishing such rates and terms, the copyright arbitration royalty panel may consider the rates and terms under voluntary license agreements negotiated as provided in paragraphs (3) and (4). The Librarian of Congress shall also establish requirements by which copyright owners may receive reasonable notice of the use of their sound recordings under this section, and under which records of such use shall be kept and made available by transmitting organizations entitled to obtain a statutory license under this subsection.

"(6) License agreements voluntarily negotiated at any time between 1 or more copyright owners of sound recordings and 1 or more transmitting organizations entitled to obtain a statutory license under this subsection shall be given effect in lieu of any determination by a copyright arbitration royalty panel or decision by the Librarian of Congress.

"(7) Publication of a notice of the initiation of voluntary negotiation proceedings as specified in paragraph (4) shall be repeated, in accordance with regulations that the Librarian of Congress shall prescribe, in the first week of January 2000, and at 2-year intervals

44

thereafter, except to the extent that different years for the repeating of such proceedings may be determined in accordance with paragraph (4). The procedures specified in paragraph (5) shall be repeated, in accordance with regulations that the Librarian of Congress shall prescribe, upon filing of a petition in accordance with section 803(a)(1), during a 60-day period commencing on July 1, 2000, and at 2-year intervals thereafter, except to the extent that different years for the repeating of such proceedings may be determined in accordance with paragraph (4). The procedures specified in paragraph (5) shall be concluded in accordance with section 802.

"(8)(A) Any person who wishes to make a phonorecord of a sound recording under a statutory license in accordance with this subsection may do so without infringing the exclusive right of the copyright owner of the sound recording under section 106(1)—

"(i) by complying with such notice requirements as the Librarian of Congress shall prescribe by regulation and by paying royalty fees in accordance with this subsection; or

"(ii) if such royalty fees have not been set, by agreeing to pay such royalty fees as shall be determined in accordance with this subsection.

"(B) Any royalty payments in arrears shall be made on or before the 20th day of the month next succeeding the month in which the royalty fees are set.

"(9) If a transmitting organization entitled to make a phonorecord under this subsection is prevented from making such phonorecord by reason of the application by the copyright owner of technical measures that prevent the reproduction of the sound recording, the copyright owner shall make available to the transmitting organization the necessary means for permitting the making of such phonorecord as permitted under this subsection, if it is technologically feasible and economically reasonable for the copyright owner to do so. If the copyright owner fails to do so in a timely manner in light of the transmitting organization's reasonable business requirements, the transmitting organization shall not be liable for a violation of section 1201(a)(1) of this title for engaging in such activities as are necessary to make such phonorecords as permitted under this subsection.

"(10) Nothing in this subsection annuls, limits, impairs, or otherwise affects in any way the existence or value of any of the exclusive rights of the copyright owners in a sound recording, except as otherwise provided in this subsection, or in a musical work, including the exclusive rights to reproduce and distribute a sound recording or musical work, including by means of a digital phonorecord delivery, under section 106(1), 106(3), and 115, and the right to perform publicly a sound recording or musical work, including by means of a digital audio transmission, under sections 106(4) and 106(6).".

(c) SCOPE OF SECTION 112(a) OF TITLE 17 NOT AFFECTED.— Nothing in this section or the amendments made by this section shall affect the scope of section 112(a) of title 17, United States Code, or the entitlement of any person to an exemption thereunder.

(d) PROCEDURAL AMENDMENTS TO CHAPTER 8.—Section 802 of title 17, United States Code, is amended—

(1) in subsection (f)—

45

    (A) in the first sentence by striking "60" and inserting "90"; and

    (B) in the third sentence by striking "that 60-day period" and inserting "an additional 30-day period"; and

    (2) in subsection (g) by inserting after the second sentence the following: "When this title provides that the royalty rates or terms that were previously in effect are to expire on a specified date, any adjustment by the Librarian of those rates or terms shall be effective as of the day following the date of expiration of the rates or terms that were previously in effect, even if the Librarian's decision is rendered on a later date.".

    (e) CONFORMING AMENDMENTS.—(1) Section 801(b)(1) of title 17, United States Code, is amended in the second sentence by striking "sections 114, 115, and 116" and inserting "sections 114(f)(1)(B), 115, and 116".

    (2) Section 802(c) of title 17, United States Code, is amended by striking "section 111, 114, 116, or 119, any person entitled to a compulsory license" and inserting "section 111, 112, 114, 116, or 119, any transmitting organization entitled to a statutory license under section 112(f), any person entitled to a statutory license".

    (3) Section 802(g) of title 17, United States Code, is amended by striking "sections 111, 114" and inserting "sections 111, 112, 114".

    (4) Section 802(h)(2) of title 17, United States Code, is amended by striking "section 111, 114" and inserting "section 111, 112, 114".

    (5) Section 803(a)(1) of title 17, United States Code, is amended by striking "sections 114, 115" and inserting "sections 112, 114, 115".

    (6) Section 803(a)(5) of title 17, United States Code, is amended—

    (A) by striking "section 114" and inserting "section 112 or 114"; and

    (B) by striking "that section" and inserting "those sections".

SEC. 406. ASSUMPTION OF CONTRACTUAL OBLIGATIONS RELATED TO TRANSFERS OF RIGHTS IN MOTION PICTURES.

    (a) IN GENERAL.—Part VI of title 28, United States Code, is amended by adding at the end the following new chapter:

"CHAPTER 180—ASSUMPTION OF CERTAIN CONTRACTUAL OBLIGATIONS

"*Sec. 4001. Assumption of contractual obligations related to transfers of rights in motion pictures.*

"§ 4001. Assumption of contractual obligations related to transfers of rights in motion pictures

    "(a) ASSUMPTION OF OBLIGATIONS.—(1) In the case of a transfer of copyright ownership under United States law in a motion picture (as the terms 'transfer of copyright ownership' and 'motion picture' are defined in section 101 of title 17) that is produced subject to 1 or more collective bargaining agreements negotiated under the laws of the United States, if the transfer is executed on or after the effective date of this chapter and is not limited to public performance rights, the transfer instrument shall be deemed to incorporate the

46

assumption agreements applicable to the copyright ownership being transferred that are required by the applicable collective bargaining agreement, and the transferee shall be subject to the obligations under each such assumption agreement to make residual payments and provide related notices, accruing after the effective date of the transfer and applicable to the exploitation of the rights transferred, and any remedies under each such assumption agreement for breach of those obligations, as those obligations and remedies are set forth in the applicable collective bargaining agreement, if—

"(A) the transferee knows or has reason to know at the time of the transfer that such collective bargaining agreement was or will be applicable to the motion picture; or

"(B) in the event of a court order confirming an arbitration award against the transferor under the collective bargaining agreement, the transferor does not have the financial ability to satisfy the award within 90 days after the order is issued.

"(2) For purposes of paragraph (1)(A), 'knows or has reason to know' means any of the following:

"(A) Actual knowledge that the collective bargaining agreement was or will be applicable to the motion picture.

"(B)(i) Constructive knowledge that the collective bargaining agreement was or will be applicable to the motion picture, arising from recordation of a document pertaining to copyright in the motion picture under section 205 of title 17 or from publication, at a site available to the public on-line that is operated by the relevant union, of information that identifies the motion picture as subject to a collective bargaining agreement with that union, if the site permits commercially reasonable verification of the date on which the information was available for access.

"(ii) Clause (i) applies only if the transfer referred to in subsection (a)(1) occurs—

"(i) after the motion picture is completed, or

"(ii) before the motion picture is completed and—

"(I) within 18 months before the filing of an application for copyright registration for the motion picture under section 408 of title 17, or

"(II) if no such application is filed, within 18 months before the first publication of the motion picture in the United States.

"(C) Awareness of other facts and circumstances pertaining to a particular transfer from which it is apparent that the collective bargaining agreement was or will be applicable to the motion picture.

"(b) SCOPE OF EXCLUSION OF TRANSFERS OF PUBLIC PERFORMANCE RIGHTS.—For purposes of this section, the exclusion under subsection (a) of transfers of copyright ownership in a motion picture that are limited to public performance rights includes transfers to a terrestrial broadcast station, cable system, or programmer to the extent that the station, system, or programmer is functioning as an exhibitor of the motion picture, either by exhibiting the motion picture on its own network, system, service, or station, or by initiating the transmission of an exhibition that is carried on another network, system, service, or station. When a terrestrial broadcast station, cable system, or programmer, or other transferee, is also func-

47

tioning otherwise as a distributor or as a producer of the motion picture, the public performance exclusion does not affect any obligations imposed on the transferee to the extent that it is engaging in such functions.

"(c) EXCLUSION FOR GRANTS OF SECURITY INTERESTS.—Subsection (a) shall not apply to—

"(1) a transfer of copyright ownership consisting solely of a mortgage, hypothecation, or other security interest; or

"(2) a subsequent transfer of the copyright ownership secured by the security interest described in paragraph (1) by or under the authority of the secured party, including a transfer through the exercise of the secured party's rights or remedies as a secured party, or by a subsequent transferee.

The exclusion under this subsection shall not affect any rights or remedies under law or contract.

"(d) DEFERRAL PENDING RESOLUTION OF BONA FIDE DISPUTE.—A transferee on which obligations are imposed under subsection (a) by virtue of paragraph (1) of that subsection may elect to defer performance of such obligations that are subject to a bona fide dispute between a union and a prior transferor until that dispute is resolved, except that such deferral shall not stay accrual of any union claims due under an applicable collective bargaining agreement.

"(e) SCOPE OF OBLIGATIONS DETERMINED BY PRIVATE AGREEMENT.—Nothing in this section shall expand or diminish the rights, obligations, or remedies of any person under the collective bargaining agreements or assumption agreements referred to in this section.

"(f) FAILURE TO NOTIFY.—If the transferor under subsection (a) fails to notify the transferee under subsection (a) of applicable collective bargaining obligations before the execution of the transfer instrument, and subsection (a) is made applicable to the transferee solely by virtue of subsection (a)(1)(B), the transferor shall be liable to the transferee for any damages suffered by the transferee as a result of the failure to notify.

"(g) DETERMINATION OF DISPUTES AND CLAIMS.—Any dispute concerning the application of subsections (a) through (f) shall be determined by an action in United States district court, and the court in its discretion may allow the recovery of full costs by or against any party and may also award a reasonable attorney's fee to the prevailing party as part of the costs.

"(h) STUDY.—The Comptroller General, in consultation with the Register of Copyrights, shall conduct a study of the conditions in the motion picture industry that gave rise to this section, and the impact of this section on the motion picture industry. The Comptroller General shall report the findings of the study to the Congress within 2 years after the effective date of this chapter.".

(b) CONFORMING AMENDMENT.—The table of chapters for part VI of title 28, United States Code, is amended by adding at the end the following:

"180. Assumption of Certain Contractual Obligations .... 4001".

SEC. 407. EFFECTIVE DATE.

Except as otherwise provided in this title, this title and the amendments made by this title shall take effect on the date of the enactment of this Act.

48

TITLE V—PROTECTION OF CERTAIN ORIGINAL DESIGNS

SEC. 501. SHORT TITLE.

This Act may be referred to as the "Vessel Hull Design Protection Act".

SEC. 502. PROTECTION OF CERTAIN ORIGINAL DESIGNS.

Title 17, United States Code, is amended by adding at the end the following new chapter:

"CHAPTER 13—PROTECTION OF ORIGINAL DESIGNS

"§ 1301. Designs protected

"(a) DESIGNS PROTECTED.—

"(1) IN GENERAL.—The designer or other owner of an original design of a useful article which makes the article attractive or distinctive in appearance to the purchasing or using public may secure the protection provided by this chapter upon complying with and subject to this chapter.

"(2) VESSEL HULLS.—The design of a vessel hull, including a plug or mold, is subject to protection under this chapter, notwithstanding section 1302(4).

"(b) DEFINITIONS.—For the purpose of this chapter, the following terms have the following meanings:

"(1) A design is 'original' if it is the result of the designer's creative endeavor that provides a distinguishable variation over prior work pertaining to similar articles which is more than merely trivial and has not been copied from another source.

"(2) A 'useful article' is a vessel hull, including a plug or mold, which in normal use has an intrinsic utilitarian function that is not merely to portray the appearance of the article or to convey information. An article which normally is part of a useful article shall be deemed to be a useful article.

"(3) A 'vessel' is a craft, especially one larger than a rowboat, designed to navigate on water, but does not include any such craft that exceeds 200 feet in length.

"(4) A 'hull' is the frame or body of a vessel, including the deck of a vessel, exclusive of masts, sails, yards, and rigging.

"(5) A 'plug' means a device or model used to make a mold for the purpose of exact duplication, regardless of whether the device or model has an intrinsic utilitarian function that is not only to portray the appearance of the product or to convey information.

"(6) A 'mold' means a matrix or form in which a substance for material is used, regardless of whether the matrix or form has an intrinsic utilitarian function that is not only to portray the appearance of the product or to convey information.

"§ 1302. Designs not subject to protection

"Protection under this chapter shall not be available for a design that is—

"(1) not original;

"(2) staple or commonplace, such as a standard geometric figure, a familiar symbol, an emblem, or a motif, or another shape, pattern, or configuration which has become standard, common, prevalent, or ordinary;

"(3) different from a design excluded by paragraph (2) only in insignificant details or in elements which are variants commonly used in the relevant trades;

"(4) dictated solely by a utilitarian function of the article that embodies it; or

"(5) embodied in a useful article that was made public by the designer or owner in the United States or a foreign country more than 1 year before the date of the application for registration under this chapter.

"§ 1303. Revisions, adaptations, and rearrangements

"Protection for a design under this chapter shall be available notwithstanding the employment in the design of subject matter excluded from protection under section 1302 if the design is a substantial revision, adaptation, or rearrangement of such subject matter. Such protection shall be independent of any subsisting protection in subject matter employed in the design, and shall not be construed as securing any right to subject matter excluded from protection under this chapter or as extending any subsisting protection under this chapter.

"§ 1304. Commencement of protection

"The protection provided for a design under this chapter shall commence upon the earlier of the date of publication of the registration under section 1313(a) or the date the design is first made public as defined by section 1310(b).

50

"§ 1305. Term of protection

"(a) IN GENERAL.—Subject to subsection (b), the protection provided under this chapter for a design shall continue for a term of 10 years beginning on the date of the commencement of protection under section 1304.

"(b) EXPIRATION.—All terms of protection provided in this section shall run to the end of the calendar year in which they would otherwise expire.

"(c) TERMINATION OF RIGHTS.—Upon expiration or termination of protection in a particular design under this chapter, all rights under this chapter in the design shall terminate, regardless of the number of different articles in which the design may have been used during the term of its protection.

"§ 1306. Design notice

"(a) CONTENTS OF DESIGN NOTICE.—(1) Whenever any design for which protection is sought under this chapter is made public under section 1310(b), the owner of the design shall, subject to the provisions of section 1307, mark it or have it marked legibly with a design notice consisting of—

"(A) the words 'Protected Design', the abbreviation 'Prot'd Des.', or the letter 'D' with a circle, or the symbol *D*;

"(B) the year of the date on which protection for the design commenced; and

"(C) the name of the owner, an abbreviation by which the name can be recognized, or a generally accepted alternative designation of the owner.

Any distinctive identification of the owner may be used for purposes of subparagraph (C) if it has been recorded by the Administrator before the design marked with such identification is registered.

"(2) After registration, the registration number may be used instead of the elements specified in subparagraphs (B) and (C) of paragraph (1).

"(b) LOCATION OF NOTICE.—The design notice shall be so located and applied as to give reasonable notice of design protection while the useful article embodying the design is passing through its normal channels of commerce.

"(c) SUBSEQUENT REMOVAL OF NOTICE.—When the owner of a design has complied with the provisions of this section, protection under this chapter shall not be affected by the removal, destruction, or obliteration by others of the design notice on an article.

"§ 1307. Effect of omission of notice

"(a) ACTIONS WITH NOTICE.—Except as provided in subsection (b), the omission of the notice prescribed in section 1306 shall not cause loss of the protection under this chapter or prevent recovery for infringement under this chapter against any person who, after receiving written notice of the design protection, begins an undertaking leading to infringement under this chapter.

"(b) ACTIONS WITHOUT NOTICE.—The omission of the notice prescribed in section 1306 shall prevent any recovery under section 1323 against a person who began an undertaking leading to infringement under this chapter before receiving written notice of the design protection. No injunction shall be issued under this chapter

51

with respect to such undertaking unless the owner of the design re-imburses that person for any reasonable expenditure or contractual obligation in connection with such undertaking that was incurred before receiving written notice of the design protection, as the court in its discretion directs. The burden of providing written notice of design protection shall be on the owner of the design.

"§ 1308. *Exclusive rights*

"The owner of a design protected under this chapter has the exclusive right to—

"(1) make, have made, or import, for sale or for use in trade, any useful article embodying that design; and

"(2) sell or distribute for sale or for use in trade any useful article embodying that design.

"§ 1309. *Infringement*

"(a) ACTS OF INFRINGEMENT.—Except as provided in subjection (b), it shall be infringement of the exclusive rights in a design protected under this chapter for any person, without the consent of the owner of the design, within the United States and during the term of such protection, to—

"(1) make, have made, or import, for sale or for use in trade, any infringing article as defined in subsection (e); or

"(2) sell or distribute for sale or for use in trade any such infringing article.

"(b) ACTS OF SELLERS AND DISTRIBUTORS.—A seller or distributor of an infringing article who did not make or import the article shall be deemed to have infringed on a design protected under this chapter only if that person—

"(1) induced or acted in collusion with a manufacturer to make, or an importer to import such article, except that merely purchasing or giving an order to purchase such article in the ordinary course of business shall not of itself constitute such inducement or collusion; or

"(2) refused or failed, upon the request of the owner of the design, to make a prompt and full disclosure of that person's source of such article, and that person orders or reorders such article after receiving notice by registered or certified mail of the protection subsisting in the design.

"(c) ACTS WITHOUT KNOWLEDGE.—It shall not be infringement under this section to make, have made, import, sell, or distribute, any article embodying a design which was created without knowledge that a design was protected under this chapter and was copied from such protected design.

"(d) ACTS IN ORDINARY COURSE OF BUSINESS.—A person who incorporates into that person's product of manufacture an infringing article acquired from others in the ordinary course of business, or who, without knowledge of the protected design embodied in an infringing article, makes or processes the infringing article for the account of another person in the ordinary course of business, shall not be deemed to have infringed the rights in that design under this chapter except under a condition contained in paragraph (1) or (2) of subsection (b). Accepting an order or reorder from the source of

52

the infringing article shall be deemed ordering or reordering within the meaning of subsection (b)(2).

"*(e) Infringing Article Defined.*—As used in this section, an 'infringing article' is any article the design of which has been copied from a design protected under this chapter, without the consent of the owner of the protected design. An infringing article is not an illustration or picture of a protected design in an advertisement, book, periodical, newspaper, photograph, broadcast, motion picture, or similar medium. A design shall not be deemed to have been copied from a protected design if it is original and not substantially similar in appearance to a protected design.

"*(f) Establishing Originality.*—The party to any action or proceeding under this chapter who alleges rights under this chapter in a design shall have the burden of establishing the design's originality whenever the opposing party introduces an earlier work which is identical to such design, or so similar as to make prima facie showing that such design was copied from such work.

"*(g) Reproduction for Teaching or Analysis.*—It is not an infringement of the exclusive rights of a design owner for a person to reproduce the design in a useful article or in any other form solely for the purpose of teaching, analyzing, or evaluating the appearance, concepts, or techniques embodied in the design, or the function of the useful article embodying the design.

"§ 1310. *Application for registration*

"*(a) Time Limit for Application for Registration.*—Protection under this chapter shall be lost if application for registration of the design is not made within two years after the date on which the design is first made public.

"*(b) When Design Is Made Public.*—A design is made public when an existing useful article embodying the design is anywhere publicly exhibited, publicly distributed, or offered for sale or sold to the public by the owner of the design or with the owner's consent.

"*(c) Application by Owner of Design.*—Application for registration may be made by the owner of the design.

"*(d) Contents of Application.*—The application for registration shall be made to the Administrator and shall state—

"(1) the name and address of the designer or designers of the design;

"(2) the name and address of the owner if different from the designer;

"(3) the specific name of the useful article embodying the design;

"(4) the date, if any, that the design was first made public, if such date was earlier than the date of the application;

"(5) affirmation that the design has been fixed in a useful article; and

"(6) such other information as may be required by the Administrator.

The application for registration may include a description setting forth the salient features of the design, but the absence of such a description shall not prevent registration under this chapter.

"*(e) Sworn Statement.*—The application for registration shall be accompanied by a statement under oath by the applicant or the

53

applicant's duly authorized agent or representative, setting forth, to the best of the applicant's knowledge and belief—

"(1) that the design is original and was created by the designer or designers named in the application;

"(2) that the design has not previously been registered on behalf of the applicant or the applicant's predecessor in title; and

"(3) that the applicant is the person entitled to protection and to registration under this chapter.

If the design has been made public with the design notice prescribed in section 1306, the statement shall also describe the exact form and position of the design notice.

"(f) EFFECT OF ERRORS.—(1) Error in any statement or assertion as to the utility of the useful article named in the application under this section, the design of which is sought to be registered, shall not affect the protection secured under this chapter.

"(2) Errors in omitting a joint designer or in naming an alleged joint designer shall not affect the validity of the registration, or the actual ownership or the protection of the design, unless it is shown that the error occurred with deceptive intent.

"(g) DESIGN MADE IN SCOPE OF EMPLOYMENT.—In a case in which the design was made within the regular scope of the designer's employment and individual authorship of the design is difficult or impossible to ascribe and the application so states, the name and address of the employer for whom the design was made may be stated instead of that of the individual designer.

"(h) PICTORIAL REPRESENTATION OF DESIGN.—The application for registration shall be accompanied by two copies of a drawing or other pictorial representation of the useful article embodying the design, having one or more views, adequate to show the design, in a form and style suitable for reproduction, which shall be deemed a part of the application.

"(i) DESIGN IN MORE THAN ONE USEFUL ARTICLE.—If the distinguishing elements of a design are in substantially the same form in different useful articles, the design shall be protected as to all such useful articles when protected as to one of them, but not more than one registration shall be required for the design.

"(j) APPLICATION FOR MORE THAN ONE DESIGN.—More than one design may be included in the same application under such conditions as may be prescribed by the Administrator. For each design included in an application the fee prescribed for a single design shall be paid.

"§ 1311. Benefit of earlier filing date in foreign country

"An application for registration of a design filed in the United States by any person who has, or whose legal representative or predecessor or successor in title has, previously filed an application for registration of the same design in a foreign country which extends to designs of owners who are citizens of the United States, or to applications filed under this chapter, similar protection to that provided under this chapter shall have that same effect as if filed in the United States on the date on which the application was first filed in such foreign country, if the application in the United States

54

is filed within 6 months after the earliest date on which any such foreign application was filed.

"§ 1312. Oaths and acknowledgments

"(a) IN GENERAL.—Oaths and acknowledgments required by this chapter—
  "(1) may be made—
    "(A) before any person in the United States authorized by law to administer oaths; or
    "(B) when made in a foreign country, before any diplomatic or consular officer of the United States authorized to administer oaths, or before any official authorized to administer oaths in the foreign country concerned, whose authority shall be proved by a certificate of a diplomatic or consular officer of the United States; and
  "(2) shall be valid if they comply with the laws of the State or country where made.
  "(b) WRITTEN DECLARATION IN LIEU OF OATH.—(1) The Administrator may by rule prescribe that any document which is to be filed under this chapter in the Office of the Administrator and which is required by any law, rule, or other regulation to be under oath, may be subscribed to by a written declaration in such form as the Administrator may prescribe, and such declaration shall be in lieu of the oath otherwise required.
  "(2) Whenever a written declaration under paragraph (1) is used, the document containing the declaration shall state that willful false statements are punishable by fine or imprisonment, or both, pursuant to section 1001 of title 18, and may jeopardize the validity of the application or document or a registration resulting therefrom.

"§ 1313. Examination of application and issue or refusal of registration

"(a) DETERMINATION OF REGISTRABILITY OF DESIGN; REGISTRATION.—Upon the filing of an application for registration in proper form under section 1310, and upon payment of the fee prescribed under section 1316, the Administrator shall determine whether or not the application relates to a design which on its face appears to be subject to protection under this chapter, and, if so, the Register shall register the design. Registration under this subsection shall be announced by publication. The date of registration shall be the date of publication.
  "(b) REFUSAL TO REGISTER; RECONSIDERATION.—If, in the judgment of the Administrator, the application for registration relates to a design which on its face is not subject to protection under this chapter, the Administrator shall send to the applicant a notice of refusal to register and the grounds for the refusal. Within 3 months after the date on which the notice of refusal is sent, the applicant may, by written request, seek reconsideration of the application. After consideration of such a request, the Administrator shall either register the design or send to the applicant a notice of final refusal to register.
  "(c) APPLICATION TO CANCEL REGISTRATION.—Any person who believes he or she is or will be damaged by a registration under this

chapter may, upon payment of the prescribed fee, apply to the Administrator at any time to cancel the registration on the ground that the design is not subject to protection under this chapter, stating the reasons for the request. Upon receipt of an application for cancellation, the Administrator shall send to the owner of the design, as shown in the records of the Office of the Administrator, a notice of the application, and the owner shall have a period of 3 months after the date on which such notice is mailed in which to present arguments to the Administrator for support of the validity of the registration. The Administrator shall also have the authority to establish, by regulation, conditions under which the opposing parties may appear and be heard in support of their arguments. If, after the periods provided for the presentation of arguments have expired, the Administrator determines that the applicant for cancellation has established that the design is not subject to protection under this chapter, the Administrator shall order the registration stricken from the record. Cancellation under this subsection shall be announced by publication, and notice of the Administrator's final determination with respect to any application for cancellation shall be sent to the applicant and to the owner of record.

"§ 1314. Certification of registration

"Certificates of registration shall be issued in the name of the United States under the seal of the Office of the Administrator and shall be recorded in the official records of the Office. The certificate shall state the name of the useful article, the date of filing of the application, the date of registration, and the date the design was made public, if earlier than the date of filing of the application, and shall contain a reproduction of the drawing or other pictorial representation of the design. If a description of the salient features of the design appears in the application, the description shall also appear in the certificate. A certificate of registration shall be admitted in any court as prima facie evidence of the facts stated in the certificate.

"§ 1315. Publication of announcements and indexes

"(a) PUBLICATIONS OF THE ADMINISTRATOR.—The Administrator shall publish lists and indexes of registered designs and cancellations of designs and may also publish the drawings or other pictorial representations of registered designs for sale or other distribution.

"(b) FILE OF REPRESENTATIVES OF REGISTERED DESIGNS.—The Administrator shall establish and maintain a file of the drawings or other pictorial representations of registered designs. The file shall be available for use by the public under such conditions as the Administrator may prescribe.

"§ 1316. Fees

"The Administrator shall by regulation set reasonable fees for the filing of applications to register designs under this chapter and for other services relating to the administration of this chapter, taking into consideration the cost of providing these services and the benefit of a public record.

56

"§ 1317. Regulations

"The Administrator may establish regulations for the administration of this chapter.

"§ 1318. Copies of records

"Upon payment of the prescribed fee, any person may obtain a certified copy of any official record of the Office of the Administrator that relates to this chapter. That copy shall be admissible in evidence with the same effect as the original.

"§ 1319. Correction of errors in certificates

"The Administrator may, by a certificate of correction under seal, correct any error in a registration incurred through the fault of the Office, or, upon payment of the required fee, any error of a clerical or typographical nature occurring in good faith but not through the fault of the Office. Such registration, together with the certificate, shall thereafter have the same effect as if it had been originally issued in such corrected form.

"§ 1320. Ownership and transfer

"(a) PROPERTY RIGHT IN DESIGN.—The property right in a design subject to protection under this chapter shall vest in the designer, the legal representatives of a deceased designer or of one under legal incapacity, the employer for whom the designer created the design in the case of a design made within the regular scope of the designer's employment, or a person to whom the rights of the designer or of such employer have been transferred. The person in whom the property right is vested shall be considered the owner of the design.

"(b) TRANSFER OF PROPERTY RIGHT.—The property right in a registered design, or a design for which an application for registration has been or may be filed, may be assigned, granted, conveyed, or mortgaged by an instrument in writing, signed by the owner, or may be bequeathed by will.

"(c) OATH OR ACKNOWLEDGEMENT OF TRANSFER.—An oath or acknowledgment under section 1312 shall be prima facie evidence of the execution of an assignment, grant, conveyance, or mortgage under subsection (b).

"(d) RECORDATION OF TRANSFER.—An assignment, grant, conveyance, or mortgage under subsection (b) shall be void as against any subsequent purchaser or mortgagee for a valuable consideration, unless it is recorded in the Office of the Administrator within 3 months after its date of execution or before the date of such subsequent purchase or mortgage.

"§ 1321. Remedy for infringement

"(a) IN GENERAL.—The owner of a design is entitled, after issuance of a certificate of registration of the design under this chapter, to institute an action for any infringement of the design.

"(b) REVIEW OF REFUSAL TO REGISTER.—(1) Subject to paragraph (2), the owner of a design may seek judicial review of a final refusal of the Administrator to register the design under this chapter by bringing a civil action, and may in the same action, if the

57

court adjudges the design subject to protection under this chapter, enforce the rights in that design under this chapter.

"(2) The owner of a design may seek judicial review under this section if—

"(A) the owner has previously duly filed and prosecuted to final refusal an application in proper form for registration of the design;

"(B) the owner causes a copy of the complaint in the action to be delivered to the Administrator within 10 days after the commencement of the action; and

"(C) the defendant has committed acts in respect to the design which would constitute infringement with respect to a design protected under this chapter.

"(c) ADMINISTRATOR AS PARTY TO ACTION.—The Administrator may, at the Administrator's option, become a party to the action with respect to the issue of registrability of the design claim by entering an appearance within 60 days after being served with the complaint, but the failure of the Administrator to become a party shall not deprive the court of jurisdiction to determine that issue.

"(d) USE OF ARBITRATION TO RESOLVE DISPUTE.—The parties to an infringement dispute under this chapter, within such time as may be specified by the Administrator by regulation, may determine the dispute, or any aspect of the dispute, by arbitration. Arbitration shall be governed by title 9. The parties shall give notice of any arbitration award to the Administrator, and such award shall, as between the parties to the arbitration, be dispositive of the issues to which it relates. The arbitration award shall be unenforceable until such notice is given. Nothing in this subsection shall preclude the Administrator from determining whether a design is subject to registration in a cancellation proceeding under section 1313(c).

§ 1322. Injunctions

"(a) IN GENERAL.—A court having jurisdiction over actions under this chapter may grant injunctions in accordance with the principles of equity to prevent infringement of a design under this chapter, including, in its discretion, prompt relief by temporary restraining orders and preliminary injunctions.

"(b) DAMAGES FOR INJUNCTIVE RELIEF WRONGFULLY OBTAINED.—A seller or distributor who suffers damage by reason of injunctive relief wrongfully obtained under this section has a cause of action against the applicant for such injunctive relief and may recover such relief as may be appropriate, including damages for lost profits, cost of materials, loss of good will, and punitive damages in instances where the injunctive relief was sought in bad faith, and, unless the court finds extenuating circumstances, reasonable attorney's fees.

"§ 1323. Recovery for infringement

"(a) DAMAGES.—Upon a finding for the claimant in an action for infringement under this chapter, the court shall award the claimant damages adequate to compensate for the infringement. In addition, the court may increase the damages to such amount, not exceeding $50,000 or $1 per copy, whichever is greater, as the court determines to be just. The damages awarded shall constitute com-

58

pensation and not a penalty. The court may receive expert testimony as an aid to the determination of damages.

"(b) INFRINGER'S PROFITS.—As an alternative to the remedies provided in subsection (a), the court may award the claimant the infringer's profits resulting from the sale of the copies if the court finds that the infringer's sales are reasonably related to the use of the claimant's design. In such a case, the claimant shall be required to prove only the amount of the infringer's sales and the infringer shall be required to prove its expenses against such sales.

"(c) STATUTE OF LIMITATIONS.—No recovery under subsection (a) or (b) shall be had for any infringement committed more than 3 years before the date on which the complaint is filed.

"(d) ATTORNEY'S FEES.—In an action for infringement under this chapter, the court may award reasonable attorney's fees to the prevailing party.

"(e) DISPOSITION OF INFRINGING AND OTHER ARTICLES.—The court may order that all infringing articles, and any plates, molds, patterns, models, or other means specifically adapted for making the articles, be delivered up for destruction or other disposition as the court may direct.

"§ 1324. Power of court over registration

"In any action involving the protection of a design under this chapter, the court, when appropriate, may order registration of a design under this chapter or the cancellation of such a registration. Any such order shall be certified by the court to the Administrator, who shall make an appropriate entry upon the record.

"§ 1325. Liability for action on registration fraudulently obtained

"Any person who brings an action for infringement knowing that registration of the design was obtained by a false or fraudulent representation materially affecting the rights under this chapter, shall be liable in the sum of $10,000, or such part of that amount as the court may determine. That amount shall be to compensate the defendant and shall be charged against the plaintiff and paid to the defendant, in addition to such costs and attorney's fees of the defendant as may be assessed by the court.

"§ 1326. Penalty for false marking

"(a) IN GENERAL.—Whoever, for the purpose of deceiving the public, marks upon, applies to, or uses in advertising in connection with an article made, used, distributed, or sold, a design which is not protected under this chapter, a design notice specified in section 1306, or any other words or symbols importing that the design is protected under this chapter, knowing that the design is not so protected, shall pay a civil fine of not more than $500 for each such offense.

"(b) SUIT BY PRIVATE PERSONS.—Any person may sue for the penalty established by subsection (a), in which event one-half of the penalty shall be awarded to the person suing and the remainder shall be awarded to the United States.

59

"§ 1327. Penalty for false representation

"Whoever knowingly makes a false representation materially affecting the rights obtainable under this chapter for the purpose of obtaining registration of a design under this chapter shall pay a penalty of not less than $500 and not more than $1,000, and any rights or privileges that individual may have in the design under this chapter shall be forfeited.

"§ 1328. Enforcement by Treasury and Postal Service

"(a) REGULATIONS.—The Secretary of the Treasury and the United States Postal Service shall separately or jointly issue regulations for the enforcement of the rights set forth in section 1308 with respect to importation. Such regulations may require, as a condition for the exclusion of articles from the United States, that the person seeking exclusion take any one or more of the following actions:

"(1) Obtain a court order enjoining, or an order of the International Trade Commission under section 337 of the Tariff Act of 1930 excluding, importation of the articles.

"(2) Furnish proof that the design involved is protected under this chapter and that the importation of the articles would infringe the rights in the design under this chapter.

"(3) Post a surety bond for any injury that may result if the detention or exclusion of the articles proves to be unjustified.

"(b) SEIZURE AND FORFEITURE.—Articles imported in violation of the rights set forth in section 1308 are subject to seizure and forfeiture in the same manner as property imported in violation of the customs laws. Any such forfeited articles shall be destroyed as directed by the Secretary of the Treasury or the court, as the case may be, except that the articles may be returned to the country of export whenever it is shown to the satisfaction of the Secretary of the Treasury that the importer had no reasonable grounds for believing that his or her acts constituted a violation of the law.

"§ 1329. Relation to design patent law

"The issuance of a design patent under title 35 for an original design for an article of manufacture shall terminate any protection of the original design under this chapter.

"§ 1330. Common law and other rights unaffected

"Nothing in this chapter shall annul or limit—

"(1) common law or other rights or remedies, if any, available to or held by any person with respect to a design which has not been registered under this chapter; or

"(2) any right under the trademark laws or any right protected against unfair competition.

"§ 1331. Administrator; Office of the Administrator

"In this chapter, the 'Administrator' is the Register of Copyrights, and the 'Office of the Administrator' and the 'Office' refer to the Copyright Office of the Library of Congress.

60

"§ 1332. No retroactive effect

"*Protection under this chapter shall not be available for any design that has been made public under section 1310(b) before the effective date of this chapter.*".

SEC. 503. CONFORMING AMENDMENTS.

(a) T<small>ABLE OF</small> C<small>HAPTERS.</small>—*The table of chapters for title 17, United States Code, is amended by adding at the end the following:*

"**13. Protection of Original Designs** .... **1301**".

(b) J<small>URISDICTION OF</small> D<small>ISTRICT</small> C<small>OURTS</small> O<small>VER</small> D<small>ESIGN</small> A<small>C-TIONS.</small>—*(1) Section 1338(c) of title 28, United States Code, is amended by inserting* ", *and to exclusive rights in designs under chapter 13 of title 17,*" *after* "*title 17*".

(2)(A) The section heading for section 1338 of title 28, United States Code, is amended by inserting "**designs,**" *after* "**mask works,**".

(B) The item relating to section 1338 in the table of sections at the beginning of chapter 85 of title 28, United States Code, is amended by inserting "*designs,*" *after* "*mask works,*".

(c) P<small>LACE FOR</small> B<small>RINGING</small> D<small>ESIGN</small> A<small>CTIONS.</small>—*(1) Section 1400(a) of title 28, United States Code, is amended by inserting* "*or designs*" *after* "*mask works*".

(2) The section heading for section 1400 of title 28, United States Code is amended to read as follows:

"§ Patents and copyrights, mask works, and designs".

(3) The item relating to section 1400 in the table of sections at the beginning of chapter 87 of title 28, United States Code, is amended to read as follows:

"*1400.   Patents and copyrights, mask works, and designs.*".

(d) A<small>CTIONS</small> A<small>GAINST THE</small> U<small>NITED</small> S<small>TATES.</small>—*Section 1498(e) of title 28, United States Code, is amended by inserting* ", *and to exclusive rights in designs under chapter 13 of title 17,*" *after* "*title 17*".

SEC. 504. JOINT STUDY OF THE EFFECT OF THIS TITLE.

(a) I<small>N</small> G<small>ENERAL.</small>—*Not later than 1 year after the date of the enactment of this Act, and not later than 2 years after such date of enactment, the Register of Copyrights and the Commissioner of Patents and Trademarks shall submit to the Committees on the Judiciary of the Senate and the House of Representatives a joint report evaluating the effect of the amendments made by this title.*

(b) E<small>LEMENTS</small> F<small>OR</small> C<small>ONSIDERATION.</small>—*In carrying out subsection (a), the Register of Copyrights and the Commissioner of Patents and Trademarks shall consider*—

(1) the extent to which the amendments made by this title has been effective in suppressing infringement of the design of vessel hulls;

(2) the extent to which the registration provided for in chapter 13 of title 17, United States Code, as added by this title, has been utilized;

(3) the extent to which the creation of new designs of vessel hulls have been encouraged by the amendments made by this title;

61

(4) the effect, if any, of the amendments made by this title on the price of vessels with hulls protected under such amendments; and

(5) such other considerations as the Register and the Commissioner may deem relevant to accomplish the purposes of the evaluation conducted under subsection (a).

SEC. 505. EFFECTIVE DATE.

The amendments made by sections 502 and 503 shall take effect on the date of the enactment of this Act and shall remain in effect until the end of the 2-year period beginning on such date of enactment. No cause of action based on chapter 13 of title 17, United States Code, as added by this title, may be filed after the end of that 2-year period.

Amend the title so as to read: "A bill to amend title 17, United States Code, to implement the World Intellectual Property Organization Copyright Treaty and Performances and Phonograms Treaty, and for other purposes.".

And the Senate agree to the same.

From the Committee on Commerce, for consideration of the House bill, and the Senate amendment, and modifications committed to conference:

TOM BLILEY,
BILLY TAUZIN,
JOHN D. DINGELL,

From the Committee on the Judiciary, for consideration of the House bill, and the Senate amendment, and modifications committed to conference:

HENRY J. HYDE,
HOWARD COBLE,
BOB GOODLATTE,
JOHN CONYERS, JR.,
HOWARD L. BERMAN,
Managers on the Part of the House.

ORRIN G. HATCH,
STROM THURMOND,
PATRICK J. LEAHY,
Managers on the Part of the Senate.

JOINT EXPLANATORY STATEMENT OF THE COMMITTEE OF CONFERENCE

The managers on the part of the House and the Senate at the conference on the disagreeing votes of the two Houses on the amendment of the Senate to the bill (H.R. 2281) to amend title 17, United States Code, to implement the World Intellectual Property Organization Copyright Treaty and Performances and Phonograms Treaty, and for other purposes, submit the following joint statement to the House and the Senate in explanation of the effect of the action agreed upon by the managers and recommended in the accompanying conference report:

The Senate amendment struck all of the House bill after the enacting clause and inserted a substitute text.

The House recedes from its disagreement to the amendment of the Senate with an amendment that is a substitute for the House bill and the Senate amendment. The differences between the House bill, the Senate amendment, and the substitute agreed to in conference are noted below, except for clerical corrections, conforming changes made necessary by agreements reached by the conferees, and minor drafting and clerical changes.

TITLE I—WIPO TREATIES IMPLEMENTATION

This title implements two new intellectual property treaties, the WIPO Copyright Treaty and the WIPO Performances and Phonograms Treaty, signed in Geneva, Switzerland in December 1996.

SECTION 101. SHORT TITLE

The House recedes to the Senate section 101. This section sets forth the short title of the Act. As between the short titles in the House bill and the Senate amendment, it is believed that the title in Section 101 of the Senate amendment more accurately reflects the effect of the Act.

SECTION 102. TECHNICAL AMENDMENTS

The Senate recedes to House section 102. This section makes technical and conforming amendments to the U.S. Copyright Act in order to comply with the obligations of the two WIPO treaties.

SECTION 103. COPYRIGHT PROTECTION SYSTEMS AND COPYRIGHT MANAGEMENT INFORMATION

The Senate recedes to House section 103 with modification. The two new WIPO Treaties include substantively identical provisions on technological measures of protection (also commonly referred to as the "black box" or "anticircumvention" provisions). These provisions require contracting parties to provide "adequate

(63)

64

legal protection and effective legal remedies against the circumvention of effective technological measures that are used by authors in connection with the exercise of their rights under this Treaty or the Berne Convention and that restrict acts, in respect of their works, which are not authorized by the authors concerned or permitted by law."

Both of the new WIPO treaties also include substantively identical provisions requiring contracting parties to protect the integrity of copyright management information. The treaties define copyright management information as "information which identifies the work, the author of the work, the owner of any right in the work, or information about the terms and conditions of use of the work, and any numbers or codes that represent such information, when any of these items of information is attached to a copy of a work or appears in connection with the communication of a work to the public."

Legislation is required to comply with both of these provisions. To accomplish this, both the House bill and the Senate amendment, in section 103, would add a new chapter (chapter twelve) to title 17 of the United States Code. This new chapter twelve includes five sections—(1) section 1201, which prohibits the circumvention of technological measures of protection; (2) section 1202, which protects the integrity of copyright management information; (3) section 1203, which provides for civil remedies for violations of sections 1201 and 1202; (4) section 1204, which provides for criminal penalties for violations of sections 1201 and 1202; and (5) section 1205, which provides a savings clause to preserve the effectiveness of federal and state laws in protecting individual privacy on the Internet. The House bill and the Senate amendment differ in several respects, primarily related to the scope and availability of exemptions from the prohibitions under section 1201.

Section 1201(a)(1)—Rulemaking by the Librarian of Congress. Section 1201(a)(1)(C) provides that the determination of affected classes of works described in subparagraph (A) shall be made by the Librarian of Congress "upon the recommendation of the Register of Copyrights, who shall consult with the Assistant Secretary for Communications and Information of the Department of Commerce and report and comment on his or her views in making such recommendation." The determination will be made in a rulemaking proceeding on the record. It is the intention of the conferees that, as is typical with other rulemaking under title 17, and in recognition of the expertise of the Copyright Office, the Register of Copyrights will conduct the rulemaking, including providing notice of the rulemaking, seeking comments from the public, consulting with the Assistant Secretary for Communications and Information of the Department of Commerce and any other agencies that are deemed appropriate, and recommending final regulations in the report to the Librarian.

Section 1201(a) and 1202—technological measures. It is the understanding of the conferees that technological measures will most often be developed through consultative, private sector efforts by content owners, and makers of computers, consumer electronics and telecommunications devices. The conferees expect this consultative approach to continue as a constructive and positive method.

65

One of the benefits of such consultation is to allow testing of proposed technologies to determine whether there are adverse effects on the ordinary performance of playback and display equipment in the marketplace, and to take steps to eliminate or substantially mitigate those effects before technologies are introduced. The public interest is well-served by such activities.

Persons may also choose to implement a technological measure without vetting it through an inter-industry consultative process, or without regard to the input of affected parties. Under such circumstances, such a technological measure may materially degrade or otherwise cause recurring appreciable adverse effects on the authorized performance or display of works. Steps taken by the makers or servicers of consumer electronics, telecommunications or computing products used for such authorized performances or displays solely to mitigate these adverse effects on product performance (whether or not taken in combination with other lawful product modifications) shall not be deemed a violation of sections 1201(a) or (b).

However, this construction is not meant to afford manufacturers or servicers an opportunity to give persons unauthorized access to protected content, or to exercise the rights under the Copyright Act of copyright owners in such works, under the guise of "correcting" a performance problem that results from the implementation of a particular technological measure. Thus, it would violate sections 1201(a) or (b) for a manufacturer or servicer to take remedial measures if they are held out for or undertaken with, or result in equipment with only limited commercially significant use other than, the prohibited purpose of allowing users to gain unauthorized access to protected content or to exercise the rights under the Copyright Act of copyright owners in such works.

With regard to section 1202, product adjustments made to eliminate recurring appreciable adverse effects on the authorized performance or display of works caused by copyright management information will not be deemed a violation of section 1202 unless such steps are held out for or undertaken with a prohibited purpose, or the requisite knowledge, of inducing, enabling, facilitating or concealing infringement of rights of copyright owners under the Copyright Act.

Section 1201(e) and 1202(d)—Law enforcement, intelligence, and other government activities. Sections 1201(e) and 1202(d) create an exception to the prohibitions of sections 1201 and 1202 for the lawfully authorized investigative, protective, or intelligence activities of an officer, agent, or employee of, the United States, a State, or a political subdivision of a State, or of persons acting pursuant to a contract with such an entity. The anticircumvention provisions of this legislation might be read to prohibit some aspects of the information security testing that is critical to preventing cyber attacks against government computers, computer systems, and computer networks. The conferees have added language to sections 1201(e) and 1202(d) to make it clear that the anticircumvention prohibition does not apply to lawfully authorized information security activities of the federal government, the states, political subdivisions of states, or persons acting within the scope of their government information security contract. In this way, the bill will

66

permit the continuation of information security activities that protect the country against one of the greatest threats to our national
security as well as to our economic security.

At the same time, this change is narrowly drafted so that it
does not open the door to the very piracy the treaties are designed
to prevent. For example, the term "information security" activities
is intended to include presidential directives and executive orders
concerning the vulnerabilities of a computer, computer system, or
computer network. By this, the conferees intend to include the re-
cently-issued Presidential Decision Directive 63 on Critical Infrastructure Protection. PDD–63 contains a number of initiatives to
ensure that the United States takes all necessary measures to
swiftly eliminate any significant vulnerability to both physical and
cyber attacks on the nation's critical infrastructures, including especially our cyber systems.

The Term "computer system" has the same definition for purposes of this section as that term is defined in the Computer Security Act, 15 U.S.C. § 278g–3(d)(1).

Subsection 1201(g)—Encryption Research. Subsection (g) permits the circumvention of access control technologies in certain circumstances for the purpose of good faith encryption research. The
conferees note that section 1201(g)(3)(A) does not imply that the results of encryption research must be disseminated. There is no requirement that legitimate encryption researchers disseminate their
findings in order to quality for the encryption research exemption
in section 1201(g). Rather, the subsection describes circumstances
in which dissemination, if any, would be weighed in determining
eligibility.

Section 1201(j)—Security Testing. Subsection (j) clarifies the intended effect of the bill with respect to information security. The
conferees understand this act to prohibit unauthorized circumvention of technological measures applied to works protected under
title 17. The conferees recognize that technological measures may
also be used to protect the integrity and security of computers,
computer systems or computer networks. It is not the intent of this
act to prevent persons utilizing technological measures in respect
of computers, computer systems or networks from testing the security value and effectiveness of the technological measures they employ, or from contracting with companies that specialize in such security testing.

Thus, in addition to the exception for good faith encryption research contained in Section 1201(g), the conferees have adopted
Section 1201(j) to resolve additional issues related to the effect of
the anti-circumvention provision on legitimate information security
activities. First, the conferees were concerned that Section 1201(g)'s
exclusive focus on encryption-related research does not encompass
the entire range of legitimate information security activities. Not
every technological means that is used to provide security relies on
encryption technology, or does so to the exclusion of other methods.
Moreover, an individual who is legitimately testing a security technology may be doing so not to advance the state of encryption research or to develop encryption products, but rather to ascertain
the effectiveness of that particular security technology.

67

The conferees were also concerned that the anti-circumvention provision of Section 1201(a) could be construed to inhibit legitimate forms of security testing. It is not unlawful to test the effectiveness of a security measure before it is implemented to protect the work covered under title 17. Nor is it unlawful for a person who has implemented a security measure to test its effectiveness. In this respect, the scope of permissible security testing under the Act should be the same as permissible testing of a simple door lock: a prospective buyer may test the lock at the store with the store's consent, or may purchase the lock and test it at home in any manner that he or she sees fit—for example, by installing the lock on the front door and seeing if it can be picked. What that person may not do, however, is test the lock once it has been installed on someone else's door, without the consent of the person whose property is protected by the lock.

In order to resolve these concerns, Section 1201(j) creates an exception for "security testing." Section 1201(j)(1) defines "security testing" as obtaining access to a computer, computer system, or computer network for the sole purpose of testing, investigating, or correcting a security flaw or vulnerability, provided that the person engaging in such testing is doing so with the consent of the owner or operator of the computer, computer system, or computer network. Section 102(j)(2) provides that, notwithstanding the provisions of Section 1201(a), a person may engage in such testing, provided that the act does not constitute infringement or violate any other applicable law. Section 1201(j)(3) provides a non-exclusive list of factors that a court shall consider in determining whether a person benefits from this exception.

Section 1201(j)(4) permits an individual, notwithstanding the prohibition contained in Section 1201(a)(2), to develop, produce, distribute, or employ technological means for the sole purpose of performing acts of good faith security testing under Section 1201(j)(2), provided the technological means do not otherwise violate section 1201(a)(2). It is Congress' intent for this subsection to have application only with respect to good faith security testing. The intent is to ensure that parties engaged in good faith security testing have the tools available to them to complete such acts. The conferees understand that such tools may be coupled with additional tools that serve purposes wholly unrelated to the purposes of this Act. Eligibility for this exemption should not be precluded because these tools are coupled in such a way. The exemption would not be available, however, when such tools are coupled with a product or technology that violates section 1201(a)(2).

Section 1201(k)—Certain Analog Devices and Certain Technological Measures. The conferees included a provision in the final legislation to require that analog video cassette recorders must conform to the two forms of copy control technology that are in wide use in the market today—the automatic gain control copy control technology and the colorstripe copy control technology. Neither are currently required elements of any format of video recorder, and the ability of each technology to work as intended depends on the consistency of design of video recorders or on incorporation of specific response elements in video recorders. Moreover, they do not employ encryption or scrambling of the content being protected.

68

As a consequence, these analog copy control technologies may be rendered ineffective either by redesign of video recorders or by intervention of "black box" devices or software "hacks". The conferees believe, and specifically intend, that the general circumvention prohibition in Section 1201(b)(2) will prohibit the manufacture and sale of "black box" devices that defeat these technologies. Moreover, the conferees believe and intend that the term "technology" should be read to include the software "hacks" of this type, and that such "hacks" are equally prohibited by the general circumvention provision. Devices have been marketed that claim to "fix" television picture disruptions allegedly caused by these technologies. However, as described in more detail below, there is no justification for the existence of any intervention device to "fix" such problems allegedly caused by these technologies, including "fixes" allegedly related to stabilization or clean up of the picture quality. Such devices should be seen for what they are—circumvention devices prohibited by this legislation.

The conferees emphasize that this particular provision is being included in this bill in order to deal with a very specific situation involving the protection of analog television programming and prerecorded movies and other audiovisual works in relation to recording capabilities of ordinary consumer analog video cassette recorders. The conferees also acknowledge that numerous other activities are underway in the private sector to develop, test, and apply copy control technologies, particularly in the digital environment. Subject to the other requirements of this section, circumvention of these technologies may be prohibited under this Act. Moreover, in some cases, these technologies are subject to licensing arrangements that provide legally enforceable obligations. The conferees applaud these undertakings and encourage their continuation, including the inter-industry meetings and working groups that are essential to their success. If, as a result of such activities, the participants request further Congressional action, the conferees expect that the Congress, and the committees involved in this Conference specifically, will consider whether additional statutory requirements are necessary and appropriate.

Before agreeing to include this requirement in the final legislation, the conferees assured themselves in relation to two critical issues—that these analog copy control technologies do not create "playability" problems on normal consumer electronics products and that the intellectual property necessary for the operation of these technologies will be available on reasonable and non-discriminatory terms.

In relation to the playability issue, the conferees have received authoritative assurances that playability issues have already been resolved in relation to the current specifications for these technologies and that an inter-industry forum will be established to resolve any playability issues that may arise in the future in relation to either revisions to the copy control specifications or development of new consumer technologies and products.

As further explanation on the playability issue, the conferees understand that the existing technologies were the subject of extensive testing that included all or virtually all of the major consumer electronics manufacturers and that this testing resulted in modi-

69

fication of the specifications to assure that the technologies do not produce noticeable adverse effects on the normal display of content that is protected utilizing these technologies. Currently, all manufacturers are effectively "on notice" of the existence of these technologies and their specifications and should be able to design their products to avoid any adverse effects.

In relation to the intellectual property licensing issues, the owner of the analog copy control intellectual property—Macrovision Corporation—has written a letter to the Chairman of the Conference Committee to provide the following assurances in relation to the licenses for intellectual property necessary to implement these analog copy control technologies: (1) that its intellectual property is generally available on reasonable and non-discriminatory terms, as that phrase is used in normal industry parlance; (2) that manufacturers of the analog video cassette recorders that are required by this legislation to conform to these technologies will be provided royalty-free licenses for the use of its relevant intellectual property in any device that plays back packaged, prerecorded content, or that reads and responds to or generates or carries forward the elements of these technologies associated with such content; (3) in the same circumstances as described in (2), other manufacturers of devices that generate, carry forward, or read and respond to these technologies will be provided licenses carrying only modest fees (in the range of $25,000—in current dollars—initial payment and lesser amounts as recurring annual fees); (4) that manufacturers of other products, including set-top-boxes and devices that perform similar functions (including integrated devices containing such functionality), will receive licenses on reasonable and non-discriminatory terms, including royalty terms and other considerations; and (5) that playability issues will not be the subject of license requirements but rather will be handled through an inter-industry forum that is being established for this purpose. The conferees emphasize the need for the technology's proprietor to adhere to these assurances in all future licensing.

With regard to the specific elements of this provision:

First, these technologies operate within the general NTSC television signal environment, and the conferees understand that this means that they work in relation to television signals that are of the 525/60 interlaced type, i.e., the standard definition television signal that has been used in the United States. The S-video and Hi-8 versions of covered devices are, of course, included within the coverage. Further, the new format analog video cassette recorders that are covered by paragraph (1)(A)(v) are those that receive the 525/60 interlaced type of input.

Second, it is the conferees understanding that not all analog video signals will utilize this technology, and, obviously, a device that receives a signal that does not contain these technologies need not read and respond to what might have been there if the signal had utilized the technology.

Third, a violation of paragraph (1) is a form of circumvention under Section 1201(b)(1). Accordingly, the enforcement of this provision is through the penalty provisions applicable to Section 1201 generally. A violation of paragraph (2) is also a violation of Section 1201 and hence subject to those penalty provisions. The inclusion

70

of paragraph (5) with regard to enforcement of paragraph (2) is intended merely to allow the particular statutory damage provisions of Section 1203 to apply to violations of this subsection.

Fourth, the conferees understand that minor modifications may be necessary in the specifications for these technologies and intend that any such modifications (and related new "revised specifications") should not negate in any way the requirements imposed by this subsection. The modifications should, however, be sufficiently minor that manufacturers of analog video cassette recorders should be free to continue to design products to conform to these technologies on the basis of the specifications existing, or actually implemented by manufacturers, as of the date of enactment of this Act.

Fifth, the provisions of paragraph (2) are intended to operate to allow copyright owners to use these technologies to prevent the making of a viewable copy of a pay-per-view, near video on demand, or video on demand transmission or prerecorded tape or disc containing one or more motion pictures or other audiovisual works, at the same time as consumers are afforded their customary ability to make analog copies of programming offered through other channels or services. Copyright owners may utilize these technologies to prevent the making of a "second generation" copy where the original transmission was through a pay television service (such as HBO, Showtime, or the like). The basic and extended basic tiers of programming services, whether provided through cable or other wireline, satellite, or future over the air terrestrial systems, may not be encoded with these technologies at all. The inclusion of paragraph (2)(D) is not intended to be read to authorize the making of a copy by consumers or others in relation to pay-per-view, near video on demand or video-on-demand transmissions or prerecorded media.

Sixth, the exclusion of professional analog video cassette recorders is necessary in order to allow the motion picture, broadcasting, and other legitimate industries and individual businesses to obtain and use equipment that is essential to their normal, lawful business operations. As a further explanation of the types of equipment that are to be subject to this exception, the following factors should be used in evaluating whether a specific product is a "professional" product:

(1) whether, in the preceding year, only a small number of the devices that are of the same kind, nature, and description were sold to consumers other than professionals employing such devices in a lawful business or industrial use;

(2) whether the device has special features designed for use by professionals employing the device in a lawful business or industrial use;

(3) whether the advertising, promotional and descriptive literature or other materials used to market the device were directed at professionals employing such devices in a lawful business or industrial use;

(4) whether the distribution channels and retail outlets through which the device is distributed and sold are ones used primarily to make sales to professionals employing such devices in a lawful business or industrial use; and

71

(5) whether the uses to which the device is most commonly put are those associated with the work of professionals employing the device in a lawful business or industrial use.

Seventh, paragraph (1)(B) contains a number of points worthy of explanation. In general, the requirement in paragraph (1)(B) is that manufacturers not materially reduce the responsiveness of their existing products and is also intended to be carried forward in the introduction of new models. This is particularly important in relation to the four-line colorstripe copy control technology, where the basic requirement in the statute is that a model of a recorder not be modified to eliminate conformance with the four-line colorstripe technology and where the standard for "conformance" is simply that the lines be visible and distracting in the display of a copy of material that was protected with the technology when the copy is played back, in normal viewing mode, by the recorder that made the copy and displayed on a reference display device. Specific elements of that requirement include:

(1) "Normal viewing mode" is intended to mean the viewing of a program in its natural sequence at the regular speed for playback and is not intended to allow "AGC-stripping viewing modes" to be developed. It is intended to exclude still frame or slow motion viewing from this definition.

(2) The "reference display device" concept is used in the legislation to acknowledge that manufacturers of analog video cassette recorders may use a specific display device to test their responsiveness to the colorstripe technology and then may use the level of such responsiveness as their baseline to achieve compliance. The reference display device for manufacturers that make televisions is intended to be a television set also made by that manufacturer. Where an analog video cassette recorder manufacturer does not make display devices, that manufacturer may choose a display device made by another manufacturer to serve as a reference. In general, a reference display device should be one that is generally representative of display devices in the U.S. market at the time of the testing.

(3) The conferees intend that the word "model" should be interpreted broadly and is not to be determined exclusively by alphabetic, numeric, name, or other label. Courts should look with suspicion at "new models" that reduce or eliminate conformance with this technology, as compared with that manufacturer's "previous models." Further, a manufacturer should not replace a previous model that showed intense lines with a model that shows weak lines in the played back picture.

For any new entrant into the VHS format analog video cassette recorder manufacturing business, the legislation provides that such a manufacturer will build its initial devices so as to be in conformance with the four-line colorstripe copy control technology based on the playback on a reference display device and thereafter not modify the design so that its products no longer conform to this technology.

Finally, the proprietor of the colorstripe copy control technology has supplied the Committee with a description of how the technology should work so as to provide the desired copy protection

72

benefits. That description is as follows: the colorstripe copy control technology works as intended if a recorder records a signal that, when played back by the playback function of that recorder in the normal viewing mode, exhibits on a reference display device a significant distortion of color on the lines which begin with a colorstripe colorburst, or a complete or intermittent loss of color throughout at least 50% of the visible image. While the conferees realize that there may be variations among recorders in relation to this technology, the conferees expect the affected manufacturers to work with the proprietor of the technology to ensure that the basic goal of content protection through this technology is achieved. The conferees understand that content protection through this technology is to the manufacturers' benefit, as well, since it encourages content providers to release more valuable content than they might otherwise release without such protection. The conferees further intend that manufacturers should seek to respond to the colorstripe technology at the highest feasible level and should not modify their recorder designs, or substitute weaker responding recorders for stronger responding recorders in order to avoid the requirements of this subsection.

Eighth, the type of colorstripe copy control technology to which the legislation requires conformance is the four-line "half burst" type version of this technology. The content provider may shift, in an adaptive fashion, from no colorstripe encoding to the two-line version to the four-line version, in order to balance the copy control features of the technology against the possible playback distortion that the four-line technology occasionally creates. This legislation requires conformance only to the four-line version, but prohibits any effort to eliminate or reduce materially the effectiveness of the two-line version in relation to any particular analog video cassette recorder that, in fact, provides a response to the two-line version. The legislation also applies the "encoding rules" in paragraph (2) to either the two-line or four-line versions of this technology.

SECTION 104. EVALUATION OF IMPACT OF COPYRIGHT LAW AND AMENDMENTS ON ELECTRONIC COMMERCE AND TECHNOLOGICAL DEVELOPMENT

The Senate recedes to House section 105 with modification.

SECTION 105. EFFECTIVE DATE

The Senate recedes to House section 106. This section sets forth the effective date of the amendments made by this title. The corresponding sections of the House bill and the Senate amendment are substantively identical.

TITLE II—ONLINE COPYRIGHT INFRINGEMENT LIABILITY LIMITATION

Title II preserves strong incentives for service providers and copyright owners to cooperate to detect and deal with copyright infringements that take place in the digital networked environment. At the same time, it provides greater certainty to service providers concerning their legal exposure for infringements that may occur in the course of their activities.

SECTION 201. SHORT TITLE

The Senate recedes to House section 201. This section sets forth the short title of the Act. The Senate accepts the House formulation.

SECTION 202. LIMITATIONS ON LIABILITY FOR COPYRIGHT INFRINGEMENT

The Senate recedes to House section 202 with modification. This section amends chapter 5 of the Copyright Act (17 U.S.C. 501, *et seq.*) to create a new section 512, titled "Limitations on liability relating to material online." New Section 512 contains limitations on service providers' liability for five general categories of activity set forth in subsections (a) through (d) and subsection (g). As provided in subsection (l), Section 512 is not intended to imply that a service provider is or is not liable as an infringer either for conduct that qualifies for a limitation of liability or for conduct that fails to so qualify. Rather, the limitations of liability apply if the provider is found to be liable under existing principles of law. This legislation is not intended to discourage the service provider from monitoring its service for infringing material. Courts should not conclude that the service provider loses eligibility for limitations on liability under section 512 solely because it engaged in a monitoring program.

The limitations in subsections (a) through (d) protect qualifying service providers from liability for all monetary relief for direct, vicarious and contributory infringement. Monetary relief is defined in subsection (k)(2) as encompassing damages, costs, attorneys' fees, and any other form of monetary payment. These subsections also limit injunctive relief against qualifying service providers to the extent specified in subsection (j). To qualify for these protections, service providers must meet the conditions set forth in subsection (i), and service providers' activities at issue must involve a function described in subsection (a), (b), (c), (d) or (g), respectively. The liability limitations apply to networks "operated by or for the service provider," thereby protecting both service providers who offer a service and subcontractors who may operate parts of, or an entire, system or network for another service provider.

Subsection (b) provides for a limitation on liability with respect to certain acts of "system caching". Paragraphs (5) and (6) of this subsection refer to industry standard communications protocols and technologies that are only now in the initial stages of development and deployment. The conferees expect that the Internet industry standards setting organizations, such as the Internet Engineering Task Force and the World Wide Web Consortium, will act promptly and without delay to establish these protocols so that subsection (b) can operate as intended.

Subsection (e) is included by the conferees in order to clarify the provisions of the bill with respect to the liability of nonprofit institutions of higher learning that act as service providers. This provision serves as a substitute for section 512(c)(2) of the House bill and for the study proposed by section 204 of the Senate amendment.

74

In general, Title II provides that a university or other public or nonprofit institution of higher education which is also a "service provider" (as that term is defined in title II) is eligible for the limitations on liability provided in title II to the same extent as any other service provider.

However, the conferees recognize that the university environment is unique. Ordinarily, a service provider may fail to qualify for the liability limitations in Title II simply because the knowledge or actions of one of its employees may be imputed to it under basic principles of respondeat superior and agency law. The special relationship which exists between universities and their faculty members (and their graduate student employees) when they are engaged in teaching or research is different from the ordinary employer-employee relationship. Since independence—freedom of thought, word and action—is at the core of academic freedom, the actions of university faculty and graduate student teachers and researchers warrant special consideration in the context of this legislation. This special consideration is embodied in new subsection (e), which provides special rules for determining whether universities, in their capacity as a service provider, may or may not be liable for acts of copyright infringement by faculty members or graduate students in certain circumstances.

Subsection (e)(1) provides that the online infringing actions of faculty members or graduate student employees, which occur when they are "performing a teaching or research function," will not be attributed to an institution of higher education in its capacity as their employer for purposes of section 512, if certain conditions are met. For the purposes of subsections (a) and (b) of section 512, such faculty member or graduate student shall be considered to be a person other than the institution, and for the purposes of subsections (c) and (d) of section 512 the faculty member's or graduate student's knowledge or awareness of his or her infringing activities will not be attributed to the institution, when they are performing a teaching or research function and the conditions in paragraphs (A)–(C) are met.

When the faculty member or the graduate student employee is performing a function other than teaching or research, this subsection provides no protection against liability for the institution if infringement occurs. For example, a faculty member or graduate student is performing a function other than teaching or research when the faculty member or graduate student is exercising institutional administrative responsibilities, or is carrying out operational responsibilities that relate to the institution's function as a service provider. Further, for the exemption to apply on the basis of research activity, the research must be a genuine academic exercise—i.e. a legitimate scholarly or scientific investigation or inquiry—rather than an activity which is claimed to be research but is undertaken as a pretext for engaging in infringing activity.

In addition to the "teaching or research function" test, the additional liability protections contained in subsection (e)(1) do not apply unless the conditions in paragraphs (A) through (C) are satisfied. First, paragraph (A) requires that the infringing activities must not involve providing online access to instructional materials that are "required or recommended" for a course taught by the in-

75

fringing faculty member and/or the infringing graduate student within the last three years. The reference to "providing online access" to instructional materials includes the use of e-mail for that purpose. The phrase "required or recommended" is intended to refer to instructional materials that have been formally and specifically identified in a list of course materials that is provided to all students enrolled in the course for credit; it is not intended, however, to refer to the other materials which, from time to time, the faculty member or graduate student may incidentally and informally bring to the attention of students for their consideration during the course of instruction.

Second, under paragraph (B) the institution must not have received more than two notifications of claimed infringement with respect to the particular faculty member or particular graduate student within the last three years. If more than two such notifications have been received, the institution may be considered to be on notice of a pattern of infringing conduct by the faculty member or graduate student, and the limitation of subsection (e) does not apply with respect to the subsequent infringing actions of that faculty member or that graduate student. Where more than two notifications have previously been received with regard to a particular faculty member or graduate student, the institution will only become potentially liable for the infringing actions of that faculty member or that graduate student. Any notification of infringement that gives rise to a cause of action for misrepresentation under subsection (f) does not count for purposes of paragraph (B).

Third, paragraph (C) states that the institution must provide to the users of its system or network—whether they are administrative employees, faculty, or students—materials that accurately describe and promote compliance with copyright law. The legislation allows, but does not require, the institutions to use relevant informational materials published by the U.S. Copyright Office in satisfying the condition imposed by paragraph (C).

Subsection (e)(2) defines the terms and conditions under which an injunction may be issued against an institution of higher education that is a service provider in cases to which subsection (e)(1) applies. First, all the factors and considerations taken into account by a court under 17 U.S.C. § 502 will apply in the case of any application for an injunction in cases covered by this subsection. In addition, the court is also required to consider the factors of particular significance in the digital environment listed in subsection (j)(2). Finally, the provisions contained in (j)(3), concerning notice to the service provider and the opportunity to appear, are also applicable in cases to which subsection (e)(1) applies.

The conferees also want to emphasize that nothing contained in subsection (e) should be interpreted to establish new liability for institutions of higher education, including under the doctrines of respondeat superior, or of contributory liability, where liability does not now exist. Further, subsection (e) does not alter any of the existing limitations on the rights of copyright owners that are already contained in the Copyright Act. So, for example, subsection (e) has no impact on the fair use (section 107) doctrine or the availability of fair use in a university setting; similarly, section 110 of the Copyright Act dealing with classroom performance and distance

76

learning is not changed by subsection (e). In this regard, subsection (e) is fully consistent with the rest of section 512, which neither creates any new liabilities for service providers, nor affects any defense to infringement available to a service provider. Finally, subsection (e) has no applicability to any case asserting that a university is liable for copyright infringement in any capacity other than as a service provider.

SECTION 203. EFFECTIVE DATE

The Senate recedes to House section 203. This section sets forth the effective date of the amendments made by this title. The corresponding sections of the House bill and the Senate amendment are substantively identical.

TITLE III—COMPUTER MAINTENANCE OR REPAIR COPYRIGHT EXEMPTION

SECTIONS 301–302

The Senate recedes to the House sections 301–302. These sections effect a minor, yet important clarification in section 117 of the Copyright Act to ensure that the lawful owner or lessee of a computer machine may authorize an independent service provider—a person unaffiliated with either the owner or lessee of the machine—to activate the machine for the sole purpose of servicing its hardware components. When a computer is activated, certain software or parts thereof is automatically copied into the machine's random access memory, or "RAM". A clarification in the Copyright Act is necessary in light of judicial decisions holding that such copying is a "reproduction" under section 106 of the Copyright Act (17 U.S.C. 106),[1] thereby calling into question the right of an independent service provider who is not the licensee of the computer program resident on the client's machine to even activate that machine for the purpose of servicing the hardware components. This section does not in any way alter the law with respect to the scope of the term "reproduction" as it is used the Copyright Act. Rather, this section it is narrowly crafted to achieve the objectives just described—namely, ensuring that an independent service provider may turn on a client's computer machine in order to service its hardware components, provided that such service provider complies with the provisions of this section designed to protect the rights of copyright owners of computer software. The corresponding sections of the House bill and the Senate amendment are substantively identical.

TITLE IV—MISCELLANEOUS PROVISIONS

SEC. 401. PROVISIONS RELATING TO THE COMMISSIONER OF PATENTS AND TRADEMARKS AND THE REGISTER OF COPYRIGHTS

The Senate recedes to the House sections 401–402 with modification. This section provides parity in compensation between the Register of Copyrights and the Commissioner of Patent and Trade-

---

[1] *See MAI Sys. Corp.* v. *Peak Computer,* 991 F.2d 511 (9th Cir. 1993), cert. denied, 114 S. Ct. 671 (1994).

marks and clarifies the duties and functions of the Register of Copyrights.

The new subsection to be added to 17 U.S.C. § 701 sets forth in express statutory language the functions presently performed by the Register of Copyrights under her general administrative authority under subsection 701(a). Like the Library of Congress, its parent agency, the Copyright Office is a hybrid entity that historically has performed both legislative and executive or administrative functions. *Eltra Corp. v. Ringer,* 579 F.2d 294 (4th Cir. 1978). Existing subsection 701(a) addresses some of the latter functions. New subsection 701(b) is intended to codify the other traditional roles of the Copyright Office and to confirm the Register's existing areas of jurisdiction.

Paragraph (1) of new subsection 701(b) reflects the Copyright Office's longstanding role as advisor to Congress on matters within its competence. This includes copyright and all matters within the scope of title 17 of the U.S. Code. Such advice, which often takes the form of testimony of pending legislation, is separate from testimony or other recommendations by the Administration pursuant to the President's concurrent constitutional power to make recommendations to Congress.

Paragraph (2) reflects the Copyright Office's longstanding role in advising federal agencies on matters within its competence. For example, the Copyright Office advises the U.S. Trade Representative and the State Department on an ongoing basis on the adequacy of foreign copyright laws, and serves as a technical consultant to those agencies in bilateral, regional and multilateral consultations or negotiations with other countries on copyright-related issues.

Paragraph (3) reflects the Copyright Office's longstanding role as a key participant in international meetings of various kinds, including as part of U.S. delegations as authorized by the Executive Branch, serving as substantive experts on matters within the Copyright Office's competence. Recent examples of the Copyright Office acting in the capacity include its central role on the U.S. delegation that negotiated the two new WIPO treaties at the 1996 Diplomatic Conference in Geneva, and its ongoing contributions of technical assistance in the TRIPS Council of the World Trade Organization and the Register's role as a featured speaker at numerous WIPO conferences.

Paragraph (4) describes the studies and programs that the Copyright Office has long carried out as the agency responsible for administering the copyright law and other chapters of title 17. Among the most important of these studies historically was a series of comprehensive reports on various issues produced in the 1960's as the foundation of the last general revision of U.S. copyright law, enacted as the 1976 Copyright Act. Most recently the Copyright Office has completed reports on the cable and satellite compulsory licenses, legal protection for databases, and the economic and policy implications of term extension. Consistent with the Copyright Office's role as a legislative branch agency, these studies have often included specific policy recommendations to Congress. The reference to "programs" includes such projects as the conferences the Copyright Office cosponsored in 1996–97 on the

78

subject of technology-based intellectual property management, and the International Copyright Institutes that the Copyright Office has conducted for foreign government officials at least annually over the past decade, often in cooperation with WIPO.

Paragraph (5) makes clear that the functions and duties set forth in this subsection are illustrative, not exhaustive. The Register of Copyrights would continue to be able to carry out other functions under her general authority under subsection 701(a), or as Congress may direct. The latter may include specific requests by Committees for studies and recommendations on subjects within the Copyright Office's area of competence. It may also include, when appropriate or required for constitutional reasons, directions to the Office in separate legislation.

SEC. 402. EPHEMERAL RECORDINGS

The Senate recedes to House section 411 with modification. This section amends section 112 of the Copyright Act (17 U.S.C. 112) to address two issues concerning the application of the ephemeral recording exemption in the digital age. The first of these issues is the relationship between the ephemeral recording exemption and the Digital Performance Right in Sound Recordings Act of 1995 ("DPRA"). The DPRA granted sound recording copyright owners the exclusive right to perform their works publicly by means of digital audio transmission, subject to certain limitations, particularly those set forth in section 114(d). Among those limitations is an exemption for nonsubscription broadcast transmissions, which are defined as those made by terrestrial broadcast stations licensed as such by the FCC. 17 U.S.C. §§ 114(d)(1)(A)(iii) and (j)(2). The ephemeral recording exemption presently privileges certain activities of a transmitting organization when it is entitled to transmit a performance or display under a license or transfer of copyright ownership or under the limitations on exclusive rights in sound recordings specified by section 114(a). The House bill and the Senate amendment propose changing the existing language of the ephemeral recording exemption (redesignated as 112(a)(1)) to extend explicitly to broadcasters the same privilege they already enjoy with respect to analog broadcasts.

The second of these issues is the relationship between the ephemeral recording exemption and the anticircumvention provisions that the bill adds as section 1201 of the Copyright Act. Concerns were expressed that if use of copy protection technologies became widespread, a transmitting organization might be prevented from engaging in its traditional activities of assembling transmission programs and making ephemeral recordings permitted by section 112 for purposes of its own transmissions within its local service area and of archival preservation and security. To address this concern, the House bill and the Senate amendment propose adding to section 112 a new paragraph that permits transmitting organizations to engage in activities that otherwise would violate section 1201(a)(1) in certain limited circumstances when necessary for the exercise of the transmitting organization's privilege to make ephemeral recordings under redesignated section 112(a)(1). By way of example, if a radio station could not make a permitted ephemeral recording from a commercially available phonorecord without violating section 1201(a)(1), then the radio station could request from the copyright owner the necessary means of making a permitted ephemeral recording. If the copyright owner did not then either provide a phonorecord that could be reproduced or otherwise provide the necessary means of making a permitted ephemeral recording from the phonorecord already in the possession of the radio station, the radio station would not be liable for violating section 1201(a)(1) for taking the steps necessary for engaging in activities permitted under section 112(a)(1). The radio station would, of course, be liable for violating section 1201(a)(1) if it engaged in activities prohibited by that section in other than the limited circumstances permitted by section 112(a)(1).

House section 411 is modified in two respects. First, the House provision is modified by adding a new paragraph (3) to include specific reference to section 114(f) in section 112(a) of the Copyright Act. The addition to section 112(a) of a reference to section 114(f) is intended to make clear that subscription music services, webcasters, satellite digital audio radio services and others with statutory licenses for the performance of sound recordings under section 114(f) are entitled to the benefits of section 112(a) with respect to the sound recordings they transmit.

Second, the House provision is modified in paragraph (4). This amendment to section 112(a) is intended to clarify the application of section 112(a) to FCC-licensed broadcasters with respect to digital nonsubscription broadcast transmissions. Notwithstanding this clarification, neither the amendment in paragraph (4) of section 411 nor the creation of a statutory license in section 112(e) is in any manner intended to narrow the scope of section 112(a) or the entitlement of any transmitting entity to the exemption provided thereunder with respect to copies made for other transmissions.

SECTION 403. LIMITATIONS ON EXCLUSIVE RIGHTS; DISTANCE EDUCATION

The Senate recedes to House section 412. The corresponding sections of the House bill and the Senate amendment are substantively identical.

SECTION 404. EXEMPTION FOR LIBRARIES AND ARCHIVES

The Senate recedes to House section 413. The corresponding sections of the House bill and the Senate amendment are substantively identical.

SECTION 405. SCOPE OF EXCLUSIVE RIGHTS IN SOUND RECORDINGS; EPHEMERAL RECORDINGS

The Senate recedes to section 415 of the House bill with modification.

The amendments to sections 112 and 114 of the Copyright Act that are contained in this section of the bill are intended to achieve two purposes: first, to further a stated objective of Congress when it passed the Digital Performance Right in Sound Recordings Act of 1995 ("DPRA") to ensure that recording artists and record companies will be protected as new technologies affect the ways in which their creative works are used; and second, to create fair and

80

efficient licensing mechanisms that address the complex issues facing copyright owners and copyright users as a result of the rapid growth of digital audio services. This section contains amendments to sections 112 and 114 of Title 17 as follows:

Section 114(d)(1). Exempt Transmissions and Retransmissions. Section 114(d)(1)(A) is amended to delete two exemptions that were either the cause of confusion as to the application of the DPRA to certain nonsubscription services (especially webcasters) or which overlapped with other exemptions (such as the exemption in subsection (A)(iii) for nonsubscription broadcast transmissions). The deletion of these two exemptions is not intended to affect the exemption for nonsubscription broadcast transmissions.

Section 114(d)(2). Statutory Licensing of Certain Transmissions. The amendment to subsection (d)(2) extends the availability of a statutory license for subscription transmissions to cover certain eligible nonsubscription transmissions. "Eligible nonsubscription transmission" are defined in subsection (j)(6). The amendment subdivides subsection (d)(2) into three subparagraphs ((A), (B), and (C)), each of which contains conditions of a statutory license for certain nonexempt subscription and eligible nonsubscription transmissions.

The conferees note that if a sound recording copyright owner authorizes a transmitting entity to take an action with respect to that copyright owner's sound recordings that is inconsistent with the requirements set forth in section 114(d)(2), the conferees do not intend that the transmitting entity be disqualified from obtaining a statutory license by virtue of such authorized actions.

The conferees intend that courts considering claims of infringement involving violation of the requirements set forth in section 114(d)(2) should judiciously apply the doctrine of de minimis non curat lex. A transmitting entity's statutory license should not be lost, and it become subject to infringement damages for transmissions that have been made as part of its service, merely because, through error, it has committed nonmaterial violations of these conditions that, once recognized, are not repeated. Similarly, if a service has multiple channels, the transmitting entity's statutory license should not be lost, and it become subject to infringement damages for transmissions that have been made on other channels, merely because of a violation in connection with one channel. Conversely, courts should not apply such doctrine in cases in which repeated or intentional violations occur.

Subparagraph (A) sets forth three conditions of a statutory license applicable to all nonexempt subscription and eligible nonsubscription transmissions. These three conditions are taken from previous subsection (d)(2).

Subparagraphs (B) and (C) are alternatives: a service is subject to the conditions in one or the other in addition to those in subparagraph (A). Subparagraph (B) contains conditions applicable only to nonexempt subscription transmissions made by a preexisting subscription service in the same transmission medium as was used by the service on July 31, 1998 or a preexisting satellite digital audio radio service. A preexisting subscription service is defined in subsection (j)(11); a preexisting satellite digital audio radio service is defined in (j)(10). The purpose of distinguishing preexisting

81

subscription services making transmissions in the same medium as on July 31, 1998, was to prevent disruption of the existing operations by such services. There was only three such services that exist: DMX (operated by TCI Music), Music Choice (operated by Digital Cable Radio Associates), and the DiSH Network (operated by Muzak). As of July 31, 1998, DMX and Music Choice made transmissions via both cable and satellite media; the DiSH Network was available only via satellite. The purpose of distinguishing the preexisting satellite digital audio radio services is similar. The two preexisting satellite digital audio radio services, CD Radio and American Mobile Radio Corporation, have purchased licenses at auction from the FCC and have begun developing their satellite systems.

The two conditions contained in subparagraph (B) are taken directly from previous subsection (d)(2). Thus, preexisting satellite digital audio radio services and the historical operations of preexisting subscription services are subject to the same five conditions for eligibility for a statutory license, as set forth in subparagraphs (A) and (B), as have applied previously to these services.

Subparagraph (C) sets forth additional conditions for a statutory license applicable to all transmissions not subject to subparagraph (B), namely all eligible nonsubscription transmissions, subscription transmissions made by a new subscription service, and subscription transmissions made by a preexisting subscription service other than those made in the same transmission medium. Subparagraph (C) contains nine conditions.

Subparagraph (C)(i) requires that transmissions subject to a statutory license cannot exceed the sound recording performance complement defined in subsection (j)(13), which is unchanged by this amendment. Subparagraph (C)(i) eliminates this requirement for retransmissions of over-the-air broadcast transmissions by a transmitting entity that does not have the right or ability to control the programming of the broadcast station making the initial broadcast transmission, subject to two limitations.

First, the retransmissions are not eligible for statutory licensing if the retransmitted broadcast transmissions are in digital format and regularly exceed the sound recording performance complement. Second, the retransmissions are not eligible for statutory licensing if the retransmitted broadcast transmissions are in analog format and a substantial portion of the transmissions, measured on a weekly basis, violate the sound recording performance complement. In both cases, however, the retransmitter is disqualified from making its transmissions under a statutory license only if the sound recording copyright owner or its representative notifies the retransmitter in writing that the broadcast transmissions exceed the sound recording performance complement. Once notification is received, the transmitting entity making the retransmissions must cease retransmitting those broadcast transmissions that exceed the sound recording performance complement.

Subparagraph (C)(ii) imposes limitations on the types of prior announcements, in text, video or audio, that may be made by a service under the statutory license. Services may not publish advance program schedules or make prior announcements of the titles of specific sound recordings or the featured artists to be performed

82

on the service. Moreover, services may not induce or facilitate the advance publication of schedules or the making of prior announcements, such as by providing a third party the list of songs or artists to be performed by the transmitting entity for publication or announcement by the third party. The conferees do not intend that the term "prior announcement" preclude a transmitting entity from identifying specific sound recordings immediately before they are performed.

However, services may generally use the names of several featured recording artists to illustrate the type of music being performed on a particular channel. Subparagraph (C)(iii) addresses limitations for archived programs and continuous programs, which are defined in subsections (j)(2) and (j)(4), respectively. Subparts (I) and (II) address archived programs. Archived programs often are available to listeners indefinitely or for a substantial period of time, thus permitting listeners to hear the same songs on demand any time the visitor wishes. Transmissions that are part of archived programs that are less than five hours long are ineligible for a statutory license. Transmissions that are part of archived programs more than five hours long are eligible only if the archived program is available on the webcaster's site or a related site for two weeks or less. The two-week limitation is to be applied in a reasonable manner to achieve the objectives of this subparagraph, so that, for example, archived programs that have been made available for two weeks are not removed from a site for a short period of time and then made available again. Furthermore, altering an archived program only in insignificant respects, such as by replacing or reordering only a small number of the songs comprising the program, does not render the program eligible for statutory licensing.

Subparagraph (C)(iii) also limits eligibility for a statutory license to transmissions that are not part of a continuous program of less than three hours duration (subparagraph (C)(iii)(III)). A listener to a continous program hears that portion of the program that is being transmitted to all listeners at the particular time that the listener accesses the program, much like a person who tunes in to an over-the-air broadcast radio station.

Finally, subparagraph (C)(iii)(IV) limits eligibility for a statutory license to transmissions that are not part of an identifiable program in which performances of sound recordings are rendered in a predetermined order that is transmitted at (a) more than three times in any two week period, which times have been publicly announced in advance, if the program is of less than one hour duration, or (b) more than four times in any two week period, which times have been publicly announced in advance, if the program is one hour or more. It is the conferee's intention that the two-week limitation in subclause (IV) be applied in a reasonable manner. consistent with its purpose so that, for example, a transmitting entity does not regularly make all of the permitted repeat performances within several days.

Subparagraph (C)(iv) states that the transmitting entity may not avail itself of a statutory license if it knowingly performs a sound recording, as part of a service that offers transmissions of visual images contemporaneous with transmissions of sound re-

83

cordings, in a manner that is likely to cause a listener to believe that there is an affiliation or association between the sound recording copyright owner or featured artist and a particular product or service advertised by the transmitting entity. This would cover, for example, transmitting an advertisement for a particular product or service every time a particular sound recording or artist is transmitted; it would not cover more general practices such as targeting advertisements of particular products or services to specific channels of the service according to user demographics. If, for example, advertisements are transmitted randomly while sound recordings are performed, this subparagraph would be satisfied.

Subparagraph (C)(v) provides that, in order to qualify for a statutory license, a transmitting entity must cooperate with sound recording copyright owners to prevent a transmission recipient from scanning the transmitting entity's transmissions to select particular sound recordings. In the future, a device or software may be developed that would enable its user to scan one or more digital transmissions to select particular sound recordings or artists requested by its user. Such devices or software would be the equivalent of an on demand service that would not be eligible for the statutory license. Technology may be developed to defeat such scanning, and transmitting entities taking a statutory license are required to cooperate with sound recording copyright owners to prevent such scanning, provided that such cooperation does not impose substantial costs or burdens on the transmitting entity. This requirement does not apply to a satellite digital audio service, including a preexisting satellite digital audio radio service, that is in operation, or that is licensed by the FCC, on or before July 31, 1998.

Subparagraph (C)(vi) requires that if the technology used by the transmitting entity enables the transmitting entity to limit the making by the transmission recipient of phonorecords in a digital format directly of the transmission, the transmitting entity sets such technology to limit such making of phonorecords to the extent permitted by such technology. The conferees note that some software used to "stream" transmissions of sound recordings enables the transmitting entity to disable such direct digital copying of the transmitted data by transmission recipients. In such circumstances the transmitting entity must disable that direct copying function. Likewise, a transmitting entity may not take affirmative steps to cause or induce the making of any copies by a transmission recipient. For example, a transmitting entity may not encourage a transmission recipient to make either digital or analog copies of the transmission such as by suggesting that recipients should record copyrighted programming transmitted by the entity.

Subparagraph (C)(vii) requires that each sound recording transmitted by the transmitting entity must have been distributed to the public under authority of the copyright owner or provided to the transmitting entity with authorization that the transmitting entity may perform such sound recording. The conferees recognize that a disturbing trend on the Internet is the unauthorized performance of sound recordings not yet released for broadcast or sale to the public. The transmission of such pre-released sound recordings is not covered by the statutory license unless the sound recording copyright owner has given explicit authorization to the

84

transmitting entity. This subparagraph also requires that the transmission be made from a phonorecord lawfully made under the authority of the copyright owner. A phonorecord provided by the copyright owner or an authorized phonorecord purchased through commercial distribution channels would qualify. However, the transmission of bootleg sound recordings (e.g., the recording of a live musical performance without the authority of the performer, as prohibited by Chapter 11) is ineligible for a statutory license.

Subparagraph (C)(viii) conditions a statutory license on whether a transmitting entity has accommodated and does not interfere with technical measures widely used by sound recording copyright owners to identify or protect their copyrighted works. Thus, the transmitting entity must ensure that widely used forms of identifying information, embedded codes, encryption or the like are not removed during the transmission process, provided that accommodating such measures is technologically feasible, does not impose substantial costs or burdens on the transmitting entity, and does not result in perceptible degradation of the digital audio or video signals being transmitted. This requirement shall not apply to a satellite digital audio service, including a preexisting satellite digital audio radio service, that is in operation, or that is licensed under the authority of the Federal Communications Commission, on or before July 31, 1998, to the extent that such service has designed, developed or made commitments to procure equipment or technology that is not compatible with such technical measures before such technical measures are widely adopted by sound recording copyright owners.

Subparagraph (C)(ix) requires transmitting entities eligible for the statutory license to identify in textual data the title of the sound recording, the title of the album on which the sound recording appears (if any), and the name of the featured recording artist. These titles and names must be made during, but not before, the performance of the sound recording. A transmitting entity must ensure that the identifying information can easily be seen by the transmission recipient in visual form. For example, the information might be displayed by the software player used on a listener's computer to decode and play the sound recordings that are transmitted. Many webcasters already provide such information, but in order to give those who do not an adequate opportunity to do so this obligation does not take effect until one year after the effective date of the amendment. This requirement does not apply to the retransmission of broadcast transmissions by a transmitting entity that does not have the right or ability to control the programming of the broadcast station making the broadcast transmission, or where devices or technology intended for receiving the service that have the capability to display the identifying information are not common in the marketplace.

Section 114(f). Licenses for Certain Nonexempt Transmissions. Section 114(f) is amended to set forth procedures for determining reasonable rates and terms for those transmissions that qualify for statutory licensing under section 114(d)(2). Section 114(f) is divided into two parts: one applying to transmissions by preexisting subscription services and preexisting satellite digital audio radio services (subsection (f)(1)), and the other applying to transmissions by

85

new subscription services (including subscription transmissions made by a preexisting subscription service other than those that qualify under subsection (f)(1)) as well as eligible nonsubscription transmissions (subsection (f)(2)).

Subsection (f)(1) provides for procedures applicable to subscription transmission by preexisting subscription services and preexisting satellite digital audio radio services. The conferees note that this subsection applies only to the three services considered preexisting subscription services, DMX, Music Choice and the DiSH Network, and the two services considered preexisting satellite digital audio radio services, CD Radio and American Mobile Radio Corporation. The procedures in this subsection remain the same as those applicable before the amendment, except that the rate currently in effect under prior section 114(f) is extended from December 31, 2000 until December 31, 2001. That rate currently applies to the three preexisting subscription services, and the Conferees take no position on its applicability to the two preexisting satellite digital audio radio services. Likewise, the initiation of the next voluntary negotiation period shall take place in the first week of January 2001 instead of January 2000 (subsection (f)(1)(C)(i)). These extensions are made purely to facilitate the scheduling of proceedings.

Subsection (f)(1)(B), which sets forth procedures for arbitration in the absence of negotiated license agreement, continues to provide that a copyright arbitration royalty panel should consider the objectives set forth in section 801(b)(1) as well as rates and terms for comparable types of subscription services.

Subsection (f)(2) addresses procedures applicable to eligible nonsubscription transmissions and subscription transmissions by new subscription services. The first such voluntary negotiation proceeding is to commence within 30 days after the enactment of this amendment upon publication by the Librarian of Congress of a notice in the Federal Register. The terms and rates established will cover qualified transmissions made between the effective date of this amendment and December 31, 2000, or such other date as the parties agree.

Subsection (f)(2) directs that rates and terms must distinguish between the different types of eligible nonsubscription transmission services and new subscription services then in operation. The conferees recognize that the nature of qualified transmissions may differ significantly based on a variety of factors. The conferees intend that criteria including, but not limited to, the quantity and nature of the use of sound recordings, and the degree to which use of the services substitutes for or promotes the purchase of phonorecords by consumers may account for differences in rates and terms between different types of transmissions.

Subsection (f)(2) also directs that a minimum fee should be established for each type of service. A minimum fee should ensure that copyright owners are fairly compensated in the event that other methodologies for setting rates might deny copyright owners an adequate royalty. For example, a copyright arbitration royalty panel should set a minimum fee that guarantees that a reasonable royalty rate is not diminished by different types of marketing practices or contractual relationships. For example, if the base royalty for a service were a percentage of revenues, the minimum fee might be a flat rate per year (or a flat rate per subscriber per year for a new subscription service).

Also, although subsection (f)(1) remains silent on the setting of a minimum fee for preexisting subscription services and preexisting satellite digital audio radio services, the Conferees do not intend that silence to mean that a minimum fee may or may not be established in appropriate circumstances when setting rates under subsection (f)(1) for preexisting subscription services and preexisting satellite digital audio radio services. Likewise, the absence of criteria that should be taken into account for distinguishing rates and terms for different services in subsection (f)(1) does not mean that evidence relating to such criteria may not be considered when adjusting rates and terms for preexisting subscription services and preexisting satellite digital audio radio services in the future.

Subsection (f)(2)(B) sets forth procedures in the absence of a negotiated license agreement for rates and terms for qualifying transmissions under this subsection. Consistent with existing law, a copyright arbitration proceeding should be empaneled to determine reasonable rates and terms. The test applicable to establishing rates and terms is what a willing buyer and willing seller would have arrived at in marketplace negotiations. In making that determination, the copyright arbitration royalty panel shall consider economic, competitive and programming information presented by the parties including, but not limited to, the factors set forth in clauses (i) and (ii).

Subsection (f)(2)(C) specifies that rates and terms for new subscription and eligible nonsubscription transmissions should be adjusted every two years, unless the parties agree as to another schedule. These two-year intervals are based upon the conferees' recognition that the types of transmission services in existence and the media in which they are delivered can change significantly in a short period of time.

Subsection (j)(2)—"archived program." A program is considered an "archived program" if it is prerecorded or preprogrammed, available repeatedly on demand to the public and is performed in virtually the same order from the beginning.

The exception to the definition of "archived program" for a recorded event or broadcast transmission is intended to allow webcasters to make available on demand transmissions of recorded events or broadcast shows that do not include performances of entire sound recordings or feature performances of sound recordings (such as a commercially released sound recording used as a theme song), but that instead use sound recordings only in an incidental manner (such as in the case of brief musical transitions in and out of commercials and music played in the background at sporting events). Some broadcast shows may be part of series that do not regularly feature performances of sound recordings but that occasionally prominently include a sound recording (such as a performance of a sound recording in connection with an appearance on the show by the recording artist). The recorded broadcast transmission of the show should not be considered an "archived program" merely because of such a prominent performance in a show that is part of a series that does not regularly feature performances of sound recordings. The inclusion of this exception to the definition of "archived program" is not intended to impose any new license requirement where the broadcast programmer or syndicator grants the webcaster the right to transmit a sound recording, such as may be the case where the sound recording has been specially created for use in a broadcast show.

Subsection 114(j)(4)—"continuous program." A "continuous program" is one that is continuously performed in the same predetermined order. Such a program generally takes the form of a loop whereby the same set of sound recordings is performed repeatedly; rather than stopping at the end of the set, the program automatically restarts generally without interruption. In contrast to an archived program (which always is accessed from the beginning of the program), a transmission recipient typically accesses a continuous program in the middle of the program. Minor alterations in the program should not render a program outside the definition of "continuous program."

Subsection 114(j)(6)—"eligible nonsubscription transmission". An "eligible nonsubscription transmission" is one that meets the following criteria. First, the transmission must be noninteractive and nonsubscription in nature. Second, the transmission must be made as part of a service that provides audio programming consisting in whole or in part of performances of sound recordings. Third, the purpose of the transmission service must be to provide audio or entertainment programming, not to sell, advertise or promote particular goods or services. Thus, for example, an ordinary commercial Web site that was primarily oriented to the promotion of a particular company or to goods or services that are unrelated to the sound recordings or entertainment programming, but that provides background music would not qualify as a service that makes eligible nonsubscription transmissions. The site's background music transmissions would need to be licensed through voluntary negotiations with the copyright owners. However, the sale or promotion of sound recordings, live concerts or other musical events does not disqualify a service making a nonsubscription transmission. Furthermore, the mere fact that a transmission service is advertiser-based or may promote itself or an affiliated entertainment service does not disqualify it from being considered an eligible nonsubscription transmission service.

Subsection 114(j)(7)—"interactive service." The definition of "interactive service" is amended in several respects. First, personalized tranmissions—those that are specially created for a particular individual—are to be considered interactive. The recipient of the transmission need not select the particular recordings in the program for it to be considered personalized, for example, the recipient might identify certain artists that become the basis of the personal program. The conferees intend that the phrase "program specially created for the recipient" be interpreted reasonably in light of the remainder of the definition of "interactive service." For example, a service would be interactive if it allowed a small number of individuals to request that sound recordings be performed in a program specially created for that group and not available to any individuals outside of that group. In contrast, a service would not be interactive if it merely transmitted to a large number of recipients of

88

the service's transmissions a program consisting of sound recordings requested by a small number of those listeners.

Second, a transmission of a particular sound recording on request is considered interactive "whether or not [the sound recording is] part of a program." This language clarifies that if a transmission recipient is permitted to select particular sound recordings in a prerecorded or predetermined program, the transmission is considered interactive. For example, if a transmission recipient has the ability to move forward and backward between songs in a program, the transmission is interactive. It is not necessary that the transmission recipient be able to select the actual songs that comprise the program. Additionally, a program consisting only of one sound recording would be considered interactive.

Third, the definition of "interactive service" is amended to clarify that certain channels or programs are not considered interactive provided that they do not substantially consist of requested sound recordings that are performed within one hour of the request or at a designated time. Thus, a service that engaged in the typical broadcast programming practice of including selections requested by listeners would not be considered interactive, so long as the programming did not substantially consist of requests regularly performed within an hour of the request, or at a time that the transmitting entity informs the recipient it will be performed.

The last sentence of the definition is intended to make clear that if a transmitting entity offers both interactive and noninteractive services then the noninteractive components are not to be treated as part of an interactive service, and thus are eligible for statutory licensing (assuming the other requirements of the statutory license are met). For example, if a Web site offered certain programming that was transmitted to all listeners who chose to receive it at the same time and also offered certain sound recordings that were transmitted to particular listeners on request, the fact that the latter are interactive transmissions would not preclude statutory licensing of the former.

Subsection 114(j)(8)—"new subscription service." A "new subscription service" is any service that is not a preexisting subscription service as defined in subsection (j)(11) or a preexisting satellite digital audio radio service as defined in subsection (j)(10).

Subsection 114(j)(10)—"preexisting satellite digital audio radio service." A "preexisting satellite digital audio service" is a subscription digital audio radio service provided pursuant to a satellite digital audio radio service license issued by the Federal Communications Commission on or before July 31, 1998. Subscription services offered by these licensed entities do not qualify as "preexisting subscription services" under section 114(j)(11) because they had not commenced making transmissions to the public for a fee on or before July 31, 1998. Only two entities received these licenses: CD Radio and American Mobile Radio Corporation.

A "preexisting satellite digital audio radio service" and "preexisting subscription service" may both include a limited number of sample channels representative of the subscription service that are made available on a nonsubscription basis in order to promote the subscription service. Such sample channels are to be treated as part of the subscription service and should be considered in determining the royalty rate for such subscription service. The conferees do not intend that the ability to offer such sample channels be used as a means to offer a nonsubscription service under the provisions of section 114 applicable to subscription services. The term "limited number" should be evaluated in the context of the overall service. For example, a service consisting of 100 channels should have no more than a small percentage of its channels as sample channels.

Subsection 114(j)(11)—"preexisting subscription service." A "preexisting subscription service" is a noninteractive subscription service that was in existence and was making transmissions to the public on or before July 31, 1998, and which is making transmissions similar in character to such transmissions made on or before July 31, 1998. Only three services qualify as a preexisting subscription service—DMX, Music Choice and the DiSH Network. As of July 31, 1998, DMX and Music Choice made transmissions via both cable and satellite media; the DiSH Network was available only via satellite.

In grandfathering these services, the conferee's objective was to limit the grandfather to their existing services in the same transmission medium and to any new services in a new transmission medium where only transmissions similar to their existing service are provided. Thus, if a cable subscription music service making transmissions on July 31, 1998, were to offer the same music service through the Internet, then such Internet service would be considered part of a preexisting subscription service.

If, however, a subscription service making transmissions on July 31, 1998, were to offer a new service either in the same or new transmission medium by taking advantages of the capabilities of that medium, such new service would not qualify as a preexisting subscription service. For example, a service that offers video programming, such as advertising or other content, would not qualify as a preexisting service, provided that the video programming is not merely information about the service itself, the sound recordings being transmitted, the featured artists, composers or songwriters, or an advertisement to purchase the sound recording transmitted.

Section 114 in General. These amendments are fully subject to all the existing provisions of section 114. Specifically, these amendments and the statutory licenses they create are all fully subject to the safeguards for copyright owners of sound recordings and musical works contained in sections 114(c), 114(d)(4) and 114(i), as well as the other provisions of section 114. In addition, the conferees do not intend to affect any of the rights in section 115 that were clarified and confirmed in the DPRA.

Section 112(e)—Statutory License. Section 112(e) creates a statutory license for the making of an "ephemeral recording" of a sound recording by certain transmitting organizations. The new statutory license in section 112(e) is intended primarily for the benefit of entities that transmit performances of sound recordings to business establishments pursuant to the limitation on exclusive rights set forth in section 114(d)(1)(C)(iv). However, the new section 112(e) statutory license also is available to a transmitting entity with a statutory license under section 114(f) that chooses to avail itself of the section 112(e) statutory license to make more than the one pho-

90

norecord it is entitled to make under section 112(a). For example, the conferees understand that a webcaster might wish to reproduce multiple copies of a sound recording to use on different servers or to make transmissions at different transmission rates or using different transmission software. Under section 112(a), as amended by this bill, a webcaster with a section 114(f) statutory license is entitled to make only a single copy of the sound recording. Thus, the webcaster might choose to obtain a statutory license under section 112(e) to allow it to make such multiple copies. The conferees intend that the royalty rate payable under the statutory license may reflect the number of phonorecords of a sound recording made under a statutory license for use in connection with each type of service.

Ephemeral recordings of sound recordings made by certain transmitting organizations under section 112(e) may embody copyrighted musical compositions. The making of an ephemeral recording by such a transmitting organization of each copyrighted musical composition embodied in a sound recording it transmits is governed by existing section 112(a) (or section 112(a)(1) as revised by the Digital Millennium Copyright Act), and, pursuant to that section, authorization for the making of an ephemeral recording is conditioned in part on the transmitting organization being entitled to transmit to the public the performance of a musical composition under a license or transfer of the copyright.

The conditions listed in section 112(e)(1), most of which are also found in section 112(a), must be met before a transmitting organization is eligible for statutory licensing in accordance with section 112(e). First, paragraph (1)(A) provides that the transmitting organization may reproduce and retain only one phonorecord, solely for its own use (unless the terms and conditions of the statutory license allow for more). Thus, trafficking in ephemeral recordings, such as by preparing prerecorded transmission programs for use by third parties, is not permitted. This paragraph provides that the transmitting organization may reproduce and retain more than one ephemeral recording, in the manner permitted under the terms and conditions as negotiated or arbitrated under the statutory license. This provision is intended to facilitate efficient transmission technologies, such as the use of phonorecords encoded for optimal performance at different transmission rates or use of different software programs to receive the transmissions.

Second, paragraph (1)(B) requires that the phonorecord be used only for the transmitting organization's own transmissions originating in the United States, and such transmissions must be made under statutory license pursuant to section 114(f) or the exemption in section 114(d)(1)(C)(iv). Third, paragraph (1)(C) mandates that, unless preserved exclusively for archival purposes, the phonorecord be destroyed within six months from the time that the sound recording was first performed publicly by the transmitting organization. Fourth, paragraph (1)(D) limits the statutory license to reproductions of sound recordings that have been distributed to the public and that are made from a phonorecord lawfully made and acquired under the authority of the copyright owner.

Subsection (e)(3) clarifies the applicability of the antitrust laws to the use of common agents in negotiations and agreements relat-

91

ing to statutory licenses and other licenses. Under this subsection, the copyright owners of sound recordings and transmitting organizations entitled to obtain the statutory license in this section may negotiate collectively regarding rates and terms for the statutory license or other licenses. This subsection provides that such copyright owners and transmitting organizations may designate common agents to represent their interests to negotiate or administer such license agreements. This subsection closely follows the language of existing antitrust exemptions in copyright law, including the exemption found in the statutory licenses for transmitting sound recordings by digital audio transmission found in section 114(f).

Subsections (e)(4) and (5) address the procedures for determining rates and terms for the statutory license provided for in this section. These procedures are parallel to the procedures found in section 114(f)(2) for public performances of sound recordings by digital audio transmission by new subscription services and services making eligible Nonsubscription transmissions.

Subsection (e)(4) provides that the Librarian of Congress should publish notice of voluntary negotiation proceedings 30 days after enactment of this amendment. Such voluntary negotiation proceedings should address rates and terms for the making of ephemeral recordings under the conditions of this section for the period beginning on the date of enactment and ending on December 31, 2000. This subsection requires that a minimum fee be established as part of the rates and terms.

In the event that interested parties do not arrive at negotiated rates and terms during the voluntary negotiation proceedings, subsection (e)(5) provides for the convening of a copyright arbitration royalty panel to determine reasonable rates and terms for the making of ephemeral recordings under this subsection. This paragraph requires the copyright arbitration royalty panel to establish rates that reflect the fees that a willing buyer and seller would have agreed to in marketplace negotiations. In so doing, the copyright arbitration royalty panel should base its decision on economic, competitive and programming information presented by the parties, including, but not limited to, such evidence as described in subparagraphs (A) and (B).

Subseciton (e)(7) states that rates and terms either negotiated or established pursuant to arbitration shall be effective for two-year periods, and the procedures set forth in subsections (e)(4) and (5) shall be repeated every two years unless otherwise agreed to by the parties.

The conferees intend that the amendments regarding the statutory licenses in sections 112 and 114 contained in section 415 of this bill apply only to those statutory licenses.

SECTION 406. ASSUMPTION OF CONTRACTUAL OBLIGATIONS RELATED TO TRANSFERS OF RIGHTS IN MOTION PICTURES

The Senate recedes to House section 416 with modification.

Paragraph (a)—Assumption of obligations. The conferees have added to paragraph (a) language that defines more specifically the meaning of the "knows or has reason to know" standard in subsection (a)(1). There are three ways to satisfy this standard. The

92

first is actual knowledge that a motion picture is or will be covered by a collective bargaining agreement. Subparagraph (ii) provides for constructive knowledge, established through two alternative mechanisms: recordation with the Copyright Office or identification of the motion picture on an online web site maintained by the relevant Guild, where the site makes it possible for users to verify their access date in a commercially reasonable way. In order to ensure that the transferee has a reasonable opportunity to obtain the relevant information, these mechanisms for providing constructive notice apply with respect to transfers that take place after the motion picture is completed. They also apply to transfer that take place before the motion picture is completed, but only if the transfer is within eighteen months prior to the filing of an application for copyright registration for the motion picture or, if there is no application for registration, within eighteen months of its first publication in the United States.

The constructive notice established by recordation for purposes of application of this section is entirely separate and independent from the constructive notice established by recordation under section 205(c) of the Copyright Act. This section does not condition constructive notice on prior registration of the motion picture with the Copyright Office, and does not have any hearing on the issue of priority between conflicting transfers as described in section 205(d) of the Copyright Act.

Subparagraph (iii) provides a more general standard for circumstances where the transferee does not have actual knowledge or constructive knowledge through one of the two mechanisms set out in subparagraph (ii), but is aware of facts and circumstances about the transfer that make it apparent that the motion picture is subject to a collective bargaining agreement. Such facts and information might include, for example, budget, location of principal photography, the identity of the talent associated with a project, or the existence of a personal service contract that references terms or conditions of collective bargaining agreements.

Paragraph (b)—Scope of exclusion of transfer of public performance rights.—New paragraph (b) clarifies that the "public performance" exclusion from the operation of paragraph (a) is intended to include performances described in paragraph (b) that reach viewers through transmission or retransmission of programming or program services via satellite, MMDS, cable, and other means of carriage. This paragraph does not expand or restrict in any way what constitutes a "public performance" for any other purpose. The public performance exclusion would not be rendered inoperable simply because a transfer of public performance rights is accompanied by a transfer of limited, incidental other rights necessary to implement or facilitate the exercise of the performance rights.

Paragraph (c)—Exclusion for grants of security interests.—The purpose of this paragraph is to ensure that banks and others providing financing for motion pictures will not be made subject to the assumption of obligations required by this section merely because they obtain a security interest in the motion picture. Because the term "transfer of copyright ownership" is defined in section 101 of the Copyright Act to include a "mortgage . . . or hypothecation" of any exclusive copyright right, this could be the unintended result

93

of the statutory language. Under this exclusion, a bank or other party would not be subject to the application of paragraph (a) based solely on the acts of taking a security interest in a motion picture, foreclosing on that interest or otherwise exercising its rights as a secured party, or transferring or authorizing transfer of copyright ownership rights secured by its security interest to a third party. Neither would any subsequent transferee downstream from the initial secured party be subject to paragraph (a). The exclusion would apply irreespective of the form or language used to grant or create the security interest.

It should be clear that the only agreements whose terms are enforced by this section are collective bargaining agreements and assumption agreements. In the course of financing a motion picture, a lender, other financier or completion guarantor may execute an inter-creditor or subordination agreement with a union including obligations with respect to the payment of residuals or the obtaining of assumption agreements. Such agreements are not within the scope of this section, and nothing in this section obligates lenders, other financiers or completion guarantors to enter into these agreements, enforces any terms thereof or diminishes any rights that the parties may have under these agreements.

Paragraph (d)—Deferral pending resolution of bona fide dispute. Paragraph (d) allows a remote transferee obligated under paragraph (a)(1) to stay enforcement of this section while there exists a bona fide dispute between the applicable union and a prior transferor regarding obligations under this section. It contemplates that union claims not subject to bona fide dispute will be payable when due under the applicable collective bargaining agreement or through application of this section. Such disputes may be manifested through grievance or arbitration claims, litigation, or other claims resolution procedures in effect between the applicable parties.

Paragraph (e)—Scope of obligations determined by private agreement. Paragraph (e) states explicitly the basic principle of operation of this section. It makes clear that the section simply provides an enforcement mechanism for obligations that have already been agreed to in a collective bargaining agreement. It is not intended to affect in any way the scope or interpretation of the provisions of, or the acts required by, any collective bargaining agreement. The rights and obligations themselves, as well as the remedies for breach, are those that have been agreed to among the parties. Accordingly, they can be changed at any time by agreement.

The collective bargaining agreements contemplate that producers will obtain assumption agreements from distributors in certain circumstances. The statute states that where a producer does not comply with the obligation and obtain an assumption agreement where required, the law will act as though the producer has in fact done so. Thus, it removes the possibility of noncompliance with the obligation to obtain an assumption agreement. It does not require assumption agreements to be obtained in circumstances where the collective bargaining agreement would not require it. If there is a dispute over the meaning and applicabiity of provisions in the collective bargaining agreement, for example over the question of which distributors must be required to execute an assumption

94

agreement, the statue does not resolve the dispute. It only requires whatever the collective bargaining agreement would require, and relegates the parties to the dispute mechanisms set out in that agreement.

This section does not expand or diminish rights or obligations under other laws that might regulate contractual obligations beyond the purpose of enforcing assumption agreements required by applicable collective bargaining agreements. Nor does this section prevent a person or entity that is subject to obligations under an assumption agreement (whether through application of this section or otherwise) from transferring any such obligations to a subsequent transferee of the applicable copyright rights, and thereby being relieved of its own obligations under the assumption agreement, to the extent permitted by, and under the conditions established in, the applicable assumption agreements.

TITLE V—PROTECTION OF CERTAIN ORIGINAL DESIGNS

Sections 501–505. The Senate recedes to House sections 601–602 with modification.

From the Committee on Commerce for consideration of the House bill, and the Senate amendment, and modifications committed to conference:

TOM BLILEY,
BILLY TAUZIN,
JOHN D. DINGELL,

From the Committee on the Judiciary for consideration of the House bill, and the Senate amendment, and modifications committed to conference:

HENRY J. HYDE,
HOWARD COBLE,
BOB GOODLATTE,
JOHN CONYERS, Jr.,
HOWARD L. BERMAN,
Managers on the Part of the House.

ORRIN G. HATCH,
STROM THURMOND,
PATRICK J. LEAHY,
Managers on the Part of the Senate.

○

Statement on Signing the Digital Millennium Copyright Act

1998 Public Papers of the Presidents--Vol. 2

October 28, 1998

STATEMENT BY PRESIDENT WILLIAM J. CLINTON UPON SIGNING H.R. 2281

Today I am pleased to sign into law H.R. 2281, the "Digital Millennium Copyright Act." This Act implements two landmark treaties that were successfully negotiated by my Administration in 1996 and to which the Senate gave its advice and consent to ratification on October 21, 1998. The Act also limits the liability of online service providers for copyright infringement under certain conditions.

The World Intellectual Property Organization (WIPO) Copyright Treaty and the WIPO Performances and Phonogram Treaty mark the most extensive revision of international copyright law in over 25 years. The treaties will grant writers, artists, and other creators of copyrighted material global protection from piracy in the digital age.

These treaties will become effective at a time when technological innovations present us with great opportunities for the global distribution of copyrighted works. These same technologies, however, make it possible to pirate copyrighted works on a global scale with a single keystroke. The WIPO treaties set clear and firm standards—obligating signatory countries to provide "adequate legal protection" and "effective legal remedies" against circumvention of certain technologies that copyright owners use to protect their works, and against violation of the integrity of copyright management information. This Act implements those standards, carefully balancing the interests of both copyright owners and users.

I am advised by the Department of Justice that certain provisions of H.R. 2281 and the accompanying Conference Report regarding the Register of Copyrights raise serious constitutional concerns. Contrary to assertions in the Conference Report, the Copyright Office is, for constitutional purposes, an executive branch entity. Accordingly, the Congress may exercise its constitutionally legitimate oversight powers to require the Copyright Office to provide information relevant to the legislative process. However, to direct that Office's operations, the Congress must act in accord with the requirements of bicameralism and presentment prescribed in Article I of the Constitution. Further, the Congress may not require the Register to act in a manner that would impinge upon or undermine the President's discretion under Article II, section 3 of the Constitution to determine which, if any, executive branch recommendations to the Congress would be "necessary and expedient." Accordingly, I will construe sections 103(a), 104(b), 410(b), and 403(a) of H.R. 2281 to require the Register to perform duties only insofar as such requirements are consistent with these constitutional principles.

From the efforts of the Assistant Secretary of Commerce and Commissioner of Patents and Trademarks who acted as the lead negotiator for these treaties, to the agreement reached by interests affected by online service provider liability, to the improvements added by two House Committees and one Senate Committee, this Act reflects the diligence and talents of a great many people. Through enactment of the Digital Millennium Copyright Act, we have done our best to protect from digital piracy the copyright industries that comprise the leading export of the United States.

William J. Clinton

THE WHITE HOUSE
October 28, 1998.

The Digital Millennium Copyright Act
Text, History, and Caselaw

IV. POST-ENACTMENT HISTORY & PROPOSED LEGISLATION

Public Law 106–44
106th Congress

An Act

To make technical corrections in title 17, United States Code, and other laws.

Aug. 5, 1999
[S. 1260]

Copyrights.

Be it enacted by the Senate and House of Representatives of the United States of America in Congress assembled,

SECTION 1. TECHNICAL CORRECTIONS TO TITLE 17, UNITED STATES CODE.

(a) EXEMPTION OF CERTAIN PERFORMANCES AND DISPLAYS ON EXCLUSIVE RIGHTS.—Section 110(5) of title 17, United States Code, is amended—

(1) by striking "(A) a direct charge" and inserting "(i) a direct charge"; and

(2) by striking "(B) the transmission" and inserting "(ii) the transmission".

(b) EPHEMERAL RECORDINGS.—Section 112(e) of title 17, United States Code, is amended—

(1) by redesignating paragraphs (3) through (10) as paragraphs (2) through (9), respectively;

(2) in paragraph (3), as so redesignated, by striking "(2)" and inserting "(1)";

(3) in paragraph (4), as so redesignated—

(A) by striking "(3)" and inserting "(2)";

(B) by striking "(4)" and inserting "(3)";

(C) by striking "(6)" and inserting "(5)"; and

(D) by striking "(3) and (4)" and inserting "(2) and (3)"; and

(4) in paragraph (6), as so redesignated—

(A) by striking "(4)" each place it appears and inserting "(3)"; and

(B) by striking "(5)" each place it appears and inserting "(4)".

(c) DETERMINATION OF REASONABLE LICENSE FEES FOR INDIVIDUAL PROPRIETORS.—Chapter 5 of title 17, United States Code, is amended—

(1) by redesignating the section 512 entitled "**Determination of reasonable license fees for individual proprietors**" as section 513 and placing such section after the section 512 entitled "**Limitations on liability relating to material online**"; and

(2) in the table of sections at the beginning of that chapter by striking

"512. Determination of reasonable license fees for individual proprietors."

and inserting

"513. Determination of reasonable license fees for individual proprietors."

and placing that item after the item entitled

"512. Limitations on liability relating to material online.".

(d) ONLINE COPYRIGHT INFRINGEMENT LIABILITY.—Section 512 of title 17, United States Code, is amended—

(1) in subsection (e)—

(A) by amending the caption to read as follows: "(e) LIMITATION ON LIABILITY OF NONPROFIT EDUCATIONAL INSTITUTIONS.—"; and

(B) in paragraph (2), by striking "INJUNCTIONS.—"; and

(2) in paragraph (3) of subsection (j), by amending the caption to read as follows:

"(3) NOTICE AND EX PARTE ORDERS.—".

(e) INTEGRITY OF COPYRIGHT MANAGEMENT INFORMATION.—Section 1202(e)(2)(B) of title 17, United States Code, is amended by striking "category or works" and inserting "category of works".

(f) PROTECTION OF DESIGNS.—(1) Section 1302(5) of title 17, United States Code, is amended by striking "1 year" and inserting "2 years".

(2) Section 1320(c) of title 17, United States Code, is amended in the subsection caption by striking "ACKNOWLEDGEMENT" and inserting "ACKNOWLEDGMENT".

(g) MISCELLANEOUS CLERICAL AMENDMENTS.—

(1) Section 101 of title 17, United States Code, is amended—

(A) by transferring and inserting the definition of "United States work" after the definition of "United States"; and

(B) in the definition of "proprietor", by striking "A 'proprietor'" and inserting "For purposes of section 513, a 'proprietor'".

(2) Section 106 of title 17, United States Code, is amended by striking "120" and inserting "121".

(3) Section 118(e) of title 17, United States Code, is amended—

(A) by striking "subsection (b)." and all that follows through "Owners" and inserting "subsection (b). Owners"; and

(B) by striking paragraph (2).

(4) Section 119(a)(8)(C)(ii) of title 17, United States Code, is amended by striking "network's station" and inserting "network station's".

(5) Section 501(a) of title 17, United States Code, is amended by striking "118" and inserting "121".

(6) Section 511(a) of title 17, United States Code, is amended by striking "119" and inserting "121".

PUBLIC LAW 106–44—AUG. 5, 1999   113 STAT. 223

SEC. 2. OTHER TECHNICAL CORRECTIONS.

(a) Cʟᴇʀɪᴄᴀʟ Aᴍᴇɴᴅᴍᴇɴᴛ ᴛᴏ Tɪᴛʟᴇ 28, U.S.C.—The section heading for section 1400 of title 28, United States Code, is amended to read as follows:

"§ 1400. Patents and copyrights, mask works, and designs".

(b) Eʟɪᴍɪɴᴀᴛɪᴏɴ ᴏꜰ Cᴏɴꜰʟɪᴄᴛɪɴɢ Pʀᴏᴠɪsɪᴏɴ.—Section 5316 of title 5, United States Code, is amended by striking "Commissioner of Patents, Department of Commerce.".

(c) Cʟᴇʀɪᴄᴀʟ Cᴏʀʀᴇᴄᴛɪᴏɴ ᴛᴏ Tɪᴛʟᴇ 35, U.S.C.—Section 3(d) of title 35, United States Code, is amended by striking ", United States Code".

Approved Aug. 5, 1999.

LEGISLATIVE HISTORY—S. 1260 (H.R. 1189):

HOUSE REPORTS: No. 106–84 accompanying H.R. 1189 (Comm. on the Judiciary).
CONGRESSIONAL RECORD, Vol. 145 (1999):
    July 1, considered and passed Senate.
    July 26, considered and passed House.

O

107TH CONGRESS
2D SESSION

S. 2048

To regulate interstate commerce in certain devices by providing for private sector development of technological protection measures to be implemented and enforced by Federal regulations to protect digital content and promote broadband as well as the transition to digital television, and for other purposes.

IN THE SENATE OF THE UNITED STATES

MARCH 21, 2002

Mr. HOLLINGS (for himself, Mr. STEVENS, Mr. INOUYE, Mr. BREAUX, Mr. NELSON of Florida, and Mrs. FEINSTEIN) introduced the following bill; which was read twice and referred to the Committee on Commerce, Science, and Transportation

---

A BILL

To regulate interstate commerce in certain devices by providing for private sector development of technological protection measures to be implemented and enforced by Federal regulations to protect digital content and promote broadband as well as the transition to digital television, and for other purposes.

1 *Be it enacted by the Senate and House of Representa-*
2 *tives of the United States of America in Congress assembled,*

2

1 **SECTION 1. SHORT TITLE; TABLE OF SECTIONS.**

2   (a) SHORT TITLE.—This Act may be cited as the

3 "Consumer Broadband and Digital Television Promotion

4 Act".

5   (b) TABLE OF SECTIONS.—The table of sections for

6 this Act is as follows:

7 **SEC. 2. FINDINGS.**

8   The Congress finds the following:

9   (1) The lack of high quality digital content con-

10   tinues to hinder consumer adoption of broadband

11   Internet service and digital television products.

12   (2) Owners of digital programming and content

13   are increasingly reluctant to transmit their products

14   unless digital media devices incorporate technologies

15   that recognize and respond to content security meas-

16   ures designed to prevent theft.

17   (3) Because digital content can be copied quick-

18   ly, easily, and without degradation, digital program-

19   mers and content owners face an exponentially in-

20   creasing piracy threat in a digital age.

•S 2048 IS

3

1   (4) Current agreements reached in the market-
2 place to include security technologies in certain dig-
3 ital media devices fail to provide a secure digital en-
4 vironment because those agreements do not prevent
5 the continued use and manufacture of digital media
6 devices that fail to incorporate such security tech-
7 nologies.

8   (5) Other existing digital rights management
9 schemes represent proprietary, partial solutions that
10 limit, rather than promote, consumers' access to the
11 greatest variety of digital content possible.

12   (6) Technological solutions can be developed to
13 protect digital content on digital broadcast television
14 and over the Internet.

15   (7) Competing business interests have frus-
16 trated agreement on the deployment of existing tech-
17 nology in digital media devices to protect digital con-
18 tent on the Internet or on digital broadcast tele-
19 vision.

20   (8) The secure protection of digital content is
21 a necessary precondition to the dissemination, and
22 on-line availability, of high quality digital content,
23 which will benefit consumers and lead to the rapid
24 growth of broadband networks.

4

1   (9) The secure protection of digital content is

2 a necessary precondition to facilitating and has-

3 tening the transition to high-definition television,

4 which will benefit consumers.

5   (10) Today, cable and satellite have a competi-

6 tive advantage over digital television because the

7 closed nature of cable and satellite systems permit

8 encryption, which provides some protection for dig-

9 ital content.

10   (11) Over-the-air broadcasts of digital television

11 are not encrypted for public policy reasons and thus

12 lack those protections afforded to programming de-

13 livered via cable or satellite.

14   (12) A solution to this problem is techno-

15 logically feasible but will require government action,

16 including a mandate to ensure its swift and ubiq-

17 uitous adoption.

18   (13) Consumers receive content such as video

19 or programming in analog form.

20   (14) When protected digital content is con-

21 verted to analog for consumers, it is no longer pro-

22 tected and is subject to conversion into unprotected

23 digital form that can in turn be copied or redistrib-

24 uted illegally.

5

1   (15) A solution to this problem is techno-

2   logically feasible but will require government action,

3   including a mandate to ensure its swift and ubiq-

4   uitous adoption.

5   (16) Unprotected digital content on the Inter-

6   net is subject to significant piracy, through illegal

7   file sharing, downloading, and redistribution over the

8   Internet.

9   (17) Millions of Americans are currently

10 downloading television programs, movies, and music

11 on the Internet and by using "file-sharing" tech-

12 nology. Much of this activity is illegal, but dem-

13 onstrates consumers' desire to access digital content.

14   (18) This piracy poses a substantial economic

15 threat to America's content industries.

16   (19) A solution to this problem is techno-

17 logically feasible but will require government action,

18 including a mandate to ensure its swift and ubiq-

19 uitous adoption.

20   (20) Providing a secure, protected environment

21 for digital content should be accompanied by a pres-

22 ervation of legitimate consumer expectations regard-

23 ing use of digital content in the home.

24   (21) Secure technological protections should en-

25 able content owners to disseminate digital content

6

1 over the Internet without frustrating consumers' le-

2 gitimate expectations to use that content in a legal

3 manner.

4   (22) Technologies used to protect digital con-

5 tent should facilitate legitimate home use of digital

6 content.

7   (23) Technologies used to protect digital con-

8 tent should facilitate individuals' ability to engage in

9 legitimate use of digital content for educational or

10 research purposes.

11 **SEC. 3. ADOPTION OF SECURITY SYSTEM STANDARDS AND**

12   **ENCODING RULES.**

13   (a) PRIVATE SECTOR EFFORTS.—

14   (1) IN GENERAL.—The Federal Communica-

15 tions Commission, in consultation with the Register

16 of Copyrights, shall make a determination, not more

17 than 12 months after the date of enactment of this

18 Act, as to whether—

19   (A) representatives of digital media device

20   manufacturers, consumer groups, and copyright

21   owners have reached agreement on security sys-

22   tem standards for use in digital media devices

23   and encoding rules; and

•S 2048 IS

7

1   (B) the standards and encoding rules con-

2   form to the requirements of subsections (d) and

3   (e).

4   (2) REPORT TO THE COMMERCE AND JUDICI-

5   ARY COMMITTEES.—Within 6 months after the date

6   of enactment of this Act, the Commission shall re-

7   port to the Senate Committee on Commerce, Science

8   and Transportation, the Senate Committee on the

9   Judiciary, the House of Representatives Committee

10 on Commerce, and the House of Representatives

11 Committee on the Judiciary as to whether—

12   (A) substantial progress has been made to-

13   ward the development of security system stand-

14   ards and encoding rules that will conform to

15   the requirements of subsections (d) and (e);

16   (B) private sector negotiations are con-

17   tinuing in good faith;

18   (C) there is a reasonable expectation that

19   final agreement will be reached within 1 year

20   after the date of enactment of this Act; and

21   (D) if it is unlikely that such a final agree-

22   ment will be reached by the end of that year,

23   the deadline should be extended.

24   (b) AFFIRMATIVE DETERMINATION.—If the Commis-

25 sion makes a determination under subsection (a)(1) that

8

1   an agreement on security system standards and encoding

2   rules that conform to the requirements of subsections (d)

3   and (e) has been reached, then the Commission shall—

4   (1) initiate a rulemaking, within 30 days after

5   the date on which the determination is made, to

6   adopt those standards and encoding rules; and

7   (2) publish a final rule pursuant to that rule-

8   making, not later than 180 days after initiating the

9   rulemaking, that will take effect 1 year after its pub-

10   lication.

11 (c) NEGATIVE DETERMINATION.—If the Commission

12 makes a determination under subsection (a)(1) that an

13 agreement on security system standards and encoding

14 rules that conform to the requirements of subsections (d)

15 and (e) has not been reached, then the Commission—

16   (1) in consultation with representatives de-

17   scribed in subsection (a)(1)(A) and the Register of

18   Copyrights, shall initiate a rulemaking, within 30

19   days after the date on which the determination is

20   made, to adopt security system standards and en-

21   coding rules that conform to the requirements of

22   subsections (d) and (e); and

23   (2) shall publish a final rule pursuant to that

24   rulemaking, not later than 1 year after initiating the

9

1   rulemaking, that will take effect 1 year after its pub-

2   lication.

3   (d) SECURITY SYSTEM STANDARDS.—In achieving

4 the goals of setting open security system standards that

5 will provide effective security for copyrighted works, the

6 security system standards shall ensure, to the extent prac-

7 ticable, that—

8   (1) the standard security technologies are—

9   (A) reliable;

10   (B) renewable;

11   (C) resistant to attack;

12   (D) readily implemented;

13   (E) modular;

14   (F) applicable to multiple technology plat-

15   forms;

16   (G) extensible;

17   (H) upgradable;

18   (I) not cost prohibitive; and

19   (2) any software portion of such standards is

20 based on open source code.

21   (e) ENCODING RULES.—

22   (1) LIMITATIONS ON THE EXCLUSIVE RIGHTS

23   OF COPYRIGHT OWNERS.—In achieving the goal of

24   promoting as many lawful uses of copyrighted works

25   as possible, while preventing as much infringement

10

1   as possible, the encoding rules shall take into ac-

2   count the limitations on the exclusive rights of copy-

3   right owners, including the fair use doctrine.

4   (2) PERSONAL USE COPIES.—No person may

5   apply a security measure that uses a standard secu-

6   rity technology to prevent a lawful recipient from

7   making a personal copy for lawful use in the home

8   of programming at the time it is lawfully performed,

9   on an over-the-air broadcast, premium or non-pre-

10   mium cable channel, or premium or non-premium

11   satellite channel, by a television broadcast station

12   (as defined in section 122(j)(5)(A) of title 17,

13   United States Code), a cable system (as defined in

14   section 111(f) of such title), or a satellite carrier (as

15   defined in section 119(d)(6) of such title).

16   (f) MEANS OF IMPLEMENTING STANDARDS.—The se-

17 curity system standards adopted under subsection (b), (c),

18 or (g) shall provide for secure technical means of imple-

19 menting directions of copyright owners for copyrighted

20 works.

21   (g) COMMISSION MAY REVISE STANDARDS AND

22 RULES THROUGH RULEMAKING.—

23   (1) IN GENERAL.—The Commission may con-

24   duct subsequent rulemakings to modify any security

25   system standards or encoding rules established

11

1 under subsection (b) or (c) or to adopt new security

2 system standards that conform to the requirements

3 of subsections (d) and (e).

4 (2) CONSULTATION REQUIRED.—The Commis-

5 sion shall conduct any such subsequent rulemaking

6 in consultation with representatives of digital media

7 device manufacturers, consumer groups, and copy-

8 right owners described in subsection (a)(1)(A) and

9 with the Register of Copyrights.

10 (3) IMPLEMENTATION.—Any final rule pub-

11 lished in such a subsequent rulemaking shall—

12 (A) apply prospectively only; and

13 (B) take into consideration the effect of

14 adoption of the modified or new security system

15 standards and encoding rules on consumers'

16 ability to utilize digital media devices manufac-

17 tured before the modified or new standards take

18 effect.

19 (h) MODIFICATION OF TECHNOLOGY BY PRIVATE

20 SECTOR.—

21 (1) IN GENERAL.—After security system stand-

22 ards have been established under subsection (b), (c),

23 or (g) of this section, representatives of digital

24 media device manufacturers, consumer groups, and

25 copyright owners described in subsection (a)(1)(A)

12

1 may modify the standard security technology that

2 adheres to the security system standards rules estab-

3 lished under this section if those representatives de-

4 termine that a change in the technology is necessary

5 because—

6   (A) the technology in use has been com-

7   promised; or

8   (B) technological improvements warrant

9   upgrading the technology in use.

10   (2) IMPLEMENTATION NOTIFICATION.—The

11 representatives described in paragraph (1) shall no-

12 tify the Commission of any such modification before

13 it is implemented or, if immediate implementation is

14 determined by the representatives to be necessary,

15 as soon thereafter as possible.

16   (3) COMPLIANCE WITH SUBSECTION (d) RE-

17 QUIREMENTS.—The Commission shall ensure that

18 any modification of standard security technology

19 under this subsection conforms to the requirements

20 of subsection (d).

21 **SEC. 4. PRESERVATION OF THE INTEGRITY OF SECURITY.**

22 An interactive computer service shall store and trans-

23 mit with integrity any security measure associated with

24 standard security technologies that is used in connection

25 with copyrighted material such service transmits or stores.

•S 2048 IS

13

**SEC. 5. PROHIBITION ON SHIPMENT IN INTERSTATE COM-
MERCE OF NONCONFORMING DIGITAL MEDIA
DEVICES.**

(a) IN GENERAL.—A manufacturer, importer, or seller of digital media devices may not—

(1) sell, or offer for sale, in interstate commerce, or

(2) cause to be transported in, or in a manner
affecting, interstate commerce,

a digital media device unless the device includes and utilizes standard security technologies that adhere to the security system standards adopted under section 3.

(b) EXCEPTION.—Subsection (a) does not apply to
the sale, offer for sale, or transportation of a digital media
device that was legally manufactured or imported, and
sold to the consumer, prior to the effective date of regulations adopted under section 3 and not subsequently modified in violation of section 6(a).

**SEC. 6. PROHIBITION ON REMOVAL OR ALTERATION OF SE-
CURITY TECHNOLOGY; VIOLATION OF EN-
CODING RULES.**

(a) REMOVAL OR ALTERATION OF SECURITY TECH-
NOLOGY.—No person may—

(1) knowingly remove or alter any standard security technology in a digital media device lawfully
transported in interstate commerce; or

14

1   (2) knowingly transmit or make available to the

2   public any copyrighted material where the security

3   measure associated with a standard security tech-

4   nology has been removed or altered, without the au-

5   thority of the copyright owner.

6   (b) COMPLIANCE WITH ENCODING RULES.—No per-

7 son may knowingly apply to a copyrighted work, that has

8 been distributed to the public, a security measure that

9 uses a standard security technology in violation of the en-

10 coding rules adopted under section 3.

11 **SEC. 7. ENFORCEMENT.**

12   (a) IN GENERAL.—The provisions of section 1203

13 and 1204 of title 17, United States Code, shall apply to

14 any violation of this Act as if—

15   (1) a violation of section 5 or 6(a)(1) of this

16   Act were a violation of section 1201 of title 17,

17   United States Code; and

18   (2) a violation of section 4 or section 6(a)(2) of

19   this Act were a violation of section 1202 of that

20   title.

21   (b) STATUTORY DAMAGES.—A court may award

22 damages for each violation of section 6(b) of not less than

23 $200 and not more than $2,500, as the court considers

24 just.

15

1 **SEC. 8. FEDERAL ADVISORY COMMITTEE ACT EXEMPTION.**

2 The Federal Advisory Committee Act (5 U.S.C. App.)

3 does not apply to any committee, board, commission, coun-

4 cil, conference, panel, task force, or other similar group

5 of representatives of digital media devices and representa-

6 tives of copyright owners convened for the purpose of de-

7 veloping the security system standards and encoding rules

8 described in section 3.

9 **SEC. 9. DEFINITIONS.**

10 In this Act:

11 (1) STANDARD SECURITY TECHNOLOGY.—The

12 term "standard security technology" means a secu-

13 rity technology that adheres to the security system

14 standards adopted under section 3.

15 (2) INTERACTIVE COMPUTER SERVICE.—The

16 term "interactive computer service" has the meaning

17 given that term in section 230(f) of the Communica-

18 tions Act of 1934 (47 U.S.C. 230(f)).

19 (3) DIGITAL MEDIA DEVICE.—The term "digital

20 media device" means any hardware or software

21 that—

22 (A) reproduces copyrighted works in digital

23 form;

24 (B) converts copyrighted works in digital

25 form into a form whereby the images and

26 sounds are visible or audible; or

16

1   (C) retrieves or accesses copyrighted works

2   in digital form and transfers or makes available

3   for transfer such works to hardware or software

4   described in subparagraph (B).

5   (4) COMMISSION.—The term "Commission"

6 means the Federal Communications Commission.

7 **SEC. 10. EFFECTIVE DATE.**

8   This Act shall take effect on the date of enactment

9 of this Act, except that sections 4, 5, and 6 shall take

10 effect on the day on which the final rule published under

11 section 3(b) or (c) takes effect.

○

107TH CONGRESS
2D SESSION

H. J. RES. 116

To recognize the rights of consumers to use copyright protected works, and
for other purposes.

IN THE HOUSE OF REPRESENTATIVES

OCTOBER 7, 2002

Mr. COX introduced the following joint resolution; which was referred to the
Committee on the Judiciary, and in addition to the Committee on Energy
and Commerce, for a period to be subsequently determined by the Speaker, in each case for consideration of such provisions as fall within the jurisdiction of the committee concerned

---

JOINT RESOLUTION

To recognize the rights of consumers to use copyright
protected works, and for other purposes.

1 *Resolved by the Senate and House of Representatives*

2 *of the United States of America in Congress assembled,*

3 **SECTION 1. SHORT TITLE.**

4   This Joint Resolution may be referred to as the

5 "Consumer Technology Bill of Rights".

6 **SEC. 2. RECOGNITION OF RIGHTS.**

7   It is the sense of Congress that, with respect to all

8 electronic media in United States commerce, consumers

9 who legally acquire copyrighted and non-copyrighted

2

1 works should be free to use these works in non-commercial

2 ways. The enumeration of rights in section 3, which shall

3 be known as the Consumer Technology Bill of Rights, sets

4 forth the rights of all Americans to personal control of

5 information and entertainment content they have lawfully

6 acquired and from which they do not intend to profit.

7 **SEC. 3. ENUMERATION OF RIGHTS.**

8   The following are the rights of consumers in legally

9 acquired copyrighted and non-copyrighted works:

10   (1) Users have the right to record legally ac-

11   quired video or audio for later viewing or listening

12   (popularly referred to as "time-shifting").

13   (2) Users have the right to use legally acquired

14   content in different places (popularly referred to as

15   "space-shifting").

16   (3) Users have the right to archive or make

17   backup copies of their content for use in the event

18   that the original copies are destroyed.

19   (4) Users have the right to use legally acquired

20   content on the electronic platform or device of their

21   choice.

22   (5) Users have the right to translate legally ac-

23   quired content into comparable formats.

•HJ 116 IH

3

1   (6) Users have the right to use technology in
2 order to achieve the rights enumerated in para-
3 graphs (1) through (5).

○

107TH CONGRESS
2D SESSION

S. J. RES. 51

To recognize the rights of consumers to use copyright protected works, and for other purposes.

IN THE SENATE OF THE UNITED STATES

OCTOBER 17, 2002

Mr. WYDEN introduced the following joint resolution; which was read twice and referred to the Committee on the Judiciary

---

JOINT RESOLUTION

To recognize the rights of consumers to use copyright protected works, and for other purposes.

1 *Resolved by the Senate and House of Representatives*
2 *of the United States of America in Congress assembled,*

3 **SECTION 1. SHORT TITLE.**

4   This Joint Resolution may be referred to as the
5 "Consumer Technology Bill of Rights".

6 **SEC. 2. RECOGNITION OF RIGHTS.**

7   It is the Sense of the Congress that United States
8 copyright law should not prohibit a consumer of informa-
9 tion or entertainment content distributed via electronic
10 media from engaging in the reasonable, personal, and non-

2

1 commercial exercise of the rights described in section 3

2 with respect to works that the consumer has legally ac-

3 quired.

4 **SEC. 3. ENUMERATION OF RIGHTS.**

5 The following rights are the rights to which section

6 2 refers:

7 (1) The right to record legally acquired video or

8 audio for later viewing or listening (popularly re-

9 ferred to as "time-shifting").

10 (2) The right to use legally acquired content in

11 different places (popularly referred to as "space-

12 shifting").

13 (3) The right to archive or make backup copies

14 of legally acquired content for use in the event that

15 the original copies are destroyed.

16 (4) The right to use legally acquired content on

17 the electronic platform or device of the consumer's

18 choice.

19 (5) The right to translate legally acquired con-

20 tent into comparable formats.

21 (6) The right to use technology in order to

22 achieve the rights enumerated in paragraphs (1)

23 through (5).

○

•SJ 51 IS

107TH CONGRESS
2D SESSION

H. R. 5522

To amend title 17, United States Code, to safeguard the rights and expectations of consumers who lawfully obtain digital entertainment.

IN THE HOUSE OF REPRESENTATIVES

OCTOBER 2, 2002

Ms. LOFGREN (for herself and Mr. HONDA) introduced the following bill; which was referred to the Committee on the Judiciary

---

A BILL

To amend title 17, United States Code, to safeguard the rights and expectations of consumers who lawfully obtain digital entertainment.

1 *Be it enacted by the Senate and House of Representa-*

2 *tives of the United States of America in Congress assembled,*

3 **SECTION 1. SHORT TITLE.**

4 This Act may be cited as the "Digital Choice and

5 Freedom Act of 2002".

6 **SEC. 2. FINDINGS.**

7 The Congress makes the following findings:

8 (1) The law of copyright is often described as

9 a "difficult balance between the interests of authors

10 . . . in the control and exploitation of their writings

2

1   . . . on the one hand, and society's competing inter-

2   est in the free flow of ideas, information, and com-

3   merce on the other hand." Sony Corp. v. Universal

4   City Studios, Inc., 464 U.S. 417, 429 (1984).

5   (2) Copyright seeks to encourage and reward

6   creative efforts by securing a fair return for an au-

7   thor's labor. Twentieth Century Music Corp. v.

8   Aiken, 422 U.S. 151, 156 (1975). At the same time,

9   "[f]rom the infancy of copyright protection, some

10 opportunity for fair use of copyrighted materials has

11 been thought necessary to fulfill copyright's very

12 purpose, '[t]o promote the Progress of Science and

13 useful Arts . . .'" Campbell v. Acuff-Rose Music,

14 Inc., 510 U.S. 569, 575 (1994).

15   (3) "[P]rivate motivation must ultimately serve

16 the cause of promoting broad public availability of

17 literature, music, and the other arts . . . When

18 technological change has rendered its literal terms

19 ambiguous, the Copyright Act must be construed in

20 light of this basic purpose." Twentieth Century

21 Music Corp., 422 U.S. at 156.

22   (4) Advances in technology have often prompted

23 changes to the copyright laws to maintain the bal-

24 ance. For example, the development of player pianos

25 preceded the enactment of the Copyright Act of

3

1   1909. The development of cable television prompted

2   complex reforms to section 111 of title 17, United

3   States Code. Sony, 464 U.S. at 430–31.

4   (5) The development of digital technology and

5   the rise of the Internet have once again altered the

6   balance. On the one hand, digital technology threat-

7   ens the rights of copyright holders. Perfect digital

8   copies of songs and movies can be publicly trans-

9   mitted, without authorization, to thousands of people

10 at little or no cost. On the other hand, technological

11 control measures give copyright holders the capacity

12 to limit nonpublic performances and threaten soci-

13 ety's interests in the free flow of ideas, information,

14 and commerce.

15   (6) The Digital Millennium Copyright Act

16 ("DMCA") was enacted as an attempt to safeguard

17 the traditional balance in the face of these new chal-

18 lenges. It gave copyright holders the ability to fight

19 digital piracy by employing technical restrictions

20 that prevent unlawful access and copying. In prac-

21 tice, however, the DMCA also endangered the rights

22 and expectations of legitimate consumers.

23   (7) Contrary to the intent of Congress, section

24 1201 of title 17, United States Code, has been inter-

25 preted to prohibit all users—even lawful ones—from

4

1 circumventing technical restrictions for any reason.

2 As a result, the lawful consumer cannot legally cir-

3 cumvent technological restrictions, even if he or she

4 is simply trying to exercise a fair use or to utilize

5 the work on a different digital media device. See,

6 e.g., Universal City Studios, Inc. v. Reimerdes, 111

7 F. Supp. 2d 294, 321–24 (S.D.N.Y. 2000) (DMCA

8 failed to give consumers the technical means to

9 make fair uses of encrypted copyrighted works).

10 (8) The authors of the DMCA never intended

11 to create such a dramatic shift in the balance. As

12 the report of the Committee of the Judiciary of the

13 House of Representatives accompanying the DMCA

14 stated: "[A]n individual [should] not be able to cir-

15 cumvent in order to gain unauthorized access to a

16 work, but [should] be able to do so in order to make

17 fair use of a work which he or she has acquired law-

18 fully." House Report 105–551, Part I, Section-by-

19 Section Analysis of section 1201(a)(1) (emphasis

20 added).

21 (9) It is now necessary to restore the traditional

22 balance between copyright holders and society, as in-

23 tended by the 105th Congress. Copyright laws in the

24 digital age must prevent and punish digital pirates

25 without treating every consumer as one.

5

SEC. 3. PROTECTING FAIR USE AND CONSUMER EXPECTA-
TIONS IN THE DIGITAL WORLD.

(a) FAIR USE.—The first sentence of section 107 of title 17, United States Code, is amended by inserting after "or by any other means specified in that section," the following: "and by analog or digital transmissions,".

(b) PERMISSIBLE USES OF DIGITAL WORKS.—

(1) IN GENERAL.—Chapter 1 of title 17, United States Code, is amended by adding after section 122 the following:

"§ 123. Limitations on exclusive rights; Permissible uses of digital works

"(a) USE OF LAWFULLY OBTAINED DIGITAL WORKS.—Notwithstanding the provisions of section 106, it is not an infringement of copyright for a person who lawfully obtains a copy or phonorecord of a digital work, or who lawfully receives a transmission of a digital work, to reproduce, store, adapt, or access the digital work—

"(1) for archival purposes, if all such archival copies are destroyed or rendered permanently inaccessible in the event that continued possession of the work should cease to be rightful; and

"(2) in order to perform or display the work, or an adaptation of the work, on a digital media device, if such performance or display is not public.

6

1   "(b) EFFECT OF LICENSES.—When a digital work is

2 distributed to the public subject to nonnegotiable license

3 terms, such terms shall not be enforceable under the com-

4 mon laws or statutes of any State to the extent that they

5 restrict or limit any of the limitations on exclusive rights

6 under this title.

7   "(c) DEFINITIONS.—As used in this section, the fol-

8 lowing terms have the following meanings:

9   "(1) A 'digital work' is any literary work (ex-

10   cept a computer program), sound recording or musi-

11   cal work, or a dramatic work, motion picture, or

12   other audiovisual work, in whole or in part in a dig-

13   ital or other nonanalog format.

14   "(2) A 'digital media device' is any hardware or

15   software that converts copyrighted works in digital

16   form into a form whereby the images and sounds are

17   visible or audible, or retrieves or accesses copy-

18   righted works in digital form and transfers or makes

19   available for transfer such works to such hardware

20   or software.

21   "(d) CONSTRUCTION.—Nothing in this section shall

22 enlarge or diminish any of the other limitations on exclu-

23 sive rights contained in this title, including any limitations

24 that relate to archival activities by a library or an archives

25 under sections 107 and 108.".

•HR 5522 IH

7

1   (2) CONFORMING AMENDMENT.—The table of

2   sections for chapter 1 of title 17, United States

3   Code, is amended by adding at the end the following

4   new item:

"123. Limitations on exclusive rights; Permissible uses of digital works.".

5 **SEC. 4. DIGITAL FIRST SALE.**

6   Section 109 of title 17, United States Code, is

7 amended by adding at the end the following:

8   "(f) The privileges prescribed by subsections (a) and

9 (c) apply where the owner of a particular copy or phono-

10 record of a work in a digital or other nonanalog format,

11 or any person authorized by such owner, sells or otherwise

12 disposes of the work by means of a transmission to a sin-

13 gle recipient, if the owner does not retain his or her copy

14 or phonorecord in a retrievable form and the work is sold

15 or otherwise disposed of in its original format.".

16 **SEC. 5. PERMISSIBLE CIRCUMVENTION TO ENABLE FAIR**

17   **USE AND CONSUMER EXPECTATIONS.**

18   Section 1201 of title 17, United States Code, is

19 amended—

20   (1) by redesignating subsections (c) through (k)

21 as subsections (d) through (l), respectively; and

22   (2) by inserting after subsection (b) the fol-

23 lowing:

24   "(c) CIRCUMVENTION FOR NONINFRINGING USES.—

25 (1) Notwithstanding any other provision in this title, a

8

1 person who lawfully obtains a copy or phonorecord of a

2 work, or who lawfully receives a transmission of a work,

3 may circumvent a technological measure that effectively

4 controls access to the work or protects a right of the copy-

5 right holder under this title if—

6   "(A) such act is necessary to make a non-

7   infringing use of the work under this title; and

8   "(B) the copyright owner fails to make publicly

9   available the necessary means to make such non-

10   infringing use without additional cost or burden to

11   such person.

12   "(2) Notwithstanding the provisions of subsections

13 (a)(2) and (b), any person may manufacture, import, offer

14 to the public, provide, or otherwise make available techno-

15 logical means to circumvent a technological measure that

16 effectively controls access to a work protected under this

17 title or protects a right of a copyright holder under this

18 title, if—

19   "(A) such means are necessary to make a non-

20   infringing use under paragraph (1)(A);

21   "(B) such means are designed, produced, and

22   marketed to make a noninfringing use under para-

23   graph (1)(A); and

•HR 5522 IH

9

1   "(C) the copyright owner fails to make available

2   the necessary means referred to in paragraph

3   (1)(B).".

○

I

107TH CONGRESS
2D SESSION
H. R. 5544

To amend the Federal Trade Commission Act to provide that the advertising or sale of a mislabeled copy-protected music disc is an unfair method of competition and an unfair and deceptive act or practice, and for other purposes.

IN THE HOUSE OF REPRESENTATIVES

OCTOBER 3, 2002

Mr. BOUCHER (for himself and Mr. DOOLITTLE) introduced the following bill; which was referred to the Committee on Energy and Commerce, and in addition to the Committee on the Judiciary, for a period to be subsequently determined by the Speaker, in each case for consideration of such provisions as fall within the jurisdiction of the committee concerned

---

A BILL

To amend the Federal Trade Commission Act to provide that the advertising or sale of a mislabeled copy-protected music disc is an unfair method of competition and an unfair and deceptive act or practice, and for other purposes.

1   *Be it enacted by the Senate and House of Representa-*
2 *tives of the United States of America in Congress assembled,*
3 **SECTION 1. SHORT TITLE.**
4   This Act may be cited as the "Digital Media Con-
5 sumers' Rights Act of 2002".

2

1 **SEC. 2. FINDINGS.**

2   Congress finds the following:

3   (1) The limited introduction into commerce of

4 "copy-protected compact discs" has caused con-

5 sumer confusion and placed increased, unwarranted

6 burdens on retailers, consumer electronics manufac-

7 turers, and personal computer manufacturers re-

8 sponding to consumer complaints, conditions which

9 will worsen as larger numbers of such discs are in-

10 troduced into commerce.

11   (2) Recording companies introducing new forms

12 of copy protection should have the freedom to inno-

13 vate, but should also be responsible for providing

14 adequate notice to consumers about restrictions on

15 the playability and recordability of "copy-protected

16 compact discs".

17   (3) The Federal Trade Commission should be

18 empowered and directed to ensure the adequate la-

19 beling of prerecorded digital music disc products.

20 **SEC. 3. INADEQUATELY LABELED COPY-PROTECTED COM-**

21   **PACT DISCS.**

22   The Federal Trade Commission Act (15 U.S.C. 41

23 et seq.) is amended by inserting after section 24 the fol-

24 lowing new section:

3

1 "INADEQUATELY LABELED COPY-PROTECTED COMPACT

2 DISCS

3 "SEC. 24A. (a) DEFINITIONS.—In this section:

4 "(1) The term 'Commission' means the Federal

5 Trade Commission.

6 "(2) The term 'audio compact disc' means a

7 substrate packaged as a commercial prerecorded

8 audio product, containing a sound recording or re-

9 cordings, that conforms to all specifications and re-

10 quirements for Red Book Audio and bears a duly li-

11 censed and authorized 'Compact disc Digital Audio'

12 logo.

13 "(3) The term 'prerecorded digital music disc

14 product' means a commercial audio product com-

15 prised of a substrate in the form of a disc in which

16 is recorded a sound recording or sound recordings

17 generally in accordance with Red Book Audio speci-

18 fications but that does not conform to all licensed

19 requirements for Red Book Audio: *Provided*, That a

20 substrate containing a prerecorded sound recording

21 that conforms to the licensing requirements applica-

22 ble to a DVD-Audio disc or a Super Audio Compact

23 Disc is not a prerecorded digital music disc product.

24 "(4) The term 'Red Book Audio' means audio

25 data digitized at 44,100 samples per second (44.1

4

1   kHz) with a range of 65,536 possible values as de-

2   fined in the 'Compact Disc-Digital Audio System

3   Description' (first published in 1980 by Philips N.V.

4   and Sony Corporation, as updated from time to

5   time).

6   "(b) PROHIBITED ACTS.—(1) The introduction into

7 commerce, sale, offering for sale, or advertising for sale

8 of a prerecorded digital music disc product which is mis-

9 labeled or falsely or deceptively advertised or invoiced,

10 within the meaning of this section or any rules or regula-

11 tions prescribed by the Commission pursuant to subsection

12 (d), is unlawful and shall be deemed an unfair method of

13 competition and an unfair and deceptive act or practice

14 in commerce under section 5(a)(1).

15   "(2) Prior to the time a prerecorded digital music

16 disc product is sold and delivered to the ultimate con-

17 sumer, it shall be unlawful to remove or mutilate, or cause

18 or participate in the removal or mutilation of, any label

19 required by this section or any rules or regulations pre-

20 scribed by the Commission pursuant to subsection (d) to

21 be affixed to such prerecorded digital music disc product.

22 Any person violating this subsection shall be deemed to

23 have engaged in an unfair method of competition and an

24 unfair and deceptive act or practice in commerce under

25 this Act.

•HR 5544 IH

5

1   "(c) MISLABELED DISCS.—For purposes of this sec-

2 tion, a prerecorded digital music disc product shall be con-

3 sidered to be mislabeled if it—

4   "(1) bears any logo or marking which, in ac-

5   cordance with common practice, identifies it as an

6   audio compact disc;

7   "(2) fails to bear a label on the packaging in

8   which it is sold at retail in words that are prominent

9   and plainly legible on the front of the packaging

10   that—

11   "(A) it is not an audio compact disc;

12   "(B) it might not play properly in all de-

13   vices capable of playing an audio compact disc;

14   and

15   "(C) it might not be recordable on a per-

16   sonal computer or other device capable of re-

17   cording content from an audio compact disc; or

18   "(3) fails to provide the following information

19   on the packaging in which it is sold at retail in

20   words that are prominent and plainly legible—

21   "(A) any minimum recommended software

22   requirements for playback or recordability on a

23   personal computer;

6

1   "(B) any restrictions on the number of

2   times song files may be downloaded to the hard

3   drive of a personal computer; and

4   "(C) the applicable return policy for con-

5   sumers who find that the prerecorded digital

6   music disc product does not play properly in a

7   device capable of playing an audio compact disc.

8   "(d) RULEMAKING.—(1) The Commission may de-

9   velop such rules and regulations as it deems appropriate

10   to prevent the prohibited acts set forth in subsection (b)

11   and to require the proper labeling of prerecorded digital

12   music disc products under subsection (c).

13   "(2)(A) The Commission may develop such additional

14   rules and regulations as it deems necessary to establish

15   appropriate labeling requirements applicable to new audio

16   discs, using new playback formats (including DVD-Audio

17   discs and Super Audio Compact Discs), if the Commission

18   finds, with respect to a particular type of disc, that—

19   "(i) the manner in which the discs are displayed

20   at retail, packaged, or marketed results in substan-

21   tial consumer confusion about the playability and re-

22   cordability of such discs;

23   "(ii) the discs are not appropriately labeled with

24   respect to their playability on standard audio com-

25   pact disc playback devices; and

7

1   "(iii)(I) the discs are not recordable on a per-

2 sonal computer; or

3   "(II) if the discs are recordable, a recording

4 made from such a disc is bound to a particular de-

5 vice.

6   "(B) To the maximum extent practicable, the Com-

7 mission shall seek to ensure that any rules and regulations

8 developed under this paragraph impose labeling require-

9 ments comparable to the requirements imposed under the

10 rules and regulations developed under paragraph (1).".

11 **SEC. 4. REPORT TO CONGRESS.**

12   Not later than 2 years after the date of enactment

13 of this Act, the Federal Trade Commission shall submit

14 to Congress a report detailing the following:

15   (1) The extent to which prerecorded digital

16   music disc products (as defined in section 24A of

17   the Federal Trade Commission Act, as added by sec-

18   tion 3 of this Act) have entered the market over the

19   preceding 2 years.

20   (2) The extent to which the Commission has re-

21   ceived complaints from consumers about the imple-

22   mentation of return policies for consumers who find

23   that a prerecorded digital music disc product does

24   not play properly in a device capable of playing an

8

1   audio compact disc (as defined in section 24A of

2   such Act).

3   (3) The extent to which manufacturers and re-

4   tailers have been burdened by consumer returns of

5   devices unable to play prerecorded digital music disc

6   products.

7   (4) The number of enforcement actions taken

8   by the Commission pursuant to section 24A of such

9   Act.

10   (5) The number of convictions or settlements

11   achieved as a result of enforcement actions taken by

12   the Commission pursuant to section 24A of such

13   Act.

14   (6) Any proposed changes to this Act, with re-

15   spect to prerecorded digital music disc products,

16   that the Commission believes would enhance enforce-

17   ment, eliminate consumer confusion, or otherwise

18   address concerns raised by consumers with the Com-

19   mission.

20 **SEC. 5. FAIR USE AMENDMENTS.**

21   (a) SCIENTIFIC RESEARCH.—Subsections (a)(2)(A)

22 and (b)(1)(A) of section 1201 of title 17, United States

23 Code, are each amended by inserting after "title" in sub-

24 section (a)(2)(A) and after "thereof" in subsection

25 (b)(1)(A) the following: "unless the person is acting solely

9

1 in furtherance of scientific research into technological pro-

2 tection measures".

3   (b) FAIR USE RESTORATION.—Section 1201(c) of

4 title 17, United States Code, is amended—

5   (1) in paragraph (1), by inserting before the pe-

6   riod at the end the following: "and it is not a viola-

7   tion of this section to circumvent a technological

8   measure in connection with access to, or the use of,

9   a work if such circumvention does not result in an

10   infringement of the copyright in the work"; and

11   (2) by adding at the end the following new

12   paragraph:

13   "(5) It shall not be a violation of this title to manu-

14 facture, distribute, or make noninfringing use of a hard-

15 ware or software product capable of enabling significant

16 noninfringing use of a copyrighted work.".

○

I

107TH CONGRESS
2D SESSION
H. R. 5211

To amend title 17, United States Code, to limit the liability of copyright owners for protecting their works on peer-to-peer networks.

IN THE HOUSE OF REPRESENTATIVES

JULY 25, 2002

Mr. BERMAN (for himself, Mr. COBLE, Mr. SMITH of Texas, and Mr. WEXLER) introduced the following bill; which was referred to the Committee on the Judiciary

---

A BILL

To amend title 17, United States Code, to limit the liability of copyright owners for protecting their works on peer-to-peer networks.

1   *Be it enacted by the Senate and House of Representa-*

2   *tives of the United States of America in Congress assembled,*

3   **SECTION 1. LIMITATION ON LIABILITY FOR PROTECTION**

4   **OF COPYRIGHTED WORKS ON PEER-TO-PEER**

5   **NETWORKS.**

6   (a) IN GENERAL.—Chapter 5 of title 17, United

7   States Code, is amended by adding at the end the fol-

8   lowing new section:

2

1 **"§ 514. Remedies for infringement: use of tech-**
2   **nologies to prevent infringement of copy-**
3   **righted works on peer-to-peer computer**
4   **networks**

5   "(a) IN GENERAL.—Notwithstanding any State or
6 Federal statute or other law, and subject to the limitations
7 set forth in subsections (b) and (c), a copyright owner
8 shall not be liable in any criminal or civil action for dis-
9 abling, interfering with, blocking, diverting, or otherwise
10 impairing the unauthorized distribution, display, perform-
11 ance, or reproduction of his or her copyrighted work on
12 a publicly accessible peer-to-peer file trading network, if
13 such impairment does not, without authorization, alter,
14 delete, or otherwise impair the integrity of any computer
15 file or data residing on the computer of a file trader.

16   "(b) EXCEPTIONS.—Subsection (a) shall not apply to
17 a copyright owner in a case in which—

18   "(1) in the course of taking an action permitted
19   by subsection (a), the copyright owner—

20   "(A) impairs the availability within a pub-
21   licly accessible peer-to-peer file trading network
22   of a computer file or data that does not contain
23   a work, or portion thereof, in which the copy-
24   right owner has an exclusive right granted
25   under section 106, except as may be reasonably
26   necessary to impair the distribution, display,

•HR 5211 IH

3

1   performance, or reproduction of such a work, or

2   portion thereof, in violation of any of the exclu-

3   sive rights of the copyright owner under section

4   106;

5   "(B) causes economic loss to any person

6   other than affected file traders; or

7   "(C) causes economic loss of more than

8   $50.00 per impairment to the property of the

9   affected file trader, other than economic loss in-

10 volving computer files or data made available

11 through a publicly accessible peer-to-peer file

12 trading network that contain works in which

13 the owner has an exclusive right granted under

14 section 106; or

15 "(2) the copyright owner fails to comply with

16 the requirements of subsection (c).

17 "(c) NOTIFICATION REQUIREMENT.—(1) A copyright

18 owner shall not be liable under subsection (a) for an act

19 to which subsection (a) applies only if—

20   "(A) the copyright owner has notified the De-

21 partment of Justice, in such manner as the Attorney

22 General shall specify, of the specific technologies the

23 copyright owner intends to use to impair the unau-

24 thorized distribution, display, performance, or repro-

4

1   duction of the owner's copyrighted works over a pub-

2   licly accessible peer-to-peer file trading network; and

3   "(B) the notification under paragraph (1) was

4   made at least 7 days before the copyright owner en-

5   gaged in the act.

6   "(2) At the request of an affected file trader or the

7   assignee of an Internet Protocol address used by an af-

8   fected file trader, a copyright owner shall provide notice

9   to the affected file trader or assignee (as the case may

10   be) of—

11   "(A) the reason for impairing trading in the

12   computer file or data containing the copyrighted

13   work of the copyright owner;

14   "(B) the name and address of the copyright

15   owner; and

16   "(C) the right of the affected file trader to

17   bring an action described in subsection (d).

18   "(3) The notification by a copyright owner under

19   paragraph (1) shall not be construed for any purpose as

20   an admission of an unlawful act.

21   "(d) CAUSE OF ACTION FOR WRONGFUL IMPAIR-

22   MENT.—(1) If, pursuant to the authority provided by sub-

23   section (a), a copyright owner knowingly and intentionally

24   impairs the distribution, display, performance, or repro-

25   duction of a particular computer file or data, and has no

5

1 reasonable basis to believe that such distribution, display,

2 performance, or reproduction constitutes an infringement

3 of copyright, and an affected file trader suffers economic

4 loss in excess of $250 as a result of the act by the copy-

5 right owner, the affected file trader may seek compensa-

6 tion for such economic loss in accordance with the fol-

7 lowing:

8   "(A) The affected file trader may file a claim

9   for such compensation with the Attorney General

10   not later than 1 year after the date on which the

11   claim accrues. The Attorney General shall, not later

12   than 10 days after the claim is filed, serve notice of

13   the claim on the copyright owner against whom the

14   claim is brought, and shall investigate the claim.

15   The claim shall be in writing under oath or affirma-

16   tion and shall contain such information and be in

17   such form as the Attorney General requires. The

18   claim shall not be made public by the Attorney Gen-

19   eral.

20   "(B) If the Attorney General determines after

21   such investigation that there is not reasonable cause

22   to believe that the facts alleged in the claim are

23   true, the Attorney General shall dismiss the claim

24   and promptly notify the affected file trader and the

6

1   copyright owner against whom the claim is brought

2   of the Attorney General's action.

3   "(C) If the Attorney General determines after

4   such investigation that there is reasonable cause to

5   believe that the facts alleged in the claim are true,

6   the Attorney General shall promptly notify the af-

7   fected file trader and the copyright owner of the At-

8   torney General's determination.

9   "(D) The Attorney General shall make the de-

10   termination on reasonable cause as promptly as pos-

11   sible, but in no case later than 120 days after the

12   date on which the claim is filed.

13   "(E) The affected file trader may seek com-

14   pensation for the economic loss that is the subject

15   of the claim, plus reasonable attorney's fees, in the

16   appropriate United States district court by filing an

17   action in such court—

18   "(i) not later than 60 days after being no-

19   tified of the Attorney General's determination

20   under subparagraph (C); or

21   "(ii) if the Attorney General has not made

22   a determination on the claim within the 120-

23   day period specified in subparagraph (D), not

24   later than 60 days after the end of that 120-

25   day period.

7

1   "(2) The cause of action established by this sub-
2 section shall only be available as a remedy against impair-
3 ing actions that would not be lawful but for subsection
4 (a).

5   "(e) SUITS BY UNITED STATES.—The Attorney Gen-
6 eral of the United States may seek injunctive relief in the
7 appropriate United States district court to prevent a copy-
8 right owner from engaging in impairing activities that
9 would not be lawful but for subsection (a) if that owner
10 has engaged in a pattern or practice of impairing the dis-
11 tribution, display, performance, or reproduction of com-
12 puter files or data without a reasonable basis to believe
13 that infringement of copyright has occurred.

14   "(f) CONSTRUCTION WITH OTHER STATUTES.—(1)
15 Nothing in this section shall be construed as limiting the
16 authority of a copyright owner to take any otherwise law-
17 ful action to enforce any of the exclusive rights granted
18 by section 106.

19   "(2) Nothing in this section shall limit any remedies
20 available to a person under section 1030 of title 18, or
21 under any other State or Federal statute or any other law,
22 against a copyright owner who fails to qualify for the pro-
23 tections afforded under subsection (a).

24   "(3) Actions taken by a copyright owner pursuant to
25 subsection (a) shall not be considered by a court for any

8

1 other purpose under this title, including in determining

2 whether a particular use of a work is infringing.

3   "(g) NONDISCLOSURE OF INFORMATION.—Informa-

4 tion contained in any notification under subsection

5 (c)(1)(A) may not be made available to the public under

6 section 552 of title 5.

7   "(h) DEFINITIONS.—In this section—

8   "(1) the term 'economic loss' means monetary

9   costs only;

10   "(2) 'peer-to-peer file trading network' means

11   two or more computers which are connected by com-

12   puter software that—

13   "(A) is primarily designed to—

14   "(i) enable the connected computers

15   to transmit files or data to other connected

16   computers;

17   "(ii) enable the connected computers

18   to request the transmission of files or data

19   from other connected computers; and

20   "(iii) enable the designation of files or

21   data on the connected computers as avail-

22   able for transmission; and

23   "(B) does not permanently route all file or

24   data inquiries or searches through a designated,

25   central computer located in the United States;

9

1   "(3) a peer-to-peer file trading network is 'pub-

2 licly accessible' if—

3   "(A) participation in the network is sub-

4   stantially open to the public; and

5   "(B) the network enables the transmission

6   of computer files or data over the Internet or

7   any other public network of computers;

8   "(4) the term 'file trader' means an individual

9 who is utilizing a publicly accessible, peer-to-peer file

10 trading network to transmit, make available for

11 transmission, or download computer files or data, or

12 the owner of a computer that is connected to a pub-

13 licly accessible, peer-to-peer file trading network and

14 is engaged in the transmission of computer files or

15 data through the peer-to-peer file trading network;

16   "(5) the term 'distribution', in the case of a

17 computer connected to a peer-to-peer file trading

18 network, includes the placement of a computer file

19 or data in an area of a computer that is accessible

20 to other computers connected to the peer-to-peer file

21 trading network; and

22   "(6) the term 'copyright owner' means a legal

23 or beneficial owner of an exclusive right under sec-

24 tion 106 and any party authorized to act on the

25 owner's behalf.".

10

1   (b) CONFORMING AMENDMENT.—The table of sec-

2 tions for chapter 5 of title 17, United States Code, is

3 amended by adding at the end the following new item:

"514. Remedies for infringement: use of technologies to prevent infringement of copyrighted works on peer-to-peer computer networks.".

○

I

108TH CONGRESS
1ST SESSION

H. R. 107

To amend the Federal Trade Commission Act to provide that the advertising or sale of a mislabeled copy-protected music disc is an unfair method of competition and an unfair and deceptive act or practice, and for other purposes.

IN THE HOUSE OF REPRESENTATIVES

JANUARY 7, 2003

Mr. BOUCHER (for himself, Mr. DOOLITTLE, Mr. BACHUS, and Mr. KENNEDY of Rhode Island) introduced the following bill; which was referred to the Committee on Energy and Commerce, and in addition to the Committee on the Judiciary, for a period to be subsequently determined by the Speaker, in each case for consideration of such provisions as fall within the jurisdiction of the committee concerned

---

A BILL

To amend the Federal Trade Commission Act to provide that the advertising or sale of a mislabeled copy-protected music disc is an unfair method of competition and an unfair and deceptive act or practice, and for other purposes.

1   *Be it enacted by the Senate and House of Representa-*
2 *tives of the United States of America in Congress assembled,*

3 **SECTION 1. SHORT TITLE.**

4   This Act may be cited as the "Digital Media Con-
5 sumers' Rights Act of 2003".

2

1 **SEC. 2. FINDINGS.**

2   Congress finds the following:

3   (1) The limited introduction into commerce of

4 "copy-protected compact discs" has caused con-

5 sumer confusion and placed increased, unwarranted

6 burdens on retailers, consumer electronics manufac-

7 turers, and personal computer manufacturers re-

8 sponding to consumer complaints, conditions which

9 will worsen as larger numbers of such discs are in-

10 troduced into commerce.

11   (2) Recording companies introducing new forms

12 of copy protection should have the freedom to inno-

13 vate, but should also be responsible for providing

14 adequate notice to consumers about restrictions on

15 the playability and recordability of "copy-protected

16 compact discs".

17   (3) The Federal Trade Commission should be

18 empowered and directed to ensure the adequate la-

19 beling of prerecorded digital music disc products.

20 **SEC. 3. INADEQUATELY LABELED COPY-PROTECTED COM-**

21   **PACT DISCS.**

22   The Federal Trade Commission Act (15 U.S.C. 41

23 et seq.) is amended by inserting after section 24 the fol-

24 lowing new section:

3

1 "SEC. 24A. INADEQUATELY LABELED COPY-PROTECTED

2   COMPACT DISCS.

3   "(a) DEFINITIONS.—In this section:

4   "(1) The term 'Commission' means the Federal

5 Trade Commission.

6   "(2) The term 'audio compact disc' means a

7 substrate packaged as a commercial prerecorded

8 audio product, containing a sound recording or re-

9 cordings, that conforms to all specifications and re-

10 quirements for Red Book Audio and bears a duly li-

11 censed and authorized 'Compact disc Digital Audio'

12 logo.

13   "(3) The term 'prerecorded digital music disc

14 product' means a commercial audio product com-

15 prised of a substrate in the form of a disc in which

16 is recorded a sound recording or sound recordings

17 generally in accordance with Red Book Audio speci-

18 fications but that does not conform to all licensed

19 requirements for Red Book Audio: *Provided,* That a

20 substrate containing a prerecorded sound recording

21 that conforms to the licensing requirements applica-

22 ble to a DVD-Audio disc or a Super Audio Compact

23 Disc is not a prerecorded digital music disc product.

24   "(4) The term 'Red Book Audio' means audio

25 data digitized at 44,100 samples per second (44.1

26 kHz) with a range of 65,536 possible values as de-

4

1   fined in the 'Compact Disc-Digital Audio System

2   Description' (first published in 1980 by Philips N.V.

3   and Sony Corporation, as updated from time to

4   time.

5   "(b) P<small>ROHIBITED</small> A<small>CTS</small>.—

6   "(1) The introduction into commerce, sale, of-

7   fering for sale, or advertising for sale of a

8   prerecorded digital music disc product which is mis-

9   labeled or falsely or deceptively advertised or

10 invoiced, within the meaning of this section or any

11 rules or regulations prescribed by the Commission

12 pursuant to subsection (d), is unlawful and shall be

13 deemed an unfair method of competition and an un-

14 fair and deceptive act or practice in commerce under

15 section 5(a)(1).

16   "(2) Prior to the time a prerecorded digital

17 music disc product is sold and delivered to the ulti-

18 mate consumer, it shall be unlawful to remove or

19 mutilate, or cause or participate in the removal or

20 mutilation of, any label required by this section or

21 any rules or regulations prescribed by the Commis-

22 sion pursuant to subsection (d) to be affixed to such

23 prerecorded digital music disc product. Any person

24 violating this subsection shall be deemed to have en-

25 gaged in an unfair method of competition and an

•HR 107 IH

5

1 unfair and deceptive act or practice in commerce

2 under this Act.

3 "(c) MISLABELED DISCS.—For purposes of this sec-

4 tion, a prerecorded digital music disc product shall be con-

5 sidered to be mislabeled if it—

6   "(1) bears any logo or marking which, in ac-

7 cordance with common practice, identifies it as an

8 audio compact disc;

9   "(2) fails to bear a label on the packaging in

10 which it is sold at retail in words that are prominent

11 and plainly legible on the front of the packaging

12 that—

13   "(A) it is not an audio compact disc;

14   "(B) it might not play properly in all de-

15   vices capable of playing an audio compact disc;

16   and

17   "(C) it might not be recordable on a per-

18   sonal computer or other device capable of re-

19   cording content from an audio compact disc; or

20   "(3) fails to provide the following information

21 on the packaging in which it is sold at retail in

22 words that are prominent and plainly legible—

23   "(A) any minimum recommended software

24   requirements for playback or recordability on a

25   personal computer;

6

1   "(B) any restrictions on the number of

2   times song files may be downloaded to the hard

3   drive of a personal computer; and

4   "(C) the applicable return policy for con-

5   sumers who find that the prerecorded digital

6   music disc product does not play properly in a

7   device capable of playing an audio compact disc.

8   "(d) RULEMAKING.—(1) The Commission may de-

9 velop such rules and regulations as it deems appropriate

10 to prevent the prohibited acts set forth in subsection (b)

11 and to require the proper labeling of prerecorded digital

12 music disc products under subsection (c).

13   "(2)(A) The Commission may develop such additional

14 rules and regulations as it deems necessary to establish

15 appropriate labeling requirements applicable to new audio

16 discs, using new playback formats (including DVD-Audio

17 discs and Super Audio Compact Discs), if the Commission

18 finds, with respect to a particular type of disc, that

19   "(i) the manner in which the discs are displayed

20   at retail, packaged, or marketed results in substan-

21   tial consumer confusion about the playability and re-

22   cordability of such discs;

23   "(ii) the discs are not appropriately labeled with

24   respect to their playability on standard audio com-

25   pact disc playback devices; and

7

1   "(iii)(I) the discs are not recordable on a per-

2 sonal computer; or

3   "(II) if the discs are recordable, a recording

4 made from such a disc is bound to a particular de-

5 vice.

6   "(B) To the maximum extent practicable, the Com-

7 mission shall seek to ensure that any rules and regulations

8 developed under this paragraph impose labeling require-

9 ments comparable to the requirements imposed under the

10 rules and regulations developed under paragraph (1).".

11 **SEC. 4. REPORT TO CONGRESS.**

12   Not later than 2 years after the date of enactment

13 of this Act, the Federal Trade Commission shall submit

14 to Congress a report detailing the following:

15   (1) The extent to which prerecorded digital

16   music disc products (as defined in section 24A of

17   the Federal Trade Commission Act, as added by sec-

18   tion 3 of this Act) have entered the market over the

19   preceding 2 years.

20   (2) The extent to which the Commission has re-

21   ceived complaints from consumers about the imple-

22   mentation of return policies for consumers who find

23   that a prerecorded digital music disc product does

24   not play properly in a device capable of playing an

8

1   audio compact disc (as defined in section 24A of

2   such Act).

3   (3) The extent to which manufacturers and re-

4   tailers have been burdened by consumer returns of

5   devices unable to play prerecorded digital music disc

6   products.

7   (4) The number of enforcement actions taken

8   by the Commission pursuant to section 24A of such

9   Act.

10   (5) The number of convictions or settlements

11   achieved as a result of enforcement actions taken by

12   the Commission pursuant to section 24A of such

13   Act.

14   (6) Any proposed changes to this Act, with re-

15   spect to prerecorded digital music disc products,

16   that the Commission believes would enhance enforce-

17   ment, eliminate consumer confusion, or otherwise

18   address concerns raised by consumers with the Com-

19   mission.

20 **SEC. 5. FAIR USE AMENDMENTS.**

21   (a) SCIENTIFIC RESEARCH.—Subsections (a)(2)(A)

22 and (b)(1)(A) of section 1201 of title 17, United States

23 Code, are each amended by inserting after "title" in sub-

24 section (a)(2)(A) and after "thereof" in subsection

25 (b)(1)(A) the following: "unless the person is acting solely

9

1 in furtherance of scientific research into technological pro-

2 tection measures".

3   (b) FAIR USE RESTORATION.—Section 1201(c) of

4 title 17, United States Code, is amended—

5   (1) in paragraph (1), by inserting before the pe-

6   riod at the end the following: "and it is not a viola-

7   tion of this section to circumvent a technological

8   measure in connection with access to, or the use of,

9   a work if such circumvention does not result in an

10   infringement of the copyright in the work"; and

11   (2) by adding at the end the following new

12   paragraph:

13   "(5) It shall not be a violation of this title to

14   manufacture, distribute, or make noninfringing use

15   of a hardware or software product capable of ena-

16   bling significant noninfringing use of a copyrighted

17   work.".

○

I

108TH CONGRESS
1ST SESSION

H. R. 1066

To amend title 17, United States Code, to safeguard the rights and
expectations of consumers who lawfully obtain digital entertainment.

IN THE HOUSE OF REPRESENTATIVES

MARCH 4, 2003

Ms. LOFGREN (for herself and Mr. BOUCHER) introduced the following bill;
which was referred to the Committee on the Judiciary

A BILL

To amend title 17, United States Code, to safeguard the
rights and expectations of consumers who lawfully obtain
digital entertainment.

1   *Be it enacted by the Senate and House of Representa-*

2   *tives of the United States of America in Congress assembled,*

3   **SECTION 1. SHORT TITLE.**

4   This Act may be cited as the "Benefit Authors with-

5   out Limiting Advancement or Net Consumer Expectations

6   (BALANCE) Act of 2003".

7   **SEC. 2. FINDINGS.**

8   The Congress makes the following findings:

9   (1) The law of copyright is often described as

10   a "difficult balance between the interests of authors

2

1   . . . in the control and exploitation of their writings

2   . . . on the one hand, and society's competing inter-

3   est in the free flow of ideas, information, and com-

4   merce on the other hand." Sony Corp. v. Universal

5   City Studios, Inc., 464 U.S. 417, 429 (1984).

6   (2) Copyright seeks to encourage and reward

7   creative efforts by securing a fair return for an au-

8   thor's labor. Twentieth Century Music Corp. v.

9   Aiken, 422 U.S. 151, 156 (1975). At the same time,

10   "[f]rom the infancy of copyright protection, some

11   opportunity for fair use of copyrighted materials has

12   been thought necessary to fulfill copyright's very

13   purpose, '[t]o promote the Progress of Science and

14   useful Arts . . .'" Campbell v. Acuff-Rose Music,

15   Inc., 510 U.S. 569, 575 (1994).

16   (3) "[P]rivate motivation must ultimately serve

17   the cause of promoting broad public availability of

18   literature, music, and the other arts . . . When

19   technological change has rendered its literal terms

20   ambiguous, the Copyright Act must be construed in

21   light of this basic purpose." Twentieth Century

22   Music Corp., 422 U.S. at 156.

23   (4) Advances in technology have often prompted

24   changes to the copyright laws to maintain the bal-

25   ance. For example, the development of player pianos

•HR 1066 IH

3

1   preceded the enactment of the Copyright Act of

2   1909. The development of cable television prompted

3   complex reforms to section 111 of title 17, United

4   States Code. Sony, 464 U.S. at 430–31.

5   (5) The development of digital technology and

6   the rise of the Internet have once again altered the

7   balance. On the one hand, digital technology threat-

8   ens the rights of copyright holders. Perfect digital

9   copies of songs and movies can be publicly trans-

10   mitted, without authorization, to thousands of people

11   at little or no cost. On the other hand, technological

12   control measures give copyright holders the capacity

13   to limit nonpublic performances and threaten soci-

14   ety's interests in the free flow of ideas, information,

15   and commerce.

16   (6) The Digital Millennium Copyright Act

17   ("DMCA") was enacted as an attempt to safeguard

18   the traditional balance in the face of these new chal-

19   lenges. It gave copyright holders the ability to fight

20   digital piracy by employing technical restrictions

21   that prevent unlawful access and copying. In prac-

22   tice, however, the DMCA also endangered the rights

23   and expectations of legitimate consumers.

24   (7) Contrary to the intent of Congress, section

25   1201 of title 17, United States Code, has been inter-

4

1   preted to prohibit all users—even lawful ones—from

2   circumventing technical restrictions for any reason.

3   As a result, the lawful consumer cannot legally cir-

4   cumvent technological restrictions, even if he or she

5   is simply trying to exercise a fair use or to utilize

6   the work on a different digital media device. See,

7   e.g., Universal City Studios, Inc. v. Reimerdes, 111

8   F. Supp. 2d 294, 321–24 (S.D.N.Y. 2000) (DMCA

9   failed to give consumers the technical means to

10   make fair uses of encrypted copyrighted works).

11   (8) The authors of the DMCA never intended

12   to create such a dramatic shift in the balance. As

13   the report of the Committee of the Judiciary of the

14   House of Representatives accompanying the DMCA

15   stated: "[A]n individual [should] not be able to cir-

16   cumvent in order to gain unauthorized access to a

17   work, but [should] be able to do so in order to make

18   fair use of a work which he or she has acquired law-

19   fully." House Report 105–551, Part I, Section-by-

20   Section Analysis of section 1201(a)(1).

21   (9) It is now necessary to restore the traditional

22   balance between copyright holders and society, as in-

23   tended by the 105th Congress. Copyright laws in the

24   digital age must prevent and punish digital pirates

25   without treating every consumer as one.

5

1 SEC. 3. PROTECTING FAIR USE AND CONSUMER EXPECTA-

2   TIONS IN THE DIGITAL WORLD.

3   (a) FAIR USE.—The first sentence of section 107 of

4 title 17, United States Code, is amended by inserting after

5 "or by any other means specified in that section," the fol-

6 lowing: "including by analog or digital transmissions,".

7   (b) PERMISSIBLE USES OF DIGITAL WORKS.—

8   (1) IN GENERAL.—Chapter 1 of title 17, United

9   States Code, is amended by adding after section 122

10   the following:

11 "§123. Limitations on exclusive rights; Permissible

12   uses of digital works

13   "(a) USE OF LAWFULLY OBTAINED DIGITAL

14 WORKS.—Notwithstanding the provisions of section 106,

15 it is not an infringement of copyright for a person who

16 lawfully obtains a copy or phonorecord of a digital work,

17 or who lawfully receives a transmission of a digital work,

18 to reproduce, store, adapt, or access the digital work—

19   "(1) for archival purposes, if all such archival

20   copies are destroyed or rendered permanently inac-

21   cessible in the event that continued possession of the

22   work should cease to be rightful; and

23   "(2) in order to perform or display the work, or

24   an adaptation of the work, on a digital media device,

25   if the work is not so performed or displayed publicly.

6

1   "(b) EFFECT OF LICENSES.—When a digital work is

2 distributed to the public subject to nonnegotiable license

3 terms, such terms shall not be enforceable under the com-

4 mon laws or statutes of any State to the extent that they

5 restrict or limit any of the limitations on exclusive rights

6 under this title.

7   "(c) DEFINITIONS.—As used in this section, the fol-

8 lowing terms have the following meanings:

9   "(1) A 'digital work' is any literary work (ex-

10   cept a computer program), sound recording, musical

11   work, dramatic work, or motion picture or other

12   audiovisual work, in whole or in part in a digital or

13   other nonanalog format.

14   "(2) A 'digital media device' is any hardware or

15   software that converts copyrighted works in digital

16   form into a format whereby the images and sounds

17   are visible or audible, or retrieves or accesses copy-

18   righted works in digital format and transfers or

19   makes available for transfer such works to such

20   hardware or software.

21   "(d) CONSTRUCTION.—Nothing in this section shall

22 enlarge or diminish any of the other limitations on exclu-

23 sive rights contained in this title, including any limitations

24 that relate to archival activities by a library or an archives

25 under sections 107 and 108.".

7

1   (2) CONFORMING AMENDMENT.—The table of
2   sections for chapter 1 of title 17, United States
3   Code, is amended by adding at the end the following
4   new item:

"123. Limitations on exclusive rights; Permissible uses of digital works.".

SEC. 4. DIGITAL FIRST SALE.

6   Section 109 of title 17, United States Code, is
7   amended by adding at the end the following:

8   "(f) The privileges prescribed by subsections (a) and
9   (c) apply in a case in which the owner of a particular copy
10   or phonorecord of a work in a digital or other nonanalog
11   format, or any person authorized by such owner, sells or
12   otherwise disposes of the work by means of a transmission
13   to a single recipient, if the owner does not retain the copy
14   or phonorecord in a retrievable form and the work is so
15   sold or otherwise disposed of in its original format.".

SEC. 5. PERMISSIBLE CIRCUMVENTION TO ENABLE FAIR USE AND CONSUMER EXPECTATIONS.

18   Section 1201 of title 17, United States Code, is
19   amended—

20   (1) by redesignating subsections (c) through (k)
21   as subsections (d) through (l), respectively; and

22   (2) by inserting after subsection (b) the fol-
23   lowing:

24   "(c) CIRCUMVENTION FOR NONINFRINGING USES.—
25   (1) Notwithstanding any other provision in this title, a

8

1 person who lawfully obtains a copy or phonorecord of a

2 work, or who lawfully receives a transmission of a work,

3 may circumvent a technological measure that effectively

4 controls access to the work or protects a right of the copy-

5 right holder under this title if—

6   "(A) such act is necessary to make a non-

7   infringing use of the work under this title; and

8   "(B) the copyright owner fails to make publicly

9   available the necessary means to make such non-

10   infringing use without additional cost or burden to

11   such person.

12   "(2) Notwithstanding the provisions of subsections

13 (a)(2) and (b), any person may manufacture, import, offer

14 to the public, provide, or otherwise make available techno-

15 logical means to circumvent a technological measure that

16 effectively controls access to a work protected under this

17 title or protects a right of a copyright holder under this

18 title, if—

19   "(A) such means are necessary to make a non-

20   infringing use under paragraph (1)(A);

21   "(B) such means are designed, produced, and

22   marketed to make a noninfringing use under para-

23   graph (1)(A); and

9

1   ''(C) the copyright owner fails to make available

2   the necessary means referred to in paragraph

3   (1)(B).''.

○

The Digital Millennium Copyright Act
Text, History, and Caselaw

V. AGENCY INTERPRETATION

THE DIGITAL MILLENNIUM COPYRIGHT ACT OF 1998
U.S. Copyright Office Summary

December 1998

INTRODUCTION

The Digital Millennium Copyright Act (DMCA)[1] was signed into law by President Clinton on October 28, 1998. The legislation implements two 1996 World Intellectual Property Organization (WIPO) treaties: the WIPO Copyright Treaty and the WIPO Performances and Phonograms Treaty. The DMCA also addresses a number of other significant copyright-related issues.

The DMCA is divided into five titles:

- Title I, the "**WIPO Copyright and Performances and Phonograms Treaties Implementation Act of 1998**," implements the WIPO treaties.
- Title II, the "**Online Copyright Infringement Liability Limitation Act**," creates limitations on the liability of online service providers for copyright infringement when engaging in certain types of activities.
- Title III, the "**Computer Maintenance Competition Assurance Act**," creates an exemption for making a copy of a computer program by activating a computer for purposes of maintenance or repair.
- Title IV contains six **miscellaneous provisions**, relating to the functions of the Copyright Office, distance education, the exceptions in the Copyright Act for libraries and for making ephemeral recordings, "webcasting" of sound recordings on the Internet, and the applicability of collective bargaining agreement obligations in the case of transfers of rights in motion pictures.
- Title V, the "**Vessel Hull Design Protection Act**," creates a new form of protection for the design of vessel hulls.

This memorandum summarizes briefly each title of the DMCA. It provides merely an overview of the law's provisions; for purposes of length and readability a significant amount of detail has been omitted. **A complete understanding of any provision of the DMCA requires reference to the text of the legislation itself.**

---

[1]Pub. L. No. 105-304, 112 Stat. 2860 (Oct. 28, 1998).

The Digital Millennium Copyright Act of 1998

Title I: WIPO Treaty Implementation

Title I implements the WIPO treaties. First, it makes certain technical amendments to U.S. law, in order to provide appropriate references and links to the treaties. Second, it creates two new prohibitions in Title 17 of the U.S. Code—one on circumvention of technological measures used by copyright owners to protect their works and one on tampering with copyright management information—and adds civil remedies and criminal penalties for violating the prohibitions. In addition, Title I requires the U.S. Copyright Office to perform two joint studies with the National Telecommunications and Information Administration of the Department of Commerce (NTIA).

Technical Amendments

National Eligibility

The WIPO Copyright Treaty (WCT) and the WIPO Performances and Phonograms Treaty (WPPT) each require member countries to provide protection to certain works from other member countries or created by nationals of other member countries. That protection must be no less favorable than that accorded to domestic works.

Section 104 of the Copyright Act establishes the conditions of eligibility for protection under U.S. law for works from other countries. Section 102(b) of the DMCA amends section 104 of the Copyright Act and adds new definitions to section 101 of the Copyright Act in order to extend the protection of U.S. law to those works required to be protected under the WCT and the WPPT.

Restoration of Copyright Protection

Both treaties require parties to protect preexisting works from other member countries that have not fallen into the public domain in the country of origin through the expiry of the term of protection. A similar obligation is contained in both the Berne Convention and the TRIPS Agreement. In 1995 this obligation was implemented in the Uruguay Round Agreements Act, creating a new section 104A in the Copyright Act to restore protection to works from Berne or WTO member countries that are still protected in the country of origin, but fell into the public domain in the United States in the past because of a failure to comply with formalities that then existed in U.S. law, or due to a lack of treaty relations. Section 102(c) of the DMCA amends section 104A to restore copyright protection in the same circumstances to works from WCT and WPPT member countries.

The Digital Millennium Copyright Act of 1998

Registration as a Prerequisite to Suit

The remaining technical amendment relates to the prohibition in both treaties against conditioning the exercise or enjoyment of rights on the fulfillment of formalities. Section 411(a) of the Copyright Act requires claims to copyright to be registered with the Copyright Office before a lawsuit can be initiated by the copyright owner, but exempts many foreign works in order to comply with existing treaty obligations under the Berne Convention. Section 102(d) of the DMCA amends section 411(a) by broadening the exemption to cover all foreign works.

Technological Protection and Copyright Management Systems

Each of the WIPO treaties contains virtually identical language obligating member states to prevent circumvention of technological measures used to protect copyrighted works, and to prevent tampering with the integrity of copyright management information. These obligations serve as technological adjuncts to the exclusive rights granted by copyright law. They provide legal protection that the international copyright community deemed critical to the safe and efficient exploitation of works on digital networks.

Circumvention of Technological Protection Measures

General approach

Article 11 of the WCT states:

> Contracting Parties shall provide adequate legal protec-
> tion and effective legal remedies against the circumven-
> tion of effective technological measures that are used
> by authors in connection with the exercise of their
> rights under this Treaty or the Berne Convention and
> that restrict acts, in respect of their works, which are
> not authorized by the authors concerned or permitted
> by law.

Article 18 of the WPPT contains nearly identical language.

Section 103 of the DMCA adds a new chapter 12 to Title 17 of the U.S. Code. New section 1201 implements the obligation to provide adequate and effective protection against circumvention of technological measures used by copyright owners to protect their works.

Section 1201 divides technological measures into two categories: measures that prevent unauthorized *access* to a copyrighted work and measures that prevent unauthorized *copying*[2] of a copyrighted work. Making or selling devices or services that are used to circumvent either category of technological measure is prohibited in certain circumstances, described below. As to the act of circumvention in itself, the provision prohibits circumventing the first category of technological measures, but not the second.

This distinction was employed to assure that the public will have the continued ability to make fair use of copyrighted works. Since copying of a work may be a fair use under appropriate circumstances, section 1201 does not prohibit the act of circumventing a technological measure that prevents copying. By contrast, since the fair use doctrine is not a defense to the act of gaining unauthorized access to a work, the act of circumventing a technological measure in order to gain access is prohibited.

Section 1201 proscribes devices or services that fall within any one of the following three categories:

- they are primarily designed or produced to circumvent;
- they have only limited commercially significant purpose or use other than to circumvent; or
- they are marketed for use in circumventing.

No mandate

Section 1201 contains language clarifying that the prohibition on circumvention devices does not require manufacturers of consumer electronics, telecommunications or computing equipment to design their products affirmatively to respond to any particular technological measure. (Section 1201(c)(3)). Despite this general 'no mandate' rule, section 1201(k) does mandate an affirmative response for one particular type of technology: within 18 months of enactment, all analog videocassette recorders must be designed to conform to certain defined technologies, commonly known as Macrovision, currently in use for preventing unauthorized copying of analog videocassettes and certain analog signals. The provision prohibits rightholders from applying these specified technologies to free television and basic and extended basic tier cable broadcasts.

---

[2]"Copying" is used in this context as a short-hand for the exercise of any of the exclusive rights of an author under section 106 of the Copyright Act. Consequently, a technological measure that prevents unauthorized distribution or public performance of a work would fall in this second category.

The Digital Millennium Copyright Act of 1998

Savings clauses

Section 1201 contains two general savings clauses. First, section 1201(c)(1) states that nothing in section 1201 affects rights, remedies, limitations or defenses to copyright infringement, including fair use. Second, section 1201(c)(2) states that nothing in section 1201 enlarges or diminishes vicarious or contributory copyright infringement.

Exceptions

Finally, the prohibitions contained in section 1201 are subject to a number of exceptions. One is an exception to the operation of the entire section, for law enforcement, intelligence and other governmental activities. (Section 1201(e)). The others relate to section 1201(a), the provision dealing with the category of technological measures that control access to works.

The broadest of these exceptions, section 1201(a)(1)(B)-(E), establishes an ongoing administrative rule-making proceeding to evaluate the impact of the prohibition against the act of circumventing such access-control measures. This conduct prohibition does not take effect for two years. Once it does, it is subject to an exception for users of a work which is in a particular class of works if they are or are likely to be adversely affected by virtue of the prohibition in making noninfringing uses. The applicability of the exemption is determined through a periodic rulemaking by the Librarian of Congress, on the recommendation of the Register of Copyrights, who is to consult with the Assistant Secretary of Commerce for Communications and Information.

The six additional exceptions are as follows:

1. *Nonprofit library, archive and educational institution exception* (section 1201(d)). The prohibition on the act of circumvention of access control measures is subject to an exception that permits nonprofit libraries, archives and educational institutions to circumvent solely for the purpose of making a good faith determination as to whether they wish to obtain authorized access to the work.
2. *Reverse engineering* (section 1201(f)). This exception permits circumvention, and the development of technological means for such circumvention, by a person who has lawfully obtained a right to use a copy of a computer program for the sole purpose of identifying and analyzing elements of the program necessary to achieve interoperability with other programs, to the extent that such acts are permitted under copyright law.
3. *Encryption research* (section 1201(g)). An exception for encryption research permits circumvention of access control measures, and the

The Digital Millennium Copyright Act of 1998

development of the technological means to do so, in order to identify flaws and vulnerabilities of encryption technologies.

4. *Protection of minors* (section 1201(h)). This exception allows a court applying the prohibition to a component or part to consider the necessity for its incorporation in technology that prevents access of minors to material on the Internet.

5. *Personal privacy* (section 1201(i)). This exception permits circumvention when the technological measure, or the work it protects, is capable of collecting or disseminating personally identifying information about the online activities of a natural person.

6. *Security testing* (section 1201(j)). This exception permits circumvention of access control measures, and the development of technological means for such circumvention, for the purpose of testing the security of a computer, computer system or computer network, with the authorization of its owner or operator.

Each of the exceptions has its own set of conditions on its applicability, which are beyond the scope of this summary.

Integrity of Copyright Management Information

Article 12 of the WCT provides in relevant part:

> Contracting Parties shall provide adequate and effective legal remedies against any person knowingly performing any of the following acts knowing, or with respect to civil remedies having reasonable grounds to know, that it will induce, enable, facilitate or conceal an infringement of any right covered by this Treaty or the Berne Convention:
>
> (i) to remove or alter any electronic rights management information without authority;
>
> (ii) to distribute, import for distribution, broadcast or communicate to the public, without authority, works or copies of works knowing that electronic rights management information has been removed or altered without authority.

Article 19 of the WPPT contains nearly identical language.

New section 1202 is the provision implementing this obligation to protect the integrity of copyright management information (CMI). The scope of the protection

The Digital Millennium Copyright Act of 1998

is set out in two separate paragraphs, the first dealing with false CMI and the second with removal or alteration of CMI. Subsection (a) prohibits the knowing provision or distribution of false CMI, if done with the intent to induce, enable, facilitate or conceal infringement. Subsection (b) bars the intentional removal or alteration of CMI without authority, as well as the dissemination of CMI or copies of works, knowing that the CMI has been removed or altered without authority. Liability under subsection (b) requires that the act be done with knowledge or, with respect to civil remedies, with reasonable grounds to know that it will induce, enable, facilitate or conceal an infringement.

Subsection (c) defines CMI as identifying information about the work, the author, the copyright owner, and in certain cases, the performer, writer or director of the work, as well as the terms and conditions for use of the work, and such other information as the Register of Copyrights may prescribe by regulation. Information concerning users of works is explicitly excluded.

Section 1202 is subject to a general exemption for law enforcement, intelligence and other governmental activities. (Section 1202(d)). It also contains limitations on the liability of broadcast stations and cable systems for removal or alteration of CMI in certain circumstances where there is no intent to induce, enable, facilitate or conceal an infringement. (Section 1202(e)).

Remedies

Any person injured by a violation of section 1201 or 1202 may bring a civil action in Federal court. Section 1203 gives courts the power to grant a range of equitable and monetary remedies similar to those available under the Copyright Act, including statutory damages. The court has discretion to reduce or remit damages in cases of innocent violations, where the violator proves that it was not aware and had no reason to believe its acts constituted a violation. (Section 1203(c)(5)(A)). Special protection is given to nonprofit libraries, archives and educational institutions, which are entitled to a complete remission of damages in these circumstances. (Section 1203(c)(5)(B)).

In addition, it is a criminal offense to violate section 1201 or 1202 wilfully and for purposes of commercial advantage or private financial gain. Under section 1204 penalties range up to a $500,000 fine or up to five years imprisonment for a first offense, and up to a $1,000,000 fine or up to 10 years imprisonment for subsequent offenses. Nonprofit libraries, archives and educational institutions are entirely exempted from criminal liability. (Section 1204(b)).

The Digital Millennium Copyright Act of 1998

Copyright Office and NTIA Studies Relating to Technological Development

Title I of the DMCA requires the Copyright Office to conduct two studies jointly with NTIA, one dealing with encryption and the other with the effect of technological developments on two existing exceptions in the Copyright Act. New section 1201(g)(5) of Title 17 of the U.S. Code requires the Register of Copyrights and the Assistant Secretary of Commerce for Communications and Information to report to the Congress no later than one year from enactment on the effect that the exemption for encryption research (new section 1201(g)) has had on encryption research, the development of encryption technology, the adequacy and effectiveness of technological measures designed to protect copyrighted works, and the protection of copyright owners against unauthorized access to their encrypted copyrighted works.

Section 104 of the DMCA requires the Register of Copyrights and the Assistant Secretary of Commerce for Communications and Information to jointly evaluate (1) the effects of Title I of the DMCA and the development of electronic commerce and associated technology on the operation of sections 109 (first sale doctrine) and 117 (exemption allowing owners of copies of computer programs to reproduce and adapt them for use on a computer), and (2) the relationship between existing and emergent technology and the operation of those sections. This study is due 24 months after the date of enactment of the DMCA.

TITLE II: ONLINE COPYRIGHT INFRINGEMENT LIABILITY LIMITATION

Title II of the DMCA adds a new section 512 to the Copyright Act[3] to create four new limitations on liability for copyright infringement by online service providers. The limitations are based on the following four categories of conduct by a service provider:

1. Transitory communications;
2. System caching;
3. Storage of information on systems or networks at direction of users; and
4. Information location tools.

New section 512 also includes special rules concerning the application of these limitations to nonprofit educational institutions.

---

[3]The Fairness in Musical Licensing Act, Title II of Pub. L. No. 105-298, 112 Stat. 2827, 2830-34 (Oct. 27, 1998) also adds a new section 512 to the Copyright Act. This duplication of section numbers will need to be corrected in a technical amendments bill.

The Digital Millennium Copyright Act of 1998

Each limitation entails a complete bar on monetary damages, and restricts the availability of injunctive relief in various respects. (Section 512(j)). Each limitation relates to a separate and distinct function, and a determination of whether a service provider qualifies for one of the limitations does not bear upon a determination of whether the provider qualifies for any of the other three. (Section 512(n)).

The failure of a service provider to qualify for any of the limitations in section 512 does not necessarily make it liable for copyright infringement. The copyright owner must still demonstrate that the provider has infringed, and the provider may still avail itself of any of the defenses, such as fair use, that are available to copyright defendants generally. (Section 512(l)).

In addition to limiting the liability of service providers, Title II establishes a procedure by which a copyright owner can obtain a subpoena from a federal court ordering a service provider to disclose the identity of a subscriber who is allegedly engaging in infringing activities. (Section 512(h)).

Section 512 also contains a provision to ensure that service providers are not placed in the position of choosing between limitations on liability on the one hand and preserving the privacy of their subscribers, on the other. Subsection (m) explicitly states that nothing in section 512 requires a service provider to monitor its service or access material in violation of law (such as the Electronic Communications Privacy Act) in order to be eligible for any of the liability limitations.

Eligibility for Limitations Generally

A party seeking the benefit of the limitations on liability in Title II must qualify as a "service provider." For purposes of the first limitation, relating to transitory communications, "service provider" is defined in section 512(k)(1)(A) as "an entity offering the transmission, routing, or providing of connections for digital online communications, between or among points specified by a user, of material of the user's choosing, without modification to the content of the material as sent or received." For purposes of the other three limitations, "service provider" is more broadly defined in section 512(k)(l)(B) as "a provider of online services or network access, or the operator of facilities therefor."

In addition, to be eligible for any of the limitations, a service provider must meet two overall conditions: (1) it must adopt and reasonably implement a policy of terminating in appropriate circumstances the accounts of subscribers who are repeat infringers; and (2) it must accommodate and not interfere with "standard technical measures." (Section 512(i)). "Standard technical measures" are defined as measures that copyright owners use to identify or protect copyrighted works, that have been developed pursuant to a broad consensus of copyright owners and service providers in an open, fair and voluntary multi-industry process, are available to anyone on

The Digital Millennium Copyright Act of 1998

reasonable nondiscriminatory terms, and do not impose substantial costs or burdens on service providers.

Limitation for Transitory Communications

In general terms, section 512(a) limits the liability of service providers in circumstances where the provider merely acts as a data conduit, transmitting digital information from one point on a network to another at someone else's request. This limitation covers acts of transmission, routing, or providing connections for the information, as well as the intermediate and transient copies that are made automatically in the operation of a network.

In order to qualify for this limitation, the service provider's activities must meet the following conditions:

- The transmission must be initiated by a person other than the provider.
- The transmission, routing, provision of connections, or copying must be carried out by an automatic technical process without selection of material by the service provider.
- The service provider must not determine the recipients of the material.
- Any intermediate copies must not ordinarily be accessible to anyone other than anticipated recipients, and must not be retained for longer than reasonably necessary.
- The material must be transmitted with no modification to its content.

Limitation for System Caching

Section 512(b) limits the liability of service providers for the practice of retaining copies, for a limited time, of material that has been made available online by a person other than the provider, and then transmitted to a subscriber at his or her direction. The service provider retains the material so that subsequent requests for the same material can be fulfilled by transmitting the retained copy, rather than retrieving the material from the original source on the network.

The benefit of this practice is that it reduces the service provider's bandwidth requirements and reduces the waiting time on subsequent requests for the same information. On the other hand, it can result in the delivery of outdated information to subscribers and can deprive website operators of accurate "hit" information — information about the number of requests for particular material on a website — from which advertising revenue is frequently calculated. For this reason, the person making the material available online may establish rules about updating it, and may utilize technological means to track the number of "hits."

The Digital Millennium Copyright Act of 1998

The limitation applies to acts of intermediate and temporary storage, when carried out through an automatic technical process for the purpose of making the material available to subscribers who subsequently request it. It is subject to the following conditions:

- The content of the retained material must not be modified.
- The provider must comply with rules about "refreshing" material—replacing retained copies of material with material from the original location— when specified in accordance with a generally accepted industry standard data communication protocol.
- The provider must not interfere with technology that returns "hit" information to the person who posted the material, where such technology meets certain requirements.
- The provider must limit users' access to the material in accordance with conditions on access (e.g., password protection) imposed by the person who posted the material.
- Any material that was posted without the copyright owner's authorization must be removed or blocked promptly once the service provider has been notified that it has been removed, blocked, or ordered to be removed or blocked, at the originating site.

Limitation for Information Residing on Systems or Networks at the Direction of Users

Section 512(c) limits the liability of service providers for infringing material on websites (or other information repositories) hosted on their systems. It applies to storage at the direction of a user. In order to be eligible for the limitation, the following conditions must be met:

- The provider must not have the requisite level of knowledge of the infringing activity, as described below.
- If the provider has the right and ability to control the infringing activity, it must not receive a financial benefit directly attributable to the infringing activity.
- Upon receiving proper notification of claimed infringement, the provider must expeditiously take down or block access to the material.

In addition, a service provider must have filed with the Copyright Office a designation of an agent to receive notifications of claimed infringement. The Office provides a suggested form for the purpose of designating an agent (http://www.loc.gov/copyright/onlinesp/) and maintains a list of agents on the Copyright Office website (http://www.loc.gov/copyright/onlinesp/list/).

The Digital Millennium Copyright Act of 1998

Under the knowledge standard, a service provider is eligible for the limitation on liability only if it does not have actual knowledge of the infringement, is not aware of facts or circumstances from which infringing activity is apparent, or upon gaining such knowledge or awareness, responds expeditiously to take the material down or block access to it.

The statute also establishes procedures for proper notification, and rules as to its effect. (Section 512(c)(3)). Under the notice and takedown procedure, a copyright owner submits a notification under penalty of perjury, including a list of specified elements, to the service provider's designated agent. Failure to comply substantially with the statutory requirements means that the notification will not be considered in determining the requisite level of knowledge by the service provider. If, upon receiving a proper notification, the service provider promptly removes or blocks access to the material identified in the notification, the provider is exempt from monetary liability. In addition, the provider is protected from any liability to any person for claims based on its having taken down the material. (Section 512(g)(1)).

In order to protect against the possibility of erroneous or fraudulent notifications, certain safeguards are built into section 512. Subsection (g)(1) gives the subscriber the opportunity to respond to the notice and takedown by filing a counter notification. In order to qualify for the protection against liability for taking down material, the service provider must promptly notify the subscriber that it has removed or disabled access to the material. If the subscriber serves a counter notification complying with statutory requirements, including a statement under penalty of perjury that the material was removed or disabled through mistake or misidentification, then unless the copyright owner files an action seeking a court order against the subscriber, the service provider must put the material back up within 10-14 business days after receiving the counter notification.

Penalties are provided for knowing material misrepresentations in either a notice or a counter notice. Any person who knowingly materially misrepresents that material is infringing, or that it was removed or blocked through mistake or misidentification, is liable for any resulting damages (including costs and attorneys' fees) incurred by the alleged infringer, the copyright owner or its licensee, or the service provider. (Section 512(f)).

Limitation for Information Location Tools

Section 512(d) relates to hyperlinks, online directories, search engines and the like. It limits liability for the acts of referring or linking users to a site that contains infringing material by using such information location tools, if the following conditions are met:

The Digital Millennium Copyright Act of 1998

- The provider must not have the requisite level of knowledge that the material is infringing. The knowledge standard is the same as under the limitation for information residing on systems or networks.
- If the provider has the right and ability to control the infringing activity, the provider must not receive a financial benefit directly attributable to the activity.
- Upon receiving a notification of claimed infringement, the provider must expeditiously take down or block access to the material.

These are essentially the same conditions that apply under the previous limitation, with some differences in the notification requirements. The provisions establishing safeguards against the possibility of erroneous or fraudulent notifications, as discussed above, as well as those protecting the provider against claims based on having taken down the material apply to this limitation. (Sections 512(f)-(g)).

Special Rules Regarding Liability of Nonprofit Educational Institutions

Section 512(e) determines when the actions or knowledge of a faculty member or graduate student employee who is performing a teaching or research function may affect the eligibility of a nonprofit educational institution for one of the four limitations on liability. As to the limitations for transitory communications or system caching, the faculty member or student shall be considered a "person other than the provider," so as to avoid disqualifying the institution from eligibility. As to the other limitations, the knowledge or awareness of the faculty member or student will not be attributed to the institution. The following conditions must be met:

- the faculty member or graduate student's infringing activities do not involve providing online access to course materials that were required or recommended during the past three years;
- the institution has not received more than two notifications over the past three years that the faculty member or graduate student was infringing; and
- the institution provides all of its users with informational materials describing and promoting compliance with copyright law.

TITLE III: COMPUTER MAINTENANCE OR REPAIR

Title III expands the existing exemption relating to computer programs in section 117 of the Copyright Act, which allows the owner of a copy of a program to make reproductions or adaptations when necessary to use the program in conjunction with a computer. The amendment permits the owner or lessee of a computer to make or authorize the making of a copy of a computer program in the course of maintaining or repairing that computer. The exemption only permits a copy that is made automatically when a computer is activated, and only if the computer already lawfully contains an authorized copy of the program. The new copy cannot be used in any other manner and must be destroyed immediately after the maintenance or repair is completed.

Title IV: Miscellaneous Provisions

Clarification of the Authority of the Copyright Office

Section 401(b), adds language to section 701 of the Copyright Act confirming the Copyright Office's authority to continue to perform the policy and international functions that it has carried out for decades under its existing general authority.

Ephemeral Recordings for Broadcasters

Section 112 of the Copyright Act grants an exemption for the making of "ephemeral recordings." These are recordings made in order to facilitate a transmission. Under this exemption, for example, a radio station can record a set of songs and broadcast from the new recording rather than from the original CDs (which would have to be changed "on the fly" during the course of a broadcast).

As it existed prior to enactment of the DMCA, section 112 permitted a transmitting organization to make and retain for up to six months (hence the term "ephemeral") no more than one copy of a work if it was entitled to transmit a public performance or display of the work, either under a license or by virtue of the fact that there is no general public performance right in sound recordings (as distinguished from musical works).

The Digital Performance Right in Sound Recordings Act of 1995 (DPRA) created, for the first time in U.S. copyright law, a limited public performance right in sound recordings. The right only covers public performances by means of digital transmission and is subject to an exemption for digital broadcasts (i.e., transmissions by FCC licensed terrestrial broadcast stations) and a statutory license for certain subscription transmissions that are not made on demand (i.e. in response to the specific request of a recipient).

Section 402 of the DMCA expands the section 112 exemption to include recordings that are made to facilitate the digital transmission of a sound recording where the transmission is made under the DPRA's exemption for digital broadcasts or statutory license. As amended, section 112 also permits in some circumstances the circumvention of access control technologies in order to enable an organization to make an ephemeral recording.

The Digital Millennium Copyright Act of 1998

Distance Education Study

In the course of consideration of the DMCA, legislators expressed an interest in amending the Copyright Act to promote distance education, possibly through an expansion of the existing exception for instructional broadcasting in section 110(2). Section 403 of the DMCA directs the Copyright Office to consult with affected parties and make recommendations to Congress on how to promote distance education through digital technologies. The Office must report to Congress within six months of enactment.

The Copyright Office is directed to consider the following issues:

- The need for a new exemption;
- Categories of works to be included in any exemption;
- Appropriate quantitative limitations on the portions of works that may be used under any exemption;
- Which parties should be eligible for any exemption;
- Which parties should be eligible recipients of distance education material under any exemption;
- The extent to which use of technological protection measures should be mandated as a condition of eligibility for any exemption;
- The extent to which the availability of licenses should be considered in assessing eligibility for any exemption; and
- Other issues as appropriate.

Exemption for Nonprofit Libraries and Archives

Section 404 of the DMCA amends the exemption for nonprofit libraries and archives in section 108 of the Copyright Act to accommodate digital technologies and evolving preservation practices. Prior to enactment of the DMCA, section 108 permitted such libraries and archives to make a single facsimile (i.e., not digital) copy of a work for purposes of preservation or interlibrary loan. As amended, section 108 permits up to three copies, which may be digital, provided that digital copies are not made available to the public outside the library premises. In addition, the amended section permits such a library or archive to copy a work into a new format if the original format becomes obsolete—that is, the machine or device used to render the work perceptible is no longer manufactured or is no longer reasonably available in the commercial marketplace.

Webcasting Amendments to the Digital Performance Right in Sound Recordings

As discussed above, in 1995 Congress enacted the DPRA, creating a performance right in sound recordings that is limited to digital transmissions. Under that legislation, three categories of digital transmissions were addressed: broadcast transmissions, which were exempted from the performance right; subscription transmissions, which were generally subject to a statutory license; and on-demand transmissions, which were subject to the full exclusive right. Broadcast transmissions under the DPRA are transmissions made by FCC-licensed terrestrial broadcast stations.

In the past several years, a number of entities have begun making digital transmissions of sound recordings over the Internet using streaming audio technologies. This activity does not fall squarely within any of the three categories that were addressed in the DPRA. Section 405 of the DMCA amends the DPRA, expanding the statutory license for subscription transmissions to include webcasting as a new category of "eligible nonsubscription transmissions."

In addition to expanding the scope of the statutory license, the DMCA revises the criteria that any entity must meet in order to be eligible for the license (other than those who are subject to a grandfather clause, leaving the existing criteria intact). It revises the considerations for setting rates as well (again, subject to a grandfather clause), directing arbitration panels convened under the law to set the royalty rates at fair market value.

This provision of the DMCA also creates a new statutory license for making ephemeral recordings. As indicated above, section 402 of the DMCA amends section 112 of the Copyright Act to permit the making of a single ephemeral recording to facilitate the digital transmission of sound recording that is permitted either under the DPRA's broadcasting exemption or statutory license. Transmitting organizations that wish to make more than the single ephemeral recording of a sound recording that is permitted under the outright exemption in section 112 are now eligible for a statutory license to make such additional ephemeral recordings. In addition, the new statutory license applies to the making of ephemeral recordings by transmitting organizations other than broadcasters who are exempt from the digital performance right, who are not covered by the expanded exemption in section 402 of the DMCA.

Assumption of Contractual Obligations upon Transfers of Rights in Motion Pictures

Section 416 addresses concerns about the ability of writers, directors and screen actors to obtain residual payments for the exploitation of motion pictures in situations where the producer is no longer able to make these payments. The guilds' collective bargaining agreements currently require producers to obtain assumption agreements from distributors in certain circumstances, by which the distributor assumes the producer's obligation to make such residual payments. Some production companies apparently do not always do so, leaving the guilds without contractual privity enabling them to seek recourse from the distributor.

The Digital Millennium Copyright Act of 1998

The DMCA adds a new chapter to Title 28 of the U.S. Code that imposes on transferees those obligations to make residual payments that the producer would be required to have the transferee assume under the relevant collective bargaining agreement. The obligations attach only if the distributor knew or had reason to know that the motion picture was produced subject to a collective bargaining agreement, or in the event of a court order confirming an arbitration award under the collective bargaining agreement that the producer cannot satisfy within ninety days. There are two classes of transfers that are excluded from the scope of this provision. The first is transfers limited to public performance rights, and the second is grants of security interests, along with any subsequent transfers from the security interest holder.

The provision also directs the Comptroller General, in consultation with the Register of Copyrights, to conduct a study on the conditions in the motion picture industry that gave rise to this provision, and the impact of the provision on the industry. The study is due two years from enactment.

TITLE V: PROTECTION OF CERTAIN ORIGINAL DESIGNS

Title V of the DMCA, entitled the Vessel Hull Design Protection Act (VHDPA), adds a new chapter 13 to Title 17 of the U.S. Code. It creates a new system for protecting original designs of certain useful articles that make the article attractive or distinctive in appearance. For purposes of the VHDPA, "useful articles" are limited to the hulls (including the decks) of vessels no longer than 200 feet.

A design is protected under the VHDPA as soon as a useful article embodying the design is made public or a registration for the design is published. Protection is lost if an application for registration is not made within two years after a design is first made public, but a design is not registrable if it has been made public more than one year before the date of the application for registration. Once registered, protection continues for ten years from the date protection begins.

The VHDPA is subject to a legislative sunset: the Act expires two years from enactment (October 28, 2000). The Copyright Office is directed to conduct two joint studies with the Patent and Trademark Office—the first by October 28, 1999 and the second by October 28, 2000—evaluating the impact of the VHDPA.

EFFECTIVE DATES

Most provisions of the DMCA are effective on the date of enactment. There are, however, several exceptions. The technical amendments in Title I that relate to eligibility of works for protection under U.S. copyright law by virtue of the new WIPO treaties do not take effect until the relevant treaty comes into force. Similarly, restoration of copyright protection for such works does not become effective until the relevant treaty comes into force. The prohibition on the act of circumvention of access

The Digital Millennium Copyright Act of 1998

control measures does not take effect until two years from enactment (October 28, 2000).

O

[FR Doc. 99–13499 Filed 5–26–99; 8:45 am]
BILLING CODE 3510–22–P

DEPARTMENT OF COMMERCE

National Telecommunications and Information Administration

LIBRARY OF CONGRESS

Copy Right Office

[Docket No. 990428110–9110–01]

RIN 0660–ZA09

Request for Comments on Section 1201(g) of the Digital Millennium Copyright Act

AGENCIES: The National Telecommunications and Information Administration, United States Department of Commerce; and the United States Copyright Office, Library of Congress.

ACTION: Request for public comment.

SUMMARY: The National Telecommunications and Information Administration of the United States Department of Commerce and the United States Copyright Office invite interested parties to submit comments on the effects of Section 1201(g) of Title 17, United States Code, as adopted in the Digital Millennium Copyright Act, Pub. L. No. 105–304, 112 Stat. 2860 (Oct. 28, 1998) ("DMCA") on encryption research and the development of encryption technology; the adequacy and effectiveness of technological measures designed to protect copyrighted works; and the protection of copyright owners against unauthorized access to their encrypted copyrighted works.

The DMCA, enacted on October 28, 1998, directs the Register of Copyrights and the Assistant Secretary for Communications and Information of the Department of Commerce to prepare a report for the Congress examining the impact of Section 1201(g) on encryption research and including legislative recommendations—if any—no later than one year after enactment of the DMCA. This **Federal Register** Notice is intended to solicit comments from interested parties on the effects of section 1201(g) of the DMCA. More specifically, how will the provisions of section 1201(g) of the DMCA affect encryption research?

The DMCA defines "encryption research" as identification and analysis of flaws and vulnerabilities of encryption technologies applied to copyrighted works. This activity must promote understanding of encryption technology or advance the development of encryption products.

DATES: Comments must be received by July 26, 1999.

ADDRESSES: The Department of Commerce and the Copyright Office invite the public to submit written comments in paper or electronic form. Comments may be mailed to Paula J. Bruening, Office of Chief Counsel, National Telecommunications and Information Administration (NTIA), Room 4713, U.S. Department of

---

Federal Register / Vol. 64, No. 102 / Thursday, May 27, 1999 / Notices   28803

Commerce, 14th Street and Constitution Avenue, N.W., Washington, DC 20230; and Jesse M. Feder, Office of Policy and International Affairs, U.S. Copyright Office, Copyright GC/I&R, P.O. Box 70400, Southwest Station, Washington, D.C. 20024. Paper submissions should include a version on diskette in PDF, ASCII, Word Perfect (please specify version), or Microsoft Word (please specify version) format. Comments should be sent to both the Department of Commerce and Copyright Office addresses.

Comments submitted in electronic form should be sent to dmca@ntia.doc.gov and crypto@loc.gov. Electronic comments should be submitted in the formats specified above and should be sent to both the Department of Congress and Copyright Office addresses.

FOR FURTHER INFORMATION CONTACT: Paula J. Bruening, National Telecommunications and Information Administration (202) 482–1816; and Jesse M. Feder, Office of Policy and International Affairs, US Copyright Office, Library of Congress (202) 707–8350.

SUPPLEMENTARY INFORMATION: The National Telecommunications and Information Administration, United States Department of Commerce and the United States Copyright Office, Library of Congress invite interested parties to submit comments on the effects of the Digital Millennium Copyright Act (DMCA) on encryption research and development of encryption technology; the adequacy and effectiveness of technological measures designed to protect copyrighted works; and, protection of copyright owners against unauthorized access to their encrypted copyrighted works.

The objective of Title I of the Digital Millennium Copyright Act was to revise U.S. copyright law to comply with two recent World Intellectual Property Organization (WIPO) Treaties and to strengthen copyright protection for motion pictures, sound recordings, computer software and other copyrighted works in electronic formats. The DMCA establishes a prohibition on the act of circumventing technological measures that effectively control access to a copyrighted work protected under the U.S. Copyright Act. The prohibition, found in Section 1201 of Title 17, U.S. Code, takes effect October 28, 2000, two years from the date of enactment of the DMCA.

The DMCA also makes it illegal for a person to manufacture, import, offer to the public, provide, or otherwise traffic in any technology, product, service, device, component or part thereof which is primarily designed or produced to circumvent a technological measure that effectively controls access to or unauthorized copying of a work protected by copyright, has only a limited commercially significant purpose or use other than circumvention of such measures, or marketed for use in circumventing such measures.

Despite the general prohibitions of Section 1201, the DMCA permits certain specified activities that include the circumvention of access control technologies in limited circumstances. One such specified activity is good faith encryption research. The DMCA defines "encryption research" as identification and analysis of flaws and vulnerabilities of encryption technologies applied to copyrighted works. This activity must promote understanding of encryption technology or advance the development of encryption products.

The DMCA exempts from the general prohibition certain good faith activities of circumvention when: (a) The person circumventing the protection system lawfully obtained the encrypted copy of the work; (b) circumvention is necessary to conduct the encryption research; (c) the person circumventing the protection system made a good faith effort to obtain authorization prior to the circumvention; and, (d) such circumvention does not constitute copyright infringement or a violation of any otherwise applicable law. The DMCA also lists additional factors to be considered when determining whether a person qualifies for the exemption.

The DMCA also includes several additional exemptions from the general prohibition or circumvention. One such exemption is for security testing. Section 1201(j) of Title 17, U.S. Code permits circumvention of access control technologies in order to test the effectiveness of a security measure. Comments on Subsection 1201(j), the exemption for "security testing," and comments on exemptions other than the exemption for encryption research, are not being solicited by this Notice and will not be considered.

Information collected from responses to this **Federal Register** Notice will be considered when preparing the required report for Congress.

Kathy D. Smith,
Acting Chief Counsel, National Telecommunications and Information Administration.

Marybeth Peters,
Register of Copyrights, United States Copyright Office.

[FR Doc. 99–13439 Filed 5–26–99; 8:45 am]

BILLING CODE 3510–60–P

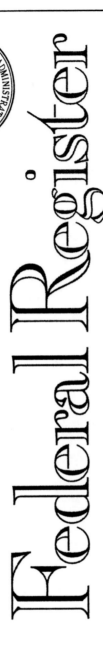

Friday,
October 27, 2000

Part V

Library of Congress

Copyright Office

37 CFR Part 201
Exemption to Prohibition on
Circumvention of Copyright Protection
Systems for Access Control Technologies;
Final Rule

LIBRARY OF CONGRESS

Copyright Office

37 CFR Part 201

[Docket No. RM 99–7D]

Exemption to Prohibition on Circumvention of Copyright Protection Systems for Access Control Technologies

AGENCY: Copyright Office, Library of Congress.

ACTION: Final Rule.

SUMMARY: This rule designates the classes of copyrighted works that the Librarian of Congress has determined shall be subject to exemption from the prohibition against circumvention of a technological measure that effectively controls access to a work protected under title 17 of the U.S. Code. In title I of the Digital Millennium Copyright Act, Congress established that this prohibition against circumvention will become effective October 28, 2000. The same legislation directed the Register of Copyrights to conduct a rulemaking procedure and to make recommendations to the Librarian as to whether any classes of works should be subject to exemptions from the prohibition against circumvention. The exemptions set forth in this rule will be in effect until October 28, 2003.

EFFECTIVE DATE: October 28, 2000.

FOR FURTHER INFORMATION CONTACT: Charlotte Douglass or Robert Kasunic, Office of the General Counsel, Copyright GC/I&R, P.O. Box 70400, Southwest Station, Washington, DC 20024. Telephone (202) 707–8380; telefax (202) 707–8366.

SUPPLEMENTARY INFORMATION:

Recommendation of the Register of Copyrights

I. Background

A. Legislative Requirements for Rulemaking Proceeding

The WIPO Copyright Treaty (WCT) and the WIPO Performances and Phonograms Treaty (WPPT) require that Contracting Parties provide adequate legal protection and effective legal remedies against the circumvention of effective technological measures that authors or other copyright owners (or, in the case of the WPPT, performers and producers of phonograms) use in connection with the exercise of their rights and that restrict acts which they

have not authorized and are not permitted by law. [1]

In fulfillment of these treaty obligations, on October 28, 1998, the United States enacted the Digital Millennium Copyright Act ("DMCA"), Pub. L. 105–304 (1998). Title I of the Act added a new Chapter 12 to Title 17 U.S.C., which among other things prohibits circumvention of access control technologies employed by or on behalf of copyright owners to protect their works. Specifically, new subsection 1201(a)(1)(A) provides, inter alia, that "No person shall circumvent a technological measure that effectively controls access to a work protected under this title." Congress found it appropriate to modify the prohibition to assure that the public will have continued ability to engage in noninfringing uses of copyrighted works, such as fair use. See the Report of the House Committee on Commerce on the Digital Millennium Copyright Act of 1998, H.R. Rep. No. 105–551, pt. 2, at 36 (1998) (hereinafter Commerce Comm. Report). Subparagraph (B) limits this prohibition. It provides that the prohibition against circumvention "shall not apply to persons who are users of a copyrighted work which is in a particular class of works, if such persons are, or are likely to be in the succeeding 3-year period, adversely affected by virtue of such prohibition in their ability to make noninfringing uses of that particular class of works under this title" as determined in this rulemaking. This prohibition on circumvention becomes effective on October 28, 2000, two years after the date of enactment of the DMCA.

During the 2-year period between the enactment and the effective date of the provision, the Librarian of Congress must make a determination as to classes of works exempted from the prohibition. This determination is to be made upon the recommendation of the Register of Copyrights in a rulemaking proceeding. The determination thus made will remain in effect during the succeeding three years. In making her recommendation, the Register of Copyrights is to consult with the Assistant Secretary for Communications and Information of the Department of Commerce and report and comment on

---

[1] The treaties were adopted on December 20, 1996 at a World Intellectual Property Organization (WIPO) Diplomatic Conference on Certain Copyright and Neighboring Rights Questions. The United States ratified the treaties in September, 1999. The treaties will go into effect after 30 instruments of ratification or accession by States have been deposited with the Director General of WIPO.

the Assistant Secretary's views. 17 U.S.C. 1201(a)(1)(C).

A more complete explanation of the development of the legislative requirements is set out in the Notice of Inquiry published on November 24, 1999, 64 FR 66139, and is also available on the Copyright Office's website at : http://www.loc.gov/copyright/1201/ anticirc.html. See also the discussion in section III.A. below.

B. Responsibilities of Register of Copyrights and Librarian of Congress

The prohibition against circumvention is subject to delayed implementation in order to permit a determination whether users of particular classes of copyrighted works are likely to be adversely affected by the prohibition in their ability to make noninfringing uses. By October 28, 2000, upon the recommendation of the Register of Copyrights in a rulemaking proceeding, the Librarian of Congress must determine whether to exempt certain classes of works (which he must identify) from the application of the prohibition against circumvention during the next three years because of such adverse effects.

The Register was directed to conduct a rulemaking proceeding, soliciting public comment and consulting with the Assistant Secretary of Commerce for Communications and Information, and then to make a recommendation to the Librarian, who must make a determination whether any classes of copyrighted works should be exempt from the statutory prohibition against circumvention during the three years commencing on that date.

The primary responsibility of the Register and the Librarian in this respect is to assess whether the implementation of technological protection measures that effectively control access to copyrighted works (hereinafter "access control measures") is diminishing the ability of individuals to use copyrighted works in ways that are otherwise lawful. Commerce Comm. Report, at 37. As examples of technological protection measures in effect today, the Commerce Committee offered the use of "password codes" to control authorized access to computer programs and encryption or scrambling of cable programming, videocassettes, and CD–ROMs. *Id.*

The prohibition becomes effective on October 28, 2000, and any exemptions to that prohibition must be in place by that time. Although it is difficult to measure the effect of a future prohibition, Congress intended that the Register solicit input that would enable consideration of a broad range of current or likely future adverse impacts. The nature of the inquiry is delineated in the statutory areas to be examined, as set forth in section 1201(a)(1)(C):

(i) The availability for use of copyrighted works;

(ii) The availability for use of works for nonprofit archival, preservation, and educational purposes;

(iii) The impact that the prohibition on the circumvention of technological measures applied to copyrighted works has on criticism, comment, news reporting, teaching, scholarship, or research;

(iv) The effect of circumvention of technological measures on the market for or value of copyrighted works; and

(v) Such other factors as the Librarian considers appropriate.

II. Solicitation of Public Comments and Hearings

On November 24, 1999, the Office initiated the rulemaking procedure with publication of a Notice of Inquiry. 64 FR 66139. The Notice of Inquiry requested written comments from all interested parties, including representatives of copyright owners, educational institutions, libraries and archives, scholars, researchers and members of the public. The Office devoted a great deal of attention in this Notice to setting out the legislative parameters and developing questions related to the criteria Congress had established. The Office was determined to make the comments it received available immediately in order to elicit a broad range of public comment; therefore, it stated a preference for submission of comments in certain electronic formats. *Id.* In response to some commenters' views that the formats permitted were not sufficient, the Office expanded the list of formats in which comments could be submitted. 65 FR 6573 (February 10, 2000). In the same document, the Office extended the comment period: comments would be due by February 17, 2000 and reply comments by March 20, 2000. On March 17, the Office extended the reply comment period to March 31; scheduled hearings to take place in Washington, DC on May 2–4 and in Palo Alto, California, at Stanford University on May 18–19; and set a June 23, 2000 deadline for submission of post-hearing comments. 65 FR 14505 (March 17, 2000). All of these notices were published not only in the **Federal Register**, but also on the Office's website.

In response to the Notice of Inquiry, the Office received 235 initial comments and 129 reply comments. Thirty-four witnesses representing over 50 groups testified at five days of hearings held in either Washington, DC or Palo Alto, California. The Office placed all initial comments, reply comments, optional

written statements of the witnesses and the transcripts of the two hearings on its website shortly after their receipt. Following the hearings, the Office received 28 post-hearing comments, which were also posted on the website. All of these commenters and witnesses are identified in the indexes that appear on the Office's website.

The comments received represent a broad perspective of views ranging from representatives or individuals who urged there should be broad exemptions to those who opposed any exemption; they also included a number of comments about various other aspects of the Digital Millennium Copyright Act. The Copyright Office has now exhaustively reviewed and analyzed the entire record, including all of the comments and the transcripts of the hearings in order to determine whether any class of copyrighted works should be exempt from the prohibition against circumvention during the next three years.[2]

III. Discussion

A. *The Purpose and Focus of the Rulemaking*

1. Purpose of the Rulemaking

As originally reported out of the Senate Judiciary Committee on May 11, 1998, S. Rep. No. 105–190 (1998), and the House Judiciary Committee on May 22, 1998, H.R. Rep. No. 105–551, pt. I (1998), section 1201(a)(1) consisted of only one sentence—what is now the first sentence of section 1201(a)(1): "No person shall circumvent a technological measure that effectively controls access to a work protected under this title." Section 1201(a)(2), like the provision finally enacted, prohibited the manufacture, importation, offering to the public, providing or otherwise trafficking in any technology, product, service, device, or component to circumvent access control measures. Section 1201(a) thus addressed "access control" measures, prohibiting both the conduct of circumventing those measures and devices that circumvent them. Thus, section 1201(a) prohibits both the conduct of circumventing access control measures and trafficking

in products, services and devices that circumvent access control measures.

In addition to section 1201(a)(1)'s prohibition on circumvention of access control measures, section 1201 also addressed circumvention of a different type of technological measure. Section 1201(b), in the versions originally reported by the House and Senate Judiciary Committees and in the statute finally enacted, prohibited the manufacture, importation, offering to the public, providing or otherwise trafficking in any technology, product, service, device, or component to circumvent protection afforded by a technological measure that effectively protects a right of a copyright owner under title 17 in a copyrighted work. The type of technological measure addressed in section 1201(b) includes copy-control measures and other measures that control uses of works that would infringe the exclusive rights of the copyright owner. They will frequently be referred to herein as copy controls. But unlike section 1201(a), which prohibits both the conduct of circumvention and devices that circumvent, section 1201(b) does not prohibit the conduct of circumventing copy control measures. The prohibition in section 1201(b) extends only to devices that circumvent copy control measures. The decision not to prohibit the conduct of circumventing copy controls was made, in part, because it would penalize some noninfringing conduct such as fair use.

In the House of Representatives, the DMCA was sequentially referred to the Committee on Commerce after it was reported out of the Judiciary Committee. The Commerce Committee was concerned that section 1201, in its original form, might undermine Congress' commitment to fair use. Commerce Comm. Report, at 35. While acknowledging that the growth and development of the Internet has had a significant positive impact on the access of students, researchers, consumers, and the public at large to information and that a "plethora of information, most of it embodied in materials subject to copyright protection, is available to individuals, often for free, that just a few years ago could have been located and acquired only through the expenditure of considerable time, resources, and money," *Id.*, the Committee was concerned that "marketplace realities may someday dictate a different outcome, resulting in less access, rather than more, to copyrighted materials that are important to education, scholarship, and other socially vital endeavors." *Id.* at 36. Possible measures that might lead to

---

[2] In referring to the comments and hearing materials, the Office will use the following abbreviations: C-Comment, R-Reply Comment, PH-Post Hearing Comments, T + speaker and date—Transcript (ex. "T Laura Gasaway, 5/18/00") and WS + speaker—Written statements (ex. "WS Vaidhyanathan"). Citations to page numbers in hearing transcripts are to the hard copy transcripts at the Copyright Office. For the hearings in Washington, DC, the pagination of those transcripts differs from the pagination of the versions of the transcript available on the Copyright Office website.

64558   **Federal Register** / Vol. 65, No. 209 / Friday, October 27, 2000 / Rules and Regulations

such an outcome included the elimination of print or other hard-copy versions, permanent encryption of all electronic copies and adoption of business models that restrict distribution and availability of works. The Committee concluded that "[i]n this scenario, it could be appropriate to modify the flat prohibition against the circumvention of effective technological measures that control access to copyrighted materials, in order to ensure that access for lawful purposes is not unjustifiably diminished." *Id.*

In order to address such possible developments, the Commerce Committee proposed a modification of section 1201 which it characterized as a "'fail-safe' mechanism." *Id.* As the Committee Report describes it, "This mechanism would monitor developments in the marketplace for copyrighted materials, and allow the enforceability of the prohibition against the act of circumvention to be selectively waived, for limited time periods, if necessary to prevent a diminution in the availability to individual users of a particular category of copyrighted materials." *Id.*

The "fail-safe" mechanism is this rulemaking. In its final form as enacted by Congress, slightly modified from the mechanism that appeared in the version of the DMCA reported out of the Commerce Committee, the Register is to conduct a rulemaking proceeding and, after consulting with the Assistant Secretary for Communications and Information of the Department of Commerce, recommend to the Librarian whether he should conclude "that persons who are users of a copyrighted work are, or are likely to be in the succeeding 3-year period, adversely affected by the prohibition under [section 1201(a)(1)(A)] in their ability to make noninfringing uses under [Title 17] of a particular class of copyrighted works." 17 U.S.C. 1201(a)(1)(C). "The Librarian shall publish any class of copyrighted works for which the Librarian has determined, pursuant to the rulemaking conducted under subparagraph (C), that noninfringing uses by persons who are users of a copyrighted work are, or are likely to be, adversely affected, and the prohibition contained in subparagraph (A) shall not apply to such users with respect to such class of works for the ensuing 3-year period." 17 U.S.C. 1201(a)(1)(C).

The Commerce Committee offered additional guidance as to the task of the Register and the Librarian in this rulemaking. "The goal of the proceeding is to assess whether the implementation of technological protection measures that effectively control access to copyrighted works is adversely affecting the ability of individual users to make lawful uses of copyrighted works * * *. The primary goal of the rulemaking proceeding is to assess whether the prevalence of these technological protections, with respect to particular categories of copyrighted materials, is diminishing the ability of individuals to use these works in ways that are otherwise lawful." Commerce Comm. Report, at 37. Accord: Staff of House Committee on the Judiciary, 105th Cong., Section-By-Section Analysis of H.R. 2281 as Passed by the United States House of Representatives on August 4, 1998, (hereinafter House Manager's Report) (Rep. Coble)(Comm. Print 1998), at 6. The Committee observed that the effective date of section 1201(a)(1) was delayed for two years in order "to allow the development of a sufficient record as to how the implementation of these technologies is affecting availability of works in the marketplace for lawful uses." Commerce Comm. Report, at 37.

Thus, the task of this rulemaking appears to be to determine whether the availability and use of access control measures has already diminished or is about to diminish the ability of the public to engage in the lawful uses of copyrighted works that the public had traditionally been able to make prior to the enactment of the DMCA. As the Commerce Committee Report stated, in examining the factors set forth in section 1201(a)(1)(C), the focus must be on "whether the implementation of technological protection measures (such as encryption or scrambling) has caused adverse impact on the ability of users to make lawful uses." *Id.*

2. The Necessary Showing

The language of section 1201(a)(1) does not offer much guidance as to the respective burdens of proponents and opponents of any classes of works to be exempted from the prohibition on circumvention. Of course, it is a general rule of statutory construction that exemptions must be construed narrowly in order to preserve the purpose of a statutory provision, and that rule is applied in interpreting the copyright law. *Tasini v. New York Times Co.*, 206 F.3d 161, 168 (2d Cir. 2000). Moreover, the burden is on the proponent of the exemption to make the case for exempting any particular class of works from the operation of section 1201(a)(1). See 73 Am. Jur. 2d 313 (1991) ("[s]tatutes granting exemptions from their general operation [to] be strictly construed, and any doubt must be resolved against the one asserting the exemption.") Indeed, the House Commerce Committee stated that "The regulatory prohibition is *presumed to apply* to any and all kinds of works, including those as to which a waiver of applicability was previously in effect, unless, and until, the Secretary makes a new determination that the *adverse impact criteria have been met* with respect to a particular class and therefore issues a new waiver." Commerce Comm. Report, at 37 (emphasis added).[3]

The legislative history makes clear that a determination to exempt a class of works from the prohibition on circumvention must be based on a determination that the prohibition has a substantial adverse effect on noninfringing use of that particular class of works. The Commerce Committee noted that the rulemaking proceeding is to focus on "distinct, verifiable, and measurable impacts, and should not be based upon de minimis impacts." Commerce Comm. Report, at 37. "If the rulemaking has produced insufficient evidence to determine whether there have been adverse impacts with respect to particular classes of copyrighted works, the circumvention prohibition should go into effect with respect to those classes." *Id.* at 38. Similarly, the House Manager's Report stated that "[t]he focus of the rulemaking proceeding must remain on whether the prohibition on circumvention of technological protection measures (such as encryption or scrambling) has caused any substantial adverse impact on the ability of users to make non-infringing uses," and suggested that "mere inconveniences, or individual cases * * * do not rise to the level of a substantial adverse impact." House Manager's Report, at 6.[4] See also *Connecticut Department of Public Utility Control v. Federal Communications Commission*, 78 F.3d 842, 851 (2d Cir. 1996) ("It is reasonable

---

[3] The Commerce Committee proposal would have placed responsibility for the rulemaking in the hands of the Secretary of Commerce. As finally enacted, the DMCA shifted that responsibility to the Librarian, upon the recommendation of the Register.

[4] Some commenters have suggested that the House Manager's Report is entitled to little deference as legislative history. See, *e.g.*, PH18, p. 3. However, because that report is consistent with the Commerce Committee Report, there is no need in this rulemaking to determine whether the Manager's Report is entitled to less weight than the Commerce Committee Report. Some critics of the Manager's Report have objected to its statement that the focus of this proceeding should be on whether there is a "substantial adverse impact" on noninfringing uses. However, they have failed to explain how this statement is anything other than another way of saying what the Commerce Committee said when it said the determination should be based on "distinct, verifiable, and measurable impacts, and should not be based upon de minimis impacts."

Federal Register / Vol. 65, No. 209 / Friday, October 27, 2000 / Rules and Regulations   64559

to characterize as 'substantial' the burden faced by a party seeking an exemption from a general statutory rule").

Although future adverse impacts may also be considered, the Manager's Report states that "the determination should be based upon anticipated, rather than actual, adverse impacts only in extraordinary circumstances in which the evidence of likelihood of future adverse impact during that time period is highly specific, strong and persuasive. Otherwise, the prohibition would be unduly undermined." *Id.* Although the Commerce Committee Report does not state how future adverse impacts are to be evaluated (apart from a single reference stating that in categories where adverse impacts have occurred or "are likely to occur," an exemption should be made, Commerce Comm. Report at 38), the Committee's discussion of "distinct, verifiable and measurable impacts" suggests that it would require a similar showing with respect to future adverse impact.

The legislative history also requires the Register and Librarian to disregard any adverse effects that are caused by factors other than the prohibition against circumvention. The House Manager's Report is instructive:

The focus of the rulemaking proceeding must remain on whether the prohibition on circumvention of technological protection measures (such as encryption or scrambling) has caused any substantial adverse impact on the ability of users to make non-infringing uses. Adverse impacts that flow from other sources * * * or that are not clearly attributable to such a prohibition, are outside the scope of the rulemaking.

House Manager's Report, at 6. The House Commerce Committee came to a similar conclusion, using similar language. Commerce Comm. Report, at 37.

In fact, some technological protection measures may mitigate adverse effects. The House Manager's Report notes that:

In assessing the impact of the implementation of technological measures, and of the law against their circumvention, the rule-making proceedings should consider the positive as well as the adverse effects of these technologies on the availability of copyrighted materials. The technological measures—such as encryption, scrambling, and electronic envelopes—that this bill protects can be deployed, not only to prevent piracy and other economically harmful unauthorized uses of copyrighted materials, but also to support new ways of disseminating copyrighted materials to users, and to safeguard the availability of legitimate uses of those materials by individuals.

House Manager's Report, at 6.

Another mitigating factor may arise when a work as to which the copyright

owner has instituted a technological control is also available in formats that are not subject to technological protections. For example, a work may be available in electronic format only in encrypted form, but may also be available in traditional hard copy format which has no such technological restrictions on access. The availability without restriction in the latter format may alleviate any adverse effect that would otherwise result from the technological controls utilized in the electronic format. The availability of works in such other formats is to be considered when exemptions are fashioned. *Id.* at 7.

3. Determination of "Class of Works"

One of the key issues discussed in comments and testimony was how a "class" of works is to be defined. The Office's initial notice of inquiry highlighted this issue, asking for comments from the public on the criteria to be used in determining what a "class of works" is and on whether works could be classified in part based on the way in which they are being used. See questions 16, 17 and 23, 64 FR at 66143. A joint submission by a number of library associations took the position that the Librarian should adopt a "'function-based" definition of classes of works." C162, p. 32. The same submission stated that "the class of works should be defined, in part, according to the ways they are being used because that is precisely how the limitations on the otherwise exclusive rights of copyright holders are phrased," *Id.*, p. 36, and concluded that "all categories of copyrighted works should be covered by this rulemaking." *Id.*, p. 38. In contrast, a coalition of organizations representing copyright owners argued for a narrower approach, rejecting a focus on particular types of uses of works or on particular access control technologies. R112, p. 10. One association of copyright owners argued that a "class" should not be defined by reference to any particular medium (such as digital versatile discs, or DVD's), but rather by reference to "a type or types of works." R59, p. 8. Many representatives of copyright owners repeated the legislative history that "the 'particular class of copyrighted works' be a narrow and focused subset of the broad categories of works of authorship than is [sic] identified in section 102 of the Copyright Act (17 U.S.C. 102)." *See, e.g., Id.*, (quoting Commerce Comm. Report, at 38). A representative of a major copyright owner took the position that "defining 'classes' of works is neither feasible nor appropriate" and that "[b]efore there is any movement in

the direction of exempting certain works or 'classes' of works from the prohibition against circumvention, those who support such exemption should come forward with proof that users who desire to make non-infringing uses or avail themselves of the fair use defense are prevented from doing so by the technological protections." C43, p.6.

Based on a review of the statutory language and the legislative history, the view that a "class" of works can be defined in terms of the status of the user or the nature of the intended use appears to be untenable. Section 1201(a)(1)(B) refers to "a copyrighted work which is in a particular class of works." Section 1201(a)(1)(C) refers to "a particular class of copyrighted works." Section 1201(a)(1)(D) "any class of copyrighted works." This statutory language appears to require that the Librarian identify a "class of works" based upon attributes of the works themselves, and not by reference to some external criteria such as the intended use or users of the works. The dictionary defines "class" as "a group, set or kind sharing common attributes." Webster's New Collegiate Dictionary 211 (1995).

Moreover, the phrase "class of works" connotes that the common attributes relate to the nature of authorship in the works. Although the Copyright Act does not define "work," the term is used throughout the copyright law to refer to a work of authorship, rather than to a material object on which the work appears or to the readers or users of the work. *See, e.g.*, 17 U.S.C. 102(a) ("Copyright protection subsists, in accordance with this title, in original *works of authorship* fixed in any tangible medium of expression, * * *) (emphasis added) and the catalog of the types of works protected by copyright set forth in section 102(a)(1)–(8) ("literary works," "musical works," "dramatic works," *etc.*).

Nevertheless, the statutory language is arguably ambiguous, and one could imagine an interpretation of section 1201(a)(1) that permitted a class of works to be defined in terms of criteria having nothing to do with the intrinsic qualities of the works. In such a case, resort to legislative history might clarify the meaning of the statute. In this case, the legislative history appears to leave no other alternative than to interpret the statute as requiring a "class" to be defined primarily, if not exclusively, by reference to attributes of the works themselves.

The Commerce Committee Report addressed the issue of determining a class of works:

64560 **Federal Register**/Vol. 65, No. 209/Friday, October 27, 2000/Rules and Regulations

The issue of defining the scope or boundaries of a "particular class" of copyrighted works as to which the implementation of technological protection measures has been shown to have had an adverse impact is an important one to be determined during the rulemaking proceedings. In assessing whether users of copyrighted works have been, or are likely to be adversely affected, the Secretary shall assess users' ability to make lawful uses of works "within each particular class of copyrighted works specified in the rulemaking." The Committee intends that the "particular class of copyrighted works" be a narrow and focused subset of the broad categories of works of authorship than [sic] is identified in section 102 of the Copyright Act (17 U.S.C. 102).

Commerce Comm. Report, at 38.[5]

A "narrow and focused subset of the broad categories of works of authorship * * * identified in section 102" presumably must use, as its starting point, the categories of authorship set forth in section 102: literary works; musical works; dramatic works; pantomimes and choreographic works; pictorial, graphic, and sculptural works; motion pictures and other audiovisual works; sound recordings; and architectural works.

Moreover, the Commerce Committee Report states that the task in this rulemaking proceeding is to determine whether the prevalence of access control measures, "with respect to *particular categories* of copyrighted materials, is diminishing the ability of individuals to use these works in ways that are otherwise lawful." Commerce Comm. Report, at 37 (emphasis added). In fact, the Report refers repeatedly to "categories" of works in connection with the findings to be made in this rulemaking. *See Id.*, at 36 ("individual users of a particular category of copyrighted materials") ("whether enforcement of the regulation should be temporarily waived with regard to particular categories of works") ("any particular category of copyrighted materials") ("assessment of adverse impacts on particular categories of works"), and 38 ("Only in categories as to which the Secretary finds that adverse impacts have occurred"). Because the term "category" of works

has a well-understood meaning in the copyright law, referring to the categories set forth in section 102, the conclusion is inescapable that the starting point for any definition of a "particular class" of works in this rulemaking must be one of the section 102 categories.[6]

The views of the Judiciary Committee are in accord with those expressed in the Commerce Committee Report. The House Manager's Report uses very similar words to describe how a "class of works" is to be determined:

Deciding the scope or boundaries of a "particular class" of copyrighted works as to which the prohibition contained in section 1201(a)(1) has been shown to have had an adverse impact is an important issue to be determined during the rulemaking proceedings. The illustrative list of categories appearing in section 102 of Title 17 is only a starting point for this decision. For example, the category of "literary works" (17 USC 102(a)(1)) embraces both prose creations such as journals, periodicals or books, and computer programs of all kinds. It is exceedingly unlikely that the impact of the prohibition on circumvention of access control technologies will be the same for scientific journals as it is for computer operating systems; thus, these two categories of works, while both "literary works," do not constitute a single "particular class" for purposes of this legislation. Even within the category of computer programs, the availability for fair use purposes of PC-based business productivity applications is unlikely to be affected by laws against circumvention of technological protection measures in the same way as the availability for those purposes of videogames distributed in formats playable only on dedicated platforms, so it is probably appropriate to recognize different "classes" here as well.

House Manager's Report, at 7.

The House Manager's Report continues:

At the same time, the Secretary should not draw the boundaries of "particular classes" too narrowly. For instance, the section 102 category "motion pictures and other audiovisual works" may appropriately be subdivided, for purposes of the rulemaking, into classes such as "motion pictures," "television programs," and other rubrics of similar breadth. However, it would be inappropriate, for example, to subdivide overly narrowly into particular genres of motion pictures, such as Westerns, comedies, or live action dramas. Singling out specific types of motion pictures by creating in the rulemaking process "particular classes" that are too narrow would be inconsistent with the intent of this bill.

Id.

The conclusion to be drawn from the legislative history is that the section 102 categories of works are, at the very least, the starting point for any determination of what a "particular class of work" might be. That is not to say that a "class" of works must be identical to a "category." In fact, that usually will not be the case. A "class" of works might include works from more than one category of works; one could imagine a "class" of works consisting of certain sound recordings and musical compositions, for example. More frequently, a "class" would constitute some subset of a section 102 category, such as the Judiciary Committee's example of "television programs."

A rigid adherence to defining "class" solely by reference to section 102 categories or even to inherent attributes of the works themselves might lead to unjust results in light of the fact that the entire "class" must be exempted from section 1201(a)(1)'s anticircumvention provision if the required adverse impact is demonstrated. For example, if a showing had been made that users of motion pictures released on DVD's are adversely affected in their ability to make noninfringing uses of those works, it would be unfortunate if the Librarian's only choice were to exempt motion pictures. Limiting the class to "motion pictures distributed on DVD's," or more narrowly to "motion pictures distributed on DVD's using the content scrambling system of access control" would be a more just " and permissible " classification. Such a classification would begin by reference to attributes of the works themselves, but could then be narrowed by reference to the medium on which the works are distributed, or even to the access control measures applied to them. But classifying a work solely by reference to the medium on which the work appears, or the access control measures applied to the work, seems to be beyond the scope of what "particular class of work" is intended to be. And classifying a work by reference to the type of user or use (*e.g.*, libraries, or scholarly research) seems totally impermissible when administering a statute that requires the Librarian to create exemptions based on a "particular class of works." If Congress had wished to provide for exemptions based on the status of the user or the nature of the use—criteria that would be very sensible—Congress could have said so clearly. The fact that the issue of noninfringing uses was before Congress and the fact that Congress clearly was seeking, in section 1201, to create exemptions that would permit noninfringing uses, make it clear that

---

[5] A leading treatise draws the following conclusion from this language:

It would seem, therefore, that the language should be applied to discrete subgroups. If users of physics textbooks or listeners to Baroque concerti, for example, find themselves constricted in the new Internet environment, then some relief will lie. If, on the other hand, the only unifying feature shared by numerous disgruntled users is that each is having trouble accessing copyrighted works, albeit of different genres, then no relief is warranted. 1 Nimmer on Copyright § 12A.03[A][[2][b] (Copyright Protection Systems Special Pamphlet).

[6] The legislative history of the Copyright Act of 1976 supports the conclusion that there is a close relation between the section 102 categories and a "class" of work. The authoritative report of the House Judiciary Committee, in discussing the section 102 categories of works, used the term "class" as a synonym for "category." See H.R. Rep. No. 94–1476, at 53 (1976).

Federal Register / Vol. 65, No. 209 / Friday, October 27, 2000 / Rules and Regulations   **64561**

Congress had every opportunity and motive to clarify that such uses could be ingredients of the definition of "class" if that was what Congress intended. Yet the fact that Congress selected language in the statute and legislative history that avoided suggesting that classes of works could be defined by reference to users or uses is strong evidence that such classification was not within Congress' contemplation.

In this rulemaking, exemptions for two classes of works are recommended. The first class, "Compilations consisting of lists of websites blocked by filtering software applications," fits comfortably within the approach to classification outlined herein. The second class, "Literary works, including computer programs and databases, protected by access control mechanisms that fail to permit access because of malfunction, damage or obsoleteness," is a somewhat less comfortable fit. It includes all literary works (a section 102 category) and specifically mentions two subclasses of literary works, but narrows the exemption by reference to attributes of the technological measures that control access to the works. Such classification probably reaches the outer limits of a permissible definition of "class" under the approach adopted herein.

B. Consultation With Assistant Secretary of Commerce for Communications and Information

As is required by section 1201(a)(1)(C), the Register has consulted with the Assistant Secretary for Communications and Information in the Department of Commerce. The Assistant Secretary is the Administrator of the National Telecommunciations and Information Administration (NTIA). Discussions with the Assistant Secretary and the NTIA staff have taken place throughout this rulemaking process. In furtherance of the consultative process, on September 29, 2000, the Assistant Secretary presented a letter to the Register detailing his views. That letter has been forwarded to the Librarian. After full and thorough consideration of and discussions with the Assistant Secretary's office on these views, the Register includes the following report and comment on the Assistant Secretary's perspective in this recommendation to the Librarian.

The Assistant Secretary stated that his principal concern is to ensure that the Librarian will preserve fair use principles in this new digital age. The concerns expressed in his letter quoted from and restated many of the concerns that were presented in the House Commerce Committee Report. The

Assistant Secretary noted that the Commerce Committee was concerned that the anticircumvention prohibition of section 1201(a)(1) might have adverse consequences on fair uses of copyrighted works protected by technological protection measures, particularly by librarians and educators. He echoed the fears of the Commerce Committee that a legal framework may be developing that would "inexorably create a pay-per-use society." He stated that the "right" to prohibit circumvention should be qualified in order to maintain a balance between the interests of content creators and information users, by means of carefully drawn exemptions from the anticircumvention provision.

Since fair use, as codified in 17 U.S.C. 107, is not a defense to the cause of action created by the anticircumvention prohibition of section 1201, the Assistant Secretary urges the Register to follow the House Commerce Committee's intent to provide for exemptions analogous to fair use. He advises the Register to preserve fair use principles by crafting exemptions that are grounded in these principles in order to promote inclusion of all parts of society in the digital economy and prevent a situation in which information crucial to supporting scholarship, research, comment, criticism, news reporting, life-long learning, and other related lawful uses of copyrighted information is available only to those with the ability to pay or the expertise to negotiate advantageous licensing terms.

The Assistant Secretary expresses support for commenters in this proceeding who believed that the term "class" should not be interpreted as "coextensive" with categories of original works of authorship, as that term is used in section 102(a) of the Copyright Act. He states that since the statute and legislative history provide little guidance on the meaning of the term "class of works" and since section 1201(a)(1)(C) instructs the Librarian to examine considerations of use that are similar to fair use analysis, the classes of exempted works should be fashioned based on a factual examination of the uses to which copyrighted materials are put.

In order to craft an exemption that will preserve fair uses, he concludes that the determination of exempted classes of works should include a factual examination of the uses to which copyrighted materials are put. With this in mind, he endorses, "as a starting point, the exception proposed by the library and academic communities." In particular, he would support the

crafting of the following exemption: "Works embodied in copies that have been lawfully acquired by users or their institutions who subsequently seek to make noninfringing uses thereof."

The Register has subsequently sought and received clarification of some of the points made in the Assistant Secretary's letter. In particular, the Register has asked (1) for the Assistant Secretary's views on whether a "class of works" can be defined or determined by reference to the uses of the works in that class, rather than by reference to attributes of the works themselves, and (2) that the Assistant Secretary identify any comments or testimony in the record of this rulemaking proceeding that he believes presented any evidence that technological measures that control access to copyrighted works actually have caused or in the next three years will cause substantial adverse impacts on the ability of users to make noninfringing uses of works in the proposed class of works that he has endorsed.

With respect to how a "class of works" is to be defined or determined, NTIA responded by stating that fair use has to be a part of any discussion focusing on exemptions to the DMCA's anticircumvention prohibition, and that because the principle of fair use is grounded in a factual examination of the use to which copyrighted materials are put, it would be reasonable to include a similar examination in fashioning a class of excepted works under 1201(a)(1)(C).

In response to the request to identify comments and testimony that present evidence of substantial adverse impacts on the ability of users to make noninfringing uses of "works embodied in copies that have been lawfully acquired by users or their institutions who subsequently seek to make noninfringing uses thereof," NTIA cited one comment and the testimony of several witnesses. NTIA also questioned whether a showing of "substantial" adverse impact is required, observing that "Nowhere in section 1201(a)(1)(C) does the word "substantial" appear" and asserting that a showing of "reasonably anticipated impacts" should be sufficient.

The views of the Assistant Secretary have been seriously considered in the preparation of these recommendations to the Librarian. Because the exemption endorsed by the Assistant Secretary (see discussion above) is not supported in this recommendation, an explanation of the reasons is in order.

At the outset of these comments on the Assistant Secretary's views, it should be understood that there is no

64562 Federal Register / Vol. 65, No. 209 / Friday, October 27, 2000 / Rules and Regulations

disagreement with the Assistant Secretary or the Commerce Committee on the need to preserve the principles of fair use and other noninfringing uses in the digital age. The Register's disagreement with the Assistant Secretary's proposals arises from the interpretation of both the statutory language of section 1201(a)(1)(C) and a review of the record in this proceeding.

First, the Assistant Secretary's proposals are based on—and necessarily require adoption of—an interpretation of the statutory phrase "particular class of copyrighted works" that the Register cannot support. As stated above in section III.A.3, a "particular class of copyrighted works" must relate primarily to attributes of the copyrighted works themselves and not to factors that are external to the works, e.g., the material objects on which they are fixed or the particular technology employed on the works. Similarly, neither the language of the statute nor the legislative history provide a basis for an interpretation of an exemption of a class of works that is "use-oriented." While the Register was required to "examine" the present or likely adverse effects on uses, and in particular noninfringing uses, that inquiry had the express goal of designating exemptions that were based on classes of copyrighted works. The only examples cited and guidance provided in the legislative history lead the Register to conclude that a class must be defined primarily by reference to attributes of the works themselves, typically based upon the categories set forth in section 102(a) or some subset thereof, e.g., motion pictures or video games.

As NTIA observes, it is appropriate to examine the impact of access control measures on fair use in determining what classes of works, if any, should be subject to an exemption. But the Assistant Secretary has not explained how a "class of works" can be defined or determined without any reference whatsoever to attributes of the works themselves, and solely by reference to the status of the persons who acquire copies of those works. While fair use is relevant in determining what classes should be exempted, its relevance relates to the inquiry whether users of a particular class of works (as defined above, in section III.A.3.) are adversely affected in their ability to make noninfringing uses (such as fair use) of works in that class.

The specific exemption endorsed by the Assistant Secretary, and the reasons why that exemption cannot be adopted, are discussed below. See section III.E.9. Those reasons will not be repeated at length here. As already noted, the proposal does not constitute a "particular class of copyrighted work" as required by the statute. Moreover, the record does not reveal that there have been adverse effects on noninfringing uses that such an exemption would remedy. Finally, this approach would, in effect, revive a version of section 1201(a)(1) focusing on persons who have gained initial lawful access that was initially enacted by the House of Representatives but ultimately rejected by Congress.

NTIA's observation that the word "substantial" does not appear in section 1201(a)(1)(C) does not require the conclusion, suggested by NTIA, that a showing of substantial harm is not required. As noted above (section III.A.2) the House Manager's Report states that the focus of this rulemaking should be on whether the prohibition on circumvention of technological protection measures has had a substantial adverse impact on the ability of users to make non-infringing uses. Although the Commerce Committee Report does not use the word substantial, its direction to make exemptions based upon "distinct, verifiable, and measurable impacts, and * * * not * * * upon de minimis impacts' requires a similar showing. Moreover, while NTIA asserts that an exemption may be made based on a finding of "likely adverse effects" or "reasonably anticipated impacts," it appears that a similar showing of substantial likelihood is required with respect to such future harm. See section III.A.2 above. "Likely"—the term used in section 1201 to describe the showing of future harm that must be made— means "probable," "in all probability," or "having a better chance of existing or occurring than not." Black's Law Dictionary 638 (Abridged 6th ed. 1991).

The comments and testimony identified by NTIA in support of the exemption are discussed below in section III.E.9.

For the foregoing reasons, the Assistant Secretary, in supporting this exemption proposed by libraries and educators, endorses an exemption that is beyond the scope of the Librarian's authority. While the proposed exemption addresses important concerns, it is a proposal that would be more appropriately suited for legislative action rather than for the regulatory process set forth in section 1201(a)(1)(C) and (D). In the absence of clarification by Congress, a "particular class of works" cannot be interpreted so expansively.

Some of the issues raised by the Assistant Secretary are also likely to be addressed in a joint study by the Assistant Secretary and the Register pursuant to section 104 of the DMCA. See 65 FR 35673 (June 5, 2000). It is possible that this study will result in legislative recommendations that might more appropriately resolve the issues raised by the Assistant Secretary.

C. Conclusions Regarding This Rulemaking and Summary of Recommendations

After reviewing all of the comments and the testimony of the witnesses who appeared at the hearings, the Register concludes that a case has been made for exemptions relating to two classes of works:

(1) Compilations consisting of lists of websites blocked by filtering software applications; and

(2) Literary works, including computer programs and databases, protected by access control mechanisms that fail to permit access because of malfunction, damage or obsolescence.

These recommendations may seem modest in light of the sweeping exemptions proposed by many commenters and witnesses, but they are based on a careful review of the record and an application of the standards governing this rulemaking procedure. While many commenters and witnesses made eloquent policy arguments in support of exemptions for certain types of works or certain uses of works, such arguments in most cases are more appropriately directed to the legislator rather than to the regulator who is operating under the constraints imposed by section 1201(a)(1).

Many of the proposed classes do not qualify for exemption because they are not true "classes of works" as described above in section III.A.3. The proposed exemptions discussed below in section III.E.2, 5, 6, 7, 8, and 9 all suffer from that frailty to varying degrees. In many cases, proponents attempted to define classes of works by reference to the intended uses to be made of the works, or the intended user. These criteria do not define a "particular class of copyrighted work."

For almost all of the proposed classes, the proponents failed to demonstrate that there have been or are about to be adverse effects on noninfringing uses that have "distinct, verifiable, and measurable impacts." See Commerce Comm. Report, at 37. In most cases, those proponents who presented actual examples or experiences with access control measures presented, at best, cases of "mere inconveniences, or individual cases, that do not rise to the level of a substantial adverse impact." See House Manager's Report, at 6. As one leading proponent of exemptions

Federal Register / Vol. 65, No. 209 / Friday, October 27, 2000 / Rules and Regulations   64563

admitted, the inquiry into whether users of copyrighted works are likely to be adversely effected by the full implementation of section 1201(a)(1) is necessarily "speculative since it entails a prediction about the future." T Jaszi, 5/2/00, pp. 11–12.

It should come as no surprise that the record supports so few exemptions. The prohibition on circumventing access control measures is not yet even in effect. Witnesses who asserted the need to circumvent access control measures were unable to cite any actual cases in which they or others had circumvented access controls despite the fact that such circumvention will not be unlawful until October 28, 2000. T Neal, 5/4/00, p. 103; T Cohen, 5/4/00, pp. 100–01.[7]

The legislative history reveals that Congress anticipated that exemptions would be made only in exceptional cases. See House Manager's Report, at 8 (it is "not required to make a determination under the statute with respect to any class of copyrighted works. In any particular 3-year period, it may be determined that the conditions for the exemption do not exist. Such an outcome would reflect that the digital information marketplace is developing in the manner which is most likely to occur, with the availability of copyrighted materials for lawful uses being enhanced, not diminished, by the implementation of technological measures and the establishment of carefully targeted legal prohibitions against acts of circumvention."); Commerce Comm. Report, at 36 ("Still, the Committee is concerned that marketplace realities *may someday* dictate a different outcome, resulting in less access * * *. In this scenario, *it could be appropriate* to modify the flat prohibition against the circumvention of effective technological measures that control access to copyrighted materials * * *."; "a "*fail-safe mechanism*" is required'; "This mechanism would * * * allow the enforceability of the prohibition against the act of circumvention to be *selectively* waived, for limited time periods, *if necessary* to prevent a diminution in the availability to individual users of a particular category of copyrighted materials.") (emphasis added).

The two recommended exemptions do constitute "particular classes of copyrighted works," and genuine harm to the ability to engage in noninfringing

activity has been demonstrated. These exemptions will remain in effect for three years. In the next rulemaking, they will be examined *de novo*, as will any other proposed exemption including exemptions that were rejected in this proceeding. If, in the next three years, copyright owners impose access controls in unreasonable ways that adversely affect the ability of users to engage in noninfringing uses, it is likely that the next rulemaking will result in more substantial exemptions.

Ultimately, the task in this rulemaking proceeding is to balance the benefits of technological measures that control access to copyrighted works against the harm caused to users of those works, and to determine, with respect to any particular class of works, whether an exemption is warranted because users of that class of works have suffered significant harm in their ability to engage in noninfringing uses. See House Managers Report at 7 (decision "should give appropriate weight to the deployment of such technologies in evaluating whether, on balance, the prohibition against circumvention of technological measures has caused an adverse impact on the specified categories of users of any particular class of copyrighted materials"). The four factors specified in section 1201(a)(1)(C) reflect some of the significant considerations that must be balanced: Are access control measures increasing or restricting the availability of works to the public in general? What impact are they having on the nonprofit archival, preservation, and educational activities? What impact are they having on the ability to engage in fair use? To what extent is circumvention of access controls affecting the market for and value of copyrighted works?

The information submitted in this, the first rulemaking proceeding under section 1201(a)(1), indicates that in most cases thus far the use of access control measures has sometimes enhanced the availability of copyrighted works and has rarely impeded the ability of users of particular classes of works to make noninfringing uses. With the exception of the two classes recommended for exemption, the balance of all relevant considerations favors permitting the prohibition against circumvention to go into effect as scheduled.

Licensing

Many of the complaints aired in this rulemaking actually related primarily to licensing practices rather than technological measures that control access to works. Some witnesses expressed concerns about overly restrictive licenses, unwieldy licensing

terms, restrictions against use by unauthorized users, undesirable terms and prices, and other licensing restrictions enforced by technological protection measures. *See, e.g.,* T Gasaway, 5/18/00; T Coyle, 5/18/00; T Weingarten, 5/19/00. One of these witnesses admitted that "some of the concerns today are just pure licensing concerns." T Gasaway, 5/18/00, p. 65.

It appears that in those cases, the licensees often had the choice of negotiating licenses for broader use, but did not choose to do so. See T. Clark, 5/3/00, p. 99, T Neal, 5/4/00, p. 133, T Gasaway, 5/18/00, p. 38. Commenters and witnesses who complained about licensing terms did not demonstrate that negotiating less restrictive licenses that would accommodate their needs has been or will be prohibitively expensive or burdensome. Nor has there been a showing that unserved persons not permitted to gain access under a particular license (*e.g.,* a member of the public wishing to gain access to material at a university library when the library's license restricts access to students and faculty) could not obtain access to the restricted material in some other way or place.

It is appropriate to consider harm emanating from licensing in determining whether users of works have been adversely affected by the prohibition on circumvention in their ability to make noninfringing uses. This triennial rulemaking is to "monitor developments in the marketplace for copyrighted materials," Commerce Comm. Report, at 36, and developments in licensing practices are certainly relevant to that inquiry. If, for example, licensing practices with respect to particular classes of works make it prohibitively burdensome or expensive for users, such as libraries and educational institutions, to negotiate terms that will permit the noninfringing uses, and if the effect of such practices is to diminish unjustifiably access for lawful purposes, see Commerce Comm. Report, at 36, exemptions for such classes may be justified. If copyright owners flatly refuse to negotiate licensing terms that users need in order to engage in noninfringing uses, an exemption may be justified. But such a case has not been made in this proceeding.

Many commenters expressed concerns that, in the words of one witness, we are "on the brink of a pay-per-use universe." T Jaszi, 5/2/00, p. 70. The Assistant Secretary for Communications and Information shares that concern, observing that the Commerce Committee Report had warned against the development of a

---

[7] One witness testified that "there have been times that we've had to circumvent," but on examination, it appears that the example the witness gave would not constitute circumvention of an access control measure. See T Gasaway, 5/18/00, pp. 49–50.

64564 Federal Register / Vol. 65, No. 209 / Friday, October 27, 2000 / Rules and Regulations

"legal framework that would inexorably create a 'pay-per-use' society." See Commerce Comm. Report, at 26.

However, a "pay-per-use" business model may be, in the words of the House Manager's Report, "use-facilitating." House Manager's Report, at 7. The Manager's Report refers to access control technologies that are "designed to allow access during a limited time period, such as during a period of library borrowing" or that allow "a consumer to purchase a copy of a single article from an electronic database, rather than having to pay more for a subscription to a journal containing many articles the consumer does not want." *Id.* For example, if consumers are given a choice between paying $100 for permanent access to a work or $2 for each individual occasion on which they access the work, many will probably find it advantageous to elect the "pay-per-use" option, which may make access to the work much more widely available than it would be in the absence of such an option. The comments and testimony of SilverPlatter Information Inc., demonstrate that the flexibility offered by such "persistent" access controls can actually enhance use. Of course, one can imagine pay-per-use scenarios that are likely to make works less widely available as well.

The record in this proceeding does not reveal that "pay-per-use" business models have, thus far, created the adverse impacts on the ability of users to make noninfringing uses of copyrighted works that would justify any exemptions from the prohibition on circumvention. If such adverse impacts occur in the future, they can be addressed in a future rulemaking proceeding.

D. The Two Exemptions

1. Compilations Consisting of Lists of Websites Blocked by Filtering Software Applications

Certain software products, often known as "filtering software" or "blocking software," restrict users from visiting certain internet websites. These software products include compilations consisting of lists of websites to which the software will deny access. Schools, libraries, and parents may choose to use such software for the purpose of preventing juveniles' access to pornography or other explicit or inappropriate materials on their computers. R56. At least one court that has addressed the use of such software has concluded that requiring use of the software in public libraries offends the First Amendment. *See, e.g., Mainstream*

Loudoun v. *Board of Trustees of the Loudoun County Library*, 24 F. Supp. 2d 552 (E.D. Va. 1998). See also Tenn. Op. Atty. Gen. No. 00–030 (2000). On the other hand, the Supreme Court has suggested that availability of such software for use by parents to prevent their children from gaining access to objectionable websites is a positive development. *Reno* v. *American Civil Liberties Union*, 521 U.S. 844, 876–77 (1997); *United States* v. *Playboy Entertainment Group, Inc.*, 120 S.Ct. 1878, 1887 (2000).

Critics charge that some filtering programs unfairly block sites that do not contain undesirable material and therefore should not be filtered. One commenter alleged that such programs have an error rate of 76%. R56 at 6. Another commenter described the "long history of errors in blocking sites," and asserted that the software manufacturers have not responded appropriately. R26. The names of blocked websites are compiled into lists which are protected by copyright as compilations. Several commenters assert that manufacturers of filtering software encrypt the lists naming the targeted sites and that they are not made available to others, including the operators of the targeted sites themselves. R56. These commenters assert that they have no alternative but to decrypt the encrypted lists in order to learn what websites are included in those lists. Persons have already decrypted the lists for the purpose of commenting on or criticizing them. R56. One commenter cites an injunction against authors of a program decrypting the list of blocked websites. R26. See *Microsystems Software, Inc.* v. *Scandinavia Online AB*, No. 00–1503 (1st Cir. Sept. 27, 2000). Such acts of decryption would appear to violate 1201(a)(1) if it took effect without an exemption for these activities.

This does appear to present a problem for users who want to make noninfringing uses of such compilations, because reproduction or display of the lists for the purpose of criticizing them could constitute fair use. The interest in accessing the lists in order to critique them is demonstrated by court cases, websites devoted to the issue, and a fair number of commenters. See generally R73 (Computer Professionals for Social Responsibility); R38; PH20; and PH5 (California Association of Library Trustees and Commissioners, reverse filtering); WS Vaidhyanathan. There is uncontroverted evidence in this record that the lists are not available elsewhere. No evidence has been presented that there is not a problem with respect to lists of websites blocked by filtering software, or that

permitting circumvention of technological measures that control access to such lists would have a negative impact on any of the factors set forth in section 1201(A)(1)(C). The commenters assert that there is no other legitimate way to obtain access to this information. No one else on the record has asserted otherwise.

A review of the factors listed in 1201(a)(1)(C) supports the creation of this exemption. Although one can speculate that the availability of technological protection measures that deny access to the lists of blocked websites might be of benefit to the proprietors of filtering software, and might even increase the willingness of those proprietors to make the software available for use by the public, no commenters or witnesses came forward to make such an assertion. No information was presented relating to the use of either the filtering software or the lists of blocked websites for nonprofit archival, preservation and educational purposes. Nor was any information presented relating to whether the circumvention of technological measures preventing access to the lists has had an impact on the market for or value of filtering software or the compilations of objectionable websites contained therein. However, a persuasive case was made that the existence of access control measures has had an adverse effect on criticism and comment, and most likely news reporting, and that the prohibition on circumvention of access control measures will have an adverse effect.

Thus, it appears that the prohibition on circumvention of technological measures that control access to these lists of blocked sites will cause an adverse effect on noninfringing users since persons who wish to criticize and comment on them cannot ascertain which sites are contained in the lists unless they circumvent. The case has been made for an exemption for compilations consisting of lists of websites blocked by filtering software applications.

2. Literary Works, Including Computer Programs and Databases, Protected by Access Control Mechanisms That Fail to Permit Access Because of Malfunction, Damage or Obsoleteness

This designation of class of works is intended to exempt users of software, databases and other literary works in digital formats who are prevented from accessing such works because the access control protections are not functioning in the way that they were intended. In the course of this rulemaking

Federal Register / Vol. 65, No. 209 / Friday, October 27, 2000 / Rules and Regulations   64565

proceeding, a number of users, and in particular consumers of software and users of compilations, expressed concerns about works which they could not access even though they were authorized users, due to the failure of access control mechanisms to function properly.

Substantial evidence was presented on this issue, in particular relating to the use of "dongles," hardware locks attached to a computer that interact with software programs to prevent unauthorized access to that software. C199. One commenter attached numerous letters and news articles to his submission and testimony, documenting the experience of users whose dongles become damaged or malfunction. It appears that in such instances, the vendors of the software may be nonresponsive to requests to replace or repair the dongle, or may require the user to purchase either a new dongle or an entirely new software package, usually at a substantial cost. In some cases, the vendors have gone out of business, and the user has had no recourse for repair or replacement of the dongle.

Libraries and educational institutions also stated that they have experienced instances where materials they obtained were protected by access controls that subsequently malfunctioned, and they could not obtain timely relief from the copyright owner. R34, R75 (National Library of Medicine), R111 (National Agricultural Library). Similarly, libraries stated that there have been instances where material has been protected by technological access protections that are obsolete or are no longer supported by the copyright owner. *Id.*

No evidence has been presented to contradict the evidence of problems with malfunctioning, damaged or obsolete technological measures. Nor has evidence been presented that the marketplace is likely to correct this problem in the next three years.

This appears to be a genuine problem that the market has not adequately addressed, either because companies go out of business or because they have insufficient incentive to support access controls on their products at some point after the initial sale or license. In cases where legitimate users are unable to access works because of damaged, malfunctioning or obsolete access controls, the access controls are not furthering the purpose of protecting the work from unauthorized users. Rather, they are preventing authorized users from getting the access to which they are entitled. This prevents them from making the noninfringing uses they

could otherwise make. This situation is particularly troubling in the context of libraries and educational institutions, who may be prevented from engaging in noninfringing uses of archiving and preservation of works protected by access controls that are obsolete or malfunctioning. In effect, it puts such users in a position where they cannot obtain access; nor, under 1201(a)(1), would they be permitted to circumvent the access controls to make non-infringing uses of the work unless they fall within an exemption.

Not only does such a result have an adverse impact on noninfringing uses, but it also does not serve the interests of copyright owners that 1201(a)(1) was meant to protect. In almost all cases where this exemption will apply, the copyright owner will already have been compensated for access to the work. It is only when the access controls malfunction that the exemption will come into effect. This does not cause significant harm to the copyright owner. Moreover, authorized users of such works are unlikely to circumvent the access controls unless they have first sought but failed to receive assistance from the copyright owner, since circumvention is likely to be more difficult and time-consuming than obtaining assistance from a copyright owner who is responsive to the needs of customers. Only as a fallback will most users attempt to circumvent the access controls themselves.

Although it might be tempting to describe this class as "works protected by access control mechanisms that fail to permit access because of malfunction, damage or obsoleteness," that would not appear to be a legitimate class under section 1201 because it would be defined only by reference to the technological measures that are applied to the works, and not by reference to any intrinsic qualities of the works themselves. See the discussion of "works" above in section III.A.3. The evidence in this rulemaking of malfunctioning, damaged or obsolete technological protection measures has related to software (dongles) and, in the cases raised by representatives of libraries, to compilations of literary works and databases. Therefore, this class of works is defined primarily in terms of such literary works, and secondarily by reference to the faulty technological protection measures.

Although this exemption fits within the parameters of the term "class of works" as described by Congress, it probably reaches the limits of those parameters. The definition of the class does start with a section 102 category of works—literary works. It then narrows

that definition by reference to attributes of access controls that sometimes protect those works—i.e., the failure of those access controls to function as intended. But in reality, this exemption addresses a problem that could be experienced by users in accessing all classes of copyrighted works. This subject matter is probably more suitable for a legislative exemption, and the Register recommends that Congress consider amending section 1201 to provide a statutory exemption for all works, regardless of what class of work is involved, that are protected by access control mechanisms that fail to permit access because of malfunction, damage or obsoleteness. Meanwhile, because genuine harm has been demonstrated in this rulemaking proceeding and because it is possible to define a class of works that fits within the framework of section 1201(a)(1)(B), (C) and (D), the Register recommends that the Librarian exempt this class of works during the first three years in which section 1201(a)(1) is in effect. But the fact that sufficient harm has been found to justify this exemption for this three-year period will not automatically justify a similar exemption in the next triennial rulemaking. In fact, if there were a showing in the next rulemaking proceeding that faulty access controls create adverse impacts on noninfringing uses of all categories of works, such a showing could, paradoxically, result in the conclusion that the problem is not one that can be resolved pursuant to section 1201(a)(1)(C) and (D), which anticipates exemptions only for "a particular class of works." A legislative resolution of this problem is preferable to a repetition of the somewhat ill-fitting regulatory approach adopted herein.

The class of works covers literary works—and is applicable in particular to computer programs, databases and other compilations—protected by access controls that fail to permit access because of damage, malfunction or obsoleteness. The terms "damage" and "malfunction" are fairly self-explanatory, and would apply to any situation in which the access control mechanism does not function in the way in which it was intended to function. For definition of the term "obsolete," it is instructive to look to section 108(c), which also addresses the issue of obsoleteness. For the purposes of section 108, "a format shall be considered obsolete if the machine or device necessary to render perceptible a work stored in that format is no longer manufactured or is no longer reasonably available in the commercial marketplace." In the context of this rulemaking, an access control should be considered obsolete in analogous circumstances.

An exemption for this class, however, would not cover several other types of problems that commenters presented. For example, a commenter describing the problems experienced by users of damaged or malfunctioning dongles noted that similar problems occur when dongles become lost or are stolen. C199. That is, vendors of the software are often reluctant to replace the dongle, or insist that the user purchase a new dongle at a high cost. While this may be a problem, exempting works in this situation could unfairly prejudice the interests of copyright owners, who have no way of ascertaining whether the dongle was in fact lost or stolen, or whether it has been passed on to another user along with an unauthorized copy of the software, while the original user obtains a replacement by claiming the original dongle was lost. This exemption also would not cover situations such as those described by certain libraries, who expressed the fear that they would be prevented by 1201(a)(1) from reformatting materials that are in obsolete formats. If the materials did not contain access control protections, but were merely in an obsolete format, 1201(a)(1) would not be implicated. To the extent that technological protections prevented the library from converting the format, those protections would seem to be copy controls, the act of circumvention of which is not prohibited by section 1201.

The factors listed in 1201(a)(1)(C) support the creation of this exemption. In cases such as those described above, access controls actually decrease the availibility of works for any use, since works that were intended to be available become unavailable due to damage, malfunction or obsoleteness. This decrease in availability is felt particularly by the library and educational communities, who have been prevented from making non-infringing uses, including archiving and preservation, by malfunctioning or obsolete access controls. Circumvention of access controls in these instances should not have a significant effect on the market for or value of the works, since copyright owners typically will already have been compensated for the use of the work.

E. Other Exemptions Considered, But Not Recommended

A number of other proposed exemptions were considered, but for the reasons set forth below the Register does not recommend that any of them be adopted.

1. "Thin Copyright" Works

Many commenters have urged the exemption of a class of works consisting of what they term "thin copyright works." These are works consisting primarily (but not entirely) of matter unprotected by copyright, such as U.S. government works or works whose term of copyright protection has expired, or works for which copyright protection is "thin," such as factual works. As one proponent, the Association of American Universities, described the class, it includes "works such as scholarly journals, databases, maps, and newspapers [which] are primarily valuable for the information they contain, information that is not protected by copyright under Section 102(b) of the Copyright Act." C161. Most often this argument is made in the context of databases that contain a significant amount of uncopyrightable material. These databases may nonetheless be covered by copyright protection by virtue of the selection, coordination and arrangement of the materials. They may also incorporate copyrightable works or elements, such as a search engine, headnotes, explanatory texts or other contributions that represent original, creative authorship. While this proposal is frequently made with reference to databases, it is not limited to them, and would apply to any works that contain a mixture of copyrightable and uncopyrightable elements.

Proponents of such an exemption make two related arguments. First, some commenters argue that using Section 1201(a)(1) to prohibit circumvention of access controls on works that are primarily factual, or in the public domain, bootstraps protection for material that otherwise would be outside the scope of protection. It would, in effect, create legal protection for even the uncopyrightable elements of the database, and go beyond the scope of what Section 1201(a)(1) was meant to cover. An exemption for these kinds of works, proponents argue, is necessary to preserve an essential element of the copyright balance " that copyright does not protect facts, U.S. government works, or other works in the public domain. Without such an exemption, users will be legally prevented from circumventing access controls to, and subsequently making noninfringing uses of, material unprotected by copyright.

A related worry of commenters is that, in practice, section 1201(a)(1) will be used to "lock up" works unprotected by copyright. They predict that compilers of factual databases will have an incentive to impose a thin veneer of copyright on a database, by adding, for example, some graphics or an introduction, and thus take unfair advantage of the protection afforded by Section 1201. In addition, they fear that access to works such as databases, encyclopedias, and statistical reports, which are a mainstay of the educational and library communities, will become increasingly and prohibitively expensive.

On the record developed in this proceeding, the need for such an exemption has not been demonstrated. First, although proponents argue that 1201(a)(1)(A) bootstraps protection for uncopyrightable elements in copyrightable databases, the copyrightable elements in databases and compilations usually create significant added value. Indeed, in most cases the uncopyrightable material is available elsewhere in "raw" form, but it is the inclusion of that material in a copyrightable database that renders it easier to use. Search engines, headnotes, selection, and arrangement, far from being a thin addition to the database, are often precisely the elements that database users utilize, and which make the database the preferred means to access and use the uncopyrightable material it contains. Because it is the utility of those added features that most users wish to access, it is appropriate to protect them under Section 1201(a)(1)(A). Moreover, all copyrightable works are likely to contain some uncopyrightable elements, factual or otherwise. This does not undermine their protection under copyright or under 1201(a)(1)(A).[8]

Second, the fear that 1201(a)(1)(A) will disadvantage users by "locking up" uncopyrightable material, while understandable, does not seem to be borne out in the record of this proceeding. Commenters have not provided evidence that uncopyrightable material is becoming more expensive or difficult to access since the enactment of Section 1201, nor have they shown that works of minimal copyright authorship

[8] One commenter suggested an exemption for "compilations and other works that incorporate works in the public domain, unless the compilation or work was marked in such a way as to allow identification of public domain elements and separate circumvention of the technological measures that controlled access to those elements." PH4 (Ginsburg). While this approach could address some of the concerns raised by proponents, it is unclear whether it would be technologically feasible for copyright owners to implement. Furthermore, as discussed below, the Register has not yet been presented with evidence that there have been or are likely to be adverse impacts in this area.

are being attached to otherwise unprotectible material to take advantage of the 1201 prohibitions. The examples presented in this rulemaking proceeding of databases that mix copyrightable and uncopyrightable elements seem to be operating in a way that minimizes the impact on noninfringing uses, such as the LEXIS/NEXIS database and databases produced by a witness in the Washington DC hearings, SilverPlatter Information Inc. These databases provide business models that allow users to pay for different levels of access, and to choose different payment schedules depending on the way they would like to use the database. Finally, although the fear that material will be "locked up" is most compelling with respect to works that are the "sole source" of uncopyrightable material, most of the uncopyrightable material in these databases can be found elsewhere, albeit not with the access and use-enhancing features provided by the copyrightable contributions. Where users can reasonably find these materials in other places, their fears that it will be "locked up" are unwarranted.

In applying the four factors in Section (a)(1)(C), the impact of access control technologies on the availability of works in general, and their impact on the library and educational communities in particular, must be evaluated. In general, it appears that the advent of access control protections has increased the availability of databases and compilations. Access controls provide an increased incentive for database producers to create and maintain databases. Often, the most valuable commodity of a database producer is access to the database itself. If a database producer could not control access, it would be difficult to profit from exploitation of the database. Fewer databases would be created, resulting in diminished availability for use. If there were evidence that technological access protections made access to these works prohibitively expensive or burdensome, it would weigh against increased availability. However, as discussed above, such evidence has not been presented in this proceeding. Nor has there been a showing of any significant adverse impact thus far on nonprofit archival, preservation and educational activities or on criticism, comment, news reporting, teaching, scholarship or research. There is no evidence that the use of technological measures that control access to "thin copyright" works has made those works less accessible for such purposes than they were prior to the introduction of such measures. Finally, in assessing the effect of

circumvention on the market for or value of the works, it appears likely that if circumvention were permitted, the ability of database producers to protect their investment would be seriously undermined and the market would be harmed.

2. Sole Source Works

A number of commenters proposed an exemption for a class of "sole source works," that is, works that are available from a single source, which makes the works available only in a form protected by access controls.[9] C162 (American Library Association et al.); C213; C234. Proponents fear that works will increasingly become available only in digital form, which will be subject to access controls that prohibit users who want to make noninfringing uses from accessing the work, either because access will be too costly or will be refused. In such cases, where there is no other way to get access to the work, all noninfringing uses of the work will be adversely impacted.

Again, it is questionable whether proponents of an exemption have identified a genuine "class" of works. The only thing the works in this proposed class have in common is that each is available from a single source. Moreover, the case has not been made for an exemption for this proposed class.

Commenters submitted different examples of works that were available only in digital form. These included a number of databases and indexes. C162 (ALA). In addition, several commenters noted that digital versions of works, such as motion pictures in DVD format, often contain material, such as interviews, film clips or search engines, not found in the analog versions of the same works. C162, C234.[10]

The concerns of proponents of this type of exemption are understandable. However, there has been no evidence submitted in this rulemaking that access to works available only in a secured format is being denied or has become prohibitively difficult. Even considering the examples presented by various commenters, they merely establish that there are works that exist only in digital form. They have not established that access controls on those works have adversely impacted their ability to make noninfringing uses, or, indeed, that access controls impede their use of

those works at all. In the case of databases and indexes, the Register heard no evidence that licenses to those works were not available or were available only on unreasonable and burdensome terms. For example, in the case of motion pictures on DVDs, anyone with the proper equipment can access (view) the work. If there were evidence that technological access controls were being used to lock up material in such a way that there was effectively no means for a user wanting to make a noninfringing use to get access, it could have a substantial adverse impact on users.[11] No such evidence has been presented in this proceeding. If such evidence is presented in a subsequent proceeding, the case for an exemption may be made.

With respect to this proposed class, little evidence has been presented relating to any of the factors set forth in Section 1201(a)(1)(C). However, a review of those factors confirms that no exemption is justified in this case. If, as the proponents of this exemption assert, there are works that are available only in digital form and only with access control protections, many if not most of those works presumably would not have been made available at all if access control measures had not been available. Indeed, it appears that many of the "sole source" works identified by the American Library Association are works that most likely did not exist in the predigital era. See C162, p. 24. As with "thin copyright" works, no showing has been made of an adverse impact on the purposes set forth in 1201(a)(1)(C)(ii) and (iii).

3. Audiovisual Works on Digital Versatile Discs (DVDs)

More comments and testimony were submitted on the subject of motion pictures on digital versatile discs (DVDs) and the technological measures employed on DVDs, primarily Content Scrambling System ("CSS"), than on any other subject in this rulemaking. DVDs are digital media, similar to compact discs but with greater capacity, on which motion pictures and other audiovisual and other works may be stored. DVDs have recently become a

---

[9] This subject has been discussed briefly above, in reference to databases that contain uncopyrightable material not available elsewhere. This section, however, refers mainly to copyrightable sole source works.

[10] The DVD issue is addressed below, Section III.E.3.

[11] Nonetheless, that evidence would have to be balanced against an author's right to grant access to a work. By definition, any unpublished creative work is almost certain to be available only from a single source—the author. Historically, there has never been a right to access an unpublished work, and the law has guarded an author's right to control first publication. Even when material has already been published, there is no absolute right of access. Even with nondigital formats, one must either purchase a copy of the work or go to someone who has purchased a copy (e.g., a library) in order to obtain access to it.

major medium, although not yet the predominant medium, for the distribution of motion pictures in the "home video" market. CSS is an encryption system used on most commercially distributed DVDs of motion pictures. DVDs with CSS may be viewed only on equipment licensed by the DVD Copy Control Association (DVD CCA). PH25. The terms of the DVD CCA license permits licensed devices to decrypt and play—but not to copy—the films. For a more complete discussion of DVDs and CSS, see *Universal City Studios, Inc.* v. *Reimerdes*, 111 F. Supp.2d 294 (S.D.N.Y. 2000), 55 U.S.P.Q.2d 1873 (S.D.N.Y. 2000).

Proponents of an exemption for motion pictures on DVDs raised four general arguments. First, they asserted that CSS represents a merger of access and use controls,[12] such that one of those two control functions of the technology cannot be circumvented without also circumventing the other. PH11. Since Congress prohibited only the conduct of circumventing access measures and declined to enact a comparable prohibition against circumvention of measures that protect the rights of the copyright owner under § 1201(b), they argued that a merger of controls exceeds the scope of the congressional grant. In this view, the merger of access and use controls would effectively bootstrap the legal prohibition against circumvention of access controls to include copy controls and thereby prevents a user from making otherwise noninfringing uses of lawfully acquired copies, such as excerpting parts of the material on a DVD for a film class, which might be a fair use.

While this is a significant concern, there are a number of considerations to be balanced. From the comments and testimony presented, it is clear that, at present, most works available in DVD format are also available in analog format (VHS tape) as well. R123, T Marks, 5/19/00, p. 301. When distributed in analog formats—formats in which distribution is likely to continue for the foreseeable future— these works are not protected by any technological measures controlling access. WS Sorkin, p. 5. Therefore, any harm caused by the existence of access control measures used in DVDs can be

avoided by obtaining a copy of the work in analog format. See House Manager's Report, at 7 ("in assessing the impact of the prohibition on the ability to make noninfringing uses, the Secretary should take into consideration the availability of works in the particular class in other formats that are not subject to technological protections.").[13]

Thus far, no proponents of this argument for an exemption have come forward with evidence of any substantial or concrete harm. Aside from broad concerns, there have been very few specific problems alleged. The allegations of harm raised were generally hypothetical in nature, involved relatively insignificant uses, or involved circumstances in which the noninfringing nature of the desired use was questionable (*e.g.*, backup copies of the DVD) or unclear. T Robin Gross, 5/19/00, pp. 314–15. This failure to demonstrate actual harm in the years since the implementation of the CSS measures tends to undermine the fears of proponents of an exemption.

Similarly, in all of the comments and testimony on this issue, no explanation has been offered of the technological necessity for circumventing the access controls associated with DVDs in order to circumvent the copy controls. If the copy control aspects of CSS may be circumvented without circumventing its access controls, this is clearly not a violation of Section 1201(a)(1)(A). There was no showing that copy or use controls could not be circumvented without violating Section 1201(a)(1). In contrast, there was specific testimony that an analog output copy control on DVD players, Macrovision, could be circumvented by an individual without circumventing the CSS protection measures and without violating section 1201(a)(1). T Marks, 5/19/00, pp.345– 46. It would appear that circumvention

of the Macrovision control, conduct not prohibited by any of the provisions of section 1201, would enable many of the noninfringing uses alleged to be prevented. If in a subsequent rulemaking proceeding one could show that a particular "copy" or "use" control could not in fact be circumvented on a legitimately acquired copy without also circumventing the access measure, one might meet the required burden on this issue.

The merger of technological measures that protect access and copying does not appear to have been anticipated by Congress.[14] Congress did create a distinction between the conduct of circumvention of access controls and the conduct of circumvention of use controls by prohibiting the former while permitting the latter, but neither the language of section 1201 nor the legislative history addresses the possibility of access controls that also restrict use. It is unclear how a court might address this issue. It would be helpful if Congress were to clarify its intent, since the implementation of merged technological measures arguably would undermine Congress's decision to offer disparate treatment for access controls and use controls in section 1201.

At present, on the current record, it would be imprudent to venture too far on this issue in the absence of congressional guidance. The issue of merged access and use measures may become a significant problem. The Copyright Office intends to monitor this issue during the next three years and hopes to have the benefit of a clearer record and guidance from Congress at the time of the next rulemaking proceeding.

Another argument raised in the comments and testimony regarding DVDs is that users of Linux and other operating systems who own computers with DVD drives and who purchase legitimate copies of audiovisual works on DVDs should be able to view these works. Many Linux users have complained that they are unable to view the works on their computers because a licensed player has not yet been developed for the Linux OS platform. R56, PH11, PH3. While this situation created frustration for legitimate users,

---

[12] In this discussion, the term "use controls" is used as a shorthand term for technological measures that effectively protect rights of copyright owners under title 17 (*e.g.*, copy controls)—the controls that are the subject of the prohibition against certain technologies, products, services, devices and components found in section 1201(b)(1).

[13] Perhaps the best case for actual harm in this context was made with respect to matter that is available along with the motion picture in DVD format but not available in videotape format, such as outtakes, interviews with actors and directors, additional language features, etc. See C204, p. 4. However, this ancillary material traditionally has not been available in copies for distribution to the general public, and it appears that it is only with the advent of the DVD format that motion picture producers have been willing or able to include such material along with copies of the motion pictures themselves. Because of this and because motion picture producers are generally unwilling to release their works in DVD format unless they are protected by access control measures, it cannot be said that enforcing section 1201(a)(1) would, in the words of the Commerce Committee, result "in less access, rather than more, to copyrighted materials that are important to education, scholarship, and other socially vital endeavors." See Commerce Comm. Report, at 35. Thus, it appears that the availability of access control measures has resulted in greater availability of these materials.

[14] However, CSS was already in development in 1998 when the DMCA was enacted. It cannot be presumed that the drafters of section 1201(a) were unaware of CSS. If CSS does involve a merger of access controls and copy controls, it is conceivable that the drafters of section 1201(a)(1) were aware of that. And it is quite possible that they anticipated that CSS would be a "technological measure that effectively controls access to a work."

Federal Register / Vol. 65, No. 209 / Friday, October 27, 2000 / Rules and Regulations   64569

the problem requires balancing of other considerations.

The reasonable availability of alternate operating systems (dual bootable) or dedicated players for televisions suggests that the problem is one of preference and inconvenience, and leads to the conclusion that an exemption is not warranted. T Metalitz, 5/19/00, pp. 298–99. Moreover, with the rapidly growing market of Linux users, it is commercially viable to create a player for this particular operating system. T Metalitz, 5/19/00, pp. 297–98. DVD CSS has expressed its willingness to license such players, and in fact has licensed such players. PH25. There is evidence that Linux players are currently being developed (Sigma Designs and Intervideo) and should be available in the near future. It appears likely that the market place will soon resolve this particular concern. PH123 (MPAA).

While it does not appear that Congress anticipated that persons who legitimately acquired copies of works should be denied the ability to access these works, there is no unqualified right to access works on any particular machine or device of the user's choosing. There are also commercially available options for owners of DVD ROM drives and legitimate DVD discs. Given the market alternatives, an exemption to benefit individuals who wish to play their DVDs on computers using the Linux operating system does not appear to be warranted.

It appears from the comments and testimony presented in this proceeding that the motion picture industry relied on CSS in order to make motion pictures available in digital format. R123. An exemption for motion pictures on DVDs would lead to a decreased incentive to distribute these works on this very popular new medium. It appears that technological measures on DVDs have increased the availability of audiovisual works to the general public, even though some portions of the public have been inconvenienced.

A third argument raised relating to DVDs was the asserted need to reverse engineer DVDs in order to allow them to be interoperable with other devices or operating systems. C10, C18, C221. While there has been limited judicial recognition of a right to reverse engineer for purposes of interoperability of computer programs in the video game industry, see *Sega Enterprises, Inc. v. Accolade, Inc.*, 977 F.2d 1510 (9th Cir. 1992); *Sony Computer Entertainment, Inc. v. Connectix*, 203 F.3d 596 (9th Cir. 2000), this rulemaking proceeding is not an appropriate forum in which to extend the recognition of such a right

beyond the scope recognized thus far by the courts or by Congress in section 1201(f). In section 1201 itself, Congress addressed the issue of reverse engineering with respect to computer programs that are reverse engineered for the purpose of interoperability under certain circumstances to the "extent any such acts of identification and analysis do not constitute infringement under this title." One court has rejected the applicability of section 1201(f) to reverse engineering of DVDs. *Universal City Studios, Inc. v. Reimerdes*, 82 F.Supp.2d 211, 217–18 (S.D.N.Y. 2000); see also *Universal City Studios, Inc. v. Reimerdes*, 111 F. Supp.2d 294 (S.D.N.Y. 2000), 55 U.S.P.Q.2d 1873 (S.D.N.Y. 2000). That decision is on appeal. If subsequent developments in that case or future cases lead to judicial recognition that section 1201(f) does apply to a case such as this, then presumably there would be no need to fashion an exemption pursuant to section 1201(a)(1)(C). If, as the *Reimerdes* court has held, section 1201(f) does not apply in such a situation, an agency fashioning exemptions pursuant to section 1201(a)(1)(C) should proceed with caution before creating an exemption to accommodate reverse engineering that goes beyond the scope of a related exemption enacted by Congress expressly for the purpose of reverse engineering in another subsection of the same section of the DMCA. In any event, a more compelling case must be made before an exemption for reverse engineering of DVDs could be justified pursuant to section 1201(a)(1)(C).

The final argument in support of an exemption for audiovisual works on DVDs was based on the motion picture industry's use of region coding as an access control measure. Proponents of an exemption argued that region coding prevents legitimate users from playing foreign films on DVDs which were purchased abroad on their machines that are encoded to play only DVDs with region coding for the region that includes the United States. C133, C231, C234, R92, PH11. There was also some showing that foreign releases of American and foreign motion pictures may contain content that is not available on the American releases and that circumvention may be necessary in order to access this material. T Gross, 5/19/00, p. 314.

While the use of region coding may restrict unqualified access to all movies, the comments and testimony presented on this issue did not demonstrate that this restriction rises to the level of a substantial adverse effect. The problem appears to be confined to a relatively

small number of users. The region coding also seems to result in inconvenience rather than actual or likely harm, because there are numerous options available to individuals seeking access to this foreign content (PAL converters to view foreign videotapes, limited reset of region code option on DVD players, or purchase of players set to different codes). Since the region coding of audiovisual works on DVDs serves legitimate purposes as an access control,[15] and since this coding encourages the distribution and availability of digital audiovisual works, on balance, the benefit to the public exceeds the *de minimis* harm alleged at this time. If, at some time in the future, material is available only in digital format protected by region codes and the availability of alternative players is restricted, a more compelling case for an exemption might be made.

Consideration of the factors enumerated in subsection 1201(a)(1)(C) supports the conclusion that no exemption is warranted for this proposed class. The release of audiovisual works on DVDs was predicated on the ability to limit piracy through the use of technological access control measures. R123. These works are widely available in digital format and are also readily available in analog format. R123 and WS Sorkin, p. 5. The digital release of motion pictures has benefitted the public by providing better quality and enhanced features on DVDs. While Linux users represent a significant and growing segment of the population and while these users have experienced inconveniences, the market is likely to remedy this problem soon. PH25. See the discussion of the Linux players being developed by Sigma Designs and Intervideo, above. Moreover, there are commercially reasonable alternatives available to these users. R123. The restrictions on DVDs are presently offset by the overall benefit to the public resulting from digital release of audiovisual works. Therefore, at present the existence of technological measures that control access to motion pictures on DVDs has not had a significant adverse impact on the availability of those works to the public at large.

On the question of the availability for use of works for nonprofit archival, preservation, and educational purposes, there was minimal evidence presented that these uses have been or are likely to be adversely affected during the

---

[15] Among other purposes, it prevents the marketing of DVDs of a motion picture in a region of the world where the motion picture has not yet been released in theatres, or is still being exhibited in theatres. See PH12, pp. 3–4.

ensuing three year period. As stated above, facts relating to the issue of the existence of merged access and use controls may be presented in the next triennial rulemaking proceeding to determine whether the prohibition on circumvention of access controls is being employed in such a manner that it also restricts noninfringing uses.

The impact that the prohibition on the circumvention of technological measures applied to copyrighted works has had or is likely to have on criticism, comment news reporting, teaching, scholarship, or research is uncertain. At present, the concerns expressed were speculative and the examples of the prohibition's likely adverse effects were minimal. At this time it appears likely that these concerns will be tempered by the market. If the market does not effectively resolve problems and sufficient evidence of substantial adverse effects are presented in the next triennial rulemaking proceeding, the Register will re-assess the need for an exemption.

At this time it appears clear from the evidence that the circumvention of technological protection measures would be likely to have an adverse effect on the availability of digital works on DVDs to the public. The music industry's reluctance to distribute works on DVDs as a consequence of circumvention of CSS is a specific example of the potential effect on availability: "In fact, it was the very hack of CSS that caused a delay in introduction of DVD audio into the marketplace." T Sherman, 5/3/2000, p. 18. Since the circumvention of technological access control measures will delay the availability of "use-facilitating" digital formats that will benefit the public and that are proving to be popular with the public, the promulgation of an exemption must be carefully considered after a balancing of all the foregoing considerations. At present, the evidence weighs against an exemption for audiovisual works on DVDs.

4. Video Games in Formats Playable Only on Dedicated Platforms

A number of comments and one witness at the hearings sought an exemption for video games that are playable only on proprietary players. T Hangartner, 5/17/00, p. 247, R73, R109. The arguments in support of an exemption for video games included three issues: reverse engineering of the games for interoperability to other platforms, merger of access and use controls, and region coding of the games.

The existence of video games playable on dedicated platforms is not a new phenomenon in the marketplace. The Computer Software Rental Amendments Act of 1990 expressly provides for different treatment of video games sold only for use with proprietary platforms and those licensed for use on a computer capable of reproduction, recognizing the lower risk that the former will be copied to the detriment of the copyright owner. 17 U.S.C. 109(b)(1)(B)(ii). In the few comments addressing the need for interoperability of video games, there was very little evidentiary support for this alleged need. In fact, the testimony on behalf of Bleem, Inc. demonstrated that in cases involving interoperability of video games, courts have held either that section 1201 is inapplicable or that the exemption in 1201(f) shields this activity for purposes of discovering functional elements necessary for interoperability. T Hangartner, 5/19/00, p. 250; T Russell, 5/19/00, p. 332. Since the Basic Input Output System (BIOS) in these dedicated platforms is a computer program, section 1201(f) would appear to address the problem. To the extent that an identifiable problem exists that is outside the scope of section 1201(f), and therefore potentially within the scope of this rulemaking, its existence has not been sufficiently articulated to support the recommendation for an exemption. See also the discussion of reverse engineering below in Section III.E.5.

The claim that the technological measures protecting access to video games also restrict noninfringing uses of the games also has not been supported by any verifiable evidence. For example, while the backup of such a work may be a noninfringing use, no evidence has been presented that access control measures, as distinguished from copy control measures, have caused an inability to make a backup, and the latter is the more likely cause. Nor has there been any showing that any copy or use control has been merged with an access control, such that the former cannot be circumvented without the latter.

The paucity of evidence supporting an exemption on the basis of region coding similarly precludes a recommendation for an exemption. The few comments that mentioned this issue do not rise to the level of substantial adverse affect that would warrant an exemption for video games.

The factors set forth in section 1201(a)(1)(C) do not support an exemption. There is no reason to believe that there has been any reduction in the availability of video games for use despite the fact that video games have incorporated access controls and dedicated platforms for many years. To the extent there has been a need for interoperability, it appears that section 1201(f) will allow functional features to be determined as the courts have allowed in the past. There has been insufficient evidence presented to indicate that video games have or will become less available after § 1201(a)(1) goes into effect. There was no evidence offered that the prohibition on circumvention will adversely effect nonprofit archival, preservation, or educational uses of these works. There was also no evidence presented that the prohibition would have an adverse effect on criticism, comment, news reporting, teaching, scholarship, or research. On the other hand, there was little evidence that circumvention would have a negative impact on the market for or value of these copyrighted works, but this is of little consequence given the *de minimis* showing of any adverse impact access control measures have had on availability of the works for noninfringing uses.

5. Computer Programs and Other Digital Works for Purposes of Reverse Engineering

A number of commenters asserted that reverse engineering is a noninfringing use that should be exempted for all classes of digital works. C143, R82. As already noted, reverse engineering was also raised as a basis for an exemption in relation to audiovisual works on DVDs and video games. C221. The arguments raised in support of a reverse engineering exemption for such works are addressed above. To the extent that reverse engineering is proposed for all classes of digital works, it does not meet the criteria of a class. A "class of works" cannot be defined simply in terms of the purpose for which circumvention is desired. See the discussion above, Section III.A.3.

Moreover, to the extent that commenters seek an exemption to permit reverse engineering of computer programs, the case has not been made even if it is permissible to designate a class of "computer programs for the purpose of reverse engineering." When it enacted section 1201, Congress carved out a specific exemption for reverse engineering of computer programs, section 1201(f). That exemption permits circumvention of an access control measure in order to engage in reverse engineering of a computer program with the purpose of achieving interoperability of an independently created computer program with other

Federal Register / Vol. 65, No. 209 / Friday, October 27, 2000 / Rules and Regulations   64571

programs, under certain circumstances set forth in the statute. When Congress has specifically addressed the issue by creating a statutory exemption for reverse engineering in the same legislation that established this rulemaking process, the Librarian should proceed cautiously before, in effect, expanding the section 1201(f) statutory exemption by creating a broader exemption pursuant to section 1201(a)(1)(C).

The proponents of an exemption for reverse engineering have expressed their dissatisfaction with the limited circumstances under which section 1201(f) permits reverse engineering (C13, C30), but the case they have made is for the legislator rather than for the Librarian. If, in the next three years, there is evidence that access control measures are actually impeding noninfringing uses of works that should be permitted, that evidence can be presented in the next triennial rulemaking proceeding. Such evidence was not presented in the current proceeding.

To the extent that commenters have sought an exemption to permit reverse engineering for purposes of making digitally formatted works other than computer programs interoperable (i.e., accessible on a device other than the device selected by the copyright owner), it seems likely that the work will incorporate a computer program or reside on a medium along with a computer program and that it will be the computer program that must be reverse engineered in order to make the work interoperable. In such cases, section 1201(f) would appear to resolve the issue. To the extent that reverse engineering of something other than a computer program may be necessary, proponents of a reverse engineering exemption would be asking the Librarian to do what no court has ever done: to find that reverse engineering of something other than a computer program constitutes fair use or some other noninfringing use. It is conceivable that the courts may address that issue one day, but it is not appropriate to address that issue of first impression in this rulemaking proceeding without the benefit of judicial or statutory guidance.

The factors set forth in section 1201(a)(1)(C) have already been discussed in the context of audiovisual works on DVDs and video games, the two specific classes of works for which a reverse engineering exemption has been sought. Those factors do not support an exemption for reverse engineering.

6. Encryption Research Purposes

A number of commenters urged that a broader encryption research exemption is needed than is contained in section 1201(g). See, e.g., C185, C30, R55, R70. Dissatisfaction was expressed with the restrictiveness of the requirement to attempt to secure the copyright owner's permission before circumventing. C153. See 17 U.S.C. 1201(g)(2)(C). Most of the references to statutory deficiencies regarding encryption research, however, merely state that the provisions are too narrow. See, e.g., PH20.

As with reverse engineering, proponents of an exemption for encryption research are asking the Librarian to give them a broader exemption than Congress was willing to enact. But they have not carried their burden of demonstrating that the limitations of section 1201(g) have prevented them or are likely in the next three years to prevent them from engaging in noninfringing uses. With respect to encryption research, the DMCA required the Copyright Office and the National Telecommunications and Information Administration of the Department of Commerce to submit a joint report to Congress on the effect the exemption in section 1201(g) has had on encryption research and the development of encryption technology, the adequacy and effectiveness of technological measures designed to protect copyrighted works; and protection of copyright owners against the unauthorized access to their encrypted copyrighted works. The Copyright Office and NTIA submitted that report in May, 2000. Report to Congress: Joint Study of Section 1201(g) of The Digital Millennium Copyright Act (posted at http://www.loc.gov/copyright/reports/studies/dmca_report.html and http://www.ntia.doc.gov/reports/dmca). In that report, NTIA and the Copyright Office concluded that "[o]f the 13 comments received in response to the Copyright Office's and NTIA's solicitation, not one identified a current, discernable impact on encryption research and the development of encryption technology; the adequacy and effectiveness of technological protection for copyrighted works; or protection of copyright owners against the unauthorized access to their encrypted copyrighted works, engendered by Section 1201(g)." That conclusion is equally applicable to the comments on encryption research submitted in this proceeding.

Moreover, an exemption for encryption research is not focused on a class of works. See discussion above, Section III.A.3.

7. "Fair Use" Works

A large number of commenters urged the Register to recommend an exemption to circumvent access control measures for fair use purposes. Responding to the statutory requirement of designating a "particular classes of works," the Higher Education Associations (the Association of American Universities, the National Association of State Universities and Land Grant Colleges, and the American Council on Education) put forth within a broad class of "fair use works" the specific classes that are most likely to be used by libraries and educational institutions for purposes of fair use. PH24. The classes are scientific and social databases, textbooks, scholarly journals, academic monographs and treatises, law reports and educational audio/visual works. A witness testifying on behalf of the Higher Education Associations explained that these works should be exempted where the purpose of using the works is fair use. T Gasaway, 5/18/00, p. 74. The Higher Education Associations also suggested that the exemption could be further limited to specific classes of persons who were likely to be fair users. PH24, at 12.

To the extent that proponents of such an exemption seek to limit its applicability to certain classes of users or uses, or to certain purposes, such limitations are beyond the scope of this rulemaking. It is the Librarian's task to determine whether to exempt any "particular class of works." 17 U.S.C. 1201(a)(1)(B), (C) (emphasis added). See the discussion above, Section III.A.3.

The merits of an exemption for scientific and social databases have already been discussed to some extent in the treatment of "thin copyright" works and sole source works. To the extent that these works are not in these previously addressed classes, even though scientific and social databases can be seen to present an appropriate class, the case for an exemption has not been presented. No evidence was submitted that specific works in these named classes have been or are likely to be inaccessible because educational institutions or libraries have been prevented from circumventing them. Although the proponents of this exemption allege that if they are prevented from circumventing these particular classes of works, they and those they represent will not be able to exercise fair use as to this class of works, they have not demonstrated that

64572   Federal Register / Vol. 65, No. 209 / Friday, October 27, 2000 / Rules and Regulations

they have been unable to engage in such uses because of access control measures.

Many of the concerns raised by proponents of such an exemption are actually related to copy control measures rather than access control measures. *See, e.g.,* R75 (National Library of Medicine). If a library or higher education institution has access to a work, section 1201 does not prevent the conduct of circumventing technological measures that prevent the copying of the work.

Although textbooks, scholarly journals, academic monographs and treatises, law reports and educational audiovisual works have been mentioned as candidates for this proposed class of "fair use" works, proponents have failed to demonstrate how technological measures that control access to such works are preventing noninfringing uses or will in the next three years prevent such uses. In fact, it is not even clear whether technological measures that control access are actually used with respect to some of these types of works, *e.g.,* textbooks. While it is easy to agree that if access control measures were creating serious difficulties in making lawful uses of these works, an exemption would be justified, the case has not been made that this is a problem or is about to be a problem.

Application of the factors set forth in section 1201(a)(1)(C) to this proposed class of works is identical to the analysis of those factors with respect to "thin copyright" works discussed above (Section III.E.1) and will not be repeated here.

8. Material that Cannot be Archived or Preserved

A number of library associations expressed concern about the general impact of the prohibition against circumvention on the future of archiving and preservation. *See, e.g.,* C175, R75, R80, C162, p.26–29, 31–32; R83, p. 2–4; PH18, p.5. To some extent, these concerns may be addressed in the second of the two recommended exemptions, to the degree that faulty or obsolete access control measures may be preventing libraries and others from gaining authorized access to works in order to archive them. But more generally, libraries expressed concerns that digital works for which there are no established non-digital alternatives may not be archived. C162, p.26–29.

Because materials that libraries and others desire to archive or preserve cut across all classes of works, these works do not constitute a particular class.[16]

See the discussion above, Section III.A.3. The Office is limited to recommending only particular classes, and then only when it has been established that actual harm has occurred, or that harm will likely occur. Such a showing of adverse effect on all materials that may need to be archived or preserved has not been made. Demonstration of the inability to archive or preserve materials tied to a more particular class of works would be needed to establish an adverse effect in this rulemaking. Application of the relevant factors cannot take place in gross, without reference to a specified class of works.

Even if such materials were to constitute a particular class, and harm were shown, adverse causes other than circumvention must be discounted in balancing the relevant factors. House Manager's Report, at 6. The libraries and Higher Education Associations provided examples of problems due to numerous other factors—licensing restrictions, cost, lack of technological storage space, and uncertainty whether publishers will preserve their own materials. These are adverse effects caused by something other than the prohibition on circumvention of access control measures.

The Higher Education Associations cite the frequent phenomenon of "disappearing" works—those appearing online or on disk today that may be gone tomorrow, *e.g.,* because they may be removed from an online database or because the library or institution has access to them only during the term of its license to use the work. See T Gasaway, 5/18/00, p. 38. This rulemaking proceeding cannot force copyright owners to archive their own works. Moreover, assuming that libraries and other institutions are unable to engage in such archiving themselves today, they have not explained how technological measures that control access to those works are preventing them from doing so. Rather, it would appear that restrictions on copying are more likely to be responsible for the problem. See R75 (National Library of Medicine's inability to preserve Online Journal of Current Clinical Trials and videotapes, apparently because of restrictions on copying); C162, pp. 25–29 (American Library Association *et al.*). Section 1201

does not prohibit libraries and archives from the conduct of circumventing copy controls. Therefore, it is difficult to understand how an exemption from the prohibition on circumvention of access controls would resolve this problem.

Some commenters have also complained that licensing terms have required them to return CD–ROMs to vendors in order to obtain updated versions, thereby losing the ability to retain the exchanged CD–ROM as an archival copy. See, *e.g.,* C162, p. 27. But they have failed to explain how technological measures that control access to the works on the CD–ROMS play any role in their inability to archive something that they have returned to the vendor.[17] In a future rulemaking proceeding, libraries and archives may be able to identify particular classes of works that they are unable to archive or preserve because of access control measures, and thereby establish the requisite harm.

Because this proposed exemption does not really address a particular class of works, application of the factors set forth in section 1201(a)(1)(C) is difficult. If particular classes of works were in danger of disappearing due to access control measures, then presumably all of the factors (with the possible exception of the factor relating to the effect of circumvention on the market for or value of the copyrighted works) would favor such an exemption. But the current record does not support an exemption.

9. Works Embodied in Copies Which Have Been Lawfully Acquired by Users Who Subsequently Seek to Make Non-infringing Uses Thereof

An exemption for "works embodied in copies which have been lawfully acquired by users who subsequently seek to make non-infringing uses thereof" was put forward by Peter Jaszi, a witness representing the Digital Future Coalition, and was subsequently endorsed by many members of the academic and library communities. T Peter Jaszi, 5/3/00; T Julie Cohen, 5/4/00, PH22, T Diana Vogelsong, 5/3/00. In addition, it was endorsed by the comments of the Assistant Secretary of Commerce for Communications and Information. See discussion above, Section III.B. Similar exemptions were independently proposed by other commenters. PH24 (AAU); PH18 (ALA), PH21. These proposed exemptions focus on allowing circumvention by users for

---

[16] The National Digital Library and the Motion Picture Broadcasting and Recorded Sound Division

of the Library of Congress addressed the class of audiovisual works when it stated that, to carry out their mission, they may need to circumvent access controls to preserve these materials for the long term. However, they did not state that they have thus far had such a need or that they are aware of circumstances likely to require them to engage in such circumvention in the next three years.

[17] A related issue, CD–ROMS with faulty access controls that erroneously exclude authorized users from access, is addressed in the second exemption recommended by the Register.

noninfringing purposes after they have gained initial lawful access, although the Association of American Universities' proposal would limit the ability to circumvent after the period of lawful access to users possessing a physical copy of the work.

The proponents for this exemption fear that pay-per-use business models (using what are sometimes called "persistent access controls") will be used to lock up works, forcing payment for each time the work is accessed. In addition, they fear that persistent access controls will be used to constrain the ability of users, subsequent to initial access, to make uses that would otherwise be permissible, including fair uses. Without this exemption, they assert, the traditional balance of copyright would be upset, tipping it drastically in favor of the copyright owners and making it more difficult and/or expensive for users to engage in uses that are permitted today.

Therefore, these commenters propose an exemption for a class of "works embodied in copies which have been lawfully acquired by users who subsequently seek to make non-infringing uses thereof." In substance, the proposal would exempt all users who wish to make noninfringing uses, regardless of the type of work, provided that they either lawfully acquire a copy or, in some versions of the proposal, lawfully acquire access privileges. This exemption, commenters argue, will equitably maintain the copyright balance. It would allow copyright owners to control the distribution of, and initial authorization of access to, copies of their works, while allowing users to circumvent those access controls for noninfringing uses after they have lawfully accessed or acquired them.

However, for several reasons, the "class" they propose is not within the scope of this rulemaking. First, none of the proposals adequately define a "class" of the type this rulemaking allows the Librarian to exempt. As discussed above in Section III.A.3, "a particular class of work" must be determined primarily by reference to qualities of the work itself. It cannot be defined by reference to the class of users or uses of the work, as these proposals suggest. Second, although the commenters have persuasively articulated their fears about how these business models will develop and affect their ability to engage in noninfringing uses, they have not made the case that these fears are now being realized, or that they are likely be realized in the next three years.

The Assistant Secretary for Communications and Information has endorsed this proposed exemption. In support of this proposal, NTIA made only general references to one comment, RC113, and to the testimony of Julie Cohen, Siva Vaidyanathan, Sarah Wiant, James Neal, Frederick Weingarten, and the Consortiums of College and University Media Centers (CCUMC). NTIA did not specifically identify what evidence these witnesses and commenters had provided, apart from noting that they provided "numerous examples regarding the manner in which persistent access controls restrict the flow of information" and testimony about "impediments to archiving and preservation of digital works, teaching, and digital divide concerns." The latter concern is addressed in Section III.E.8.

The one comment cited by NTIA related to medical records that are stored in proprietary formats. RC113. It does not appear from that single comment—the only comment or testimony submitted on the issue—that the problem identified by the commenter related to technological measures that control access to copyrighted works. The commenter raised legitimate concerns about difficulties in converting data from one format to another. One can speculate that in the future, access control measures might be applied to medical data and prevent health care workers from obtaining needed access, but the commenter did not make the case that this is happening or is likely to happen in the next three years.

The testimony cited by NTIA relating to access controls that restrict the flow of information raised many fears and concerns but minimal distinct, verifiable, or measurable impacts. Of course, it is a tautology that any measure that controls access to a work will, by definition, at least to some degree restrict the flow of the information in the work. But although many of the witnesses complained about "persistent access controls," they did not present specific examples of any evidence of present or likely nontrivial adverse effects causally related to such controls.[18] The testimony relating to noninfringing uses that could be adversely affected has not been specifically shown to be caused by access controls as opposed to other

---

[18] In fact, one of those witnesses admitted that "the law has caused little harm yet" and that "my fears are speculative and alarmist." T Vaidyanathan, 5/18/00, p. 11. Another of the witnesses admitted that librarians have not yet experienced the "persistent access controls" feared by proponents of this exemption. T Neal, 5/4/00, p. 42.

technological or licensing measures. There appears to be no support in the record for a finding that the cited testimony rises to the level of distinct, verifiable and measurable impacts justifying an exemption at this time.

Finally, the proposed exemption parallels elements of an approach that was considered, and ultimately rejected, by Congress during the drafting of the law. The version of the DMCA that was passed by the House of Representatives on August 4, 1998, contained a provision that required a rulemaking proceeding that would determine classes of works for which, inter alia, users "who have gained lawful initial access to a copyrighted work" would be adversely affected in their ability to make noninfringing uses. HR 2281 EH, Section 1201(a)(1)(B):

The prohibition contained in subparagraph (A) shall not apply to persons with respect to a copyrighted work which is in a particular class of works and to which such persons have gained initial lawful access, if such persons are, or are likely to be in the succeeding 3-year period, adversely affected by virtue of such prohibition in their ability to make noninfringing uses of that particular class of works under this title, as determined under subparagraph (C)."

See also section 1201(a)(1)(D).

Thus, when it first passed the DMCA the House of Representatives appears to have agreed with much of the approach taken by the proponents of this exemption. But the fact that Congress ultimately rejected this approach when it enacted the DMCA and, instead, deleted the provision that had limited the applicability of the exemptions to persons who have gained initial lawful access, is clear indication that the Librarian does not have the power to fashion a class of works based upon such a limitation. Such an exemption is more properly a subject of legislation, rather than of a rulemaking the object of which is to determine what classes of works are to be exempted from the prohibition on circumvention of access controls.

10. Exemption for Public Broadcasting Entities

The Public Broadcasting Service, National Public Radio, and the Association of America's Public Television Stations described the public broadcasting entities' need to use sound recordings, published musical works and published pictorial, graphic and sculptural works in accordance with exemptions and statutory licenses under section 114(b) and 118(d) of the Copyright Act. R106. They observe that if copyright owners encrypted these classes of works, they would not be able to make noninfringing uses of them pursuant to the statute. But their submission addressed potential adverse effects of the prohibition on circumvention, not current or even likely adverse effects. There has been no allegation that public broadcasters have encountered or are about to encounter technological protection measures that prevent them from exercising their rights pursuant to sections 114 and 118.

If public broadcasting entities were able to demonstrate such adverse impact, a strong case might be made for an exemption for sound recordings, published musical works and published pictorial, graphic and sculptural works. In part for that very reason, public broadcasters may not experience serious adverse impacts on their ability to use such works pursuant to the compulsory licenses, because copyright owners will have every incentive to facilitate those permitted uses. Indeed, the public broadcasters stated that they "believe that the developing methods of technological protection will be deployed "to support new ways of disseminating copyrighted materials to users, and to safeguard the availability of "works to the public." *Id.*

In any event, there is no need at present for an exemption to accommodate the needs of public broadcasters.

IV. Conclusion

Pursuant to the mandate of 17 U.S.C. 1201 (b) and having considered the evidence in the record, the contentions of the parties, and the statutory objectives, the Register of Copyrights recommends that the Librarian of Congress publish two classes of copyrighted works where the Register has found that noninfringing uses by users of such copyrighted works are, or are likely to be, adversely affected, and the prohibition found in 17 U.S.C. 1201 (a) should not apply to such users with respect to such class of work for the ensuing 3-year period. The classes of work so identified are:

1. Compilations consisting of lists of websites blocked by filtering software applications; and
2. Literary works, including computer programs and databases, protected by access control mechanisms that fail to permit access because of malfunction, damage or obsoleteness.

The Register notes that any exemption of classes of copyrighted works published by the Librarian will be effective only until October 28, 2003. Before that period expires, the Register will initiate a new rulemaking to consider de novo what classes of copyrighted works, if any, should be exempt from § 1201(a)(1)(A) commencing October 28, 2003.

Marybeth Peters,
Register of Copyrights.

Determination of the Librarian of Congress

Having duly considered and accepted the recommendation of the Register of Copyrights concerning what classes of copyrighted works should be exempt from 17 U.S.C. 1201(a)(1)(A), the Librarian of Congress is exercising his authority under 17 U.S.C. 1201(a)(1)(C) and (D) and is publishing as a new rule the two classes of copyrighted works that shall be subject to the exemption found in 17 U.S.C. 1201(a)(1)(B) from the prohibition against circumvention of technological measures that effectively control access to copyrighted works set forth in 17 U.S.C. 1201(a)(1)(A) for the period from October 28, 2000 to October 28, 2003. The classes are:

1. Compilations consisting of lists of websites blocked by filtering software applications; and
2. Literary works, including computer programs and databases, protected by access control mechanisms that fail to permit access because of malfunction, damage or obsoleteness.

List of Subjects in 37 CFR Part 201

Copyright, Exemptions to prohibition against circumvention.

For the reasons set forth in the preamble, the Library amends 37 CFR part 201 as follows:

PART 201—GENERAL PROVISIONS

1. The authority citation for part 201 continues to read as follows:

Authority: 17 U.S.C. 702.

2. A new § 201.40 is added to read as follows:

§ 201.40 Exemption to prohibition against circumvention.

(a) *General.* This section prescribes the classes of copyrighted works for which the Librarian of Congress has determined, pursuant to 17 U.S.C. 1201(a)(1)(C) and (D), that noninfringing uses by persons who are users of such works are, or are likely to be, adversely affected. The prohibition against circumvention of technological measures that control access to copyrighted works set forth in 17 U.S.C. 1201(a)(1)(A) shall not apply to such users of the prescribed classes of copyrighted works.

(b) *Classes of copyrighted works.* Pursuant to the authority set forth in 17 U.S.C. 1201(a)(1)(C) and (D), and upon the recommendation of the Register of copyrights, the Librarian has determined that two classes of copyrighted works shall be subject to the exemption found in 17 U.S.C. 1201(a)(1)(B) from the prohibition against circumvention of technological measures that effectively control access to copyrighted works set forth in 17 U.S.C. 1201(a)(1)A) for the period from October 28, 2000 to October 28, 2003. The exempted classes of works are:

(1) Compilations consisting of lists of websites blocked by filtering software applications; and

(2) Literary works, including computer programs and databases, protected by access control mechanisms that fail to permit access because of malfunction, damage or obsoleteness.

Dated: October 23, 2000.

James H. Billington,
The Librarian of Congress
[FR Doc. 00–27714 Filed 10–26–00; 8:45 am]
BILLING CODE 1410–30–P

Report to Congress: Study Examining 17 USC Sections 109 and 117 Pursuant to Section 104 of the Digital Millennium Copyright Act

National Telecommunications and Information Administration

March 2001

INTRODUCTION

Congress enacted the Digital Millennium Copyright Act (the "DMCA" or "the Act")[1] as part of an effort "to begin updating national laws for the digital era."[2] It was designed to "facilitate the robust development and world-wide expansion of electronic commerce, communications, research, development, and education in the digital age."[3]

The DMCA seeks to advance two mutually supportive goals: the protection of intellectual property rights in today's digital environment and the promotion of continued growth and development of electronic commerce.[4] The Act attempts to accomplish these priorities through, *inter alia*, the interaction of two carefully crafted imperatives. First, as a means of preventing the theft of copyrighted works, the Act affords copyright owners legal protection and remedies against unauthorized circumvention of technological measures employed to prevent unauthorized access to copyrighted works.[5] Second, as a means of advancing a more efficient electronic marketplace, the Act guides legitimate consumers and businesses to create and use appropriate devices, conduct, and models in the course of their electronic transacting.[6] The DMCA reflects Congress' understanding that the melding of these concepts into workable legislation was critical to determining the extent to which electronic commerce realized its potential.

To ensure the continued enactment of policies that promoted both overarching goals, Congress recognized the need for current information that examined the intricate relationship between electronic commerce and the laws governing intellectual property. Such material must not only define that relationship, but also explain its "practical implications on the development of technology to be used in promoting electronic commerce."[7] To this end, Congress explicitly included in the Act a means of acquiring this crucial data. Section 104 of the DMCA directs the Register of Copyrights and the Assistant Secretary for Communications and Information of the Department of Commerce to submit to the Congress a report evaluating the effects of the amendments made by title 1 of the DMCA and the development of electronic commerce and associated technology on the operation of sections 109 and 117 of the Copyright Act, and the relationship between existing and emerging technology and the operation of those sections.[8]

In order to fulfill the mandate established by Congress and to assist in development of a factual basis for this report, on June 5, 2000, the Copyright Office and the National Telecommunications and Information Administration ("NTIA") published a *request for public comment* in the Federal Register.[9] Thereafter, on October 24, 2000, the agencies published a notice of public hearing, conducted on November 29, 2000, that would amplify the record and permit inquiry into specific areas of concern presented in the written comments.[10]

Part I of this report presents a brief overview of the current state of electronic commerce in the United States and the legislative background of Sections 109 and 117 of the Copyright Act. *Part II* presents an explanation of the operation of Sections 109 and 117 of the Copyright Act. *Part III* summarizes the substance of the public comments received by the Copyright Office and NTIA in response to the request for comment and in oral testimony at the hearing. *Part IV* concludes that it is premature for NTIA to draw any conclusions or make any legislative recommendations at this time with respect to either section, but describes areas of consideration for further Congressional inquiry.

PART I – ELECTRONIC COMMERCE IN THE UNITED STATES

The United States has found itself in the midst of a technological revolution propelled by digital processing. New digitally-based economic arrangements are changing how the nation works, communicates, consumes, and relaxes. Two facets of the digital economy, e-commerce [11] and the information technology ("IT") industries that make e-commerce possible, are maturing at breathtaking speeds, outstripping estimates that only recently appeared merely optimistic.

In 1995, it was nearly impossible to foresee how advances in IT would profoundly alter the manner in which business was conducted and value, created. That year marked the beginning of appreciable commerce over the Internet, with sales generated totaling just over $435 million. [12] Over the next five years, the potential for conducting business electronically was recognized and tapped. Remarkably, recently released estimates of e-commerce sales by retail establishments for 2000 total $25.8 billion. [13]

The impact of e-commerce on the economy extends far beyond simply the dollar value of business activity. The growth of e-commerce has fueled the nation's sustained economic growth and restrained a core inflation rate that remains low despite record employment and the lowest jobless rate in a generation. Despite a modest 8.3 percent share of the economy, IT-producing industries powered the nation's economic performance, contributing approximately 30 percent of U.S. economic growth since 1995. [14] These industries also have accounted for half or more of the recent acceleration in U.S. productivity growth, from 1.4 percent per year during 1973-1995 to 2.8 percent during 1995-1999. [15] IT appears to make it possible for the U.S. economy to grow without sparking increased inflation.

From the consumer's point of view, the most significant potential impact of e-commerce may be on the pricing and delivery of goods and services. Potential buyers can check price and availability of products from a variety of sites in far less time than it would take to conduct a store-to-store comparison. Auction sites have become popular, and "reverse auctions" (where the consumer names the price and the seller decides whether or not to accept it) have grown rapidly. Pricing has been directly influenced by consumers who now have in their control a repository of information on product and service information, previously unattainable before the advent of the World Wide Web. Buyers now can access detailed product, warranty, and repair information, along with comparisons of competitive prices, before finalizing sales.

The Internet also provides new mechanisms for the delivery of goods and services, permitting the immediate downloading of music, photographs, software, books, news reports, and a host of other products. Recent reports on the state of electronic commerce and the digital delivery of goods reveal astonishing estimates.

According to Forrester Research, while only 3 percent of all current online [business-to-consumer] sales consist of digitally-downloaded products, this level could reach 22 percent of all online sales by 2004. The most dramatic growth in direct, digital download sales will probably be in the music sector, while sales could rise from 0.1 percent of online sales in 1999 to 25 percent in 2004, followed by software (rising from 7 percent of online sales in 1999 to 40 percent in 2004) and books (rising from 1 percent of book sales online in 1999 to 13 percent in 2004). [16]

The technologies that drive e-commerce and its operating environment are still evolving. In fact, this new business model and the technologies that support it offer new challenges, as the ability to deliver digital products has, in many ways, outpaced the resolution of contentious yet inseparable legal and policy questions. [17] Given this, full realization of the promise of e-commerce depends, in large measure, on the development of "the same safeguards and predictable legal environment that individuals and businesses have come to expect in the offline world." [18]

PART II - SUMMARY OF SECTIONS 109 AND 117 OF THE COPYRIGHT ACT

Section 109 of the Copyright Act, 17 USC §109, permits the owner of a particular copy or phonorecord lawfully made under title 17 to sell or otherwise dispose of possession of that copy or phonorecord without the authority of the copyright owner; notwithstanding the copyright owner's exclusive right of distribution under 17 USC §106(3). Commonly referred to as the "first sale doctrine," this provision permits such activities as the sale of used books. The first sale doctrine is subject to limitations that permit a copyright owner to prevent the unauthorized commercial rental of computer programs and sound recordings.

Section 117 of the Copyright Act, 17 USC §117, permits the owner of a copy of a computer program to make a copy or adaptation of the program for archival purposes or as an essential step in the utilization of the program in conjunction with a machine. In addition, pursuant to an amendment contained in title III of the DMCA, section 117 permits the owner or lessee of a machine to make a temporary copy of a computer program if such copy is made solely by virtue of the activation of a machine that lawfully contains an authorized copy of the computer program, for purposes of maintenance or repair of that machine.

PART III - SUMMARY OF PUBLIC COMMENTS AND TESTIMONY CONCERNING THE SECTION 104 STUDY

As noted above, on June 5, 1999, the Copyright Office and NTIA issued a *joint Federal Register* notice soliciting public comment on the effects of the amendments made by title 1 of the DMCA and the development of electronic commerce and associated technology on the operation of sections 109 and 117 of the Copyright Act, and the relationship between existing and emerging technology and the operation of those sections. The *submissions received in response* to the Federal Register notice made clear both the complexity of the issues and the depth of the division between different stakeholders and the public. [19] At the request of members of Congress, the agencies conducted a public hearing on November 29, 2000, to amplify the record and permit inquiry into specific areas of concern presented in the written comments. [20] Presented below is a summary of the substantive issues raised in the 49 total responses submitted during the comment period, and a synopsis of pertinent testimony presented at the November Hearing. [21]

A. Section 109

Initial Comments - Proponents of a Digital First Sale Doctrine

The proponents of a digital first sale doctrine, led in large measure by the Digital Media Association ("DiMA"), premised their arguments regarding the need for legislative clarification of section 109 on electronic commerce concerns:

> To create a level playing field for ecommerce in digitally-delivered audio, video and other media, the first sale doctrine of 17 USC §109(a) must be extended, either by judicial interpretation or amendment, to apply to content lawfully acquired by digital transmission. Unless consumers receive from digital media the same quality, value and convenience they receive from physical media, ecommerce will be left stranded at the starting gate. [22]

In the proponents' view, two policies underlie any discussion of whether or how to adapt the Copyright Act to the digital networked environment. [23] First, the proponents noted that copyright exists to promote the public interest. Securing the rights of authors is intended to provide incentives to support that greater public good, not to be an end in itself. As such, statutory changes and interpretations of copyright law should balance the impact of the law upon the copyright owner against the paramount public interest in the dissemination and proliferation of copyrighted works. Second, the proponents argued that copyright law should respond to technological progress, not hinder it. Generally, the competitive market should be given time to evolve before making "pre-emptive" changes to copyright law. Over time, the proponents suggested, existing exemptions created for the "physical" world likely would be adapted to the digital realm by judicial interpretation, or justified under doctrines such as fair use. "Nevertheless, the public interest and the evolution of the marketplace often are better served by laws that clearly address and define the rules for a new technological environment." [24] Thus, the proponents believed that legal certainty in applying copyright to new digital technologies benefit the copyright owner and user alike, and prepares the market for compelling technologies and business models. [25] They concluded that the very issues addressed in this study and which threaten digital media companies are ripe for resolution.

The proponents further noted that the first sale doctrine balances the economic rights of the copyright owner and the consumer with respect to copyrighted works. Copyright law secures to the copyright owner the exclusive right of first distribution, to provide an incentive for the creation and dissemination of works. However, once the copyright holder has been compensated for the initial distribution of the work, no further incentive is required. As such, the copyright owner should be unable to extract further profits from that particular copy of the work. After that first sale, the right to vend has been fully exercised and further limitations cannot be imposed on the disposition of those goods. The proponents argued that these rationales apply with equal force in today's digital world. Although a court could justifiably interpret the existing language of Section 109 to protect digital retransmissions of digitally-acquired content, some copyright owners have disputed this interpretation. To this end, the proponents supported a legislative clarification of Section 109 so as to firmly establish that the first sale doctrine applies to digital retransmissions of digitally-acquired copies and phonorecords of copyrighted works. [26]

In order to meet this objective, the proponents recommended that the Copyright Office and NTIA endorse the provisions of the Ashcroft and Boucher-Campbell bills that seek to update current law for the digital era. First introduced in November 1997 by Representatives Rick Boucher and Tom Campbell, H.R. 3048, the Digital Era Copyright Enhancement Act, would have added to Title 17 a new Section 109(f) that would have permitted the operation of the first sale doctrine by transmission of copyrighted work to a single recipient, if the person effectuating the transfer erases or destroys his or her copy or phonorecord at substantially the same time. As Mr. Boucher explained in his statement accompanying introduction of the bill, "[T]his legislation best advances the interest of both creators and users of copyrighted works in the digital era by modernizing the Copyright Act in a way that will preserve the fundamental balance built into the act by our predecessors throughout the analog era." [27]

According to the proponents, when H.R. 3048 was originally introduced, content owners opposed to a digital first sale privilege contended that such a doctrine would promote widespread copying and redistribution of copyrighted works, and that consumers could not be trusted to delete their copies once transferred. Questions were raised regarding whether technology existed to ensure that the proposed amendment could be implemented as intended. The proponents insisted such technology exists. [28] Copyrighted content can be delivered to consumers with digital rights management ("DRM") systems that enable secure electronic transfers of possession or ownership, and that protect against unauthorized retention of the transferred copy. "Through technological processes such as encryption, authentication, and password-protection, copyright owners can ensure that digitally downloaded copies and phonorecords are either deleted after being transferred or are disabled (such as by permanently transferring with the content the only copy of the decryption key)." [29] In fact, the proponents propounded that DRM technology actually provides a more secure media for digitally-transmitted content than for today's physical media, and that clarification of the law will provide the incentive for development of newer and more efficient DRM tools. [30]

The proponents further noted that any extension of the first sale doctrine cannot apply only to content protected using DRM tools, as several online businesses are successfully marketing digital downloaded media in unprotected or open formats such as MP3. Lastly, "the digital sale right favored by DiMA encompasses electronic transfers of possession only for media lawfully acquired by digital transmission." [31]

Initial Comments - Copyright Community

The copyright community's initial comments were brief, focusing in large measure on the legislative history of Section 109 and a "plain reading" of the statute. In short, it argued that the moniker "digital first sale doctrine" is a faulty construct, aimed not at merely applying the doctrine to digital works, but rather promoting "wholesale expansion of the . . . doctrine in derogation of the rights of copyright owners." [32] In its view, the first sale doctrine was developed with respect to *tangible* copies, and was (and will continue to be) applicable to such *tangible* copies made under authority of the copyright owners whatever the nature of the technology. However, to the extent that emerging technology "deals not with tangible copies but with streaming and/or downloading of digitized programming, the first sale doctrine neither can nor should have any application." [33]

To support this view, several members of the copyright community examined the first sale doctrine's origin and its current statutory application. Each recognized that the doctrine has as its underlying purpose to prevent untoward use of copyright law to impose price or other conditions on the ability of the owner of a copy of a work to dispose of that copy. That objective was accomplished by providing an exception to the rights granted by Section 106 of the Copyright Act. But of crucial importance to these commenters was that the first sale doctrine does not provide any exception to the exclusive right of reproduction, nor does it apply to copies not "lawfully made under this title." Given this, the copy owner has only the right to transfer possession of the copy/original he holds, and no right to make or distribute additional second generation copies. Stated differently, the copyright community asserts that the first sale doctrine only applies when a particular tangible copy of a work changes hands, and possession of that very copy is surrendered.[34] According to the copyright community, any other formulation (in which the giver and receiver both have copies) would exceed the scope of the first sale doctrine.

Under the copyright community's schema, Section 109 could not apply to works distributed by transmission over the Internet because such action would involve both the reproduction of the initial copy (as to which no exception is provided and, accordingly, the copy being transferred is not "'lawfully made") as well as its distribution.[35] Moreover, the owner of the original/copy of the work would not be surrendering his possession of the initial copy as contemplated by the first sale doctrine.[36] To compound the problem, commenters noted that the copy generated during the distribution is a perfect copy — one that could serve as a "master for the production of an unlimited number of additional perfect copies, all of which can conveniently be redistributed over digital networks to a virtually limitless class of recipients."[37] Given the foregoing, the consequences of an "unjustified expansion" of the first sale doctrine could easily overwhelm the incentives for production of creative works provided by the copyright law.

While acknowledging recent technical advances in the past five years, at least one commenter rejected the "promise" offered by these developments. That commenter maintained that throughout the "digitally networked environment," distribution of copyrighted material "virtually never occurs without a prior reproduction of the [copyrighted] material," and it is that copy, not the original, that is distributed.[38] According to this commenter, that fact alone would push the distribution action outside the parameters of the first sale doctrine.

Another commenter argued that the development of e-commerce has actually resulted in a reduced need for the first sale doctrine. The creation of new licensing and delivery mechanisms will likely permit computer uses to obtain copies of virtually any work easily and quickly. "In fact, these new licensing and delivery mechanisms will promote alienation and trade in copyrighted works to such a degree that individuals will have less of a need to avail themselves of the first sale exception because they will easily be able to get a copy of a work online. Accordingly, there is no need for the first sale exception to apply to the Internet and related digital distribution systems."[39] Yet another commenter went further, suggesting that the absence of a digital first sale doctrine has actually had the positive effect of encouraging the growth of markets for works in digital form.[40]

Reply Comments - Proponents of a Digital First Sale Doctrine

Proponents of a digital first sale doctrine noted that the comments received in response to the request for comments demonstrate the need for legislative clarification of Section 109 so as to ensure its proper application to digital works. They reiterated that the first sale doctrine is a specific application of the general economic and public policy against restraints on the alienation of property or trade in lawfully-acquired copyrighted works. Moreover, the economic incentive to create such works is satisfied by the first sale of the copy, and therefore, any restraint on alienation was unnecessary to provide that incentive.[41]

At the outset, one commenter took exception to copyright community assertions that the first sale doctrine is unnecessary because e-commerce will enable anyone to buy a copy of works online. This assertion relegates the doctrine to be nothing more than a means to satisfy consumer demand and copyright owners' ability to sell.[42] The commenter argued that the absence of a digital first sale doctrine will impede the free flow of information, including the ability of libraries and others to provide access to digital works to those parts of the public that lack the resources and opportunities that at least one member of the copyright community touts as diminishing the need for a first-sale doctrine. [43]

Proponents claimed that a digital copy authorized by the copyright owner that is downloaded by a consumer is conceptually no different than a copy made by the copyright owner and then sold to the consumer. [44] In both instances, a copy was lawfully made with the copyright holder's permission. Given that several members of the copyright community agreed with this assertion, proponents thought it curious that not one community member would offer a "rationale as to why consumers should not have full possessory rights in a digital file that was created on their computer with the permission of the copyright holder." [45]

The proponents argued that extending to consumers the right to resell the digitally delivered works that they have lawfully acquired will neither encourage nor lead to unlimited reproductions and distribution of copyrighted works. Technology, they stated, exists to secure the first sale privilege in a digital environment, ensuring that the original/initial digital copy is deleted (or made permanently inaccessible) from the transferor's computer upon digitally transferring the data to the transferee. [46] This system, along with digital rights management systems, authentication, encryption, and password-protections, will foster new innovations that will actually decrease the piracy risks that concern these commenters, while concurrently ensuring consumers of their possessory rights. [47]

Lastly, the proponents contended that, although new licensing and delivery mechanisms may enable more consumers to access works via electronic means, the absence of a first sale doctrine may increase the likelihood of abuse of copyrighted works.

> [W]ith respect to digital downloading, if you build it, consumers will come; but if copyright owners won't build it, someone else will. If digital delivery satisfies consumer needs, including a means to transfer ownership, then ecommerce will succeed. But if there is no first sale right for digitally-delivered media, consumers will find some other way to exercise these privileges. Without a first sale right, [the proponents] fear that circumvention technologies like DeCSS, DivX, and others, will gain popularity among otherwise law-abiding consumers who cannot abide overly-restrictive licensing terms and hypertechnical copyright laws. [48]

More than one commenter argued that unless copyright law adapts essential consumer privileges such as first sale to the new e-commerce environment, existing onerous licensing restrictions may be merely the harbinger of even more invasive conditions in the offing. Unless Congress acts, the proponents' fear that the copyright owners' use of their copyright monopoly in conjunction with technological measures to circumvent the first sale doctrine and to restrain competition (through the purported licensing of "rights" not recognized by copyright) may well be realized. [49]

Reply Comments – Copyright Community

The copyright community contended that proposals to amend section 109 as suggested by the advocates for a digital first sale doctrine do not update, reaffirm, or extend the doctrine to a new technological environment. Rather, the proposals propound "completely new limits upon the exclusive rights of copyright owners other than the distribution right (the only right which the first sale doctrine limits) . . . undermin[ing] the exclusive reproduction right, the fundamental cornerstone of the edifice of copyright protection." [50] The copyright community noted that the "forward-and-delete" proposal, embodied in the amendments to section 109 proposed by Representative Boucher, among others, had been "consistently rejected" in various fora, and while "superficially attractive," cannot withstand close scrutiny as a justification for a broad expansion of section 109 at this time. [51] The copyright community set forth five overarching concerns.

First, the copyright community asserted that Digital Rights Management systems and technology that allow copyright owners to use encryption, authentication, and password protection, are "not yet so ubiquitous and so secure that it can provide the foundation for the substantial diminution of the reproduction right which the H.R. 3048 language represents. Whether this technology ever achieves that status is a decision that will turn on future developments in the marketplace." Moreover, they argue that, at present, it is still too expensive for general application.

Second, the copyright community claimed that the proponents have attempted to expand the first sale doctrine even into areas in which DRM technologies are not in use. The community believes that this fall-back position, tantamount to an honor system for determining whether the original of a forwarded digital copy, was, in fact simultaneously deleted, is "not practical and no more palatable now than it was years ago when it was rejected by Congress . . . ."

Third, the community noted that "[e]ven if an expanded section 109 were to apply only to copies or phonorecords to which DRM tools had been applied, it is virtually certain that some users would seek to disable those tools in order to carry out broader unauthorized distribution than the 'forward and delete' model contemplates." [52]

Fourth, the copyright community reiterated its opposition to the language of H.R. 3048 as a threat that would undermine not just one, but four, of the five exclusive rights that copyright owners have historically enjoyed. "[T]he H.R. 3048 language would deny the copyright owner any control over the reproduction needed to carry out an unauthorized performance or display, even though these activities (unlike an authorized distribution) could not plausibly be characterized as ever coming within the first sale doctrine. We must assume as well that the advocates of this approach believe (although the language they support does not explicitly say so) that the public performance or display which is enabled by the (immunized) reproduction should also be free from the control of the copyright owner." [53]

Lastly, the proposal espoused by the advocates of the digital first sale doctrine ignores the flexibility that licensing arrangements can provide to allow trade or selling under certain circumstances without tampering with the statutory first sale doctrine. The community argued that predictions that consumers will become dissatisfied with e-commerce if they cannot trade or sell via transmissions the works they acquire digitally are simply that — predictions.

The copyright community remarked that "technological developments, including DRM tools, will significantly affect the environment within which the first sale doctrine — as well as the rest of the Copyright Act — is operative. . . . We cannot rule out the possibility that the further development of these technologies will, at some point in the future, justify changes to section 109 that can advance the mutually supportive goals of providing adequate incentives for creativity and innovation, and promoting electronic commerce and other digital dissemination of works of authorship. But clearly such changes are not justified at this time." [54]

B. Section 117

Initial Comments – Proponents for a Revision to Section 117

Proponents for a revision to section 117 maintained that the growth and promise of e-commerce call for an expansion of this section to address all forms of digital content, new technologies, and new uses. Three specific suggestions were posited, each based on an examination of how the concepts underlying Section 117 ought to be applied to new technologies and uses. One commenter noted that section 117 was first enacted some twenty years ago upon the recommendation of the National Commission on New Technological Uses of Copyrighted Works. (It has remained essentially unchanged until 1998, when it was amended by the DMCA.) According to this commenter, Congress could not have possibly foreseen the potential applications of the underlying principles of Section 117 to as yet not conceived types of devices and media. Currently, digital media other than software programs and computing devices are pervasive. Content, other than computer programs, is available to the consumer, is susceptible to loss, and cannot be used by the purchaser without temporary copying into device memory. In short, "although the language of Section 117 may have been premised upon a particular technological environment, the conceptual justifications for the exemption were founded on principles that have general application to the digital environment." [55]

Two commenters acknowledged that the growing popularity of digital downloading necessitates that the law continue to guarantee consumers the right to secure their investments in digital media. Consumers must be certain that their lawfully-acquired content will not be lost in the event of a server or hard disk crash. Similarly, consumers who upgrade their computer systems need some means of transferring media to their new computers. Given this, Section 117 must permit archival or back-up copying of media acquired digitally, without the threat of copyright infringement litigation.

Secondly, these commenters observed that "virtually all devices that playback content recorded in a digital format must process that content by first loading all or some portion of it into memory." All devices that perform such digital media effectively are computers, including CD players, DVD players, and HD television receivers. Consumers have begun purchasing these items, as well as a new generation of portable playback devices — and yet more will come to market in the next year. Ephemeral copies made in the course of viewing or lawfully gaining access to a work have nothing to do with piracy. Given this, these commenters believed that in order to advance the interests of information consumers, while protecting the legitimate interests of copyright owners, Congress should exempt temporary copies of recorded content made in the course of playback (through buffering, caching, or other means) from claims of infringement. [56]

Lastly, proponents asserted that the technical process of Internet webcasting requires that the receiving device temporarily store a few seconds of data transmitted by the webcaster, before playing back the audio or video to the consumer. The small temporary buffer memory copies used in today's webcasting technology have no intrinsic or economic value apart from the performance. In the proponents' view, where the webcaster makes an authorized performance of copyrighted material, the temporary buffers necessary to enable the performance should be exempt from any claim of copyright infringement. [57] The proponents believed this exemption from the reproduction right is "all the more warranted for webcasting, where the same copyright owners of the musical composition, audiovisual work, or the sound recording already will have authorized, and been compensated for, the performance of the work." [58]

To this end, the proponents, especially HRRC and DiMA, expressed support for the legislative models proffered by H.R. 3048 (Boucher-Campbell Bill) and S. 1146 (the Digital Copyright Clarification and Technology Education Act of 1997, introduced by Senator John Ashcroft). [59]

Initial Comments – Copyright Community

Commenters from the copyright community were unaware of any "significant impediments to electronic commerce which have arisen as a result of Section 117." They, too, acknowledged the history of the provision, including recent amendments by the DMCA. In their view, "those amendments appear to be functioning as intended." However, the copyright community did express concerns regarding "misinterpretations of other aspects of Section 117," employed by some not as a defense to infringement "but as an enticement to engage in online piracy." [60] To this end, the copyright community suggested that this report could serve to educate the general public regarding the parameters of the exception provided by Section 117. Four specific discussion topics were envisioned by the copyright community:

First, the archival copying exception applies only to computer programs. No exception exists that would allow the creation of "back-up" copies of any other kind of work, including sound recordings, music, audio-visual works, or databases, except by libraries, archives, broadcasters, and other specifically identified institutions under circumstances defined by law. "Anyone offering unauthorized copies of works other than computer programs as 'back-up copies' is in violation of the law."

Second, the archival copying exception of Section 117 does not apply to contemporary personal computer, videogame console, or online gaming environments, where threats of damage or destruction by mechanical or electrical failure are minimal and archival copying is not needed to prepare for them.

Third, only the legitimate owner of a copy of a computer program can make or authorize the making of an archival copy under Section 117 and only from a legitimate copy that he or she owns. A web site or other source offering "back-up copies" for distribution to the public falls outside the exception and is committing copyright infringement.

Lastly, according to the copyright community, the law forbids the transfer of an archival copy except in conjunction with the transfer of an original the transfer of all rights in that original. [61]

Reply Comments – Proponents of a Revision to Section 117

In their Reply Comments, proponents responded to arguments set forth by the copyright community regarding the application and scope of Section 117. At the outset, one commenter argued that miseducation concerning the scope and proper application of Section 117 cannot justify limiting the ownership rights of legitimate consumers, "particularly when case law has upheld laws such as 17 USC §1201 against the types of fallacious arguments of concern" to the copyright community. In that commenter's view, there is simply no reason why extending Section 117 to other digital works cannot (nor should not) coexist with a process of educating the public as advocated by the copyright community. [62]

Proponents further assert that arguments that technological changes have made the archival copy exemption largely unnecessary for the purposes for which it was enacted overlook circumstances that necessitate creation of an archival copy to protect one's investment in a copyrighted work, especially when obtained by digital delivery. Suggestions that new business models (such as application service providers that permit access to software any time and anywhere) and other strategies have eliminated the need for Section 117 are misplaced, serving only to misguide and detract from the focus of the section under review. "Section 117 addresses the case where a copy must permanently reside with the user in order for the user to use the product. That may not be necessary for networked or thin client computing, but most definitely is required for digitally-downloaded content . . . ." [63]

In their reply comments, the proponents renewed their call for extending Section 117 to apply to other digital devices and media forms beyond merely software. The technical functionality of the Internet makes it:

[L]ogical and reasonable to extend the principles underlying Section 117 to the 'statements and instructions' in new digital media. The transmission of all digital data, whether software or copyrighted works sold or webcast via the Internet, necessarily involves the moving of packets of information from the RAM of one server to the RAM of the next, making at each stage certain reproductions necessary for the system to function. In short, temporary copying is inherent to digital technology. Particularly in the case of Internet webcasting, streaming audio or video requires temporary storage of data before it is reassembled and played for the consumer. . . . **[T]he temporary buffer storage of a few seconds of content during webcasting is merely a technological means of facilitating smooth performance of real-time transmissions. The data are not recorded or accessed for other purposes and have no economic value apart from the performances themselves** (emphasis added). [64]

Thus, the proponents contended that for both downloading and webcasting to become viable modes of e-commerce, the law should be clarified to assure web businesses and consumers that these actions will not expose them to potential copyright liability.

Ecommerce promises to revolutionize the market for copyrighted works, and to give consumers even greater flexibility and control over their own acquired content. Yet, the promises of ecommerce are not guarantees. Indeed, some have argued, not entirely without justification, that copyright owners' first shots fired in the ecommerce revolution have caught them squarely in the foot. Ecommerce will gain acceptance only if and when consumers obtain from lawfully-acquired digital downloads the same full value that they receive from physical media — including first sale rights and archival and temporary copying. This only can occur in a legal environment that supports and facilitates ecommerce, and that adapts reasonably and timely to new technological and economic models. [65]

Reply Comments - Copyright Community

The copyright community maintained that the incidental copying amendment advocated by the proponents is not justified by technological developments and would not promote the healthy growth of electronic commerce, but would "dramatically expand the scope of section 117 and drastically cut back on the exclusive reproduction right in all works."[66] Two years ago, the community argued, the proponents of H.R. 3048 called upon Congress to overturn the holdings of *MAI Systems Corp. v. Peak Computer, Inc.*,[67] by adopting the "incidental copying exception" that the proponents now seek to "revive."[68] The copyright community stated that Congress did not merely spurn this suggestion, but rather drew the opposite conclusion, passing legislation endorsing and reaffirming the principles of the case, its progeny, and related policy decisions. In fact, Title III of the DMCA added a new Section 117(c) that spells out the specific and limited circumstances under which the reproduction of a computer program in memory for the purpose of computer maintenance or repair is not an infringement of the reproduction right. The copyright community remarked that none of the proponents addressed this change to the law, but rather sought:

> [T]o employ section 117 as a convenient starting point for a much more comprehensive attack on the exclusive reproduction right. They resurrect a proposal that . . . undercuts the reproduction right in all works, not just computer programs; that applies to copies made in any kind of 'device,' not just in a computer; and that purposes to solve a 'problem' whose seriousness has never been demonstrated and that is, in any case, already adequately addressed by other provisions of the DMCA.[69]

The copyright community argued that Congress, in enacting the DMCA, already addressed the "flash points" to which the proponents of H.R. 3048 make reference. For example Title II of the DMCA (now section 512 of the Copyright Act) fashions limitations of remedies that apply to infringements, including notably incidently copying "that may occur in the course of activities that are essential to the smooth functioning of the Internet, such as linking, storing, caching, or providing conduit services."[70] Given this, "the proposed incidental copying exception remains a drastic ... solution in search of something more than a largely theoretical problem."[71]

The copyright community took exception to the suggestion that the narrow exception to the reproduction right set forth in Section 117(a)(2) should somehow be expanded to include back-up copies of sound recordings, music, audiovisual works, or databases — or for that matter, any other content that consumers lawfully acquire through digital downloading. Adoption of the proponents' request would likely encourage malevolent behavior on the part of certain actors, and mislead the public generally.[72]

C. Hearing Testimony

The testimony presented at the November 29, 2000 hearing supplemented the submissions provided to NTIA and the Copyright Office during the comment period. Summaries of individual testimony provided by the witnesses can be found in Appendix B. This section will highlight selected portions of the hearing that provided additional explication of arguments set forth in the comments and reply comments.

SECTION 109

Forward and Delete Technology

Much discussion during the hearing centered on "forward and delete technology" and its ability to undergird the Boucher-Campbell proposal to amend Section 109. Even assuming the existence of this or similar technology that could reliably restrict the consumer to transmitting a single version of a copyrighted work to a single end-user (with the original copy being rendered unaccessible/unuseable to the initial consumer), representatives of the copyright community were steadfast in their opposition to both the amendment and technology associated with it. Several concerns were raised throughout the course of the day, including quality of the digital transfer;[73] impact on contractual licensing arrangements;[74] and evidentiary, procedural,[75] and privacy[76] considerations. One representative, who agreed that he would not have an objection to amending section 109 if appropriate technologies were extant, [77] set forth "minimum standards" which would have to be satisfied prior to any adoption of new policy with respect to Section 109. These would include the following:

1.   the technology must be exempted by section 1201 of the DMCA;

2.   the use of the technology must be voluntary and should not impose substantial costs on the copyright owners; [78]

3.   use should not impede the incentives underlying the Copyright Act to create and distribute new works of authorship;

4.   the technology should not burden or adversely affect the copyright owner's interest in exploiting the work itself;

5.   the technology should be developed pursuant to a broad consensus of copyright owners and other relevant industry representatives and should be made available to those parties on reasonable terms;

6.   the technology must attach to any generational copy;

7.   the technology should prevent the source copy from being transferred unless the transferor retains no electronic or nonelectronic copy of the work regardless of the format; and

8.   the source copy must be destroyed simultaneously. [79]

Technology and E-Commerce

Testimony was presented that technology is currently available to protect digital goods in such a way as to prevent unauthorized copying. In fact, technology exists (and had been used by the company providing testimony) that permitted digital copies to have as much, if not more, copy protection as the same copyrighted work delivered on a physical medium such as a compact disk. [80] The company, a supporter of a digital first sale doctrine, noted that when digital goods are treated differently from physical goods, content owners are free to apply different rules to those goods, in a manner having a direct negative impact on consumers. [81]

> These differences are not consumer friendly and the rules imposed by content owners are often hostile to consumers. . . . Consumers expect to have the same rights of ownership they have with physical goods. We found that they don't understand why they can't do the same thing with digital goods as they could with the same product in a physical format. . . . The key to digital commerce is acceptance by consumers. Consumers won't accept digital commerce until it is ubiquitous, easy to access, and can be used, consumed, in a manner that is satisfying. ... If consumers aren't buying, there is no market. Without a market, content owners won't be paid for a product they have a right to sell. Everyone loses. [82]

Sentiments expressed by one commenter attempted to encapsulate the reality of the situation:

> [Consumers] have for decades bought physical CDs, bought physical books, and have been able to do with them as they wish. When a time comes, and we hope the time never comes that a consumer bumps smack up against a restriction imposed on them because the first sale doctrine was not updated, there is going to be a tremendous human cry and the human cry is not necessarily going to be first to Congress. It's going to be a backlash against e-commerce companies that are selling them something that they think is insufficient, inadequate, and does not deliver to them the full value and flexibility that they expect from CDs, from books, and from hard copies of goods, as well as from digital media which inherently people view as being more flexible and capable. [83]

The copyright community expressed disagreement with this outlook, noting that the marketplace should be given an opportunity to "help us see a little more clearly what it is that consumers want and what is most important to them." [84]

Marketplace Determination of Business Models or Applications to Effect a Digital First Sale

Many within the copyright community argued that the market should determine the type of business model or application to be used. In their view, the marketplace should be allowed to do so without being placed in a "statutory straight jacket" of requiring use of a particular technology. [85] The proponents countered that the doctrine of first sale has never been a creation or function of the marketplace. Rather, it has been a legal limitation on what the marketplace could achieve. "To say that the market ought to control on the question of whether we should have the functional equivalent of first sale in the digital environment seems to be to perhaps wrongly characterize what that first sale functionality has always been; that is, as a limitation on market function. This is essentially a cultural as well as a commercial issue . . . ." [86]

SECTION 117

A Practical View of "Back-Up Copying" of Computer Programs

Testimony was provided addressing "back-up" copying of computer programs. According to one witness, Section 117 assumes that only computer programs need to be backed up to guard against a failure of the disk drive normally holding the computer program or a similar catastrophic failure that will require the restoration of the computer program, and that archival backups are done on a program-by-program basis. In many common backup situations, neither is the case. One witness summarized his testimony on this issue as follows:

> Backup operations on file servers copy an entire file system or selected directories to the archive medium. Between full backups, incremental backups are made comprising those files that have been changed since the last backup was made. Such backup operations generally do not discriminate between computer programs and other types of files. They make a copy of every file on the particular file system or directory. These backup are generally performed by a system administrator, who can't reasonably be aware of whether a file is a computer program or a data file, whether the limits on backup copies in software licenses have been exceeded, or even whether the user has rightful use of the programs and files. With the advent of CD-ROM drives on personal computers, many users are writing similar backup disks of their personal directories. Although such file backups are done (or should be done) at every computer installation, there is nothing in Section 117 that sanctions them. These backups should be addressed by Section 117, so that people will respect its other limits.
>
> Section 117 is also unrealistic in its requirement of destroying all archive copies when a license to a software package has expired. It would be exceeding difficult to delete such program files from a tape backup, even if it were clear which files to delete. It is impossible to selectively delete files from a CD-ROM, which can't be changed after it has been written. But that inability to delete such files will not result in any hardship for copyright owners, since system administrators or users are unlikely to give their backups to others because of the personal information and other files that they also contain.
>
> Amending Section 117 to permit the creation of archive files containing not only computer programs but any digital information, and removing the requirement that files on the archive must be destroyed, will not provide a loophole for copyright infringement of digital material. It would still be an infringement of copyright to use the backed-up information without authorization, since the archive right only covers the creation of the backup, not any reading of information from the backup. But it will recognize the realities in file backup procedures. [87]

Streaming

Testimony was presented by a number of web companies engaged in the business of Internet webcasting or streaming, all of whom sought legislation clarifying that temporary copies inherent to digital transmissions do not implicate copyrights. This group urged that temporary buffer memory copies for lawful streaming should be explicitly placed outside the copyright owners' monopoly power and right to demand compensation. [88] These copies in buffer memory are technically required for the transmission and playback of streams of music on the Internet both during transmission through the Internet infrastructure and also at the ultimate destination, the user's personal computer. [89] According to these web companies, there is "no practical way to transmit and play back streams without [buffer copies]. These buffer memory copies are not permanent. They bring no value to consumers and consumers will not pay for them. They are mere technical necessities no different . . . from the buffer copies made every day in CD players, in e-book readers, and other electronic players of digital material. . . . [T]he clarification we request should be precise about exempting buffer memory copies for all lawful transmissions and playback, not just those that are licensed." [90] Absent such clarification, the streamers contended that they "would continue to be exposed to the threats from owners of copyrights and their representatives who contend that we who stream audio files online must not only pay public performance fees (music performance rights and the sound recording performance rights), but also must pay again for the fleeting buffer memory copies as if such were the equivalent of permanent downloads." [91]

The copyright community responded to this line of reasoning by noting that it was not their role to "subsidize certain types of business models by refraining from enforcing, or seeking no compensation for the exercise of, one of their exclusive rights." [92] In short, amending section 117 would compel the copyright owner, the composer, the record copyright or "whatever copyright owner is involved to be forced to forego compensation for exercise of those rights." [93] The web companies pointed out that the resultant copying is purely a "technological accident" of the way that the Internet protocol is created. [94] Choice of business model does not enter into the discussion. The web businesses concluded that "copyright laws should avoid needlessly placing obstacles in the way of commerce and consumer enjoyment, particularly hurdles on the most trivial of technicalities. This is particularly advisable when clarifications of the law will have virtually no effect on a copyright owner's reasonable and just expectations for compensation." [95]

On a related topic, proponents were of one voice in rejecting application of Section 512 of the Copyright Act to their activities. [96] That section, which fashions limitations on the remedies that apply to infringement including all the incidental copying that may occur in the course of activities that are essential to the functioning of the Internet, was thought to be particularly helpful for those who qualified as Internet service providers within the meaning of Section 512. Many webcasters and Internet broadcasters, however, do not claim to be Internet service providers. Moreover, Section 512 does not provide a solution for those at the "end of the process after you get through the ISPs," where the end-users' personal computer is generating a buffer copy that is used in order to facilitate the streamed performance. [97]

Licenses

Several participants at the hearing were concerned regarding the use of terms incorporated in licenses (including click-thru and shrink wrap licenses) that would "override consumer privileges codified in the Copyright Act such as the Section 109 first-sale doctrine or the Section 117 adaptation and archiving rights." [98] The proponents advocated new legislation, "perhaps in the form of amendments to Section 301 of Title 17 that would provide a clear statement as to the supremacy of federal law providing for consumer privileges under copyright over state contract rules which might be employed to enforce overriding terms and shrink wrap and clink-thru licenses." [99] One commenter attempted to sum up these arguments in the following manner:

The trend toward the displacement of the provisions of a uniform federal law (the United States Copyright Act) with licenses (or contracts) for digital information is of great concern. College and university administrators, faculty, and students who previously turned to a single source of law and experience for determining legal and acceptable use must now evaluate and interpret thousands of independent license terms. A typical license agreement will limit if not eliminate the availability of fundamental copyright provisions (such as "fair use" and the ability for libraries to "archive and preserve" information) by characterizing the information transaction as a "license" rather than a "sale." It is misleading to contend that "freedom of contract" will prevail and that license negotiations are between entities with equal bargaining power, especially when non-profit educational institutions are usually presented with standard license agreements developed by the information providers. The enforceability of "shrinkwrap" or "clickthrough" licenses also poses the same restrictive use regime on individual students, faculty, and researchers. I am not convinced that copyright protections for authors and creators of digital materials is [sic] so much in peril that we must resort to a (non-uniform) system of individual licenses that also opens the floodgates for restrictions on otherwise legitimate uses. [100]

The copyright community responded to these arguments, noting that the intent of the first sale doctrine has never been to "restrict the ability of copyright owners to enter into contracts that [certain communities] find objectionable." [101]

We think that it's important for parties voluntarily to write licenses about what can and cannot be done with copies. They can dispose of them, transfer them, lend them. . . . The point I'm making is whatever you chose to do, it's important to ensure that private parties retain the right to write licenses as they see fit and as they freely agree to do so. [102]

Another member of the copyright community addressed these concerns in the following manner:

[C]opyright is a form of property and copyright owners like other property owners must be able to capture the value of that property through the use of licenses and other contracts. Indeed, the rapid development of new digital music business models will require the flexibility of contractual arrangements to meet the expectations of all the parties involve which includes consumers, distributors, recording artists and record companies. This is especially true in this new environment where the needs and desires of these groups can change quickly. Furthermore, the use of technological measures to support the contractual agreements of the parties is also essential to the deployment of new music delivery methods. For this reason, we strongly object to the suggestions of some commentors that Section 109 should be amended to place limits on copyright owner's ability to contract freely with respect to their intellectual property. . . . Moreover, other areas of the law such as contract and antitrust are available to resolve any concerns about licensing practices. Section 109 simply is not the place to address these matters. [103]

Additionally, of particular concern to the copyright community was the proponents' views regarding the Uniform Computer Information Transactions Act ("UCITA") and efforts to ensure its passage in every state. The copyright community was concerned that certain proponents for a change to Section 109 would mislead the general public into believing that UCITA ignores the supremacy of federal law.

While . . . UCITA provisions may not meet the over zealous demands of the DFC and the libraries for new statutory creation of rights for users of computer information, it is clear that state-based law properly defers to the supremacy of federal law on issues involving fundamental public policies including the applicability of the Copyright Act's fair-use exceptions and the latest provisions of the DMCA. To do otherwise would have risked disturbing or even destroying the delicate but deliberate balance that U.S. law has always maintained between the federal system of copyright protection and the state role in determining agreements among private parties including contracts and licenses. [104]

PART IV – CONCLUSION

The record compiled in this matter reveals deep divisions between the proponents of legislative changes to Sections 109 and 117 and the copyright community. Very little consensus appears to exist with respect to the possible application of Sections 109 and 117 to the digital world, and the effect on the development of electronic commerce and associated technologies. The record does contain information about some exciting new technologies that in the near future may assist in resolving some of the more difficult issues presented by the need to adequately protect the rights of the copyright community in the digital world. Thus, NTIA believes that it would be premature to draw any conclusions or make any legislative recommendations at this time with respect to either Section 109 or 117, but believes there are several areas that warrant further Congressional inquiry.

With respect to Section 109, there does appear to be limited consensus with respect to one particular application to digitally downloaded files. Both the proponents and the copyright community seem to agree that if the files are downloaded with the consent of the copyright owner, a "lawfully made copy or phonorecord" will have been created on the PC hard drive or tangible portable medium (such as a writeable CD). Thus, Section 109 would apply to the owner of that new digital copy or phonorecord. With respect to other applications of Section 109 to digitally downloaded files, however, there was considerable divergence between the stakeholders with respect to whether a copyright owner's interest could be adequately protected. There was significant information in the record to suggest, however, that DRM systems and other like developments hold some promise of offering a technological solution.

With respect to Section 117, the record does reflect considerable information about the technical functionality of the Internet and the practical reality of the way, during the course of Internet webcasting, Internet protocols require the temporary storage of data, before reassembling and playing it in real time for the consumer. According to the record, this data is eliminated once the playback actually begins. There was also significant information in the record to suggest that the temporary storage of a few seconds of content during webcasting had no separable economic value apart from the value of the performance itself for which copyright owners would be compensated. Thus, it appears further Congressional consideration of whether an extension of the principles underlying Section 117 to buffered content stored in RAM, as required for playback of Internet webcasting, is warranted.

Similar focus might also be given to examining whether Section 117 principles should be extended to the temporary copies of recorded content made in the course of playback. Virtually all devices that playback content recorded in a digital format must process such content by first loading all or some portion of it into memory. This is an essential and critical step for all computing devices that allow playback, including CD-players, DVD-players, HD television receivers, and a host of new portable devices. Again, while there is considerable division among the stakeholders, further consideration might be given to whether an extension of Section 117 is warranted given the above-cited technological imperatives.

One other issue emerged from the Section 117 examination, not arising out of the reality of "how the technology operates," but rather from a review of practical computing in everyday life. The record contains descriptions of the manner in which some "backup" or "archival" copies are made. First, in connection with an archiving of the data from a computer, most people will likely copy every file on a particular file system or directory. Second, given the growing popularity of digital downloading, the making of a single backup copy of lawfully acquired digital content to protect against server or hard drive crashes (or to transfer to an updated computer system) is not surprising. Thus, Congress might consider further examination of real-world practices raised during comment period and November hearing.

Appendix A

. . . . . .

Appendix B

. . . . . .

---

[1]   P.L. No. 105-304, 112 Stat 2860 (October 28, 1998).

[2]   H.R. Rep. No. 105-551, pt. 2, at 21 (1998). The objective of Title I of the DMCA was to revise U.S. copyright law to comply with two recent World Intellectual Property Organization treaties and to strengthen copyright protection for motion pictures, sound recordings, computer software, and other copyrighted works in electronic formats. To this end, the Act prohibits the circumvention of copyright protections measures; proscribes the falsification of copyright management information accompanying a copyrighted work; limits the liability of Internet service

providers for the infringing activity of their users; and exempts from prohibition the copying of a computer program for the purpose of maintenance or repair.

[3] S. Rep. No. 105-190, at 1, 8 (1998).

[4] H.R. Rep. No. 105-551, pt. 2, at 23 (1998).

[5] "Due to the ease with which digital works can be copied and distributed worldwide virtually instantaneously, copyright owners will hesitate to make their works readily available on the Internet without reasonable assurance that they will be protected against massive piracy. Legislation implementing the [World Intellectual Property Organization treaties on copyright and on performers and phonograms] provides this protection and creates the legal platform for launching the global digital on-line marketplace for copyrighted works." S. Rep. No. 105-190, at 8 (1998).

[6] H.R. Rep. No. 105-551, pt. 2, at 22 (1998). "A thriving electronic marketplace provides new and powerful ways for the creators of intellectual property to make their works available to legitimate consumers in the digital environment. And a plentiful supply of intellectual property—whether in the form of software, music, movies, literature, or other works—drives the demand for a more flexible and efficient electronic marketplace." *Id.*

[7] *Id.* at 23.

[8] 17 USC §104. This report focuses on the electronic commerce aspects of the evaluation consistent with NTIA's mission. The Copyright Office will provide its views in a separate report to follow.

[9] Report to Congress Pursuant to Section 104 of the Digital Millennium Copyright Act – Request for Public Comment, 65 FR 35673 (2000).

[10] Report to Congress Pursuant to Section 104 of the Digital Millennium Copyright Act – Notice of Public Hearing, 65 FR 63626 (2000).

[11] "Electronic commerce is a means of conducting transactions that, prior to the evolution of the Internet as a business tool in 1995, would have been completed in more traditional ways – by telephone, mail, facsimile, proprietary electronic data interchange systems, or face-to-face contact." U.S. Department of Commerce, Economic and Statistics Administration, Office of Policy Development, *The Emerging Digital Economy II,* (June 1999), p. 1.

[12] The U.S. Government Working Group on Electronic Commerce, *Leadership for the New Millennium: Delivering on Digital Progress and Prosperity,* (2000) Third Annual Report (2001), ("Leadership Report 2000"), p. vi.

[13] Press Release, United States Department of Commerce, Economic and Statistics Administration, U.S. Census Bureau, *Retail E-Commerce Sales in Fourth Quarter 2000 were $8.7 Billion, Up 67.1 Percent from Fourth Quarter 1999, Census Bureau Reports* (Feb. 16, 2001).

[14] U.S. Department of Commerce, Economics and Statistics Administration, *Digital Economy 2000,* p. vi.

[15] *Id.*

[16] U.S. Department of Commerce, Economics and Statistics Administration, *Digital Economy 2000,* p. 21, referencing Forrester Research, *Spectacular Growth for Digital Delivery,* February 7, 2000 reported by *Nua Internet Surveys* (http://www.nua.ie).

[17] "Efforts are underway within the U.S. government, multilateral organizations, and within the private sector, to resolve thorny issues related to privacy, safeguards for children, consumer protection, information security, authentications, intellectual property rights, jurisdiction, taxes, and tariffs." *Id.,* at 22.

[18] *Id.*

[19] The comments that were received during the comment period are available at the Register of Copyrights, Index of Submissions (visited February 26, 2001) <http://www.loc.gov/copyrights/reports/104*study/comments.html*> and at the National Telecommunications and Information Administration, Index of Comments (visited February 26, 2001) <http://www.ntia.doc.gov/ntiahome/occ/dmca/commentssindex.htm>.

[20] Letter from the Honorable Patty Murray to Marybeth Peters, Register of Copyrights, and Gregory L. Rohde, Assistant Secretary of Commerce and Administrator, National Telecommunications and Information Administration,

dated September 21, 2000. Letter from the Honorable Jay Inslee to Gregory L. Rohde, dated September 27, 2000. Letter from the Honorable Slade Gorton to Marybeth Peters and Gregory L. Rohde, Dated September 28, 2000.

[21] Although 46 comments and reply comments were received during the comment period and 40 persons presented testimony at the November hearing, two distinct coalitions emerged, based on continuity of views. The first group, the proponents of extending sections 109 and 117 to digital media, included the Digital Media Association (a coalition of more than 50 technology developers, webcasters, and retailers) (DiMA); the Digital Futures Coalition (DFC); the Home Recording Rights Coalition (HRRC); the National Association of Recording Merchandisers (NARM); the Computer & Communications Industry Association (CCIA); the Video Software Dealers Associations (VSDA); and the Library Associations. The second group, the copyright community, included the Copyright Industry Organizations (the American Film Marketing Association, Association of Music Publishers, Business Software Alliance, Interactive Digital Software Association, Motion Picture Association of America, National Music Publishers' Association, and the Recording Industry of America, collectively and individually); Time Warner, Inc.; Software & Information Industry Association, Broadcast Music, Inc.; and Reed Elsevier Inc. The report will use the terms "proponents for change" and "copyright community" for ease of reference. A complete list of commenters and witnesses at the November 29, 2000 hearing is available at *Appendix A*.

[22] Comments of the Digital Media Association (DiMA Comments) (August 4, 2000).

[23] To lend support to its line of reasoning, DiMA references *Twentieth Century Music Corp. v. Aiken*, 422 U.S. 151 (1975). The commenter notes that in *Twentieth Century*, the Court held:

The limited scope of the copyright holder's statutory monopoly, like the limited copyright duration required by the Constitution, reflects a balance of competing claims upon the public interest: Creative work is to be encouraged and rewarded, but private motivation must ultimately serve the cause of promoting broad public availability of literature, music, and the other arts. The immediate effect of our copyright law is to secure a fair return for an 'author's' creative labor. But the ultimate aim is, by this incentive, to stimulate artistic creativity for the general public good. *'The sole interest of the United States and the primary object in conferring the monopoly,' this Court has said, 'lie in the general benefits derived by the public from the labors of authors.' When technological change has rendered its literal terms ambiguous, the Copyright Act must be construed in light of this basic purpose.*

DiMA Comments (citing *Twentieth Century*, at 156 (citations and footnotes omitted); emphasis added).

[24] This commenter notes that the principle was also recognized by the Copyright Office in a recently published report concerning digital distance education.

Where a statutory provision that was intended to implement a particular policy is written in such a way that it becomes obsolete due to changes in technology, the provision may require updating if that policy is to continue. Doing so may be seen not as preempting a new market, but as accommodating existing markets that are being tapped by new methods.

DiMA Comments (quoting *Report on Copyright and Digital Distance Education*, at 144 (May 1999)).

[25] Another commenter, the Home Recording Rights Coalition, went further, noting that legal certainty in applying copyright to new digital technologies will benefit copyright owners and consumers alike, and will open the market to more exciting and compelling technologies and business models. Comments of the Home Recording Rights Coalition (HRRC Comments) (August 4, 2000).

[26] Both the National Association of Recording Merchandisers and the Video Software Dealers Association contend that the first sale doctrine already applies to digital media, and the appropriate inquiry for this study is whether the DMCA or electronic commerce may have an effect on it, such as to weaken its salutary purposes. *See* Joint Comments of the National Association of Recording Merchandisers and Video Software Dealers Association (NARM and VSDA Comments) (August 4, 2000). NARM and VSDA are concerned by the trend of some major copyright owners to use technological measures to circumvent the operation of the first sale doctrine. "Although technological measures may lawfully be used to prevent copyright infringement and to effectuate the licensing of copyrights, they should not be used to permanently control the lawful distribution and use of copies or phonorecords once the legal right to do so has been exhausted." NARM and VSDA Comments. *See also* Comments of Robert S. Thau and Bryan Taylor (Thau and Taylor Comments) (August 4, 2000). The Library Associations have called for a uniform federal policy that sets minium standards respecting limitations on the exclusive rights of ownership and that

set aside state statutes and contractual terms which unduly restrict access rights. *See* Comments of American Library Association et al.(Library Association Comments) (August 4, 2000).

[27] HRRC Comments (citing Cong. Rec. at E2352 (Nov. 13, 1997) (daily ed.)).

[28] *See* DiMA Comments and Comments of NARM and VSDA.

[29] HRRC Comments.

[30] "CDs and books are resold freely; yet, the consumer/reseller may have copied these physical media using cassette or CD recorders, scanners, and photocopy equipment. Denying the first sale doctrine for digitally-delivered media ironically would deprive consumers of traditional privileges in a far more secure environment." DiMA Comments.

[31] "DRM systems can protect against any threat posed by file-sharing technologies. If such files may be shared, they either cannot be accessed by the downloader, or (in the case of DRM systems that promote paid superdistribution models) cannot be accessed without payment of a fee." DiMA Comments.

[32] Comments of Time Warner (Time Warner Comments) (August 4, 2000).

[33] *Id.*

[34] For example, the first sale doctrine would be available for both traditional media in which works are fixed (VHS tapes), as well as tangible digital media (DVDs). The fact that the tangible medium contains works embodied in digital form does not affect the application of the first sale doctrine. *Id.*

[35] *See* Comments of the Software & Information Industry Association (SIIA Comments) (August 4, 2000). *See also,* Time Warner Comments, n. 1 ("We note that the initial downloading of a copy, from an authorized source to a purchaser's computer, can result in lawful ownership of a copy stored in a tangible medium. If the purchaser does not make and retain a second copy, further transfer of that particular copy on such medium would fall within the scope of the first sale doctrine.").

[36] *See* Time Warner Comments. *See also* Comments of the Copyright Industry Organizations (CIO Comments) (August 4, 2000).

The first sale doctrine does not readily apply in the digital networked environment because the owner of a particular digital copy usually does not sell or otherwise dispose of the possession of that copy. Rather, "disposition" of a digital copy by its owner normally entails reproduction and transmission of that reproduction to another person. The original copy may then be retained or destroyed.

CIO Comments (citing House Manager's Report at 24, 46 J. Copyr. Soc. 631, 657 (1999)).

[37] *See* CIO Comments. *See also* Time Warner Comments and Comments of Patrice A. Lyons, Esq. (August 4, 2000).

[38] *See* CIO Comments.

[39] *See* SIIA Comments.

[40] "Because content owners are not faced with the dangers that would result from application (in our view, misapplication) of the first sale doctrine to digital transmissions, content owners are encouraged to make their works available in digital form. They can make those works available for downloading, for streaming and for whatever other new technology develops in a variety of pricing and other arrangements so as to meet diverse consumer needs and desires. Misapplying the first sale doctrine to these businesses would quickly discourage them." CIO Comments.

[41] *See* DiMA Reply Comments (September 5, 2000).

[42] "Copyright policy exists primarily to serve the public good, not only to establish economic rights for copyright owners." "In order to promote e-commerce, consumers that purchase copyrighted works via digital delivery should be ensured that they received the same value for their investment as when they by a book, compact disc, or video game from a traditional retail outlet, which necessarily includes the right to resell, lend or give away that particular item." DiMA Reply Comments.

[43] DiMA Reply Comments.

[44] *See* DiMA Reply Comments.

[45] DiMA Reply Comments.

[46] *See* DiMA Reply Comments; Library Associations Reply Comments (September 5, 2000).

[47] *See* DiMA Reply Comments.

[48] DiMA Reply Comments.

[49] *See* DiMA Reply Comments. *See also* NARM and VSDA Comments. DiMA notes that other commenters, including the Library Associations and the Digital Future Coalition, suggest that these problems should be addressed by the adoption of the digital first sale doctrine and an amendment to Section 301 of the Copyright Act confirming the supremacy over state laws (and non-negotiated license terms) of these federal law exemptions and privileges. *See* Library Associations Comments; Library Associations Reply Comments (September 5, 2000); and Comments of the Digital Future Coalition (DFC Comments) (August 2, 2000).

[50] CIO Reply Comments (September 5, 2000).

[51] *Id.*

[52] *Id.*

[53] *Id. See also,* Reply Comments of Broadcast Music, Inc. (BMI Reply Comments) (September 5, 2000).

[54] *Id. See also,* BMI Reply Comments. The copyright community takes exception to the views proposed by some advocates for a digital first sale doctrine when they argue that the tranferees of copies or phonorecords in digital formats should be "free to ignore contractual or licensing restrictions on further redistribution of these materials, or that technological measures employed by copyright owners should be stripped of all legal protections if they have an impact on such redistribution." The copyright community notes that no cogent reason has been forwarded why a contract or license should not be enforced simply because it restricts the redistribution right that the transferee would otherwise enjoy under section 109 when applied to traditional media in which works are fixed, as well as tangible digital media. "Indeed, to the extent that the terms of a transfer include redistribution restrictions, it may well be that the transfer does not constitute a sale, the tranferree is not the owner of the copy in question, and the first sale doctrine is completely inapplicable. . . . [I]t is hard to understand how the interest of consumers could possibly be served by shutting down particular e-commerce business models because of the particular status and perquisites they offer to the recipient of digital copyrighted products." *Id.*

[55] DiMA Comments.

[56] *See* HRRC Comments.

[57] DiMA Comments. This commenter notes the Copyright Office appears to have "reached a similar conclusion in its study of distance education, resulting in the recommendation that the scope of the Section 110(2) exemption should be expanded to encompass 'transient copies created as part of the automatic technical process of the digital transmission of an exempted performance or display.' Report on Copyright and Digital Distance Education (citation omitted)." *Id.*

[58] *Id.*

[59] Section 117(b) as proposed would provide as follows:

Notwithstanding the provisions of section 106, it is not an infringement to make a copy of a work in digital format if such copying—

(1) is incidental to the operation of a device in the course of the use of a work otherwise lawful under this title; and

(2) does not conflict with the normal exploitation of the work and does not unreasonably prejudice the legitimate interests of the author.

This language, proposed by then-Senator Ashcroft in S.1146 during September 1997, is also found in the 1997 Boucher-Campbell bill, H. 3048.

[60] *See* CIO Comments. *See also* SIIA Comments and the Comments of the Interactive Digital Software Association (IDSA Comments) (August 4, 2000).

[61] IDSA Comments.

[62] DiMA Reply Comments.

[63] *Id.*

[64] DiMA Reply Comments.

[65] DiMA Reply Comments.

[66] CIO Reply Comments.

[67] 991 F2d 4511 *[1 ILR (P&F) 71]* (9th Cir 1993), *cert. dismissed,* 510 US 1033 (1994). According to the Reply Comments submitted by the copyright community, the central holding of *MAI* is its reaffirmation that copies of computer programs made in the memory of a computer – in that case, temporary copies made in Random Access Memory (RAM) – are reproductions that fall within the scope of the exclusive reproduction right of the Copyright Act. *MAI,* 991 F2d at 518-19. "The second major holding in *MAI* simply restricted the benefit of the section 117 exceptions to the sole party designated by Congress to enjoy it – the owner of a copy of a computer program, as distinguished from a licensee." *MAI,* 991 F2d at 519 n. 5. CIO Reply Comments.

[68] *Id.*

[69] *Id.*

[70] *Id. But cf.* Comments of the Computer & Communications Industry Association (CCIA Comments) (August 4, 2000) ("The potential exposure of Internet service providers for activities initiated by third parties led to the lengthy and costly negotiations that culminated in the [DMCA's] safe harbor provisions. Service providers now often find themselves modifying the structure of their services in order to comply with the safe harbors' complex legal requirements rather than deploying the most technologically efficient solutions. When the activity can not be squeezed into the DMCA's safe harbors, service providers and users alike must really [sic] on uncertain legal doctrines such as fair use, copyright misuse, and implied license to avoid legal liability").

[71] *Id.* Other commenters were more direct in their approach. "Section 117 has nothing to do with the broadcasting of music and any attendant reproduction rights issues, and there is no indication in Section 104 of the DMCA that Congress intended that this inquiry should involve music or broadcasting-related issues on the Internet. In view of the explosion of webcasting since 1988 . . . it is difficult to see how a brand new exemption is necessary to foster webcasting over the next several years. The Office and the NTIA should therefore decline the . . . invitation to address these matters in the context of this proceeding." BMI Reply Comments.

[72] *Id.*

[73] "Quality of the digital transfer" refers to the speed, convenience, and potential global reach of the proposed first sale transaction. This term also references the ability to transmit, with the copyrighted work, the forward and delete technology such that any subsequent sale/retransmission would be similarly limited.

[74] Assuming that technology to effectuate the Boucher amendment existed, one commenter noted that "the testimony and comments of the library communique indicate quite clearly that that would only shift the argument to the question of whether or not the digital first-sale doctrine trumps any kind of contractual licensing arrangement that may be involved with respect to the work." Testimony of Allan Adler, Association of American Publishers, Hearing Transcript, at 71.

[75] Advocates of a digital first sale argued that the Boucher-Campbell amendment would not create significant new enforcement problems for copyright owners.

> Detecting unauthorized transmissions of copyright works is an inevitable and necessary first step in any enforcement effort involving the Internet and such detection would be no more difficult if some of those transmissions were, in fact, potentially privileged by virtue of an amended Section 109. If copyright owners object to being required to show the absence of first sale in connection with proving a claim of Internet-based infringement, the burden of demonstrating that the copy previously acquired by the person making the transmission was, in fact, erased or destroyed might fairly be assigned to whoever is claiming the benefit of the privilege.

Testimony of Professor Peter Jaszi, Digital Future Coalition, Hearing Transcript, at 225. The copyright community retorted that shifting the burden of proof "is really cold comfort here. This is not enforceable and it would be very easy for the end-user to say, 'Yes, I deleted it.' And then what do you do, conduct discovery about when he deleted it and look at his hard drive?" Testimony of Steven J. Metalitz, Esq., Copyright Industry Organizations, Hearing Transcript, at 289.

[76] "Yet, when you look at the recommendation that they make in support of Mr. Boucher's approach to amending the first-sale doctrine, which would depend upon some notion of the practical enforceability of a simultaneous deletion concept which would be extremely intrusive in terms of personal privacy if anyone was to attempt to try to see if, in fact, it worked on a practical basis, you are left to try to figure out how to deal with privacy issues which were not even the subject of the study as the Congress set it forth in the requirements of the DMCA." Adler Testimony, Hearing Transcript, at 27-28. (The proponents noted, however, that the same kind of evidentiary privacy issues would arise in a non-digital world (*i.e.*, photocopying a book before selling it to another and/or not destroying the photocopied version). *See*, Testimony of Rodney Peterson. Library Associations, Hearing Transcript, at 42.)

Another commenter from the copyright community noted that it would be neither possible, nor practical for the copyright owner or the courts "to verify that the source copy was discarded. Even if it was [sic] possible to determine that a source copy had been discarded, it would not be possible the verify that it was done so simultaneously." Testimony of Keith Kupferschmidt, Esq., Software & Information Industry Association, Hearing Transcript, at 87.

[77] *See also*, Testimony of Bernard Sorkin, Esq., Time Warner, Inc., Hearing Transcript, at 59.

[78] *See also*, Testimony of Susan Mann, National Music Publishers' Association, Hearing Transcript, at 213.

[79] Kupferschmidt Testimony, Hearing Transcript, at 124-127. One commenter questioned the reason for the change to Section 109 if the forward and delete technology were ever to become ubiquitous, perfect, and met all necessary assumptions. "If copyright owners and everybody else used this technology, I think the best way to look at it would be as either an implied or explicit license to make copies of the material that had been transmitted on the condition that the technology was also employed to delete the original copy." Metalitz Testimony, Hearing Transcript, at 245.

[80] "It is more difficult to reproduce those works in violation of the valid purposes of the copyright law than it would be to reproduce a book via a Xerox machine." Testimony of Charles Jennings, Supertracks, Hearing Transcript, at 344.

[81] This sentiment was similarly held by other participants at the hearing. "Some commentors appear to contend that consumers who lawfully acquire electronic books or music via digital downloading should not have a first-sale privilege. This, in my view, constitutes a radical expansion of copyright principles." Testimony of Seth Greenstein, Esq., Digital Media Association, Hearing Transcript, at 232.

[82] Jennings Testimony, Hearing Transcript, at 345-346.

[83] Greenstein Testimony, Hearing Transcript, at 268-269.

[84] Metalitz Testimony, Hearing Transcript, at 270.

[85] Metalitz Testimony, Hearing Transcript, at 245-246, 270. *See also* Adler Testimony, at 66.

[86] Jaszi Testimony, Hearing Transcript, at 265.

[87] Summary of Intended Testimony of Dr. David Hollar, University of Utah (provided in its entirety at Appendix B).

[88] "It is, of course, possible that a real time transmission could be listened to or perceived as well as recorded, and, in that case, yes, both the performance and a reproduction right have been implicated. It is also possible for those to be implicated separately." Greenstein Testimony, Hearing Transcript at 236.

[89] For a detailed explanation of the manner in which streaming is effected, *see* Albin Testimony, Hearing Transcript, at 311 -316.

[90] Greenstein Testimony, Hearing Transcript, at 329-330. *See also* CCIA Comments. Of major importance to the web business was that the proposed clarification would address **lawful** uses and copies as opposed to those **authorized** by a specific copyright owner. "This formulation is the best way to preserve consumer rights under fair use or consumer rights under exemptions with respect to private performances, *i.e.*, nonpublic performance such as

personal streaming from a locker service, and other exceptions and exemptions under the Copyright Act." Greenstein Testimony, Hearing Transcript, at 239. Members of the copyright community could not accept this language. "I would much prefer a term that says authorized because that would say that I have now licensing terms and conditions that are enforceable and the law is enforceable. The extent to which I have imposed, through the license, restrictions on what can and cannot be done are fully enforceable. The problem that we run into is that "lawful" term which sweeps in concepts as intended by Mr. Boucher of fair use which then are intended and interpreted as trumping those licensing terms and conditions. That's where we run into a problem." Testimony of Emery Simon, Business Software Alliance, Hearing Transcript, at 142-143.

[91] Testimony of David Pakman, MyPlay, Inc., Hearing Transcript, at 330. After having conducted a study of 4 million customer usage patterns and the economic benefit that could be derived from that usage, MyPlay concluded that an amendment to Section 117 would be beneficial to copyright owners as well. The web business' study concludes that there was no rational business model that allows for payments by consumers or advertisers for mere buffer memory copies. "Royalties and payments due for use of copyrighted works are made possible only when an economically rational business can be built in accordance with the use of such works. We believe strongly that significant profitable businesses can be built from the use of copyrighted works. However, no business can be built or expanded solely by commercializing temporary buffer memory copies. Conversely, if royalties were due on the creation of purely transient copies, there is a substantial danger that presently viable business models would be fatally undermined." *Id.* at 331-332.

[92] Metalitz Testimony, Hearing Transcript, at 276.

[93] "Now there may well be good business reasons to do that and that is why we want negotiation over these fees and whatever other mechanisms are used to set these fees. That's why this is a business decision. There may well be good business reasons to do that but I don't think it's appropriate to amputate part of the reproduction right because the business model for webcasters isn't working out the way they told their venture capitalist it would." Metalitz Testimony, Hearing Transcript, at 277.

[94] "But there is a technological necessity because of the way the Internet is designed to operate efficiently that causes this RAM buffer copy to be made. It is not captured in other ways. It evaporates. It is evanescent once the playback occurs. It has no independent commercial significance and we consider it ludicrous that we would be asked to pay for it twice." Greenstein Testimony, Hearing Transcript, at 278.

[95] Pakman Testimony, Hearing Transcript, at 332.

[96] Jaszi Testimony, Hearing Transcript, at 273; and Greenstein Testimony, Hearing Transcript, at 274. *But see* Metalitz Testimony, Hearing Transcript, 247.

[97] Greenstein Testimony, Hearing Transcript, at 274.

[98] Jaszi Testimony, Hearing Transcript, at 228. *See also* Testimony of Rodney Peterson, Director of Policy and Planning , University of Maryland, Office of Information Technology, Hearing Transcript, at 22-24, and Testimony of James Neal, Dean of University Libraries, Johns Hopkins University, Hearing Transcript, at 16 ("The first sale doctrine is being undermined by contract and restrictive licensing. . . . We believe that no review of the first sale doctrine and computer licensing rules should be completed without the Congress giving favorable consideration to a new federal preeemption provision affecting these rules."

[99] Jaszi Testimony, Hearing Transcript, at 228. *See* Greenstein Testimony, Hearing Transcript, at 239.

[100] Summary of Intended Testimony by Rodney J. Peterson, November 29, 2000 (*see* Appendix B).

[101] Adler Testimony, Hearing Transcript, at 36. The copyright community has taken the view that Section 109 does not prevent them from entering into end-user license agreements and enforcing them through technology, including access control devices. *See* CIO Reply Comments, at 6 (first sale doctrine would apply to lawfully made copies only "in the absence of licensing or technological restrictions to the contrary"), and Testimony of Cary Sherman, Recording Industry Association of America, Hearing Transcript, at 300. *But see,* Testimony of Scott Moskowitz, Blue Spike, Inc., Hearing Transcript, at 100 ("[L]eaving digital works uncovered by [the] first sale doctrine gives copyright holders and the technologists who develop copyright security schemes little impetus to develop more nuanced and context-appropriate means of securing their works against infringement that access restriction systems").

[102] Adler Testimony, Hearing Transcript, at 36.

[103] Sherman Testimony, Hearing Transcript, at 300. One member of the copyright community expressed that community's displeasure with the proposed changes advocated for Sections 109 and 117, arguing that they would create "substantial disruption to the marketplace calling into question the viability of well-established business models" for the software community. (Of particular importance to this witness was the impact proposed legislative changes would have to the emergence of application service providers (ASPs), who permit companies to use a software product without having to buy it or having to install it on a local computer. According to this witness, the demand for such services is expected to grow rapidly, by some estimates exceeding $21 billion by next year.) His comments attempted to meld licensing issues and concerns regarding the "reproduction right" as it applies to temporary copies. *See* Testimony of Emory Simon, Business Software Alliance, Hearing Transcript, at 108-115; 134-135 ("[u]nless we have a cause of action against those portions of copies being made, even on a temporary basis we have no reproduction right-based cause of action to go against now all those people that have exceeded the licensed authorized use of the work").

Another member of the copyright community did not endorse this attempt at melding the two concepts. *See* Testimony of Keith Kupferschmidt, Software & Information Industry Alliance, Hearing Transcript, at 135-136 ("the thing he brings up on a limited license where someone has licensed 10 copies or the simultaneous use of 10 copies. Because they are on a server and there's more than 10 people using it is a question of whether the person is a rightful user at that time. It's not a thing about whether it's in RAM at the time"). Indeed that comment would be supported in large measure by proponents who have argued that BSA's concerns with respect to ASPs and the proposed changes to Section 117 are mismatched. "Section 117 addresses the case where a copy must permanently reside with the user in order for the user to use the product. That may not be necessary for networked or thin client computing, but most definitely is required for the digitally-downloaded content" addressed by DiMA in its proposal. *See* DiMA Reply Comments. Another proponent approached BSA's testimony in yet a different manner. *See* Testimony of John Mitchell, Esq., Video Software Dealers' Association, Hearing Transcript, at 193 ("[t]he Business Software Alliance has indicated that . . . they claim not to sell software but only to license the software. If that is the case, then logically if they haven't sold it and they still own it, the first-sale doctrine never applies, which begs the question why they are here? Why they are here is because I think they do recognize that, in fact, they do sell it . . .").

[104] Testimony of Daniel Duncan, Digital Commerce Coalition, Hearing Transcript, at 255.

DMCA
Section 104 Report

U.S. Copyright Office
August 2001

A Report of the Register of Copyrights
Pursuant to §104 of the Digital Millennium Copyright Act

DIGITAL MILLENNIUM COPYRIGHT ACT OF 1998, § 104
Pub. L. No. 105-304, 112 Stat. 2860, 2876

SEC. 104. EVALUATION OF IMPACT OF COPYRIGHT LAW AND AMENDMENTS ON ELECTRONIC COMMERCE AND TECHNOLOGICAL DEVELOPMENT.

(a) EVALUATION BY THE REGISTER OF COPYRIGHTS AND THE ASSISTANT SECRETARY FOR COMMUNICATIONS AND INFORMATION.–The Register of Copyrights and Assistant Secretary for Communications and Information of the Department of Commerce shall jointly evaluate–

(1) the effects of the amendments made by this title and the development of electronic commerce and associated technology on the operation of sections 109 and 117 of title 17, United States Code; and

(2) the relationship between existing and emergent technology and the operation of sections 109 and 117 of title 17, United States Code.

(b) REPORT TO CONGRESS.–The Register of Copyrights and the Assistant Secretary for Communications and Information of the Department of Commerce shall, not later than 24 months after the date of the enactment of this Act, submit to the Congress a joint report on the evaluation conducted under subsection (a), including any legislative recommendations the Register and the Assistant Secretary may have.

**DMCA
Section 104 Report
U.S. Copyright Office
August 2001**

A Report of the
Register of Copyrights
Pursuant to §104 of the Digital
Millennium Copyright Act

Library of Congress Cataloging-in-Publication Data

Library of Congress. Copyright Office.
    DMCA section 104 report a report of the Register of Copyrights pursuant to
[section] 104 of the Digital Millennium Copyright Act.
        p. cm.
    1. United States. Digital Millennium Copyright Act. 2. Copyright--
Electronic information resources--United States--Legislative history. 3.
Copyright and electronic data processing--United
States--Legislative history.   I. Title.
    KF2989.573.A15 2001
    346.7304'82--dc21

                                                              2001042373

8-29-01

The Register of Copyrights
of the
United States of America

Library of Congress
Department 17
Washington, D.C. 20540

(202) 707-8350

August 29, 2001

Dear Mr. Speaker:

I am pleased to present the Copyright Office's "DMCA Section 104 Report."

As required under section 104 of Public Law No. 105-304, the Report evaluates the effects of title I of the Digital Millennium Copyright Act of 1998 and the development of electronic commerce and associated technology on the operation of sections 109 and 117 of title 17, U.S.C. It also evaluates the relationship between existing and emergent technology and the operation of those sections.

Respectfully,

Marybeth Peters

Marybeth Peters
Register of Copyrights

Enclosure

The Honorable J. Dennis Hastert
Speaker
United States House of Representatives
Washington, D.C. 20515

ACKNOWLEDGMENTS

This report is the result of the expertise, skills and dedication of many people. I was fortunate to be able to draw on many talented staff, and I am grateful to all of them. However, I especially thank and acknowledge the efforts of two officials of the Office. The first is Jesse Feder, Acting Associate Register for Policy and International Affairs, who served as the project manager and who was also a primary drafter of the report; the second is David O. Carson, General Counsel of the Copyright Office, whose wise counsel and sound advice was present throughout the process. Also, worthy of special praise are the others who drafted the report; they are Marla Poor, Attorney Advisor, Office of Policy and International Affairs, Steven Tepp, Policy Planning Advisor, Office of Policy and International Affairs, and Robert Kasunic, Senior Attorney-Advisor, Office of the Copyright General Counsel. Their efforts went well beyond writing sections of the report and they played important roles in the review process.

Others in the Office assisted the "report team" in numerous ways, including sharing their insight and advice. These individuals are Robert Dizard, Staff Director and Chief Operating Officer of the Copyright Office, Tanya Sandros, Senior Attorney, Office of the Copyright General Counsel; William Roberts Senior Attorney-Advisor for Compulsory Licenses, Office of the Copyright General Counsel; and Sayuri Rajapakse, Attorney-Advisor, Office of Policy and International Affairs. I also thank Kelly Lacey, our intern from Georgetown University Law Center, for her first-rate substantive help.

Numerous and important contributions were made by many others in the Copyright Office. I thank, Marylyn Martin of the Register's Office, for her assistance in organizing our public hearing; Shirada Harrison of the Office of Policy and International Affairs, and Guy Echols and Sandra Jones of the General Counsel's Office for their assistance in completing the final document; Helen Hester-Ossa, Teresa McCall and Charles Gibbons of the Information and Reference Division for their excellent assistance in the design and layout of the Report and in getting it printed; Denise Prince of the General Counsel's Office for her assistance in getting it delivered to Congress; and Ed Rogers and George Thuronyi, our webmasters, for their expert contributions both during the study and in getting our Report out to the public via the Internet. Special thanks also to Xue Fei Li of our Automation Group for her technical assistance in receiving comments from the public by email.

Finally, just prior to completing the process, I asked June Besek, Director of Studies and Director of the International Program of the Kernochan Center for Law, Media and the Arts at Columbia Law School, to review the penultimate draft text. I appreciate her exceptional efforts (she had less than 48 hours) and her invaluable suggestions and comments.

Marybeth Peters
Register of Copyrights

TABLE OF CONTENTS

iv

EXECUTIVE SUMMARY

INTRODUCTION

The Digital Millennium Copyright Act of 1998 (DMCA) was the foundation of an effort by Congress to implement United States treaty obligations and to move the nation's copyright law into the digital age. But as Congress recognized, the only thing that remains constant is change. The enactment of the DMCA was only the beginning of an ongoing evaluation by Congress on the relationship between technological change and U.S. copyright law. This Report of the Register of Copyrights was mandated in the DMCA to assist Congress in that continuing process.

Our mandate was to evaluate "the effects of the amendments made by [title I of the DMCA] and the development of electronic commerce and associated technology on the operation of sections 109 and 117 of title17, United States Code; and the relationship between existing and emergent technology and the operation of sections 109 and 117. . . ." Specifically, this Report focuses on three proposals that were put forward during our consultations with the public: creation of a "digital first sale doctrine;" creation of an exemption for the making of certain temporary incidental copies; and the expansion of the archival copying exemption for computer programs in section 117 of the Act.

Part I of this Report describes the circumstances leading up to the enactment of the DMCA and the genesis of this study. Part I also examines the historical basis of sections 109 and

v

117 of the Act. Part II discusses the wide range of views expressed in the public comments and testimony. This input from the public, academia, libraries, copyright organizations and copyright owners formed the core information considered by the Office in its evaluation and recommendations. Part III evaluates the effect of title I of the DMCA and the development of electronic commerce and associated technology on the operations of sections 109 and 117 in light of the information received and states our conclusions and recommendations regarding the advisability of statutory change.

I.   BACKGROUND

A. THE DIGITAL MILLENNIUM COPYRIGHT ACT

The World Intellectual Property Organization (WIPO) treaties were the impetus for the U.S. legislation. In order to facilitate the development of electronic commerce in the digital age, Congress implemented the WIPO treaties by enacting legislation to address those treaty obligations that were not adequately addressed under existing U.S. law. Legal prohibitions against circumvention of technological protection measures employed by copyright owners to protect their works, and against the removal or alteration of copyright management information, were required in order to implement U.S. treaty obligations.

The congressional determination to promote electronic commerce and the distribution of digital works by providing copyright owners with legal tools to prevent widespread piracy was tempered with concern for maintaining the integrity of the statutory limitations on the exclusive

vi

rights of copyright owners. In addition to the provisions adopted by Congress in 1998, there were other proposals – including amendments to sections 109 and 117, that were not adopted, but were the subjects of a number of studies mandated by the DMCA. Section 104 of the DMCA requires the Register of Copyrights and the Assistant Secretary for Communications and Information to report on the effects of the DMCA on the operation of sections 109 and 117 and the relationship between existing and emergent technology on the operation of sections 109 and 117 of title 17 of the United States Code.

The inclusion of section 109 in the study has a clear relationship to the digital first sale proposal contained in a bill introduced in 1997 by Congressmen Rick Boucher and Tom Campbell. The reasons for including section 117 in the study are less obvious. While there is no legislative history explaining why section 117 is included in the study, it appears that the reference was intended to include within the scope of the study a proposed exemption for incidental copies found in the Boucher-Campbell bill, which would have been codified in section 117 of the Copyright Act.

B. SECTION 109(a) AND THE FIRST SALE DOCTRINE

The common-law roots of the first sale doctrine allowed the owner of a particular copy of a work to dispose of that copy. This judicial doctrine was grounded in the common-law principle that restraints on the alienation of tangible property are to be avoided in the absence of clear congressional intent to abrogate this principle. This doctrine appears in section 109 of the Copyright Act of 1976. Section 109(a) specified that this notwithstanding a copyright owner's exclusive distribution right under section 106 the owner of a particular copy or phonorecord that was lawfully made under title 17 is entitled to sell or further dispose of the possession of that copy or phonorecord.

C. Section 117 Computer Program Exemptions

Section 117 of the Copyright Act of 1976 was enacted in the Computer Software Copyright Amendments of 1980 in response to the recommendations of the National Commission on New Technological Uses of Copyrighted Works' (CONTU). Section 117 permits the owner of a copy of a computer program to make an additional copy of the program for purely archival purposes if all archival copies are destroyed in the event that continued possession of the computer program should cease to be rightful, or where the making of such a copy is an essential step in the utilization of the computer program in conjunction with a machine and that it is used in no other manner.

II.   VIEWS OF THE PUBLIC

Section II of the report summarizes the views received from the public through comments, reply comments and hearing testimony. The summaries are grouped into three categories: views concerning section 109, views concerning section 117, and views on other miscellaneous issues.

viii

A. VIEWS CONCERNING SECTION 109

Most of the comments dealt with section 109 whether of not they addressed section 117. While there was a broad range of views on the effect of the DMCA on the first sale doctrine, most of the commenters believed that the anticircumvention provisions of 17 U.S.C. section 1201 allowed copyright owners to restrict the operation of section 109. Of particular concern to many commenters was the Content Scrambling System (CSS) and the "region coding" used to protect motion pictures on Digital Versatile Disks (DVDs). They argued that use of CSS forces a consumer to make two purchases in order to view a motion picture on DVD: the DVD and the authorized decryption device. In the view of these commenters, this system reduces or eliminates the value of and market for DVDs by interfering with their free alienability on the market. A similar argument was advanced for the region coding on DVDs in that the geographic market for resale is restricted by this technological protection measure.

Another concern expressed by a number of commenters was the growing use of non-negotiable licenses accompanying copyrighted works that are written to restrict or eliminate statutorily permitted uses, including uses permitted under section 109. In some cases, these license restrictions are enforced through technological measures. It was argued that these licensing practices and the prohibition on circumvention frustrate the goals of the first sale doctrine by allowing copyright owners to maintain control on works beyond the first sale of a particular copy. These commenters stated that this interference with the operation of the first sale doctrine has the capacity to inhibit the function of traditional library operations, such as interlibrary loan, preservation, and use of donated copies of works.

Other commenters rebutted these claims, arguing that over-restrictive technological protection measures or licenses would not survive in the marketplace, since competition would be a limiting principle. It was also argued that the effect of licensing terms on the first sale doctrine is beyond the scope of this study.

Commenters generally viewed section 1202 of the DMCA, which prohibits the alteration or removal of copyright management information, as having no impact of the operation of the first sale doctrine.

The greatest area of contention in the comments was the question of whether to expand the first sale doctrine to permit digital transmission of lawfully made copies of works. Although some proponents argued that such transmissions are already permitted by the current language of section 109, most thought that clarification of this conclusion by Congress would be advisable since the absence of express statutory language could lead to uncertainty.

The proponents of revising section 109 argued that the transmission of a work that was subsequently deleted from the sender's computer is the digital equivalent of giving, lending, or selling a book. Allowing consumers to transfer the copy of the work efficiently by means of

X

online transmission would foster the principles of the first sale doctrine. These principles have promoted economic growth and creativity in the analog world and should be extended to the digital environment. Proponents of this argument sought amendment to section 109 to allow a person to forward a work over the Internet and then delete that work from his computer.

Others opposed such an amendment for a number of reasons. Opponents pointed out that the first sale doctrine is a limitation on the distribution right of copyright owners and has never implicated the reproduction right which is, in their view, a "cornerstone" of copyright protection. In addition, the impact of the doctrine on copyright owners was also limited in the off-line world by a number of factors, including geography and the gradual degradation of books and analog works. The absence of such limitations would have an adverse effect on the market for digital works. Opponents also believed that proposals that depend on the user deleting his copy would be unverifiable, leading to virtually undetectable cheating. Given the expanding market for digital works without a digital first sale doctrine, opponents questioned the consumer demand for such a change in the law.

B. VIEWS CONCERNING SECTION 117

The comments related to section 117 fell into two main categories: those addressing the status of temporary copies in RAM and those concerning the scope of the archival exemption.

xi

Many commenters advocated a blanket exemption for temporary copies that are incidental to the operation of a device in the course of use of a work when that use is lawful under title 17. Such an exemption was originally proposed in the Boucher-Campbell bill as an amendment to section 117.

Other commenters vigorously opposed any exemption for incidental copies at this time. They argued that such an exemption would dramatically expand the scope of section 117 in contrast to the carefully calibrated adjustment made to section 117 in the DMCA to address the problems experienced by independent computer service organizations at issue in *MAI Systems Corp. v. Peak Computer, Inc.* These commenters stated that Congress' narrow adjustment to section 117 in the DMCA reaffirmed the conclusion that temporary copies in random access memory (RAM) are copies that are subject to the copyright owner's exclusive reproduction right. Further change would undercut the reproduction right in all works and endanger international treaty obligations.

There was disagreement on the economic value of temporary copies. Proponents of an amendment argued that temporary buffer copies are necessary to carry out streaming of performances of works on the Internet and have no value apart from that performance. They argued that the limitations under other sections of the Copyright Act, including sections 107 and 512, were insufficient to sustain the operation of businesses that stream audio performances to the public.

xii

Opponents, on the other hand, argued that these copies are within the scope of the copyright owner's exclusive rights and do possess value. Particular emphasis was placed on the value of temporary copies of computer programs. It was also argued that as streaming performances become more common, these temporary copies will increase in value because of the adverse effect of the performances on the market for purchases of copies of these works. Opponents believed it would be premature to change the law because of the absence of specific evidence of harm and the high potential for adverse unintended consequences. It was noted that when Congress was presented with concrete evidence of harm to independent service organizations after the *MAI v. Peak* decision, Congress took steps to remedy the situation. Similarly, section 512 of the DMCA created limitations on the remedies available against Internet service providers for incidental copying that is essential to the operation of the Internet.

The other major concern involving section 117 concerned the scope of the archival exemption. Proponents of amending section 117 raised two primary points. First, they argued that the policy behind the archival exemption needs to be updated to encompass all digital works rather than just computer programs. Since computers are vulnerable to crashes, viruses, and other failures, downloaded music, electronic books and other works face the same risks that precipitated the exemption for computer programs. Some argued that all digital media is susceptible to accidental deletion or corruption. Consumers should be permitted to protect their investments in works.

xiii

Proponents of expansion of the archival exemption offered another argument – section 117 does not comport with reality. Systematic backup practices do not fit the structure of section 117, which is limited to making a copy of an individual program at the time the consumer obtains it. It was argued that such a discrepancy between the law and commonly accepted practices undermines the integrity of the law. Such a fundamental mismatch creates the perception that the law need not be literally followed, thereby creating a slippery slope.

Opponents of an expansion of the archival exemption countered that the justification behind section 117 no longer exists. Most software is distributed on CD-ROM, which is far more robust than floppy disks. Consumers need merely retain the original CD as a backup, since it is a simple operation to reinstall software that is compromised. In addition, these opponents argued that there is currently an inaccurate public perception of the scope of the backup copy exception. These commenters argue that many invoke the archival exception as a shield to commercial piracy.

Opponents of an amendment to section 117 asserted that even if there is a mismatch between actual backup practices and the current exception, no one has been harmed by it. Commenters noted that no one has been sued as a result of backing up material outside the scope of section 117, and no one has stopped performing backups. It was also argued that if a particular activity does not fall within the terms of section 117, it may nevertheless be privileged under the fair use doctrine.

xiv

C. VIEWS CONCERNING OTHER MISCELLANEOUS ISSUES

There were assorted other comments and testimony on a range of issues. There were concerns raised about the potential adverse effects of sections 1201 and 1202 on the traditional concepts of first sale, fair use, and the archival and preservation exemptions. It was argued that these prohibitions are likely to diminish, if not eliminate, otherwise lawful uses. It was asserted that copyright management information may also have the capacity to reveal user information in a manner that would chill legitimate uses of copyrighted works.

Another prevalent concern was that licenses are being used increasingly by copyright owners to undermine the first sale doctrine and restrict other user privileges under the copyright law. These commenters argue that this trend is displacing the uniformity of federal copyright law with a wide variation of contract terms that must be evaluated and interpreted. This poses a particular challenge to large institutions, such as universities and libraries, in determining legal and acceptable use in any given work. A number of commenters argued that federal copyright law should preempt such license terms.

Other commenters argued that Congress did not intend copyright law broadly to preempt contract provisions. They argue that the freedom to contract serves the interests on both copyright owners and the public by allowing greater flexibility in determining pricing, terms and conditions of use, and other options.

xv

III. EVALUATION AND RECOMMENDATIONS

We are not persuaded that title I of the DMCA has had a significant effect on the operation of sections 109 and 117 of title 17. The adverse effects that section 1201, for example, is alleged to have had on these sections cannot accurately be ascribed to section 1201. The causal relationship between the problems identified and section 1201 are currently either minimal or easily attributable to other factors such as the increasing use of license terms. Accordingly, none of our legislative recommendations are based on the effects of section 1201 on the operation of sections 109 and 117.

A. THE EFFECT OF TITLE I OF THE DMCA ON THE OPERATION OF SECTIONS 109 AND 117

The arguments raised concerning the adverse effects of the CSS technological protection measure on the operation of section 109 are flawed. The first sale doctrine is primarily a limitation on copyright owner's distribution right. Section 109 does not guarantee the existence of secondary markets for works. There are many factors which could affect the resale market for works, none of which could be said to interfere with the operation of section 109. The need for a particular device on which to view the work is not a novel concept and does not constitute an effect on section 109. VHS videocassettes for example, must be played on VHS VCRs.

A plausible argument can be made that section 1201 may have a negative effect on the operation of the first sale doctrine in the context of works tethered to a particular device. In the case of tethered works, even if the work is on removable media, the content cannot be accessed

xvi

on any device other than the one on which it was originally made. This process effectively prevents disposition of the work. However, the practice of tethering a copy of a work to a particular hardware device does not appear to be widespread at this time, at least outside the context of electronic books. Given the relative infancy of digital rights management, it is premature to consider any legislative change at this time. Should this practice become widespread, it could have serious consequences for the operation of the first sale doctrine, although the ultimate effect on consumers is unclear.

We also find that the use of technological measures that prevent the copying of a work potentially could have a negative effect on the operation of section 117. To the extent that a technological measure prohibits access to a copyrighted work, the prohibition on the circumvention of measures that protect access in section 1201(a)(1) may have an adverse impact on the operation of the archival exception in section 117. Again, however, the current impact of such a concern appears to be minimal, since licenses generally define the scope of permissible archiving of software, and the use of CD-ROM reduces the need to make backup copies.

Given the minimal adverse impact at the present time, we conclude that no legislative change is warranted to mitigate any effect of section 1201 on section 117.

xvii

B. The Effect of Electronic Commerce and Technological Change on Sections 109 and 117

There is no dispute that section 109 applies to works in digital form. Physical copies of works in a digital format, such as CDs or DVDs, are subject to section 109 in the same way as physical copies in analog form. Similarly, a lawfully made tangible copy of a digitally downloaded work, such as a work downloaded to a floppy disk, Zip™ disk, or CD-RW, is clearly subject to section 109. The question we address here is whether the transmission of a work to another person falls within – or should fall within – the scope of section 109.

1. *The First Sale Doctrine in the Digital World*

a. Evaluation of Arguments Concerning First Sale

The first sale doctrine is primarily a limitation on the copyright owner's exclusive right of distribution. It does not limit the exclusive right of reproduction. While disposition of a work downloaded to a floppy disk would only implicate the distribution right, the transmission of a work from one person to another over the Internet results in a reproduction on the recipient's computer, even if the sender subsequently deletes the original copy of the work. This activity therefore entails an exercise of an exclusive right that is not covered by section 109.

Proponents of expansion of the scope of section 109 to include the transmission and deletion of a digital file argue that this activity is essentially identical to the transfer of a physical copy and that the similarities outweigh the differences. While it is true that there are similarities, we find the analogy to the physical world to be flawed and unconvincing.

xviii

Physical copies degrade with time and use; digital information does not. Works in digital format can be reproduced flawlessly, and disseminated to nearly any point on the globe instantly and at negligible cost. Digital transmissions can adversely effect the market for the original to a much greater degree than transfers of physical copies. Additionally, unless a "forward-and-delete" technology is employed to automatically delete the sender's copy, the deletion of a work requires an additional affirmative act on the part of the sender subsequent to the transmission. This act is difficult to prove or disprove, as is a person's claim to have transmitted only a single copy, thereby raising complex evidentiary concerns. There were conflicting views on whether effective forward and delete technologies exist today. Even if they do, it is not clear that the market will bear the cost of an expensive technological measure.

The underlying policy of the first sale doctrine as adopted by the courts was to give effect to the common law rule against restraints on the alienation of tangible property. The tangible nature of a copy is a defining element of the first sale doctrine and critical to its rationale. The digital transmission of a work does not implicate the alienability of a physical artifact. When a work is transmitted, the sender is exercising control over the intangible work through its reproduction rather than common law dominion over an item of tangible personal property. Unlike the physical distribution of digital works on a tangible medium, such as a floppy disk, the transmission of works interferes with the copyright owner's control over the intangible work and the exclusive right of reproduction. The benefits to further expansion simply do not outweigh the likelihood of increased harm.

xix

507

Digital communications technology enables authors and publishers to develop new business models, with a more flexible array of products that can be tailored and priced to meet the needs of different consumers. We are concerned that these proposals for a digital first sale doctrine endeavor to fit the exploitation of works online into a distribution model – the sale of copies – that was developed within the confines of pre-digital technology. If the sale model is to continue as the dominant method of distribution, it should be the choice of the market, not due to legislative fiat.

We also examined how other countries are addressing the applicability of the first sale – or exhaustion – doctrine to digital transmissions. We found that other countries are addressing digital transmissions under the communication to the public right and are not applying the principle of exhaustion, or any other analog thereof, to digital transmissions.

b. Recommendation Concerning the Digital First Sale Doctrine

We recommend no change to section 109 at this time. Although speculative concerns have been raised, there was no convincing evidence of present-day problems. In order to recommend a change in the law, there should be a demonstrated need for the change that outweighs the negative aspects of the proposal. The Copyright Office does not believe that this is the case with the proposal to expand the scope of section 109 to include digital transmissions. The time may come when Congress may wish to address these concerns should they materialize.

xx

The fact that we do not recommend adopting a "digital first sale" provision at this time does not mean that the issues raised by libraries are not potentially valid concerns. Similarly, our conclusion that certain issues are beyond the scope of the present study does not reflect our judgment on the merits of those issues.

The library community has raised concerns about how the current marketing of works in digital form affects libraries with regard to five specifically enumerated categories: interlibrary loans, off-site accessibility, archiving/preservation, availability of works, and use of donated copies. Most of these issues arise from terms and conditions of use, and costs of license agreements. One arises because, when the library has only online access to the work, it lacks a physical copy of the copyrighted work that can be transferred. These issues arise from existing business models and are therefore subject to market forces. We are in the early stages of electronic commerce. We hope and expect that the marketplace will respond to the various concerns of customers in the library community. However, these issues may require further consideration at some point in the future. Libraries serve a vital function in society, and we will continue to work with the library and publishing communities on ways to ensure the continuation of library functions that are critical to our national interest.

2. *The Legal Status of Temporary Copies*

a. RAM Reproductions as "Copies" under the Copyright Act

All of the familiar activities that one performs on a computer, from the execution of a computer program to browsing the World Wide Web, necessarily involve copies stored in

xxi

integrated circuits known as RAM. This information can remain in memory until the power is switched off or the information is overwritten. These reproductions generally persist only for as long as the particular activity takes place.

The legal status of RAM reproductions has arisen in this study almost exclusively in the context of streaming audio delivery, including webcasting. In order to render the packets of audio information in an audio "stream" smoothly, in spite of inconsistencies in the rate of delivery, packets of audio information are saved in a portion of RAM called a buffer until they are ready to be rendered.

Based on an the text of the Copyright Act – including the definition of "copies" in section 101 – and its legislative history, we conclude that the making of temporary copies of a work in RAM implicates the reproduction right so long as the reproduction persists long enough to be perceived, copied, or communicated.

Every court that has addressed the issue of reproductions in RAM has expressly or impliedly found such reproductions to be copies within the scope of the reproduction right. The seminal case on this subject, *MAI, Sys. Corp. v. Peak Computer, Inc.*, found that the loading of copyrighted software into RAM creates a "copy" of that software. At least nine other courts have followed *MAI v. Peak* in holding RAM reproductions to be "copies" and several other cases have

xxii

held that loading a computer program into a computer entails making a copy, without mentioning RAM specifically.

b. Evaluation of Arguments Concerning Temporary Incidental Copy Exceptions

In the course of this study, arguments were advanced in support of a blanket exemption for incidental copies similar to that proposed in the Boucher-Campbell bill. Most of the arguments advanced on such a proposal focused exclusively on the specific issue of buffer copies made in the course of audio streaming, rather than the broader issue of incidental copying generally. This focus suggests that legislation tailored to address the specific problems raised in the context of audio streaming should be examined. This focus is particularly appropriate since there was no compelling evidence presented in support of a blanket exemption for incidental copies and there was evidence that such an exemption could lead to unintended adverse consequences for copyright owners.

There was compelling evidence presented, however, on the uncertainty surrounding temporary buffer copies made in RAM in the course of rendering a digital musical stream. Specifically, webcasters asserted that the unknown legal status of buffer copies exposes webcasters to demands for additional royalty payments from the owner of the sound recording, as well as potential infringement liability.

xxiii

The buffer copies identified by the webcasting industry exist for only a short period of time and consist of small portions of the work. Webcasters argue that these reproductions are incidental to the licensed performance of the work and should not be subject to an additional license for a reproduction that is only a means to an authorized end. Buffer copies implicate the reproduction right, thus potentially resulting in liability. There is, therefore, a legitimate concern on the part of webcasters and other streaming music services as to their potential liability.

We believe that there is a strong case that the making of a buffer copy in the course of streaming is a fair use. Fair use is a defense that may limit any of the copyright owner's exclusive rights, including the reproduction right implicated in temporary copies. In order to assess whether a particular use of the works at issue is a fair use, section 107 requires the consideration and balancing of four mandatory, but nonexclusive, factors on a case-by-case basis.

In examining the first factor – the purpose and character of the use – it appears that the making of buffer copies is commercial and not transformative. However, the use does not supersede or supplant the market for the original works. Buffer copies are a means to a noninfringing and socially beneficial end – the licensed performance of these works. There is no commercial exploitation intended or made of the buffer copy in itself. The first factor weighs in favor of fair use.

The second factor – the nature of the copyrighted work – weighs against a finding of fair use because musical works are generally creative. The third factor – the amount and

xxiv

512

substantiality of the portion used in relation to the copyrighted work as a whole – would also be likely to weigh against fair use since, in aggregate, an entire musical work is copied in the RAM buffer. Since this is necessary in order to carry out a licensed performance of the work, however, the factor should be of little weight.

In analyzing the fourth factor – the effect of the use on the actual or potential market for the work – the effect appears to be minimal or nonexistent. This factor strongly weighs in favor of fair use.

Two of the four statutory factors weigh in favor of fair use, but fair use is also an "equitable rule of reason." In the case of temporary buffer copies, we believe that the equities unquestionably favor the user. The sole purpose for making the buffer copies is to permit an activity that is licensed by the copyright owner and for which the copyright owner receives a performance royalty. In essence, copyright owners appear to be seeking to be paid twice for the same activity. Additionally, it is technologically necessary to make buffer copies in order to carry out a digital performance of music over the Internet. Finally, the buffer copies exist for too short a period of time to be exploited in any way other than as a narrowly tailored means to enable the authorized performance of the work. On balance, therefore, the equities weigh heavily in favor of fair use.

xxv

c. Recommendation Concerning Temporary Incidental Copies

Representatives of the webcasting industry expressed concern that the case-by-case fair use defense is too uncertain a basis for making rational business decisions. We agree. While we recommend against the adoption of a general exemption from the reproduction right to render noninfringing all temporary copies that are incidental to lawful uses, a more carefully tailored approach is desirable.

We recommend that Congress enact legislation amending the Copyright Act to preclude any liability arising from the assertion of a copyright owner's reproduction right with respect to temporary buffer copies that are incidental to a licensed digital transmission of a public performance of a sound recording and any underlying musical work.

The economic value of licensed streaming is in the public performances of the musical work and the sound recording, both of which are paid for. The buffer copies have no independent economic significance. They are made solely to enable the performance of these works. The uncertainty of the present law potentially allows those who administer the reproduction right in musical works to prevent webcasting from taking place – to the detriment of other copyright owners, webcasters and consumers alike – or to extract an additional payment that is not justified by the economic value of the copies at issue. Congressional action is desirable to remove the uncertainty and to allow the activity that Congress sought to encourage through the adoption of the section 114 webcasting compulsory license to take place.

xxvi

Although we believe that the fair use defense probably does apply to temporary buffer copies, this approach is fraught with uncertain application in the courts. This uncertainty, coupled with the apparent willingness of some copyright owners to assert claims based on the making of buffer copies, argues for statutory change. We believe that the narrowly tailored scope of our recommendation will minimize, if not eliminate, concerns expressed by copyright owners about potential unanticipated consequences.

Given our recommendations concerning temporary copies that are incidental to digital performances of sound recordings and musical works, fairness requires that we acknowledge the symmetrical difficulty that is faced in the online music industry: digital performances that are incidental to digital music downloads. Just as webcasters appear to be facing demands for royalty payments for incidental exercise of the reproduction right in the course of licensed public performances, it appears that companies that sell licensed digital downloads of music are facing demands for public performance royalties for a technical "performance" of the underlying musical work that allegedly occurs in the course of transmitting it from the vendor's server to the consumer's computer.

Although we recognize that it is an unsettled point of law that is subject to debate, we do not endorse the proposition that a digital download constitutes a public performance even when no contemporaneous performance takes place. If a court were to find that such a download can be considered a public performance within the language of the Copyright Act, we believe the that arguments concerning fair use and the making of buffer copies are applicable to this performance

xxvii

issue as well. It is our view that no liability should result from a technical "performance" that takes place in the course of a download.

3. *Archival Exemption*

a. Evaluation of Arguments Concerning the Scope of Section 117(a)(2)

Currently the archival exemption under section 117(a)(2) is limited to computer programs. This section allows the owner of a copy of a computer program to make or authorize the making of an additional copy of the program "for archival purposes," provided that "all archival copies are destroyed in the event that continued possession of the computer program should cease to be rightful." A number of arguments were advanced in the course of this study for an expansion of this archival exemption in order to cover the kind of routine backups that are performed on computers and to allow consumers to archive material in digital format other than computer programs.

Commenters asserted that consumers need to backup works in digital form because they are vulnerable. That was CONTU's rationale for recommending that Congress create an exemption to permit archival copies of computer programs. In both cases, the vulnerability stems from the digital nature of the works. It would be perfectly consistent with the rationale of CONTU's recommendations and Congress' enactment of section 117 to extend the archival exemption to protect against the vulnerabilities that may afflict all works in digital format.

xxviii

Evidence was presented to us noting that the archival exemption under section 117 does not permit the prevailing practices and procedures most people and businesses follow for backing up data on a computer hard drive. There is a fundamental mismatch between accepted, prudent practices among most system administrators and other users, on the one hand, and section 117 on the other. As a consequence, few adhere to the law.

While there is no question that this mismatch exists, nobody was able to identify any actual harm to consumers as a result of the limited scope of the archival exemption. Additionally, it was argued that the need to make archival copies of computer programs has diminished, because almost all software sold in the United States is distributed on CD-ROM, which itself serves as an archival copy in the event of hard drive problems or upgrades.

b. Recommendations Concerning the Archival Exemption

Although there has been a complete absence of any demonstrated harm to the prospective beneficiaries of an expanded archival exemption, and although we believe that a strong case could be made that most common archival activities by computer users would qualify as fair use, we have identified a potential concern – the interplay between sections 107 and 109. It appears that the language of the Copyright Act could lead a court to conclude that copies lawfully made under the fair use doctrine may be freely distributed under section 109.

Section 109 permits "the owner of a particular copy or phonorecord lawfully made" under title 17 to distribute that copy without the copyright owner's permission. To the extent that

xxix

section 107 permits a user to make a backup copy of a work stored on a hard drive, that copy is lawfully made and the user owns it. Section 109, on its face, appears to permit the user to sell or otherwise dispose of the possession of that backup copy. The legislative history can be read to support either view.

We conclude that a statutory change is desirable, and recommend that Congress amend the copyright law in one of two ways.

Given the uncertain state of authority on the issue, we cannot conclude with a satisfactory level of certainty that a court will not, in the future, find a backup copy made by virtue of section 107 to be eligible for distribution under section 109. We believe that such a result is contrary to the intent of Congress and would have the capacity to do serious damage to the copyright owner's market. We therefore recommend that Congress either (1) amend section 109 to ensure that fair use copies are not subject to the first sale doctrine or (2) create a new archival exemption that provides expressly that backup copies may not be distributed. We express no preference as between the two options, and note that they are not mutually exclusive.

The first option would entail amending section 109(a) to state that only copies lawfully made *and lawfully distributed* are subject to the first sale doctrine. This proposed change would not preclude the distribution of copies made pursuant to the fair use doctrine since the exclusive right of distribution is equally subject to the fair use doctrine. It would, however, require that a separate fair use analysis be applied to the distribution of that copy.

xxx

The second option entails creating a new exemption for making backups of lawful copies of material in digital form, and amending section 117 to delete references to archival copies. The new exemption should follow the general contours of section 117(a)(2) and (b), and include the following elements: it should permit the making of one or more backup copies of a work. The copy from which the backup copies are made must be in digital form on a medium that is subject to accidental erasure, damage, or destruction in the ordinary course of its use. It should stipulate that the copies may be made and used solely for archival purposes or for use in lieu of the original copy. It should also specify that, notwithstanding the provisions of section 109, the archival copy may not be transferred except as part of a lawful transfer of all rights in the work. Finally, it should specify that the archival copies may not be used in any manner in the event that continued possession of the work ceases to be rightful.

4. *Contract Preemption*

The question of contract preemption was raised by a number commenters who argued that the Copyright Act should be amended to insure that contract provisions that override consumer privileges in the copyright law, or are otherwise unreasonable, are not enforceable. Although the general issue of contract preemption is outside the scope of this Report, we do note that this issue is complex and of increasing practical importance, and thus legislative action appears to be premature. On the one hand, copyright law has long coexisted with contract law. On the other hand, the movement at the state level toward resolving questions as to the enforceability of non-negotiated contracts coupled with legally-protected technological measures that give right holders the technological capability of imposing contractual provisions unilaterally, increases the

xxxi

possibility that right holders, rather than Congress, will determine the landscape of consumer privileges in the future. Although market forces may well prevent right holders from unreasonably limiting consumer privileges, it is possible that at some point in the future a case could be made for statutory change.

INTRODUCTION

The Digital Millennium Copyright Act of 1998 (DMCA) was the most substantial revision of the nation's copyright law since the general revision enacted in 1976. What began as a more modest (though critically important) effort to implement two new treaties that addressed issues of copyright in the digital age became a far more comprehensive legislative project to address a range of issues, digital and non-digital. The debates, both inside and outside the Congress, that were generated by this legislation led to myriad proposals – some of which were enacted and some of which were not. As Representative Howard Coble, Chairman of the House Judiciary Subcommittee on Courts and Intellectual Property and one of the bill's chief sponsors in the House, stated when he brought the measure to the floor, the DMCA "is only the beginning of Congress' evaluation of the impact of the digital age on copyrighted works."[1]

The DMCA directed the Register of Copyrights to prepare this Report as part of Congress' continuing evaluation of the impact of the digital age on copyrighted works. It is the fourth such undertaking mandated by Congress in the DMCA. In 1999, the Copyright Office released a report on digital distance education, which included recommendations that are embodied in S. 487 in this Congress.[2] In 2000, the Copyright Office and the National Telecommunications and Information Administration of the Department of Commerce (NTIA) released a joint report on the effect of the prohibition on circumventing access control

---

[1] 144 Cong. Rec. H7092 (daily ed. Aug. 4, 1998) (statement of Rep. Coble).

[2] Copyright Office, Copyright Office Report on Copyright and Digital Distance Education (1999). The results of this study were presented to Congress on May 25, 1999 and are available at: www.loc.gov/copyright/docs/de_rprt.pdf. The text of S.487 is available at: thomas.loc.gov/cgi-bin/query/z?c107:S.487:.

1

technologies in section 1201(a)(1)(A) of title 17, and an exception to that prohibition in section 1201(g), on encryption research.[3] Also in 2000, the Office completed a rulemaking required under section 1201(a)(1)(C) concerning an exemption from the section 1201(a)(1)(A) prohibition for noninfringing uses with respect to certain classes of works.

The focus of this Report is an evaluation of "the effects of the amendments made by [title I of the DMCA] and the development of electronic commerce and associated technology on the operation of sections 109 and 117 of title 17, United States Code; and the relationship between existing and emergent technology and the operation of sections 109 and 117 . . . ."[4] It is an outgrowth of proposals that were made contemporaneously with the consideration of the DMCA, but were not adopted in the law. Specifically, this Report focuses on two proposals that were characterized as vital to the continued growth of electronic commerce by their proponents: creation of a digital first sale doctrine to permit certain retransmissions of downloaded copies of works in digital form; and an exemption for certain digital reproductions that are incidental to the use of a copyrighted work in conjunction with a machine. One additional issue that was raised during the preparation of the Report, and appears to fall within the scope set forth by Congress in section 104 of the DMCA, is the appropriate breadth and formulation of the exception for making archival copies of computer programs in section 117.

---

[3] The results of that joint Copyright Office and NTIA study were presented to Congress in May 2000 and are available at: www.loc.gov/copyright/reports/studies/dmca_report.html.

[4] DMCA, Pub. L. No. 105-304, § 104(a), 112 Stat. 2860, 2876 (1998).

2

The DMCA contemplated that, like the report on encryption research, the present effort would be a joint report of the Copyright Office and NTIA. In March 2001, however, NTIA released its own report. This Report, consequently, is exclusively the work of the Copyright Office. All of the views expressed and the recommendations made are, necessarily, solely those of the Register of Copyrights.

3

4

I. BACKGROUND

A. THE DIGITAL MILLENNIUM COPYRIGHT ACT

The DMCA was "designed to facilitate the robust development and world-wide expansion of electronic commerce, communications, research, development, and education in the digital age."[5] The DMCA grew out of legislation introduced to implement the provisions of two treaties concluded in Geneva, Switzerland in December 1996. These two treaties – which are sometimes referred to as the "Internet Treaties" – updated international copyright norms to account for the advent of digital networks. Title I of the DMCA implements the treaties, "thereby bringing the U.S. copyright law squarely into the digital age and setting a marker for other nations who must also implement these treaties."[6] Congress crafted title I to "protect property rights in the digital world."[7]

1. The WIPO Treaties

On December 20, 1996, at the conclusion of a three-week Diplomatic Conference held in Geneva, Switzerland, headquarters of the World Intellectual Property Organization (WIPO), delegations from 127 countries and the European Commission agreed on the text of two new treaties on copyright and neighboring rights: the WIPO Copyright Treaty (WCT) and the WIPO

---

[5] S. Rep. No. 105-190, at 1-2 (1998).

[6] *Id.* at 2.

[7] Staff of House Committee on the Judiciary, 105th Cong., Section-by-Section Analysis of H.R. 2281 as Passed by the United States House of Representatives on August 4, 1998, at 2 (Comm. Print 1998) (Serial No. 6) (hereinafter House Manager's Statement). As the Senate Judiciary Committee noted, "[due to the ease with which digital works can be copied and distributed worldwide virtually instantaneously, copyright owners will hesitate to make their works readily available on the Internet without reasonable assurance that they will be protected against massive piracy. Legislation implementing the treaties provides this protection and creates the legal platform for launching the global digital on-line marketplace for copyrighted works." S. Rep. No. 105-190, at 8 (1998).

5

Performances and Phonograms Treaty (WPPT). The Diplomatic Conference was the culmination of a process that began formally in 1991 when a "Committee of Experts" was convened at WIPO to discuss a possible protocol to the Berne Convention for the Protection of Literary and Artistic Works (Berne)[8].

Berne is the principal multilateral agreement for protecting copyrights internationally. Berne establishes minimum levels of protection that all member countries must grant to authors, and requires member countries to grant national treatment to authors from other member countries. The last general revision of Berne took place in 1971. Technological and legal developments during the intervening two decades made updating Berne an imperative in the international copyright community.

In addition, the United States sought to introduce the subject of improved protection for sound recordings into the early Berne Protocol discussions. Rather than incorporating the subject of protection for sound recordings in the Berne Protocol, it was placed on a parallel track that had as its goal the creation of a separate "new instrument" for the protection of performers and producers — reflecting the civil law tradition of protecting performers and producers of sound recordings under the separate rubric of neighboring rights (or related rights, as they are sometimes called), rather than copyright.

---

[8] Berne Convention for the Protection of Literary and Artistic Works (Paris Act 1971).

6

In 1993, at the urging of the United States, the Committees of Experts on the Berne Protocol and the New Instrument began considering the possible need for new international norms to address the effects on copyright owners of digital technologies and the rapid growth of digital networks.[9] The emergence and widespread use of these technologies exposed copyright owners to substantial risks of massive global piracy, while at the same time holding out the promise of new markets, new distribution channels and new means of licensing copyrighted works. In addition, digital technology created greater possibilities to use technological means to foil would-be infringers.

A central component of the "digital agenda" in the Berne Protocol and New Instrument discussions was to include in any new treaty a measure against the circumvention of technological measures employed by right holders to protect their rights. By 1993 it was widely recognized that, while use of technological measures to protect works was likely to become a critical element in a digital network environment, those measures were vulnerable to tampering. Widespread availability and use of devices or software for circumventing technological measures would imperil the right holder's reproduction right and, ultimately, could serve to dissuade right holders from making their works available in digital form.

Proposals up to and including the documents prepared for the 1996 Diplomatic Conference focused on prohibiting the making and selling of devices, or provision of services,

---

[9] *E.g.*, WIPO, Questions Concerning a Possible Protocol to the Berne Convention — Part III, New Items, WIPO Doc. No. BCP/CE/III/2-III at ¶¶74-75 (March 12, 1993).

7

for the purpose of circumvention. The obligation adopted by the Diplomatic Conference and set forth in Article 11 of the WCT and Article 18 of the WPPT is somewhat less precise. Rather than specifying the particular means of achieving the desired result — the prevention of circumvention of technological protection measures — the treaties require Contracting Parties to put in place adequate and effective legal measures for achieving that result.[10] Contracting Parties are afforded a degree of flexibility in determining precisely how to implement this obligation within their respective legal systems, provided that the implementation is adequate and effective against circumvention.

2. Implementation of the WIPO Treaties in the DMCA

The Administration proposed and Congress adopted a minimalist approach in implementing the WCT and the WPPT in U.S. law.[11] In this context, "minimalist" was understood to mean that any provision of the treaty that was already implemented in U.S. law would not be addressed in new legislation. As to treaty obligations that were not adequately

---

[10] Article 11 of the WCT states:

Contracting Parties shall provide adequate legal protection and effective legal remedies against the circumvention of effective technological measures that are used by authors in connection with the exercise of their rights under this Treaty or the Berne Convention and that restrict acts, in respect of their works, which are not authorized by the authors concerned or permitted by law.

Article 18 of the WPPT states:

Contracting Parties shall provide adequate legal protection and effective legal remedies against the circumvention of effective technological measures that are used by performers or producers of phonograms in connection with the exercise of their rights under this Treaty and that restrict acts, in respect of their performances or phonograms, which are not authorized by the performers or the producers of phonograms concerned or permitted by law.

[11] The U.S. took the same approach in implementing the Berne Convention in 1988. *See* H.R. Rep. No. 100-609, at 20 (1988).

addressed in existing U.S. law, new measures would have to be adopted in implementing

legislation in order to satisfy these obligations.

Protection against circumvention was determined not to be adequately covered by U.S.

law. Certain specific instances of circumvention were prohibited by federal law, such as

unauthorized decryption of encrypted satellite signals and trafficking in the means to do so,[12] but

coverage was not comprehensive. To the extent that circumvention requires reproduction of the

work that is protected by a technological measure, an act of circumvention can constitute

copyright infringement. In addition, some instances of providing devices that circumvent

technological measures could constitute contributory copyright infringement, but those

circumstances would be extremely narrow — confined essentially to those instances where the

device used to circumvent has *no* substantial noninfringing uses.[13] Consequently, new legislation

was deemed necessary to implement the anticircumvention obligation in Article 11 of the WCT

and Article 18 of the WPPT.[14]

a. *Section 1201 - Anticircumvention*

A principal means of addressing the risk of infringement in the digital age was to

encourage copyright owners to help themselves by using technological measures to protect works

---

[12] 47 U.S.C. § 605.

[13] *See Sony Corp. v. Universal City Studios, Inc.*, 464 U.S. 417, 442 (1984) (manufacture of a staple article of commerce such as a copying device is not contributory infringement if it is "merely . . . capable of substantial noninfringing uses").

[14] H.R. 2281, 105th Cong., 1st Sess. (1997); S. 1146, 105th Cong., 1st Sess. (1997).

9

in digital form. Section 1201 of the DMCA reinforces those technological measures through legal sanctions against those who circumvent them. Not only does section 1201 prohibit the manufacture and distribution of devices, and the rendering of services, for the purpose of circumventing technological measures that protect against unauthorized access to works, or unauthorized exercise of the rights of the copyright owner, it also addresses the conduct of circumventing a technological measure that protects access.

It was determined early in the legislative drafting process that a prohibition on the *devices and services* that enable circumvention (the original focus of the treaty proposals) would be a critical element in treaty implementation, notwithstanding the fact that the treaty obligation was formulated broadly enough to include, potentially, national laws directed at the *act* of circumventing technological protection measures. Since the act of circumvention frequently entails copyright infringement, or is immediately followed by an act of infringement, a legal prohibition focusing exclusively on the act of circumvention would add little to existing protections under copyright, and would suffer from the same practical difficulties in enforcement.[15] Whether under copyright or under a specific prohibition on circumvention, a copyright owner's only recourse would be to detect individual violations by users of copyrighted works and bring a multitude of actions against the violators unfortunate enough to get caught. From a practical standpoint this outcome was viewed as an expensive, inefficient, and ultimately ineffective means of combating on-line infringement. By contrast, a prohibition on the

---

[15] *Cf.* S. Rep. No. 105-190, at 12 (1998) ("The copyright law has long forbidden copyright infringements, so no new prohibition [on circumvention of copy control technologies] was necessary.").

10

manufacture, import or sale of devices, or rendering of services, for the circumvention of technological measures can prevent infringement by keeping the tools that enable circumvention out of the hands of individual users.

In addition to ensuring that protection against circumvention would be adequate and effective as required by the treaties, the drafters of the implementing legislation sought to protect the countervailing interest of users in their continuing ability to engage in noninfringing uses of copyrighted works. The principal means of accomplishing this goal was to divide technological protection measures into two categories — measures that control access to a work and measures that control the exercise of exclusive rights with respect to a work— and to treat these categories differently.

Fair use and other exceptions and limitations to a copyright owner's exclusive rights are defenses to copyright infringement — that is, the unauthorized exercise of the copyright owner's exclusive rights. Technological measures that control or prevent the exercise of those exclusive rights (often referred to by the shorthand phrase "copy control measures") thus have a direct relationship to fair use and other copyright exceptions. Activity that may be permitted under these exceptions could, nonetheless, result in liability under a prohibition on circumvention that included copy control measures. For this reason, the implementing legislation proposed by the Administration did not (and the DMCA does not) prohibit the conduct of circumventing of copy control measures.

11

By contrast, fair use and other copyright exceptions are not defenses to gaining unauthorized access to a copyrighted work: Quoting a manuscript may be a fair use; breaking into a desk drawer and stealing it is not.[16] Circumventing access control measures was, therefore, prohibited in the Administration's proposed implementing legislation.

As to both types of technological measures, trafficking in circumvention tools — devices and services that enable circumvention — was prohibited under the Administration proposal if those tools meet at least one of three statutory criteria relating to the purpose for which the tool is designed, the predominant commercially significant use of the tool and the purpose for which the tool is marketed. This basic structure was retained throughout the legislative process and has been enacted into law as part of the DMCA.[17]

b. *Section 1202 - Copyright Management Information*

In addition to the anticircumvention provisions of title I, Congress also found that U.S. law did not adequately meet the requirements of the WIPO treaties that require contracting states to prohibit the removal or alteration of copyright management information (CMI).[18] As a

---

[16] *See* H.R. Rep. No. 105-551, pt. 1, at 17 (1998) ("The act of circumventing a technological protection measure put in place by a copyright owner to control access to a copyrighted work is the electronic equivalent of breaking into a locked room in order to obtain a copy of a book.") (House Judiciary Committee).

[17] 17 U.S.C. § 1201

[18] Article 12 of the WCT provides in relevant part:

Contracting Parties shall provide adequate and effective legal remedies against any person knowingly performing any of the following acts knowing, or with respect to civil remedies having reasonable grounds to know, that it will induce, enable, facilitate or conceal an infringement of any right covered by this Treaty or the Berne Convention:
(i) to remove or alter any electronic rights management information without

12

consequence, Congress enacted a new section as part of title I of the DMCA implementing the

obligation to protect the integrity of CMI.[19] The scope of protection for this section is set out in

two separate paragraphs, the first addressing false CMI[20] and the second prohibiting the removal

or alteration of CMI. Subsection (a) prohibits the knowing provision or distribution of false

CMI, if done with the intent to induce, enable, facilitate or conceal infringement. Subsection (b)

bars the intentional removal or alteration of CMI without the authority of the copyright owner, as

well as the dissemination of CMI or copies of works, knowing that the CMI has been removed or

altered without authority. These provisions of the DMCA differ from other copyright provisions

in title 17 in that they require that the act be done with knowledge or, with respect to civil

remedies, with reasonable grounds to know that it will induce, enable, facilitate or conceal an

infringement.

The implementation of these provisions to protect the integrity of CMI in U.S. law go

beyond the minimum requirements in the two WIPO treaties.[21] The law does not, however,

---

authority;
      (ii) to distribute, import for distribution, broadcast or communicate to the public, without authority, works or copies of works knowing that electronic rights management information has been removed or altered without authority.

Article 19 of the WPPT contains nearly identical language.

[19] 17 U.S.C. § 1202.

[20] Provision of false CMI is not prohibited under the WIPO treaties. A prohibition on false CMI was, however, proposed in an Administration white paper in 1995, and introduced in Congress that same year. Information Infrastructure task force, Intellectual Property and the National Information Infrastructure: The Report of the Working Group on Intellectual Property Rights 235-36 (1995); H.R. 2441, 104th Cong., 1st Sess. § 4 (1995); S. 1284, 104th Cong., 1st Sess. § 4 (1995). It appears these proposals carried over into the Administration proposal for treaty implementation and, ultimately, into the DMCA as enacted.

[21] *See supra* note 20.

13

address the liability of persons who manufacture devices or provide services and it does not

mandate the use of CMI or any particular type of CMI. It "merely protects the integrity of CMI if

a party chooses to use it in connection with a copyrighted work."[22]

c. *Origin of the Present Report*

During the legislative process leading to the enactment of the DMCA, there were

concerns raised about the adverse effects of these new protections on traditional noninfringing

uses of copyrighted works that were privileged under limitations of the exclusive rights in the

Copyright Act. In particular, concerns about the future viability of, *inter alia*, fair use and the

first sale doctrine, and about liability for temporary incidental copies, were raised by segments of

the public and Members of Congress.

One remedial method of addressing these concerns was the incorporation of a triennial

rulemaking proceeding to be conducted by the Copyright Office.[23] This rulemaking process was

created to examine whether section 1201(a)(1) has had or is likely to have any adverse effect on

noninfringing uses of copyrighted works. It was intended to operate as a recurring means of

monitoring the effect of section 1201(a)(1) on the market. Congress provided the Librarian of

Congress with the regulatory authority to exempt "particular classes of works" for which users of

copyrighted works were adversely affected in their ability to make noninfringing uses. On

---

[22] House Manager's Statement, *supra* note 7 at 20.

[23] *Id.* § 1201(a)(1)(C).

14

October 27, 2000, the results of the first rulemaking proceeding were published in the Federal Register.[24]

Another response to the concerns about the continued applicability of the first sale doctrine in section 109 of the Copyright Act and the temporary reproductions that are incidental to lawful uses of works on digital equipment was a bill proposed by Representative Rick Boucher and Representative Tom Campbell (the "Boucher-Campbell bill").[25] One of the changes suggested in this bill was a modification of section 109 to make the first sale privilege apply expressly to digital transmissions of copyrighted works.[26] Another section of the bill proposed amending section 117 of the Copyright Act to allow reproductions of digital works that were incidental to the operation of a device and that did not affect the normal exploitation of the work.[27] At that time, based on the evidence available to it, Congress did not adopt this proposal.

---

[24] 65 Fed. Reg. 64,556 (October 27, 2000). Exemption to Prohibition on Circumvention of Copyright Protection Systems for Access Control Technologies. Final rule.

[25] H.R. 3048, 105th Cong., 1st Sess. (1997).

[26]
SEC. 4. FIRST SALE.

Section 109 of title 17, United States Code, is amended by adding the following new subsection at the end thereof:

`(f) The authorization for use set forth in subsection (a) applies where the owner of a particular copy or phonorecord in a digital format lawfully made under this title, or any person authorized by such owner, performs, displays or distributes the work by means of transmission to a single recipient, if that person erases or destroys his or her copy or phonorecord at substantially the same time. The reproduction of the work, to the extent necessary for such performance, display, distribution, is not an infringement.

[27]
SEC. 6. LIMITATIONS ON EXCLUSIVE RIGHTS.

(a) TITLE- The title of section 117 of title 17, United States Code, is amended to read as follows:

15

Instead Congress chose to have the Copyright Office and NTIA jointly conduct a study. In

setting the parameters of this Report, however, the legislative history demonstrates that the scope

of the Report was not intended to comprehend the full sweep of the proposals made in the

Boucher-Campbell bill.[28]

'Sec. Limitations on exclusive rights: Computer programs and digital copies';

   (b) DIGITAL COPIES–Section 117 of title 17, United States Code, is amended by inserting
'(a)' before 'Notwithstanding' and inserting the following as a new subsection (b):

   '(b) Notwithstanding the provisions of section 106, it is not an infringement to make a copy of a
work in a digital format if such copying--

      '(1) is incidental to the operation of a device in the course of the use of a work otherwise
lawful under this title; and

      '(2) does not conflict with the normal exploitation of the work and does not unreasonably
prejudice the legitimate interests of the author.'

[28] The Boucher-Campbell bill also included proposals on the following:

- expanding fair use to include uses by analog or digital transmission in connection with teaching, research,
  and other specified activities. The proposal was not acted on;

- expanding the rights of libraries and archives to reproduce and distribute copies or phonorecords to
  authorize three copies or phonorecords to be reproduced or distributed for preservation, security, or
  replacement purposes, and to permit such copies to be in digital form. This proposal, with some
  modifications, was enacted as section 404 of the DMCA;

- revising limitations on exclusive rights to provide for certain distance education activities. The DMCA
  directed the Register of Copyrights to study the issue of promoting distance education through digital
  technologies and provide recommendations to Congress. Copyright Office, "Report on Copyright and
  Digital Distance Education" (1999). Based in large part on recommendations made in the Copyright
  Office's Study, this proposal has now been taken up in S. 487, which passed the Senate and is currently
  pending in the House;

- preemption of terms in non-negotiated licenses that abrogate or restrict the limitations on exclusive rights in
  chapter 1 of the Copyright Act. This proposal was not acted on. See discussions *infra* at 69-71 and 162-
  164;

- copyright protection and management systems. These provisions were proposed as an alternative to the
  anticircumvention and CMI provisions of the DMCA. The DMCA version prevailed and was enacted.

16

In an amendment to H.R. 2281 offered by Representative Rick White and adopted by the House Commerce Committee, what was to become the joint study by the Copyright Office and NTIA was introduced into the DMCA. Section 205 of the House Commerce Committee proposal called for a broad evaluation of the copyright law and electronic commerce "to ensure that neither the copyright law nor electronic commerce inhibits the development of the other."[29]

By the time the bill reached the House floor on August 4, 1998, the language regarding the joint study by the Copyright Office and NTIA had been pared back to focus on an evaluation of "the impact of this title and the development of electronic commerce on the operation of sections 109 and 117 of title 17, and the relationship between existing and emerging technology

---

[29] *Id.* § 6 H.R. Rep.No. 105-551, pt. 2, at (1998) at 18.

SEC. 205. EVALUATION OF IMPACT OF COPYRIGHT LAW AND AMENDMENTS ON ELECTRONIC COMMERCE AND TECHNOLOGICAL DEVELOPMENT.

(a) FINDINGS–In order to maintain strong protection for intellectual property and promote the development of electronic commerce and the technologies to support that commerce, the Congress must have accurate and current information on the effects of intellectual property protection on electronic commerce and technology. The emergence of digital technology and the proliferation of copyrighted works in digital media, along with the amendments to copyright law contained in this Act, make it appropriate for the Congress to review these issues to ensure that neither copyright law nor electronic commerce inhibits the development of the other.

(b) EVALUATION BY SECRETARY OF COMMERCE–The Secretary of Commerce, in consultation with the Assistant Secretary of Commerce for Communications and Information and the Register of Copyrights, shall evaluate–

(1) the effects of this Act and the amendments made by this Act on the development of electronic commerce and associated technology; and

(2) the relationship between existing and emergent technology and existing copyright law.

(c) REPORT TO CONGRESS–The Secretary of Commerce shall, not later than 1 year after the date of the enactment of this Act, submit to the Congress a report on the evaluation conducted under subsection (b), including any legislative recommendations the Secretary may have.

17

on the operation of those provisions."[30] This change makes it clear that Congress was not seeking a broad review of copyright and electronic commerce issues, but focused instead on two particular sections of the Copyright Act.

In explaining the reasons for examining section 109, the House Manager's Statement stated that:

> [t]he first sale doctrine does not readily apply in the digital networked environment because the owner of a particular digital copy usually does not sell or otherwise dispose of the possession of that copy. Rather, "disposition" of a digital copy by its owner normally entails reproduction and transmission of that reproduction to another person. The original copy may then be retained or destroyed. The appropriate application of this doctrine to the digital environment merits further evaluation and this section therefore calls for such an evaluation and report."[31]

The reference to section 109 in the bill plainly refers back to the digital first sale proposal in the Boucher-Campbell bill. Although there is no similar legislative history explaining why section 117 is included in the Report, the most likely explanation is that it is an oblique reference to the proposed exception for incidental copies in section 6 of the Boucher-Campbell bill – particularly given the absence of any contemporaneous discussions concerning the scope of the computer program exemptions in section 117 (apart from title III of the DMCA). The Boucher-Campbell proposal on incidental copies would have been codified in section 117 of the Copyright Act.

---

[30] House Manager's Statement, *supra* note 7, at 24. The conference committee made no substantive changes to the language of this section, which was ultimately enacted as section 104 of the DMCA.

[31] *Id.*

18

As ultimately enacted, section 104 of the DMCA requires the Copyright Office and NTIA jointly to evaluate:

> (1) the effects of the amendments made by this title and the development of electronic commerce and associated technology on the operation of sections 109 and 117 of title 17, United States Code; and

> (2) the relationship between existing and emergent technology and the operation of sections 109 and 117 of title 17, United States Code.

B. SECTION 109 AND THE FIRST SALE DOCTRINE

Section 109 of the Copyright Act restates the principle commonly referred to as the "first sale doctrine." Under the first sale doctrine a copyright owner does not retain the legal right to control the resale or other distribution of copies or phonorecords of a work that have already been lawfully sold. The first sentence of section 109(a) of the Copyright Act provides:

> Notwithstanding the provisions of section 106(3), the owner of a particular copy or phonorecord lawfully made under this title, or any person authorized by such owner, is entitled, without the authority of the copyright owner, to sell or otherwise dispose of the possession of that copy or phonorecord.

It is this provision of the copyright law that permits sales of used books and CDs, lending of books and other copyrighted materials by libraries, and rentals of videocassettes, among other activities, without the need to obtain the permission of copyright owners or make royalty payments.

19

1. History of the First Sale Doctrine

The first sale doctrine was initially a judicial doctrine. In *Bobbs-Merrill Co. v. Straus*,[32] the U.S. Supreme Court held that a copyright owner's exclusive right to "vend" did not permit it to impose a price limitation on the retail sale of books in the absence of any agreement as to the future sale price. In its interpretation of the reach of the vending right, the Court expressed doubt that Congress intended to abrogate the common-law principle that restraints on the alienation of tangible property are to be avoided. It posed and answered a series of rhetorical questions:

> What does the statute mean in granting 'the sole right of vending the same'? Was it intended to create a right which would permit the holder of the copyright to fasten, by notice in a book or upon one of the articles mentioned within the statute, a restriction upon the subsequent alienation of the subject-matter of copyright after the owner had parted with the title to one who had acquired full dominion over it and had given a satisfactory price for it? It is not denied that one who has sold a copyrighted article, without restriction, has parted with all right to control the sale of it. The purchaser of a book, once sold by authority of the owner of the copyright, may sell it again, although he could not publish a new edition of it.[33]

The Court drew a sharp distinction between the reproduction right and the right to vend. It noted, as a matter of statutory construction, that the reproduction right was the "main purpose" of the copyright law, and the right to vend existed to give effect to the reproduction right.[34] Since a grant of control to the copyright owner over resales would not further this main purpose of

---

[32] 210 U.S. 339 (1908).

[33] *Id.* at 349-50.

[34] *Id.* at 350-51.

20

protecting the reproduction right, the Court was unwilling to read the statute as providing such a grant:[35]

> In our view the copyright statutes, while protecting the owner of the copyright in his right to multiply and sell his production, do not create the right to impose . . . a limitation at which the book shall be sold at retail by future purchasers, with whom there is no privity of contract. This conclusion is reached in view of the language of the statute, read in the light of its main purpose to secure the right of multiplying copies of the work . . . . True, the statute also secures, to make this right of multiplication effectual, the sole right to vend copies of the book . . . . To add to the right of exclusive sale the authority to control all future retail sales . . . would give a right not included in the terms of the statute, and, in our view, extend its operation, by construction, beyond its meaning, when interpreted with a view to ascertaining the legislative intent in its enactment.[36]

The parties in *Bobbs-Merrill* also raised, and the Court of Appeals addressed, antitrust concerns. Although the Supreme Court did not address these concerns, it was undoubtedly aware of them,[37] and competition policy is viewed as one of the underlying bases for the first sale doctrine.[38]

---

[35] *Id.*

[36] *Id.*

[37] "This conclusion renders it unnecessary to discuss other questions noticed in the opinion in the Circuit Court of Appeals, or to examine into the validity of the publisher's agreements, alleged to be in violation of the acts to restrain combinations creating a monopoly or directly tending to the restraint of trade." *Id.*

[38] *See* MELVILLE B. NIMMER & DAVID NIMMER, NIMMER ON COPYRIGHT §8.12[A] [hereinafter NIMMER].

21

2. Legislative History of Section 109

The year following the *Bobbs-Merrill* decision, Congress codified the first sale doctrine in the Copyright Act of 1909.[39] Section 109(a) of the Copyright Act of 1976 carried forward the existing federal policy of terminating a copyright owner's distribution right as to a particular lawfully-made copy or phonorecord of a work after the first sale of that copy. The House Report explains:

> Section 109(a) restates and confirms the principle that, where the copyright owner has transferred ownership of a particular copy or phonorecord of a work, the person to whom the copy or phonorecord is transferred is entitled to dispose of it by sale, rental, or any other means. Under this principle, which has been established by the court decisions and section 27 of the present law, the copyright owner's exclusive right of public distribution would have no effect upon anyone who owns "a particular copy or phonorecord lawfully made under this title" and who wishes to transfer it to someone else or to destroy it.[40]

Section 109 creates a two-prong test for eligibility for the privileges[41] under section 109. First, the person must be the owner of the copy[42] at issue. This applies to ownership of the

---

[39] Section 27 of the 1909 Copyright Act provided:

The copyright is distinct from the property in the material object copyrighted, and the sale or conveyance, by gift or otherwise, of the material object shall not of itself constitute a transfer of the copyright, nor shall the assignment of the copyright constitute a transfer of the title to the material object; *but nothing in this title shall be deemed to forbid, prevent, or restrict the transfer of any copy of a copyrighted work the possession of which has been lawfully obtained.*
17 U.S.C. § 27 (1977) (emphasis added).

[40] H.R. Rep. No. 94-1476, at 79 (1976) ["1976 House Report"].

[41] Many of the commenters referred to the first sale doctrine as a "right." This is an inartful term to describe the doctrine. Rights are guaranteed to individuals and are generally enforceable in court. The first sale doctrine is not an enforceable right from the standpoint of the owner of a copy – that is, there is no independent remedy if a person is effectively denied the benefits of section 109 through technological or contractual means. The first sale doctrine is a limitation to the scope of copyright; specifically it is a limitation to the distribution right of copyright owners.

[42] For convenience, the term "copy" will be used with the understanding that it incorporates phonorecords as well.

22

tangible item (e.g., a book, photograph, videocassette, CD, floppy disc, etc.) in which a copyrighted work is fixed.[43] While ownership may be obtained by virtue of a sale, this prong is also satisfied if ownership is obtained by virtue of gift, bequest, or other transfer of title.[44] It does not apply to mere possession, regardless of whether that possession is legitimate, such as by rental, or illegitimate, such as by theft.[45] Nor does it refer to ownership of the copyright or of any of the exclusive rights.[46]

Second, that copy must have been lawfully made. Ownership of a copy that is not authorized by either the copyright owner or the law, even if the owner is unaware of the piratical nature of the copy, does not permit the owner to avail himself of section 109.[47] Nothing in the statute limits the manner in which the making of the copy may be accomplished, so long as the resulting copy is lawful.

The statute does not distinguish between analog and digital copies. Consequently, it does not matter whether the work is embodied in an analog videocassette or a digital DVD – the copyright owner's distribution right with respect to that particular copy is extinguished once

---

[43] Nimmer, *supra* note 38, at § 8.12[B][1].

[44] *Id.*

[45] *Id.*

[46] *Id.*

[47] Nimmer, *supra* note 38, at § 8.12[B][4].

23

ownership of the copy has been transferred, and the new owner is entitled to dispose of that copy as he desires.

3. Subsequent Amendments to Section 109

Congress has seen fit on three occasions to limit the effect of the first sale doctrine. In the Record Rental Amendment of 1984,[48] Congress amended section 109 to allow copyright owners of sound recordings and the musical works embodied therein to retain the exclusive right to dispose of a particular phonorecord by rental, lease or lending for purposes of direct or indirect commercial advantage, even after a lawful first sale of that phonorecord. The purpose of the amendment was to prevent the displacement of record sales by "rentals" that were, in fact, thinly-disguised opportunities for consumers to make personal copies of records without buying them.[49] In essence the so-called "rental right" serves to guard against infringement of the reproduction right. Congress extended the same concept to computer programs in the Computer Software Rental Amendments Act of 1990.[50] Both provisions have been incorporated into multilateral agreements and are now widely-accepted international standards.[51]

---

[48] Pub. L. No. 98-450, 98 Stat. 1727 (1984).

[49] H.R. Rep. No. 98-987, at 2. (1983).

[50] Title VII of the Judicial Improvements Act of 1990, Pub. L. No. 101-650, 104 Stat. 5089, 5134 (1990). Both the Record Rental Amendment and the Computer Software Rental Amendments Act are codified at 17 U.S.C. § 109(b).

[51] Agreement on Trade-Related Aspects of Intellectual Property Rights ("TRIPS"), Articles 11 and 14.4 (1994); WIPO Copyright Treaty, Article 7 (1996); WIPO Performances and Phonograms Treaty, Articles 9 and 13 (1996).

24

Congress also limited the effect of the first sale doctrine when, in the course of implementing U.S. obligations under the TRIPS agreement in 1994, it extended copyright protection to certain preexisting works of foreign origin that had previously fallen into the public domain in the United States. Under section 109(a), as amended by the Uruguay Round Agreements Act,[52] copies embodying certain restored copyrights may not be sold or otherwise disposed of without the authorization of the copyright owner more than twelve months after the person in possession of the copies receives actual or constructive notice that the copyright owner intends to enforce his rights in the restored work.

By the same token, Congress has, on one occasion, expanded the first sale doctrine to cover not only the distribution right, but the public performance and public display rights as well.[53] Although legislatively sunsetted on October 1, 1995, section 109(e) permitted the public performance or display of an electronic videogame intended for use in coin-operated equipment.[54]

---

[52] Pub. L. No. 103-465, 108 Stat. 4809, 4981 (1994).

[53] Section 109(c) also permits public display in limited circumstances: "Notwithstanding the provisions of section 106(5), the owner of a particular copy lawfully made under this title, or any person authorized by such owner, is entitled, without the authority of the copyright owner, to display that copy publicly, either directly or by the projection of no more than one image at a time, to viewers present at the place where the copy is located." This provision permits, among other things, the display of a painting in a museum or public art gallery by the purchaser of the painting.

[54] Pub. L. No. 101-650, § 804(c), 104 Stat. 5089, 5136 (1990) was enacted as part of the Computer Software Rental Amendments of 1990 in order to overturn the result in *Red Baron-Franklin Park, Inc. v. Taito Corp.*, 883 F.2d 275 (4th Cir. 1989), *cert. denied*, 493 U.S. 1058 (1990), a case which held that a copyright owner could prevent the purchaser of gray market circuit boards containing a copyrighted videogame from performing the videogame in a video arcade.

25

C. SECTION 117 COMPUTER PROGRAM EXEMPTIONS

Section 117 of the Copyright Act limits the exclusive rights of copyright owners by allowing the lawful owner of a copy of a computer program to make or authorize the making of another copy or adaptation of that program only for archival purposes or if it is necessary as an essential step in the utilization of the program in conjunction with a machine. [55]

---

[55] In its entirety, section 117 reads as follows:

§ 117. Limitations on exclusive rights: Computer programs

(a) Making of Additional Copy or Adaptation by Owner of Copy.-Notwithstanding the provisions of section 106, it is not an infringement for the owner of a copy of a computer program to make or authorize the making of another copy or adaptation of that computer program provided:

(1) that such a new copy or adaptation is created as an essential step in the utilization of the computer program in conjunction with a machine and that it is used in no other manner, or

(2) that such new copy or adaptation is for archival purposes only and that all archival copies are destroyed in the event that continued possession of the computer program should cease to be rightful.

(b) Lease, Sale, or Other Transfer of Additional Copy or Adaptation.-Any exact copies prepared in accordance with the provisions of this section may be leased, sold, or otherwise transferred, along with the copy from which such copies were prepared, only as part of the lease, sale, or other transfer of all rights in the program. Adaptations so prepared may be transferred only with the authorization of the copyright owner.

(c) Machine Maintenance or Repair.-Notwithstanding the provisions of section 106, it is not an infringement for the owner or lessee of a machine to make or authorize the making of a copy of a computer program if such copy is made solely by virtue of the activation of a machine that lawfully contains an authorized copy of the computer program, for purposes only of maintenance or repair of that machine, if-

(1) such new copy is used in no other manner and is destroyed immediately after the maintenance or repair is completed; and

(2) with respect to any computer program or part thereof that is not necessary for that machine to be activated, such program or part thereof is not accessed or used other than to make such new copy by virtue of the activation of the machine.

(d) Definitions.-For purposes of this section-

(1) the "maintenance" of a machine is the servicing of the machine in order to make it work in accordance with its original specifications and any changes to those specifications authorized for that machine; and

26

In addition, pursuant to an amendment contained in title III of the DMCA,[56] section 117

permits the owner or lessee of a machine to make or authorize the making of a temporary copy of

a computer program if such copy is made solely by virtue of the activation of a machine that

lawfully contains an authorized copy of the computer program, for purposes of maintenance or

repair of that machine. The exemption only permits a copy that is made automatically when a

computer is activated, and only if the computer already lawfully contains an authorized copy of

the program. The new copy cannot be used in any other manner and must be destroyed

immediately after the maintenance or repair is completed.

1. Legislative History of Section 117

a. *Recommendations of CONTU*

The transformation of section 117 into its current form dealing with computer programs

began in the 1970s. When the 1976 Act took effect on January 1, 1978, Congress' approach to

problems relating to computer uses of copyright works was still "not sufficiently developed for a

definitive legislative solution."[57] Congress enacted what was commonly referred to as a

"moratorium" provision in section 117, which preserved the status quo on December 31, 1977

(i.e., the day before the 1976 Copyright Act became effective) as to use of copyrighted works in

conjunction with computers and similar information systems.[58]

---

(2) the "repair" of a machine is the restoring of the machine to the state of working in accordance with its original specifications and any changes to those specifications authorized for that machine.

[56] Computer Maintenance Competition Assurance Act, Pub. L. No. 105-304, 112 Stat. 2860, 2886 (1998), codified at 17 U.S.C. § 117.

[57] 1976 House Report, *supra* note 40, at 116.

[58] *Id.* at 19. Former section 117 provided:

Notwithstanding the provisions of sections 106 through 116 and 118, this title does not afford to

27

Congress stated at that time that it would look to the National Commission on New

Technological Uses of Copyrighted Works (CONTU) to "recommend definitive copyright

provisions to deal with the situation."[59] CONTU was created in 1974[60] to assist the President and

Congress in developing a national policy for both protecting the rights of copyright owners and

ensuring public access to copyrighted works when they are used in computer and machine

duplication systems, bearing in mind the public and consumer interest.

Between CONTU's inception in 1974 and the issuance of its final report on July 31,

1978, the 1976 Copyright Act was enacted and became effective.[61] The final report

recommended that section 117 as enacted in 1976 be repealed in its entirety to ensure that the

generally applicable copyright rules set forth in the 1976 Copyright Act apply to all computer

uses of copyrighted works.[62] In addition, CONTU proposed that the Act be amended: (1) to

define "computer program";[63] (2) to ensure that rightful possessors of copies of computer

programs may use or adapt these copies for their use, because "placement of a work into a

---

the owner of copyright in a work any greater or lesser rights with respect to the use of the work in conjunction with automatic systems capable of storing, processing, retrieving, or transferring information, or in conjunction with any similar device, machine or process, than those afforded to works under the law, whether title 17 or the common law or statutes of a State, in effect on December 31, 1977, as held applicable and construed by a court in action brought under this title.

[59] 1976 House Report, *supra* note 40, at 116.

[60] Pub. L. No. 93-573, 88 Stat. 1873 (1974).

[61] Final Report of the National Commission on New Technological Uses of Copyrighted Works 3-4 (1979) [hereinafter CONTU Report]. Although the report was issued in 1978, it was published in 1979.

[62] *Id*. at 12-13.

[63] Congress had already made it clear in legislative history that computer programs, to the extent that they embody a programmer's original expression, were protected under copyright within the category of "literary works." 1976 House Report, *supra* note 40, at 54.

28

computer is the preparation of a copy;"[64] and (3) to permit rightful possessors of computer programs to make archival (backup) copies of programs to "guard against destruction or damage by mechanical or electrical failure."[65]

b. *The 1980 Computer Software Copyright Amendments*

Congress adopted CONTU's recommendations in the Computer Software Copyright Amendments of 1980 with few changes.[66] The House Report accompanying the 1980 amendments did not explain the intent of the legislation, other than to "implement the recommendations of the [CONTU] Commission with respect to clarifying the law of copyright of computer software."[67] In the absence of a substantive discussion in the committee report, some courts have treated the CONTU Report as the legislative history of the 1980 amendments to the Copyright Act.[68] Other courts have expressed scepticism regarding the use of a report by an independent commission as evidence of congressional intent.[69]

---

[64] CONTU Report, *supra* note 61, at 13.

[65] *Id.*

[66] Pub. L. No. 96-517, 94 Stat. 3015, 3028 (1980). Congress changed "rightful possessor" to "owner."

[67] H.R. Rep No. 96-1307, pt. I (1980).

[68] *See, e.g., Apple Computer, Inc. v. Formula Int'l, Inc.*, 725 F.2d 521, 525 (9th Cir. 1984) (employing CONTU Report as legislative history of the 1980 amendments); *Apple Computer, Inc. v. Franklin Computer Corp.*, 714 F.2d 1240, 1247-48, 1252 (3d Cir. 1983)(same).

[69] *See, e.g., Lotus Dev. Corp. v. Borland Int'l., Inc.*, 788 F. Supp. 78, 93 (D. Mass. 1992), *rev'd on other grounds*, 49 F.3d 807 (1st Cir. 1995), *aff'd by an equally divided Court*, 116 S. Ct. 804 (1996).

As enacted in 1980, section 117 permits the owner of a copy of a computer program to make an additional copy of the program for archival purposes[70], or where the making of such a copy is "an essential step in the utilization of the computer program in conjunction with a machine and . . . is used in no other manner . . . ."[71]

c. *The Computer Maintenance Competition Assurance Act of 1998*

Section 117 was further amended by title III of the DMCA, the Computer Maintenance Competition Assurance Act of 1998. The amendment was intended to "provide a minor, yet important, clarification in section 117 of the Copyright Act to ensure that the lawful owner or lessee of a computer machine may authorize an independent service provider, a person unaffiliated with either the owner or lessee of the machine, to activate the machine for the sole purpose of servicing its hardware components."[72] Title III was prompted by the outcome in *MAI Systems Corp. v. Peak Computer, Inc.*[73] and other cases that had held an independent service organization liable for copyright infringement by virtue of loading operating system software into a computer's RAM when a technician switched the computer on in order to repair or maintain it. Rather than addressing the general question of temporary copies as proposed in some contemporaneous bills,[74] title III of the DMCA narrowly overturned the outcome of *MAI v. Peak*

---

[70] "Archival purposes," in this context, was intended to mean the backing up of copies by users, not for the purposes of, for example, expanding a library's archival collection.

[71] 17 U.S.C. § 117(a)(1).

[72] 144 Cong. Rec. S11890 (daily ed. Oct. 8, 1998) (statement by Sen. Leahy).

[73] 991 F.2d 511, *cert. dismissed*, 114 S. Ct. 671 (1994).

[74] *See* discussion of the Boucher-Campbell bill, *supra* at 15.

30

with respect to independent service organizations, leaving the underlying holding with respect to temporary copies intact.

2. Judicial Interpretation of Section 117

Courts have interpreted the section 117 exceptions narrowly. For example, in *Sega Enterprises Ltd. v. Accolade, Inc.*,[75] the Ninth Circuit held that copying a computer program into memory in order to disassemble it was a use that "went far beyond that contemplated by CONTU and authorized by section 117."[76] Regarding the archival exemption, one court has held that section 117 does not excuse the making of purported backup copies of a videogame embodied in ROM, because that particular storage medium is not vulnerable to "damage by mechanical or electrical failure."[77]

---

[75] 977 F.2d 1510 (9th Cir. 1992).

[76] *Id.* at 1520.

[77] *Atari, Inc. v. J S & A Group, Inc.*, 597 F. Supp. 5, 9-10 (N.D. Ill. 1983).

31

32

II. VIEWS OF THE PUBLIC

A. SOLICITATION OF PUBLIC COMMENTS

In order to focus the issues involved in this Report, and to provide information and assistance to the Copyright Office and NTIA, the two agencies sought both written comments and oral testimony from the public. This process of public consultation commenced with the publication of a Notice of Inquiry in the Federal Register on June 5, 2000.[78]

The Notice of Inquiry sought comments and reply comments in connection with the effects of the amendments made by title I of the DMCA and the development of electronic commerce on the operation of sections 109 and 117 of title 17, United States Code, and the relationship between existing and emerging technology and the operation of such sections.[79]

In response to the Notice of Inquiry, we received thirty initial comments and sixteen reply comments.[80] Of those thirty initial comments, twenty-one dealt with section 109 and twelve dealt with section 117. Of the sixteen replies (to the initial comments), thirteen dealt with section 109 and eight dealt with section 117.

---

[78] 65 Fed Reg 35,673 (June 5, 2000).

[79] *Id.* For a more complete statement of the background and purpose of the inquiry, see the Notice of Inquiry which is available on the Copyright Office's website at: www.loc.gov/copyright/fedreg/65fr35673.html.

[80] The comments and replies have been posted on the Office's website; *see* www.loc.gov/copyright/reports/studies/dmca/comments/ and www.loc.gov/copyright/reports/studies/dmca/reply/, respectively.

33

On October 24, 2000, the two agencies published a notice of public hearing in the Federal Register.[81] At this public hearing, held at the Copyright Office on November 29, 2000, the two agencies inquired into points made in the written comments and focused on a series of specific questions. The information received from the written comments, as well as from the testimony of witnesses at the November 2000 public hearing, is summarized here.[82]

B. VIEWS CONCERNING SECTION 109[83]

1. The Effect of Section 1201 Prohibitions on the Operation of the First Sale Doctrine

There was a dramatic range of opinions in the many comments addressing this question. Most commenters believed that the anticircumvention provisions of 17 U.S.C. § 1201 provided copyright owners with the ability to restrict the operation of the first sale doctrine. A few of these commenters did not elaborate on this assertion. Those who did expressed many different views on precisely how the rule against the circumvention of technological protection measures restricts the operation of the first sale doctrine, and how severe that effect is.

---

[81] 65 Fed Reg 63,626 (October 24, 2000).

[82] Summaries of testimony are available on the Copyright Office website at www.loc.gov/copyright/reports/studies/dmca/testimony/hearings.html; a full transcript of the public hearing is available at www.loc.gov/copyright/reports/studies/dmca/testimony/transcript.pdf.

[83] In referring to the comments and hearing materials, we will use the following abbreviations: C-Comment, R-Reply Comment, WST-Written Summary of Testimony, T + speaker-Hearing Transcript. Citations to page numbers in the hearing transcript are to the PDF version of the transcript on the Copyright Office website: www.loc.gov/copyright/reports/studies/dmca/testimony/transcript.pdf.

34

Among those who believed that section 1201 limits first sale, the majority of comments focused on one of two practical concerns surrounding the market for DVDs. The first addressed the proprietary encryption scheme known as the Content Scrambling System[84] (CSS) that is used on commercial DVDs, and the requirement that manufacturers be licensed to produce DVD players. The second addressed the practice known as region coding.[85]

Most commercially released motion pictures on DVD, as noted by many commenters, are encrypted using CSS. Some commenters noted further that the only devices that are authorized to decrypt DVDs are DVD players that have been manufactured under a license from the consortium (which includes the major motion picture studios) that owns the rights to CSS.[86] As a result, the commenters complained, they are required to make two purchases in order to view a single DVD (i.e., the DVD and the player).[87] Certain commenters suggested that the practice of requiring a licensed player in order to view a DVD amounts to a violation of antitrust law.[88]

But for the anticircumvention law, it would be permissible for a person to use an unauthorized decryption program to view DVDs on devices other than authorized players, such

---

[84] CSS is the technological protection measure adopted by the motion picture industry and consumer electronics manufacturers to provide security to copyrighted content of DVDs and to prevent unauthorized copying of that content. Motion Picture Association of America website: www.mpaa.org/Press, visited on May 1, 2001.

[85] See discussion infra, at 36.

[86] C-Arromdee, at 1.

[87] C-Taylor, at 1.

[88] C-National Association of Recording Merchandisers, Inc. (NARM) and the Video Software Dealers Association, Inc. (VSDA), at 29-30.

35

as personal computers, if necessary. Such a program was found in violation of section 1201 in a highly publicized court case.[89] Some commenters discussed the case in great detail in their comments.[90]

The implication of the complaint about the CSS encryption code is that by enabling copyright owners to compel users to purchase a licensed DVD player, the value of a DVD is reduced. It is, argued some commenters, a requirement that each subsequent owner of a DVD obtain a new authorization to view the contents of that work.[91] That, in turn, means that the value of the first sale doctrine as applied to DVDs is reduced or eliminated. Thus, as applied to the market for DVDs, these commenters argued that the operation of the first sale doctrine has been obstructed by the rules against circumvention of technological protection measures.[92]

The concerns about region coding of DVDs are similar in nature. Region coding is a technological means of preventing DVDs manufactured for sale in one region of the world from playing on a DVD player that is manufactured for sale in a different region of the world. The result is that a DVD purchased in Asia cannot be viewed on a licensed DVD player purchased in the United States.[93] Were unauthorized circumvention permissible, region coding could be

---

[89] *See Universal City Studios, et al. v. Reimerdes*, 82 F. Supp. 2d 211 (S.D.N.Y. 2000). The case is presently on appeal to the Second Circuit. *Universal City Studios, et al. v. Corley*, docket #00-9185.

[90] C-Thau and Taylor, at 4 *et seq.*

[91] *E.g.*, C-Taylor, at 1.

[92] *E.g.*, C-Arromdee, at 1.

[93] Some DVD players can be switched from one region setting to another, but the user may only switch a few times before being permanently locked into a region.

36

defeated. These commenters argued that region coding reduces the value of the first sale doctrine by limiting the market for resale of a DVD. And because the anticircumvention rules prevent users from defeating region coding, these commenters argued that those rules are interfering with the operation of the first sale doctrine.[94]

Others who believe that prohibitions on circumvention of technological protection measures have restricted the operation of the first sale doctrine were more general in their comments. One representative sample is a comment which noted that access controls that permit access on only a single device are likely to interfere with the exercise of the first sale doctrine.[95] This comment also addressed other situations, noting that access controls sometimes limit the amount of a work that is viewable at any time. While acknowledging that this serves a reasonable anti-piracy purpose, the comment also noted that such a practice makes it less likely that the user will exercise the first sale privilege. This is because in order to obtain a complete tangible copy of the work the user will have to separately print out numerous small portions.[96] This comment also observed that while files that require a password to gain access may not be limited to one device, transfer of the password, or "key," may be restricted in a way that prevents transfer of a file in a usable form.[97]

---

[94] *E.g.*, C-LXNY, at 1.

[95] C-Computer Professionals for Social Responsibility (CPSR), at 2.

[96] *Id.* at 3, 5.

[97] *Id.* at 4.

37

That final point was echoed by a number of commenters. Their concern was that the non-negotiable licenses which are offered to users of copyrighted works are written to reduce or eliminate the availability of statutorily permitted uses, including uses permitted under section 109.[98] These terms may be enforced through technological protection measures. Thus, they argued, the rules against circumvention of such measures hamper the operation of the first sale doctrine.[99] This concern was particularly evident among users of computer software, who decried so-called shrinkwrap and click-wrap licenses.[100] A few commenters delved into a discussion of the relative merits of the Uniform Computer Information Transactions Act[101] (UCITA) – legislation that is currently being considered in numerous state legislatures, that would validate the enforceability of shrinkwrap and click-wrap licenses.[102]

---

[98] *E.g.*, C-American Library Association, American Association of Law Libraries, Association of Research Libraries, Medical Library Association, and Special Libraries Association (Library Ass'ns), at 5-7.

[99] *Id.*

[100] Shrinkwrap and click-wrap licenses are terms used to describe the non-negotiable licensing terms that are sometimes placed on consumer packaging of copyrighted works, particularly software, in lieu of a simple sale of that copy of the work. The names derive from the practice of demonstrating users' assent to the terms by virtue of their tearing open the plastic shrinkwrap packaging or clicking an "agree" button with a mouse.

[101] The Uniform Computer Information Transactions Act (UCITA), according to the National Conference of Commissioners on Uniform State Laws, represents the first comprehensive uniform computer information licensing law. This act uses the accepted and familiar principles of contract law, setting the rules for creating electronic contracts and the use of electronic signatures for contract adoption – thereby making computer information transactions as well-grounded in the law as traditional transactions. National Conference of Commissioners on Uniform State Laws website: www.nccusl.org/uniformact_factsheets/uniformacts-fs-ucita.htm , visited on May 2, 2001.

[102] *E.g.*, C-Lyons, at 3-5; R-Software and Information Industry Association (SIIA), at 10-11.

38

Similar concerns were also raised in the submission of the library associations.[103] They expressed concern that rules against circumvention give copyright owners the ability to maintain a running control on access to and copying of their works.[104] This, they argued, frustrates the goal of the first sale doctrine, by extending the rights of the copyright owner beyond the first sale of a particular copy.[105] As tangible examples of how this interference in the operation of the first sale doctrine might inhibit the functioning of a library, they gave several examples including interlibrary loan programs, preservation, and accepting donations of works.[106] All of these, they argued, have become difficult or impossible as a result of the intersection of licensing terms, technological measures and restrictions on circumvention.[107]

Other commenters had varying explanations for their belief that anticircumvention rules have hampered the first sale doctrine. For example, one commenter argued that anticircumvention rules limit the user's ability to make copies, which effectively precludes users from benefitting from the first sale doctrine.[108]

A few commenters stated that the rules against circumvention have little or no effect on the first sale doctrine. One commenter, for example, opined that such rules are irrelevant

---

[103] C-Library Ass'ns, at 4-7.

[104] *Id.*

[105] *Id.*

[106] *Id.* at 10-19.

[107] *Id.*

[108] C-Van De Walker, at 2.

39

because they are essentially unenforceable.[109] Others argued that it is simply too soon in the

evolution of this field to know.[110] They noted, however, that with time that condition may

change.

A significant number of commenters expressed the view that prohibitions on

circumvention of technological protection measures, particularly in the online environment, have

had no effect on the operation of the first sale doctrine because the first sale doctrine is

inapplicable to digital transmissions.[111] Several of these comments sought to respond to the

concerns previously mentioned. For example, one commenter argued that concerns about

copyright owners locking up works behind technological protection measures are without merit,

because doing so would be a doomed business strategy.[112] That commenter also argued that the

licensing of DVD players in no way disadvantaged consumers.[113] Further, that commenter

asserted that analysis of the effect of licensing terms is beyond the scope of this Report.[114]

---

[109] C-Stanford Linear Accelerator Center (SLAC), at 1.

[110] C-Digital Media Association (DiMA), at 7-9; C-Anthony, at 1.

[111] *E.g.*, R-Reed Elsevier Inc., at 5-8.

[112] R-Time Warner Inc., at 1-2.

[113] *Id.* at 2.

[114] *Id.* at 4.

40

2. The Effect of Section 1202 Prohibitions on the Operation of the First Sale Doctrine

The overwhelming number of commenters that expressed a view on this issue stated that there has not been any effect on the operation of the first sale doctrine as a result of the protections for copyright management information.[115] However, the library associations argued that when combined with technological protection measures and licensing limitations, copyright management information can give the copyright owner the ability to monitor and prohibit uses that are permissible under the law.[116] They were also concerned that such technology can give the copyright owner access to personal information about users, such as 'cookies',[117] that chills use of the work.[118] One commenter argued that protections for copyright management information limit the utility of the first sale doctrine because they prevent the owner of the copy from removing what he referred to as the "packaging" of the work.[119]

---

[115] *See, e.g.*, C-SLAC, at 1; C-McGown, at 1; C-DiMA, at 9.

[116] C-Library Ass'ns, at 7-10.

[117] A "cookie" is information that is stored by Internet browsing software on a user's hard drive in response to an automated request by a web server. A subsequent automated request by a web server can instruct the browsing software to transmit that information back to the server.

[118] C-Library Ass'ns, at 7-10.

[119] C-Thomason, at 1.

41

3. The Effect of the Development of Electronic Commerce and Associated Technology on the Operation of the First Sale Doctrine.

One commenter simply found that the development of electronic commerce and associated technology has had no effect on the first sale doctrine.[120] Another believed that it was too soon to tell what the effect will be.[121]

The library associations argued that with the increase in distribution of copyrighted works online, it is less likely that a user will purchase a copy. Rather, they foresee that the user will be licensed to access a work online.[122] One result of this change, they argued, is that the first sale doctrine will not apply to online access.[123] They also argued that it permits copyright owners to create a price structure wherein entities that cannot afford the best version of the work must settle for a less expensive and less desirable version.[124]

Other commenters took that sentiment further, arguing that particularly in the e-commerce sphere, technology can now be used by copyright owners to circumvent constitutional and legislative limitations on the distribution right to the point of copyright misuse and/or antitrust violations.[125]

---

[120] C-McGown, at 1.

[121] C-DiMA, at 9-11.

[122] C-Library Ass'ns, at 10-19.

[123] *Id.*

[124] *Id.*

[125] *See* C-NARM/VSDA, at 29-30, 37.

42

One copyright owner commented that new technology has made infringement of copyright easier and that a change in the existing level of protection for copyrighted works (such as expanded first sale privilege) could be disastrous for copyright owners.[126]

4. The Relationship Between Existing and Emergent Technology, on One Hand, and the First Sale Doctrine, on the Other

Relatively few commenters addressed this issue directly. Of those who did, most commenters believed that there is no relationship between existing and emergent technology and the first sale doctrine.[127] Some argued that technology is being used to defeat the first sale doctrine, as discussed above.[128] Another commenter noted that the first sale doctrine applies to tangible copies, not to the streaming or downloading of works.[129]

5. The Extent to Which the First Sale Doctrine Is Related To, or Premised On, Particular Media or Methods of Distribution

Many comments indicated that the first sale doctrine is not premised on any particular media or methods of distribution.[130] Some noted that the first sale doctrine is premised on older

---

[126] R-Time Warner Inc., at 1.

[127] *E.g.,* C-McGown, at 1; C-Library Ass'ns, at 19.

[128] C-Library Ass'ns, at 10-19.

[129] C-Time Warner Inc., at 2-3.

[130] *E.g.,* C-McGown, at 1; C-Taylor, at 5.

43

technology which provided greater impediments to the transfer of works than modern technology.[131] Others observed that the first sale doctrine is based on tangible copies.[132]

6. The Extent, if Any, to Which the Emergence of New Technologies Alters the Technological Premises upon Which the First Sale Doctrine Is Established

As with the previous issues, many of the commenters indicated that new technology does not alter the technological premises upon which the first sale doctrine is established. One commenter stated that new technology has made copyright laws obsolete and ineffective because of the impossibility of enforcement.[133] Several commenters noted that while new technology has not altered the premises of the first sale doctrine, the legislative codification of that doctrine may need to be periodically updated to continue the proper application of the first sale doctrine to new technology.

7. The Need, if Any, to Expand the First Sale Doctrine to Apply to Digital Transmissions

The comments on this issue were both voluminous and passionate. They can be divided into two starkly contrasting groups: those arguing that section 109 should be amended to permit the digital transmission of works that were lawfully acquired (including the reproduction of the work as a part of the transmission process) and those opposing modification of section 109.

---

[131] C-SIIA, at 6; C-SLAC, at 2.

[132] C-Time Warner Inc., at 3; C-Anthony, at 2-3.

[133] C-SLAC, at 2-3.

44

Some of the commenters argued that digital transmissions are already permitted by the existing language of section 109.[134] This is because in obtaining the "source" copy, a user receives a transmission and upon completion of that transmission, there exists a copy of the work in tangible form. They dismissed concerns about additional copies being made when the first purchaser transmits the work to a second as being incidental to the transmission process. A legislative change that they seek is to amend section 1201 to allow circumvention of technological protection measures which prevent the operation of the first sale doctrine.[135]

Other commenters argued that the current language of section 109 could be read to apply to digital transmissions (although some conceded that a "formalistic" reading of section 109 does not), but sought legislative clarification to codify this conclusion.[136] Many commenters referred to the Boucher-Campbell bill[137] as a model for the changes they would like to see made to section 109.[138]

The commenters supporting changes to section 109 argued that copyright law has always been interpreted to be technology neutral, and that in order to be faithful to that tradition, the first sale doctrine should be updated to apply to digital transmissions.[139] They noted that the policy

---

[134] C-NARM/VSDA, at 36-37.

[135] *Id.*

[136] R-Library Ass'ns, at 1-2.

[137] H.R. 3048, 105th Cong., 1st Sess. (1997).

[138] *E.g.*, C-Digital Future Coalition (DFC), at 3.

[139] *Id.*

45

behind the first sale doctrine was to prevent restraints on the alienability of property in order to promote the continual flow of property in society.[140] They argued further that the first sale doctrine has, for nearly a century, promoted economic growth and creativity, and should be extended into the digital environment.[141] In anticipation of counter-arguments that such an extension would be an invitation to infringement, they argued that technological protection measures and copyright management information can be used in concert to guarantee that when a user transmits the work, the "source" copy is deleted.[142] They also asserted that this technology exists now. Additionally, some argued that without a clear application of the first sale doctrine to digital transmissions, circumvention technology will gain in popularity.[143]

The library associations sought specific amendments to section 109 to address the concerns unique to libraries relating to interlibrary loans, preservation/archiving, accepting donated works, and other activities.[144]

There were a few other views supporting such a change as well. One commenter argued that while the copyright law is no longer relevant and the expansion of section 109 is not technologically necessary, the principles of copyright law should apply evenly.[145] Another

---

[140] C-NARM /VSDA, at 9.

[141] C-Home Recording Rights Coalition (HRRC), at 2-3.

[142] *Id.* at 5.

[143] R-DiMA, at 6-7.

[144] C-Library Ass'ns, at 11-19.

[145] C-SLAC, at 3.

46

commented that first sale principles should also apply to the transmission of encryption "keys" so as to prevent technological protection measures from inhibiting exercise of the first sale right while still providing protection against infringement.[146]

Those who opposed the amendment of section 109 argued that the requested changes do not merely update the long-standing first sale doctrine to accommodate new technology, but expand the first sale doctrine well beyond its previous scope.[147] To date, the first sale doctrine has, with limited exceptions,[148] always been a limitation on only the distribution right. Commenters from the copyright industries noted that in order to transfer a copy of a work from one person to another by digital transmission it is necessary for copies to be made, thus implicating the reproduction right.[149] They asserted too that the transfer may also involve a performance of the work, implicating the public performance right or for sound recordings, the digital audio transmission right.[150]

Those opposed to amending section 109 also argued that a change along the lines proposed in the Boucher-Campbell bill would open the door to widespread unauthorized copying

---

[146] C-Thau and Taylor, at 6.

[147] C-SIIA, at 3.

[148] *See* § 109(c) (limiting the public display right) and § 109(e) (limiting the public performance and public display rights). These provisions are discussed *supra,* at 25.

[149] R-American Film Marketing Association, Association of American Publishers, Business Software Alliance, Motion Picture Association of America, National Music Publishers' Association, and Recording Industry Association of America (Copyright Industry Orgs.), at 2.

[150] *Id.* at 5.

47

of works which, in turn, would destroy the market for those works.[151] They argued that this result could occur because the technology to require simultaneous destruction of the "source" copy remains ineffective and prohibitively expensive.[152] Moreover, at least one copyright owner representative questioned the existence of any demand in the marketplace for the simultaneous destruction (also called "forward and delete") technology.[153] Opponents also argued that in the context of traditional technology, the effect of the first sale doctrine on the marketplace for unused copies was limited by geography and the gradual degradation of books and analog tapes.[154] The absence of such limitations in the context of digital technology would cause an expanded first sale doctrine to have a far greater effect on the market.[155] They also noted that copyright owners'concerns raised in the context of this Report were precisely the same concerns that persuaded the Congress not to enact the Boucher-Campbell bill in the 105th Congress, and that nothing has changed that should alter Congress' judgment.[156]

8. The Effect of the Absence of a Digital First Sale Doctrine on the Marketplace for Works in Digital Form

For those who seek an amendment to section 109 to include digital transmissions explicitly in the first sale doctrine, the absence of express statutory language is a source of

---

[151] *E.g.,* R-Time Warner Inc., at 1.

[152] R-Copyright Industry Orgs., at 3-4.

[153] T-National Music Publishers' Association (NMPA), Mann, at 157-58.

[154] R-SIIA, at 6.

[155] *Id.*

[156] R-NMPA, at 2-3.

48

uncertainty, reduced utility and/or a chilling effect on users in the marketplace, which is reducing the demand for copyrighted works.[157]

To those who oppose such an amendment, the current law provides an environment in which copyright owners are willing to offer their works in a digital form.[158] This, they argued, enhances the market for such works by providing them to consumers in the media they desire most. To counter claims that the absence of a clear application of the first sale doctrine to digital transmissions is harming the marketplace, one commenter quoted a 1997 U.S. Department of Commerce study asserting that "electronic shopping and mail order houses sold $22.9 billion in computer hardware, software, and supplies . . . more than any other types of retail businesses."[159] Another noted that according to Jupiter Communications, digital downloads will be a $1.5 billion commercial market by 2006.[160]

C. VIEWS CONCERNING SECTION 117

The public comments related to section 117 fell broadly into two categories: comments concerning the status of temporary copies in RAM and comments concerning the scope of the archival exemption.

---

[157] C-Library Ass'ns, at 25-26; C-DiMA, at 13.

[158] *E.g.*, C-Time Warner Inc., at 3.

[159] R-SIIA, at 5.

[160] R-Broadcast Music, Inc. (BMI), at 6-7.

49

1. Exemption for Temporary Buffer Copies in Random Access Memory (RAM)

a. *Legal Status of Temporary Copies and Need for an Exception.*

Most of the comments received on "section 117" related not to the computer program

exemptions provided in that section, but to the question whether an exemption for temporary

incidental copies should be enacted. One group of commenters requested an exemption from the

exclusive right of reproduction for certain kinds of temporary copies.[161] Another group of

commenters, mostly comprised of copyright owners, did not believe there is any need or basis for

an exemption for these temporary copies.[162]

Many of the commenters who support an amendment to create a general exception from

the reproduction right for temporary incidental copies supported the exemption proposed in the

Boucher-Campbell bill.[163] This bill included an exemption for digital copies that are incidental to

the operation of a device in the course of use of a work when that use is lawful under title 17,

U.S. Code. Because this exemption was originally proposed as an amendment to section 117, we

discuss it in the context of section 117.[164]

---

[161] *See generally* comments by Computer & Communications Industry Association (CCIA), DFC, HRRC, DiMA (suggesting similar but different wording), Blue Spike, Launch; *see also* R-Library Ass'ns, at 15-16.

[162] *See generally* comments by NARM and VSDA, Digital Commerce Coalition (DCC), Business Software Alliance (BSA), BMI, Copyright Industry Orgs., Reed Elsevier, Inc. (REI).

[163] H.R. 3048, 105th Cong., (1997); *see* discussion *supra* at 15.

[164] *See* discussion of the nexus between the temporary incidental copy issue and section 117 *supra* at 18.

50

The proponents of a temporary incidental copy exception argued that court decisions like *MAI Systems Corp. v. Peak Computer, Inc.*[165] and its progeny, have had the effect of invalidating the usefulness of the exemptions under section 117.[166] *MAI v. Peak* held that the loading of software into a computer's random access memory (RAM) in violation of a license agreement was an infringement because it entailed making a copy.[167] The exemption in section 117 applies to "the owner of a copy of a computer program."[168] The court in *MAI v. Peak* concluded that since the software was licensed by the copyright owner, the defendant, a third-party independent service oganization, was not an "owner" of the software and did not qualify for the exemptions under section 117.[169] The commenters argued that because most software today is acquired by license rather than purchase, few users of computer software would qualify for the exemption under section 117. Therefore, they contended, it is of little use.[170]

Other commenters generally opposed any exemption for temporary incidental copies at this time.[171] Many of them opposed the Boucher-Campbell bill, arguing that the proposed

---

[165] 991 F.2d 511 (9th Cir. 1993), *cert. dismissed*, 114 S. Ct. 671 (1994).

[166] The DFC argues, for instance, that the practical force of the section 117 exemptions has been deprived by recent case law, citing *MAI v. Peak* and subsequent decisions that hold that every temporary RAM copying of a computer program, incidental to its use on a hardware platform, constitutes a form of "reproduction". C-DFC, at 3. CCIA said that the existing 117 has "in essence . . . been repealed" by *MAI v. Peak* and decisions like it. C-CCIA, at 2.

[167] *See* discussion of *MAI v. Peak infra* at 118.

[168] 17 U.S.C. § 117(a)(1).

[169] 991 F.2d 511, 518 n. 5 (9th Cir. 1993).

[170] This argument appears to be less relevant to the proposal for a general exemption for temporary incidental copies, than to the question whether the existing exemptions under section 117 should apply only to "owners" of copies or to "rightful possessors" including licensees.

[171] *See generally* comments by the Copyright Industry Orgs., NMPA, and SIIA; T-BMI, Berenson, at 167.

51

exemption is not justified by technological developments, would dramatically expand the scope of section 117, and would drastically cut back on the exclusive reproduction right for all works.[172] In their view, the *MAI v. Peak* decision stands for two propositions relevant to section 117, both of which buttress, rather than weaken or "repeal" that statutory provision and the objectives for which it was enacted.[173] First, the Ninth Circuit's holding in *MAI v. Peak* has been followed in a number of other federal court decisions.[174] The copyright owners also argued that if the Ninth Circuit had reached the opposite conclusion – that such copying of a computer program into memory was not a reproduction falling within the scope of the reproduction right – enactment of what is now section 117(a)(1) would not have been necessary.[175] Second, the copyright owners argued that proponents of the Boucher-Campbell bill called on Congress in 1998 to overturn *MAI v. Peak* by adopting an exception for incidental copies, but that Congress did the opposite by passing title III of the DMCA, endorsing and reaffirming the conclusions of CONTU and the Ninth Circuit regarding temporary copies.[176] The copyright owners, joined by other commenters, argued that the DMCA embraced the general principle that temporary copies in RAM are copies that are subject to the copyright owner's exclusive reproduction right, and made only those carefully calibrated adjustments to the principle necessary to address the problems experienced by independent providers of computer maintenance and repair services.[177]

---

[172] R-Copyright Industry Orgs., at 9.

[173] *Id.*

[174] *See infra* at 119.

[175] R-Copyright Industry Orgs., at 9; *see infra*, at 113.

[176] *Id.*

[177] R-Copyright Industry Orgs., at 10.

52

The copyright owners were also concerned that an exception for incidental copies would undercut the reproduction right in all works, and would raise significant questions about U.S. compliance with its international obligations.[178]

b. *The Economic Value of Temporary Copies*

Commenters were divided on the question whether temporary copies have economic value. The point of view of the commenters appeared to be strongly influenced by the context in which the particular temporary copy is made. Some commenters who discussed temporary copies that are incidental to an authorized transmission placed little or no economic value on the copies. The small temporary buffer memory copies that are used in today's webcasting technology, argued one commenter, have no intrinsic or economic value apart from the performance.[179] This commenter, representing an alliance of companies that develop and deploy technologies to perform, promote and market music and video content on the web and through other digital networks, noted that this webcasting technology demonstrates why section 117 needs to be updated for the digital age. He said that it should provide that the temporary buffers necessary to enable an authorized performance of copyrighted material are exempt from any claim of copyright infringement.[180]

---

[178] WST-Copyright Industry Orgs.

[179] C-DiMA, at 19.

[180] *Id.*

53

Other commenters argued that the temporary copy has significant economic value.[181] These commenters referred to the holding in *MAI v. Peak*, and its subsequent confirmation by Congress in title III of the DMCA, as an implicit recognition that the copies have economic value since Congress deemed them worthy of protection.[182] Indeed, one commenter from a trade association that represents software and electronic commerce developers asserted that in the digital world it is possible that the full commercial value of the work is contained in that temporary copy. For example, customers are becoming less interested in possessing a permanent copy of software, and more interested in having that copy available to them as they need it.[183]

c. *Promotion of Electronic Commerce*

Some commenters asserted that the promotion and growth of electronic commerce requires a general exception for temporary incidental copies to cover all forms of digital content, not just computer software.[184]

Opposing that view was one commenter who noted that there is every indication from the marketplace to suggest that electronic commerce and the Internet continue to grow vigorously, and that in the two years since the enactment of the DMCA that growth has accelerated.[185] The commenter concluded that the evidence is simply not there to support the thesis that exemptions

---

[181] *See generally* comments by Copyright Industry Orgs., BSA.

[182] R-Copyright Industry Orgs., at 9; T-BSA, Simon, at 105.

[183] T-BSA, Simon, at 138.

[184] C-DiMA, at 15; WST-HRRC ; R-Library Ass'ns, at 14.

[185] T-BSA, Simon, at 105.

54

must be expanded to meet the demands of electronic commerce.[186] Copyright industries did not believe any changes to section 117 were necessary at this time in order to facilitate the continued growth of electronic commerce and the advance of technology for conducting electronic transactions in copyrighted materials. They professed to be unaware of any significant impediments to electronic commerce which have arisen as a result of section 117 in its current form.

d. *Changed Circumstances since Enactment of the DMCA*

A representative of the copyright industry associations observed that when Congress has dealt with the question of temporary copies, it has done so in response to real problems.[187] He noted that Congress responded in 1998 to real problems that were presented to it by independent service organizations that had been sued and were being held liable for creating temporary copies in RAM in the course of maintaining or repairing computers.[188] Congress, he also noted, took the same approach when it was presented with evidence that there was at least a credible threat of liability for online service providers, for making temporary copies in the course of carrying out functions that are at the core of the Internet.[189]

Several commenters spoke directly to this issue by addressing what has changed in the past two years that would require an exemption from the reproduction right for certain temporary

---

[186] *Id.*

[187] T-Copyright Industry Orgs., Metalitz, at 249.

[188] *Id; see supra*, at 30.

[189] T-Copyright Industry Orgs., Metalitz, at 249; *see infra*, note 201.

copies and what additional experience has been gained over the past two years that may persuade

Congress to rethink these issues. One commenter remarked that the test that should be

considered is whether something has happened to the marketplace that would justify further

changes in law.[190] He noted that Congress found no compelling evidence in 1998 that changes

were merited, and having reviewed the submissions and marketplace developments, he found

that there is no justification to come to a different conclusion today.[191]

Still another commenter argued that an amendment to section 117 to exempt temporary

copies of works that are made as part of the operation of the machine or device is not necessary

and would be inappropriate because no one can provide any evidence of harm.[192] This

commenter asserted that no concrete examples had been proffered of situations where copyright

owners have filed suit or otherwise made inappropriate claims based on such temporary copies or

where webcasters have been hampered by any alleged threats. He was not aware of any record

company that has claimed infringement or threatened litigation based on the making of temporary

copies. To the contrary, he provided examples of webcasters and other Internet music services

being licensed by copyright owners with all the permissions they need to operate their business.

Need for legislative action on this point, he said, has not been demonstrated and none should be

taken where the likelihood of unintended consequences is high.[193]

---

[190] T-BSA, Simon, at 105.

[191] *Id.*

[192] T-RIAA, Sherman, at 305.

[193] *Id.*

56

Other commenters, however, argued the problem was not theoretical. One webcaster noted that there are music publishers that are seeking mechanical royalties for temporary copies made in RAM buffers when music is streamed on the Internet, even though the performance to which the copy is incidental is fully·licensed.[194] He noted that his company had not been sued but certainly had been threatened, and the threat of suit had been used against it in negotiations over license agreements.[195] The commenter said the threat of litigation, particularly to a growing company like his, is enough to cause problems, and is enough to make such a company agree to licenses that are, perhaps, unfair.[196] He also noted that it is not in anyone's interest to resolve a perceived ambiguity through litigation; this is a clear example of an instance in which legislative action could effectively resolve any uncertainty.[197]

e. *Applicability of the Fair Use Doctrine to Temporary Copies*

Suggestions were made in the comments that the fair use doctrine, rather than a separate exemption for temporary incidental copies, could address some of the concerns that were raised about such copies. Since certain commenters proposed that language be added to section 117 that would permit the making of temporary copies when such copies are "incidental to the operation of a device . . ." and do "not conflict with the normal exploitation of the work and do not unreasonably prejudice the legitimate interests of the author," one commenter suggested instead that the fair use doctrine be used rather than expanding section 117 with such broad

---

[194] T-Launch, Goldberg, at 311.

[195] Launch has since been sued, but over issues unrelated to buffer copies.

[196] T-Launch, Goldberg, at 311.

[197] WST-Launch.

57

language. This commenter argued that this language is too broad and use of it may be dangerous by allowing acts well above and beyond any reasonable fair use.[198]

One of the commenters advocating an exemption for temporary incidental copies also recognized that fair use may address some of the concerns that were expressed. This commenter took the position that between the archival exemption set out in section 117 and the fair use doctrine, certain types of copies should already be determined not to be infringing under the law, including temporary copies of recorded content made in the course of playback through buffering, caching, or other means.[199] Library associations said that while they believe that the copying rights at issue already exist under fair use, making them explicit could help to eliminate some of the uncertainty that is currently preventing these rights from being fully and consistently exercised.[200]

---

[198] R-SIIA, at 3, 4; WST-SIIA; T-SIIA, Kupferschmid, at 132.

[199] WST-HRRC. The copies that HRRC asserts should already be determined not to be infringing under the law (because the copies fall under the archival exemption set out in section 117 or the fair use doctrine) are back-up or archival copies of works or phonorecords of content lawfully acquired through digital downloading; temporary copies of recorded content made in the course of playback through buffering, caching, or other means; and temporary copies that are stored through the technical process of Internet webcasting.

[200] R-Library Ass'ns, at 14.

f. *Liability for Making Temporary Copies under Section 512*[201]

The copyright industries questioned why the limitations on liability set out in section 512 cannot be used by the webcasters to address their problems regarding threats of litigation and noted that there have not been significant legal conflicts over incidental copying.[202] The copyright industries asserted that Congress, in enacting the DMCA, addressed and resolved some of the potential flash points. For instance, they asserted that, in what is now section 512, Congress carefully fashioned limitations on remedies that apply to infringements – including, notably "incidental copying" – that may occur in the course of activities that are essential to the smooth functioning of the Internet such as linking, storing, caching or providing conduit services, rather than creating broad exemptions to exclusive rights.[203]

Other commenters disagreed. One noted that the section 512 provisions are helpful to those who qualify as Internet service providers within the meaning of section 512 but that many webcasters are not Internet service providers and do not qualify for relief from liability under

---

[201] 17 U.S.C. § 512. Under section 512, a party that qualifies as a "service provider" may be eligible for one or more of four limitations on monetary liability for copyright infringement deriving from specified activities. For purposes of the first limitation, relating to transitory communications, "service provider" is defined in section 512(k)(1)(A) as "an entity offering the transmission, routing, or providing of connections for digital online communications, between or among points specified by a user, of material of the user's choosing, without modification to the content of the material as sent or received." For purposes of the other three limitations relating to system caching, hosting, and information location tools, "service provider" is more broadly defined in section 512(k)(l)(B) as "a provider of online services or network access, or the operator of facilities therefor."

In addition, to be eligible for any of the limitations, a service provider must meet two overall conditions: (1) it must adopt and reasonably implement a policy of terminating in appropriate circumstances the accounts of subscribers who are repeat infringers; and (2) it must accommodate and not interfere with "standard technical measures" as defined in section 512(i).

[202] T-Copyright Industry Orgs., Metalitz, at 247.

[203] R-Copyright Industry Orgs., at 10-11.

59

section 512.[204] Another commenter agreed that section 512 can be extremely helpful for intermediaries, but asserted that it does not solve the particular problem for Internet webcasters and Internet broadcasters who are the originators of the transmissions.[205]

2. Scope of the Archival Exemption

a. *Expansion of the Archival Exemption to Works Other than Computer Programs*

Although most comments received on section 117 related to an exemption for temporary copies, a number of commenters discussed the scope of section 117's archival exemption. One commented that it supports amending section 117 to allow owners of any digitally-acquired content (i.e., not just computer programs) the right to make an archival or backup copy;[206] that consumers may wish to make removable archive copies of downloaded music and video to protect their downloads against losses; and that despite the convenience of digital downloading, media collections on hard drives are vulnerable.[207] This commenter noted, for example, that when a consumer wants to upgrade to a new computer or a more capacious hard disk drive, there is no lawful means to transfer the consumer's media collection onto new equipment.

This point was echoed by other commenters who said that section 117 is too narrow and, in addition to computer programs, should apply to other works due to the fact that CDs can erode

---

[204] T-DFC, Jaszi, at 273-74.

[205] T-DiMA, Greenstein, at 274.

[206] The copyright industry organizations pointed out in reply comments that DiMA believes this narrow exception to section 117(a)(2) should be expanded to cover any "content that [consumers] lawfully acquire through digital downloading." R-Copyright Industry Orgs., at 12.

[207] T-DiMA, Greenstein, at 238-39.

60

and DVDs can also develop similar problems.[208] Another commenter representing the library associations said that more categories of works are now being published in digital formats and that section 117 should be updated to clarify that the rights apply to all rightfully possessed digital media.[209] The library associations went on to say that all digital content is prone to deletion, corruption, and loss due to system crashes and that consumers must be permitted to protect their investments; thus it is critical to recognize that archival copying rights are as important today to the growth of digital publishing as they were to the growth of the computer software industry in the 1980s.[210]

On the other side was a trade association for the software and information industries. This association suggested that an expansion of section 117 to other copyrighted works is senseless because it is being used so sparingly today for computer software and the justification for the provision no longer exists.[211]

This same trade association expressed the view that the public perception of the scope of the section 117 backup copy exception may be distorted, and that persons engaged in piracy of software and other content assert they can justify their actions by relying on section 117. That commenter contended, for example, that persons attempting to auction off their so-called backup

---

[208] C-Antony, at 4-5.

[209] R-Library Ass'ns, at 11. "Many types of works that were formerly distributed in print and analog formats are now being distributed only in digital format." *Id.* at 14.

[210] *Id.* at 15.

[211] R-SIIA, at 9.

61

copies of computer software or who make pirated software available on websites, ftp sites or chat rooms, do so under the guise of the section 117 backup copy exception.[212]

A trade association representing publishers of video and computer games stated that section 117 is used, not as a legitimate defense to infringement, but as an enticement to engage in piracy.[213] It asserted that, despite the diminishing need for an archival copy exception to protect any legitimate interest of users of computer programs, and the lack of any judicial precedent for expanding the scope of section 117(a)(2), the Internet is replete with sites purporting to offer "backup copies" of videogames containing computer programs, or the means for making them.[214] It contended that many of these sites specifically refer to section 117 as providing a legal basis for their operations; for example, one website offering such 'backup copies' reassures users that "under the copyright laws of the U.S., you are entitled to own a backup of any software you have paid for," while another proclaims: "All the games, music cd's, and computer software that you will find on this page for sale are copied because it is perfectly legal by Section 117 of the US Copyright Law, to own these cd's and use them as long as you have the original program, game, or music cd."[215] In fact, according to this commenter, these sites are not actually offering "backup copies" or even copies that they rightfully own, and in any event they offer works other than computer programs. The commenter asserted that such sites "refer to section 117(a)(2) only

---

[212] C-SIIA, at 3-4.

[213] C-Interactive Digital Software Association (IDSA), at 5.

[214] *Id.*

[215] *Id.*

to provide a patina of legitimacy to their operations, and to foster a false sense among users that a patently illicit transaction – a download of pirate product – might in fact somehow be lawful.

The same commenter recommended that the language of section 117(a)(2) be narrowed to make it clear that the provision does not allow a free-standing market in so-called "backup copies," and that it only covers the copying of computer programs to the extent required to prevent loss of use of the program when the original is damaged or destroyed due to electrical or mechanical failures. It asserted that such a statutory adjustment would not only accurately reflect the changes wrought by two decades of technological advancement, but would also promote legitimate electronic commerce. Perhaps most importantly, such an adjustment would eliminate much of the confusion created in the minds of some users by those who justify their piratical activities by reference to a supposed "right" to make "back up copies" of entertainment software products.[216]

b. *Clarification of the Archival Copy Exemption for Computer Programs*

One commenter noted that section 117 does not comport with normal practices and procedures that people use for archiving information on computers.[217] He asserted that while most businesses, and many individuals, perform periodic backups of everything on their hard

---

[216] *Id.* at 6.

[217] WST-Hollaar.

drive, section 117 prescribes a different style of archiving: making a copy of an individual program at the time the consumer obtains it.[218]

In this case, the commenter advised, the archival copy will not only contain copied data, but also copied commercial software that happened to be installed on the hard drive. Not only is the program copied but also data that came along with the program, even though section 117 does not give permission to copy that data.[219]

If the use of a particular program ceases to be rightful (primarily because the user has obtained a new version of the program – perhaps an upgraded version) the user no longer has the right to use it, but rather has the right to use the new program. The user most likely will not go back, find the CD-ROM that includes the archived data and programs and try to attempt in some way to delete the programs from the CD. Section 117, noted the commenter, does not match the reality of how file archives are made today.[220]

Another commenter agreed and said multiple backup copies are needed; programs that perform backups have no knowledge of the license status of the computer files being backed up and there is no commonly used file system that stores such status with the files, so that there is no way (within common practice) for backup programs to ascertain that status.[221] He also explained

---

[218] *Id.*

[219] *Id.* at 93-95.

[220] *Id.*

[221] C-LXNY, at 1.

64

that periodic backups are made according to schedules, and to enable recovery. For example, backups may be made daily, weekly, monthly, yearly. Each tape (of the "full backup" type) would contain a copy. Although tapes are generally recycled, there are often legitimate reasons to preserve tapes.[222]

In response to the question whether there is any evidence of actual harm resulting from this mismatch between section 117 and the way system administrators or others actually backup network systems, most commenters were not aware of any harm that had resulted in this mismatch.[223] One commenter expressed concern that when the law is so far out of step with reality that it is seldom, if ever, observed, respect for the legal system diminishes and the rule of law suffers.[224]

However, one commenter did not agree that archiving backup copies necessarily amounted to a violation of section 117. He pointed out that it would be necessary to look at section 107, stating that if the activity does not fall within the specific terms of section 117, then it may be permissible under the fair use doctrine.[225] Another commenter agreed that there was a mismatch, but questioned what the practical effect of this mismatch is. No one has been sued for backing up material that may fall outside the scope of Section 117. The commenter noted that the mission of the Report is to respond to real problems. He referred to the comment submitted

---

[222] *Id.*

[223] *Id.* at 129.

[224] *Id.* at 95.

[225] T-SIIA, Kupferschmid, at 148.

65

by the Interactive Digital Software Association, which reported that one of the easiest ways to find pirated videogames online is to search for the term "section 117," since many websites offering pirated products refer, incorrectly, to that provision as legitimizing their conduct.[226]

D. VIEWS ON MISCELLANEOUS TOPICS

A number of public comments that we received addressed issues that are not directly related to section 109 or section 117. These miscellaneous views are summarized below.

1. Effect of Technological Protection Measures and Rights Management Information on Access to Works, Fair Use, and Other Noninfringing Uses.

There were many comments relating to the effects on noninfringing uses of works of technological protection measures used by copyright owners to protect their works from unauthorized access or copying. The library associations argued that it is not in the public interest to introduce legal and technological measures that diminish, if not eliminate, otherwise lawful uses.[227] The public, they asserted, now must face licensing barriers (contractual restrictions) and legal barriers (criminal penalties for circumvention) to both private and public lending and use.[228] They fear that it will remain illegal for a library or a user to circumvent technical protection measures in order to use the underlying works in ways that have traditionally been permitted under the first sale doctrine, fair use and exemptions for preservation.[229]

---

[226] T-Copyright Industry Orgs., Metalitz, at 249.

[227] T-Library Ass'ns, Petersen, at 23.

[228] C-Library Ass'ns, at 4.

[229] *Id.* at 2.

66

The DMCA was criticized by another commenter because he said it prohibits circumvention of access control devices without requiring that the devices serve only their primary purpose.[230] This commenter believes the DMCA should not allow access control devices to act as a single entry point to a technology, thereby creating an artificially privileged group of technology providers in the market.[231]

Another commenter reached the opposite conclusion based on the premise that technological protection measures are largely ineffective. This commenter noted that despite the current illegality of circumventing technological protection measures, these measures are routinely defeated, concluding that, in practice, the law has not had a significant effect on controlling copying and distribution of digital works.[232]

Some commenters expressed concern with the effects on a user's ability to use copyrighted material under the fair use provisions when anticircumvention devices are employed. More broadly, one commenter opined that the pendulum has swung too far in the interest of copyright owners and has begun to trample the needs and rights of the copyright users.[233] The library associations noted that many librarians are reluctant to make fair use judgment calls due to accountability imposed by CMI technologies and criminal sanctions; where uncertainty about

---

[230] C-Fischer, at 1-2.

[231] *Id.*

[232] C-SLAC, at 1-5.

[233] C-Beard, at 1-3.

67

permissible use exists, liability concerns may lead librarians to forego uses that are actually permitted under license and law.[234]

Another comment regarding the anti-circumvention provisions of the DMCA related to the implementation of the Secure Digital Music Initiative (SDMI) and similar technologies that could deprive educators and researchers of access to music.[235] The commenter noted that access to music under traditional notions of fair use has always been a part of our nation's cultural and legal history.[236]

2. Privacy

The library associations expressed concern for privacy rights and noted that, with copyright management information, content owners have the ability to track ongoing use of works in digital form, and to monitor who is looking at a work and exactly what the users are doing with it despite Congress' efforts to protect privacy in the DMCA.[237] They went on to say that although the DMCA's definition of CMI specifically excludes any personally identifying information about a user of a work or a copy,[238] the way CMI technologies are actually implemented may result in the compilation and tracking of usage information.[239]

---

[234] C-Library Ass'ns, at 8.

[235] C-Future of Music Coalition, at 3.

[236] *Id.*

[237] C-Library Ass'ns, at 8.

[238] 17 U.S.C. § 1202(c).

[239] C-Library Ass'ns, at 8.

68

Another commenter noted a threat to the right to privacy since copyright holders may invade the privacy of citizens attempting to communicate privately with one another on the grounds that "violations" or "infringements" may be occurring.[240] This may lead government, said the commenter, to routine monitoring of its own citizens' communications in order to prevent the transmission of "unlicensed" information.[241]

3. Contract Preemption and Licensing

Many comments raised in both written and oral testimony related to contract preemption and licensing issues. The library associations argued that the first-sale doctrine is being undermined by contract and restrictive licensing which results in uncertainty about the application of the first sale doctrine for copies of works in digital form.[242] They noted the trend towards the displacement of provisions of the uniform federal law — the Copyright Act — with licenses or contracts for digital information. The library associations asserted that college and university administrators, faculty, and students who previously turned to a single source of law and experience for determining legal and acceptable use must now evaluate and interpret thousands of licenses.[243]

---

[240] C-Darr, at 2.

[241] *Id.*

[242] T-Library Ass'ns, Neal, at 16.

[243] *Id.* T-Library Ass'ns., Petersen, at 23.

69

Another commenter argued that the case law is in disarray concerning the effectiveness of contractual terms contained in so-called "shrink-wrap" and "click-through" licenses[244] that override consumer privileges codified in the Copyright Act. This commenter proposed that section 301 of the Copyright Act[245] be amended to provide a clear statement of the supremacy of federal copyright law provisions providing for consumer privileges over state contract rules.[246] The library associations agreed with this view. Publishers responded to this line of argumentation by characterizing it as a licensing issue, not a first-sale issue.[247] The publishers noted that Congress did not intend copyright law broadly to preempt contract provisions, citing the example of section 108(f)(4) which provides that despite the privileges otherwise provided to libraries and archives under section 108, nothing in the section is to affect any contractual obligations assumed at any time by a library or archives when it obtained a copy of a work in its collections. These privileges for libraries, according to the publishers, were written to take account of the fact that contractual licensing was going to be the primary way in which copyright owners were going exploit the rights provided to them under the law.[248] Another commenter pointed out that it is a long accepted principle of American jurisprudence that parties should be free to form contracts as they see fit.[249]

---

[244] *See supra*, note 100.

[245] 17 U.S.C. § 301. Section 301 establishes the scope of federal preemption under the Copyright Act. *See infra*, at 162.

[246] C-DFC, at 3; T-DFC, Jaszi, at 228.

[247] T-AAP, Adler, at 31, 32.

[248] *Id.*

[249] R-DCC, at 4.

70

Some commenters discussed UCITA in this context and noted that, as with the Uniform Commercial Code and other uniform state laws, UCITA is intended to help facilitate electronic commerce.[250] Concern was expressed that UCITA ignores the supremacy of federal law, and, again, recommendations were made to amend section 301. The library associations believe that ambiguity in the law harms libraries and has a stifling impact on library activities. As an example, they stated that it is unclear whether a librarian, on behalf of a patron, can secure and provide interlibrary loan copies or interlibrary loan delivery of works in this environment.[251]

4. Open Source Software

One commenter was concerned that amendments to section 109 may jeopardize the ability of open source and free software licensors to ensure that third-party transferees receive the entire product whose distribution was authorized by the licensor, including the software license rights.[252] Open source or free software licenses grant users the right to: (1) have the source code; (2) freely copy the software; (3) modify and make derivative works of the software; and (4) transfer or distribute the software in its original form or as a derivative work, without paying copyright license fees.[253] The entire open source model is premised on the enforceability of those license provisions.

---

[250] R-DCC, at 1; *see supra*, note 38 and accompanying text.

[251] T-Library Ass'ns, Neal, at 55.

[252] T-Red Hat, Kunze, at 256, 257.

[253] WST-Red Hat.

71

5. Other DMCA Concerns

Several commenters expressed opposition to the DMCA for a variety of reasons. One commented that his right to communicate freely under the First Amendment was threatened by the DMCA because it broadened the definition and scope of copyright. This, in turn, resulted in frivolous cease and desist letters being sent to those attempting to exercise fair use and other exceptions.[254]

Another commenter expressed concern that the DMCA shifted the balance of power away from consumers and gave undue leverage to corporations.[255] This commenter believes that the DMCA has hampered progress and the rights of citizens by, for example, taking down websites without due process and condoning corporate behavior that does not support fair use.[256]

Concern was expressed over the distribution of monies relating to the digital performance right in sound recordings.[257] This commenter noted that the royalties should not be distributed in the "same unfair and inaccurate way" as monies are distributed under the current formula of the Audio Home Recording Act.

---

[254] C-Darr, at 1.

[255] C-Jones, at 1.

[256] *Id.*

[257] C-Future of Music Coalition, at 2.

72

III. EVALUATION AND RECOMMENDATIONS

A. THE EFFECT OF TITLE I OF THE DMCA ON THE OPERATION OF SECTIONS 109 AND 117

We are not persuaded that title I of the DMCA has had a significant effect on the operation of sections 109 and 117 of title 17, apart from some isolated factual contexts that are discussed below. Many of the public comments received by us alleged that 17 U.S.C. § 1201, as enacted in title I of the DMCA,[258] is affecting the operation of sections 109 and 117[259] (while a significant number of others argued that it is not[260]). However, either the concerns raised cannot be accurately described as being "effects on the operation of" one of those sections, or if there is an effect on the operation of one of those sections, that effect can just as easily be ascribed to other factors (such as the existence of license terms) as to section 1201. Consequently, none of the legislative recommendations made in this Report are based on effects of section 1201 on the operation of sections 109 and 117.

1. The Effect of Section 1201 on the Operation of the First Sale Doctrine

a. *DVD Encryption*

Several commenters argued that section 1201's protection of CSS for DVDs against circumvention affects consumers' exercise of the first sale doctrine by enforcing technological limitations on the way DVDs can be used.[261] These commenters asserted that because CSS is

---

[258] No commenters indicated that any other provision of title I of the DMCA affected the operation of sections 109 and 117, and we are not aware of any issues relating to whether other provisions have an effect on those sections of the Copyright Act.

[259] See C-Fischer, C-DFC, C-NARM/VSDA.

[260] See C-Copyright Industry Orgs., C-Time Warner Inc.

[261] *See* C-Arromdee, C-Thau and Taylor.

73

proprietary technology that is licensed to device manufacturers under restrictive terms, the use of CSS limits the potential playback devices for DVDs, which, in turn, limits the potential market for resale of DVDs. Second, they argued that because licensed playback devices enforce region codes,[262] DVDs purchased in one region of the world cannot be as easily resold in other regions, again limiting the potential resale market.

This argument is without merit. The first sale doctrine codified in section 109 limits an author's distribution right so that subsequent disposition of a particular copy by its owner is not an infringement of copyright. The first sale doctrine does not guarantee the existence of a secondary market or a certain price for copies of copyrighted works. If fewer people may wish to purchase a used DVD, or if they would pay less for it due to CSS, that would not equate to interference with the operation of section 109. Many circumstances in the marketplace may affect the resale market for copies of works – improvements in technology, introduction of new formats, and the quality and cultural durability of the content of the work. None of these factors can properly be said to interfere with the operation of section 109, even though they could reduce the resale market for a work or even render it nonexistent.[263]

---

[262] Each DVD bears an embedded region code corresponding to the region of the world where the particular DVD is authorized to be sold. Licensed DVD players will only play DVDs that are coded for the region where the player is sold. Region coding is used to prevent gray market importation of DVDs from one region to another.

[263] To the extent that there is a concern that region coding may limit the number of purchasers outside North America who are willing to buy region 1 DVDs (i.e., DVDs coded for sale within North America), that concern has nothing to do with section 1201. Section 1201 of title 17, United States Code, has no effect outside the United States. Consequently, a purchaser in Hong Kong could modify a region 6 player so that it could play a region 1 DVD without fear of any repercussions under section 1201 (although there may or may not be consequences under Hong Kong law). Moreover, resale outside the U.S. has nothing to do with section 109, which only governs resale within the United States.

74

Equally without merit is the argument – essentially a corollary to the guaranteed resale market argument – that the first sale doctrine gives consumers a right to use a DVD on any electronic device. In fact, virtually all devices capable of playing a DVD that are sold in the U.S. are compliant with CSS, so there is no real effect on the resale market as a result of the application of CSS technology. Further, this argument has nothing whatever to do with the privilege under section 109 to dispose of a copy of a work. Moreover, taken one step further, that argument would lead to the absurd result of requiring that consumers be able to play Beta videocassettes on VHS players, or VHS videocassettes on personal computers.

b. *Tethering Works to a Device*

A plausible argument can be made that section 1201 may have a negative effect on the operation of the first sale doctrine in the context of tethered copies – copies that are encrypted with a key that uses a unique feature of a particular device, such as a CPU identification number, to ensure that they cannot be used on any other device.[264] Even if a tethered copy is downloaded directly on to a removable medium such as a Zip™ disk or CD-RW, the content cannot be accessed on any device other than the device on which it was made. Disposition of the copy becomes a useless exercise, since the recipient will always receive nothing more than a useless piece of plastic. The only way of accessing the content on another device would be to circumvent the tethering technology, which would violate section 1201.

---

[264] *See* C-CPSR, at 4-5.

75

The practice of using technological measures to tether a copy of a work to a particular hardware device does not appear to be widespread at the present time, at least outside the context of electronic books. We understand through informal discussions with industry that this technique is – or at least can be – employed in some cases with electronic books using digital rights management (DRM) technology. Given that DRM is in its relative infancy, and the use of DRM to tether works is not widespread, it is premature to consider any legislative change to mitigate the effect of tethered works on the first sale doctrine. Nevertheless, we recognize that if the practice of tethering were to become widespread, it could have serious consequences for the operation of the first sale doctrine, although the ultimate effect on consumers of such a development remains unclear.

2. The Effect of Section 1201 on the Operation of Section 117

The use of technological measures that prevent copying of a work could have a negative effect on users' ability to make archival copies that are permitted under section 117. If, and to the extent that, such anti-copying measures can also be considered to be access control measures that are protected against circumvention by section 1201,[265] section 1201 could be said to have an adverse impact on the operation of section 117 in this context. For several reasons, however, the actual impact on consumers appears to be minimal.

---

[265] Section 1201 does not prohibit the circumvention of technological protection measures that only prevent copying. Thus, a user could lawfully circumvent the measures to create an archival copy. However, to the extent that copy controls also function as access controls, the circumvention of which is prohibited by section 1201, the circumvention of those measures is prohibited. Moreover, because section 1201 also prohibits the creation and distribution of circumvention tools, those consumers who lack the ability to circumvent technological protection measures would be unable to circumvent those measures even when such circumvention would not be unlawful.

76

First, since the overwhelming majority of computer programs sold in the United States are sold pursuant to a license, and section 117 applies only to "owners," the terms of the license agreement generally determine whether a user has the right to make an archival copy.[266] In cases where the license does not permit the creation of an archival copy, even absent technological protection measures, the copying is prohibited. Thus, in such cases it is the license that is impairing the operation of section 117.

Second, at the present time most software is sold without copy protection. Where the license permits or does not preclude the creation of an archival copy (or in the relatively few cases where the transaction was an outright sale) the user may make an archival copy as contemplated in section 117.

Third, as of last year approximately ninety-eight percent of computer software sold in the United States was sold on CD-ROM.[267] This means that even where consumers are prevented from making an archival copy, they are still able to reinstall the work in the event of computer malfunction. In essence, the CD-ROM itself acts as the archival copy. In that case, even if consumers are prevented from making archival copies as contemplated in section 117, their software investment is protected from system malfunctions, thus fulfilling the purpose of the

---

[266] Our (admittedly unscientific) review of sixteen license agreements for software used by the Copyright Office found that fourteen of them permitted the user to make a backup copy and one was silent. Only one of the sixteen licenses prohibited the user from making a backup copy, requiring the user either to use the original media as the backup copy or to replace the original media for a twenty-five dollar fee.

[267] R-SIIA, at 9.

77

archival exemption as articulated by CONTU.[268] Accordingly, we conclude that the evidence at this time of an effect of title I of the DMCA on the operation of section 117 is not substantial, and no legislative change is warranted.

B. The Effect of Electronic Commerce and Technological Change on Sections 109 and 117

We have made no attempt in preparing this study to separate out the impact of electronic commerce on sections 109 and 117 from the impact of technological change. Such an effort would probably have been futile since, as the language of section 104 suggests, by grouping the two issues together, the issues are inextricably intertwined. In its essence, electronic commerce is commerce carried out through new technologies. This study is an outgrowth of the intersection between new technology and the new business models that it makes possible. Our evaluation is of the impact of that intersection on the specified provisions of the Copyright Act.

1. The First Sale Doctrine in the Digital World

a. *Application of Existing Law to Digital Content*

The application of section 109 to digital content is not a question of whether the provision applies to works in digital form — it does. Physical copies of works in a digital format, such as CDs or DVDs, are subject to section 109 in the same way as physical copies of works in analog form. Likewise, a lawfully made tangible copy of a digitally downloaded work, such as an image file downloaded directly to a floppy disk, is subject to section 109. The question we address here

---

[268] *See supra*, at 29.

is whether the conduct of transmitting the work digitally,[269] so that another person receives a copy of the work, falls within the scope of the defense.[270]

Section 109 limits a copyright owner's exclusive right of distribution. It does not, by its terms, serve as a defense to a claim of infringement of any of the other exclusive rights.[271] The transmissions that are the focus of proposals for a "digital first sale doctrine"[272] result in reproductions of the works involved. The ultimate product of one of these digital transmissions is a new copy in the possession of a new person. Unlike the traditional circumstances of a first sale transfer, the recipient obtains a new copy, not the same one with which the sender began. Indeed, absent human or technological intervention, the sender retains the source copy. This copying implicates the copyright owner's reproduction right as well as the distribution right.

---

[269] The transmissions discussed in this section are not broadcasts, but transmissions that, like point-to-point transmissions, involve the selection of specific recipients by the sender.

[270] Some commenters were confused between the proposal to apply the first sale doctrine to otherwise unauthorized digital transmissions of copyrighted works by lawful owners of copies of such works and the notion that a lawful copy created as a result of an authorized digital transmission is a lawful copy for purposes of section 109. The former would expand the scope of section 109 and will be discussed below. The latter is well within the current language of the statute. Regardless of whether a copy is created as a result of the nearly instantaneous transmission of digital information through broadband computer connections or as a result of months of painstaking labor of a cloistered monk working with a quill by candlelight, so long as that copy is lawfully made, it satisfies the second prong of eligibility for the section 109 defenses.

[271] 17 U.S.C. § 109(a). In limited circumstances the public display right is covered as well. 17 U.S.C. § 109(c). *See supra*, note 53.

[272] The term "digital first sale doctrine" is used here to denote a proposed copyright exception that would permit the transmission of a work from one person to another, generally via the Internet, provided the sender's copy is destroyed or disabled (whether voluntarily or automatically by virtue of a technological measure). We use the term because it has been used frequently in discourse about the subject. It is, however, a misnomer since the proposal relates not to works in digital form generally (which are, of course, already subject to section 109), but to *transmissions* of such works.

79

Section 109 provides no defense to infringements of the reproduction right. Therefore, when the owner of a lawful copy of a copyrighted work digitally transmits that work in a way that exercises the reproduction right without authorization, section 109 does not provide a defense to infringement.

Some commenters suggested that this reading of section 109 is unduly formalistic. The language of the statute, however, must be given effect. Section 109 is quite specific about the rights that are covered, and does not support a reading that would find additional rights to be covered by implication. Where Congress intended to immunize an activity, such as fair use, from infringement of any of the exclusive rights, it did so expressly.[273] It simply cannot be presumed that where Congress did enumerate specific rights, it somehow intended other rights to be included as well. In addition, our reading of section 109 is entirely consistent with the judicial origin of the first sale doctrine in the *Bobbs-Merrill* decision. The Supreme Court drew a sharp distinction between the two rights, creating an exception to the vending (i.e., distribution) right only to the extent that it didn't interfere with the reproduction right.[274] We therefore conclude that section 109 does not apply to digital transmission of works.

b. *Evaluation of Arguments Concerning Expansion of Section 109*

A number of commenters proposed that section 109 be expanded to apply expressly to the reproduction, public performance and public display rights to the extent necessary to permit the

---

[273] *E.g.,* 17 U.S.C. § 107 ("Notwithstanding the provisions of sections 106 and 106A, the fair use of a copyrighted work . . . is not an infringement of copyright.").

[274] *Bobbs-Merrill*, 210 U.S. at 350-51. *See* discussion *supra*, at 20-21.

digital transmission of a work by the owner of a lawful copy of that work, so long as that copy is destroyed. This section will review the arguments for and against such a digital first sale doctrine.

i. Analogy to the physical world

Arguments in support of a digital first sale doctrine generally proceed from an analogy to the circulation of physical goods. Whether couched as a means of achieving technological neutrality,[275] meeting consumer expectations that were formed in the off-line world,[276] or eliminating barriers to competition between e-commerce and traditional commerce,[277] an underlying basis for the argument in favor of a digital first sale doctrine is that the transmission and deletion of a digital file is essentially the same as the transfer of a physical copy.

To be sure, there is an important similarity between physical transfer, on one hand, and transmission and deletion, on the other. At the completion of each process the transferor no longer has the copy (at least in usable form) and the transferee does. Some of the proposals would enhance this similarity by requiring the use of technological measures (in some cases

---

[275] *E.g.*, C-Anthony, at 3.

[276] *E.g.*, R-DiMA, at 6 (arguing that, without a digital first sale doctrine, consumers are being short-changed when they purchase copyrighted works online because they don't get what they expect, and, consequently, will become disenchanted with the medium, decreasing legitimate demand and increasing online infringement).

The opponents of a digital first sale doctrine counter that the proposal would sharply reduce the supply of works available online because copyright owners would lack confidence that their works will be protected from piracy. In addition, they point out that there is tremendous demand for copyrighted works online, even though section 109 has not been expanded. R-SIIA, R-BMI. They view this as evidence that revision of section 109 is not a prerequisite to having robust growth in e-commerce in copyrighted works.

[277] C-HRRC, at 5-6.

referred to as "move" or "forward-and-delete" technology) that will disable access to or delete entirely the source file upon transfer of a copy of that file. Assuming the technology is effective, these proposals would ensure that the single act of sending the work to a recipient results in a copy of the work being retained by the recipient alone. They differ from the Boucher-Campbell bill, which required an additional affirmative act: the subsequent deletion of the work by the sender.

Implicit in any argument by analogy is the assertion that the similarities outweigh the differences. Whether or not the analogy outlined above is compelling from a policy perspective depends upon whether the differences between the circulation of physical copies and electronic "transfers" are more significant than the similarities.

Physical copies of works degrade with time and use, making used copies less desirable than new ones. Digital information does not degrade, and can be reproduced perfectly on a recipient's computer. The "used"[278] copy is just as desirable as (in fact, is indistinguishable from) a new copy of the same work. Time, space, effort and cost no longer act as barriers to the movement of copies, since digital copies can be transmitted nearly instantaneously anywhere in the world with minimal effort and negligible cost. The need to transport physical copies of works, which acts as a natural brake on the effect of resales on the copyright owner's market, no

---

[278] The "used" copy refers to the copy on the recipient's computer. In fact, it is not "used" in any sense of the word since it was initially created on the recipient's computer as the end result of the transmission process.

82

longer exists in the realm of digital transmissions. The ability of such "used" copies to compete for market share with new copies is thus far greater in the digital world.[279]

Even the "lending" of a fairly small number of copies of a work by digital transmission could substitute for a large number of purchases. For example, one could devise an aggregation site on the Internet that stores (or, in a peer-to-peer model, points to) multiple copies of an electronic book. A user can "borrow" a copy of the book for as long as he is actually reading it. Once the book is "closed," it is "returned" into circulation. Unlike a typical lending library, where the book, once lent to a patron, is out of circulation for days or weeks at a time, the electronic book in this scenario is available to other readers at any moment that it is not actually being read. Since, at any given time, only a limited number of readers will actually be reading the book, a small number of copies can supply the demand of a much larger audience. The effect of this activity on the copyright owner's market for the work is far greater than the effect of the analogous activity in the non-digital world.

In addition, unless a "forward-and-delete" technology is employed, transfer of a copy by transmission requires an additional affirmative act by the sender. In applying a digital first sale doctrine as a defense to infringement it would be difficult to prove or disprove whether that act had taken place, thereby complicating enforcement.[280] This carries with it a greatly increased risk

---

[279] T-SIIA, Kupferschmid, at 85.

[280] These differences have already been noted by the Register on a prior occasion. Marybeth Peters, *The Spring 1996 Horace S. Manges Lecture – The National Information Infrastructure: A Copyright Office Perspective*, 20 Colum. V.L.A. Journal 341, 355 (Spring, 1996).

of infringement in a medium where piracy risks are already orders of magnitude greater than in the physical world. Removing, even in limited circumstances, the legal limitations on retransmission of works, coupled with the lack of inherent technological limitations on rapid duplication and dissemination, will make it too easy for unauthorized copies to be made and distributed, seriously harming the market for those works.[281]

Even the use of "forward-and-delete" technology, as advocated by some commenters,[282] is not a silver bullet. Technological measures can be hacked; they are expensive; and they often encounter resistence in the marketplace. In order to achieve a result that occurs automatically in the physical world, a publisher would have to pay for an expensive (and less than 100 percent reliable) technology and pass that cost along to the consumer, while at the same time potentially making the product less desirable in the marketplace. The ability of the market to correct this imbalance would be inhibited because copyright owners would need to apply these measures or face the risk of unauthorized copying under the guise of the first sale doctrine. In addition, technological measures may inadvertently impede legitimate uses of the work, harming consumers. Further, no one has offered evidence that this technology is viable at this time.

One copyright industry representative observed in oral testimony that there had been no "hue and cry, not even so much as a suggestion, that consumers are looking for products that will

---

[281] *Accord* R-Time Warner Inc., at 2-3.

[282] *E.g.*, R-DiMA, at 5.

84

function under the forward-and-delete model."[283] To the contrary, the Napster phenomenon was cited as evidence that consumers wish to retain, not destroy, the digital copy from which the work is transmitted.[284] We encountered nothing in the course of preparing this Report that would refute this observation.

Each of these differences between circulation of tangible and intangible copies is directly relevant to the balance between copyright owners and users in section 109. In weighing the detrimental effect of a digital first sale doctrine on copyright owners' markets against the furtherance of the policies behind the first sale doctrine it must be acknowledged that the detrimental effect increases significantly in the online environment. "The ultimate question is whether an equivalent to the first sale doctrine *should* be crafted to apply in the digital environment. The answer must turn on a determination that such a new exception is needed to further the policies behind the first sale doctrine, and that it can be implemented without greater detriment to the copyright owner's market."[285] We turn now to an evaluation of the policies behind the first sale doctrine.

---

[283] T-NMPA, Mann, at 157.

[284] *Id.* at 157-58.

[285] Peters, *supra*, note 280, at 355-56 (emphasis in original).

85

ii. Policies behind the first sale doctrine

"The first sale doctrine was originally adopted by the courts to give effect to the early common law rule against restraints on the alienation of tangible property."[286] As discussed above, it appears to have been motivated as well by competition concerns – specifically, the ability of publishers to use their vending or distribution right to control not only the initial sales of books, but the aftermarket for resales.[287]

The tangible nature of the copy is not a mere relic of a bygone technology. It is a defining element of the first sale doctrine and critical to its rationale. This is because the first sale doctrine is an outgrowth of the distinction between ownership of intangible intellectual property (the copyright) and ownership of tangible personal property (the copy).[288]

The distribution right can be conceptualized as an extension of the copyright owner's exclusive rights to include an interest in the tangible copies. Under common-law principles, the owner of the physical artifact – the copy – has complete dominion over it, and may dispose of possession or ownership of it as he sees fit. The distribution right, nonetheless, enables the

---

[286] S. Rep. No. 162, 98th Cong., 1st Sess. 4 (1983). The legislative history of section 109 and of section 27 of the 1909 law, the first codification of the first sale doctrine, is quite brief. Despite its brevity, it focuses on one important and relevant concept. Repeatedly, the congressional reports refer to the ability of the owner of a *material copy* to dispose of that copy as he sees fit. H.R. Rep. No. 2222, 60th Cong., 2nd Sess. 19 (1909); H.R. 28192, 60th Cong., 2nd Sess. 26 (1909); H.R. Rep. No. 94-1476, 94th Cong., 2nd Sess. 79 (1976).

[287] *See supra*, at 21.

[288] "Ownership of a copyright, or of any of the exclusive rights under a copyright, is distinct from ownership of any material object in which the work is embodied. Transfer of ownership of any material object, including the copy or phonorecord in which the work is first fixed, does not of itself convey any rights in the copyrighted work embodied in the object; nor, in the absence of an agreement, does transfer of ownership of a copyright or of any exclusive rights under a copyright convey property rights in any material object." 17 U.S.C. § 202.

86

copyright owner to prevent alienation of the copy – up to a point. That point is when ownership of a lawfully made copy is transferred to another person – *i.e.*, first sale. The first sale doctrine upholds the distinction between ownership of the copyright and ownership of the material object by confining the effect of the distribution right's encroachment on that distinction.

The underlying connection between the two concepts is apparent in the 1909 Copyright Act. Both the first sale doctrine and the doctrine that ownership of copyright is distinct from ownership of a material object are found in section 27.[289] Notwithstanding their codification in separate sections of the 1976 Act, their origin as part of the same provision of the 1909 Act demonstrates that the concepts are two sides of the same coin.

Digital transmission of a work does not implicate the alienability of a physical artifact. When a work is transmitted, the sender is not exercising common-law dominion over an item of personal property; he is exercising the central copyright right of reproduction with respect to the intangible work. Conversely, the copyright owner's reproduction right does not interfere at all with the ability of the owner of the physical copy to dispose of ownership or possession of that copy, since the first sale doctrine applies fully with respect to the tangible object (e.g., the user's hard drive) in which the work is embodied.

Because the underlying purpose of the first sale doctrine is to ensure the free circulation of tangible copies, it simply cannot be said that a transformation of section 109 to cover digital

---

[289] The text of section 27 is quoted, *supra*, note 39.

87

transmissions furthers that purpose. The concerns that animate the first sale doctrine do not apply to the transmission of works in digital form.[290]

A number of the comments we received express the view that a digital first sale doctrine would further the purposes of section 109. We note that none of those comments are supported by a historically sound formulation of what those purposes are. For example, one commenter argued that the first sale doctrine is based on a calculation of incentives to create.[291] This view is not supported by the legislative history of section 109. Moreover, as is discussed below, the potential harm to the market and increased risk of infringement that would result from an expansion of section 109 could substantially reduce the incentive to create.[292] Thus, this argument is both historically unsound and unpersuasive as a practical matter.

Another commenter suggested that the original purpose of the first sale doctrine was "to Promote the Progress of science and Useful Arts [sic]."[293] This observation does not advance the argument. It is a given that the "Progress of Science and useful Arts"[294] is the policy

---

[290] "The first sale doctrine was developed to avoid restraints on the alienation of physical property, and to prevent publishers from controlling not only initial sales of books, but the after-market for resales. These concerns do not apply to transmissions of works on the [Internet]." Peters, *supra*, note 280, at 355-56 (emphasis in original).

[291] C-DiMA, at 5-6 ("Copyright law secures to the copyright owner the exclusive rights of first distribution to provide an incentive for the creation and dissemination of copyrighted works. Once the copyright holder has been compensated for the initial distribution of the work, no further incentive is required, so the copyright owner should not be able to extract further profits from that particular copy of the work.").

[292] *See infra*, at 97-99.

[293] C-DFC, at 2 ("Historically, the 'first sale' doctrine has contributed to the achievement of that goal by providing a means for the broad secondary dissemination of works of imagination and information.") (quoting without citation, U.S. Const. Art. I, sec. 8).

[294] U.S. Const. Art. I, sec. 8.

88

undergirding the *entire* Copyright Act. However, particular provisions of the law may have more precise purposes, as is the case here.

The library associations made the claim that the first sale doctrine is based on a right of access[295] – a right not found in the legislative history of section 109. In support of this argument, they cited to section 109(d)[296] as a demonstration that section 109 applies "according to the scope of the interest that has been transferred, rather than according to the object of that interest."[297] We understand this argument to suggest that because the lease of a tangible object is not activity to which section 109 applies, the fact that a work is embodied in a tangible object must not be the test for the application of section 109. Instead, this argument appears to suggest, the scope of the interest conveyed (ownership versus rental) is the determinative factor for the application of section 109. This interpretation is fundamentally flawed. Section 109 is conditioned on *both* ownership (as opposed to mere possession) and the requirement that such ownership be of a particular physical copy. The failure to satisfy either requirement will preclude the distribution of the copy pursuant to section 109.

The library associations supported their conclusion regarding the first sale doctrine being a proxy for a right of access by proceeding from the premise that the requirement of a particular physical copy should be jettisoned from the doctrine. To support that premise, the library

---

[295] R-Library Ass'ns, at 3-7.

[296] 17 U.S.C. § 109(d) (stipulating that the privileges of this section apply only to ownership of copies, not mere possession).

[297] *Id.* at 3.

associations claim that the requirement of a particular physical copy "was an efficient proxy for distinguishing the copyright owner's exclusive rights in his work from the right to access and use that work . . . ."[298] The argument is circular.

There is nothing to support the thesis that the first sale doctrine is a stand-in for a right of access to copyrighted works. Apart from the reference to section 109(d) discussed above, no authority was marshaled in support of this proposition. Neither the statutory text nor the legislative history of section 109 (or section 27 of the 1909 law) support the proposition. To the contrary, however, the Supreme Court's decision in *Bobbs-Merrill* and the legislative history of the 1909 Act do refer directly to alienability of tangible property.[299]

A number of the comments also made reference to socially desirable activities, such as library lending, that are furthered by the existing first sale doctrine, and argue that similarly desirable activities would be furthered by a digital first sale doctrine. Asserting that a digital first sale doctrine would have beneficial effects is not the same as arguing that it would further the purposes of the existing first sale doctrine, since there is no sound basis for asserting that those effects are related to the purpose of the first sale doctrine. This argument relates not to underlying purpose, but to a balancing of the impact of copyright rights and exceptions. Even assuming the accuracy of the assertion that a digital first sale doctrine would result in socially desirable activities, the fact that a particular limitation on a copyright owner's exclusive rights

---

[298] *Id.* at 3-4.

[299] *See supra* at 20-24.

90

will promote a public good is not, in itself, a sufficient basis for curtailing copyright protection. The social benefit must be balanced against the harm to the copyright owner's legitimate interests, and thus to the incentive to create. As discussed above, the extension, by analogy, of the first sale doctrine to the online environment has a significantly greater negative impact on copyright owners' legitimate interests than does the traditional first sale doctrine in the realm of tangible copies.

iii. Development of new business models

Reasoning by analogy always carries with it the risk of becoming captive to the analogy. Assumptions that are implicit in one situation can carry over to the analogous situation even though those assumptions no longer apply. This appears to be the case with the analogy between distribution of tangible copies and online transmissions of works.

Proposals for a digital first sale doctrine endeavor to fit the exploitation of works online within a distribution model that was developed within the confines of pre-digital technology. Digital communications technology enables authors and publishers to develop new business models, with a more flexible array of products that can be tailored and priced to meet the needs of different consumers.[300] Requiring that transmissions of digital files be treated just the same as the sale of tangible copies artificially forces authors and publishers into a distribution model based on outright sale of copies of the work. The sale model was dictated by the technological necessity of manufacturing and parting company with physical copies in order to exploit a work –

---

[300] Jane C. Ginsburg, *From Having Copies to Experiencing Works: the Development of an Access Right in U.S. Copyright Law* 10 (2000) (available online at papers.ssrn.com/paper.taf?abstract_id=222493).

neither of which apply to online distribution. If the sale model continues to be the dominant method of distribution, it should be the choice of the market, not due to legislative fiat.

iv. International considerations

In evaluating the arguments put forward to support a digital first sale doctrine, it is instructive to inquire how the international community is addressing the application of exhaustion of rights[301] to the online transmissions of works. The 1996 WIPO treaties[302] set international norms for the treatment of copyright and related rights in the Internet environment. The treaties addressed both the circulation of physical goods and the transmission of works.

---

[301] "Exhaustion" is the term that is often used in international agreements to refer to the termination of a copyright owner's distribution right with respect to a particular copy after that copy has been sold with the copyright owner's authorization — i.e., the first sale doctrine. The distribution right is said to "exhaust" after the first sale.

[302] *See supra*, at 5.

The WCT and the WPPT provide an exclusive distribution right[303] with respect to

tangible copies of works while, with respect to intangible copies (that is, transmissions),

providing a separate exclusive right of making available to the public, that was conceived as a

---

[303] WCT, art. 6:

(1) Authors of literary and artistic works shall enjoy the exclusive right of authorizing the making available to the public of the original and copies of their works through the sale or other transfer of ownership.

(2) Nothing in this Treaty shall affect the freedom of Contracting Parties to determine the conditions, if any, under which the exhaustion of the right in paragraph (1) applies after the first sale or other transfer of ownership of the original or a copy of the work with the authorization of the owner.*

*Agreed statement concerning Articles 6 and 7: As used in these Articles, the expressions "copies" and "original and copies," being subject to the right of distribution and the right of rental under the said Articles, refer exclusively to fixed copies that can be put into circulation as tangible objects.

WPPT, art. 8:

(1) Performers shall enjoy the exclusive right of authorizing the making available to the public of the original and copies of their performances fixed in phonograms through the sale or other transfer of ownership.

(2) Nothing in this Treaty shall affect the freedom of Contracting Parties to determine the conditions, if any, under which the exhaustion of the right in paragraph (1) applies after the first sale or other transfer of ownership of the original or a copy of the fixed performance with the authorization of the performer.*

*Agreed statement concerning Articles 2(e), 8, 9, 12, and 13: As used in these Articles, the expressions "copies" and "original and copies," being subject to the right of distribution and the right of rental under the said Articles, refer exclusively to fixed copies that can be put into circulation as tangible objects.;

WPPT, art. 12:

(1) Producers of phonograms shall enjoy the exclusive right of authorizing the making available to the public of the original and copies of their performances fixed in phonograms through the sale or other transfer of ownership.

(2) Nothing in this Treaty shall affect the freedom of Contracting Parties to determine the conditions, if any, under which the exhaustion of the right in paragraph (1) applies after the first sale or other transfer of ownership of the original or a copy of the phonogram with the authorization of the producer of the phonogram.*

*Agreed statement concerning Articles 2(e), 8, 9, 12, and 13: As used in these Articles, the expressions "copies" and "original and copies," being subject to the right of distribution and the right of rental under the said Articles, refer exclusively to fixed copies that can be put into circulation as tangible objects.

93

subset of a general right of communication to the public.[304] The treaties permit members to limit

the distribution right with an exhaustion principle,[305] but there is no requirement to do so. There

is no provision in either treaty regarding exhaustion of the making available or communication

rights. This is hardly surprising since exhaustion is a concept that has heretofore only applied to

the right to distribute tangible copies.

Those countries that have implemented protection for online transmissions have largely

done so through the right of communication to the public and thus provide no equivalent of the

first sale limitation to such rights. We are not aware of any country other than the United States

that has implemented the making available right through application of a combination of the

distribution, reproduction, public performance and public display rights. In a sense, the only

reason the issue of first sale arises in the U.S. is because we chose to implement the making

---

[304] WCT, art. 8:

Without prejudice to the provisions of Articles 11(1)(ii), 11bis(1)(i) and (ii), 11ter(1)(ii) and 14bis(1) of the Berne Convention, authors of literary and artistic works shall enjoy the exclusive right of authorizing any communication to the public of their works, by wire or wireless means, including the making available to the public of their works in such a way that members of the public may access these works from a place and at a time individually chosen by them.

WPPT, art. 10:

Performers shall enjoy the exclusive right of authorizing the making available to the public of their performances fixed in phonograms, by wire or wireless means, in such a way that members of the public may access them from a place and at a time individually chosen by them.;

WPPT, art. 14:

Producers of phonograms shall enjoy the exclusive right of authorizing the making available to the public of their phonograms, by wire or wireless means, in such a way that members of the public may access them from a place and at a time individually chosen by them.

[305] WCT, art. 6(2); WPPT, art. 8(2), art. 12(2).

94

available right through, *inter alia*, the distribution right. Elsewhere, online transmissions are considered communications to the public, and the first sale doctrine simply does not apply.

An important example of this is the European Union's Information Society Directive.[306] This directive, which, among other things, implements the WIPO treaties, provides for a distribution right[307] that is limited by the exhaustion principle, and a separate making available right that is not. The exhaustion principle in the Directive is expressly limited to circulation of tangible copies:

> Copyright protection under this Directive includes the exclusive right to control distribution of the work incorporated in a tangible article. The first sale in the Community of the original of a work or copies thereof by the rightholder or with his consent exhausts the right to control resale of that object in the Community.[308]

The Directive goes further, stating in clear terms that exhaustion does not apply to online transmissions:

> The question of exhaustion does not arise in the case of services and on-line services in particular. This also applies with regard to a material copy of a work or other subject-matter made by a user of such a service with the consent of the rightholder. Therefore, the same applies to rental and lending of the original and copies of works or other subject-matter which are services by nature. Unlike CD-

---

[306] Directive 2001/29/EC of the European Parliament and of the Council of 22 May 2001, on the harmonisation of certain aspects of copyright and related rights in the information society (OJ L 167/10 2001) ("Information Society Directive").

[307] Information Society Directive, art. 4:

1.   Member States shall provide for authors, in respect of the original of their works or of copies thereof, the exclusive right to authorise or prohibit any form of distribution to the public by sale or otherwise.

2.   The distribution right shall not be exhausted within the Community in respect of the original or copies of the work, except where the first sale or other transfer of ownership in the Community of that object is made by the rightholder or with his consent.

[308] Information Society Directive, art. 28.

95

ROM or CD-I, where the intellectual property is incorporated in a material medium, namely an item of goods, every on-line service is in fact an act which should be subject to authorisation where the copyright or related right so provides.[309]

The decision of the EU not to create an exception to the right of communication to the public that is similar to the doctrine of exhaustion of the right of distribution represents an informed policy decision that such an expansion is not appropriate. We are not aware of a public outcry in any of the EU countries in opposition to this decision.

The analogy that some in the U.S. have made between the downstream distribution of a tangible copy of a work and an online transmission is attractive because of the broad application of the right of distribution in U.S. copyright law. As both activities implicate the distribution right, the distinction between the distribution of physical objects and intangible transmissions may at first blush seem small. They are, however, distinct acts with distinct characteristics that ought not necessarily be treated similarly. When viewed through an international lens this distinction becomes clearer.

c. *Recommendations*

Based on the foregoing discussion, and for the reasons set forth below, we recommend no change to section 109 at this time. Although there is a great deal of speculation about what may happen in the future, we heard no convincing evidence of present-day problems. However, legitimate concerns have been raised about what may develop as the market and technology evolve. These concerns are particularly acute in the context of the potential impact on library

---

[309] Information Society Directive, art. 29.

96

operations. The time may come when Congress may wish to consider further how to address these concerns.

i. No change to section 109

In order to recommend a change in the law, there should be a demonstrated need for the change that outweighs any negative aspects of the proposal. We do not believe that this is the case with the proposal to expand the scope of section 109 to include a digital first sale doctrine.

Much of the rhetorical force behind the digital first sale proposal stems from the analogy to circulation of goods in the physical realm. On examining the nature of digital transmissions compared to the nature of transfers of material objects, we do not find this analogy compelling for several reasons.

The analogy ultimately rests on the fiction that a transmission of a work is the same as a transfer of a physical copy. In order to get around the fact that a transmission results in two copies, the analogy requires one of two things to happen: either a voluntary deletion of the sender's copy or its automatic deletion by technological means. Both are unworkable at this time.

Relying on voluntary deletion is an open invitation to virtually undetectable cheating, and there is no reason to believe there would be general compliance with such a requirement. If the burden were placed on the copyright owner to demonstrate that there was no simultaneous

97

deletion of the copy from which the transmission was made, it would erect what would probably be an impossible evidentiary burden. If the burden of establishing the defense were placed on the defendant, and had to be met by demonstrating simultaneous deletion, the defendant would have a similarly impossible evidentiary burden. If the defendant were merely required to demonstrate the absence of a copy of the work on his hard drive, then the simultaneous deletion principle would, as a practical matter, disappear, and section 109 would become a defense that could be asserted whenever a copy was deleted at any time after it had been transmitted one or more times or copied for retention on another medium. The recent phenomenon of the popularity of using Napster to obtain unauthorized copies of works strongly suggests that some members of the public will infringe copyright when the likelihood of detection and punishment is low.

Relying on a "forward-and-delete" technology is not workable either. At present such technology does not appear to be available. Even assuming that it is developed in the future, the technology would have to be robust, persistent, and fairly easy to use. As such, it would likely be expensive – an expense that would have to be borne by the copyright owner or passed on to the consumer. Even so, the technology would probably not be 100 percent effective. Conditioning a curtailment of the copyright owners' rights on the employment of an expensive technology would give the copyright owner every incentive *not* to use it. In the alternative, it would be damaging to the market to expand section 109 in anticipation of the application of technological protection measures, thus giving the copyright owner a choice between significantly increased expenses, significantly increased exposure to online infringement, or not offering works online.

Asserting, by analogy, that an online digital transmission is the same as a transfer of a material object ignores the many differences between the two events. Digital transmission has a much greater effect on the market for copies provided by the copyright owners. It is also accompanied by a greatly increased risk of piracy.

The risk that expansion of section 109 will lead to increased digital infringement weighs heavily against such an expansion. Copyright piracy in the online world is not a matter of speculation — it is, unfortunately, an established fact of life. It appears likely that expanding section 109 would encourage infringement of the reproduction right, either in the mistaken belief that the provision allows a user to retain a copy of a work after it has been transmitted one or more times, or in the belief that the defense can be asserted in bad faith to defeat, or at least complicate, an infringement lawsuit. And unlike Napster, the activity would not rely on a central server, so both the infringing activity and the evidence of infringement would be decentralized and therefore difficult to detect and remedy.[310]

Twice since the enactment of the current Copyright Act, Congress has stepped in to *narrow* the scope of the first sale doctrine to safeguard the reproduction right.[311] In both cases there was anecdotal evidence of abuses in the marketplace, combined with conditions that created the opportunity for widespread abuse. The same conditions apply to the proposals to

---

[310] *See* I. Trotter Hardy, Project Looking Forward: Sketching the Future of Copyright in a Networked World 262-63 (Copyright Office, 1998) (analyzing the difficulties involved in preventing, identifying, and remedying decentralized infringement) (available online at www.loc.gov/copyright/docs/thardy.pdf).

[311] *See* discussion *supra*, at 24-25.

99

create a digital first sale doctrine. Again, the striking popularity of Napster is a strong indication that many people will infringe copyright if the means to do so is at their disposal. And the more convenient the means, the greater the likelihood of infringements. The risk to the copyright owners' reproduction right is simply too great.

We do not ignore the claim that an expansion of section 109 would further the pro-competitive goals of the first sale doctrine. To the extent that section 109 does not permit the transmission of copyrighted works, the right holders retain the exclusive right to restrict or prohibit such activity, thereby barring resales that compete with sales of new copies. Of course, a lawfully made and owned copy of a work on a floppy disk, Zip™ disk, CD-ROM or similar removable storage medium can easily be transferred by physical transfer of the item and that activity is within the current reach of section 109. In the final analysis, the concerns about expanding first sale to limit the reproduction right, harm to the market as a result of the ease of distribution, and the lessened deterrent effect of the law that could promote piracy, outweigh the pro-competitive gains that might be realized from the creation of a digital first sale doctrine. In addition, there does not appear to be any evidence that the kind of price-fixing behavior that prompted the Supreme Court to establish the first sale doctrine is occurring. Should such behavior become widespread, and should antitrust law fail to afford an appropriate remedy, this conclusion may have to be revisited.

Implicit in several of the submissions that addressed the first sale issue is a belief that the analogy of transmissions to physical transfer is so compelling that consumer expectations about

100

transferability of downloaded material have become deeply-rooted. It is said that failure of the law to live up to this expectation will damage commerce in such material. We are aware of no empirical (or even anecdotal) evidence for this proposition, so any assessment of claims concerning consumer expectations and their effect on e-commerce is necessarily conjectural. However, it can be said with confidence that e-commerce and the market for works online has grown quite substantially despite the absence of an expanded section 109. In addition, judging from consumer trends today, there appears to be little or no evidence of desire on the part of consumers to engage in the kind of conduct — transmission and simultaneous deletion — that would be covered in a digital first sale doctrine.

In any event, these issues of consumer expectations and the growth of electronic commerce are precisely what should be left to the marketplace to determine. Straight-jacketing copyright owners into a distribution model that developed around a different technology at a different time is a formula for stifling innovative, market-driven approaches to meeting consumer demand for digital content. If, as has been asserted, the current terms by which copyright owners offer their products are unacceptable to consumers, consumers will stop buying them under those terms and competitors will step into the breach. Such self-correcting market forces should be given an opportunity to address these types of concerns before Congress alters the balance of rights and exceptions in the Copyright Act.

101

ii. Further consideration of ways to address library issues related to the first sale doctrine

The fact that we did not recommend adopting a "digital first sale" provision at this time does not mean that the issues raised by libraries are not potentially valid concerns. Similarly, our conclusion that certain issues are beyond the scope of the present study does not reflect our judgment on the merits of those issues.

The library community has raised concerns about how the current marketing of works in digital form affects libraries with regard to five specifically enumerated categories: interlibrary loans, off-site accessibility, archiving/preservation, availability of works, and use of donated copies.[312] In each case, the concern is that licensing terms for use of the works will effectively prohibit the desired activity.[313]

Concerning interlibrary lending, library associations suggest that the Copyright Act should reaffirm and strengthen rules on interlibrary loan especially for acquired digital works.[314] They state that licenses often prohibit the loaning of works in digital form. As mentioned elsewhere, the issue of licenses is beyond the scope of this study.

It should be noted that many interlibrary loans are not in fact loans – the temporary lending of a particular copy of a work – but delivery of copies. The "lending" institution

---

[312] C-Library Ass'ns, at 11-19.

[313] *Id.*

[314] *Id.* at 11-13, 23.

102

reproduces the copyrighted work and sends the reproduction to the "borrowing" library. This copy is given by the borrowing library to its patron, who becomes the owner of that copy. Clearly this activity of libraries is outside of the scope of section 109. As to the library patron, to the extent that such a reproduction and distribution is authorized by section 108,[315] the copy becomes his property and is therefore subject to section 109.

Library concerns about offsite accessibility relate chiefly to licenses that limit access to a particular work to a specific location (e.g., a single building or computer). This means that such works are not available for use offsite, including in a classroom. Libraries seek the ability to make all works in their collections available for classroom use.[316] These are contract issues that are not within the mandate for this study.

Library associations raised a related concern about licensing terms which limit the number of users of a work at any given time, the hours of the day during which works may be used, or other similar limitations.[317] Less restrictive licenses are often available, but at a higher price. As with restrictions on offsite availability of works, these limitations have the effect of reducing the general availability of those works that are subject to the limitations. The library associations believe that these restrictions create substantial burdens to research.[318] This is also a

---

[315] Section 108 was updated in the Digital Millennium Copyright Act of 1998; as updated, section 108 makes it clear that digital copies may not be given to patrons. Copies given to patrons must be in analog form – e.g., photocopies.

[316] C-Library Ass'ns, at 11-13, 23.

[317] *Id.* at 17.

[318] *Id.*

103

contract issue that is not within the mandate of the study. However, we do note that the difficulty identified by the library associations is not new, and is not unique to the digital world. Libraries have always had make difficult trade-offs between greater availability of particular works (through the purchase of more copies) and other priorities.

Concern was also raised about works that libraries can only offer by means of online access. The terms of use of a work that is accessed in this way are typically set forth in a subscription agreement. Online access is achieved by loading the work into the RAM of a computer while it is being accessed; it does not involve the making of a permanent copy. Here there is no section 109 issue – at the end of the online session the library owns no physical copy that can be transferred.

Preservation and archiving are identified as potential problems because many licenses prohibit copying for such purposes (or for any purpose) and because prohibitions on copying are enforced by technological means.[319] The library associations propose creating a national system of digital repositories, where specific libraries or institutions would be designated as custodians of specific parts of our nation's digital history and assisted in their efforts to preserve these works.[320] While these issues are beyond the scope of this study, we acknowledge that they are legitimate concerns that have been recognized as such.[321] In fact, they are being addressed. For

---

[319] C-Library Ass'ns, at 14.

[320] *Id.* at 23.

[321] Committee on Intellectual Property Rights and the Emerging Information Infrastructure, The Digital Dilemma 209-10 (2000).

104

example, the Librarian of Congress, James H. Billington, has appointed a national advisory committee to assist the Library of Congress in the development of a National Digital Information Infrastructure and Preservation Program to ensure the long-term availability of digital materials. That committee held its first meeting on May 1, 2001.

The focus of library concerns regarding donated copies is their ability to use donated CD-ROMs. Libraries are not able to use CD-ROMs donated to them because the donors are not owners of the CD-ROMs, only licensees, and thus lack the legal authority to transfer the copy of the work they possess.[322] Since the license agreement prevents the transfer, the issue is beyond the scope of this study.

Most of these issues arise from terms and conditions of use, and costs of license agreements. One arises because, when the library has only online access to the work, it lacks a physical copy of the copyrighted work that can be transferred.[323] These issues arise from existing business models and are therefore subject to market forces. We are in the early stages of electronic commerce. We hope and expect that the marketplace will respond to the various concerns of customers in the library community. However, these issues may require further consideration at some point in the future. Libraries serve a vital function in society, and we will continue to work with the library and publishing communities on ways to ensure the continuation of library functions that are critical to our national interest.

---

[322] C-Library Ass'ns, at 18-19.

[323] *See* Ginsburg *supra* note 300, at 10.

105

2. The Legal Status of Temporary Copies

a. *Relevance to this Report*

As was discussed above, this Report is a direct outgrowth of Congressional concern at the time of the enactment of the DMCA about the copyright treatment of digital reproduction and transmission.[324] Specifically, the scope of the study and Report mandated by Congress in section 104 of the DMCA can be traced to some of the proposed amendments to sections 109 and 117 of title17 made in the Boucher-Campbell bill.[325] One of these proposals was an amendment to section 117 that would allow temporary copies to be made if these copies were "incidental to the operation of a device in the course of the use of a work otherwise lawful under this title."[326] While this proposal was not adopted by Congress, section 117 was one of the provisions of title 17 that we were instructed to examine in this Report. The only context in which section 117 arose in the Boucher-Campbell bill was with respect to incidental copying.

This Report necessarily requires consideration and evaluation of temporary incidental copies made in the course of use on a computer or computer network, such as the Internet. In addition to the congressional concerns leading to the creation of this Report, the comments and testimony received in the course of our study illustrate the importance of clarifying the lawful scope of temporary copies in the current market. In order to understand the issues raised by the transmission of digital works over the Internet, it is appropriate to clarify the current state of the

---

[324] *See* discussion *supra*, at 18.

[325] H.R. 3048, 105th Congress, 1st Session, November 13, 1997. *See* discussion *supra*, at 15 & ff.

[326] *Id.* at Sec. 6(b)(1).

106

law on this issue. This section will discuss the origins of the section 117 exemption for temporary copies and examine its purpose in relation to new developments related to temporary buffer copies.

b. *RAM Reproductions as "Copies" under the Copyright Act*

i. Technical background

All instructions and data that are operated on by a computer are stored in integrated circuits known as RAM. Unlike flash memory, read-only memory (ROM)[327] and magnetic storage devices such as disk and tape drives, RAM is volatile: when power is switched off, all information stored in RAM is erased. Conversely, as long as the power remains on, information stored in RAM can be retrieved and reproduced unless it is overwritten by other information.

All of the familiar activities that one performs on a computer — e.g., execution of a computer program, retrieval and display of information, browsing the World-Wide Web — necessarily entail making reproductions in RAM. These reproductions generally are made automatically, and transparently to the user—i.e., without the user being aware that copies are being made. The copies usually persist for as long as the activity takes place.[328] For example, the instructions that comprise a computer program generally remain in RAM for as long as the

---

[327] This term includes all variants of ROM, such as programmable read-only memory (PROM), erasable programmable read-only memory (EPROM), electrically erasable programmable read-only memory (EEPROM) and so on.

[328] In many instances, as a technical matter, the information will remain in RAM even after it is no longer in use. For example, when a computer program terminates, the operating system takes note of the fact that the memory occupied by the program is now available for other use. The content of that memory, however, is unchanged until it is overwritten with new information, or the power is turned off.

107

program is running. Likewise, the data that express text and images remain in RAM for as long as the text and images are displayed. As the packets of binary information comprising works traverse computer networks, temporary copies (in RAM and on disk) are made as they move from point to point along the way from source to destination.

Although it is theoretically possible that information could be stored in RAM for such a short period of time that it could not be retrieved, displayed, copied or communicated, this is unlikely to happen in practice. A device that is capable of storing, but not retrieving, displaying, copying or communicating information would have no practical purpose, and there would be no engineering justification for making such a device.

The issue of the legal status of RAM reproductions has arisen in this study almost exclusively in the particular factual context of streaming audio.[329] In order to render[330] the packets of audio information in an audio "stream " smoothly, the rendering software maintains a "buffer" – a portion of memory set aside to store audio information until it has been rendered. Inconsistencies in the rate at which audio packets are delivered over the Internet are thus evened out, so that the software can render the information at a constant rate. As information is rendered, it is discarded and new information is put into the buffer as it is received.

---

[329] "Streaming audio" is the digital transmission of sound – often sound recordings of musical compositions – as a series of packets of audio information that are reassembled and rendered on the recipient's computer as they are received.

[330] In this context "render" means the process by which the digital representation of sounds and/or images is converted back into those sounds and/or images.

108

ii. Statutory analysis

Section 106(1) of the Copyright Act grants a copyright owner the exclusive right "to reproduce the copyrighted work in copies" and to authorize others to do so. Reproducing a work in RAM therefore falls within the scope of a copyright owner's exclusive reproduction right if it results in a "copy."

The starting point for determining whether reproductions in RAM are copies for copyright purposes is the text of the statute. "Copies" are defined in the Copyright Act as:

> material objects, other than phonorecords, in which a work is fixed by any method now known or later developed, and from which the work can be perceived, reproduced, or otherwise communicated, either directly or with the aid of a machine or device.[331]

There is no question that RAM chips are "material objects." They are electronic integrated circuits, etched and deposited on a wafer of semiconducting material (such as silicon), which are capable of storing binary information in the form of electrical impulses. A work stored in RAM can be "perceived, reproduced, or otherwise communicated" with the aid of a computer. The key issue, therefore, is whether a reproduction in RAM is "fixed."

The Copyright Act defines "fixed" as follows:

> A work is "fixed" in a tangible medium of expression when its embodiment in a copy or phonorecord . . . is sufficiently permanent or stable to permit it to be perceived, reproduced, or otherwise communicated for a period of more than transitory duration.[332]

---

[331] 17 U.S.C. § 101.

[332] *Id.*

109

As to the element of duration, the definition of "fixed" does not require that a copy be permanent or that it last for any specified period of time.[333] For a work to be fixed, is must only be "*sufficiently* permanent *or stable*, to permit it to be perceived [or] reproduced . . . for a period of more than transitory duration."[334] Although the embodiment of a work in RAM is not permanent, since loss of power results in erasure of the work, typically it is "sufficiently . . . stable" to be "perceived [or] reproduced" for an indefinite period of time — i.e., for as long as the power remains on and the memory locations storing the work are not overwritten with other information. As one court has observed, the conclusion that RAM copies are fixed

> is actually confirmed rather than refuted by [the] argument that the RAM representation of the program is not "fixed" because it disappears from RAM the instant the computer is turned off. Thus one need only imagine a scenario where the computer, with the program loaded into RAM, is left on for extended periods of time, say months or years, or indeed left on for the life of the computer. In this event, the RAM version of the program is surely not ephemeral or transient; it is, instead, essentially permanent and thus plainly sufficiently fixed to constitute a copy under the Act.[335]

Based on the definitional language in the Copyright Act, RAM reproductions are generally "fixed" and thus constitute "copies" that are within the scope of the copyright owner's reproduction right. The definition of "fixed" leaves open the possibility, however, that certain RAM reproductions that exist for only a "period of . . . transitory duration" are not copies. The statute does not define "transitory duration" directly. Since permanence is not required for

---

[333] *See Advanced Computer Services of Michigan, Inc. v. MAI Sys. Corp.*, 845 F. Supp. 356, 362-63 (E.D. Va. 1994).

[334] 17 U.S.C. § 101 (emphasis added).

[335] *Advanced Computer Services*, 845 F. Supp. at 363.

110

fixation, "transitory" must denote something shorter than "temporary." "Transitory" must also

denote something less than "ephemeral," as that term is used in the Copyright Act, since the Act

confirms that "ephemeral recordings" are fixed by providing a specific exemption for "ephemeral

recordings" lasting up to six months.[336] Courts have not attempted to formulate a general rule

defining how long a reproduction must endure to be "fixed," deciding instead on a case-by-case

basis whether the particular reproduction at issue sufficed.[337]

Nonetheless, a general rule can be drawn from the language of the statute. In establishing

the dividing line between those reproductions that are subject to the reproduction right and those

that are not, we believe that Congress intended the copyright owner's exclusive right to extend to

all reproductions from which economic value can be derived. The economic value derived from

a reproduction lies in the ability to copy, perceive or communicate it. Unless a reproduction

manifests itself so fleetingly that it cannot be copied, perceived or communicated, the making of

that copy should fall within the scope of the copyright owner's exclusive rights. The dividing

line, then, can be drawn between reproductions that exist for a sufficient period of time to be

capable of being "perceived, reproduced, or otherwise communicated" and those that do not.[338]

---

[336] 17 U.S.C. § 112.

[337] *See, e.g., MAI Sys. Corp. v. Peak Computer, Inc.*, 991 F.2d 511, 518 (9th Cir. 1993); *Advanced Computer Servs.*, 845 F. Supp. at 363.

[338] This view is consistent with the discussion of fixation in the legislative history of the Copyright Act. The legislative history is examined *infra* at 114-117.

It is also consistent with "a quite well-established position at the international level" that "fixation means sufficient stability of form so that what is 'fixed' may be perceived, reproduced or otherwise communicated." Mihály Ficsor, *Copyright for the Digital Era: The WIPO "Internet" Treaties*, 21 Colum./VLA J. L. and the Arts 197 (1997) ("Digital Era").

111

As a practical matter, as discussed above, this would cover the temporary copies that are made in RAM in the course of using works on computers and computer networks.

Drawing the line with reference to the ability to perceive, reproduce or otherwise communicate a work makes particular sense when one considers the manner in which one important category of digital works—computer programs—are utilized. Computer programs are exploited chiefly through exercise of the rights of reproduction and distribution. In order to utilize a program, it must be copied into RAM. To exercise the right to make that temporary copy in RAM is to realize the economic value of the program. That RAM copy need only exist long enough to communicate the instructions to the computer's processing unit in the proper sequence.

Exploitation of works on digital networks illustrates the same point. Digital networks permit a single disk copy of a work to meet the demands of many users by creating multiple RAM copies. These copies need exist only long enough to be perceived (e.g., displayed on the screen or played through speakers), reproduced or otherwise communicated (e.g., to a computer's processing unit) in order for their economic value to be realized. If the network is sufficiently reliable, users have no need to retain copies of the material. Commercial exploitation in a network environment can be said to be based on selling a right to perceive temporary reproductions of works.[339]

---

[339] Other exclusive rights may be involved as well. A discussion of these additional rights is beyond the scope of this Report.

112

Apart from these policy considerations, attempting to draw a line based on duration may be impossible. The language of the Copyright Act rules out drawing the line between temporary and permanent copies, as discussed above. Even if this distinction were possible under the statute, the concept of permanence is not helpful in this context. Magnetic disks and tapes can be erased; printed works decompose over time, or can be destroyed deliberately or accidentally. Separating some temporary copies from others based on their duration poses similar difficulties. How temporary is temporary? Hours? Minutes? Seconds? Nanoseconds? The line would be difficult to draw, both in theory and as a matter of proof in litigation.

The conclusion that reproductions in RAM are "copies" is reinforced by the existence of another provision of the Copyright Act: section 117. The current version of section 117 was added in 1980 at the recommendation of CONTU. In relevant part, it provides:

> Notwithstanding the provisions of section 106, it is not an infringement for the owner of a copy of a computer program to make or authorize the making of another copy or adaptation of that computer program provided:
>
> (1) that such a new copy or adaptation is created as an essential step in the utilization of the computer program in conjunction with a machine and that it is used in no other manner . . . .[340]

The "new copy" that is "created as an essential step in the utilization of the computer program in conjunction with a machine" is the copy made in RAM when the program is executed. No such exemption would have been necessary if reproductions in RAM could not be copies. It would be

---

[340] 17 U.S.C. § 117.

113

unreasonable to interpret the definitions in section 101 in such a way that it would render section 117 superfluous.[341]

iii. Legislative history

The legislative history of the Copyright Act confirms that certain temporary reproductions implicate the reproduction right, but is ambiguous as to the precise dividing line between temporary reproductions that are considered "fixed" and those that are not. In discussing the definition of "fixed," the House Report that accompanied the Copyright Act of 1976 states that copies that exist only "momentarily" in RAM may not satisfy the fixation requirement.[342] According to the 1976 House Report, "the definition of 'fixation' would exclude from the concept purely evanescent or transient reproductions such as those projected briefly on a screen, shown electronically on a television or other cathode ray tube, or captured momentarily in the 'memory' of a computer."[343]

One interpretation of that statement is that Congress viewed all reproductions in the "memory" of a computer to exist only momentarily, and thus as incapable of meeting the fixation requirement.[344] If so, then the legislative history was based on an imperfect grasp of the relevant technology. As discussed above, reproductions in RAM can exist for long periods of time — i.e.,

---

[341] *See, e.g., Pennsylvania Dept. of Public Welfare v. Davenport*, 495 U.S. 552, 562 (1990) ("Our cases express a deep reluctance to interpret a statutory provision so as to render superfluous other provisions in the same enactment.").

[342] 1976 House Report, *supra* note 40, at 53.

[343] *Id.*

[344] *See* discussion *infra*, at 120-123.

for as long as the power remains on and no other information is stored in the memory locations occupied by the reproduction. In addition, RAM reproductions are qualitatively different from the other examples cited (projection on a screen, or display on a television or cathode ray tube). RAM reproductions are stored or embodied in the RAM chip. A projection on a screen or a display on a television or cathode ray tube is not stored or embodied in the screen or TV or display tube.[345] In any event, the premise that all RAM reproductions exist only momentarily is incorrect, and cannot support a conclusion that all RAM reproductions are unfixed.[346]

Another possible interpretation of the statement in the House Report concerning computer memory is that it applies not to all RAM reproductions, but only to those "reproductions . . . captured *momentarily*" in "computer memory."[347] This interpretation implies that any reproduction in computer memory that exists more than "momentarily" is fixed. This interpretation adheres more closely to the statutory text, since, as discussed above, the statute on its face contemplates that at least some temporary copies satisfy the fixation requirement.[348] Consequently, it appears to be the better interpretation of the language in the 1976 House Report.

---

[345] *See infra*, note 369.

[346] *Accord* CONTU Report, *supra* note 61, at 22 n.111 ("Insofar as a contrary conclusion [that works in computer storage are not fixed] is suggested in one report accompanying the new law, this should be regarded as incorrect and should not be followed since legislative history need not be perused in the construction of an unambiguous statute.").

[347] 1976 House Report, *supra* note 22, at 53 (emphasis added).

[348] *See* discussion *supra,* at 109–114.

115

Stating that copies which exist only "momentarily" are not fixed (and copies that exist longer are fixed) still begs the question of precisely which RAM copies exist for too short a time to satisfy the fixation requirement, and which do not. The best guide in the legislative history for determining where Congress intended to draw the line between fixed and unfixed reproductions is elsewhere in the 1976 House Report, where it is stated that "fixation is sufficient if the work 'can be perceived, reproduced, or otherwise communicated, either directly or with the aid of a machine or device.'"[349] This statement supports the distinction drawn above between RAM copies that exist long enough to be perceived, reproduced or otherwise communicated and those that do not.

The legislative history of a subsequent amendment to the Copyright Act also supports the conclusion that temporary copies in RAM may satisfy the fixation requirement. The current text of sections 117(a) and (b) was added in 1980 as part of a package of amendments recommended by CONTU. The House report accompanying the 1980 amendments did not explain the intent of the legislation, other than to implement CONTU's recommendations.[350] The CONTU Report sets forth its reasons for recommending the statutory additions, which Congress enacted with few changes.[351]

---

[349] 1976 House Report, *supra* note 35, at 52 (quoting 17 U.S.C. § 102(a)).

[350] Referring to the portion of the bill that added the section 101 definition of "computer program" and section 117, the House committee report stated only that it "embodie[d] the recommendations of the Commission on New Technological Uses of Copyrighted Works with respect to clarifying the law of copyright of computer programs." H.R. Rep. No. 1307 (Part I), 96th Cong., 2d Sess. 23 (1980).

[351] The status of the CONTU Report as legislative history is discussed *supra*, at 29.

CONTU clearly viewed reproductions in computer memory as "copies," implicating a copyright owner's exclusive rights under section 106.[352] In 1976 Congress considered the problems associated with computer uses of copyrighted works not to be sufficiently developed for a definitive legislative solution.[353] Congress enacted what was commonly referred to as a "moratorium" provision in section 117, which preserved the status quo on December 31, 1977 as to use of copyrighted works in conjunction with computers and similar information systems.[354] In recommending the repeal of that provision, CONTU stated:

> The 1976 Act, without change, makes it clear that the placement of any copyrighted work into a computer is the preparation of a copy and, therefore, a potential infringement of copyright. . . .
>
> Because the placement of a work into a computer is the preparation of a copy, the law should provide that persons in rightful possession of copies of programs be able to use them freely without fear of exposure to copyright liability. . . . One who rightfully possesses a copy of a program, therefore, should be provided with a legal right to copy it to that extent which will permit its use by that possessor. This would include the right to load it into a computer . . . .[355]

---

[352] CONTU Report, *supra* note 61, at 13. It is reasonable to assume that in 1978, when the CONTU Report was published, reference to "placement of a work into a computer" was understood to include reproduction in volatile memory. Although early generations of computers used non-volatile ferrite core memory, volatile solid-state memory was in wide use by the early 1970s.

[353] 1976 House Report, *supra* note 35, at 116.

[354] Pub. L. No. 94-553, 90 Stat. 2541 (1976); 1976 House Report, *supra* note 35, at 116. Former section 117 read as follows:

Notwithstanding the provisions of sections 106 through 116 and 118, this title does not afford to the owner of copyright in a work any greater or lesser rights with respect to the use of the work in conjunction with automatic systems capable of storing, processing, retrieving, or transferring information, or in conjunction with any similar device, machine or process, than those afforded to works under the law, whether title 17 or the common law or statutes of a State, in effect on December 31, 1977, as held applicable and construed by a court in action brought under this title.

[355] CONTU Report, *supra* note 61, at 13.

117

iv. Judicial interpretation

Every court that has addressed the issue of reproductions in volatile RAM has expressly or impliedly found such reproductions to be copies within the scope of the reproduction right. We are aware of no cases that have reached the contrary conclusion.

The seminal case on the subject is *MAI Sys. Corp. v. Peak Computer, Inc.*,[356] in which the defendant's loading of operating system and diagnostic software into computer memory in violation of a license agreement was held to be an infringement.[357] In reaching that conclusion, the Ninth Circuit examined the definitions in section 101 and found that "loading of copyrighted software into RAM creates a 'copy' of that software."[358] The court noted that, although it was aware of no prior cases holding that reproductions in RAM were copies, "it is generally accepted that the loading of software into a computer constitutes the creation of a copy under the Copyright Act."[359] After making note of evidence in the record that, once the software was loaded into RAM, the defendant was able to view the system error log in order to diagnose a problem with the computer, the court reasoned that this evidence demonstrated "that the representation created in the RAM is 'sufficiently permanent or stable to permit it to be perceived, reproduced, or otherwise communicated for a period of more than transitory

---

[356] 991 F.2d 511 (9th Cir. 1993), *cert. dismissed*, 114 S. Ct. 671 (1994).

[357] *MAI v. Peak* has generated controversy on two fronts. As discussed *infra*, at 120, the holding regarding RAM copying has been consistently upheld by later courts, but criticized by a number of academic commentators. In addition, the implications of the case for competition in the computer repair industry led in 1998 to a specific legislative exemption for certain temporary copies in RAM. *See* discussion *infra*, at 30.

[358] *Id.* at 518.

[359] *Id.* at 519.

118

duration.'"[360] Consequently, the court affirmed the district court's conclusion that "a 'copying'

for purposes of copyright law occurs when a computer program is transferred from a permanent

storage device to a computer's RAM."[361]

At least nine other courts have followed *MAI v. Peak* in holding RAM reproductions to be

"copies," although not all have ultimately found the defendant to be liable for infringement.[362]

Even before *MAI v. Peak*, the Fifth Circuit had stated that "the act of loading a program from a

medium of storage into a computer's memory creates a copy of the program."[363] The factual

context suggests that the court was referring to RAM. Several other cases have also held that

---

[360] *Id.*

[361] *Id.*

[362] *See Stenograph L.L.C. v. Bossard Assocs.*, 144 F.3d 96, 101-02 (D.C. Cir. 1998) (holding that "a RAM reproduction constitutes a copy"); *DSC Communications Corp. v. DGI Technologies, Inc.*, 81 F.3d 597, 600 (5th Cir. 1996) (citing *MAI v. Peak*, holding that copy is made when software is loaded into computer's RAM; defendant is not enjoined from making such copies, however, because it is likely to prevail on its defense of copyright misuse); *Triad Sys. Corp. v. Southeastern Express Co.*, 64 F.3d 1330, 1335 (9th Cir.), *cert. denied*, 116 S. Ct. 1015 (1995) (loading of software into RAM is "copying" for purposes of the Copyright Act); *Intellectual Reserve, Inc. v. Utah Lighthouse Ministry, Inc.*, 75 F. Supp. 2d 1290, 1294 (D. Utah 1999); *Wilcom Pty. Ltd. v. Endless Visions*, 1998 U.S. Dist. LEXIS 20583, *9 (E.D. Mich. Dec. 2, 1998) ("a temporary copy of the program's object code in . . . RAM . . . is sufficiently 'fixed in a tangible medium of expression' to constitute an infringing copy under the Copyright Act"); *In re Independent Serv. Orgs. Antitrust Litigation*, 23 F. Supp. 2d 1242, 1245 (D. Kan. 1998) ("use (and hence reproduction into random access memory ('RAM')) of diagnostic software . . . was not authorized by [plaintiff] and hence constituted infringement"); *Marobie-FL, Inc. v. National Assoc. of Fire Equip. Dists.*, 983 F. Supp. 1167, 1176-78 (N.D. Ill. 1997) (citing *MAI v. Peak*, finding RAM copies to be fixed as long as they are capable of being perceived); *Religious Tech. Center v. Netcom On-line Comm.*, 907 F. Supp 1361, 1368 (N.D. Cal. 1995) ("In the present case, there is no question after *MAI* that 'copies' were created . . . ."; preliminary injunction denied, however, because plaintiff did not demonstrate a substantial likelihood of success on the merits); *In re Independent Serv. Orgs. Litigation*, 910 F. Supp. 1537, 1541 (D. Kan. 1995) ("We agree with the court in [*MAI v. Peak*], that transferring a computer program from a storage device to a computer's RAM constitutes a copy for purposes of copyright law."); *Advanced Computer Servs. of Mich., Inc. v. MAI Systems Corp.*, 845 F. Supp. 356, 363 (E.D. Va. 1994) (where "a copyrighted program is loaded into RAM and maintained there for minutes or longer, the RAM representation of the program is sufficiently 'fixed' to constitute a 'copy' under the Act"). See also, *Ohio v. Perry*, 41 U.S.P.Q.2d (BNA) 1989 (Ohio App. 1997) (following *MAI v. Peak* in concluding that state charge of unauthorized use of property stemming from the unauthorized posting of software on a computer bulletin board service was preempted by the Copyright Act because the defendant's acts constituted copyright infringement).

[363] *Vault Corp. v. Quaid Software Ltd.*, 847 F.2d 255, 260 (5th Cir. 1988).

loading a computer program into a computer entails making a copy, without mentioning RAM specifically.[364]

v. Commentary

In contrast to the apparent unanimity among courts that have considered the issue of RAM copying, legal scholars are divided on the question – which may account for the characterization of *MAI v. Peak* by at least one commenter as "controversial."[365] Although some academics have expressed support for the conclusion that the reproduction right can embrace RAM copies,[366] much commentary on the subject has criticized the holding of *MAI v. Peak*.[367]

---

[364] *See, e.g., Sega Enterprises Ltd. v. MAPHIA*, 948 F. Supp. 923, 931-32 (N.D. Cal. 1996) (following *MAI v. Peak*); *NLFC, Inc. v. Devcom Mid-America, Inc.*, 45 F.3d 231, 235 (7th Cir. 1995) ("Neither party disputes that loading software into a computer constitutes the creation of a copy under the Copyright Act"; nonetheless, court affirms summary judgment for defendant because of plaintiff's failure to establish copying as a factual matter); *Roeslin v. District of Columbia*, 921 F. Supp. 793, 800 (D.D.C. 1995) ("The placement of a copyrighted program into a computer, or the loading of a copyrighted program into a computer (which occurs every time [one] uses the program), constitutes 'copying' the program for purposes of the Copyright Act."); *Tricom, Inc. v. Electronic Data Sys. Corp.*, 902 F. Supp. 741, 745 (E.D. Mich. 1995) (loading software onto mainframe computer constitutes copying under the copyright law); *Hubco Data Prods. Corp. v. Management Assistance, Inc.*, 219 U.S.P.Q. (BNA) 450, 456 (D. Idaho 1983) (statutory definition of "copy" "makes clear that the input of a work into a computer results in the making of a copy, and hence that such unauthorized input infringes the copyright owner's reproduction right").

[365] C-DFC, at 3.

[366] *See, e.g.,* 1 William F. Patry, Copyright Law and Practice 171(1994); David Nimmer, *Brains and Other Paraphernalia of the Digital Age*, 10 Harv. J. of Law & Tech. 1, 10-11 (1996); Jane C. Ginsburg, *Putting Cars on the "Information Superhighway": Authors, Exploiters, and Copyright in Cyberspace*, 95 Colum L. Rev. 1466, 1475-77 (1995); I. Trotter Hardy, *Symposium: Copyright Owners' Rights and Users' Privileges on the Internet: Computer RAM "Copies": A Hit or a Myth? Historical Perspectives on Caching as a Microcosm of Current Copyright Concerns*, 22 Dayton L. Rev. 423, 427-28, 456-60 (1997).

[367] *See, e.g.,* Mark A. Lemley, *Symposium: Copyright Owners' Rights and Users' Privileges on the Internet: Dealing with Overlapping Copyrights on the Internet*, 22 Dayton L. Rev. 547, 550-51 (1997); James Boyle, *Intellectual Property Policy Online: A Young Person's Guide*, 10 Harv. J. Law and Tech. 47, 88-94 (1996); Fred H. Cate, *The Technological Transformation of Copyright Law*, 81 Iowa L. Rev. 1395, 1452-53; Niva Elkin-Koren, *Cyberlaw and Social Change: A Democratic Approach to Copyright Law in Cyberspace*, 14 Cardozo Arts & Ent. L.J. 215, 269-74 (1996); Pamela Samuelson, *Legally Speaking: The NII Intellectual Property Report*, Communications of the ACM, Dec. 1994, at 21, 22 ("*Legally Speaking*"); Jessica Litman, *The Herbert Tenzer Memorial Conference: Copyright in the Twenty-First Century: The Exclusive Right to Read*, 13 Cardozo Arts & Ent. L.J. 29, 42-43 (1994).

120

The criticism of *MAI* has rested mainly on three arguments: (1) that the text and legislative history of the Copyright Act indicate that Congress did not intend that "the temporary storage of a copyrighted work in a computer's memory . . . be regarded as an infringing reproduction";[368] (2) that the reasoning employed in *MAI v. Peak*, if carried to its logical extreme, would lead to absurd results ; and (3) that *MAI v. Peak* is merely the decision of one appellate court, and should not be followed.

The first argument — that Congress did not intend RAM reproductions to be copies — is addressed in the foregoing analysis. Except for reproductions that do not persist long enough to be perceived, reproduced or otherwise communicated, the text and legislative history of the Copyright Act support the conclusion that Congress intended temporary reproductions in RAM to be "copies." In particular, the argument fails to explain Congress' view that it was necessary to adopt section 117(a)(1) to permit the making of temporary RAM copies in the course of using a computer program.

The second argument — that the reasoning employed in *MAI v. Peak* would lead to absurd results — is based on the implicit assumption that a finding of *copying* leads inevitably to a finding of *infringement*.[369] But determining that a reproduction in RAM implicates the

---

[368] Pamela Samuelson, *The Copyright Grab*, Wired, Jan. 1996, at 4.

[369] One example that has been made to support this argument is that, by the logic of *MAI v. Peak*, "holding a mirror up to a book would be infringement because the book's image could be perceived there for more than a transitory duration, i.e., however long one has the patience to hold the mirror." *Legally Speaking, supra,* n.13; *see also* Litman, *supra,* at 42 n.63 (quoting *Legally Speaking*). *MAI v. Peak* does not compel a finding of copying in this hypothetical, however. A reflection on a mirror is not fixed. This conclusion flows not from its temporary nature, but from the fact that the work reflected off the mirror's surface is not "embodied" in the mirror. By contrast, there was no question that the work in *MAI v. Peak* was "embodied" in RAM by virtue of the electrical charges stored in

121

reproduction right does not mean that there is liability every time a RAM copy is made.[370] As

discussed in the following section, many uses of works that entail RAM copying are expressly or

impliedly licensed. In addition, exemptions, such as fair use, that apply to copying in other

contexts apply in this context as well. Several recent exemptions have been adopted into U.S.

law specifically to address RAM copying in particular contexts.[371] If existing exceptions are

determined to be insufficient and current law could still lead to inappropriate results, additional

exceptions could be adopted in the future to deal with those circumstances.

The third argument — that *MAI v. Peak* is merely the decision of one appellate court, and

therefore should not be followed — has been overtaken by events. As discussed above, a judicial

consensus has formed around the holding in *MAI v. Peak* since these commentators' articles were

written. The D.C. Circuit, the Fifth Circuit and several trial courts have endorsed the Ninth

Circuit's holding, without contradiction by any other court.[372]

An additional argument (not related specifically to *MAI v. Peak*) has been leveled at the

application of the reproduction right to transient copies made in the course of transmitting

material on a packet-switched digital network. The crux of this argument is that, since the

---

the RAM circuitry. The issue was whether the embodiment in RAM was sufficiently permanent or stable to satisfy the fixation requirement.

[370] For example, liability was not imposed in several of the cases cited above that followed *MAI v. Peak*. *See, e.g., Religious Tech. Center*, 907 F. Supp. 1361; *DSC Communications*, 81 F.3d 597.

[371] *See, e.g.*, titles II and III of the DMCA, Pub. L. No. 105-304, 112 Stat. 2860, 2886-2905 (1998).

[372] Moreover, two Courts of Appeals appear to have reached the same conclusion, at least implicitly, before the *MAI v. Peak* decision. *See NLFC, Inc. v. Devcom Mid-America, Inc.*, 45 F.3d 231, 235 (7th Cir. 1995); *Vault Corp. v. Quaid Software, Ltd.*, 847 F.2d 255, 260 (5th Cir. 1988).

122

material is broken down into packets for transmission across the network, it is only those packets representing portions of the work that are copied. No copies of the entire work will exist at any intermediate point between the sender and the recipient. Therefore there are no "copies" of the work except in the recipient's computer where the packets are reassembled (and not even there in the case of streaming audio, where the packets are rendered in real time and discarded).[373]

There are a number of problems with this argument. To determine whether the reproduction right is implicated, the focus is on whether there has been a fixation in a material object, not on the quantity of material that has been so fixed. The reproduction right is not limited to copies of an entire work. Photocopying a page or paragraph out of an encyclopedia implicates the reproduction right and may, in appropriate circumstances, be an infringement. Whether or not a copy of a portion of a work is infringing is a question not of whether the reproduction right is implicated, but of whether the copying is substantial.

In addition, this argument fails to account for the fact that in many instances, transient copies of a number of packets may be made on a single machine in the course of transmission, that, in aggregate, represent a large portion or even the entirety of a work.

---

[373] *See, e.g.*, David L. Hayes, *Advanced Copyright Issues on the Internet*, at 5 (May 1998) (available on the Internet at www.fenwick.com/pub/copyright.pdf).

123

vi. International considerations

The treatment of temporary copies under U.S. law that is described above is consistent with the scope of the reproduction right that is mandated in Berne. Berne establishes the reproduction right in broad and general terms:

> Authors of literary and artistic works protected by this convention shall have the exclusive right of authorizing the reproduction of these works, in any manner or form.[374]

On its face, the plain language of Article 9(1) includes temporary copies in RAM. Article 9(1) does not restrict the coverage of the right by the duration of a reproduction, and explicitly covers "any manner or form." As one "manner or form" of reproduction, temporary copies in RAM are covered by this formulation. This view has been advanced by Dr. Mihály Ficsor, then-Assistant Director General of WIPO, in a statement to Congress:

> It would be in conflict with the Berne Convention to deny the application of the right of reproduction just because a reproduction is not in tangible form, or because it is only temporary. . . . There is only one criterion, namely whether or not there is any fixation of the work in a computer memory, even for a very short time, but still for a sufficient time, so that it may serve as a basis for the perception of the signs, images and/or sounds in which the work is expressed, or for a parallel or subsequent reproduction.[375]

---

[374] Berne, Art. 9(1). This provision is among those that are incorporated by reference in the WTO Agreement on Trade-Related Aspects of Intellectual Property Rights ("TRIPS"), and is thus a part of the U.S. obligations under its WTO commitments. Similarly, the WIPO Copyright Treaty ("WCT") also incorporates the Berne reproduction right by reference, and articles 7 and 11 of the WIPO Performances and Phonograms Treaty ("WPPT") give performers and producers of phonograms (sound recordings) the exclusive right to reproduce their sound recordings "in any manner or form." Neither the WCT nor the WPPT has yet come into force, although both are expected to enter into force during 2001. The WIPO Copyright Treaty is discussed further *infra* at pages 125-127.

[375] *Joint Hearing before the Subcommittee on Courts and Intellectual Property of the House Committee on the Judiciary and the Senate Committee on the Judiciary on H.R. 2441 and S. 1284* (Serial No. 38 (Part 1)), 104th Cong., 1st Sess. 57 (1995) (statement of Mihály Ficsor); see also, WIPO, *Basic Proposal for the Substantive Provisions of the Treaty on Certain Questions Concerning The Protection of Literary and Artistic Works to Be Considered by the Diplomatic Conference*, Art. 7, explanatory notes 7.05-7.06 (Doc. No. CRNR/DC/4) (1996) (memorandum prepared by the Chairman of the Committees of Experts) ("Draft WIPO Copyright Treaty").

124

A similar conclusion was reached by a committee of governmental experts convened by WIPO and UNESCO in 1982 to examine copyright issues arising from the use of computers in creating or accessing works. In its report of the meeting, the committee stated:

> As for the act of input of protected subject-matter for storage purposes, it was generally agreed that it included at least reproduction of works on a machine-readable material support and their fixation in memory of a computer system. The Committee agreed that whatever this act may be, it involves fixation of works in a form sufficiently stable to permit their communication to an individual, and therefore it should be considered as governed by the international conventions and national legislation on copyright and therefore was subjected to the author's exclusive rights.[376]

Nonetheless, since temporary reproductions in RAM were not considered in the deliberations over the last revision of Berne in 1971, the principal treatise on the Berne Convention argues that Article 9(1) does not compel member states to include RAM copies within the scope of the reproduction right.[377] Events in the intervening decade and a half since that treatise was written, however, cast serious doubt on that conclusion.

In 1996 an effort was made to clarify the scope of the Berne reproduction right in the WCT (or, as it was styled up until its conclusion, the Berne Protocol). Article 7 of the draft copyright treaty that served as the basis for negotiations stated that "[t]he exclusive right accorded to authors of literary and artistic works in Article 9(1) of the Berne Convention of

---

[376] *Second Committee of Governmental Experts on Copyright Problems Arising from the Use of Computers for Access to or the Creation of Works* ¶33 (1982) (*reprinted in* UNESCO Copyright Bulletin, vol. XVI, no. 4, at 39, 43 (1982)).

[377] Sam Ricketson, *The Berne Convention for the Protection of Literary and Artistic Works: 1886-1986*, at 373-74 (1987).

125

authorizing the reproduction of their works shall include direct and indirect reproduction of their works, whether permanent or temporary, in any manner or form."[378] The second paragraph of draft Article 7 would have permitted parties to adopt exceptions to the reproduction right as applied to temporary copies

> in cases where a temporary reproduction has the sole purpose of making the work perceptible or where the reproduction is of a transient or incidental nature, provided that such reproduction takes place in the course of use of the work that is authorized by the author or permitted by law.[379]

The Diplomatic Conference did not adopt proposed Article 7, but adopted the following Agreed Statement patterned, in part, on the joint WIPO/UNESCO statement from 1982 that is quoted above:[380]

> The reproduction right, as set out in Article 9 of the Berne Convention, and the exceptions permitted thereunder, fully apply in the digital environment, in particular to the use of works in digital form. It is understood that the storage of a protected work in digital form in an electronic medium constitutes a reproduction within the meaning of Article 9 of the Berne Convention.[381]

While the outcome of the 1996 Diplomatic Conference does not go as far in clarifying the reach of Article 9(1) of Berne as originally proposed, the statement that was adopted tends to confirm that Article 9(1) covers temporary copies in computer memory: "It follows from [the] first sentence [of the agreed statement] that Article 9(1) of the Convention, which extends to reproduction 'in any manner of [sic] form,' must not be restricted just because a reproduction is

---

[378] Draft WIPO Copyright Treaty, *supra* note 124, Art. 7(1).

[379] *Id.*, Art. 7(2).

[380] *Supra*, at 125.

[381] WIPO, *Agreed Statements Concerning the WIPO Copyright Treaty* (WIPO Doc. No. CRNR/DC/96) (1996) (Agreed Statement concerning Article 1(4)).

126

in digital form, through storage in an electronic memory, and just because a reproduction is of a temporary nature."[382]

Lending support to this interpretation of the Berne obligation, the national laws of a number of Berne countries (in addition to the United States) consider the making of temporary RAM copies to be within the reproduction right, either generally or in the context of computer programs. Although some countries expressed concern about applying the reproduction right to all temporary copies in RAM in the context of the debate at the December 1996 Diplomatic Conference, we are aware of no country that has excluded such copies from the reproduction right in its legislation.[383]

In 1991, the European Union[384] adopted a directive on software protection that required each of the member states[385] to protect computer programs under copyright law.[386] The Directive

---

[382] Ficsor, Digital Era, *supra* note 338, at 8.

[383] A court in Japan has, however, considered the absence of an explicit statement in that country's copyright statute to preclude protection for temporary copies. The court took the unusual step of noting the inequitable outcome of the case and suggested that a legislative response may be warranted. RIAJ v. Dai-Ichi Kosho (Tokyo Dist. Ct. 2000).

[384] The term "European Union" did not actually come into use until the Treaty of Maastricht came into force, after the adoption of the Software Directive.

[385] The EU presently consists of the following fifteen Member States: Austria, Belgium, Denmark, Finland, France, Germany, Greece, Ireland, Italy, Luxembourg, The Netherlands, Portugal, Spain, Sweden and the United Kingdom. The European Economic Area (EEA) consists of the following three Member States: Iceland, Liechtenstein and Norway. The EU and EEA Member States participate in one single market – EU Single Market – and are governed by the same basic rules (Acquis Communiautaire). EEA members are thus obliged to implement EU directives. Countries of Central and Eastern Europe that are seeking EU membership also generally conform their intellectual property laws to the relevant EU directives. Consequently, the directives have a direct impact beyond the fifteen Member States.

[386] *Council Directive on the Legal Protection of Computer Programs*, 91/250/EEC, 1991 O.J. (L 122) 42 (the "European Software Directive").

127

expressly requires that rightholders be granted the exclusive right to make temporary copies such as those made in RAM:

> Subject to the provisions of Articles 5 and 6, the exclusive rights of the rightholder within the meaning of Article 2, shall include the right to do or to authorize:

> (a) the permanent or temporary reproduction of a computer program by any means and in any form, in part or in whole. Insofar as loading, displaying, running, transmission or storage of the computer program necessitate such reproduction, such acts shall be subject to authorization by the rightholder . . . .[387]

The exclusive reproduction right is subject to an exemption that parallels section 117(1) of the U.S. Copyright Act, permitting acts that "are necessary for the use of the computer program by the lawful acquirer in accordance with its intended purpose."[388] The Directive has been implemented in each of the member countries of the European Union.

Earlier this year the EU finalized a Directive on Copyright and Related Rights in the Information Society[389] that had been under consideration since 1997 and is intended, *inter alia*, to implement the WIPO treaties in the EU. The Directive includes temporary copies generally within the reproduction right,[390] but then mandates that Member States enact an exemption for:

---

[387] *Id.*, Art. 4.

[388] *See id.*, Art. 5(1) .

[389] Directive 2001/29/EC of the European Parliament and of the Council of 22 May 2001, on the harmonisation of certain aspects of copyright and related rights in the information society (OJ L 167/10 2001) ("Information Society Directive").

[390] "Member States shall provide for the exclusive right to authorise or prohibit direct or indirect, temporary or permanent reproduction by any means and in any form, in whole or in part . . . ." *Id.*, Art. 2.

128

Temporary acts of reproduction . . . which are transient or incidental, which are an integral and essential part of a technological process whose sole purpose is to enable:

(a) a transmission in a network between third parties by an intermediary or

(b) a lawful use of a work or other subject matter . . . and which have no independent economic significance . . . .[391]

Member States must implement the Directive in their national laws within 18 months from the date it was published in the Official Journal of the European Communities – June 22, 2001.[392]

Australian copyright law also considers RAM copies of at least computer programs to implicate the reproduction right. In recommending to Parliament an exception to permit reproduction of computer programs for normal use,[393] the Australian Copyright Law Review Committee (CLRC) stated:

> [B]ecause most computer programs operate by reproduction in whole or in part in the random access memory (RAM) of the computer, each time the purchaser of a copy of a computer program uses the program he or she arguably exercises the copyright owner's right to reproduce the program in material form. Unless the user has the permission of the copyright owner, this will constitute an infringement of copyright and, although permission may be implied by the very act of marketing the program, the lack of express statutory sanction has been commented on.[394]

---

[391] *Id.*, Art. 5(1).

[392] *Id.*, Art. 13(1).

[393] Copyright Act (1968), § 47B(1), as added by Copyright Amendment (Computer Programs) Act 1999.

[394] CLRC, *Computer Software Protection* 139 (1995). See also, *Ricketson*, at 374 & n.28 (discussing this aspect of Australian copyright law).

129

c. *Temporary Digital Copies Incidental to any Lawful Use*

Although many of the comments supported adoption of the blanket exception for incidental copies that was proposed in the Boucher-Campbell bill,[395] most of the arguments advanced in support of that proposal focused only on the specific issue of buffer copies made in the course of streaming transmissions of performances of musical works, including webcasting, rather than the broader issue of incidental copies generally. This suggests that another possible approach – legislation tailored to address the specific problems raised in the context of such streaming – should be examined.

In fact, no compelling evidence was presented to us during the course of our study that would support a blanket exception for incidental copies. Under current law, without any broad exception for incidental copies, we can discern no harm to users of copyrighted works. Nor does there appear to be any discernable evidence that electronic commerce is being impeded by the absence of a general exception for incidental copies. In fact, the opposite was shown – that electronic commerce is thriving. Moreover, we were presented with no evidence, outside the context of buffer copies of streaming audio, that consumers or businesses were facing claims for compensation or refraining from any activities as a result of legal uncertainty concerning the status of incidental copies.

On the other hand, we were presented with evidence that a blanket exception for incidental copies could have the unintended consequence of harming copyright owners and

---

[395] *See* discussion *supra*, at 15.

130

threatening new business models. For example, we heard testimony regarding the emerging

practice of delivering software on demand, not for retention but for immediate use and

subsequent disposal.[396] The software exists as a temporary copy on the user's computer while it

is used, then the copy is discarded. The users never possess a permanent copy of the software;

rather, copies of software are available to them as they need them. The only event in this model

that has copyright significance is the making of the temporary copy that is incidental to the use of

the software. In essence, the entire economic value of the transaction is in that temporary copy of

the software.

Another, somewhat more prosaic example that was cited is the use of software on a local

area network (LAN) beyond the scope of the applicable license.[397] Each user on the LAN can

realize the full economic value of the software by running the software on his individual

computer – an activity that entails making a temporary incidental copy in the PC's RAM.

In light of the lack of factual arguments to support a blanket exception for incidental

copies, and the significant risks that such an exception would immunize copying that

appropriates the economic value of the work, we do not recommend such an exception. We turn

instead to an examination of a tailored approach that focuses on the specific problems that were

brought to our attention.[398]

---

[396] T-BSA, Simon, at 111-13.

[397] T-BSA, Simon, at 111.

[398] We note that similar problems were raised during the debates in Europe over the Information Society Directive. Recall that the Information Society Directive, *infra* at 23, provides an exception in Article 5(1) to the exclusive right of reproduction to allow certain acts of temporary reproduction subject to a number of conditions.

131

d. *Temporary Copies Incidental to a Licensed Digital Performance of a Musical Work*

One factual context for the temporary copying issue was repeatedly brought to our attention during the preparation of this Report: temporary buffer copies made in RAM in the course of rendering a digital music stream.[399] The buffer copies identified by the webcasting industry have the following characteristics: they exist for only a short period of time; at any given time they consist of only a small portion of the work; and they are incidental to a performance of the work that has been licenced by the copyright owner. Webcasters asserted that lack of clarity as to the legal status of buffer copies casts a shadow over their nascent industry, exposing them to demands for additional royalty payments and potential infringement liability. As we will discuss below, it appears that their concerns have merit.

The exception in Article 5(1) would appear to be broader than the exception we are recommending in this Report. Member States of the European Union have 18 months from the publishing date in the Official Journal of the European Communities – June 22, 2001 – to implement the Information Society Directive. What scope courts actually give this exception then remains to be seen.

Article 5 is to be read in conjunction with Recital 33, which reads as follows:

(33)   The exclusive right of reproduction should be subject to an exception to allow certain acts of temporary reproduction, which are transient or incidental reproductions, forming an integral and essential part of a technological process and carried out for the sole purpose of enabling either efficient transmission in a network between third parties by an intermediary, or a lawful use of a work or other subject-matter to be made. The acts of reproduction concerned should have no separate economic value on their own. To the extent that they meet these conditions, this exception should include acts which enable browsing as well as acts of caching to take place, including those which enable transmission systems to function efficiently, provided that the intermediary does not modify the information and does not interfere with the lawful use of technology, widely recognised and used by industry, to obtain data on the use of the information. A use should be considered lawful where it is authorised by the rightholder or not restricted by law.

Some Member States give no legal weight to recitals, however, so it will be necessary to await and look to their implementing legislation to see whether, and to what degree, those Member States put this language into effect.

[399] *See supra*, at 108.

132

i. Do buffer copies implicate the reproduction right?

The fact that the copies made in the course of streaming are of very small portions of a work does not necessarily render them noninfringing.[400] Even if each individual copy were to be considered a *de minimis* portion under the test for substantial similarity, the aggregate effect is the copying of the entire work. Moreover, increases in broadband use by consumers could ultimately result in the use of buffers that store the entire work for the duration of the performance. There does appear to be at least some risk that making buffer copies in the course of streaming infringes the reproduction right.

The fact that the copies are incidental to a licensed performance does not bear upon either the applicability of the reproduction right or the test for substantial similarity. It could, however, affect a fair use analysis.[401]

ii. Is the making of buffer copies in the course of streaming a fair use?

The webcasters have asserted that the making of buffer copies in the course of streaming should be considered a fair use, and one copyright owner representative has suggested that it is.[402] While we agree that there is, in fact, a strong case that the making of a buffer copy in this context is a fair use, we note that whether a use is fair is determined on a case-by-case basis by the courts.

---

[400] *See supra*, at 122-123.

[401] *Cf. Sega Enterprises Ltd. v. Accolade, Inc.*, 977 F.2d 1510, 1522-23 (9ᵗʰ Cir. 1992) (first factor weighed in favor of a defendant who engaged in disassembly of a computer program because the use was intermediate in the process of developing a noninfringing program).

[402] *See generally* comments and testimony by SIIA.

133

The judicially-created doctrine of fair use that is codified in section 107 of the Copyright Act[403] limits the copyright owner's exclusive rights, including the reproduction right as it applies to temporary copies. Section 107 sets out four nonexclusive factors to be considered in determining whether or not a particular use is fair: (1) the purpose and character of the use, including whether such use is of a commercial nature or is for nonprofit educational purposes; (2) the nature of the copyrighted work; (3) the amount and substantiality of the portion used in relation to the copyrighted work as a whole; and (4) the effect of the use upon the potential market for or value of the copyrighted work.[404] In addition, as a doctrine that has its origins in equity, other equitable considerations may be brought to bear in a fair use analysis.

In analyzing the purpose and character of the use, courts inquire, *inter alia*, whether the use merely supplants the original work or instead adds a further purpose or different character. In other words, this factor asks "whether and to what extent the new work is 'transformative.'"[405]

---

[403] § 107. Limitations on exclusive rights: Fair use

Notwithstanding the provisions of sections 106 and 106A, the fair use of a copyrighted work, including such use by reproduction in copies or phonorecords or by any other means specified by that section, for purposes such as criticism, comment, news reporting, teaching (including multiple copies for classroom use), scholarship, or research, is not an infringement of copyright. In determining whether the use made of a work in any particular case is a fair use the factors to be considered shall include-

(1) the purpose and character of the use, including whether such use is of a commercial nature or is for nonprofit educational purposes;
(2) the nature of the copyrighted work;
(3) the amount and substantiality of the portion used in relation to the copyrighted work as a whole; and
(4) the effect of the use upon the potential market for or value of the copyrighted work.

The fact that a work is unpublished shall not itself bar a finding of fair use if such finding is made upon consideration of all the above factors.

[404] 17 U.S.C. § 107.

[405] *Campbell v. Acuff-Rose Music, Inc.*, 510 U.S. 569, 579 (1994).

134

Although "transformative use is not absolutely necessary for a finding of fair use, the goal of

copyright, to promote science and the arts, is generally furthered by the creation of transformative

works. Such works thus lie at the heart of the fair use doctrine's guarantee of breathing space

within the confines of copyright, and the more transformative the new work, the less will be the

significance of other factors, like commercialism, that may weigh against a finding of fair use."[406]

The making of a buffer copy is not transformative. The portion of the work that is copied

into the buffer is an identical reproduction of the corresponding portion of the original. "There is

neither new expression, new meaning nor new message."[407] While the copy is made in order to

effectuate a performance, this fact, in itself, would not render the use transformative.[408]

Another element that courts examine under this factor is whether the use is commercial or

noncommercial.[409] Uses that are of a "commercial nature" are generally disfavored under fair

use.[410] However, the commercial nature of a particular use does not necessarily lead to the

conclusion that an activity is not fair use.[411] Moreover, the characteristics of a particular

---

[406] *Id.* (citations omitted).

[407] *Infinity Broadcast Corp. v. Kirkwood,* 150 F.3d 104, 108 (2d Cir. 1994) (quoting the District Court opinion, 965 F. Supp. 553, 557 (S.D.N.Y. 1997)).

[408] *Cf. Id.* (difference in purpose is not the same thing as transformation).

[409] *Campbell,* 510 U.S. at 584-85 (1994). In fact, 17 U.S.C. § 107 expressly includes "including whether such use is of a commercial nature or is for nonprofit educational purposes" as a consideration under the first fair use factor.

[410] 17 U.S.C. § 107 (first factor). *See, e.g., Harper & Row, Publishers, Inc. v. Nation Enters.,* 471 U.S. 539, 562 (1985); *Sony Corp. of America v. Universal City Studios, Inc.,* 464 U.S. 417, 451 (1984); *Triangle Publications, Inc. v. Knight-Ridder Newspapers, Inc.,* 626 F.2d 1171, 1175 (5th Cir. 1980).

[411] *Campbell,* 510 U.S. 569, 584-85 (1994).

135

commercial use should be considered in determining whether the first factor weighs in favor of the copyright owner.[412]

Inasmuch as the buffer copy is made to further a commercial activity (commercial streaming of music) it is a commercial use. However, it is not a superseding use that supplants the original. It is a necessary incident to carrying out streaming. The purpose of making the copy is solely to render a performance that is fully licensed. There is no separate exploitation of the buffer copy. It is a productive use that serves a socially beneficial end – bringing a licensed performance to a consumer. As such, it can be readily concluded that the use is for "a legitimate, essentially non-exploitative purpose, and that the commercial aspect of [the] use can best be described as of minimal significance."[413]

Notwithstanding the commercial and non-transformative nature of the making of a buffer copy, the essentially "non-exploitative" purpose of the use — i.e., to enable a use that has been authorized by the copyright owner and for which the copyright owner typically has been compensated — persuades us that the first factor favors the user.

---

[412] *Sega Enters. Ltd. v. Accolade, Inc.*, 977 F.2d 1510, 1522-23 (1992); *Maxtone-Graham v. Burtchaell*, 803 F.2d 1253, 1262 (2d Cir. 1986), *cert. denied*, 481 U.S. 1059 (1987).

[413] *Sega*, 977 F.2d at 1523. A parallel can be drawn to "time-shifting," which the Supreme Court held to be "a noncommercial, nonprofit activity" in *Sony*. In *Sony*, the Court noted that "time-shifting merely enables viewer to see such a work which he has been invited to witness in its entirety free of charge . . . ." *Sony*, 464 U.S. at 449. The buffer copy merely enables the user to listen to a work that the transmitting entity is licensed to stream to him. *Campbell*, 510 U.S. at 591 (No "presumption" or inference of market harm that might find support in Sony is applicable to a case involving something beyond mere duplication for commercial purposes.)

136

It is generally accepted that in analyzing the second fair use factor — the nature of the copyrighted work — creative works are subject to a more limited scope of fair use than informational works.[414] Musical works that are copied into buffers while they are streamed are generally at the creative end of the spectrum that is generally subject to a narrower scope of fair use. Of course, the same can be said of the motion pictures and television programs, the copying of which for time-shifting purposes the Supreme Court held to be a fair use. This factor would appear to favor the copyright owner, but, as demonstrated by the *Sony* case, it by no means precludes the conclusion that the making of a buffer copy is a fair use.

In analyzing the third factor — the amount and substantiality of the portion used in relation to the copyrighted work as a whole — copying an entire work generally weighs against a finding of fair use.[415] "While 'wholesale copying does not preclude fair use per se,' copying an entire work 'militates against a finding of fair use.'"[416]

At any given time, the content of the buffer comprises only a small, fairly insubstantial portion of the work. In aggregate, though, the buffer copies constitute the entire work. Even if the making of buffer copies is considered to be a reproduction of the entire work, that does not preclude a finding of fair use. There are a number of circumstances where courts have considered copying of an entire work to be fair use. For example, in *Sony* the time-shifting of

---

[414] *Campbell*, 510 U.S. at 586; *Diamond v. Am-Law Corp.*, 745 F.2d 142, 148 (2d Cir. 1984).

[415] *Infinity Broadcast Corp. v. Kirkwood*, 150 F.3d 104, 109 (2d Cir 1998).

[416] *Worldwide Church*, 227 F.3d at 1118 (quoting *Hustler Magazine, Inc. v. Moral Majority, Inc.*, 796 F.2d 1148, 1155 (9th Cir. 1986)).

137

entire motion pictures or television programs was held to be a fair use.[417] In *Sega v. Accolade*, the court, recognizing that disassembly of a computer program necessarily entailed making digital reproductions of the entire work, found this factor to weigh in favor of the copyright owner, but to be "of very little weight."[418]

To the extent that the portion residing in the buffer at any given time is examined in isolation, it represents a *de minimis* portion of the entire work and this factor would weigh in favor of the user. If, however, all the buffer copies are aggregated to constitute the entire work, this factor would favor the copyright owner. But this factor would be of very little weight in the overall analysis. Although the entire work is reproduced, in the aggregate, the entire work must be copied to achieve its productive purpose – to render the performance of the work over the Internet. In achieving this purpose, the individual packets buffered contain no more than is reasonably necessary to effectuate that function.[419]

"Fair use, when properly applied, is limited to copying by others which does not materially impair the marketability of the work which is copied."[420] In analyzing the fourth fair use factor with regard to the making of a temporary buffer copy, the effect of the use on the

---

[417] *Sony Corp. v. Universal City Studios, Inc.*, 464 U.S. 417, 449-50 (1984) (acknowledging that time-shifting necessarily involved making a complete copy of a protected work).

[418] *Sega*, 977 F.2d at 1527.

[419] *See Campbell*, 510 U.S. 569, 588 (1994) ("Once enough has been taken to assure identification, how much more is reasonable will depend, say, on the extent to which the song's overriding purpose and character is to parody the original or, in contrast, the likelihood that the parody may serve as a market substitute for the original".)

[420] *Harper & Row*, 471 U.S. 539, 566-67 (1985).

actual or potential market for the work appears to be minimal, if indeed there is any effect at all. The buffer copy has no economic value independent of the performance that it enables, so there appears to be no conceivable effect upon the market for or value of the copyrighted work. In *Sony*, the Supreme Court directs us to inquire whether "if [the use] should become widespread, it would adversely affect the potential market for the copyrighted work."[421] There is no market for buffer copies other than as a means to block an authorized performance of the musical works.[422] Nor can it be said that record sales are being reduced because of the making of buffer copies. The copy merely facilitates an already existing market for the authorized and lawful streaming of works. This factor strongly favors the user.

Of the four statutory factors, the first and fourth favor the user, and the second factor appears to favor the copyright owner. The third factor favors the copyright owner, but should be accorded little weight. Of course, fair use is not determined simply by tallying up the factors that favor either party. Rather, fair use is an "equitable rule of reason."[423] It is especially appropriate where, as here, the statutory factors do not favor either the copyright owner or the user lopsidedly, to weigh other equitable considerations in carrying out the balancing inherent in an equitable rule of reason. We identified three.

---

[421] *Sony*, 464 U.S. at 451.

[422] *Campbell*, 510 U.S. at 592. This could be analogized to requiring a license for a parody of a work – a successful noninfringing parody is lawful notwithstanding a copyright owner's subsequent willingness to offer a license.

[423] *Sony*, 464 U.S. at 448 (quoting 1976 House Report, supra note 40, at 65).

139

First, the sole purpose for making these buffer copies is to permit an activity that is licensed by the copyright owner and for which the copyright owner receives a performance royalty. In essence, there appears to be some truth to the allegation made by some commenters that copyright owners are seeking to be paid twice for the same activity.[424] Demanding a separate payment for the copies that are an inevitable by-product of that activity appears to be double-dipping, and is not a sound equitable basis for resisting the invocation of the fair use doctrine.

Second, it is technologically necessary (at least given the nature of the Internet today, and quite possibly well into the future) to make buffer copies in order to carry out a digital performance of music over the Internet. The work cannot be experienced without copying it. This circumstance appears analogous to facts that were before the Ninth Circuit in *Sega v. Accolade.* There the court found that a computer program could not be read and understood by a programmer without disassembling it, and it could not be disassembled without copying it.[425] Those elements favored the court's holding that disassembly in that case was a fair use.

Third, the buffer copies exist for too short a period of time to be exploited in any way other than to enable the performance of the work. Absent intervention by the consumer and use of technologies to get around the normal functioning of the rendering software, the buffer copy is continually overwritten and ceases to exist once the song is finished playing. No further use can be made of the buffer copy because it is not retained: at the end of the transmission the consumer

---

[424] T-DIMA, Greenstein, at 275; T-Launch, Goldberg, at 307.

[425] *Sega,* 977 F.2d at 1525-26.

140

is left with nothing but the fond memory of a favorite song. The use of the copy is narrowly

tailored to the licensed performance of the work. This circumstance favors a finding of fair use.

On balance, we find the case that the making of temporary buffer copies to enable a

licensed performance of a musical work by streaming technology is a fair use to be a strong one.

We do recognize, however, that fair use is determined on a case-by-case basis and, as such, lacks

the certainty of a specific exception. Representatives of the webcasting industry expressed

concern in their comments that, given copyright owners' willingness to assert claims based on

the making of temporary buffer copies, the fair use defense in this context may be too uncertain a

basis for making rational business decisions.

e. *Recommendations*

i. A blanket exception for temporary copies incidental to a lawful use is not warranted

We recommend against the adoption of a general exception from the reproduction right to

render noninfringing all temporary copies that are incidental to lawful uses. Outside the context

of buffer copies that are incidental to a licensed performance of a work,[426] no compelling case has

been made that a broad exception is needed.[427] However, the risks of a blanket exception appear

significant.[428]

---

[426] *See* discussion *infra*, at 142-145.

[427] *See* discussion *supra*, at 131.

[428] *See* discussion *supra*, at 130-131.

141

Copyright owners have pointed out with justification that the reproduction right is the "cornerstone of the edifice of copyright protection"[429] and that exceptions from that right should not be made lightly. In the absence of specific, identifiable harm, the risk of foreclosing legitimate business opportunities based on copyright owners' exploitation of their exclusive reproduction right counsels against creating a broad exception to that right.

The risks associated with a narrowly defined exception are less significant. We believe that Congress' tailored approach taken in the Computer Maintenance Competition Assurance Act[430] to the question of temporary copies to be the appropriate model. Presented with specific examples of identifiable harm to competition in the computer repair and maintenance industry in the form of infringement suits premised on temporary copying, Congress created a narrow exemption to deal with that specific problem.[431] We believe the same approach should be taken here.

ii. Temporary copies incidental to a licensed digital performance should result in no liability

We recommend that Congress enact legislation amending the Copyright Act to preclude any liability arising from the assertion of a copyright owner's reproduction right with respect to

---

[429] T-Copyright Industry Orgs., at 243.

[430] Title III of the DMCA, Pub. L. No. 105-304, 112 Stat. 2860, 2887 (1998).

[431] *See supra*, at 30.

142

temporary buffer copies that are incidental to a licensed digital transmission of a public performance of a sound recording and any underlying musical work.

The economic value of licensed streaming is in the public performances of the musical work and the sound recording, both of which are paid for. The buffer copies have no independent economic significance. They are made solely to enable the performance. The same copyright owners appear to be seeking a second compensation for the same activity merely because of the happenstance that the transmission technology implicates the reproduction right, and the reproduction right of songwriters and music publishers is administered by a different collective than the public performance right.[432]

The uncertainty of the present law potentially allows those who administer the reproduction right in musical works to prevent webcasting from taking place — to the detriment of copyright owners, webcasters, and consumers alike — or to extract an additional payment that is not justified by the economic value of the copies at issue. Congressional action is desirable to remove the uncertainty and to allow the activity that Congress sought to encourage through the adoption of the section 114 webcasting compulsory license to take place.

---

[432] It seems unlikely that this particular problem would arise in other industries where the copyright owner's public performance right and reproduction right are administered by the same entity. We note, for example, that the issue of temporary buffer copies of sound recordings has not been raised as an issue, and does not appear to be the subject of any demands for additional royalties. In the recording industry, the reproduction right and digital public performance right are generally held by the same entity.

143

A close analogy to the present circumstances can be found in the adoption of an exemption for so-called ephemeral recordings in section 112 of the Copyright Act. Ephemeral recordings are copies that are made and used by a transmitting organization to facilitate its transmitting activities. Congress saw fit to exempt those copies when the transmission is either made under license (including the compulsory license for webcasting and subscription digital transmissions) or under an exemption from exclusive rights (as in the case of analog public performances of sound recordings). As with temporary buffer copies, ephemeral recordings are made for the sole purpose of carrying out a transmission. If they are used strictly in accordance with the restrictions set forth in section 112,[433] they have no economic value independent of the public performance that they enable.[434]

We note the suggestion by one copyright owner group that statutory change is unnecessary because the issue of buffer copies can be addressed under the aegis of the fair use

---

[433] An ephemeral recording may be retained and used only by the transmitting organization that made it, and no further copies may be reproduced from it; it may be used only for the transmitting organization's own transmissions or for archival preservation or security; and it must be destroyed within six months from the date that it was first transmitted to the public unless it is preserved exclusively for archival purposes. 17 U.S.C. § 112(a)(1). The use of temporary buffer copies is even more limited, since they are used only in the course of a single transmission, and do not endure any longer than the transmission.

[434] The webcasting amendments in section 405 of the DMCA created a new compulsory license to make ephemeral recordings of sound recordings under specified circumstances. 17 U.S.C. § 112(e). In light of the original purpose of section 112, and a subsequent legislative proposal to exempt certain ephemeral recordings used to facilitate the transmission of digital distance education materials, *see* S. 487, 107th Cong., 1st Sess. § 1(c) (2001), section 112(e) can best be viewed as an aberration. As we indicated in 1998 to the affected parties who championed this provision as part of an overall compromise, we saw no justification for the disparate treatment of broadcasters and webcasters regarding the making of ephemeral recordings. Nor did we see any justification for the imposition of a royalty obligation under a statutory licence to make copies that have no independent economic value and are made solely to enable another use that is permitted under a separate compulsory license. Our views have not changed in the interim, and we would favor repeal of section 112(e) and the adoption of an appropriately-crafted ephemeral recording exemption.

144

doctrine.[435] While we agree that the fair use defense probably does apply to such buffer copies,[436] this approach is fraught with uncertainty. It is conceivable that a court confronted with the issue could conclude that the making of buffer copies is not fair use. This risk, coupled with the apparent willingness of some copyright owners to assert claims based on the making of buffer copies, argues for statutory change.

A number of the copyright owners expressed concerns about the potential unintended consequences of an exception from the reproduction right for temporary copies. We note that most of those comments were addressed to the proposal for a broader exception covering all temporary, incidental copies – a proposal that we have declined to endorse. We believe that the much narrower scope of our recommendation addresses these concerns.

We also note the criticism leveled at proponents of a temporary copy exception for webcasting – that they are seeking to have copyright owners subsidize certain types of business models by refraining from enforcing, or seeking compensation for one of their exclusive rights.[437] This is not a case where an additional use is being made of a work beyond the use that has been compensated. The making of buffer copies is a part of the same use. It is integral to the performance, and would not take place but for the performance. Permitting such incidental copies cannot be considered a "subsidy" by copyright owners.

---

[435] T-SIIA, Kupferschmid, at 83-84, 131-32.

[436] *See supra*, at 133-141.

[437] T-Copyright Industry Orgs., p. 276.

145

Finally, we note that in informal communications with representatives of music publishers we have been apprised of concerns that streaming technology renders musical works vulnerable to digital copying.[438] A mechanical royalty on audio streams (based on the buffer copy) is viewed as a necessary protection against lost revenues from unauthorized copying. Although we are sympathetic to the concerns expressed by copyright owners about such technology, we find this reasoning flawed and unpersuasive.

Whether or not consumers make unauthorized copies of audio streams has nothing to do with temporary buffer copies. Those copies are not directly involved in the making of the unauthorized copy.[439] Requiring payment for a copy with no economic value because an unrelated copy with economic value might be made would be inappropriate.

iii. Public performances incidental to licensed music downloads should result in no liability

Given our recommendations concerning temporary copies that are incidental to digital performances of sound recordings and musical works, fairness requires that we acknowledge the symmetrical difficulty that is faced in the online music industry: digital performances that are incidental to digital music downloads.

---

[438] "Total Recorder" is an example of one software product, available on the Internet, that permits unauthorized copying of streaming audio. Devices such as Total Recorder may violate section 1201(b). *See, e.g.*, 17 U.S.C. § 1201(b) and 17 U.S.C. § 114(d)(2)(C)(vi), (viii). If they do not, consideration should be given to amending section 1201(b) to prohibit such devices.

[439] The data in the stream buffer is compressed and may be subject to technological protections such as encryption. Consequently, it makes far more sense to capture the audio data after it has been rendered by the player software and is uncompressed and unprotected. Total Recorder works in this fashion, capturing the audio data on its trip from the player software to the sound card.

146

Just as webcasters appear to be facing demands for royalty payments for incidental exercise of the reproduction right in the course of licensed public performances, it appears that companies that sell digital downloads of music under either voluntary licenses from music publishers or the section 115 compulsory license, and voluntary licenses from record companies, are facing demands for public performance royalties for a technical "performance" of the underlying musical work that allegedly occurs in the course of transmitting it from the vendor's server to the consumer's PC.[440]

As with the issue of buffer copies made in the course of streaming, this appears to be an issue driven as much by the structure of the administration of copyright rights in the music industry as by technology. The issue simply would not seem to arise in other industries where the public performance and reproduction rights are exercised by the same entity.

We view this issue as the mirror image of the question regarding buffer copies. We recognize that the proposition that a digital download constitutes a public performance even when no contemporaneous performance takes place is an unsettled point of law that is subject to debate. However, to the extent that such a download can be considered a public performance, the performance is merely a technical by-product of the transmission process that has no value separate from the value of the download. If it is a public performance, then, we believe that arguments concerning fair use and the making of buffer copies apply to that performance.[441] In

---

[440] T-BMI, Berenson, at 163-65.

[441] *See* discussion of the application of fair use to buffer copies, *supra*, at 133-141.

147

any case, for the reasons articulated above, it is our view that no liability should result under U.S. law from a technical "performance" that takes place in the course of a download.

3. Scope of Archival Exemption

Currently the archival exemption under section 117(a)(2) is limited to computer programs. This section allows the owner of a copy of a computer program to make or authorize the making of an additional copy of the program "for archival purposes," provided that "all archival copies are destroyed in the event that continued possession of the computer program should cease to be rightful."[442] A number of arguments were advanced in the course of the study for an expansion of this archival exception in order to cover the kind of routine backups that are performed on computers and to allow consumers to archive material in digital format other than computer programs. The arguments for and against such an expansion are discussed below.

a. *Arguments in Favor of Expanding the Archival Exemption*

i. General vulnerability of content in digital form

Commenters asserted that consumers need to back up works in digital form because they are vulnerable. CONTU recommended that Congress create an exemption to permit archival (backup) copies of computer programs because they are vulnerable to "destruction or damage by mechanical or electrical failure."[443] This vulnerability stems not from the fact that they are computer programs, but because they are stored in digital form. The rationale given by CONTU

---

[442] 17 U.S.C. § 117(a)(2).

[443] CONTU Report, *supra* note 61 at 13.

148

for adopting an archival exemption for computer programs would apply equally to any work stored in digital format.[444]

It would be perfectly consistent with CONTU's recommendations and Congress' enactment of section 117 to extend the archival exemption to protect against technical vulnerabilities that afflict the present day use of digital files. The digital media collection on a hard drive is also vulnerable to technical failure such as hard disk crashes, virus infection, or file corruption.

ii. Mismatch between section 117 and current archival practices

Evidence has been presented noting that the archival exemption under section 117 does not permit the practices and procedures most people follow for backing up data on a computer hard drive. The commenters stated that an amendment to section 117 would be necessary for it to reflect the reality of how many computer users (and most business users) actually back up information.

Section 117 appears to have been written to address a particular style of archiving: the making of a copy of an individual program at the time the consumer obtains it. However, we were told that most businesses, and many individuals, perform periodic backups of everything on

---

[444] It would have been well within CONTU's mandate (to make recommendations concerning "the reproduction and use of copyrighted works of authorship. . . . in conjunction with automatic systems capable of storing, processing, retrieving, and transferring information") to have proposed an archival exemption applicable to all works in digital form. CONTU Report, *supra* note 61, at 4. It did not do so, for reasons that were not articulated in the Report.

149

their disk (and not just one backup copy upon purchase of the computer program). This backup copy includes all installed computer programs, together with any related data files, various configuration files, and all of the user's own data, including any copyrighted works that have been downloaded. Section 117 does not permit the copying of anything other than the computer programs.[445]

Section 117 requires the destruction of any archived copy once possession of the program ceases to be rightful. Possession – or at least use – of a program typically ceases to be rightful once the user acquires an upgraded version.[446] A literal reading of section 117 would require the user to go through all of the backup tapes, CD-Rs and other archival media, identify each of the files that constitute the earlier version of the computer program, and attempt to delete them. This is neither practical nor reasonable.

Based on the evidence presented during the course of preparing this Report, there is a fundamental mismatch between accepted, prudent practice among most system administrators and other users, on one hand, and section 117 on the other. As a consequence, few adhere to the letter of the law.

---

[445] It was suggested by one commenter that even data files associated with a computer program could not be archived under section 117. WST-Hollaar.

[446] T-Hollaar, at 94, 150. For example, the Symantec License and Warranty for Norton SystemWorks™ provides that "YOU MAY NOT: . . . use a previous version or copy of the Software after you have received a disk replacement set or an upgraded version as a replacement of the prior version, . . . ".

150

b. *Arguments Against Expanding the Archival Exemption*

i. Lack of demonstrated harm

While the mismatch between section 117 and sound backup practices is indisputable, nobody was able to identify any instance where a consumer has suffered any harm as a result of the limited scope of the archival exemption. There are two principal ways that consumers could be harmed: by refraining, to their detriment, from activities because they do not fall within the scope of the exemption; and by being subject to legal claims from copyright owners for conduct that falls outside the scope of the exemption. Neither appears to be occurring.

It was pointed out several times during the course of this study that the backup copies that consumers make from their hard drives generally embody all files, including digital downloads. If this activity is so commonplace, it does not appear that consumers are risking their investment in digital media to conform their conduct to section 117. Nor has anyone provided any evidence that any consumer has ever faced litigation, or even the threat of litigation, for making a backup copy of a hard drive containing material that fell outside the scope of the archival exception under section 117. To the contrary, evidence was presented that consumers who back up their hard drives generally do so outside the parameters of section 117 with no repercussions whatsoever.

ii. Justification for section 117(a)(2) has diminished

The need to make backup copies of computer programs has diminished. It was pointed out in the comments that today section 117(a)(2) has little, if any, utility. Almost all the software

151

sold in the United States is sold on CD-ROM.[447] The CD-ROM serves as the backup copy once a computer program is loaded from the CD-ROM to one's computer. CD-ROMs have an estimated failure rate of significantly less than 1%.

It has been argued that there would seem to be little point to expanding section 117(a)(2) to other copyrighted works when current law does not appear to be causing any real-world problems and the justification for the provision may no longer exist. While this may be the case today, we acknowledge that the sale of computer software as digital downloads is on the rise, and that may increase the need for an archival exemption.

iii. Bad faith use of the section 117 defense

It was brought to our attention during the course of this study that section 117 is being used by some members of the public to justify conduct that it does not permit because of the public's misunderstanding of the purpose of the section. We were told that persons engaged in software and content piracy are also using section 117 to justify their activities. For example, one of the commenters noted that people auction off their so-called backup copies of their computer software or make pirate software available on websites, ftp sites or chat rooms under the guise of the section 117 back-up copy exception.[448]

---

[447] According to PC Data, in 1999, ninety-seven percent of all the software sold in the United States was sold on CD-ROM and in 2000, ninety-eight percent of all software was sold on CD-ROM. R-SIIA, at 9.

[448] C-SIIA, at 4.

152

c. *Recommendations*

We recommend that Congress amend the copyright law in one of the two ways that we outline below. We acknowledge that persuasive arguments were presented on both sides of the question whether to expand the archival copy exemption that is currently in section 117(a)(2). On balance, after examining those arguments and taking into consideration the additional concerns that we discuss below, we conclude that a statutory change is desirable.

In support of a recommendation to revise the archival exemption, it has been demonstrated to our satisfaction that there is a fundamental mismatch between section 117 and current archival practices. Those practices – to which copyright owners have not objected – do not harm right holders, are necessary for consumers to protect their investment in digital materials, and should be permitted to continue.

In support of making no change to the scope of the exemption, there has been a complete absence of any demonstrated harm to the prospective beneficiaries of an expanded archival exemption.[449] Any dramatic expansion of a fairly modest copyright exemption carries with it the risk of causing unintended consequences. Moreover, we believe that a strong case can be made that most common archival activities by computer users[450] would qualify as fair use.

---

[449] This factor is an element that distinguishes the archival exemption issue from the buffer copy issue discussed *supra*.

[450] We are assuming for purposes of this fair use analysis that the activity consists of backing up all or a portion of the contents of a hard drive on a removable medium for retention against the possibility of accidental destruction of that material *and for no other purpose*. Of course, this analysis would not apply to any infringing material on a hard drive.

The purpose of the use – backing up the material on a computer's hard drive – is merely to safeguard lawfully-obtained copies against accidental destruction. Although the use is not transformative, it probably would not be considered commercial either.[451] The use does not supplant the original because it does not entail a separate exploitation of the work – or any exploitation unless that original copy is damaged or destroyed. As with time-shifting, backing up is "a legitimate, essentially non-exploitative purpose." This factor appears to favor the user.

The second factor – nature of the work – would appear to favor copyright owners since many of the works being copied are clearly very creative in nature, and are thus subject to a more limited scope of fair use than informational works.[452] But this by no means precludes the conclusion that making backup copies is a fair use.[453]

The third factor – the amount and substantiality of the portion used – might also appear to weigh against a finding of fair use since the entire work is copied.[454] However, this too does not preclude a finding of fair use.[455] Here, since the purpose of the activity being engaged in is to protect one's legally obtained copy through archiving, copying the entire work is necessary.

---

[451] *See Campbell*, 510 U.S. at 579 (discussing transformative use); *id.* at 584-85 (discussing commercial use).

[452] *Id.* at 586; *Diamond*, 745 F.2d 142, at 148 (2d Cir. 1984).

[453] For example, copying of entire motion pictures for time-shifting purposes was considered a fair use in *Sony*. Motion pictures generally fall at the creative end of the spectrum.

[454] *Infinity Broadcast Corp.*, 150 F.3d 104, at 109 (2d. Cir. 1998).

[455] *Sony*, 464 U.S. 417, 449-50 (1984).

154

The fourth factor – effect of the use on the market – weighs strongly in favor of fair use. The effect on the market for the copyrighted work will be nonexistent. The copies being made under this fair use analysis are being made for the sole purpose of safeguarding one's investment – a vulnerable investment due to susceptibility of digital media to accidental damage or destruction. The archival copies do not enter the market at any point and since they are copies of works for which the copyright owner has already been compensated, there is no harm to the owner in lost revenue. It is our conclusion that a strong case can be made that the use being made is fair.

If the analysis ended there, recommending no statutory change could be a viable option. Another element to consider, however, is the interplay between sections 107 and 109. It appears that the language of the Copyright Act could lead a court to conclude that, by operation of section 109, copies of works made lawfully under the fair use doctrine may be freely distributed.

Section 109 permits "the owner of a particular copy or phonorecord lawfully made" under title 17 to distribute that copy without the copyright owner's permission.[456] To the extent that section 107 permits a user to make backup copies of works stored on a hard drive, those backup copies are lawfully made and the user owns them. Section 109, on its face, appears to permit the

---

[456] 17 U.S.C. § 109(a).

155

user, as the owner of a lawfully made backup copy, to "sell or otherwise dispose of the possession" of that backup copy.[457]

Authority is unclear over the application of the first sale doctrine to lawfully made copies that have not been distributed with the copyright owner's consent. Section 109 is commonly understood to codify the "first sale doctrine," which implies that an actual sale, or at least an authorized distribution, must occur before the doctrine applies. However, the statutory text only requires that the copy be lawfully made, and makes no reference to a prior authorized sale or other distribution.[458]

The legislative history of section 109 can be read to support both views. In one sentence, the 1976 House Report suggests that an actual first sale is required to trigger section 109, which it asserts "restates and confirms the principle that, where the copyright owner has transferred ownership of a particular copy or phonorecord of a work, the person to whom the copy or phonorecord is transferred is entitled to dispose of it by sale, rental, or any other means . . . ."[459] But this position is undercut by a passage on the same page, which asserts that "the disposition of a phonorecord legally made under the compulsory licensing provisions of Section 115 would not

---

[457] *Id.* Backup copies made pursuant to § 117(a)(2), though "lawfully made," are subject to the limitations on distribution contained in § 117(b) and the requirement in § 117(a)(2) that they be destroyed once possession of the original is no longer rightful. Since § 117 is both the more specific and the later enacted provision, these limitations would prevail over the general language of § 109(a) under basic canons of statutory interpretation.

[458] 17 U.S.C. § 109(a).

[459] 1976 House Report, *supra* note 40, at 79 (1976).

156

[be outside the scope of Section 109(a)]."[460] A leading copyright treatise concludes that "on balance, it would seem that the literal text of Section 109(a) should be followed, so that its immunity may be claimed by any 'owner of a particular copy or phonorecord lawfully made,' and not just by those who acquired such ownership via a prior transfer from the copyright owner."[461]

Given our view that, in the typical situation,[462] the making of backup copies is probably a fair use, we see a risk to copyright owners under current law that those backup copies could then be distributed without legal consequence. We believe that outcome would be fundamentally unfair[463] and, notwithstanding the ambiguity of the 1976 House Report on this point, contrary to congressional intent. Nonetheless, we cannot overlook the possibility that a court would hold this way. When added into the balance, this element tips the scale in favor of statutory change.

We therefore recommend that Congress either (1) amend section 109(a) to ensure that fair use copies are not subject to the first sale doctrine; or (2) create a new archival exemption that provides expressly that backup copies may not be distributed. We express no preference as between the two options, and note that they are not mutually exclusive.

---

[460] *Id.*

[461] Nimmer, *supra* note 21, at § 8.12[B][3][c].

[462] *See supra*, note 450.

[463] Apart from the obvious detrimental effect this outcome would have on the copyright owner's market, we note that the initial determination of fair use that permitted the making of the copy may have been premised on the fact that the copy was not made for distribution. *See infra*, note 468.

The first option would entail amending section 109(a) to state that only copies that have been lawfully made *and lawfully distributed* are subject to the first sale doctrine. We believe that this change would be consistent with what Congress intended in section 109.

As noted above, the text of section 109 does not refer to any previous transfer of a lawfully owned copy (although the condition that the person be an owner could be argued to presuppose a sale or other transfer of ownership from the copyright owner) and the 1976 House Report is ambiguous on the question whether a first sale must occur to trigger the application of section 109 to a particular copy. Section 109 was intended by Congress to "restate[] and confirm[]" a principle that had been "established by the court decisions and section 27" of the 1909 law. Section 27 refers not to "lawful copies" but to copies "the possession of which has been lawfully obtained." This language arguably requires a lawful sale or other distribution (otherwise the copy would be lawfully "made" not lawfully "obtained"q).[464] The seminal court decision on first sale, *Bobbs-Merrill Co. v. Straus*,[465] went even further, holding that the copyright owner parted with all right to control sale of a copy after it "had parted with the title to one who had acquired full dominion over it and had given a satisfactory price . . . ."[466] Given this chronology of the development of the first sale doctrine, it seems very unlikely that Congress intended a radical departure from the requirement of a "first sale" or other authorized distribution by the copyright owner. A likelier explanation for the particular wording in the statute is that it

---

[464] *See Platt & Munk Co. v. Republic Graphics, Inc.*, 513 F.2d 847 (2d. Cir. 1963).

[465] 210 U.S. 339 (1908). The case is discussed *supra*, at 20.

[466] 210 U.S. at 350.

158

was drafted to avoid any potential conflict with the ability of a compulsory licensee's, or subsequent purchaser's, ability to sell phonorecords made under the section 115 compulsory license "to make and distribute phonorecords" of nondramatic musical works.[467]

We note that this proposed change to section 109 would not preclude the distribution of copies made pursuant to section 107 in all cases, since (like all of the exclusive rights in section 106) the distribution right is subject to the fair use doctrine. It would, however, require that a separate fair use analysis be applied to the distribution of that particular copy. The fair use copy could be transferred only in those cases where the distribution itself qualified as a fair use.[468]

The second option entails creating a new exemption for making backups of lawful copies of material in digital form, and amending section 117 to delete references to archival copies.[469] The new exemption should follow the general contours of section 117 (a)(2) and (b), and include the following elements: It should permit the making of one or more backup copies of a work.

---

[467] 1976 House Report, *supra* note 40, at 79 ("[A]ny resale of an illegally 'pirated' phonorecord would be an infringement, but the disposition of a phonorecord legally made under the compulsory licensing provisions of section 115 would not."). Our proposal would also meet this concern since a phonorecord that is manufactured and sold under the section 115 license would be both lawfully made and lawfully distributed.

[468] In some cases, the making of a copy may be a fair use in large part because the copy is not disseminated to third parties. For example, in *Sony*, the Supreme Court held that it was a fair use for a private citizen to record a television program off-the-air for purposes of "time-shifting," which the Court described as "the practice of recording a program to view it once at a later time, and thereafter erasing it." 464 U.S. at 423. The personal nature of that use was critical to the Court's analysis. *See, e.g.*, 464 U.S. at 449 ("the District Court's findings plainly establish that time-shifting for private home use must be characterized as a noncommercial, nonprofit activity"). The fact that the making of a personal copy for purposes of time-shifting (and with the anticipation of subsequent destruction of the copy) is fair use should not make it lawful subsequently to sell, rent or give that "lawfully made" copy to a third party.

[469] We recommend this approach in order to preserve section 117's present character as a computer program exemption and at the same time ensure that computer programs and other materials in digital form are subject to the same rules concerning the making of backup copies.

159

The copy from which the backup copies are made must be in digital form on a medium that is subject to accidental erasure, damage or destruction in the ordinary course of its use. It should stipulate that the copies may be made and used solely for archival purposes or for use in lieu of the original copy. It should also specify that, notwithstanding the provisions of section 109, the archival copy may not be transferred except as part of a lawful transfer of all rights in the work. Finally, it should specify that the archival copies may not be used in any manner in the event that continued possession of the work ceases to be rightful.

Permitting the making of multiple copies is necessary because prudent backup practice requires it. For example, a typical approach to backing up would entail making both on-site and off-site copies of the entire contents of a hard drive on a regular basis, in addition to making incremental backups of just those files on the hard drive that have changed.

The requirement that the work be stored in digital form on a medium that is subject to accidental erasure, damage or destruction in the ordinary course of its use is intended to avoid claims like that faced by the court in *Atari, Inc. v. J S & A Group, Inc.*,[470] without unduly limiting the exemption to current technology.[471] The exemption would also not be limited, as the *Atari* court suggested, to damage or destruction by electrical or mechanical failure. Media that are subject to accidental erasure by human error would qualify as well. Digital media that are subject

---

[470] 597 F. Supp. 5, 9-10 (N.D. Ill. 1983) (rejecting assertion that making of 'backup' copies of a videogame embodied in ROM is permitted under section 117 because ROM is not vulnerable to "damage by mechanical or electrical failure," court holds device for copying videogames in ROM not to have substantial noninfringing uses under *Sony* analysis of contributory infringement)

[471] Currently, the exception would be limited primarily to backups made from copies on a hard drive, floppy disk, or other magnetic medium.

160

to accidental destruction outside the ordinary course of use (e.g., by fire or other catastrophe), however, would not qualify, since there would no longer be a basis for treating them any differently from traditional hard-copy media for purposes of archiving.

The proposal that archival copies may be made and used solely for archival purposes or for use in lieu of the original copy is derived from section 117(a)(2). It has been modified in recognition of the fact that, in certain instances, the original copy is used as the backup, and the backup becomes the use copy.[472]

The requirement that archival copies not be transferable (except as part of a lawful transfer of all of the transferor's rights in the work) is derived from section 117(b). This takes care of the concern addressed above regarding the intersection of sections 107 and 109 in the context of backup copies.

The requirement that archival copies not be used in any manner in the event that continued possession of the work ceases to be rightful is a substitute for the requirement in section 117(a)(2) that any such backup copies be destroyed. Since backup copies frequently include many works on a single medium, and since erasure or destruction of individual files on such a medium is often impossible, the proposal would not require destruction. It would instead require that the archival copies not be used in any manner.

---

[472] *See* Copyright Office, The Computer Software Rental Amendments Act of 1990: The Nonprofit Library Lending Exemption to the "Rental Right" 77-78 (1994).

161

4. Contract Preemption

Several commenters proposed that the Copyright Act should be amended to ensure that contractual provisions that override consumer privileges in the copyright law, or are otherwise unreasonable, are not enforceable.[473] In essence, this is a request to amend section 301 of the Copyright Act, which governs the scope of federal preemption of state law (including state contract law). Section 301 states that

> all legal or equitable rights that are equivalent to any of the exclusive rights within the general scope of copyright as specified by section 106 in works of authorship that are fixed in a tangible medium of expression and come within the subject matter of copyright as specified by sections 102 and 103, . . . whether published or unpublished, are governed exclusively by this title. . . . [N]o person is entitled to any such right or equivalent right in any such work under the common law or statutes of any State.

There appears to be consensus among courts that enforcement of contracts is not prohibited as a general matter.[474] However, there is disagreement among courts respecting the degree to which the Copyright Act may preclude the enforcement of specific contractual provisions that would otherwise be enforceable under state law. At least one court has taken a nearly categorical approach to contract preemption, holding that rights created by contract are not "rights equivalent to any of the exclusive rights within the general scope of copyright."

> Rights "equivalent to copyright" are rights established by law – rights that restrict the options of persons who are strangers to the author. . . . A copyright is a right against the world. Contracts, by contrast, generally affect only their parties; strangers may do as they please, so contracts do not create "exclusive rights."[475]

---

[473] *See, e.g.,* C-DFC, at 4; T-Library Ass'ns, Neal, at 16; T-DiMA, Greenstein, at 239.

[474] *Architectronics, Inc. v. Control Systems, Inc.*, 935 F. Supp 425, 441 (S.D.N.Y. 1996); *see also Selby v. New Line Cinema Corp.*, 96 F. Supp. 2d 1053, 1059 (C.D. Cal. 2000) (a majority of courts have found that breach of contract claims generally are not preempted).

[475] *ProCD, Inc. v. Zeidenberg*, 86 F.3d 1447, 1454 (7th Cir. 1996).

162

Consequently, "a simple two-party contract . . . may be enforced."[476]

Other courts have found contract rights preempted to the extent that they essentially restate one or more of the exclusive rights under section 106 of the Copyright Act (e.g., reproduction) with no "extra element."[477] No case, however, has applied preemption broadly enough to nullify contractual provisions that vary or override exceptions and limitation in the Copyright Act.

Section 7 of the Boucher-Campbell bill would have amended section 301 to apply the broad scope of preemption of contract rights advocated by some of the commenters.[478] Unlike the proposals concerning the first sale doctrine and temporary copies, however, section 104 of the DMCA does not include any statutory reference that arguably brings this proposal within the scope of the Report. Consequently, we conclude that the issue of preemption of contractual provisions is outside the scope of the Report.

---

[476] *Id.*

[477] *National Car Rental Sys. v. Computer Assocs. Int'l*, 991 F.2d 426, 433 (8th Cir. 1993); *Frontline Test Equip. v. Greenleaf Software, Inc.*, 10 F. Supp. 2d 583, 593 (W.D. Va. 1998).

[478]
SEC. 7. PREEMPTION.

Section 301(a) of title 17, United States Code, is amended by inserting the following at the end thereof:
"When a work is distributed to the public subject to non-negotiable license terms, such terms shall not be enforceable under the common law or statutes of any state to the extent that they–
"(1) limit the reproduction, adaptation, distribution, performance, or display, by means of transmission or otherwise, of material that is uncopyrightable under section 102(b) or otherwise; or
"(2) abrogate or restrict the limitations on exclusive rights specified in sections 107 through 114 and sections 117 and 118 of this title.".

H.R. 3048, 105th Cong., 1st Sess., § 7 (1997).

163

We do note, however, that the issue is complex and of increasing practical importance, and, as such, may be worthy of further consideration at some point in the future.[479] On one hand, copyright has long coexisted with contract law, providing a background of default provisions against which parties are generally free to order their own commercial dealings to suit their needs and the realities of the marketplace. On the other hand, movement at the state level toward resolving uncertainties that have existed about the enforceability of non-negotiated license agreements, coupled with legally-protected technological measures that give right holders the technical capability of imposing contractual provisions unilaterally, increases the likelihood that right holders, and not the copyright policies established by Congress, will determine the landscape of consumer privileges in the future. Although market forces may well prevent right holders from unreasonably limiting consumer privileges, it is possible that at some point in the future a case could be made for statutory change.

5. Miscellaneous Additional Issues Beyond the Scope of the Report

a. *Impact of Section 1201 on Fair Use and other Copyright Exceptions*

Several commenters expressed general opposition to the prohibitions on circumvention of technological protection measures contained in 17 U.S.C. § 1201, and noted their concerns about

---

[479] We note that in Australia the CLRC published an issues paper in June 2001 seeking information regarding the prevalence, effects and desirability of contracts that purport to override copyright exceptions granted under the *Copyright Act 1968*. In particular, the CLRC is investigating the extent to which such agreements occur in the online and offline environments and whether these agreements are and should be valid and enforceable. In all, the CLRC seeks views on nine issues. Details can be found on the CLRC website at www.law.gov.au/clrc.

164

the adverse impact that section 1201 may have on fair use and other copyright exceptions.[480] Given the express language of section 104, which requires an evaluation of the impact of, *inter alia*, section 1201 on the operation of two specific provisions of the copyright law – sections 109 and 117 – it seems unlikely that Congress intended this Report to delve into the general relationship between section 1201 and all of the other copyright exceptions and limitations. Moreover, the fact that Congress expressly directed us to evaluate this precise issue every three years as part of the rulemaking under section 1201(a)(1)(C), tends to support the conclusion that the impact of section 1201 on fair use and other copyright exceptions is outside the scope of this Report.

b. *Impact of Section 1201 on Users of DVDs*

Several sets of comments were focused on the litigation[481] concerning software tools for circumventing the CSS that is used to encrypt motion pictures distributed on DVD.[482] Some of these comments offered a point-by-point rebuttal of the plaintiffs' case; others expressed concern that section 1201 had an adverse effect on users of DVDs by limiting the playback of DVD movies to devices that are licensed by the consortium holding the rights to the CSS technology.

Only the courts have the authority to determine the outcome of the *Reimerdes* case; our mandate is to evaluate the impact of section 1201 on the operation of sections 109 and 117.

---

[480] *See, e.g.,* C-NARM/VSDA, at 37. *See generally* C-Fischer; C-Darr; C-Jones; C-Klosowski; C-Love.

[481] *See supra,* note 89.

[482] *See, e.g.,* C-Arromdee; C-Thau and Taylor.

165

Although some of the comments tried to recast the DeCSS controversy as a first sale issue,[483] this effort reflected a misconception of the nature of the first sale doctrine.[484]

Apart from the foregoing issue, the general questions concerning the relationship between section 1201 and users of DVDs are outside the scope of this Report.

R:\104 Study\Report\Report Master Document.wpd

---

[483] *See, e.g.,* C-LXNY, at 1.

[484] *See supra,* at 74.

166

whether there are particular classes of works as to which users are, or are likely to be, adversely affected in their ability to make noninfringing uses due to the prohibition on circumvention. This notice requests written comments from all interested parties, including representatives of copyright owners, educational institutions, libraries and archives, scholars, researchers and members of the public, in order to elicit evidence on whether noninfringing uses of certain classes of works are, or are likely to be, adversely affected by this prohibition on the circumvention of measures that control access to copyrighted works.

DATES: Written comments are due by December 18, 2002. Reply comments are due by February 19, 2003.

ADDRESSES: Electronic Internet submissions must be made through the Copyright Office Web site: *http:// www.copyright.gov/1201/ comment_forms; See* section 3 of the **SUPPLEMENTARY INFORMATION** section for file formats and other information about electronic and non-electronic filing requirements. If delivered by hand, comments should be delivered to the Office of the General Counsel, Copyright Office, LM–403, James Madison Memorial Building, 101 Independence Avenue, SE., Washington, DC. If delivered by means of the United States Postal Service (*see* section 3 of the **SUPPLEMENTARY INFORMATION** about continuing mail delays), comments should be addressed to David O. Carson, General Counsel, Copyright GC/I&R, PO Box 70400, Southwest Station, Washington, DC 20024–0400. See **SUPPLEMENTARY INFORMATION** section for information about requirements and formats of submissions.

FOR FURTHER INFORMATION CONTACT: Rob Kasunic, Office of the General Counsel, Copyright GC/I&R, PO Box 70400, Southwest Station, Washington, DC 20024–0400. Telephone (202) 707–8380; telefax (202) 707–8366.

SUPPLEMENTARY INFORMATION:

1. Mandate for Rulemaking Proceeding

On October 28, 1998, President Clinton signed into law the Digital Millennium Copyright Act, Pub. L. 105–304 (1998). Section 103 (subtitled "Copyright Protection Systems and Copyright Management Information") of Title I of the Act added a new Chapter 12 to title 17 United States Code, which among other things prohibits circumvention of access control technologies employed by or on behalf of copyright owners to protect their works. Specifically, subsection 1201(a)(1)(A) provides, inter alia, that

"No person shall circumvent a technological measure that effectively controls access to a work protected under this title." Subparagraph (B) limits this prohibition. It provides that prohibition against circumvention "shall not apply to persons who are users of a copyrighted work which is in a particular class of works, if such persons are, or are likely to be in the succeeding 3-year period, adversely affected by virtue of such prohibition in their ability to make noninfringing uses of that particular class of works under this title" as determined in this rulemaking. This prohibition on circumvention became effective two years after the date of enactment, on October 28, 2000.

At the end of the 2-year period between the enactment and effective date of the provision, the Librarian of Congress made an initial determination as to classes of works to be exempted from the prohibition for the first triennial period. Exemption to Prohibition on Circumvention of Copyright Protection Systems for Access Control Technologies, 65 FR 64556, 64574 (2000) (hereinafter Final Reg.). This determination was made upon the recommendation of the Register of Copyrights following an extensive rulemaking proceeding. The exemptions promulgated by the Librarian in the first rulemaking will remain in effect until October 28, 2003. At that point, the exemptions created in the first anticircumvention rulemaking will expire and any exemptions promulgated in this second anticircumvention rulemaking will take effect for a new 3-year period.

2. Background

Title I of the Digital Millennium Copyright Act was, inter alia, the congressional fulfillment of obligations of the United States under the WIPO Copyright Treaty and the WIPO Performances and Phonograms Treaty. For additional information on the historical background and the legislative history of Title I, See Exemption to Prohibition on Circumvention of Copyright Protection Systems for Access Control Technologies, 64 FR 66139, 66140 (1999) (*http://www.loc.gov/ copyright/fedreg/1999/64fr66139.html*).

Section 1201 of title 17 of the United States Code prohibits two general types of activity: (1) The conduct of "circumvention" of technological protection measures that control access and (2) trafficking in any technology, product, service, device, component, or part thereof that protects either access to a copyrighted work or that protects the "rights of the copyright owner," if that

LIBRARY OF CONGRESS

Copyright Office

37 CFR Part 201

[Docket No. RM 2002–4]

Exemption to Prohibition on Circumvention of Copyright Protection Systems for Access Control Technologies

AGENCY: Copyright Office, Library of Congress.

ACTION: Notice of inquiry.

SUMMARY: The Copyright Office of the Library of Congress is preparing to conduct proceedings mandated by the Digital Millennium Copyright Act, which provides that the Librarian of Congress may exempt certain classes of works from the prohibition against circumvention of technological measures that control access to copyrighted works. The purpose of this rulemaking proceeding is to determine device or service meets one of three conditions. The first type of activity, the conduct of circumvention, is prohibited in section 1201(a)(1). The latter activities, trafficking in devices or services that circumvent (1) access or (2) the rights of the copyright owner are contained in sections 1201(a)(2) and 1201(b) respectively. In addition to these prohibitions, section 1201 also includes a series of section-specific limitations and exemptions to the prohibitions of section 1201.

The Anticircumvention Provision at Issue

Subsection 1201(a)(1) applies when a person who is not authorized by the copyright owner to gain access to a work does so by circumventing a technological measure put in place by the copyright owner to control access to the work. See the Report of the House Committee on Commerce on the Digital Millennium Copyright Act of 1998, H.R. Rep. No. 105–551, pt. 2, at 36 (1998) (hereinafter Commerce Comm. Report).

That section provides that "No person shall circumvent a technological measure that effectively controls access to a work protected under this title." 17 U.S.C. 1201(a)(1)(A) (1998). The relevant terms are defined:

(3) As used in this subsection—

(A) To "circumvent a technological measure" means to descramble a scrambled work, to decrypt an encrypted work, or otherwise to avoid, bypass, remove, deactivate, or impair a technological measure, without the authority of the copyright owner; and

(B) A technological measure "effectively controls access to a work" if the measure, in the ordinary course of its operation, requires the application of information, or a process or a treatment, with the authority of the copyright owner, to gain access to the work. 17 U.S.C. 1201(a)(3).

Scope of the Rulemaking

The statutory focus of this rulemaking is limited to one subsection of section 1201: The prohibition on the conduct of circumvention of technological measures that control access to copyrighted works. 17 U.S.C. 1201(a)(1)(C). The Librarian has no authority to limit either of the anti-trafficking provisions contained in subsections 1201(a)(2) or 1201(b). This narrow focus was the subject of a great deal of confusion during the first rulemaking and, therefore, demands some clarification.

This rulemaking addresses only the prohibition on the conduct of circumventing measures that control "access" to copyrighted works, e.g.,

decryption or hacking of access controls such as passwords or serial numbers. The structure of section 1201 is such that there exists no comparable prohibition on the conduct of circumventing technological measures that protect the "rights of the copyright owner," e.g., the section 106 rights to reproduce, adapt, distribute, publicly perform, or publicly display a work. Circumventing a technological measure that protects these section 106 rights of the copyright owner is governed not by section 1201, but rather by the traditional copyright rights and the applicable limitations in the Copyright Act. For example, if a person circumvents a measure that prohibits printing or saving an electronic copy of an article, there is no provision in section 1201 that precludes this activity. Instead, it would be actionable as copyright infringement of the section 106 right of reproduction unless an applicable limitation applied, e.g., fair use. The trafficking in, inter alia, any device or service that allowed others to circumvent such a technological protection measure may, however, be actionable under section 1201(b).

Since section 1201 contains no prohibition on the circumvention of technological measures that protect the "rights of the copyright owner," sometimes referred to as "use" or "copy" control measures, any effect these measures may have on noninfringing uses would not be attributable to a section 1201 prohibition. Since there is a prohibition on the act of circumventing a technological measure that controls access to a work, and since traditional Copyright Act limitations are not defenses to the act of circumventing a technological measure that controls access, Congress chose to create the current rulemaking proceeding as a "fail-safe mechanism" to monitor the effect of the anticircumvention provision in 1201(a)(1)(A). Commerce Comm. Report, at 36. This anticircumvention rulemaking is authorized to monitor the effect of the prohibition on "access" circumvention on noninfringing uses of copyrighted works. In this triennial rulemaking proceeding, effects on noninfringing uses that are unrelated to section 1201(a)(1)(A) may not be considered. See 1201(a)(1)(C).

Burden of Proof

In the last rulemaking, the Register concluded from the language of the statute and the legislative history that a determination to exempt a class of works from the prohibition on circumvention must be based on a

showing that the prohibition has a substantial adverse effect on noninfringing uses of a particular class of works. It was determined that proponents of an exemption bear the burden of proof that an exemption is warranted for a particular class of works and that the prohibition is presumed to apply to all classes of works unless an adverse impact has been shown. See Commerce Comm. Report, at 37; see also Final Reg., 65 FR 64556, 64558.

In order to meet the burden of proof, proponents of an exemption must provide evidence either that actual harm exists or that it is "likely" to occur in the ensuing 3-year period. Actual instances of verifiable problems occurring in the marketplace are necessary to satisfy the burden with respect to actual harm and a compelling case will be based on first-hand knowledge of such problems. While "likely" adverse effects will also be examined in this rulemaking, this standard requires proof that adverse effects are more likely than not to occur and cannot be based on speculation alone. The House Manager's Report stated that an exemption based on "likely" future adverse impacts during the applicable period should only be made "in extraordinary circumstances in which the evidence of likelihood is highly specific, strong and persuasive." Staff of the House Committee on the Judiciary, 105th Cong., Section-By-Section Analysis of H.R. 2281 as passed by the United States House of Representatives on August 4, 1998 (hereinafter House Manager's Report) at 6. While such a statement could be interpreted as raising the burden beyond a standard of a preponderance of the evidence, the statutory language enacted—"whether persons who are users of a copyrighted work are, or are likely to be in the succeeding 3-year period, adversely affected by the prohibition"—does not specify a standard beyond more likely than not. Nevertheless, as the Register's final recommendation explained, the expectation of "distinct, verifiable and measurable impacts" in the legislative history as actual harm suggests that conjecture alone would be insufficient to support a finding of "likely" adverse effect. Final Reg., 65 FR 64556, 64559. A showing of "likely" adverse impact will necessarily involve prediction, but the burden of proving that the expected adverse effect is more likely than other possible outcomes is on the proponent of the exemption.

The identification of a specific problem and the meeting of a burden of proof as to a problem is not, however, the end of the analysis. For an

63580 Federal Register / Vol. 67, No. 199 / Tuesday, October 15, 2002 / Proposed Rules

exemption to be warranted in a particular class of works, a proponent must show that such problems are or are likely to become of such significance that they would constitute a substantial adverse effect. De minimis or isolated problems would be insufficient to warrant an exemption for a class of works. Similarly, mere inconveniences to noninfringing uses or theoretical critiques of Section 1201 would not satisfy the requisite showing. House Manager's Report, at 6. There is a presumption that the prohibition will apply to any and all classes of works, including those as to which an exemption of applicability was previously in effect, unless a new showing is made that an exemption is warranted. Final Reg., 65 FR 64556, 64558. Exemptions are reviewed de novo and prior exemptions will expire unless the case is made in the rulemaking proceeding that the prohibition has or will more likely than not have an adverse effect on noninfringing uses. A prior argument that resulted in an exemption may be less persuasive within the context of the marketplace in the next 3-year period. Similarly, proposals that were not found to warrant an exemption in the last rulemaking could find factual support in the present rulemaking.

Availability of Works in Unprotected Formats

Other factors must also be balanced with any adverse effects attributable to the prohibition on circumvention of technological protection measures that protect access to copyrighted works. In making her recommendation to the Librarian, the Register is instructed to consider the availability for use of copyrighted works. 17 U.S.C. 1201(a)(1)(C)(i). The Register must also consider whether works protected by technological measures that control access are also available in the marketplace in formats that are unprotected. The fact that a work is available in a format without technological protection measures would allow the public to make noninfringing uses of the work even if that is not the preferred or optimal format for use. For example, in the last rulemaking, although many users claimed that the technological measures on motion pictures contained on Digital Versatile Disks (DVDs) restricted noninfringing uses of works, a balancing consideration was that the vast majority of these works were also available in analog format on VHS tapes. Final Reg., 65 FR 64554, 64568. Such availability is a factor to consider in assessing the

need for an exemption to the prohibition on circumvention.

Another consideration relating to the availability for use of copyrighted works is whether the measure supports a model that is likely to benefit the public. For example, while a measure may limit the length of time of access to a work or may limit access to only a portion of work, those limitations may benefit the public by providing "use-facilitating" models that will allow users to obtain access to works at a lower cost than they would otherwise be able to obtain were such restrictions not in place. Similarly, if there is compelling evidence that particular classes of works would not be offered at all without the protection afforded by technological protection measures that control access, this use-facilitating factor must be considered. House Manager's Report, at 6. Accord: Final Reg., 65 FR 64556, 64559.

The Scope of the Term "Class of Works"

Section 1201 does not define a critical term for the rulemaking process: "class of works." In the first rulemaking, the Register elicited views on the scope and meaning of this term. After review of the statutory language, the legislative history and the extensive record in the proceeding,[1] the Register reached certain conclusions on the scope of this term. For a more detailed discussion, see Final Reg., 65 FR 64556, 64559.

The Register found that the statutory language required that the Librarian identify a "class of works" primarily based upon attributes of the works themselves, and not by reference to some external criteria such as the intended use or the users of the works. The phrase "class of works" connotes that the shared, common attributes of the "class" relate to the nature of authorship in the "works." Thus a "class of works" was intended to be a "narrow and focused subset of the the broad categories of works of authorship * * * identified in section 102." Commerce Comm. Report, at 38. The starting point for a proposed exemption of a particular class of works must be the section 102 categories of authorship: literary works; musical works; dramatic works; pantomimes and choreographic works; pictorial, graphic and sculptural works; motion pictures and other audiovisual works; sound recordings; and architectural works.

This determination is supported by the House Manager's Report which

discussed the importance of appropriately defining the proper scope of the exemption. House Manager's Report, at 7. The legislative history stated that it would be highly unlikely for all literary works to be adversely affected by the prohibition and therefore, determining an appropriate subcategory of the works in this category would be the goal of the rulemaking. Id.

Therefore, the Register concluded that the starting point for identifying a particular "class of works" to be exempted must be one of the section 102 categories. Final Reg., 65 FR 64559–64561. From that starting point, it is likely that the scope or boundaries of a particular class would need to be further limited to remedy the particular harm to noninfringing uses identified in the rulemaking.

In the first anticircumvention rulemaking, the Register recommended and the Librarian agreed that two classes of works should be exempted:

(1) Compilations consisting of lists of websites blocked by filtering software applications; and

(2) Literary works, including computer programs and databases, protected by access control mechanisms that fail to permit access because of malfunction, damage or obsoleteness.

While the first class exempted fits comfortably within the approach to classification discussed above, the second class includes the entire category of literary works, but narrows the exemption by reference to attributes of the technological measures that controls access to the works. The Register found that this second class probably reached the outer limits of a permissible definition of "class" under the approach adopted in the first rulemaking.

Commenters should familiarize themselves with the Register's recommendation in the first rulemaking, since many of these issues which were unsettled at the start of that rulemaking have been addressed in the final decision. Since the bases of those determinations were the statute and the legislative history relevant to these issues, and since Congress has not provided any additional guidance to the Register or the Librarian since that rulemaking's conclusion, interested parties should presume that these determinations will be applied to the evidence submitted during this second anticircumvention rulemaking as well. Of course, commenters may argue for adoption of alternative approaches, but a persuasive case will have to be made to warrant reconsideration of decisions regarding interpretation of section 1201.

---

[1] See Final Reg., 65 FR 64556, 64557 for a description of the record in the last rulemaking proceeding.

Federal Register / Vol. 67, No. 199 / Tuesday, October 15, 2002 / Proposed Rules **63581**

The exemptions that were published for the first 3-year period of the effective date of section 1201(a)(1)(A) are temporary and will expire on the last day of such 3-year period, October 27, 2003. This rulemaking will examine adverse effects in the current marketplace and in the next 3-year period to determine whether any exemptions to the prohibition on circumvention of technological protection measures that effectively control access to copyrighted works are warranted by the evidence raised during this rulemaking.

This notice requests written comments from all interested parties. In addition to the necessary showing discussed above, in order to make a *prima facie* case for a proposed exemption, certain critical points must be established. First, a proponent must identify the technological measure that is the ultimate source of the alleged problem, and the technological measure must effectively control access to a copyrighted work. Second, a proponent must specifically explain what noninfringing activity the prohibition on circumvention is preventing. Third, a proponent must establish that the prevented activity is, in fact, a noninfringing use under current law. The nature of the Librarian's inquiry is further delineated by the statutory areas to be examined:

(i) The availability for use of copyrighted works;

(ii) The availability for use of works for nonprofit archival, preservation, and educational purposes;

(iii) The impact that the prohibition on the circumvention of technological measures applied to copyrighted works has on criticism, comment, news reporting, teaching, scholarship, or research;

(iv) The effect of circumvention of technological measures on the market for or value of copyrighted works; and

(v) Such other factors as the Librarian considers appropriate.

17 U.S.C. 1201(a)(1)(C).

These statutory considerations require examination and careful balancing. The harm identified by a proponent of an exemption must be balanced with the harm that would result from an exemption. In some circumstances, an exemption could have a greater adverse effect on the public than would the adverse effects identified. The ultimate determination of the Librarian must take all of these factors into consideration.

Proponents and opponents of exemptions should address each of these statutory factors. Because the statute invites the Librarian to take into account "such other factors as the Librarian considers appropriate," commenters are invited to identify any such factors, explain why any factors identified should be considered, and discuss how such factors would affect the analysis relating to any proposed class of works that the commenters are addressing.

For the entire record of the first anticircumvention rulemaking, including all comments, testimony and notices published, See the Copyright Office's Web site at: *http://www.loc.gov/copyright/1201/anticirc.html.*

3. Written Comments

In the last rulemaking the Register determined that the burden of proof is on the proponent of an exemption to come forward with evidence supporting an exemption for a particular class of works. Therefore, the initial comment period in this rulemaking specifically seeks the identification of this information from proponents of exemptions. First, the commenter should identify the particular class of works that is being proposed as an exemption, followed by a summary of the argument for the exemption. The commenter should then specify the facts and evidence providing a basis for this exemption and any legal arguments in support of the exemption. Finally, the commenter may include in the comment any additional information or documentation which supports the commenter's position.

If a commenter proposes that more than one class of works be exempted, each individual class proposed should be numbered and followed by a summary of the argument for that proposed class and the factual support and legal arguments in support of that class. This format of class/summary/facts/argument should be sequentially followed for each class of work proposed as necessary.

As discussed above, the best evidence in support of an exemption would consist of concrete examples or cases of specific instances in which the prohibition on circumvention of technological measures controlling access has had or is likely to have an adverse effect on noninfringing uses. It would also be useful for the commenter to quantify the adverse effects in order to explain the scope of the problem, e.g., evidence of widespread or substantial impact through data or supplementary material.

In the reply comments, persons who oppose or support any exemptions proposed in the initial comments will have the opportunity to respond to the proposals made in the initial comments

and to provide factual information and legal argument addressing whether a proposed exemption should be adopted. Since the reply comments are intended to be responsive to the initial comments, reply commenters must identify what proposed class they are responding to, whether in opposition, support, amplification or correction. As with initial comments, reply comments should first identify the proposed class, provide a summary of the argument, and then provide the factual and/or legal support for their argument. This format of class/summary/facts and/or legal argument should be repeated for each reply to a particular class of work proposed.

The Copyright Office intends to place the comments and reply comments that are submitted in this proceeding on its Web site (*http://www.copyright.gov/1201*). Regardless of the mode of submission, all comments must, at a minimum, contain the legal name of the submitter and the entity on whose behalf the comment was submitted, if any. If persons do not wish to have their address, telephone number, or email address publicly displayed on the Office's website, the comment itself should not include such information, but should only include the name of the commenter. The Office prefers that comments and reply comments be submitted in electronic form and strongly encourages commenters to submit their comments electronically. However, the Office recognizes that it must provide a means of delivery for persons who are unable to submit their comments through the Office's website or to deliver their comments in person. Therefore, comments may also be delivered through the United States Postal Service, addressed to the General Counsel, Copyright GC/I&R, PO Box 70400, Southwest Station, Washington, DC 20024–0400. Because private carriers such as Airborne Express, DHL Worldwide Express, Federal Express, and United Parcel Service cannot deliver to post office boxes or directly to the office of the General Counsel, commenters are cautioned not to use such services to deliver their comments. Moreover, due to continuing mail delays at the Library of Congress, submission by means of the United States Postal Service is strongly discouraged and the submitter assumes the risk that the comment will not be received at the Copyright Office by the due date. Comments submitted by means of the United States Postal Service must be physically received by an employee of the General Counsel's Office of the Copyright Office by the applicable

63582   Federal Register / Vol. 67, No. 199 / Tuesday, October 15, 2002 / Proposed Rules

deadline to be considered. Commenters who use the postal service should consider using Express Mail. Electronic filing or hand-delivery will help insure timely receipt of comments by the Office. Electronic comments successfully submitted through the Office's website will generate a confirmation receipt to the submitter and submitters hand-delivering comments may request a date stamp on an extra copy provided by the submitter.

If submitted through the Copyright Office's website: The Copyright Office's website will contain a submission page at: *http://www.copyright.gov/1201/comment_forms*. Approximately thirty days prior to each applicable deadline (*see* DATES), a form will be activated on the Copyright Office website allowing information to be entered into the required fields, including the name of the person making the submission, his or her title, organization, mailing address, telephone number, and email address. For initial comments, there will be two additional fields required: (1) The proposed class or classes of copyrighted work(s) to be exempted, and (2) a brief summary of the argument(s). The comment or reply comment itself must be sent as an attachment, and must be in a single file in either Adobe Portable Document File (PDF) format (preferred), in Microsoft Word Version 2000 or earlier, or in WordPerfect 9 or earlier, or in ASCII text. There will be a browse button on the form that will allow submitters to attach the comment file to the form and then to submit the completed form to the Office. The personal information entered in the required fields will not be publicly posted on the website, but the Office intends to post on its website the proposed class and the summary of the argument, as well as the entire comment. Only the commenter's name (and, if applicable, the entity on whose behalf the comment is submitted) is required on the comment document itself and a commenter who does not want other personal information posted on the Office's website should avoid including other private information on the comment itself. Except in exceptional circumstances, changes to the submitted comment will not be allowed and it will become a part of the public record of this rulemaking.

If by means of the United States Postal Service or hand delivery: Send, to the appropriate address listed above, two copies, each on a 3.5-inch write-protected diskette or CD–ROM, labeled with the name of the person making the submission and the entity on whose behalf the comment was submitted, if any. The document itself must be in a single file in either Adobe Portable Document File (PDF) format (preferred), or in Microsoft Word Version 2000 or earlier, in WordPerfect Version 9 or earlier, or in ASCII text. If the comment is hand delivered or mailed to the Office and the submitter does not wish to have the address, telephone number, or email address publicly displayed on the Office's website, the comment should not include such information on the document itself, but only the name and affiliation, if any, of the commenter. In that case, a cover letter should be included that contains the commenter's address, telephone number, email address, and for initial comments, the proposed class of copyrighted work to be exempted and another field for a brief summary of the argument.

Anyone who is unable to submit a comment in electronic form (on the website as an attachment or by means of hand delivery or the United States Postal Service on disk or CD–ROM) should submit an original and fifteen paper copies by hand or by means of the United States Postal Service to the appropriate address listed above. It may not be feasible for the Office to place these comments on its website.

General Requirements for all submissions: All submissions (in either electronic or non-electronic form delivered through the website, by means of hand delivery or the United States Postal Service) must contain on the comment itself, the name of the person making the submission and, if applicable, the entity on whose behalf the comment is submitted. The mailing address, telephone number, telefax number, if any, and email address need not be included on the comment itself, but must be included in some form, *e.g.*, on the website form or in a cover letter, with the submission. All submissions must also include the class/summary/factual and/or legal argument format in the comment itself for each class of work proposed or for each reply to a proposal. Initial comments and reply comments will be accepted for a 30-day period in each round, and a form will be placed on the Copyright Office website at least 30 days prior to the deadline for submission. Initial comments will be accepted from November 19, 2002, until December 18, 2002, at 5 P.M. Eastern Standard Time, at which time the submission form will be removed from the website. Reply comments will be accepted from January 21, 2003, until February 19, 2003, at 5 P.M. Eastern Standard Time.

4. Hearings and Further Comments

The Register intends to hold hearings in this rulemaking in the spring of 2003.

Following these hearings, the Register will make a determination as to whether there is a need for additional written comments in the form of post-hearing comments specifically addressing matters raised in the record of this proceeding. Details on hearings and any post-hearing comments will be announced at a future date.

In order to provide flexibility in this proceeding to take into account unforeseen developments that may occur and that would significantly affect the Register's recommendation, an opportunity to petition the Register for consideration of new information will be made available after the deadlines specified. A petition, including proposed new classes of works to be exempted, must be in writing and must set forth the reasons why the information could not have been made available earlier and why it should be considered by the Register after the deadline. A petition must also set forth the proposed class of works to be exempted, a summary of the argument, the factual basis for such an exemption and the legal argument supporting such an exemption. Fifteen copies of the petition must be hand-delivered to the Office of the General Counsel of the Copyright Office at the address listed above. The Register will make a determination whether to accept such a petition based on the stage of the rulemaking process at which the request is made and the merits of the petition. If a petition is accepted, the Register will announce deadlines for comments in response to the petition.

Dated: October 4, 2002.

Marybeth Peters,
Register of Copyrights.

James H. Billington,
The Librarian of Congress.
[FR Doc. 02–26183 Filed 10–11–02; 8:45 am]
BILLING CODE 1410–30–P

LIBRARY OF CONGRESS

Copyright Office

37 CFR Part 201

[Docket No. RM 2002–4A]

Exemption to Prohibition on Circumvention of Copyright Protection Systems for Access Control Technologies

AGENCY: Copyright Office, Library of Congress.

ACTION: Notice of inquiry.

SUMMARY: The Copyright Office of the Library of Congress has granted a petition by Static Control Components, Inc. to consider a newly-proposed class of works to be exempted from the prohibition on circumvention of technological measures that control access to copyrighted works as part of a pending rulemaking pursuant to the Digital Millennium Copyright Act. The Office has posted Static Control's comment in support of the proposed exemption on its website and seeks reply comments on the proposed exemption.

DATES: Reply comments must be received by the Copyright Office General Counsel no later than 5 pm Eastern Standard Time on March 10, 2003.

ADDRESSES: Electronic Internet submissions must be made through the Copyright Office Web site at *http://www.copyright.gov/1201/comment_forms. See* Exemption to Prohibition on Circumvention of Copyright Protection Systems for Access Control Technologies, 67 FR 63578, 63582 (October 15, 2002), for file formats and other information about electronic and non-electronic filing requirements. If delivered by hand, comments should be delivered to the Office of the General Counsel, Copyright

Federal Register / Vol. 68, No. 27 / Monday, February 10, 2003 / Proposed Rules 6679

Office, LM–403, James Madison Memorial Building, 101 Independence Avenue, SE., Washington, DC. If delivered by means of the United States Postal Service, comments should be addressed to David O. Carson, General Counsel, Copyright GC/I&R, PO Box 70400, Southwest Station, Washington, DC 20024–0400.

FOR FURTHER INFORMATION CONTACT: Rob Kasunic, Office of the General Counsel, Copyright GC/I&R, PO Box 70400, Southwest Station, Washington, DC 20024–0400. Telephone (202) 707–8380; telefax (202) 707–8366.

SUPPLEMENTARY INFORMATION: The Copyright Office of the Library of Congress is currently conducting proceedings mandated by the Digital Millennium Copyright Act, which provides that the Librarian of Congress may exempt certain classes of works from the prohibition against circumvention of technological measures that control access to copyrighted works. *See* 17 U.S.C. 1201(a)(1)(C). The purpose of this rulemaking proceeding is to determine whether there are particular classes of works as to which users are, or are likely to be, adversely affected in their ability to make noninfringing uses due to the prohibition on circumvention. If there are, the Librarian may exempt such classes from the statutory prohibition.

Comments proposing classes of works to be exempted were due December 18, 2002. However, in order to provide flexibility in this rulemaking proceeding and to take into account unforeseen developments that might significantly affect the recommendation of the Register of Copyrights, the Office's October 15, 2002 Notice of Inquiry provided an opportunity to petition the Register for consideration of new information that could not reasonably have been known prior to the December 18 deadline. *See* Exemption to Prohibition on Circumvention of Copyright Protection Systems for Access Control Technologies, 67 FR 63578, 63582 (October 15, 2002). The Notice of Inquiry states that a petition to consider new classes of works proposed for exemption must be in writing and must set forth the reasons why the information could not have been made available earlier and why it should be considered by the Register after the deadline. A petition must also set forth the proposed class or classes of works to be exempted, a summary of the argument, the factual basis for such an exemption and the legal argument supporting such an exemption. The Register's determination whether to accept such a petition is based on the stage of the rulemaking process at which the request is made and the merits of the petition.

Static Control Components, Inc. ("Static Control") has petitioned for consideration of the following classes of works:

1. Computer programs embedded in computer printers and toner cartridges and that control the interoperation and functions of the printer and toner cartridge;

2. Computer programs embedded in a machine or product and which cannot be copied during the ordinary operation or use of the machine or product; and

3. Computer programs embedded in a machine or product and that control the operation of a machine or product connected thereto, but that do not otherwise control the performance, display or reproduction of copyrighted works that have an independent economic significance.

The Register of Copyrights has determined that Static Control has adequately explained why the information set forth in its petition could not have been made available earlier, and that Static Control has set forth sufficiently serious arguments on the merits to warrant consideration of its proposal after the initial deadline. Accordingly, the "Petition of Static Control Components, Inc. for Consideration of New Information" has been accepted as a comment proposing three classes of works to be exempted from the prohibition on circumvention, and interested parties are invited to submit reply comments responsive to this comment, either in support of or opposition to the Static Control proposal. Static Control's comment is available on the Copyright Office Web site at *http://www.copyright.gov/1201/2003/petitions/*.

Reply comments responsive to this new comment will be accepted from February 24, 2003 until March 10, 2003, at 5 pm Eastern Standard Time. Commenters are encouraged to file their comments electronically. *See* **ADDRESSES**, above. Please review the initial Notice of Inquiry for format requirements for comments. *See* 67 FR at 63582 (October 15, 2002).

Dated: February 5, 2003.

David O. Carson,

General Counsel, Copyright Office.

[FR Doc. 03–3256 Filed 2–7–03; 8:45 am]

BILLING CODE 1410–30–P

The Digital Millennium Copyright Act
Text, History, and Caselaw

VI. JUDICIAL INTERPRETATION

A&M Records, Inc.
v.
Napster, Inc.
(Applicability of DMCA Safe Harbor)

**United States District Court,
Northern District of California**

May 5, 2000

5 ILR (P&F) 418, 2000 WL 573136

No. 99-05183 MHP

DMCA's liability exemptions do not apply to online music system.

The Napster online music system is not a "passive conduit" entitled to the copyright infringement liability exemptions provided to online service providers under Section 512(a) of the Digital Millennium Copyright Act (DMCA). Defendant Napster makes its proprietary MusicShare software freely available for Internet users who use it to share CD-quality MP3 files with others logged on to the Napster system. Napster "enables or facilitates" connections between its users, but does not "transmit, route, or provide connections through its system," as required for the exemption. The legislative history of §512 demonstrates that Congress intended the §512(a) safe harbor to apply only to activities "in which a service provider plays the role of a 'conduit' for the communications of others." In any event, even if Napster met the criteria outlined in §512(a), summary adjudication in favor of Napster is inappropriate due to genuine issues of fact about Napter's compliance with the threshold eligibility requirements of §512(i), which a service provider must satisfy to enjoy the protection of any of the safe harbors of §512. Subsection 512(i) requires service providers to adopt and "reasonably implement" a policy of terminating repeat infringers. Napster did not make its users aware of such a policy until two months after the filing of the instant suit, and plaintiffs raised genuine issues of material fact about whether Napster's practice of blocking IP addresses is a reasonable means of terminating infringers. — **A&M Records, Inc. v. Napster, Inc. (Applicability of DMCA Safe Harbor), 5 ILR (P&F) 418 [ND Cal, 2000].**

OPINION

MARILYN HALL PATEL, *Chief Judge.* On December 6, 1999, plaintiff record companies filed suit alleging contributory and vicarious federal copyright infringement and related state law violations by defendant Napster, Inc. ("Napster"). Now before this court is defendant's motion for summary adjudication of the applicability of a safe harbor provision of the Digital Millennium Copyright Act ("DMCA"), 17 USC section 512(a), to its business activities. Defendant argues that the entire Napster system falls within the safe harbor and, hence, that plaintiffs may not obtain monetary damages or injunctive relief, except as narrowly specified by subparagraph 512(j)(1)(B). In the alternative, Napster asks the court to find subsection 512(a) applicable to its role in downloading MP3 music files,[1] as opposed to searching for or indexing

such files. Having considered the parties' arguments and for the reasons set forth below, the court enters the following memorandum and order.

BACKGROUND

Napster—a small Internet start-up based in San Mateo, California—makes its proprietary MusicShare software freely available for Internet users to download. Users who obtain Napster's software can then share MP3 music files with others logged-on to the Napster system. MP3 files, which reproduce nearly CD-quality sound in a compressed format, are available on a variety of websites either for a fee or free-of-charge. Napster allows users to exchange MP3 files stored on their own computer hard-drives directly, without payment, and boasts that it "takes the frustration out of locating servers with MP3 files." Def. Br. at 4.

Although the parties dispute the precise nature of the service Napster provides, they agree that using Napster typically involves the following basic steps: After downloading MusicShare software from the Napster website, a user can access the Napster system from her computer. The MusicShare software interacts with Napster's server-side software when the user logs on, automatically connecting her to one of some 150 servers that Napster operates. The MusicShare software reads a list of names of MP3 files that the user has elected to make available. This list is then added to a directory and index, on the Napster server, of MP3 files that users who are logged-on wish to share. If the user wants to locate a song, she enters its name or the name of the recording artist on the search page of the MusicShare program and clicks the "Find It" button. The Napster software then searches the current directory and generates a list of files responsive to the search request. To download a desired file, the user highlights it on the list and clicks the "Get Selected Song(s)" button. The user may also view a list of files that exist on another user's hard drive and select a file from that list. When the requesting user clicks on the name of a file, the Napster server communicates with the requesting user's and host user's [2] MusicShare browser software to facilitate a connection between the two users and initiate the downloading of the file without any further action on either user's part.

According to Napster, when the requesting user clicks on the name of the desired MP3 file, the Napster server routes this request to the host user's browser. The host user's browser responds that it either can or cannot supply the file. If the host user can supply the file, the Napster server communicates the host's address and routing information to the requesting user's browser, allowing the requesting user to make a connection with the host and receive the desired MP3 file. *See* Declaration of Edward Kessler ("Kessler Dec."), Exh. B; Reply Declaration of Edward Kessler ("Kessler Reply Dec.") ¶22. The parties disagree about whether this process involves a hypertext link that the Napster server-side software provides. *Compare* Pl. Br. at 9 *with* Def. Reply Br. at 10 n. 12. However, plaintiffs admit that the Napster server gets the necessary IP address information from the host user, enabling the

requesting user to connect to the host. *See* Declaration of Daniel Farmer ("Farmer Dec.") ¶17; Declaration of Russell. J. Frackman ("Frackman Dec."), Exh. 1 (Kessler Dep.) at 103-05. The MP3 file is actually transmitted over the Internet, *see, e.g.*, Def. Reply Br. at 3, but the steps necessary to make that connection could not take place without the Napster server.

The Napster system has other functions besides allowing users to search for, request, and download MP3 files. For example, a requesting user can play a downloaded song using the MusicShare software. Napster also hosts a chat room.

Napster has developed a policy that makes compliance with all copyright laws one of the "terms of use" of its service and warns users that:

> Napster will terminate the accounts of users who are repeat infringers of the copyrights, or other intellectual property rights, of others. In addition, Napster reserves the right to terminate the account of a user upon any single infringement of the rights of others in conjunction with use of the Napster service.

Kessler Dec. ¶19. However, the parties disagree over when this policy was instituted and how effectively it bars infringers from using the Napster service. Napster claims that it had a copyright compliance policy as early as October 1999, but admits that it did not document or notify users of the existence of this policy until February 7, 2000.

LEGAL STANDARD

The court may grant summary adjudication of a particular claim or defense under the same standards used to consider a summary judgment motion. *See* Fed. R. Civ. P. 56(a), (b); *Pacific Fruit Express Co. v. Akron, Canton & Youngstown R.R. Co.*, 524 F2d 1025, 1029-30 (9th Cir 1975). Summary judgment shall be granted when there is no genuine issue of material fact and the movant is entitled to judgment as a matter of law. *See* Fed. R. Civ. 56(c).

The moving party bears the initial burden of identifying those portions of the record that demonstrate the absence of a genuine issue of material fact. The burden then shifts to the nonmoving party to "go beyond the pleadings, and by [its] own affidavits, or by the 'depositions, answers to interrogatories, or admissions on file,' designate 'specific facts showing that there is a genuine issue for trial.' " *Celotex Corp. v. Catrett*, 477 US 317, 324 (1986) (citations omitted). A dispute about a material fact is genuine "if the evidence is such that a reasonable jury could return a verdict for the nonmoving party." *Anderson v. Liberty Lobby, Inc.*, 477 US 242, 248 (1986). The moving party discharges its burden by showing that the nonmoving party has not disclosed the existence of any "significant probative evidence tending to support the complaint." *First Nat'l Bank v. Cities Serv. Co.*, 391 US 253, 290 (1968). The court does not make credibility determinations in considering a motion for summary judgment. *See Anderson*, 477 US at 249. Rather, it views the inferences drawn from the facts in the light most favorable to the party opposing the motion. *See T.W. Elec. Serv., Inc. v. Pacific Elec. Contractor's Ass'n*, 809 F2d 626, 631 (9th Cir 1987).

DISCUSSION

Section 512 of the DMCA addresses the liability of online service and Internet access providers for copyright infringements occurring online. Subsection 512(a) exempts qualifying service providers from monetary liability for direct, vicarious, and contributory infringement and limits injunctive relief to the degree specified in subparagraph 512(j)(1)(B). Interpretation of subsection 512(a), or indeed any of the section 512 safe harbors, appears to be an issue of first impression.[3]

Napster claims that its business activities fall within the safe harbor provided by subsection 512(a). This subsection limits liability "for infringement of copyright by reason of the [service] provider's transmitting, routing, or providing connections for, material through a system or network controlled or operated by or for the service provider, or by reason of the intermediate and transient storage of that material in the course of such transmitting, routing, or providing connections," if five conditions are satisfied:

(1) the transmission of the material was initiated by or at the direction of a person other than the service provider;

(2) the transmission, routing, provision of connections, or storage is carried out through an automatic technical process without selection of the material by the service provider;

(3) the service provider does not select the recipients of the material except as an automatic response to the request of another person;

(4) no copy of the material made by the service provider in the course of such intermediate or transient storage is maintained on the system or network in a manner ordinarily accessible to anyone other than the anticipated recipients, and no such copy is maintained on the system or network in a manner ordinarily accessible to such anticipated recipients for a longer period than is reasonably necessary for the transmission, routing, or provision of connections; and

(5) the material is transmitted through the system or network without modification of its content.

17 USC §512(a).

Citing the "definitions" subsection of the statute, Napster argues that it is a "service provider" for the purposes of the 512(a) safe harbor. *See* 17 USC §512(k)(1)(A).[4] First, it claims to offer the "transmission, routing, or providing of connections for digital online communications" by enabling the connection of users' hard-drives and the transmission of MP3 files "directly from the Host hard drive and Napster browser through the Internet to the user's Napster browser and hard drive." Def. Reply Br. at 3. Second, Napster states that users choose the online communication points and the MP3 files to be transmitted with no direction from Napster. Finally, the Napster system does not modify the content of the transferred files. Defendant contends that, because it meets the definition of "service provider,"[5] it need only satisfy the five remaining requirements of the safe harbor to prevail in its motion for summary adjudication.

Defendant then seeks to show compliance with these requirements by arguing: (1) a Napster user, and never Napster itself, initiates the transmission of MP3 files; (2) the transmission occurs through an automatic, technical process without any editorial input from Napster; (3) Napster does not choose the recipients of the MP3 files; (4) Napster does not make a copy of the material during transmission; and (5) the content of the material is not modified during transmission. Napster maintains that the 512(a) safe harbor thus protects its core function—

"transmitting, routing and providing connections for sharing of the files its users choose." Def. Reply Br. at 2.

Plaintiffs disagree. They first argue that subsection 512(n) requires the court to analyze each of Napster's functions independently and that not all of these functions fall under the 512(a) safe harbor. In their view, Napster provides information location tools—such as a search engine, directory, index, and links—that are covered by the more stringent eligibility requirements of subsection 512(d), rather than subsection 512(a).

Plaintiffs also contend that Napster does not perform the function which the 512(a) safe harbor protects because the infringing material is not transmitted or routed *through* the Napster system, as required by subsection 512(a). They correctly note that the definition of "service provider" under subparagraph 512(k)(1)(A) is not identical to the prefatory language of subsection 512(a). The latter imposes the additional requirement that transmitting, routing, or providing connections must occur "through the system or network." Plaintiffs argue in the alternative that, if users' computers are part of the Napster system, copies of MP3 files are stored on the system longer than reasonably necessary for transmission, and thus subparagraph 512(a)(4) is not satisfied.

Finally, plaintiffs note that, under the general eligibility requirements established in subsection 512(i), a service provider must have adopted, reasonably implemented, and informed its users of a policy for terminating repeat infringers. Plaintiffs contend that Napster only adopted its copyright compliance policy after the onset of this litigation and even now does not discipline infringers in any meaningful way. Therefore, in plaintiffs' view, Napster fails to satisfy the DMCA's threshold eligibility requirements or show that the 512(a) safe harbor covers any of its functions.

I. *Independent Analysis of Functions*

Subsection 512(n) of the DMCA states:

Subsections (a), (b), (c), and (d) describe separate and distinct functions for purposes of applying this section. Whether a service provider qualifies for the limitation on liability in any one of those subsections shall be based solely on the criteria in that subsection and shall not affect a determination of whether that service provider qualifies for the limitations on liability under any other such subsections.

Citing subsection 512(n), plaintiffs argue that the 512(a) safe harbor does not offer blanket protection to Napster's entire system. Plaintiffs consider the focus of the litigation to be Napster's function as an information location tool—eligible for protection, if at all, under the more rigorous subsection 512(d). They contend that the system does not operate as a passive conduit within the meaning of subsection 512(a). In this view, Napster's only possible safe harbor is subsection 512(d), which applies to service providers "referring or linking users to an online location containing infringing material or infringing activity, by using information location tools, including a directory, index, reference, pointer, or hypertext link . . . ." Subsection 512(d) imposes more demanding eligibility requirements because it covers active assistance to users.

Defendant responds in two ways. First, it argues that subsection 512(a), rather than 512(d), applies because the information location tools it provides are incidental to its core function of automatically transmitting, routing, or providing connections for the MP3 files users select. In the alternative, defendant maintains that, even if the court decides to analyze the information location functions under 512(d), it should hold that the 512(a) safe harbor protects other aspects of the Napster service.

Napster undisputedly performs some information location functions. The Napster server stores a transient list of the files that each user currently logged-on to that server wants to share. *See, e.g.*, Kessler Dec. ¶12. This data is maintained until the user logs off, but the structure of the index itself continues to exist. *See* Frackman Dec., Exh. 1 (Kessler Dep.), at 71:3-4, 16-21; 77:8. If a user wants to find a particular song or recording artist, she enters a search, and Napster looks for the search terms in the index. *See id.* at 76:17-25, 77:1-2. Edward Kessler, Napster's Vice President of Engineering, admitted in his deposition that, at least in this context, Napster functions as a free information location tool. *See id.* at 21:12-19; *cf.* Farmer Dec. ¶16 (stating that "Napster operates exactly like a search engine or information location tool to the user"). Napster software also has a "hot list" function that allows users to search for other users' log-in names and receive notification when users with whom they might want to communicate have connected to the service. *See* Frackman Dec., Exh. 1 (Kessler Dep.), at 59:16-18. In short, the parties agree on the existence of a searchable directory and index, and Napster representatives have used the phrase "information location tool," which appears in the heading for subsection 512(d), to characterize some Napster functions.

There the agreement ends. According to Napster, the information location tools upon which plaintiffs base their argument are incidental to the system's core function of transmitting MP3 music files, and for this reason, the court should apply subsection 512(a). Napster also disputes the contention that it organizes files or provides links to other Internet sites in the same manner as a search engine like Yahoo!. *See* Kessler Reply Dec. ¶¶16-20 (discussing differences between Napster and other search engines). Consequently, it deems subsection 512(d) inapplicable to its activities. *Cf.* H.R. Rep. No. 105-551 (II), 105th Cong., 2d Sess. (1998), 1998 WL 414916, at *147 (using Yahoo! as an example of an information location tool covered by 512(d)). Napster contrasts its operations, which proceed automatically after initial stimuli from users, with search engines like Yahoo! that depend upon the "human judgment and editorial discretion" of the service provider's staff. *Id.*

Napster's final and most compelling argument regarding subsection 512(d) is that the DMCA safe harbors are not mutually exclusive. According to subsection 512(n), a service provider could enjoy the 512(a) safe harbor even if its information location tools were also protected by (or failed to satisfy) subsection 512(d). *See* 17 USC §512(n) ("Whether a service provider qualifies for the limitation on liability in any one of those subsections . . . shall not affect a determination of whether that service provider qualifies for the limitations on liability under any other such subsections.") Similarly, finding *some* aspects of the system outside the scope of subsection 512(a) would not preclude a ruling that *other* aspects *do* meet 512(a) criteria.

Because the parties dispute material issues regarding the operation of Napster's index, directory, and search engine, the court declines to hold that these functions are peripheral to the alleged infringement, or that they should not be analyzed separately under subsection 512(d).[6] Indeed, despite its contention that its search engine and indexing functions are incidental to the provision of connections and transmission of MP3 files, Napster has advertised the ease with which its users can locate "millions of songs" online without "wading through page after page of unknown artists." Frackman Dec., Exh. 5, 4. Such statements by Napster to promote its service are tantamount to an admission that its search and indexing functions are essential to its marketability. Some of these essential functions—including but not limited to the search engine and index—should be analyzed under subsection 512(d).

However, the potential applicability of subsection 512(d) does not completely foreclose use of the 512(a) safe harbor as an affirmative defense. *See* 17 USC §512(n). The court will now turn to Napster's eligibility for protection under subsection 512(a). It notes at the outset, though, that a ruling that subsection 512(a) applies to a given function would not mean that the DMCA affords the service provider blanket protection.

II. *Subsection 512(a)*

Plaintiffs' principal argument against application of the 512(a) safe harbor is that Napster does not perform the passive conduit function eligible for protection under this subsection. As defendant correctly notes, the words "conduit" or "passive conduit" appear nowhere in 512(a), but are found only in the legislative history and summaries of the DMCA. The court must look first to the plain language of the statute, "construing the provisions of the entire law, including its object and policy, to ascertain the intent of Congress." *United States v. Hockings*, 129 F3d 1069, 1071 (9th Cir 1997) (quoting *Northwest Forest Resource Council v. Glickman*, 82 F3d 825, 830 (9th Cir 1996)) (internal quotation marks omitted). If the statute is unclear, however, the court may rely on the legislative history. *See Hockings*, 129 F3d at 1071. The language of subsection 512(a) makes the safe harbor applicable, as a threshold matter, to service providers "transmitting, routing or providing connections for, material *through a system or network* controlled or operated by or for the service provider . . . ." 17 USC §512(a) (emphasis added). According to plaintiffs, the use of the word "conduit" in the legislative history explains the meaning of "through a system."

Napster has expressly denied that the transmission of MP3 files ever passes through its servers. *See* Kessler Dec. ¶14. Indeed, Kessler declared that "files reside on the computers of Napster users, and are transmitted directly between those computers." *Id.* MP3 files are transmitted "from the Host user's hard drive and Napster browser, *through the Internet* to the recipient's Napster browser and hard drive." Def. Reply Br. at 3 (citing Kessler Dec. ¶12-13) (emphasis added). The Internet cannot be considered "a system or network controlled or operated by or for the service provider," however. 17 USC §512(a). To get around this problem, Napster avers (and plaintiffs seem willing to concede) that "Napster's servers and Napster's MusicShare browsers on its users' computers are all part of Napster's overall system." Def. Reply Br. at 5. Defendant narrowly defines its system to include the browsers on users' computers. *See* Kessler Dec. ¶13. In contrast, plaintiffs argue that either (1) the system does not include the browsers, or (2) it includes not only the browsers, but also the users' computers themselves. *See* Farmer Dec. ¶17.

Even assuming that the system includes the browser on each user's computer, the MP3 files are not transmitted "through" the system within the meaning of subsection 512(a). Napster emphasizes the passivity of its role—stating that "[a]ll files transfer directly from the computer of one Napster user *through the Internet* to the computer of the requesting user." Def. Br. at 5 (emphasis added); *see also id.* at 12 (citing Kessler Dec. ¶13-15). It admits that the transmission bypasses the Napster server. *See* Kessler Dec. ¶14; Def. Reply Br. at 6. This means that, even if each user's Napster browser is part of the system, the transmission goes *from* one part of the system *to* another, or *between* parts of the system, but not "through" the system. The court finds that subsection 512(a) does not protect the transmission of MP3 files.

The prefatory language of subsection 512(a) is disjunctive, however. The subsection applies to "infringement of copyright by reason of the provider's transmitting, routing, *or* providing connections through a system or network controlled or operated by or for the service provider." 17 USC §512(a) (emphasis added). The court's finding that transmission does not occur "through" the system or network does not foreclose the possibility that

subsection 512(a) applies to "routing" or "providing connections." Rather, each of these functions must be analyzed independently.

Napster contends that providing connections between users' addresses "constitutes the value of the system to the users and the public." Def. Br. at 15. This connection cannot be established without the provision of the host's address to the Napster browser software installed on the requesting user's computer. *See* Kessler Dec. ¶10-13. The central Napster server delivers the host's address. *See id.* While plaintiffs contend that the infringing material is not *transmitted* through the Napster system, they provide no evidence to rebut the assertion that Napster supplies the requesting user's computer with information necessary to facilitate a connection with the host.

Nevertheless, the court finds that Napster does not provide connections "through" its system. Although the Napster server conveys address information to establish a connection between the requesting and host users, the connection itself occurs through the Internet. The legislative history of section 512 demonstrates that Congress intended the 512(a) safe harbor to apply only to activities "in which a service provider plays the role of a 'conduit' for the communications of others." H.R. Rep. No. 105-551 (II), 105th Cong., 2d Sess. (1998), 1998 WL 414916, at *130. Drawing inferences in the light most favorable to the non-moving party, this court cannot say that Napster serves as a conduit for the connection itself, as opposed to the address information that makes the connection possible. Napster enables or facilitates the initiation of connections, but these connections do not pass through the system within the meaning of subsection 512(a).

Neither party has adequately briefed the meaning of "routing" in subsection 512(a), nor does the legislative history shed light on this issue. Defendant tries to make "routing" and "providing connections" appear synonymous—stating, for example, that "the central Napster server *routes* the transmission by providing the Host's address to the Napster browser that is installed on and in use by User1's computer." Def. Br. at 16. However, the court doubts that Congress would have used the terms "routing" and "providing connections" disjunctively if they had the same meaning.[7] It is clear from both parties' submissions that the route of the allegedly infringing material goes through the Internet from the host to the requesting user, not through the Napster server. *See, e.g.*, Def. Br. at 13 ("Indeed, the content of the MP3 files are routed without even passing through Napster's Servers."). The court holds that routing does not occur through the Napster system.

Because Napster does not transmit, route, or provide connections through its system, it has failed to demonstrate that it qualifies for the 512(a) safe harbor. The court thus declines to grant summary adjudication in its favor.

III. *Copyright Compliance Policy*

Even if the court had determined that Napster meets the criteria outlined in subsection 512(a), subsection 512(i) imposes additional requirements on eligibility for *any* DMCA safe harbor. This provision states:

> The limitations established by this section shall apply to a service provider only if the service provider—
>
> > (A) has adopted and reasonably implemented, and informs subscribers and account holders of the service provider's system or network of, a policy that provides for the termination in appropriate circumstances of subscribers and account holders of the service provider's system or network who are repeat infringers; and
> >
> > (B) accommodates and does not interfere with standard technical measures.

17 USC §512(i).

Plaintiffs challenge Napster's compliance with these threshold eligibility requirements on two grounds. First, they point to evidence from Kessler's deposition that Napster did not adopt a written policy of which its users had notice until on or around February 7, 2000—two months after the filing of this lawsuit. *See* Frackman Dec., Exh. 1 (Kessler Dep.) at 189:17-25, 190:1-25, 191:1-12. Kessler testified that, although Napster had a copyright compliance policy as early as October 1999, he is not aware that this policy was reflected in any document, *see id.* at 191:22-24, 192:9-11, or communicated to any user. *See id.* at 192:15-16. Congress did not intend to require a service provider

to "investigate possible infringements, monitor its service or make difficult judgments as to whether conduct is or is not infringing," but the notice requirement is designed to insure that flagrant or repeat infringers "know that there is a realistic threat of losing [their] access." H.R. Rep. 105-551(II), 1998 WL 414916, at *154.

Napster attempts to refute plaintiffs' argument by noting that subsection 512(i) does not specify when the copyright compliance policy must be in place. Although this characterization of subsection 512(i) is facially accurate, it defies the logic of making formal notification to users or subscribers a prerequisite to exemption from monetary liability. The fact that Napster developed and notified its users of a formal policy *after* the onset of this action should not moot plaintiffs' claim to monetary relief for past harms. Without further documentation, defendant's argument that it has satisfied subsection 512(i) is merely conclusory and does not support summary adjudication in its favor.

Summary adjudication is also inappropriate because Napster has not shown that it *reasonably* implemented a policy for terminating repeat infringers. *See* 17 USC §512(i)(A) (requiring "reasonable" implementation of such a policy). If Napster is formally notified of infringing activity, it blocks the infringer's password so she cannot log on to the Napster service using that password. *See* Kessler Dec. ¶23. Napster does not block the IP addresses of infringing users, however, and the parties dispute whether it would be feasible or effective to do so. *See* Frackman Dec., Exh. 1 (Kessler Dep.), at 205:4-7.

Plaintiffs aver that Napster wilfully turns a blind eye to the identity of its users—that is, their real names and physical addresses—because their anonymity allows Napster to disclaim responsibility for copyright infringement. Hence, plaintiffs contend, "infringers may readily reapply to the Napster system to recommence their infringing downloading and uploading of MP3 music files." Pl. Br. at 24. Plaintiffs' expert, computer security researcher Daniel Farmer, declared that he conducted tests in which he easily deleted all traces of his former Napster identity, convincing Napster that "it had never seen me or my computer before." Farmer Dec. ¶29. Farmer also cast doubt on Napster's contention that blocking IP addresses is not a reasonable means of terminating infringers.

He noted that Napster bans the IP addresses of users who runs "bots" [8] on the service. *See id.* ¶27.

Hence, plaintiffs raise genuine issues of material fact about whether Napster has reasonably implemented a policy of terminating repeat infringers. They have produced evidence that Napster's copyright compliance policy is neither timely nor reasonable within the meaning of subparagraph 512(i)(A).

CONCLUSION

This court has determined above that Napster does not meet the requirements of subsection 512(a) because it does not transmit, route, or provide connections for allegedly infringing material through its system. The court also finds summary adjudication inappropriate due to the existence of genuine issues of material fact about Napster's compliance with subparagraph 512(i)(A), which a service provider must satisfy to enjoy the protection of *any* section 512 safe harbor. Defendant's motion for summary adjudication is DENIED.

IT IS SO ORDERED.

---

[1] The Motion Picture Experts Group first created MP3 in the early 1980s as the audio layer 3 of the MPEG-1 audiovisual format. MP3 technology allows for the fast and efficient conversion of compact disc recordings into computer files that may be downloaded over the Internet. *See generally Recording Industry Ass'n of America v. Diamond Multimedia Systems Inc.*, 180 F3d 1072, 1073-74 *[3 ILR (P&F) 66]* (9th Cir 1999) (discussing MP3 technology).

[2] Napster uses the term "host user" to refer to the user who makes the desired MP3 file available for downloading.

[3] In *Universal City Studios, Inc. v. Reimerdes*, 82 F Supp 2d 211, 217 & n. 17 *[4 ILR (P&F) 399]* (SD NY 2000), one defendant sought protection under subsection 512(c). Although the court noted in passing that the defendant offered no evidence that he was a service provider under subsection 512(c), it held that he could not invoke the safe harbor because plaintiffs claimed violations of 17 USC section 1201(a), which applies to circumvention products and technologies, rather than copyright infringement.

[4] Subparagraph 512(k)(1)(A) provides:

As used in subsection (a), the term "service provider" means an entity offering the transmission, routing, or providing of connections for digital online communications, between or among points specified by a user, of material of the user's choosing, without modification to the content of the material sent or received.

Subparagraph 512(k)(1)(B) states:

As used in this section, other than subsection (a), the term "service provider" means a provider of online services or network access, or the operator of facilities therefor, and includes an entity described in subparagraph (A).

[5] It is not entirely clear to the court that Napster qualifies under the narrower subparagraph 512(k)(1)(A). However, plaintiffs appear to concede that Napster is a "service provider" within the meaning of subparagraph 512(k)(1)(A), arguing instead that Napster does not satisfy the additional limitations that the prefatory language of subsection 512(a) imposes. The court assumes, but does not hold, that Napster is a "service provider" under subparagraph 512(k)(1)(A).

[6] The court need not rule on the applicability of subsection 512(d) to the functions plaintiffs characterize as information location tools because defendant does not rely on subsection 512(d) as grounds for its motion for summary adjudication.

[7] Napster sometimes appears to recognize a distinction between the two terms. For example, it states that "the system provides remote users with connection to each other and allows them to transmit and route the information as they choose." Def. Reply Br. at 2.

[8] Farmer informed that court that "A 'bot' is a robot, or program, that performs actions continuously, in a sort of manic or robotic fashion." Farmer Dec. ¶27.

A&M Records, Inc.

v.

Napster, Inc.
(Opinion Granting
Preliminary Injunction)

United States District Court,
Northern District of California

August 10, 2000

5 ILR (P&F) 745, 114 F Supp 2d 896

No. C 99-5183 MHP, C 00-0074 MHP

Distribution of MP3 files warrants preliminary injunction; no fair use.

Plaintiff record companies, which hold the copyrights to various sound recordings, have shown a strong likelihood of success on the merits of their claims that defendant is contributorily and vicariously liable for copyright infringement by encouraging and facilitating the distribution and reproduction of digital music (MP3) files. In establishing defendant's liability, plaintiffs successfully establish direct infringement by third parties, namely, those individuals who use defendant's service to download and upload copyrighted music. Defendant fails to show that such use is either a fair use or a substantial noninfringing use. Although downloading and uploading MP3 files is not paradigmatic commercial activity, it is not personal use in the traditional sense, and the court rejects defendant's proffers that sampling, space shifting, and authorized distribution of the work of new artists constitute fair uses. In particular, plaintiffs have demonstrated a meaningful likelihood that the activity defendant calls sampling actually decreases retail sales of their music. The court also rejects defendant's reliance on the Audio Home Recording Act (AHRA). AHRA is irrelevant because plaintiffs have not brought any claims under it. Furthermore, the Ninth Circuit did not hold in *RIAA v. Diamond Multimedia*, 3 ILR (P&F) 33, that the AHRA covers the downloading of MP3 files. Accordingly, because plaintiffs have made a convincing showing with regard to the elements of both contributory and vicarious copyright infringement, plaintiffs are entitled to preliminary injunctive relief. — **A&M Records, Inc. v. Napster, Inc. (Opinion Granting Preliminary Injunction), 5 ILR (P&F) 745 [ND Cal, 2000].**

Distribution of MP3 files warrants preliminary injunction; no free speech defense.

Plaintiff record companies are entitled to a preliminary injunction to prevent defendant from facilitating the distribution and reproduction of digital music (MP3) files by consumers over the Internet. The injunction does not violate the First Amendment free speech rights of defendant or of defendant's users. Free speech concerns are protected by and coextensive with the fair use doctrine, and plaintiffs do not seek to enjoin any fair uses that are not completely contrived or peripheral to the existence of the service. — **A&M Records, Inc. v. Napster, Inc. (Opinion Granting Preliminary Injunction), 5 ILR (P&F) 745 [ND Cal, 2000].**

Distribution of MP3 files warrants preliminary injunction; misuse of copyright defense rejected.

Plaintiff record companies are entitled to a preliminary injunction to prevent defendant from facilitating the distribution and reproduction of digital music (MP3) files by consumers over the Internet. The court rejects defendant's misuse of copyright defense, which is essentially an antitrust argument, *i.e.*, that plaintiffs seek to aggrandize their monopoly beyond the scope of their copyrights by controlling the distribution of music over the Internet. Alleged antitrust violations by a copyright plaintiff generally do not afford a valid defense against an infringement action and ought not to dissuade a court from granting injunctive relief. — **A&M Records, Inc. v. Napster, Inc. (Opinion Granting Preliminary Injunction), 5 ILR (P&F) 745 [ND Cal, 2000].**

Distribution of MP3 files warrants preliminary injunction; waiver defense rejected.

Plaintiff record companies are entitled to a preliminary injunction to prevent defendant from facilitating the distribution and reproduction of digital music (MP3) files by consumers over the Internet. The court rejects defendant's waiver defense, *i.e.*, that plaintiffs waived their entitlement to copyright protection because (a) they hastened the proliferation of MP3 files on the Internet, and (b) they plan to enter the market for digital downloading themselves. Although defendant has submitted deposition excerpts related to plaintiffs' business dealings with Internet and software companies that provide ripping software, custom CDs, and players capable of playing unencrypted MP3 files, none of plaintiffs' online partners is a party to this action. Only one plaintiff sells a device capable of playing downloaded MP3 files, regardless of whether the distribution of such files is authorized, but this limited evidence fails to convince the court that plaintiffs created the monster that is now devouring their intellectual property rights. Defendant fails to show that, in hastening the proliferation of MP3 files, plaintiffs did more than seek partners for their commercial downloading ventures and develop music players for files they planned to sell over the Internet. Nor did plaintiffs invite wholesale infringement when they distributed a small number of free MP3 files for promotional purposes, especially since many of these files automatically "timed-out." — **A&M Records, Inc. v. Napster, Inc. (Opinion Granting Preliminary Injunction), 5 ILR (P&F) 745 [ND Cal, 2000].**

OPINION

MARILYN HALL PATEL, *Chief Judge.* The matter before the court concerns the boundary between sharing and theft, personal use and the unauthorized worldwide distribution of copyrighted music and sound recordings.[1] On December 6, 1999, A&M Records and seventeen other record companies ("record company plaintiffs") filed a complaint for contributory and vicarious copyright infringement, violations of the California Civil Code section 980(a)(2), and unfair competition against Napster, Inc.,[2] an Internet start-up that enables users to download MP3 music files without payment. On January 7, 2000, plaintiffs Jerry Leiber, Mike Stoller, and Frank Music Corporation filed a complaint for vicarious and contributory copyright infringement on behalf of a putative class of similarly-situated music publishers ("music publisher plaintiffs") against Napster, Inc. and former CEO Eileen Richardson. The music publisher plaintiffs filed a first amended complaint on April 6, 2000, and on May 24, 2000, the court entered a stipulation of dismissal of all claims against Richardson.[3] Now before this court is the record company and music publisher plaintiffs' joint motion [*5 ILR (P&F) 2096*] to preliminarily enjoin Napster, Inc. from engaging in or assisting others in copying, downloading, uploading, transmitting, or distributing copyrighted music without the express permission of the rights owner. In opposition to this motion [*5 ILR (P&F)*

2130], defendant seeks to expand the "fair use" doctrine articulated in *Sony Corp. of America v. Universal City Studios, Inc.*, 464 US 417 (1984), to encompass the massive downloading of MP3 files by Napster users. Alternatively, defendant contends that, even if this third-party activity constitutes direct copyright infringement, plaintiffs have not shown probable success on the merits of their contributory and vicarious infringement claims. Defendant also asks the court to find that copyright holders are not injured by a service created and promoted to facilitate the free downloading of music files, the vast majority of which are copyrighted.

Having considered the parties' arguments, the court grants plaintiffs' motion for a preliminary injunction against Napster, Inc. The court makes the following Findings of Fact and Conclusions of Law to support the preliminary injunction under Federal Rules of Civil Procedure 65(d).

I. FINDINGS OF FACT

A. MP3 Technology

1. Digital compression technology makes it possible to store audio recordings in a digital format that uses less memory and may be uploaded and downloaded over the Internet. *See* David M. Lisi Dec. (Tygar Rep.) at 11. MP3 is a popular, standard format used to store such compressed audio files. *See* Edward Kessler Dec. ¶3;[4] Lisi Dec. (Tygar Rep.)

at 11. Compressing data into MP3 format results in some loss of sound quality. *See* List Dec. (Tygar Rep.) at 12. However, because MP3 files are smaller, they require less time to transfer and are therefore better suited to transmission over the Internet. *See id.* at 11.

2. Consumers typically acquire MP3 files in two ways. First, users may download audio recordings that have already been converted into MP3 format by using an Internet service such as Napster. *See* Lisi Dec. (Tygar Rep.) at 11. Second, "ripping" software makes it possible to copy an audio compact disc ("CD") directly onto a computer hard-drive; ripping software compresses the millions of bytes of information on a typical CD into a smaller MP3 file that requires a fraction of the storage space. *See id.*; Kessler Dec. ¶32; 1 Laurence F. Pulgram Dec., Exh. A (Conroy Dep.) at 13: 19-24.

B. Defendant's Business

1. Napster, Inc. is a start-up company based in San Mateo, California. It distributes its proprietary file-sharing software free of charge via its Internet website. People who have downloaded this software can log-on to the Napster system and share MP3 music files with other users who are also logged-on to the system. *See* Kessler Dec. ¶6. It is uncontradicted that Napster users currently upload or download MP3 files without payment to each other, defendant, or copyright owners. According to a Napster, Inc. executive summary, the Napster service gives its users the unprecedented ability to "locate music by their favorite artists in MP3 format." 1 Frackman Dec., Exh. A (Richardson Dep.), Exh. 127 at ER000131.[5] Defendant boasts that it "takes the frustration out of locating servers with MP3 files" by providing a peer-to-peer file-sharing system that allows Napster account holders to conduct relatively sophisticated searches for music files on the hard drives of millions of other anonymous users. *See A&M Records, Inc. v. Napster, Inc.*, 2000 WL 573136, at *1 (ND Cal. May 12, 2000) (citing Def.'s Mot. for Summ. Adjud.) at 4.

2. Although Napster was the brainchild of a college student who wanted to facilitate music-swapping by his roommate, *see* 1 Frackman Dec., Exh. B (Fanning Dep.) at 31:10-35:1, it is far from a simple tool of distribution among friends and family. According to defendant's internal documents, there will be 75 million Napster users by the end of 2000. *See* 1 Frackman Dec., Exh. A (Richardson Dep.) at 318:19-319:1, Exh. 166 at 002725. At one point, defendant estimated that even without marketing, its "viral service" was growing by more than 200 percent per month. *Id.*, Exh. 127 at ER00130. Approximately 10,000 music files are shared per second using Napster, and every second more than 100 users attempt to connect to the system. *See* Kessler Dec. ¶29.

3. Napster, Inc. currently collects no revenues and charges its clientele no fees; it is a free service. *See, e.g.*, 1 Frackman Dec., Exh. A (Richardson Dep.) at 179:15. However, it has never been a non-profit organization. *See id.* at 116:10. It plans to delay the maximization of revenues while it attracts a large user base. *See id.*, Exh. 127 at ER00130; 1 Frackman Dec., Exh. C (Parker Dep.) at 160:1-162:14, Exh. 254 at SF00099. The value of the system grows as the quantity and quality of available music increases. *See id.* at 112:18-113:2, Exh. 127 at ER00130; David J. Teece Rep. at 4. Defendant's internal documents reveal a strategy of attaining a "critical mass" of music in an "ever-expanding library" as new members bring their MP3 collections online. *See* 1 Frackman Dec. (Richardson Dep.), Exh. 127 at ER00130; Exh. C (Parker Dep.) at 160:1-162:14, Exh. 254 at SF00099. Defendant eventually plans to "monetize" its user base. *See id.* at 115:24-116:13; Teece Rep. at 4, 7-11. Potential revenue sources include targeted email; advertising; commissions from links to commercial websites; and direct marketing of CDs, Napster products, and CD burners and rippers. *See* 1 Frackman Dec., Exh. C (Parker Dep.) at 160:1-162:14, Exh. 254 at SF00099-100; Teece Rep. at 2-3. Defendant also may begin to charge fees for a premium or commercial version of its software. *See* Teece Rep. at 8; *cf.* 1 Frackman Dec., Exh. A (Richardson Dep.) at 179:6-25. The existence of a large user base that increases daily and can be "monetized" makes Napster, Inc. a potentially attractive acquisition for larger, more established firms. *See* Teece Rep. at 7.

4. Napster Inc.'s value—which is measured, at least in part, by the size of its user base—lies between 60 and 80 million dollars. *See* Teece Rep. at 11-12; Def.'s Opp. at 35. Defendant obtained substantial capital infusions after the onset of this litigation. For example, in May 2000, the venture

firm Hummer Winblad purchased a twenty-percent ownership interest in the company for 13 million dollars; other investors simultaneously invested 1.5 million dollars. *See* Hank Barry Dec. ¶7.

5. The evidence shows that virtually all Napster users download or upload copyrighted files and that the vast majority of the music available on Napster is copyrighted. Eighty-seven percent of the files sampled by plaintiffs' expert, Dr. Ingram Olkin, "belong to or are administered by plaintiffs or other copyright holders."[6] Olkin Rep. at 7. After analyzing Olkin's data, Charles J. Hausman, anti-piracy counsel for the RIAA, determined that 834 out of 1,150 files in Olkin's download database belong to or are administered by plaintiffs; plaintiffs alone own the copyrights to more than seventy percent of the 1,150 files. *See* Charles J. Hausman Dec. ¶8. Napster users shared these files without authorization. *See id.*

6. Napster, Inc. has never obtained licenses to distribute or download, or to facilitate others in distributing or downloading, the music that plaintiffs own. *See* Kevin Conroy Dec. ¶4; Richard Cottrell Dec. ¶5; Mark R. Eisenberg Dec. ¶21; Lawrence Kenswil Dec. ¶15; Paul Vidich Dec. ¶8; Mike Stoller Dec. ¶11.

7. Defendant's internal documents indicate that it seeks to take over, or at least threaten, plaintiffs' role in the promotion and distribution of music. *See, e.g.*, 1 Frackman Dec., Exh. C (Parker Dep.), 160:1-162:14, Exh. 254, at SF00099 (declaring that "[u]ltimately Napster could evolve into a full-fledged music distribution platform, usurping the record industry as we know it today and allowing us to digitally promote and distribute emerging artists at a fraction of the cost" but noting that "we should focus on our realistic short-term goals while wooing the industry before we try to undermine it").[7]

8. Defendant's internal documents also demonstrate that its executives knew Napster users were engaging in unauthorized downloading and uploading of copyrighted music. *See, e.g.* 1 Frackman Dec., Exh. C (Parker Dep.) at 160:1-162:14, Exh. 254 at SF00100 (stating that Napster users "are exchanging *pirated* music."); *id.* at SF00102 ("[W] e are not just making *pirated* music available but also pushing demand"). Several Napster executives admitted in their depositions that they believed many of the millions of MP3 music

files available on Napster were copyrighted. *See, e.g.*, 1 Frackman Dec., Exh. B (Fanning Dep.) at 105:10-108:2.

9. At least on paper, the promotion of new artists constituted an aspect of defendant's plan as early as October 1999. *See* Sean F. Parker Dec. ¶5 & Exh. B[8]; Scott Krause Dec. ¶6. New or unsigned artists now may promote their works and distribute them in MP3 format via the Napster service. *See* Krause Dec. ¶¶8-15. Napster, Inc. has sought business alliances and developed both Internet- and software-based technologies to support its New Artist Program. *See* Parker Dec. ¶6.

However, the court finds that the New Artist Program accounts for a small portion of Napster use and did not become central to defendant's business strategy until this action made it convenient to give the program top billing. An early version of the Napster website advertised the ease with which users could find their favorite popular music without "wading through page after page of unknown artists." 1 Frackman Dec., Exh. C (Parker Dep.) at 104:16-105:10, Exh. 235. Defendant did not even create the New Artist Program that runs on its Internet website until April 2000—well after plaintiffs filed this action.[9] *See* Krause Dec. ¶9, Exh. A. Moreover, in Olkin's sample of 1,150 files (which were randomly selected from over 550,000), only 232 files matched *any* of the 19,440 names that were listed in defendant's new artist database as of July 2000. *See* Olkin Reply Dec. ¶¶3-5; Hausman Reply Dec. ¶¶3-6. An RIAA representative who analyzed the data also noted that the list of so-called new artists actually contained many popular stars represented by major record labels—among them teen sensation Britney Spears and the legendary alternative rock band Nirvana. *See* Hausman Reply Dec. ¶5. Once established artists were eliminated from the results, only eleven new artists and fourteen of their music files remained in Olkin's sample of 1,150 files. *See id.* ¶6.

10. Defendant employs the term "space-shifting" to refer to the process of converting a CD the consumer already owns into MP3 format and using Napster to transfer the music to a different computer—from home to office, for example.[10] *See* Def. Opp. at 12. The court finds that space-shifting accounts for a *de minimis* portion of Napster use and is not a significant aspect of defendant's business. According to the court's understanding

of the Napster technology, a user who wanted to space-shift files from her home to her office would have to log-on to the system from her home computer, leave that computer online, commute to work, and log-on to Napster from her office computer to access the desired file. In the meantime, many users might download it before she reached the office. Common sense dictates that this use does not draw users to the system. Defendant fails to cite a single Napster, Inc. document indicating that the company saw space-shifting as an attraction for its user base, and survey evidence shows that almost half of college-student survey respondents previously owned less than ten percent of the songs they have downloaded. *See* E. Deborah Jay Rep. at 4, 21 & Tbl. 7.

C. The Napster Technology

1. Internet users may download defendant's proprietary MusicShare software free of charge from the Napster website. This free software enables users to access the Napster computer network. *See* Kessler Dec. ¶6.

2. The software becomes fully functional after users register with Napster by selecting an account name, or "user name," and a password. *See* Kessler Dec. ¶¶6, 23. Persons who register may include biographical data, but registration does not require a real name or address. *See* 2 Frackman Dec., Exh. E (Kessler Dep.) at 255:20-257:22. Napster does not associate user names with the biographical information that individuals provide at registration. *See id.* Indeed, after a user logs-on, her physical address information is no longer available to the Napster server. *See id.* 3. The software features a browser interface, search engine, and chat functions that operate in conjunction with defendant's online network of servers. *See id.* ¶¶6, 13. The software also contains a "hotlist" tool that allows users to compile and store lists of other account holders' user names. *See id.* ¶8. In addition, the Napster software may be used to play and categorize audio files, which users can store in specific file directories on their hard drives. *See id.* ¶¶6-7. Those directories, which allow account holders to share files on Napster, constitute the "user library." *Id.* Some users store their MP3 files in such directories; others do not. *See id.*

4. Defendant maintains clusters of servers that compose its network or system. *See* Kessler Dec.

¶13. Account holders who access the Napster network may communicate, share files, and learn of designated hotlist names only within the cluster to which they are assigned. *See id.* Users can access the network of servers free of charge.

5. Once an account holder signs on to the Napster network, the Napster browser interacts with its proprietary server-side software. *See id.* ¶¶7, 8; 2 Frackman Dec., Exh. E (Kessler Dep.) at 54:16-56:10. If a user sets the "allowable uploads" function of the MusicShare software above zero, all of the MP3 file names she stores in her user library automatically become available to other online Napster users. *See* Kessler Dec. ¶7.

However, before the client software uploads MP3 file names to defendant's master servers, it "validates" the files stored in the user library directories. *See* 2 Frackman Dec., Exh. E (Kessler Dep.) at 145:2-18. The client software reads those files to ensure they are indeed MP3 files, checking to see whether they contain the proper syntax specification and content. *See id.* If the files are not properly formatted, their file names will not be not [*sic*] uploaded to the Napster servers. *See id.*

Once the file names are successfully uploaded to the servers, each user library, identified by a user name, becomes a "location" on the servers. Kessler Dec. ¶8. Napster locations are short-lived; they are respectively added or purged every time a user signs on or off of the network. *See id.* Thus, a user's MP3 files are only accessible to other users while she is online.

6. A user who is logged-on to the Napster servers via the client software may access the content of other users' uploaded "locations" in one of two ways: (a) by utilizing defendant's proprietary search engine, or (b) by employing the hotlist tool featured in the client software. *See id.* ¶12.

7. An account holder may use the search tools included in the Napster client software to find MP3 files. *See id.* ¶10. The server-side application software maintains a search index that is updated in real time as users log-on and -off of the system. *See id.*; 2 Frackman Dec., Exh. E (Kessler Dep.) at 56:3-10. The file-name index contains the names of MP3 files that on-line users save in their designated user library directories. *See* Kessler Dec. ¶¶7, 14; 2 Frackman Dec., Exh. E (Kessler Dep.) at 55:14-56:10; Exh. 2. Users who wish to search for a song

or artist may do so by entering the name of the song or artist in the search fields of the client software and then clicking the "Find It" button. When the search form is transmitted to the Napster network, the Napster servers send the requesting user a list of files that include the same term(s) she entered on the search form. *See* Kessler Dec. ¶5; 2 Frackman Dec., Exh. E (Kessler Dep.) at 56:3-10.

After the application software returns a list of specific MP3 file names to the requesting user, the user then must peruse the list to determine whether she desires any of those files. *See id.* ¶10. She must read through the list because the Napster application software does not search for a particular song or recording artist *per se*. Napster does not organize MP3 files based on content because, currently, they are not designed for such indexing. *See id.* ¶11. Instead, Napster performs a text search of the file names indexed in a particular cluster. Those file names may contain typographical errors or otherwise inaccurate descriptions of the content of the files since they are designated by other users. *See id.* ¶¶13, 10, 27; 2 Pulgram Dec. Exh. B (Fanning Dep.) at 116:8-19.

In addition to listed text results from an executed search, Napster's servers provide other information about particular MP3 files. For instance, the client software can sort the results of "echo packets" or "ping requests" that it sends out to host users; these requests help gauge the "responsiveness value" of a transmission between two users by calculating the amount of time it takes for ping responses to be returned to the client software. *See* 2 Frackman Dec., Exh. E (Kessler Dep.) at 56:3-10, Exh. 5 at 3; Shawn Fanning Dec. ¶8. Users can also search for files that meet certain technical criteria, such as the host user's bandwidth. *See id.* Finally, the file name or "data object description" includes the size and bytes stored and "attributes of quality," such as bit rate. *See* 2 Frackman Dec., Exh. E (Kessler Dep.) at 153:16-154:24; Fanning Dec. ¶8. These Napster options contribute to the ease with which the user can locate and obtain the music she wants.

8. Alternatively, users may access MP3 files via the hotlist function. This function enables a Napster user to archive other user names and learn whether account holders who access the network under those names are online. *See* Kessler Dec. ¶¶8-9. A requesting user can access or browse all files listed in the user libraries of hotlisted users. *See id.*

¶9. Then she can request a particular file in a host user's user library by selecting, or clicking on, that file name. *See id.* The hotlist function is a feature that helps make Napster users a virtual community—they are not only able to download the music they desire, but also to obtain files from particular individuals whom they know by user name.

9. The Napster network facilitates the same mode of file-transfer, whether a requesting user accesses a specific MP3 file with the search engine or the hotlist. *See id.* ¶12. Once a requesting user locates and selects the file she wishes to download, the server-side software engages in a dialogue with her browser and that of the "host user" (that is, the user who makes the MP3 available for downloading). *See* Kessler Dec. ¶12; 2 Frackman Dec., Exh. E (Kessler Dep.) at 80:19-22; 56:3-10. Napster servers obtain the necessary IP address information from the host user. *See* Daniel Farmer Dec. ¶17; Frackman Dec., Exh. 1 (Kessler Dep.) at 103-05. The servers then communicate the host user's address or routing information to the requesting user; the requesting user's computer employs this information to establish a connection with the host user's browser software and download the MP3 file from the host user's library. *See* Kessler Dec. ¶¶10-13; 2 Frackman Dec., Exh. E (Kessler Dep.) at 56:3-10. The content of the actual MP3 file is transferred over the Internet between users, not through the Napster servers. *See* Kessler Dec. ¶12; *A & M Records, Inc. v. Napster, Inc.*, 2000 WL 573136, at *7 (N D Cal. May 12, 2000). However, users would not be able to access the uploaded file names and corresponding routing data without signing on to the Napster system. *See* Kessler Dec. ¶23.

10. In some instances, a requested file is not immediately ready for download. Those files are "queued" or deferred until the host user is able to transmit the file. *See* 2 Frackman Dec., Exh. E (Kessler Dep. at 80:2-22). The request may be deferred, for example, because the host user has limited the number of downloads she can provide simultaneously, or because the host user has signed off the Napster network. *See id.*

Defendant employs technology that permits users to resume queued downloads at a later time. *See* 2 Frackman Dec., Exh. E (Kessler Dep.) at 112:3-13. Every MP3 file has a mathematically-generated and unique fingerprint or "checksum."

See Kessler Dec. ¶32; 2 Frackman Dec., Exh. E (Kessler Dep.) at 112:3-13. Any requesting user who is unable to download a particular MP3 file may use the client software to send the file's checksum and full intended size to the Napster servers and attempt to locate a match for download. *See* 2 Frackman Dec., Exh. E (Kessler Dep.) at 112:3-13.

11. Defendant also provides Napster users with a chat service. Its central servers permit users who are logged-on to communicate with other online users, including those whose user names comprise the hotlist. *See* Kessler Dec. ¶13. Aside from communicating with specific online users logged-on to the same cluster of servers, the chat service allows users to communicate in groups. Defendant organizes these groups within "channels" or "chat rooms" named after particular musical genres. *See id.*; 2 Pulgram Dec., Exh. B (2 Fanning Dep.) at 219:4-14. Alternatively, users can create their own channels in which to communicate. *See* Kessler Dec. ¶13.

12. Defendant's New Artist Program technology functions in two interrelated environments: (a) on its Internet website and (b) through its network-client browser and search technology. *See* Krause Dec. ¶¶9-15. The website version performs several functions. It allows new or unsigned artists to create a "profile" that consists of certain biographical and descriptive data including artist and band names, similar artists or influences, and news about the band. *See id.* ¶¶9-10, Exh. C. Defendant only accepts completed forms if the submitting artist authorizes Napster users to share his music. *See id.* ¶10, Exh. D. Once defendant accepts the profile, it stores all of the relevant information in a database linked to its Internet website. *See id.* ¶11. Defendant has accepted several thousand such profiles. *See id.* ¶¶9, 16.

Members of the public can then search the new artist database in several ways: (1) by artist name, (2) by artist influence, or (3) by browsing the different genres of music and then scrolling down lists of new artists categorized in those genres. *See id.* ¶12. The Napster site does not store any of the new artists' music, however. *See id.* ¶9. Instead, those who access the website-based service acquire information about an artist, such as his name. *See id.*, Exh. E. Once an individual obtains this data, she is directed to switch to Napster's software-and network-based service to search for and download the new artist's music. *See id.* ¶15.

Napster account holders who use MusicShare software and log-on to the Napster system can locate and download new artists' songs in the same manner they would find and download any other files: by utilizing the search engine, or by browsing user libraries. *See id.* ¶9. While on the Napster network, both new artists and other users may use the chat function to market music directly or learn about new artists. *See id.* ¶¶8, 15.

D. Plaintiffs' Business

1. The music publisher plaintiffs compose music and write songs. *See, e.g.*, Stoller Dec. ¶2. They depend financially upon the sale of sound recordings because they earn royalties from such sales. *See id.* at ¶¶2, 11, 13. However, they do not get a royalty when a Napster user uploads or downloads an MP3 file of their compositions without payment or authorization. *See id.* ¶11. The record company plaintiffs' sound recordings also result from a substantial investment of money, time, manpower, and creativity. *See* Conroy Dec. ¶5; Cottrell Dec. 5; Eisenberg Dec. ¶¶5, 21; Kenswil Dec. ¶5.

In contrast, defendant invests nothing in the content of the music which means that, compared with plaintiffs, it incurs virtually no costs in providing a wide array of music to satisfy consumer demand. *See* Teece Rep. at 14.

2. To make a profit, the record company plaintiffs largely rely on the success of "hit" or popular recordings, which may constitute as little as ten or fifteen percent of albums released. *See, e.g.*, Eisenberg Dec. ¶7. Many, or all, of their top recordings have been available for free on Napster. *See* Frank Creighton Dec. ¶5.

3. The record company plaintiffs have invested substantial time, effort, and funds in actual or planned entry into the digital downloading market. BMG Music ("BMG")[11] began to explore digital downloading in early 1996 and has made more than twenty tracks commercially available for downloading through the digital service providers ("DSPs") Amplified.com and the Liquid Music Network. *See* Conroy Dec. ¶9. BMG has entered several business partnerships, strategic marketing agreements, and clearinghouse relationships to develop a plan for secure, commercial digital

downloading; July 2000 was the target date for BMG's launch. *See id.* at ¶¶10-17.

Plaintiffs Capitol Record, Inc. and Virgin Records America are affiliated with EMI Recorded Music, North America ("EMI"). *See* Cottrell Dec. ¶1. EMI has developed business plans to distribute its music through several DSPs which represent more than 800 retail websites. *See id.* ¶7. All digital downloads that EMI offers will be encrypted and watermarked. *See id.* ¶12.

Sony Music Entertainment ("Sony") has already begun to make selected singles available through its websites and those of its artists; to obtain a permanent copy of this music, consumers must pay for the download. *See* Eisenberg Dec. ¶13. As of May 31, 2000, Sony also began selling downloadable music through a distribution network of about thirty-five retail sites. *See id.* at ¶17.

Plaintiffs A&M Records, Geffen Records, Interscope Records, Island Records, MCA Records, Motown Records, UMG Records, and Universal Records (collectively, "Universal") have spent millions of dollars preparing a secure digital distribution system scheduled for launch in mid-summer 2000. *See* Kenswil Dec. ¶9-16.

Warner Music Group and its associated labels—plaintiffs Atlantic Recording Corp., London-Sire Records Inc. (f/k/a Sire Records Group Inc.), Elektra Entertainment Group Inc., and Warner Bros. Records (collectively, "Warner")—have done due diligence and dedicated a substantial budget to digital distribution. *See* Vidich Dec. ¶7(a)-(e). Warner expects to launch its commercial digital distribution of hundreds of recordings by the fourth quarter of 2000. *See id.* at ¶7(e)

4. Promotional samples offered by plaintiffs and other retail sites differ significantly from using Napster to decide whether to buy a CD. The record company plaintiffs have made some free downloads available but have limited them in amount and duration. They have not provided entire albums, and the downloads typically have been "timed-out" so that users can only play them for a finite period of time—often less than a month. *See* Conroy Dec. ¶¶9-17; Cottrell Dec. ¶15; Eisenberg Dec. ¶13; Kenswil Dec. ¶12; Vidich Dec. ¶¶7(d), 8. Although plaintiffs have not been completely successful in managing the rights to promotional downloads, record company executives accord importance to the security of music distributed in this manner. [12] *See* Conroy Dec. ¶¶9-17; Cottrell Dec. ¶15; Eisenberg Dec. ¶13; Kenswil Dec. ¶12; Vidich Dec. ¶¶7(d), 8. Retail sites, such as Amazon.com, offer thirty-to-sixty-second song samples in streaming audio format, rather than as downloads. *See* David Lambert Reply Dec. ¶2. Unlike downloading, streaming does not copy the music onto the listener's computer hard drive; it merely allows her to hear it. *See id.* Because companies like DiscoverMusic that provide song samples to these Internet retailers enter licensing agreements, rights holders earn royalties from this form of sampling. *See id.* ¶3.

In contrast, persons who obtain MP3 files for free using Napster can retain and play them indefinitely—and, even if they download a song to make a purchasing decision, they may decide *not* to buy the music. While Napster users can burn CDs comprised of unauthorized downloads they obtained to "sample" new songs, sampling on sites affiliated with plaintiffs does not substitute for purchasing the entire disc. *See* Teece Rep. at 17.

E. Effect of Napster on the Market for Plaintiffs' Copyrighted Works

1. The court finds that Napster use is likely to reduce CD purchases by college students, whom defendant admits constitute a key demographic. *See* Jay Rep. at 4, 18; Michael Fine Rep. at 1; Julia Greer Reply Dec. (Brooks Dep.) at 145: 10-12 ("We believes [sic] ourselves to have a high college demographic, and beyond that to be primarily [ages] 12 to 24."). Plaintiffs' expert, Dr. E. Deborah Jay, opined that forty-one percent of her college-student survey respondents "gave a reason for using Napster or described the nature of its impact on their music purchases in a way which either explicitly indicated or suggested that Napster displaces CD sales." Jay Rep. at 4, 18. She also found that twenty-one percent of the college students surveyed revealed that Napster helped them make a better selection or decide what to buy. *See id.*, Tbl. 4. However, Jay's overall conclusion was that "[t]he more songs Napster users have downloaded," the more likely they are to admit or imply that such use has reduced their music purchases. *See id.* at 4, 18. The report of Soundscan CEO Michael Fine lends support to Jay's findings. After examining data culled from three types of retail stores near college or university campuses, [13] Fine concluded that "on-line file sharing

has resulted in a loss of album sales within college markets." [14] Fine Rep. at 1.

For the reasons discussed in the court's separate order, the report by defendant's expert, Dr. Peter S. Fader, does not provide credible evidence that music file-sharing on Napster stimulates more CD sales than it displaces. [15] Nor do the recording industry documents that defendant cites reliably show increased music sales due to Napster use. One such memorandum deals with the effect of Warner's promotional downloads, which are "timed-out" and thus differ from MP3 files obtained using Napster. *See* 1 Pulgram Dec., Exh. N (Vidich Dep.), Exh. 279 at T3122-23; Vidich Dec. ¶¶7(d), 8 (stating that free, promotional downloads are "timed-out."). Another purported "smoking gun" is a Universal survey on music-purchasing by people who download MP3 files. *See* 1 Pulgram Dec., Exh. F (Kenswil Dep.) at 110:22-111:15. However, the court has too little information about this survey to rely on it, and the deponent, Universal representative Lawrence Kenswil, declined to vouch for the survey's accuracy. *See id.* at 111:8, 14-15.

2. Because plaintiffs entered the digital download market very recently, or plan to enter it in the next few months, they are especially vulnerable to direct competition from Napster, Inc. *See* Teece Rep. at 15-16. The court finds that, in choosing between the free Napster service and pay-per-download sites, consumers are likely to choose Napster. *See id.* at 14; Jay Rep. at 4, 18 (reaching this conclusion with regard to a survey sample of college students).

Defendant's economic expert, Dr. Robert E. Hall, opines that plaintiffs' music could still command a high price after a period when the price has been zero due to Napster use; thus, he concludes, plaintiffs will not suffer irreparable harm between now and a trial verdict against defendant. *See* Lisi Dec. (Hall Rep.) ¶¶39, 54. This argument does not square with Hall's assertion that preliminarily enjoining defendant will put it out of business because users will switch to services offered by "kindred spirits." Hall Rep. ¶15-19, 73; *see also* Barry Dec. ¶13. If this is true, consumers will not necessarily resume *buying* music if Napster is enjoined; rather, they will go to other sites offering free MP3 files. [16] Indeed, as Dr. David J. Teece avers, defendant has contributed to a new attitude that digitally-downloaded songs ought to be free—

an attitude that creates formidable hurdles for the establishment of a commercial downloading market. *See* Teece Rep. at 14-18.

Hall also maintains that Napster, Inc. will increase the volume of plaintiffs' online sales by stimulating consumer investment in the hardware and software needed to obtain and play MP3 files. *See* Hall Rep. ¶¶45-49. However, he ignores evidence of reduced CD-buying among college students due to Napster use, *see* Jay Rep. at 18, and the data upon which he relies to argue that Napster has enhanced sales is either weak (in the case of the Fader Report) or unavailable for the court's review. *See, e.g., id.* ¶17 (relying on IDC and Forrester Research studies), ¶¶27-28 (discussing reports by Student Monitor and Andersen Consulting), ¶34 (citing a study by the University of Southern California). The court therefore finds that the barriers to commercial distribution posed by an emerging sense of entitlement to free music probably outweigh the benefits that defendant purports to confer.

3. Downloading on Napster also has the potential to disrupt plaintiffs' promotional efforts because it does not involve any of the restrictions on timing, amount, or selection that plaintiffs impose when they offer free music files. *See* Conroy Dec. ¶9-17; Cottrell Dec. ¶15; Eisenberg Dec. ¶13; Kenswil Dec. ¶12; Vidich Dec. ¶¶7(d), 8; *see also* Teece Rep. at 18. Even if Napster users sometimes download files to determine whether they want to purchase a CD, sampling on Napster is vastly different than that offered by plaintiffs. On Napster, the user—not the copyright owner—determines how much music to sample and how long to keep it.

II. CONCLUSIONS OF LAW
A. Legal Standard

1. The Ninth Circuit authorizes preliminary injunctive relief for "a party who demonstrates either (1) a combination of probable success on the merits and the possibility of irreparable harm, or (2) that serious questions are raised and the balance of hardships tips in its favor." *Prudential Real Estate Affiliates, Inc. v. PPR Realty, Inc.*, 204 F3d 867, 874 (9th Cir 2000).

2. The standard is a sliding scale which requires a greater degree of harm the lesser the probability of success. *See id.* In a copyright infringement case, demonstration of a reasonable likelihood of success

on the merits creates a presumption of irreparable harm.[17] *See Micro Star v. Formgen, Inc.*, 154 F3d 1107, 1109 (9th Cir 1998).

B. Proof of Direct Infringement

1. To prevail on a contributory or vicarious copyright infringement claim, a plaintiff must show direct infringement by a third party. *See Sony Corp. of Am. v. Universal City Studios, Inc.*, 464 US 417, 434 (1984). As a threshold matter, plaintiffs in this action must demonstrate that Napster users are engaged in direct infringement.

2. Plaintiffs have established a prima facie case of direct copyright infringement. As discussed above, virtually all Napster users engage in the unauthorized downloading or uploading of copyrighted music; as much as eighty-seven percent of the files available on Napster may be copyrighted, and more than seventy percent may be owned or administered by plaintiffs. *See* Olkin Rep. at 7; Hausman Dec. ¶8.

C. Affirmative Defense of Fair Use and Substantial Non-Infringing Use

1. Defendant asserts the affirmative defenses of fair use and substantial non-infringing use. The latter defense is also known as the staple article of commerce doctrine. *See Sony*, 464 US at 442. *Sony* stands for the rule that a manufacturer is not liable for selling a "staple article of commerce" that is "capable of commercially significant noninfringing uses." *Id.* The Supreme Court also declared in *Sony*, "Any individual may reproduce a copyrighted work for a 'fair use'; the copyright holder does not possess the exclusive right to such a use." *Id.* at 433. Defendant bears the burden of proving these affirmative defenses. *See Bateman v. Mnemonics, Inc.*, 79 F3d 1532, 1542 n. 22 (11th Cir 1996) ("[I]t is clear the burden of proving fair use is always on the putative infringer.").

2. For the reasons set forth below, the court finds that any potential non-infringing use of the Napster service is minimal or connected to the infringing activity, or both. The substantial or commercially significant use of the service was, and continues to be, the unauthorized downloading and uploading of popular music, most of which is copyrighted.

3. Section 107 of the Copyright Act provides a non-exhaustive list of fair use factors. These factors include:

(1) the purpose and character of the use, including whether such use is of a commercial nature or is for nonprofit educational purposes;

(2) the nature of the copyrighted work;

(3) the amount and substantiality of the portion used in relation to the copyrighted work as a whole; and

(4) the effect of the use upon the potential market for or value of the copyrighted work.

17 USC §107.

4. In the instant action, the purpose and character of the use militates against a finding of fair use. Ascertaining whether the new work transforms the copyrighted material satisfies the main goal of the first factor. *See Campbell v. Acuff-Rose Music, Inc.*, 510 US 569, 579 (1994). Plaintiff persuasively argues that downloading MP3 files does not transform the copyrighted music. *See UMG Recordings, Inc. v. MP3.com, Inc.*, 92 F Supp 2d 349, 351 [5 ILR (P&F) 415] (SD NY 2000) (concluding that repackaging copyrighted recordings in *MP3* format suitable for downloading "adds no 'new aesthetics, new insights and understandings' to the original").

5. Under the first factor, the court must also determine whether the use is commercial. In *Acuff-Rose*, the Supreme Court clarified that a finding of commercial use weighs against, but does not preclude, a determination of fairness. *See Acuff-Rose*, 510 US at 584.

6. If a use is non-commercial, the plaintiff bears the burden of showing a meaningful likelihood that it would adversely affect the potential market for the copyrighted work if it became widespread. *See Sony*, 464 US at 451.

7. Although downloading and uploading MP3 music files is not paradigmatic commercial activity, it is also not personal use in the traditional sense. Plaintiffs have not shown that the majority of Napster users download music to sell—that is, for profit. However, given the vast scale of Napster use among anonymous individuals, the court finds that downloading and uploading MP3 music files with the assistance of Napster are not private uses. At the very least, a host user sending a file cannot be said to engage in a personal use when distributing that file to an anonymous requester. Moreover, the

fact that Napster users get for free something they would ordinarily have to buy suggests that they reap economic advantages from Napster use. *See Sega Enters. Ltd. v. MAPHIA*, 857 F Supp 679, 687 (ND Cal. 1994) ("*Sega I*") (holding that copying to save users expense of purchasing authorized copies has commercial character and thus weighs against finding of fair use); *cf. American Geophysical Union v. Texaco, Inc.*, 60 F3d 913, 922 (2d Cir 1994) (holding that for-profit enterprise which made unauthorized copies of scholarly articles to facilitate scientific research reaped indirect economic advantage from copying and, hence, that copying constituted commercial use).

8. The court finds that the copyrighted musical compositions and sound recordings are creative in nature; they constitute entertainment, which cuts against a finding of fair use under the second factor. *See Harper & Row Publishers, Inc. v. Nation Enters.*, 471 US 539, 563 (1985); *Sega I*, 857 F Supp at 687; *Playboy Enters., Inc. v. Frena*, 839 F Supp 1552, 1558 (MD Fla. 1993) (citing *In re New Era Publications Int'l v. Carol Publ'g*, 904 F2d 152, 157-58 (2d Cir), *cert. denied*, 498 US 921 (1990)).

9. With regard to the third factor, it is undisputed that downloading or uploading MP3 music files involves copying the entirety of the copyrighted work. The Ninth Circuit held prior to *Sony* that "wholesale copying of copyrighted material precludes application of the fair use doctrine." *Marcus v. Rowley*, 695 F2d 1171, 1176 (9th Cir 1983). Even after *Sony*, wholesale copying for private home use tips the fair use analysis in plaintiffs' favor if such copying is likely to adversely affect the market for the copyrighted material. *See Sony*, 464 US at 449-50, 456.

10. The fourth factor, the effect on the potential market for the copyrighted work, also weighs against a finding of fair use. Plaintiffs have produced evidence that Napster use harms the market for their copyrighted musical compositions and sound recordings in at least two ways. First, it reduces CD sales among college students. *See* Jay Rep. at 4, 18; *cf.* Fine Rep. at 1. Second, it raises barriers to plaintiffs' entry into the market for the digital downloading of music. *See* Teece Rep. at 12-18.

11. Defendant asserts several potential fair uses of the Napster service—including sampling, space-shifting, and the authorized distribution of new artists' work. Sampling on Napster is not a personal use in the traditional sense that courts have recognized—copying which occurs within the household and does not confer any financial benefit on the user. *See, e.g,* Sony, 464 US at 423, 449-50. Instead, sampling on Napster amounts to obtaining permanent copies of songs that users would otherwise have to purchase; it also carries the potential for viral distribution to millions of people. Defendant ignores critical differences between sampling songs on Napster and VCR usage in *Sony*. First, while "time-shifting [TV broadcasts] merely enables a viewer to see . . . a work which he ha[s] been invited to witness in its entirety free of charge," plaintiffs in this action almost always charge for their music—even if it is downloaded song-by-song. *Sony*, 464 US at 449-50; *see e.g.*, Conroy Dec. ¶9; Eisenberg Dec. ¶16. They only make promotional downloads available on a highly restricted basis. *See* Conroy Dec. ¶¶9-17; Cottrell Dec. ¶15; Eisenberg Dec. ¶13; Kenswil Dec. ¶12; Vidich Dec. ¶¶7(d), 8. Copyright owners also earn royalties from streamed song samples on retail websites like Amazon.com. *See* Lambert Reply Dec. ¶3. Second, the majority of VCR purchasers in *Sony* did not distribute taped television broadcasts, but merely enjoyed them at home. *See id.* at 423. In contrast, a Napster user who downloads a copy of a song to her hard drive may make that song available to millions of other individuals, even if she eventually chooses to purchase the CD. So-called sampling on Napster may quickly facilitate unauthorized distribution at an exponential rate.

Defendant's argument that using Napster to sample music is akin to visiting a free listening station in a record store, or listening to song samples on a retail website, fails to convince the court because Napster users can *keep* the music they download. Whether or not they decide to buy the CD, they still obtain a permanent copy of the song. In contrast, many retail sites only offer thirty-to-sixty-second samples in streaming audio format, *see* Lambert Reply Dec. ¶2, and promotional downloads from the record company plaintiffs are often "timed-out." *See* Cottrell Dec. ¶15; Eisenberg Dec. ¶13; Kenswil Dec. ¶12; Vidich Dec. ¶¶7(d), 8.

The global scale of Napster usage and the fact that users avoid paying for songs that otherwise would not be free militates against a determination that sampling by Napster users constitutes personal or home use in the traditional sense.[18]

12. Even if the type of sampling supposedly done on Napster were a non-commercial use, plaintiffs have demonstrated a substantial likelihood that it would adversely affect the potential market for their copyrighted works if it became widespread. *See Sony*, 464 US at 451. Plaintiffs claim three general types of harm: a decrease in retail sales, especially among college students; an obstacle to the record company plaintiffs' future entry into the digital downloading market; and a social devaluing of music stemming from its free distribution. With regard to sampling, twenty-one percent of the Jay survey respondents indicated that Napster helps them decide what music to purchase. *See* Jay Rep., Tbl. 4. Nevertheless, Jay reached the overarching conclusion that the more songs Napster users download, the more likely they are to reveal that such use reduces their music buying. *See id.* at 4, 18. Jay's evidence suggests that sampling and building a free music library through unauthorized downloading are not mutually exclusive: it is likely that survey respondents who sample are primarily direct infringers. Napster users—not the record companies—control the music selection, the amount and the timing of the sampling activity, and they may keep many songs after deciding not to purchase the entire CD.

Defendant maintains that sampling does not decrease retail music sales and may even stimulate them. To support this assertion, it relies heavily on the Fader Report, which concludes that consumers do not view MP3 files as perfect substitutes for CDs. *See* Lisi Dec. (Fader Rep.) ¶63. Fader cites a survey that he did not conduct for the assertion that "60% of online users who download free digital music do so to preview music before buying the CD." Fader Rep. ¶74. Examining the results of a different survey that he purportedly designed, but did not carefully supervise, he reports that about twenty-eight percent of Napster users indicate that their music purchases have increased since they began using the Napster software. *See id.* ¶43. For reasons explained in the court's evidentiary order, the Fader Report is unreliable and fails to rebut plaintiffs' showing of harm. Plaintiffs have demonstrated a meaningful likelihood that the activity defendant calls sampling actually decreases retail sales of their music.

13. Any potential enhancement of plaintiffs' sales due to sampling would not tip the fair use analysis conclusively in favor of defendant. Indeed, courts have rejected the suggestion that a positive impact on sales negates the copyright holder's entitlement to licensing fees or access to derivative markets. *See Ringgold v. Black Entertainment Television*, 126 F3d 70, 81 n. 16 (2d Cir 1997) (noting that, even if allegedly infringing use of plaintiff's poster in television program increased poster sales, plaintiff retained right to licensing fee); *DC Comics, Inc. v. Reel Fantasy, Inc.*, 696 F2d 24, 28 (2d Cir 1982) (stating that speculated increase in plaintiff's comic book sales due to unauthorized use of Batman and Green Arrow figures on advertising flyers did not establish fair use defense as matter of law); *MP3.com*, 92 F Supp 2d at 352 (holding that allegedly positive impact on plaintiffs' prior market "in no way frees defendant to usurp a further market that directly derives from reproduction of [the] copyrighted works.").

The *MP3.com* opinion is especially instructive. Although MP3.com's activities arguably stimulated CD sales, the plaintiffs "adduced substantial evidence that they . . . [had] taken steps to enter [the digital downloading market]." *MP3.com*, 92 F Supp 2d at 352. The fourth factor thus weighed against a finding of fair use. Plaintiffs in the instant action similarly allege that Napster use impedes their entry into the online market. The record company plaintiffs have already expended considerable funds and effort to commence Internet sales and licensing for digital downloads. *See* Conroy Dec. ¶¶9-18; Cottrell Dec. ¶¶6-17; Eisenberg Dec. ¶¶9-22; Vidich Dec. ¶¶7-10. Plaintiffs' economic expert opined that the availability of free MP3 files will reduce the market for authorized, commercial downloading. *See* Teece Dec. at 14-18. This point is corroborated by the fact that all forty-nine songs available for purchase on Sony's website can be obtained for free using Napster. *See* Eisenberg Dec. ¶16. If consumers choose to buy, rather than burn, entire CDs they are still more likely to obtain permanent copies of songs on Napster than buy them from Sony's site or listen to streamed samples at other online locations.

The court concludes that, even assuming the sampling alleged in this case is a non-commercial use, the record company plaintiffs have demonstrated a meaningful likelihood that it would adversely affect their entry into the online market if it became widespread. *See Sony*, 464 US at 451. Moreover, it deprives the music publisher plaintiffs of royalties for individual songs. The unauthorized downloading of plaintiffs' music to sample songs would not constitute a fair use, even if it enhanced CD sales.

14. The court is also unconvinced that *Sony* applies to space-shifting. Defendant erroneously relies on the Ninth Circuit's assertion, in a case involving an inapplicable statute, that space-shifting constitutes non-commercial personal use. *See Recording Indus. Ass'n of Am. v. Diamond Multimedia Sys., Inc.*, 180 F3d 1072, 1079 (9th Cir 1999) (discussing the applicability of the Audio Home Recording Act of 1992 to the Rio MP3 player). [19] Defendant also implies that space-shifting music is sufficiently analogous to time-shifting television broadcasts to merit the protection of *Sony*. According to the gravely flawed Fader Report, space-shifting—like time-shifting—leaves the value of the copyrights unscathed because it does not displace sales. *See* Fader Rep. ¶77; *Sony*, 464 US at 421 (concluding that plaintiffs did not prove that time-shifting created any likelihood of harm). Defendant again cites Fader for the statistic that seventy percent of Napster users at least sometimes engage in space-shifting. *See* Lisi Dec. (Fader Rep.) ¶77. In contrast, Jay opined that approximately forty-nine percent of her college-student survey respondents previously owned less than ten percent of the songs they downloaded, and about sixty-nine percent owned less than a quarter. *See* Jay Rep. at 4, 21 & Tbl. 7. The court has already held that the Jay Report bears greater indicia of reliability than the Fader Report. Moreover, under either analysis, the instant matter is distinguishable from *Sony* because the Supreme Court determined in *Sony* that time-shifting represented the *principal,* rather than an occasional use of VCRs. *See Sony*, 464 US at 421.

15. Defendant argues that, if space-shifting is deemed a fair use, the staple article of commerce doctrine precludes liability for contributory or vicarious infringement. Under *Sony*, the copyright holder cannot extend his monopoly to products "capable of substantial noninfringing uses." *Sony*, 464 US at 442. Defendant fails to show that space-shifting constitutes a commercially significant use of Napster. Indeed, the most credible explanation

for the exponential growth of traffic to the website is the vast array of free MP3 files offered by other users—*not* the ability of each individual to space-shift music she already owns. Thus, even if space-shifting is a fair use, it is not substantial enough to preclude liability under the staple article of commerce doctrine. *See Cable/Home Communication Corp. v. Network Prods., Inc.*, 902 F2d 829, 846 (11th Cir 1990) (affirming finding of contributory infringement where defendant primarily promoted pirate computer chips and other devices capable of descrambling pay-TV broadcasts as infringement aids); *A& M Records v. General Audio Video Cassettes, Inc.*, 948 F Supp 1449, 1456 (CD Cal. 1996) (rejecting *Sony* defense because counterfeiting was chief purpose of time-loaded cassettes that defendant sold). [20]

16. This court also declines to apply the staple article of commerce doctrine because, as paragraphs (D)(6) and (E)(2) of the legal conclusions explain, Napster exercises ongoing control over its service. In *Sony*, the defendant's participation did not extend past manufacturing and selling the VCRs: "[t]he only contact between Sony and the users of the Betamax . . . occurred at the moment of sale." *Sony*, 464 US at 438. Here, in contrast, Napster, Inc. maintains and supervises an integrated system that users must access to upload or download files. Courts have distinguished the protection *Sony* offers to the manufacture and sale of a device from scenarios in which the defendant continues to exercise control over the device's use. *See General Audio Video*, 948 F Supp at 1456-57 (finding *Sony* doctrine inapplicable to seller of blank tapes who "acted as a contact between his customers and suppliers of other material necessary for counterfeiting"); *RCA Records v. All-Fast Sys., Inc.*, 594 F Supp 335, 339 (SD NY 1984) (holding that defendant in position to control cassette-copying machine could not invoke *Sony*); *see also Columbia Pictures Indus., Inc. v. Aveco, Inc.*, 800 F2d 59, 62 & n. 3 (3d Cir 1986) (holding that business which rented rooms where public viewed copyrighted video cassettes engaged in contributory infringement, even when it was not source of cassettes). Napster, Inc.'s facilitation of unauthorized file-sharing smacks of the contributory infringement in these cases, rather than the legitimate conduct of the VCR manufacturers. Given defendant's control over the service, as opposed to

mere manufacturing or selling, the existence of a potentially unobjectionable use like space-shifting does not defeat plaintiffs' claims.

17. Nor do other potential non-infringing uses of Napster preclude contributory or vicarious liability. Defendant claims that it engages in the authorized promotion of independent artists, ninety-eight percent of whom are not represented by the record company plaintiffs. *See* Def.'s Opp. at 10 (citing, *inter alia,* Krause Dec. ¶16), 27. However, the New Artist Program may not represent a substantial or commercially significant aspect of Napster. The evidence suggests that defendant initially promoted the availability of songs by major stars, as opposed to "page after page of unknown artists." *See* 1 Frackman Dec., Exh. C (Parker Dep.) at 104:16-105:10, Exh. 235. Its purported mission of distributing music by artists unable to obtain record-label representation appears to have been developed later. Other facts point to the conclusion that the New Artists Program was an afterthought, not a major aspect of the Napster business plan. Former CEO Eileen Richardson claimed in her deposition that she told the press Napster is not about known artists like Madonna. But, tellingly, discovery related to downloads by Napster executives reveals that Richardson's own computer contained about five Madonna files obtained using Napster. *See* 1 Frackman Dec., Exh. A (Richardson Dep.) at 238:2-240:25. Defendant did not launch the website aspect of its New Artist Program until *after* plaintiffs filed suit, and as recently as July 2000, bona fide new artists constituted a very small percentage of music available on Napster. *See* Krause Dec. ¶9, Exh. A; Olkin Reply Dec. ¶¶3-5; Hausman Reply Dec. ¶¶3-6.

In any event, Napster's primary role of facilitating the unauthorized copying and distribution established artists' songs renders *Sony* inapplicable. *See General Audio Video*, 948 F Supp at 1456-57; *RCA Records*, 594 F Supp at 339.

18. Plaintiffs do not object to *all* of the supposedly non-infringing uses of Napster. They do not seek an injunction covering chat rooms or message boards, the New Artist Program or any distribution authorized by rights holders. *See* Pl.'s Reply at 19. Nor do they seek to enjoin applications unrelated to the music recording industry.[21] *See id.* Because plaintiffs do not ask the court to shut down such satellite activities, the fact that these activities

may be non-infringing does not lessen plaintiffs' likelihood of success. The court therefore finds that plaintiffs have established a reasonable probability of proving third-party infringement.

D. Contributory Copyright Infringement

1. Once they have shown direct infringement by Napster users, plaintiffs must demonstrate a likelihood of success on their contributory infringement claim. A contributory infringer is "one who, with knowledge of the infringing activity, induces, causes or materially contributes to the infringing conduct of another." *Gershwin Publ'g Corp. v. Columbia Artists Management, Inc.*, 443 F2d 1159, 1162 (2d Cir 1971); *see Fonovisa, Inc. v. Cherry Auction, Inc.*, 76 F3d 259, 264 (9th Cir 1996). Courts do not require actual knowledge; rather, a defendant incurs contributory copyright liability if he has reason to know of the third party's direct infringement. *See Cable/Home Communication Corp.*, 902 F2d at 846; *Sega Enter. Ltd. v. MAPHIA*, 948 F Supp 923, 933 [2 *ILR (P&F) 168*] (ND Cal. 1996) ("*Sega II*").

2. Plaintiffs present convincing evidence that Napster executives actually knew about and sought to protect use of the service to transfer illegal MP3 files. For example, a document authored by co-founder Sean Parker mentions the need to remain ignorant of users' real names and IP addresses "since they are exchanging *pirated* music." 1 Frackman Dec., Exh. C (Parker Dep.) at 160:1-162:14, Exh. 254 at SF00100 (emphasis added). The same document states that, in bargaining with the RIAA, defendant will benefit from the fact that "we are not just making *pirated* music available but also pushing demand." *Id.* at 160:1-162:14, Exh. 254 at SF00102 (emphasis added). These admissions suggest that facilitating the unauthorized exchange of copyrighted music was a central part of Napster, Inc.'s business strategy from the inception.

Plaintiff [*sic*] also demonstrate that defendant had actual notice of direct infringement because the RIAA informed it of more than 12,000 infringing files. *See* Creighton 12/3/99 Dec., Exh. D. Although Napster, Inc. purportedly terminated the users offering these files, the songs are still available using the Napster service, as are the copyrighted works which the record company plaintiffs identified in Schedules A and B of their complaint. *See* Creighton Supp. Dec. ¶¶3-4.

3. The law does not require actual knowledge of specific acts of infringement. *See Gershwin*, 443 F2d at 1163 (holding that general knowledge that third parties performed copyrighted works satisfied knowledge element of contributory infringement); *Sega I*, 857 F Supp at 686-87 (concluding that plaintiffs established knowledge element, even though electronic bulletin board company did not know exactly when infringing video games would be uploaded to or downloaded from bulletin board). Accordingly, the court rejects defendant's argument that titles in the Napster directory cannot be used to distinguish infringing from non-infringing files and thus that defendant cannot know about infringement by any particular user of any particular musical recording or composition. *See* Lisi Dec. (Tygar Rep.) at 29 (offering expert opinion about difficulty of identifying copyrighted works by file name); Lars Ulrich Dep. at 36:16-37:2 (stating that in the past he did not object to individuals taping his band's concerts and making MP3 files of such concerts available via Napster); Sanders Dep. at 24:23-29:13 (discussing complex process for determining chain of title for copyright owners).[22]

4. Defendant's reliance on *Religious Technology Center v. Netcom Online Communication Services, Inc.*, 907 F Supp 1361 [*1 ILR (P&F) 778*] (ND Cal. 1995), does not alter the court's conclusion that plaintiffs have a reasonable likelihood of proving contributory liability. The cited passage from *Religious Technology Center* states:

> Where a BBS [bulletin board service] operator cannot reasonably verify a claim of infringement, either because of a possible fair use defense, the lack of copyright notices on the copies, or the copyright holder's failure to provide the necessary documentation to show that there is likely infringement, the operator's lack of knowledge will be found reasonable and there will be no liability for contributory infringement for allowing the continued distribution of the works on its system.

Id. at 1374. This language is dicta because the plaintiffs in *Religious Technology Center* raised a genuine issue of material fact regarding knowledge. More importantly, Napster is not an Internet service provider that acts as a mere conduit for the transfer of files. *See A& M Records v. Napster, Inc.*, 2000 WL 57136, at *6, 8 (ND Cal. May 12, 2000). Rather,

it offers search and directory functions specifically designed to allow users to locate music, the majority of which is copyrighted. *See id.* at *6. Thus, even if dicta from another federal district court were binding, *Religious Technology Center* would not mandate a determination that Napster, Inc. lacks the knowledge requisite to contributory infringement.

5. At the very least, defendant had constructive knowledge of its users' illegal conduct. Some Napster executives boast recording industry experience, *see* 1 Frackman Dec. (Richardson Dep.), Exh. 129 at ER00138, and defendant does not dispute that it possessed enough sophistication about intellectual property laws to sue a rock band that copied its logo. *See* 2 Frackman Dec., Exh. M (online news article about court proceedings to halt The Offspring's use of Napster logo).[23] The evidence indicates that Napster executives downloaded infringing material to their own computers using the service and promoted the website with screen shots listing infringing files. *See* 2 Frackman Dec., Exh. D (Brooks Dep.) at 51:8-24, 54:25-56:11, Exh. 64 at 2-4, Exh. 126 at 002260, 002263; 1 Frackman Dec., Exh. A (Richardson Dep.) at 20:5-22: 10, 25: 2-26:1; Exh. C (Parker Dep.) at 70:14-16, Exh. 230, ¶3-5; Exh. B (Fanning Dep.), Exhs. 174-76. Such conduct satisfies the objective test for constructive knowledge—defendant had reason to know about infringement by third parties. *See Cable/Home Communication Corp.*, 902 F2d at 846.[24]

6. Plaintiffs have also shown that defendant materially contributed to the infringing activity. In *Fonovisa*, the owners of copyrights for musical recordings stated a contributory infringement claim against the operators of a swap meet at which independent vendors sold counterfeit recordings. *See Fonovisa*, 76 F3d at 264. The Ninth Circuit held the copyright owners' allegations were "sufficient to show material contribution" because "it would have been difficult for the infringing activity to take place in the massive quantities alleged without the support services provided by the swap meet." *Id.* According to plaintiffs in the instant action, "Napster is essentially an Internet swap meet—more technologically sophisticated but in many ways indistinguishable from the [defendant] in *Fonovisa*." Pl.'s Br. at 6. The court largely agrees with this characterization.

Unlike the swap meet vendors, Napster users offer their infringing music for free. However, defendant's material contribution is still analogous to that of the swap meet in *Fonovisa*. The swap meet provided support services like parking, booth space, advertising, and clientele. *See Fonovisa*, 76 F3d at 264. Here, Napster, Inc. supplies the proprietary software, search engine, servers, and means of establishing a connection between users' computers. Without the support services defendant provides, Napster users could not find and download the music they want with the ease of which defendant boasts.

Several contributory infringement cases involving online services are in accord with the court's conclusion that defendant materially contributes to the infringing activity. For example in *Sega II*, an electronic bulletin board service acted as a central depository for unauthorized copies of computer games and materially contributed to infringement because it provided software, hardware, and phone lines needed for uploading and downloading copyrighted material. *See Sega II*, 948 F Supp at 933. Similarly, in *Religious Technology Center*, a case defendant ignores when convenient, a court in this district stated that an Internet access provider is not a mere landlord; rather, it exerts control akin to a radio station replaying infringing broadcasts. *See Religious Tech. Ctr.*, 907 F Supp at 1375 (holding that plaintiffs raised genuine issue of material fact as to service provider's substantial participation).

Defendant marshals two district court cases in an attempt to rebut plaintiffs' argument about material contribution. *See Intellectual Reserve, Inc. v. Utah Lighthouse Ministry*, 75 F Supp 2d 1290, 1293 [*4 ILR (P&F) 303*] (D Utah 1999) (holding that posting links to infringing websites did not contribute to infringement by those websites' operators); *Bernstein v. J. C. Penny, Inc.*, 50 USPQ 2d 1063 (CD Cal. 1998) (paraphrasing defendant's apparently successful argument that "multiple linking does not constitute substantial participation in any infringement where the linking website does not mention the fact that Internet users could, by following the links, find infringing material on another website"). The *Bernstein* court offered no reasoning for its dismissal of the complaint. Neither case is factually apposite, for Napster provides its users with much more than hyperlinking; Napster is an integrated service designed to enable users to locate and download MP3 music files. In keeping with its view that Napster, Inc. plays a more active role in facilitating file-sharing than an Internet service provider acting as a passive conduit, this court finds it probable that defendant materially contributed to unlawful conduct.

7. Because they have made a convincing showing with regard to both the knowledge and material contribution elements, plaintiffs have established a reasonable likelihood of success on their contributory infringement claims.

E. Vicarious Copyright Infringement

1. Even in the absence of an employment relationship, a defendant incurs liability for vicarious copyright infringement if he "has the right and ability to supervise the infringing activity and also has a direct financial interest in such activities." *Fonovisa*, 76 F3d at 262 (quoting *Gershwin*, 443 F2d at 1162).

2. In *Fonovisa*, the swap meet operator satisfied the first element of vicarious liability because it had the right to terminate vendors at will; it also controlled customers' access and promoted its services. *See id.* Although Napster, Inc. argues that it is technologically difficult, and perhaps infeasible, to distinguish legal and illegal conduct, plaintiffs have shown that defendant supervises Napster use. Indeed, Napster, Inc. itself takes pains to inform the court of its improved methods of blocking users about whom rights holders complain. *See* Def.'s Opp. Br. at 19 (citing Kessler Dec. ¶22), 33 (citing Kessler Dec. ¶¶23-24). This is tantamount to an admission that defendant can, and sometimes does, police its service. *See Religious Tech. Ctr.*, 907 F Supp at 1376 (concluding that evidence that Internet access provider acted to suspend subscribers' accounts and could delete specific postings raised genuine issue of material fact about vicarious liability).

Moreover, a defendant need not exercise its supervisory powers to be deemed capable of doing so. *See Gershwin*, 443 F2d at 1161-63. The court therefore finds that Napster, Inc. has the right and ability to supervise its users' infringing conduct.

3. Plaintiffs have shown a reasonable likelihood that Napster, Inc. has a direct financial interest in the infringing activity. Citing several non-governing cases from other districts, they contend that direct financial benefit does not require earned revenue,

so long as the defendant has economic incentives for tolerating unlawful behavior. For instance, in *Major Bob Music v. Stubbs*, 851 F Supp 475 (SD Ga. 1994), a bar derived direct financial benefit from infringing musical performances on its premises. The court noted that "an enterprise is considered to be 'profit-making' even if it never actually yields a profit." *Id.* at 480; *see also Walden Music, Inc. v. C. H. W., Inc.*, 1996 WL 254654, at *5 (D Kan. 1996) ("The fact that defendant' entrepreneurial enterprise is not profiting is not a defense to the plaintiffs' copyright infringement claims."); *Broadcast Music, Inc. v. Hobi, Inc.*, 1993 WL 404152, at *3 (MD La. 1993) (holding defendant vicariously liable because it operated with goal of making a profit, even though it did not actually make one), *aff'd* 20 F3d 1171 (5th Cir 1994).

Although Napster, Inc. currently generates no revenue, its internal documents state that it "will drive [sic] revenues directly from increases in userbase." 1 Frackman Dec. (Parker Dep.), Exh. 251.[25] The Napster service attracts more and more users by offering an increasing amount of quality music for free. *See, e.g*, 1 Frackman Dec., Exh. A (Richardson Dep.) at 112:18-113:2. It hopes to "monetize" its user base through one of several generation revenue models noted in the factual findings.

This is similar to the type of direct financial interest the Ninth Circuit found sufficient for vicarious liability in *Fonovisa*, where the swap meet's revenues flowed directly from customers drawn by the availability of music at bargain basement prices. *See Fonovisa*, 76 F3d at 263-64; *see also Famous Music Corp. v. Bay State Harness Horse Racing and Breeding Ass'n*, 554 F2d 1213, 1214 (1st Cir 1977) (holding racing association vicariously liable for infringing broadcast of music to entertain race-goers "when they were not absorbed in watching the races"); *Playboy Enters., Inc. v. Webbworld, Inc.*, 968 F Supp 1171, 1177 [2 ILR (P&F) 58] (ND Tex. 1997) (holding defendant vicariously liable because "plaintiff's photographs enhanced the attractiveness of the Neptics' website to potential customers"); *Polygram Int'l Publ'g, Inc. v. Nevada/ TIG, Inc.*, 855 F Supp 1314, 1332 (D Mass. 1994) (finding that music used to cultivate trade show attendees' interest provided direct financial benefit to trade show).

Napster, Inc.'s cursory discussion of the second element of vicarious liability does little to rebut this line of reasoning. Relying on *Religious Technology Center*, 907 F Supp at 1376-77, defendant maintains that it does not have a policy of ignoring infringement, and that even if it did, its non-infringing uses lure consumers to its service. The latter contention, for which it provides no factual support, does not square with its prediction that "the requested injunction would effectively put Napster out of business." Def.'s Opp. Br. at 31. If many of defendant's commercially significant uses were non-infringing, an injunction limited to unlawful activity would not have such a dire impact. Defendant's representations about the primacy of its legitimate uses thus appear disingenuous. The ability to download myriad popular music files without payment seems to constitute the glittering object that attracts Napster's financially-valuable user base.

4. Plaintiffs have shown a reasonable likelihood of success on their vicarious infringement claims.

F. Defendant's First Amendment Challenge

1. According to Napster, Inc., the requested injunction would impose a prior restraint on its free speech, as well as that of its users and the unsigned artists that depend upon its service. This First Amendment argument centers on the fact that defendant offers an electronic directory, which does not itself contain copyrighted material. Directories have been accorded First Amendment protection. *See Princeton Community Phone Book, Inc. v. Bate*, 582 F2d 706, 710-11 (3d Cir) (holding that First Amendment affords as much protection to listing in directory as it does to newspaper advertisement), *cert. denied*, 439 US 966 (1978).

2. Although an overbroad injunction might implicate the First Amendment, free speech concerns "are protected by and coextensive with the fair use doctrine." *Nihon Keizai Shimbun, Inc. v.comline Bus. Data, Inc.*, 166 F3d 65, 74 (2d Cir 1999); *Religious Tech. Ctr.*, 907 F Supp at 1377 (stating that, where otherwise appropriate, imposing liability for copyright infringement does not necessarily create First Amendment concerns because the fair use defense encompasses this issue). This court has already determined that plaintiffs do not seek to enjoin any fair uses of the Napster service that are not completely contrived or peripheral to its existence.

3. The parties dispute the extent to which infringing and non-infringing aspects of the service are separable. Napster, Inc's interim CEO Hank Barry and Vice President of Engineering Edward Kessler both opine that the requested injunction would have the practical effect of compelling defendant to exclude all songs from its system, including those which plaintiffs do not own. *See* Barry Dec. ¶13; Kessler Dec. ¶39. In this view, the injunction would destroy the Napster service, or if the service did not shut down completely, forcibly supplant peer-to-peer file-sharing with a model under which defendant dictated the content. *See* Kessler Dec. ¶39. Barry avers that, as a result of the injunction, Napster would lose its competitive edge *vis-a-vis* similar services. *See* Barry Dec. ¶13.

In contrast, plaintiffs contend that Napster's New Artist Program, message boards, chat rooms, and file-sharing applications for business and scientific research would remain viable if the court granted the requested relief. *See* Pl.'s Reply at 19; Daniel Farmer Dec. ¶¶3-4. Plaintiffs expert Daniel Farmer suggests several potentially viable methods of limiting the Napster service to music files authorized for sharing. First, defendant could compile a database of authorized music and then write a software program to read the files on users' hard drives when they log-on to the Napster service. The program would compare those file names with the authorized list, and only those files that matched could be uploaded onto Napster. *See* Farmer Dec. ¶3. Alternatively, defendant could write a software program that prevented users from successfully searching for file names excluded from the authorized list. *See id.*

In the event that Napster, Inc. cannot separate the infringing and non-infringing aspects of its service, its First Amendment argument still fails. Courts will not sustain a First Amendment challenge where the defendant entraps itself in an "all-or-nothing predicament." *Dr. Seuss Enters., L. P. v. Penguin Books USA, Inc.*, 109 F3d 1394, 1406 (9th Cir) (enjoining entire book that included parody in style of Dr. Seuss poem because defendant proceeded with book production after onset of litigation), *cert. dismissed*, 118 S Ct 27 (1997). Even if it is technologically impossible for Napster, Inc. to offer such functions as its directory without facilitating infringement, the court still must take action to protect plaintiffs' copyrights. *See, e.g.,*

Orth-O-Vision, Inc. v. Home Box Office, 474 F Supp 672, 686 n. 14 (SD NY 1979).

G. Misuse of Copyright Defense

1. Defendant essentially raises an antitrust argument as an equitable defense against the preliminary injunction motion. Under the rubric of misuse of copyright, Napster, Inc. argues that plaintiffs seek to aggrandize their monopoly beyond the scope of their copyrights by (1) restricting the flow of unsigned artists' music, which competes with their own, and (2) controlling the distribution of music over the Internet. Alleged antitrust violations by a copyright plaintiff generally do not afford a valid defense against an infringement action and ought not to dissuade a court from granting injunctive relief. *See* 4 Nimmer on Copyright §13.09[A], at 13-286 (citing, *inter alia, Orth-O-Vision*, 474 F Supp at 689).

2. Furthermore, most of the cases defendant cites deal with improper attempts to enlarge a copyright monopoly through restricted or exclusive licensing. *See, e.g., Practice Management Info. Corp. v. American Med. Ass'n*, 121 F3d 516, 521 (9th Cir) (1997), as amended 133 F3d 1140 (9th Cir 1998) (finding licensing agreement precluding use of competitor's products to be misuse), and *cert. denied*, 522 US 933 (1997); *see also, e.g., Alcatel USA, Inc. v. DGI Tech., Inc.*, 166 F3d 772, 792-95 (overturning district court's rejection of misuse defense based on licensing agreement allowing plaintiff to gain control over uncopyrighted products), *reh'g* and *reh'g en banc denied*, 180 F3d 267 (5th Cir 1999); *Lasercomb Am., Inc. v. Reynolds*, 911 F2d 970, 978-79 (4th Cir 1990) (concluding that exclusive licensing clause inhibiting licensees from developing own products constituted misuse). Plaintiffs have granted no licenses to defendant, let alone impermissibly restrictive ones. *See* Conroy Dec. ¶4; Cottrell Dec. ¶5; Eisenberg Dec. ¶21; Kenswil Dec. ¶15; Vidich Dec. ¶8; Stoller Dec. ¶11.

3. Accordingly, this court rejects the misuse of copyright defense.

H. Waiver

1. Napster, Inc. also avers that plaintiffs waived their entitlement to copyright protection because (a) they hastened the proliferation of MP3 files on the Internet, and (b) they plan to enter the market for

digital downloading themselves. These arguments are unavailing.

Defendant has submitted deposition excerpts related to the record company plaintiffs' business dealings with Internet and software companies that provide ripping software, custom CDs,[26] and players capable of playing unencrypted MP3 files.[27] *See, e.g.*, 1 Pulgram Dec., Exh. A (Conroy Dep.) at 51:8-52:16, Exh. B (Cottrell Dep.) at 141:10-142:142. None of plaintiffs' online partners is a party to this action. But at least one plaintiff—Sony—sells a device capable of playing downloaded MP3 files, regardless of whether the distribution of such files is authorized. *See id.*, Exh. E (Eisenberg Dep.) at 44:5-48:10, Exh. 220.

This limited evidence fails to convince the court that the record companies created the monster that is now devouring their intellectual property rights.[28] Although plaintiffs have not sued their business partners for contributory infringement, they typically have asked them to discourage unauthorized ripping and have made security part of their agreements. *See, e.g.*, Exh. A (Conroy Dep.) at 17:13-23, 18:22-19:6, 38:3-22, 51:8-14; Exh. B (Cottrell Dep.) at 135:24-136:7. Defendant fails to show that, in hastening the proliferation of MP3 files, plaintiffs did more than seek partners for their commercial downloading ventures and develop music players for files they planned to sell over the Internet.[29] Nor did plaintiffs invite wholesale infringement when they distributed a small number of free MP3 files for promotional purposes, especially since many of these files automatically "timed-out." *See* Conroy Dec. ¶¶9-17; Cottrell Dec. ¶15; Eisenberg Dec. ¶13; Kenswil Dec. ¶12; Vidich Dec. ¶¶7(d), 8.

To support its waiver argument, defendant primarily cites inapposite cases involving implied licenses. *See, e.g., Effects Assocs., Inc. v. Cohen*, 908 F2d 555, 559-60 (9th Cir 1990) (finding implied license where plaintiff created work at defendant's request and gave work to defendant with intent that defendant copy and distribute it), *cert. denied,* 498 US 1103 (1991). The evidence here does not reveal the existence of an implied license; indeed, the RIAA gave defendant express notice that it objected to the availability of its members' copyrighted music on Napster. *See* Creighton 12/3/99 Dec., Exh. D.

I. Failure to Present Evidence of Copyright Registration

1. Defendant argues that, to claim infringement of multiple works, plaintiffs must specify the works with particularity and provide proof of copyright registration. The cited statutory subsection, 17 USC section 411(a), provides with certain exceptions: "[N]o action for infringement of the copyright in any work shall be instituted until registration of the copyright claim has been made in accordance with this title." 17 USC §411(a); *see also Kodadek v. MTV Networks, Inc.*, 152 F3d 1209, 1211 (9th Cir 1998). A copyright infringement claim consists of two elements: (a) ownership of a valid copyright, and (b) copying of original elements of the copyrighted work. *See Feist Publications, Inc. v. Rural Telephone Serv. Co.*, 499 US 340, 361 (1991).

2. Napster, Inc. exaggerates the import of a non-governing case, *Cole v. Allen*, 3 FRD 236, 237 (SD NY 1942). In *Cole*, the defendant allegedly copied episodes from six books. Cole failed to plead her infringement claim with sufficient particularity because she merely listed the books' titles without specifying which portions were copied. Here, plaintiffs have attached two schedules listing works allegedly infringed in their *entirety*. Schedule A includes proof of registration; Schedule B (works recorded before 1972) does not because this material is governed by state law. Thus, despite their claim that it would be burdensome or even impossible to identify all of the copyrighted music they own, plaintiffs have made at least a minimal effort to describe the works in suit.

3. Furthermore, in *Walt Disney Co. v. Powell*, 897 F2d 565, 568 (DC Cir 1990), the DC Circuit allowed a permanent injunction covering works owned by the plaintiff but not in suit. The *Walt Disney* court found such a broad injunction appropriate where "liability has been determined adversely to the infringer, there has been a history of continuing infringement and a significant threat of future infringement remains." *Id.* Here, the evidence establishes that unauthorized sharing of plaintiffs' copyrighted music occurred on a massive scale in the past; Napster continues to be used to download and upload files illegally despite defendant's purportedly enhanced ability to terminate infringers; and the court anticipates a hemorrhage of plaintiffs' copyrighted material as users rush to obtain free music before trial. The

courts therefore finds it necessary to issue an injunction covering both plaintiffs' copyrighted works in suit and those not yet named.

J. Irreparable Harm

1. Because plaintiffs have shown a reasonable likelihood of success on the merits of their contributory and vicarious copyright infringement claims, they are entitled to a presumption of irreparable harm. *See Micro Star*, 154 F3d at 1109.

2. The court rejects defendant's contention that it has rebutted this presumption by demonstrating that any harm is *de minimis*. The declarations of record company executives, combined with the Teece Report, establish that plaintiffs have invested in the digital downloading market and that their business plans are threatened by a service that offers the same product for free. *See* Conroy Dec. ¶¶9-18; Cottrell Dec. ¶¶6-17; Eisenberg Dec. ¶¶9-22; Teece Rep. at 14-18 ; Vidich Dec. ¶¶7-10. Moreover, while the court recognizes the limitations of a survey that only targets college students, the Jay Report suggests the tendency of Napster use to suppress CD purchases, especially among heavy users. *See* Jay Rep. at 4, 18.

K. Balance of the Hardships

1. The court cannot give much weight to defendant's lament that the requested relief will put it out of business. *See Sun Microsystems, Inc. v. Microsoft Corp.*, 188 F3d 1115, 1119 (9th Cir 1999). Although even a narrow injunction may so fully eviscerate Napster, Inc. as to destroy its user base [30] or make its service technologically infeasible, the business interests of an infringer do not trump a rights holder's entitlement to copyright protection. Nor does defendant's supposed inability to separate infringing and non-infringing elements of its service constitute a valid reason for denying plaintiffs relief or for issuing a stay. *See Dr. Seuss*, 109 F3d at 1406.

Any destruction of Napster, Inc. by a preliminary injunction is speculative compared to the statistical evidence of massive, unauthorized downloading and uploading of plaintiffs' copyrighted works—as many as 10,000 files per second, by defendant's own admission. *See* Kessler Dec. ¶29. The court has every reason to believe that, without a preliminary injunction, these numbers will mushroom as Napster users, and newcomers attracted by the publicity, scramble to obtain as much free music as possible before trial.

2. Napster, Inc. contends that its service poses no harm to plaintiffs because future SDMI specifications will protect their music releases in both CD and downloadable formats. [31] Defendant purportedly intends to support SDMI-compliant formats when they become available. *See* Kessler Dec. ¶37. However, this argument suffers from two fatal flaws. First, assuming SDMI protections work, they will only affect plaintiffs' *new* releases; neither the copyrighted material in Schedules A and B of the complaint nor any other existing music that plaintiffs own will be covered. *See* 1 Pulgram Dec. (Vidich Dep.) at 54:6-55:4, 59:8-62:10. Second, because the SDMI specifications have not yet taken effect, they cannot shield plaintiffs from irreparable harm at this moment—the moment in which the preliminary injunction is sought. *See id.* at 59:8-62:10. A rights-friendly regime scheduled for implementation, at the earliest, by the end of 2000 does nothing to staunch the illegal flow of plaintiffs' copyrighted material over the Internet in the summer and autumn of this year.

3. Thus, even if the court were required to balance the hardships, which it is not because plaintiffs have raised serious questions and shown a strong likelihood of success on the merits, plaintiffs would prevail in their motion for a preliminary injunction.

III. CONCLUSION

For the foregoing reasons, the court GRANTS plaintiffs' motion for a preliminary injunction against Napster, Inc. Defendant is hereby preliminarily ENJOINED from engaging in, or facilitating others in copying, downloading, uploading, transmitting, or distributing plaintiffs' copyrighted musical compositions and sound recordings, protected by either federal or state law, without express permission of the rights owner. This injunction applies to all such works that plaintiffs own; it is not limited to those listed in Schedules A and B of the complaint.

Plaintiffs have shown persuasively that they own the copyrights to more than seventy percent of the music available on the Napster system. *See* Hausman Dec. ¶8. Because defendant has contributed to illegal copying on a scale that is without precedent, it bears the burden of developing a means to comply with the injunction. Defendant must insure that no work owned by plaintiffs which neither defendant nor Napster users have permission to use or distribute is uploaded or downloaded on Napster. The court ORDERS plaintiffs to cooperate with defendant in identifying the works to which they own copyrights. To this end, plaintiffs must file a written plan no later than September 5, 2000, describing the most expedient method by which their rights can be ascertained. The court also ORDERS plaintiffs to post a bond for the sum of $5,000,000.00 to compensate defendant for its losses in the event that this injunction is reversed or vacated. [32]

IT IS SO ORDERED.

---

[1] Hereafter, the court will use the term "music" to encompass both musical compositions and sound recordings, unless otherwise specifically noted.

[2] For the sake of clarity, the court will refer to the defendant Internet company as "Napster, Inc." The term "Napster" will be used to denote Napster, Inc.'s integrated service, including but not limited to its software, servers, search functions, and indexing functions. Where "Napster" appears as an adjective, the aspect of the service to which the adjective refers should be clear from the context. The term "Napster user" refers to any individual who uses Napster software to download and/or upload files.

[3] Although the parties sporadically include Eileen Richardson as a defendant in the caption, the court notes that she was dismissed from this action pursuant to the May 24, 2000 stipulation of dismissal.

[4] In this Memorandum and Order, the court will cite to and quote from any declaration, deposition, or other material filed under protective order if the parties relied upon it, or it is necessary to explain the court's findings and conclusions. Documents unsealed on this ground include: Russell Frackman Declaration (vols. 1 & 2), Kevin Conroy Declaration, Richard Cottrell Declaration, Mark Eisenberg Declaration, Lawrence Kenswil Declaration, Paul Vidich Declaration, David J. Teece Declaration, Edward Kessler Declaration, Laurence F. Pulgram Declaration (vols. 1 & 2), Daniel Farmer Declaration, Russell Frackman Reply Declaration, Julia Greer Reply Declaration, and David Lambert Reply Declaration. This list includes any, or all, supporting exhibits that may contain internal company plans, deposition transcripts, or other material upon which the court has relied. Any other document formerly covered by protective order but cited in this Memorandum and Order is also deemed to be unsealed.

[5] Defendant objects to this exhibit to former CEO Eileen Richardson's deposition on the grounds that it is neither properly authenticated nor "relevant to Napster work today." Def.'s Objections to Pl.'s Evidence at 10. The court does not intend to rule directly on each of defendant's myriad objections, many of which are unfounded; however, it notes that Richardson testified that she reviewed this document and that it dated from October 1999. She confirmed much of its content under oath, and defendant's counsel failed to object to the document during the deposition on relevancy, foundational, or authentication grounds. Defendant's early business plans are relevant to this action because they reveal facts about the early operation of the Napster service, as well as the knowledge and goals of Napster, Inc. executives. Accordingly, Exhibit 127 to the Richardson Deposition is admissible.

[6] Plaintiffs' expert Dr. Ingram Olkin, a professor of statistics at Stanford University, divided his study into two projects. In the User Project, a sample list of users and file names was taken every hour for four days. Researchers culled a random sub-sample of 1,150 users from 28,000 sampled and determined that all 1,150 users offered to share at least two copyrighted songs. See id. at 4-5, 7. The Download Project performed downloads at eight separate times for a five-minute period and generated a list of 1,150 songs from a population of approximately 574,185 files. See id. at 6. Olkin found that plaintiffs or other copyright holders own or administer the rights to 1,002 (or 87.1 percent) of the 1,150 files. Thirty-seven (or 3.2 percent) of the files are likely to copyrighted and distributed without authorization. Dr. Olkin identified only three files (or .26 percent) which were clearly offered without objection from the rights holder, while 108 (or 9.4 percent) of the files did not present enough data to yield a conclusion. See id. at 7. Charles J. Hausman, anti-piracy counsel for the RIAA, determined that 834 out of 1,150 files in Olkin's download database belonged to or were administered by plaintiffs and were exchanged on Napster without permission. See Charles J. Hausman Dec. ¶8.

[7] Defendant's objection to Exhibit 254 of the Parker Deposition exemplifies a strategy, in which both parties have engaged, of indiscriminately challenging unfavorable evidence. This approach is both fruitless and burdensome for the court. Defendant characterizes Exhibit 254 as irrelevant to how the company "actually operates;" yet the early business strategies of Napster, Inc. are plainly relevant to such issues as defendant's knowledge of the infringing activity and its intended effect on the market.

While defendant raises many meritless objections, it also correctly notes that plaintiffs failed to authenticate some of the documents upon which they rely. For example, plaintiffs did not get Shawn Fanning to authenticate

Exhibits 186 and 188 to his deposition. They have paid a price for this oversight. The court cannot rely on documents that would otherwise be "smoking guns" indicating that Napster, Inc. sought to "bypass the record industry entirely," make record stores obsolete, and "bring[] about the death of the CD." 1 Frackman Dec. (Fanning Dep.), Exh. 186 at 00017; Exh. 188.

[8]   Sean Parker appears to have mistakenly identified this document, numbered NAP003687—an October 28, 1999 email from Stephanie Norton to other Napster employees, including Parker—as Exhibit A to his declaration. In fact, it is Exhibit B. Although the email indicates that defendant planned to solicit interest among unsigned artists, it contains a cryptic statement regarding the creation of indexes listing available MP3s: "For now, we should do this for UNSIGNED artists only so the RIAA *thinks* we are not infringing on copyright." Parker Dec., Exh. B (second emphasis added). As is often the case with defendant's internal documents, whether defendant viewed the promotion of new artists as a genuine goal or a smokescreen remains ambiguous.

[9]   *See infra* at section (C)(12) of the Findings of Fact for a description of the two aspects of defendant's New Artist Program—a website version and a software-based version.

[10]   Defendant also provides an audio player capable of playing MP3 files on a user's hard drive, regardless of how those files were obtained. *See* Edward Kessler Reply Dec. in Support of Def.'s Mot. for Summ. Adjud. ¶29. Neither party has briefed the function of the audio player in support of its position on the necessity of a preliminary injunction. However, the player has little or no connection to the alleged copying that occurs when Napster users upload or download music and, hence, is not relevant to the requested relief. *See id.* While a consumer might rip CDs and then play the resultant MP3 files on the Napster player, the court rejects any suggestion that this activity constitutes a substantial, non-infringing use of Napster for the same reasons it dismisses defendant' [sic] argument about space-shifting from home to office. The court also notes that, because the audio player can only play music files which a user already possesses, it cannot be used for sampling.

[11]   BMG's labels include plaintiffs Arista Records, LaFace Records, and RCA Records. *See* Conroy Dec. ¶1. BMG Music is also a plaintiff in this action.

[12]   If such music is not protected technologically, an individual consumer may become a worldwide distributor of copyrighted material after obtaining a single, promotional copy in digital format. *See* Teece Rep. at 13.

[13]   Fine's study tracked retail music sales trends in three types of stores in the United States: (1) all stores located within one mile of any college or university on a list acquired from Quality Education Data; (2) all stores located within one mile of any college or university on a list of colleges and universities that have banned Napster use; (3) all stores within one mile of any college or university listed among the "Top 40 Most Wired Colleges in 1999," according to Yahoo Internet Life. Researchers working on the Fine Report used Soundscan Point of Sale data to compare music sales totals from the latter two categories with (1) national totals and (2) sales from the first category, "All College Stores." The report tracked retail sales in the first quarter (" Q1") of 1997, 1998, 1999, and 2000. *See* Fine Rep. at 2-4.

[14]   Fine's conclusions were not limited to Napster, but rather assessed the effects of online music file-sharing in general. *See id.* While national sales grew "significantly and consistently" in the quarters Fine studied, sales at stores near colleges or universities declined, with sales in the "Top 40 Most Wired Colleges" and "Napster-banned" subsets showing an even sharper decline than those in the "All College Stores" category. *See id.*

The court has noted the limitations of the Jay and Fine Reports in its separate order regarding the admissibility of expert opinions. Despite flaws in each report, the court relies on Jay's insights into the music purchasing and downloading habits of college students, as opposed to all Napster users, and considers the Fine Report relevant to corroborate Jay's findings.

[15]   The court's memorandum and order regarding the admissibility of expert reports includes a detailed discussion of flaws in the Fader Report. Among the shortcomings the court noted are Fader's heavy reliance on journalistic articles and studies that he did not conduct, the fact the centerpiece of his report is a survey that he only distantly supervised, and the lack of tables offering statistical breakdowns of survey respondents and their answers.

[16]   The availability of free MP3 music files elsewhere in cyberspace means that enjoining Napster fails to provide a complete panacea for plaintiffs' problems. However, arguing that third-parties also facilitate unlawful activity does not constitute valid defense to claims of contributory and vicarious copyright infringement.

[17]   Defendant cites *Cadence Design Systems, Inc. v. Avant! Corp.*, 125 F3d 824, 829 (9th Cir 1997), *cert. denied*, 523 US 1118 (1998), for the proposition that showing a plaintiff has suffered no injury, or *de minimis* injury, rebuts the presumption of irreparable harm. Such language in *Cadence* constitutes pure dicta. Moreover, the passage from *Nimmer on Copyright* to which the *Cadence* court refers deals with defeating an allegation of substantial similarity by demonstrating that the amount of copying was *de minimis*. Defendant does not suggest

that downloading entire copyrighted songs is *de minimis* copying, but rather that obtaining music using Napster does not displace CD sales. *See* Def.'s Opp. at 29.

[18] Defendant cites the Office of Technology Assessment ("OTA") report on home taping to bolster its misguided argument about the Audio Home Recording Act of 1992. *See infra* note 19. Plaintiffs note that the OTA Report expressly contemplates use by "a household and its normal circle of friends, rather than the public." Pl.'s Reply at 4 (citing U.S. Cong., OTA, Copyright and Home Copying: Technology Challenges the Law). Although this definition of home use does not control, it nevertheless suggests flaws in defendant's position.

[19] Defendant's opposition brief opens with a perplexing argument. It cites *Recording Industry Association of America v. Diamond Multimedia Systems, Inc.*, 180 F3d 1072, 1079 [*3 ILR (P&F) 66*] (9th Cir 1999), for the proposition that the Audio Home Recording Act of 1992, 17 USC sections 1001-1010 (" AHRA"), immunizes the non-commercial use of Napster to space-shift music. The AHRA is irrelevant to the instant action. Neither the record company nor music publisher plaintiffs have brought claims under the AHRA; moreover, the Ninth Circuit did not hold in *Diamond Multimedia* that the AHRA covers the downloading of MP3 files.

Diamond Multimedia involved a suit under the AHRA by the Recording Industry Association of America (" RIAA") to enjoin the manufacture and distribution of the Rio portable music player—a hand-held device that can receive, store, and re-play MP3 files. *See Diamond Multimedia*, 180 F3d at 1074. The Ninth Circuit held that the Rio player is not a digital audio recording device subject to the AHRA's restrictions. *See id.* at 1081. Nor are computers and their hard drives digital audio recording devices. *See id.* at 1078. The *Diamond Multimedia* court *did* opine that making copies with the Rio to space-shift, or make portable, files already on a user's hard drive constitutes "paradigmatic noncommercial personal use entirely consistent with the purposes of the Act [*i.e.* the facilitation of personal use]." *Id.* at 1079. However, this dicta is of limited relevance. Because plaintiffs have not made AHRA claims, the purposes and legislative history of the AHRA do not govern the appropriateness of a preliminary injunction against Napster, Inc. Furthermore, as explained below, the court is not persuaded that space-shifting constitutes a substantial, non-infringing use of the Napster service. The Ninth Circuit did not discuss the fair use doctrine in *Diamond Multimedia*.

This court denies defendant's request for judicial notice of the legislative history of the AHRA, filings in *Diamond Multimedia*, and certain other materials deemed irrelevant or inappropriate for judicial notice.

[20] Relying on *Vault Corp. v. Quaid Software, Ltd*, 847 F2d 255 (5th Cir 1988), defendant argues that even one substantial non-infringing use precludes contributory liability. RAMKEY, one feature of Quaid's computer diskette, had an unobjectionable use because consumers could use it to make archival copies of Vault's anti-piracy software if Vault's program were inadvertently destroyed. Based on this one use, the Fifth Circuit held that there was no contributory copyright infringement, even though third parties *did* engage in direct infringement. *See id.* at 262. Other jurisdictions have disagreed with the *Vault* approach where the product's primary purpose is unlawful. *See Cable/Home Communication Corp.* 902 F2d at 846; *General Audio Video*, 948 F Supp at 1456. A Fifth Circuit opinion does not bind this court. Moreover, even the Fifth Circuit declined to consider the legitimate functions of Copywrite, another feature of Quaid's product, because "without RAMKEY, Copywrite would have no commercial value." *Vault*, 847 F2d at 264 n. 16. The Napster service arguably has little commercial value without the availability of copyrighted popular music.

[21] For example, defendant notes that its technology might be used for collaborative working relationships in business, education, and research. *See* Def.'s Opp. at 9 n. 10.

[22] MP3 files do not bear a copyright notice or watermark. *See* Lisi Dec. (Tygar Rep.) at 37-47. More than one artist may use a song title; and multiple recordings of the same work may carry different authorizations. *See id.* at 29.

[23] Defendant objects to Exhibit M to the Frackman Declaration because press articles constitute hearsay and statements reported within them are double hearsay. *See* Def.'s Objections to Pl.'s Evidence at 12. However, defendant does not appear to dispute the truth of the matter asserted—that Napster, Inc. sued The Offspring for violating its intellectual property rights. Indeed, defendant's second ground for objecting indicates that it admits such a lawsuit was filed. *See id.* If the exhibit should be excluded because the suit involved trademark, rather than copyright, defendant effectively concedes that it brought a trademark action.

[24] This finding also puts an end to defendant's persistent attempts to invoke the protection of the Digital Millennium Copyright Act, 17 USC section 512. In its opposition brief, Napster, Inc. attempts to persuade the court that subsection 512(d) provides an applicable safe harbor. However, this subsection expressly excludes from protection any defendant who has "[a]ctual knowledge that the material or activity is infringing," §512(d)(1)(A), or "is aware of facts or circumstances from which infringing activity is apparent." §512(d)(1)(B). Defendant has failed to persuade this court that subsection 512(d) shelters contributory infringers.

[25] Although defendant appears to object to Exhibit 251 to the Parker Deposition, it does not assert any grounds for doing so. *See* Def.'s Objections to Pl.'s Evidence at 11. The court declines to speculate about defendant's reasons for objecting. Exhibit 251 is deemed admissible due to defendant's failure to make a proper objection.

[26] Custom CDs can be created using a CD burner, a device that allows consumers to convert MP3 files from a computer hard drive to CD format. *See, e.g.*, 1 Pulgram Dec., Exh. A (Conroy Dep.) at 14:10-17.

[27] Player software enables consumers to play MP3 files. Such software is available on the Internet, possibly free of charge, and may be part of the bundled software sold by PC manufacturers. *See, e.g.*, 1 Pulgram Dec., Exh. A (Conroy Dep.) at 14:21-17:12.

[28] For example, such plaintiffs as BMG and Sony have entered into agreements with Listen.com, a site that provides links to CD-ripping applications. *See* Exh. A (Conroy Dep.) at 49: 22-51: 20, Exh. 295; Exh. E (Eisenberg Dep.) at 135: 2-24. However, BMG representative Kevin Conroy stated in his deposition that BMG encourages its online partners "to provide only for authorized ripping" and that BMG has agreements with such sites "to legitimately and securely market, promote, and sell [BMG] artists' music." *Id.* at 43:20-24, 51:8-14.

In the case of Musicmaker.com, in which EMI owns an equity stake, consumers can *purchase* single tracks and have them burned into a custom CD. *See id.*, Exh. B (Cottrell Dep.) at 141:10-142:17. It is not clear that Musicmaker.com promotes the use of pirated music. Similarly, Universal has entered agreements related to commercial downloading with Real Jukebox, which the first phase of the Secure Digital Music Initiative ("SDMI") did not cover. *See id.*, Exh. F (Kenswil Dep.) at 54:8-56:25; *see also infra* note 31 (discussing SDMI specifications). Under its agreement with Universal, RealJukebox will become SDMI-compliant, but still will be able to play unencrypted files to the extent the SDMI specifications allow. Defendant provides no conclusive evidence that Universal has encouraged the use of Real Jukebox to play copyrighted music for which no authorization has been obtained.

Finally, Sony VAIO Music Clip appears to be a Sony product that facilitates the downloading, arrangement, storage, and playback of MP3, ATRAC3, or WAV files. However, while the VAIO Music Clip may not be able to screen out unauthorized files, one advertisement promotes the "secure music download capability of the software" and indicates that consumers should "purchase the wave of titles for major artists and record labels that are soon to come" on music websites. *See id.*, Exh. E (Eisenberg Dep.) at 44:5-48:10, Exh. 220 (emphasis added).

[29] An internal Universal document that mentions "superdistribution" constitutes the most compelling evidence of defendant's position. *See id.*, Exh. F (Kenswil Dep), Exh. 257 at U0866. "Superdistribution" means viral distribution through a chain of consumers and their friends. *See id.* at 45:1-4, 19-25. However, in his deposition, Lawrence Kenswil indicated that Universal envisioned a model of viral distribution in which consumers would pay for the product and permission of the rights holder would be obtained prior to transmission. *See id.* at 45:5-46:7. That such a system eventually might encompass some version of Napster does not demonstrate a waiver of plaintiffs' copyrights.

According to another internal Universal plan, the "[g]oal is not just to equal Napster et al. but to surpass them." *Id.*, Exh. 258 at U0840. Defendant argues that Universal intended to commandeer Napster for its own benefit. Yet the strategic plan repeatedly employs the word "secure"— emphasizing its "secure . . . core technology" and referring to the "perceived attractiveness of *secure* content by users" as a barometer of success. *Id.* (emphasis added). Nowhere does this document state or imply that Universal planned to promote unrestricted downloading of its music for free.

[30] Because the Napster service appears to enjoy a cult following, the court doubts that a preliminary injunction would destroy defendant's user base. If users switch to other services like Gnutella while Napster is temporarily enjoined, there is a reasonable likelihood that they will switch back, especially considering defendant's claim to offer more music and more efficient search tools than its competitors.

[31] The Secure Digital Music Initiative, "SDMI," is a forum that brings together interested parties to develop technology specifications for protecting the distribution of digital media. *See* Kessler Dec. ¶36. Some time in the future, but no earlier than the end of the year 2000, SDMI will select certain specifications for content media, such as CDs and digital file formats. *See* 1 Pulgram Dec., Exh. N (Vidich Dep.) at 59:8-62:10. The first phase of SDMI covered portable physical devices, but still allowed these devices to play unencrypted files. *See* 1 Pulgram Dec., Exh. F (Kenswil Dep.) at 54:8-54:19.

Generally speaking, the next phase of SDMI will concern two forms of digital rights management technology: encryption and watermarking. *See* Kessler Dec. ¶¶35, 36;1 Pulgram Dec., Exh. N (Vidich Dep.) at 59:8-62:10. Encryption codes files in a way that requires "keys," such as the consumer's hardware serial numbers, to access the files' content. *See* Kessler Dec. ¶36; 1 Pulgram Dec., Exh. N (Vidich Dep.) at 53:10-56:8. Encryption technology has limitations, however. For example, encrypted CDs will not function in existing CD players because the players will not be able to read them. *See* 1 Pulgram Dec., Exh. N (Vidich Dep.) at 52:21-53:2. Thus, consumers will have to purchase new CD players to listen to encrypted CD music. *See id.* at 53:22-54:4. Also, encryption technology will provide only prospective protection because it will not affect existing discs. *See id.* 54:6-55:4.

Watermarking imbeds "bits" or inaudible marks on content media; future SDMI-compliant devices or software players will be able to read the presence or absence of those bits and control copying accordingly. *See* Pulgram Dec., Exh. N (Vidich Dep.) at 57:2-9; 59:8-62:10. One form of copy control will allow consumers to copy CDs onto their SDMI-compliant devices, but will prevent further copying or transmission over the Internet. *See id.* at 60:14-25; 61:11-62:10; Exh. 227 at TW 0556742. Some time in the future, but not before year's end, several record company plaintiffs intend to implement watermarking technology that complies with SDMI specifications. *See, e.g.*, Pulgram Dec., Exh. N (Vidich Dep.) at 59:8-62:10); Exh. B (Cottrell Dep.) at 99:24-101:4 (EMI)). However, watermarking technology also has limitations. For instance, the first phase of SDMI-compliant devices and popular digital music software like the Real Jukebox can play formats that do not contain watermarking. *See* Pulgram Dec., Exh. N (Vidich Dep. at 59:8-60:25), Exh. F (Kenswil Dep.) at 54:8-56:19. Finally, like encryption, watermarking only offers prospective copy protection; it will not affect existing media because (a) such media cannot be "queried" to determine if the copy is legitimate, and (b) only future SDMI-compliant players will be able to make that query. *See* 1 Pulgram Dec., Exh. N (Vidich Dep.) at 59:8-62:10.

[32] On July 26, 2000, the court ordered defendant to comply with the preliminary injunction by midnight on July 28, 2000; however, on July 28, a Ninth Circuit panel stayed the injunction. That same day, plaintiffs posted their bond.

A&M Records, Inc.

v.

Napster, Inc.

**United States Court of Appeals,
Ninth Circuit**

**February 12, 2001
As amended April 3, 2001**

7 ILR (P&F) 1, 239 F3d 1004

Nos. 00-16401 and 00-16403

Napster users directly infringe copyrights; fair use defense properly rejected.

The district court [5 ILR (P&F) 745] properly concluded that users of an online music file sharing system (known as Napster) directly infringed plaintiffs' copyrighted musical compositions and sound recordings; such users are not engaged in a fair use of the material. Napster users infringe at least two of the copyright holders' exclusive rights: the right of distribution (by uploading file names to the search index for others to copy) and the right of reproduction (by downloading files containing copyrighted music). As for the fair use defense, the district court judge properly rejected the specific alleged fair uses of sampling (where users make temporary copies of a work before purchasing) and space-shifting (where users access a sound recording through the Napster system that they already own in audio CD format). The district court did not err in concluding that sampling remains a commercial use even if some users eventually purchase the music or that Napster has an adverse impact on the audio CD and digital download markets. Nor did the district court err when it refused to apply the "shifting" analyses of *Sony Corp. v. Universal City Studios, Inc.*, 464 US 417 (1984), and *RIAA v. Diamond Multimedia Sys., Inc.*, 3 ILR (P&F) 66 (9th Cir 1999). Both cases are inapposite because the methods of shifting involved there did not also simultaneously involve distribution of the copyrighted material to the general public; the time or space-shifting of copyrighted material exposed the material only to the original user. — **A&M Records Inc. v. Napster Inc., 7 ILR (P&F) 1 [9th Cir, 2001].**

Napster likely liable for contributory infringement.

The district court [5 ILR (P&F) 745] properly concluded that plaintiff record companies would likely prevail in establishing that the operator of an online music file sharing system (Napster) is liable as a contributory infringer. Napster, by its conduct, knowingly encourages and assists the direct infringement of plaintiffs' copyrights. Although the district court placed undue weight on the proportion of current infringing use as compared to current and future noninfringing use, the evidentiary record nevertheless supports the district court's conclusion. If a computer system operator learns of specific infringing material available on his system and fails to purge such material from the system, the operator knows of and contributes to direct infringement. Conversely, absent any specific information which identifies infringing activity, a computer system operator cannot be liable for contributory infringement merely because the structure of the system allows for the exchange of copyrighted material. To enjoin simply because a computer network allows for infringing use would violate *Sony Corp. v. Universal City Studios, Inc.*, 464 US 417 (1984), and potentially restrict activity unrelated to infringing use. Nevertheless, sufficient knowledge exists to impose contributory liability when linked to demonstrated infringing use of the Napster system. The record supports the district court's finding that Napster has *actual* knowledge that *specific* infringing material is available using its system, that it could block access to the system by suppliers of the infringing material, and that it failed to remove the material. Furthermore, Napster materially contributes to the infringing activity inasmuch as it provides the site and facilities for direct infringement. — **A&M Records Inc. v. Napster Inc., 7 ILR (P&F) 1 [9th Cir, 2001].**

Napster likely liable for vicarious infringement.

The district court [5 ILR (P&F) 745] properly concluded that plaintiff record companies would likely prevail in establishing that the operator of an online music file sharing system (Napster) is liable for vicarious copyright infringement. Napster has a direct financial interest in the infringing activity, and it has the right and ability to supervise its users' conduct. Although Napter's ability to police its system is limited—Napster does not "read" the content of indexed files other than to check that they are in the proper MP3 format—it nevertheless has the ability to locate infringing material listed on its search indices and the right to terminate users' access to the system. — **A&M Records Inc. v. Napster Inc., 7 ILR (P&F) 1 [9th Cir, 2001].**

AHRA does not insulate Napster from liability for copyright infringement.

The Audio Home Recording Act (AHRA), 17 USC §1008, does not insulate the operator of an online music file sharing system (Napster) from contributory or vicarious copyright liability. AHRA does not cover the downloading of MP3 files to computer hard drives. Under the plain meaning of the Act's definition of digital audio recording devices, computers (and their hard drives) are not digital audio recording devices because their primary purpose is not to make digital audio copied recordings. Moreover, notwithstanding Napster's claim that computers are "digital audio recording devices," computers do not make "digital music recordings" as defined by AHRA. [Affirming 5 ILR (P&F) 745.] — **A&M Records Inc. v. Napster Inc., 7 ILR (P&F) 1 [9th Cir, 2001].**

Applicablity of DMCA's safe harbor.

The district court [5 ILR (P&F) 745] erred in concluding that the Digital Millennium Copyright Act (DMCA), 17 USC §512(d), which exempts "Internet service providers" from suits for copyright infringement, will never protect secondary infringers, such as defendant, the operator of an online music file sharing system (Napster). Consequently, Napster's potential liability for contributory and vicarious infringement does not render the DMCA's safe harbor inapplicable per se. This issue will be more fully developed at trial. Nevertheless, for purposes of a preliminary injunction, the plaintiff record companies have raised significant questions, including: (1) whether Napster is an Internet service provider as defined by 17 USC §512(d); (2) whether copyright owners must give a service provider "official" notice of infringing activity in order for it to have knowledge or awareness of infringing activity on its system; and (3) whether Napster complies with §512(i), which requires a service provider to timely establish a detailed copyright compliance policy. Furthermore, the district court considered ample evidence to support its determination that the balance of hardships tips in plaintiffs' favor. — **A&M Records Inc. v. Napster Inc., 7 ILR (P&F) 1 [9th Cir, 2001].**

Affirmative defenses properly rejected.

In finding the operator of an online music file sharing system (Napster) contributorily and vicariously liable for copyright infringement, the district court [5 ILR (P&F) 745] did not improperly reject the affirmative defenses of waiver, implied license, and copyright misuse. In hastening the proliferation of MP3 files, the plaintiff record companies did not, as Napster suggests, waive legal authority to exercise control over the creation and distribution of MP3 files. Rather, they did nothing more than seek partners for their commercial downloading ventures and develop music players for files they planned to sell over the Internet. As for the contention that plaintiffs granted Napster an implied license by encouraging MP3 file exchange over the Internet, the district court properly observed that no evidence supported such a defense; courts have found implied licenses only where one party created a work at the other's request and handed it over, intending that the other copy and distribute it. Nor is there any evidence of copyright misuse, for plaintiffs seek only to control reproduction and distribution of their copyrighted works; there is no evidence that plaintiffs seek to control areas outside of their grant of monopoly. — **A&M Records Inc. v. Napster Inc., 7 ILR (P&F) 1 [9th Cir, 2001].**

Preliminary injunction overbroad.

A district court order [5 ILR (P&F) 745] preliminarily enjoining the operator of an online music file sharing system (Napster) from "copying, downloading, uploading, transmitting, or distributing" plaintiffs' copyrighted works is overbroad because it places on Napster the entire burden of ensuring that no infringement of plaintiffs' works occurs on the system. Plaintiffs must provide notice to Napster of copyrighted works and files containing such works available on the Napster system before Napster has the duty to disable access to the offending content. Napster, however, bears the burden of policing the system within the limits of the system. In crafting the injunction on remand, the district court should recognize that the MP3 files are named by the users themselves and that Napster's system does not currently appear to allow Napster access to the content of users' MP3 files. — **A&M Records Inc. v. Napster Inc., 7 ILR (P&F) 1 [9th Cir, 2001].**

First Amendment inapplicable to uses of copyrighted material that are not fair uses.

A district court order [5 ILR (P&F) 745] preliminarily enjoining the operator of an online music file sharing system (Napster) from "copying, downloading, uploading, transmitting, or distributing" plaintiffs' copyrighted works, though overbroad, does not violate the First Amendment. First Amendment concerns in copyright are allayed by the presence of the fair use doctrine. Based on the preliminary determination that Napster users are not fair users, uses of copyrighted material that are not fair uses are rightfully enjoined. — **A&M Records Inc. v. Napster Inc., 7 ILR (P&F) 1 [9th Cir, 2001].**

Compulsory royalty payment inappropriate.

The district court [5 ILR (P&F) 745] properly refused to impose a monetary penalty by way of a compulsory royalty in place of an injunction against the operator of an online music file sharing system (Napster). Notwithstanding Napster's argument that a compulsory royalty may be appropriate in "special circumstances," the appellate court is at a loss to find any "special circumstances" simply because the case requires it to apply well-established doctrines of copyright law to a new technology. Neither does the court agree with Napster that an injunction would cause "great public injury." Imposing a compulsory royalty payment schedule would give Napster an "easy out." If such royalties were imposed, Napster would avoid penalties for any future violation of an injunction, statutory copyright damages, and any possible criminal penalties for continuing infringement. The royalty structure would also grant Napster the luxury of either choosing to continue and pay royalties or shut down. On the other hand, the wronged parties would be forced to do business with a company that profits from the wrongful use of intellectual properties. Plaintiffs would lose the power to control their intellectual property: they could not make a business decision *not* to license their property to Napster, and, in the event they planned to do business with Napster, compulsory royalties would take away the copyright holders' ability to negotiate the terms of any contractual arrangement. — **A&M Records Inc. v. Napster Inc., 7 ILR (P&F) 1 [9th Cir, 2001].**

Appeals from the United States District Court for the Northern District of California *[5 ILR (P&F) 745]*, **MARILYN HALL PATEL, Chief District Judge**, Presiding.

Before: **MARY M. SCHROEDER, Chief Judge, ROBERT R. BEEZER and RICHARD A. PAEZ, Circuit Judges.** Opinion by **Judge Beezer.**

COUNSEL

David Boies, Jonathan Schiller and *Robert Silver*, Boies, Schiller & Flexner, Armonk, New York, *Laurence F. Pulgram, David L. Hayes, Daniel Johnson, Jr.* and *Darryl M. Woo*, Fenwick & West, Palo Alto, California, for defendant-appellant.

Russell J. Frackman, George M. Borkowski, Jeffrey D. Goldman, Roy L. Shults and *Peter B. Gelblum*, Mitchell, Silberberg & Knupp, Los Angeles, California; *Carey R. Ramos*, Paul, Weiss, Rifkind, Wharton & Garrison, New York, New York, for the plaintiffs-appellees.

Hannah Bentley, San Anselmo, California, for amicus Casanova Records.

Andrew P. Bridges, Wilson, Sonsini, Goodrich & Rosati, Palo Alto, California, for amicus Digital Media Association.

Scott E. Bain, Wiley, Rein & Fielding, Washington, D.C., for amici Ad Hoc Copyright Coalition; Commercial Internet Exchange; Computer & Communications Industry Association; Information Technology Association of America; Netcoalition.com; United States Internet Industry Association, and United States Telecommunications Association.

Scott R. McIntosh, Civil Division, Department of Justice, Washington, D.C., for amicus United States.

Ann Brick, San Francisco, California, for amici American Civil Liberties Union and the American Civil Liberties Union of Northern California.

Judith B. Jennison, Perkins Coie, San Francisco, California, for amicus Scour, Inc.

Ralph Oman, Dechert, Price & Rhoads, Washington, D.C., as amicus. *Christopher Tayback*, Quinn, Emanuel, Urquhart, Oliver & Hedges, Los Angeles, California, for amicus National Academy of Recording Arts & Sciences.

E. Edward Bruce, Covington & Burling, Washington, D.C., for amicus Business Software Alliance.

Kevin T. Baine, Williams & Connolly, Washington, D.C., for amici Motion Picture Association of America, Inc., Software & Information Industry Association, American Film Marketing Association, Association of American Publishers, American Society of Media Photographers, Professional Photographers Association, Graphic Artists Guild, Interactive Digital Software Association, American Society of Composers, Authors and Publishers, Broadcast Music, Inc., Producers Guild of America, Directors Guild of America, Inc., Writers Guild of America, West, Inc., American Federation of Musicians of the United States and Canada, Reed Elsevier, Inc., American Federation of Television and Radio Artists, Office of the Commissioner of Baseball, Songwriters Guild of America, and AmSong, Inc.; *Joel M. Litvin*, New York, New York, for amicus National Basketball Association.

Salvatore A. Romano, Seyfarth, Shaw, Washington, D.C., for amici National Association of Recording Merchandisers, Inc. and Video Software Dealers Association.

Erwin Chemerinsky, University of Southern California School of Law, Los Angeles, California, for amicus Law Professors Erwin Chemerinsky, Kenneth L. Karst, Steven Shiffrin, Rodney A. Smolla and Marcy Strauss.

Barry I. Slotnick, Richards & O'Neil, New York, New York, for amicus Association for Independent Music.

Morton David Goldberg, Cowan, Liebowitz & Latman, New York, New York, for amici Alliance Entertainment Corp., Audible Inc., Blue Spike, Inc., The Clandestine Group, Inc., Digimarc Corporation, Digital Media on Demand, Inc., FullAudio Corporation, InterTrust Technologies Corporation, Oak Technology, Inc., Reciprocal, Inc., RioPort, Inc., RPK SecureMedia Inc., Verance Corporation, and VNU USA, Inc.

Richie T. Thomas, Squire, Sanders & Dempsey, Washington, D.C., for amici Consumer Electronics Association, Digital Future Coalition, and Computer & Communications Industry Association.

Karen B. Tripp, Houston, Texas, for amici Association of American Physicians & Surgeons, Inc. and Eagle Forum Education and Legal Defense Fund.

Professor *Jessica Litman*, Wayne State University Law School, Detroit, Michigan; Professor *Keith Aoki*, University of Oregon School of Law; Professor Ann Bartow, University of South Carolina School of Law; Professor *Dan Burk*, University of Minnesota; Professor Julie Cohen, Georgetown University School of Law; Professors *Christine Haight Farley* and *Peter Jaszi*, Washington College of Law, American University; Professor *Lydia Pallas Loren*, Lewis and Clark College Northwestern School of Law; Professor *Pamela Samuelson*, Boalt Hall School of Law, University of California Berkeley; Professor *Shubha Ghosh*, University at Buffalo, SUNY; Professors *Paul J. Heald*, Allen Post Professor of Law, *L. Ray Patterson*, Pope Brock Professor of Law, and *Laura N. Gasaway*, University of Georgia School of Law; Professor *Michael Madison*, University of Pittsburgh School of Law; *Professor Ruth Okediji*, University of Oklahoma Law School; *Alfred C. Yen*, Associate Dean for Academic Affairs and Professor of Law, Boston College Law School; *Professor*

Diane Zimmerman, New York University School of Law, and Professor *Dennis Karjala*, Arizona State University College of Law, for amicus Copyright Law Professors.

OPINION

BEEZER, Circuit Judge. Plaintiffs are engaged in the commercial recording, distribution and sale of copyrighted musical compositions and sound recordings. The complaint alleges that Napster, Inc. ("Napster") is a contributory and vicarious copyright infringer. On July 26, 2000, the district court granted plaintiffs' motion for a preliminary injunction *[5 ILR (P&F) 663]*. The injunction was slightly modified by written opinion on August 10, 2000. *A&M Records, Inc. v. Napster, Inc.*, 114 F Supp 2d 896 *[5 ILR (P&F) 745]* (ND Cal. 2000). The district court preliminarily enjoined Napster "from engaging in, or facilitating others in copying, downloading, uploading, transmitting, or distributing plaintiffs' copyrighted musical compositions and sound recordings, protected by either federal or state law, without express permission of the rights owner." *Id.* at 927. Federal Rule of Civil Procedure 65(c) requires successful plaintiffs to post a bond for damages incurred by the enjoined party in the event that the injunction was wrongfully issued. The district court set bond in this case at $5 million.

We entered a temporary stay of the preliminary injunction pending resolution of this appeal. We have jurisdiction pursuant to 28 USC §1292(a)(1). We affirm in part, reverse in part and remand.

I

We have examined the papers submitted in support of and in response to the injunction application and it appears that Napster has designed and operates a system which permits the transmission and retention of sound recordings employing digital technology.

In 1987, the Moving Picture Experts Group set a standard file format for the storage of audio recordings in a digital format called MPEG-3, abbreviated as "MP3." Digital MP3 files are created through a process colloquially called "ripping." Ripping software allows a computer owner to copy an audio compact disk ("audio CD") directly onto a computer's hard drive by compressing the audio information on the CD into the MP3 format. The MP3's compressed format allows for rapid transmission of digital audio files from one computer to another by electronic mail or any other file transfer protocol.

Napster facilitates the transmission of MP3 files between and among its users. Through a process commonly called "peer-to-peer" file sharing, Napster allows its users to: (1) make MP3 music files stored on individual computer hard drives available for copying by other Napster users; (2) search for MP3 music files stored on other users' computers; and (3) transfer exact copies of the contents of other users' MP3 files from one computer to another via the Internet. These functions are made possible by Napster's MusicShare software, available free of charge from Napster's Internet site, and Napster's network servers and server-side software. Napster provides technical support for the indexing and searching of MP3 files, as well as for its other functions, including a "chat room," where users can meet to discuss music, and a directory where participating artists can provide information about their music.

A. Accessing the System

In order to copy MP3 files through the Napster system, a user must first access Napster's Internet site and download [1] the MusicShare software to his individual computer. *See http://www.Napster.com.* Once the software is installed, the user can access the Napster system. A first-time user is required to register with the Napster system by creating a "user name" and password.

B. Listing Available Files

If a registered user wants to list available files stored in his computer's hard drive on Napster for others to access, he must first create a "user library" directory on his computer's hard drive. The user then saves his MP3 files in the library directory, using self-designated file names. He next must log into the Napster system using his user name and password. His MusicShare software then searches his user library and verifies that the available files are properly formatted. If in the correct MP3 format, the names of the MP3 files will be uploaded from the user's computer to the Napster servers. The content of the MP3 files remains stored in the user's computer.

Once uploaded to the Napster servers, the user's MP3 file names are stored in a server-side "library" under the user's name and become part of a "collective directory" of files available for transfer during the time the user is logged onto the Napster system. The collective directory is fluid; it tracks users who are connected in real time, displaying only file names that are immediately accessible.

C. Searching For Available Files

Napster allows a user to locate other users' MP3 files in two ways: through Napster's search function and through its "hotlist" function.

Software located on the Napster servers maintains a "search index" of Napster's collective directory. To search the files available from Napster users currently connected to the network servers, the individual user accesses a form in the MusicShare software stored in his computer and enters either the name of a song or an artist as the object of the search. The form is then transmitted to a Napster server and automatically compared to the MP3 file names listed in the server's search index. Napster's server compiles a list of all MP3 file names pulled from the search index which include the same search terms entered on the search form and transmits the list to the searching user. The Napster server does not search the contents of any MP3 file; rather, the search is limited to "a text search of the file names indexed in a particular cluster. Those file names may contain typographical errors or otherwise inaccurate descriptions of the content of the files since they are designated by other users." *Napster*, 114 F Supp 2d at 906.

To use the "hotlist" function, the Napster user creates a list of other users' names from whom he has obtained MP3 files in the past. When logged onto Napster's servers, the system alerts the user if any user on his list (a "hotlisted user") is also logged onto the system. If so, the user can access an index of all MP3 file names in a particular hotlisted user's library and request a file in the library by selecting the file name. The contents of the hotlisted user's MP3 file are not stored on the Napster system.

D. Transferring Copies of an MP3 file

To transfer a copy of the contents of a requested MP3 file, the Napster server software obtains the Internet address of the requesting user and the Internet address of the "host user" (the user with the available files). *See generally Brookfield Communications, Inc. v. West Coast Entm't Corp.*, 174 F3d 1036, 1044 *[2 ILR (P&F) 492]* (9th Cir 1999) (describing, in detail, the structure of the

Internet). The Napster servers then communicate the host user's Internet address to the requesting user. The requesting user's computer uses this information to establish a connection with the host user and downloads a copy of the contents of the MP3 file from one computer to the other over the Internet, "peer-to-peer." A downloaded MP3 file can be played directly from the user's hard drive using Napster's MusicShare program or other software. The file may also be transferred back onto an audio CD if the user has access to equipment designed for that purpose. In both cases, the quality of the original sound recording is slightly diminished by transfer to the MP3 format.

This architecture is described in some detail to promote an understanding of transmission mechanics as opposed to the content of the transmissions. The content is the subject of our copyright infringement analysis.

II

We review a grant or denial of a preliminary injunction for abuse of discretion. *Gorbach v. Reno*, 219 F3d 1087, 1091 (9th Cir 2000) (*en banc*). Application of erroneous legal principles represents an abuse of discretion by the district court. *Rucker v. Davis*, __ F3d __, 2001 WL 55724, at *4 (9th Cir Jan. 24, 2001) (*en banc*). If the district court is claimed to have relied on an erroneous legal premise in reaching its decision to grant or deny a preliminary injunction, we will review the underlying issue of law *de novo. Id.* at *4 (citing *Does 1-5 v. Chandler*, 83 F3d 1150, 1152 (9th Cir 1996)).

On review, we are required to determine, "whether the court employed the appropriate legal standards governing the issuance of a preliminary injunction and whether the district court correctly apprehended the law with respect to the underlying issues in the case." *Id.* "As long as the district court got the law right, 'it will not be reversed simply because the appellate court would have arrived at a different result if it had applied the law to the facts of the case.' " *Gregorio T. v. Wilson*, 59 F3d 1002, 1004 (9th Cir 1995) (quoting *Sports Form, Inc. v. United Press, Int'l*, 686 F2d 750, 752 (9th Cir 1982)).

Preliminary injunctive relief is available to a party who demonstrates either: (1) a combination of probable success on the merits and the possibility of irreparable harm; or (2) that serious questions are raised and the balance of hardships tips in its favor. *Prudential Real Estate Affiliates, Inc. v. PPR Realty, Inc.*, 204 F3d 867, 874 (9th Cir 2000). "These two formulations represent two points on a sliding scale in which the required degree of irreparable harm increases as the probability of success decreases." *Id.*

III

Plaintiffs claim Napster users are engaged in the wholesale reproduction and distribution of copyrighted works, all constituting direct infringement.[2] The district court agreed. We note that the district court's conclusion that plaintiffs have presented a prima facie case of direct infringement by Napster users is not presently appealed by Napster. We only need briefly address the threshold requirements.

A. Infringement

Plaintiffs must satisfy two requirements to present a prima facie case of direct infringement: (1) they must show ownership of the allegedly infringed material and (2) they must demonstrate that the alleged infringers violate at least one exclusive right granted to copyright holders under 17 USC §106. *See* 17 USC §501(a) (infringement occurs when alleged infringer engages in activity listed in §106); *see also Baxter v. MCA, Inc.*, 812 F2d 421, 423 (9th Cir 1987); *see, e.g., S.O.S., Inc. v. Payday, Inc.*, 886 F2d 1081, 1085 n. 3 (9th Cir 1989) ("The word 'copying' is shorthand for the infringing of any of the copyright owner's five exclusive rights . . . ."). Plaintiffs have sufficiently demonstrated ownership. The record supports the district court's determination that "as much as eighty-seven percent of the files available on Napster may be copyrighted and more than seventy percent may be owned or administered by plaintiffs." *Napster*, 114 F Supp 2d at 911.

The district court further determined that plaintiffs' exclusive rights under §106 were violated: "here the evidence establishes that a majority of Napster users use the service to download and upload copyrighted music. . . . And by doing that, it constitutes—the uses constitute direct infringement of plaintiffs' musical compositions, recordings." *A&M Records, Inc. v. Napster, Inc.*, Nos. 99-5183, 00-0074, 2000 WL 1009483, at *1 *[5 ILR (P&F) 663]* (ND Cal. July 26, 2000) (transcript of proceedings). The district court also noted that "it is pretty much acknowledged . . . by Napster that this is infringement." *Id.* We agree that plaintiffs have shown that Napster users infringe at least two of the copyright holders' exclusive rights: the rights of reproduction, §106(1); and distribution, §106(3). Napster users who upload file names to the search index for others to copy violate plaintiffs' distribution rights. Napster users who download files containing copyrighted music violate plaintiffs' reproduction rights.

Napster asserts an affirmative defense to the charge that its users directly infringe plaintiffs' copyrighted musical compositions and sound recordings.

B. Fair Use

Napster contends that its users do not directly infringe plaintiffs' copyrights because the users are engaged in fair use of the material. *See* 17 USC §107 ("[T]he fair use of a copyrighted work . . . is not an infringement of copyright."). Napster identifies three specific alleged fair uses: sampling, where users make temporary copies of a work before purchasing; space-shifting, where users access a sound recording through the Napster system that they already own in audio CD format; and permissive distribution of recordings by both new and established artists.

The district court considered factors listed in 17 USC §107, which guide a court's fair use determination. These factors are: (1) the purpose and character of the use; (2) the nature of the copyrighted work; (3) the "amount and substantiality of the portion used" in relation to the work as a whole; and (4) the effect of the use upon the potential market for the work or the value of the work. *See* 17 USC §107. The district court first conducted a general analysis of Napster system uses under §107, and then applied its reasoning to the alleged fair uses identified by Napster. The district court concluded that Napster users are not fair users.[3] We agree. We first address the court's overall fair use analysis.

1. Purpose and Character of the Use

This factor focuses on whether the new work merely replaces the object of the original creation or instead adds a further purpose or different character. In other words, this factor asks "whether and to what extent the new work is 'transformative.' " *See Campbell v. Acuff-Rose Music, Inc.*, 510 US 569, 579 (1994).

The district court first concluded that downloading MP3 files does not transform the copyrighted work. *Napster*, 114 F Supp 2d at 912. This conclusion is supportable. Courts have been reluctant to find fair use when an original work is merely retransmitted in a different medium. *See, e.g., Infinity Broadcast Corp. v. Kirkwood*, 150 F3d 104, 108 (2d Cir 1994) (concluding that retransmission of radio broadcast over telephone lines is not transformative); *UMG Recordings, Inc. v. MP3.com, Inc.*, 92 F Supp 2d 349, 351 *[5 ILR (P&F) 415]* (SD NY) (finding that reproduction of audio CD into MP3 format does not "transform" the work), *certification denied*, 2000 WL 710056 (SD NY June 1, 2000) ("Defendant's copyright infringement was clear, and the mere fact that it was clothed in the exotic webbing of the Internet does not disguise its illegality.").

This "purpose and character" element also requires the district court to determine whether the allegedly infringing use is commercial or noncommercial. *See Campbell*, 510 US at 584-85. A commercial use weighs against a finding of fair use but is not conclusive on the issue. *Id.* The district court determined that Napster users engage in commercial use of the copyrighted materials largely because (1) "a host user sending a file cannot be said to engage in a personal use when distributing that file to an anonymous requester" and (2) "Napster users get for free something they would ordinarily have to buy." *Napster*, 114 F Supp 2d at 912. The district court's findings are not clearly erroneous.

Direct economic benefit is not required to demonstrate a commercial use. Rather, repeated and exploitative copying of copyrighted works, even if the copies are not offered for sale, may constitute a commercial use. *See Worldwide Church of God v. Philadelphia Church of God*, 227 F3d 1110, 1118 (9th Cir 2000) (stating that church that copied religious text for its members "unquestionably profit[ed]" from the unauthorized "distribution and use of [the text] without having to account to the copyright holder"); *American Geophysical Union v. Texaco, Inc.*, 60 F3d 913, 922 (2d Cir 1994) (finding that researchers at for-profit laboratory gained indirect economic advantage by photocopying copyrighted scholarly articles). In the

record before us, commercial use is demonstrated by a showing that repeated and exploitative unauthorized copies of copyrighted works were made to save the expense of purchasing authorized copies. *See Worldwide Church*, 227 F3d at 1117-18; *Sega Enters. Ltd. v. MAPHIA*, 857 F Supp 679, 687 (ND Cal. 1994) (finding commercial use when individuals downloaded copies of video games "to avoid having to buy video game cartridges"); *see also American Geophysical*, 60 F3d at 922. Plaintiffs made such a showing before the district court. [4]

We also note that the definition of a financially motivated transaction for the purposes of criminal copyright actions includes trading infringing copies of a work for other items, "including the receipt of other copyrighted works." *See No Electronic Theft Act ("NET Act")*, P.L. No. 105-147, 18 USC §101 (defining "Financial Gain").

2. The Nature of the Use

Works that are creative in nature are "closer to the core of intended copyright protection" than are more fact-based works. *See Campbell*, 510 US at 586. The district court determined that plaintiffs' "copyrighted musical compositions and sound recordings are creative in nature . . . which cuts against a finding of fair use under the second factor." *Napster*, 114 F Supp 2d at 913. We find no error in the district court's conclusion.

3. The Portion Used

"While 'wholesale copying does not preclude fair use per se,' copying an entire work 'militates against a finding of fair use.' " *Worldwide Church*, 227 F3d at 1118 (quoting *Hustler Magazine, Inc. v. Moral Majority, Inc.*, 796 F2d 1148, 1155 (9th Cir 1986)). The district court determined that Napster users engage in "wholesale copying" of copyrighted work because file transfer necessarily "involves copying the entirety of the copyrighted work." *Napster*, 114 F Supp 2d at 913. We agree. We note, however, that under certain circumstances, a court will conclude that a use is fair even when the protected work is copied in its entirety. *See, e.g., Sony Corp. v. Universal City Studios, Inc.*, 464 US 417, 449-50 (1984) (acknowledging that fair use of time-shifting necessarily involved making a full copy of a protected work).

4. Effect of Use on Market

"Fair use, when properly applied, is limited to copying by others which does not materially impair the marketability of the work which is copied." *Harper & Row Publishers, Inc. v. Nation Enters.*, 471 US 539, 566-67 (1985). "[T]he importance of this [fourth] factor will vary, not only with the amount of harm, but also with the relative strength of the showing on the other factors." *Campbell*, 510 US at 591 n. 21. The proof required to demonstrate present or future market harm varies with the purpose and character of the use:

> A challenge to a noncommercial use of a copyrighted work requires proof either that the particular use is harmful, or that if it should become widespread, it would adversely affect the potential market for the copyrighted work. . . . *If the intended use is for commercial gain, that likelihood [of market harm] may be presumed. But if it is for a noncommercial purpose, the likelihood must be demonstrated.*

Sony, 464 US at 451 (emphases added).

Addressing this factor, the district court concluded that Napster harms the market in "at least" two ways: it reduces audio CD sales among college students and it "raises barriers to plaintiffs' entry into the market for the digital downloading of music." *Napster*, 114 F Supp 2d at 913. The district court relied on evidence plaintiffs submitted to show that Napster use harms the market for their copyrighted musical compositions and sound recordings. In a separate memorandum and order regarding the parties' objections to the expert reports, the district court examined each report, finding some more appropriate and probative than others. *A&M Records, Inc. v. Napster, Inc.*, Nos. 99-5183 & 00-0074, 2000 WL 1170106 (ND Cal. August 10, 2000). Notably, plaintiffs' expert, Dr. E. Deborah Jay, conducted a survey (the "Jay Report") using a random sample of college and university students to track their reasons for using Napster and the impact Napster had on their music purchases. *Id.* at *2. The court recognized that the Jay Report focused on just one segment of the Napster user population and found "evidence of lost sales attributable to college use to be probative of irreparable harm for purposes of the preliminary injunction motion." *Id.* at *3.

Plaintiffs also offered a study conducted by Michael Fine, Chief Executive Officer of Soundscan, (the "Fine Report") to determine the effect of online sharing of MP3 files in order to show irreparable harm. Fine found that online file sharing had resulted in a loss of "album" sales within college markets. After reviewing defendant's objections to the Fine Report and expressing some concerns regarding the methodology and findings, the district court refused to exclude the Fine Report insofar as plaintiffs offered it to show irreparable harm. *Id.* at *6.

Plaintiffs' expert Dr. David J. Teece studied several issues ("Teece Report"), including whether plaintiffs had suffered or were likely to suffer harm in their existing and planned businesses due to Napster use. *Id.* Napster objected that the report had not undergone peer review. The district court noted that such reports generally are not subject to such scrutiny and overruled defendant's objections. *Id.*

As for defendant's experts, plaintiffs objected to the report of Dr. Peter S. Fader, in which the expert concluded that Napster is beneficial to the music industry because MP3 music file-sharing stimulates more audio CD sales than it displaces. *Id.* at *7. The district court found problems in Dr. Fader's minimal role in overseeing the administration of the survey and the lack of objective data in his report. The court decided the generality of the report rendered it "of dubious reliability and value." The court did not exclude the report, however, but chose "not to rely on Fader's findings in determining the issues of fair use and irreparable harm." *Id.* at *8.

The district court cited both the Jay and Fine Reports in support of its finding that Napster use harms the market for plaintiffs' copyrighted musical compositions and sound recordings by reducing CD sales among college students. The district court cited the Teece Report to show the harm Napster use caused in raising barriers to plaintiffs' entry into the market for digital downloading of music. *Napster*, 114 F Supp 2d at 910. The district court's careful consideration of defendant's objections to these reports and decision to rely on the reports for specific issues demonstrates a proper exercise of discretion in addition to a correct application of the fair use doctrine. Defendant has failed to show any basis for disturbing the district court's findings.

We, therefore, conclude that the district court made sound findings related to Napster's deleterious effect on the present and future digital download market. Moreover, lack of harm to an established market cannot deprive the copyright holder of the right to develop alternative markets for the works. *See L.A. Times v. Free Republic*, 54 USPQ 2d 1453, 1469-71 *[5 ILR (P&F) 4]* (CD Cal. 2000) (stating that online market for plaintiff newspapers' articles was harmed because plaintiffs demonstrated that "[defendants] are attempting to exploit the market for viewing their articles online"); *see also UMG Recordings*, 92 F Supp 2d at 352 ("Any allegedly positive impact of defendant's activities on plaintiffs' prior market in no way frees defendant to usurp a further market that directly derives from reproduction of the plaintiffs' copyrighted works."). Here, similar to *L.A. Times* and *UMG Recordings*, the record supports the district court's finding that the "record company plaintiffs have already expended considerable funds and effort to commence Internet sales and licensing for digital downloads." 114 F Supp 2d at 915. Having digital downloads available for free on the Napster system necessarily harms the copyright holders' attempts to charge for the same downloads.

Judge Patel did not abuse her discretion in reaching the above fair use conclusions, nor were the findings of fact with respect to fair use considerations clearly erroneous. We next address Napster's identified uses of sampling and space-shifting.

5. Identified Uses

Napster maintains that its identified uses of sampling and space-shifting were wrongly excluded as fair uses by the district court.

a. Sampling

Napster contends that its users download MP3 files to "sample" the music in order to decide whether to purchase the recording. Napster argues that the district court: (1) erred in concluding that sampling is a commercial use because it conflated a noncommercial use with a personal use; (2) erred in determining that sampling adversely affects the market for plaintiffs' copyrighted music, a requirement if the use is noncommercial; and (3) erroneously concluded that sampling is not a fair use because it determined that samplers may also engage in other infringing activity.

The district court determined that sampling remains a commercial use even if some users eventually purchase the music. We find no error in the district court's determination. Plaintiffs have established that they are likely to succeed in proving that even authorized temporary downloading of individual songs for sampling purposes is commercial in nature. *See Napster*, 114 F Supp 2d at 913. The record supports a finding that free promotional downloads are highly regulated by the record company plaintiffs and that the companies collect royalties for song samples available on retail Internet sites. *Id.* Evidence relied on by the district court demonstrates that the free downloads provided by the record companies consist of thirty-to-sixty second samples or are full songs programmed to "time out," that is, exist only for a short time on the downloader's computer. *Id.* at 913-14. In comparison, Napster users download a full, free and permanent copy of the recording. *Id.* at 914-15. The determination by the district court as to the commercial purpose and character of sampling is not clearly erroneous.

The district court further found that both the market for audio CDs and market for online distribution are adversely affected by Napster's service. As stated in our discussion of the district court's general fair use analysis: the court did not abuse its discretion when it found that, overall, Napster has an adverse impact on the audio CD and digital download markets. Contrary to Napster's assertion that the district court failed to specifically address the market impact of sampling, the district court determined that "[e]ven if the type of sampling supposedly done on Napster were a non-commercial use, plaintiffs have demonstrated a substantial likelihood that it would adversely affect the potential market for their copyrighted works if it became widespread." *Napster*, 114 F Supp 2d at 914. The record supports the district court's preliminary determinations that: (1) the more music that sampling users download, the less likely they are to eventually purchase the recordings on audio CD; and (2) even if the audio CD market is not harmed, Napster has adverse effects on the developing digital download market.

Napster further argues that the district court erred in rejecting its evidence that the users' downloading of "samples" increases or tends to increase audio CD sales. The district court, however, correctly noted that "any potential enhancement of plaintiffs' sales . . . would not tip the fair use analysis conclusively in favor of defendant." *Id.* at 914. We agree that increased sales of copyrighted material attributable to unauthorized use should not deprive the copyright holder of the right to license the material. *See Campbell*, 510 US at 591 n. 21 ("Even favorable evidence, without more, is no guarantee of fairness. Judge Leval gives the example of the film producer's appropriation of a composer's previously unknown song that turns the song into a commercial success; the boon to the song does not make the film's simple copying fair."); *see also L.A. Times*, 54 USPQ 2d at 1471-72. Nor does positive impact in one market, here the audio CD market, deprive the copyright holder of the right to develop identified alternative markets, here the digital download market. *See id.* at 1469-71.

We find no error in the district court's factual findings or abuse of discretion in the court's conclusion that plaintiffs will likely prevail in establishing that sampling does not constitute a fair use.

b. Space-Shifting

Napster also maintains that space-shifting is a fair use. Space-shifting occurs when a Napster user downloads MP3 music files in order to listen to music he already owns on audio CD. *See id.* at 915-16. Napster asserts that we have already held that space-shifting of musical compositions and sound recordings is a fair use. *See Recording Indus. Ass'n of Am. v. Diamond Multimedia Sys., Inc.*, 180 F3d 1072, 1079 *[3 ILR (P&F) 66]* (9th Cir 1999) ("Rio [a portable MP3 player] merely makes copies in order to render portable, or 'space-shift,' those files that already reside on a user's hard drive. . . . Such copying is a paradigmatic noncommercial personal use."). *See also generally Sony*, 464 US at 423 (holding that "time-shifting," where a video tape recorder owner records a television show for later viewing, is a fair use).

We conclude that the district court did not err when it refused to apply the "shifting" analyses of *Sony* and *Diamond*. Both *Diamond* and *Sony* are inapposite because the methods of shifting in these cases did not also simultaneously involve distribution of the copyrighted material to the general public; the time or space-shifting of copyrighted material exposed the material only to the original user. In *Diamond*, for example, the copyrighted music was transferred from the user's computer hard drive to the user's portable MP3 player. So too *Sony*, where "the majority of VCR purchasers . . . did not distribute taped television broadcasts, but merely enjoyed them at home." *Napster*, 114 F Supp 2d at 913. Conversely, it is obvious that once a user lists a copy of music he already owns on the Napster system in order to access the music from another location, the song becomes "available to millions of other individuals," not just the original CD owner. *See UMG Recordings*, 92 F Supp 2d at 351-52 (finding space-shifting of MP3 files not a fair use even when previous ownership is demonstrated before a download is allowed); cf. *Religious Tech. Ctr. v. Lerma*, No. 95-1107A, 1996 WL 633131, at *6 *[2 ILR (P&F) 158]* (ED Va. Oct. 4, 1996) (suggesting that storing copyrighted material on computer disk for later review is not a fair use).

c. Other Uses

Permissive reproduction by either independent or established artists is the final fair use claim made by Napster. The district court noted that plaintiffs did not seek to enjoin this and any other noninfringing use of the Napster system, including: chat rooms, message boards and Napster's New Artist Program. *Napster*, 114 F Supp 2d at 917. Plaintiffs do not challenge these uses on appeal.

We find no error in the district court's determination that plaintiffs will likely succeed in establishing that Napster users do not have a fair use defense. Accordingly, we next address whether Napster is secondarily liable for the direct infringement under two doctrines of copyright law: contributory copyright infringement and vicarious copyright infringement.

IV

We first address plaintiffs' claim that Napster is liable for contributory copyright infringement. Traditionally, "one who, with knowledge of the infringing activity, induces, causes or materially contributes to the infringing conduct of another, may be held liable as a 'contributory' infringer." *Gershwin Publ'g Corp. v. Columbia Artists Mgmt., Inc.*, 443 F2d 1159, 1162 (2d Cir 1971); *see also Fonovisa, Inc. v. Cherry Auction, Inc.*, 76 F3d 259, 264 (9th Cir 1996). Put differently, liability exists if the defendant engages in "personal conduct that encourages or assists the infringement." *Matthew Bender & Co. v. West Publ'g Co.*, 158 F3d 693, 706 (2d Cir 1998).

The district court determined that plaintiffs in all likelihood would establish Napster's liability as a contributory infringer. The district court did not err; Napster, by its conduct, knowingly encourages and assists the infringement of plaintiffs' copyrights.

A. Knowledge

Contributory liability requires that the secondary infringer "know or have reason to know" of direct infringement. *Cable/Home Communication Corp. Network Prods., Inc.*, 902 F2d 829, 845 & 846 n. 29 (11th Cir 1990); *Religious Tech. Ctr. v. Netcom On-Line Communication Servs., Inc.*, 907 F Supp 1361, 1373-74 *[1 ILR (P&F) 778]* (ND Cal. 1995) (framing issue as "whether Netcom knew or should have known of" the infringing activities). The district court found that Napster had both actual and constructive knowledge that its users exchanged copyrighted music. The district court also concluded that the law does not require knowledge of "specific acts of infringement" and rejected Napster's contention that because the company cannot distinguish infringing from noninfringing files, it does not "know" of the direct infringement. 114 F Supp 2d at 917.

It is apparent from the record that Napster has knowledge, both actual and constructive,[5] of direct infringement. Napster claims that it is nevertheless protected from contributory liability by the teaching of *Sony Corp. v. Universal City Studios, Inc.*, 464 US 417 (1984). We disagree. We observe that Napster's actual, specific knowledge of direct infringement renders Sony's holding of limited assistance to Napster. We are compelled to make a clear distinction between the architecture of the Napster system and Napster's conduct in relation to the operational capacity of the system.

The *Sony* Court refused to hold the manufacturer and retailers of video tape recorders liable for contributory infringement despite evidence that such machines could be and were used to infringe plaintiffs' copyrighted television shows. *Sony* stated that if liability "is to be imposed on petitioners in this case, it must rest on the fact that they have sold equipment with constructive knowledge of the fact that their customers may use that equipment to make unauthorized copies of copyrighted material." *Id.*

at 439 (emphasis added). The *Sony* Court declined to impute the requisite level of knowledge where the defendants made and sold equipment capable of both infringing and "substantial noninfringing uses." *Id.* at 442 (adopting a modified "staple article of commerce" doctrine from patent law). *See also Universal City Studios, Inc. v. Sony Corp.*, 480 F Supp 429, 459 (CD Cal. 1979) ("This court agrees with defendants that their knowledge was insufficient to make them contributory infringers."), *rev'd*, 659 F2d 963 (9th Cir 1981), *rev'd*, 464 US 417 (1984); Alfred C. Yen, Internet Service Provider Liability for Subscriber Copyright Infringement, Enterprise Liability, and the First Amendment, 88 Geo. L.J. 1833, 1874 & 1893 n. 210 (2000) (suggesting that, after *Sony*, most Internet service providers lack "the requisite level of knowledge" for the imposition of contributory liability).

We are bound to follow *Sony*, and will not impute the requisite level of knowledge to Napster merely because peer-to-peer file sharing technology may be used to infringe plaintiffs' copyrights. *See* 464 US at 436 (rejecting argument that merely supplying the "'means' to accomplish an infringing activity" leads to imposition of liability). We depart from the reasoning of the district court that Napster failed to demonstrate that its system is capable of commercially significant noninfringing uses. *See Napster*, 114 F Supp 2d at 916, 917-18. The district court improperly confined the use analysis to current uses, ignoring the system's capabilities. *See generally Sony*, 464 US at 442-43 (framing inquiry as whether the video tape recorder is "capable of commercially significant noninfringing uses") (emphasis added). Consequently, the district court placed undue weight on the proportion of current infringing use as compared to current and future noninfringing use. *See generally Vault Corp. v. Quaid Software Ltd.*, 847 F2d 255, 264-67 (5th Cir 1997) (single noninfringing use implicated Sony). Nonetheless, whether we might arrive at a different result is not the issue here. *See Sports Form, Inc. v. United Press Int'l, Inc.*, 686 F2d 750, 752 (9th Cir 1982). The instant appeal occurs at an early point in the proceedings and "the fully developed factual record may be materially different from that initially before the district court . . . ." *Id.* at 753. Regardless of the number of Napster's infringing versus noninfringing uses, the evidentiary record here supported the district court's finding that plaintiffs would likely prevail in establishing that Napster knew or had reason to know of its users' infringement of plaintiffs' copyrights.

This analysis is similar to that of *Religious Technology Center v. Netcom On-Line Communication Services, Inc.*, which suggests that in an online context, evidence of actual knowledge of specific acts of infringement is required to hold a computer system operator liable for contributory copyright infringement. 907 F Supp at 1371. *Netcom* considered the potential contributory copyright liability of a computer bulletin board operator whose system supported the posting of infringing material. *Id.* at 1374. The court, in denying *Netcom*'s motion for summary judgment of noninfringement and plaintiff's motion for judgment on the pleadings, found that a disputed issue of fact existed as to whether the operator had sufficient knowledge of infringing activity. *Id.* at 1374-75.

The court determined that for the operator to have sufficient knowledge, the copyright holder must "provide the necessary documentation to show there is likely infringement." 907 F Supp at 1374; cf. *Cubby, Inc. v. Compuserve, Inc.*, 776 F Supp 135, 141 *[1 ILR (P&F) 571]* (SD NY 1991) (recognizing that online service provider does not and cannot examine every hyperlink for potentially defamatory material). If such documentation was provided, the court reasoned that Netcom would be liable for contributory infringement because its failure to remove the material "and thereby stop an infringing copy from being distributed worldwide constitutes substantial participation" in distribution of copyrighted material. *Id.*

We agree that if a computer system operator learns of specific infringing material available on his system and fails to purge such material from the system, the operator knows of and contributes to direct infringement. *See Netcom*, 907 F Supp at 1374. Conversely, absent any specific information which identifies infringing activity, a computer system operator cannot be liable for contributory infringement merely because the structure of the system allows for the exchange of copyrighted material. *See Sony*, 464 US at 436, 442-43. To enjoin simply because a computer network allows for infringing use would, in our opinion, violate *Sony* and potentially restrict activity unrelated to infringing use.

We nevertheless conclude that sufficient knowledge exists to impose contributory liability when linked to demonstrated infringing use of the Napster system. *See Napster*, 114 F Supp 2d at 919 ("*Religious Technology Center* would not mandate a determination that Napster, Inc. lacks the knowledge requisite to contributory infringement."). The record supports the district court's finding that Napster has *actual* knowledge that *specific* infringing material is available using its system, that it could block access to the system by suppliers of the infringing material, and that it failed to remove the material. *See Napster*, 114 F Supp 2d at 918, 920-21.[6]

B. Material Contribution

Under the facts as found by the district court, Napster materially contributes to the infringing activity. Relying on *Fonovisa*, the district court concluded that "[w]ithout the support services defendant provides, Napster users could not find and download the music they want with the ease of which defendant boasts." *Napster*, 114 F Supp 2d at 919-20 ("Napster is an integrated service designed to enable users to locate and download MP3 music files."). We agree that Napster provides "the site and facilities" for direct infringement. *See Fonovisa*, 76 F3d at 264; cf. *Netcom*, 907 F Supp at 1372 ("Netcom will be liable for contributory infringement since its failure to cancel [a user's] infringing message and thereby stop an infringing copy from being distributed worldwide constitutes substantial participation."). The district court correctly applied the reasoning in *Fonovisa*, and properly found that Napster materially contributes to direct infringement.

We affirm the district court's conclusion that plaintiffs have demonstrated a likelihood of success on the merits of the contributory copyright infringement claim. We will address the scope of the injunction in part VIII of this opinion.

V

We turn to the question whether Napster engages in vicarious copyright infringement. Vicarious copyright liability is an "outgrowth" of respondeat superior. *Fonovisa*, 76 F3d at 262. In the context of copyright law, vicarious liability extends beyond an employer/employee relationship to cases in which a defendant "has the right and ability to supervise the infringing activity and also has a direct financial interest in such activities." *Id.* (quoting *Gershwin*, 443 F2d at 1162); *see also Polygram Int'l Publ'g, Inc. v. Nevada/TIG, Inc.*, 855 F Supp 1314, 1325-26 (D Mass. 1994) (describing vicarious liability as a form of risk allocation).

Before moving into this discussion, we note that *Sony*'s "staple article of commerce" analysis has no application to Napster's potential liability for vicarious copyright infringement. *See Sony*, 464 US at 434-435; *see generally* 3 Melville B. Nimmer & David Nimmer, *Nimmer on Copyright* §§ 12.04[A][2] & [A][2][b] (2000) (confining *Sony* to contributory infringement analysis: "Contributory infringement itself is of two types—personal conduct that forms part of or furthers the infringement and contribution of machinery or goods that provide the means to infringe"). The issues of *Sony*'s liability under the "doctrines of 'direct infringement' and 'vicarious liability' " were not before the Supreme Court, although the Court recognized that the "lines between direct infringement, contributory infringement, and vicarious liability are not clearly drawn." *Id.* at 435 n. 17. Consequently, when the *Sony* Court used the term "vicarious liability," it did so broadly and outside of a technical analysis of the doctrine of vicarious copyright infringement. *Id.* at 435 ("[V]icarious liability is imposed in virtually all areas of the law, and the concept of contributory infringement is merely a species of the broader problem of identifying the circumstances in which it is just to hold one individual accountable for the actions of another."); *see also Black's Law Dictionary* 927 (7th ed. 1999) (defining "vicarious liability" in a manner similar to the definition used in *Sony*).

A. Financial Benefit

The district court determined that plaintiffs had demonstrated they would likely succeed in establishing that *Napster* has a direct financial interest in the infringing activity. *Napster*, 114 F Supp 2d at 921-22. We agree. Financial benefit exists where the availability of infringing material "acts as a 'draw' for customers." *Fonovisa*, 76 F3d at 263-64 (stating that financial benefit may be shown "where infringing performances enhance the attractiveness of a venue"). Ample evidence supports the district court's finding that Napster's future revenue is directly dependent upon "increases in userbase." More users register with the Napster system as the "quality and quantity of available music increases." 114 F Supp 2d at 902. We conclude that the district court did not err in determining that Napster financially benefits from the availability of protected works on its system.

B. Supervision

The district court determined that Napster has the right and ability to supervise its users' conduct. *Napster*, 114 F Supp 2d at 920-21 (finding that Napster's representations to the court regarding "its improved methods of blocking users about whom rights holders complain . . . is tantamount to an admission that defendant can, and sometimes does, police its service"). We agree in part.

The ability to block infringers' access to a particular environment for any reason whatsoever is evidence of the right and ability to supervise. *See Fonovisa*, 76 F3d at 262 ("Cherry Auction had the right to terminate vendors for any reason whatsoever and through that right had the ability to control the activities of vendors on the premises."); cf. *Netcom*, 907 F Supp at 1375-76 (indicating that plaintiff raised a genuine issue of fact regarding ability to supervise by presenting evidence that an electronic bulletin board service can suspend subscriber's accounts). Here, plaintiffs have demonstrated that Napster retains the right to control access to its system. Napster has an express reservation of rights policy, stating on its website that it expressly reserves the "right to refuse service and terminate accounts in [its] discretion, including, but not limited to, if Napster believes that user conduct violates applicable law . . . or for any reason in Napster's sole discretion, with or without cause."

To escape imposition of vicarious liability, the reserved right to police must be exercised to its fullest extent. Turning a blind eye to detectable acts of infringement for the sake of profit gives rise to liability. *See, e.g., Fonovisa*, 76 F3d at 261 ("There is no dispute for the purposes of this appeal that Cherry Auction and its operators were aware that vendors in their swap meets were selling counterfeit recordings."); *see also Gershwin*, 443 F2d at 1161-62 (citing *Shapiro, Bernstein & Co. v. H.L. Greene Co.*, 316 F2d 304 (2d Cir 1963), for the proposition that "failure to police the conduct of the primary infringer" leads to imposition of vicarious liability for copyright infringement).

The district court correctly determined that Napster had the right and ability to police its system and failed to exercise that right to prevent the exchange of copyrighted material. The district court, however, failed to recognize that the boundaries of the premises that Napster "controls and patrols" are limited. *See, e.g., Fonovisa*, 76 F2d at 262-63 (in addition to having the right to exclude vendors, defendant "controlled and patrolled" the premises); *see also Polygram*, 855 F Supp at 1328-29 (in addition to having the contractual right to remove exhibitors, trade show operator reserved the right to police during the show and had its "employees walk the aisles to ensure 'rules compliance' "). Put differently, Napster's reserved "right and ability" to police is cabined by the system's current architecture. As shown by the record, the Napster system does not "read" the content of indexed files, other than to check that they are in the proper MP3 format.

Napster, however, has the ability to locate infringing material listed on its search indices, and the right to terminate users' access to the system. The file name indices, therefore, are within the "premises" that Napster has the ability to police. We recognize that the files are user-named and may not match copyrighted material exactly (for example, the artist or song could be spelled wrong). For Napster to function effectively, however, file names must reasonably or roughly correspond to the material contained in the files, otherwise no user could ever locate any desired music. As a practical matter, Napster, its users and the record company plaintiffs have equal access to infringing material by employing Napster's "search function."

Our review of the record requires us to accept the district court's conclusion that plaintiffs have demonstrated a likelihood of success on the merits of the vicarious copyright infringement claim. Napster's failure to police the system's "premises," combined with a showing that Napster financially benefits from the continuing availability of infringing files on its system, leads to the imposition of vicarious liability. We address the scope of the injunction in part VIII of this opinion.

VI

We next address whether Napster has asserted defenses which would preclude the entry of a preliminary injunction.

Napster alleges that two statutes insulate it from liability. First, Napster asserts that its users engage in actions protected by §1008 of the Audio Home Recording Act of 1992, 17 USC §1008. Second, Napster argues that its liability for contributory and vicarious infringement is limited by the Digital Millennium Copyright Act, 17 USC §512. We address the application of each statute in turn.

A. Audio Home Recording Act

The statute states in part:

No action may be brought under this title alleging infringement of copyright based on the manufacture, importation, or distribution of a digital audio recording device, a digital audio recording medium, an analog recording device, or an analog recording medium, or *based on the noncommercial use by a consumer of such a device or medium* for making digital musical recordings or analog musical recordings.

17 USC §1008 (emphases added). Napster contends that MP3 file exchange is the type of "noncommercial use" protected from infringement actions by the statute. Napster asserts it cannot be secondarily liable for users' nonactionable exchange of copyrighted musical recordings.

The district court rejected Napster's argument, stating that the Audio Home Recording Act is "irrelevant" to the action because: (1) plaintiffs did not bring claims under the Audio Home Recording Act; and (2) the Audio Home Recording Act does not cover the downloading of MP3 files. *Napster*, 114 F Supp 2d at 916 n. 19.

We agree with the district court that the Audio Home Recording Act does not cover the downloading of MP3 files to computer hard drives. First, "[u]nder the plain meaning of the Act's definition of digital audio recording devices, computers (and their hard drives) are not digital audio recording devices because their 'primary purpose' is not to make digital audio copied recordings." *Recording Indus. Ass'n of Am. v. Diamond Multimedia Sys., Inc.*, 180 F3d 1072, 1078 *[3 ILR (P&F) 66]* (9th Cir 1999). Second, notwithstanding Napster's claim that computers are "digital audio recording devices," computers do not make "digital music recordings" as defined by the Audio Home Recording Act. *Id.* at 1077 (citing S. Rep. 102-294) ("There are simply no grounds in either the plain language of the definition or in the legislative history for interpreting the term 'digital musical recording' to include songs fixed on computer hard drives.").

B. Digital Millennium Copyright Act

Napster also interposes a statutory limitation on liability by asserting the protections of the "safe harbor" from copyright infringement suits for "Internet service providers" contained in the Digital Millennium Copyright Act, 17 USC §512. *See Napster*, 114 F Supp 2d at 919 n. 24. The district court did not give this statutory limitation any weight favoring a denial of temporary injunctive relief. The court concluded that Napster "has failed to persuade this court that subsection 512(d) shelters contributory infringers." *Id.*

We need not accept a blanket conclusion that §512 of the Digital Millennium Copyright Act will never protect secondary infringers. *See* S. Rep. 105-190, at 40 (1998) ("The limitations in subsections (a) through (d) protect qualifying service providers from liability for all monetary relief for direct, vicarious, and contributory infringement."), *reprinted in* Melville B. Nimmer & David Nimmer, *Nimmer on Copyright: Congressional Committee Reports on the Digital Millennium Copyright Act and Concurrent Amendments (2000); see also* Charles S. Wright, *Actual Versus Legal Control: Reading Vicarious Liability for Copyright Infringement Into the Digital Millennium Copyright Act of 1998*, 75 Wash. L. Rev. 1005, 1028-31 (July 2000) ("[T]he committee reports leave no doubt that Congress intended to provide some relief from vicarious liability").

We do not agree that Napster's potential liability for contributory and vicarious infringement renders the Digital Millennium Copyright Act inapplicable per se. We instead recognize that this issue will be more fully developed at trial. At this stage of the litigation, plaintiffs raise serious questions regarding Napster's ability to obtain shelter under §512, and plaintiffs also demonstrate that the balance of hardships tips in their favor. *See Prudential Real Estate*, 204 F3d at 874; *see also Micro Star v. Formgen, Inc.* 154 F3d 1107, 1109 (9th Cir 1998) ("A party seeking a preliminary injunction must show . . . 'that serious questions going to the merits were raised and the balance of hardships tips sharply in its favor.' ").

Plaintiffs have raised and continue to raise significant questions under this statute, including: (1) whether Napster is an Internet service provider as defined by 17 USC §512(d); (2) whether copyright owners must give a service provider "official" notice of infringing activity in order for it to have knowledge or awareness of infringing activity on its system; and (3) whether Napster complies with §512(i), which requires a service provider to timely establish a detailed copyright compliance policy. *See A&M Records, Inc. v. Napster, Inc.*, No. 99-05183, 2000 WL 573136 (ND Cal. May 12, 2000) (denying summary judgment to Napster under a different subsection of the Digital Millennium Copyright Act, §512(a)).

The district court considered ample evidence to support its determination that the balance of hardships tips in plaintiffs' favor:

> Any destruction of Napster, Inc. by a preliminary injunction is speculative compared to the statistical evidence of massive, unauthorized downloading and uploading of plaintiffs' copyrighted works— as many as 10,000 files per second by defendant's own admission. *See* Kessler Dec. ¶29. The court has every reason to believe that, without a preliminary injunction, these numbers will mushroom as Napster users, and newcomers attracted by the publicity, scramble to obtain as much free music as possible before trial.

114 F Supp 2d at 926.

VII

Napster contends that even if the district court's preliminary determinations that it is liable for facilitating copyright infringement are correct, the district court improperly rejected valid affirmative defenses of waiver, implied license and copyright misuse. We address the defenses in turn.

A. Waiver

"Waiver is the intentional relinquishment of a known right with knowledge of its existence and the intent to relinquish it." *United States v. King Features Entm't, Inc.*, 843 F2d 394, 399 (9th Cir 1988). In copyright, waiver or abandonment of copyright "occurs only if there is an intent by the copyright proprietor to surrender rights in his work." 4 Melville B. Nimmer & David Nimmer, *Nimmer*

On Copyright ¶13.06 (2000); *see also Micro Star v. Formgen, Inc.*, 154 F3d 1107, 1114 (9th Cir 1998) (discussing abandonment).

Napster argues that the district court erred in not finding that plaintiffs knowingly provided consumers with technology designed to copy and distribute MP3 files over the Internet and, thus, waived any legal authority to exercise exclusive control over creation and distribution of MP3 files. The district court, however, was not convinced "that the record companies created the monster that is now devouring their intellectual property rights." *Napster*, 114 F Supp 2d at 924. We find no error in the district court's finding that "in hastening the proliferation of MP3 files, plaintiffs did [nothing] more than seek partners for their commercial downloading ventures and develop music players for files they planned to sell over the Internet." *Id.* [7]

B. Implied License

Napster also argues that plaintiffs granted the company an implied license by encouraging MP3 file exchange over the Internet. Courts have found implied licenses only in "narrow" circumstances where one party "created a work at [the other's] request and handed it over, intending that [the other] copy and distribute it." *SmithKline Beecham Consumer Healthcare, L.P. v. Watson Pharms., Inc.*, 211 F3d 21, 25 (2d Cir 2000) (quoting *Effects Assocs., Inc. v. Cohen*, 908 F2d 555, 558 (9th Cir 1990)), *cert. denied*, 121 S Ct 173 (2000). The district court observed that no evidence exists to support this defense: "indeed, the RIAA gave defendant express notice that it objected to the availability of its members' copyrighted music on Napster." *Napster*, 114 F Supp 2d at 924-25. The record supports this conclusion.

C. Misuse

The defense of copyright misuse forbids a copyright holder from "secur[ing] an exclusive right or limited monopoly not granted by the Copyright Office." *Lasercomb Am., Inc. v. Reynolds*, 911 F2d 970, 977-79 (4th Cir 1990), *quoted in Practice Mgmt. Info. Corp. v. American Med. Ass'n*, 121 F3d 516, 520 (9th Cir), *amended by* 133 F3d 1140 (9th Cir 1997). Napster alleges that online distribution is not within the copyright monopoly. According to Napster, plaintiffs have colluded to "use their copyrights to extend their control to online distributions."

We find no error in the district court's preliminary rejection of this affirmative defense. The misuse defense prevents copyright holders from leveraging their limited monopoly to allow them control of areas outside the monopoly. *See Lasercomb*, 911 F2d at 976-77; *see also Religious Tech. Ctr. v. Lerma*, No. 95-1107A, 1996 WL 633131, at *11 [2 ILR (P&F) 158]* (ED Va. Oct. 4, 1996) (listing circumstances which indicate improper leverage). [8] There is no evidence here that plaintiffs seek to control areas outside of their grant of monopoly. Rather, plaintiffs seek to control reproduction and distribution of their copyrighted works, exclusive rights of copyright holders. 17 USC §106; *see also, e.g., UMG Recordings*, 92 F Supp 2d at 351 ("A [copyright holder's] 'exclusive' rights, derived from the Constitution and the Copyright Act, include the right, within broad limits, to curb the development of such a derivative market by refusing to license a copyrighted work or by doing so only on terms the copyright owner finds acceptable."). That the copyrighted works are transmitted in another medium—MP3 format rather than audio CD—has no bearing on our analysis. *See id.* at 351 (finding that reproduction of audio CD into MP3 format does not "transform" the work).

VIII

The district court correctly recognized that a preliminary injunction against Napster's participation in copyright infringement is not only warranted but required. We believe, however, that the scope of the injunction needs modification in light of our opinion. Specifically, we reiterate that contributory liability may potentially be imposed only to the extent that Napster: (1) receives reasonable knowledge of specific infringing files with copyrighted musical compositions and sound recordings; (2) knows or should know that such files are available on the Napster system; and (3) fails to act to prevent viral distribution of the works. *See Netcom*, 907 F Supp at 1374-75. The mere existence of the Napster system, absent actual notice and Napster's demonstrated failure to remove the offending material, is insufficient to impose contributory liability. *See Sony*, 464 US at 442-43.

Conversely, Napster may be vicariously liable when it fails to affirmatively use its ability to patrol its system and preclude access to potentially infringing files listed in its search index. Napster has both the ability to use its search function to identify infringing musical recordings and the right to bar participation of users who engage in the transmission of infringing files.

The preliminary injunction which we stayed is overbroad because it places on Napster the entire burden of ensuring that no "copying, downloading, uploading, transmitting, or distributing" of plaintiffs' works occur on the system. As stated, we place the burden on plaintiffs to provide notice to Napster of copyrighted works and files containing such works available on the Napster system before Napster has the duty to disable access to the offending content. Napster, however, also bears the burden of policing the system within the limits of the system. Here, we recognize that this is not an exact science in that the files are user named. In crafting the injunction on remand, the district court should recognize that Napster's system does not currently appear to allow Napster access to users' MP3 files.

Based on our decision to remand, Napster's additional arguments on appeal going to the scope of the injunction need not be addressed. We, however, briefly address Napster's First Amendment argument so that it is not reasserted on remand. Napster contends that the present injunction violates the First Amendment because it is broader than necessary. The company asserts two distinct free speech rights: (1) its right to publish a "directory" (here, the search index) and (2) its users' right to exchange information. We note that First Amendment concerns in copyright are allayed by the presence of the fair use doctrine. *See* 17 USC §107; *see generally Nihon Keizai Shimbun v. Comline Business Data, Inc.*, 166 F.3d 65, 74 (2d Cir 1999); *Netcom*, 923 F Supp at 1258 (stating that the Copyright Act balances First Amendment concerns with the rights of copyright holders). There was a preliminary determination here that Napster users are not fair users. Uses of copyrighted material that are not fair uses are rightfully enjoined. *See Dr. Seuss Enters. v. Penguin Books USA, Inc.*, 109 F.3d 1394, 1403 (9th Cir 1997) (rejecting defendants' claim that injunction would constitute a prior restraint in violation of the First Amendment).

IX

We address Napster's remaining arguments: (1) that the court erred in setting a $5 million bond, and (2) that the district court should have imposed a constructive royalty payment structure in lieu of an injunction.

A. Bond

Napster argues that the $5 million bond is insufficient because the company's value is between $1.5 and $2 billion. We review objections to the amount of a bond for abuse of discretion. *Walczak v. EPL Prolong, Inc.*, 198 F3d 725 (9th Cir 1999).

We are reluctant to dramatically raise bond amounts on appeal. *See GoTo.com, Inc. v. The Walt Disney Co.*, 202 F3d 1199, 1211 *[4 ILR (P&F) 393]* (9th Cir 2000); *see also* Fed. R. Civ. P. 65(c). The district court considered competing evidence of Napster's value and the deleterious effect that any injunction would have upon the Napster system. We cannot say that Judge Patel abused her discretion when she fixed the penal sum required for the bond.

B. Royalties

Napster contends that the district court should have imposed a monetary penalty by way of a compulsory royalty in place of an injunction. We are asked to do what the district court refused.

Napster tells us that "where great public injury would be worked by an injunction, the courts might . . . award damages or a continuing royalty instead of an injunction in such special circumstances." *Abend v. MCA, Inc.*, 863 F2d 1465, 1479 (9th Cir 1988) (quoting 3 Melville B. Nimmer & David Nimmer, *Nimmer On Copyright* §14.06[B] (1988)), *aff'd*, 495 US 207 (1990). We are at a total loss to find any "special circumstances" simply because this case requires us to apply well-established doctrines of copyright law to a new technology. Neither do we agree with Napster that an injunction would cause "great public injury." Further, we narrowly construe any suggestion that compulsory royalties are appropriate in this context because Congress has arguably limited the application of compulsory royalties to specific circumstances, none of which are present here. *See* 17 USC §115.

The Copyright Act provides for various sanctions for infringers. *See, e.g.,* 17 USC §§502 (injunctions); 504 (damages); and 506 (criminal penalties); *see also* 18 USC §2319A (criminal penalties for the unauthorized fixation of and trafficking in sound recordings and music videos of live musical performances). These statutory sanctions represent a more than adequate legislative solution to the problem created by copyright infringement.

Imposing a compulsory royalty payment schedule would give Napster an "easy out" of this case. If such royalties were imposed, Napster would avoid penalties for any future violation of an injunction, statutory copyright damages and any possible criminal penalties for continuing infringement. The royalty structure would also grant Napster the luxury of either choosing to continue and pay royalties or shut down. On the other hand, the wronged parties would be forced to do business with a company that profits from the wrongful use of intellectual properties. Plaintiffs would lose the power to control their intellectual property: they could not make a business decision *not* to license their property to Napster, and, in the event they planned to do business with Napster, compulsory royalties would take away the copyright holders' ability to negotiate the terms of any contractual arrangement.

X

We affirm in part, reverse in part and remand.

We direct that the preliminary injunction fashioned by the district court prior to this appeal shall remain stayed until it is modified by the district court to conform to the requirements of this opinion. We order a partial remand of this case on the date of the filing of this opinion for the limited purpose of permitting the district court to proceed with the settlement and entry of the modified preliminary injunction.

Even though the preliminary injunction requires modification, appellees have substantially and primarily prevailed on appeal. Appellees shall recover their statutory costs on appeal. *See* Fed. R. App. P. 39(a)(4) ("[i]f a judgment is affirmed in part, reversed in part, modified, or vacated, costs are taxed only as the court orders.").

AFFIRMED IN PART, REVERSED IN PART AND REMANDED.

---

[1] "To download means to receive information, typically a file, from another computer to yours via your modem . . . . The opposite term is upload, which means to send a file to another computer." *United States v. Mohrbacher*, 182 F3d 1041, 1048 *[3 ILR (P&F) 165]*

(9th Cir 1999) (quoting Robin Williams, Jargon, An Informal Dictionary of Computer Terms 170-71 (1993)).

[2] Secondary liability for copyright infringement does not exist in the absence of direct infringement by a third party. *Religious Tech. Ctr. v. Netcom On-Line Communication Servs., Inc.*, 907 F Supp 1361, 1371 *[1 ILR (P&F) 778]* (ND Cal. 1995) ("[T]here can be no contributory infringement by a defendant without direct infringement by another."). It follows that Napster does not facilitate infringement of the copyright laws in the absence of direct infringement by its users.

[3] Napster asserts that because plaintiffs seek injunctive relief, they have the burden of showing a likelihood that they would prevail against any affirmative defenses raised by Napster, including its fair use defense under 17 USC §107. *See Atari Games Corp. v. Nintendo*, 975 F2d 832, 837 (Fed. Cir 1992) (following Ninth Circuit law, and stating that plaintiff must show likelihood of success on *prima facie* copyright infringement case and likelihood that it would overcome copyright misuse defense); *see also Dr. Seuss Enters. v. Penguin Books USA*, 924 F Supp 1559, 1562 (SD Cal. 1996) ("The plaintiff's burden of showing a likelihood of success on the merits includes the burden of showing a likelihood that it would prevail against any affirmative defenses raised by the defendant."), *aff'd*, 109 F3d 1394 (9th Cir 1997); *Religious Tech. Ctr. v. Netcom On-Line Communication Servs.*, 923 F Supp 1231, 1242 n. 12 (1995) (same); 2 William W. Schwarzer *et al.*, *California Practice Guide, Federal Civil Procedure Before Trial* ¶13:47 (2000) (advising that when a preliminary injunction is sought "plaintiff must demonstrate a likelihood of prevailing on any affirmative defense as well as on plaintiff's case in chief"). *But see Fair Use of Copyrighted Works*, H.R. Rep. 102-836 n. 3 (criticizing a Northern District of New York case in which "the district court erroneously held that where the copyright owner seeks a preliminary injunction, the copyright owner bears the burden of disproving the [fair use] defense"); *see also* 1 William F. Patry, *Copyright Law & Practice*, 725, 725 n. 27 (1994) (citing cases placing burden on defendant at preliminary injunction stage).

The district court stated that "defendant bears the burden of proving . . . affirmative defenses." *Napster*, 114 F Supp 2d at 912. Plaintiffs assert that the district court did not err in placing the burden on Napster. We conclude that even if plaintiffs bear the burden of establishing that they would likely prevail against Napster's affirmative defenses at the preliminary injunction stage, the record supports the district court's conclusion that Napster users do not engage in fair use of the copyrighted materials.

[4] Napster counters that even if certain users engage in commercial use by downloading instead of purchasing

the music, space-shifting and sampling are nevertheless *non*commercial in nature. We address this contention in our discussion of these specific uses, *infra*.

⁵ The district court found actual knowledge because: (1) a document authored by Napster co-founder Sean Parker mentioned "the need to remain ignorant of users' real names and IP addresses 'since they are exchanging pirated music' "; and (2) the Recording Industry Association of America ("RIAA") informed Napster of more than 12,000 infringing files, some of which are still available. 114 F Supp 2d at 918. The district court found constructive knowledge because: (a) Napster executives have recording industry experience; (b) they have enforced intellectual property rights in other instances; (c) Napster executives have downloaded copyrighted songs from the system; and (d) they have promoted the site with "screen shots listing infringing files." *Id.* at 919.

⁶ As stated by the district court:

Plaintiff[s] . . . demonstrate that defendant had actual notice of direct infringement because the RIAA informed it of more than 12,000 infringing files. *See* Creighton 12/3/99 Dec., Exh. D. Although Napster, Inc. purportedly terminated the users offering these files, the songs are still available using the Napster service, as are the copyrighted works which the record company plaintiffs identified in Schedules A and B of their complaint. *See* Creighton Supp. Dec. PP 3-4.

114 F Supp 2d at 918.

⁷ Napster additionally asserts that the district court improperly refused to allow additional discovery into affirmative defenses and also erroneously failed to hold an evidentiary hearing. The denial of an evidentiary hearing is reviewed for abuse of discretion, *Kenneally v. Lungren*, 967 F2d 329, 335 (9th Cir 1992), as is the court's decision to deny further discovery. *See Sablan v. Dep't of Finance*, 856 F2d 1317, 1321 (9th Cir 1988) (stating that decision to deny discovery will not be disturbed except upon a clear showing "that the denial of discovery results in actual and substantial prejudice"). We conclude that the court did not abuse its discretion in denying further discovery and refusing to conduct an evidentiary hearing.

⁸ The district court correctly stated that "most of the cases" that recognize the affirmative defense of copyright misuse involve unduly restrictive licensing schemes. *See Napster*, 114 F Supp 2d at 923; *see also Lasercomb*, 911 F2d at 973 (stating that "a misuse of copyright defense is inherent in the law of copyright"). We have also suggested, however, that a unilateral refusal to license a copyright may constitute wrongful exclusionary conduct giving rise to a claim of misuse,

but assume that the "desire to exclude others . . . is a presumptively valid business justification for any immediate harm to consumers." *See Image Tech. Servs. v. Eastman Kodak Co.*, 125 F3d 1195, 1218 (9th Cir 1997). *But see Intergraph Corp. v. Intel Corp.*, 195 F3d 1346, 1362 (Fed. Cir 1999) ("[M]arket power does not 'impose on the intellectual property owner an obligation to license the use of that property to others.' " (quoting United States Dep't of Justice & Fed. Trade Comm'n, *Antitrust Guidelines for the Licensing of Intellectual Property* 4 (1995)).

In re Aimster Copyright Litigation

United States District Court,
Northern District of Illinois

September 4, 2002

11 ILR (P&F) 786, 2002 ILRWeb (P&F) 1899, 2002 WL 31006142

Master File No. 01 C 8933

AHRA not an affirmative defense to P2P service's liability for copyright infringement.

The Audio Home Recording Act (AHRA), which forbids actions based on the noncommercial use of a device to record digital or analog musical recordings, does not shield the operator of a peer-to-peer file-sharing service (Aimster) from liability for vicarious and contributory copyright infringement. The ongoing, massive, and unauthorized distribution and copying of plaintiffs' copyrighted works by Aimster's users does not constitute "personal use" within the meaning of the AHRA. [Distinguishing *RIAA v. Diamond Multimedia Systems, Inc.*, 3 ILR (P&F) 66.] — **In re Aimster Copyright Litigation, 11 ILR (P&F) 786 [ND Ill, 2002].**

Likely success on contributory infringement claim against Aimster.

Record companies and music publishers that brought suit against the operator of a peer-to-peer file-sharing service (Aimster) are likely to succeed on the merits of their claim of contributory copyright infringement, given the overwhelming evidence that Aimster knew of the direct infringement of its users. Although Aimster's system encrypts the data sent between users' computers so that Aimster is unaware of which users are transferring which files, there is no indication that such specificity of knowledge is required in the contributory infringement context. It is disingenuous of Aimster to suggest that it lacks the requisite level of knowledge when its putative ignorance is due entirely to an encryption scheme that Aimster itself put in place. In any event, the encryption scheme would not prevent Aimster from having constructive knowledge. Moreover, Aimster has materially contributed to the infringement by providing the software and support services necessary for individual users to connect with each other. Although Aimster argues that its service is capable of substantial non-infringing uses as identified by the Supreme Court in its *Sony* decision, *Sony* is distinguishable: (1) whereas *Sony* found that the *principal* use of video recorders was non-infringing, Aimster has provided no evidence that its service is *actually* used for non-infringing purposes; (2) *Sony* applies only to a "staple article of commerce," which Aimster is not; (3) nothing suggests that *Sony* extends to protect the unauthorized and widespread *distribution* of infringing works; (4) *Sony*'s protection is not available when the product at issue is specifically manufactured for infringing activity; and (5) the defendant in *Sony* had not influenced or encouraged unlawful copying. — **In re Aimster Copyright Litigation, 11 ILR (P&F) 786 [ND Ill, 2002].**

Likely success on vicarious infringement claim against Aimster.

Record companies and music publishers that brought suit against the operator of a peer-to-peer file-sharing service (Aimster) are likely to succeed on the merits of their claim of vicarious copyright infringement. Evidence shows that Aimster has the right and ability to supervise infringing activity and that it has a direct financial interest in such activities. Aimster's own posted Terms of Service state that Aimster will "take down" "infringing material" and that repeat violators of copyright law "may have their access to all services terminated." Inasmuch as each user must pay a $4.95 monthly fee, Aimster's direct financial interest in the infringing activities is without question. The financial benefit element is also satisfied where, as here, the existence of infringing activities act as a draw for potential customers. — **In re Aimster Copyright Litigation, 11 ILR (P&F) 786 [ND Ill, 2002].**

Unclean hands no defense to entry of injunction against Aimster.

The doctrine of unclean hands would not prevent plaintiff record companies and music publishers from securing a preliminary injunction against the operator of a peer-to-peer file-sharing service (Aimster). Aimster argued that America Online's Instant Messaging (IM) service permits the same type of file-sharing service as Aimster, but AOL's conduct is not relevant to the case. First, Aimster and AOL IM are quite difference services. More importantly, however, AOL is not even a party to the suit. Although AOL shares a common corporate parent with one of the record companies, no authority suggests that where multiple plaintiffs are seeking equitable relief, the unclean hands of one plaintiff should serve to prevent all of the other plaintiffs from receiving their due relief. — **In re Aimster Copyright Litigation, 11 ILR (P&F) 786 [ND Ill, 2002].**

Failure to implement repeat infringer policy prevents application of DMCA safe harbor.

The operator of a peer-to-peer file-sharing service (Aimster) cannot escape liability for contributory or vicarious copyright infringement under the safe harbor provisions of the Digital Millennium Copyright Act (DMCA) because it fails to satisfy the threshold requirements of 17 USC §512(i). Although Aimster fits within the statutory definition of a "service provider," and although it has adopted a repeat infringer policy, it has failed to reasonably implement that policy. Aimster, in fact, acknowledges that its policy *cannot* be implemented because of an encryption system built into its system that prevents Aimster from knowing which users are transferring which files. Adopting a repeat infringer policy and then purposely eviscerating any hope that such a policy could ever be carried out is not an "implementation" as required by §512(i) of the DMCA. Consequently, Aimster's failure to comply with the threshold requirements of §512(i) renders it ineligible for any of the DMCA's safe harbor protections. — **In re Aimster Copyright Litigation, 11 ILR (P&F) 786 [ND Ill, 2002].**

Aimster does not qualify for protections of DMCA safe harbor.

Even if the operator of a peer-to-peer file-sharing service (Aimster) were able to satisfy the threshold requirements of 17 USC §512(i), it nevertheless would not escape liability for contributory or vicarious copyright infringement under any of the relevant safe harbor provisions of the Digital Millennium Copyright Act (DMCA). Specifically, Aimster would not qualify for the transitory communications safe harbor, §512(a), because that provision requires the infringing material to be routed or transmitted *through* a system. As a true peer-to-peer service, Aimster allows the transfer of information between individual users; it does not pass "through" Aimster at all. Nor does Aimster qualify for the system caching safe harbor, §512(b)(1), which limits liability only that may arise "by reason of" the caching of material. Aimster also fails to meet the conditions of the Information Location Tools Safe Harbor, 17 USC §512(d), because Aimster has actual and constructive knowledge of the infringing activity and because Aimster receives a financial benefit. — **In re Aimster Copyright Litigation, 11 ILR (P&F) 786 [ND Ill, 2002].**

Delay in seeking injunction against Aimster not unreasonable.

Copyright holders' delay in seeking to enjoin the operator of a peer-to-peer file-sharing service (Aimster) from continuing its operations was not unreasonable and is not enough to rebut the presumption of irreparable harm. Although plaintiffs first became aware of Aimster's service 17 months prior to seeking the injunction, they sent a cease-and-desist letter to Aimster within eight months' time. Aimster cannot therefore claim that it had been lulled into a false sense of security after receipt of the cease-and-desist letter. As to the period prior to that letter, Aimster's system had been plagued with technical glitches, making it impossible for plaintiffs to pass judgment on Aimster's activities. — **In re Aimster Copyright Litigation, 11 ILR (P&F) 786 [ND Ill, 2002].**

Preliminary injunction against Aimster P2P service.

The operator of a peer-to-peer file-sharing service (Aimster) is preliminarily enjoined from continuing contributory infringement of plaintiffs' copyrighted sound recordings. The balance of the hardships tips in plaintiffs' favor, given the exceptionally strong likelihood of plaintiffs' success on the merits. The court rejects Aimster's argument that an injunction will put it out of business. If the court were to accept the going-out-of-business argument, a blatant copyright infringer would be encouraged to go into an infringing business because it can later argue to a court that enjoining the blatant infringement would sink the business. The court also rejects Aimster's argument that since it represents a small portion of the total amount of the file-sharing traffic on the Internet, plaintiffs would not suffer any hardship without an injunction. This argument is specious, given the unrebutted presumption of irreparable harm. — **In re Aimster Copyright Litigation, 11 ILR (P&F) 786 [ND Ill, 2002].**

MEMORANDUM OPINION AND ORDER

MARVIN E. ASPEN, *Chief Judge*: On November 17, 2001, the Judicial Panel on Multidistrict Litigation consolidated eleven cases in this court for pretrial proceedings under Multi-District Litigation number 1425 (master file 01-c-8933). Presently before us is a joint motion for preliminary injunction filed by several of those Plaintiffs (from cases 01-c-8940, 01-c-8941, and 01-c-8942) against the owner and operator of an Internet file sharing service called Aimster.[1] At issue is a service whose very *raison d'etre* appears to be the facilitation of and contribution to copyright infringement on a massive scale. Plaintiffs seek an injunction to prevent the contributory and vicarious infringement of their copyrighted works on Defendants' system and, for the following reasons, we grant their motion.

I. FACTUAL BACKGROUND

A. Defendants

Aimster is a file sharing service that allows its members to identify large numbers of similarly situated users with whom they can transfer files in encrypted form and send instant messages. Aimster is the brain child of Defendant John A. Deep, who also founded Defendant BuddyUSA, Inc. ("BuddyUSA") to develop the software and Defendant AbovePeer, Inc. ("AbovePeer") to operate the system (collectively, "Defendants"). Deep Decl. ¶2, n.1[2]; Pla. Brief at 3. Deep is the President and Chief Executive Officer of AbovePeer. Deep Decl. ¶1.

B. Plaintiffs

The instant joint motion for preliminary injunction was filed by three sets of plaintiffs from three of the eleven cases currently pending under this multidistrict litigation. Most of the plaintiffs can be grouped into two broad categories. First, a number of plaintiffs representing various record companies (the "Record Company Plaintiffs") have invested substantial time, money, and resources to create, produce, manufacture, and sell recorded music. The myriad Record Company Plaintiffs (including, *inter alia*, BMG Music, Capitol Records, Inc., and New Line Cinema Corporation) own or control the copyrights in their sound recordings and are listed in an Appendix attached to Plaintiffs' Brief. Pla. Brief at 2. The Record Company Plaintiffs are each a member of the Recording Industry Association of America, Inc. ("RIAA"), a trade organization whose members account for approximately 90% of the sound recordings produced, manufactured, or distributed in the United States. Creighton Decl. ¶2. The second broad group of plaintiffs includes a number of songwriters and music publishers (the "Music Publisher Plaintiffs," including, *inter alia*, Jerry Lieber Music, Mike Stoller Music, and Famous Music Corporation) who compose and publish musical compositions and own the copyrights to the underlying music and lyrics of those musical works. The Music Publisher Plaintiffs own or control the copyrights to some very recognizable musical compositions, including "Jailhouse Rock," "My Favorite Things," and "Moon River."[3]

Together, the Music Publisher Plaintiffs and the Record Company Plaintiffs own or license the copyrights to a vast repository of music, including hit music by hugely popular artists like Madonna, Garth Brooks, the Backstreet Boys, the Beatles and Bob Dylan. Pla. Brief at 2. *See, e.g.,* Cotrell Decl. ¶¶3-6 (attaching many examples of Certificates of Copyright Registration on behalf of EMI Music Distribution); Eisenberg Decl. ¶¶3-6 (attaching many examples of Certificates of Copyright Registration on behalf of Sony Music); Ostroff Decl. ¶¶3-6 (attaching many examples of Certificates of Copyright Registration on behalf of Universal Music Group). According to Plaintiffs, the vast majority of their copyrighted musical works are available on the Aimster system for unauthorized transfer among its users in the manner described below. The Music Publisher Plaintiffs bring suit based upon the alleged infringement of underlying music and lyrics of their copyrighted songs. The Record Company Plaintiffs bring suit based upon their copyrighted sound recordings.

C. General Background

Some of the basic technology underlying the present dispute is a matter of common knowledge and has been the subject of extensive factual findings by other courts. As such, it is not necessary to go into a detailed explanation of the nature and inner workings of the Internet, the World Wide Web, and digital compression technology (such as the widely used MP3 format). A full description can be found, by way of example, in *A&M Records, Inc. v. Napster, Inc.*, 114 F Supp 2d 896 *[5 ILR (P&F) 745]* (ND Ca 2000) ("*Napster I*"),[4] *RIAA v. Diamond Multimedia Systems, Inc.*, 180 F3d 1072 *[3 ILR (P&F) 66]* (9th Cir 1999) ("*Diamond Multimedia*"), or *Reno v. American Civil Liberties Union*, 521 US 844 *[1 ILR (P&F) 1]* (1997).

Before delving into a full description of the Aimster service, it is useful to describe some underlying concepts and technology. The first of such concepts is instant messaging. Instant messaging ("IM") is a way for people to communicate instantly over the computer to one or more 'buddies' that they specify. *See generally,* Mujica Decl. ¶¶5-7. There are several different IM networks, including America Online's Instant Messenger ("AOL IM"), ICQ, and Yahoo IM. Instant Messaging works through the use of a computer program that each individual user downloads to his or her machine. With the program installed, the computer connects to the IM network and the user can specify friends that also have the IM program installed on their computers. The system then alerts the user in real time whenever those friends are online. When a friend is online, the user can send that person an instant message that will pop up on their screen. The users can then chat back and forth in real time using their keyboards. As such, instant messaging is much faster than e-mail. An instant message pops up on the screen unbidden as soon as it is sent from a friend's computer.

AOL IM also has a feature that allows buddies to transfer files to each other.[5] There are two ways a AOL IM user can transfer files: by using a file transfer or AOL IM's "get file" functionality. A simple file transfer on AOL IM requires a user to specify a file on his hard drive to send to one of his IM buddies. The buddy, after signaling his acceptance of the transfer, would then receive the file onto his hard drive. This method of file transfer can be used to send any kind of files over the AOL IM network, including documents, digital pictures, and MP3 music.

Another aspect of AOL IM's file transfer feature is the "get file" functionality. This function is the ability of a user to specify certain files or directories that are available for other users to freely take at their leisure. So, for instance, if an AOL IM user wanted to allow his friends to download any of the pictures located on his computer, he would simply specify to the AOL IM program that those buddies have access to those files. Anytime thereafter, the buddies could retrieve those files. That is, the user does not have to actually send those files to his buddies; the buddies could, rather, retrieve the files for themselves. According to Raul Mujica, Vice President and General Manager of the AOL service, AOL IM's "get file" functionality is limited in two respects. First, an AOL IM user can only access the files of an AOL IM user whose identity (or unique screen name) is already known to that user. Second, since AOL IM has no capability to search the files of other users, the user must know the particular file that is being sought from the other user's hard drive before that file can be fetched. Mujica Decl. ¶10. There is dispute between the parties as to the real differences between AOL IM's file transfer functionality and the functionality of Aimster. An analysis of that dispute can be found in Section III.B.4 below.

D. The Aimster Service

1. Basic Operations

According to Deep, Aimster performs two fundamental functions. *See generally,* Deep Decl. ¶¶4-6. First, it allows its users to send messages or transfer files to other users by facilitating the creation of direct user-to-user (or peer-to-peer) networks. Through the use of encryption technology contained within the Aimster software, the individual users are assured of complete privacy in their online transaction. In particular, Deep claims that Defendants have no knowledge whatsoever of when its users are exchanging files, who are exchanging files, or what files are being exchanged. Deep Decl. ¶4. Aimster encrypts all the information that is transferred between its users on their private networks. Even the identities of such users are encrypted. Deep Decl. ¶8. While Deep admits that Aimster can be used to transfer musical works (just as it can be used to transfer any other information or data) from one user to another, the subject matter of the transfer and the recipient are determined entirely by the users themselves. Deep Decl. ¶10. In short, Defendants go to great pains to characterize the Aimster service as merely an innocent provider of "infrastructure services" to end users, id., with the implication being that Aimster is not and should not be held responsible for the malfeasance, if any, of its end users. According to Deep, virtually all "of the copyrighted musical works that Plaintiffs claim are being infringed by Defendants are songs that are transferred by individual users from one hard drive to another using Aimster solely as an internet service provider, in much the same way that such files can be and are transferred on AOL and other internet service providers." Deep Decl. ¶22.

Aimster's second fundamental function, according to Deep, is to allow users to identify other "buddies" who have similar interests and who may wish to correspond and exchange files. Deep Decl. ¶5. Users of the Aimster system locate buddies by searching the user profiles on the system. The user profile identifies other users by subject matter of interest or "by the name of the file or files that user has available on his or her hard drive." Id.

If Deep's declaration were the only means by which we could evaluate the Aimster system, we might be convinced that it is as innocent as Defendants claim. Unfortunately for Defendants, however, Plaintiffs have submitted numerous declarations to demonstrate that Deep's description of the Aimster service is less than complete.

Plaintiffs' characterization of the Aimster service is understandably more sinister than Deep's: "Aimster is a highly integrated system that connects people throughout the world (who otherwise would likely have no contact with one another) and *encourages* and *enables* them to make their music files, among other copyrighted works, available for copying and distribution in a single database index."

Creighton Decl. ¶3 (emphasis supplied). [6] The following description of the Aimster system (from Plaintiffs' perspective) is culled from the declarations of several individuals. *See* Creighton Decl. (from the RIAA); Farmer Decl. (Plaintiffs' independent computer expert); Forrest Decl. (Plaintiffs' attorney attaching hundreds of pages of screen shots from the Aimster system in action); Schafer Decl. (Plaintiff paralegal attaching screen shots of Aimster message boards and chat rooms); Cheng Decl. (Plaintiffs' attorney attaching Certificates of Copyright Registration and Aimster screen shots showing each corresponding copyrighted song available for download).

In order to use Aimster, prospective users must download the Aimster software from its website. Downloading and using the software (known as Classic Aimster) is free. [7] Once the software is installed and executed, Aimster piggybacks onto America Online's IM network and allows its users to communicate and share files with any other Aimster user currently online. Essentially, Aimster greatly expands the file transferring capability of AOL IM described above by designating every Aimster user as the "buddy" of every other Aimster user. In this way, every Aimster user has the ability to search for and download files contained on the hard drives of any other Aimster user (provided that the user has previously designated those files to be available for searching). The Aimster website also posts Terms of Service, to which every Aimster user putatively agrees before using Aimster. The Terms of Service specifically state that Aimster will disable the access of users who repeatedly violate copyright law. *See* Forrest Decl. Ex. 19 (screen shot of Copyright Notice).

The method by which Aimster accomplishes its purpose is quite simple. Once logged onto the Aimster system, a user need only type in a file search to be presented with a list of all Aimster users currently online (up to 500) who have files meeting the search criteria on their hard drive available for download. For example, a user seeking an MP3 of Paula Cole's "I Don't Want to Wait" (a song whose copyright is owned or controlled by Plaintiffs, *see* Cheng Decl. Ex. 1) need only type in "I Don't Want To Wait" into the Aimster search field to be presented with all buddies online that currently offer that song for download. *See* Cheng Decl. Ex. 2 (showing screenshot of the "I Don't Want To Wait" search and a listing of available files for download). Users also have the ability to do more advanced searches. The Aimster software allows searching to be restricted by file type and bit rate. The search results provided by the Aimster software show the file name and other file characteristics directly pertinent to the distribution of MP3 files (such as file size, bit rate, frequency, and song length). Notably, the software also provides the unique screenname of the buddy who currently possesses the file. [8]

Once the search for a suitable file is complete, a user need only click on the file name title and then click on the "Download" button to obtain a copy of the song. At that moment, the Aimster system facilitates the connection of its two users through a private, encrypted network and the file is transferred between them. During the copying of a file, the Aimster system provides a constant update about the status (including the progress, the rate of transfer, the time remaining) of each download or upload.

While any Aimster user is on the Aimster system, the files that that user previously designated as available for transfer are available for searching and downloading by any other Aimster users. Thus, while an Aimster user is searching for files to transfer *into* his or her harddrive, other Aimster users are able to search for and download files *from* that user's harddrive. In this way, an Aimster user with copyrighted music files on his harddrive available for download can thereafter become an unauthorized *distributor* of that copyrighted music as soon as another Aimster user initiates a transfer of that file. All of the searching for and transfers of files on the Aimster system is accomplished without a searching user needing to know the location or identity of any other individual or specific Aimster users.

In addition, Aimster provides the ability to automatically resume transfers of files that, for whatever reason, are interrupted. For example, in a transfer between two Aimster users of the Paula Cole song described above, it is a requirement that both users remain online during the entire transfer. The transfer is interrupted if the source user goes offline or otherwise terminates the transfer at any time before its completion. Aimster solves this problem by automatically reconnecting the searching user to a identical song or file located elsewhere on the hard drive of a different Aimster user and automatically resuming the transfer at the point at which it was previously terminated.

After a file transfer is completed, the transferred song or file is copied to the retrieving user's hard drive. At that point, both the retrieving user and the source user have a copy of the file that is thereafter further available for searching and transfer by other Aimster users.

2. Guardian Tutorial

Also located for a time on Aimster's website was a feature or utility called "Aimster's Guardian Tutorial." [9] This tutorial, located on (but since removed from) Defendants' web site, methodically demonstrated how to transfer and copy copyrighted works over the Aimster system. It accomplished this goal by using, as illustrative on-screen examples, some of the very copyrighted works that Defendants had previously been informed were being infringed on the Aimster system. *See* Creighton Decl. ¶13, Ex. 12 (including screen shots of the Guardian tutorial printed from the Aimster web page); Farmer Decl. ¶25. [10]

3. Chat Rooms and Bulletin Boards

Aimster's service includes message (or bulletin) boards on which Aimster users would regularly post messages to each other. Schafer Decl. ¶3, Ex. 1 (containing screen shots of bulletin board messages). The discussions on these bulletin boards generally fell into a range of particular topics, including: (1) Aimster users seeking to download copyrighted recordings ("I'm trying to find downloads from the Purafunalia album. Specifically the song Blast" (posted by SeanKoury, July 4, 2001)); (2) Aimster users offering recordings for download ("I have a lot of hip hop shared at all times when I'm on, usually over 500 MP3s . . . [F]eel free to get whatever you want" (posted by biggvince, July 17, 2001)); (3) Aimster as an alternative to Napster ("I'm a long time Napster user, with about 900 MP3s . . . like everyone else, the RIAA has forced me to try other mp3 websites, so here I am" (posted by honey, March 17, 2001), "Use Aimster like Napster" (posted by Marcella42, May 27, 2001)); (4) comments on the illegality of sharing copyrighted music files ("What you have with Aimster is a way to share, copy, listen to, and basically in a nutshell break the law using files from other people's computers. . . . I suggest you accept aimster for what it is, an unrestricted music file sharing database" (posted by zhardoum, May 18, 2001)); and (5) bashing of the music industry and the RIAA ("LET'S ALL FUCK OVER THE MUSIC INDUSTRY . . . LETS CHEAT THE VERY ARTISTS WE LISTEN TO" (posted by poiuytrewqm May 20, 2001), "I AM NOT GOING TO BUY CDS ANYMORE!" (posted by OKOK, October 9, 2001)). *See, generally*, Schafer Decl. Ex. 1 (attaching screen shots).

In addition, Aimster allows for real-time chatting between buddies on online chat rooms in the Aimster system. Screen shots of the conversations in these chat rooms reveal that a frequent discussion among the users is the exchange of music files. *See* Schafer Decl. Ex. 2.

4. Club Aimster

Around November 2001, Aimster launched a new service called Club Aimster. Club Aimster is a repackaged version of the basic Aimster service that great enhances the ability of its members to locate and download copyrighted music. It accomplishes this goal by providing, for a $4.95 monthly fee), "All the Hot New Releases All The Time." Forrest Decl. Ex. 18 (screen shot of Club Aimster introductory page).

To use Club Aimster, members must pay their monthly fee, download the Club Aimster software, and log-on to the site with a unique member name and password. Forrest Decl. Ex. 19 (screen shots of the log-in page and download page). Users are thereafter presented with a list of "The Aimster Top-40" a list of the 40 "hot new releases" most frequently downloaded by Aimster users, virtually all of which are owned by Plaintiffs. Creighton Decl. ¶14 and Ex. 13. *See also* Forrest Decl. Ex. 19 (screen shots of the Aimster Top 40). The Aimster Top 40 includes the song and artist name of each selection, a review of the selection (apparently written by Defendants), the Aimster ranking, and the current "Labels" ranking.[11] Finally, each Aimster Top 40 selection includes a "Play" button that a user can click to automatically begin the copying and transfer of that particular song to the member's computer. In this way, Club Aimster seamlessly allows for the distribution of copyrighted music without even the inconvenience of having to type in an Aimster search request Club Aimster, in short, "takes the search out of searching." Farmer Decl. ¶26.[12]

Several screen shots from the Club Aimster service are found in the Forrest Declaration at Exhibit 19. The number one selection on the Aimster Top 40 on the date listed (October 25, 2001) is the song "Hero," by Enrique Iglesias. The current "Label" ranking of the song is listed as number nine but the written review of the song states that "This song will be #1 on the Labels' Chart in about 2-4 weeks." Forrest Decl. Ex. 19. To download "Hero," a user need only click on the Play button situated next to the listing. Other songs available through one-click downloading on Club Aimster (as of October 25, 2001) include "I am a Slave 4 U," by Britney Spears, "Family Affair," by Mary J. Blige, "Turn Off the Light," by Nelly Fertado, and "You Rock my World" by Michael Jackson.

The vast majority, if not all of the music available for copying on Club Aimster is owned by Plaintiffs and is listed in the Billboard Hot 100. Creighton Decl. ¶14.

5. Commercial Aspects

Defendants, according to Deep, "do not sell anything on or through their service. Except for the services provided through Club Aimster, which accounts for a very small portion of the traffic on Defendants' service, there is not money exchanged for any service and there is no paid advertising on the site." Deep Decl. ¶20. This description of Aimster's commercial aspect is inaccurate.

In the time since the filing of Deep's original Declaration, it appears that Club Aimster now accounts for significantly more than "a very small portion of the traffic on Defendants' service." On the contrary, any attempt to download the Aimster software now requires that a prospective user join Club Aimster and pay the $4.95 monthly membership fee. This limitation exists despite text on the Aimster homepage stating that one need not be an Aimster member to download and use Classic Aimster. *See* Farmer Supp. Decl. ¶9, Ex. 1 (including description of thwarted attempt to download the Aimster software for free and appropriate screen shots). As such, it now appears that every user of the Aimster system is required to join Club Aimster and pay the monthly fee. Aimster is very much a commercial enterprise. Users are expected to pay $4.95 per month for the privilege of "hours of entertainment every day." Forrest Decl. Ex. 19.

As further evidence of Aimster's commercial nature, Plaintiffs also attach screen shots from the Aimster web page offering various merchandise for sale. This merchandise includes Aimster Jeans, Designer Fragrance, Nutritional Supplements, and bottles of "Fat Metabolizer." *See* Creighton Decl. Ex. 23 (attaching screen shots).

There is another, if minor, commercial aspect to Aimster. Defendants' website actively solicits for $10 "voluntary payments" to benefit Aimster's "Fight For Freedom" against "the Recording Industry, the Motion Picture Association and America Online in court to protect [Aimster users'] rights to privacy and free speech." In return for their $10 payment, contributors were to receive an Aimster "Fight for Freedom" poster. *See* Forrest Decl. Ex. 2 (screen shot of the "Fight For Freedom" web page).

6. Availability of Music on Aimster

Plaintiffs have provided abundant documentary evidence of the vast amounts of copyrighted music available on Aimster system. By way of example, Plaintiffs' representatives on the Aimster system conducted searches for and downloaded the music of every single recording on the November 3, 2001 Billboard Hot 100. Creighton ¶18, Ex. 19. Plaintiffs also searched for and downloaded every single Top 10 recording from the period between November 5, 2000 and November 3, 2001. Creighton ¶18, Ex. 20. Furthermore, Plaintiffs demonstrate that at least one recording from every album certified as Gold or Diamond between November 1, 2000 and October 31, 2001 was available on the Aimster system. Creighton ¶18, Exs. 21-22. Virtually all of the referenced recordings are owned or controlled by Plaintiffs. *Id.*

II. PROCEDURAL BACKGROUND

Following threatened legal action by the RIAA against Defendants for the rampant copyright infringement on the Aimster system, Defendants AbovePeer and BuddyUSA each filed separate complaints for declaratory relief against the RIAA in the United States District Court for the Northern District of New York on April 30, 2001. Thereafter, between May 24, 2001 and November 2001, numerous additional actions were commenced in the Southern District of New York, the Central District of California, the Middle District of Tennessee, and the Southern District of Florida. In July 2001,

Plaintiffs, according to Deep, moved to consolidate and coordinate for pretrial proceedings all of the actions regarding Aimster before the Judicial Panel on Multidistrict Litigation ("MDL Panel"). On November 16, 2001, the MDL Panel found that consolidation of the cases would "serve the convenience of the parties and witnesses and promote the just and efficient conduct of [the Aimster litigation]." Transfer Order at 2. The MDL Panel further concluded that this court would be a convenient, central forum given that the forums for the underlying cases were scattered throughout the country.

On December 21, 2001, Plaintiffs filed the instant motion for preliminary injunction. Defendants filed their opposition to the preliminary injunction on January 22, 2002. Both parties thereafter filed numerous pleadings and supporting material. The motion for preliminary injunction and Defendants' opposition has now been fully briefed since March 2002.

A status conference was set in this court for March 19, 2002 to discuss the parties' proposals for a case management plan and schedule a date for oral argument on the preliminary injunction. On March 11, 2002, however, prior to the status conference, Defendant John Deep filed for bankruptcy protection under Chapter 13 of the United States Bankruptcy Code. Thereafter, both corporate Defendants filed for bankruptcy under Chapter 11. With all Defendants in bankruptcy proceedings, these proceedings were stayed under the automatic stay provisions of the Bankruptcy Code pending a determination of Debtors' rights in the Bankruptcy Court for the Northern District of New York.

On May 1, 2002, Plaintiffs herein filed a motion with the Bankruptcy Court for relief from the automatic stay provisions to the extent necessary to allow our court to rule on the pending and fully briefed motion for preliminary injunction. On May 23, 2002, the Bankruptcy Court, Judge Littlefield, held a hearing on the motion and, on June 18, 2002, granted the motion by written opinion and order.

Bankruptcy Judge Littlefield's order lifting the automatic stay limits us in the manner we are permitted to proceed. His order specifies that the automatic stay is lifted "for the limited purpose of permitting [the movants, Plaintiffs herein] to request the MDL Court to issue its decision on the pending preliminary injunction motion, without any further hearings other than oral argument of or conferences regarding the merits of the motion." *In Re John A. Deep, In Re AbovePeer, Inc., In Re BuddyUSA, Inc.*, Nos. 02-11552, 02-11745, 02-11755, slip op. at 12 (Bankr ND NY June 18, 2002). As such, by the very terms of Judge Littlefield's order we were precluded from holding any evidentiary hearings on the pending motion.

Seizing on this language, Defendants, on June 21, 2002, moved that we refer the motion for preliminary injunction back to the Bankruptcy Court in the Northern District of New York. The basis for Defendants' motion to transfer was that the preliminary injunction could not be decided without an evidentiary hearing to better determine the facts of the case and that such an evidentiary hearing was specifically prohibited by the Bankruptcy Court. On July 18, 2002, however, we denied Defendants' motion to transfer finding that the "evidence presently before us is sufficient at this preliminary stage of the proceedings." In short, we felt that, given the length and comprehensive nature of the parties' submissions, an evidentiary hearing was unnecessary. In fact, we would likely have decided the present motion without an evidentiary hearing even in the absence of Judge Littlefield's limiting order.

On July 24, 2002, the parties presented oral argument on the motion for preliminary injunction. All that remains is a decision by this court on the motion and the parties can return to the Bankruptcy Court for further proceedings.

III. ANALYSIS

A. Preliminary Injunction Standard

A preliminary injunction "is an extraordinary and drastic remedy." *Mazurek v. Armstrong*, 520 US 968, 972 (1997). Its purpose is to minimize the hardship to the parties pending the ultimate resolution of their lawsuit. *Anderson v. U.S.F. Logistics, Inc.*, 274 F3d 470, 474 *[10 ILR (P&F) 78]* (2001). Generally, a party moving for a preliminary injunction must show that (1) its case has some likelihood of success on the merits; (2) that no adequate remedy at law exists; and (3) it will suffer irreparable harm if the injunction is not granted. *Ty, Inc. v. Jones Group, Inc.*, 237 F3d 891, 895 (7th Cir 2001). If all three conditions have been

met, we must balance the harms the non-moving party will suffer if the injunction is granted against the irreparable harm the moving party will suffer if the injunctive relief is denied. *Id.* Finally, we must consider whether granting or denying the injunction will harm the public interest. *Id.*

The Copyright Act authorizes injunctive relief in situations where it is reasonable for the purposes of restraining or preventing infringement of copyright. 17 USC §502(a). Irreparable injury may normally be presumed from a showing of copyright infringement. *Atari Inc. v. North Am. Phillips Consumer Elec. Corp.*, 672 F2d 607, 620 (7th Cir), *cert. denied*, 459 US 880 (1982). In addition, the public interest may favor the grant of a preliminary injunction because copyright laws embody a policy of encouraging creativity. *See, e.g., ISC-Bunker Ramo Corp. v. Altech, Inc.*, 765 F Supp 1310, 1333 (ND Ill 1990) *citing Atari*, 672 F2d at 620.

B. Likelihood of Success on the Merits

Musical compositions and sound recordings are protected by the Copyright Act. 17 USC §102(a)(2); *Goldstein v. California*, 412 US 546, 552 (1973). Copyright owners, by definition, have the exclusive rights to copy and distribute their copyrighted works. 17 USC §106(1) & (3). To establish direct copyright infringement, a plaintiff must prove two elements: (1) ownership in the applicable copyright(s) and (2) unauthorized copying by the defendant of the constituent elements of the work that are original. *Feist Pub., Inc. v. Rural Tel. Serv. Co., Inc.*, 499 US 340, 361 *[1 ILR (P&F) 180]* (1991). Contributory copyright infringement, by contrast, stems from the notion that one who contributes to another's direct infringement should be held accountable. *Fonovisa, Inc. v. Cherry Auction, Inc.*, 76 F3d 259, 264 (9th Cir 1995). As such, the first step in assessing the existence of contributory infringement is determining the existence of the underlying and direct infringing activity by a third party in this case, Aimster's users.

1. The Existence of Direct Infringement

As a threshold matter, Plaintiffs must demonstrate that Aimster's end users are themselves engaged in direct copyright infringement. Copyright infringement, as noted above, requires a showing by the Plaintiffs that (1) they own the applicable copyrights and (2) there was unauthorized copying of the elements of the work that are original. *Feist*

Pub., 499 US at 361. Furthermore, there is no doubt that input of a copyrighted work onto a computer constitutes the making of a copy under the Copyright Act. *NLFC, Inc. v. Devcom Mid-America, Inc.*, 45 F3d 231, 235 (7th Cir), *cert. denied*, 515 US 1104 (1995).

Plaintiffs have unequivocally established that Aimster's users are engaged in direct copyright infringement. Plaintiffs have submitted convincing evidence that they own or control the copyrights for works copied and distributed using the Aimster system. Plaintiffs' declarants have attached copyright registration certificates demonstrating their ownership or control of the copyrights for hundreds of works found to be available through the Aimster system. *See* Agnew Decl. ¶3; Cottrell Decl. ¶¶3-6; Eisenberg Decl. ¶¶3-6; Leak Decl. ¶¶3-5; Ostroff Decl. ¶¶3-6; Seklir Decl. ¶¶3-7.

Defendants, in their brief and at oral argument, do not dispute that unauthorized copying of copyrighted works occurs on the Aimster system by Aimster's end users. Indeed, during oral argument, Defendants' counsel, George Carpinello, admitted several times that the Aimster system is used to transfer music. *See, e.g.*, Oral Argument Tr. at 32 ("Granted, [Aimster is] also being used to transfer music. There's no question about that. Again, like any other peer-to-peer system, it's being used for that.").

Instead of disputing the existence of direct infringement by Aimster's users, Defendants assert that the provisions of the Audio Home Recording Act of 1992 (the "AHRA") act as an affirmative defense.

The AHRA forbids actions based on the non-commercial use of a device to record digital or analog music recordings. 17 USC §1008. The main purpose of the AHRA was "to ensure the right of consumers to make analog or digital audio recordings of copyrighted music for their private, noncommercial use." *Diamond Multimedia*, 180 F3d at 1079 (quoting S. Rep. 102-294 (1992) *reprinted in* 1992 WL 133198).

According to Defendants, the AHRA shields them from liability because the AHRA was intended to immunize from liability personal use of copyrighted material by "protecting *all* noncommercial copying by consumers of digital and analog musical recordings." Def. Brief at 8, *citing*

Diamond Multimedia, 180 F3d at 1079. While Defendants do not elucidate this argument in their brief, they apparently believe that the ongoing, massive, and unauthorized distribution and copying of Plaintiffs' copyrighted works by Aimster's end users somehow constitutes "personal use." This contention is specious and unsupported by the very case on which Defendants rely.

In *Diamond Multimedia* the Ninth Circuit affirmed the denial of a preliminary injunction against the manufacturer of a hand held device, called the Rio, capable of receiving, storing, and re-playing MP3 music files. 180 F3d 1072. Users of the Rio were able to transfer MP3 files already located on their computer to the Rio so that the songs could then be played elsewhere without the need for the computer. The Rio was not capable of further distributing the music to other computers. Rather, it was solely used as a means by which a user of MP3 files could make further private and personal use of those files away from his or her computer. The RIAA brought suit to enjoin the Rio, claiming it did not meet the requirements of the AHRA. Specifically, the RIAA wanted to prevent the sale of the Rio because it did not employ a Serial Copyright Management System as required by the AHRA. In finding that the RIAA did not have a likelihood of success on the merits, the Ninth Circuit found, *inter alia*, that the Rio was not a "digital audio recording device" under subject to the AHRA.

The facts of the instant case and *Diamond Multimedia* are markedly different. The activity at issue in the present case is the copying of MP3 files from one user's hard drive onto the hard drive of another user. The Rio in *Diamond Multimedia*, by contrast, "merely [made] copies in order to render portable, or 'space shift,' those files that already reside on a user's hard drive." 180 F3d at 1079. The difference is akin to a owner of a compact disc making a copy of the music onto a tape for that owner's sole use while away from home versus the owner making thousands of copies of the compact disk onto a tape for distribution to all of his friends. Furthermore, *Diamond Multimedia* had nothing whatsoever to do with whether the MP3 files on the owner's computers themselves infringed copyrights. Rather, the decision was limited solely to the infringement issue regarding the act of shifting files from a computer to a personal device and whether that copying was subject to the particular requirements of the AHRA. In short, Defendant's reliance on *Diamond Multimedia* is entirely misplaced.

2. Contributory Infringement by Aimster

Having shown direct infringement by Aimster users, Plaintiffs must next demonstrate a likelihood of success on their contributory infringement claim. A party can be liable for contributory infringement where the party "with knowledge of the infringing activity, induces, causes, or materially contributes to the infringing conduct of another." *Design Craft Fabric Corp. v. K-Mart Corp.*, 98 C 5698, 1999 WL 1256258, at *4 (ND Ill 1999) (*quoting Gershwin Publ'g Corp. v. Columbia Artists Mgt., Inc.*, 443 F2d 1159, 1162 (2d Cir 1971)).

a. Knowledge of Infringing Activity

The imposition of contributory liability requires that the secondary infringer know or have reason to know of the direct infringement. *See A&M Records, Inc. v. Napster, Inc.*, 239 F3d 1004, 1020 *[7 ILR (P&F) 1]* (9th Cir 2001) (*"Napster II"*); *Cable/ Home Comm. v. Network Prods., Inc.*, 902 F2d 829, 846 (11th Cir 1990).

There is no doubt that Defendants either know or should know of the direct infringement occurring on the Aimster system. Plaintiffs have sent repeated notices to Defendants of the obvious infringing activity on Aimster. On April 3, 2000, Frank Creighton of the RIAA sent a cease-and-desist letter to Defendants in which he detailed the availability of copyrighted works on Aimster. Creighton Decl. ¶7, Ex. 8. Again, on May 9, 2001, Mr. Creighton sent a cease-and-desist letter to Defendants, this time including screen shots showing approximately 2900 sound recordings owned or controlled by RIAA members available for download through Aimster. Creighton Decl. ¶10, Ex. 11. On November 26, 2001, Mr. Creighton sent a third letter to Defendants again demonstrating the existence of unauthorized sound recordings available through Aimster and specifically mentioning Club Aimster. Creighton Decl. ¶14, Ex. 13.

Aimster's Guardian Tutorial is further evidence of Defendants' knowledge of infringing activity. The Tutorial was available on the Aimster web site and methodically demonstrated how to infringe Plaintiff's copyrights by using specific copyrighted titles as pedagogical examples. Defendants' service, moreover, included online chat rooms and bulletin

board systems in which Aimster users openly discussed trafficking in copyrighted material and "screwing" the RIAA. Each of these elements, taken together or even individually, would conclusively demonstrate Defendants' knowledge of the infringing activity taking place on the Aimster system. *See, e.g., Fonovisa, Inc. v. Cherry Auction, Inc.*, 76 F3d 259, 261 (9th Cir 1996) ("no question" that plaintiff adequately alleged the element of knowledge in contributory copyright infringement claim where the sheriff had sent letters notifying the defendant that infringing materials were being sold at defendant's swap meet).

Club Aimster provides further evidence of Defendant's knowledge of infringement. With Club Aimster, Defendants actually comment upon and track the top copyrighted sound recordings available on Aimster. The "Aimster Top 40," available to users through Club Aimster, not only provides users with an easy way to locate and download copyrighted material, but it even makes reference to where each particular song is ranked on the Aimster list *vis-à-vis* the music labels' lists. *See* Forrest Decl. Ex 19.

In short, the letters to Defendants by the RIAA, the existence of the Guardian Tutorial, the activity on Aimster's chat rooms and bulletin boards, and the operation of Club Aimster all demonstrate that Defendants have actual knowledge of the infringing activity.

Despite this overwhelming evidence, Defendants point to a technical attribute of the Aimster system that, they say, prevents them from having such knowledge. According to Deep, the Aimster system encrypts the data sent between the users' computers such that Defendants are never aware of which users are actually transferring which files. Defendants argue that, "every communication between and among users is encrypted. Just like an electronic bank or financial transaction, only the parties to the transaction have access to the transmission." Def. Brief at 10. The crux this *[sic]* argument is that, while Plaintiffs may be able to point to specific users on the Aimster system that have copyrighted material available on their individual hard drives, Plaintiff cannot show, nor can Defendants actually be aware of, specific transfers of such material between Aimster's users. This limitation exists because Aimster itself encrypts the communications between its users so that no one but those users are aware of what files are being transferred. Thus, according to Deep, "Defendants have no knowledge of when an exchange takes place, who is exchanging information[,] or what information is being exchanged." Deep. Decl. ¶4.

Defendants' encryption argument, clever though it may be, does not convince us that they lack actual knowledge of infringement. It may be true that, due to Aimster's encryption scheme, Defendants are unaware of the actual specific transfers of specific copyrighted music between specific users of the Aimster system. However, there is absolutely no indication in the precedential authority that such *specificity* of knowledge is required in the contributory infringement context. Plaintiffs have provided defendants with screen shots of the Aimster system showing the availability of Plaintiffs' copyrighted sound recordings on those users' hard drives. Forrest Decl. Ex. 20. The screen shots unequivocally identify the individual users ("buddies") who possess the offending files. *Id.* Each of these individually identified users must log on to the Aimster system with a password and user name provided by Aimster. Forrest Decl. Ex. 19 (screen shot of the Aimster login screen). While it may be true that the actual transfers between users are unknown to Defendants due to Aimster's encryption scheme, it is disingenuous of Defendants to suggest that it is unaware of which users are using its system and what files those users are offering up for other users to download at their whim. It is also disingenuous of Defendants to suggest that they lack the requisite level of knowledge when their putative ignorance is due entirely to an encryption scheme *that they themselves put in place.*

Even if we were to agree that the encryption on Defendants' system prevents them from having actual knowledge of infringement, the encryption scheme would not prevent Defendants from having constructive knowledge. Constructive knowledge may also meet the knowledge requirement of a contributory infringement claim. *See Gershwin Publ'g Corp.*, 443 F2d at 1162. Here, given the facts described above, Defendants clearly should have been aware of the infringing activity. Such constructive knowledge suffices for our purposes.

b. Induce, Cause, or Materially Contribute To The Infringing Activity of Another

Plaintiffs have also successfully shown that Defendants materially contribute to the underlying infringement by Aimster's users. Here, the Ninth Circuit's reasoning in *Fonovisa*, 76 F3d 259, is illustrative. In that case, the court held that the owners of a swap meet or flea market could be held contributorily liable for the infringement of individual vendors in the swap meet when those vendors were trafficking in counterfeit musical recordings. In finding that the swap meet organizers materially contributed to the infringing activity of the vendors, the court reasoned that "it would be difficult for the infringing activity to take place in the massive quantities alleged without the support services provided by the swap meet." *Id.* at 264. Those services included "the provision of space, utilities, parking, advertising, plumbing, and customers." *Id.* Relying on *Fonavisa*, the district court in *Napster I* (dealing with a file sharing service, Napster, markedly similar to the Aimster service) found that the provision of services by Napster were analogous to the provision of services in *Fonovisa*. *Napster I*, 114 F Supp 2d at 919. Such services provided by Napster included supplying "the proprietary software, search engine, servers, and means of establishing a connection between users' computers." *Id.* Furthermore, without the support services offered by Napster, its users "could not find and download the music they want." *Id.*

Here, too, we rely on *Fonovisa* to support our finding that Defendants have materially contributed to infringing activities. Instead of parking spaces, advertisement, and plumbing, Defendants in this case have provided the software and the support services necessary for individual Aimster users to connect with each other. Without Aimster's services, Aimster's infringing users would need to find some other way to connect. We need not solely rely on such "but for" causation, however, for Defendants go much further. The very existence of Club Aimster demonstrates the extent to which Defendants contribute to infringing activity. The Aimster Top 40 catalogues and presents for Aimster users the top copyrighted music that they may wish to transfer. It comments upon that music and, in some cases, even suggests that the user *should* have it. *See, e.g.,* Forrest Decl. Ex. 19C ("Aimster Sayz (sic): Anybody that oWns this, maybe you could be my hero. . .”). What's more, users wishing to download music using Club Aimster need merely click on a play button and the Aimster software automatically creates a connection with another users' computer to facilitate the transfer. As stated by Plaintiffs in their brief, "Aimster predicates its entire service upon furnishing a 'road map' for users to find, copy, and distribute copyrighted music." Pla. Brief at 13. We agree. Defendants manage to do everything but actually steal the music off the store shelf and hand it to Aimster's users.

i. Unintended Effect

Instead of directly arguing against this point, Defendants urge us to consider that Plaintiffs reasoning would have the collateral, unintended effect of making liable *every* Internet service provider as long as the provider's service could be said to be the "but for" cause of the infringing activity of some of its users. "If Aimster were held to materially cause infringement," say Defendants, "so would every search engine, instant messenger[,] and internet service provider." Def. Brief at 11. Yet this argument ignores the reality of Defendants' service as compared to the search engines and instant messengers to which they claim such similarity. A search engine does not entice its users to infringe others' copyrights. Instant Messaging programs (like AOL IM) do not index, rank, and comment upon MP3 music for its users to browse and copy. Aimster is different. [13]

ii. Substantial Non-Infringing Uses

As another defense to the contributory infringement claim, Defendants argue that Aimster is capable of "substantial non-infringing uses" as identified by the Supreme Court in *Sony Corp. of Am. v. Universal City Studios*, 464 US 417 (1984). In *Sony*, the Supreme Court rejected the efforts of the entertainment industry to enjoin the sale and distribution of Betamax video cassette recorders that were being used by their users to record copyrighted television broadcasts. Finding that the video recorders were capable of substantial non-infringing uses, the Court declined to extend contributory liability to the recorders' manufacturer. Defendants argue that, like the Betamax video recorder, Aimster is capable of substantial non-infringing uses. Such uses include the ability of Aimster users to transfer any number and type of non-copyrighted files and messages to other users, [14] and the ability of users to

identify other users with similar interests, share information, and develop clubs. Def. Brief at 9. In addition, businesses without a network administrator may use Aimster to exchange business records securely and efficiently. Deep Decl. ¶16-18.

Sony is plainly distinguishable from the present case. First, in *Sony*, the court found that the *principal* use of video recorders was non-infringing (mere "time shifting"). 464 US at 421. By contrast, Defendants here have provided no evidence whatsoever (besides the unsupported declaration of Deep) that Aimster is *actually* used for any of the stated non-infringing purposes. Absent is any indication from real-life Aimster users that their primary use of the system is to transfer non-copyrighted files to their friends or identify users of similar interests and share information. Absent is any indication that even a single business without a network administrator uses Aimster to exchange business records as Deep suggests. Indeed, the mere inclusion of such evidence would not suffice unless it tended to show that such use constituted Aimster's primary use. Instead, the evidence leads to the inescapable conclusion that the *primary* use of Aimster is the transfer of copyrighted material among its users.

Second, *Sony* applied only to a "staple article of commerce." 464 US at 442. The Court opined that copyright law must look beyond actual duplication of a publication and look also to "the products or activities that make such duplication possible." *Id.* "Accordingly," said the Court, "the sale of copying equipment, like the sale of other articles of commerce, does not constitute contributory infringement if the product is widely used for legitimate, unobjectionable purposes." *Id.* The Court noted that contributory infringement is usually reserved for cases "involving an ongoing relationship between the direct infringer and the contributory infringer at the time the infringing conduct occurred," and observed that the Betamax VCR "plainly does not fall into that category." *Id.* at 437-8 ("[T]he only contact between Sony and the users of the Betamax . . . occurred at the moment of sale."). Here, Aimster cannot be said to be such a staple article of commerce. It is not discrete product, like a Betamax VCR, to be sold to customers who thereafter use the machine as they see fit. Instead, Aimster is a *service* more closely akin to the swap meet in *Fonavisa*. Like the swap meet organizers in *Fonavisa*, Defendants provide an ongoing service to their users, including the provision of software, the maintenance of the Aimster system, and the continuing control of editorial content (*i.e.*, Club Aimster). Unlike the case in *Sony*, the instant case involves an ongoing relationship between the direct infringers (the users) and the contributory infringers (the Defendants).

Third, there is nothing to suggest that *Sony* extends to protect the unauthorized and widespread *distribution* of infringing works. The conduct of the Betamax users at issue was the "private, home use of VTR's for recording programs broadcast on the public airwaves without charge to the viewer." *Sony*, 464 US at 425. There was simply "[n]o issue concerning the transfer of tapes to other persons." *Id.* By stark contrast, Aimster has virtually nothing to do with private, home use copying (or time shifting). Instead, Aimster makes each of its users a global distributor of Plaintiff's copyrighted music for copying by any number of other Aimster users. Much like the AHRA argument discussed above, Defendants cannot successfully contend that Aimster involves merely private, home use.

Fourth, there is authority to suggest that *Sony*'s protection is not available when the products at issue are specifically manufactured for infringing activity, even if those products have substantial noninfringing uses. *See, e.g., Cable/Home Comm.*, 902 F2d at 846 (even though "other uses" existed, defendants liable where they "utilized and advertised these devices primarily as infringement aids and not for legitimate, noninfringing uses."); *A&M Records, Inc. v. Abdallah.*, 948 F Supp 1449, 1456 (CD Cal 1996). Here, it is our finding that Aimster is a service specifically designed to aid the infringing activities of its users and, on that basis alone, should not be eligible for *Sony*'s protections.

Finally, the court in *Sony* approvingly cited the district court's finding that Sony had not "influenced or encouraged" the unlawful copies. *Sony*, 464 US at 438. Aimster does not fall into this category of innocent enabler. Indeed, our factual findings demonstrate that Aimster actually goes to great lengths to both influence and encourage the direct infringement among its users.

We are convinced that Defendants had knowledge of and materially contributed to the infringing activity of Aimster's users. We are further convinced that the protections of *Sony* are simply not applicable to the instant case. As such, Plaintiffs have adequately demonstrated a likelihood of success on the merits for the contributory infringement claim.

3. Vicarious Infringement

Even if we were to find that Plaintiffs did not have a likelihood of success on the contributory infringement claim, we would, as an alternative, find a likelihood of success on the vicarious infringement claim. Vicarious copyright infringement is established when a defendant has "the right and ability to supervise infringing activity and also has direct financial interest in such activities." *Hard Rock Café Licensing Corp. v. Concession Services, Inc.*, 955 F2d 1143, 1150 (7th Cir 1992) (citing *Gershwin Publ'g Corp.*, 443 F2d at 1162). Unlike contributory liability, one can be liable for vicarious copyright infringement even without knowledge of the infringement. *F.E.L. Pub., Ltd. v. Nat'l Conference of Catholic Bishops*, 466 F Supp 1034, 1040 (ND Ill 1978) (citing *Dreamland Ball Room, Inc. v. Shapiro, Bernstein & Co.*, 36 F2d 354 (7th Cir 1929)).

a. Right and Ability to Supervise

Defendants have the right and ability to supervise Aimster's users. On this point, the Ninth Circuit's reasoning in *Fonovisa* is again instructive.[15] In *Fonovisa*, 76 F3d at 262, the swap meet organizers had the right to terminate individual vendors at any time and controlled the access of customers to the swap meet area. These facts, among others, were integral to the court's finding that the swap meet organizers had the right and ability to control the infringing activities of the vendors. *Id.* at 263.

Here, Defendants have largely the same abilities as the defendants in *Fonovisa*. Defendants, according to their own posted Terms of Service, have the right to terminate individual users. The Terms of Service state that Aimster will "take down" "infringing material" and that repeat violators of copyright law "may have their access to all services terminated." Forrest Decl. Ex. 8. Furthermore, Defendants control the access of Aimster's users. Users of the system are required to log on after paying their monthly fee to join Club Aimster. This log in requires the user to supply a "Member Name" and password. Forrest Decl. Ex. 19.

We are not convinced by Defendants' argument that, due to the encryption on the Aimster system, they do not have the ability to block user's access to the service without shutting the whole system down. Def. Brief at 11. This argument, even if it were true, would not prove that Defendants did not have the right and ability to supervise. The fact that users must log in to the system in order to use it also demonstrates that Defendants know full well who their users are. Defendants argue that Aimster's architecture prevents them from discovering the "physical internet address" of their users. Def. Brief at 11. Yet, there is nothing about the right and ability to control which requires Defendants to have such precise identifying knowledge.

b. Direct Financial Interest

Defendants' direct financial interest in the infringing activities of its users is without question. Each Club Aimster user must pay $4.95 per month to use the service. Credible evidence (described in Section I.D.5) even suggests that *every* Aimster user must now pay this fee. Defendants solicit monetary contributions on the Aimster site to help fund their involvement in this litigation. Defendants sell various Aimster-related merchandise on their site, including Aimster "Fight For Justice" posters apparently intended as a rallying call for the free availability of copyrighted music. In short, Aimster is very much a commercial enterprise and Defendants have a direct financial interest in the infringement by its users.

The financial benefit element is also satisfied where, as here, the existence of infringing activities act as a draw for potential customers. *See, e.g., Napster II*, 239 F3d at 1023 ("Financial benefit exists where the availability of infringing material 'acts as a draw' for customers." (quoting *Fonovisa*, 76 F3d at 263-264)). The facts demonstrate that Aimster's users were drawn to the service in this manner. Aimster's bulletin boards and chat rooms are replete with examples of users drawn there simply because they know it is a place where they can obtain infringing material.

Plaintiffs have thus shown a reasonable likelihood of success on the vicarious infringement claim.

4. Unclean Hands

Defendants next contend that the preliminary injunction should be denied due to AOL's unclean hands. AOL, claim Defendants, "engages in the same conduct that it and the other Plaintiffs rail against here." Def. Brief at 6. Defendants argue that AOL, through AOL IM, "has now become one of the largest purveyors of file sharing in the entire world" and "provides the *exact same service* as Defendants." *Id.* at 7 (emphasis supplied). Defendants are mistaken that unclean hands should prevent injunctive relief, however, because AOL's conduct simply is not relevant to this case.

The doctrine of unclean hands prevents plaintiffs from obtaining relief for conduct in which they themselves participated. *Precision Instrument Mfg. Co. v. Automotive Maint. Mach. Co.*, 324 US 806, 814-15 (1945). The maxim applies "to one tainted with inequitableness or bad faith relative to the matter in which he seeks relief, however improper may have been the behavior of the defendant." *Packers Trading Co. v. Commodity Futures Trading Comm'n*, 972 F2d 144, 148 (7th Cir 1992). While we have wide discretion to refuse to aid an unclean litigant, *id.*, "the doctrine is not to be used as a loose cannon, depriving a plaintiff of an equitable remedy to which he is otherwise entitled merely because he is guilty of unrelated misconduct." *Am. Hosp. Supply Corp. v. Hosp. Prods. Ltd.*, 780 F2d 589, 601 (7th Cir 1986).

Deep's declaration provides a detailed account (including a series of screen shots) of the means by which one can download and transfer copyrighted music through AOL's service. In addition, Deep filed a supplemental declaration on this issue after the Time Warner Music Group Plaintiffs filed a separate reply brief dealing specifically with differences between AOL IM and Aimster.

These materials convince us unequivocally that Aimster and AOL IM are quite different in the means by which they allow file transfers between users. In short, Aimster's system makes the process of locating and copying an infringing file extremely easy while the file transfer capabilities of AOL's system are clearly of secondary importance. Even more important than the mere functionality of the two systems is the fact that Aimster clearly encourages, entices, and contributes to the infringement of its users (witness, for example, Club

Aimster and the 'Fight for Freedom' posters), while AOL's service does nothing of the sort.

Putting aside the differences or similarities of Aimster versus AOL IM, however, there is a more important issue. Defendants go to great pains to describe the conduct of AOL, but *AOL is not even a party to this case.* At best, AOL can be described as having a tenuous relationship with only one group of Plaintiffs the Warner Music Group Plaintiffs. As described by counsel to the Warner Music Group Plaintiffs at oral argument, "Time Warner, the AOL Time Warner parent, owns AOL" and AOL is the Internet Service Provider that owns AOL IM. Oral Arg. at 37 & Warner Reply Brief at 9. AOL, in turn, is not the owner of the Warner Music Group plaintiffs. Indeed, the only relationship between AOL and some of the Plaintiffs in this case is that some of them share a common corporate parent. *Id.*

Furthermore, even assuming *arguendo* that AOL did have unclean hands and did have some significant relationship with some of the Plaintiffs, we fail to see how that relationship would be the least bit relevant *vis-à-vis* all of the other Plaintiffs currently seeking a preliminary injunction in this case. We can find no authority to suggest that where multiple plaintiffs are seeking equitable relief, the unclean hands of one plaintiff should serve to prevent all of the other plaintiffs from receiving their due relief.

5. DMCA

Defendants next argue that they are eligible for the liability limitations found in the Digital Millennium Copyright Act ("DMCA"), 17 USC §512, enacted in 1998. The DMCA was "enacted both to preserve copyright enforcement on the Internet and to provide immunity to service providers from copyright infringement liability for 'passive,' 'automatic' actions in which a service provider's system engages through a technological process initiated by another without the knowledge of the service provider." *ALS Scan, Inc. v. RemarQ Communities, Inc.*, 239 F3d 619, 625 *[7 ILR (P&F) 69]* (4th Cir 2001) (citing H.R. Conf. Rep. No. 105-796, at 72 (1998)). [16] This immunity is not presumptive, but granted only to "innocent" service providers who can show that they do not have a defined level of knowledge regarding the infringement on their system. *Id.* The DMCA's protection of an innocent service provider

disappears "at the moment the service provider loses its innocence, *i.e.*, at the moment it becomes aware that a third party is using its system to infringe." *Id.* Liability protection under the DMCA is an affirmative defense and, as such, Defendants bear the burden of establishing its applicability.

The DMCA provides internet service providers with four possible safe harbors from liability for direct, vicarious, and contributory copyright infringement. The first safe harbor, §512(a) (the "Transitory Communication Safe Harbor"), applies in certain situations where liability would otherwise be predicated on the service provider's providing connections for infringing material through its network. The second safe harbor, §512(b) (the "System Caching Safe Harbor"), provides a limitation on liability in certain circumstances for the intermediate and temporary storage (or caching) of material on the service provider's system. Both parties agree that the third safe harbor, §512(c), is not relevant in this case. The fourth safe harbor under the DMCA, §512(d) (the "Information Location Tools Safe Harbor"), provides for a limitation on the liability of service providers who, under certain circumstances, refer or link users to infringing material or infringing activity.

The applicability (or inapplicability) of the DMCA's safe harbor provisions does not affect the availability of any other defense under the Copyright Act, such that service providers are free to establish defenses in addition to, and independent from, the DMCA provisions. 17 USC §512(l). Furthermore, the DMCA specifically sets forth that the applicability of its safe harbor provisions are not conditioned upon a service provider "monitoring its service or affirmatively seeking facts indicating infringing activity." 17 USC §512(m). In this way, the DMCA represents a legislative determination that copyright owners must themselves bear the burden of policing for infringing activity—service providers are under no such duty.

Before a service provider can take advantage of the safe harbor provisions, it must satisfy two threshold determinations. First, the potential defendant must meet the DMCA's definition of "service provider." Second, the potential defendant must adopt and reasonably implement a policy which terminates the access of users who are identified as repeat infringers. Each of these threshold determinations are examined in turn.

a. Service Provider

The DMCA defines "service provider" in two different ways, depending upon which safe harbor is at issue. For the purpose of the Transitory Communication Safe Harbor, "service provider" is defined as "an entity offering the transmission, routing, or providing of connections for digital online communications, between or among parties specified by a user, of material of the user's choosing, without modification of the content of the material as sent or received." 17 USC §512(k)(1)(A). For the purposes of the remaining safe harbors, the "service provider" definition is even more broad: a service provider is "a provider of online services or network access, or the operator of facilities therefor." 17 USC §512(k)(1)(B). The second definition further provides that it includes any entity that qualifies under the first definition. *Id.*

A plain reading of both definitions reveals that "service provider" is defined so broadly that we have trouble imagining the existence of an online service that *would not* fall under the definitions, particularly the second. In any event, Aimster certainly qualifies under the first version (and, by extension, the second). As described by Defendants,

> Aimster connects digital signals from one user to another so that they may identify each other as "buddies" or for the purpose of sending information and data from one user to another. The material to be sent and the "buddies" are chosen wholly by the user without modification by Defendants. . . . Aimster operates in the standard way that many infrastructure providers do, such as providers of email gateways, instant messaging and caching servers, by providing a backbone or infrastructure through a contractual relationship with other intermediate service providers, who in turn have commercial relationships with other infrastructure providers on down the line to the provider that has a relationship with the end user.

Def. Brief at 14. This description (uncontroverted by Plaintiffs) plainly shows that Aimster is a service provider under the DMCA's definition in that it provides the routing of digital communication between its users. Plaintiffs retort that internet service providers "generally provide a way to connect to the Internet (*e.g.*, phone or cable modem) as well as a mechanism that tells a computer how and where to access information on the Internet," and that Aimster provides none of these services. Farmer Decl. ¶28. Plaintiffs are probably correct that Aimster would not be considered an internet service provider under the commonly accepted usage of that term. However, the DMCA has provided two specific definitions of "service provider" and those broad definitions must control.

b. Repeat Infringer Policy

The second threshold determination of an entity's eligibility for the DMCA's safe harbors is the adoption and reasonable implementation of a policy to disable the access of repeat infringers. 17 USC §512(i)(1)(A) states in part that the DMCA's liability limitations shall apply to a service provider only if the provider "has adopted and reasonably implemented, and informs subscribers and account holders of the service provider's system or network of, a policy that provides for the termination in appropriate circumstances of subscribers and account holders of the service provider's system or network who are repeat infringers." Defendants cannot jump this hurdle.

Aimster has adopted a repeat infringer policy. The copyright notice on the Aimster site informs users that they "respect copyright law and expects our users to do the same." Forrest Decl. Ex. 8 (screen shot of Aimster copyright notice). The copyright notice goes on to provide a detailed form that an aggrieved copyright owner can fill out to identify the work that is being infringed and the "user name under which such material is available through the AbovePeer service, and the path and the file name." *Id.* The notice goes on to explain the procedure for taking down or disabling access to the infringing material and the procedure for reestablishing access in the event of a mistake.[17] Finally, the notice provides that "uses who are found to repeatedly violate copyright rights of others may have their access to all services terminated." *Id.* These facts support a finding that Aimster has adopted a repeat infringer policy.[18]

The problem, Plaintiffs and Defendants agree, is in the method the repeat infringer policy is *implemented* that is to say, the policy is *not* implemented. Where the parties differ is as to what significance we should attach to this lack of implementation. Defendants point out, and we are inclined to believe them, that the policy is not implemented because it *cannot* be implemented. As described in Section III.B.2.a, *supra*, the encryption on Aimster renders it impossible to ascertain which users are transferring which files. Thus, while Plaintiffs have identified many Aimster users who may have copyrighted works residing on their individual hard drives (itself probably not an infringing activity), Plaintiffs cannot demonstrate that any particular user is actually *transferring* any of those files (which *would* be an infringing activity). Defendants point out that the Plaintiffs have yet to identify a single repeat infringer whose access should be terminated. Indeed, say Defendants, once they "are notified that a particular internet protocol address is identified with any infringing use, Defendants will notify the primary internet service provider to terminate their access." Def. Brief at 16. This statement is not nearly so helpful and agreeable as it seems, however, because, according to Defendants themselves, such identification would be impossible.

We are not convinced by Defendants' arguments on this issue for two reasons. First, we note that the repeat infringer language of §512(i) does not require a copyright holder to provide the sort of notice sought by Defendants. Nowhere in that subsection is there the requirement that a copyright holder provide the Defendants with the internet protocol address of a particular copyright infringer on the Aimster system. Rather, the statute merely provides that the service provider implement a policy that provides for the termination of access to repeat infringers in "appropriate circumstances." 17 USC §512(i). Second, as noted previously in this opinion, we remain nonplused with Defendants' argument that the Aimster encryption scheme absolves them of responsibility when that scheme is voluntarily instituted by the Defendants themselves. Adopting a repeat infringer policy and then purposely eviscerating any hope that such a policy could ever be carried out is not an "implementation" as required by §512(i).

Defendants' failure to comply with §512(i) renders them ineligible for any of the DMCA's safe harbor protections. Nonetheless and for the sake of completeness, we will briefly address the relevant safe harbors arguments and Defendants' ineligibility for each.

c. Transitory Communications Safe Harbor

The Transitory Communications Safe Harbor holds that a service provider shall not be liable for copyright infringement by "reason of the provider's transmitting, routing, or providing connections for, materials *through* a system or network controlled or operated by or for the service provider . . ." provided a number of conditions are satisfied. 17 USC §512(a) (emphasis supplied). Noting that the safe harbor specifically requires the putatively infringing material be routed or transmitted *through* the Aimster system, Plaintiffs argue that Aimster would not qualify. We agree. According to Deep, the Aimster system works by allowing users to communicate and transfer files via "privately created network[s.]" *See* Deep Decl. ¶4. Aimster is a "peer-to-peer service," Oral Arg. Tr. at 18, that is, it allows for the transfer of information directly between one user and another user through the Internet. If the transaction between the users is truly peer-to-peer, then the information transferred between individual users does not pass "through" Aimster's system at all. *See, e.g., A&M Records, Inc. v. Napster*, No. C 99-05183, 2000 WL 573136 *[5 ILR (P&F) 418]* (ND Cal 2000) ("even if each user's Napster browser is part of the system, the transmission goes *from* one part of the system *to* another, or *between* parts of the system, but not 'through' the system."); Farmer Decl ¶28 ("Aimster has been designed so that the download itself does not pass through Aimster's own servers."). In this way, Plaintiffs urge that the word "through" in the statute should be read to mean "as a conduit."

Defendants, in their brief, do not directly disagree with Plaintiffs' argument that material does not pass through Aimster's own servers. Instead, Defendants argue that "through" should be given a broader meaning, such as "be means of" or "by the help or agency of." Def. Brief at 14. Defendants' brief tacitly accepts that Aimster could qualify for the Transitory Communications Safe Harbor only if we were apply these broader definitions of "through." The legislative history, however, reveals that Plaintiffs' interpretation is correct: the Transitory Communications Safe Harbor is limited to situations "in which a service provider plays the role of a 'conduit' for the communications of others." H.R. Rep. No. 105-551(II) (1998), *reprinted in* 1998

WL 414916, *130. Aimster cannot fairly be said to be a mere "conduit" of the information transferred between its users. The system provides broad search capabilities to its users, allows for the automatic resumption of interrupted downloads, provides for easy one-click downloading of the system's most popular titles, and offers editorial comment on popular titles. These features do not a mere conduit make.[19]

d. System Caching Safe Harbor

The System Caching Safe Harbor holds that a service provider shall not be liable for copyright infringement "by reason of the intermediate and temporary storage of material on a system or network controlled or operated by or for the service provider." 17 USC §512(b)(1). Defendants provide ample explanation of how and why certain information is cached on their system. *See* Deep Decl. ¶14.[20] However, Defendants' brief reveals a fundamental misunderstanding of the nature of the System Caching Safe Harbor. Defendants assert that the System Caching Safe Harbor "provides a safe harbor to service providers that temporarily store material on a system and meet certain other conditions." Def. Brief at 16. Apparently, Defendants believe that the safe harbor protects service providers from liability for copyright infringement *so long as* the material in question is cached on the system. Yet, the language of the safe harbor is quite clear that the liability limitation applies to liability that may arise *"by reason of"* the caching of material. 17 USC §512(b)(1) (emphasis supplied).

The difference between these two interpretations is substantial. By Defendants' reading of the safe harbor, a service provider is cleansed of liability for infringing material whenever, during a transfer of material between its users, the material in question happens to be cached on the service provider's system. That reading is an impossibly broad interpretation of the safe harbor. Instead, the plain language of the safe harbor provides that a service provider, having met the other requirements of the safe harbor, is safe from liability *when that liability results from the act of caching itself.*

Here, Plaintiffs do not assert that Defendants are liable as a result of the caching of material of their system. Rather, Defendants' putative liability is a result of their material contribution to the infringing activities of others. The System Caching Safe Harbor is simply not applicable in this case.[21]

e. Information Location Tools Safe Harbor

The Information Location Tools Safe Harbor provides that a service provider shall not be liable "by reason of the provider referring or linking users to an online location containing infringing material or infringing activity, by using information location tools, including a directory, index, reference, pointer, or hypertext link," if the service provider meets three other specified conditions. 17 USC §512(d).

Defendants fail to meet the conditions outlined by the Information Location Tools Safe Harbor. First, a service provider cannot have actual knowledge of the infringing material or activity, or, in the absence of actual knowledge, the service provider cannot be aware of facts or circumstances from which the infringing activity is apparent. 17 USC §512(d)(1). In the alternative, if a service provider does have actual or constructive knowledge, the service provider must "act[ ] expeditiously to remove, or disable access to, the material." 17 USC §512(d)(1)(C). As described in Section III.B.2.a, however, Defendants do have actual and constructive knowledge of the infringing activity. Furthermore, there is no evidence whatsoever that Defendants have taken steps to remove or disable access to infringing material.

Second, a service provider cannot "receive a financial benefit directly attributable to the infringing activity, in a case in which the service provider has the right and ability to control such activity." 17 USC §512(d)(2). As more fully described in Section III.B.3, however, we find that Defendants do receive the sort of financial benefit described by this condition and Defendants do have the right and ability to control the infringing activity (even if they purposely avoid such ability through a self-imposed encryption scheme).[22]

C. No Adequate Remedy at Law and Irreparable Harm

In the context of a preliminary injunction, we must consider the equitable defense of laches as a mitigating factor with regard to Plaintiffs' claim of irreparable harm. While irreparable harm may normally be presumed in the copyright infringement context, *Atari, Inc. v. North Am. Phillips Consumer Elec. Corp.*, 672 F2d 607, 620 (7th Cir 1982), that presumption can be overcome when the Plaintiff is inexcusably tardy in seeking relief and such tardiness weighs against the Plaintiffs' claim of irreparable harm. *See, e.g., Ideal Industries, Inc. v. Gardner Bender, Inc.*, 612 F2d 1018, 1025 (7th Cir 1979), *cert. denied*, 447 US 924 (1980).

In assessing the excusability of delay in seeking a preliminary injunction, the relevant issue is whether a defendant has been "lulled into a false sense of security or had acted in reliance on the plaintiff's delay." *Ty, Inc.*, 237 F3d at 903. In *Ty*, the manufacturer of the popular "Beanie Babies" toys sought to preliminarily enjoin the manufacture and marketing of confusingly similar "Beanie Racers" toys. In addressing the defendant's argument that the plaintiffs waited too long to bring their motion, the Seventh Circuit affirmed the magistrate judge's decision that "it cannot be said that this minimal [eight month] delay lulled Defendant into a false sense of security, nor that the delay was unreasonable." *Id*. Of note was the dearth of "affirmative evidence that [Plaintiff's] delay . . . caused [Defendant] to be lulled into a false sense of security or that [Defendant] in any way relied on [Plaintiff's] delay." *Id*.

We are therefore instructed to search the record before us for any affirmative evidence that the Defendants in this case were lulled into a false sense of security or relied on Plaintiff's delay in continuing their operations. Like the court in *Ty*, we find such evidence to be wholly lacking.

The parties agree that Plaintiffs became aware of the Aimster system around August or September 2000. The present motion for preliminary injunction was filed with this court on December 21, 2001, about sixteen or seventeen months later. Such a lengthy delay, however, is not dispositive in and of itself because the issue is not merely the exact number of days between an injury and a motion. Rather, the delay must be assessed in the context of the parties' situation and in its affect on the Defendants.

Examined in the context of the parties' situation, the delay suddenly seems less objectionable. In his declaration, Deep catalogues various contacts he had with some of the record company plaintiffs in the months following Aimster's release. He asserts that he met with several product managers of AOL on September 3, 2000 to discuss the possibility of a business relationship between Aimster and AOL.

Deep Decl. ¶26. On October 2000, Aimster formed a business relationship with EMI/Capital Records (one of the Plaintiffs) to market the copyrighted work "Radiohead Kid A." Furthermore, Deep alleges that representatives of Aimster held at least four separate meetings with representatives of Bertelsmann AG (a RIAA member) to discuss possible investments in Aimster. [23] Deep claims that in these discussions he explained in detail how Aimster worked and how music could be distributed in encrypted form over the Aimster system. Deep Decl. ¶28. During this entire period from approximately August 2000 to March 2001, according to Deep, neither the RIAA nor any of its members raised any issues with regard to the Aimster's alleged copyright infringement. Deep Decl. ¶29. The rattling of legal sabers began on April 3, 2001, according to Deep, two weeks after a senior executive for Transworld Entertainment Corp., a retailer of musical recordings, contacted Edgar Bronfman of Vivendi/Universal about the possibility of Transworld selling musical recordings through Aimster under a license from the major record companies. Deep Decl. ¶29. On April 3, 2001, the RIAA sent its first of two cease and desist letters to Defendants threatening legal action unless Defendants took steps to eliminate the rampant copyright infringement on Aimster system. Thereafter, Defendants commenced their own declaratory judgment actions in the Northern District of New York and the procedural history of this case commenced in manner outlined above in Section II culminating, in November 2001, with all actions consolidated and transferred to this court for pretrial proceedings. Even fully accepting Defendants' recitation of events, it is obvious that the actual relevant period in our analysis of the Plaintiff's delay is from August 2000 to April 3, 2001 eight months rather than seventeen. Defendants could not and cannot claim that they were lulled into a false sense of security or reasonably relied upon Plaintiff's delay after April 3, 2001 because it is on that date that they definitively became aware of Plaintiff's intentions. After all, the April 3, 2001 cease and desist letter specifically notified Defendants that continued infringing activities on the Aimster system may force the RIAA to "seek additional legal remedies." Creighton Decl., Ex. 8. Such additional legal remedies undoubtedly included, in due course of time, a motion for preliminary injunction or other equitable relief. *See, e.g., Ty, Inc. v. Softbelly's, Inc.*, No. 00-C-5230, 2001 WL 125321 *8 (ND Ill 2001)

(Norgle, J.) ("[T]he very fact that Ty sent a cease and desist letter should have placed Softbelly on notice that the instant action and motion could result."). Therefore, the time period between April 3, 2001 and the eventual filing of the preliminary injunction is simply not relevant to our analysis of the appropriateness of Plaintiffs' delay in seeking the preliminary injunction.

In assessing whether Defendants were lulled into a false sense of security, we therefore need only focus on the happenings in the time period between August 2000 and April 3, 2001. For their part, Plaintiffs contend that until March 2001 the Aimster system was difficult to ascertain because it was prone to technical problems and frequently inaccessible for lengthy periods. Pla. Reply at 11. In a supplemental declaration, Frank Creighton, Executive Vice President and Director of Anti-Piracy for the RIAA, states that during the months following September 2000 when his staff became aware of the Aimster system, their attempts to monitor the system were thwarted by Aimster's technical problems. In fact, he says, "there were days (and even weeks) during which we could not log on to the system." Creighton Supp. Decl. ¶3. Screen shots of the Aimster web page during this time support Plaintiffs' contention that the service was prone to technical problems. Dated news updates on the web site specifically refer to "connection hassles and download glitches" on October 17, 2000 and promising that "a new version of Aimster is on the way." Forrest Decl. Ex. 3. The web page further notified Aimster users on November 17, 2000 that service would be suspended pending the release of a new version of the software. *Id.* According to the screen shots of Aimster's own web page, that new version was not released until February 2, 2001. *Id.* ("Long Awaited AIMSTER 3 Debuts!").

Defendants reject the notion that Plaintiffs were unaware of the Aimster system prior to March 2001. They point to the many contacts and meetings (described above) they had with various representatives of the Plaintiffs. But the contacts that Defendants describe are not evidence that Plaintiffs were fully aware of the Aimster system or what it would become nor are they evidence that Plaintiffs were implicitly condoning Defendants' activities. At best, it seems clear that Plaintiffs, prior to April 3, 2001, were intrigued by Aimster and trying learn more about it. *See, e.g.,* Mujica Decl.

¶23. Discussions of possible investment, even if true, are not, by themselves, sufficient to lull Defendants into a false sense of security. Deep furthermore makes much of the business relationship between Aimster and EMI/Capital Records. This "relationship," however, consisted solely of an agreement to place an advertisement for Radiohead on the Aimster web page and a hyperlink to the EMI web page. Deep Decl. ¶27. Despite what Defendants may argue, this "relationship" as such was hardly a definitive indication that EMI/Capital Records knew about and condoned the wide scale unauthorized transfer of Plaintiffs' copyrighted works, nor was the advertisement a reasonable indication to Defendants that they were safe from liability. [24]

Finally, Defendants have repeatedly referred to a newspaper quotation in which Barry Schuler, chairman and Chief Executive of America Online, Inc., says that Aimster is "not doing anything illegal." Deep Decl. Ex. D. Defendants imply that this assertion contributed to their false sense of security and indicates Plaintiffs' full knowledge of Aimster activities as early as February 2001. Deep Decl. ¶26 and Oral Argument Tr. 25. Assuming for a moment that the quotation attributed to AOL (which is not directly a party to this action) is both relevant and admissible, it is taken grossly out of context. Defendants would have us believe that AOL's chairman was explicitly condoning the illegal distribution of copyrighted music over the Internet through the Aimster system. However, it is quite clear from the context of the Washington Post article at issue that Mr. Schuler was referring specifically to Aimster's activity of piggybacking onto the AOL IM network and noting that the piggybacking practice was not itself illegal. [25] The mischaracterization of Mr. Schuler's words does not help Defendants' cause.

Plaintiffs' delay in bringing the motion for preliminary injunction was not unreasonable and is not enough the *[sic]* rebut the presumption of irreparable harm. Furthermore, there is insufficient affirmative evidence that Defendants were lulled into a false sense of security or that they reasonably relied on Plaintiffs' delay in assuming that a day of legal reckoning would somehow never come. In short, it is inconceivable that Defendants' had any *reasonable* belief that Plaintiffs' would not take all appropriate action to protect their intellectual property.

D. Balance of Hardships and Public Interest

The next step in the preliminary injunction analysis is to "consider the irreparable harm that the nonmoving party will suffer if preliminary relief is granted, balancing such harm against the irreparable harm the moving party will suffer if relief is denied." *Ty, Inc.*, 237 F3d at 895. This step requires us to engage in a "sliding scale approach; the more likely the plaintiff will succeed on the merits, the less the balance of irreparable harms need favor the plaintiff's position." *Id.*

Defendants urge that the balance of hardships tips in their favor because a preliminary injunction would preemptively destroy their business before they had the opportunity for a full hearing on the merits. Defendants' argument, however, distorts the meaning of the balance of hardships test. If we were to accept the going-out-of-business argument, a blatant copyright infringer "would be encouraged to go into an infringing business because it can later argue to a court that enjoining the blatant infringement would sink the business." *See Horn Abbott Ltd. v. Sarsaparilla Ltd.*, 601 F Supp 360, 369-70 (ND Ill 1984) (Aspen, J.). We do not accept such reasoning. Defendants further argue that, because Aimster represents such a small portion of the total amount of the file sharing traffic on the Internet, Plaintiffs would not suffer any hardship without an injunction. This argument is specious, however, given our (here unrebutted) presumption of irreparable harm.

Using the sliding scale approach, therefore, we find that the balance of hardships tips in favor of Plaintiffs. This finding is especially apt considering our belief that Plaintiffs have an exceptionally strong likelihood of success on the merits of their contributory infringement claim.

The preliminary injunction analysis also requires us to "consider the public interest (non-parties) in denying or granting the injunction." *Ty, Inc.*, 237 F3d at 895. Defendants urge that the public will be harmed "by the overextension of copyright laws." Def. Brief at 20. However, given our finding regarding Plaintiffs likelihood of success of the merits, we do not agree that a preliminary injunction in this case will result in such an overextension. To the contrary, the public interest is served by

upholding copyright protections against those who would seek to misappropriate protected works.

IV. CONCLUSION

For the foregoing reasons, we grant the Plaintiffs' motion for preliminary injunction. Plaintiffs are hereby ordered to submit proposed language for the preliminary injunction within 5 business days of this opinion. Defendants thereafter have two business days with which to submit any response to the proposed language. Plaintiffs' submission should be narrowly tailored, to the extent possible, to achieve the primary goal of preventing Defendants' continuing contributory infringement of Plaintiffs' copyrighted works while allowing non-infringing uses of the Aimster system, if any, to continue. To this end, and by way of example, we invite the parties to study the Ninth Circuit's reasoning and proposed modifications to the injunction in the Napster case, *Napster II*, 239 F3d at 1027-1028 (Section VIII), and the resulting modified injunction from the district court. *A&M Records, Inc. v. Napster, Inc.*, No. C 99-05183, 00-1369, 2001 WL 227083 *[7 ILR (P&F) 244]* (ND Cal March 5, 2001). Like Napster, Aimster presents a unique problem with regard to the identification of infringing material and the transitory nature of its end-users. Plaintiffs' submission should reflect a sensitivity to these issues by including a practical method by which they can be overcome.

Pursuant to Rule 65(c), we also order Plaintiffs to post a bond for the sum of $500,000 to compensate Defendants for their losses in the event this injunction is reversed or vacated.

It is so ordered.

---

[1] The Aimster software and service, which used to be provided through its website at *www.aimster.com*, has now been renamed "Madster," and is located at *www.madster.com*. To avoid confusion, however, this opinion will continue to refer to the software and system as Aimster.

[2] Deep has filed a detailed declaration describing the Aimster system and various other facts pertinent to this case. Similarly, Plaintiffs have filed many (some quite lengthy) declarations with exhibits setting forth additional relevant facts. Throughout this opinion, declarations will be cited with the last name of the declarant followed by

"Decl." and the paragraph or exhibit number. In some instances, declarants have filed supplemental declarations. Those supplemental declarations are cited with a "Supp."

³ *See* Complaint, *Jerry Lieber et al. v. AbovePeer et al.*, No. 01 c 8942.

⁴ We note in passing that the *Napster* decision, while certainly persuasive on some points, is simply not precedential authority in this circuit. The parties expend a great deal of time and effort to convince us as to Aimster's similarities or differences *vis-à-vis* Napster. However, our decision today need not rest on the legal reasoning or factual findings of the *Napster* courts.

⁵ The file transfer functionality of AOL IM service is relevant only insofar as it relates to Defendants' argument that AOL has unclean hands and shouldn't be able to pursue a preliminary injunction. The crux of Defendants' argument is that AOL IM allows for substantially the same file transfer abilities of which the Plaintiffs now complain about Aimster. As explain in Section III.B.4, herein however, this claim is a red herring.

⁶ The concept that Aimster catalogues all available files for download in a single, centralized database is hotly contested by the parties. The reason for this debate is that a critical aspect of the *Napster* decision was that Napster operated a central directory of all the files available on its system. According to Deep, "Aimster contains no such central database." Deep Decl. ¶15. Plaintiffs disagree. *See* Creighton Decl. ¶3; Farmer Decl. ¶21-22. In the absence of an evidentiary hearing (which, as described below, we were precluded from holding by the Bankruptcy Court), we find that there is insufficient evidence to resolve this conflict. However, our decision today can be and is based upon considerations independent of this evidentiary insufficiency. In other words, the reasoning in this opinion would hold regardless of whether or not Aimster maintains a central database of files available for transfer.

⁷ Evidence suggests, however, that this is no longer the case. Efforts to download the software for free now bring a user to a page requiring registration with Club Aimster (described below) and the payment of a $4.95 fee. *See* Farmer Supp. Decl. ¶9.

⁸ It is important to remember throughout this discussion that Aimster does not itself store all of the music (or other) files made available through a search on its system. Rather, each file is stored on the individual hard drive of the Aimster user's computer itself. There is, however, some question as to the amount of file "caching" (or temporary storage of material to facilitate further distribution) on the Aimster system. This activity, to the extent it is relevant, is described below in Section III.B.5.d.

⁹ It is unclear from both parties' submissions whether "Guardian" was another version of the Aimster software, or merely a separate feature of the existing code.

¹⁰ In a declaration filed by Deep subsequent to oral argument on this motion, he has reiterated his position that the "Guardian Tutorial" was not prepared or placed on the Aimster website by any Defendant or their agents. Rather, the "Guardian Tutorial," according to Deep, appeared on a website called "Our Aimster" created by an individual who was not an employee or agent of Defendants. Deep claims that the creators of "Our Aimster" asked, and Defendants agreed, that the "Our Aimster" site contents would be cached onto the Aimster web site. But, claims Deep, it was not until Plaintiffs submitted their papers on this motion that he was aware of the contents of that site. Upon becoming so aware, he immediately disabled access to the "Our Aimster" material through the Aimster website. But Plaintiffs, in their response to Deep's additional declaration, point out the Guardian Tutorial was accessible from and existed on the Aimster system from at least August 16, 2001 until at least January 2002. Moreover, the screen shots of the "Guardian Tutorial" unequivocally show that it was accessible from, and was a part of, Aimster's web page. We find Deep's contention that the Defendants "were unaware of the content of the tutorial" (Deep 7/25/02 Supp. Decl. ¶6) simply unbelievable.

¹¹ Presumably, the "Labels" ranking is based upon the song's current ranking on the Billboard Hot 100. *Billboard* is a leading periodical in the music field, is widely available, and is used by music professionals worldwide. On a weekly basis, *Billboard* prepares a list of 100 recordings receiving the most radio air play and retail sales. *See* Creighton Decl. ¶18.

¹² By stark contrast, Deep's description of Club Aimster leaves out these most egregious details and describes the service in purely innocuous terms. While "Plaintiffs make much of the existence of Club Aimster," he says, it is "merely reporting to Aimster users the popularity of individual songs. . . Those individuals who wish to listen to songs listed on Club Aimster must still click onto a search request for the song title." Deep. Decl. ¶21.

¹³ Nonetheless, Defendants persist in their argument that AOL IM allows for the transfer of copyrighted music just as Aimster does. This argument is more fully discussed below in Section III.B.4.

¹⁴ In fact, during oral argument Defendants' counsel contended that a large number of the files transferred through Aimster are adult photographs rather than copyrighted music. Oral Arg. at 21.

[15] The court in *Fonovisa* addressed both contributory and vicarious infringement.

[16] Given the DMCA's relatively recent enactment, there is a dearth of Seventh Circuit precedent interpreting its provisions.

[17] The copyright notice appears to track the irrelevant (for our purposes) notice, take-down, and counter notice procedures of §512(g).

[18] It is, as we shall see, an absolute mirage, but it is a stated policy nonetheless.

[19] Defendants would not be eligible for the Transitory Communications Safe Harbor for an additional reason. §512(a)(5) requires that material be "transmitted through the system or network *without modification of its content.*" However, by Defendants' own admission, Aimster *does* modify the content: "Aimster encrypts all the information that is transferred between users." Deep Decl. ¶8. This modification further belies the notion of Aimster as a mere conduit.

[20] Notably, however, Deep's declaration is careful to avoid claiming that Aimster ever caches the actual infringing files. He instead refers to "data," "messages," and "attributes." Deep Decl. ¶14.

[21] Defendants would not be eligible for the System Caching Safe Harbor for two additional reasons. First, just like the Transitory Communications Safe Harbor, the System Caching Safe Harbor requires that the material in question be transmitted "through" the Aimster system, §512(b)(1)(B), when it is not. Second, the material must be transmitted without modification to its content. §512(b)(2)(A). As noted above in footnote 19, however, Aimster's encryption scheme belies this assumption.

[22] The third condition of the Information Location Tools Safe Harbor requires the expeditious take-down of infringing material after the service provider receives proper notice from the copyright holder that complies with §512(c)(3). Because Defendants do not meet the first two conditions, however, we find it unnecessary to delve into this third condition. We note in passing, however, that the notice requirements of §512(c)(3) probably have not been met by Plaintiffs. The RIAA sent its notice of infringement and cease and desist letters to Deep personally. However, the DMCA contains a technical requirement that such notice be sent to a service provider's designated agent. *See* 17 USC §512(c)(2) & (3). Defendants' designated agent to receive such notification appears to be Melissa Fass of AbovePeer, not Deep. *See* Forrest Decl. Ex. 8 (screen shot of Aimster Copyright Notice page providing contact information for designated agent Melissa Fass).

[23] There is dispute as to whether these meetings took place. Plaintiffs have filed a Declaration by Deirdre McDonald, Vice President of Legal and Business Affairs for BMG Music in which Ms. McDonald refutes Deeps assertion that anyone from the Bertelmann New Media Group or Bertelsmann Random House New Media Group ever met with Aimster to discuss possible investment. McDonald Decl. ¶2. Deep thereafter filed a supplemental declaration further describing his meetings with members of Bertelsmann and Random House staff and attaching various e-mails that appear to discuss the scheduling of meetings between Aimster and Bertelsmann. Notwithstanding Ms. McDonald's declaration, we have little doubt that Deep met with some if not all of the parties as he has described. We do doubt, however, that these meetings have any relevance vis-à-vis Plaintiffs' delay.

[24] Indeed, Ted Cohen, Vice-President for New Media for EMI, had filed a declaration further describing the relationship between EMI and Defendants. He recounts a meeting with Deep at which Deep sought business from the record companies by trumping up Aimster's ability to protect copyrights. The agreement reached between EMI and Defendants as a result of this meeting was a mere linking arrangement in which no money changed hands. *See* Cohen Decl. ¶2-4.

[25] This obvious interpretation is supported by Mr. Shuler himself. *See* Shuler Decl. ¶3 ("This statement simply meant that the act of piggybacking on the AOL IM service did not appear to constitute a trespass of the AOL network.").

ALS Scan, Inc.

v.

RemarQ Communities, Inc.

**United States Court of Appeals,
Fourth Circuit**

February 6, 2001

7 ILR (P&F) 69, 239 F3d 619

No. 00-1351

'Substantial' notice by copyright holder blocks safe harbor for infringing ISP.

An Internet service provider that receives a notice of infringing activities that "substantially" complies with the requirements of the Digital Millennium Copyright Act (DMCA) may not rely on a claim of defective notice to maintain the immunity defense provided by that statute's "safe harbor" provisions. The DMCA requires that a copyright owner put the service provider on notice in a detailed manner, but allows notice by means that comport with the prescribed format only "substantially," rather than perfectly. 17 USC §512(c)(3)(A). In addition, with respect to multiple works, not all must be identified—only a "representative" list. §512(c)(3)(A)(ii). With respect to location information, the copyright holder must provide information that is "*reasonably* sufficient" to permit the service provider to "locate" this material. §512(c)(3)(A)(iii). In this case, plaintiff provided defendant with information that (1) identified two sites created for the sole purpose of publishing plaintiff's copyrighted works, (2) asserted that virtually all the images at the two sites were its copyrighted material, and (3) referred defendant to two web addresses where defendant could find pictures of plaintiff's models and obtain plaintiff's copyright information. In addition, it noted that material at the site could be identified as plaintiff's material because the material included plaintiff's name and/or copyright symbol next to it. With this information, plaintiff substantially complied with the notification requirement of providing a representative list of infringing material as well as information reasonably sufficient to enable defendant to locate the infringing material. — **ALS Scan Inc. v. RemarQ Communities Inc., 7 ILR (P&F) 69 [4th Cir, 2001].**

Appeal from the United States District Court for the District of Maryland, at Baltimore. J. Frederick Motz, Chief District Judge. (CA-99-2594-JFM).

Before **WIDENER, WILKINS,** and **NIEMEYER, Circuit Judges**. Affirmed in part, reversed in part, and remanded by published opinion.

COUNSEL

ARGUED: *Harry Brett Siegel*, Law Office of Joel Marc Abramson, Columbia, Maryland, for Appellant. *Robert R. Vieth*, Cooley Godward, L.L.P., Reston, Virginia, for Appellee.

ON BRIEF: *Robert T. Cahill*, Cooley Godward, L.L.P., Reston, Virginia, for Appellee.

OPINION

NIEMEYER, Circuit Judge. We are presented with an issue of first impression—whether an Internet service provider enjoys a safe harbor from copyright infringement liability as provided by Title II of the Digital Millennium Copyright Act ("DMCA") when it is put on notice of infringement activity on its system by an imperfect notice. Because we conclude that the service provider was provided with a notice of infringing activity that *substantially* complied with the Act, it may not rely on a claim of defective notice to maintain the immunity defense provided by the safe harbor. Accordingly, we reverse the ruling of the district court that found the notice fatally defective, and affirm its remaining rulings.

I

ALS Scan, Inc., a Maryland corporation, is engaged in the business of creating and marketing "adult" photographs. It displays these pictures on the Internet to paying subscribers and also sells them through the media of CD ROMs and videotapes. ALS Scan is holder of the copyrights for all of these photographs.

RemarQ Communities, Inc., a Delaware corporation, is an online Internet service provider that provides access to its subscribing members. It has approximately 24,000 subscribers to its newsgroup base and provides access to over 30,000 newsgroups which cover thousands of subjects. These newsgroups, organized by topic, enable subscribers to participate in discussions on virtually any topic, such as fine arts, politics, religion, social issues, sports, and entertainment. For example, RemarQ provides access to a newsgroup entitled "Baltimore Orioles," in which users share observations or materials about the Orioles. It claims that users post over one million articles a day in these newsgroups, which RemarQ removes after about 8-10 days to accommodate its limited server capacity. In providing access to newsgroups, RemarQ does not monitor, regulate, or censor the content of articles posted in the newsgroup by subscribing members. It does, however, have the ability to filter information contained in the newsgroups and to screen its members from logging onto certain newsgroups, such as those containing pornographic material.

Two of the newsgroups to which RemarQ provides its subscribers access contain ALS Scan's name in the titles. These newsgroups—"alt.als" and "alt.binaries.pictures.erotica.als"—contain hundreds of postings that infringe ALS Scan's copyrights. These postings are placed in these newsgroups by RemarQ's subscribers.

Upon discovering that RemarQ databases contained material that infringed ALS Scan's copyrights, ALS Scan sent a letter, dated August 2, 1999, to RemarQ, stating:

> Both of these newsgroups ["alt.als" and "alt.binaries.pictures.erotica.als"] were created for the sole purpose of violating our Federally filed Copyrights and Tradename. These newsgroups contain virtually all Federally Copyrighted images. . . . Your

servers provide access to these illegally posted images and enable the illegal transmission of these images across state lines.

> This is a cease and desist letter. You are hereby ordered to cease carrying these newsgroups within twenty-four (24) hours upon receipt of this correspondence . . . .

> America Online, Erol's, Mindspring, and others have all complied with our cease and desist order and no longer carry these newsgroups.

> * * *

> Our ALS Scan models can be identified at *http://www.alsscan.com/modlinf2.html*[.] Our copyright information can be reviewed at *http://www.alsscan.com/copyrite.html*[.]

RemarQ responded by refusing to comply with ALS Scan's demand but advising ALS Scan that RemarQ would eliminate individual infringing items from these newsgroups if ALS Scan identified them "with sufficient specificity." ALS Scan answered that RemarQ had included over 10,000 copyrighted images belonging to ALS Scan in its newsgroups over the period of several months and that

> [t]hese newsgroups have apparently been created by individuals for the express sole purpose of illegally posting, transferring and disseminating photographs that have been copyrighted by my client through both its websites and its CD-ROMs. The newsgroups, on their face from reviewing messages posted thereon, serve no other purpose.

When correspondence between the parties progressed no further to resolution of the dispute, ALS Scan commenced this action, alleging violations of the Copyright Act and Title II of the DMCA, as well as unfair competition. In its complaint, ALS Scan alleged that RemarQ possessed actual knowledge that the newsgroups contained infringing material but had "steadfastly refused to remove or block access to the material." ALS Scan also alleged that RemarQ was put on notice by ALS Scan of the infringing material contained in its database. In addition to injunctive relief, ALS Scan demanded actual and statutory damages, as well as attorneys fees. It attached to its complaint affidavits establishing the essential elements of its claims.

In response, RemarQ filed a motion to dismiss the complaint or, in the alternative, for summary judgment, and also attached affidavits, stating that RemarQ was prepared to remove articles posted in its newsgroups if the allegedly infringing articles were specifically identified. It contended that because it is a provider of access to newsgroups, ALS Scan's failure to comply with the DMCA notice requirements provided it with a defense to ALS Scan's copyright infringement claim.

The district court ruled on RemarQ's motion, stating, "[RemarQ's] motion to dismiss or for summary judgment is treated as one to dismiss and, as such, is granted." In making this ruling, the district court held: (1) that RemarQ could not be held liable for *direct* copyright infringement merely because it provided access to a newsgroup containing infringing material; and (2) that RemarQ could not be held liable for *contributory* infringement because ALS Scan failed to comply with the notice requirements set forth in the DMCA, 17 USC 512(c)(3)(A). This appeal followed.

II

ALS Scan contends first that the district court erred in dismissing its direct copyright infringement claim. It contends that it stated a cause of action for copyright infringement when it alleged (1) the "ownership of valid copyrights," and (2) RemarQ's violation of its copyrights "by allowing its members access to newsgroups containing infringing material." [1] *See generally Keeler Brass Co. v. Continental Brass Co.*, 862 F2d 1063, 1065 (4th Cir 1988) (describing the requirements of a direct infringement claim). In rejecting ALS Scan's direct infringement claim, the district court relied on the decision in *Religious Technology Center v. Netcom On-Line Communication Services, Inc.*, 907 F Supp 1361, 1368-73 *[1 ILR (P&F) 778]* (ND Cal. 1995), which concluded that when an Internet provider serves, without human intervention, as a passive conduit for copyrighted material, it is not liable as a direct infringer. The *Netcom* court reasoned that "it does not make sense to adopt a rule that could lead to liability of countless parties whose role in the infringement is nothing more than setting up and operating a system that is necessary for the functioning of the Internet." *Id.* at 1372. That court

observed that it would not be workable to hold "the entire Internet liable for activities that cannot reasonably be deterred." *Id.*; *see also Marobie-FL, Inc. v. National Ass'n of Fire Equip. Distribs.*, 983 F Supp 1167, 1176-79 (ND Ill. 1997) (agreeing with *Netcom*'s reasoning). ALS Scan argues, however, that the better reasoned position, contrary to that held in *Netcom*, is presented in *Playboy Enterprises, Inc. v. Frena*, 839 F Supp 1552, 1555-59 *[1 ILR (P&F) 770]* (MD Fla. 1993), which held a computer bulletin board service provider liable for the copyright infringement when it failed to prevent the placement of plaintiff's copyrighted photographs in its system, despite any proof that the provider had any knowledge of the infringing activities.

Although we find the *Netcom* court reasoning more persuasive, the ultimate conclusion on this point is controlled by Congress' codification of the *Netcom* principles in Title II of the DMCA. As the House Report for that Act states,

> The bill distinguishes between direct infringement and secondary liability, treating each separately. This structure is consistent with evolving case law, and appropriate in light of the different legal bases for and policies behind the different forms of liability.

> As to direct infringement, liability is ruled out for passive, automatic acts engaged in through a technological process initiated by another. Thus the bill essentially codifies the result in the leading and most thoughtful judicial decision to date: *Religious Technology Center v. Netcom On-Line Communications Services, Inc.*, 907 F Supp 1361 *[1 ILR (P&F) 778]* (ND Cal. 1995). In doing so, it overrules these aspects of *Playboy Enterprises, Inc. v. Frena*, 839 F Supp 1552 *[1 ILR (P&F) 770]* (MD Fla. 1993), insofar as that case suggests that such acts by service providers could constitute direct infringement, and provides certainty that *Netcom* and its progeny, so far only a few district court cases, will be the law of the land.

H.R. Rep. No. 105-551(I), at 11 (1998). Accordingly, we address only ALS Scan's claims brought under the DMCA itself.

III

For its principal argument, ALS Scan contends that it substantially complied with the notification requirements of the DMCA and thereby denied RemarQ the "safe harbor" from copyright infringement liability granted by that Act. *See* 17 USC §512(c)(3)(A) (setting forth notification requirements). It asserts that because its notification was sufficient to put RemarQ on notice of its infringement activities, RemarQ lost its service-provider immunity from infringement liability. It argues that the district court's application of the DMCA was overly strict and that Congress did not intend to permit Internet providers to avoid copyright infringement liability "merely because a cease and desist notice failed to technically comply with the DMCA."

RemarQ argues in response that it did not have "knowledge of the infringing activity as a matter of law," stating that the DMCA protects it from liability because "ALS Scan failed to identify the infringing works in compliance with the Act, and RemarQ falls within the 'safe harbor' provisions of the Act." It notes that ALS Scan never provided RemarQ or the district court with the identity of the pictures forming the basis of its copyright infringement claim.

These contentions of the parties present the issue of whether ALS Scan complied with the notification requirements of the DMCA so as to deny RemarQ the safe-harbor defense to copyright infringement liability afforded by that Act.

Title II of the DMCA, designated the "Online Copyright Infringement Limitation Act," DMCA, §201, P.L. 105-304, 112 Stat 2877 (1998) (codified at 17 USC §101 note), defines limitations of liability for copyright infringement to which Internet service providers might otherwise be exposed. The Act defines a service provider broadly to include any provider of "online services or network access, or the operator of facilities therefor," including any entity providing "digital online communications, between or among points specified by user, of material of the user's choosing, without modification to the content of the material as sent or received." 17 USC §512(k). Neither party to this case suggests that RemarQ is not an Internet service provider for purposes of the Act.

The liability-limiting provision applicable here, 17 USC §512(c), gives Internet service providers a safe harbor from liability for "infringement of copyright by reason of the storage at the direction of a user of material that resides on a system or network controlled or operated by or for the service provider" as long as the service provider can show that: (1) it has neither actual knowledge that its system contains infringing materials nor an awareness of facts or circumstances from which infringement is apparent, or it has expeditiously removed or disabled access to infringing material upon obtaining actual knowledge of infringement; (2) it receives no financial benefit directly attributable to infringing activity; *and* (3) it responded expeditiously to remove or disable access to material claimed to be infringing after receiving from the copyright holder a notification conforming with requirements of §512(c)(3). *Id.* §512(c)(1).[2] Thus, to qualify for this safe harbor protection, the Internet service provider must demonstrate that it has met all three of the safe harbor requirements, and a showing under the first prong—the lack of actual or constructive knowledge—is prior to and separate from the showings that must be made under the second and third prongs.

In this case, the district court evaluated the adequacy given to RemarQ under the third prong only. Despite the fact the district court stated it was treating RemarQ's motion as a motion to dismiss, rather than as a motion for summary judgment, the court's memorandum opinion fails to mention the allegation made in ALS Scan's complaint that RemarQ had *actual* knowledge of the infringing nature of the two subject newsgroups even before being contacted by ALS Scan, an allegation denied by RemarQ. Clearly, had the court truly been evaluating ALS Scan's complaint under a 12(b)(6) standard of review, it would necessarily have had to accept ALS Scan's allegation as proven for purposes of testing the adequacy of the complaint, *see Eastern Shore Markets, Inc. v. J.D. Assoc. Ltd. P'ship*, 213 F3d 175, 180 (4th Cir. 2000), and consequently been required to rule in favor of ALS Scan under the first prong.

Even if we were to treat the district court's order as disposing of a motion for summary judgment, and not a motion to dismiss, the court still could not, as a matter of law, have resolved the conflicting affidavits about actual knowledge. Resolving whether the court actually treated the motion as one to dismiss or for summary judgment is not necessary, however, because we conclude that ALS Scan substantially complied with the third prong, thereby denying RemarQ its safe harbor defense.

In evaluating the third prong, requiring RemarQ to remove materials following "notification," the district court concluded that ALS Scan's notice was defective in failing to comply strictly with two of the six requirements of a notification—(1) that ALS Scan's notice include "a list of [infringing] works" contained on the RemarQ site and (2) that the notice identify the infringing works in sufficient detail to enable RemarQ to locate and disable them. 17 USC §512(c)(3)(A)(ii), (iii). [3]

In support of the district court's conclusion, RemarQ points to the fact that ALS Scan never provided it with a "representative list" of the infringing photographs, as required by §512(c)(3)(A)(ii), nor did it identify those photographs with sufficient detail to enable RemarQ to locate and disable them, as required by §512(c)(3)(A)(iii). RemarQ buttresses its contention with the observation that not all materials at the offending sites contained material to which ALS Scan held the copyrights. RemarQ's affidavit states in this regard:

> Some, but not all, of the pictures users have posted on these sites appear to be ALS Scan pictures. It also appears that users have posted other non-ALS Scan's erotic images on these newsgroups. The articles in these newsgroups also contain text messages, many of which discuss the adult images posted on the newsgroups.

ALS Scan responds that the two sites in question— "alt.als" and "alt.binaries.pictures.erotica.als"— were created solely for the purpose of publishing and exchanging ALS Scan's copyrighted images. It points out that the address of the newsgroup is defined by ALS Scan's name. As one of its affidavits states:

> [RemarQ's] subscribers going onto the two offending newsgroups for the purpose of violating [ALS Scan's] copyrights, are actually aware of the copyrighted status of [ALS Scan's] material because (1) each newsgroup has "als" as part of its title, and (2) each photograph belonging to [ALS Scan] has [ALS Scan's] name and/or the copyright symbol next to it.

Each of these two newsgroups was created by unknown persons for the illegal purpose of trading the copyrighted pictures of [ALS Scan] to one another without the need for paying to either (1) become members of [ALS Scan's] web site(s) or (2) purchasing the CD-ROMs produced by [ALS Scan].

ALS Scan presses the contention that these two sites serve no other purpose than to distribute ALS Scan's copyrighted materials and therefore, by directing RemarQ to these sites, it has directed RemarQ to a representative list of infringing materials.

The DMCA was enacted both to preserve copyright enforcement on the Internet and to provide immunity to service providers from copyright infringement liability for "passive," "automatic" actions in which a service provider's system engages through a technological process initiated by another without the knowledge of the service provider. H.R. Conf. Rep. No. 105-796, at 72 (1998), *reprinted in* 1998 USCCAN 649; H.R. Rep. No. 105-551(I), at 11 (1998). This immunity, however, is not presumptive, but granted only to "innocent" service providers who can prove they do not have actual or constructive knowledge of the infringement, as defined under any of the three prongs of 17 USC §512(c)(1). The DMCA's protection of an innocent service provider disappears at the moment the service provider loses its innocence, *i.e.*, at the moment it becomes aware that a third party is using its system to infringe. At that point, the Act shifts responsibility to the service provider to disable the infringing matter, "preserv[ing] the strong incentives for service providers and copyright owners to cooperate to detect and deal with copyright infringements that take place in the digital networked environment." H.R. Conf. Rep. No. 105-796, at 72 (1998), *reprinted in* 1998 USCCAN 649. In the spirit of achieving a balance between the responsibilities of the service provider and the copyright owner, the DMCA requires that a copyright owner put the service provider on notice in a detailed manner but allows notice by means that comport with the prescribed format only "substantially," rather than perfectly. The Act states: "To be effective under this subsection, a notification of claimed infringement must be a written communication provided to the designated agent of a service provider that includes *substantially* the following . . . ." 17 USC §512(c)(3)(A) (emphasis added). In addition to substantial compliance, the notification requirements are relaxed to the extent that, with respect to multiple works, not all must be identified—only a "representative" list. *See id.* §512(c)(3)(A)(ii). And with respect to location information, the copyright holder must provide information that is *"reasonably* sufficient" to permit the service provider to "locate" this material. *Id.* §512(c)(3)(A)(iii) (emphasis added). This subsection specifying the requirements of a notification does not seek to burden copyright holders with the responsibility of identifying every infringing work—or even most of them—when multiple copyrights are involved. Instead, the requirements are written so as to reduce the burden of holders of multiple copyrights who face extensive infringement of their works. Thus, when a letter provides notice equivalent to a list of representative works that can be easily identified by the service provider, the notice substantially complies with the notification requirements.

In this case, ALS Scan provided RemarQ with information that (1) identified two sites created for the sole purpose of publishing ALS Scan's copyrighted works, (2) asserted that virtually all the images at the two sites were its copyrighted material, and (3) referred RemarQ to two web addresses where RemarQ could find pictures of ALS Scan's models and obtain ALS Scan's copyright information. In addition, it noted that material at the site could be identified as ALS Scan's material because the material included ALS Scan's "name and/or copyright symbol next to it." We believe that with this information, ALS Scan substantially complied with the notification requirement of providing a representative list of infringing material as well as information reasonably sufficient to enable RemarQ to locate the infringing material. To the extent that ALS Scan's claims about infringing materials prove to be false, RemarQ has remedies for any injury it suffers as a result of removing or disabling noninfringing material. *See* 17 USC §512(f), (g).

Accordingly, we reverse the district court's ruling granting summary judgment in favor of RemarQ on the basis of ALS Scan's non-compliance with the notification provisions of 17 USC §512(c)(3)(A)(ii) and (iii). Because our ruling only removes the safe harbor defense, we remand for

further proceedings on ALS Scan's copyright infringement claims and any other affirmative defenses that RemarQ may have.

IV

ALS Scan also appeals the district court's decision not to enter summary judgment on its behalf with respect to its infringement claim. Because there is a dispute as to several material facts, however, we affirm the district court's ruling on ALS Scan's motion for summary judgment. If ALS Scan is able to prove that in fact the offending newsgroups' "sole purpose" is infringement of ALS Scan's copyrights, it may be entitled to a remedy. However, because it is contested both that such is, in fact, the "sole" purpose of the newsgroups, and that "virtually all" the images posted in the newsgroups are infringing, we are unable to come to any legal conclusions. Final disposition must await further development of the record and further proceedings.

V

Accordingly, for the reasons given, we reverse the district court's decision to grant summary judgment in favor of RemarQ, affirm the district court's decision not to grant summary judgment in favor of ALS Scan, and remand this case for further proceedings consistent with this opinion.

AFFIRMED IN PART, REVERSED
IN PART, AND REMANDED

---

[1] It would appear that ALS Scan's allegations amount more to a claim of contributory infringement in which a defendant, "with knowledge of the infringing activity, induces, causes or materially contributes to the infringing conduct of another," *Gershwin Publ'g Corp. v. Columbia Artists Mgmt., Inc.*, 443 F2d 1159, 1162 (2d Cir 1971), than to a claim of direct infringement.

[2] Section 512(c)(1) provides in full:

(c) Information residing on systems or networks at direction of users.—

(1) In general.—A service provider shall not be liable for monetary relief, or, except as provided in subsection (j), for injunctive or other equitable relief, for infringement of copyright by reason of the storage at the direction of a user of material that resides on a system or network controlled or operated by or for the service provider, if the service provider—

(A)(i) does not have actual knowledge that the material or an activity using the material on the system or network is infringing;

(ii) in the absence of such actual knowledge, is not aware of facts or circumstances from which infringing activity is apparent; or

(iii) upon obtaining such knowledge or awareness, acts expeditiously to remove, or disable access to, the material;

(B) does not receive a financial benefit directly attributable to the infringing activity, in a case in which the service provider has the right and ability to control such activity; and

(C) upon notification of claimed infringement as described in paragraph (3), responds expeditiously to remove, or disable access to, the material that is claimed to be infringing or to be the subject of infringing activity.

³   Section 512(c)(3)(A)(ii), (iii) provides:

(3) Elements of notification.—

(A) To be effective under this subsection, a notification of claimed infringement must be a written communication provided to the designated agent of a service provider that includes substantially the following:

* * *

(ii) Identification of the copyrighted work claimed to have been infringed, or, if multiple copyrighted works at a single online site are covered by a single notification, a representative list of such works at that site.

(iii) Identification of the material that is claimed to be infringing or to be the subject of infringing activity and that is to be removed or access to which is to be disabled, and information reasonably sufficient to permit the service provider to locate the material.

Arista Records, Inc.
v.
MP3Board, Inc.

**United States District Court,
Southern District of New York**

August 29, 2002

11 ILR (P&F) 700, 2002 ILRWeb (P&F) 1897, 2002 WL 1997918

No. 00 CIV. 4660 (SHS)

Issues of fact preclude entry of judgment against music search engine.

Notwithstanding defendant's acknowledgment that its music search engine site "may" facilitate copyright infringement by directing Internet users to pirated copies of plaintiffs' sound recordings, plaintiffs' motion for summary judgment is denied because material issues of fact exist regarding whether any direct infringement occurred with the aid of defendant's site. While the structure of defendant's site and the scale of the operation certainly give rise to a strong statistical inference that Internet users downloaded files containing copyrighted music in violation of plaintiffs' reproduction rights, plaintiffs have failed to eliminate all genuine issues of material fact. In particular, they have failed to set forth any direct evidence of infringement, such as user logs or other technical data showing the downloading of copyrighted and unauthorized files. At the summary judgment stage, plaintiffs cannot rely solely upon circumstantial evidence and admissions by defendant's officers that it is statistically "likely" that direct infringement occurred. — **Arista Records, Inc. v. MP3Board, Inc., 11 ILR (P&F) 700 [SD NY, 2002].**

Issues of fact preclude entry of judgment in favor of music search engine as to contributory infringement.

Defendant, which operates a music search engine site that enables Internet users to locate allegedly pirated versions of plaintiff's copyrighted sound recordings, cannot obtain summary judgment on plaintiffs' infringement claims because material issues of fact exist regarding whether defendant has engaged in contributory copyright infringement. There is sufficient evidence from which a factfinder could determine that defendant engaged in an overall course of conduct which materially contributed to copyright infringement. Not only could a jury find that defendant provided the facilities to promote infringing activity, but also that it directly assisted users in locating and downloading infringing files. Additional issues of fact exist regarding defendant's constructive knowledge, as well as whether defendant obtained actual knowledge of infringement occurring via its site. — **Arista Records, Inc. v. MP3Board, Inc., 11 ILR (P&F) 700 [SD NY, 2002].**

Demand letter may have given MP3 site actual notice of infringement of copyrights.

A cease-and-desist letter listing specific sound recordings that were available through defendant's musical search engine site may have given defendant actual knowledge of infringing activity being facilitated by its service. Defendant's service enables Internet users to locate music files from publicly available web sites. A trade association representing the interests of the plaintiff record companies sent defendant three notification letters pursuant to the Digital Millennium Copyright Act (DMCA). The first two letters, which merely listed a handful of performers whose works were allegedly being infringed, fell short of the DMCA's standard in providing defendant with knowledge of infringement. The third letter, however, not only named particular artists along with specified songs, but was accompanied by printouts of screen shots of defendant's web site, on which 662 links were highlighted, identifying those files believed to infringe upon plaintiffs' copyrights. That letter provided information reasonably sufficient to permit defendant to located the links. Defendant's argument, that it was not required to disable access to or even investigate the links because the trade association did not submit the links in electronic form or accompanied with the URLs of the pages to which the links connected, is baseless and not grounded in the text of the DMCA or any judicial interpretation of that statute. — **Arista Records, Inc. v. MP3Board, Inc., 11 ILR (P&F) 700 [SD NY, 2002].**

Issues of fact preclude entry of judgment in favor of music search engine as to vicarious infringement.

Defendant, which operates a music search engine site that enables Internet users to locate allegedly pirated versions of plaintiff's copyrighted sound recordings, cannot obtain summary judgment on plaintiffs' infringement claims because material issues of fact exist regarding whether defendant has engaged in vicarious copyright infringement. A company may be found vicariously liable for copyright infringement if it has the right and ability to supervise infringing activity and also has a direct financial interest in that activity. There are material issues of fact on both these points. There are also material issues of fact as to whether defendant qualifies as a "service provider" entitled to the "safe harbor" protections of the Digital Millennium Copyright Act (DMCA), 17 USC §512(d). Defendant contends that it is a "traditional search engine," while plaintiffs contend that defendant provides a host of services not provided by traditional search engines. Even if defendant meets the definition of a "service provider," it must still surmount the other hurdles of §512—a proposition of doubtful certainty—to qualify for the liability limitations the statute affords. Notably, the statute limits liability rather than providing a complete exemption. Moreover, because there are material issues of fact regarding defendant's knowledge of the infringing activity— another factor weighed in the availability of the "safe harbor" provision—defendant cannot obtain summary judgment pursuant to the defense of lack of knowledge. — **Arista Records, Inc. v. MP3Board, Inc., 11 ILR (P&F) 700 [SD NY, 2002].**

First Amendment, fair use does not shield music search engine from copyright liability.

Defendant's operation of a music search engine site, which enables Internet users to locate allegedly pirated versions of plaintiffs' copyrighted sound recordings, is not entitled to First Amendment protection since First Amendment concerns are protected by and coextensive with the fair use doctrine. In its summary judgment papers, defendant has not asserted that the activities in question constitute "fair use" and therefore do not violate plaintiffs' copyrights. Moreover, even if it had, the evidence indicates that such a claim would fail because the four specific factors courts must consider in deciding fair use all weigh against such a finding in the present case. Regarding the first factor, "the purpose and character of the use," the purpose of defendant and its users was commercial, as they were allegedly profiting from the exploitation of the copyrighted work without paying the customary prices. Regarding the second factor, "the nature of the copyrighted work," the published creative sound recordings copied are close to the core of intended copyright protection. Regarding the third factor, "the amount and substantiality of the portion used in relation to the copyrighted work as a whole," plaintiffs contend that entireties of copyrighted works were infringed rather than small portions. Regarding the fourth factor, "the effect of the use upon the potential market for or value of the copyrighted work," the alleged activities of defendant and its users on their face could harm the market for the original works. Thus, because all four factors weigh against a finding of fair use, and there are no other relevant factors apparent, defendant's motion for summary judgment based upon the theory that its activities are protected by the First Amendment is denied. — **Arista Records, Inc. v. MP3Board, Inc., 11 ILR (P&F) 700 [SD NY, 2002].**

Faulty DMCA notice does not generate liability for author of notice.

A trade association representing the interests of record companies is not liable for violating the Digital Millennium Copyright Act (DMCA) or for tortious interference with contractual relations. The record companies had sued defendant for copyright infringement, based on defendant's music search engine that enables Internet users to locate allegedly pirated versions of copyrighted sound recordings. Defendant, in turn, filed a third-party complaint against the trade association based on its actions in serving a notice and subpoena on defendant's Internet service provider directing the ISP to shut down defendant's site pursuant to the DMCA. The ISP complied. Defendant claimed that the association's DMCA notice contained a knowing and material misrepresentation of infringement. Although the notice did not substantially comply with the DMCA's requirements for effective notification—it had listed solely artists' names and neglected to specify any links or particular songs—liability cannot be incurred under §512(f) for merely sending insufficient notification. The DMCA standard is whether the copyright owner's agent "knowingly materially misrepresents . . . that material or activity is infringing," and there is no evidence of that here. Furthermore, the resulting disruption of defendant's Internet service does not render the association liable for tortious interference with contract because the association was justified in sending the infringement notice to the ISP. Absent a showing that the ISP was immune from liability pursuant to DMCA §512(a), and that the association knew the ISP to be immune, liability cannot be grounded on the association's statement that the ISP could be liable for hosting defendant's activities if the ISP knew of defendant's infringement but failed to disable access. — **Arista Records, Inc. v. MP3Board, Inc., 11 ILR (P&F) 700 [SD NY, 2002].**

OPINION & ORDER

STEIN, *District Judge.* Plaintiffs, several leading record companies, have sued MP3Board, Inc. for contributory and vicarious copyright infringement, 17 USC §§101 *et seq.*, and state law unfair competition. The record companies allege that MP3Board operates an Internet site which provides users with links to pirated copies of the record companies' copyrighted musical recordings, thereby facilitating the users' infringement of the record companies' copyrights. MP3Board has instituted a third-party claim against the Recording Industry Association of America ("RIAA"), a trade association of record companies, for tortious interference and knowing material misrepresentation of infringement in violation of the Digital Millennium Copyright Act ("DMCA"), stemming from the RIAA's sending copyright infringement notices to MP3Board's Internet Service Providers ("ISPs").

The record companies have moved for summary judgment pursuant to Federal Rule of Civil Procedure 56, seeking an order finding MP3Board liable for contributory and vicarious copyright infringement and unfair competition. MP3Board has moved for summary judgment on the grounds that its activities are protected by the First Amendment to the United States Constitution, and has alternatively moved for partial summary judgment on each of the counts of the complaint for a variety of reasons and on the grounds that the record companies have failed to show damages. The RIAA has also moved for summary judgment with respect to MP3Board's third party claims against it.

The record companies' motion for summary judgment is denied because material issues of fact exist regarding whether any direct infringement occurred with the aid of the MP3Board site. MP3Board's motion for summary judgment is denied because its activities are not protected by the First Amendment and because material issues of fact exist regarding whether MP3Board has engaged in contributory or vicarious copyright infringement. The RIAA's motion for summary judgment is granted because its actions were justified and it did not materially misrepresent that links to infringing material were posted on the MP3Board site.

OVERVIEW

Several major record companies have brought suit against MP3Board for operating a Web site, located at http://www.mp3board.com, which provides Internet users with resources enabling them to locate sound recording files from publicly available Web sites. Such audio files can be created by using computer software to digitally copy an audio recording directly onto a computer's hard drive, compressing the digital information via a technology such as MP3 in order to allow for more efficient storage and transmission of the file over the Internet. The record companies have alleged that many of the audio files which can be located with the assistance of MP3Board's Web site are pirated copies of the record companies' copyrighted works.

During the relevant time period, no music files were located on the MP3Board Web site; rather, the Web site featured an automated search engine that searched for, aggregated and organized links to media files on the Web, and provided a tutorial offering users instruction in how to locate and download such files. (MP3Board's Objections to

Pls.' Resp. Ex. A; Eli Mapstead Dep. at 118, 227, 304, 308; Mathewson Dep. at 79-80; Pls.' Exs. 24, 25, 35, 36; Am. Answer ¶41.) MP3Board additionally solicited users to post links on the MP3Board site to other sites containing audio files and provided a link to a third party named Freedrive where users could store audio files online. (MP3Board's Objections to Pls.' Resp. Ex. A; Pls.' Exs. 8, 9, 10; Am. Answer ¶39.) The MP3Board site also featured a message board which allowed users to post questions or song requests to be replied to by other users or MP3Board staff. (MP3Board's Objections to Pls.' Resp. Ex. A.) In response to users' posted requests, MP3Board personnel personally searched for links to songs and posted the links on the message board, solicited other users to provide the requested works, and obtained and posted passwords to enable users to access certain music files. (Eli Mapstead Dep. at 199-200, 202-03, 205-06, 342; Mathewson Dep. at 52; MP3Board's Objections to Pls.' Resp. Exs. A, B; Am. Answer ¶41; Pls.' Ex. 22.)

On October 27, 1999, the RIAA, acting on behalf of its member record companies, served a subpoena and notice letter to AboveNet Communications, Inc., the ISP that connected MP3Board's Web site to the Internet. The letter identified artists whose work was being allegedly infringed and requested that AboveNet remove or disable access to the MP3Board site or MP3Board's links to infringing works. (Creighton Decl. ¶7 and Ex. A; McDevitt Decl. ¶4; McDevitt Dep. at 8-10.) AboveNet did not substantially interrupt MP3Board's service as a result of this letter, and MP3Board suffered no injury. (Eli Mapstead RIAA Dep. at 26, 27; see also Lars Mapstead RIAA Dep. at 385-86.) MP3Board did not dismantle access to any links to the identified artists' works. (Noah Mapstead Dep. at 175-77, 194-98 .)

On April 18, 2000, the RIAA sent a notice to Metromedia Fiber Network, Inc., AboveNet's corporate successor. (Creighton Decl. ¶8.) Like the October 1999 notice, the April 2000 notice also named representative artists whose works were allegedly being infringed and requested that Metromedia remove MP3Board site or the infringing links from its system. (Creighton Decl. Ex. B.) Moreover, the letter warned Metromedia that failure to comply could subject it to liability pursuant to the DMCA. (Creighton Decl. Ex. B.)

In response, Metromedia disabled Internet access to the MP3Board Web site beginning on April 19, 2000. (Eli Mapstead RIAA Dep. at 37-38, 40.) MP3Board requested that Metromedia restore its service, and Metromedia replied that it would only restore MP3Board's service if MP3Board supplied a counter notification in accordance with the DMCA. On April 21, 2000, MP3Board supplied a counter notification to Metromedia asserting that it had removed the infringing material identified in the RIAA's notice. (Lars Mapstead RIAA Dep. at 498; Knowles Decl. Ex. K.) Metromedia restored MP3Board's Internet connectivity on May 5, 2000. (Eli Mapstead RIAA Dep. at 197.)

On May 25, 2000, the RIAA wrote directly to MP3Board and demanded that MP3Board remove all infringing links from its site by June 2, 2000, naming twenty-one artists and twenty-two song titles which were representative of the titles being infringed, and also attaching printouts of screen shots of MP3Board's Web site on which the RIAA identified 662 links which the RIAA believed to lead to material infringing upon the record companies' copyrights. (Pls.' Ex. 36, Ex. C.) MP3Board failed to dismantle access to any of the identified links in response to this letter. (Noah Mapstead Dep. at 175-77, 194-98.) On June 23, 2000, the record companies filed suit against MP3Board in the Southern District of New York *[5 ILR (P&F) 2161]*.

DISCUSSION

Summary judgment may be granted "only when the moving party demonstrates that 'there is no genuine issue as to any material fact and that the moving party is entitled to a judgment as a matter of law.' " *Allen v. Coughlin*, 64 F3d 77, 79 (2d Cir 1995) (quoting Fed. R. Civ. P. 56(c)); *see also Celotex Corp. v. Catrett*, 477 US 317, 322 (1986). The Court must "view the evidence in the light most favorable to the nonmoving party and draw all reasonable inferences in its favor, and may grant summary judgment only when 'no reasonable trier of fact could find in favor of the nonmoving party.' " *Allen*, 64 F3d at 79 (citation omitted) (quoting *Lund's, Inc. v. Chemical Bank*, 870 F2d 840, 844 (2d Cir 1989)).

Once the moving party meets its initial burden of demonstrating the absence of a genuine issue of material fact, the nonmoving party must come forward with specific facts to show there is a factual question that must be resolved at trial. Fed. R. Civ. P. 56(e); *see also Legal Aid Soc'y v. City of New York*, 114 F Supp 2d 204 (SD NY 2000). A nonmoving party must produce evidence in the record and "may not rely simply on conclusory statements or on contentions that the affidavits supporting the motion are not credible." *Ying Jing Gan v. City of New York,* 996 F2d 522, 532 (2d Cir 1993). In short, a nonmoving party must "do more than simply show there is some metaphysical doubt as to the material facts." *Matsushita Elec. Indus. Co. v. Zenith Radio Corp.*, 475 US 574, 586 (1986).

I. The Record Companies' Motion for Summary Judgment is Denied Because Issues of Material Fact Exist Regarding Whether the Record Companies' Copyrights Were Infringed by MP3Board's Users.

In order to establish liability for contributory or vicarious copyright infringement, a plaintiff must first prove that direct infringement of its works occurred by showing that it owned a valid copyright and unauthorized infringement of its protected material occurred. *See Sony Corp. of Amer. v. Universal City Studios*, 464 US 417, 434 (1984); *Feist Publ'ns v. Rural Tel. Serv. Co.*, 499 US 340, 361 *[1 ILR (P&F) 180]* (1991); *Rogers v. Koons,* 960 F2d 301, 306 (2d Cir 1992). The record companies' ownership of the sound recordings at issue has not been disputed. (Plts.' Rule 56.1 Stmt. ¶¶23-24.) The RIAA has also confirmed that the 58 files listed in the complaint as available through MP3Board's Web site constituted unauthorized copies of the copyrighted recordings. (Creighton Reply Decl. ¶8.)

However, the record companies have failed to prove that any direct infringement resulted from MP3Board's operations. Pursuant to 17 USC §501(a), infringement occurs when one of the exclusive rights granted to copyright holders by 17 USC §106 is violated. *See A&M Records, Inc. v. Napster, Inc.*, 239 F3d 1004, 1014 *[7 ILR (P&F) 1]* (9th Cir 2001). While the structure of MP3Board's site and the scale of the operation certainly give rise to a strong statistical inference that MP3Board users downloaded files containing copyrighted music in violation of the record companies' reproduction rights under Section 106(1), the record companies have failed to eliminate all genuine issues of material fact.

MP3Board freely acknowledges the possibility that infringement is conducted with the aid of its site. MP3Board has stated that it "is generally aware that some of the music files . . . may contain infringing material," and it admits that it "allows" and "generally encourages" site visitors to download music files, thus promoting the "highly effective facilitation of access to popular music." (Am. Answer ¶¶2, 3, 40, 52.) "MP3Board acknowledges that users *may* use its systems for purposes of infringement." (MP3Board's Statement of Material Facts in Opp'n to Pls.' Mot. for Summ. J. ¶56 (emphasis in original).) MP3Board's principals also testified that they were aware that some of MP3Board's links connected to copyrighted works, and they assumed that those unauthorized copies were downloaded by users of the service through those links. (Eli Mapstead Dep. at 313, 316; Lars Mapstead Dep. at 249.). One principal admitted that it was "particularly likely" that MP3Board's users have used links on MP3Board's Web site to download full-length copies of major record labels' songs. (Noah Mapstead Dep. at 107.) There is also evidence that MP3Board personally assisted users in obtaining particular songs that the users requested, *see* Section II(A)(1) *infra*, and a finder of fact could certainly infer that it is likely that those users subsequently downloaded the songs they had requested. However, the record companies have not eliminated all issues of material fact by setting forth any direct evidence of infringement, such as user logs or other technical data showing the downloading of copyrighted and unauthorized files. At the summary judgment stage, the record companies cannot rely solely upon circumstantial evidence and admissions by MP3Board officers that it is statistically "likely" that direct infringement occurred.

Additionally, while the record companies and the RIAA have conclusively established that links to unauthorized infringing files were posted on the MP3Board Web site by describing how the RIAA investigators followed the links on the MP3Board Web site and determined that they lead to audio files that infringed upon plaintiffs' copyrights, (Creighton Decl. ¶10; McDevitt Decl. ¶5), to show the unlawful "distribution" of a copyrighted work pursuant to 17 USC §106(3) the record companies must show that an unlawful copy was disseminated "to the public." *Hotaling v. Church of Jesus Christ of Latter-Day*

Saints, 118 F3d 199, 203 (4th Cir 1997) (internal quotations omitted). "Infringement of the distribution right requires an actual dissemination of . . . copies." *National Car Rental Sys. v. Computer Assocs. Int'l, Inc.*, 991 F2d 426, 434 (8th Cir 1993) (citing 2 Nimmer on Copyright §8.11[A], at 8-124.1); *see also Napster*, 239 F3d at 1014. While a copyright holder may not be required to prove particular instances of use by the public when the proof is impossible to produce because the infringer has not kept records of public use, *see Hotaling*, 118 F3d at 204, in the present case there has been no showing that the record companies did not have access to such data. Accordingly, the record companies' motion for summary judgment regarding contributory and vicarious copyright infringement and unfair competition is denied.

II. MP3Board's Motion for Summary Judgment is Denied Because Issues of Material Fact Exist Regarding Whether MP3Board is Liable for Contributory Copyright Infringement, Vicarious Infringement, and Unfair Competition.

A. Issues of Material Fact Exist Regarding Whether MP3Board is Liable for Contributory Copyright Infringement.

"A party 'who, with knowledge of . . . infringing activity . . . materially contributes to the infringing conduct of another, may be held liable as a 'contributory' infringer.' " *Matthew Bender & Co., Inc. v. West Publ'g Co.*, 158 F3d 693, 706 *[1 ILR (P&F) 38]* (2d Cir 1998) (quoting *Gershwin Publ'g Corp. v. Columbia Artists Mgmt., Inc.*, 443 F2d 1159, 1162 (2d Cir 1971)); *see also Ex-Tixz, Inc. v. Hit Tix, Inc.*, 919 F Supp 728, 732 (SD NY 1996). In order to carry its burden, MP3Board must demonstrate the absence of material facts regarding (1) the noninfringing conduct of MP3Board's users, (2) MP3Board's lack of material contribution to that infringement, or (3) MP3Board's lack of knowledge of the infringing activity. MP3Board has failed to demonstrate the absence of material facts with respect to any of the elements. As an initial matter, for the reasons set forth in Section I, *supra*, material facts exist regarding the first element of direct infringement; while the record companies did not eliminate all issues of material fact, they showed statements by MP3Board's officers and circumstantial evidence regarding MP3Board's Web

site which suffice to defeat summary judgment against them on the issue of direct infringement.

1. Issues of Material Fact Exist Regarding Whether MP3Board Materially Contributed to Any Infringement.

MP3Board cannot obtain summary judgment on the contributory infringement claim on the grounds that no material issues of fact exist regarding MP3Board's material contribution to any infringement. Liability for contributory infringement exists if the defendant engages in "personal conduct that encourages or assists the infringement." *Matthew Bender*, 158 F3d at 706. Merely supplying the " 'means' to accomplish an infringing activity" cannot give rise to the imposition of liability for contributory copyright infringement. *Sony*, 464 US at 436; *see also Napster*, 239 F3d at 1020-21. "Participation in the infringement must be substantial. The . . . assistance must bear a direct relationship to the infringing acts, and the contributory infringer must have acted in concert with the direct infringer." *ZVI Livnat v. Shai Bar Lavi*, No. 96 Civ. 4967, 1998 WL 43221, at *3 (SD NY Feb. 2, 1998) (internal quotation marks and citations omitted). MP3Board argues that the record companies have not shown that MP3Board substantially participated in any infringement. MP3Board styles itself a "passive" tool, contending that "[a]ny participation by MP3Board in its users' infringement is tangential to their direct downloading from a third-party website." (MP3Board Mem. in Opp'n at 14, 15.)

However, there is sufficient evidence from which a factfinder could determine that MP3Board engaged in an overall course of conduct which materially contributed to copyright infringement. The MP3Board site featured a search engine: an automated system devoted to searching for, aggregating and organizing links. (MP3Board's Objections to Pls.' Resp. Ex. A.) The site also solicited third parties to post links to sites containing audio files. (MP3Board's Objections to Pls.' Resp. Ex. A; Pls.' Exs. 8, 9, 10; Am. Answer ¶39.) MP3Board provided a link to a third party named Freedrive where users could store audio files online. (MP3Board's Objections to Pls.' Resp. Ex. A.) MP3Board offered new users "getting started" information and a tutorial containing instructions on how to locate and download audio files via MP3Board—actually using one of the record companies' copyrighted recordings as an example. (Eli Mapstead Dep. at 118, 227, 304, 308; Mathewson Dep. at 79-80; Pls.' Exs. 24, 25, 35, 36; Am. Answer ¶41.)

The site also contained a message board which allowed users to post questions to be answered by other users or MP3Board staff. (MP3Board's Objections to Pls.' Resp. Ex. A.) Significantly, when individual users posted messages on the message board requesting particular songs which they could not find links to on the MP3Board site, MP3Board personnel personally searched for links to the requested song files and posted the links on the message board. (Eli Mapstead Dep. at 202-03, 205-06; Mathewson Dep. at 52; MP3Board's Objections to Pls.' Resp. Ex. B; Am. Answer ¶41.) When one MP3Board employee could not find any links to one particular work, he solicited users to provide the work. (Pls.' Ex. 22.) MP3Board also obtained and posted passwords to enable users to access certain music files. (Eli Mapstead Dep. at 199-200, 342.)

Thus, based upon all the foregoing facts, genuine issues of material fact exist regarding whether MP3Board materially contributed to infringement. Not only could a jury find that MP3Board provided the facilities to promote infringing activity, *see, e.g., Fonovisa, Inc. v. Cherry Auction, Inc.*, 76 F3d 259, 261, 264 (9th Cir 1996); *Sega Enters. v. Maphia*, 857 F Supp 679, 687 *[2 ILR (P&F) 168]* (ND Cal 1994); *Sega Enters. Ltd. v. Sabella*, No. 93 Civ. 4260, 1996 WL 780560, at *8 (ND Cal Dec. 18, 1996), but also that it directly assisted users in locating and downloading infringing files, *see Intellectual Reserve, Inc. v. Utah Lighthouse Ministry, Inc.*, 75 F Supp 2d 1290, 1294-95 *[4 ILR (P&F) 303]* (D Utah 1999). Viewed in totality, the record companies have introduced evidence that raises a material issue of fact regarding whether MP3Board's active role in facilitating its users' copying constituted substantial material participation in infringement.

2. Issues of Material Fact Exist Regarding Whether MP3Board Knew that Infringing Activity Was Taking Place.

A defendant must possess either actual or constructive knowledge of the infringing activity to be found contributorily liable. *See ZVI Livnat*, 1998 WL 43221, at *3; *see also Napster*, 239 F3d at 1020 (requiring that the secondary infringer "know or have

reason to know" of direct infringement). Issues of fact exist regarding MP3Board's constructive knowledge as well as whether MP3Board obtained actual knowledge of infringement occurring via its site.

a. Issues of Material Fact Exist Concerning Whether MP3Board Possessed Constructive Knowledge of Infringing Activity.

As an initial matter, it is axiomatic that without any knowledge of infringing activity, a defendant cannot be found strictly liable for contributory infringement simply for providing a technology that may allow others to exchange copyrighted material. A court may not impute constructive knowledge of infringement to a defendant "merely because . . . [a] technology may be used to infringe plaintiffs' copyrights," where the system is "capable of commercially significant noninfringing uses." *Napster*, 239 F3d at 1020-21 (citing *Sony*, 464 US at 436, 442-43). In *Sony*, the U.S. Supreme Court refused to permit liability to be imposed upon Sony for providing customers with equipment (the Betamax video cassette recorder) with "constructive knowledge . . . that their customers may use that equipment to make unauthorized copies of copyrighted material." *Sony*, 464 US at 439. Rather, a plaintiff must actually show the defendant knew that infringing activity was taking place instead of simply relying on the technology's potential. At this stage of the litigation, material facts exist regarding whether the Court can impute constructive knowledge to MP3Board based upon its technology's capabilities; the parties have not set forth sufficient facts for the Court to determine whether MP3Board's activities are covered by the *Sony* doctrine and whether MP3Board's Web site is "capable of commercially significant noninfringing uses."

However, the record companies have introduced direct evidence that MP3Board should have known of any infringement. There is evidence from which a jury could find that MP3Board possessed constructive knowledge of infringement, despite the fact that this case does not share the same strong indicia of constructive knowledge as in the cases cited by the record companies. *See Fonovisa*, 76 F3d at 261; *Napster*, 114 F Supp 2d at 919; *Playboy Enters., Inc. v. Russ Hardenburgh, Inc.*, 982 F Supp 503, 513, 514 *[2 ILR (P&F) 13]* (ND Ohio 1997) (the defendant had an active screening procedure by which the defendant's employees personally viewed all files posted on the bulletin board service); *Maphia*, 857 F Supp at 683 ("the uploading and downloading of unauthorized copies of Sega's copyrighted video games is particularly known to defendant"); *Sabella*, 1996 WL 780560, at *8 (the defendant, the operator of the bulletin board service, read the user log containing files labeled as Sega Genesis games several times a day, advertised copiers which played unauthorized copies of Sega games, gave downloading privileges to customers that bought copiers, and offered a gift award that would enable users to 'get started right away with [their] collection of games' "). Nor does the operating of an audio file search engine have "no other imaginable [noninfringing] use," thus inevitably suggesting infringement to a rational person. *RSO Records, Inc. v. Peri*, 596 F Supp 849 (SD NY 1984) (where the defendant was engaged in photographing the packaging of copyrighted records and tapes).

The record companies contend that evidence of MP3Board's knowledge can be found in the fact that MP3Board created 16 genre categories on its site, such as "Pop" and "Classical," in which link contributors could display their posted links, and one of these categories was entitled "Legal MP3s." (Eli Mapstead Dep. at 153.) The record companies urge that the category heading "Legal MP3s" constitutes evidence that MP3Board recognized that the other categories contained MP3s which were *not* legal. MP3Board responds that the genre heading "Legal MP3s" does not constitute an admission as to the contents of the other genres, particularly because Epitonic, a third-party MP3 supplier, specifically requested the title "Legal MP3" to describe the category, which contained exclusively Epitonic content. (Eli Mapstead Dep. at 105; Lars Mapstead Dep. at 128.) The record companies also argue that a substantial number of the posted links themselves promoted their illegal nature, as the posters of the links gave themselves such names as "SUPERiLLEGAL MP3z," "FREE ILLEGAL MP3 FILES DIRECT DOWNLOAD," "FREE FAST ILLEGAL MP3 DIRECT DOWNLOAD," "The BIGGEST Archive of ILLEGAL MP3 FLZ," "100% ILLEGAL FAST DOWNLOADS," "a HUGE Archive of Illegal MP3 Files!!" and "any song you want." (Pls.' Ex. 23.) MP3Board contends in response that there is no evidence that it monitored

the posting of links, and it has stated that it does not investigate the links, and perceived the names of the posters to be the site-owners' efforts to boost traffic on their sites by means of attention-getting methods. (Lars Mapstead Decl. ¶11; Lars Mapstead Dep. at 129.)

Nonetheless, the above-stated facts, combined with the fact that MP3Board's principals acknowledged a statistical possibility that some of the links found on MP3Board's Web site went to copyrighted works and that users had downloaded unauthorized copies of copyrighted sound recordings through the links, (Lars Mapstead Dep. at 249, 451; Eli Mapstead Dep. at 313, 355; Noah Mapstead Dep. at 107), give rise to triable issues of fact regarding whether MP3Board possessed constructive knowledge of the infringing nature of links.

b. Issues of Material Fact Exist Regarding Whether MP3Board Acquired Actual Knowledge of Infringement.

There is also much stronger evidence that MP3Board acquired actual knowledge of infringement from a notice that the RIAA sent to MP3Board pursuant to the DMCA. In order for a notice to be considered effective pursuant to the DMCA, it must provide "identification of the reference or link, to material or activity claimed to be infringing . . . and information reasonably sufficient to permit the service provider to locate that reference or link." 17 USC §512(d)(1)(C)(3). The RIAA sent notification letters on October 27, 1999 and April 18, 2000 to MP3Board's ISPs, who forwarded copies of the letters to MP3Board, and also sent a notification letter on May 25, 2000 directly to MP3Board. While the letters dated October 27, 1999 and April 18, 2000 fell short of the DMCA's standard in providing MP3Board with knowledge of infringement, the letter dated May 25, 2000 did provide MP3Board with sufficient knowledge.

The letter from the RIAA to AboveNet dated October 27, 1999 failed to put MP3Board on notice of any infringement. It stated that the MP3Board site:

> offers over one thousand direct links to sound files on other Internet sites for download. Many of these files contain recordings owned by our member companies, including songs

by such artists as Sugar Ray, Ricky Martin, Radiohead, TLC, Red Hot Chili Peppers, Madonna, Shania Twain, Lou Bega, the Fugees and Ace of Base. We have a good belief that the above-described activity is not authorized by the copyright owner, its agent, or the law.

(Pls.' Ex. 34.) By solely listing artists' names, and neglecting to specify any infringing links or even particular songs, the letter did not include "identification of the reference or link, to material or activity claimed to be infringing . . . and information reasonably sufficient to permit the service provider to locate that reference or link." 17 USC §512(d)(1)(C)(3).

The record companies' citation to the Fourth Circuit's decision in *ALS Scan, Inc. v. RemarQ Communities, Inc.*, 239 F3d 619, 622 *[7 ILR (P&F) 69]* (4th Cir 2001), cannot save this letter. *ALS Scan* set forth that "[w]hen a letter provides notice equivalent to a list of representative works that can be easily identified by the service provider, the notice substantially complies with the notification requirements." 239 F3d at 622. The plaintiff in *ALS Scan* alerted the defendant to infringement in sufficient detail when it

(1) identified two sites created for the sole purpose of publishing ALS Scan's copyrighted works, (2) asserted that virtually all the images at the two sites were [ALS Scan's] copyrighted material, . . . (3) referred RemarQ to two web addresses where RemarQ could find pictures of ALS Scan's models and obtain ALS Scan's copyright information . . . [and (4)] noted that material at the site could be identified as ALS Scan's material because the material included ALS Scan's 'name and/or copyright symbol next to it.' *Id.*

However, by merely listed ten artists in the October 27 letter, the RIAA fell short of "substantially compl[ying] with the notification requirement." *Id.* The citation to a handful of performers does not constitute a representative list of infringing material, and certainly did not provide information reasonably sufficient to enable MP3Board to locate the particular infringing works. Therefore, MP3Board's failure to delete links to sites containing music files of the enumerated artists

in response to the October 1999 letter, (Lars Mapstead Dep. at 399), cannot give rise to any liability. *C.f. Religious Tech. Ctr. v. Netcom On-Line Communication Servs., Inc.*, 907 F Supp 1361, 1374 *[1 ILR (P&F) 778]* (ND Cal 1995) (where a bulletin board service operator cannot reasonably verify a claim of infringement due to the copyright holder's failure to provide the necessary documentation to show that there is likely infringement, the operator's lack of knowledge is reasonable and there is no liability for contributory infringement for allowing the continued distribution of the works).

The email from the RIAA to Metromedia dated April 18, 2000, and subsequently forwarded to MP3Board, similarly stated that the MP3Board site:

is offering direct links to files on other Internet sites containing full-length sound recordings for other users to download, including songs by such artists as Third Eye Blind, Rage Against the Machine, No Doubt, Rammstein and the Bloodhound Gang. We have a good faith belief that the above-described activity is not authorized by the copyright owner, its agent, or the law.

(Pls.' Ex. 35.) This email, nearly identical in form to the October 27, 1999 letter, similarly failed to put MP3Board on notice of any infringement because it listed solely artists' names, and neglected to specify any links or even particular songs.

However, in contrast with the earlier letters, the letter from the RIAA to MP3Board dated May 25, 2000 substantially complied with the DMCA notification requirements. The letter not only named particular artists along with specified songs, but was accompanied by printouts of screen shots of MP3Board's Web site, on which the RIAA highlighted and placed an asterisk next to 662 links which the RIAA believed to infringe upon the record companies' copyrights. (Pls.'s Ex. 36, Ex. C.) Despite the fact that the RIAA did not provide MP3Board with the specific Universal Resource Locators ("URLs") of the pages to which the links connected, the RIAA provided MP3Board with the pages on MP3Board's own site where the links appeared. (Pls.'s Ex. 36, Ex. C.) Overall, the letter and its attachments identified the material or activity claimed to be infringing and provided information reasonably sufficient to permit MP3Board to locate the links and thus complied with the DMCA. *See* 17 USC §512(d)(1)(C)(3); *ALS Scan*; 239 F3d at 622; *see also Napster*, 239 F3d at 1021-22 & n. 6; *Fonovisa*, 76 F3d at 261, 264; *Olan Mills, Inc. v. Linn Photo Co.*, 23 F3d 1345, 1348 (8th Cir 1994); *Napster*, 114 F Supp 2d at 918.

MP3Board failed to dismantle access to any of the identified links in response to these letters. (Noah Mapstead Dep. at 175-77, 194-98.) MP3Board's argument, that it was not required to disable access to or even investigate the links because the RIAA did not submit the links in electronic form or accompanied with the URLs of the pages to which the links connected, are baseless and not grounded in the text of the DMCA or any judicial interpretation of that statute. Despite the fact that the RIAA did not provide MP3Board with specific URLs, it provided MP3Board with the pages on MP3Board's own site where the links appeared, thus identifying the links to material or activity claimed to be infringing and information reasonably sufficient to permit MP3Board to locate the links. Therefore, because issues of material fact exist regarding whether MP3Board materially contributed to infringing activity and had acquired knowledge of the infringement, summary judgment in favor of MP3Board with respect to the claim of contributory copyright infringement is denied.

B. Issues of Material Fact Exist Regarding Whether MP3Board is Liable for Vicarious Infringement.

A company may be found vicariously liable for copyright infringement if it has the right and ability to supervise infringing activity and also has a direct financial interest in that activity. *See Gershwin Publ'g*, 443 F2d at 1162. Vicarious liability, "commonly imposed upon publishers, printers, and vendors of copyrighted materials," is appropriate where a company is "in a position to police the conduct of the 'primary' infringer." *Shapiro, Bernstein & Co. v. H.L. Green Co.*, 316 F2d 304, 308 (2d Cir 1963) (citations omitted).

As an initial matter, although the record companies correctly state that, in general, vicarious infringement is a tort of strict liability and hence the vicarious infringer need not possess knowledge of the infringement, the record companies do not address the additional limitations upon copyright infringement liability relating to online material

provided by the DCMA—albeit an affirmative defense only vaguely raised in MP3Board's answer. Nonetheless, the DMCA provides that a service provider:

> shall not be liable . . . for infringement of copyright by reason of the provider referring or linking users to an online location containing infringing material or infringing activity, by using information location tools, including a directory, index, reference, pointer, or hypertext link, if the service provider does not have actual knowledge that the material or activity is infringing [or] in the absence of such actual knowledge, is not aware of facts or circumstances from which infringing activity is apparent.

17 USC §512(d)(1). There are material issues of fact as to whether MP3Board qualifies as a "service provider" entitled to the "safe harbor" protections of section 512(d). MP3Board contends that it is a "traditional search engine," (Def.'s Statement of Material Facts ¶20), while plaintiffs contend that MP3Board provides a host of services not provided by traditional search engines, (Pls.' Resp. to Def.'s Statement of Material Facts ¶20). Even if MP3Board meets the definition of a "service provider" it must still surmount the other hurdles of section 512—a proposition of doubtful certainty— to qualify for the liability limitations the statute affords. Notably, the statute limits liability rather than providing a complete exemption. *See* 17 USC §512(d); *see also Perfect 10, Inc. v. Cybernet Ventures, Inc.*, No. CV 01-2595, 2002 U.S. Dist. LEXIS 7333, at *77 [10 ILR (P&F) 483] (CD Cal Apr. 22, 2002); 3 Nimmer on Copyright §12B.01[C][2], at 12B-18. Moreover, because there are material issues of fact regarding MP3Board's knowledge of the infringing activity—another factor weighed in the availability of the "safe harbor" provision—MP3Board cannot obtain summary judgment pursuant to the defense of lack of knowledge. *See* 17 USC §512(d); *see also* Section II(A)(2), *supra*.

1. Issues of Material Fact Exist Regarding Whether MP3Board Had the Right and the Ability to Supervise the Infringing Activities.

The record companies have introduced evidence showing that MP3Board possessed the right and the ability to supervise its users and the information displayed on its site. A defendant's "ability to block infringers' access to a particular environment for any reason" constitutes proof of its right and ability to supervise and control the infringing activities. *Napster*, 239 F3d at 1023; *see also Fonovisa*, 76 F3d at 262-63 (a swap-meet operator could exclude vendors for any reason); *Shapiro*, 316 F2d at 306-08. The facts have shown that MP3Board had the right and ability to police those who posted links to the site, as well as the ability to delete the links themselves from being displayed to users.

While there is no evidence that MP3Board could control which links were initially found by its automated procedures, MP3Board could delete links from its database and thus prevent them from being displayed in response to user queries. (Lars Mapstead Dep. at 338, 488-89.) Moreover, MP3Board had stated a policy of restricting users from posting certain types of links, such as those linking to pornography, hate, and hacker and "warez" (illegally copied and distributed commercial software) sites, and did in fact remove offending links from the site and banned repeat offenders of MP3Board's rules from posting any additional links. (Lars Mapstead Dep. at 338; Eli Mapstead Dep. at 328-31, 408-08.) Thus, there is evidence that MP3Board had the right and ability to remove links to infringing works and bar the participation of users who transmitted those infringing files. *See Napster*, 239 F3d at 1024; *see also Fonovisa*, 76 F3d at 260, 262.

2. Issues of Material Fact Exist Regarding Whether MP3Board Possessed a Direct Financial Interest in the Infringing Activities.

The record companies have also introduced evidence indicating that MP3Board possessed a direct financial interest in the exchange of infringing files. Infringement which increases a defendant's user base or otherwise acts as a draw for customers constitutes a direct financial interest. *See Napster*, 239 F3d 1023; *Fonovisa*, 76 F3d at 262-64 (financial benefit exists where "infringing performances enhance the attractiveness of a venue"); *Shapiro*, 316 F2d at 307. MP3Board's principals testified that the revenue MP3Board received from banner advertisements on the site was directly tied to the number of users who were exposed to those ads. (Lars Mapstead Dep. at 173, 219, 507-08; Eli Mapstead Dep. at 383; Eli Mapstead RIAA Dep. at 87.) Furthermore, the

RIAA's letter dated May 25, 2000 set forth that an extremely high proportion of the links on MP3Board's site went to infringing works. (Pls.'s Ex. 36, Ex. C.) The MP3Board site is exclusively and consciously devoted to locating audio files, and its financial interest in the locating and copying of music files is thus far more substantial and direct than the general interest, content neutral search engines with which MP3 wishes to compare itself. A jury could certainly find that MP3Board possessed a direct financial interest in infringing activities.

C. Issues of Material Fact Exist Regarding Whether MP3Board Is Liable for Unfair Competition.

The record companies have also sued MP3Board for unfair competition pursuant to New York common law with respect to the record companies' pre-1972 sound recordings, which are not subject to federal statutory copyright protection. *See* 17 USC §301(c); *Firma Melodiya v. ZYX Music, GmbH*, 882 F Supp 1306, 1316 (SD NY 1995). Summary judgment on this claim in favor of MP3Board is also denied.

In New York, an unfair competition claim may be grounded in the appropriation of the exclusive property of the plaintiff by the defendant. *See H.L. Hayden Co. v. Siemens Med. Sys., Inc.*, 879 F2d 1005, 1025 (2d Cir 1989). Pursuant to New York common law, "[a]n unfair competition claim involving misappropriation usually concerns the taking and use of the plaintiff's property to compete against the plaintiff's own use of the same property." *Roy Export Co. v. CBS*, 672 F2d 1095, 1105 (2d Cir 1982). Due to the legal overlap between the New York tort of unfair competition based upon misappropriation and federal copyright infringement, *see Kregos v. Associated Press*, 3 F3d 656, 666 (2d Cir 1993), summary judgment in favor of MP3Board is denied for the reasons stated above denying summary judgment on the copyright infringement claims.

D. Summary Judgment is Denied with Respect to MP3Board's Argument That Its Activities Are Entitled to First Amendment Protection.

MP3Board's argument that its activities are protected by the First Amendment to the U.S. Constitution is without merit. The U.S. Court of Appeals for the Second Circuit has held that "the fair use doctrine encompasses all claims of first amendment in the copyright field." *New Era Pubs. Int'l, ApS v. Henry Holt & Co.*, 873 F2d 576, 584 (2d Cir 1989); *see also* 17 USC §107; *Napster*, 239 F3d at 1028 (rejecting Napster's asserted free speech right to publish a "directory" in the form of a music file search index because Napster's users were not fair users); *Nihon Keizai Shimbun v. Comline Business Data, Inc.*, 166 F3d 65, 74 (2d Cir 1999) ("First Amendment concerns are protected by and coextensive with the fair use doctrine"); *Netcom*, 923 F Supp at 1258 (stating that the Copyright Act balances First Amendment concerns with the rights of copyright holders).

In its summary judgment papers, MP3Board has not asserted that the activities in question constitute "fair use" and therefore do not violate plaintiffs' copyrights. Moreover, even if it had, the evidence indicates that such a claim would fail. In analyzing the defense of "fair use," the Copyright Act specifies four factors that must be considered:

> (1) the purpose and character of the use, including whether such use is of a commercial nature or is for nonprofit educational purposes; (2) the nature of the copyrighted work; (3) the amount and substantiality of the portion used in relation to the copyrighted work as a whole; and (4) the effect of the use upon the potential market for or value of the copyrighted work.

17 USC §107. Other relevant factors may also be considered in order to apply the test in light of the overall purposes of the Copyright Act. *See Harper & Row, Publishers, Inc. v. Nation Enters.*, 471 US 539, 549 (1985); *Sony*, 464 US at 448, 454.

Assuming plaintiffs' allegations to be true, all four mandatory factors weigh against a finding of fair use in the present case. Regarding the first factor, "the purpose and character of the use," the purpose of MP3Board and its users was commercial, as they were allegedly "profit[ing] from the exploitation of the copyrighted work without paying the customary prices." *Harper & Row*, 471 US at 562. Moreover, the copied works were simply retransmitted, not transformed. *See Napster*, 239 F3d at 1015. Regarding the second factor, "the nature of the copyrighted work," the published creative sound recordings copied are "close to the core of intended copyright protection," and, conversely, far removed from the more factual or

descriptive type of work that is more amenable to fair use. *See UMG Recordings, Inc. v. MP3.com, Inc.*, 92 F Supp 2d 349, 351-52 *[5 ILR (P&F) 415]* (SD NY 2000) (citations omitted). Regarding the third factor, "the amount and substantiality of the portion used in relation to the copyrighted work as a whole," plaintiffs contend that entireties of copyrighted works were infringed rather than small portions. Regarding the fourth factor, "the effect of the use upon the potential market for or value of the copyrighted work," the alleged activities of MP3Board and its users on their face could harm the market for the original works. *See Napster*, 239 F3d at 1017. Thus, because all four factors weigh against a finding of fair use, and there are no other relevant factors apparent, MP3Board's motion for summary judgment based upon the theory that its activities are protected by the First Amendment is denied.

E. Issues of Material Fact Exist Regarding Damages.

MP3Board briefly argues that the record companies have not shown that they have suffered actual damages, or that MP3Board obtained any profits as a result of any infringement. MP3Board is correct: the amount of damages has not been litigated or established at this juncture. However, MP3Board also summarily—and incorrectly—argues that the record companies cannot prove statutory damages. The Copyright Act permits a copyright owner to elect to recover an award of statutory damages simply upon a showing of infringement. 17 USC §504(c). Should the record companies establish copyright infringement, they may elect to pursue an award of statutory damages.

III. The RIAA's Motion for Summary Judgment with Respect to MP3Board's Claims Against the RIAA Is Granted.

MP3Board has asserted two claims against the RIAA stemming from the RIAA's notices of copyright infringement sent to MP3Board's ISPs: (a) knowing material misrepresentation of infringement in violation of the DMCA, and (b) tortious interference with contractual relations and prospective economic advantage. The RIAA is entitled to summary judgment on those claims.

On October 27, 1999, the RIAA served a subpoena and DMCA notice letter to AboveNet that identified representative artists and requested AboveNet's "immediate assistance in stopping this unauthorized activity. Specifically, we request that you remove the site, delete the infringing links or that you disable access to this site or the infringing links being offered via your system." (Creighton Decl. ¶7 and Ex. A; McDevitt Decl. ¶4; McDevitt Dep. at 8-10.) However, the October 27, 1999 letter caused at most a very short-term interruption in MP3Board's service and, by MP3Board's own statements, no injury to MP3Board. (Eli Mapstead RIAA Dep. at 26-27; Lars Mapstead RIAA Dep. at 385-86.)

On April 18, 2000, the RIAA sent a second DMCA notice to Metromedia, identifying a URL of an MP3Board page, naming representative artists whose works were allegedly being infringed, and requesting Metromedia's

> immediate assistance in stopping this unauthorized activity. Specifically, we request that you remove the site or the infringing links from your system and that you inform the site operator of the illegality of his or her conduct. You should understand that this letter constitutes notice to you that this site operator may be liable for the infringing activity occurring on your server. In addition, under the Digital Millennium Copyright Act, if you ignore this notice, you and/or your company may be liable for any resulting infringement.

(Creighton Decl. ¶8 and Ex. B.) In response to this letter, Metromedia disabled Internet access to the MP3Board Web site beginning April 19, 2000 and did not restore service until May 5, 2000. (Eli Mapstead RIAA Dep. at 37-38, 40, 197.) As an initial matter, because MP3Board was only damaged by the April 18, 2000 notice, only that notice is potentially actionable.

A. The RIAA Is Entitled to Summary Judgment with Respect to MP3Board's Claim of "Knowing Material Misrepresentation of Infringement" in Violation of the DMCA.

MP3Board asserts that the RIAA's notice contained knowing and material misrepresentation. Pursuant to 17 USC §512(f),

> Any person who knowingly materially misrepresents . . . that material or activity is

infringing . . . shall be liable for any damages . . . incurred by the alleged infringer . . . who is injured by such misrepresentation, as the result of the service provider relying upon such misrepresentation in removing or disabling access to the material or activity claimed to be infringing.

As set forth in Section II(A)(2)(b), *supra,* the RIAA's letter dated April 18, 2000 did not constitute an effective notification to MP3Board pursuant to the DMCA because it listed solely artists' names, and neglected to specify any links or even particular songs. For the same reasons, the letter did not substantially comply with the notification requirements for Metromedia, as it did not provide location information reasonably sufficient to permit Metromedia to locate the material pursuant to 17 USC §512(c)(3)(A). *See ALS Scan,* 239 F3d at 625; *see also Netcom,* 907 F Supp at 1374.

The April 2000 letter was simply not specific enough to provide adequate notice. Although the DMCA permits a copyright owner to identify a "representative" list of works, 17 USC §512(c)(3)(A)(ii), in this case, a bare list of musical artists whose songs were allegedly linked to did not constitute a representative list of works, or notice equivalent to a list of representative works that can be easily identified by the service provider. *See ALS Scan,* 239 F3d at 625. While the DMCA only requires that a copyright owner need only comply "substantially" with the prescribed format, the RIAA's April notice fell short of even that standard. 17 USC §512(c)(3)(A); *see also ALS Scan,* 239 F3d at 625. The RIAA cannot shift the DMCA's duty to identify infringing material from the copyright holders or their agents to ISPs, which is what the April 18, 2000 letter seeks to do.

Nonetheless, liability cannot be incurred by the RIAA pursuant to Section 512(f) for merely sending a letter that constitutes insufficient notification; rather, the DMCA standard is whether the copyright owner's agent "knowingly materially misrepresents . . . that material or activity is infringing." There is no evidence that the RIAA incorrectly stated that MP3Board was "offering direct links to files on other Internet sites containing full-length sound recordings for other users to download, including songs by [the listed] artists." The sole evidence of any misrepresentation in this notice consists of the fact that Eli Mapstead stated that he later found one link on the MP3Board site leading to a song by one of the listed artists that was authorized to be on the Internet. (Eli Mapstead Dep. at 481-87.) However, the presence of one authorized song file does not constitute a material misrepresentation in light of the facts of this case. Moreover, MP3Board's claim must fail because there is no evidence that any misrepresentation by the RIAA was made knowingly.

MP3Board also contends that the RIAA's notification constituted "knowing material misrepresentation" because it improperly threatened a suit for money damages against a service provider that was immune from suit pursuant to 17 USC §512(a). However, Section 512 only penalizes copyright holders for knowingly materially misrepresenting "that material or activity is infringing." It does not provide a cause of action for knowingly materially misrepresenting that a service provider may be liable for hosting certain material.

In addition, MP3Board appears to seek liability for vagueness in the RIAA's notice, and the possibility that vagueness may have induced Metromedia to take the entire MP3Board site offline because Metromedia could not reasonably ascertain which of MP3Board's activities constituted infringing activity. However, vagueness does not constitute a material misrepresentation "that material or activity is infringing" pursuant to Section 512(f). MP3Board stretches Section 512 beyond its breaking point.

B. The RIAA Is Entitled to Summary Judgment with Respect to MP3Board's Claims of Tortious Interference with Contractual Relations and Prospective Economic Advantage.

MP3Board contends in its third claim for relief that when the RIAA caused Metromedia to disrupt MP3Board's service, the RIAA thereby tortiously interfered with MP3Board's contracts with Metromedia as well as MP3Board's expectation of prospective economic advantage from future visitors to its site. (Am. Countercl. ¶¶80-81.) By applying the New York choice of law rules, *see Arochem Int'l Inc. v. Buirkle*, 968 F2d 266, 269 (2d Cir 1993), the Court finds that California tort law applies in this matter; California has the greater interest in the litigation of this issue due to the fact that MP3Board is located in California and its contractual relationship with another California corporation was allegedly interfered with in California.

The elements of intentional interference with contractual relations are (1) a valid contract between the plaintiff and a third party; (2) the defendant's knowledge of this contract; (3) intentional acts designed to induce a breach or disruption of the contractual relationship; (4) actual breach or disruption of the relationship; and (5) resulting damage. *Quelimane Co. v. Stewart Title Guar. Co.*, 960 P2d 513, 530 (Cal 1998).

The RIAA contends that MP3Board cannot assert a claim for tortious interference with contract because MP3Board never had a contract with Metromedia, but only had an arrangement with Lars Mapstead's company, Cyberzine, which in turn had a preexisting relationship with AboveNet (later Metromedia). (Noah Mapstead RIAA Dep. at 17-23; Lars Mapstead RIAA Dep. at 33, 407-08.) However, because there is evidence that the contract or a later modification of it was made expressly for MP3Board's benefit—for example, AboveNet/Metromedia assigned a static IP address to MP3Board and agreed to serve as the contact for MP3Board in connection with MP3Board's registration with Network Systems, Inc., (Mapstead Decl. in Opp'n to RIAA's Mot. For Summ. J. ¶¶2, 4-5),—at this juncture the Court cannot conclude that there was no valid contract with AboveNet/Metromedia that MP3Board could enforce as a third party beneficiary.

The RIAA also contends that the letter to Metromedia on April 18, 2000 was a simple pre-litigation demand letter. However, to assert the litigation privilege—an affirmative defense—the RIAA must prove that its statements were made in good faith contemplating a suit. *See Sade Shoe Co. v. Oschin & Snyder*, 162 Cal App 3d 1174, 1180, 209 Cal Rptr 124 (1984); *Aronson v. Kinsella*, 58 Cal App 4th 254, 263-65, 68 Cal Rptr 2d 305 (1997); *see also Matsushita Electronics Corp. v. Loral Corp.*, 974 F Supp 345, 354-55 (SD NY 1997). Material issues of fact exist regarding whether the RIAA contemplated filing a suit against Metromedia in "good faith and on serious consideration." *Aronson*, 58 Cal App 4th at 266; 68 Cal Rptr 2d 305.

Nonetheless, no material issues of fact exist regarding the RIAA's justification for its actions. Pursuant to California state law, justification is an affirmative defense to a charge of tortious interference with contract. *See Echazabal v. Chevron U.S.A., Inc.*, 221 F3d 1347 (9th Cir 2000) (unpublished); *Seaman's Direct Buying Serv., Inc. v. Standard Oil Co.*, 686 P2d 1158, 1165 (Cal 1984) (overruled on other grounds). Seeking to protect a copyright by alerting a third party that the copyright is being infringed constitutes a justification defense to that claim. *See, e.g., Shapiro & Son Bedspread Corp. v. Royal Mills Assoc.*, 764 F2d 69, 75 (2d Cir 1985); *Montgomery County Ass'n of Realtors, Inc. v. Realty Photo Master Corp.*, 878 F Supp 804, 818 (D Md 1995) (notifying customers of an alleged copyright infringement in good faith is justified and does not constitute tortious interference with contractual relations). There have been no material issues of fact raised regarding whether the RIAA acted in good faith in notifying Metromedia of the infringement. Accordingly, the RIAA cannot be subjected to liability for tortious interference with contract and summary judgment should issue in its favor on this claim.

The elements in California of the tort of intentional interference with prospective economic advantage are (1) the existence of a prospective economic relationship containing the probability of future economic rewards for the plaintiff; (2) the defendant's knowledge of this relationship; (3) intentional acts designed to disrupt the relationship; (4) actual causation; and (5) proximate damages. *PMC, Inc. v. Saban Entm't, Inc.*, 52 Cal Rptr 2d 877, 886 (1996). The tort, which is also called interference with prospective economic relations, "imposes liability for improper methods of disrupting or diverting the business relationship of another which fall outside the boundaries of fair competition." *Settimo Assocs. v. Environ Sys., Inc.*, 17 Cal Rptr 2d 757, 758 (1993).

Because the general wrong inherent in intentional interference with prospective economic advantage is the interference with a business opportunity through methods which are not within the privilege of fair competition, a plaintiff must also prove that the defendant "engaged in conduct that was wrongful by some legal measure other than the fact of interference itself." *Della Penna v. Toyota Motor Sales, U.S.A., Inc.*, 902 P2d 740, 751 (Cal 1995). For tortious interference with prospective economic advantage, a plaintiff must prove that the defendant's conduct was not privileged; the defendant does not need to prove privilege as an affirmative defense. *See Bed, Bath & Beyond of La Jolla, Inc. v. La Jolla Square Venture Partners*, 60 Cal Rptr 2d 830, 839 (1997). As set forth above, the RIAA was justified in sending Metromedia the April 18 notification of infringement and no liability can lie for tortious interference with prospective economic advantage.

Moreover, MP3Board has not shown the additional element of wrongful conduct required for a claim of intentional interference with prospective economic advantage. *See Della Penna*, 902 P2d at 751. While threatening to litigate against a party who is known to be immune from suit—as MP3Board alleges—may sufficiently constitute wrongful conduct, *see PMC*, 52 Cal Rptr 2d at 891; *see also Matsushita*, 974 F Supp at 354, MP3Board's claim that Metromedia was known to be immune from suit pursuant to 17 USC §512(a) has no support. There is no evidence showing that the RIAA believed that Metromedia was engaged in "transitory digital network communications," pursuant to Section 512(a), which deals with the transient storage of material in the course of transmitting, routing or providing connections.

Rather, by all outward appearances Metromedia was hosting MP3Board's site on its network, leaving the RIAA to conclude that Metromedia was not merely transmitting, routing or providing connections for infringing material but that infringing activities were being conducted on Metromedia's system at MP3Board's direction. Pursuant to Section 512(c), entitled "information residing on systems or networks at direction of users," a service provider is "liable for monetary relief . . . for infringement of copyright by reason of the storage at the direction of a user of material that resides on a system or network controlled or operated by or for the service provider," unless the service provider does not have knowledge or reason to know of infringing activity and fails to expeditiously to remove or disable access to the infringing material. 17 USC §512(c)(1). Absent a showing that Metromedia was immune from liability pursuant to Section 512(a), and that the RIAA knew that Metromedia was immune, liability cannot be grounded on the RIAA's statement that Metromedia could be liable for hosting MP3Board's activities if Metromedia knew of MP3Board's infringement but failed to disable access. MP3Board has pointed to no evidence whatsoever in support of its claim that the RIAA threatened legal action against a party that it knew to be immune from liability and therefore the RIAA is entitled to summary judgment on this claim.

CONCLUSION

For the reasons stated forth above, the record companies' motion for summary judgment is denied, MP3Board's motion for summary judgment is denied, and the RIAA's motion for summary judgment is granted.

SO ORDERED.

CoStar Group, Inc.
v.
LoopNet, Inc.

**United States District Court,
District of Maryland**

September 28, 2001

9 ILR (P&F) 720, 164 F Supp 2d 688

Civil Action No. DKC 99-2983

No liability for direct infringement.

Plaintiff, a company that provides a copyrighted commercial real estate database on the Internet, cannot maintain a cause of action for direct copyright infringement against defendant, which offers a free service for real estate brokers to list properties on the Internet. Plaintiff alleges that many of its copyrighted photographs of properties appear on defendant's web site, but defendant, as a passive conduit for copyrighted material posted by third parties (*i.e.*, the real estate brokers), cannot be liable as a direct infringer. [Following *Religious Technology Center v. Netcom On-Line Communications Services, Inc.*, 1 ILR (P&F) 778, and *ALS Scan, Inc. v. RemarQ Communities, Inc.*, 7 ILR (P&F) 69. — **CoStar Group, Inc. v. LoopNet, Inc., 9 ILR (P&F) 720 [D Md, 2001].**

Real estate listing service satisfies definition of "online service provider" for purposes of DMCA safe harbor.

Defendant, which offers a free service for real estate brokers to list properties on the Internet, meets the definition of an "online service provider" under the Digital Millennium Copyright Act (DMCA). Plaintiff, a company that provides a copyrighted commercial real estate database on the Internet, alleges that many of its copyrighted photographs of properties appear on defendant's web site, thereby rendering defendant vicariously liable for copyright infringement. For purposes of determining whether defendant qualifies for the DMCA's safe harbor, 17 USC §512(c), defendant clearly satisfies the broad definition of "online service provider" found in §512(k)(1)(B): "a provider of online services or network access, or the operator of facilities therefor." [Citing *Hendrickson v. eBay, Inc.*, 8 ILR (P&F) 573.] — **CoStar Group, Inc. v. LoopNet, Inc., 9 ILR (P&F) 720 [D Md, 2001].**

Real estate listing service falls within DMCA safe harbor where third party uploads infringing material.

Defendant, which offers a free service for real estate brokers to list properties on the Internet, is not disqualified from the Digital Millennium Copyright Act (DMCA) safe harbor, 17 USC §512(c), because it reviewed allegedly infringing photographs of properties before posting them on its web site. Plaintiff, a company that provides a copyrighted commercial real estate database on the Internet, alleges that many of its copyrighted photographs appear on defendant's web site, thereby rendering defendant vicariously liable for copyright infringement. The DMCA protects a service provider from liability "for infringement of copyright by reason of its storage at the direction of a user of material." 17 USC §512(c)(1). Plaintiff argues that photographs are uploaded to the site only after review and selection by defendant, so they are not stored at the instance of the user. That, however, is a mischaracterization of the process. Photographs are uploaded at the volition of the user and are subject, not to a review and selection process, but to a mere screening to assess whether they are commercial property and to catch any obvious infringements. Although humans are involved rather than mere technology, they serve only as a gateway and are not involved in a selection process. — **CoStar Group, Inc. v. LoopNet, Inc., 9 ILR (P&F) 720 [D Md, 2001].**

Fact issues preclude summary ruling on eligibility for DMCA safe harbor.

Material issues of fact prevent a summary ruling on whether defendant, which offers a free service for real estate brokers to list properties on the Internet, has adopted and reasonably implemented a "take down" policy under 17 USC §512(i)(1)(A) so as to be eligible for the safe harbor defense under the Digital Millennium Copyright Act (DMCA). Plaintiff, a company that provides a copyrighted commercial real estate database on the Internet, alleges that many of its copyrighted photographs appear on defendant's web site, thereby rendering defendant vicariously liable for copyright infringement. There are several material factual disputes, however, as to whether the removal of allegedly infringing photographs was satisfactorily expeditious and whether defendant's termination policy was reasonable and effective. Moreover, plaintiff's infringement claims are based on the posting of specific photographs, and defendant's knowledge of the alleged infringements and its "take down" and termination policies have changed over time in fairly significant ways. In order to resolve this issue, the fact finder will have to focus on each photo and the policy in effect prior to the posting of each photo. Hence, neither party is entitled to summary judgment on this issue. — **CoStar Group, Inc. v. LoopNet, Inc., 9 ILR (P&F) 720 [D Md, 2001].**

Direct financial benefit on eligibility for DMCA safe harbor.

Defendant, which offers a free service for real estate brokers to list properties on the Internet, is not disqualified from the Digital Millennium Copyright Act (DMCA) safe harbor, 17 USC §512(c), on grounds it obtains a direct financial benefit from the infringing photographs appearing on its web site. Plaintiff, a company that provides a copyrighted commercial real estate database on the Internet, alleges that many of its copyrighted photographs appear on defendant's web site, thereby rendering defendant vicariously liable for copyright infringement. Defendant, however, does not have the "right and ability" to control its users commensurate with the standard for vicarious infringement, nor does it derive a direct financial benefit. Defendant does not charge a fee for posting any real estate listing, with or without a photograph. The legislative history of the DMCA indicates that it would not be a considered a direct financial benefit "where the infringer makes the same kind of payment as non-infringing users of the provider's service." In this case, neither infringing or non-infringing users made any kind of payment. Furthermore, for purposes of the DMCA, the financial benefit must be "directly attributable to the infringing activity." 17 USC §512(c)(1)(B). [Distinguishing *Playboy Ent. v. Russ Hardenburgh, Inc.*, 2 ILR (P&F) 13.] — **CoStar Group, Inc. v. LoopNet, Inc., 9 ILR (P&F) 720 [D Md, 2001].**

Fact issues preclude summary ruling on contributory infringement.

Material issues of fact prevent a summary ruling on whether defendant, which offers a free service for real estate brokers to list properties on the Internet, is liable for contributory infringement. Plaintiff, a company that provides a copyrighted commercial real estate database on the Internet, alleges that many of its copyrighted photographs appear on defendant's web site and that it adequately notified defendant of the infringing activity. In the context of assessing liability for contributory infringement, the question is not whether defendant adequately removed the infringing material, but whether, at some point, it created an inducement to put infringing material up on the site. The situation in the current case resides in that gray middle range of cases in which the service provider has information suggesting, but not conclusively demonstrating, that subscribers committed infringement. Thus, in order to prove its claim, plaintiff needs to establish that the notice it gave to defendant comprised at least constructive knowledge of specific infringing activity which defendant materially contributed to or induced by its alleged failure to halt the activity. There remain too many material factual disputes for the court to decide on summary judgment either that such a level of knowledge did or did not exist or that defendant's actions in trying to stop the infringement were or were not insufficient to the point of comprising inducement as a matter of law. — **CoStar Group, Inc. v. LoopNet, Inc., 9 ILR (P&F) 720 [D Md, 2001].**

Defense of misuse rejected.

Defendant, which offers a free service for real estate brokers to list properties on the Internet, may not rely on misuse of copyright as an affirmative defense to plaintiff's claim of copyright infringement. Plaintiff provides a copyrighted commercial real estate database on the Internet and alleges that many of its copyrighted photographs appear on defendant's web site. The gravamen of defendant's misuse claim is that plaintiff seeks to restrict brokers from distributing photographs and data over which, by its own admission, it has no claim of ownership. In this case, however, there is no allegation that plaintiff has misled the court over the scope of its copyrights. Furthermore, there is no allegation of tying or abuse of copyright serious enough to offend the public policy behind copyright and rise to the level of misuse. — **CoStar Group, Inc. v. LoopNet, Inc., 9 ILR (P&F) 720 [D Md, 2001].**

Statutory damages.

If defendant, which offers a free service for real estate brokers to list properties on the Internet, is found to have infringed plaintiff's copyrights by using photographs of commercial properties from plaintiff's real estate database, plaintiff will only be eligible for 13 statutory damages awards, corresponding to the number of registered compilations of the database information. Plaintiff argued that each of the 348 photographs at issue constitutes a separate work for purposes of the damages award, but plaintiff did not register the photographs separately from the compilations. The registrations make no mention of the numbers of separate photographs plaintiff meant to register on each application. Use of the term "photographs" without further explication is insufficient evidence that plaintiff registered copyrights for the photographs separate from its database compilations. — **CoStar Group, Inc. v. LoopNet, Inc., 9 ILR (P&F) 720 [D Md, 2001].**

State law claims preempted.

Plaintiff's state law claims for unfair competition, unjust enrichment, and intentional interference with business relations—all based on the posting of plaintiff's copyrighted photographs on defendant's web site—are preempted by the Copyright Act; none of the state law claims satisfy the "extra-element" test, and each is therefore equivalent to plaintiff's copyright infringement claim. Plaintiff's Lanham Act claims, however, are not preempted because the Copyright Act does not repeal or otherwise affect other federal statutes. — **CoStar Group, Inc. v. LoopNet, Inc., 9 ILR (P&F) 720 [D Md, 2001].**

Modification of preliminary injunction.

Defendant, accused of accepting copyrighted photographs of commercial properties from real estate brokers who list properties on defendant's web site, had been preliminarily enjoined, in part, to require *prima facie* evidence of copyright ownership from all brokers identified as having previously posted infringing photographs. The preliminary injunction is modified to require that all brokers in that same office should be subject to the *prima facie* evidence requirement. Moreover, for the purposes of the preliminary injunction, the brokerage office should remain in that status pending completion of the lawsuit. — **CoStar Group, Inc. v. LoopNet, Inc., 9 ILR (P&F) 720 [D Md, 2001].**

MEMORANDUM OPINION

DEBORAH K. CHASANOW, *District Judge.*

Presently pending and ready for resolution in this copyright infringement action are (1) Plaintiffs' motion and Defendant's cross-motion for summary judgment on the safe harbor defense under the Digital Millennium Copyright Act (paper nos. 70 and 87); (2) Plaintiffs' motion and Defendant's cross-motion for summary judgment on copyright infringement liability (paper nos. 71 and 87); (3) Defendant's motion and Plaintiffs' cross-motion for partial summary judgment on misuse and statutory damages (paper nos. 87 and 95); and (4) Plaintiffs' motions to modify the preliminary injunction (paper nos. 66, 105, and 121).[1] Hearings were held separately on the preliminary injunction and the summary judgment motions.

I. Background

Plaintiffs CoStar Group, Inc. and CoStar Realty Information, Inc. (collectively CoStar) filed suit against LoopNet, Inc. (LoopNet) alleging copyright infringement. CoStar is a national provider of commercial real estate information services. It maintains a copyrighted commercial real estate database which includes photographs. Some of the photographs are taken by professional photographers hired by CoStar either as employees or as independent contractors. CoStar licenses users of its database.

LoopNet is an internet based company offering a service through which a user, usually a real estate broker, may post a listing of commercial real estate available for lease. The user accesses and fills out a form at LoopNet's site, with the property name, type, address, square footage, age, description, identifying information, and password. The property is listed once the user submits the form. To include a photograph, however, the user must fill out another form. A photograph, once submitted, is not immediately available to the public. Instead, it is uploaded into a separate "folder," elsewhere in LoopNet's system, where it is reviewed by a LoopNet employee to determine that it is in fact a photograph of commercial property and that there is no obvious indication that the photograph was submitted in violation of LoopNet's terms and conditions. If the photograph meets LoopNet's criteria, the employee accepts the photograph and it is automatically posted along with the property listing. The listing is then made available to any user upon request.

LoopNet does not charge a fee for posting real estate listings or for accessing those listings.[2]

In the initial complaint, CoStar claims that over 300 of its copyrighted photographs have appeared on LoopNet's site (the number has increased over time). CoStar contends that LoopNet is liable for direct or contributory copyright infringement as a matter of law, asserting that there is no material dispute of fact (1) that it owns the copyrights in the photographs; (2) that LoopNet is copying, distributing, and displaying; and/or (3) contributing to the copying, distributing, and displaying of the photographs without authorization. LoopNet's

position on those issues is (1) that CoStar authorized its customers to use the photographs on the internet through the license agreements; (2) that its activities do not constitute direct infringement; and (3) that it is not liable for contributory infringement because it lacked knowledge and did not induce, cause, or materially contribute to the infringing conduct of others.

In addition, LoopNet contends that CoStar misused its copyright and that it is entitled to the "safe harbor" protections provided under the Digital Millennium Copyright Act (DMCA) as an "online service provider." In response to this aspect of their dispute, CoStar contends that LoopNet does not qualify as an "online service provider," does not provide a "web page hosting service," and is not entitled to the protection of the DMCA because (1) the photographs are stored at the direction of LoopNet rather than its users; (2) its review of the photographs prior to permanent storage disqualifies it from protection; (3) LoopNet has not reasonably implemented a termination policy; (4) it obtains a direct financial benefit from the infringing photographs that appear on its web site; and (5) it has not acted expeditiously to remove infringing material. CoStar contends, and LoopNet agrees, that there is no safe harbor for photographs posted prior to December 8, 1999, the date on which LoopNet appointed an agent to receive notices of infringement.

LoopNet also asserts that the copyright act preempts CoStar's non-copyright claims, and that CoStar's statutory damages are limited to, at most, 11 (now 13) infringements.

II. Standard of Review

It is well established that a motion for summary judgment will be granted only if there exists no genuine issue as to any material fact and the moving party is entitled to judgment as a matter of law. Fed. R. Civ. P. 56(c); *Anderson v. Liberty Lobby, Inc.*, 477 US 242, 250 (1986); *Celotex Corp. v. Catrett*, 477 US 317, 322 (1986). In other words, if there clearly exist factual issues "that properly can be resolved only by a finder of fact because they may reasonably be resolved in favor of either party," then summary judgment is inappropriate. *Anderson*, 477 US at 250; *see also Pulliam Inv. Co. v. Cameo Properties*, 810 F2d 1282, 1286 (4th Cir 1987); *Morrison v. Nissan Motor Co.*, 601 F2d 139, 141

(4th Cir 1979); *Stevens v. Howard D. Johnson Co.*, 181 F2d 390, 394 (4th Cir 1950). The moving party bears the burden of showing that there is no genuine issue as to any material fact. Fed. R. Civ. P. 56(c); *Pulliam Inv. Co.*, 810 F2d at 128 (citing *Charbonnages de France v. Smith*, 597 F2d 406, 414 (4th Cir 1979)).

When ruling on a motion for summary judgment, the court must construe the facts alleged in the light most favorable to the party opposing the motion. *United States v. Diebold, Inc.*, 369 US 654, 655 (1962); *Gill v. Rollins Protective Servs. Co.*, 773 F2d 592, 595 (4th Cir 1985). A party who bears the burden of proof on a particular claim must factually support each element of his or her claim. "[A] complete failure of proof concerning an essential element . . . necessarily renders all other facts immaterial." *Celotex Corp.*, 477 US at 323. Thus, on those issues on which the nonmoving party will have the burden of proof, it is his or her responsibility to confront the motion for summary judgment with an affidavit or other similar evidence. *Anderson*, 477 US at 256. In *Celotex Corp.*, the Supreme Court stated:

> In cases like the instant one, where the nonmoving party will bear the burden of proof at trial on a dispositive issue, a summary judgment motion may properly be made in reliance solely on the "pleadings, depositions, answers to interrogatories, and admissions on file." Such a motion, whether or not accompanied by affidavits, will be "made and supported as provided in this rule," and Rule 56(e) therefore requires the nonmoving party to go beyond the pleadings and by her own affidavits, or by the "depositions, answers to interrogatories, and admissions on file," designate "specific facts showing that there is a genuine issue for trial."

Celotex Corp., 477 US at 324. However, " 'a mere scintilla of evidence is not enough to create a fact issue.' " *Barwick v. Celotex Corp.*, 736 F2d 946, 958-59 (4th Cir 1984) (quoting *Seago v. North Carolina Theaters, Inc.*, 42 FRD 627, 632 (ED NC 1966), *aff'd*, 388 F2d 987 (4th Cir 1967)). There must be "sufficient evidence favoring the nonmoving party for a jury to return a verdict for that party. If the evidence is merely colorable, or is not significantly probative, summary judgment may be

granted." *Anderson*, 477 US at 249-50 (citations omitted).

III. Analysis

Application of copyright law in cyberspace is elusive and perplexing. The world wide web has progressed far faster than the law and, as a result, courts are struggling to catch up. Legislatures and courts endeavor in this growing area to maintain the free flow of information over the internet while still protecting intellectual property rights. The DMCA is one attempt by Congress to strike the proper balance. Understanding the interplay between basic copyright jurisprudence and the DMCA presents an additional challenge for the courts.

A. Direct Copyright Infringement

A *prima facie* case of direct infringement consists of proof of ownership of the allegedly infringed material and violation of at least one of the exclusive rights granted to copyright holders under 17 USC §106. *A&M Records, Inc. v. Napster, Inc.*, 239 F3d 1004, 1013 *[7 ILR (P&F) 1]* (9th Cir 2001).

1. Ownership

LoopNet does not contest CoStar's assertion that it owns, in the first instance, the photographs. Rather, in resisting summary judgment on this threshold issue, LoopNet claims that the license agreements, or some of them, grant the licensees the right to publish the photographs on the internet.[3]

Maryland adheres to the law of objective interpretation of contracts and, thus, where the language is clear and unambiguous, the plain meaning is given effect and no further construction is needed. The question of contract interpretation is one of law for the court. *Auction & Estate Representatives, Inc. v. Ashton*, 731 A2d 441, 444-45 (Md 1999). LoopNet suggests that the following language grants the licensee permission to upload photographs onto its web site:

> Licensee may use the Database only for its internal market research purposes and to produce reports for Licensee's in-house use or for its clients in the course of Licensee's normal brokerage operations . . . ; provided however, that Licensee may not generally reproduce or republish all or substantial portions of the Database or Images, without the prior written consent of RIP [predecessor

to CoStar], for any other purpose or in any other form . . . Licensee may not distribute any Image file in electronic format, except for use in presentation or marketing format for distribution to client. Licensee is explicitly prohibited from publishing or posting CoStar data or compilations based upon CoStar data on, or providing access to CoStar via, the Internet, a public or private bulletin board system or other electronic network, without the express prior written permission of RIG.

Paper No. 87, at 13, ex. 18.

Assuming the quoted language is in a pertinent agreement, LoopNet's strained interpretation depends on finding that the use granted in the first sentence broadly grants the right to post the photographs and then that the limitations on Internet use apply to data, and not to images. The contract language itself does not support that interpretation. There is no broad right to use any portion of the database; rather, the licensee's use is restricted to research, in house reports, and for clients. There is no broad right to use the database for wider, indiscriminate dissemination. Thus, LoopNet's premise is lacking and it is not necessary to parse the remaining language.

2. LoopNet's Conduct

CoStar asserts that LoopNet directly copies and distributes its photographs on its web site. LoopNet contends, however, by relying on *Religious Tech. Center v. Netcom On-Line Communication Servs., Inc.*, 907 F Supp 1361 *[1 ILR (P&F) 778]* (ND Cal 1995), that it cannot be liable for direct infringement absent "some element of volition or causation." Paper 87 at 18. LoopNet also argues that it does not "reproduce" CoStar's photographs on its web site, but rather only allows another to upload or download them. *Id.* at 23-24. Similarly, LoopNet challenges CoStar's contention that it directly distributes or displays the photographs.

In this case, as in *ALS Scan, Inc. v. RemarQ Cmtys., Inc.*, 239 F3d 619, 621-22 *[7 ILR (P&F) 69]* (4th Cir 2001), there is insufficient basis for a claim of direct infringement:

ALS Scan contends first that the district court erred in dismissing its direct copyright infringement claim. It contends that it stated a cause of action for copyright infringement

when it alleged (1) the "ownership of valid copyrights," and (2) RemarQ's violation of its copyrights "by allowing its members access to newsgroups containing infringing material." [FN1] *See generally Keeler Brass Co. v. Continental Brass Co.*, 862 F2d 1063, 1065 (4th Cir 1988) (describing the requirements of a direct infringement claim). In rejecting ALS Scan's direct infringement claim, the district court relied on the decision in *Religious Technology Center v. Netcom On-Line Communication Services, Inc.*, 907 F Supp 1361, 1368-73 *[1 ILR (P&F) 778]* (ND Cal 1995), which concluded that when an Internet provider serves, without human intervention, as a passive conduit for copyrighted material, it is not liable as a direct infringer. The *Netcom* court reasoned that "it does not make sense to adopt a rule that could lead to liability of countless parties whose role in the infringement is nothing more than setting up and operating a system that is necessary for the functioning of the Internet." *Id.* at 1372. That court observed that it would not be workable to hold "the entire Internet liable for activities that cannot reasonably be deterred." *Id.*; *see also Marobie-Fl, Inc. v. National Ass'n of Fire and Equipment Distributors*, 983 F Supp 1167, 1176-79 (ND Ill 1997) (agreeing with *Netcom*'s reasoning). ALS Scan argues, however, that the better reasoned position, contrary to that held in *Netcom*, is presented in *Playboy Enterprises, Inc. v. Frena*, 839 F Supp 1552, 1555-59 *[1 ILR (P&F) 770]* (MD Fla 1993), which held a computer bulletin board service provider liable for the copyright infringement when it failed to prevent the placement of plaintiff's copyrighted photographs in its system, despite any proof that the provider had any knowledge of the infringing activities.

FN1. It would appear that ALS Scan's allegations amount more to a claim of contributory infringement in which a defendant, "with knowledge of the infringing activity, induces, causes or materially contributes to the infringing conduct of another," *Gershwin Pub. Corp. v. Columbia Artists Management, Inc.*, 443 F2d 1159,

1162 (2d Cir 1971), than to a claim of direct infringement.

In the 1995 *Netcom* decision, Judge Whyte applied pre-DMCA law to the operator of a computer bulletin board service, which gained access to the internet through Netcom, a large internet access provider. The court was careful to distinguish between the system at issue there, where the copying of material was initiated by a third party, from that in *MAI Systems Corp. v. Peak Computer, Inc.*, 991 F2d 511 *[1 ILR (P&F) 71]* (9th Cir 1993), where the defendant itself initiated the creation of temporary copies. It was in that context that the court observed: "Although copyright is a strict l i a b i l i t y statute, there should still be some element of volition or causation which is lacking where a defendant's system is merely used to create a copy by a third party." 907 F Supp at 1370.

In *ALS Scan*, 239 F3d at 622, the Fourth Circuit resolved the dichotomy as follows:

> Although we find the *Netcom* court reasoning more persuasive, the ultimate conclusion on this point is controlled by Congress' codification of the *Netcom* principles in Title II of the DMCA. As the House Report for the Act states,
>
> > The bill distinguishes between direct infringement and secondary liability, treating each separately. This structure is consistent with evolving case law, and appropriate in light of the different legal bases for and policies behind the different forms of liability.
> >
> > As to direct infringement, liability is ruled out for passive, automatic acts engaged in through a technological process initiated by another. Thus the bill essentially codifies the result in the leading and most thoughtful judicial decision to date: *Religious Technology Center v. Netcom On-Line Communications Services, Inc.*, 907 F Supp 1361 *[1 ILR (P&F) 778]* (ND Cal 1995). In doing so, it overrules these aspects of *Playboy Enterprises Inc. v. Frena*, 839 F Supp 1552 *[1 ILR (P&F) 770]* (MD Fla

1993), insofar as that case suggests that such acts by service providers could constitute direct infringement, and provides certainty that *Netcom* and its progeny, so far only a few district court cases, will be the law of the land.

> H.R. Rep. No. 105-551(I), at 11 (1998). Accordingly, we address only ALS Scan's claims brought under the DMCA itself.

Thus, the Fourth Circuit found that Congress had decided the issue, adopting the *Netcom* approach, which it found more persuasive in any event. CoStar nevertheless continues to urge a finding of direct infringement here, by pointing out that the version of the DCMA actually enacted was NOT the one described in the referenced House Report. Then, it urges the court to adopt the reasoning of the *Playboy* line of cases instead.

The undersigned finds that this case does not present a valid claim of direct copyright infringement. As observed by the Fourth Circuit, the *Netcom* approach is more persuasive, even if not mandated by the DCMA. Rather, contributory infringement is the proper rubric under which to analyze the case.

B. Contributory Copyright Infringement

1. Overview

It is, today, a given that:

> "one who, with knowledge of the infringing activity, induces, causes or materially contributes to the infringing conduct of another, may be held liable as a 'contributory' infringer." *Gershwin Publ'g Corp. v. Columbia Artists Mgmt, Inc.*, 443 F2d 1159, 1162 (2d Cir 1971); *see also Fonovisa, Inc. v. Cherry Auction, Inc.*, 76 F3d 259, 264 (9th Cir 1996). Put differently, liability exists if the defendant engages in "personal conduct that encourages or assists the infringement." *Matthew Bender & Co. v. West Publ'g Co.*, 158 F3d 693, 706 *[1 ILR (P&F) 38]* (2d Cir 1998).

A&M Records, 239 F3d at 1019.

CoStar argues that LoopNet is liable because of its own conduct in operating the system, and not merely because it made technology available that others might use to infringe. According to CoStar, once it gave notice of specific alleged infringements to LoopNet, LoopNet had knowledge of ongoing infringements by its users. CoStar asserts that this knowledge, coupled with the lack of more drastic measures to prevent infringement, constitutes inducement and so renders LoopNet liable for contributory infringement.

CoStar attempts to distinguish this case from *Sony Corp. v. Universal City Studios, Inc.*, 464 US 417 (1984), where the mere provision of means, capable of substantial noninfringing uses, was not a basis for contributory infringement. Instead, CoStar seeks to bring the current case under the analysis in *Fonovisa v. Cherry Auction*, 76 F3d 259, 264 (9th Cir 1996) (holding that the knowing provision of swap meet facilities necessary to the sale and distribution of infringing works was a "material contribution" to the infringement of others) and *A&M Records v. Napster*, 239 F3d 1004, 1020 *[7 ILR (P&F) 1]* (9th Cir 2001) (distinguishing *Sony* on the basis of Napster's "actual, specific knowledge" of direct infringement).

The difference between *Sony*, in which the court found no contributory infringement, and *Fonovisa* and its ilk, where it did, is a matter of time frame and the retention of some control by the party providing facilities. In *Sony*, the only connection between Sony and the potential direct infringers was at the point of sale, after which Sony had no control over the use of its Betamax. In contrast, in *Fonovisa*, the operators of the swap meet not only rented the premises, but provided other facilities. Furthermore, they continued to retain control over the facilities and were in a position to deny access once they had actual knowledge of infringement. *Fonovisa*, 76 F3d at 264.

The court in *Napster* picked up on this and found that Napster had actual knowledge of specific infringements by its users, *Napster*, 239 F3d at 1020, whereas in *Sony*, it was a matter of imputing knowledge of possible infringements. Although fact issues precluded summary judgment on contributory infringement in *Netcom*, that case supports this characterization of the difference between *Fonovisa* and *Sony* because the court held that the time to assess infringement was when the services were provided, not when the parties entered into an agreement. *Netcom*, 907 F Supp at 1373, 1374. Thus, CoStar seeks to analogize LoopNet's role vis à vis the infringements to that of the swap meet

operator in *Fonovisa*, where ongoing services were provided and in which the operators had actual or constructive knowledge of direct infringements.

LoopNet, in turn, contends that is *[sic]* not liable for contributory infringement because (1) it had no knowledge of the infringement prior to notice from CoStar and (2) it has not induced, caused, or materially contributed to the infringing conduct of its users because it discontinued access to the infringing material immediately upon discovery. It asserts that its policy for removal of infringing material and of denying access to repeat infringers is sufficient to avoid liability because its conduct does not rise to the level of inducement.

In addition, LoopNet argues that, for any infringements occurring after December 8, 1999[4], it is protected from liability in damages for contributory infringement by the DMCA's safe harbor for online service providers (OSP's). The DMCA was enacted to strike a new balance between the viable operations of OSP's and the need to enforce copyright protection. It shields service providers from damages unless they have knowledge of infringement by users or are notified by copyright owners of alleged infringements. The liability shield remains, however, only as long as the service provider follows the Act's "take down" provisions and expeditiously removes or blocks access to infringing (or allegedly infringing) material. LoopNet contends that it is protected by the safe harbor, that it maintains an adequate policy for the termination of repeat offenders, and that, once notified by CoStar of alleged infringements, it complied sufficiently with the "take down" provisions to remain shielded from liability. CoStar, on the other hand, maintains that LoopNet is not protected by the safe harbor and that, even if it is, its removal procedures do not satisfy the "take down" requirements for staying within the safe harbor once it has knowledge of actual or potential infringements.

CoStar does not claim that LoopNet had knowledge of its users' infringements prior to its giving notice.[5] Paper no. 71, at 26. In *Netcom*, the court found that Netcom was unable to screen out the allegedly infringing postings before they were made and that there was a factual dispute over whether Netcom had knowledge apart from that gained when it received notice of specific infringements from the plaintiff. *Netcom*, 907 F

Supp at 1374. Given the nature of the infringements in this case, it was impossible for LoopNet to have knowledge of the alleged infringement before receiving notice from CoStar. CoStar does not attach a copyright notice to its photos and even CoStar's own expert could not identify a CoStar photo simply by reviewing it. Paper no. 87, at 26, Ex. 20. Additionally, prior to receiving notice from CoStar, LoopNet did not have knowledge about the status of CoStar's licensing agreements with its clients. Although exceeding the scope of a license constitutes copyright infringement (*see Tasini v. New York Times Co.,* 206 F3d 161, 170 *[3 ILR (P&F) 542]* (2d Cir 2000)), even if LoopNet suspected that some photographs posted on its site were copyrighted, as with the user's fair use claim in *Netcom*, there was no way for LoopNet to know whether the copyright owners' licensing agreements would allow the photographs to be used in such a way. In the case of a service provider, knowledge giving rise to liability only exists when there is no colorable claim of users' noninfringement. *Netcom*, 907 F Supp at 1374. Thus, LoopNet cannot be charged with any form of knowledge before receiving claims of infringement from CoStar.

Although CoStar does not claim that LoopNet had knowledge of infringement prior to receiving notice from CoStar, there remain factual disputes about the type of knowledge with which it can be charged after receiving the claims of infringement. CoStar alleges that once it gave LoopNet notice that its photographs were being infringed, LoopNet can be charged with knowledge of continuing infringements. Additionally, there is a dispute over whether LoopNet's policies to deter infringement, remove infringing works, and prevent repeat infringement were inadequate. CoStar claims that if, as it asserts, those policies were not adequate, LoopNet can be found to have induced or materially contributed to continuing infringements by its users of which, CoStar argues, it had knowledge.

The existence of the safe harbor convolutes the analysis of copyright infringement which, theoretically, should proceed in a straight line. Ideally, CoStar would have to make a *prima facie* showing that LoopNet was liable of contributory infringement and then the court would turn to the question of whether the "safe harbor" provided a defense. However, because the parameters of the liability protection provided by the "safe harbor" are not contiguous with the bounds of liability for contributory infringement, the analysis may proceed more efficiently if issues are decided a bit out of order. On summary judgment, it is often appropriate for a court to decide issues out of the traditional order because a dispute of fact is only material if it can affect the outcome of a proceeding. *Anderson*, 477 US at 248. Thus, to the extent, if at all, that LoopNet is entitled to summary judgment in its safe harbor defense, all other issues concerning damages liability for contributory infringement would be rendered immaterial.

2. The Digital Millennium Copyright Act

The court now turns to its analysis of LoopNet's status under the DMCA and whether it remains in the safe harbor provided by that act with regard to damages for infringements occurring after December 8, 1999.

In 1998, Congress enacted the DMCA. Title II of the Act, the Online Copyright Infringement Liability Limitation Act, is codified at 17 USC §512. It provides, in part, that:

(c) **Information residing on systems or networks at direction of users—**

(1) **In general.**—A service provider shall not be liable for monetary relief, or, except as provided in subsection (j), for injunctive or other equitable relief, for infringement of copyright by reason of the storage at the direction of a user of material that resides on a system or network controlled or operated by or for the service provider, if the service provider—

(A)(i) does not have actual knowledge that the material or an activity using the material on the system or network is infringing;

(ii) in the absence of such actual knowledge, is not aware of the facts or circumstances from which infringing activity is apparent;

(iii) upon obtaining such knowledge or awareness, acts expeditiously to remove, or disable access to, the material;

(B) does not receive a financial benefit directly attributable to the infringing activity, in a case in which the service provider has the right and ability to control such activity; and

(C) upon notification of claimed infringement as described in paragraph (3), responds expeditiously to remove, or disable access to, the material that is claimed to be infringing or to be the subject of infringing activity.

17 USC §512(c)(1) (1998). The service provider must also designate an agent to receive notifications. 17 USC §512(c)(2) (1998).

As a relatively recently enacted statute, there is little interpretative case law, although there is a growing body of commentary and reports. Amy P. Bunk, J.D., *Validity, Construction and Application of Digital Millennium Copyright Act*, 2001 ALR Fed 2 (2001) (unpublished annotation); *see also* Alfred C. Yen, *Internet Service Provider Liability for Subscriber Copyright Infringement, Enterprise Liability, and the First Amendment*, 88 Geo LJ 1833 (2000). To the extent that the statutory language may be unclear, the legislative history of the DMCA can be useful in fleshing out its meaning given the paucity of precedent interpreting the statute. Congress has traditionally defined the scope of copyright protections:

> Sound policy, as well as history, supports our consistent deference to Congress when major technological innovations alter the market for copyrighted materials. Congress has the constitutional authority and the institutional ability to accommodate fully the varied permutations of competing interests that are inevitably complicated by such new technology.

Sony, 464 US at 431. In light of the courts' traditional deference to Congress and the lack of precedent interpreting the Digital Millennium Copyright Act, it is appropriate to turn to the legislative history of that act, as well as precedent, in order to define the relationship between contributory infringement and the safe harbor provisions of the Act.

The Fourth Circuit has decided one case dealing with the relationship of the DMCA and contributory infringement: *ALS Scan*, 239 F3d at 625, *citing* H.R. Rep. No. 105-796, at 72 (1998):

The DMCA was enacted both to preserve copyright enforcement in the Internet and to provide immunity to service providers from copyright infringement liability for "passive," "automatic" actions in which a service provider's system engages through a technological process initiated by another without the knowledge of the service provider. . . . The DMCA's protection of an innocent service provider disappears at the moment the service provider loses its innocence, *i.e.*, at the moment it becomes aware that a third party is using its system to infringe. At that point, the Act shifts responsibility to the service provider to disable the infringing matter, "preserv[ing] the strong incentives for service providers and copyright owners to cooperate to detect and deal with copyright infringements that take place in the digital networked environment."

The DMCA seeks to strike a balance by shielding online service providers from liability in damages as long as they remove or prevent access to infringing material.[6] The initial inquiry is whether LoopNet can be considered a service provider for the purposes of the DMCA.

a. Service Provider

In order to qualify for the safe harbor in the DMCA, LoopNet must meet the definition of "online service provider." Under §512(k)(1)(A), a service provider is "an entity offering the transmission, routing, or providing of connections for digital online communications, between or among points specified by a user, of material of the user's choosing, without modification to the content of the material as sent or received." 17 USC §512(k)(1)(A) (1998). For the other safe harbor provisions, including (c), which is at issue here, the definition is broader: "a provider of online services or network access, or the operator of facilities therefor." *Id.* at (B).

CoStar challenges LoopNet's ability to qualify as a service provider, contending that LoopNet is not a web page hosting service limited to the "provision of Internet infrastructure." Paper no. 96, at 12. LoopNet contends that it is a web page hosting service, but also, more generally, that it falls within the Act's broad definition of "online service provider." Paper no. 87, at 35.

Statutory interpretation principles direct the court to consider, first, the plain language of the statute. If there is no ambiguity, then no resort to extrinsic aids is appropriate.[7] A court must harmonize all portions of a statute, and not read any single provision out of context. "The plainness or ambiguity of statutory language is determined by reference to the language itself, the specific context in which the language is used, and the broader context of the statute as a whole." *Robinson v. Shell Oil Co.*, 519 US 337, 341 (1997), *citing Estate of Cowart v. Nicklos Drilling Co.*, 505 US 469, 477 (1992).

It is not necessary to decide, at this time, just how far the definition of "online service provider" extends. CoStar turns to the legislative history of the DMCA for support for its proposed limitation of the term "online service provider," but that limitation is simply not commensurate with the language of the act. "The Act defines a service provider broadly." *ALS Scan*, 239 F3d at 623. In *ALS Scan*, neither party suggested that RemarQ was not a service provider under that definition. In another recent case, it was also undisputed that internet auction site eBay "clearly meets the DMCA's broad definition of online 'service provider.' " *Hendrickson v. eBay, Inc.*, 165 F Supp 2d 1082, No. CV 01-0495 RJK, 2001 WL 1078981, at *5 [8 ILR (P&F) 573] (CD Cal Sept 4 2001). Therefore, it is simply not possible to read the definition of service provider as narrowly or as technically restrictive as CoStar would have it. "Online services" is surely broad enough to encompass the type of service provided by LoopNet that is at issue here. The term is, of course, only a threshold to the protections of the Act. Even if LoopNet qualifies as a service provider, it must meet the other criteria.

b. Stored at the instance of the user

A service provider is only protected from liability by the DMCA, "for infringement of copyright by reason of its storage at the direction of a user of material." 17 USC §512(c)(1). The legislative history indicates that this does not include material "that resides on the system or network operated by or for the service provider through its own acts or decisions and not at the direction of a

user." H.R. Rep. No. 105-551, at 53 (1998). CoStar argues that photographs are uploaded to the site only after review and selection by LoopNet and so they are not stored at the instance of the user. However, that is a mischaracterization of the process by which the photographs are uploaded. They are uploaded at the volition of the user and are subject, not to a review and selection process, but to a mere screening to assess whether they are commercial property and to catch any obvious infringements. Paper no. 87, at 52. Although humans are involved rather than mere technology, they serve only as a gateway and are not involved in a selection process. *See supra* note 6.

The ability to remove or block access to materials cannot mean that those materials are not stored at the user's discretion or it would render the DMCA internally illogical. The "take down" procedures of §512 mandate that the service provider remove or block access to materials in order to stay in the safe harbor. It would be inconsistent, then, if in order to get into the safe harbor, the provider needed to lack the control to remove or block access. *See Hendrickson*, 2001 WL 1078981 at *9 (making analogous argument regarding the standard for direct financial benefit in §512(c)(1)(B)), *see also infra* note 9. Therefore, this threshold requirement is met and LoopNet is not disqualified from the safe harbor on these grounds.

c. Knowledge

The safe harbor protects service providers from liability unless they have knowledge of copyright infringement. There are three types of knowledge of infringement that can take a service provider out of the safe harbor: (1) the service provider can have actual knowledge of infringement; (2) it can be aware of facts which raise a "red flag" that its users are infringing; or (3) the copyright owner can notify the service provider in a manner "substantially" conforming with §512 (c)(3) that its works are being infringed. *See* H.R. Rep. No. 105-551, Part 2, at 53 (describing the "red flag" test). The service provider does not automatically lose its liability shield upon receiving notice, but "the Act shifts responsibility to the service provider to disable the infringing matter. . . ." *ALS Scan*, 239 F3d at 625.

The question at this stage of the analysis is whether LoopNet had sufficient knowledge of its users' copyright infringement to trigger the "take down" provisions of the DMCA. If sufficient knowledge is established, then the analysis shifts to whether LoopNet complied with the language of the DMCA's "take down" provisions. Although different DMCA sub-sections control "take down" procedures for actual or "red flag" knowledge than those necessitated when the service provider receives notification of a claimed infringement,[8] the language of both sub-sections is the same: whether the service provider acted, "expeditiously to remove, or disable access to, the material," so as to stay in the safe harbor. 17 USC §512(c)(1)(A)(iii) or §512(c)(1)(C). If LoopNet did not adequately remove or block access to the claimed infringing material, it loses its DMCA liability shield, but is not necessarily liable for contributory infringement. As will be seen, proof that LoopNet had knowledge of and induced the infringements are necessary elements of CoStar's contributory infringement claim. These elements are slightly different from those applicable to LoopNet's safe harbor defense and so require a separate determination if LoopNet fails to remain in the safe harbor.

LoopNet has not challenged the sufficiency of CoStar's notification of claimed infringement. Furthermore, under Fourth Circuit law, notice is adequate to trigger the safe harbor "take down" protocols when it "substantially complies with the notification requirements" of §512(c)(3)(A). *ALS Scan*, 239 F3d at 625. Therefore, LoopNet received notification of claimed infringement that complies with §512(c)(3)(A) and so the adequacy of LoopNet's removal policy must be assessed to determine whether LoopNet is protected by the safe harbor.

d. Adequacy of Termination and "Take Down" Policy

Once a service provider has received notification of a claimed infringement as described in §512(c)(3), the service provider can remain in the safe harbor if it "responds expeditiously to remove, or disable access to, the material that is claimed to be infringing or to be the subject of infringing activity." 17 USC §512(c)(1)(C) (1998). CoStar claims that LoopNet has not acted expeditiously or effectively in removing infringing material once it has received notification and so has not satisfied §512(c)(1)(C). Furthermore, there is a related, though not identical, requirement that limitations on

liability only apply to a service provider if that provider:

> has adopted and reasonably implemented, and informs subscribers and account holders of the service provider's system or network of, a policy that provides for the termination in appropriate circumstances of subscribers and account holders of the service provider's system or network who are repeat infringers.

17 USC §512(i)(1)(A) (1998). This requirement is designed so that flagrant repeat infringers, who "abuse their access to the Internet through disrespect for the intellectual property rights of others should know there is a realistic threat of losing . . . access." H.R. Rep. No. 105-551, Part 2, at 61. CoStar argues that LoopNet has not adopted and reasonably implemented a policy and so should lose its liability shield according to §512(i)(1). Although the satisfaction of each of these provisions have different requirements, they each turn on similar factual determinations. With respect to each, there are material factual disputes that preclude summary judgment.

In making its claim that LoopNet's "take down" of infringing material following notification was inadequate, CoStar points to LoopNet's failure to remove several photographs after being notified by CoStar that they were infringing and claims that several photographs have been posted more than once after notification. Paper no. 96, at 34. In attacking LoopNet's termination policy for repeat infringers, CoStar asserts that there is no evidence that LoopNet has ever terminated any user's access despite the fact that some of them have an extensive history as repeat infringers. Paper no. 70, at 29, 20, ex.5, 23.

LoopNet argues in contrast that §512(i)(1)(A) does not require that it terminate access, but that it reasonably implement a policy for termination of repeat infringers in appropriate circumstances. Paper no. 87, at 45. LoopNet's policy includes "Terms and Conditions" that include the removal of listings alleged to have infringed copyrights, the possibility of additional evidence demonstrating compliance with the noninfringement policy for repeat infringers, and the possibility of termination. *Id.* at 45, ex. 7. In addition, LoopNet claims that it promptly removes photographs once it receives notice of alleged infringement, sends an e-mail to brokers explaining the potential consequences of repeat infringement and investigates brokers it suspects to be repeat infringers. *Id.* at 46, ex.16, 2, 3. Specifically, LoopNet challenges the designation by CoStar of certain brokers as repeat infringers and claims that it has limited the access of some brokers. *Id.* at 47-49, ex. 2, 3, 24. Finally, LoopNet counters CoStar's assertion that it has not acted expeditiously to remove allegedly infringing photographs in compliance with §512(c)(1)(C) when it receives notice and claims to have implemented additional precautions to avoid reposting of infringing photographs in the future. *Id.* at 56, ex. 2.

There are several material factual disputes remaining as to whether the removal of allegedly infringing photographs was satisfactorily expeditious and whether LoopNet's termination policy was reasonable and effective. CoStar's infringement claims are based on the posting of specific photographs. Additionally, LoopNet's knowledge of the alleged infringements and its "take down" and termination policies have changed over time in fairly significant ways. In order to resolve this issue, the factfinder will have to focus on each photo and the policy in effect prior to the posting of each photo. Hence, neither party is entitled to summary judgment on this issue.

e. Direct financial benefit

CoStar argues that LoopNet does not qualify for the safe harbor because it obtains a direct financial benefit from the infringing photographs that appear on its website. Paper no. 96, at 30. Regardless of whether LoopNet complied with the "take down" requirements, a finding that it received a direct financial benefit from the infringement automatically would remove it from the safe harbor. To stay in the safe harbor, LoopNet has to show that it "does not receive a financial benefit directly attributable to the infringing activity, in a case in which the service provider has the right and ability to control such activity." 17 USC §512(c)(1)(B) (1998). Basically, the DMCA provides no safe harbor for vicarious infringement because it codifies both elements of vicarious liability. 3 Melville B. Nimmer and David Nimmer, *Nimmer on Copyright*, §12B.04[A][2], at 12B-38 (2001).

LoopNet meets neither element of this test. CoStar does not assert that LoopNet has any right to control its users beyond merely the ability to control or block access to its site. As such, LoopNet does not have the "right and ability" to control its users commensurate with the standard for vicarious infringement. "[T]he 'right and ability to control' the infringing activity, as the concept is used in the DMCA, cannot simply mean the ability of a service provider to remove or block access to materials posted on its website or stored in its system." *Hendrickson*, 2001 WL 1078981 at *9.[9]

Furthermore, LoopNet does not meet the other element for direct financial benefit. LoopNet does not charge a fee for posting any real estate listing, with or without a photograph. While CoStar correctly asserts that the legislative history of the DMCA supports the use of a common-sense rather than a formalistic approach, that same Senate Report stated that it would not be a considered a direct financial benefit "where the infringer makes the same kind of payment as non-infringing users of the provider's service." H.R. Rep. No. 105-551, Part 2, at 54. In this case, neither infringing or non-infringing users made any kind of payment.

CoStar attempts to bolster its argument for a broader conception of benefit by relying on *Playboy Ent. v. Russ Hardenburgh, Inc.*, 982 F Supp 503 *[2 ILR (P&F) 13]* (ND Oh 1997). In that case, the defendant operator of an electronic bulletin board (BBS) was found liable for contributory infringement when it encouraged subscribers to upload photographs and benefitted indirectly from having more files available to customers. *Hardenburgh* was based in part on *Fonovisa*, in which "contributory liability could attach where 'infringing performances enhance the attractiveness of the venue to potential customers.' " *Hardenburgh*, 982 F Supp at 514, *citing Fonovisa*, 76 F3d at 263. However, that assessment of a benefit to the defendant was not for the purposes of §512(c)(1)(B) of the DMCA, but rather was a part of the court's determination that the defendant met the standard for contributory infringement. Both the language and the purpose of the test for direct financial benefit are different from the test for contributory infringement. Whereas in *Playboy* and *Fonovisa*, the finding of added value to the defendant was evidence that the defendant induced the infringement, for the purposes of the DMCA, the financial benefit must be "directly attributable to the infringing activity." 17 USC §512(c)(1)(B) (1998). CoStar might make an argument that the indirect type of benefit cited in *Hardenburgh* is also present here. However, such a benefit does not fit within the plain language of the statute. Accordingly, §512(c)(1)(B) does not present a barrier to LoopNet remaining in the safe harbor.

3. Liability for Contributory Infringement

With regard to the photographs that were infringed before the safe harbor applied, [10] and in case LoopNet's termination policy and take down of infringing photographs is found to be inadequate so as to remove it from the safe harbor, the analysis shifts from the DMCA back to contributory infringement. The determination of contributory infringement liability turns on a different issue of knowledge than the standard used to determine LoopNet's eligibility for the safe harbor. Here, the question is whether CoStar's notice of claimed infringement was sufficient to satisfy the knowledge prong of the test for contributory infringement either by providing actual knowledge, a "red flag" that infringement was occurring, or constructive knowledge. Additionally, to prevail on its claim for contributory infringement, CoStar must prove that LoopNet induced, caused or materially contributed to the infringement. *Gershwin*, 443 F2d at 1162.

It is necessary to assess this claim along two dimensions. The first is whether notice by CoStar to LoopNet satisfies the knowledge prong of the test for contributory infringement. More specifically, there are questions as to the scope of the notice given and the corresponding scope of knowledge. CoStar alleges that once it gave LoopNet notice of specific infringements, LoopNet was on notice that ongoing infringements were occurring and had a duty to prevent repeat infringements. LoopNet does not deny that it was on notice that specific photographs were allegedly infringed, but asserts that it cannot be charged with imputed knowledge of future infringements. This first dimension of knowledge flows into the second assessment, determining whether inducement occurred. There is a critical interplay between the level of knowledge possessed by LoopNet as a result of CoStar's notices and the amount of policing, deterrence and removal demanded of LoopNet to avoid being liable for contributory infringement. If CoStar's notice to LoopNet gave LoopNet a broad scope of knowledge that infringements were occurring, then it creates a high level of policing necessary by LoopNet to avoid inducing infringement.

The issue of the adequacy of LoopNet's removal policy is different at this stage than it was when assessing its adequacy for the purposes of the DMCA safe harbor. In the safe harbor context, the removal policy had adequately to remove infringing or allegedly infringing material. If LoopNet met the standard following notice it was shielded from damages liability by the safe harbor. In the context of assessing liability for contributory infringement, the question is not whether LoopNet adequately removed the infringing material, but whether, at some point, it created an inducement to put infringing material up on the site. CoStar argues that the fact that it gave LoopNet notice meant that when LoopNet, as it alleges, did not adequately police infringement and create disincentives to infringing, it actually induced the infringing. Therefore, it argues, LoopNet is liable because it had knowledge of infringement and induced the infringers to use its site. *See Gershwin*, 443 F2d at 1162.

While liability for contributory infringement can be based on "merely providing the means for infringement," *Fonovisa*, 76 F3d at 264, *citing* 2 William F. Patry, Copyright Law & Practice 1147, merely providing means is not always sufficient to prove infringement. CoStar is correct that its claims for contributory infringement against LoopNet are not analogous to *Sony*, in which the court found that the mere provision of means was an insufficient basis for contributory infringement when those means were capable of substantial noninfringing use. In *Sony*, the only connection between Sony and the direct infringers was at the point of sale; Sony retained no access control similar to that of a service provider. Furthermore, the Betamax buyers were capable of potential infringements, but, at the time of the sale, Sony could not have notice of any actual infringements because they did not yet exist. In the current case, unlike *Sony*, LoopNet maintained control over access to the site and could deny access or block materials after gaining knowledge of infringement. It is unclear, however, when and to what extent LoopNet gained knowledge of infringement.

Instead, CoStar seeks to draw comparisons between the current case and *Fonovisa*, in which the owner of a swap meet who provided support services and took rental payments materially contributed to the underlying infringing activity.

There was no question in that case that the swap meet owner had actual knowledge of the infringements. *Fonovisa* differs from *Sony* in the time frame involved; the owner had continued control over access to the swap meet, provided ongoing support through the use of facilities and knew of actual infringements, but did not block access. *See Fonovisa*, 76 F3d at 264. CoStar also draws comparisons between the current case and *Sega Enters. Ltd. v. Maphia*, 948 F Supp 923 *[2 ILR (P&F) 168]* (ND Cal 1996). In *Sega*, the operator of a BBS was found liable for contributory infringement of copyrighted video games when he knew users were uploading and copying games, provided the site and facilities for the infringing conduct, actively solicited users to upload games and highlighted the location of unauthorized games on his site. *Sega*, 948 F Supp at 933.

While LoopNet's continued control over access to its site is more similar to that of the BBS operator in *Sega* or the swap meet owner in *Fonovisa* than to the mere seller of goods in *Sony*, there are elements of knowledge in those cases which the court is not satisfied have been proven here. The current case seems more factually similar to *Netcom*, in which the court held that when a BBS operator could not "reasonably verify a claim of infringement" because it was beyond the ability of a BBS operator quickly and fairly to determine the validity of the user's fair use claim, the operator's lack of knowledge was reasonable. *Netcom*, 907 F Supp at 1374. In *Netcom*, the court found that a triable issue of fact existed with respect to the degree of knowledge Netcom possessed about its subscriber's infringement where the subscriber had "at least a colorable claim" of noninfringement. *Netcom*, 907 F Supp 1374. As in *Netcom*, the situation in the current case resides in that gray middle range of cases in which the service provider has information suggesting, but not conclusively demonstrating, that subscribers committed infringement. *See* Yen, *supra*, at 1875 (stating that *Netcom* holds that knowledge is necessary for contributory liability).

In the analysis of LoopNet's safe harbor defense to liability, mere notification of claimed infringement by CoStar was enough to trigger one of two scenarios. Either LoopNet could comply with the "take-down" provisions of the DMCA and remain in the safe harbor or refuse to remove the allegedly infringing material and expose itself to the choppier waters of contributory infringement liability. However, that notification did not automatically equate to knowledge for the purpose of assessing liability. *Netcom* stands for the proposition that the bare claim of infringement by a copyright holder does not necessarily give rise to knowledge of an infringement.

CoStar needs to prove not only that LoopNet had knowledge of the infringements by its users, but that, as it asserts, LoopNet's alleged failure effectively to remove infringing photographs and dissuade infringers at some point began to comprise inducement or material contribution. In *Hardenburgh* and *Sega*, BBS operators not only had actual knowledge of its users' infringement, but encouraged subscribers to upload infringing works. While *Napster* and *Fonovisa* did not require actual encouragement of infringement, in both cases the defendant had actual, specific knowledge of infringements and continued to provide support and facilities to infringers. Thus, in order to prove its claim, CoStar needs to establish that the notice it gave to LoopNet comprised at least constructive knowledge of specific infringing activity which LoopNet materially contributed to or induced by its alleged failure to halt the activity. There remain too many material factual disputes for the court to decide on summary judgment either that such a level of knowledge did or did not exist or that LoopNet's actions in trying to stop the infringement were or were not insufficient to the point of comprising inducement as a matter of law. Again, CoStar has alleged the infringement of specific photographs posted at different times. Over the same time, LoopNet's knowledge of the alleged infringements and policies regarding removal and termination have shifted significantly. As a result, the factfinder must determine along a continuum the adequacy of the policy in place prior to the posting of each specific photograph. Therefore, neither party is entitled to summary judgment on this issue.

C. Misuse

LoopNet argues that CoStar misused its copyrights by extending them beyond their intended reach to limit its licensees from distributing the entire database, including data and photographs in which it has no copyright. Paper no. 87, at 31, 32. Misuse of copyright is an affirmative defense to a claim of copyright infringement. The misuse defense, which is rarely asserted, stems from an analogous misuse of patent defense recognized by the Supreme Court in *Morton Salt Co. v. G.S. Suppiger*, 314 US 488 (1942), and was adapted to copyright in *Lasercomb America, Inc. v. Reynolds*, 911 F2d 970, 973-74 (4th Cir 1990). Basically, this defense is an assertion that the copyright holder is using his copyright, "to secure an exclusive right or limited monopoly not granted by the [Copyright] Office and which it is contrary to public policy to grant." *Id.* at 977, *citing Morton Salt*, 314 US at 492.

Although misuse is a claim of anticompetitive behavior, *Lasercomb* distinguished misuse from an antitrust violation when it held that:

> a misuse need not be a violation of antitrust law in order to comprise an equitable defense to an infringement action. The question is not whether the copyright is being used in a manner violative of antitrust law ... but whether the copyright is being used in a manner violative of the public policy embodied in the grant of a copyright.

Lasercomb, 911 F2d at 978. In *Lasercomb*, the Fourth Circuit examined plaintiff's use of anticompetitive language in its licensing agreements to determine whether the language was adverse to the public policy embodied in copyright law. It found that "[t]he misuse arises from Lasercomb's attempt to use its copyright in a particular expression, the Interact software, to control competition in an area outside the copyright, *i.e.*, the idea of computer-assisted die manufacture, regardless of whether such conduct amounts to an antitrust violation." *Id.* at 979. Despite the fact that conduct need not rise to the level of an antitrust violation to constitute misuse, the Fourth Circuit has been hesitant to find misuse. For example, in *Service & Training, Inc. v. Data General Corp.*, 963 F2d 680, 690 (4th Cir 1992), the court rejected the appellant's effort to establish copyright misuse where appellant failed to establish that appellee did anything more than limit the use of its software to the repair and maintenance of specific computer hardware. Such activity, it held, was protected as an exclusive right of a copyright owner.

The gravamen of LoopNet's misuse claim is that CoStar seeks to restrict licensees from distributing photographs and data over which, by its own admission, it has no claim of ownership. Paper no. 87, at 32. However, this case bears little similarity to *Lasercomb*, where the software licensing agreement in question precluded the development of even non-infringing software. The establishment of this defense depends on a determination that the holder of a copyright is using that copyright in an anticompetitive manner against the public policy behind copyright. One case relied upon by LoopNet, *QAD, Inc. v. ALN Assocs., Inc.*, 770 F Supp 1261 (ND Ill 1991), demonstrates that the misuse defense is only applied in situations that are sufficiently abusive of copyright's grant of exclusivity.

LoopNet seeks to compare CoStar's use of its licensing agreement to the plaintiff's attempt in *QAD* to restrain the defendant's use of material over which it held no copyright. In that case, however, the plaintiff deceived the court over the copyrighted and uncopyrighted elements of its software and, "further used that confusion to wield the heavy sword of litigation under the guise of legitimate copyright enforcement in areas in which it had no rights." *Id.* at 1267, n. 17. In this case, there is no allegation that CoStar has misled the court over the scope of its copyrights. Furthermore, there is no allegation of tying or abuse of copyright serious enough to offend the public policy behind copyright and rise to the level of misuse. Accordingly, LoopNet's defense of copyright misuse is rejected.

D. Statutory Damages

LoopNet contends that, even if CoStar can establish infringement, it may, as a matter of law, recover no more than 11 statutory damage awards, corresponding to each of the then 11 (now 13) copyright registrations on which CoStar registered its photograph copyrights. Paper no. 87, at 62, 63. In contrast, CoStar contends that each of its 348 photographs constitutes a separate work and, therefore, it is entitled to 348 separate statutory damage awards should the court find infringement. Paper no. 94, at 25. 17 USC §504 (c)(1) states, in relevant part:

> the copyright owner may elect, at any time before final judgment is rendered, to recover, instead of actual damages and profits, an award of statutory damages for all infringements involved in the action, with respect to any one work, for which any one infringer is liable individually ... in a sum of not less than $500 or more than $20,000, as the court considers just. For the purposes

of this subsection, all the parts of a compilation or derivative work constitute one work.

17 USC §504(c)(1) (1996). Each side agrees that the number of statutory damage awards should be determined on summary judgment, so both parties have moved for summary judgment on this issue.

The court's determination of the correct number of statutory damage awards will depend on what constitutes a "work" for the purposes of §504(c)(1) and, more particularly, on whether CoStar registered its photographs as a compilation or as separate works on the same registration. There appears to be a division of authority over whether the copyright registration is determinative of the number of works or whether the determinative factor is whether each work is independently copyrightable. However, this division can be reconciled by looking beyond the language used by the courts to the actual result in each case.

LoopNet seeks to establish that the number of registration certificates should be determinative of the number of statutory damage awards. In *Phillips v. Kidsoft*, 52 USPQ2d 1102, 1106-07 (D Md 1999), a recent case in this district, the court held that the plaintiff was entitled only to 5 statutory damage awards for each registered maze book as opposed to 30 awards for each separate maze. That case seems to support the proposition that the copyright registrations were dispositive of the issue of statutory damage awards. The *Phillips* court appeared to disregard the economic viability test articulated in *Walt Disney Co. v. Powell*, 897 F2d 565, 569 (DC Cir 1990), and *Gamma Audio & Video, Inc. v. Ean-Chea*, 11 F3d 1106, 1116 (1st Cir 1993), and said, "In this case, whether or not the mazes copied by Kidsoft possess separate economic value is irrelevant because they are not individually copyrighted." *Phillips*, 52 USPQ2d at 1106. This seems to place the onus on the number of copyrights registered to determine the number of statutory damage awards.

The court in *Stokes Seeds Ltd. v. Geo. W. Park Seed Co.*, 783 F Supp 104, 107 (WD NY 1991), seems to take the same approach in holding that the plaintiff could get only a single statutory damage award for a book of photographs. The photographs constitute only one work, even though the photographs were separately copyrightable, because

they were assembled into a collective whole and registered as a compilation. As in *Phillips*, the *Stokes Seed* court seems to look only to the number of registrations and eschews the "independent copyright life" test. *Id.; see also Xoom, Inc. v. Imageline, Inc.*, 93 F Supp 2d 688, 693 (ED Va 1999) (holding that for a compilation or derivative work, "there should be only one award of statutory damages per registration.")

However, other courts have just as clearly recognized that multiple copyrights may be registered on the same form and, so, the registration is not dispositive. CoStar looks to authority which establishes an economic viability test for determining what constitutes a "work" for the purposes of statutory damages. In *Gamma Audio*, 11 F3d at 1116, the First Circuit stated that "separate copyrights are not distinct 'works' unless they can 'live their own copyright life.' " (internal citations omitted). Further, the court stated:

Under regulations promulgated by the Copyright Office, the copyrights in multiple works may be registered on a single form, and thus considered one work for the purposes of registration, *see* CFR §202.3(b)(3)(A), while still qualifying as separate "works" for the purposes of awarding statutory damages. We are unable to find any language in either the statute or the corresponding regulations that precludes a copyright owner from registering the copyrights in multiple works on a single registration form while still collecting an award of statutory damages for the infringement of each work's copyright."

Gamma Audio, 11 F3d at 1117 (internal citations omitted).

In another case, *Playboy Enters., Inc. v. Sanfilippo*, 46 USPQ2d (BNA) 1350 *[1 ILR (P&F) 445]* (1998), the court cited three main factors in its decision that each photograph should be considered a separate work for statutory damages: (1) each photograph had independent economic value and was viable on its own (as evidenced by licensing agreements for the redistribution of individual photographs subsequent to publication as a group in the magazine); (2) each photograph represents a singular and copyrightable effort concerning a particular model, photographer, and location; and (3) the defendant marketed each image separately on his web site. *Id.* at 1354-1356. The economic value of the work has also been determinative in the Eleventh Circuit, which held that whether a work is distinct is determined by whether each unit would have "independent economic value." *MCA Television Ltd. v. Feltner,* 89 F3d 766, 769 (11th Cir 1996).

Although these courts use language that makes them seem at odds, the approach has actually been consistent and so provides a clear guide for the current case. In cases like *Phillips* where each "work" was considered one registration, the plaintiff had actually registered a compilation, not separate copyrights on the same form. Therefore, even though the court in that case said the fact of the single registration obviated the need to assess the independent viability of each maze, the crucial fact was not the single registration, but the nature of what was registered. The photographs in *Sanfilippo* and the video tapes in *Gamma Audio* were never registered as compilations while the maze book in *Phillips* and the seed books in *Stokes Seeds* were. The critical fact, then, is not that CoStar registered multiple photographs on the same registration form, but whether it registered them as compilations or as individual copyrights.

The court, then, must look at how CoStar registered the photographs to determine whether they are separate works. CoStar asserts that it "has consistently registered the photographs collectively (that is, as a group) separately from the compilation." Paper no. 94, at 26, 27. It asserts that it is irrelevant that the photographs were registered together with compilations because they were not a "part of the compilation" and, thus, should be considered separate works like the photographs in *Gamma Audio. Id.* at 27. However, it would stretch the bounds of credulity to read the evidence CoStar supplies as supporting its claim that the photographs are registered separately from the compilation.

While CoStar claims it makes a separate reference to the photographs in addition to its registration of the database compilation (*see* Paper no. 94, at 26), the language on the registration under "Nature of Authorship" on all but the first registration reads, "REVISED COMPILATION OF DATABASE INFORMATION; SOME ORIGINAL TEXT AND PHOTOGRAPHS." Paper no. 94, Ex. H. This same language is repeated when the form

asks the registrant to give a brief, general statement of the material added to the work. On those same forms, where the registrant is asked to identify any previous works that the current work is based on or incorporates, the registration reads only, "previously registered database." *Id.* The registration makes no mention of the number or any specific features of the photographs it claims it sought to register. If CoStar registered these photographs without any other reference or description, as it claims to have done, it theoretically could have registered any number of photographs on those registrations. The bare reference to "photographs" only has efficacy as a description of the work to be copyrighted if it was made with reference to the other elements being copyrighted—the compilation of work. In other words, without the presence of the compilation as a limiting feature providing explication of which photographs CoStar sought to include in the registration, the word "photographs" is inadequate to describe the works to be registered.

CoStar refers to the slightly different language in its April 17, 1998, registration to support its assertion that it made separate mention of the photographs apart from the compilation. CoStar's registration does differ from its later registrations stating under "Nature of Authorship" that it is copyrighting "Compilation, text, and photographs." *Id.* On that same registration, when asked to describe briefly the work to be copyrighted, CoStar stated, "Compilation of public domain material, substantial original text, and original photographs." *Id.* Admittedly, there is some ambiguity resulting from the placement of punctuation. For example, there could plausibly be some significance to the difference between having a comma separate the word "compilation" from the words "text" and "photographs" on the April 17, 1998 registration as opposed to the semicolon it used in later registrations. Additionally, it is not entirely clear whether CoStar meant to describe the work as a compilation of the material, text and photographs or, as it seeks to argue, a compilation of material and also text and photographs. However, these arguments are not sufficient where CoStar makes no mention of the numbers of separate photographs it meant to register on each application. For the reasons stated above, an interpretation of the registrations in which CoStar registered "photographs" without further explication makes no sense and is rejected.

CoStar seeks to bolster its interpretation of the language on the registrations by pointing to a letter from the Copyright Office which, it claims, "specifically recognized that CoStar is registering its compilation, photographs, and text collectively." Paper no. 94, at 27. CoStar is incorrect. The letter refers only to a copyright application for a "database" and authorizes "special relief" from the requirement that a complete database be filed with the Library of Congress so that CoStar could file a single registration for "*a group of updates*." Paper no. 94, Ex. I. No mention is made of text or photographs in the latter and the only reference to any collective registration is to the "group of updates." CoStar has not provided sufficient evidence that it registered copyrights for the photographs on the registration forms separate from its database compilations. Therefore, the court finds that CoStar registered only a compilation on each form.

As in *Phillips*, 52 USPQ2d at 1106, it is irrelevant whether the photographs have independent economic value because they have not been separately registered, but registered only as the components of a compilation. Accordingly, CoStar will only be eligible for 13 statutory damage awards, corresponding to the number of registered compilations, if LoopNet is found to have infringed on CoStar's copyright.

E. Preemption of Non-Copyright Claims

LoopNet asserts that the Copyright Act preempts CoStar's non-copyright claims for reverse passing off, false designation of origin, unfair competition under federal and state law, intentional interference with business relations, and unjust enrichment under common law. Paper no. 87, at 61. The Copyright Act preempts state law that is "equivalent to any of the exclusive rights within the general scope of copyright as specified by section 106." 17 USC §301(a) (1996). "The Fourth Circuit Court of Appeals has interpreted the 'equivalency' test to mean that state law claims involving an act that would infringe rights under the Copyright Act are preempted unless they are 'qualitatively different.' " *Wharton v. Columbia Pictures Indus., Inc.*, 907 F Supp 144, 145 (D Md 1995), *citing Roscizewski v. Arete Associates, Inc.*, 1 F3d 225, 230 (4th Cir

1993). LoopNet argues that since the gravamen of CoStar's complaint is that LoopNet violated CoStar's exclusive right to reproduce, distribute, and display its copyrighted materials, this court should follow the court in *Wharton* which held that claims were "equivalent" when they concerned the "central allegation" of copyright infringement. Paper no. 87, at 62, citing 17 USC §106 and *Wharton*, 907 F Supp at 146.

As a preliminary matter, LoopNet's argument that the Lanham Act claims are preempted, Paper no. 87, at 61, is without merit. Section 301(d) of Title 17 states: "Nothing in this title annuls or limits any right or remedies under any other Federal statute." Thus, the Copyright Act, by its terms, does not preempt plaintiff's Lanham Act claims. *See Tracy v. Skate Key, Inc.*, 697 F Supp 748 (SD NY 1988); *see also D.C. Comics, Inc. v. Filmation Assoc.*, 486 F Supp 1273, 1277 (SD NY 1980); 1 Melville B. Nimmer and David Nimmer, *Nimmer on Copyright* §1.01[D], at 1-66.6 (2001) ("[T]he current Copyright Act does not in any manner repeal or otherwise affect other federal statutes.").

"To determine whether a state claim is preempted by the Act, courts must make a two-part inquiry: (1) the work must be within the scope of the subject matter of copyright, and (2) the state law rights must be equivalent to any exclusive rights within the scope of federal copyright." *Fischer v. Viacom Intern. Corp.*, 115 F Supp 2d 535, 540 (D Md 2000) (internal citation omitted). The scope of the subject matter of copyright encompasses "original works of authorship fixed in any tangible medium of expression" including literary, pictorial, and audiovisual works. 17 USC §102(a) (1996). The first prong of this test is met since all of Plaintiff's claims involve the alleged infringement of its photographs, and photographs are pictorial works fixed in a tangible medium and so, within the scope of the subject matter of copyright. "The second prong of the preemption inquiry requires a court to examine the rights a plaintiff claims under state law to determine whether these rights are equivalent to the exclusive rights granted by the Copyright Act." *Fischer*, 115 F Supp 2d at 541. In order to demonstrate that the claims are not equivalent and "[t]o avoid preemption, a cause of action defined by state law must incorporate elements beyond those necessary to prove copyright infringement, and must regulate conduct qualitatively different from the conduct governed by federal copyright law." *Trandes Corp. v. Guy F. Atkinson Co.*, 996 F2d 655, 659 (4th Cir 1993).

CoStar asserts that its state law claims meet the burden of being "qualitatively different" from the copyright claims because they include elements not found in the copyright claims. Paper no. 94, at 35, *citing Avtec Sys., Inc. v. Peiffer*, 21 F3d 568, 574 (4th Cir 1994). In both *Avtec* and *Trandes*, defendants' claims that §301 of the Copyright Act preempted trade secret claims failed because recovery for trade secret misappropriation requires proof of breach of confidence, which is an additional element of proof beyond those necessary to recover for copyright infringement. *See Avtec*, 21 F3d at 574; *see also Trandes*, 996 F2d at 660.

However, similar additional elements are not found in CoStar's common law unfair competition claims. The *Trandes* court distinguished the trade secret violation from a copyright infringement claim by holding that it was "the employment of improper means to procure the trade secret, rather than the mere copying or use, which is the basis of [liability]." *Trandes*, 966 F2d at 660 (emphasis omitted), *citing* Restatement (First) of Torts §757 cmt. A (1939). The distinction between those unfair competition claims that are not preempted and those that are is that "claims based upon breaches of confidential relationships, breaches of fiduciary duty and trade secrets have been held to satisfy the extra-element test," *American Movie Classics Co. v. Turner Entm't Co.*, 922 F Supp 926, 933 (SD NY 1996), *citing Kregos v. Associated Press*, 3 F3d 656, 666 (2d Cir 1993), whereas claims of misappropriation and unfair competition based solely on the copying of the plaintiff's protected expression fail that test. The critical question, then, is whether CoStar's unfair competition claim contains an additional element or whether it is based solely on the alleged copying.

The basis of CoStar's argument that its unfair competition claim should not be preempted is that LoopNet did not merely copy its photographs, but passed them off as its own photographs. In doing so, CoStar alleges, LoopNet caused separate injury than by the mere act of copying because it caused its users to believe it had photographs equivalent to CoStar's or that it had authorization to use CoStar's photographs. Paper no. 94, at 34-35. Furthermore, CoStar asserts that *Waldman Pub. Corp. v. Landoll, Inc.*, 43 F3d 775, 780 (2d Cir 1994), stands for the proposition that this kind of "reverse passing off," where a party passes off the goods of another party as its own, is not preempted by the Copyright Act. However, *Waldman* did not state that claims of reverse passing off are not preempted. Rather, it vacated on other grounds a district court decision holding that "[a] claim that a defendant has reproduced the plaintiff's work and sold it under the defendant's name—even if denominated 'passing off' by the plaintiff—is preempted by the Copyright Act." *American Movie Classics*, 922 F Supp at 934 (internal citation omitted). Essentially, CoStar's claim is that LoopNet is exhibiting as its own photographs on its web site that CoStar has an exclusive right to exhibit or license for exhibition. This type of reverse passing off is, in effect, a "disguised copyright infringement claim." 1 *Nimmer on Copyright*, §1.01[B][1][e], at 1-28 (2001); *see also American Movie Classics*, 922 F Supp at 934. The same act which constitutes LoopNet's alleged copyright infringement, the unauthorized copying of CoStar's photographs, also constitutes CoStar's unfair competition claim. Therefore, this claim does not satisfy the "extra-element" test and so is equivalent to CoStar's claim under the Copyright Act. Accordingly, it is preempted.

The determination of whether CoStar's remaining state claims are preempted similarly turns on whether they arise solely from copying or whether they require additional elements. CoStar characterizes its unjust enrichment claim as based not on the copyright infringement, but rather upon misattribution of source arising from its Lanham Act claims. Paper no. 94, at 36. In *Wharton*, however, the court held that the plaintiff's claim of unjust enrichment was preempted by the Copyright Act because it "concerns the central allegation that Defendants plagiarized his copyrighted screenplay." *Wharton*, 907 F Supp at 146; *see also American Movie Classics*, 922 F Supp at 934 (holding preemption is appropriate where unjust enrichment claim does not allege that the defendants were enriched by anything other than copyright infringement). CoStar seeks to distinguish the present case from *Wharton* and *American Movie Classics* by asserting that those cases do not deal with a claim of passing off. Paper no. 94, at 36. However, as with CoStar's unfair competition claims, the court fails to discern a true claim for passing off and instead sees only a disguised copyright claim. Accordingly, CoStar's unjust enrichment claims are preempted.

Finally, CoStar seeks to rescue its intentional interference with business relations claim by asserting that LoopNet interfered with existing licenses as opposed to prospective business relationships as in *Wharton*. Paper no. 94, at 37, citing *Wharton*, 907 F Supp at 145-46. According to CoStar, in contrast to interference with prospective business relationships, interference with existing contracts is akin to a breach of contract claim, which is not preempted. *See Architectronics, Inc. v. Control Systems, Inc.*, 935 F Supp 425, 440-41 *[2 ILR (P&F) 394]* (SD NY 1996) (breach of contract claims are different and not preempted). However, in *Harper & Row, Publishers, Inc. v. Nation Enters.*, 723 F2d 195, 201 (2d Cir 1983), *rev'd on other grounds*, 471 US 539 (1985), the Second Circuit held that a plaintiff's claim of tortious interference with contractual relations was preempted when it was based on the unauthorized publication of a work protected by the Copyright Act. It stated:

> The enjoyment of benefits from derivative use is so intimately bound up with the right itself that it could not possibly be deemed a separate element. *See* 1 Nimmer on Copyright §1.01[B], at n. 46 (1983). As the trial court noted, the fact that cross-appellants pleaded additional elements of awareness and intentional interference, not part of a copyright infringement claim, goes merely to the scope of the right; it does not establish qualitatively different conduct on the part of the infringing party, nor a fundamental nonequivalence between the state and federal rights implicated.

Id.

Therefore, as with CoStar's other state claims, the critical question to be decided is whether the alleged tortious interference depends on an extra element. In *National Car Rental Sys., Inc. v. Computer Assocs. Int'l, Inc.*, 991 F2d 426, 433-34 (8th Cir 1993), the Eighth Circuit found that a tortious interference claim was not preempted where a contractual restriction on the use of a computer program constituted an additional element. Similarly, in *Telecomm Tech. Servs., Inc. v. Siemens Rolm Communications, Inc.*, 66 F Supp 2d 1306,

1326 (ND Ga 1998), a case relied upon by CoStar for the proposition that the Copyright Act does not preempt intentional interference claims, the court found that claims were not preempted where the violation of licensing agreements and contractual provisions comprised an extra element. Even accepting CoStar's claims that LoopNet's alleged interference was with existing licenses as opposed to prospective relationships, the present case does not present an additional element similar to the the the *[sic]* violation of contractual agreements by defendants in *Telecomm* or *National Car Rental*. Accordingly, CoStar's intentional interference claim is also preempted by the Copyright Act.

IV. Modification of Preliminary Injunction

On March 14, 2000, the court entered a preliminary injunction, directing LoopNet to (1) remove from its web site all photographs for which it received notification of claimed infringement from CoStar; (2) notify the user who uploaded the photograph of CoStar's claim of the removal and that repeat acts of infringement might result in restrictions on the user's (or the brokerage firm's) access to the web site; and (3) with regard to identified brokers, require *prima facie* evidence of copyright ownership prior to posting a photograph. The injunction also required that other brokerage firms or offices later shown to the court's satisfaction to be repeat offenders after notice would similarly be subject to the *prima facie* showing requirement.

Dissatisfied with LoopNet's performance, and troubled by what it sees as escalating repeat infringements, CoStar seeks substantial modifications to the preliminary injunction. Specifically, CoStar seeks to require LoopNet to obtain a hand-signed written declaration of copyright ownership prior to any posting, to direct that any repeat infringer thereafter be prohibited from submitting any further photographs, to add to its database the address and property identification number of the 306 photographs thus far identified as infringing, and to order that failure to remove a photograph within 24 hours of notification from all locations and the reposting of any photograph will constitute evidence of direct contempt. In part, CoStar seeks to add additional firms or offices to the list of repeat infringers who are subject to the *prima facie* proof requirement. LoopNet disputes CoStar's factual recitations, and asserts that it has not only complied with the terms of the preliminary injunction, but has itself initiated further measures designed to prevent further unauthorized postings of CoStar's photographs. In a supplemental filing, CoStar claims that the *prima facie* evidence requirement is not inhibiting brokers from submitting non-infringing photographs, that LoopNet has posted a photograph without obtaining such evidence as required, and that there are additional repeat infringers. Again, LoopNet disputes both the facts and the conclusions drawn.

The court has reviewed the arguments and supporting material concerning LoopNet's compliance *vel non* with the preliminary injunction, as well as CoStar's requested enhancements. As discussed at the hearing on December 15, 2000, CoStar would have to meet the standard for issuance of preliminary injunctive relief to obtain relief in the form of enhancements. It has not done so. The facts are sufficiently disputed that the court cannot conclude that additional irreparable harm will befall CoStar if LoopNet is not required, for example, to obtain signed authorizations, or that such a requirement would not cause irreparable harm to LoopNet. Furthermore, in light of the court's resolution of the contributory infringement/safe harbor issues above, CoStar's likelihood of success has not been substantially demonstrated with regard to the potential enhancements being requested. Finally, the public interest in access to the commercial information weighs against imposing any further impediments during the pendency of this litigation. Accordingly, CoStar's request to modify the preliminary injunction IS DENIED to the extent that it seeks enhancements to the types of actions required of LoopNet.

On the other hand, application of the injunction requires the court to direct LoopNet to require *prima facie* evidence from those brokers or firms who post an alleged infringing photograph after notice that a previously posted photograph is claimed to infringe a CoStar copyright. During the course of these proceedings, LoopNet has implemented a probation/termination policy designed to deal with those brokers or offices that post an allegedly infringing photograph after removal of an earlier posting and accompanying notice. The court concludes that the policy, while helpful, does not go quite far enough in two ways. First, all brokers in an office in which any broker posted an allegedly infringing photograph after notice to any broker in that same office should be subject to the *prima facie* evidence requirement. And, for the purposes of the preliminary injunction, the brokerage office should remain in that status pending completion of this lawsuit.

When an office receives notice that one of its brokers has posted an allegedly infringing photograph, that office can be expected to monitor its own activities more vigilantly. Accordingly, if any broker in that office, whether or not the original offender, posts a second allegedly infringing photograph, then it is appropriate to require any broker in that office to provide *prima facie* evidence of the right to post a photograph. Thus, the gradations of "probation" cut too fine a distinction at this time. Furthermore, the discontinuance of probationary status in three, six, or twelve month intervals poses an enforcement problem for the court. The time necessary to review allegations of violations of either the policy or the injunction has become burdensome, not only to the parties, but to the court as well. With the resolution of the issues set forth above, the case will move toward what, it is hoped, will be the final stages of the proceedings at this level. Accordingly, the court concludes that the status of "repeat infringer," once achieved, will remain during the pendency of these proceedings.

V. Conclusion

For the foregoing reasons, by separate order, both motions concerning the safe harbor defense of the DMCA will be denied, summary judgment will be granted in favor of LoopNet on direct infringement, both motions concerning contributory infringement will be denied, summary judgment will be granted in favor of CoStar on LoopNet's misuse defense, summary judgment will be granted in favor of LoopNet on the issues of statutory damages and preemption of the state law claims of unfair competition, unjust enrichment, and intentional interference with business relations, and the preliminary injunction will be particularized regarding repeat violators.

ORDER

For the reasons stated in the foregoing Memorandum Opinion, it is this 28th day of September, 2001, by the United States District Court for the District of Maryland, ORDERED that:

1. The cross-motions for summary judgment on the safe harbor defense of the Digital Millennium Copyright Act ARE DENIED;

2. CoStar's motion for summary judgment on liability IS DENIED;

3. LoopNet's cross-motion for summary judgment on liability IS GRANTED as to direct infringement and DENIED as to contributory infringement;

4. LoopNet's motion as to copyright misuse IS DENIED, while CoStar's cross-motion IS GRANTED;

5. CoStar's motion as to statutory damages IS DENIED, while LoopNet's motion IS GRANTED;

6. LoopNet's motion to dismiss claims as preempted IS GRANTED as to the common law unfair competition, unjust enrichment, and intentional interference with business relations claims and DENIED as to the Lanham Act claims;

7. CoStar's motions to modify preliminary injunction ARE DENIED, except that *prima facie* evidence of authorization to post a photograph must be obtained from any broker at an office of a brokerage house once a second allegedly infringing photograph is posted by any broker after removal of and notice concerning the first allegedly infringing photograph has been sent to any broker in the same office;

8. A status and scheduling telephone conference will be held on Monday, October 22, 2001, at 4:00 p.m. Counsel for CoStar is directed to arrange for and initiate the call to counsel for LoopNet and the court; and

9. The clerk will transmit copies of the Memorandum Opinion and this Order to counsel for the parties.

---

[1] The parties have also filed motions to seal all of the motion papers because they contain proprietary or confidential information subject to protective order. See paper nos. 67, 72, 97, 104, 108, 110, 118, and 125. No oppositions have been received. Those motions are GRANTED. The parties have also moved for leave to file supplemental memoranda and responses, see paper nos. 90, 105, 109, 115, 116, 121, 122 and 127, and one to exceed the page limit, paper no. 106. Those motions are GRANTED.

[2] LoopNet provides other services, some generating income, and it sells advertising space on the public areas of its site.

[3] LoopNet has not identified which licensing agreements pertain to which alleged infringing photographs. Accordingly, it would not be appropriate to grant it summary judgment on this issue, even were the court to find that any of the agreements contained a sufficient consent by CoStar to the internet use of the photographs.

[4] The DMCA states: "The limitations on liability . . . apply to a service provider only if the service provider has designated an agent to receive notifications of claimed infringement described in paragraph (3)." 17 USC 512(c)(2) (1998). It is undisputed that LoopNet did not designate an agent until December 8, 1999. Paper no. 96, at 33. Therefore, the safe harbor is only available to LoopNet with regard to its liability (if any) arising after that date.

[5] LoopNet first received at least some notice of infringements from CoStar in the form of a letter on February 16, 1998. Paper no. 1, at 7, ex. G. CoStar refers in one brief to the first of its seven notices to LoopNet occurring on February 28, 1999. Paper no. 71, at 26. However, all other briefs and exhibits show no evidence of a February 28, 1999 notice, but prove the existence of the February 16, 1998 letter.

[6] CoStar makes an argument both here and when addressing the issue of contributory infringement directly that LoopNet's use of humans to check photographs as opposed to the mere use of an automated process distinguishes it from the "technology" line of cases, notably *Napster*. While CoStar is correct in that ongoing, active control over the facilities used by infringers is the critical issue, whether the uploading process is controlled by technological or human barriers is irrelevant. LoopNet has people checking photographs for purposes other than copyright infringement (Paper no. 87, at 52) and CoStar's own experts could not distinguish between a CoStar and non-CoStar photograph upon inspection. *Id.* at 26, Ex. 20. Essentially, the difference between human or computer control does not change the calculus that LoopNet only had notice, if ever, when informed of alleged infringements by CoStar and that the existence of ongoing, active control is proven without reference to the human/technology dichotomy.

[7] The parties concentrate on the legislative history which reports that the definition includes "providing Internet access, e-mail, chat room and web page hosting services." H.R. Rep. No. 105-551, at 64 (1998). They then debate whether LoopNet provides webpage hosting services.

[8] If the service provider has actual knowledge under §512(c)(1)(A)(i) or "red flag" knowledge under §512(c)(1)(A)(ii), the "take down" provisions of §512(c)(1)(A)(iii) must be met to stay in the safe harbor. Alternatively, if it receives notification of claimed infringement in accordance with §512(c)(3), the "take down" provisions of §512(c)(1)(C) must be met.

[9] A finding that the "right and ability to control" standard could be met merely by the ability to remove or block access to materials would render the DMCA internally inconsistent. The result would be that the very policy mandated by the DMCA in §512(c)(1)(C) to remain in the safe harbor, terminating infringers and blocking access, would force service providers to lose their immunity by violating §512(c)(1)(B). *See Hendrickson,* 2001 WL 1078981, at *9.

[10] It is undisputed that "LoopNet does not claim immunity for damages prior to LoopNet's registration under the DMCA." Paper no. 87, at 35 n. 20. CoStar identifies 179 photographs that fall in that category of photographs identified before safe harbor took effect. Paper. No. 96, at 33. However, CoStar does not claim that LoopNet is liable for the contributory infringement of its photographs before it sent the first notification of alleged infringement to LoopNet on February 16, 1998. Paper no. 1, at 7. The issues of liability addressed in this section pertain to those photographs that were alleged to be infringed between that first notice and the safe harbor.

Ellison

v.

Robertson

**United States District Court,
Central District of California**

March 13, 2002

10 ILR (P&F) 386, 189 F Supp 2d 1051

CV 00-04321 FMC (RCx)

ISP not liable for direct copyright infringement.

An Internet service provider cannot be liable for direct copyright infringement based upon copies of works made and uploaded by a third party and stored on the ISP's Usenet servers. Following *Religious Technology Center v. Netcom On-Line Communications Services, Inc.*, 1 ILR (P&F) 778 (ND Cal 1995); *ALS Scan, Inc. v. RemarQ Communities, Inc.*, 7 ILR (P&F) 69 (4th Cir 2001); and *Costar Group, Inc. v. Loopnet, Inc.*, 9 ILR (P&F) 720 (D Md 2001). — **Ellison v. Robertson, 10 ILR (P&F) 386 [CD Cal, 2002].**

Question of fact as to whether ISP is liable for contributory copyright infringement.

Plaintiff, an author whose works had been digitally copied and uploaded by a direct infringer, demonstrates a triable issue of fact as to whether an Internet service provider is liable for contributory copyright infringement based upon its storage of the infringing works on its Usenet servers. Plaintiff presents evidence suggesting that the ISP should have known of the infringement prior to the initiation of the present suit because the ISP had changed its e-mail address for copyright complaints without notifying the Copyright Office. Therefore, e-mails from individuals, such as plaintiff's counsel, who obtained the ISP's e-mail address from the Copyright Office and attempted to notify the ISP of infringing works were routed to a defunct account. Plaintiff also presents a triable issue of fact as to whether the ISP materially contributed to the copyright infringement. Relevant precedent [1 ILR (P&F) 778] holds that providing a service that allows for the automatic distribution of all Usenet postings, infringing and noninfringing, can constitute a material contribution when the ISP knows or should know of infringing activity on its system yet continues to aid in the accomplishment of the direct infringer's purpose of publicly distributing the postings. The ISP, however, successfully argues that it qualifies for the safe harbor provision under §512(a) of the Digital Millennium Copyright Act. — **Ellison v. Robertson, 10 ILR (P&F) 386 [CD Cal, 2002].**

ISP's ability to block infringing material after-the-fact is insufficient to show "control" for purposes of vicarious copyright infringement.

An Internet service provider's ability to delete or block access to postings of infringing material after those postings have already found their way onto the ISP's Usenet servers is insufficient to constitute "the right and ability to control the infringing activity" as that term is used in the context of vicarious copyright infringement. [Distinguishing *A&M Records, Inc. v. Napster, Inc.*, 7 ILR (P&F) 1, and *Religious Technology Center v. Netcom On-Line Communications Services, Inc.*, 1 ILR (P&F) 778.] — **Ellison v. Robertson, 10 ILR (P&F) 386 [CD Cal, 2002].**

Failure to derive financial benefit precludes liability for vicarious copyright infringement.

Even if an Internet service provider had the right and ability to control the infringing activity of third parties on a Usenet newsgroup, it would not be liable for vicarious copyright infringement because it did not derive a direct financial benefit from that activity. Financial benefit exists where the availability of infringing material acts as a "draw" for customers. While plaintiff, an author whose works had been digitally copied and uploaded onto the newsgroup, argues that the ISP's provision of access to Usenet newsgroups acts as a draw for customers, that argument ignores the requirement that any alleged financial benefit must be direct. The ISP does not receive any financial compensation from its peering agreements and participation in Usenet, and Usenet usage constitutes a very small percentage of the ISP's total member usage; any "draw" to one particular newsgroup, such as the one at issue here, is minuscule. Moreover, the relevant subset of activity is not simply Usenet newsgroup usage, but that portion of Usenet usage which is related to copyright infringement. Usenet postings containing infringing copies of copyrighted works cannot be characterized as a significant "draw" for customers. Furthermore, the Digital Millennium Copyright Act provides at least persuasive support for interpreting "direct financial benefit" to require something more than the indirect, insignificant financial benefits that may have accrued to the ISP as a result of copyright infringement on its Usenet servers. — **Ellison v. Robertson, 10 ILR (P&F) 386 [CD Cal, 2002].**

ISP adopted policy that satisfies statutory prerequisite for DMCA safe harbor.

An Internet service provider, seeking to qualify for the safe harbor provisions of the Digital Millennium Copyright Act (DMCA), satisfies the statutory prerequisite laid out in 17 USC §512(i): the ISP adopted, reasonably implemented, and notified its members of a repeat infringer termination policy at the time the allegedly infringing activity occurred. Subsection 512(i) requires only the adoption and reasonable implementation of a such a policy; it does not require ISPs to actually terminate repeat infringers, or even to investigate potential infringement so as to identify the responsible individuals. — **Ellison v. Robertson, 10 ILR (P&F) 386 [CD Cal, 2002].**

ISP qualifies for DMCA safe harbor under §512(a).

An Internet service provider's storage of Usenet messages containing binary files on its servers for fourteen days in order to make those messages accessible to the ISP's users constitutes "intermediate and transient storage" for purposes of the Digital Millennium Copyright Act's safe harbor provision in 17 USC §512(a). Thus, where an author's copyrighted works had been digitally copied and uploaded onto a Usenet newsgroup, which caused them to be automatically transmitted to and received by the ISP's Usenet servers, the ISP's storage of those infringing works on its servers for 14 days (in accordance with its retention policy for Usenet messages containing binary files) falls within the §512(a) safe harbor. Although subsection (a)(2) mandates that the storage of material be made "without selection" by the ISP, that refers to the selection of *infringing* material, not material generally. Thus, the ISP's decision not to carry every single newsgroup is not the relevant inquiry. Even if it were, however, the ISP's failure to carry every newsgroup still would not disqualify it from subsection (a)(2). An ISP would need to take on a greater editorial role—such as choosing specific postings or blocking certain messages—before forfeiting the protections of (a)(2)'s safe harbor. — **Ellison v. Robertson, 10 ILR (P&F) 386 [CD Cal, 2002].**

ORDER GRANTING DEFENDANT AOL'S MOTION FOR SUMMARY JUDGMENT

Introduction

FLORENCE-MARIE COOPER, *District Judge.* When an overenthusiastic fan uploads his favorite author's novels to a newsgroup on the internet, what is the liability of an internet service provider, such as AOL, for allowing the books to reside for two weeks on their USENET server? The impact of the Digital Millennium Copyright Act on this issue presents a question of first impression in the Ninth Circuit.

I. Procedural Posture

This matter is before the Court on (1) Defendant AOL's Motion for Summary Adjudication, filed June 4, 2001; (2) Defendant AOL's Motion for Summary Judgment, filed November 26, 2001; and (3) Plaintiff's Motion for Summary Adjudication, filed November 27, 2001. This matter came on for hearing on February 4, 2002. The parties were in possession of the Court's tentative decision to grant Summary Judgment to Defendant AOL. Following oral argument, the matter was taken under submission. For the reasons set forth below, the

Court hereby **GRANTS** summary judgment in favor of AOL.[1]

II. Background

A. Factual History

Plaintiff Harlan Ellison is the author of many works of fact and fiction, particularly science fiction. He is the owner of the valid copyrights to most if not all of those works and has registered his copyrights in accordance with all applicable laws. Some of his fictional works, however, have been copied and distributed on the internet without his permission.

Some time in late March or early April 2000, Stephen Robertson scanned a number of Ellison's fictional works in order to convert them to digital files. Thereafter, Robertson uploaded and copied the files onto the USENET newsgroup "alt.binaries.e-book." Robertson accessed the internet through his local internet services provider, Tehama County Online ("TCO"); his USENET service was provided by RemarQ Communities, Inc. ("RemarQ"). The USENET, an abbreviation of "User Network," is an international collection of organizations and individuals (known as 'peers') whose computers connect to each other and exchange messages posted by USENET users.[2] Messages are organized into "newsgroups," which are topic-based discussion forums where individuals exchange ideas and information.[3] Users' messages may contain the users' analyses and opinions, copies of newspaper or magazine articles, and even binary files containing binary copies of musical and literary works. "Alt.binaries.e-book", the newsgroup at issue in this case, seems to have been used primarily to exchange pirated and unauthorized digital copies of text material, primarily works of fiction by famous authors, including Ellison.

Peers in USENET enter into peer agreements, whereby one peer's servers automatically transmit and receive newsgroup messages from another peer's servers. As most peers are parties to a large number of peer agreements, messages posted on one USENET peer's servers are quickly transmitted around the world. The result is a huge informational exchange system whereby millions of users can exchange millions of messages every day.

AOL has been a USENET peer since 1994, and its USENET servers automatically transmit and receive newsgroup messages from at least 41 other peers. AOL estimates that its peer servers receive 4.5 terabytes of data in more than twenty-four million messages each week from AOL's peers. This data is automatically transmitted to and received by AOL's USENET servers, which are computers that are accessed by AOL's users when they reach the USENET system through AOL's newsgroup service. In late March and early April 2000, when Robertson posted the infringing copies of Ellison's works, AOL's retention policy provided for USENET messages containing binary files to remain on the company's servers for fourteen days.

After Robertson uploaded the infringing copies of Ellison's works to the alt.binaries.e-book newsgroup, they were then forwarded and copied throughout USENET onto servers all over the world, including those belonging to AOL. As a result, AOL users had access to the alt.binaries.e-book newsgroup containing the infringing copies of Ellison's works. As these infringing copies were in binary file form, they would have remained on AOL's servers for approximately fourteen days.

On or about April 13, 2000, Plaintiff learned of the infringing activity and contacted counsel. After researching the notification procedures of 17 USC §512, the Digital Millennium Copyright Act ("DMCA"), Plaintiff's counsel sent an e-mail on April 17, 2000, to TCO's and AOL's agents for notice of copyright infringement. Plaintiff received an acknowledgement of receipt from TCO, but no response from AOL, which claims never to have received that e-mail.

On April 24, 2000, Plaintiff filed suit against AOL and other Defendants. After having been served by Plaintiff on April 26, 2000, AOL blocked its users' access to alt.binaries.e-book.

B. Procedural History

On April 24, 2000, Plaintiff filed his original complaint with this Court. Shortly thereafter, on May 30, 2000, Plaintiff filed a First Amendment Complaint. On June 1, 2000, a consent judgment was entered in which one of the Defendants, Stephen Robertson, agreed to pay Plaintiff the sum of $3,648.96. Plaintiff in turn dismissed Robertson from the lawsuit. On July 27, 2000, the Court issued an Order granting in part and denying in part Defendant AOL's Motion to dismiss.

On September 26, 2000, Plaintiff filed a second amended complaint ("SAC") against America

Online, Inc. ("AOL"), RemarQ Communities, Inc. (RemarQ), Critical Path, Inc. ("CP") (RemarQ's parent company), Citizen 513, and Does on October 27, 2000, alleging the following causes of action:

(1) Direct Copyright Infringement against all Defendants;

(2) Contributory Infringement against all Defendants;

(3) Vicarious Infringement against RemarQ, CP, and AOL;

(4) Unfair Competition in Violation of Section 43(a) of the Lanham Act against all Defendants; and

(5) Trademark Dilution under Section 43(c) of the Lanham Act against all Defendants except Robertson and AOL.

On November 28, 2001, Plaintiff dismissed his Lanham Act claims as against AOL. On January 18, 2002, Plaintiff dismissed Defendant RemarQ from the case, the two parties having reached a settlement agreement. And on January 25, 2002, Plaintiff similarly dismissed his action against Defendant Critical Path.

On November 26, 2001, AOL filed a Motion for summary judgment, alleging that Plaintiff had failed to set forth prima facie cases of copyright infringement, and also claiming various defenses under the DMCA. On November 27, 2001, Plaintiff filed his own motion for summary adjudication of his contributory and vicarious copyright infringement claims against AOL. This Order addresses all three of those Motions. [4]

III. Standard

Summary judgment is proper only where "the pleadings, depositions, answers to interrogatories, and admissions on file, together with the affidavits, if any, show that there is no genuine issue as to any material fact and that the moving party is entitled to judgment as a matter of law." Fed. Rule Civ. Pro. 56(c); *see also Matsushita Elec. Indus. Co. v. Zenith Radio Corp.*, 475 US 574, 106 S Ct 1348, 89 L Ed 2d 538 (1986).

The moving party bears the initial burden of demonstrating the absence of a genuine issue of material fact. *Anderson v. Liberty Lobby, Inc.*, 477 US 242, 256, 106 S Ct 2505, 91 L Ed 2d 202 (1986). Whether a fact is material is determined by looking

to the governing substantive law; if the fact may affect the outcome, it is material. *Id.* at 248, 106 S Ct 2505.

If the moving party meets its initial burden, the "adverse party may not rest upon the mere allegations or denials of the adverse party's pleading, but the adverse party's response, by affidavits or as otherwise provided in this rule, must set forth specific facts showing that there is a genuine issue for trial." Fed. R. Civ. P. 56(e). Mere disagreement or the bald assertion that a genuine issue of material fact exists does not preclude the use of summary judgment. *Harper v. Wallingford*, 877 F2d 728 (9th Cir 1989).

The Court construes all evidence and reasonable inferences drawn therefrom in favor of the non-moving party. *Anderson*, 477 US at 255; *Brookside Assocs. v. Rifkin*, 49 F3d 490, 492-93 (9th Cir 1995).

IV. Discussion

A. Plaintiff's case against AOL for copyright infringement

AOL contends that Plaintiff cannot establish the prima facie elements of his direct, contributory, and vicarious copyright infringement claims against it, and therefore summary adjudication is appropriate. Plaintiff disputes AOL's contentions and asserts that he is entitled to summary adjudication of his contributory and vicarious copyright infringement claims.

1. Direct copyright infringement

"Plaintiffs must satisfy two requirements to present a prima facie case of direct infringement: (1) they must show ownership of the allegedly infringed material and (2) they must demonstrate that the alleged infringers violated at least one exclusive right granted to copyright holders under 17 USC §106." *A&M Records, Inc. v. Napster, Inc.*, 239 F3d 1004, 1013 *[7 ILR (P&F) 1]* (2001).

It is undisputed that Plaintiff owns valid copyrights for most, if not all, of the allegedly infringed works identified in his Complaint. [5] And if AOL were found to have copied any of Ellison's works then it might have violated, for example, his exclusive rights to reproduction and distribution. *See* 17 USC §106(1), (3). AOL contends, however, that it has not in any way copied Ellison's works. In his second amended complaint Plaintiff alleges that AOL made copies of his works on its USENET servers after receiving the USENET messages posted by Robertson, and that one binary file containing a copied work remained on AOL's servers for ten days after Plaintiff's counsel sent the company a Notification of Infringement e-mail.[6]

In his Opposition to AOL's Motion for summary judgment, however, Ellison does not respond to AOL's argument that there was no direct copyright infringement. Accordingly, it appears that he has abandoned his direct infringement claim against AOL. Regardless, AOL's role in the infringement as a passive provider of USENET access to AOL users cannot support direct copyright infringement liability. *See Religious Technology Center v. Netcom On-Line Communications Services, Inc.,* 907 F Supp 1361, 1372-73 *[1 ILR (P&F) 778]* (ND Cal 1995). In *Netcom,* the court held that the defendant, an internet services provider like AOL, could not be found guilty of direct copyright infringement based on copies of works that were made and stored on its USENET servers. *See id; accord ALS Scan, Inc. v. RemarQ Communities, Inc.,* 239 F3d 619, 622 *[7 ILR (P&F) 69]* (4th Cir 2001); *Costar Group, Inc. v. Loopnet, Inc.,* 164 F Supp 2d 688, 696 [9 ILR (P&F) 720] (D Md 2001). The *Netcom* Court stated that assigning direct copyright infringement liability to ISPs would be pointless:

> These parties [the ISPs], who are liable under plaintiff's theory, do no more than operate or implement a system that is essential if Usenet messages are to be widely distributed. There is no need to construe the [Copyright] Act to make all of these parties infringers.

Id. at 1369-70. The Court based this decision on its conclusion that "[t]he court does not find workable a theory of direct infringement that would hold the entire Internet liable for activities that cannot reasonably be deterred." *Id.* at 1372. While the *Netcom* court left open the possibility that an ISP with USENET messages on its servers might be guilty of contributory infringement under certain circumstances, it held that direct infringement liability should be limited to those users, like Robertson, who are responsible for the actual copying. *See id.* at 1372-73.

The Court agrees with the analysis of the court in *Netcom.* Accordingly, summary adjudication of Plaintiff's direct copyright infringement claim against AOL is granted.

2. Contributory copyright infringement

"[O]ne who, with knowledge of the infringing activity, induces, causes or materially contributes to the infringing conduct of another, may be liable as a 'contributory' infringer . . . Put differently, liability exists if the defendant engages in personal conduct that encourages or assists the infringement." *A&M Records, Inc. v. Napster, Inc.,* 239 F3d 1004, 1019 *[7 ILR (P&F) 1]* (2001) (internal quotations and citations omitted). "The absence of such language in the copyright statute does not preclude the imposition of liability for copyright infringement on certain parties who have not themselves engaged in the infringing activity. For vicarious liability is imposed in virtually all areas of the law, and the concept of contributory infringement is merely a species of the broader problem of identifying the circumstances in which it is just to hold one individual accountable for the actions of another." *Sony Corp. v. Universal City Studios, Inc.,* 464 US 417, 435 (1984).

(i) Knowledge

The knowledge requirement means that the contributory infringer must "know or have reason to know of direct infringement." *Id.* at 1020 (internal quotations omitted). Plaintiff argues that AOL actually knew about the infringing copies of his works on their USENET servers based on the e-mail that his attorney sent to AOL on April 17, 2000. But AOL claims never to have received that e-mail and asserts that it was first put on notice of infringement when it was served with a copy of Plaintiff's initial complaint. The Court accepts AOL employees' assurances that they never received the e-mail,[7] and finds Plaintiff's argument somewhat puzzling given his professed belief, supported in detail in his briefs, that his attorney's e-mail was not received because AOL had provided the Copyright Office with an incorrect e-mail contract address, and his attorney had relied on that address when trying to contact AOL. Accordingly, the Court finds that AOL did not have actual knowledge of the infringement before being served by Ellison.

On the other hand, Ellison presents substantial evidence suggesting that AOL should have known about the infringement prior to being served. First, AOL's failure to receive the April 17, 2000, e-mail is its own fault. Inexplicably, AOL had changed its contact e-mail address from "copyright@aol.com" to "aolcopyright@aol.com" in fall 1999, but waited until April 2000 to notify the Copyright Office of this change. As a result, the complaints of individuals such as Ellison's attorney, who obtained AOL's e-mail address from the Copyright Office and attempted to notify AOL of infringement occurring on its servers were routed to the defunct account. Nor did AOL make provision for forwarding to the new address e-mails sent to the defunct account. AOL has declined to explain why it delayed months before notifying the Copyright Office of its change in e-mail addresses. If AOL could avoid the knowledge requirement through this oversight or deliberate action, then it would encourage other ISPs to remain willfully ignorant in order to avoid contributory copyright infringement liability. Based upon the record before the Court, a reasonable trier of fact could certainly find that AOL had reason to know that infringing copies of Ellison's works were stored on their Usenet servers.

In addition, AOL received further information about the infringement occurring on the USENET newsgroup accessible to AOL users from John J. Miller. Miller noticed a number of apparently unauthorized copies of various authors' works on the newsgroup and called AOL to report the suspicious activity, although he probably mentioned only works by authors other than Ellison. Even though it is not clear that Miller's phone call can be fairly said to have put AOL on notice of the infringing activity (he spoke only with low-level customer service representatives, it's not clear whether he expressly mentioned the alt.binaries.e-book newsgroup, and he did not follow up on the customer service representatives' advice by sending AOL an e-mail setting forth the details of his complaint), it is another piece of evidence which might lead a reasonable trier of fact to conclude that AOL should have known about the infringement of Ellison's copyrights occurring in its newsgroup. For example, a reasonable trier of fact might conclude that AOL should have transferred Miller to speak with an employee with knowledge of AOL's copyright infringement policies instead of directing him to an e-mail address. [8]

(ii) Material contribution to the infringement

AOL correctly points out that it did not induce or encourage Robertson to directly infringe Ellison's copyrights. Plaintiff, however, maintains that AOL materially contributed to infringement by participating in USENET peering agreements which resulted in making the infringing copies of Ellison's works available to millions of AOL users. Plaintiff analogizes AOL's conduct to that of Napster, which was held to constitute a material contribution to infringement. See *Napster*, 239 F3d at 1022. The Court of Appeals in *Napster* based its holding on the district court's finding that "[w]ithout the support services defendant provides, Napster users could not find and download the music they want with the ease of which defendant boasts." *Id.* (quoting *A&M Records, Inc. v. Napster, Inc.,* 114 F Supp 2d 896, 919-920 *[5 ILR (P&F) 745]* (ND Cal 2000). As such, Napster was providing the " 'site and facilities' for direct infringement." *Napster*, 239 F2d at 1022. By analogy, Plaintiff alleges that AOL provided the site and facilities for direct infringement by storing infringing copies of Ellison's works on its USENET servers and providing its users with access to those copies.

In response, AOL contends that its mere provision of USENET access to its users, as a matter of law, is far too attenuated from the actual infringing activity to constitute a material contribution. In support it points to section 512(m) of the DMCA, which provides that an ISP does not have to monitor its service or affirmatively search for infringing activity on its network in order to qualify for any of the limitation-on-liability safe harbors.

The Court agrees with the findings of the court in *Netcom* that "[p]roviding a service that allows for the automatic distribution of all Usenet postings, infringing and noninfringing" can constitute a material contribution when the ISP knows or should know of infringing activity on its system "yet continues to aid in the accomplishment of Erlich's [the direct infringer's] purpose of publicly distributing the postings." *Netcom*, 907 F Supp at 1375. The court noted that "Netcom allows Erlich's infringing messages to remain on its system and be further distributed to other Usenet servers worldwide." *Id.*; *see also Napster*, 239 F3d at 1021 (approving the *Netcom* Court's conclusion regarding Netcom's potential liability for contributory infringement); 3 NIMMER ON COPYRIGHT §12B.01[A], at 12B-9 n. 50 ("Given that Netcom declined to cancel Erlich's messages, if plaintiffs could show that it had knowledge of their infringing character, it would make a strong showing for contributory infringement.").

In *Netcom* the court dealt with a situation in which the ISP had actual knowledge of the presence of infringing material on its USENET servers. Here, by contrast, there is a triable issue of fact as to whether AOL should have known of the infringing material on the alt.binaries.e-books newsgroup based on the e-mail sent to it by Plaintiff's counsel and the Miller phone call. Although there is some difference between an ISP actually knowing of infringement and ignoring requests to remedy the situation and an ISP remaining ignorant of infringement through its own fault and taking no action, the *Netcom* decision cannot be distinguished on that basis. To do so would invite ISPs to remain willfully ignorant of infringement on their servers (through the creation of unchecked notification e-mail addresses and other means), and would frustrate the careful balance struck by Congress when it enacted the DMCA.

In addition, *Netcom* is not legally distinguishable on the basis that AOL had no real connection with Robertson, whereas Netcom played a significant role in connecting Erlich, the direct infringer, to the Internet. Although a trier of fact might consider this difference in reaching the conclusion that AOL did not make a material contribution to Robertson's underlying infringement, that difference cannot alone transform a triable issue of fact into a determination suitable for summary adjudication. *Netcom* analyzed the ISP's behavior after the infringement had already occurred, and with regard to contributory infringement, the court's central concern was the ISP's decision to leave the infringing messages on its system even after receiving the plaintiff's infringement complaint. Similar concerns provide the basis for plaintiff's contributory infringement claim against AOL.

Accordingly, the Court finds that Plaintiff has demonstrated a triable issue of fact as to whether AOL materially contributed to the direct infringement of Ellison's copyrights by others.

3. Vicarious copyright infringement

"In the context of copyright law, vicarious liability extends beyond an employer/employee relationship to cases in which a defendant 'has the right and ability to supervise the infringing activity and also has a direct financial interest in such activities.'" *Napster*, 239 F3d at 1022 (quoting *Gershwin Publ'g Corp. v. Columbia Artists Mgmt.*, *Inc.*, 443 F2d 1159, 1162 (2d Cir 1971)). "Unlike contributory infringement, knowledge is not an element of vicarious liability." *Netcom*, 907 F Supp at 1375 (citing to 3 NIMMER ON COPYRIGHT §12.04[A][1], at 12070).

1. Right and ability to supervise the infringing activity

AOL maintains that it did not possess the right or ability to supervise Robertson's infringing acts because of the automated nature of its participation in the USENET system. Robertson never used the AOL system to upload the infringing copies of Plaintiff's works, and his posting was just one of millions of USENET postings that AOL servers automatically receive from peers each week.

Plaintiff, on the other hand, contends that the Ninth Circuit's recent decision in *Napster* defeats AOL's position. In *Napster*, the Court found that Napster's "ability to block infringers' access to a particular environment for any reason whatsoever is evidence of the right and ability to supervise." *Id.* at 1023. AOL had the same capacity to block infringers' access to its USENET servers, Plaintiff argues, as demonstrated by AOL's successful blocking of the alt.binaries.e-book newsgroup from access by AOL users upon receiving notice of Plaintiff's lawsuit. Further support comes from *Netcom*. In *Netcom*, the court found there was a triable issue of fact as to an ISP's right and ability to control and supervise infringement on its system. The court also stated that whether the ISP's ability to terminate the accounts of infringers and to block access to or delete infringing material "occurred before or after the abusive conduct is not material to whether Netcom can exercise control." *Id.* at 1376.

AOL disputes the *Napster* analogy. The Napster system, AOL argues, was closed and afforded Napster the right and ability to control infringing parties because only Napster members could access and commit infringement on the system. By contrast, AOL's after-the-fact ability to remove or block access to infringing activities by non-AOL users such as Robertson does not constitute an ability to control or supervise. Robertson accessed USENET from outside of AOL, and AOL had no ability to effectively control his infringement.

AOL also points to the recent decision in *Hendrickson v. eBay* in support of its contention that it did not possess the right and ability to control the infringing activity. *See Hendrickson v. eBay,* 165 F Supp 2d 1082 *[8 ILR (P&F) 573]* (CD Cal 2001). In *eBay,* the district court held that "the 'right and ability to control' the infringing activity, as the concept is used in the DMCA, cannot simply mean the ability of a service provider to remove or block access to materials posted on its website or stored on its system." *Id.* at 1093. The court reasoned that because DMCA specifically requires ISPs to remove or block access to infringing materials in order to avail themselves of the limitation on liability found in subsection 512(c), the "right and ability to control" must mean something more than the ability to delete or block access to infringing materials after the fact. *See id.* Otherwise, "a service provider loses immunity under the safe-harbor provision of the DMCA because it engages in acts that are specifically required by the DMCA." *Id.* at 1094.

The *eBay* court's analysis somewhat overstates the predicament (ISPs not receiving a financial benefit directly attributable to the infringing activity would not face this "catch-22"), but it does raise an interesting point, namely: ISPs that do receive a financial benefit directly attributable to the infringement activity and that wish to avail themselves of subsection (c)'s safe harbor are required by 512(c)(1)(C) to delete or block access to infringing material. Yet in taking such action they would, in Plaintiff's analysis, be admitting that they have the "right and ability to control" infringing activity, which under 512(c)(1)(B) would prevent them from qualifying for the subsection (c) safe harbor. It is conceivable that Congress intended that ISPs which receive a financial benefit directly attributable to the infringing activity would not, under any circumstances, be able to qualify for the subsection (c) safe harbor. But if that was indeed their intention, it would have been far simpler and much more straightforward to simply say as much. The Court does not accept that Congress would express its desire to do so by creating a confusing, self-contradictory catch-22 situation that pits 512(c)(1)(B) and 512(c)(1)(C) directly at odds with one another, particularly when there is a much simpler explanation: the DMCA requires more than the mere ability to delete and block access to infringing material after that material has been posted in order for the ISPs to be said to have "the right and ability to control such activity."

The DMCA did not simply rewrite copyright law for the on-line world. Rather it crafted a number of safe harbors which insulate ISPs from most liability should they be accused of violating traditional copyright law.[9] And the legislative history expressly states that "new Section 512 does not define what is actionable copyright infringement in the on-line environment . . . [t]he rest of the Copyright Act sets those rules." H.R. Rep. 105-551(II), at p. 64 (July 22, 1998). Nonetheless, there is much to be gained from defining and analyzing certain terms and concepts consistently throughout copyright law, including the DMCA. And when Congress chooses to utilize exact phrases that have a specialized legal meaning under copyright law (*i.e.,* "the right and ability to control infringing activity"),[10] and gives those phrases a certain meaning in one context (*i.e.,* under the DMCA, the ability to delete or block access to infringing materials after the infringement has occurred is not enough to constitute "the right and ability to control"), Congress's choice provides at least persuasive support in favor of giving that phrase a similar meaning when used elsewhere in copyright law.

Moreover, the right and ability to control the infringing behavior in AOL's case was substantially less than that enjoyed by the ISP in *Netcom.* There, the ISP was one of the two entities responsible for providing the direct infringer with access to the Internet. *See Netcom,* 907 F Supp at 1365-66. As a result, by taking affirmative steps against the other entity involved, the ISP had the ability to target the infringer himself and deny him access to the Internet. By contrast, AOL had no such ability to go after Robertson personally here. Rather, it found itself in the same situation as every other ISP in the world that had entered into peer agreements which included the alt.binaries.e-book newsgroup. It could delete or block users' access to the infringing postings, but it could not do anything to restrict the infringing activity at the root level.

The Court holds that AOL's ability to delete or block access to Robertson's postings of infringing material after those postings had already found their way onto AOL's USENET servers was insufficient to constitute "the right and ability to control the infringing activity" as that term is used in the context of vicarious copyright infringement.

2. Direct financial benefit

Even if AOL had the right and ability to control Robertson's infringing activity, it would not be liable for vicarious copyright infringement because it did not derive a direct financial benefit from that activity. "Financial benefit exists where the availability of infringing material 'acts as a "draw" for customers.'" *Napster*, 239 F3d at 1023 (quoting *Fonovisa, Inc. v. Cherry Auction, Inc.*, 76 F3d 259 (9th Cir 1996)).

Ellison maintains that AOL's provision of access to USENET newsgroups does act as a draw for customers. Like e-mail or instant messaging, USENET access is one of the many services AOL provides in order to lure new customers and retain old ones, Ellison urges. According to Plaintiff, AOL's situation is indistinguishable from that in *Napster*, where the Court of Appeals held that "[a]mple evidence supports the district court's finding at Napster's future revenue is directly dependent upon 'increases in userbase.'" *Id.* at 1023.

Plaintiff's argument ignores the requirement that any alleged financial benefit must be direct. AOL did not receive any financial compensation from its peering agreements and participation in USENET. And USENET usage constitutes a very small percentage, 0.25%, of AOL's total member usage; any "draw" to one particular newsgroup, such as alt.binaries.e-book, is minuscule and remote, as the pro rata "draw" of any single newsgroup (AOL carries more than 43,000 total) constitutes approximately 0.00000596% of AOL's total usage. Moreover, the relevant subset of activity is not simply USENET newsgroup usage, but that portion of USENET usage which is related to copyright infringement. By way of example, only ten of AOL's more than 20 million users inquired when AOL blocked all access to alt.binaries.e-book on April 28, 2000.

USENET postings containing infringing copies of copyrighted works cannot be characterized as a significant "draw" for customers. USENET usage constitutes a very small percentage of total AOL usage, and Plaintiff has failed to produce any evidence suggesting that a significant portion of even that minimal usage entails the illegal exchange of files containing copyrighted material. In this way AOL's situation is radically different from that of Napster, whose service was devoted to the exchange from mp.3 music files which usually contained unauthorized copies of copyrighted material. Making it easier to exchange infringing copies of music files was Napster's main draw:

> And here the evidence establishes that a majority of Napster users use the service to download and upload copyrighted music. This, in fact, should come as no surprise to Napster since that really, it's clear from the evidence in this case and the early records that were divulged in discovery, was the purpose of it.

A&M Records, Inc. v. Napster, Inc., 2000 WL 1009483, at *1 [5 ILR (P&F) 663] (ND Cal July 26, 2000) (transcript of the proceedings). By contrast, only a tiny fraction of AOL usage has anything to do with USENET, and only a substantially smaller subset of that usage appears to have anything to do with infringing copyrights.

Fonovisa presents another case in which courts have required that the sale or distribution of infringing materials must be a significant draw to customers in order for vicarious copyright liability to apply. In *Fonovisa*, the defendant operated a swap meet at which third-party vendors routinely sold counterfeit recordings that infringed on that plaintiff's copyrights. *Id.* at 260. For example, a single 1991 Sheriff's department raid had netted more than 38,000 pirated recordings. "The facts alleged by Fonovisa . . . reflect that the defendants reap substantial financial benefits from admission fees, concession stand sales and parking fees, all of which flow directly from customers who want to buy the counterfeit recordings at bargain basement prices." *Id.* at 263. "In short, in *Fonovisa*, a symbiotic relationship existed between the infringing vendors and the landlord." *Adobe Systems Incorporated v. Canus Productions, Inc.*, 173 F Supp 2d 1044 (CD Cal 2001) (discussing *Fonovisa*).[11]

By contrast, the record before the Court demonstrates that USENET usage related to copyright infringement constitutes a minuscule portion of AOL usage. The financial benefit accruing to AOL from such infringing usage, if any benefit exists at all, is too indirect and constitutes far too small a "draw" to fairly support the imposition of vicarious copyright liability on AOL.

Moreover, as with the discussion of AOL's "right and ability to control,", the DMCA provides at least persuasive support for interpreting "direct financial benefit" to require something more than the indirect, insignificant financial benefits that may have accrued to AOL as a result of copyright infringement on its USENET servers. The legislative history of the DMCA provides:

> In determining whether the financial benefit criterion [of section 512(c)(1)(B)] is satisfied, courts should take a common-sense, fact-based approach, not a formalistic one. In general, a service provider conducting a legitimate business would not be considered to receive a 'financial benefit directly attributable to the infringing activity' where the infringer makes the same kind of payment as non-infringing users of the provider's service.

H.R. Rep. 105-51(II), at p. 54 (July 22, 1998). Accordingly, summary adjudication for AOL of Plaintiff's claim for vicarious copyright infringement is granted.

B. DMCA Limitations on Liability

AOL claims to qualify for two of the DMCA's "safe-harbor" provisions, subsection (a), Transitory digital network communications, and subsection (c), Information residing on systems or networks at direction of users. *See* 17 USC §512(a), (c). These safe harbors do not confer absolute immunity upon ISPs, but do drastically limit their potential liability based on specific functions they perform (*e.g.*, user-directed information storage). *See generally* 17 USC §512. A party satisfying the requirements for one of the safe harbors cannot be liable for monetary relief, or, with the exception of the rather narrow relief available under subsection (j), for injunctive or other equitable relief for copyright infringement. *See id.*

1. Section 512(i)

In order to avail itself of any of section 512's limitation-on-liability safe harbors, AOL must also satisfy the two requirements laid out in section 512(i). Section 512(i) provides that all safe-harbor provisions established by the DMCA shall apply to a service provider only if the service provider:

(A) has adopted and reasonably implemented, and informs subscribers and account holders of the service provider's system or network of, a policy that provides for the termination in appropriate circumstances of subscribers and account holders of the service provider's system or network who are repeat infringers; and

(B) accommodates and does not interfere with standard technical measures.

17 USC §512(i)(1).

Furthermore, in order for an ISP to comply with subsection (i) and avail itself of one of the DMCA's safe harbors, the ISP must have adopted, reasonably implemented, and notified its members of the repeat infringer termination policy at the time the allegedly infringing activity occurred. Doing so after the infringing activity has already occurred is insufficient if the ISP seeks a limitation of liability in connection with that infringing activity. As explained by the district court in *Napster,* to hold otherwise would be defeat the whole purpose of subsection (i):

> Napster attempts to refute plaintiffs' argument by noting that subsection (i) does not specify when the copyright compliance policy must be in place. Although this characterization of subsection (i) is factually accurate, it defies the logic of making formal notification to users or subscribers a prerequisite to exemption from monetary liability. The fact that Napster developed and notified its users of a formal policy *after* the onset of this action should not moot plaintiffs' claim to monetary relief for past harms.

Napster, 2000 WL 573136 at *9 (original emphasis).

On its face, subsection (i) is only concerned with repeat-infringer termination policies, and not with copyright infringement in general. Nonetheless, Plaintiff urges that any reasonable policy whose goal is to put repeat infringers on notice that they face possible termination must necessarily include some procedures for actually identifying such individuals in the first place, such as a mechanism whereby the public can notify an ISP of copyright infringement occurring on its system. A termination policy could not be considered "reasonably implemented" if the ISP remained willfully ignorant of users on its system who infringe copyrights repeatedly. Although the text of section 512(i) could conceivably support such an interpretation, the legislative history demonstrates that Congress's intent was far more limited regarding subsection (i): [12]

> the Committee does not intend this provision to undermine the principles of new subsection (1) [13] or the knowledge standard of new subsection (c) by suggesting that a provider *must investigate possible infringements, monitor its service, or make difficult judgments as to whether conduct is or is not infringing.* However, those who repeatedly or flagrantly abuse their access to the Internet through disrespect for the intellectual property rights of others should know that there is a realistic threat of losing that access.

H.R. Rep. 105-551(II), at p. 61 (July 22, 1998) (emphasis added); *see also* S. Rep. 105-190, at p. 51-52 (May 11, 1998) (providing *verbatim* the same explanation of subsection (i)). In the face of such clear guidance from the legislative history of the DMCA, subsection (i) cannot be interpreted to require ISPs to take affirmative steps to investigate potential infringement and set up notification procedures in an attempt to identify the responsible individuals. Accordingly, many of Plaintiff's argument *[sic]* regarding subsection (i) are irrelevant to determining whether AOL had reasonably implemented a policy for termination of repeat infringers. [14]

It is undisputed that AOL satisfies prong (B) based on its accommodation and non-interference with standard technical measures. And AOL presents evidence to support the conclusion that it has also met the requirements of prong (A). AOL's Terms of Service, to which every AOL member must agree before becoming a member, includes a notice that AOL members may not make unauthorized copies of content protected by copyrights, trademarks, or any other intellectual property rights. They also notify members that their AOL accounts could be terminated for making such unauthorized copies.

Plaintiff contends, however, that AOL cannot satisfy prong (A) of subsection 512(i)(1) because although the ISP has presented substantial evidence of compliance, most of that evidence comes from March 2001, nearly a year after the infringing conduct occurred. AOL's percipient witness, Elizabeth Compton, testified that AOL's procedures for notifying its users that their access could be terminated if they were to infringe others' copyrights has not changed substantively since April 2000. However, Plaintiff challenges the credibility and competency of Ms. Compton, whose grasp of the technical side of AOL's copyright infringement procedures was decidedly less than expert.

In addition, Plaintiff notes that although AOL claims to have complied with subsection (i) and adopted and reasonably implemented polices aimed at terminating repeat infringers, Compton testified that no individual has ever been terminated for being a repeat infringer. Given the millions of AOL users, Plaintiff argues, this lack of even a single termination for repeat infringement is evidence that AOL has failed to fulfill its obligation to reasonably implement its subsection (i) termination policy. Moreover, Compton testified at her deposition that at the time of the infringement, AOL had not precisely defined how many times a user had to be guilty of infringement before that user could be classified as a "repeat infringer." Plaintiff claims this is further evidence that AOL had failed to comply with the reasonable-implementation requirement of subsection (i).

As noted above in the discussion of the legislative history of the DMCA, however, subsection (i) does not require AOL to actually terminate repeat infringers, or even to investigate infringement in order to determine if AOL users are behind it. [15] That is the province of subsection (c), which provides detailed requirements related to notification of infringement and the ISPs' responsibility to investigate and, in some instances, delete or block access to infringing material on their systems. Subsection (i) only requires AOL to put its users on notice that they face a realistic threat of having their Internet access terminated if they repeatedly violate intellectual property rights.

Plaintiff has attacked the credibility of competence of Elizabeth Compton, and in particular challenges her assertion that the AOL's procedures for compliance with subsection (i) have not changed substantively since April 2000. But most of Plaintiff's "attacks" only demonstrate that Ms. Compton did not understand the technical means by which access to infringing material on AOL's servers may be blocked or by which an AOL user's

Internet access could be terminated. While such shortcomings might be relevant when weighing her testimony regarding AOL's compliance with subsection (c), they are not relevant when considering the much less stringent (and less technical) requirements of subsection (i). And although Plaintiff disputes Compton's claim that AOL's notification policy has not changed, he has not produced any evidence to the contrary. "When a motion for summary judgment is made and supported as provided in this rule, an adverse party may not rest upon the mere allegations or denials of the adverse party's pleading, but the adverse party's response, by affidavits or as otherwise provided in this rule, must set forth specific facts showing that there is a genuine issue for trial." Fed. R. Civ. Proc. 56(e).

Accordingly, the Court holds that AOL had satisfied the requirements of 17 USC §512(i) at the time of the alleged infringement of Ellison's copyrights.

2. Section 512's limitation on liability (a) through (d)

Section 512(n) explicitly provides that each of the four limitation-on-liability safe harbors found in subsections (a) through (d) "describe separate and distinct functions for purposes of applying this section." *Id.* As a result, "[w]hether a service provider qualifies for the limitation of liability in any one of the subsections shall be based solely on the criteria in that subsection, and shall not affect a determination of whether the service provider qualifies for the limitations on liability under any other such subsection." *Id.* The DMCA's legislative history provides the following instructional example:

> Section 512's limitations on liability are based on functions, and each limitation is intended to describe a separate and distinct function. Consider, for example, a service provider that provides a hyperlink to a site containing infringing material which it then caches on its system in order to facilitate access to it by its users. This service provider is engaging in at least three functions that may be subject to the limitation on liability: transitory digital network communications under subsection (a), system caching under

subsection (b), and information locating tools under subsection (d).

H.R. Rep. 105-551(II), at p. 65 (July 22, 1998). In this example, if the service provider met the threshold requirements of subsection (i), "then for its acts of system caching it is eligible for that limitation on liability with corresponding narrow injunctive relief. But if the same company is committing an infringement by using information locating tools to link its users to infringing material, then its fulfillment of the requirements to claim the system caching liability limitation does not affect whether it qualifies for the liability limitation for information location tools." 3 NIMMER ON COPYRIGHT §12B.06[A], at 12B-53, 54.

Although AOL performs many Internet-service-provider-related functions, Plaintiff's claims against AOL are based solely on its storage of USENET messages on its servers and provision of access to those USENET messages to AOL users and others accessing the AOL system from outside.

AOL claims that it is eligible under both subsections (a) and (c) for a limitation on liability regarding Plaintiff's claims against it.

3. Subsection (a)'s limitation on liability

AOL contends that it meets all the criteria for the limitation-on-liability safe harbor found in subsection (a), which provides:

> (a) Transitory digital network communications.—A service provider shall not be liable for monetary relief, or, except as provided in subsection (j), for injunctive or other equitable relief, for the infringement of copyright by reason of the provider's transmitting, routing, or providing connections for, material through a system or network controlled or operated by or for the service provider, or by reason of the intermediate and transient storage of that material in the course of transmitting, routing, or providing connections, if —
>
> (1) the transmission of the material was initiated by or at the direction of a person other than he service provider;
>
> (2) the transmission, routing, provision of connections, or storage is carried out though an automatic technical process without

selection of the material by the service provider;

(3) the service provider does not select the recipients of the material except as an automatic response to the request of another person;

(4) no copy of the material made by the service provider in the course of such intermediate or transient storage is maintained on the system or network in a manner ordinarily accessible to anyone other than anticipated recipients, and no such copy is maintained on the system or network in a manner ordinarily accessible to such anticipated recipients for a longer period than is reasonably necessary for the transmission, routing, or provision of connections; and

(5) the material is transmitted through the system without modification of its content.

Subsection (a) does not require ISPs to remove or block access to infringing materials upon receiving notification of infringement, as is the case with subsections (c) and (d).

On the other hand, the term "service provider" is defined more restrictively for subsection (a) than it is throughout the rest of section 512. *See* 17 USC §512(k). "As used in subsection (a), the term 'service provider' means an entity offering the transmission, routing, or providing of connections for digital online communication, between or among points specified by a user, of material of the user's choosing, without modification to the content of the material as sent or received."[16] *Id.* In effect, this definition merely restates a number of the requirements that are already set forth in subsection (a). Therefore, Plaintiff's contention that AOL does not meet the restrictive definition of a "service provider" as subsection (k) defines that term for subsection (a) does not need to be addressed separately from Plaintiff's arguments that AOL cannot satisfy the requirements of subsection (a). The Court addresses each of those requirements in turn.

Plaintiff argues that AOL's USENET servers do not engage in "intermediate and transient storage" of USENET messages such as the one posted by Robertson. Instead, AOL stores USENET messages containing binary files on its servers for up to fourteen days."[17] AOL, however, claims that the USENET message copies are "intermediate." AOL's role is an intermediary between the original USENET user who posts a message, such as Robertson, and the recipient USENET users who later choose to view the message.

By itself, the term "intermediate and transient storage" is rather ambiguous. And it is unclear from reading the DMCA whether AOL's storage of USENET messages containing binary files on its servers for fourteen days in order to make those messages accessible to AOL users constitutes "intermediate and transient storage." Certain functions such as the provision of e-mail service or Internet connectivity clearly fall under the purview of subsection (a); other functions such as hosting a web site or chatroom fall under the scope of subsection (c). The question presented by this case is which subsection applies to the function performed by AOL when it stores USENET messages in order to provide USENET access to users. Faced with the ambiguous language in the statute itself, the Court looks to the DMCA's legislative history for guidance in interpretation. The only real guidance is provided in the House Judiciary Committee Report. *See* H.R. Rep. 105-551 (May 22, 1998).

The Court is mindful that reliance on the Report issued by the House Judiciary Committee, "the body that traditionally vets copyright legislation,"[18] is somewhat problematic. The Report's section-by-section analysis was based on an early version of the DMCA which differs in a number of ways from the final version that was eventually enacted by Congress. And the Court recognizes that "even if the language of a given feature [in the earlier version of the bill] does ultimately follow through to the Digital Millennium Copyright Act, the meaning may be different in the context of a law containing vastly more provisions than the [earlier version]." 3 NIMMER ON COPYRIGHT §12B.01[C], at 12B-19. Nonetheless, the Court believes that the analysis in the House Judiciary Committee Report provides the clearest guidance concerning Congress' intent.

At the time the first House Report was issued, the Committee was considering a version of the bill that differs in many ways from the final version that was eventually enacted into law as the DMCA. However, the previous version's language regarding "the intermediate storage and transmission of material" is very similar to the "intermediate and transient storage of that material" language that is found in the final version of the DMCA. Moreover, the portion of subsection (a) in the previous version, having to do with maintaining material on the system, is also extremely similar to the corresponding language found in the enacted version of the DMCA at 512(a)(4).[19] Although other aspects of the bill changed substantially before the final version was enacted into law, the language dealing with the "intermediate storage" did not. Accordingly, the section-by-section analysis found in the First House Report is relevant to interpreting whether AOL's storage of USENET messages in order to provide USENET access to AOL users constitutes (1) "intermediate and transient storage" of (2) copies that are not "maintained on the system or network . . . for a longer period than is reasonably necessary for the transmission, routing, or provision of connections." 17 USC §512(a), (a)(4).

The First House Report answers both of those questions with a resounding yes:

> The exempted storage and transmissions are those carried out through an automatic technological process that is indiscriminate—*i.e.*, the provider takes no part in the selection of the particular material transmitted—where the copies are retained no longer than necessary for the purpose of carrying out the transmission. This conduct would ordinarily include forwarding of customers' Usenet postings to other Internet sites in accordance with configuration settings that apply to all such postings. . .

This exemption codifies the result of *Religious Technology Center v. Netcom On-line Communications Services, Inc.*, 907 F Supp 1361 *[1 ILR (P&F) 778]* (ND Cal 1995) ("Netcom"), with respect to liability of providers for direct copyright infringement.[20] *See id.* at 1368-70. In *Netcom* the court held that a provider is not liable for direct infringement where it takes no "affirmative action that [directly results] in copying . . . works other than by installing and maintaining a system whereby software automatically forwards messages received from subscribers . . . and temporarily stores copies on its system." *By referring to temporary storage of copies, Netcom recognizes implicitly that intermediate*

copies may be retained without liability for only a limited period of time. The requirement in 512(a)(1) that "no copy be maintained on the system or network . . . for a longer period than reasonably necessary for the transmission" is drawn from the facts of the Netcom case, and is intended to codify this implicit limitation in the Netcom holding.

H.R. Rep. 105-551(I), at p. 24. (emphasis added).

In *Netcom*, infringing USENET postings were stored on Netcom's servers for up to *eleven days*, during which those postings were accessible to Netcom users. *See Netcom*, 907 F Supp at 1368. In AOL's case, messages containing binary files, such as the message posted by Robertson, were stored on AOL's servers for up to *fourteen days*. While "intermediate copies may be retained without liability for only a limited period of time," the three-day difference between AOL's USENET storage and that of Netcom is insufficient to distinguish the two cases.

Accordingly, the Court finds that AOL's storage of Robertson's posts on its USENET servers constitutes "intermediate and transient storage" that was not "maintained on the system or network . . . for a longer period than is reasonably necessary for the transmission, routing, or provision of connections."

While this issue presented the central disagreement regarding AOL's qualifications for subsection (a)'s limitation-on-liability safe harbor, the parties also dispute whether AOL satisfies other requirements set forth in subsection (a).

(1) the transmission of the material was initiated by or at the direction of a person other than the service provider

It is clear that the transmission of Robertson's newsgroup message was not initiated by or at the direction of AOL. In fact, Plaintiff does not appear to even dispute this conclusion. (Plaintiff's Separate Statement of Genuine Issues at II(3), 6/4/2001 Motion for summary judgment).

(2) the transmission, routing, provision of connections, or storage is carried out through an automatic technical process without selection of the material by the service provider

Plaintiff claims that AOL selects the material that is transmitted, routed, and stored in its USENET groups. Namely, AOL decides which newsgroups its subscribers may access through its newsgroup service.

AOL did not select the individual postings on the alt.binaries.e-book newsgroup, let alone the handful of infringing Robertson posts. 512(a)(2) is concerned with "selection of the material," meaning the allegedly infringing material, not material generally. By focusing on AOL's decision to not carry every single newsgroup conceivably available, Plaintiff is attempting to slip from the specific to the general, despite the fact that subsection (a) is concerned with the specific material giving rise to the Plaintiff's claims against AOL.

Even if Plaintiff were right, and AOL's treatment of USENET messages in general was the relevant inquiry, AOL's failure to carry every newsgroup available would not disqualify it from subsection (a)(2). Although this would present a closer call, the Court thinks that an ISP would need to take a greater editorial role than merely choosing not to carry certain newsgroups. Although the legislative history states that "subsection (a)(2) means the editorial function of determining what material to send, or the specific sources of material to place on-line," H.R. Rep. 105-551(II) (July 22, 1998), the better interpretation of (a)(2) is that the ISP would have to choose specific postings, or perhaps block messages sent by users expressing opinions with which the ISP disagrees. If an ISP forfeits its ability to qualify for subsection (a)'s safe harbor by deciding not to carry every USENET newsgroup or web site possible, then the DMCA would have the odd effect of punishing ISPs that choose not to carry, for example, newsgroups devoted to child pornography and prostitution, or web sites devotes to ritual torture.[21] Given the concern Congress has shown in other bills for children's access to obscene materials on-line, it would be absurd to conclude that Congress intended such a result with regard to the DMCA.

(3) the service provider does not select the recipients of the material except as an automatic response to the request of another person

Plaintiff argues that AOL selects the recipients of the material because it chooses to engage in USENET peering agreements with some entities but not with others. First, as with (a)(2), Plaintiff's argument fails because section 512(a) is concerned with AOL's selection of the recipients of the material in question in this lawsuit, *i.e.*, Robertson's infringing posts. It is clear that AOL did not select certain recipients for that material. Rather, it was accessible to any AOL user through AOL's USENET newsgroup server. Second, and also analogous to (a)(2), the better interpretation is that AOL would have to direct material to certain recipients (*e.g.*, all AOL members whose names start with "G") but not others. If AOL were to lose its ability to qualify for subsection (a)'s safe harbor because it has peer agreements with some entities but not with others, then the DMCA would appear to place an affirmative obligation on AOL to enter into peering arrangements with every conceivable peering entity in the world. This could not have been what Congress' intent *[sic]*.

(5) *[sic]* the material is transmitted through the system without modification of its content

Plaintiff does not seriously contest that AOL does not modify the content of newsgroup messages stored on its servers and transmitted through its system. Moreover, Plaintiff has presented no evidence that AOL in any way modified the content of Robertson's infringing posts.

The Court hereby finds that and/or qualifies for the limitation-on-liability provider under subsection 512(a).[22]

V. Conclusion

The Court hereby **GRANTS** Defendant AOL's Motion for summary judgment. This Order disposes of Motions #109, 152, and 156 on the Court's Docket for this Matter.

---

[1]   AOL also filed a fourth Motion for summary judgment or adjudication focusing on the extent of damages that would be available to Ellison if he were to

prevail on his copyright infringement claims against AOL. Because the Court grants AOL's Motion for summary judgment on the merits, we need not reach the issue of damages.

[2] Although the USENET is closely affiliated to the internet, the two are distinct. There is no specific network that is the USENET. Instead, Usenet traffic flows over a wide range of networks, including the internet.

[3] There are newsgroups devoted to such diverse topics as "science fiction writers" and "New York Mets baseball."

[4] Plaintiff claims that AOL's motion for summary judgment is improper because its arguments regarding its compliance with subsections 512(a) and (i) were raised for the first time in its first summary judgment Motion's Reply brief, which was filed on September 5, 2001. Even assuming arguendo that AOL raised certain issues for the first time in its Reply Brief, Plaintiff cannot claim that he was prejudiced in any way. First, Plaintiff had ample opportunity to respond in connection with AOL's second Motion for summary judgment (filed November 26, 2001) and with Plaintiff's own Motion for summary adjudication (filed November 27, 2001). And second, the Court granted Plaintiff permission to file a supplemental brief specifically in response to AOL's September 5, 2001 Reply, and Plaintiff did so, filing its supplemental brief on December 10, 2001. At this point, all the issues before the Court have been fully briefed, and no party can claim surprise, prejudice, or unfair treatment. Moreover, if the Court were to reject AOL's Motion for summary judgment on the grounds that certain matters were raised for the first time in its September 5, 2001, Reply brief, that would merely delay the inevitable and force the parties to file the same boxes of papers with the Court yet again.

[5] AOL claims that Ellison does not own a valid registered copyright for the audiowork "The Voice From the Edge," and that Ellison only registered his copyright for "Count the Clock That Tells the Time" two months after AOL blocked access to the alt.binaries.e-book site in late April 2000, but makes no similar allegations relating to any of the other works cited by Plaintiff.

[6] In its Opposition to Ellison's Motion for summary judgment and its Reply brief to its own Motion for summary judgment, AOL for the first time contends that Ellison has produced no evidence indicating that infringing copies of his works were located on AOL's USENET servers. In particular, AOL argues that the consent decree entered into by Ellison and co-Defendant Robertson cannot be asserted against AOL as evidence of Robertson's placing of infringing materials onto the alt.binaries.e-book newsgroup where, per AOL's USENET peer agreements' protocol, they were transferred and copied onto AOL's servers. Even assuming arguendo

that the consent decree does not have any preclusive effect as against AOL, it does constitute evidence that a reasonable trier of fact could rely on. And although AOL labels the consent decree inadmissible hearsay, it is an order entered and signed by the Court, and therefore qualifies as a hearsay exception under, at least, Fed. R. Evid. Rule 803(8).

In addition, the deposition testimony of Susan Paris presents extremely strong circumstantial evidence that infringing copies of works (including some of Ellison's works) were, in fact, posted on and downloaded from the alt.binaries.e-book newsgroup.

[7] Plaintiff has provided no evidence that AOL actually did receive the e-mail. To the contrary, Plaintiff's former counsel states that while she received an acknowledgment of receipt for her April 17, 2000, e-mail from TCO, no such acknowledgment came from AOL.

[8] It is not clear if Miller was directed by AOL customer service representatives to the correct e-mail address or the same defunct address where Ellison's attorney sent her e-mail.

[9] The DMCA provides that "[t]he failure of a service provider's conduct to qualify for limitation of liability under this section shall not bear adversely upon the consideration of a defense by the service provider that the service provider's conduct is not infringing under this title or any other defense." 17 USC §512(1); *see also* 3 NIMMER ON COPYRIGHT §12B.06[B].

[10] *See* 3 NIMMER ON COPYRIGHT §12B.04[A][2] ("The combination of each of these twin factors of financial benefit and ability to control [found in section 512(c)(1)(B)] codifies both elements of vicarious liability").

[11] In *Adobe,* the district court reasoned that although some of the language in *Fonovisa* is quite broad, the Ninth Circuit had implicitly recognized that vicarious copyright liability was only appropriate where the infringing activity was a *substantial* draw, *i.e.*, "substantial numbers of customers are drawn to a venue with the explicit purpose of [obtaining] counterfeit goods." *Adobe,* 173 F Supp 2d at 1050. The *Adobe* Court noted that unless the counterfeit goods constituted "the main customer 'draw' to the venue, *Fonovisa* would provide essentially for the limitless expansion of vicarious liability into spheres wholly unintended by the court." *Id.* at 1051. While the provision of unauthorized copies of copyrighted material need not necessarily be *the main* customer draw, the infringing activity must be least a *substantial* draw. As the *Adobe* decision points out, to hold otherwise would provide essentially for the limitless expansion of vicarious liability. For ISPs, the vicarious copyright infringement doctrine might start to resemble strict liability for any material that somehow finds its way onto the ISP's servers.

[12] The House Report was analyzing a version of the DMCA that was slightly different from the version finally enacted by Congress and signed by President Clinton in late 1998. Accordingly, what is now subsection (i) was then subsection (h). However, subsection (i) is not substantively different from subsection (h), and both contain the same requirement that ISPs adopt, implement, and inform subscribers of a termination policy for repeat infringers. Therefore, the legislative history analyzing subsection (h) is equally relevant to subsection (i).

[13] In the version of the DMCA actually enacted, subsection (l)'s equivalent is now found at subsection (m).

[14] These arguments are, however, relevant to determining whether AOL complied with the requirements of subsection (c).

[15] As such, the "realistic threat of losing [Internet] access" that Congress wishes ISPs to impress upon would-be infringers remains just that—a mere threat—unless the ISP decides to implement procedures aimed at identifying, investigating, and remedying infringement in hopes of meeting the requirements of subsection (c)'s safe harbor. Such an arrangement makes a certain amount of sense. If subsection (i) obligated ISPs to affirmatively seek out information regarding infringement and then investigate, eradicate, and punish infringement on their networks, then most if not all of the notice and takedown requirements of the subsection (c) safe harbor would be indirectly imported and applied to subsections (a) and (b) as well. This would upset the carefully balanced, "separate function—separate safe harbor—separate requirements" architecture of the DMCA.

[16] By contrast, for the purposes of the rest of section 512, the term "service provider" is defined more broadly as "a provider of online services or network access, or the operator of facilities therefor." 17 USC §512(k)(2).

[17] Plaintiff has presented evidence suggesting that despite AOL's 14-day storage protocol, certain USENET messages containing binary files might have resided on AOL's servers for up to thirty-one days, but he makes no claim that such was the case with the messages containing infringing copies of his works (nor with any other infringing messages in the alt.binaries.e-book newsgroup). When deciding whether AOL qualifies for subsection (a)'s limitations on liability, the Court considers only the allegedly infringing postings.

[18] 3 NIMMER ON COPYRIGHT §12B.01[C], at 12-18

[19] The version considered by the House Judiciary Committee, at 512(a)(C) states that "(C) no copy of the material thereby made by the provider is maintained on the provider's system or network in a manner ordinarily

accessible to anyone other than the recipient anticipated by the person who initiated the transmission, and no such copy is maintained on the system or network in a manner ordinarily accessible to such recipients for a longer period than is reasonably necessary for the transmission."

The final version of the DMCA provides, at subsection 512(a)(4), that "(4) no copy of the material made by the service provider in the course of such intermediate and transient storage is maintained on the system or network in a manner ordinarily accessible to anyone other than anticipated recipients, and no such copy is maintained on the system or network in a manner ordinarily accessible to such anticipated recipients for a longer period than is reasonably necessary for the transmission, routing, or provision of connections."

[20] Any argument that this codification of *Netcom*'s facts regarding intermediate storage was only meant to apply to direct infringement, and not to vicarious or contributory infringement, is forestalled by subsection (2) of the version of the bill then under consideration by the Judiciary Committee. For subsection (2) makes it clear that the same limitations on liability that apply under subsection (1) for direct infringement also apply to "contributory infringement or vicarious liability, based solely on conduct described in paragraph (1)." *See* H.R. Rep. 105-551(1), at p. 8. In effect, subsection (2) provided that regardless of a plaintiff's theory of infringement—direct, contributory, or vicarious—it was the underlying conduct of the ISP, *i.e.*, the function it was performing, that is central to determining whether the ISP qualifies for a limitation on liability. This section-by-section analysis said this of subsection (2): "Paragraph 512(a)(2) exempts a provider from any type of monetary relief under theories of contributory infringement or vicarious liability for the same activities for which providers are exempt from liability for direct infringement under paragraph 512(a)(1). This provision extends the *Netcom* holding with respect to direct infringement to remove monetary exposure for such limited activities for claims arising under doctrines of secondary liability. Taken together, paragraphs (1) and (2) mean that providers will never be liable for any monetary damages for this type of transmission of material at the request of third parties or for intermediate storage of such material in the course of the transmission." H.R. Rep. 105-551(I), at p. 25.

[21] ISPs would also be punished for making the economic decision not to provide access to newsgroup and other sites for which there was no user demand.

[22] Accordingly, we need not reach the arguments presented by the parties regarding AOL's satisfaction of the requirements of subsection 512(c).

Felten

v.

Recording Industry Association of America, Inc. (First Amended Complaint)

**United States District Court,
District of New Jersey**

June 26, 2001

8 ILR (P&F) 2083

No. CV-01-2660 (GEB)

[Plaintiffs' original Complaint is reported at 8 ILR (P&F) 2073. The court granted defendants' motions to dismiss on November 28, 2001. Plaintiffs announced on February 6, 2002 that they will not appeal the court's decision. — Ed.]

Researchers amend complaint seeking court order allowing presentation of encryption research.

Plaintiffs, a group of university professors, students, and computer scientists working on digital music access control technologies, amend their original complaint [8 ILR (P&F) 2073] that seeks a declaration that they have a First Amendment right to present their research at a scientific conference. The amendments to the complaint allege that Plaintiffs also have ongoing and future research projects that will be chilled by the litigation threats allegedly made by Defendants, a recording industry trade association and an Internet content security company. Plaintiffs also assert that the Digital Millenium Copyright Act, 17 USC §1201, under which Defendants allegedly threaten to sue, exceeds the enumerated powers of Congress. — **Felten v. Recording Industry Association of America, Inc. (First Amended Complaint), 8 ILR (P&F) 2083 [D NJ, 2001].**

FIRST AMENDED COMPLAINT FOR DECLARATORY JUDGMENT AND INJUNCTIVE RELIEF

INTRODUCTION

"So here's the invitation: Attack the proposed technologies. Crack them."

"Open Letter to the Digital Community," available on the Internet at: *http://www.sdmi.org/pr/ OL_Sept_6_2000.htm.*

1. The private Defendants, relying on a relatively new and unclear statute, have chilled Plaintiffs from engaging in core scientific speech. The private Defendants dared, and specifically invited, the entire Internet world to attempt to crack certain technologies which they were proposing to use to protect digital music from copyright infringement. The individual Plaintiffs, researchers from Princeton University, Rice University and elsewhere took up the challenge as part of their normal scientific research and defeated most of the technologies. They then did exactly what scientific researchers normally do: they wrote a paper discussing their work; they submitted it to a peer-reviewed scientific conference which accepted it for publication; they planned to present the paper at the conference. But then, in a brazen attempt to squelch Plaintiffs' research, the private Defendants threatened to sue, claiming (among other things) violations of the Digital Millennium Copyright Act (DMCA)—even though they had specifically authorized Plaintiffs to attack their technologies.

2. Unfortunately, the private Defendants successfully accomplished their short-sighted objective. The conference at which the paper was to be presented was thrown into chaos, and the researchers felt compelled to withdraw their paper for fear of having to defend baseless litigation. Their

speech was chilled, to their detriment and to the detriment of the scientific community.

3. The individual Plaintiffs (all but one of the original researchers) still desire to present the results of their research, but fear that they will be sued. Plaintiff USENIX Association has accepted their research for its Security Symposium in mid-August, but fears that, because it benefits financially from holding conferences, it may be subject to criminal as well as civil liability under the relevant provision of the DMCA. Plaintiffs are forced to seek a Declaration from this Court that publication and presentation of the paper is lawful, since they have no other reasonable way to assure themselves, in the face of the serious threats made by the private Defendants, that they will not be sued or prosecuted for publishing mainstream and valuable scientific research.

> The Declaratory Judgment Act was designed to relieve potential defendants from the Damoclean threat of impending litigation which a harassing adversary might brandish, while initiating suit at his leisure—or never. The Act permits parties so situated to forestall the accrual of potential damages by suing for a declaratory judgment, once the adverse positions have crystallized and the conflict of interests is real and immediate.

Japan Gas Lighter Ass'n v. Ronson Corp., 257 F Supp 219, 237 (D NJ 1966).

THE PARTIES

4. Plaintiff Edward W. Felten is an Associate Professor of Computer Science at Princeton University, and resides in Princeton, New Jersey.

5. Plaintiff Bede Liu is a Professor of Electrical Engineering at Princeton University, and resides in Princeton, New Jersey.

6. Plaintiff Scott A. Craver is a graduate student in the Department of Electrical Engineering at Princeton University, and resides in Princeton, New Jersey.

7. Plaintiff Min Wu recently completed her Ph.D. studies in the Department of Electrical Engineering at Princeton University, and resides in Princeton, New Jersey. She has just been appointed to the faculty at the University of Maryland.

8. Plaintiff Dan S. Wallach is an Assistant Professor in the systems group of the Rice University

Department of Computer Science, and resides in Houston, Texas.

9. Plaintiff Ben Swartzlander recently completed his Masters program in the Department of Computer Science at Rice University in Houston, Texas, and currently resides in San Jose, CA.

10. Plaintiff Adam Stubblefield is an undergraduate student majoring in mathematics at Rice University, and resides in Houston, Texas.

11. Plaintiff Richard Drews Dean, Ph.D. is a computer scientist who resides in Cupertino, California. The Plaintiffs referred to in paragraphs 4-11 will sometimes be referred to collectively as the "individual Plaintiffs."

12. Plaintiff USENIX Association (USENIX) is a Delaware non-profit non-stock corporation, with its executive office in Berkeley, California. Since 1975, USENIX has brought together the community of engineers, system administrators, scientists, and technicians working on the cutting edge of the computing world. Its conferences have become the essential meeting grounds for the presentation and discussion of the most advanced information on the developments of all aspects of computing systems. USENIX routinely publishes conference proceedings, including presented papers. Proceedings at least a year old are published for free public access on the USENIX web site. Proceedings less than a year old are accessible online by USENIX members, see *http://www.usenix.org/publications/library/proceedings/index.html*. Proceedings are also published on paper and sold to conference attendees and the general public.

13. Upon information and belief, Defendant Recording Industry Association of America, Inc. (RIAA) is a New York not-for-profit corporation with a place of business in Washington D.C. It represents entities which manufacture and distribute sound recordings, including the five major labels and many of their subsidiary labels.

14. Upon information and belief, Defendant Secure Digital Music Initiative Foundation (SDMI) is a multi-industry consortium, business form unknown, established to create specifications for the secure delivery of digital music. In September and October 2000, SDMI ran the SDMI Public Challenge, which is at the root of this action. SDMI's mailing address is SDMI Secretariat, c/o

SAIC (Science Applications International Corporation, a Delaware corporation), 10260 Campus Point Drive, San Diego, California, 92121.

15. Upon information and belief, Defendant Verance Corporation (Verance) is a Delaware corporation that maintains its principal place of business in San Diego, California. According to the Verance web site, *http://www.verance.com/*, it "offers innovative audio watermarking solutions to protect, manage, and monitor your audio and audio visual content . . . ." At least one of Verance's technologies was among the ones involved in the SDMI Public Challenge. Upon information and belief, that technology was Technology A in the SDMI Public Challenge. The Defendants referred to in paragraphs 13 through 15 will sometimes be referred to collectively as the "private Defendants."

16. Defendant Attorney General John Ashcroft heads the United States Department of Justice, which is the agency of the United States government responsible for enforcement of federal criminal laws, including 17 USC §1204, the criminal provision of the DMCA, as well as defending constitutional challenges to federal statutes. Attorney General Ashcroft is sued only in his official capacity.

17. Defendant Doe 1, whose identity is unknown to Plaintiffs, was the proponent of Technology B in the SDMI Public Challenge, as more fully described in paragraph 34, *infra*. Some of the relief which Plaintiffs seek cannot be fully afforded in the absence of this defendant, and thus this defendant, when identified, should be joined if feasible in accordance with F.R.C.P. 19(a).

18. Defendant Doe 2, whose identity is unknown to Plaintiffs, was the proponent of Technology C in the SDMI Public Challenge, as more fully described in paragraph 34, *infra*. Some of the relief that Plaintiffs seek cannot be fully afforded in the absence of this defendant, and thus this defendant, when identified, should be joined if feasible in accordance with F.R.C.P. 19(a).

19. Defendant Doe 3, whose identity is unknown to Plaintiffs, was the proponent of Technology D in the SDMI Public Challenge, as more fully described in paragraph 34, *infra*. Some of the relief that Plaintiffs seek cannot be fully afforded in the absence of this defendant, and thus this defendant, when identified, should be joined if feasible in accordance with F.R.C.P. 19(a).

20. Defendant Doe 4, whose identity is unknown to Plaintiffs, was the proponent of Technology F in the SDMI Public Challenge, as more fully described in paragraph 34, *infra*. Some of the relief that Plaintiffs seek cannot be fully afforded in the absence of this defendant, and thus this defendant, when identified, should be joined if feasible in accordance with F.R.C.P. 19(a).

JURISDICTION AND VENUE

21. This Court has jurisdiction over this action pursuant to 28 USC §1331 and 1338(a) because this action arises under the First Amendment to the United States Constitution and under the Digital Millennium Copyright Act, 17 USC §§1201 *et seq*. This Court also has supplemental jurisdiction of the state law claims pursuant to 28 USC §1367.

22. Venue is proper in this Court pursuant to 28 USC §§1391(b) and 1391(e) in that a substantial part of the events giving rise to the claim occurred in this District, and pursuant to §1391(e) in that half of the individual Plaintiffs reside in this District and the Attorney General is a Defendant.

THE FACTS

23. SDMI is "a forum that brings together more than 180 companies and organizations representing information technology, consumer electronics, security technology, the worldwide recording industry, and Internet service providers. SDMI's charter is to develop open technology specifications that protect the playing, storing, and distributing of digital music such that a new market for digital music may emerge." *http://www.sdmi.org/*

24. On September 6, 2000, SDMI issued an "Open Letter to the Digital Community," available on the Internet at *http://www.sdmi.org/pr/OL_Sept_6_2000.htm*. A true and complete copy of the Open Letter, printed from that web page, was filed with the Court as Exhibit A to the Complaint (June 6, 2001) and incorporated herein by this reference. The Open Letter provided in part:

> Here's an invitation to show off your skills, make some money, and help shape the future of the online digital music economy.

> The Secure Digital Music Initiative is a multi-industry initiative working to develop a secure framework for the digital distribution of music. SDMI protected content will be embedded with an inaudible,

robust watermark or use other technology that is designed to prevent the unauthorized copying, sharing, and use of digital music.

We are now in the process of testing the technologies that will allow these protections. The proposed technologies must pass several stringent tests: they must be inaudible, robust, and run efficiently on various platforms, including PCs. They should also be tested by you.

So here's the invitation: Attack the proposed technologies. Crack them.

By successfully breaking the SDMI protected content, you will play a role in determining what technology SDMI will adopt.

25. The details of what became known as the SDMI Public Challenge, including the technologies offered as part of the challenge, were made available by SDMI on or about September 18, 2000 at the web site *http://www.hacksdmi.org* (which no longer exists).

26. The home page, or top page, of the hacksdmi.org web site was located at *http://www. hacksdmi.org/default.asp.* Entitled "Secure Digital Music Initiative Public Challenge," it stated, in part:

The Challenge

Several proposals are currently being considered for the Phase Two screening technology. Some are digital watermarking technologies; others use a different technology to provide the screening functionality. The challenge is to defeat the screening technology. For example, where the proposed technology is a watermark, the challenge is to remove or alter the watermark while not significantly degrading the quality of a digital music sample. Marked samples and files may be downloaded from this site. If you believe you have successfully defeated the security technology you may upload the attacked sample or file to this web site. We will evaluate your submission. Under certain conditions, challengers may be able to receive compensation for describing and providing to SDMI their successful attack.

27. At the bottom of the home page was a button labeled "Continue". If a viewer clicked on that

button, then the viewer would be taken to the next page on the hacksdmi.org web site, which was located at the URL *http://www.hacksdmi.org/hacksClickThrough.asp* and entitled "Click-Through Agreement for the SDMI Public Challenge" (hereinafter the "Click-Through Agreement"). A true and complete copy of the Click-Through Agreement was filed with the Court as Exhibit B to the Complaint (June 6, 2001) and incorporated herein by this reference.

28. The Click-Through Agreement purported to be a binding legal agreement between SDMI on the one hand, and those who chose to participate in the Public Challenge, on the other. Additionally, it gave an overview of how the Public Challenge was to work. The first paragraph stated that the Public Challenge was "open to everyone . . ." with limited exceptions not applicable to any of the Plaintiffs.

29. Digital music file formats such as the MP3 format compress files so that they take up less space on storage media like a computer hard disk and can be transmitted more quickly on the Internet without overly degrading sound quality. The second paragraph of the Click-Through Agreement provided that four different digital watermark technologies were included in the Public Challenge. It said that each was designed to detect compression in a digital music file, though it was not clear to the individual Plaintiffs that the watermarks actually were designed for that purpose. Additionally, two other technologies were included in the Public Challenge, each designed to prevent separation of individual tracks on a CD from the rest of the CD, thus attempting to prevent, for example, a hit single from a CD from being played apart from the original CD.

30. The third and fourth paragraphs of the Click-Through Agreement generally explained how to test the four watermark technologies and the two other technologies. In the case of each watermark, for example, the participant would download from the hacksdmi.org web site a "triplet," or three music samples. The first two would be the same music sample, one with the watermark, one without, while the third would be an unrelated watermarked sample. Using whatever information one could glean from the triplet, as well as other legitimate sources of information, the object was to "determine if the watermark can be removed from the entire sample

without significantly reducing the sound quality of the digital music . . . ."

31. The fifth paragraph described how a challenger would know if his or her attack on one or more of the technologies was successful. Briefly, the challenger would upload the attacked file(s) to the "oracle" at the hacksdmi.org site, which would automatically test the submission and notify the challenger if the attack was successful. If so, then the oracle might ask for additional information concerning how the attack was accomplished, and might give the challenger additional music samples in order to determine if the attack was reproducible.

32. Those who successfully attacked one or more of the Public Challenge technologies were eligible for compensation of up to $10,000 per successful attack, provided they agreed to additional terms. The individual Plaintiffs' attacks on five of the technologies were successful, but they elected not to seek compensation for their success. Since the provisions of the Click-Through Agreement meaningfully varied depending on whether the successful challenger did or did not seek compensation, we set forth those provisions in full:

> Compensation of $10,000 will be divided among the persons who submit a successful unique attack on any individual technology during the duration of the SDMI Public Challenge. In exchange for such compensation, all information you submit, and any intellectual property in such information (including source code and other executables) will become the property of the SDMI Foundation and/or the proponent of that technology. In order to receive compensation, you will be required to enter into a separate agreement, by which you will assign your rights in such intellectual property. The agreement will provide that (1) you will not be permitted to disclose any information about the details of the attack to any other party, (2) you represent and warrant that the idea for the attack is yours alone and that the attack was not devised by someone else, and (3) you authorize us to disclose that you submitted a successful challenge. If you are a minor, it will be necessary for you and your parent or guardian to sign this document, and any

compensation will be paid to your parent or guardian.

> *You may, of course, elect not to receive compensation, in which event you will not be required to sign a separate document or assign any of your intellectual property rights, although you are still encouraged to submit details of your attack.*

(Emphasis added.)

> The SDMI Foundation will also analyze the information you have submitted in detail to determine the reproducibility of your attack. To be clear, you will be eligible for compensation for reasonably reproducible attacks only if you have not disclosed the trade secrets in your submission to anyone other than the SDMI Foundation, have assigned all your intellectual property rights in your attack to the SDMI Foundation, and have kept your submission, and all information relating to your submission, confidential. All decisions relating to the success of your challenge, the timing of your submission and all other matters pertaining to the SDMI Public Challenge shall be within the discretion of the SDMI Foundation or its designee and shall be final and binding in all respects.

Stated simply, successful challengers who received compensation were required to assign all of their intellectual property rights and to agree to confidentiality and other terms. Successful challengers such as Plaintiffs who eschewed compensation were not required to assign any of their rights or make any further agreements with SDMI; and in fact, Plaintiffs did not assign any of their rights or make any further agreements with SDMI.

33. Finally, the Click-Through Agreement provided:

> **What else do I need to know?** By releasing encoded digital music samples for attack and other digital files, the SDMI Foundation and the technology proponents are only providing permission, under U.S. or other applicable law, to attack those particular samples and files during the duration of this SDMI Public Challenge. No permission is granted to attack or make any other use of

content protected by SDMI outside of this SDMI Public Challenge. In addition, neither the SDMI Foundation, copyright owners nor the proponent of the technology being attacked, waive any rights that it or they may have under any applicable law including, without limitation, the U.S. Digital Millennium Copyright Act, for any acts not expressly authorized by this Agreement. Moreover, no permission is granted to attack content encoded with any technology proponent outside of this SDMI Public Challenge. You are prohibited from reproducing, modifying, distributing, performing or making any other use of the samples other than as specifically authorized by this Agreement. A list of persons who have submitted successful attacks and received compensation therefor [sic] will be provided if you mail a self-addressed, stamped envelope to the SDMI Secretariat, c/o SAIC at 10260 Campus Point Drive, San Diego, California 92121 USA. We are not responsible for lost, incomplete or misdirected submissions. This offer is void where prohibited.

By clicking on the "I Agree" button below you agree to be bound by the terms of this Agreement.

34. Clicking on the "I Agree" button took viewers to the next page on the hacksdmi.org web site, *http://www.hacksdmi.org/hackDownload.asp*, entitled "Download and Upload the Files." From that page, challengers could, and the individual Plaintiffs did, download each of the four audio watermark technologies that were included in the Public Challenge (technologies A, B, C and F) and the two additional technologies (technologies D and E). From that same page, challengers could, and the individual Plaintiffs did, upload their attacks to the hacksdmi.org oracle.

35. Plaintiffs' attacks on each of the four watermark technologies were successful. Plaintiffs also believe that they successfully attacked one of the two other technologies, technology D. However, the oracle for technology D was defective, and thus did not indicate whether Plaintiffs' attack on that technology succeeded. Plaintiffs did not attack technology E, the other non-watermark technology,

because they determined that SDMI did not give them enough information to mount a credible attack.

36. At no time did Plaintiffs attack "content protected by SDMI" outside of the Public Challenge, or attack content encoded with any technology proponent outside of the Public Challenge.

37. Having successfully attacked five of the six Public Challenge technologies, the individual Plaintiffs, who had not assigned any of their rights to SDMI and had not entered into any other agreements with SDMI, chose to write a paper describing their research and their attacks, to submit the paper to a peer-reviewed scientific conference, and if accepted, to publish the paper in the proceedings of the conference. Plaintiffs selected the Fourth International Information Hiding Workshop ("IHW"), to be held in Pittsburgh on April 25-27, 2001, and proceeded to write their paper, entitled "Reading Between the Lines: Lessons from the SDMI Challenge" (hereinafter simply the "SDMI Paper"). The SDMI Paper was submitted to IHW in late November or December, 2000.

38. After the SDMI Paper went through the peer review process, the Plaintiffs were notified in February 2001 that it had been accepted for presentation at IHW, on April 26. As is customary, the reviews were anonymous, but as is also customary, the authors were provided with the anonymous reviews, which they could, and did, use to improve the SDMI Paper. The revised paper was submitted to IHW in late March 2001 for inclusion in the IHW proceedings.

39. On November 1, 2000, Professor Felten received an e-mail from Joseph M. Winograd, the Executive Vice President and Chief Technology Officer of Defendant Verance. He stated that Verance was the proponent of one of the watermark technologies in the Public Challenge (which Plaintiffs believe is technology A), and that he wished to speak by phone with Professor Felten about the subject. Professor Felten was out of the country at a computer security conference at the time, but after he returned to New Jersey, he and Dr. Winograd spoke cordially about the subject on November 9, 2000. On a few occasions between then and mid-December, Dr. Winograd made inquiries about the paper, but because it still was in the early draft stage, Professor Felten did not feel

comfortable giving a draft to Dr. Winograd at that time.

40. On March 30, 2001, apparently having learned that the SDMI Paper had been accepted by IHW, Dr. Winograd e-mailed Professor Felten requesting a pre-publication copy of the SDMI Paper. (As with all e-mails from Dr. Winograd to Professor Felten, the e-mail was addressed to Professor Felten's Princeton University e-mail address in New Jersey.) Though under no obligation to provide Dr. Winograd with such a copy, on March 31 Professor Felten e-mailed an electronic copy of the SDMI Paper to Dr. Winograd. In the e-mail, Professor Felten specifically stated "Please do not circulate this outside of Verance."

41. On April 6, 2001, Dr, Winograd sent an e-mail back to Professor Felten. He stated that he had not circulated the SDMI Paper outside of Verance, but that he took ". . . the precautionary step of alerting the SDMI Foundation, our commercial partner the 4C Entity, and our recording company licensees about the pending conference and provided each with a brief general description of your paper's contents." Among other things, Dr. Winograd wrote:

> Speaking only for myself and for Verance, I am most concerned that your paper provides unnecessarily detailed information, in particular relating to detailed numerical measurements (such as frequencies, numeric parameters, etc.) that you and your colleagues obtained through analysis of the samples provided by SDMI and/or employed in your proposed attacks. It is not clear to me that the inclusion of these specific numeric details either advances your stated goals of furthering the academic body of knowledge regarding security technologies or any other cause, other than facilitating the use of your results by others seeking to circumvent the legitimate use of these technologies for copyright protection purposes. I urge you to reconsider your decision to include this information in your publication.

> I believe that there could be ways in which our individual objectives can be met without potentially compromising the academic value of your work or the security of any of the technologies that were included in the SDMI Challenge. I would welcome the opportunity to discuss these further with you while there is still time to do so.

42. Only three days later, and without Professor Felten having received anything specific from Dr. Winograd about how his concerns might be addressed, Professor Felten received a letter at Princeton dated April 9, 2001 from Matthew Oppenheim, Esq. The pre-printed letterhead is that of Defendant RIAA, and identifies Oppenheim as the Senior Vice President, Business and Legal Affairs, of RIAA. The letter's signature block additionally identifies Oppenheim as the Secretary of Defendant SDMI. The letter shows copies to Dr. Ira S. Moskowitz of the Naval Research Laboratory, who was the Program Chair of IHW; Cpt. Douglas H. Rau, USN, Commanding Officer, National Research Laboratory; Mr. Howard Ende, General Counsel of Princeton; and Mr. David Dobkin, Computer Science Department Head of Princeton. A true and complete copy of the letter was filed with the Court as Exhibit C to the Complaint (June 6, 2001) and incorporated herein by this reference.

43. Acting as the agent for Verance and possibly others, Oppenheim wrote, among other things:

> As you are aware, at least one of the technologies that was the subject of the Public Challenge, the Verance Watermark, is already in commercial use and the disclosure of any information that might assist others to remove this watermark would seriously jeopardize the technology and the content it protects.[1] Other technologies that were part of the Challenge are either likewise in commercial use or could be utilized in this capacity in the near future. Therefore, any disclosure of information that would allow the defeat of those technologies would violate both the spirit and the terms of the Click-Through Agreement (the "Agreement"). In addition, any disclosure of information gained from participating in the Public Challenge would be outside the scope of activities permitted by the Agreement and could subject you and your research team to actions under the Digital Millennium Copyright Act ("DMCA"). [Footnote omitted.]

. . . Unfortunately, the disclosure that you are contemplating could result in significantly broader consequences and could directly lead to the illegal distribution of copyrighted material. Such disclosure is not authorized in the Agreement, would constitute a violation of the Agreement and would subject your research team to enforcement actions under the DMCA and possibly other federal laws.

As you are aware, the Agreement covering the Public Challenge narrowly authorizes participants to attack the limited number of music samples and files that were provided by SDMI. The specific purpose of providing these encoded files and for setting up the Challenge was to assist SDMI in determining which of the proposed technologies are best suited to protect content in Phase II products. The limited waiver of rights (including possible DMCA claims) that was contained in the Agreement specifically prohibits participants from attacking content protected by SDMI technologies outside the Public Challenge. If your research is released to the public this is exactly what could occur. In short, you would be facilitating and encouraging the attack of copyrighted content outside the limited boundaries of the Public Challenge and thus places you and your researchers in direct violation of the Agreement.

In addition, because public disclosure of your research would be outside the limited authorization of the Agreement, you could be subject to enforcement actions under federal law, including the DMCA. The Agreement specifically reserves any rights that proponents of the technology being attacked may have "under any applicable law, including, without limitation, the U.S. Digital Millennium Copyright Act, for any acts not expressly authorized by their Agreement." The Agreement simply does not "expressly authorize" participants to disclose information and research developed through participating in the Public Challenge and thus such disclosure could be the subject of a DMCA action.

44. Chaos quickly ensued. Though Professor Felten was the only author of the SDMI Paper to whom Oppenheim sent the letter directly, it affected all of the authors, and copies quickly were circulated among them. Plaintiffs had no idea of what to make of Oppenheim's threats, their research being standard scientific fare. In the meantime, the IHW organizers were equally confused, and did not know how to proceed.

45. Shortly thereafter, talks began between various combinations of Professor Felten, attorneys for Princeton, Rice, Xerox and Dr. Dean on the one hand, and Oppenheim, Dr. Winograd, David Liebowitz (Chairman of the Board of Verance, and former Executive Vice President and General Counsel of Defendant RIAA) and a team of outside attorneys for Verance, on the other. Oppenheim's role in those talks was limited. Verance was left to determine, from the private Defendants' side, whether an acceptable solution could be reached.

46. On April 16, Dr. Winograd e-mailed Professor Felten, stating that he believed that, "with some minor modifications," the SDMI Paper could meet Verance's desires while still maintaining academic integrity. But only a day later, on April 17, Dr, Winograd e-mailed to Professor Felten a document entitled "Recommendations on 'Reading Between the Lines: Lessons from the SDMI Challenge." Dr. Winograd's "recommendations" consisted of 25 separate requests for changes in the SDMI Paper (some of which were compound), and included removal of several text sections and entire diagrams. Indeed, though only one Verance watermark (technology A) was apparently included among the five technologies which Plaintiffs successfully hacked, more than half of Dr. Winograd's recommendations were addressed to the attacks on watermarks of presumed competitors of Verance, technologies B, C and F, as well as to the other non-watermark technology, technology D. At no time did Dr. Winograd or any other representative of the private Defendants indicate that any technology other than watermark technology A was a technology propounded by Verance.

47. Though talks continued, both on a group basis and one-on-one between Professor Felten and Dr. Winograd, right up until the day before the SDMI Paper was to have been presented at IHW, at no time did Dr. Winograd or any other representative of the private Defendants indicate that Dr.

Winograd's recommendations, including those involving technologies in which Verance had no direct interest, were offered on anything other than a take it or leave it basis. Had Plaintiffs accepted Dr. Winograd's recommendations, the resultant paper would have been rejected by any respectable scientific conference.

48. During the same time period, it was clear that IHW was not of one mind regarding how to proceed. On April 19, Dr. Ira Moskowitz, the Program Chair of IHW, sent an e-mail saying that the SDMI Paper could not be presented at IHW without a written agreement by all concerned parties. That e-mail, which imposed a deadline of April 23, was sent not only to each of the individual Plaintiffs, but also to Oppenheim and Bruce Block of RIAA, but not to anyone from Verance. Also on or about April 19, Dr. Moskowitz phoned Professor Felten, expressing concerns that he and IHW would get embroiled in litigation. However, on April 24, only two days before the SDMI Paper was to be presented, and the day after the deadline which Dr. Moskowitz had set, Ross Anderson, a member of the IHW Program Committee, sent an e-mail saying that the Committee had met that morning, and that the presentation of the paper could proceed.

49. However, there was never any indication from Oppenheim, SDMI, RIAA, Verance or any of their representatives that Oppenheim's threat of suit was anything other than one to be taken with great seriousness. The pressure on all of the authors to withdraw the SDMI Paper from IHW increased, and the pressure was particularly intense on Professor Felten, the only one of the authors who was in regular, direct communication with the private Defendants or their representatives. Finally, the authors decided that the threat of litigation against them, the IHW organizers and their employers was all too credible. With great reluctance the decision was made to withdraw the SDMI Paper from IHW, for no reason other than the fear of having to defend a lawsuit. The private Defendants set out to chill the researchers' scientific speech, and they succeeded.

50. After the SDMI paper was withdrawn, Defendant RIAA issued a press release claiming that they had not intended to sue the researchers. This came as a surprise to the researchers, who had been led to believe that they and the others involved would be sued if the paper was presented. Neither RIAA nor SDMI nor Verance ever informed the researchers directly that they had changed their position and now did not intend to sue if the paper was published.

51. The authors still desire to publish their research, and in that regard, the SDMI Paper has been accepted for publication and presentation at the 10th USENIX Security Symposium, to be held in Washington, D.C. on August 13-17, 2001. However, Plaintiffs, including USENIX, cannot be certain that the cycle will not repeat itself, that the private Defendants will not once again threaten to sue, or simply go forward with an action, or that the Doe Defendants will not make their presence felt. Further, as an entity which stands to gain commercially from the publication of the SDMI Paper, USENIX is concerned about potential criminal liability under 17 USC §1204 if the SDMI Paper should be found to violate the DMCA. Thus, Plaintiffs are forced to bring this Declaratory Judgment action as their only reasonable method of publishing the SDMI Paper without fear of civil or criminal liability.

52. The SDMI paper Plaintiffs wish to present at the USENIX Security Conference was filed under seal with the Court as Exhibit D to the Complaint (June 6, 2001) and is incorporated herein by this reference.

53. Two additional papers have been written about the work of the individual Plaintiffs during the SDMI Public Challenge. The first, written primarily by Plaintiff Min Wu, is entitled "Analysis of Attacks on SDMI Audio Watermarks" and was submitted to and accepted for publication at the IEEE Signal Processing Society 26th International Conference on Acoustics, Speech and Signal Processing, which was held in Salt Lake City on May 7-11, 2001 (the "ICASSP Paper"). The ICASSP Paper was both shorter and had a different technical emphasis than the SDMI Paper, and it was submitted and accepted before the researchers received the Oppenheim letter. However, after the decision to pull the SDMI Paper from the IHW, Dr. Wu and her advisor, Plaintiff Bede Liu, became concerned that the ICASSP Paper might also draw fire from the private Defendants. Professor Liu attempted to have it removed from the conference proceedings, but it was too late. As set forth below, Dr. Wu and her co-authors now seek a judicial Declaration that the ICASSP Paper does not violate the law or any rights that Defendants may assert. A

true and complete copy of the ICASSP Paper was filed under seal with the Court as Exhibit E to the Complaint (June 6, 2001) and is incorporated herein by this reference.

54. Additionally, in her Doctoral Dissertation, entitled "Multimedia Data Hiding," Dr. Wu included Chapter 10, entitled "Attacks on Unknown Data Hiding Algorithms," which further discussed the work done during the Public Challenge. Until the events leading to the withdrawal of the SDMI Paper from the IHW, Dr. Wu had no reason to believe that Chapter 10 would be found objectionable by anyone, but in the light of those events, Dr. Wu now has a credible fear of being sued if she should publish that chapter. In accordance with standard practice, she has made her dissertation available on the Internet, at *http://www.ee.princeton.edu/~minwu /research/phd_thesis.html*. However, because she has felt the chill of her scientific speech, she has removed Chapter 10, an act that varies markedly from standard research publication practice. As with the ICASSP Paper, she now seeks a judicial Declaration that Chapter 10 does not violate the law or any rights that Defendants may assert. A true and complete copy of Chapter 10 was filed under seal with the Court as Exhibit F to the Complaint (June 6, 2001) and is incorporated herein by this reference.

55. Several of the Plaintiffs have current projects underway that are subject to the same chilling effects experienced as a result of the claims made by Defendants surrounding the SDMI challenge noted above and the facial reach of the DMCA.

56. Plaintiff Scott Craver is currently working on a portion of his PhD project that could be chilled by the DMCA. He has discovered a better way to detect and characterize certain types of modifications, such as the addition of echoes, to digital music. Mr. Craver's discovery could have significant applications outside the realm of digital music, including geophysics and other disciplines that rely on echo detection.

57. Using this discovery, Mr. Craver is in the process of creating a software program that can more efficiently perform the forensic analysis of music. That is, it can detect digital watermarks as well as other modifications to digital music files better than previous computer programs. The program would

be useful to people designing or testing watermarking systems.

58. Mr. Craver believes that his computer program would be a boon to both data hiding research as well as those studying audio compression or other aspects of signal processing. Since it can be used to detect watermarks, however, he is concerned that he will be prevented from publishing or presenting it due to threats from the Defendants and others that it violates the DMCA.

59. As a result of this uncertainty, Mr. Craver is reluctant to follow his normal practice of asking others to join him in working on the project. This will delay completion of the project. Also, the scientific value of the project may be negatively affected if it cannot benefit from the contributions of others.

60. Mr. Craver is concerned that the development, distribution or presentation of his PhD project will be chilled or prevented by the Defendants or others based upon the DMCA.

61. Plaintiff Min Wu's areas of interest involve multimedia technologies. Her new employer, the University of Maryland, hired her to continue her research into multimedia security among other fields.

62. Dr. Wu has been approached by a prestigious publishing house, Kluwer Academic Publishers, with an offer to publish her dissertation as a book. On May 16, 2001, the Kluwer publishing manager sent Dr. Wu a prospectus questionnaire and invited her to suggest reviewers for the peer-review process. Dr. Wu replied that she would be interested, but she put the proposal on hold and explained that she was concerned about liability under DMCA.

63. Dr. Wu received a reply e-mail on June 13, 2001, from the Kluwer publishing manager stating that Kluwer would like to proceed with the process.

64. To publish Dr. Wu's dissertation as a book, some revisions may be required based on the technical peer review and marketing review conducted by the publisher. She may also make additions or revisions in the book manuscript.

65. It is important for faculty members, especially new Ph.D.'s, to be active in publishing and to have peer-reviewed book publications by prestigious publishers. Publication of her thesis as

a monograph would enhance Dr. Wu's professional reputation and opportunities for advancement.

66. In addition, to disseminate Dr. Wu's research results would contribute to the enhancement of technical knowledge generally.

67. Despite the benefits that the publication of her dissertation as a book would bring to her and to the scientific community, Dr. Wu has withheld the proposal from Kluwer because she is afraid of prosecution under the DMCA, both on its face and in light of the threats of April 2001.

68. Dr. Wu also plans to continue research on digital multimedia in the areas of (1) multimedia security, (2) multimedia representation and content analysis, and (3) multimedia communication over network and wireless channels, all of which are directly implicated by the DMCA.

69. These areas require the study and discussion of strengths and weaknesses of technological protection measures. Dr. Wu is concerned that her proposals for this future research will be thwarted by threats of litigation under the Digital Millennium Copyright Act. She cannot tell whether she would be allowed to pursue these avenues of study, and does not know how to advise graduate student who intend to undertake research into these areas on the legal implications of their research, which they should be aware of.

70. Plaintiff Daniel Wallach is currently developing two proposals that are likely to be impacted by the DMCA. First, he has planned to finish the work on Technologies D and E (the non-watermark technologies), if and when he is able to study them again. The research team was not able to complete its study because the SDMI oracle was broken. When the technology appears in production, he intends to continue his study to test the theories developed by the team during the SDMI Challenge.

71. In addition, Professor Wallach is developing a proposal to study and publish the results of research into new technologies being marketed as making it more difficult to "rip" consumer audio CDs, that is, to copy the music files from the CD to a personal computer. The goal of the research, as with the SDMI research, is to investigate the strength of the technological protection measures and to write a publishable paper about his findings.

72. Professor Wallach is concerned that both of these projects will be subject to threats and other chilling effects due to the DMCA.

73. Professor Bede Liu is currently continuing his research into watermarks and attacking technologies. His research on watermarks and attacks is supported by one current research grant, two proposals pending final decision by the funding agency. One of the pending proposal is in collaboration with another researcher on studying how a specific watermarking method for digital video can survive intentional attacks.

74. Professor Liu hopes to follow the traditional course of presenting any new research result at conferences and publishing it in the conference proceedings. In addition, his manuscripts will be submitted to archival scholarly journals for publication. He may also present the results at seminars at other academic institutions and industrial research labs. Without clarity about the scope of the DMCA, he is uncertain about whether this research and publication can go forward.

75. The researchers are fearful not only of losing in litigation, but of the cost of litigation and the time such litigation would take away from their research and professional responsibilities. They are also concerned about the damage to their reputations and opportunities for advancement that would result from involvement in litigation over their professional actions, regardless of the outcome of that litigation.

76. In addition to the researcher Plaintiffs, Plaintiff USENIX, just like any other sponsor of scientific conferences, will continue to face uncertainty and chilling effects under the DMCA. USENIX has long published papers in fields that necessarily involve so-called "technical protection measures" and their vulnerabilities.

77. USENIX sponsors 8-10 conferences per year. Of those, at least six have a security component where an issue about the anti-dissemination provisions could arise. Since papers for USENIX Conferences are not reviewed by USENIX until approximately six months prior to a particular conference and are not chosen until after that, USENIX will not know of specific future papers that could cause DMCA difficulties until shortly before they are to be published or presented. This means that in order to avoid potential litigation

USENIX will either have to ask Defendants or the other copyright holders and creators of the relevant technologies for permission each time such a paper is presented or seek emergency relief from the courts.

78. USENIX could adopt a policy of steering clear of papers that might subject it to liability under DMCA. If it were forced to do so, its reputation would be irreparably harmed.

79. The threat of DMCA liability is harmful to scientific and technical innovation in the United States. If conferences like those sponsored by USENIX are chilled from publishing papers discussing the merits of technological protection measures, such conferences will probably be held in other countries where the risk of liability is smaller. The movement of forums for scientific discussion overseas will damage scientific discussion in the United States.

80. The problem for scientific conferences reaches individual scientists as well. For example, Professor Felten was appointed to the program committee of the Workshop on Security and Privacy in Digital Rights Management ("DRM Workshop"), which will be held in Philadelphia in November 2001. ("Digital Rights Management" refers to technologies to control access to, or use of, digital works.) As a program committee member he would be partially responsible for the choice of papers to be published at each conference.

81. In addition, Professor Felten was appointed as Publications Chair of the ACM Conference on Computer and Communications Security, which will also be held in Philadelphia in November 2001. His duties as Publications Chair include assembling the authors' papers, having them printed into a bound "Proceedings" document, and distributing the Proceedings at the conference.

82. Both of these conferences cover subject areas that are affected by the DMCA. CCS covers all areas of computer security, and has published papers related to copy-protection mechanisms in the past. The DRM Workshop is specifically about technologies that control access and copying of copyrighted materials—that is the main topic of the conference.

83. The DRM Workshop's Call for Papers requests the submission of papers on "all theoretical and practical aspects of [Digital Rights Management]", on "experimental studies of fielded systems", and on "threat and vulnerability assessment", among other topics. These topics all involve the evaluation, publication and presentation of information about the vulnerabilities of technological protection measures as defined in the DMCA.

84. Professor Felten is concerned that his involvement in choosing and publishing the papers to be presented at these two conferences will subject him to liability or threats by the Defendants and others under the DMCA

85. The threats against the researchers who volunteered to organize the IHW conference have been discussed widely among computer security researchers. Professor Felten is informed and believes that many other people are worried about the consequences of volunteering to help organize conferences.

86. Conferences such as CCS and the DRM Workshop rely on researchers who work, on a volunteer basis, as program committee members, as Publications Chair, and in other positions. If researchers are unwilling to volunteer for these positions, the conferences cannot be held.

FIRST CAUSE OF ACTION
(No DMCA Violation)

87. The Plaintiffs reallege and incorporate all of the previous paragraphs as if set forth here in full.

88. The DMCA prohibits a number of activities that interfere with "technological measures" designed to control access and limit the copying of works protected by the Copyright Act, including the dissemination and distribution of technologies that can be used to circumvent technological measures.

89. The DMCA makes it unlawful to "offer to the public . . . any technology . . . that . . . is primarily designed or produced for the purpose of circumventing a technological measure that effectively controls access to a [copyrighted] work . . ." 17 USC § 1201(a)(2). The DMCA also makes it unlawful to disseminate technology that can be used to circumvent "a technological measure that effectively protects a right of a copyright owner . . . . in a [copyrighted] work or a portion thereof." 17 USC § 1201(b).

90. The DMCA also prohibits (1) the intentional removal or alteration of "copyright management information" without the authority of the copyright owner or the law and (2) the distribution of copyright management information that has been removed or altered without the authority of the copyright owner or the law, if the person removing, altering or distributing the information has "reasonable grounds to know, that it will induce, enable, facilitate, or conceal an infringement of any right under [the Copyright Act]." *See* 17 USC §1202(b). "Copyright management information" is defined as information that can identify a copy of a work and which is conveyed along with the copy (including such information as the title and the terms and conditions for use of the work). *See* 17 USC §1202(c).

91. The individual Plaintiffs did not violate the DMCA by submitting the SDMI Paper to the IHW or the USENIX Security Symposium, and no Plaintiff will violate the DMCA by presenting or publishing the SDMI Paper at the USENIX Security Symposium or elsewhere.

92. Plaintiffs Wu, Craver, Liu and Felten did not violate the DMCA by submitting the ICASSP Paper to ICASSP, did not violate the DMCA by presenting the ICASSP Paper and having it published in the conference proceedings and will not violate the DMCA by publishing the ICASSP Paper elsewhere.

93. Plaintiff Min Wu did not violate the DMCA by writing and defending Chapter 10 of her dissertation and will not violate the DMCA by publishing Chapter 10 on her website or elsewhere.

94. The DMCA is not violated by the conduct, publication or presentation of future research projects such as those described above by the Plaintiffs or others related to technological protection measures.

SECOND CAUSE OF ACTION
(First Amendment)

95. The Plaintiffs reallege and incorporate paragraphs all of the previous paragraphs as if set forth here in full.

96. Any person who violates sections 1201 or 1202 of the DMCA is subject to civil liability under 17 USC §1203. Persons who, for financial or commercial interests, willfully violate sections 1201 or 1202 of the DMCA are subject to criminal liability under 17 USC §1204.

97. Since USENIX receives revenues from organizing conferences and publishing papers presented at its conferences, it is subject to criminal liability under 17 USC §1204 for violations of the DMCA.

98. All of the Plaintiffs fear having to defend against future threats of liability under the DMCA. Most, if not all, of the individual Plaintiffs will continue to work in areas of research that involve digital music and other technologies protected by the DMCA. But they desire to continue their research and publish in this area without fear of liability and currently feel chilled by the DMCA.

99. The primary institutional activity of USENIX is to hold scientific and technical conferences and publish conference proceedings. USENIX has a history of receiving and publishing papers that examine, describe, evaluate and defeat cryptographic and watermarking and other technologies. It expects to receive such papers in the future. Many technologies addressed by these papers can be used as access or copy control measures in copyright management information systems. Some papers, such as the SDMI Paper, may even examine the technologies in a context of technological controls over copyrighted works. Accepting and publishing these papers would therefore subject USENIX, its referees, and the authors of the papers to civil and criminal liability under the DMCA. USENIX desires to publish and present all papers accepted by its referees, including those that raise the specter of liability under the DMCA.

100. Because of the fear of civil and criminal liability, the DMCA has chilled, and will continue to chill, the Plaintiffs and others from engaging in activities protected by the First Amendment.

101. In chilling publication and presentation of scientific speech, the DMCA wreaks havoc in the marketplace of ideas, not only the right to speak, but the right to receive information—the right to learn. The main mission of USENIX is to organize forums where scientists and researchers learn from each other. By intimidating the individual plaintiffs into withdrawing their paper from the IHW, however, the private Defendants prevented people from learning. If the source of Defendants' power

to threaten, the DMCA, is not dispelled, Plaintiffs will not be the only victims. Without full and open access to research in areas potentially covered by the DMCA, scientists and programmers working in those areas cannot exchange ideas and fully develop their own research. As a consequence, the DMCA will harm science.

102. By imposing civil and criminal liability for publishing speech (including computer code) about technologies of access and copy control measures and copyright management information systems, the challenged DMCA are provisions impermissibly restrict freedom of speech and of the press, academic freedom and other rights secured by the First Amendment to the United States Constitution in that, among others, they are overbroad, vague and discriminate as to content.

103. Application of DMCA to speech protected by the First Amendment, including its application to the SDMI Paper and other work by the Plaintiffs related to the SDMI Public Challenge, violates the First Amendment rights of the Plaintiffs and of their readers, of other scientists, programmers and publishers, and of others similarly situated.

104. Unless the Department of Justice is restrained from enforcing the challenged provisions against Plaintiff USENIX and the private and Doe Defendants are enjoined from seeking to impose civil liability on all of the Plaintiffs, the speech of the Plaintiffs and others will continue to be restrained and will continue to cause Plaintiffs and others irreparable harm.

THIRD CAUSE OF ACTION
(No Violation of Click-Through Agreement— Private Defendants Only)

105. The Plaintiffs reallege and incorporate paragraphs all of the previous paragraphs as if set forth here in full.

106. The individual Plaintiffs did not violate the Click-Through Agreement by submitting the SDMI Paper to the IHW or the USENIX Security Symposium, and no Plaintiff will violate the Click-Through Agreement by presenting or publishing the SDMI Paper at the USENIX Security Symposium or elsewhere.

107. Plaintiffs Wu, Craver, Liu and Felten did not violate the Click-Through Agreement by writing the ICASSP Paper or by submitting it to ICASSP

and presenting it and having it published in the ICASSP proceedings, and will not violate the Click-Through Agreement by publishing it elsewhere.

108. Dr. Wu did not violate the Click-Through Agreement by writing and defending Chapter 10 of her dissertation, and will not violate the Click-Through Agreement by publishing it on her website or elsewhere.

109. In the alternative, to the extent the Click-Through Agreement would preclude the Plaintiffs from engaging in any of the actions identified in paragraphs 73 through 75 above, the Click-Through Agreement is invalid and/or unenforceable with respect to the Plaintiffs.

FOURTH CAUSE OF ACTION
(DMCA Exceeds Congress' Enumerated Powers)

110. The Plaintiffs reallege and incorporate all of the previous paragraphs as if set forth here in full.

111. Congress may legislate only pursuant to a power specifically enumerated in the Constitution. Neither the text nor the legislative history of the DMCA indicates which power Congress relied on to enact the statute.

112. The DMCA prohibits the distribution of technology without regard for originality, duration of copyright, or infringement of copyright in the underlying, technologically-protected work. It therefore is not a valid exercise of the intellectual property power of the Constitution.

113. The DMCA is not a valid exercise of the necessary and proper power or the commerce power, because it contravenes specific limits on Congress' power under the intellectual property clause.

114. Unless the Department of Justice is restrained from enforcing the challenged provisions and the private and Doe Defendants are enjoined from seeking to impose civil liability, the Plaintiffs and others will continue to be restrained in their abilities to make lawful and constitutionally protected uses of technology and of material that has been subjected to technological protection, and will continue to suffer irreparable harm.

115. Plaintiffs have no adequate remedy at law to resolve all of the disputes raised in this Complaint.

PRAYER FOR RELIEF

WHEREFORE, Plaintiffs request the following relief:

Declaratory Relief
(First Cause of Action)

A. A declaration that the individual Plaintiffs are not liable under the DMCA for (1) submitting the SDMI Paper to IHW or the USENIX Security Symposium, or for presenting or publishing the SDMI Paper at the USENIX Security Symposium or elsewhere; (2) submitting the ICASSP Paper to the ICASSP conference and presenting or publishing it in the ICASSP proceedings or elsewhere; and (3) publishing or presentations based on Chapter 10 of Dr. Wu's dissertation in electronic form or otherwise.

B. A declaration that Plaintiff USENIX is not civilly liable under the DMCA and is not subject to criminal liability for publishing the SDMI Paper or presentations based upon the paper at the USENIX Security Symposium, or elsewhere.

C. A declaration that the Plaintiffs are not liable under the DMCA for the presentation or publication of any research resulting from, or related to, the SDMI Public Challenge.

D. A declaration that the DMCA is not violated by the publication or presentation by the Plaintiffs or others of future scientific and technical information (including computer code) related to access and copy control measures and copyright management information systems.

Declaratory Relief
(Second Cause of Action)

E. A declaration that the application of the DMCA to the publication or presentation of the SDMI Paper, the ICASSP Paper, Chapter 10 of Dr. Wu's dissertation and/or any scientific, technical or academic research related to the SDMI Public Challenge violates the First Amendment to the United States Constitution.

F. A declaration that the DMCA is unconstitutional on its face because it violates the First Amendment to the United States Constitution.

G. A declaration that the application of the DMCA to the publication or presentation of scientific, academic or technical speech, including the publication of computer programs, violates the First Amendment to the United States Constitution.

Declaratory Relief
(Third Cause of Action)

H. A declaration that the individual Plaintiffs did not and will not violate the Click-Through Agreement by (1) submitting the SDMI Paper to IHW or the USENIX Security Symposium, or for presenting or publishing the SDMI Paper at the USENIX Security Symposium or elsewhere; and (2) submitting the ICASSP Paper to the ICASSP conference and presenting or publishing it in the ICASSP proceedings or elsewhere; and (3) by Dr. Wu writing, defending and publishing Chapter 10 of her dissertation in electronic form or otherwise.

Declaratory Relief
(Fourth Cause of Action)

I. A declaration that the DMCA is unconstitutional because it is not a valid exercise of any of Congress' enumerated powers.

Injunctive Relief

J. A preliminary and permanent injunction enjoining the private Defendants, the Doe Defendants and their respective agents, employees, attorneys, successors in office, assistants and all persons acting in concert with them from initiating an action against the Plaintiffs under the DMCA or for violating the Click-Through Agreement, where applicable, for the presentation, publication or discussion of (1) the SDMI Paper, (2) the ICASSP Paper, (3) Dr. Wu's dissertation, (4) any revisions, changes or amendments to any of those documents, and (5) any academic or scientific work by the Plaintiffs, including works in progress or future works.

K. A preliminary and permanent injunction enjoining the Department of Justice and its agents, employees, attorneys, successors in office, assistants and all persons and agencies acting in concert with them from enforcing the DMCA against Plaintiff USENIX for violating the DMCA by (1) allowing the individual Plaintiffs to present the SDMI Paper at the USENIX Security Symposium and publishing the SDMI Paper in electronic form or otherwise; or (2) allowing others to resent their work (including computer code) at future USENIX Conferences and publishing their work, in electronic form or otherwise.

L. A preliminary and permanent injunction enjoining all of the Defendants from enforcing, or threatening to enforce the DMCA to prevent protected expression under the First Amendment, including scientific, academic or technical papers, presentations and computer programs.

M. A permanent injunction enjoining enforcement of the DMCA because it is in excess of Congress' enumerated powers.

Other Relief

N. For costs and disbursements incurred in this action, including reasonable attorneys' fees, and such other and further relief as the Court deems proper.

Grayson Barber (GB 0034)
(FLC 9895)
Grayson Barber, L.L.C.
Grassi, PC
68 Locust Lane
Princeton, NJ 08540
phone (609) 921-0391
fax (609) 921-7405

Gino J. Scarselli
664 Allison Drive Blvd.
Richmond Hts., OH 44143
phone & fax (216) 291-8601

Cindy A. Cohn
Lee Tien
Robin D. Gross
Electronic Frontier Foundation
454 Shotwell St.
San Francisco, CA 94110
phone (415) 436-9333
fax (415) 436-9993

Frank L. Corrado (FLC 9895)
Rossi, Barry, Corrado & Grassi, PC
Wildwood, NJ 08260
phone (609) 522-4927
fax (609) 522-4927

James S. Tyre
10736 Jefferson Blvd., #512
Culver City, CA 90230-4969
phone (310) 839-4114
fax (310) 839-4602

Joseph P. Liu
Boston College Law School
885 Centre Street
Newton, MA
phone (617) 552-8550

Attorneys for Plaintiffs

Felten

v.

Recording Industry Association of America, Inc.
(Transcript of 11/28/01 Proceedings)

United States District Court,
District of New Jersey

November 28, 2001

10 ILR (P&F) 730

Case No. 01 CV 2669

[The original complaint is located at 8 ILR (P&F) 2073. The first amended complaint is reported at 8 ILR (P&F) 2083. The RIAA memorandum in support of motion to dismiss may be found at 8 ILR (P&F) 2096. Plaintiffs announced on February 6, 2002, that they would not appeal the court's decision.—Ed.]

No case or controversy exists in researchers' lawsuit claiming right to report encryption findings.

No case or controversy exists between plaintiffs, scientists seeking to publish the results of their research on digital music access control technologies in current and future research papers, and defendants, sponsors of the Secure Digital Music Initiative (SDMI) under which the research was conducted and the U.S. Attorney General, because defendants have not taken action against plaintiffs for publishing their work and have not expressed any intent to do so in the future. The SDMI defendants, including the Recording Industry Association of America (RIAA), initially threatened litigation pursuant to the Digital Millennium Copyright Act (DMCA), 17 USC §1201 *et seq.*, in a letter from RIAA counsel to plaintiffs under the theory that publication of SDMI research would jeopardize copyright control technologies. In their amended complaint, plaintiffs sought a declaration affirming their First Amendment right to publish their work, as well as a declaration that the DMCA violates the First Amendment and exceeds the enumerated powers of Congress. All defendants subsequently stated, in public and to the court, that the RIAA letter was mistaken and that they have no intention of bringing any civil or criminal action against plaintiffs. Certain plaintiffs ultimately published their papers without action being taken against them. With plaintiffs suffering no injury or credible threat of future injury at the hands of defendants, no adversity of interests exists to create a case or controversy within the meaning of Article III, §2 of the U.S. Constitution for the court to adjudicate.—**Felten v. Recording Industry Association of America, Inc. (Transcript of 11/28/01 Proceedings), 10 ILR (P&F) 730 [D NJ, 2001].**

TRANSCRIPT OF MOTIONS BEFORE HONORABLE GARRETT E. BROWN UNITED STATES DISTRICT COURT JUDGE

APPEARANCES

For the Plaintiffs: Grayson Barber, L.L.C., *GRAYSON BARBER, ESQ.,.,68 Locust Lane,* Princeton, New Jersey 08540.

Local co-counsel for the Plaintiffs: Rossi Barry Corrado & Grassi, *FRANK L. CORRADO, ESQ.,* 2700 Pacific Avenue, Wildwood, New Jersey 08260.

Pro Hac Vice Counsel for Plaintiffs: Electronic Frontier Foundation, *LEE TIEN, ESQ.,* 454 Shotwell Street, San Francisco, California 94110, *JAMES S. TYRE, ESQ.,* 10736 Jefferson Boulevard, 512, Culver City, California 90230-4969, *GINO J. SCARSELLI, ESQ.,* 664 Allison Drive, Richmond Heights, Ohio 44143.

For the Defendants: Sterns & Weinroth, *KAREN A. CONFOY, ESQ.,* 50 West State Street, Suite 1400, Trenton, New Jersey 08607.

Pro Hac Vice Counsel For the Defendants: Williams & Connolly, LLP, *DAVID E. KENDALL,*

ESQ., KEVIN HARDY, ESQ., 725 Twelfth Street, NW, Washington, D.C. 20005.

LYNDA BRAUN, ESQ.

THOMAS WACK, ESQ.

For the Government: U.S. Department of Justice, Civil Division, *RICHARD G. PHILLIPS, JR., ESQ.*, 901 E. Street, NW, Washington, D.C. 20530.

Audio Operator: Christopher Wright

Proceedings recorded by electronic sound recording, transcript produced by transcription service.

TRANSCRIPT

THE COURT: Who do we have on the line?

MR. WACK: Your Honor, this is Thomas Wack [phonetic] on behalf of defendant, Secured Digital Music and Instrument Foundation.

MS. BRAUN: And Lynda Braun on behalf of the Verance Corporation.

THE COURT: Could you give the reporter the spelling of your last names?

MS. BRAUN: Sure. Lynda, L-Y-N-D-A, Braun, B-R-A-U-N.

THE COURT: All right. The case is *Felten, et al., v. Recording Industry Association, et al.* Let me have appearances first by the plaintiff.

MS. BARBER: Thank you, Your Honor. I'm the local counsel for the plaintiffs. My name is Grayson Barber. And I'd like to introduce my co-local counsel, Frank Corrado of Rossi, Barry, Corrado and Grassi.

And we have three out-of-state counsel who have been admitted pro hac vice. Gino Scarselli will be presenting argument today. With him are Jim Tyre and Lee Tien of the Electronic Frontier Foundation.

THE COURT: So, who is the lawyer who will actually be speaking when called upon by the plaintiff.

MR. BARBER: This will be Gino Scarselli, Your Honor.

THE COURT: Thank you very much. And for the defense?

MS. CONFOY: Your Honor, Karen Confoy, Sterns & Weinroth as local counsel for the defendants, Recording Industry Association of America, Secured Digital Music Initiative Foundation and Verance Corporation.

And with me to my left is David Kendall, Kevin Hardy, both admitted pro hac vice from the firm of Williams and Connolly for Recording Industry Association of American. Mr. Kendall will be leading the argument today for the defendants.

THE COURT: All right. Now, I assume that you also—you'll also be speaking on behalf of Secured Digital Musical Initiative and Verance Corporation, is that right?

MR. KENDALL: Your Honor, they

MR. WACK: Your Honor, this is Thomas Wack.

THE COURT: Okay.

MR. WACK: Mr.—Mr. Kendall's argument, I believe, will be—I won't have much to add to what he has to say, although I will have a few comments.

THE COURT: And you're representing whom, Mr. Wack?

MR. WACK: Secured Digital Music Initiative Foundation.

THE COURT: Who's representing Verance?

MS. BRAUN: I am, Lynda Braun, Your Honor. And I will defer to Mr. Kendall's argument.

THE COURT: Okay. And representing the Attorney General?

MR. PHILLIPS: Richard Phillips, Your Honor, from the Justice Department.

THE COURT: Is there anyone else whose appearance hasn't been noted? All right.

MS. CONFOY: Your Honor, I just have with me representatives from Recording Industry Association of America, Dean Garfield and Matthew Oppenheim, also from the SDMI.

THE COURT: All right. Now we start out with an order permitting filing under seal sought by the plaintiff. Is there any opposition by the defense to their motion to file under seal a computer program entitled Tiny Warp Dot C, the Source Code Used to Defeat Technology F During the SDMI Public Challenge, according to the letter of October 24th of Ms. Barber. Anyone have any opposition to it being filed under seal?

All right, I will sign the order by consent. And the Clerk will file it.

The plaintiffs filed a complaint, and then a first amended complaint. All defendants move to dismiss the letter. We have two sets of motion papers. The defendants—the private defendants, Recording Industry, Verance and Secure Digital Music move in one set of papers, which the defense has responded to and which we have a series of declarations filed by both sides. And also, the Attorney General has moved to dismiss, as well.

And, again, the plaintiffs have responded and filed declarations and we have a full set of briefing on both sides.

I have read the briefs and I do not desire to have any party repeat the arguments in their briefs. I think the matter has been fully briefed by both sides. Nonetheless, if either side wishes to be heard briefly on points raised since the briefing, I will permit it.

Perhaps the wisest thing to do since the moving parties have had the last brief is to ask Mr. Scarselli whether he has any response to the briefs.

MR. SCARSELLI: Yes, Your Honor, I have a number of responses to particular points.

THE COURT: All right. Don't repeat your brief and only respond to the last brief that was filed. I've read the rest of it several times.

MR. SCARSELLI: Yes.

THE COURT: Shall we turn first to the private defendant's motions?

MR. SCARSELLI: Yes. May I?

THE COURT: Proceed.

MR. SCARSELLI: May it please the Court, I am Gino Scarselli and I represent the plaintiffs in this action.

Your Honor, with respect to the private defendants' briefs, the reply brief, the last brief, what I would like to point out are simply two things:

One is our concern over the three papers to which the private defendants have represented to the Court—

THE COURT: They say they have no problem, correct? If it weren't for the one Oppenheim letter, you wouldn't be here, would you?

MR. SCARSELLI: No, because of the whole series of events, Your Honor, that took place leading up to the Oppenheim letter—

THE COURT: So, you have one letter which they withdrew before the seminar took place. And since then, they have been saying over and over again we're not going to sue in these papers, we're not going to sue in these papers, we're not going to sue in these papers. Indeed, back last summer you came in for injunctive relief and I told you it didn't make sense.

MR. SCARSELLI: Your Honor, there was no retraction from the other side prior to the filing of the complaint. All there was was a press statement—

THE COURT: Well, that's a matter of dispute. They say that they issued it before but you didn't get it before.

MR. SCARSELLI: No—

THE COURT: Let's talk about the stipulation that you—

MR. SCARSELLI: Yes.

THE COURT:—entered into with them or were going to enter into with them. Why wasn't that signed?

MR. SCARSELLI: We didn't—it wasn't signed because the private defendants refused to sign it. It was a stipulation, first of all, to avoid a need for preliminary relief or extraordinary relief.

THE COURT: And what was it that the private defendants found troubling about that proposed stipulation?

MR. SCARSELLI: I honestly don't know, Your Honor. I don't know the answer to that question.

THE COURT: Then we'll have to ask them when it comes to be their turn. Okay.

MR. SCARSELLI: So—

THE COURT: Go ahead.

MR. SCARSELLI: So what we tried to do—but, Your Honor, if I may clarify, it wasn't just a matter of a single letter by Mr. Oppenheim that was sent on April 9th. It was a matter of events that occurred post letter, that occurred over the span of two weeks leading up to the date of the conference.

THE COURT: You're talking about the negotiation between the lawyers?

MR. SCARSELLI: Those were—Your Honor, they—they can be construed as negotiations. But they're—they were clearly considered threats, not just by these plaintiffs, but by University counsels for Princeton or Rice Universities, by the Program Chair of the Information Hiding Workshop who pulled the papers, the decision was reversed by a higher committee the following day. But he actually pulled the paper.

It's not just a matter of these plaintiffs looking and feeling threatened or chilled by the letter and the ensuing negotiations.

In those negotiations, Mr. Turnbull [phonetic] of Verance's outside counsel referred to the paper as a recipe for circumventing technological measures, what would put it clearly under the—under the Statute.

Mr. Liebowitz [phonetic], Verance's CEO, claimed that the plaintiffs have violated the DMCA strictly by submitting the paper to the conference. Those events—

THE COURT: That one letter is what you seem to be hanging your hat on.

MR. SCARSELLI: It was the negotiations also, and it was also the—these were—Mr. Endy [phonetic] of Rice—of Princeton University—Princeton's general counsel describes daily and sometimes hourly conversations. Now, they occurred over a short span of time, but they occurred over a short span of time because there was a date certain when the paper was supposed to be published.

And during that time, threats were—I mean there's different ways of saying that. We could say that the same threat was reiterated, were—that other threats were made. But the point is that it was absolutely clear to everyone present on our side of the table, along with the University counsels of two major universities, along with outside counsel of Rice University, because Rice retained outside counsel in anticipation of litigation.

THE COURT: Well, since that time, you've published everything you want to publish without a peep out of the defense, except to say go to it, correct?

MR. SCARSELLI: We have published—I want to be very specific here.

THE COURT: Okay.

MR. SCARSELLI: There was—there were three papers we attached to the complaint.

THE COURT: Um-hum.

MR. SCARSELLI: All right? After the paper was pulled, the only—the plaintiffs had heard nothing from the private defendants. General counsels of Princeton and Rice heard nothing from the private defendants.

Mr. Endy and Mr. Zanzitus [phonetic], both counsels of Rice, stated that they were still concerned at that point. This is after the paper was pulled and after RIAA/SDMI issued that press statement on that same day. That was all that happened, that was all that the other side did.

So, the concern—the—that there still was a live threat of litigation persisted that entire time. One of the papers—the ICAS [phonetic] paper, this is a paper that Professor Wu, who just graduated from Princeton and is now at University of Maryland College Park, had written principally with Mr. Craver, who's still a graduate student at Princeton. That paper was submitted to another conference. It was a similar paper, but it had—it wasn't exactly the same. There was some technical details that were different.

What happens, Your Honor, is with all the focus on the SDMI paper, the paper—excuse me—the paper that was ultimately pulled from the Pittsburgh conference, this one just sort of—it fell through the cracks. When they realized it after the paper was pulled, they tried—they tried to pull it from that conference also.

Professor Liu, who's Professor Wu's advisor, contacted the organizers of the second conference—

THE COURT: I read your submissions. Most of what you're saying is in your submissions, is it not?

MR. SCARSELLI: Yes. Yes.

THE COURT: All right.

MR. SCARSELLI: Excuse me, Your Honor.

THE COURT: Let's not repeat things that we already have.

MR. SCARSELLI: So,—

THE COURT: I mean I've spent hours going over this, I don't intend to spend hours listening to it.

MR. SCARSELLI: I'm sorry, Your Honor. Let me just move on. But that paper has been published. There was an effort to pull it, but it was too late because that conference didn't just—didn't just present the paper—publish the papers in paper form, they burn CD's, and they had already burned CD's at that time, so it was too late to pull that paper.

The paper—the other paper, the paper that was pulled from the Pittsburgh conference was re-advised—

THE COURT: You still haven't answered my question. My question is: Is there anything as of now that these plaintiffs have prepared for publication and sought to publish which has not been published?

MR. SCARSELLI: Well, there is the program Tiny Warp, which we submitted and you've just granted the motion to file under seal. That is written and that's ready for publication.

THE COURT: Have the—

MR. SCARSELLI: But the problem—

THE COURT: Have the defendants said that they will sue you if you publish that?

MR. SCARSELLI: No, Your Honor. But the initial threat was—excuse me—wasn't about one paper. Mr. Oppenheim's letter of April 9th refers to the public discussion of information gained during the—

THE COURT: We're back to the—

MR. SCARSELLI:—SDMI public challenge.

THE COURT:—original Oppenheim letter again, aren't we?

MR. SCARSELLI: Well—well, I mean, yes, we're back there. We're back at those negotiations because that's when the threat occurred.

THE COURT: Maybe it would be profitable to turn to your response to the Attorney General's—

MR. SCARSELLI: Yes.

THE COURT:—submissions at this point.

MR. SCARSELLI: Yes, sir.

THE COURT: Now, you're asserting that I suppose USENIX fears criminal prosecution by the Attorney General, is that what you're saying?

MR. SCARSELLI: USENIX has a credible— faces a credible threat of prosecution from the Attorney—

THE COURT: The other plaintiffs have a credible threat of prosecution by the Attorney General?

MR. SCARSELLI: Professor Felten does because the paper that he wants to write for *Scientific American*, he was invited to write it, would place him under the criminal provisions because *Scientific American*, unlike peer review journals, actually pays for articles.

THE COURT: Okay. In your injunctive relief request at Paragraph K, you seek a preliminary and permanent injunction against the Department of Justice—

MR. SCARSELLI: Yes.

THE COURT:—from enforcing the DMCA against plaintiffs USENIX for violating the Act. But you don't seek it as to the other plaintiffs. Are you saying that they don't fear prosecution by the Attorney General?

MR. SCARSELLI: Your Honor, we have—this is a very difficult—it's a complicated Statute and we believed at that time that the only—the only plaintiff that faced criminal prosecution because of Section 1204, which is the criminal provision, and requires that a violation be done for commercial— a commercial advantage or private financial gain only apply to USENIX because they gain money through the conference.

Since the arrest of Mr. Sklyarov, we're not sure where that line is drawn any longer.

THE COURT: Well, I'm looking at the amended complaint, you're not seeking that relief. Now, are you saying that these defendants—the defendant Attorney General would prosecute your plaintiffs? It seems to me there's a tremendous difference between Mr. Sklyarov and your plaintiffs, isn't there?

MR. SCARSELLI: I don't—

THE COURT: You don't see it?

MR. SCARSELLI: We don't see that—no, Your Honor.

THE COURT: Okay.

MR. SCARSELLI: He's a grad—

THE COURT: Well—

MR. SCARSELLI:—student at Moscow State University.

THE COURT: Okay.

MR. SCARSELLI: He came to the United States—

THE COURT: Well, if you don't see it, enough said. We'll deal—

MR. SCARSELLI: Okay.

THE COURT:—with that later. I mean I—I see the difference as being night and day, you don't. Let's move on then.

MR. SCARSELLI: Yes, sir. If I could say just one—if I may follow-up just one more thing.

THE COURT: All right, go ahead.

MR. SCARSELLI: Under the Statute, our point is that under the Statute, the lines aren't clear between Mr. Sklyarov's case and our case. We don't know all of the facts of that case yet. And reviewing the Government's indictment is just not clear to us.

The other point, though—and really what is relevant about the Sklyarov case, sir, is that it shows that the Government is intent on enforcing the Statute. This is not a Statute that the Attorney General has dismissed that refuses to enforce. He will enforce it. But exactly—

THE COURT: Does that mean that anyone—

MR. SCARSELLI: Exactly the—

THE COURT:—can seek an injunction against prosecution, regardless of the circumstance? Regardless of asserting that they are actually going to engage in prohibited acts?

MR. SCARSELLI: Sir, we would—Your Honor, we would have to amend that complaint because I don't believe injunctive relief is warranted now.

THE COURT: I'm dealing with the complaint as you have amended it the first time.

MR. SCARSELLI: Correct.

THE COURT: That's what they've moved to dismiss.

MR. SCARSELLI: Correct. And I don't think injunctive relief is appropriate against the Government for the USENIX conference, I do believe though that declaratory relief is still appropriate.

THE COURT: Okay. So, you concede that you don't have standing to bring an injunction action against the Government to stop it from contemplating a prosecution against you that they have not even contemplated, is that what you're saying?

MR. SCARSELLI: Only with respect to the USENIX conference.

THE COURT: Otherwise you think you do?

MR. SCARSELLI: Absolutely.

THE COURT: Okay.

MR. SCARSELLI: Under—under controlling Third Circuit law, Your Honor. Because under Third Circuit law, if—I mean a threat from the Attorney General is not required. All that is required is that the plaintiffs want to engage in conduct that's constitutionally protected and that the Statute proscribes their conduct. That's all that's required.

THE COURT: And you assert the Statute—

MR. SCARSELLI: Then a presumption is created.

THE COURT:—proscribes your conduct, is that what you're saying?

MR. SCARSELLI: I'm saying that the Statute absolutely proscribes the—proscribes the publication of the Tiny Warp Program.

And as far as the plaintiffs' other conduct—

THE COURT: Even though all your adversaries disagree with you on that.

MR. SCARSELLI: Your Honor, the private defendants threatened—threatens to sue under the DMCA for the publication and presentation of an academic paper. They obviously must read the Statute and to help draft the Statute so that it covers papers. And it makes sense, though, it's a reasonable reading of the Statute and it's a reasonable reading of part of the intent behind the Statute, which is to prevent the disclosure of information that can be used to circumvent measures that are intended to protect copying and access to copyrighted works.

THE COURT: Anything else?

MR. SCARSELLI: With respect to the—

THE COURT: Either of those two points, then I'm going to give your adversaries no more than five minutes a piece to respond and then I'll rule.

MR. SCARSELLI: Yes, sir. Your Honor, may I comment—may I have just a moment?

(Pause)

MR. SCARSELLI: Nothing, Your Honor.

THE COURT: Okay. All right, counsel for the private defendants. You heard my injunction to your adversary, I've read the papers, don't repeat them, no more than five minutes, and please confine yourself to what we've been hearing from your adversary.

MR. KENDALL: May it please the Court, David Kendall—

THE COURT: This is just designed to supplement your papers. No more.

MR. KENDALL: David Kendall for defendant, RIAA. The Court asked why the stipulation was not signed, that stipulation is attached as Exhibit J to Mr. Hardy's declaration in support of our motion to dismiss.

THE COURT: That's right.

MR. KENDALL: The only reason it wasn't signed, Your Honor, is one word. You'll note that there's a signature line for the Court. The one word that is missing from the stipulation is dismissed.

We believe—and I think—I thought that the plaintiffs believed that that stipulation resolved both past and present questions. It resolved past questions by giving them assurances from not only—

THE COURT: Who prepared the stipulation?

MR. KENDALL: Excuse me?

THE COURT: Who prepared the stipulation?

MR. KENDALL: It was really prepared by both sides and it's so recites in it—

THE COURT: But you were the ones that wouldn't sign it, you wouldn't sign it because they wouldn't agree to dismiss this action, as well as everything else that was agreed in there, is that right?

MR. KENDALL: That's correct.

THE COURT: Okay.

MR. KENDALL: And we thought that we had dealt with the three papers in Paragraphs 1, 2 and 3, which gave them categorical assurances, not only RIAA, but SDMI and Verance that no action on those papers would be taken.

They recognize our point in Paragraph 6 that as to the future, nobody knows. We can't—you know, nobody can give assurances about the future. We thought that ended the case. I said so in my letter sent back to Mr. Scarselli the same day, that we only had one problem, and that was we wanted a dismissal on it. So, that's why the stipulation wasn't signed.

I think it does end the case. I think the case—for reasons set forth in our papers, is moot. And there's no actual controversy.

As to Mr. Scarselli's second point, he referred to papers. And I think that the short answer to them is that every—

THE COURT: Is it moot or is the issue not ripe? Or do the plaintiffs lack standing?

MR. KENDALL: I think you could say either one of those, Your Honor. My feeling is that the plaintiffs probably lack standing. I think moot suggests that there was at one time a controversy.

So, I would say that probably they lack standing and the issue isn't ripe. But I think also, if—even if you gave them the benefit of the doubt, it's been mooted by the stipulation and our assurances.

THE COURT: All right. Anything else?

MR. KENDALL: The only thing I—in Mr. Scarselli's second point, he mentioned papers. We responded to every paper identified in their amended complaint. They were filed under seal, there's no reason to seal them anymore, Your Honor, because they've been published on the Internet by regular paper and given at conferences.

Thank you.

THE COURT: All right. Mr. Wack, do you have anything on that?

MR. WACK: I have nothing to add, Your Honor.

THE COURT: Ms. Braun?

MS. BRAUN: No, Your Honor.

THE COURT: All right. Mr. Phillips, for the Government?

MR. PHILLIPS: Actually, Your Honor— Richard Phillips from the Justice Department.

Actually, Your Honor, I appreciate the five minutes, but I believe the briefs covered the waterfront. If the Court has questions, I'd be happy to answer them.

THE COURT: Okay. All right, very well.

MR. PHILLIPS: Thank you.

THE COURT: All right. Well, I certainly have had an opportunity to read the various briefs submitted by the parties and the declarations submitted by the parties, and I have reviewed the first amended complaint in some detail with the attachments.

It's tempting to reserve decision and write a definitive opinion here, but it's unnecessary because the United States Supreme Court—the United States Court of Appeals for the Third Circuit, among others, have already conclusively spoken on the issues presented. And this would serve no purpose other than to delay this matter further.

I will discuss the issues raised in somewhat of an abbreviated fashion. The question presented is, as the parties have annunciated, do we have a case or controversy. That limitation on the Federal Courts is both a Separation of Powers limitation and a Prudential limitation. We don't have roving commissions to go about and consider any statute passed by the Congress, which some party may wish to question. The reasons for that are set forth in the briefs submitted, and I will hopefully go into that in some greater detail.

But an abstract review of the constitutionality of statutes passed by Congress is beyond the powers of this Court and, of course, is certainly limited by prudential concerns, as well.

The Courts of the United States are quite busy handling real, rather than theoretical cases, between true adversaries with an adequately developed factual record.

I feel that if I were to delay my ruling, it would be unfortunate. I think right now, it's necessary to speak and avoid further expenditure of the resources of the parties and of the Court where we do not have an actual case or controversy.

As Dorothy Parker said in another context, "there is no there there." Looking at the repeated assurances given by the defendants that there is no dispute, that there is no controversy, the plaintiffs seem unwilling to accept that.

You'll have to bear with me and don't interrupt me, I have a series of notes and references here and I will try to dictate an abbreviated opinion into the record, which I think will assist the parties. And when and if they do have a case or controversy, they are certainly free to come back to this Court. But at this point, as I say, they do not.

I think everybody has given me a form of order here if I'm not mistaken, let me just make sure.

(Pause)

THE COURT: Yes, I have a form of order here from the United States and I have one from the Recording Industry Association, one from SDMI and one from Verance.

(Pause)

THE COURT: My apologies to the attorneys that are present by telephone. I'm going to keep you for a while. Is that inconvenient? Are you someplace where you can't stay on the phone for a while?

MR. WACK: No. We—I can certainly stay on the phone, Your Honor.

MS. BRAUN: So can I, Your Honor.

THE COURT: All right.

(Pause)

THE COURT: The claim here arises out of what is called the SDMI initiative, a letter to the digital community to attack certain technologies, which is referred to in the beginning of the amended complaint, which also sets forth the parties.

The plaintiffs assert that they did enter this contest. They assert that they were successful, at least in part, the defendants assert they were not, but that is irrelevant to the matters that are before us.

In any event, the claim is that the plaintiffs, as scholars and researchers, intended to publish the results of their examination. And that they were met with a response by Mr. Oppenheim, which is set forth at Paragraph 43 of the complaint. This goes on after allegedly Professor Felten was in correspondence with Mr. Winograd of Verance. And Dr. Winograd said at Paragraph 41 that, "I am most concerned that your paper provides unnecessarily detailed information, in particular relating to detailed numerical measurements, such as frequencies, numeric parameters, etc., you and your colleagues obtain through analysis of the samples provided by SDMI and/or employ in your proposed attacks. It's not clear to me that the inclusion of these specific numeric details either advances your stated goal for furthering the academic body of knowledge regarding security technologies or any other cause other than facilitating the use of your results by others seeking to circumvent the legitimate use of these technologies for copyright protection purposes. I urge you to reconsider your decision to include this information in your publication, I believe that there could be ways in which our individual objectives can be met without potentially compromising the academic value of your work or the security of any of the technologies that were included in the SDMI challenge.

"I welcome the opportunity to discuss these further with you while there is still time to do so."

And it's alleged that three days later, Professor Felten received a letter from Matthew Oppenheim, Esquire, Senior Vice President of Business and Legal Affairs of the Recording Institute of America—Industry Association of America, Inc., one of the defendants here. And this is the letter which seems to be the crux of the plaintiffs' claimed fears, together with the claimed negotiations thereafter.

Oppenheim said, "As you are aware, at least one of the technologies that was the subject of the public challenge, the Verance Watermark is already in commercial use. A disclosure of any information that might assist others to remove this watermark would seriously jeopardize the technology and content it protects.

"Other technologies that were part of the challenge are either likewise in commercial use or could be utilized in this capacity in the near future.

"Therefore, any disclosure of the information that would allow the defeat of those technologies would violate both the spirit and the terms of the click-through agreement. In addition, any disclosure of information gained from participating in the public challenge would be outside the scope of activities permitted by the agreement and could subject you and your research team to action under the Digital Millennium Copyright Act, DMCA.

"Unfortunately, the disclosure that you are contemplating could result in significantly broader consequences and could directly lead to the illegal distribution of copyrighted materials." Material, singular.

"Such disclosure is not authorized in the agreement, would constitute a violation of the agreement and would subject your research team to enforcement actions under the DMCA and possibly other Federal laws.

"As you are aware, the agreement covering the public challenge narrowly authorizes participants to attack the limited number of music samples and files that were provided by the SDMI. The specific purpose of providing these encoded files and for setting up the challenge was to assist the SDMI in determining which proposed technologies are best suited to protect the content in phase two products." It talks about the limited waiver.

And then goes on—and I won't read all of it, but what he is saying it would—you'd be in direct violation of the agreement and would be outside the limited authorization of the agreement, could be subject to the enforcement under Federal laws, including the DMCA. And disclosure could be subject to a DMCA action.

And it's alleged that thereafter, the plaintiffs were concerned, negotiated with the defendants, both themselves and counsel for the universities, and while finally the paper was cleared for a publication by the presenting organization, the plaintiff, specifically Dr. Felten, decided not to present it.

The plaintiffs have four causes of action here, and I will not read the entire amended complaint, which is lengthy. I need not do that, it's part of the record.

They're seeking, first, declaratory judgment, that they're not liable under the Act for submitting the referenced papers. And going beyond that, that they would not be liable for presentation of publication of any research resulting from or relating to the public challenge. And also, a declaration of the Act is not violated by the publication or presentation by plaintiffs or others of future scientific or technical information, including computer code, related to access and copy control measures and copyright management information systems.

They're also seeking a declaration, a second cause of action, that the Act violates the First Amendment of the United States Constitution on its face and as applied.

And, third, a declaration that they will not violate the click-through agreement by certain designated acts.

And, fourth, a declaration that the act is in fact unconstitutional because it's not a valid exercise of any of Congress' enumerated powers.

The injunctive relief is set forth thereafter. I referred to the claim for an injunction against the Department of Justice from initiating criminal prosecutions. I understand from counsel that maybe that is not what they're seeking right now, but that's what the complaint says.

Now, when we look at this complaint, of course, the first thing the Court must consider is its own jurisdiction or lack thereof. And as I said initially, we have jurisdiction under Article 3 only for actual cases and controversies. Indeed, early in the founding of the republic, there were some consideration of whether the Court, specifically the Supreme Court, should have advisory powers to pass on the constitutionality of acts of Congress. And, of course, that view was soundly rejected.

What we have here is a situation where we don't have any justiciable case or controversy. We don't have the necessary adversity, which is required for this Court's subject matter jurisdiction. On one side you have people saying we are afraid things are going to happen. On the other side, we have people saying, no, they're not, we're not going to do any such thing. This leads to, at best, a collusive lawsuit, and at worst . . . almost a default situation.

We're not here to abstractly consider the merits of legislation, the wisdom of legislation. And I know that the plaintiffs' attack of the wisdom of the legislation is a matter for the Congress and not for the courts.

The plaintiffs seek a declaration of their rights to publish and present three, and sometimes it's characterized as four if you look at permutations of one of them, specifically identified academic papers.

And the private defendants repeatedly expressed publicly and in correspondence, you can see it in the record and the declarations, they have no objection whatsoever to them publishing or presenting these three papers. And if you look at the proposed stipulation, you'll see how narrow the issue between the parties is. And it basically comes down to is there a present judicable controversy or not? Can this action be dismissed or not?

The plaintiffs don't say, well, it's not true, they really say they are going to sue us. They haven't said that. They rely on the Oppenheim letter, which, as we know, disavowed quite early on.

Now, as far as papers that may be written in the future, again, we have a non-justiciable dispute. It's unripe and speculative.

An analogy came to mind and, of course, all analogies should be approached with caution and are, by nature, imprecise and probably misleading. If we had a party who said I wish to enter into agreements with banks, but I'm afraid of the bank fraud laws, I'm afraid that my good faith submissions to the bank will be considered as bank fraud and I will be prosecuted for it. Therefore, I would like a declaration in advance.

Well, if the bank says, I'm not going to have any civil remedy under bank fraud. And the Attorney General says, we're not going to prosecute you under that one. I don't see how they can do it then.

If the plaintiff says, well, how about any papers I ever submit to a bank? I think, again, we have something that's unripe and speculative. And one could hardly expect the Attorney General to say any papers you ever submit to a bank or anyone ever submits to a bank will not be prosecuted for bank fraud. It may well be, we don't know.

I'm not in a position to rule on hypotheticals, that's why we try to sharpen the record by adverse interest so I can deal with real cases and real controversies.

The factual scenario is set forth in the declarations of the parties and in the briefs submitted. And I don't think I need to go over all of those.

What we do know, and it's clear, is that the Oppenheim letter, which seems to be the catalyst, has been explained by the RIAA and the SDMI saying that the response was far too strong and threatening, and that there was no intent at any time to sue, nor did they overtly say we are going to sue you. It could be seen in the Oppenheim letter, but it was not expressed there.

It talks about the possibility of violations, but it doesn't say we're going to sue you.

Now, the counsel of Princeton and Rice were concerned about a lawsuit, and did discuss them at the time. But the plaintiffs received permission to present this paper in the academic conference which had been notified of the controversy, and they decided to withdraw it. They've subsequently decided to present it.

And we know that the private defendant said that SDMI does not, nor did it ever intend to bring any legal action against Professor Felten or his coauthors.

The record is clear as to whether or not there is a case or controversy that this Court could consider whether it has jurisdiction that the private defendants have plainly, unequivocally, over and over again stated repeatedly that they have no objection to presenting or publishing the Felten paper or the Wu paper.

And, of course, they said that it was never our intention to bring any kind of action against Felten. And this—we're going back before this lawsuit was filed. The irony is that the defendants having said we're not going to sue you, the plaintiffs decided apparently to catalyze this action by bringing a suit themselves.

And one thing that I noted was that Mr. Oppenheim, in a letter to plaintiffs' counsel, said that the RIAA and the SDMI do not object to the publication of the academic papers identified in the complaint, and gave a list of published statements, which they've expressly disavowed any intention of initiating litigation and said we, frankly, don't know how we could have been any clearer. Or to paraphrase a popular phrase, what part of the word yes don't you understand?

Of course, after that, we had this request for emergent relief, and I could see no basis for the emergent relief back in June. And specifically expressed my concern about the lack of an actual case or controversy between the parties.

Of course, we have the negotiation of the stipulation. When you look at the stipulation as to the terms, of course the parties can't stipulate as to future events. But as to present events, I agree with the defense that the only dispute between the parties is the justiciability of this case, which is a question of law, and one that I think is not particularly difficult. We're just not here to give advisory opinions on abstract or hypothetical issues. This is an Article 3 limitation.

We can't declare an act of Congress unconstitutional in such a context. We need true adverse interest and standing.

I can't find any adversity of interest with respect to the Felten paper or the Wu papers. And I would note that the defendants never said they were going to do anything at any time against the Wu paper. That is only Ms. Wu's statement that she felt that she was in danger of being sued.

As the parties focus on the key case in the Third Circuit, *Step-Saver Data Systems, Inc. v. Wyse Technology*, 912 F2d 643, Third Circuit, 1990, the question in each declaratory judgment case is whether the facts alleged under all the circumstances show there's a substantial controversy between parties having adverse legal interest of sufficient immediacy and reality to warrant the issuance of a declaratory judgment. I cannot find that those questions are met in this case.

As the defendants note in their brief, there's another principle applicable here, avoiding the ruling on Federal Constitutional matters in advance of a necessity for deciding them, which is a factor also to be considered in justiciability.

As I said, we don't have some roving commission to go around declaring acts of Congress unconstitutional because some party would like us to look at them.

The plaintiffs say, well, this is a First Amendment case and, therefore, it is different. Well, as the Third Circuit has noted in the *Salvation Army* case, again referred to by both sides, 919 F2d 183, Third Circuit, 1990, where a plaintiff seeks a declaratory judgment with respect to constitutionality of a State Statute, even when the attack is on First Amendment grounds, there must be a real and immediate threat of enforcement against the plaintiff. And this threat must remain throughout the course of the litigation.

Well, the clear and uncontested record here indicates that there is not a real and immediate threat of enforcement against the plaintiffs, much less one that remains throughout the course of the litigation.

The fact that the plaintiffs assert that they feel chilled, their subjective views are insufficient unless we find evidence that there is an actual immediate threat.

As to the hypothetical future academic papers, I don't think that those provide a sufficient ground for the immediacy asserted by the plaintiffs. The plaintiffs, of course, bear the burden of establishing the elements of the jurisdiction of this Court. I don't see any injury, in fact, here.

Not only would it be premature adjudication, but it is ephemeral adjudication. It is speculative adjudication. It is by analogy. Sort of adjudication that would let the Court peer into the future to determine whether any loan application by a putative plaintiff could conceivably be a fraud. Courts are ill-equipped to engage in that sort of speculation.

Indeed, the absence of a controversy can be seen by the fact that there are no mentions of any threat by any private defendant, or the Attorney General with respect to the plaintiffs' future works at all, even if we knew what those works were.

As the defense notes, pre-enforcement review of a statute is the exception, rather than the rule, *Artway v. Attorney General* [phonetic], 81 F3d 1235, 1247, Third Circuit, 1996. Pre-enforcement review of a statute may occur only where the plaintiff has alleged an intention to engage in a course of conduct, arguably affected with the constitutional interest, but proscribed by the Statute, and there exists a credible threat of the prosecution thereunder.

Here, the plaintiffs have not alleged that they plan to violate the Statute, only that the Statute appears unclear to them.

I can't see any credible threat of any imminent prosecution, either civilly or criminally. There's no real immediate threat of enforcement.

Indeed, because the papers have not even been written, it's impossible to know whether they will or will not violate the Act, or any other law for that matter. And the Court declines to engage in feudal speculation.

Plaintiffs are also seeking, in addition to the claim based upon the past papers as to which there is no objection to them publishing them, or future papers that they may prepare seeking to have me invalidate the Act as it applies to, according to the amended complaint, publication or presentation of all scientific, academic or technical speech, including the publication of computer programs. A rather broad and ephemeral, at best and one that would require the Court to engage in useless speculation.

I don't know that I need to further discuss the claims against the individual defendants. I will say that I think that the position taken by the individual defendants as to Third Circuit and Supreme Court law is correct. And that there is no basis for me to

find a case or controversy here. Of course, the *Salvation Army* case from the Third Circuit is particularly instructive here.

Step-Saver factors, which are not met here, are particularly the instructive here, as well.

I can't find any injury in fact here. So, therefore, a pre-enforcement review of a Statute would be inappropriate.

I can't say that the plaintiffs have alleged an intention to engage in a course of conduct arguably affected with a Constitutional interest, but proscribed by the Statute. Indeed, the defendants assert that it's not proscribed by the Statute.

Indeed, the Attorney General, when he talks about the Statute, explains why it is not. There's certainly no credible threat of prosecution here, much less one that is impending.

To feel—fear or concern asserted by the plaintiffs, again, is subjective. Threats claimed derived from the Oppenheim letter, which the defendants clarified and explained that they were not threatening any lawsuit. Whether it was withdrawn before the complaint or after the complaint, it was—I don't think we need to reach at this point.

The Wu papers, nobody ever made any reference to the Act concerning the Wu papers.

And, indeed, as I noted, all the papers have since been published. Thus, arguing against the claimed chill and the—there's an assertion by the defense that the Felten paper was not out of circulation, even if withdrawn from the information hiding workshop because it was already publicly released on the Internet.

So, we have all these repeated protestations that, you know, we're not threatening you, and I don't understand how this one letter or the—even the negotiations thereafter, in light of the record here, can show me any real case or controversy here.

Certainly the plaintiffs have not demonstrated that the conduct that they seek to engage in is clearly proscribed by the relevant Statute. To the contrary, the plaintiffs say the Statute is ambiguous and uncertain.

I—even if there were a case or controversy, which there is not, I would note that the Declaratory Judgment Act gives me discretion. And if I had discretion here, I would not exercise it to consider the constitutionality or applicability of a recent act of Congress in this area where the facts are not developed and where there is no adversity between the parties. But I don't think I need to reach that issue because it seems to me it would be a clear Article 3 violation for me to do that.

Now, I'm going to turn to the suit against the Attorney General. The plaintiffs admit that they haven't been prosecuted nor threatened with prosecution under the Act by the Attorney General. The Attorney General does not indicate that he plans to do so.

The fact that he will not give in advance a non-prosecution agreement or waiver as to any conduct that the plaintiffs or any other party may engage in in the future does not mean that there is a case or controversy here.

The analogy or the concern as to the criminal case that has been brought does not seem to assist the plaintiffs.

The defendants have referred to, I think it's Sklyarov, S-K-L-Y-A-R-O-V, indictment, against Dmitry Sklyarov and Elcom[soft] Ltd., and it's clear distinction between what is alleged there and anything that the plaintiffs say they are doing or intend to do.

The indictment charges that these defendants designed a program that circumvents a restriction on copying, distributing and printing of certain electronic books and offered—and I believe it was Adobe Acrobat, and offered the program for sale to the general public on the Internet specifically for the purpose of circumventing these restrictions.

The plaintiffs do not allege that they have [engaged] or intend to engage in piracy of that nature. They don't assert that they are trying to prepare programs to circumvent restrictions on copying and that they have a constitutional right to do so or that they intend to sell them to the public or have sold them to the public.

Rather, they're saying they published them to fellow scientists as part of a scientific process of improving access controls. I can't see how the prosecution of Mr. Sklyarov assists them in their effort to have the criminal portion of the Statute declared unconstitutional. I'm not sure entirely that that is what they're seeking at this time based upon

counsel's argument. But I certainly can't find any adverse legal interest here between the Attorney General and the plaintiffs.

Of course, the other factors of the *Step-Saver* analysis—and I cited that case previously—the case is susceptible if it concludes a judgment, the judgment would be a practical utility of the parties are as inapplicable here as they are in the case of the private defendants.

The Act which was entered—passed by the Congress, pursuant to an international copyright treaty, prohibits the manufacturing offering the public and the like of any technology, et cetera, and is primarily designed or produced for the purpose of circumventing the technological measure that effectively controls the access to work protected under the Copyright Act, that's 17 U.S. Code 1201(A)(2), or has only limited commercial significant purpose or use other than to circumvent, and I'm paraphrasing here, or is marketed for use in circumventing. Language such as is primarily designed or produced.

As the Attorney General notes, seven exceptions here. If you look at 1201(D) through J, including conduct which is necessary to engage in encryption research or conduct which is necessary to engage in security testing of computer system. Also, provides for innocent violations where the violator neither knew nor should have known that its acts constituted a violation.

If someone were prosecuted under these, would these exceptions apply? I don't know. I can't speculate. I can't create an intellectual dichotomy with myself where there is no adversity of—between the parties.

The Attorney General argues that the plaintiffs' claims are not ripe. So, we don't have an actual case of controversy.

Of course, the doctrines of ripeness and standing, while different, are certainly intertwined. And they're both founded on concerns on the proper limited role of the unelected third branch, Democratic Society.

The Supreme Court has repeatedly admonished us not to entertain constitutional questions in advance of the strictest necessity. And the parties cite *Poe v. Allman* [phonetic] for that, 367 US 497, 503, 1961, but it has been said on numerous occasions. And, of course, the Attorney General says, again, these are truisms really from the first year of constitutional law. The ability of the judiciary to declare a law unconstitutional does not amount to an unlimited power to survey the statute books and pass judgment on laws before the courts are called upon to enforce them, citing *Younger v. Harris* 401 US 37 52, 1971. Of course, power is legitimate only as a last resort, as a necessity to determine real earnest and vital controversy between individuals, which we don't have here.

There is a danger of premature adjudication. Entangling the Court in abstract disagreements, as the Third Circuit said in the *Artway* case that I've previously referred to, 81 F3d at 1246.

I can't find that the Attorney General has an adverse legal interest to the plaintiffs at this time. He hasn't prosecuted them, or threatened them with prosecution under the Statute. There's no substantial threat of real harm of prosecution. There's no chill that is objectively reasonable. It's not enough for an individual to say I feel chilled. There's no objective reasonableness chilling here. The Attorney General says the mere existence of the Act without more is insufficient here to create a concrete adversity of interest.

Nor does the prosecution, which I believe is in California, Northern District of California, which is completely distinguishable, as I state here. That, on the other hand, I will just note as a footnote. There the Court will have adversity of interest. They will have a real controversy. And any constitutional issues which Mr. Sklyarov or Elcom could raise will properly be before the Court for determination. That is not the case here.

The plaintiffs, on the other hand, allege their conduct falls outside the scope of the Act, that they are not violating the Act. They say, as the Attorney General says, by their own allegations, their purpose is not to circumvent any access control measures, but rather to study and assist others in bolstering those access controls. They don't say they're going to manufacture or offer any product designed to circumvent access controls or sell them.

The Attorney General also says that the plaintiffs' claim did not admit a conclusive relief as the applicability of the act of their conduct is contingent on the precise papers they intend to publish, which the plaintiff have not yet articulated.

Now, I discussed that in connection with the private plaintiffs, and I don't need to discuss it that much further here. Again, we can't forecast the future, nor can we give an overall determination that anything the plaintiffs may wish to do or that anyone else may wish to do in the future will not violate the Statute or some provision thereof. All we know is at the present time, plaintiffs have published and they have not been prosecuted and don't have any realistic fear of being prosecuted.

Now, the plaintiffs, again, argue, as they did with the private defendants, that this is a First Amendment case and a question of ripeness should be less stringently applied here. But as the Attorney General says, the slender First Amendment exception only applies to those who have suffered some cognizable injury whose conduct is not protected by the First Amendment to assert the Constitutional Rights of others.

Plaintiffs here haven't demonstrated they themselves suffered an injury. In fact, the Statute has never been applied to the plaintiffs. They had— cannot show that they had at least a substantial threat of real harm from prosecution under the Statute. They haven't shown that their conduct is proscribed by the Statute or they face a credible threat of prosecution under it.

They assert that the Attorney General's view that the plaintiffs' academic pursuits are not proscribed by the Act, seeking to thus create some adversity between the two parties. If you look at the primarily designed language, look at the language in the Statute and look at the Attorney General saying this is the way I interpret it, I certainly can't find any realistic threat of prosecution here whatsoever. Certainly not to speculate as to what may happen in the future.

Now, the plaintiffs take the position that no threat is required. The Attorney General disagrees and says that you can presume a credible threat of prosecution if a reasonable reading of the Statute would include the plaintiffs' conduct, and there's no compelling evidence against that presumption.

Here, plaintiffs' conduct is clearly not covered by the Act which the plaintiffs say is ambiguous. They don't say we plan to violate the Act, please declare the Act unconstitutional. They say it's unclear. The Attorney General says it's clear, it doesn't apply to them. No credible threat that prosecution can be presumed.

Consider also the fact that much of what the plaintiffs propose to do has been done. And, again, without any repercussions whatsoever from the Attorney General.

The parties' subjective fear that they may be prosecuted for engaging in expressive activity will not be held to constitute an injury for standing purposes unless the fear is objectively reasonable. And here, I can't find that it is.

The Attorney General concludes the only pattern you can glean from plaintiffs' conduct—this is at his brief, Page 12 of the reply brief, is that they are willing to and, in fact, continue to engage in the very conduct they claim is proscribed by the Act. The decision to publish certain speech and to delay or possibly forego other identical speech does not reflect a fear of prosecution. If it did, then logically plaintiffs would be publishing none of the material. Therefore, any alleged refusals to publish cannot be considered a chill and do not evince a need or basis for declaratory judgment in this case.

Now, a few other points.

(Pause)

THE COURT: The plaintiffs liken themselves to modern Galileos persecuted by authorities. I fear that a more apt analogy would be to modern day Don Quixotes feeling threatened by windmills which they perceive as giants. There is no real controversy here.

The plaintiffs may wish to strike down the Statute, but their concern is, as the defendants say, political, rather than a legal concern, one that can best be pursued in the halls of the Legislature until they have a real case or controversy to bring before this Court.

At this stage, they do not. That constitutes the opinion of the Court. And I reserve the right to extend or modify it as set forth in the local rules of this Court, but I thought that for the interest of all parties, prompt resolution would assist all of you.

I have entered orders reflecting this opinion as submitted by counsel for the defense. Court stands in recess.

[end]

CERTIFICATION

I, KAREN HARTMANN, certify that the foregoing is a correct transcript to the best of my ability, from the electronic sound recording of the proceedings in the above-entitled matter.

J&J COURT TRANSCRIBERS, INC.

Date: December 12, 2001

[Some obvious transcription errors were corrected by the Electronic Frontier Foundation, Dec. 21, 2001.]

Hendrickson

v.

eBay, Inc.

**United States District Court,
Central District of California**

September 4, 2001

8 ILR (P&F) 573, 165 F Supp 2d 1082

**Case No. CV 01-0495 RJK (RNBx),
consolidated with Case Nos. CV 01-3412 RJK and CV 01-3412 RJK**

Failure to comply with DMCA notice provision dooms infringement claim.

The Digital Millennium Copyright Act's "safe harbor," 17 USC §512(c), protects the operator of an Internet auction house (eBay) from vicarious copyright infringement where the copyright owner failed to provide eBay with proper notice of the allegedly infringing materials (*i.e.*, pirated copies of a motion picture). Section 512(c)(3) sets forth the required elements for proper notification by copyright holders, many of which plaintiff did not satisfy in the instant case. Specifically, plaintiff's "cease and desist" letter and e-mails failed to include a written statement attesting to the accuracy of the notice's information, §512(c)(3)(A)(vi), and the good faith belief that the materials were unauthorized, §512(c)(3)(A)(v). Plaintiff also failed to provide eBay with sufficient information to identify the various listings that purportedly offered pirated copies of the movie, §512(c)(3)(A)(iii). While there may be circumstances when a copyright holder need not provide specific item numbers to satisfy the identification requirement, in this case such specification was necessary because plaintiff never explained what distinguished an authorized copy from an unauthorized copy. The limited information provided by plaintiff could not, as a matter of law, give eBay actual or constructive knowledge of infringement within the meaning of the first prong of the §512(c) safe harbor, and eBay's mere technical ability to remove or block access to infringing materials does not constitute the "right and ability to control" infringing activity within the meaning of the safe harbor's second prong. Accordingly, eBay meets the test for safe harbor under §512(c) and is entitled to summary judgment. — **Hendrickson v. eBay, Inc., 8 ILR (P&F) 573 [CD Cal, 2001].**

DMCA safe harbor extends to employees of service provider.

The Digital Millennium Copyright Act's "safe harbor," 17 USC §512(c), extends not only to a service provider, but to the service provider's employees as well. Thus, where a copyright holder's infringement claims against the employees of an Internet auction house (eBay) were based solely upon acts and omissions committed within the scope of their employment, eBay's immunity from liability (pursuant to the safe harbor) also extends to the employees. — **Hendrickson v. eBay, Inc., 8 ILR (P&F) 573 [CD Cal, 2001].**

No duty to monitor site for potential trade dress violation.

Plaintiff, asserting certain trademark/trade dress rights in a motion picture, is not entitled to an injunction that restrains an Internet auction house (eBay) from displaying any *new* listings of pirated copies of the motion picture. Such an injunction would effectively require eBay to monitor the millions of new listings posted on its web site each day and determine, on its own, which of those listings infringe plaintiff's Lanham Act rights. No law imposes an affirmative duty on companies such as eBay to engage in such monitoring. — **Hendrickson v. eBay, Inc., 8 ILR (P&F) 573 [CD Cal, 2001].**

ORDER GRANTING DEFENDANTS EBAY INC., MARGARET C. WHITMAN AND MICHAEL RICHTER'S MOTION FOR SUMMARY JUDGMENT OR, ALTERNATIVELY, MOTION FOR PARTIAL SUMMARY JUDGMENT

ROBERT J. KELLEHER, District Judge.

This case involves a matter of first impression in the federal courts: whether one of the "safe harbor" provisions of the Digital Millennium Copyright Act ("DMCA") affords protection to the operator of the popular Internet auction web service, www.ebay.com, when a copyright owner seeks to hold the operator secondarily liable for copyright infringement by its sellers. On August 20, 2001, the Court heard Defendants eBay, Inc. ("eBay"), Margaret Whitman and Michael Richter's (collectively, the "eBay Defendants") motion for summary judgment on the copyright and trademark claims in the consolidated *Hendrickson v. eBay, Inc. et al*, cases. After the hearing, the Court took the motion under submission. After considering the papers submitted by the parties, the case file and oral argument, the Court hereby GRANTS the motion.

I. FACTUAL BACKGROUND

eBay provides an Internet website service where over 25 million buyers and sellers of consumer goods and services have come together to buy and sell items through either an auction or a fixed-price format. Pursuant to their agreement with eBay, users set up user IDs or "screen names" to conduct business on eBay's website in a semi-anonymous fashion.[1] Buyers and sellers reveal their real identities to each other in private communications to complete sales transactions.

eBay's website allows sellers to post "listings" (or advertisements) containing descriptions of items they wish to offer for sale; and it allows buyers to bid for items they wish to buy. People looking to buy items can either browse through eBay's 4,700 categories of goods and services or search for items by typing words into eBay's search engine. Every day, eBay users place on average over one million new listings on eBay's website. At any given time, there are over six million listings on the website.[2]

On or about December 20, 2000, eBay received a "cease and desist" letter from *pro se* Plaintiff Robert Hendrickson. The letter advised eBay that

Plaintiff dba Tobann International Pictures is the copyright owner of the documentary "Manson." The letter also stated that pirated copies of "Manson" in digital video disk ("DVD") format were being offered for sale on eBay. However, the letter did not explain which copies of "Manson" in DVD format were infringing copies; nor did it fully describe Plaintiff's copyright interest. The letter demanded that eBay cease and desist "from any and all further conduct considered an infringement(s) of [Plaintiff's] right" or else face prosecution "to the fullest extend *[sic]* provided by law." (*See* Richter Decl., Ex. C.)

Promptly after receiving this letter, eBay sent Plaintiff e-mails asking for more detailed information concerning his copyright and the alleged infringing items. (*See id.*, Exs. D-G.) eBay advised Plaintiff that he has to submit proper notice under the DMCA. For example, on December 20, 2000, eBay sent the following e-mail to Plaintiff:

> [R]ecognizing that some posted items may infringe certain intellectual property rights, we have set up specific procedures which enable verified rights owners to identify and request removal of allegedly infringing auction listings. These procedures are intended to substantially comply with the requirements of the [DMCA], 17 USC section 512. Click on the following link to access the [DMCA].

(*Id.*, Ex. D.) In that e-mail, eBay also encouraged Plaintiff to join its Verified Rights Owner ("VeRO") program, by submitting eBay's Notice of Infringement form.[3] As eBay explained, some of the benefits of the VeRO program include, among other things: (1) access to a customer support group dedicated to servicing the VeRO participants; (2) dedicated priority email queues for reporting alleged infringing activities; and (3) ability to use a special feature called "Personal Shopper," which allows users to conduct automatic searches for potentially infringing item. (*Id.*, Ex. D.)

On December 28, 2000, Defendant Richter, eBay's Intellectual Property Counsel, followed up with another e-mail:

> We have tried to contact you numerous times concerning your letter dated December 14, 2000. [¶] We would like to assist you in removing items listed by third parties on our

site which you claim infringe your rights. However, in order to do so, we would need proper notice under the [DMCA]. Specifically, we would need you to, among other things, identify the exact items[4] which you believe infringe your rights. In addition, we would need a statement from you, under penalty of perjury, that you own (or are the agent of the owner) the copyrights in the documentary. As you can understand, a statement that 'we immediately CEASE and DESIST from any and all further conduct considered an infringement(s) of my right granted under Copyright and other laws of the land' gives us no indication of what your rights are, and gives us no indication as to which items infringe such rights.

(*Id.*, Ex. G.) Plaintiff refused to join eBay's VeRO program and refused to fill out eBay's Notice of Infringement form.[5] Before filling suit, Plaintiff never provided eBay the specific item numbers that it sought.

II. PROCEDURAL BACKGROUND

On January 17, 2001, Plaintiff filed the first of three lawsuits against eBay. In CV 01-0495 ("Case No. 1"), Plaintiff sued eBay and two eBay sellers, asserting a claim for copyright infringement. The Complaint in Case No. 1 alleges, among other things, that eBay is liable for the sale of unauthorized copies of the film "Manson" by users on eBay's website.

On February 12, 2001, Plaintiff filed the second lawsuit. In CV 01-1371 ("Case No. 2"), Plaintiff sued eBay, David Durham (another third party seller) and Margaret C. Whitman ("Whitman"), eBay's President and CEO. In this case, Plaintiff alleges that eBay and Whitman are liable for copyright infringement because they allowed Defendant Durham to sell unauthorized copies of the film "Manson" on or after January 17, 2001, the date Plaintiff filed Case No. 1.

On April 13, 2001, Plaintiff filed his third lawsuit against eBay. In CV 01-3412 ("Case No. 3"), Plaintiff added several other defendants, including eBay's senior Intellectual Property Counsel, Michael Richter ("Richter"). Plaintiff alleges, among other things, that eBay and Richter are liable for copyright infringement because they wrongfully continued to allow the sale of unauthorized copies of the film

"Manson" by eBay users after February 25, 2001, the date Plaintiff commenced Case No. 2. In addition, Plaintiff alleges a Lanham Act claim and a state claim for tortuous interference with prospective economic advantage.

On April 30, 2001, the Court denied Plaintiff's motion for preliminary injunction in Case No. 1. On the same day, the Court granted eBay's motion to consolidate the three actions for all purposes. On July 2, 2001, the Court issued an order granting, in part, the eBay Defendants' first motion for summary judgment. The Court denied the eBay Defendants' motion for summary judgment on the copyright claims without prejudice to its refiling. However, the Court granted eBay and Richter's motion for summary adjudication of the application of the Lanham Act's "innocent infringer" provision. The Court also granted the motion for summary judgment on Plaintiff's state claim on the ground that it is preempted by the Copyright Act.

On July 27, 2001, the eBay Defendants filed the pending motion for summary judgment. Plaintiff filed his opposition on August 6, 2001 and the eBay Defendants filed their reply on August 13, 2001.

III. DISCUSSION

A. Standard

Summary judgment is proper if "the pleadings, depositions, answers to interrogatories, and admissions on file, together with the affidavits, if any, show that there is no genuine issue as to any material fact and that the moving party is entitled to judgment as a matter of law," Fed. R. Civ. P. 56(c). A fact is material only if it is relevant to a claim or defense and its existence might affect the suit's outcome. *See T.W. Elec. Serv., Inc. v. Pacific Elec. Contractors Assoc.*, 809 F2d 626, 630 (9th Cir 1987). A court may not, on a motion for summary judgment, evaluate the credibility of the evidence submitted by the parties. *See Leslie v. Grupo ICA*, 198 F3d 1152, 1157-59 (9th Cir 1999).

The moving party bears the burden of demonstrating the absence of a genuine issue of material fact for trial. *See Anderson v. Liberty Lobby, Inc.*, 477 US 242, 256 (1986). "[T]he burden on the moving party may be discharged by 'showing'—that is, pointing out to the district court—that there is an absence of evidence to support the nonmoving party's case." *Celotex Corp.*

v. Catrett, 477 US 317, 325 (1986); *see Musick v. Burke*, 913 F2d 1390, 1394 (9th Cir 1990). To demonstrate that the non-moving party lacks sufficient evidence to entitle it to judgment, the moving party must affirmatively show the absence of such evidence in the record, either by deposition testimony, the inadequacy of documentary evidence or by any other form of admissible evidence. *See Celotex*, 477 US at 322. The moving party has no burden to negate or disprove matters on which the opponent will have the burden of proof at trial. *See id.* at 325.

A non-moving party's allegation that factual disputes persist between the parties will not automatically defeat an otherwise properly supported motion for summary judgment. *See* Fed. R. Civ. P. 56(e) (non-moving party "may not rest upon the mere allegations or denials of the adverse party's pleadings, but . . . must set forth specific facts showing that there is a genuine issue for trial."). "[A] mere 'scintilla' of evidence will be insufficient to defeat a properly supported motion for summary judgment; instead, the nonmoving party must introduce some 'significant probative evidence tending to support the complaint.' " *Fazio v. City and County of San Francisco*, 125 F3d 1328, 1331 (9th Cir 1997), *quoting Anderson*, 477 US at 249, 252. In judging evidence at the summary judgment stage, courts must draw all reasonable inferences in favor of the party against whom summary judgment is sought. *See Matsushita Elec. Indus. Co. v. Zenith Radio Corp.*, 475 US 574, 587 (1986); *Chaffin v. United States*, 176 F3d 1208, 1213 (9th Cir 1999).

B. The Copyright Claims Against eBay

1. The Infringing Activity

Plaintiff alleges that eBay participated in and facilitated the unlawful sale and distribution of pirated copies of "Manson" DVDs by providing an online forum, tools and services to the third party sellers. (*See* Opp. at 3; *see also* Complaint in Case No. 1, ¶¶18, 20, 21 & 30.) Plaintiff does not allege that the advertisements that sellers posted on eBay's website violate his copyright in "Manson." The type of secondary liability that Plaintiff seeks to impose on the eBay defendants is similar to the type of secondary liability the Ninth Circuit allowed in *Fonovisa, Inc. v. Cherry Auction, Inc.*, 76 F3d 259 (9th Cir 1996). There, the court held that the complaint stated causes of action for vicarious and contributory copyright infringement against the operators of a traditional swap meet for sales of counterfeit recordings by independent vendors.[6] Thus, the issue raised by Plaintiff's copyright claim is not whether eBay can be held secondarily liable for "third party advertisements." (*See* Reply at 3.) Rather, the question is whether eBay can be held secondarily liable for providing the type of selling platform/forum and services that it provided, however limited or automated in nature, to sellers of counterfeit copies of the film "Manson." Before the Court reaches the merits of that question, the Court must address a preliminary issue: whether the DMCA shields eBay from liability for copyright infringement.

2. The DMCA

The DMCA "is designed to facilitate the robust development and world-wide expansion of electronic commerce, communications, research, development, and education." S. Rep. No. 105-190, at 1 (105th Congress, 2d Session 1998). Title II of the DMCA, set forth in 17 USC §512, "protects qualifying Internet service providers from liability for all monetary relief direct, vicarious and contributory infringement." *Id.* at 20. "Title II preserves strong incentives for service providers and copyright owners to cooperate to detect and deal with copyright infringements that take place in the digital networked environment." *Id.* at 40.

There is no dispute over whether eBay is an Internet "service provider" within the meaning of Section 512. eBay clearly meets the DMCA's broad definition of online "service provider." *See* 17 USC §512(k)(1)(B) ("the term 'service provider' means a provider of online services or network access, or the operator of facilities therefor").

To qualify for one of the safe harbor provisions, the service provider's activities at issue must involve functions described in one of four separate categories set forth in subsections (a) through (d) of Section 512. *See* 17 USC §512(n). eBay argues that it qualifies for protection under the third and fourth categories. Because the record establishes that eBay qualifies for protection under Section 512(c), the Court need not address the applicability of Section 512(d).

3. Safe Harbor Under Section 512(c)

Subsection (c) limits liability for "infringement of copyright by reason of the *storage* at the direction of a user of *material* that resides on a system or network controlled or operated by or for the service provider." 17 USC §512(c) (emphasis added). This section applies where a plaintiff seeks to hold an Internet service provider responsible for either (1) infringing "material" stored and displayed on the service provider's website *or* (2) infringing "activity using the material on the [service provider's computer] system." 17 USC §512(c)(1)(A)(i). Here, because the focus of the copyright claims against eBay concerns infringing activity—the sale and distribution of pirated copies of "Manson"—using "materials" posted eBay's website, Section 512(c) would provide eBay a safe harbor from liability if eBay meets the conditions set forth therein.

Three requirements for safe harbor are delineated in Section 512(c)(1). First, the service provider must demonstrate that it does not have actual knowledge that an activity using the material stored on its website is infringing *or* an awareness of "facts or circumstances from which infringing activity is apparent." 17 USC §512(c)(1)(A)(i)-(ii). Alternatively, the service provider must show that it expeditiously removed or disabled access to the problematic material upon obtaining knowledge or awareness of infringing activity. *See* 17 USC §512(c)(1)(A)(iii). Second, the service provider must show it "does not receive a financial benefit directly attributable to the infringing activity" *if* the service provider has "the right and ability to control such activity." 17 USC §512(c)(1)(B). Third, the service provider must show that it responded expeditiously to remove the material that is the subject of infringing activity upon receiving notification of the claimed infringement in the manner described in Section 512(c)(3). 17 USC §512(c)(1)(C).

a. The Third Prong of the Test: Notification of the Alleged Infringing Activity

Under the third prong of the test, the service provider's duty to act is triggered only upon receipt of proper notice. *See id.* Section 512(c)(3) sets forth the required elements for proper notification by copyright holders. First, rights holders must provide *written* notification to the service provider's designated agent. *See* 17 USC §512(c)(3). In addition, the notification must include "substantially" the following six elements:

(1) a physical or electronic signature of a person authorized to act on behalf of the owner of an exclusive right that is allegedly infringed;

(2) identification of the copyrighted work claimed to have been infringed;

(3) identification of the material that is claimed to be infringing or to be the subject of infringing activity and that is to be removed or access to which is to be disabled, and information reasonably sufficient to permit the service provider to locate the material;

(4) information reasonably sufficient to permit the service provider to contact the complaining party;

(5) a statement that the complaining party has a good faith belief that use of the material in the manner complained of is not authorized by the copyright owner, its agent, or the law; and

(6) a statement that the information in the notification is accurate, and under penalty of perjury, that the complaining party is authorized to act on behalf of the copyright owner.

Id.

Preliminary, the Court rejects Plaintiff's argument that he need not submit written notification in the manner described above (*i.e.*, provide the notification referenced in the third prong of the safe harbor test) as long as other facts show the service provider received actual or constructive knowledge of infringing activity. (*See* Opp. at 8.) Plaintiff refers to the first prong of the safe harbor test set forth in Section 512(c)(1)(ii) and (iii) in support of this argument. Plaintiff's argument has no merit.

The DMCA expressly provides that if the copyright holder's attempted notification fails to "comply substantially" with the elements of notification described in subsection (c)(3), that notification "shall *not* be considered" when evaluating whether the service provider had actual or constructive knowledge of the infringing activity under the first prong set forth in Section 512(c)(1). 17 USC §512(c)(3)(B)(i) (emphasis added). Here, Plaintiff does not dispute that he has not strictly complied with Section 512(c)(3). (*See, e.g.,* Opp. at 8-9.) The question is whether Plaintiff's *imperfect* attempts to give notice satisfy Section 512(c)(3)'s "substantial[]" compliance requirement.

(1) No Statement Attesting to Good Faith And Accuracy of Claim

Plaintiff's pre-suit "cease and desist" letter and e-mails to eBay do not include several of the key elements for proper notice required by Section 513(c)(3). (*See* Richter Decl., Exs. C, E, F, H & I.) None of these writings includes a written statement under "penalty of perjury" attesting to the fact "that the information in the notification is accurate . . . [and] the complaining party is authorized to act on behalf of the owner" of the copyright at issue. 17 USC §512(c)(3)(A)(vi). Additionally, none of these writings includes a written statement that Plaintiff "has a good faith belief that use of the material in the manner complained of is not authorized." 17 USC §512(c)(3)(A)(v). The complete failure to include these key elements in his written communications to eBay, even after eBay specifically asked for these items, renders Plaintiff's notification of claimed infringement deficient under Section 512(c)(3).

(2) Inadequate Identification of Material Claimed to be the Subject of Infringing Activity

Moreover, the record shows that Plaintiff failed to comply substantially with the requirement that he provide eBay with sufficient information to identify the various listings that purportedly offered pirated copies of "Manson" for sale. *See* 17 USC §512(c)(3)(A)(iii). It is true that Plaintiff has informed eBay in writing that counterfeit copies of "Manson" were being offered and sold on eBay's website. However, when eBay requested that Plaintiff identify the alleged problematic listings by the eBay item numbers, Plaintiff refused. (*See, e.g.,* Kim Decl., Ex. P [Plaintiff's Response to First Request for Admissions], RFA Nos. 21 and 22.) Plaintiff contends that it is not his job to do so once he had notified eBay of the existence of infringing activity by eBay sellers. (*See id.* at 3.)

The Court recognizes that there may be instances where a copyright holder need not provide eBay with specific item numbers to satisfy the identification requirement. For example, if a movie studio advised eBay that *all* listings offering to sell a new movie (*e.g.,* "Planet X,") that has not yet been released in VHS or DVD format are unlawful, eBay could easily search its website using the title "Planet X" and identify the offensive listings. However, the record in this case indicates that specific item numbers were necessary to enable eBay to identify problematic listings.

Plaintiff has never explained what distinguishes an authorized copy of "Manson" from an unauthorized copy. Initially, in his December 2000 cease and desist letter, Plaintiff only complained about pirated copies of "Manson" in DVD format. (*See* Richter Decl., Ex. C.) Plaintiff did not inform eBay that *all* DVD copies were unauthorized copies; he merely asserted that pirated copies of "Manson" DVDs were being sold on eBay. (*See id.*) Subsequently, Plaintiff sent an e-mail to eBay complaining about a seller who was selling a pirated copy of "Manson" in VHS format. (*See id.* at ¶24 & Ex. I.)[7] But Plaintiff's e-mail did not identify the basis for his claim that the seller was selling a pirated copy of "Manson."

During oral argument, Plaintiff stated that he notified eBay that *all* copies of "Manson" in DVD format are unauthorized. However, the undisputed record in this case shows that Plaintiff did not provide this notification *in writing* before filing suit.[8] A copyright holder must comply with the "written communication" requirement. *See* 17 USC §512(3)(A). The writing requirement is not one of the elements listed under the substantial compliance category. *See id.* Therefore, the Court disregards all evidence that purports to show Plaintiff gave notice that all DVDs violate his copyright in "Manson."[9]

With respect to "Manson" VHS tapes, Plaintiff has admitted that authorized copies of "Manson" have been released in VHS format. (*See* Hendrickson Decl., ¶11 ("certain VHS tapes were infringing[] because some of those had been authorized"; Kim Decl., ¶7.) Therefore, authorized copies of "Manson" in VHS format are available in the marketplace. Plaintiff has offered no explanation to eBay or this Court as to how eBay could determine which "Manson" VHS tapes being offered for sale are unauthorized copies.[10]

Plaintiff raises two more arguments in support of his claim that he need not provide eBay with specific item numbers to satisfy the "identification" requirement under the DMCA. Neither argument has merit.

First, Plaintiff points out that he has sent an e-mail to eBay identifying the eBay user IDs of four alleged infringers. Plaintiff asserts that the identification of user names provides eBay with sufficient information to locate the listings that offered pirated copies of "Manson." (*See* Hendrickson Decl., ¶9(b).) The e-mail in question, dated December 21, 2000, does not satisfy the DMCA's identification requirement. (*See id.*, Ex. G)[11] The e-mail does not identify the listings that are claimed to be the subject of infringing activity; it does not even describe the infringing activity. Moreover, it contains none of the other requisite elements of a proper notification under Section 512(c)(3)(A), *e.g.*, a statement attesting to the good faith and accuracy of the allegations.

Second, Plaintiff contends that eBay can identify listings offering infringing copies of "Manson" for sale without particular item numbers because eBay previously removed two listings even though Plaintiff did not provide the item numbers. (*See* Hendrickson Decl., ¶¶7 & 10.) The first listing, item number 1401275408, was the one that offered a VHS for sale by the seller "vidjointnyc@hotmail.com." (*See id.*, Richter Decl., Ex. J.) As discussed above, eBay found and removed this listing after Plaintiff sent an email complaining about this seller; this seller only had one active advertisement at the time. (*See* Richter Decl., ¶24.) At the time, eBay had no evidence that seller vidjointnyc@hotmail.com was engaging in infringing activity; eBay simply removed the listing out of an abundance of caution. (*See id.*) With respect to the second listing, item number 525181519, the record is not clear as to why eBay removed the listing. Plaintiff's only "evidence" concerning this listing is a single page printout from some unidentified Internet message board that contains a post submitted by an unknown user. (*See* Hendrickson Decl., ¶10 & Ex. J.) Plaintiff's evidence is inadmissible and his conclusion is unsubstantiated.

In sum, the record in this case shows that proper identification under Section 512(c)(3)(A)(iii) should include the specific item numbers of the listings that are allegedly offering pirated copies of "Manson" for sale. It is undisputed that Plaintiff refused to provide specific item numbers of problematic listings before filing suit.[12] Accordingly, the Court holds that Plaintiff failed to comply substantially with Section 512(c)(3)'s identification requirement.[13]

Consequently, eBay did not have a duty to act under the third prong of the safe harbor test. *See* 17 USC §512(c)(1)(C). Thus, if eBay establishes that it meets the remaining prongs of the safe harbor test, eBay would be entitled to judgment in its favor on the copyright claims.

b. The First Prong of the Test: Actual or Constructive Knowledge

Under the DMCA, a notification from a copyright owner that fails to comply substantially with Section 512(c)(3)(A)(ii), (iii) or (iv) "*shall not be considered* under [the first prong of the safe harbor test] in determining whether a service provider has actual knowledge or is aware of the facts or circumstances from which infringing activity is apparent." *See* 17 USC §512(c)(3)(B)(i) & (ii) (emphasis added). As discussed above, Plaintiff's written notifications do not comply substantially with Section (c)(3)(A)(ii)'s adequate identification requirement. Therefore, the Court does not consider those notices when evaluating the actual or constructive knowledge prong of the safe harbor test.

eBay's evidence shows that prior to this lawsuit, it did not have actual or constructive knowledge that particular listings were being used by particular sellers to sell pirated copies of "Manson." The limited information that Plaintiff provided to eBay cannot, as a matter of law, establish actual or constructive knowledge that particular listings were involved in infringing activity. Accordingly, the Court holds that eBay has satisfied the first prong of the safe harbor test under Section 512(c). *See* 17 USC §512(c)(1)(A).

c. The Second Prong of the Test: Right and Ability to Control Infringing Activity

To satisfy the second prong of the test, eBay must show that it "does not receive a financial benefit directly attributable to the infringing activity, *in a case in which the service provider has the right and ability to control such activity*." 17 USC §512(c)(1)(B) (emphasis added). Because the undisputed facts establish that eBay does not have the right and ability to control the infringing activity, the Court need not evaluate the financial benefit element of this prong.

Plaintiff's *only* argument on the "ability to control" issue centers on eBay's ability to remove infringing listings (1) after it receives proper notification of infringing activity and (2) upon detecting an "apparent" infringement on its own. [14] (*See* Opp. at 7.) Plaintiff argues that the record shows eBay has the right and ability to control the infringing activity because it has removed the listings for the sale of various items in the past, including the listings offering pirated copies of "Manson" (in response to Plaintiff's complaints). Plaintiff's argument has no merit.

First, the "right and ability to control" the infringing activity, as the concept is used in the DMCA, cannot simply mean the ability of a service provider to remove or block access to materials posted on its website or stored in its system. To hold otherwise would defeat the purpose of the DMCA and render the statute internally inconsistent. The DMCA specifically requires a service provider to remove or block access to materials posted on its system when it receives notice of claimed infringement. *See* 17 USC §§512(c)(1)(C). The DMCA also provides that the limitations on liability *only* apply to a service provider that has "adopted and reasonably implemented . . . a policy that provides for the termination in appropriate circumstances of [users] of the service provider's system or network who are repeat infringers." *See* 17 USC §512(i)(1)(A). Congress could not have intended for courts to hold that a service provider loses immunity under the safe harbor provision of the DMCA because it engages in acts that are specifically required by the DMCA.

Second, eBay's voluntary practice of engaging in limited monitoring of its website for "apparent" infringements under the VeRO program cannot, in and of itself, lead the Court to conclude that eBay has the right and ability to control infringing activity within the meaning of the DMCA. The legislative history shows that Congress did not intend for companies such as eBay to be penalized when they engage in voluntary efforts to combat piracy over the Internet:

> This legislation is not intended to discourage the service provider from monitoring its service for infringing material. Courts should not conclude that the service provider loses eligibility for limitations on liability under section 512 solely because it engaged in a monitoring program.

House Report 105-796 at 73 (Oct. 8, 1998).

Moreover, as Plaintiff acknowledges, the infringing activities at issue are the sale and distribution of pirated copies of "Manson" by various eBay sellers—which are consummated "offline"—and not the display of any infringing material on eBay's website. (Reply at 3.) Viewing the term "infringing activity" in this context, the undisputed facts demonstrate that eBay does not have the right and ability to control such activity.

Unlike a traditional auction house, eBay is not actively involved in the listing, bidding, sale and delivery of any item offered for sale on its website. eBay's evidence shows that it does not have any control over the allegedly infringing items—the pirate films. (*See* Richter Decl., ¶¶7, 33 & 34.) The evidence also shows that eBay never has possession of, or opportunity to inspect, such items because such items are only in the possession of the seller. (*See id.*) When auctions end, eBay's system automatically sends an email to the high bidder and the seller identifying each other as such. (*See id.* at ¶7.) After that, all arrangements to consummate the transaction are made directly between the buyer and seller. (*See id.*) eBay has no involvement in the final exchange and generally has no knowledge whether a sale is actually completed (*i.e.*, whether payment exchanges hands and the goods are delivered). (*See id.*) If an item is sold, it passes directly from the seller to the buyer without eBay's involvement. (*See id.*) eBay makes money through the collection of an "insertion fee" for each listing and a "final value fee" based on a percentage of the highest bid amount at the end of the auction. (*See id.* at ¶8.)

Plaintiff offers no evidence that establishes the existence of a triable issue of fact on the "ability to control the infringing activity" issue. Accordingly, the Court hold *[sic]* that the record shows that eBay does not have the right and ability to control the infringing activity at issue.

Because eBay has established that it meets the test for safe harbor under Section 512(c), eBay is entitled to summary judgment in its favor on the copyright claims.

C. Plaintiff's Copyright Claims Against Richter and Whitman

The copyright claims against eBay's employees, Richter and Whitman, are based solely on alleged acts and omissions committed in the course and scope of their employment with eBay. Consequently, eBay's immunity from liability for copyright infringement should also extend to Defendants Richter and Whitman. To hold that the safe harbor provision of the DMCA protects the company but not its employees for the same alleged bad acts would produce an absurd result. Congress could not have intended to shift the target of infringement actions from the Internet service providers to their employees when it enacted the safe harbor provisions. Accordingly, the Court holds that Richter and Whitman are also entitled to summary judgment in their favor.

D. Plaintiff's Lanham Act Claim Against eBay and Richter

In Case No. 3, Plaintiff alleges that eBay, Richter and over a dozen third party sellers violated his rights under the Lanham Act, 15 USC §1125. This claim is premised on a "printer-publisher" liability for trademark/trade dress infringement. The Court recently held that eBay and Defendant Richter would be "innocent infringers" within the meaning of 15 USC §1114(2) even if Plaintiff were to establish infringement. *See* July 3, 2001 Order at 17. The Court reached this ruling in part because the undisputed facts showed that eBay had no knowledge of a potential trade dress violation before Plaintiff filed suit. *See id.* Because eBay and Richter are "innocent infringers," Plaintiff's remedy is limited to an injunction against the future publication or transmission of the infringing advertisements on eBay's website. *See* 15 USC §1114(2)(B).

Now, eBay argues that Plaintiff's need for such an injunction has been obviated because eBay has stopped running all the advertisements claimed to be infringing and it has no intention of running the identified advertisements in the future. *See, e.g., Brown v. Armstrong*, 957 F Supp 1293, 1303 n. 8 (D Mass 1997) (Lanham Act false advertisement claim for injunctive relief based on false statements in an infomercial was moot where the infomercial had stopped running and there were no plans to air

it in the future); *Stephen W. Boney Servs. Inc.*, 127 F3d 821, 827 (9th Cir 1997) (grocery store operator's claim for declaratory judgment that it had priority in use of trade name was moot where the competitor had announced that it would rename its stores). eBay's evidence shows that it has removed from its website the allegedly false and misleading advertisements identified by Plaintiff. (*See* Richter Decl., ¶¶38-44.) Plaintiff has offered no evidence that contradicts this showing.

Rather, Plaintiff argues that he is entitled to an injunction that restrains eBay "from *any* further displaying and or transmitting of *any* false and or misleading advertisements in connection with the sale/distribution of 'counterfeit' MANSON DVD's via its websites." (Opp. at 11 (emphasis added).) In short, Plaintiff seeks an injunction enjoining any and all false and/or misleading advertisements that may be posted on eBay's website by users in the future, regardless of whether they are the basis of this lawsuit and whether they have been identified by Plaintiff.

No authority supports Plaintiff's position. Indeed, such an injunction would effectively require eBay to monitor the millions of new advertisements posted on its website each day and determine, on its own, which of those advertisements infringe Plaintiff's Lanham Act rights. As the Court previously noted, "no law currently imposes an affirmative duty on companies such as eBay to engage in such monitoring." July 3, 2001 Order at 15. Further, the Court's recent "innocent infringer" ruling was premised on the Court's determination that eBay has no affirmative duty to monitor its own website for potential trade dress violation and Plaintiff had failed to put eBay on notice that particular advertisements violated his Lanham Act rights before filing suit. The Court holds that Plaintiff is not entitled to the remedy that he seeks. The undisputed facts show that Plaintiff's Lanham Act claim for injunctive relief is moot.

IV. DISPOSITION

Because no triable issues of material fact exist with respect to the eBay Defendants' entitlement to immunity under the DMCA, the Court hereby GRANTS the eBay Defendants' motion for summary judgment on the copyright claims. Additionally, because the undisputed facts establish that Plaintiff's Lanham Act claim is now moot, the

Court hereby GRANTS eBay and Richter's motion for summary judgment on the Lanham Act claim.

IT IS SO ORDERED.

---

[1] This is akin to what users of CB radios do when they give themselves a handle that identifies themselves over the radio waves. Some eBay user IDs referenced in the records of this case include "emailtales" and "luckyboyentertainment," and "vidjointnyc."

[2] In this case, eBay repeatedly characterizes its website as merely an online venue that publishes "electronic classified ads." (*See, e.g.*, Motion at 3.) However, eBay's description grossly oversimplifies the nature of eBay's business. A review of eBay's website shows eBay operates far more than a sophisticated online classified service. (To the extent some of the descriptions about eBay's website are not in the record, the Court takes judicial notice of www.eBay.com and the information contained therein pursuant to Federal Rule of Evidence 201.) Indeed, eBay's website is known first and foremost as an Internet *auction* website. *See, e.g.*, Leslie Walker, *Ebay Goes Off-Line To Train Its Next Block of Dealers*, Wash. Post, Aug. 9, 2001, *available at* 2001 WL 23185584 ("eBay, the giant Internet auction house"); Pradnya Joshi & Charles V. Zehren, *Bidders' Remorse Online Auctions Now No. 1 Source of Internet Fraud*, Newsday, Aug. 30, 2000, *available at* 2000 WL 10031214 ("eBay, the world's largest online auction service"). eBay's own website describes itself as "the world's largest online marketplace." *See* "Overview" page, *at* http://pages.ebay.com/community/aboutebay/overview/index.html. eBay "enables trade on a local, national and international basis" and "features a variety of . . . sites, categories and services that aim to provide users with the necessary tools for efficient online trading in the auction-style and fixed price formats." *Id.* eBay's Internet business features elements of both traditional swap meets—where sellers pay for use of space to display their goods—and traditional auction houses—where goods are sold via the highest bid process.

[3] eBay's Notice of Infringement form quotes the notification provision of the DMCA, as set forth in 17 USC §512(c)(3)(A). (*See* Richter Decl., Ex. B.)

[4] Each listing on eBay's website has its own item number.

[5] In his response to eBay's First Set of Requests for Admissions, Plaintiff explained why he refused to join the VeRO program:

Knowing that EBAY's so called VeRO program is nothing more than a wickedly concealed scheme to defraud unknowledgeable proprietors of Copyrights, out of their LAWFUL rights, Plaintiff refuses to join in, become a member of, participate in, act in concert with, be associated with, lend his name to, or in any way, be a part of a scheme intended to deprive anyone of their hard earned LAWFUL rights.

(Richter Decl., Ex. P at 2.)

[6] In April of this year, the Ninth Circuit in *A&M Records, Inc. v. Napster, Inc.*, 239 F3d 1004 *[7 ILR (P&F) 1]* (9th Cir 2001) extended *Fonovisa* to the Internet context. Napster operates an Internet service that facilitates the transmission and retention of digital audio files by its users. The Ninth Circuit affirmed the district court's conclusion that the plaintiffs—record companies and music publishers—have demonstrated a likelihood of success on the merits of their contributory and vicarious copyright infringement claims against Napster under the standards set forth in *Fonovisa*. The Ninth Circuit declined to reach the question of whether the safe harbor provisions of the DMCA applied, concluding that "this issue will be more fully developed at trial." 239 F3d at 1025.

[7] On January 4, 2001, Plaintiff sent eBay an e-mail complaining about a seller named "vidjointnyc@hotmail.com." who was "still selling pirated copies of my film MANSON in YOUR 'Thieves Market'." (*See* Richter Decl., Ex. I.) After receiving Plaintiff's e-mail, eBay discovered that this seller had one active listing on eBay's website; that listing offered "Charles Manson Family Footage VHS New!!" (*See id.* at ¶24 & Ex. J.) Nowhere in the listing did the seller state he was offering a copy of a film entitled "Manson." (*See id.*) eBay removed the listing at the risk of exposing itself to a lawsuit from the seller even though up until that time Plaintiff had only complained about pirated DVDs, the seller was clearly offering a VHS tape for sale, and the listing made no reference to the title "Manson." (*See id.* at ¶24 & n.1.)

[8] Plaintiff contends that during a January 2001 telephone conversation (shortly after he commenced suit), he told Richter that all copies of "Manson" in DVD format infringe on his copyright because he has never authorized the release of this movie on DVD. (Hendrickson Decl., ¶11.) There is a dispute in the record as to when Plaintiff orally advised eBay that *all* copies of "Manson" in DVD format were unauthorized. (*Compare id. with* Kim Decl., ¶7.) However, the dispute over the dates is immaterial. It is undisputed that Plaintiff has never provided this information in a written communication to eBay as required by Section 512(c)(3).

[9] The Court notes that even though Plaintiff failed to submit proper notice of his claim that all "Manson" in

DVD format are unauthorized, since March 2001, eBay has voluntarily searched its website on a daily basis for all copies of "Manson" in DVD format, removed all such listings and suspended repeat offenders. (*See* April 13, 2001 Declaration of Michael Richter filed in support of the eBay Defendants' Opp. to Motion for Prelim. Injunction, ¶24.) eBay has represented to the Court that it plans to continue to take such action during the pendency of this lawsuit. (*See id.*)

¹⁰ Plaintiff states that during a January 2001 telephone conversation, he informed Richter that all VHS tapes labeled "new" had to be counterfeit. (Hendrickson Decl., ¶11.) Because Plaintiff did not provide this information to eBay in writing, the Court need not consider the deficient notice. Nevertheless, the Court notes that Plaintiff's contention that all "new" VHS tapes must be counterfeit is wholly unsubstantiated. Perhaps Plaintiff has not authorized the release of new VHS copies in recent years. However, it is certainly possible that a seller advertised a "Manson" VHS tape as "new" because the tape remains sealed in its original package. Such a VHS could be an authorized copy.

¹¹ The e-mail states:

Hi, Kai, this is Robert Hendrickson, the copyright owner of the motion picture MANSON. Because of the copyright infringement activity conducted by the following Ebay User Names: emailtales, luckyboyentertainment, stoonod and vidjointnyc via your website, please email me any and ALL information you have on these criminals. Thanks.

(Hendrickson Decl, Ex. G)

¹² Plaintiff provided eBay a list of specific eBay item numbers of allegedly problematic listings on one occasion—he identifies them in his March 5, 2001 written response to the eBay Defendants' request for production of documents. This discovery response pre-dates the filing of Case No. 3. To the extent Plaintiff contends this discovery response constitutes sufficient notice of claims alleged in Case No. 3, the Court rejects Plaintiff's contention. The response was not under oath, it does not attest to a good faith belief that the items identified in the list are pirated copies of "Manson," and it does not attest to the accuracy of the allegations. Such a writing, without more, does not constitute adequate notice under Section 512(c)(3)(A).

¹³ In light of the above ruling, the Court need not address whether Plaintiff's notification satisfied the other elements set forth in Section 512(c)(3)(A), *e.g.*, whether Plaintiff notified eBay's "designated agent." However, during the hearing on this motion, Plaintiff raised a new argument involving the "designated agent" requirement. Plaintiff argued, for the first time, that eBay should not be able to avail itself of the protections of the DMCA because its website failed to identify a "designated agent" until recently. Based on the comments made during oral argument, the Court surmises that Plaintiff's contention is premised on the belief that eBay cannot simply designate "VeRO Department" for the submission of notices of infringement; rather, eBay must identify on its website the name of an individual "agent." Because Plaintiff failed to raise this argument in his papers and failed to submit evidence in support of this argument, the Court declines to consider it. Nevertheless, the Court notes that the record shows that at all relevant times, eBay advised Plaintiff that the notices of infringement should be submitted to the attention of eBay's "VeRo Program." In its emails to Plaintiff, eBay provided a hypertext link to the notice of infringement form on eBay's website. That form identifies the address and fax number for the VeRO Program. Nothing in the DMCA mandates that service providers must designate the name of a person as opposed to a specialized department to receive notifications of claimed infringement. *See* 17 USC §512(c)(2).

¹⁴ In December 2000, eBay voluntarily began searching its website daily, on a limited basis, for listings that appear on their faces to be infringing—"apparent" infringements. (*See* Richter Decl., ¶13.) eBay conducts these searches using generic key words such as "bootleg," "pirated," "counterfeit," and "taped off TV" that may indicate potentially infringing activity. If eBay's staff determines that a seller appears to be offering infringing goods for sale, eBay would remove the listing from its website, notify the seller that the listing has been removed, refund the fees paid for that listing and review the seller's account for possible suspension. (*See id.*)

Kelly

v.

Arriba Soft Corp.

**United States District Court,
Central District of California**

December 15, 1999

4 ILR (P&F) 306

Case No. SA CV 99-560 GLT

[Affirmed in part and reversed in part by the Ninth Circuit in an opinion reported at 9 ILR (P&F) 675, 280 F3d 934. The Ninth Circuit's decision did not address the DMCA issue, however.—Ed.]

"Thumbnail" display of copyrighted images constitutes fair use.

The display of copyrighted images by a "visual search engine" on the Internet constitutes fair use under the Copyright Act. Here, a photographer sued the operator of a visual search engine when defendant's web crawler converted plaintiff's photos into "thumbnail" images and placed them in its image database. In response to a search query, users of defendant's search engine could click on a desired thumbnail and view a window displaying the full-size version of the image, a description of its dimensions, and the URL of the host web site. While the second and third factors of the fair use inquiry (creative nature of the work and amount or substantiality of copying) weigh against fair use, the first and fourth factors (character of use and lack of market harm) weigh in favor of a fair use finding. The first factor is the most important in this case. Defendant never held plaintiff's work out as its own, or even engaged in conduct specifically directed at plaintiff's work. Plaintiff's images were swept up along with millions of others available on the Internet as part of defendant's efforts to provide users with a better way to find images on the Internet. Defendant's purposes were and are inherently transformative. Weighing all of the factors together, the court finds that defendant's conduct constituted fair use of plaintiff's images. — **Kelly v. Arriba Soft Corp., 4 ILR (P&F) 306 [CD Cal, 1999].**

Display of images on search engine does not violate DMCA.

The display of images by a "visual search engine" without their copyright management information does not violate the Digital Millennium Copyright Act (DMCA). Here, a photographer sued the operator of a visual search engine when defendant's web crawler converted plaintiff's photos into "thumbnail" images and placed them in its image database. Because plaintiff's copyright notices did not appear in the images themselves, defendant's crawler did not include them when it indexed the images. As a result, any users retrieving plaintiff's images while using defendant's web site would not see the copyright information. Users who clicked on the thumbnail images would, however, be given the address of the host web site, where any associated copyright information would be available. Section 1202(b)(1) of the DMCA, which prohibits several forms of knowing removal or alteration of copyright information, applies only to the removal of copyright information on a plaintiff's original work, so that provision does not apply here. Although §1203(b)(3) prohibits the knowing removal of copyright information from *copies* of a plaintiff's work, defendant has warned its users about the possibility of use restrictions on the images in its index and has instructed users to check with the originating web sites before copying and using any images. Thus, defendant did not have "reasonable grounds to know" it would cause its users to infringe plaintiff's copyrights. — **Kelly v. Arriba Soft Corp., 4 ILR (P&F) 306 [CD Cal, 1999].**

Steven L. Krongold, Krongold Law Firm, Costa Mesa , California, for plaintiff.

Judith Bond Jennison, Perkins Coie LLP, Menlo Park, California, for defendent.

ORDER ON CROSS-MOTIONS FOR PARTIAL SUMMARY JUDGMENT

GARY L. TAYLOR, District Judge. On apparent first impression, the Court holds the use by an Internet "visual search engine" of others' copyrighted images is a prima facia copyright violation, but it may be justified under the "fair use" doctrine. The Court finds that, under the particular circumstances of this case, the "fair use" doctrine applies, and the Digital Millennium Copyright Act is not violated.

Defendant's Motion for Partial Summary Judgment on Plaintiff's First and Second Claims for Relief is GRANTED. Plaintiff's Motion for Partial Summary Judgment is DENIED.

I. BACKGROUND

Defendant Ditto (formerly known as Arriba) operates a "visual search engine" on the Internet. Like other Internet search engines, it allows a user to obtain a list of related Web content in response to a search query entered by the user. Unlike other Internet search engines, Defendant's retrieves images instead of descriptive text. It produces a list of reduced, "thumbnail" pictures related to the user's query.

During the period when most of the relevant events in this case occurred, Defendant's visual search engine was known as the Arriba Vista Image Searcher. By "clicking" on the desired thumbnail, an Arriba Vista user could view the "image attributes" window displaying the full-size version of the image, a description of its dimensions, and an address for the Web site where it originated.[1] By clicking on the address, the user could link to the originating Web site for the image.[2]

Ditto's search engine (in both of its versions) works by maintaing an indexed database of approximately two million thumbnail images. These thumbnails are obtained through the operation of Ditto's "crawler," a computer program that travels the Web in search of images to be converted into thumbnails and added to the index.[3] Ditto's employees conduct a final screening to rank the most relevant thumbnails and eliminate inappropriate images.

Plaintiff Kelly is a photographer specializing in photographs of California gold rush country and related to the works of Laura Ingalls Wilder. He does not sell the photographs independently, but his photographs have appeared in several books. Plaintiff also maintains two Web sites, one of which (www.goldrush1849.com) provides a "virtual tour" of California's gold rush country and promotes Plaintiff's book on the subject, and the other (www.showmethegold.com) markets corporate retreats in California's gold rush country.

In January 1999, around thirty five of Plaintiff's images were indexed by the Ditto crawler and put in Defendant's image database. As a result, these images were made available in thumbnail form to users of Defendant's visual search engine.

After being notified of Plaintiff's objections, Ditto removed the images from the database, though due to various technical problems some of the images reappeared a few times. Meanwhile Plaintiff, having sent Defendant a notice of copyright infringement in January, filed this action in April. Plaintiff argues its copyrights in the images were infringed by Defendant's actions and also alleges Defendant violated the Digital Millennium Copyright Act (DMCA) by removing or altering the copyright management information associated with Plaintiff's images.[4]

II. DISCUSSION

These cross motions for summary adjudication present two questions of first impression. The first is whether the display of copyrighted images by a "visual search engine" on the Internet constitutes fair use under the Copyright Act. The second is whether the display of such images without their copyright management information is a violation of the Digital Millennium Copyright Act.

Summary judgment is proper if there is no genuine issue of fact and the moving party is entitled to a judgment as a matter of law. Fed. R. Civ. Proc. 56(c). If no material historical facts are disputed, the ultimate conclusion to be drawn on the issue of "fair use" is for the Court and not a jury. *Harper & Row, Publishers, Inc. v. Nation Enterprises*, 471 US 539, 85 L. Ed. 2d 588, 105 S. Ct. 2218 (1985); *Fisher v. Dees*, 794 F.2d 432, 436 (9th Cir. 1986).

A. Fair Use

In order to show copyright infringement, Plaintiff must show ownership of a valid copyright and invasion of one of the exclusive rights of copyright holders. 17 USC §106. Defendant does not dispute the validity of Plaintiff's copyrights or his ownership of them. Defendant also does not dispute it reproduced and displayed Plaintiff's images in thumbnail form without authorization. Plaintiff thus has shown a prima facie case of copyright infringement unless the fair use doctrine applies.

"Fair use" is a limitation on copyright owners' exclusive right "to reproduce the copyrighted work in copies." 17 USC §106(1). It is codified at 17 USC §107, which provides:

> Notwithstanding the provisions of sections 106 and 106A, the fair use of a copyrighted work, including such use by reproduction in copies or phonorecords or by any other means specified by that section, for purpose such as criticism, comment, news reporting, teaching (including multiple copies for classroom use), scholarship, or research, is not an infringement of copyright. In determining whether the use made of a work in any particular case is a fair use the factors to be considered shall include-
>
> (1) the purpose and character of the use, including whether such use is a of a commercial nature or is for nonprofit educational purposes;
>
> (2) the nature of the copyrighted work;
>
> (3) the amount and substantiality of the portion used in relation to the copyrighted work as a whole; and
>
> (4) the effect of the use upon the potential market for or [sic] value of the copyrighted work

The fact that a work is unpublished shall not itself bar a finding of fair use if such finding is made upon consideration of all the above factors.

Fair use is an affirmative defense, and defendants carry the burden of proof on the issue. *American Geophysical Union v. Texaco Inc.*, 60 F 3d 913, 918 (2d Cir 1995); *Columbia Pictures Ind. v. Miramax Films Corp.*, 11 F Supp 2d 1179, 1187 (CD Cal. 1998) ("because fair use is an affirmative defense, Defendants bear the burden of proof on al of its factors"). Based on an analysis of the factors, the Court finds there is fair use here.

1. Purpose and Character of the Use

The first factor considers the nature of the use, including whether the use is commercial or educational. This, however, does not end the inquiry. "Purpose and character" also involve an assessment of whether "the new work merely supersedes the objects of the original creation, or instead adds something new, with a further purpose or different character, altering the first with new expression, meaning, or message; it asks, in other words, whether and to what extent the new work is transformative." *Campbell v. Acuff-Rose Music,* 510 US 569, 579, 127 L. Ed. 2d 500, 114 S. Ct. 1164 (1994) (citation omitted). "The more transformative the new work, the less will be the significance of other factors, like commercialism, that may weigh against a finding of fair use." *Id.* at 579.

There is no dispute Defendant operates its Web site for commercial purposes. Plaintiff's images, however, did not represent a significant element of that commerce, nor were they exploited in any special way.[5] They were reproduced as a result of Defendant's generally indiscriminate method of gathering images. Defendant has a commercial interest in developing a comprehensive thumbnail index so it can provide more complete results to users of its search engine. The Ditto crawler is designed to obtain large numbers of images from numerous sources without seeking authorization.[6] Plaintiff's images were indexed as a result of these methods. While the use here was commercial, it was also of a somewhat more incidental and less exploitative nature than more traditional types of "commercial use."[7]

The Ditto crawler has, in the past, apparently visited sites that were supposed to be blocked. Plaintiff argues this is evidence of bad faith by Defendant and suggests the fair use defense should as a result be precluded. The record shows Defendant made efforts to correct problems of this sort when it became aware of them, and did not act in bad faith.

The most significant factor favoring Defendant is the transformative nature of its use of Plaintiff's images. Defendant's use is very different from the use for which the images were originally created.

Plaintiff's photographs are artistic works used for illustrative purposes. Defendant's visual search engine is designed to catalog and improve access to images on the Internet. Joint Stip. PP 27-29, 32. The character of the thumbnail index is not esthetic, but functional; its purpose is not to be artistic, but to be comprehensive.

To a lesser extent, the Arriba Vista image attributes page also served this purpose by allowing users to obtain more details about an image. The image attributes page, however, raises other concerns. It allowed users to view (and potentially download) full-size images without necessarily viewing the rest of the originating Web page. At the same time, it was less clearly connected to the search engine's purpose of finding and organizing Internet content for users. The presence of the image attributes page in the old version of the search engine somewhat detracts from the transformative effect of the search engine. But, when considering purpose and character of use in a new enterprise of this sort, it is more appropriate to consider the transformative purpose rather than the early imperfect means of achieving that purpose. The Court finds the purpose and character of Defendant's use was on the whole significantly transformative.

The Court finds the first factor weighs in favor of fair use.

2. Nature of the Copyrighted Work

The second factor in §107 is acknowledgment "that some works are closer to the core of intended copyright protection than others, with the consequence that fair use is more difficult to establish when the former works are copied." *Campbell, supra* 510 US at 586. Artistic works like Plaintiff's photographs are part of that core. The Court finds the second factor weighs against fair use.

3. Amount and Substantiality of the Portion Used

The third fair use factor assesses whether the amount copied was "reasonable in relation to the purpose of the copying." *Id.* The analysis focuses on "the persuasiveness of a [copier's] justification for the particular copying done, and the enquiry will harken back to the first of the statutory factors, for. . .the extent of permissible copying varies with the purpose and character of the use." *Id.* at 586-87.

In the thumbnail index, Defendant used Plaintiff's images in their entirety, but reduced them in size. Defendant argues it is necessary for a visual search engine to copy images in their entirety so users can be sure of recognizing them, and the reduction in size and resolution mitigates damage that might otherwise result from copying. As Defendant has illustrated in its brief, thumbnails cannot be enlarged into useful images. Defendant's Memo of P & A, at 3. Use of partial images or images further reduced in size would make images difficult for users to identify, and would eliminate the usefulness of Defendant's search engine as a means of categorizing and improving access to Internet resources.

As with the first factor, the Arriba Vista image attributes page presents a greater problem because it displayed a full-size image separated from the surrounding content on its originating Web page. Image attributes (e.g. dimensions and the address of the originating site) could have been displayed without reproducing the full-size image, and the display of the full image was not necessary to the main purposes of the search engine. [8]

If only the thumbnail index were at issue, Defendant's copying would likely be reasonable in light of its purposes. The image attributes page, however, was more remotely related to the purposes of the search engine. The Court finds the third factor weighs slightly against fair use.

4. Effect of the Use on the Potential Market or Value

The fourth factor inquiry examines the direct impact of the defendant's use and also considers "whether unrestricted and widespread conduct of the sort engaged in by the defendant. . .would result in a substantially adverse impact on the potential market for the original." *Campbell, supra,* 510 US at 590 (citation omitted).

The relevant market is Plaintiff's Web sites as a whole. The photographs are used to promote the products sold by Plaintiff's Web sites (including Plaintiff's books and corporate tour packages) and draw users to view the additional advertisements posted on those Web sites. The fourth factor addresses not just the potential market for a particular photo, but also its "value." The value of Plaintiff's photographs to Plaintiff could potentially be adversely affected if their promotional purposes are undermined.

Defendant argues there is no likely negative impact because its search engines does not compete with Plaintiff's Web sites and actually increases the number of users finding their way to those sites.

Plaintiff argues the market for his various products has been harmed. Defendant's conduct created a possibility that some users might improperly copy and use Plaintiff's images from Defendant's site. Defendant's search engine also enabled users to "deep link" directly to the pages containing retrieved images, and thereby bypass the "front page" of the originating Web site. As a result, these users would be less likely to view all of the advertisements on the Web sites or view the Web site's entire promotional message. However, Plaintiff has shown no evidence of any harm or adverse impact.

In the absence of any evidence about traffic to Plaintiff's Web sites or effects on Plaintiff's businesses, the Court cannot find any market harm to Plaintiff. The Defendant has met its burden of proof by offering evidence tending to show a lack of market harm, and Plaintiff has not refuted that evidence. The Court finds the fourth factor weighs in favor of fair use.

5. Conclusion—Fair Use

The Court finds two of the four factors weigh in favor of fair use, and two weigh against it. The first and fourth factors (character of use and lack of market harm) weigh in favor of a fair use finding because of the established importance of search engines and the "tranformative" nature of using reduced versions of images to organize and provide access to them. The second and third factors (creative nature of the work and amount or substantiality of copying) weigh against fair use.

The first factor of the fair use test is the most important in this case. Defendant never held Plaintiff's work out as its own, or even engaged in conduct specifically directed at Plaintiff's work. Plaintiff's images were swept up along with two million others available on the Internet, as part of Defendant's efforts to provide its users with a better way to find images on the Internet. Defendant's purposes were and are inherently transformative, even if its realization of those purposes was at times imperfect. Where, as here, a new use and new

technology are evolving, the broad transformative purpose of the use weighs more heavily than the inevitable flaws in its early stages of development.

The Court has weighed all of the §107 factors together. The Court finds Defendant's conduct constituted fair use of Plaintiff's images. There is no triable issue of material fact remaining to be resolved on the question of fair use, and summary adjudication is appropriate. Defendant's motion is GRANTED and Plaintiff's motion is DENIED as to copyright infringement claims.

B. Digital Millennium Copyright Act

Enacted on October 28, 1998, the Digital Millennium Copyright Act (DMCA) implements two earlier World Intellectual Property Organization treaties. Section 1202 of the DMCA governs "integrity of copyright management information."[9] Section 1202(a) prohibits falsification of copyright management information with the intent to aid copyright infringement. Section 1202(b) prohibits, unless authorized, several forms of knowing removal or alteration of copyright management information.[10] Section 1203 creates a federal civil action for violation of these provisions.

Plaintiff argues Defendant violated §1202(b) by displaying thumbnails of Plaintiff's images without displaying the corresponding copyright management information consisting of standard copyright notices in the surrounding text. Joint Stip. of Facts, PP 64-69. Because these notices do not appear in the images themselves, the Ditto crawler did not include them when it indexed the images.[11] *Id.* P70. As a result, the images appeared in Defendant's index without the copyright management information, and any users retrieving Plaintiff's images while using Defendant's Web site would not see the copyright management information.

Section 1202(b)(1) does not apply to this case. Based on the language and structure of the statute, the Court holds this provision applies only to the removal of copyright management information on a plaintiff's product or original work. Moreover, even if §1202(b)(1) applied, Plaintiff has not offered any evidence showing Defendant's actions were intentional, rather than merely an unintended side effect of the Ditto crawler's operation.

Here, where the issue is the absence of copyright management information from copies of Plaintiff's works, the applicable provision is §1202(b)(3). To show a violation of that section, Plaintiff must show Defendant makes available to its users the thumbnails and full-size images, which were copies of Plaintiff's work separated from their copyright management information, even though it knows or should know this will lead to infringement of Plaintiff's copyrights. There is no dispute the Ditto crawler removed Plaintiff's images from the context of Plaintiff's Web sites where their copyright management information was located, and converted them to thumbnails in Defendant's index. There is also no dispute the Arriba Vista search engine allowed full-size images to be viewed without their copyright management information.

Defendant's users could obtain a full-sized version of a thumbnailed image by clicking on the thumbnail. A user who did this was given the name of the Web site from which Defendant obtained the image, where any associated copyright management information would be available, and an opportunity to link there.[12] Users were also informed on Defendant's Web site that use restrictions and copyright limitations may apply to images retrieved by Defendant's search engine.[13]

Based on all of this, the Court finds Defendant did not have "reasonable grounds to know" it would cause its users to infringe Plaintiff's copyrights. Defendant warns its users about the possibility of use restrictions on the images in its index, and instructs them to check with the originating Web sites before copying and using those images, even in reduced thumbnail form.

Plaintiff's images are vulnerable to copyright infringement because they are displayed on Web sites. Plaintiff has not shown users of Defendant's site were any more likely to infringe his copyrights, any of these users did infringe, or Defendant should reasonably have expected infringement.

There is no genuine issue of material fact requiring a trial on Plaintiff's DMCA claims, and summary adjudication is appropriate. The Court finds there was no violation of DMCA §1202. Defendant's motion is GRANTED and Plaintiff's motion is DENIED on the DMCA claim.

---

[1] This full-size image was not technically located on Defendant's Web site. It was displayed by opening a link to its originating Web page. But only the image itself, and not any other part of the originating Web page, was displayed on the image attributes page. From the user's perspective, the source of the image matters less than the context in which it is displayed.

[2] Defendant's current search engine, ditto.com, operates in a slightly different manner. When a ditto.com user clicks on a thumbnail, two windows open simultaneously. One window contains the full-size image; the other contains the originating Web page in full.

[3] Images are briefly stored in full on Defendant's server until the thumbnail is made; they are then deleted. Joint Stip. P 32. There is no claim that Defendant provides any access to the full-sized images during this period.

[4] Defendant's request for judicial notice of a Nature article, and Plaintiff's objection to the request, are both inappropriate. The parties have already included this article as Exhibit 5 to their Joint Stipulation of Facts.

[5] The use in this case is commercial, but it is unusual and less serious than many other commercial uses. If, for example, Plaintiff's images were used without authorization in advertising for Defendant's Web site, a finding of fair use would be much less likely.

[6] The parties argue at length about the possibility of blocking the Ditto crawler from a Web site by use of a "robots.txt" file or other methods. Defendant posted instructions on its Web site for blocking the Ditto crawler in March, after Plaintiff's images had already been indexed. Plaintiff's Web sites have never used any of these blocking methods. Joint Stip. P 34.

[7] Defendant also sought to promote a now-discontinued software product called Arriba Express. Arriba Express allowed users to "vaccum" an entire originating Web site and store it on their computers simply by pointing at a thumbnail. Joint Stip. P 45-50, Exh. 18. The images would be stored along with all content from the originating Web site. Arriba Express served a function related to that of the search engine, and Defendant's promotion of it represents a related type of "commercail use."

[8] The newer search engine, ditto.com, appears to lessen this problem by eliminating the image attributes page and simultaneously opening the originating Web page along with a full-size image.

[9] "Copyright management information" is defined, in relevant part, as:

> Any of the following information conveyed in connection with copies. . .of a work. . .or displays of a work, including in digital form. . .

(1) The title and other information identifying the work, including the information set forth on a notice of copyright.

(2) The name of, and other identifying information about, the author of a work.

(3) The name of, and other identifying information about, the copyright owner of the work, including the information set forth in a notice of copyright.

17 USC §1202(c).

[10] Section 1202(b) provides, in relevant part,

No person shall, without the authority of the copyright owner or the law—

(1) intentionally remove or alter any copyright management information,. . .

(3) [sic] distribute. . .copies of works. . .knowing that copyright management information has been removed or altered without authority of the copyright owner or the law, knowing, or, with respect to civil remedies under section 1203, having reasonable grounds to know, that it will induce, enable, facilitate, or conceal an infringement of any right under [federal copyright law].

[11] There was one exception—a version of the "Shasta Rainbow" image obtained by the Ditto crawler from a third-party Web site. The copyright notice for that image was incorporated into the image itself (fine print along the edge of the picture). See Joint Stip. PP 72-73. Plaintiff's allegations of DMCA violations are inapplicable to this image.

[12] Through Defendant's current search engine, ditto.com, the user can nc longer open a full-sized image without also opening the site where its copyright management information is located.

[13] Plaintiff argues Defendant's warnings are insufficient because they do not appear with the thumbnail images on the search result pages produced by the search engine. The Arriba Vista Web site only offered a warning if users clicked on a link to it's [sic] "Copyright" page. This warning may arguably have been place in the wrong place to deter some potential copyright infringers. But this does not necessarily mean Defendant "knew" or "should have known" for purposes of a DMCA violation, especially since Plaintiff offers no evidence of any actual copyright infringement about which Defendant "should have known."

Lexmark International, Inc.
v.
Static Control Components, Inc.
(Preliminary Injunction)

United States District Court,
Eastern District of Kentucky

February 27, 2003

2003 ILRWeb (P&F) 1235

Civil Action No. 02-571-KSF

IP 1.4.4, IP 1.4.7, IP 1.5.3 — Wholesale copying of toner loading programs; infringement.

Plaintiff, a manufacturer of laser printers and toner cartridges, is likely to succeed on the merits of its copyright infringement claim against defendant, which manufactures and sells microchips designed to circumvent the "secret handshake" that ensures usage of plaintiff's authorized toner cartridges with plaintiff's printers. Defendant's microchip, which contains unauthorized copies of plaintiff's copyrighted toner loading programs, enables printer functionality with cartridges manufactured and refilled by other parties. Defendant has failed to prove the invalidity of plaintiff's copyrights covering the toner loading programs. The toner loading programs are not "lock-out" codes; they are not required as part of the authentication sequence performed between the toner cartridge and the printer. Nevertheless, even if they were lock-out codes, defendant's identical copying of plaintiff's toner loading programs went beyond that which was necessary for compatibility because defendant could have achieved a valid authentication sequence without engaging in the verbatim copying of the programs. — **Lexmark International, Inc. v. Static Control Components, Inc. (Preliminary Injunction), 2003 ILRWeb (P&F) 1235 [ED Ky, 2003].**

IP 1.6.1 — Wholesale copying of toner loading programs; fair use.

Defendant's wholesale copying of plaintiff's toner loading programs does not constitute fair use. Plaintiff manufactures laser printers and toner cartridges. Defendant manufactures a microchip containing unauthorized copies of plaintiff's copyrighted toner loading programs to enable printer functionality with cartridges manufactured and refilled by other parties. Three of the four fair use factors weigh heavily in plaintiff's favor: (1) defendant copied the toner loading programs for a commercial purpose; (2) defendant copied the programs in their entirety; and (3) in light those two findings, a likelihood of significant market harm can be presumed. The remaining factor—the nature of the protected work—weighs only slightly in defendant's favor because computer programs are still entitled to some copyright protection, even if this protection does not rise to the level afforded to more traditional literary works. On balance, defendant's actions do not fall under the protective umbrella of the fair use doctrine. — **Lexmark International, Inc. v. Static Control Components, Inc. (Preliminary Injunction), 2003 ILRWeb (P&F) 1235 [ED Ky, 2003].**

IP 1.1, IP 1.5.3 — Toner loading programs entitled to copyright protection.

Plaintiff's toner loading programs are entitled to copyright protection because they could be written in a number of different ways to perform the same function. — **Lexmark International, Inc. v. Static Control Components, Inc. (Preliminary Injunction), 2003 ILRWeb (P&F) 1235 [ED Ky, 2003].**

IP 1.6.2, IP 1.7.1 — Wholesale copying of toner loading programs; copyright misuse defense.

Defendant, which manufactures a microchip containing unauthorized copies of plaintiff's copyrighted toner loading programs, cannot withstand plaintiff's infringement claim based on the defense of copyright misuse. Although plaintiff permits consumers to purchase its toner cartridges at a substantial discount in exchange for their promise to return the cartridge to plaintiff for remanufacturing and recycling, defendant merely alleges that this practice is anticompetitive. Defendant fails to present any factual or legal basis for there being an antitrust violation by plaintiff. Furthermore, plaintiff's efforts to enforce its rights under the Digital Millennium Copyright Act (DMCA) cannot be considered an unlawful act undertaken to stifle competition. — **Lexmark International, Inc. v. Static Control Components, Inc. (Preliminary Injunction), 2003 ILRWeb (P&F) 1235 [ED Ky, 2003].**

IP 1.7.1, IP 1.7.2 — Preliminary injunction bars toner cartridge remanufacturer from making, selling chips.

Plaintiff, a manufacturer of laser printers and toner cartridges, is likely to succeed on the merits of its Digital Millennium Copyright Act (DMCA) claim against defendant, which manufactures and sells microchips designed to circumvent the authentication sequence, or "secret handshake," that ensures usage of plaintiff's authorized toner cartridges with plaintiff's printers. Defendant's microchip contains unauthorized copies of plaintiff's copyrighted toner loading programs so as to enable printer functionality with cartridges manufactured and refilled by other parties. The DMCA broadly prohibits trafficking in a product or device that circumvents "a *technological measure* that effectively *controls access* to a *work protected under this title*." 17 USC §1201(a)(2)(A). The authentication sequence that occurs between plaintiff's printers and microchips contained on authorized toner cartridges constitutes a "technological measure" that "controls access" to a copyrighted work, and plaintiff's toner loading programs and printer engine programs are works "protected under [the Copyright Act]." Defendant admits that its microchips avoid or bypass plaintiff's authentication process. Although defendant argues that the DMCA was intended only to protect copyrighted works such as books, CDs, and motion pictures from piracy, defendant's argument is unconvincing for it would render §1201(a)(2) mere surplusage. Furthermore, defendant's actions do not fall within any of the statutory exceptions. In particular, the reverse engineering exemption under §1201(f) does not apply because defendant's microchip cannot qualify as an "independently created computer program" and because defendant's conduct constitutes copyright infringement. Inasmuch as plaintiff has satisfied the other elements for the issuance of a preliminary injunction, defendant is enjoined from making, selling, distributing, or offering its microchips for sale. — **Lexmark International, Inc. v. Static Control Components, Inc. (Preliminary Injunction), 2003 ILRWeb (P&F) 1235 [ED Ky, 2003].**

KARL S. FORESTER, *Chief Judge.*

**FINDINGS OF FACT
AND CONCLUSIONS OF LAW
FINDINGS OF FACT
I. THE PARTIES**

1. The Plaintiff, Lexmark International, Inc. ("Lexmark") is a Delaware corporation with its principal place of business in Lexington, Kentucky. Lexmark is a worldwide developer, manufacturer, and supplier of, *inter alia,* laser printers and toner cartridges. Lexmark Complaint ("Complaint") ¶ 2.

2. The Lexmark products that are the focus of this dispute are Lexmark's T520/522 and T620/622 laser printers and toner cartridges, and in particular, certain computer codes resident on microchips that are within the toner cartridges. *See generally,*

Complaint ¶¶ 22-23; Declaration of Michael Robert Yaro ("Yaro Dec.") ¶ 1.

3. The Defendant, Static Control Components, Inc. ("SCC") is a North Carolina corporation with its principal place of business in Sanford, North Carolina. SCC manufactures and sells, *inter alia,* components for remanufactured toner cartridges. Affidavit of William K. Swartz ("Swartz Aff.") ¶¶ 4-5.

**II. THE CAUSES OF ACTION AND
PROCEDURAL POSTURE OF THE CASE**

4. In the complaint in this action, filed December 30, 2002, Lexmark asserts three causes of action. Count One alleges that the "SMARTEK" microchip manufactured by SCC (for use in replacement toner cartridges for the T520/522 and T620/622 ("T-Series") Lexmark printers) infringes Lexmark's copyright in its "Toner Loading Programs." Counts Two and Three assert that the SMARTEK microchip

circumvents a technological measure that controls access to Lexmark's Toner Loading Programs and its Printer Engine Program, in violation of the Digital Millennium Copyright Act of 1998, 17 USC §1201 *et seq.* ("DMCA").

5. Concurrent with the filing of its Complaint, Lexmark moved for a preliminary injunction to prevent SCC from manufacturing, distributing, selling, or marketing the SMARTEK microchips.

6. On January 8, 2003, the Court, upon agreement of the parties, entered an order that enjoined SCC from making, selling, distributing, offering for sale, or otherwise trafficking the SMARTEK microchips until the hearing on Lexmark's motion for a preliminary injunction.

7. On February 7, 2003, the Court held an evidence hearing on Lexmark's motion for a preliminary injunction, at which time the parties presented evidence and argument regarding the issue involved in the motion. At the conclusion of the hearing, the Court extended the temporary injunctive relief until February 28, 2003.

III. LEXMARK'S PRODUCTS

8. The computer programs at issue in this case are used by laser printers and are sold either within the laser printers or within toner cartridges that are used with the laser printers.

9. A toner cartridge is a device that is inserted within a laser printer and contains the toner necessary for the printer to print.

10. Lexmark sells two types of toner cartridges for use with its T-Series printers, namely regular cartridges and Prebate cartridges. Lexmark's Reply in Support of its Motion for Preliminary Injunction ("Lexmark Reply"), Ex. G, Second Declaration of Michael Robert Yaro (2nd Yaro Dec.") ¶ 2.

11. Customers can choose to buy either regular cartridges or Prebate cartridges for use with Lexmark's T-Series printers. 2nd Yaro Dec. ¶ 2.

12. Lexmark sells the Prebate cartridges at an up-front discount to consumers. Yaro Dec. ¶ 9, 2nd Yaro Dec. ¶ 2. The up-front discount could amount to approximately $50 depending on the type of toner cartridge. Yaro Dec. ¶ 5.

13. In exchange for this discount, consumers agree to use the Prebate toner cartridge only once

and return the used cartridge to Lexmark for manufacturing and recycling. Yaro Dec. ¶ 9.

14. The Prebate agreement between Lexmark and the consumer is in the form of a shrink-wrap agreement that is placed across the top of every Prebate toner cartridge box.[1] Yaro Dec. ¶ 9.

15. Consumers that find the Prebate conditions objectionable can choose to purchase regular toner cartridges instead of Prebate toner cartridges. Yaro Dec. ¶ 10; 2nd Yaro Dec. ¶ 4.

16. Regular toner cartridges do not contain the "use and return" conditions that accompany the Prebate cartridges. 2nd Yaro Dec. ¶ 4.

17. When consumers purchase regular toner cartridges, they do not receive up-front discounts and are not obligated to return the used regular cartridges to Lexmark. 2nd Yaro Dec. ¶ 4.

18. Consumers can purchase regular toner cartridges and refill them themselves or have them refilled by a third party remanufacturer. 2nd Yaro Dec. ¶ 4.

19. Consumers can purchase regular toner cartridges from numerous resellers or directly from Lexmark. 2nd Yaro Dec. ¶ 4.

20. Third party remanufacturers offer refilled versions of Lexmark's regular toner cartridges for sale. 2nd Yaro Dec. ¶ 4. SCC has sold and continues to sell products for the remanufacturing of Lexmark's regular toner cartridges. Hearing, p. 176, lines 11-20.

21. Lexmark's regular toner cartridges contain microchips that utilize a technological measure. This technological measure, however, does not prevent third parties from remanufacturing the regular cartridges. Neither does this technological measure prohibit consumers from using remanufactured regular cartridges. 2nd Yaro Dec. ¶ 5.

IV. LEXMARK'S PROGRAMS

22. Lexmark's T-Series printers utilize computer programs to control various operations of the printer and to monitor operational characteristics of its associated toner cartridge. The computer programs at issue in this case are the Printer Engine Program and the Toner Loading Programs. Lexmark's Memorandum in Support of its Motion for Preliminary Injunction ("Lexmark Memo"), Ex. B, Declaration of Douglas Able ("Able Dec.") ¶ 4.

23. Lexmark is the legal owner of the Printer Engine Program and the Toner Loading Programs. Lexmark Memo, Exs. D-F.

A. The Printer Engine Program

24. The Printer Engine Program resides within the Lexmark T-Series printers and controls various operations of the printer including, for example, paper feed, paper movement, motor control, fuser operation, and voltage control for the electrophotographic (EP) system. Able Dec. ¶ 5.

25. Slightly different Printer Engine Programs are used in each of the T-Series printers with the differences being minor variations to account for differences in operational characteristics and available options of the particular printer model. Able Dec. ¶ 5.

26. Lexmark has obtained a Certificate of Registration from the Register of Copyrights for its Printer Engine Program. The Printer Engine Program for the T620 model printers is covered by Certificate of Registration No. TX 5-624-273. Lexmark Memo, Ex. F.

27. The Printer Engine Programs used by each of the remaining T-Series models, namely the Lexmark T520/522 and T622 laser printers, are slight modifications of each other and are covered by the copyright registrations either as original or derivative works. Lexmark Memo at 2.

28. Lexmark applied for a Certificate of Registration for the Printer Engine Program under the Rule of Doubt due to trade secret information being contained in the program. Hearing, p. 68, lines 16-23. There has never been any question about the Printer Engine Program's eligibility for copyright protection. Hearing, p. 64, lines 18-25.

29. The Rule of Doubt for computer programs does not mean that it is not copyrightable. It merely means that the Copyright Office cannot determine copyrightability due to the deposit being in human-unreadable object code. Hearing, p. 64, line 18 – p. 65, line 25).

30. The Printer Engine Program contains a substantial amount of computer codes. Hearing, p. 67, lines 4-9.

31. The former head of the Copyright Office, Ralph Oman, in his expert opinion, testified at the preliminary injunction hearing that if the copyright registration application for the Printer Engine Program were filed with twenty (20) pages of its source code, there would be absolutely no question that the Printer Engine Program would have been registered without the Rule of Doubt. According to Oman, under the Copyright Office procedures, the Printer Engine Program meets the test for registrability because the Printer Engine Program contains the requisite amount of original expression. Hearing, p. 68, lines 7-15.

32. SCC does not dispute the copyrightability of the Printer Engine Program. SCC's computer programming expert, Dr. Benjamin Goldberg, has not offered any opinion on the Printer Engine Program and acknowledged at the preliminary injunction hearing that he did not review the Printer Engine Program source code. Hearing, p. 212, lines 14-17.

B. The Toner Loading Programs

33. The Toner Loading Programs reside within microchips attached to the toner cartridges for Lexmark's T-Series printers. Able Dec. ¶ 6. The Toner Loading Programs enable the printers to approximate the amount of toner remaining in the toner cartridges. Hearing, p. 88, lines 16-20; p. 101, lines 7-16. The printers, using the Printer Engine Program, use this information to display a "toner low" condition to the printer screen at the appropriate time. Able Dec. ¶ 6; Hearing, p. 102, lines 16-19.

34. The Toner Loading Programs are located on the toner cartridge for the purpose of allowing for future changes to the Toner Loading Programs should there be changes made to the toner or cartridge characteristics in future aftermarket cartridges. Hearing, p. 124, lines 1-16.

35. The T520/522 model laser printers use one Toner Loading Program and the T620/622 model laser printers use another Toner Loading Program. Different cartridge and toner characteristics dictate the differences between the two Toner Loading Programs. SCC's Opposition Memorandum ("SCC Opp."), App. 6, Tab B, p. 2.

36. The Toner Loading Program for the T520/522 printer contains an embedded "reference tag" or marker to aid Lexmark in detecting copyright infringers. In particular, the T520/522 printers' Toner Loading Program contains the ASCII code sequence "4C 58 4B" that spells out Lexmark's stock market ticker symbol, "LXK." This reference tag

does not affect Toner Loading Programs functionality. Its sole use is as an infringement detection tool. Able Dec. ¶ 7.

37. Lexmark has obtained Certificates of Registration from the Register of Copyrights for its Toner Loading Programs. The Toner Loading Program for the T520/522 model printers is covered by Certificate of Registration No. TX 5-609-284. Lexmark Memo, Ex. D. The Toner Loading Program for the T620/622 model printers is covered by Certificate of Registration No. TX 5-609-285. Lexmark Memo, Ex. E.

1. The Toner Loading Programs are not "Lock-Out Codes"

38. The size of the Toner Loading Program for the T520/522 printers is 37 bytes. None of this Toner Loading Program is used as input to the Secure Hash Algorithm-1 ("SHA-1"), a publicly available government standard, as part of Lexmark's authentication sequence between its T-Series printers and Prebate cartridges.

39. The Toner Loading Program for the T520/522 printers does not function, in whole or in part, as a lock-out code because it is not used in Lexmark's authentication sequence. Hearing, p. 115, line 12 – p. 116, line 1, lines 15-18; Lexmark Reply, Ex. E, Declaration of Bruce Maggs ("Maggs Dec.") ¶ 14.

40. The size of the Toner Loading Program for the T620/622 is 55 bytes. Only 7 of these 55 bytes are used as input to the SHA-1 as part of Lexmark's authentication sequence. Hearing, p. 112, line 22 – p. 113, line 6.

41. It does not matter what the values are for these 7 bytes of Toner Loading Program for the T620/622, which are used as an input to the SHA-1. These bytes could be any values at all. The contents of the Toner Loading Program are irrelevant to the authentication sequence. Hearing, p. 113, lines 11-25; Maggs Dec. ¶ 14.

42. The Toner Loading Program for the T620/622 printers does not function as a lock-out code because it is neither necessary nor required in Lexmark's authentication sequence.

43. For purposes of Lexmark's authentication sequence, it is irrelevant whether a Toner Loading Programs is even stored on the toner cartridge. The authentication sequence can work correctly irrespective of the existence of a Toner Loading Program on the cartridge. Hearing, p. 113, lines 11-25; Maggs Dec. ¶ 14.

44. The Toner Loading Programs for the T520/522 and the T620/622 are readable directly from the microchips on the toner cartridges. Hearing, p. 115, lines 4-11.

45. The key to understanding Lexmark's authentication sequence is an 8-byte secret code called the Derived Secret. Hearing, p. 111, lines 17-24.

2. The Toner Loading Programs may be Expressed in Different Ways

46. Lexmark made a series of design choices when writing the Toner Loading Programs for purposes of estimating the amount of toner remaining in a toner cartridge. Maggs Dec. ¶ 23.

47. The Toner Loading Programs contain creative expression because of the creative choices made by Lexmark during the development of the Toner Loading Programs. Hearing, p. 88, line 21 – p. 89, line 3; p. 102, line 20 – p. 103, line 21.

48. The Toner Loading Programs may be expressed in different ways to perform the same function, namely estimating the amount of toner remaining in toner cartridges. Hearing, p. 101, lines 17-24; Maggs Dec. ¶ 30. Lexmark's computer programming expert, Dr. Bruce Maggs, in his testimony and his declaration, outlined a number of different possible methods of performing this function. These methods include applying other mathematical equations than the ones chosen by Lexmark, using a look-up table, and even abandoning the torque reading system relied upon by Lexmark in favor of an altogether different system. Hearing, p. 89, line 4 – p. 90, line 6, Maggs Dec. ¶ 30. Dr. Maggs also demonstrated that other options exist for expressing the Toner Loading Program even when the same approximation technique is used and the same formulas and constants are employed. Hearing, p. 104, lines 13-17, p. 105, lines 11-22; Maggs Dec. ¶ 30.

49. SCC's computer programming expert, Dr. Benjamin Goldberg, acknowledged, with some reservations regarding efficiency, that other ways of writing the Toner Loading Programs were possible. Hearing, p. 206, line 6 – p. 207, line 2. Dr. Goldberg also suggested that the Toner Loading

Programs would have been expressed differently by writing the Toner Loading Programs in a programming language other than Lexmark's custom programming language. Hearing, p. 209, lines 5-20.

50. Lexmark's unique computer programming language and its selection and arrangement of appropriate approximation techniques, including the selection, arrangement, and particular expression of formulas, constants, and variables that comprise the Toner Loading Programs constitutes creative expression and is entitled to copyright protection.

3. The Copyright Office Considered Copyrightability Issues of the Toner Loading Programs

51. The Copyright Office considered copyrightability issues when it examined the Toner Loading Programs and granted Certificates of Registration for those programs. Hearing, p. 69, line 6 – p. 71, line 12; Lexmark Reply, Ex. F., Declaration of Ralph Oman ("Oman Dec.") ¶ 18, 54. The correspondence between the Copyright Office and Lexmark describes the issues that the Copyright Office addressed with Lexmark. Oman Dec. ¶ 53; SCC Opp., App. 6.

52. The Copyright Office considered whether the Toner Loading Programs were mere mathematical formulas, and informed Lexmark that mathematical formulas are not copyrightable. Oman Dec. ¶ 62; SCC Opp., App. 6, Tab A.

53. The Copyright Office reviewed the information submitted by Lexmark and determined that both Toner Loading Programs constituted more than mere mathematical formulas. Rather, the programs were determined to contain source code and a series of symbols and numerical indicia that implement a particular formula, and that "set of . . . instructions to be used directly or indirectly in a computer in order to bring about a certain result," contains enough original authorship to qualify for copyright protection. Hearing, p. 75, line 13 – p. 76, line 12; Oman Dec. ¶ 62; *see* 17 USC §101 (definition of computer program).

54. The Copyright Office's examining manual provides that a set of statements and instructions in a computer program that implement a mathematical formula or algorithm is entitled to copyright protection. For example, the Copyright Office will register "a program that calculates the orbit of a rocket" or "a program that computes wages and salaries for a payroll," even if the program uses a formula or an algorithm to perform these calculations. Hearing, p. 75, line 16 – p. 76, line 12; Lexmark Reply, Ex. C., *Compendium of Copyright Office Practices* §321 at 300-16.

55. The Copyright Office considered merger issues, and sought to determine if the expressive elements in the Toner Loading Programs were dictated by the functional aspects of the printer or the toner cartridge. Hearing, p. 76, line 24 – p. 77, line 19; Oman Dec. ¶ 65.

56. The Copyright Office reviewed the information submitted by Lexmark and determined that both Toner Loading Programs contain a sufficient amount of original expression, and that Lexmark's expression does not merge with the ideas, procedures, processes, systems, or methods of operations that it has expressed. Hearing, p. 76, line 13 – p. 77, line 19; Oman Dec. ¶ 65.

57. The Copyright Office considered the two Toner Loading Programs to be independently copyrightable when it issued the Certificates of Registration for both programs. Hearing, p. 70, lines 5-15; Oman Dec. ¶ 58.

V. LEXMARK'S AUTHENTICATION SEQUENCE

58. Lexmark's authentication sequence prevents the unauthorized access to its Printer Engine Programs and Toner Loading Programs and is the subject of the DMCA counts in this case.

59. To protect the Printer Engine Programs and Toner Loading Programs and to prevent unauthorized toner cartridges from being used with Lexmark's T-Series printers, Lexmark uses an authentication sequence that runs each time a toner cartridge is inserted into a Lexmark printer, the printer is powered on, or whenever the printer is opened or closed. Able Dec. ¶ 8.

60. The first step of the authentication sequence requires the printer and the microchip on the toner cartridge to calculate a Message Authentication Code ("MAC"). Hearing, p. 107, lines 8-12; Maggs Dec. ¶ 6.

61. The second step requires the microchip on the toner cartridge to communicate its MAC to the printer. Hearing, p. 107, lines 13-17; Maggs Dec. ¶ 6.

62. The third step requires the printer to compare the MAC that it calculated with the MAC it received from the microchip on the toner cartridge. Hearing, p. 107, lines 18-19; Maggs Dec. ¶ 6.

63. The authentication sequence succeeds if the MAC calculated by the printer matches the MAC calculated by the microchip on the toner cartridge. Hearing, p. 107, line 20 – p. 108, line 9; Maggs Dec. ¶ 6.

64. The MAC computations on both the printer and the toner cartridge are calculated by using the SHA-1. Maggs Dec. ¶ 7.

65. There are six pre-defined inputs to the SHA-1 that are used to calculate the MAC on the Lexmark microchips. Hearing, p. 110, lines 7-24; Maggs Dec. ¶ 9. Those pre-defined inputs are located in certain memory portions on the Lexmark microchip. Hearing, p. 110, line 19 – p. 111, line 14; Maggs Dec. ¶ 9.

66. The Printer Engine Program uses these same six pre-defined inputs to calculate the MAC on the printer side. Hearing, p. 116, lines 2-8.

67. The contents of the Toner Loading Program are irrelevant to the SHA-1 for calculating the MAC. Maggs Dec. ¶ 14.

68. The effectiveness of Lexmark's authentication sequence has been widely acknowledged by aftermarket cartridge microchip manufacturers. Lexmark Memo, Ex. H.

A. Lexmark's Authentication Sequence Controls Access to Lexmark's Printer Engine Program

69. If the MAC calculated by the microchip matches the MAC calculated by the printer, the cartridge is authenticated and authorized for use by the printer. Able Dec. ¶ 8. The printer is then capable of running the Printer Engine Program to thereby print. Hearing, p. 108, lines 6-9, p. 107, line 22 – p. 108, line 1, p. 128, lines 8-12; Able Dec. ¶ 8.

70. If, on the other hand, the two MAC calculations do not match, the printer will issue an error message and will not run the Printer Engine Program. Hearing, p. 108, lines 10-17; Able Dec. ¶ 8.

71. By design, unless this authentication sequence successfully occurs, the printer will not recognize the toner cartridge as being an authorized cartridge and access to the Printer Engine Program will be disabled. Able Dec. ¶ 9.

B. Lexmark's Authentication Sequence Controls Access to Lexmark's Toner Loading Programs

72. If the MAC calculated by the microchip on the toner cartridge matches the MAC calculated by the printer, then the cartridge is authenticated and authorized for use by the printer. Able Dec. ¶ 8. The printer can then access the Toner Loading Program to monitor the toner status of the authenticated toner cartridge. Hearing, p. 107, line 22 – p. 108, line 1, p. 128, lines 8-12; Able Dec. ¶ 8.

73. If, on the other hand, the MAC calculated by the printer does not match the MAC calculated by the microchip on the toner cartridge, the printer will issue an error message and the printer will not access the Toner Loading Program for toner status monitoring. Able Dec. ¶ 8.

74. By design, unless this authentication sequence successfully occurs, the printer will not recognize the toner cartridge as being an authenticated cartridge and the Toner Loading Program will not be accessed. Able Dec. ¶ 9.

C. The "Checksum" Operation is not Part of Lexmark's Authentication Sequence nor is it a Secondary Authentication Sequence

75. Following the successful completion of Lexmark's authentication sequence, the Printer Engine Program may download a copy of the Toner Loading Program from the microchip on the toner cartridge if a certain bit on the microchip is set. Hearing, p. 107, line 22 – p. 108, line 1, p. 120, line 4 – p. 121, lines 5-11.

76. In the event that the Toner Loading Program is downloaded from the toner cartridge, the Printer Engine Program will perform a checksum operation to ensure the integrity of the Toner Loading Program. Hearing, p. 117, line 24 – p. 118, line 16, p. 122, lines 8-11; Maggs Dec. ¶ 16.

77. Checksum operations are commonly used techniques to ensure data integrity when data is transmitted from one point to another. Hearing, p. 146, lines 8-16; Maggs Dec. ¶ 16.

78. The checksum operation can be summarized as follows: When a message is transmitted, a

numerical checksum value is also transmitted. This checksum value represents the result of a mathematical computation that is performed on the bits in the transmitted message. Upon receiving the transmitted message, the receiving station performs the same mathematical computation on the bits in the transmitted message and compares the computed result with the transmitted checksum value. If the result matches, then the receiving station has some assurance that the transmitted message is accurate. If not, the receiving station assumes that the message was somehow corrupted. Hearing, p. 94, line 24 – p. 95, line 15; Maggs Dec. ¶ 16.

79. The memory map for the microchips on Lexmark's toner cartridges identifies the existence of the checksum value, and specifies the checksum's location and size. Hearing, p. 118, line 23 – p. 120, line 1; Maggs Dec. ¶ 17.

80. If the checksum operation performed by the Printer Engine Program results in a value that matches the checksum value stored in the microchip on the toner cartridge, the Printer Engine Program assumes that the integrity of the Toner Loading Program was not compromised and continues operation. Hearing, p. 125, lines 12-16; Maggs Dec. ¶ 16.

81. If, on the other hand, the checksum operation performed by the Printer Engine Program results in a value that does not match the checksum value stored in the microchip on the toner cartridge, the Printer Engine Program assumes that the integrity of the Toner Loading Program was somehow compromised. Maggs Dec. ¶ 16. As a result, the Printer Engine Program issues a "32 Unsupported Print Cartridge" message. Hearing, p. 122, line 20 – p. 123, line 3; Maggs Dec. ¶ 17.

82. The "secondary authentication sequence" referred to at the hearing by SCC's computer programming expert, Dr. Benjamin Goldberg, is the checksum operation used by Lexmark to determine data integrity. Hearing, p. 192, lines 2-14, p. 197, lines 7-12, p. 203, lines 11-14.

83. The checksum process could successfully process any arbitrary computer program, whether or not toner related. The particular Toner Loading Programs used by Lexmark are not required for the checksum process to be successfully completed. The checksum process could be successfully completed for any Toner Loading Program as long

as the proper checksum value was provided in the microchip. Hearing, p. 118, line 19 – p. 119, line 3, p. 125, line 21-24; Maggs Dec. ¶ 18.

84. There was some dispute at the hearing between Dr. Goldberg and Lexmark's computer programming expert, Dr. Bruce Maggs, as to the particular computation that the Printer Engine Program performs in determining the checksum value. Dr. Maggs testified that the Printer Engine Program performs a calculation, other than an SHA-1 computation, to determine the checksum value. Dr. Goldberg, on the other hand, testified that the Printer Engine Program performs an SHA-1 computation to determine the checksum value and therefore the checksum computation was a secondary authentication sequence. Hearing, p. 194, lines 10-16.

85. The Court finds little value in this distinction because the method used to calculate the checksum value is irrelevant. Hearing, p. 148, lines 2-9. Knowledge of the particular mathematical computation performed by the checksum process would not be needed to incorporate a different Toner Loading Program. Hearing, p. 148, lines 6-9.

86. Because the checksum value used in Lexmark's microchips is only eight (8) bits long, there are only a total of 256 possible values that the checksum value could have. Hearing, p. 121, lines 15-25. Accordingly, if one wanted to use another Toner Loading Programs, the checksum value could be determined by trial and error and without having to know the actual method used to calculate the checksum value. Hearing, p. 121, lines 17-25.

87. Dr. Goldberg's byte-by-byte analysis of Lexmark's Toner Loading Programs did not pass the checksum check because Dr. Goldberg did not make a corresponding change to the checksum. If a checksum is not updated corresponding to a change in the Toner Loading Programs, the checksum operation will fail and the printer will issue a "32 Unsupported Cartridge Error" message. Hearing, p. 122, lines 1-24.

88. Dr. Goldberg does not dispute that with an understanding of the checksum, a different toner loading program having a correct checksum value could be employed. Dr. Goldberg acknowledges that with knowledge of the checksum information, it would only be a matter of 256 tries. Hearing, p. 197, lines 19-21.

89. It would be extraordinarily difficult to determine the existence and location of the checksum value on Lexmark's microchips without any contextual information to assist in determining the meaning and significance of the bytes on the microchips.

VI. SCC's SMARTEK MICROCHIPS

90. SCC manufactures and sells components for use in the remanufacturing of toner cartridges for Lexmark's T-Series printers. One such component is its SMARTEK microchip, which is used to replace the microchip found in Lexmark's toner cartridges. SCC sells one SMARTEK microchip for use with Lexmark's T520/522 toner cartridges and another SMARTEK microchip for use with Lexmark's T620/622 toner cartridges. SCC Opp. at 1.

91. SCC's Imaging Supplies Division, which is one of two divisions in SCC, manufactures and sells a multitude of other products and parts to the toner cartridge remanufacturing industry. According to William Schwartz, the president of this division, SCC's product line includes over 3,000 products. Hearing at p. 163, lines 21-24, p. 164, lines 3-5.

A. SCC's SMARTEK Microchip Contains Identical Copies of Lexmark's Toner Loading Programs

92. SCC acknowledges that it copied Lexmark's Toner Loading Programs "in the exact format and order" in its SMARTEK microchips. Hearing, p. 196, line 22 – p. 197, line 1; SCC Opp. at 4 & 19.

93. The SMARTEK microchip for use with Lexmark's T520/522 toner cartridges contains an identical copy of Lexmark's T520/522 Toner Loading Program that is covered by Registration No. TX 5-6090284. Able Dec. ¶ 12.

94. The SMARTEK microchip for use with Lexmark's T520/522 printers toner cartridges also contains the ASCII code sequence "4C 58 4B" that spells out Lexmark's stock market ticker symbol, "LXK." Able Dec. ¶ 14; SCC Opp. at 4.

95. The SMARTEK microchip for use with Lexmark's T620/622 toner cartridges contains an identical copy of Lexmark's T620/622 Toner Loading Program that is covered by Registration No. TX 5-624-273. Able Dec. ¶ 12.

96. SCC admits that it had access to Lexmark's Toner Loading Programs and that it "slavishly copied" Lexmark's Toner Loading Programs. SCC Opp., App. 2 ¶7; SCC Opp. at 11.

97. According to one SCC press release dated October 10, 2002, the "new" SMARTEK microchip was introduced to be compatible with Lexmark's new firmware release for the T-Series printers. SCC was able to introduce its SMARTEK microchip within five (5) months after this new firmware release from Lexmark. Lexmark Memo, Ex. 1.

B. SCC's SMARTEK Microchip Circumvents Lexmark's Authentication Sequence

98. SCC acknowledges that it specifically designed its SMARTEK microchip to circumvent Lexmark's authentication sequence. SCC Opp. at 2-4.

99. SCC acknowledges that its SMARTEK microchip has no commercial purpose other than to circumvent Lexmark's authentication sequence. SCC Opp. at 2-4.

100. The SMARTEK microchip's method of circumvention involves the use of technology that mimics the authentication sequence performed by an original microchip on Lexmark's T-Series toner cartridges and the printer. SCC Opp. at 2-4.

101. Each time a consumer installs an unauthorized toner cartridge containing a SMARTEK microchip into a Lexmark T-Series laser printer, powers on, or opens and closes the printer containing such an unauthorized toner cartridge, the SMARTEK microchip circumvents Lexmark's authentication sequence, the technological measure that controls access to both the Printer Engine Program and the Toner Loading Program. Hearing, p. 90, line 2 – p. 91, line 1.

102. By circumventing Lexmark's technological measure, the SMARTEK microchip enables various printer functions by providing access to both Lexmark's Printer Engine Program resident on the controller board in the Lexmark's T-Series laser printers and the unauthorized copy of Lexmark's Toner Loading Programs resident on the SMARTEK microchip. Hearing, p. 128, lines 8-16.

103. SCC sells and markets its SMARTEK microchips for use in circumventing Lexmark's authentication sequence. According to one SCC advertisement, the SMARTEK microchip circumvents the "secret code," which "even on the fastest computer available today . . . would take

Years to run through all of the possible 8-byte combinations to break . . . ." Lexmark Memo, Ex. K (emphasis in original).

104. According to another SCC advertisement, the SMARTEK microchips are "[c]hips that send the *right* messages [to Lexmark's T-Series printers]. Lexmark Memo, Ex. S (emphasis in original).

VII. SCC'S PETITION TO EXEMPT ITS SMARTEK MICROCHIPS FROM COVERAGE UNDER THE DMCA

105. On January 23, 2003, SCC applied to the Copyright Office for an exemption to cover both the specific allegations lodged in this case with respect to toner cartridges and printers and, more broadly, embedded software without independent market value.

106. On February 5, 2003, the Copyright Office granted SCC's petition and will consider SCC's request to exempt its SMARTEK microchips from the prohibitions under the DMCA. Hearing, p. 9, lines 4-18.

VIII. THE BALANCE OF POTENTIAL HARMS

A. Lexmark

107. Lexmark expended significant time and financial resources developing its Printer Engine Program, Toner Loading Programs and the authentication sequence designed to prevent unauthorized access to the programs. Yaro Dec. ¶ 15.

108. Lexmark sells a significant number of toner cartridges for its T-Series printers under the Prebate agreement with consumers where the consumers agree to use the toner cartridge only once and then return the used cartridge to Lexmark for remanufacturing and recycling. Yaro Dec. ¶ 9. Approximately 90% of the toner cartridges sold by Lexmark for its T-Series printers are Prebate cartridges. Hearing, p. 19, lines 14-18.

109. The SMARTEK microchip allows consumers to reuse refilled Prebate cartridges without returning those cartridges for remanufacturing to Lexmark in accordance with the Prebate agreement. Yaro Dec. ¶ 16.

110. Lexmark's remanufacturing program is dependent upon the return of used Prebate cartridges, and consumers' failure to return those used Prebate cartridges to Lexmark may significantly increase the cost of Lexmark's remanufacturing process and may limit Lexmark's ability to compete for remanufactured toner cartridges. Yaro Dec. ¶ 16.

111. In addition, third parties can sell reused Prebate cartridges containing the SMARTEK microchip to consumers in direct competition with Lexmark's authorized remanufactured toner cartridges. Yaro Dec. ¶ 14.

112. The sale of unauthorized toner cartridges at reduced prices to consumers could result in fewer customer orders for authorized Lexmark remanufactured toner cartridges and could significantly damage Lexmark's remanufactured toner cartridge sales for its T-Series printers. Yaro Dec. ¶ 14.

B. SCC

113. The issuance of a preliminary injunction will result in substantial lost profits for SCC on the sale of its SMARTEK microchip. Hearing, p. 161.

114. In addition to causing lost profits on the sale of the SMARTEK microchip and related components, the issuance of a preliminary injunction could affect SCC's sales of other components for older Lexmark cartridges, and have a depressing effect on the remanufacturing industry as a whole. Hearing, p. 160-61.

CONCLUSIONS OF LAW

1. This Court has subject matter jurisdiction over this action pursuant to 28 USC §§1331, 1338(a), and 17 USC §1203(a) and has personal jurisdiction over SCC.

2. Venue in this jurisdiction is proper under 28 USC §§1391 and 1400(a).

I. PRELIMINARY INJUNCTION STANDARD

3. In considering Lexmark's Motion for a Preliminary Injunction, four factors must be considered: (1) Lexmark's likelihood of success on the merits; (2) whether Lexmark will suffer irreparable harm if the injunction is not issued; (3) the public interest; and (4) the possibility of substantial harm to others. *Forry, Inc. v. Neundorfer, Inc.*, 837 F2d 259, 262 (6th Cir 1988).

4. These factors are to be balanced and the relative strength of one or more factors can offset

the weakness of another. *In re DeLorean Motor Co.,* 755 F2d 1223, 1229 (6th Cir 1985).

5. The "likelihood of success" factor should be given the strongest weight in balancing all four tests, because irreparable harm and inadequate remedies at law can be presumed in cases involving registered copyrights and violations of the anti-trafficking provisions of the DMCA. *See Forry,* 837 F2d at 267 (irreparable injury presumed in copyright infringement cases when the plaintiff establishes a likelihood of success on the merits); *Universal City Studios, Inc. v. Reimerdes,* 82 F Supp 2d 211, 215 *[4 ILR (P&F) 399]* (SD NY 2000) (irreparable injury presumed when the plaintiff establishes a likelihood of success on DMCA claims); *Tree Publishing Co., Inc. v. Warner Bros. Records,* 785 F Supp 1272, 1276-77 (MD Tenn 1991) (citing *Johnson Controls, Inc. v. Phoenix Control Sys., Inc.,* 886 F2d 1173, 1174 (9th Cir 1989)) ("plaintiff's burden for obtaining a preliminary injunction in most copyright cases collapses into the showing of a substantial likelihood of success on the merits, and that issue becomes determinative.").

II. LEXMARK HAS DEMONSTRATED A LIKELIHOOD OF SUCCESS ON THE MERITS OF ITS COPYRIGHT INFRINGEMENT CLAIM

6. The manufacture and/or sale of an unauthorized copy that is substantially similar to a protected work constitutes copyright infringement. *See* 17 USC §§106, 501(a).

7. To establish copyright infringement, Lexmark must prove (1) that it owns a valid copyright, and (2) that SCC copied protectable elements of the copyrighted work. *Feist Publ'n, Inc. v. Rural Tel. Serv. Co.,* 499 US 340, 361 *[1 ILR (P&F) 180]* (1991); *Robert R. Jones Assocs., Inc. v. Nino Homes,* 858 F2d 274, 276-77 (6th Cir 1988).

A. Lexmark's Toner Loading Programs are Entitled to Copyright Protection

8. "A 'computer program' is a set of statements of instructions to be used directly or indirectly in a computer in order to bring about a certain result." 17 USC §101.

9. A computer program, whether in object code or source code, is a "literary work" and is protected from unauthorized copying, whether from the object or source code version. *Apple Computer, Inc. v.*

Franklin Computer Corp., 714 F2d 1240, 1249 (3d Cir 1983).

10. "To qualify for copyright protection, a work must be original to the author." *Feist,* 499 US at 345. "Original, as the term is used in copyright, means only that the work was independently created by the author . . . and that it possesses at least some minimal degree of creativity." *Id.*

11. "[T]he requisite level of creativity is extremely low; even a slight amount will suffice." *Id.* Indeed, "[t]he vast majority of works made the grade quite easily, as they possess some creative spark, 'no matter how crude, humble or obvious' it might be." *Id.; SAS Inst., Inc. v. S&H Computer Sys., Inc.,* 605 F Supp 816, 825 (MD Tenn 1985) (determining that a program contained copyrightable expression and noting that "[e]ven in the case of simple statistical calculations, there is room for variation, such as the order in which arithmetic operations are performed.").

12. Lexmark's unique creative computer programming language and its selection and arrangement of appropriate approximation techniques, including the selection, arrangement, and particular expression of formulas, constants, and variables that comprise the Toner Loading Programs contain the requisite amount of creativity for the Toner Loading Programs to qualify for copyright protection.

13. The Certificates of Registration for Lexmark's Toner Loading Programs constitute *prima facie* evidence of copyright originality and validity. *See, e.g., Johnson Controls,* 866 F2d at 1175. The burden therefore rests upon SCC to demonstrate that the Toner Loading Programs are not entitled to copyright protection. *See, e.g., Ets-Hokin v. Skyy Spirits, Inc.,* 225 F3d 1068, 1075-76 (9th Cir 2000) ("A certificate of copyright registration . . . shifts to the defendant the burden to prove the invalidity of the plaintiff's copyrights.").

14. Lexmark is likely to succeed at trial on the merits of its copyright infringement claim because SCC has failed to prove the invalidity of the Lexmark copyrights covering the Toner Loading Programs.

1. The Toner Loading Programs are not Lock-Out Codes

15. SCC's primary defense to Lexmark's copyright infringement claim is that the Toner

Loading Programs are lock-out codes, and that the exact Toner Loading Program is required as a part of the authentication sequence performed between the toner cartridges and the printer.

16. The Toner Loading Programs are not required as a part of the authentication sequence. Hearing, p. 118, lines 5-18. Any Toner Loading Program could be used that would result in a valid authentication sequence and a valid checksum operation. Hearing, p. 125, lines 17-24.

17. SCC does not deny that a valid authentication sequence and valid checksum operation could occur with any Toner Loading Program being used. Rather, SCC argues that there is no way that it could have known this because of the technological complexity of the microchips on Lexmark's toner cartridges. SCC Opp. at 5.

18. Innocent infringement, however, is still infringement. *See, e.g., Repp. v. Webber*, 132 F2d 883, 889 (2d Cir 1997) ("The fact that infringement is "subconscious' or 'innocent' does not affect liability. . . ."); *Los Angeles News Serv. v. Conus Communications Co.*, 969 F Supp 579, 584 (CD Cal 1997) ("[T]he innocent intent of the defendant will not constitute a defense to a finding of liability." (quoting 3 Melville B. Nimmer & David Nimmer, *Nimmer on Copyright* §13.08 (1996))).

19. SCC's claim that it would have been extraordinarily difficult to know, without having access to Lexmark's confidential documents, that the Toner Loading Programs are not needed for a valid authentication sequence and a valid checksum operation to occur does not excuse infringement or change the fact that the Toner Loading Programs are not actually lock-out codes.

20. SCC's incomplete analysis of Lexmark's microchips is no excuse for being unable to determine that the Toner Loading Programs are not lock-out codes. *See, e.g., Brooktree Corp. v. Advanced Micro Devices, Inc.*, 977 F2d 1555, 1570 (Fed Cir 1992) (in context of the Semiconductor Chip Prevention Act, 17 USC §§901-914, declining to find that the accused infringer had, as a matter of law, a defense against infringement when it spent two and a half years and in excess of three million of dollars to reverse engineer its competitor's chip—"an element of the defense of reverse engineering [is] that the product be original . . . The statute does not reflect an intent to excuse copying as a matter

of law, if the copier had first tried and failed to do the job without copying.").

21. The Toner Loading Programs do not need to be copied in whole or in part for a valid authentication sequence and a valid checksum to occur.

22. The lock-out cases relied upon by SCC are irrelevant because Lexmark's Toner Loading Programs do not function as lock-out codes. *See Sega Enters. Ltd. v. Accolade, Inc.*, 977 F2d 1510 *[1 ILR (P&F) 450]* (9th Cir 1992); *Atari Games Corp. v. Nintendo of Am.*, No. C88-4805 FMS, C89-0027 FMS, 1993 U.S. Dist. LEXIS 8183 (ND Cal Apr. 15, 1993). *Sega* and *Atari* do not apply in the instant case because the plaintiffs' computer programs in those cases were, either in their entirety or in part, security codes that were required to circumvent the lock-out measures that prevented the use of unauthorized products with the plaintiffs' game systems. This is simply not the case here where the use of any Toner Loading Program could still result in a valid authentication sequence and a valid checksum.

23. In *Sega,* the accused infringing activity focused on "intermediate copying" engaged in by the accused infringer for the sole purpose of reverse engineering. *Sega,* 977 F2d at 1522 ("[Defendant] copied [plaintiff's] software solely in order to discover the functional requirements for compatibility."). The *Sega* Court, after a lengthy overview of the copyright fair use factors and public policy concerns, allowed this narrow exception of copying a copyrighted program for the limited purpose of allowing reverse engineering activities to analyze ideas embedded in computer programs. *Sega* did not involve allegations of an accused infringer copying a protected work and then incorporating that very work into a produced offered for sale. *Sega,* 977 F2d at 1515.

24. The instant case, on the other hand, does not deal with any intermediate copying that SCC may have engaged in for purposes of analyzing or testing Lexmark's Toner Loading Programs and creating an independent work using the ideas expressed by the Toner Loading Programs. Rather, this is a case of wholesale, identical copying of Lexmark's Toner Loading Programs for commercial exploitation and profit. Lexmark has not challenged, in this action, any reverse engineering activities SCC

may have undertaken in its attempts to understand the Toner Loading Programs.

25. Even if the Toner Loading Programs were somehow considered to be lock-out codes, copyright infringement would still exist in the instant case. "Security systems are just like any other computer program and are not inherently unprotectable." *Atari,* 1993 U.S. Dist. LEXIS 8183 at *28-29. Infringement may still be found if there is substantial similarity and "that those similarities extend beyond those necessary to produce the sequence of bits that will unlock the [copyright owner's] console." *Id.* at *29.

26. "[T]he fact that multiple ways exist to generate the necessary signal stream may provide evidence that [the accused infringer] copied more than was necessary to achieve compatibility." *Id.; see also Atari Games Corp. v. Nintendo of Am., Inc.,* 975 F2d 832, 845 (Fed Cir 1992) ("While Atari may freely reproduce the idea or process of Nintendo's 10NES code, copying of fully extraneous instructions unnecessary to the 10NES program's function strongly supports the district court's imposition of an injunction on the likelihood Nintendo will show infringement."). Public policy favors requiring competitors to carefully study security systems and discern what is truly necessary for compatibility. *Atari,* 975 F2d at 843.

27. In the instant case, SCC's identical copying of Lexmark's Toner Loading Programs went beyond that which was necessary for compatibility because SCC could have achieved a valid authentication sequence and a valid checksum operation without engaging in the verbatim copying of Lexmark's Toner Loading Programs.

2. The Fair Use Exception does not Apply

28. SCC's wholesale copying of Lexmark's Toner Loading Programs does not constitute fair use.

29. The cases relied upon by SCC do "not stand for the proposition that any form of copyright infringement is privileged as long as it is done as part of an effort to explore the operation of a product that uses copyright software." *DSC Communications Corp. v. Pulse Communications, Inc.,* 170 F3d 1354, 1363 (Fed Cir 1999). Where the accused infringer's copying is part of the ordinary operation of the accused product, fair use does not apply. *Id.; see also Cable/Home Communication Corp. v. Network Prods., Inc.* 902

F2d 829, 843-45 (11th Cir 1990) (affirming grant of summary judgment of infringement in favor of the plaintiffs and holding that the defendant's copying of the plaintiff's copyrighted cable descrambling software is not fair use); *Allen-Myland, Inc. v. Int'l Bus. Machs. Corp.,* 746 F Supp 520, 533-35 (ED Pa 1990) (holding that copying all or substantial portions of microcode was not fair use); *Compaq Computer Corp. v. Procom Tech., Inc.,* 908 F Supp 1409, 1419-21 (SD Tex 1995) (issuing judgment for the plaintiff and permanent injunction and holding that the defendants' verbatim copying of copyrighted "threshold values" was not fair use); *Princeton Univ. Press v. Mich. Document Servs.,* 99 F3d 1381, 1385-92 (6th Cir 1996) (en banc) (holding that substantial verbatim copying by a copy service of materials to be used in "coursepacks" for college students was not fair use).

30. The fair use doctrine requires the balancing of four non-exclusive factors: (1) the purpose and character of the use, including whether the use is of a commercial nature or is for nonprofit or educational purposes; (2) the nature of the copyrighted work; (3) the amount and substantiality of the portion used in relation to the copyrighted work as a whole; and (4) the effect of the use upon the potential market for or the value of the copyrighted work. 17 USC §107 (2002).

31. *Purpose and Character of the Use*—"[T]he fact that copying is for a commercial purpose weighs against a finding of fair use." *Sega,* 977 F2d at 1522, *accord Campbell v. Acuff-Rose Music, Inc.,* 510 US 569, 585 (1994). It is clear that SCC has copied Lexmark's Toner Loading Programs for the commercial purpose of developing its SMARTEK microchips for use with Lexmark's T-Series toner cartridges and printers. SCC contends that commercial gain is only one factor to consider, and that the Court is also free to consider the public interest and benefit resulting from a particular use, such as the marketing of compatible and interoperable products, notwithstanding the fact that an accused party may gain commercially. *Sega,* 977 F2d at 1522-23. While this is certainly the case, the Court finds that this factor weighs heavily in Lexmark's favor because SCC engaged in the wholesale copying of Lexmark's Toner Loading Programs for the purpose of developing the SMARTEK microchips and profiting from their sale.

32. *Nature of the Copyrighted Work*—Not all copyrighted works are entitled to the same degree of protection. Works that are essentially factual, have strong functional elements, or are essentially utilitarian articles, such as computer programs, are afforded a lower degree of copyright protection than more traditional literary works. *Sony Computer Entm't, Inc. v. Connectix*, 203 F3d 596, 603 (9th Cir 2000); *Sega;* 977 F2d at 1524-26. While computer programs are entitled to some copyright protection, the Court finds that this factor weighs slightly in SCC's favor because of the lesser degree of protection frequently provided to computer programs.

33. *Amount and Substantiality of the Portion Used in Relation to the Copyrighted Work as a Whole*—In the instant case, it is clear that SCC copied Lexmark's Toner Loading Programs in their entirety. This finding heavily favors Lexmark. *See Campbell*, 510 US at 587-88 ("[A] work composed primarily of an original . . . with little added or changed, is more likely to be a merely superseding use, fulfilling demand for the original."). SCC contends that copying an entire work can be deemed fair use. *See Sony Corp. of Am. v. Universal City Studios, Inc.*, 464 US 417 (1984); *Sega;* 977 F2d at 1523 ("The fact that an entire work was copied does not, however, preclude a finding of fair use."). While this is certainly the case in some instances, the Court finds that this factor weighs heavily in Lexmark's favor in the instant case because SCC did not have to engage in wholesale copying of the Toner Loading Programs in their entirety to enable interoperability, given that valid authentication sequences and checksum operations can occur with completely different Toner Loading Programs.

34. *The Effect of the Use upon the Potential Market for or Value of the Copyrighted Work*—Where, as here, a verbatim copy of a work is made with the intended purpose of commercial gain, a likelihood of significant market harm is presumed. *See Sony*, 464 US at 451 ("If the intended use is for commercial gain, [the] likelihood [of significant market harm may be] presumed."); *accord Campbell*, 510 US at 591 (presumption of likelihood of significant market harm is presumed for "mere duplication for commercial purposes."). Accordingly, the Court finds that this factor weighs in Lexmark's favor.

35. In sum, three of the four fair use factors weigh heavily in Lexmark's favor. The only factor that weighs in SCC's favor, the nature of the protected work, only weighs slightly in SCC's favor because computer programs are still entitled to some copyright protection, even if this protection does not rise to the level afforded to more traditional literary works. On balance, the three factors in Lexmark's favor substantially outweigh the one factor in SCC's favor. Accordingly, the Court finds that SCC's actions do not fall under the protective umbrella of the fair use doctrine.

3. The Toner Loading Programs are not Mere Formulas and Constants

36. The copyright protection for each of the Toner Loading Programs covers the unique creative computer programming language and selection and arrangement of appropriate approximation techniques, including the selection, arrangement, and particular expression of formulas, constants, and variables. *See, e.g., Feist*, 499 US at 348 ("arrangement or selection of facts can be protected by copyright . . . however, the copyright is limited to the particular selection and arrangements."); *Apple Computer, Inc. v. Formula Int'l, Inc.*, 725 F2d 521, 525 (9th Cir 1984) (a plaintiff "seeks to copyright only its particular set of instructions [*i.e.*, the source code or object code], not the underlying computer process [*i.e.*, performing a function].").

37. External factors such as compatibility requirements, industry standards, and efficiency should be considered as part of the substantial similarity analysis rather than a copyrightability analysis. *See, e.g., Liberty Am. Ins. Group, Inc. v. Westpoint Underwriters, L.L.C.*, 199 F Supp 2d 1271, 1290 (MD Fla 2001) (considering the effect of external factors during the substantial similarity analysis); *cf. Diamond Direct, L.L.C. v. Star Diamond Group, Inc.*, 116 F Supp 2d 525, 529-30 n. 29 (SD NY 2000) (noting that the idea/expression distinction is not a limitation on copyrightability but rather "a measure of the degree of similarity that must exist between a copyrightable work and an unauthorized copy, in order to constitute the latter an infringement" (quoting Melville B. Nimmer & David Nimmer, 1 *Nimmer on Copyright* §2.03[D] (2000))).

38. To determine whether Lexmark's Toner Loading Programs are entitled to copyright

protection, the Court may consider "whether other programs can be written which perform the same function as the copyrighted program." *E.F. Johnson Co. v. Uniden Corp. of Am.*, 623 F Supp 1485, 1502 (D Minn 1985). Indeed, "[i]f other programs can be written or created which perform the same function as the copyrighted program, then that program is an expression of the idea and hence copyrightable." *Id.* at 1502 (granting preliminary injunction and determining that the plaintiff's computer program was copyrightable because the plaintiff's computer program contained an "H-matrix" consisting of "a series of ones and zeroes arranged in rows and columns in a matrix format" that could "be configured in any of 32 different ways.").

39. There are a number of ways that Toner Loading Programs may be written to approximate toner level. Hearing, p. 90, lines 4-6, p. 127, lines 6-15. Alternative Toner Loading Program possibilities exist even if one were to implement the same formulas used by Lexmark. Hearing, p. 123, lines 15-20. The Toner Loading Programs were written in a custom programming language created by Lexmark. Hearing, p. 94, lines 18-21, p. 138, lines 1-7.

40. Lexmark's Toner Loading Programs are entitled to copyright protection because they could be written in a number of different ways. This conclusion is consistent with the decisions of numerous other courts. *See, e.g., Formula Int'l*, 725 F2d at 525 (affirming grant of preliminary injunction and determining that the plaintiff's computer programs were copyrightable on the basis that "[the plaintiff] introduced evidence that numerous other methods exist for writing the programs involved here, and [the defendant] does not contend to the contrary."); *Franklin Computer*, 714 F2d at 1253 ("If other programs can be written or created which perform the same function as [the plaintiff's] operating system program, then [the plaintiff's] program is an expression of the idea and hence copyrightable."); *Whelan Assocs., Inc. v. Jaslow Dental Lab, Inc.*, 797 F2d 1222, 1240 (3d Cir 1986) (A computer program is copyrightable where "there are a variety of program structures through which that idea [*i.e.*, the function performed by that program] can be expressed."); *Allen-Myland*, 770 F Supp at 1011-12 (computer microcode was copyrightable because the plaintiff could have written the microcode in a different programming language, could have chosen different verbs for the command terms and could have used different values and numeric codes).

41. SCC's reliance on *Gates Rubber Co. v. Bando Chem. Indus., Ltd.*, 9 F3d 823 (10th Cir 1993) for the proposition that constants are unprotectable facts is misplaced. Unlike the constants at issue in *Gates*, the constants at issue in the instant case are not simply observable scientific measurements that Lexmark merely recorded. Rather, substantial skill and ingenuity went into the selection of Lexmark's constants.

42. While the programs at issue in *Gates* took direct measurements, Lexmark's Toner Loading Programs do not directly measure toner level. They are expressions of creative approximation techniques. Indeed, Lexmark not only expended creative skill in selecting its hybrid approximation technique—as evidenced by the fact that numerous techniques could have been employed—but also exercised creative skill in selecting the specific constants at issue. That is, unlike the constants at issue in *Gates*, Lexmark's constants were not simply observations of fact that were "mechanical or routine." Additionally, as the United States Court of Appeals for the Tenth Circuit noted, the district court in *Gates* relied heavily upon the constants at issue in granting injunctive relief, finding that the constants "lie at the heart of the dispute." *Gates*, 9 F3d at 843.

43. In the instant case, the constants are not at the heart of the dispute. Rather, SCC copied Lexmark's entire Toner Loading Programs. *See Adobe Sys. Inc. v. S. Software, Inc.*, No. C95-20710 RMW(RPT), 1998 U.S. Dist. LEXIS 1941 at *16-17 (ND Cal Jan. 30, 1998) (selection of x and y coordinates, or reference points, for use in a font generating software met the requisite degree of creativity and constituted copyrightable expression); *Compaq*, 908 F Supp at 1418 (selection of five threshold values for use in a computer hard drive monitor met the requisite degree of creativity and constituted copyrightable expression); *Allen-Myland*, 770 F Supp at 1011-12 ("choices as to whether and how to use a table structure, how to arrange the instructions and other information within the tables and within the entries in the tables were all" copyrightable expression); *SAS Inst.*, 605 F Supp at 825 (determining that the program contained

copyrightable expressing and noting that "[e]ven in the case of simple statistical calculations, there is room for variation, such as the order in which arithmetic operations are performed.").

44. Even if, as SCC argues, there are only a limited number of ways to write a computer program that performs the same function as the Toner Loading Programs, Lexmark's Toner Loading Programs are still protected against the type of identical copying that SCC performed in the instant case. *Homan v. Clinton*, 1999 U.S. App. LEXIS 13401, at *3 (6th Cir June 14, 1999) (unpublished); *Concret Mach. Co. v. Classic Lawn Ornaments, Inc.*, 843 F2d 600, 606-07 (1st Cir 1988).

B. SCC Copied the Entire Protectable Expression of Lexmark's Toner Loading Programs

45. To prove copying, it is sufficient to show (1) that the accused work is "substantially similar" to the protected work, and (2) that the accused infringer had access to the protected work. *Robert R. Jones*, 858 F2d at 276-77; *Johnson Controls*, 886 F2d at 1176.

46. The general test for substantial similarity is "whether the accused work is so similar to the plaintiff's work that an ordinary reasonable person would conclude that the defendant unlawfully appropriated the plaintiff's protectable expression by taking material of substance and value." *Wildlife Express Corp. v. Carol Wright Sales, Inc.*, 1 F3d 502, 509 (7th Cir 1994).

47. Access need not be proven where the similarities between the protected computer program and the accused program are identical or so striking that copying may be inferred. *Ty, Inc. v. GMA Accessories, Inc.*, 132 F3d 1167, 1170-71 (7th Cir 1997).

48. The presence of non-functional elements of the protected work is evidence of access and copying. *See Williams Elecs, Inc. v. Arctic Int'l, Inc.*, 685 F2d 870, 876 n. 6 (3d Cir 1982) (the presence of identical errors in the copyrighted program and the accused program was evidence of copying); *E.F. Johnson Co.*, 623 F Supp at 1495-96 (the presence of identical, superfluous instructions in copyrighted program and the accused program was evidence of copying); *SAS Inst.*, 605 F Supp at 824 (the presence of identical, unnecessary

instructions in the copyrighted program and the accused program was evidence of copying).

1. SCC's Works are "Substantially Similar" because they are Identical Copies of Lexmark's Toner Loading Programs

49. The "substantial similarity" requirement is satisfied in the instant case because the computer programs resident on SCC's SMARTEK microchips contain exact copies of Lexmark's Toner Loading Programs. *See Ty*, 132 F3d at 1170-71.

50. Lexmark's Toner Loading Programs, in their entirety, constitute copyrightable expression. Hearing, p. 88, line 24 – p. 89, line 3. Lexmark's unique creative computer programming language and its selection and arrangement of appropriate approximation techniques, including the selection, arrangement, and particular expression of formulas, constants, and variables is entitled to copyright protection.

51. SCC admittedly copied Lexmark's Toner Loading Programs in their entireties. Moreover, the presence of the "LXK" infringement detector in SCC's SMARTEK microchips demonstrates that it engaged in wholesale copying of Lexmark's Toner Loading Programs.

2. The Abstraction-Filtration-Comparison Test

52. Because SCC admits that it engaged in the verbatim copying of Lexmark's Toner Loading Programs in its SMARTEK microchips, there is no dispute as to the copying element of the infringement analysis. The Court therefore need not perform any further analysis to determine whether SCC's copying amounts to infringement. *See, e.g., Wilcom Pty. Ltd. v. Endless Visions*, 128 F Supp 2d 1027, 1029-32 (ED Mich 1998) (finding copyright infringement by simply comparing the plaintiff's copyrighted computer program with the defendant's accused program and not applying the abstraction-filtration-comparison test), *aff'd*, 229 F3d 1155 (6th Cir 2000).

53. As other federal courts have determined, the abstraction-filtration-comparison ("AFC") test is either unnecessary or simply does not apply in cases of literal copying.[2] *See Mitek Holdings, Inc. v. Arce Eng'g Co.*, 89 F3d 1548, 1555-56 n. 16 *[1 ILR (P&F) 339]* (11th Cir 1996) (explaining that the AFC test "was designed to help assess nonliteral

copying of a nonliteral element, not nonliteral copying of computer code (a literal element")); *Lotus Dev. Corp. v. Borland Int'l, Inc.*, 49 F3d 807, 815 (1st Cir 1995) ("While the [AFC] test may provide a useful framework for assessing the alleged nonliteral copying of computer code, we find it to be of little help in assessing whether the literal copying of a menu command hierarchy constitutes copyright infringement."); *ILOG, Inc. v. Bell Logic, LLC,* 181 F Supp 2d 3, 7 (D Mass 2002) (holding that literal copying is not governed by the AFC test); *Data Gen Corp. v. Grumman Sys. Support Corp.,* 803 F Supp 487, 490-91 (D Mass 1992) ("The complex [AFC] test . . . and such a detailed code examination are not applicable to the case before this court . . . Since [the accused infringer] has directly copied [the copyright holder's object code], there is no need to confront the more difficult issue of evaluating 'non-literal' elements of a program."), *aff'd,* 36 F3d 1147 (1st Cir 1994).

54. Accordingly, the Court finds that it is unnecessary to apply the AFC test in the instant case. All this Court needs to do is determine that SCC copied the protectable expression from Lexmark's Toner Loading Programs. In the instant case, each of the Toner Loading Programs, in its entirety, is a protectable expression for approximating toner level within a toner cartridge. SCC admits that it "slavishly copied" both Toner Loading Programs in their entireties. As a result, SCC identically copied the entire protectable expression of each Toner Loading Program.

55. Application of the AFC test would result in the same result. Each of the Toner Loading Programs represents an expression (*i.e.*, the unique selection and arrangement of equations, variables, and constants written in a custom programming language created by Lexmark) of an idea (*i.e.*, approximating the amount of toner remaining in a toner cartridge based upon a sensed torque value) and SCC copied verbatim the protectable elements of both Toner Loading Programs.

C. Copyright Misuse

56. The misuse defense, while often asserted, has rarely been upheld as a defense to claim of copyright infringement. Where the misuse defense has been upheld, it has been where a party has sought to extend its limited copyright monopoly beyond

that to which it is entitled under the Copyright Act. *See* Nimmer §13.09[A].

57. To establish copyright misuse, a defendant must establish either "(1) that [the plaintiff] violated the antitrust laws, or (2) that [the plaintiff] illegally extended its monopoly beyond the scope of the copyright or violated the public policies underlying the copyright laws." *See Microsoft Corp. v. Compusource Distribs., Inc.*, 115 F Supp 2d 800, 811 (ED Mich 2000) (finding that the defendant failed to raise a genuine issue of material fact regarding copyright misuse that would preclude a grant of summary judgment in favor of the plaintiff).

58. In the instant case, other than merely accuse Lexmark's Prebate program as being anticompetitive, SCC presents no factual or legal basis for there being an antitrust violation by Lexmark.[3] SCC's misuse defense is based on the mere allegation that Lexmark is "using copyright to secure an exclusive right or limited monopoly not expressly granted by copyright law." SCC Opp. at p. 20. Contrary to SCC's allegation, however, Lexmark is not seeking to improperly extend its copyright monopoly.

59. Lexmark is simply attempting to enforce, and protect access to, its copyrighted computer programs.

60. Lexmark's copyright infringement claim against a party that has engaged in the wholesale copying of Lexmark's copyrighted computer programs cannot be considered misuse.

61. Lexmark's efforts to enforce the rights conferred to it under the DMCA cannot be considered an unlawful act undertaken to stifle competition. *Cf. Data Gen. Corp. v. Grumman Sys. Support Corp.*, 36 F3d 1147 (1st Cir 1994) ("[A]n author's desire to exclude others from use of its copyrighted work is a presumptively valid business justification for any immediate harm to consumers.").

62. SCC's argument is virtually identical to the argument asserted by the defendants and rejected by the court in *Sony Computer Entm't Am. Inc. v. GameMasters*, 87 F Supp 2d 976 *[1999 ILRW (P&F) 3001]* (ND Cal 1999). In *GameMasters*, the defendant argued that Sony was "misusing" its copyright rights by attempting to extend or enlarge those rights through use of an access control measure that precluded users from playing non-authorized

video games on the Sony console. *Id.* at 988-89. The court rejected the defense because Sony's "targeting of the [product was] based upon a sound construction of the [DMCA]." *Id.*

III. LEXMARK HAS DEMONSTRATED A LIKELIHOOD OF SUCCESS ON THE MERITS OF ITS TWO SEPARATE AND DISTINCT CLAIMS UNDER SECTION 1201(a)(2) OF THE DIGITAL MILLENNIUM COPYRIGHT ACT

63. The DMCA was enacted to prohibit, *inter alia*, the trafficking of products or devices that circumvent the technological measures used by copyright owners to restrict access to their copyrighted works. *Universal City Studios, Inc. v. Corley*, 273 F3d 429, 440-41 *[9 ILR (P&F) 330]* (2d Cir 2001).

64. Section 1201(a)(2) of the DMCA, commonly referred to as the anti-trafficking provision, prohibits any product or device that circumvents a technological measure that prevents unauthorized access to a copyrighted work. *Universal City Studios*, 273 F3d at 440-41.

65. It is a well-established rule of statutory construction that "the starting point is the language employed by Congress." *Appleton v. First Nat'l Bank of Ohio*, 62 F3d 791, 801 (6th Cir 1995); *accord United States v. Ron Pair Enters., Inc.*, 489 US 235, 241 (1989). "When a statute is unambiguous, resort to legislative history and policy consideration is improper." *In re Koenig Sporting Goods, Inc.*, 203 F3d 986, 988 (6th Cir 2000).

66. The plain meaning of the DMCA is clear and it would be inappropriate for the Court to consider the legislative history in an effort to determine the "true" congressional intent. *See United States v. Elcom, Ltd.*, 203 F Supp 2d 1111, 1124 *[10 ILR (P&F) 611]* (ND Cal 2002).

67. Section 1201(a)(2) of the DMCA contains three independent bases for liability. *RealNetworks, Inc. v. Streambox, Inc.*, No. C99-2070P, 2000 US Dist LEXIS 1889, at *20 *[5 ILR (P&F) 251]* (WD Wash Jan. 18, 2000). To establish a violation of section 1201(a)(2), a party must prove that an accused product or device satisfies just one of those tests. *Id.* Section 1201(a)(2) prohibits the manufacture, distribution, and/or sale of any product or device that:

(A) is primarily designed or produced for the purpose of circumventing a technological measure that effectively controls access to a work protected under this title;

(B) has only a limited commercially significant purpose or use other than to circumvent a technological measure that effectively controls access to a work protected under this title; or

(C) is marketed by that person or another acting in concert with that person with that person's knowledge for use in circumventing a technological measure that effectively controls access to a work protected under this title.

17 USC §1201(a)(2)(A)-(C).

68. The DMCA explains that a technological measure "controls access" to a copyrighted work if that measure "requires the application of information, or a process or a treatment, with the authority of the copyright owner, to gain access to the work." *Id.* at §1201(a)(3)(B). In addition, the statute provides that a product or device "circumvents" a technological measure by "avoid[ing], bypass[ing], remov[ing], deactivat[ing] or [otherwise] impair[ing]" the operation of that technological measure. *Id.* at §1201(a)(3)(A).

69. The DMCA does not specifically define the term "access." Thus, the term should be given its ordinary, customary meaning. *See FDIC v. Meyer*, 510 US 471, 476 (1994) (when the text of a statute contains an undefined term, that term receives its "ordinary or natural meaning."). The ordinary, customary meaning of the term "access" is the "ability to enter, to obtain, or to make use of." *Merriam-Webster's Collegiate Dictionary* 6 (10th ed 1999).

70. The authentication sequence that occurs between Lexmark's printers and the microchips contained on authorized Lexmark toner cartridges constitutes a "technological measure" that "controls access" to a copyrighted work. This authentication sequence requires the application of information and the application of a process to gain access to Lexmark's copyrighted Toner Loading Programs and Printer Engine Programs.

71. Lexmark's authentication sequence effectively "controls access" to the Toner Loading

Programs and the Printer Engine Program because it controls the consumer's ability to make use of these programs. *See GameMasters*, 87 F Supp 2d at 987 (Sony's PlayStation console contained a technological measure that controlled a consumer's ability to make use of copyrighted computer programs).

A. SCC's SMARTEK Microchips Circumvent the Technological Measure that Controls Access to Lexmark's Copyrighted Toner Loading Programs

72. SCC admits that its SMARTEK microchips avoid or bypass Lexmark's authentication sequence. SCC Opp. at p. 4. The SMARTEK microchips mimic the technology for calculating and transmitting a MAC from Lexmark's toner cartridges to Lexmark's T-Series printers and circumvents the authentication sequence. As a result, the SMARTEK microchips are able to deceive the Lexmark T-Series printers into thinking that the SMARTEK microchips are, in fact, original microchips contained on authorized Lexmark toner cartridges. After the SMARTEK microchips bypass the authentication sequence, the printers access, without Lexmark's authority, the copyrighted Toner Loading Programs.

73. Lexmark has demonstrated that SCC's SMARTEK microchips satisfy all three tests for liability under section 1201(a)(2).

74. SCC's SMARTEK microchips satisfy the first independent test for liability because SCC acknowledges that it specifically developed the SMARTEK microchips to circumvent the authentication sequence that controls access to Lexmark's copyrighted Toner Loading Programs. SCC Opp. at pp. 2-4; Lexmark Memo, Exs. R, Q.

75. SCC's SMARTEK microchips satisfy the second independent test for liability because SCC acknowledges that its SMARTEK microchips have no commercial purpose other than to circumvent the authentication sequence that controls access to Lexmark's copyrighted Toner Loading Programs. SCC Opp. at 2-4; Lemark Memo, Exs. R, Q.

76. SCC's SMARTEK microchips satisfy the third independent test for liability because SCC markets the SMARTEK microchips as being capable of circumventing the access control protections provided by the original microchips on Lexmark's T-Series toner cartridges. Lexmark Memo, Exs. J, K, S.

B. SCC's SMARTEK Microchips Circumvent the Technological Measure that Controls Access to Lexmark's Copyrighted Printer Engine Program

77. SCC admits that its SMARTEK microchips avoid or bypass the authentication sequence. SCC Opp. at p. 4. After the SMARTEK microchips bypass the authentication sequence, the printer accesses, without Lexmark's authority, the Printer Engine Program.

78. Lexmark has demonstrated that SCC's SMARTEK microchips satisfy all three tests for liability under section 1201(a)(2) of the DMCA.

79. SCC's SMARTEK microchips satisfy the first independent test for liability because SCC acknowledges that it specifically developed the SMARTEK microchips to circumvent the authentication sequence that controls access to Lexmark's copyrighted Printer Engine Program. SCC Opp. at pp. 2-4; Lexmark Memo, Exs. R, Q.

80. SCC's SMARTEK microchips satisfy the second independent test for liability because SCC acknowledges that its SMARTEK microchips have no commercial purpose other than to circumvent the authentication sequence that controls access to Lexmark's copyrighted Printer Engine Program. SCC Opp. at pp. 2-4; Lexmark Memo, Exs. R, Q.

81. SCC's SMARTEK microchips satisfy the third independent test for liability because SCC markets the SMARTEK microchips as being capable of circumventing the access control protections provided by the original microchips on Lexmark's T-Series toner cartridges. Lexmark Memo, Exs. J, K, S.

C. SCC's Actions do not Fall under any of the Exceptions to Section 1201(a)(2)

1. SCC's Manufacture, Distribution and Sale of its SMARTEK Microchips Fall within the Plain Language of the DMCA

82. Because the language of the DMCA is clear, it is unnecessary to consider the legislative history or the policy arguments raised by SCC to determine congressional intent or the scope of the DMCA. *See Elcom*, 203 F Supp 2d at 1124. In addition, SCC does not cite to any portion of the legislative history that indicates that "the literal application of [the]

statute will produce a result demonstrably at odds with the intentions of its drafters." *Koenig Sporting Goods*, 203 F3d at 988.

83. The protections provided by the DMCA are not, and were never intended to be, as limited as SCC asserts. The DMCA is clear that the right to protect against unauthorized access is a right separate and distinct from the right to protect against violations of exclusive copyright rights such as reproduction and distribution. Section 1201(b) prohibits trafficking in devices that circumvent measures that "effectively protect[ ] a right of a copyright owner under this title." 17 USC §1201(b)(1)(A). In contrast, section 1201(a)(2) more broadly prohibits trafficking in devices that circumvent measures that "effectively control[ ] access to a work protected under this title." 17 USC §1201(a)(2)(A).

84. If the DMCA were only intended to protect copyrighted works from digital piracy, that goal was accomplished through section 1201(b); SCC's argument would render section 1201(a)(2) mere surplusage. Section 1201(a) creates, and section 1201(a)(2) protects, a right of "access," the violation of which is the "electronic equivalent [of] breaking into a castle." 3 Nimmer §12A.03[D][1] at 12A-29.

85. The few cases that have applied the DMCA are in accord. *See, e.g., RealNetworks, Inc.*, 2002 US Dist LEXIS 1889 at *3 (the plaintiff's "Secret Handshake" was species of access control governed by section 1201(a)(2)); *GameMasters*, 87 F Supp 2d at 987 (enjoining sale of device that circumvented technological measure that prevented access to software embedded in Sony's PlayStation console, even though the device did not facilitate piracy).

86. The DMCA is not limited to the protection of "copies of works (such as books, CD's and motion pictures) that have an independent market value." The DMCA broadly prohibits trafficking in a product or device that circumvents "a technological measure that effectively controls access *to a work protected under this title*." 17 USC §1201(a)(2)(A), (B) (emphasis added).

87. Lexmark's Toner Loading Programs and Printer Engine Program are works protected under the Copyright Act.

88. Quite simply, if a work is entitled to protection under the Copyright Act, trafficking in a

device that circumvents a technological measure that controls access to such work constitutes a violation under section 1201(a). The few cases decided under the DMCA prove that section 1201(a) applies to the very type of computer software that Lexmark seeks to protect, and the very type of access-protection regime Lexmark has employed to protect it.

89. The authentication sequence employed by Lexmark in this case is similar to the technological measure employed by Sony in the *GameMasters* case that prevented access to the copyrighted computer software that operates with Sony's PlayStation video game console. The console employs a technological measure that verifies whether a CD-ROM game inserted into the console is "an authorized, legitimate [Sony] product licensed for distribution in the same geographical territory of the console's sale." *GameMasters*, 87 F Supp 2d at 981. If the console cannot verify that the game is, in fact, such an authorized product, the console will not operate and the game will not play. *Id*. The *GameMasters* court found that Sony was likely to succeed on the merits of its 1201(a)(2)(A) claim, and thus granted injunctive relief, because the defendant's "GameEnhancer" device circumvented the access control measure on the console "that ensures the console operates only when encrypted data is read from an authorized CD-ROM [video game]." *Id*. at 987.

90. The access control measure upheld by the *GameMasters* court is, as a technical matter, virtually identical to, and as a legal matter, indistinguishable from, the access control measure employed by Lexmark in the instant case. Like the PlayStation console, the Lexmark printer employs a technological measure—the authentication sequence—that verifies whether the toner cartridge inserted into the printer is authorized (*e.g.*, it is either a Prebate cartridge, a non-Prebate cartridge, a refilled non-Prebate cartridge, or a Lexmark remanufactured cartridge, but it is not an unauthorized third-party refilled Prebate cartridge). If the printer cannot verify that the cartridge is, in fact, such a product, the Printer Engine Program will not operate and will not "play" the Toner Loading Program. SCC's SMARTEK microchips, like the "GameEnhancer" device in *GameMasters*, circumvents the access control measure on the Lexmark printer "that ensures the [printer] operates only when encrypted data is read from an authorized

[toner cartridge]." Thus, the allegations in Lexmark's complaint are hardly, as SCC claims, "novel."

2. The Reverse Engineering Exemption under Section 1201(f) of the DMCA does not Apply

91. Sections 1201(f)(2) and (3) of the DMCA are not broad exceptions that can be employed to excuse any behavior that makes some device "interoperable" with some other device.

92. Sections 1201(f)(2) and (3) provide that a person may develop a circumvention device and make that circumvention device available to others "*solely* for the purpose of enabling interoperability *of an independently created computer program* with other programs, and *to the extent that doing so does not constitute infringement under this title or violate applicable law other than section.*" 17 USC §1201(f)(3) (emphasis added).

a. SCC's SMARTEK Microchips are not Independently Created Computer Programs

93. SCC contends that it was justified in developing the SMARTEK microchips because these circumvention devices enable independently created programs to interoperate with Lexmark's Printer Engine Program and Toner Loading Programs. The independently created programs identified by SCC are programs contained on the SMARTEK microchips.

94. SCC's SMARTEK microchips cannot be considered independently created computer programs. The SMARTEK microchips serve no legitimate purpose other than to circumvent Lexmark's authentication sequence and the SMARTEK microchips cannot qualify as independently created when they contain exact copies of Lexmark's Toner Loading Programs.

b. SCC's Conduct Constitutes Copyright Infringement

95. SCC can only take advantage of the protection afforded by section 1201(f) of the DMCA if its conduct "does not constitute infringement under this title [the Copyright Act] or violate applicable law other than this section." 17 USC §1201(f)(3).

96. For reasons set forth above, SCC's exact copying of Lexmark's Toner Loading Programs into its SMARTEK microchips constitutes copyright infringement. Accordingly, section 1201(f) of the DMCA does not offer any protection to SCC.

IV. LEXMARK HAS DEMONSTRATED THAT IT WILL SUFFER IRREPARABLE HARM IF THE COURT REFUSES TO GRANT THE PRELIMINARY INJUCNTION

A. Irreparable Harm to Lexmark is Presumed as a Matter of Law

97. Irreparable harm is presumed as a matter of law because Lexmark has shown that it is likely to succeed on the merits of its copyright infringement and DMCA claims.

98. If a plaintiff in a copyright infringement action demonstrates a likelihood of success on the merits of its copyright infringement claim, then the irreparable harm to that plaintiff as a result of the infringement is presumed. *Forry*, 837 F2d at 267. There is a well-established presumption that damages incurred by copyright infringement are, by their very nature, irreparable and not susceptible of monetary measurement, thus rendering any remedy at law inadequate. *See Atari*, 672 F2d at 620; *ISC-Bunker Ramo Corp. v. Altech, Inc.*, 765 F Supp 1310, 1329 (ND Ill 1990).

99. In copyright infringement cases, there simply is no need to prove irreparable harm. *See Concrete Mach.*, 843 F2d at 612 (discussing the presumption of irreparable harm and stating that "[t]here is . . . no need actually to prove irreparable harm when seeking an injunction against copyright infringement."). In fact, some courts have held that a failure to consider the presumption of irreparable harm is reversible error. *See Franklin Computer*, 714 F2d at 1254 (holding that the district court erred when it failed to consider the presumption of irreparable harm); *Atari*, 672 F2d at 620-21 (reversing the district court's finding of noninfringement and directing the district court to enter a preliminary injunction based upon the presumption of irreparable harm).

100. Similarly, a plaintiff that demonstrates a likelihood of success on the merits of its claim for violation of the anti-trafficking provisions of the DMCA is entitled to a presumption of irreparable injury. *See Reimerdes*, 82 F Supp 2d at 215 (determining that the plaintiff was entitled to a presumption of irreparable harm because the plaintiff demonstrated a likelihood of success on its claim for violation of section 1201(a)(2) of the DMCA). The damages incurred by violations of section 1201(a)(2) of the DMCA simply "cannot

readily be measured, suggesting that the injury truly [is] irreparable." *Id.*

101. SCC has failed to rebut the presumption that Lexmark will suffer irreparable injury as a result of SCC's copyright infringement. SCC contends that money damages could adequately compensate Lexmark, but the alleged availability of money damages is not a sufficient reason to deny injunctive relief. *See Cadence Design Sys., Inc. v. Avant! Corp.*, 125 F3d 824, 827 (9th Cir 1997) (quoting Nimmer for the proposition that if a plaintiff established a likelihood of success on the merits of a copyright infringement claim, "it would seem erroneous to deny a preliminary injunction simply because actual damages can be precisely calculated."). In any event, it would be incredibly difficult to precisely calculate Lexmark's damages in the instant case because of the possibility of Lexmark suffering the loss of customer goodwill.

B. Even without the Presumption of Irreparable Harm, Lexmark has Established the Irreparable Harm that it will Suffer Absent an Injunction against SCC

102. Lexmark has demonstrated that it expended significant time and financial resources to develop its copyrighted programs and the authentication sequence that prevents unauthorized access to those programs. Yaro Dec. ¶15. SCC copies Lexmark's Toner Loading Programs and sells identical copies of the programs to consumers in its SMARTEK microchips.

103. SCC's copyright infringement and the trafficking of the SMARTEK microchips could result in a multitude of harms to Lexmark that would be difficult to quantify. These harms include fewer customer orders, reduced margins, potential market share loss, damage to the reputation of Lexmark's products, and damage to Lexmark's relationships with consumers. *See, e.g., Basic Computer Corp. v. Scott*, 973 F2d 507, 512 (6th Cir 1992) ("The loss of customer goodwill often amounts to irreparable injury because the damages flowing from such losses are difficult to compute.").

104. Lexmark's potential damages are difficult to measure or quantify, and thus Lexmark will likely suffer irreparable injury absent an injunction against SCC.

V. THE PUBLIC INTEREST FACTOR FAVORS LEXMARK

105. In copyright infringement cases, as with the irreparable harm factor, it is ordinarily presumed that an injunction will serve the public interest if the copyright holder shows a likelihood of success on the merits. *Concrete Mach.*, 843 F2d at 612. Further, "it is virtually axiomatic that the public interest can only be served by upholding copyright protections and, correspondingly, preventing the misappropriation of the skills, creative energies, and resources which are invested in the protected work." *Franklin Computer*, 714 F2d at 1254. Moreover, a preliminary injunction is necessary "to preserve the integrity of the copyright laws which seek to encourage individual effort and creativity by granting valuable enforcement rights." *Atari*, 672 F2d at 620.

106. SCC contends that policies of the United States government favor the recycling and remanufacturing of toner cartridges and further claims that "an injunction would threaten significant and truly irreparable harm to the environment." SCC Opp. at p. 30. This argument rests primarily upon the assumption that the majority of Lexmark's Prebate toner cartridges will end up in landfills should the Court enjoin SCC from trafficking in its SMARTEK microchips. The Court finds this claim to be largely unsubstantiated. Lexmark, in fact, has an extensive remanufacturing program for all of its used Prebate cartridges. Accordingly, the Court does not accept SCC's argument that an injunction will threaten significant environmental degradation.

107. SCC contends that public policy favors competition and supports the availability of multiple remanufacturers for toner cartridges. SCC further contends that public policy opposes the use of technological measures to prevent or limit remanufacturing. The Court has no trouble accepting SCC's claim that public policy generally favors competition. The Court finds, however, that this general principle only favors legitimate competition. Public policy certainly does not support copyright infringement and violations of the DMCA in the name of competition.

VI. THE POSSIBILITY OF SUBSTANTIAL HARM TO OTHERS

A. SCC

108. "Advantages built [on] deliberately [copied software] do not . . . give [SCC] standing to complain that [its] vested interests will be disturbed." *Atari*, 672 F2d at 620. One cannot build a business based upon infringing another's intellectual property rights, and then be allowed to complain that making them stop will cause harm. *See Cadence*, 125 F3d at 829 (the district court erred by giving improper emphasis to harm to defendant that would devastate its business; "a defendant who knowingly infringes another's copyright 'cannot complain of the harm that will befall it when properly forced to desist from its infringing activities.' "); *Franklin Computer*, 714 F2d at 1255 (reversing district court's denial of a preliminary injunction because of its "devastating effect" on the defendant's business: "[i]f [the effect on the defendant] were the correct standard, then a knowing infringer would be permitted to construct its business around its infringement, a result we cannot condone.").

109. SCC intentionally copied Lexmark's Toner Loading Programs and purposely developed and sold a product that circumvents the access control measure that protects Lexmark's copyrighted works. Thus, under the circumstances, the "Court should not consider a balancing of hardships as a determining factor in granting injunctive relief in a copyright matter" because "[a]llowing for a balancing of hardships would permit a knowing infringer to construct its entire business around infringement." *Value Group, Inc. v. Mendham Lake Estates, L.P.*, 800 F Supp 1228, 1235 (D NJ 1992) (citing *Franklin Computer*, 714 F2d at 1255). In any event, the Court finds that the harm that Lexmark would likely suffer absent an injunction outweighs the harm that SCC would likely suffer because of an injunction.

B. Third Parties

110. As has been stated by SCC and various amici, the issuance of an injunction in the instant case could have a significant impact upon the toner cartridge remanufacturing industry and some impact upon the remanufacturing industries as a whole. SCC and the various amici, however, have provided little evidentiary support for these claims and any possible impact that an injunction in the instant case would have on others in the remanufacturing industry appears to be almost entirely speculative.

111. SCC also contends that the issuance of an injunction in the instant case would have a negative impact upon consumers because they will not have the opportunity to have their Prebate cartridges refilled or remanufactured by third parties. While this may be the case, the Court feels little sympathy for consumers that accept the up-front discount when purchasing Prebate cartridges and are subsequently required to comply with the Prebate agreement and return the used cartridges to Lexmark.

VII. LEGAL CONCLUSION

112. Lexmark is likely to prevail on the merits of its copyright infringement and DMCA claims. It is presumed that Lexmark will suffer irreparable harm in the absence of an injunction, and SCC has failed to rebut this presumption. Even in the absence of this presumption, Lexmark has shown that it will suffer irreparable harm. It is further presumed that the public interest favors granting the injunction, and SCC has failed to rebut this presumption. Even in the absence of this presumption, it is clear that the public interest favors discouraging copyright infringement and violations of the DMCA. SCC contends that certain third parties could be harmed should the Court issue an injunction, but the Court finds these claims to be unpersuasive. The Court has fully considered the four preliminary injunction factors, and, on balance, it is clear that injunctive relief is appropriate in the instant case.

CONCLUSION

For the reasons stated above, Lexmark's Motion for a Preliminary Injunction shall be granted by Order of this Court, contemporaneously entered in accordance with these Findings of Fact and Conclusions of Law. In announcing this decision, the Court has adopted a majority of Lexmark's Proposed Findings of Fact and Conclusions. The Court, has, however, conducted an exhaustive independent review of this matter and has made changes to Lexmark's Proposed Findings of Fact and Conclusions of Law where appropriate.

ORDER

In accordance with the Findings of Fact and Conclusions of Law entered on the same date herewith, **IT IS HEREBY ORDERED** that:

(1) Lexmark International, Inc's ("Lexmark") motion for a preliminary injunction is GRANTED;

(2) Static Control Components, Inc. ("SCC") shall cease making, selling, distributing, offering for sale or otherwise trafficking in the "SMARTEK" microchips for the Lexmark T520/522 and T620/622 toner cartridges, until further Order from this Court; and

(3) the bond previously posted by Lexmark shall remain in effect until further Order from this Court.

Entered this 27th day of February, 2003.

existence and widely publicized since 1997, well before the sale of Lexmark's T520/522 and T620/622 laser printers at issue here, and allows customers an unfettered choice in selecting remanufacturing options, *i.e.*, an upfront discount for a Prebate toner cartridge to be returned only to Lexmark for remanufacturing or a regular toner cartridge capable of being remanufactured by anyone.

---

[1] The Prebate agreement states as follows: RETURN EMPTY CARTRIDGE TO LEXMARK FOR REMANUFACTURING AND RECYCLING. Please read before opening. Opening this package or using the patented cartridge inside confirms your acceptance of the following license/agreement. This all-new cartridge is sold at a special price subject to a restriction that it may be used only once. Following this initial use, you agree to return the empty cartridge only to Lexmark for remanufacturing and recycling. If you don't accept these terms, return the unopened package to your point of purchase. A regular price cartridge without these terms is available.

[2] The terms "literal" and "non-literal" are used in two ways in copyright infringement cases involving computer software: to describe different types of elements of software and different types of copying. *See Mitek Holdings, Inc. v. Arce Eng'g Co.*, 89 F3d 1548, 1555-56 n. 16 *[1 ILR (P&F) 339]* (11th Cir 1996). "The 'literal elements' of a computer program are its source and object code." *Id.* at 1555 n. 15. The "non-literal elements" of a computer program "are the products that are generated by the code's interaction with the computer hardware and operating program[s]." *Id.* Examples of non-literal elements include "screen displays and the main menu and submenu command tree structure." *Id.* "Literal copying" means verbatim copying, whereas "non-literal copying" means non-verbatim copying. *See id.* at 1555-56 n. 16.

[3] An antitrust claim cannot succeed under an after-market antitrust theory when the accused party has not changed its policy and has been otherwise forthcoming about its policies. *See PSI Repair Serv., Inc. v. Honeywell, Inc.*, 104 F3d 811 (6th Cir), *cert. denied*, 520 US 1265 (1997). Here, Lexmark's Prebate program has been in

Perfect 10, Inc.
v.
Cybernet Ventures, Inc.

**United States District Court,
Central District of California**

April 22, 2002

10 ILR (P&F) 483, 2002 ILRWeb (P&F) 1411

CV 01-2595 LGB (SHx)

Internet exhibits properly authenticated and admissible.

In a suit alleging infringement of a large number of copyrighted photographs, certain Internet print-outs, attached as exhibits to a witness's declaration, are admissible because the declaration is sufficient to establish their authenticity. The declaration adequately establishes the prima facie case for admissibility by claiming that the attached exhibits were either: (1) true and correct copies of documents produced by defendant in discovery; (2) true and correct copies of photographs from plaintiff's magazine or plaintiff's web site; or (3) true and correct copies of pages printed from the Internet that were printed by the witness or under his direction. Those web pages that fall under category (3) contain the Internet domain address from which the image was printed and the date on which it was printed. The first category is covered by caselaw holding that discovery documents are deemed authentic when offered by a party-opponent. The second and third categories have met the prima facie burden because the declarations, particularly in combination with circumstantial indicia of authenticity (such as the dates and web addresses), would support a reasonable juror in the belief that the documents are what plaintiff says they are. Following *U.S. v. Tank*, 6 ILR (P&F) 241. Moreover, because computer printouts are the only practical method by which the allegations of the complaint can be brought before the court and because there is generally a reduced evidentiary standard in preliminary injunction motions, the declaration is sufficient to establish the exhibits' authenticity. [Distinguishing *U.S. v. Jackson*, 5 ILR (P&F) 35, and *St. Clair v. Johnny's Oyster & Shrimp, Inc.*, 4 ILR (P&F) 317.] — **Perfect 10, Inc. v. Cybernet Ventures, Inc., 10 ILR (P&F) 483 [CD Cal, 2002].**

E-mails admissible.

In a suit alleging infringement of a large number of copyrighted photographs, the court will treat e-mail communications attributable to defendant's employees as party admissions and will accept e-mail communications from third parties only insofar as they indicate notice of infringing or potentially infringing activity. — **Perfect 10, Inc. v. Cybernet Ventures, Inc., 10 ILR (P&F) 483 [CD Cal, 2002].**

Printout of web sites not hearsay.

In a suit alleging infringement of a large number of copyrighted photographs on web sites affiliated with defendant's gateway service, printouts from those web sites fall outside the ambit of the hearsay rule to the extent these images and text are being introduced to show the images and text found on the web sites. To the extent that plaintiff relies on directories and the like as assertions that the links provided actually connect to the subject matter claimed in the link, the hearsay issue is a closer question, and the court will deal with the issue, should it arise, on a case-by-case basis. As for any asserted connection between those sites and defendant, evidence of defendant's business structure and the workings of its "Adult Check" age verification program, combined with statements identifying the individual web sites as Adult Check sites, are enough to establish the sites' membership in the Adult Check program. This takes the various printouts outside the definition of hearsay, for this purpose. — **Perfect 10, Inc. v. Cybernet Ventures, Inc., 10 ILR (P&F) 483 [CD Cal, 2002].**

Age verification service not liable for direct infringement.

Plaintiff, a publisher of copyrighted pornographic images, shows little likelihood of success on its claim that defendant, which provides an age verification gateway service for pornographic web sites, is liable for direct copyright infringement based on the large number of copyrighted images found on web sites that use defendant's service. To be liable for direct infringement, a defendant must *actively* engage in one of the activities recognized in the Copyright Act. Based on the evidence before the court, it appears that defendant does not use its hardware either to store the infringing images or to move them from one location to another for display. This technical separation between its facilities and those of its webmasters prevents defendant from engaging in reproduction or distribution and makes it doubtful that defendant publicly displays the works. Further, there is currently no evidence that defendant has prepared works based upon plaintiff's copyrighted material. — **Perfect 10, Inc. v. Cybernet Ventures, Inc., 10 ILR (P&F) 483 [CD Cal, 2002].**

Age verification service may be liable under vicarious, contributory infringement claims.

Defendant, which provides an age verification gateway service (called "Adult Check") for pornographic web sites, may be liable for copyright infringement committed by its member sites under theories of vicarious and contributory copyright infringement. Plaintiff, a publisher of copyrighted pornographic images, shows a strong likelihood of success in proving defendant's knowledge of the infringement, as well as defendant's material contributions to the infringing activity. Defendant markets its Adult Check brand through advertising, pays webmasters commissions directly based upon the number of Adult Check users that register through the site, provides technical and content advice, reviews sites, and attempts to control the quality of the "product" it presents to consumers as a unified brand. Plaintiff thus established a strong likelihood of success on the merits of its contributory infringement claim. As for vicarious infringement, defendant has a sufficiently direct financial interest: all the money associated with these sites flows directly to defendant before some of it is returned to the individual site owners as "commissions." Furthermore, plaintiff has shown defendant's ability to exercise control over the directly infringing parties: defendant has a monitoring program in place to ensure that celebrity images do not oversaturate any given site and that other images (such as child porn) do not appear on any participating site. — **Perfect 10, Inc. v. Cybernet Ventures, Inc., 10 ILR (P&F) 483 [CD Cal, 2002].**

Age verification service as an "online services provider."

While the statutory language of the Digital Millennium Copyright Act (DMCA) strongly suggests that the definition of a service provider is meant to include services that only provide location service tools or that provide Internet access and such tools, it is a close question whether an age verification service, which serves as a gateway for access to affiliated pornographic web sites, qualifies as a "provider of online services" as defined in DMCA §512(k). For purposes of determining whether defendant may qualify for the DMCA's safe harbor, however, the court will assume that defendant is an online services provider. — **Perfect 10, Inc. v. Cybernet Ventures, Inc., 10 ILR (P&F) 483 [CD Cal, 2002].**

Age verification service fails to satisfy statutory prerequisite for DMCA safe harbor.

Defendant, an age verification service (AVS) that acts as a gateway for access to affiliated pornographic web sites, is not likely to qualify for the safe harbor provisions of the Digital Millennium Copyright Act (DMCA) because it fails to satisfy the statutory prerequisite laid out in 17 USC §512(i), *viz.*, and it has not "reasonably implemented" a policy directed at terminating repeat infringers, even in "appropriate circumstances." Section 512 does not endorse business practices that would encourage content providers to turn a blind eye to the source of massive copyright infringement while continuing to knowingly profit, indirectly or not, from every one of these same sources until a court orders the provider to terminate each individual account. The Court thus views 512(i) as creating room for enforcement policies less stringent or formal than the "notice and take-down" provisions of section 512(c), but still subject to 512(i)'s "reasonably implemented" requirement. It therefore respectfully parts ways with the interpretation of 512(i) in *Ellison v. Robertson*, 10 ILR (P&F) 386, in order to maintain the "strong incentives" for service providers to prevent their services from becoming safe havens or conduits for known repeat copyright infringers. The record supports the conclusion that defendant has taken great pains to avoid shouldering the burdens of the copyright regime, all the while profiting from pirates. — **Perfect 10, Inc. v. Cybernet Ventures, Inc., 10 ILR (P&F) 483 [CD Cal, 2002].**

Deficiencies in notice procedures render §512(c) and (d) safe harbors inapplicable.

Even if defendant could satisfy the statutory prerequisites of the Digital Millennium Copyright Act (DMCA), defendant would nevertheless be unlikely to qualify for the §512(c) ("information storage") or the §512(d) ("information location tool") safe harbors. Defendant is an age verification service (AVS) that acts as a gateway for access to affiliated pornographic web sites. Both the section 512(c) and (d) safe harbors contain parallel notification and counter-notification requirements in an attempt to balance the duties of service providers, the rights of copyright owners, and the rights of other users. Defendant has altered the notice requirements by not allowing copyright owners to provide a representative list in cases of multiple infringements. Defendant has also deviated from the counter-notification requirements by removing the good faith requirement that separates innocent users from those who knowingly infringe copyrights. — **Perfect 10, Inc. v. Cybernet Ventures, Inc., 10 ILR (P&F) 483 [CD Cal, 2002].**

Financial benefit and ability to control render §512(c) and (d) safe harbors inapplicable.

Even if defendant could satisfy the statutory prerequisites of the Digital Millennium Copyright Act (DMCA), defendant would nevertheless be unlikely to qualify for the §512(c) ("information storage") or the §512(d) ("information location tool") safe harbors. Defendant is an age verification service that acts as a gateway for access to affiliated pornographic web sites. Both 512(c) and (d) exclude from the safe harbor service providers that "receive a benefit directly attributable to the infringing activity, in a case in which the service provider has the right and ability to control such activity." Here, there is significant evidence that defendant receives a direct financial benefit because all the money associated with the infringing sites flows directly to defendant. With regard to the right and ability to control, defendant prescreens sites, gives them extensive advice, and prohibits the proliferation of identical sites. This combination of financial benefit and ability to control makes it highly unlikely that defendant may avail itself of the DMCA safe harbor provisions. — **Perfect 10, Inc. v. Cybernet Ventures, Inc., 10 ILR (P&F) 483 [CD Cal, 2002].**

Plaintiff likely to succeed on right to publicity claims.

Plaintiff, a publisher of pornographic photographs and the assignee of models' rights of publicity, shows a likelihood of success on its unfair competition claim against defendant, an age verification service (AVS) that acts as a gateway for access to affiliated pornographic web sites. A large number of the models' photographs appeared on sites that used defendant's AVS service. Because California law recognizes secondary liability for violations of publicity rights, and because evidence presented in the context of plaintiff's copyright infringement claim is substantial, plaintiff is likely to prevail to the extent it predicates liability on an aiding and abetting theory for the violation of publicity rights. Plaintiff is also likely to succeed in its claim that defendant is secondarily liable for violating the publicity rights of third-party celebrities who have complained to defendant about the presence of fake nude pictures that either claim to be actual pictures of the celebrities or that advertise themselves as fakes. Plaintiff, as a competitor vying for pornographic viewing dollars, has standing to assert the rights of the third-party celebrities. — **Perfect 10, Inc. v. Cybernet Ventures, Inc., 10 ILR (P&F) 483 [CD Cal, 2002].**

Insufficient showing of trademark infringement.

Plaintiff, a publisher of a pornographic magazine and web site, has not established a likelihood of success on its claim that defendant, which provides an age verification gateway service for pornographic web sites, is liable for contributory trademark infringement based on those sites' direct infringement of plaintiff's mark. — **Perfect 10, Inc. v. Cybernet Ventures, Inc., 10 ILR (P&F) 483 [CD Cal, 2002].**

Preliminary injunction granted.

Plaintiff, the publisher of a pornographic magazine and web site, is entitled to a preliminary injunction against defendant, which provides an age verification service (AVS) for pornographic web sites, based on theories of vicarious and contributory copyright infringement. Although plaintiff's hands are not "white as snow," the balance of hardships weighs significantly in favor of plaintiff. Based on the evidence before the court, it appears that defendant profits from the infringing and unlawful activities of its member web sites without shouldering any of the undesired burdens associated with protection of intellectual property rights. This willful blindness harms plaintiff, defeats the rights of third-parties who find themselves displayed on these sites against their will, and skews the online porn market. Plaintiff has already spent an inordinate amount of time researching these infringements and was forced to pay a competitor in order to discover the infringing images on the defendant's system. Defendant is not only in a position to exercise its ability to control the content of the system, but it already does when it suits its financial interests. Moreover, the tolerance of pirating behavior by the country's largest AVS system harms the public by rewarding illicit behavior. — **Perfect 10, Inc. v. Cybernet Ventures, Inc., 10 ILR (P&F) 483 [CD Cal, 2002].**

ORDER GRANTING PERFECT 10'S MOTION FOR PRELIMINARY INJUNCTION

LOURDES G. BAIRD, *District Judge*:

I. INTRODUCTION

This action springs from Perfect 10, Inc.'s ("Perfect 10") allegations that defendant Cybernet Ventures, Inc. ("Cybernet"), a corporation running a web-service called "Adult Check," and other defendants infringe Perfect 10's copyrights, violate Perfect 10's trademark rights and otherwise engage in rampant unfair business practices.

Currently before the Court is Perfect 10's Request for a Preliminary Injunction, which requests relief against a variety of defendants. The Court has received Perfect 10's motion, defendants Cybernet and Laith Alsarraf's oppositions, and Perfect 10's reply. These briefs are supported by voluminous supporting papers (and the accompanying evidentiary objections).

II. INITIAL EVIDENTIARY OBJECTIONS

In support of its motion for preliminary injunction, Perfect 10 submitted 117 exhibits attached to the declaration of Norman Zadeh, Ph.D. ("Zadeh Decl."), 16 exhibits attached to the declaration of Daniel Farmer ("Farmer Decl.") and 13 exhibits attached to the declaration of Jeffrey Mausner ("Mausner Decl."). Perfect 10 supplemented these declarations with several others. Cybernet basically objects to every exhibit attached to the Zadeh and Farmer declarations, as well as

two exhibits attached to the Mausner declaration. In addition Cybernet has raised objections to portions of declarations filed by Zadeh, Farmer, Mausner, Laurence Rudolph ("Rudolph Decl."), Selma Rubin ("Rubin Decl.") and John Baruck ("Baruck Decl.").

Perfect 10 has also raised objections to evidence submitted by Cybernet. Perfect 10 objects to a single paragraph in the declaration of Timothy Umbreit ("Umbreit Decl.") and to ten paragraphs in the declaration of Frederick Lane III ("Lane Decl."). Before the Court makes its findings of fact under Federal Rule of Procedure 65, it will address these objections. It will do so, however, only in broad strokes.

A. AUTHENTICATION OBJECTIONS

The great bulk of Cybernet's objections center on Perfect 10's exhibits printed off of the internet. See Cybernet Evidentiary Objections ("Def.Obj.") at 1-5. Cybernet argues these exhibits are insufficiently authenticated. *See, e.g., id.* at 1. In support, Cybernet points to two cases, *United States v. Jackson*, 208 F3d 633, 637 *[5 ILR (P&F) 35]* (7th Cir 2000), *cert. denied*, 531 US 973 (2000), and *St. Clair v. Johnny's Oyster & Shrimp, Inc.*, 76 F Supp 2d 773, 774 *[4 ILR (P&F) 317]* (SD Tex 1999).

The *Jackson* court upheld the exclusion of certain web postings attributed to white supremacist groups because they were insufficiently authenticated. 208 F3d at 638. As the court viewed the situation, the criminal defendant in the case had to show that the postings, in which these groups appeared to claim responsibility for a series of racist mailings, actually were posted by the groups, as opposed to being slipped on the groups' web sites by the defendant, who was a skilled computer user. *Id.*

The *St. Clair* court took a more extreme view over the admissibility of data taken from the United States Coast Guard's online vessel database concerning the ownership of a vessel. 76 F Supp 2d at 774. The court viewed the internet as "one large catalyst for rumor, innuendo, and misinformation," stated that there was "no way" the plaintiff could overcome "the presumption that the information . . . discovered on the Internet is inherently untrustworthy." *Id.* The court then excluded the information as hearsay, rather than "relying on the voodoo information taken from the Internet." *Id.*

Although these out-of-circuit cases are informative concerning the potential pitfalls of internet-based documents, this Court must look to the Ninth Circuit for guidance. In *United States v. Tank*, 200 F3d 627, 630 *[6 ILR (P&F) 241]* (9th Cir 2000), the Ninth Circuit addressed the admissibility of certain chat room logs. In *Tank*, the government initiated a prosecution against a child pornography suspect after a search of another suspect's computer files revealed "recorded" online chat room discussions among members of an internet club focused on discussing, trading, and producing child pornography. 200 F3d at 629. The recorder of these chat room discussions had deleted from his computer nonsexual conversations and extraneous material, such as date and time stamps. *Id.*

The *Tank* court observed that the foundational requirement of authentication is satisfied by evidence sufficient to support a finding that the matter in question is what its proponent claims. *See* 200 F3d at 630 (citing Fed. R. Evid. 901(a)). This burden is met when "sufficient proof has been introduced so that a reasonable juror could find in favor of authenticity." *Id.* (citations omitted). This burden was met where the producer of the logs explained how he created the logs with his computer and stated that the printouts appeared to be accurate representations. *Id.* Additionally, the government established the connection between Tank and the chat room log printouts. *Id.*

The Court finds that Zadeh's declaration adequately establishes the prima facie case for admissibility in claiming the exhibits attached to his declaration were either:

1) true and correct copies of documents produced by Cybernet in discovery (identified by a CV prefix);

2) true and correct copies of pictures from Perfect 10 Magazine or from Perfect 10's website; or

3) true and correct copies of pages printed from the Internet that were printed by Zadeh or under his direction.

Zadeh Decl. ¶7. Those webpages that fall under category (3) contain the internet domain address from which the image was printed and the date on which it was printed. *Id.* ¶8.

The first category is covered by *Maljack Prods., Inc. v. GoodTimes Home Video Corp.*, 81 F3d 881, 889 n. 12 (9th Cir 1996) (discovery documents deemed authentic when offered by party-opponent). *See also Orr v. Bank of America, NT & SA*, 285 F3d 764, 2002 WL 507525 *1, *6 n. 20 (9th Cir 2002) (citing to same). The second and third categories have met the prima facie burden because the declarations, particularly in combination with circumstantial indicia of authenticity (such as the dates and web addresses), would support a reasonable juror in the belief that the documents are what Perfect 10 says they are. *See Tank*, 200 F3d at 630. Moreover, because computer printouts are the only practical method by which the allegations of the complaint can be brought before the Court and there is generally a reduced evidentiary standard in preliminary injunction motions,[1] the Court finds that, as a general rule, Zadeh's declaration is sufficient to establish the exhibits' authenticity.[2]

This is particularly true with regard to e-mail communications attributed to Brad Estes. Mr. Estes's deposition testimony establishes that it is part of his duties to respond to posts in Adult Check's "webmasters lounge" and that he responds to e-mails from webmasters concerning aspects of Cybernet's "Adult Check" program. Mausner Decl., Ex. C at 94-97.

B. E-MAILS BETWEEN CYBERNET EMPLOYEES AND THIRD PARTIES

Cybernet does not object to the Court's consideration of the communications purportedly made by Cybernet's employees "if the Court were to accept Plaintiff's scanty authentication" but does object to consideration of the communications attributed to third parties on hearsay grounds. *See* Evid. Obj. at 3. The Court treats the communications attributable to Cybernet employees as party admissions and will accept the third party communications only insofar as they indicate notice of infringing or potentially infringing activity. [3] *See* Fed R. Evid. 801.

C. PRINTOUTS FROM THE THIRD-PARTY WEBSITES

Cybernet objects to the printouts from third-party websites as a violation of the rule against hearsay. *See* Fed. R. Evid. 801. To the extent these images and text are being introduced to show the images and text found on the websites, they are not statements at all—and thus fall outside the ambit of the hearsay rule. [4] To the extent that Perfect 10 relies on directories and the like as assertions that the links provided actually connect to the subject matter claimed in the link, the Court finds the hearsay issue to be a closer question. The Court will deal with this issue, should it arise, on a case-by-case basis. As for any asserted connection between those sites and Adult Check (Cybernet), the Court finds the evidence of Cybernet's business structure and the workings of Adult Check's age verification program combined with statements identifying the individual websites as Adult Check sites are enough to establish the sites' membership in the Adult Check program. This takes the various printouts outside the definition of hearsay, for this purpose. *See* Fed. R. Evid. 801(d)(2)(D).

D. OBJECTION TO CHART

Perfect 10 has prepared a chart ("Chart 1") outlining examples of infringing conduct it claims has been or can be found on websites affiliated with "Adult Check." Zadeh Decl., Chart 1. Cybernet argues that the Zadeh declaration has failed to adequately establish how the chart was compiled, fails to lay an adequate foundation and that its descriptions of exhibits are confusing or inaccurate. Evid. Obj. at 5. The Court finds these objections, as a general matter, to be without merit.

The chart simply reiterates information found elsewhere, including the website where the information was found, the date of download, Perfect 10's claimed infringement, a brief description, which copyright registration covers the claimed Perfect 10 images, and an assertion concerning rights of publicity. To the extent this information is found on the face of each exhibit it is unobjectionable. Further, any errors in describing the contents are easily confirmed by visual inspection of the exhibits. Finally, Perfect 10 has provided information supporting its claimed copyrights and rights of publicity. The Court finds no reason to exclude Chart 1 and has found it a helpful reference in its review of the voluminous documents provided.

E. REPLY EVIDENCE

Perfect 10 has supplied the Court with a significant volume of reply evidence. Perfect 10 claims most of this evidence is directed at arguments made by Cybernet that this motion should be barred by laches or the doctrine of "unclean hands," challenges to Perfect 10's claims of copyright ownership, and Cybernet's claims to be effectively policing the websites making use of the "Adult Check" brand. Cybernet moved ex parte for an order striking all this evidence, which the Court denied in a previous minute order. Nevertheless, for reasons that will become clear the Court has felt no need to consider any of this proposed rebuttal evidence, although isolated exceptions to this general rule will be noted as they appear.

F. OBJECTIONS TO CYBERNET'S DECLARATIONS

The Court sustains Cybernet's objections to the Lane Declaration's ¶¶ 70, 71, and 81, except to the extent they may be used as party admissions.

III. FINDINGS OF FACT

Pursuant to Fed. Rule of Procedure 52(a), the Court makes the followings *[sic]* findings of fact:

Perfect 10

1. Plaintiff Perfect 10, Inc. ("Perfect 10") was formed in 1996 by Norman Zadeh, who has occupied the post of Chief Executive Officer ("CEO") since Perfect 10's formation. Zadeh Decl., ¶ 2.

2. Mr. Zadeh received his Ph.D. in Operations Research in 1972, spent some time working in IBM's computer research department, and has taught applied mathematics as a visiting professor at Stanford, UCLA, U.C. Irvine, and Columbia Universities. Id., ¶¶ 3,4.

3. Armed with a single idea—that there was a market for "classy" pictures of nude women without breast implants, cosmetic surgery, or the like—Perfect 10 was formed. Jenal Decl., Ex. L at 94.

4. Although Mr. Zadeh did not prepare a formal business plan before launching Perfect 10, he had some idea of the costs involved and an idea of how the magazine would develop. Id. at 93; Request for Judicial Notice, Ex. 1 ("*Bacon's* article") at 4.[5]

5. Since Perfect 10's formation, it has built its circulation up to approximately 90,000 issues.[6] Zadeh Decl., ¶ 9.

6. Perfect 10 created a website, Perfect10.com, in 1996. *Id.*

7. Perfect10.com receives about 100,000 visitors each month. *Id.* There is no indication how many paid subscribers Perfect10.com has attracted.

8. Perfect 10's first magazine was published in 1997. Jenal Decl., Ex. L at 97.

9. Since Perfect 10's inception it has created approximately 3,000 photographic images. Zadeh Decl., ¶ 12.

10. Perfect 10 sells memberships allowing access to Perfect10.com at a rate of $25.50 per month to persons 18 years and older. *Id.*, ¶ 13.

11. Despite Perfect 10's costs per individual picture rising into the thousands of dollars, Perfect 10 has not been profitable. *See* Jenal Decl., Ex. L at 97-101. The company is now losing approximately $4 to $5 million per year. *Id.* at 101.

12. Some of this loss was anticipated by the CEO, Mr. Zadeh, although in retrospect those estimates were low. *Id.* at 95; *Bacon's* Article at 4-5. In an August 1997 interview, Mr. Zadeh, said that he planned to publish the magazine six times a year at $6.95 per issue. *Bacon's* Article at 5. For the interview, he stated that he'd be happy losing $500,000 a year, but that he felt he could expect to break even with a few issues. *Id.* At the time, he felt that the magazine would begin attracting advertisers when circulation reached 150,000 to 200,000 copies. *Id.*

13. Perfect 10 lost an estimated $700,000 per issue for the two issues it published in 1997. Jenal Decl., Ex. L at 99. In 1998, Perfect 10 published four issues and estimates losses around $500,000 per issue. *Id.* at 100.

14. In addition to its website and magazine, Perfect 10 has also produced calendars and model of the year videotapes. *Id.* at 101.

Age Verification Services

15. The online-pornographic industry faces the constant threat of litigation and regulation stemming from a variety of fears, including access by under-age users and violations of obscenity laws, including those against child pornography, bestiality and other such subjects that the government identifies and chooses to regulate. *See, e.g.*, Lane Decl. 25, 44.

16. Age verification services ("AVS") are meant to provide some level of reassurance to all involved.

17. An AVS places a computer script on individual webpages or websites. Farmer Decl., ¶ 15. When a visitor hits a page containing the script, it provides a prompt before allowing the visitor to view the page or other pages on the site. *Id.* AVS services sell passwords to consumers so they can gain access to materials on participating websites. Lane Decl., ¶ 47; Farmer Decl., ¶ 13.

18. Although not a perfect screen, the credit card is a relatively strong proxy for identifying those who are 18 or older. Lane Decl., ¶ 46.

AVS and Credit Card Billing

19. The growth of the online-pornographic business has been a boon to credit card companies. Lane Decl. ¶ 32. At the same time, credit card companies have had problems with a phenomenon called chargebacks as they relate to online adult businesses. *Id.* ¶¶ 51, 52.

20. Chargebacks are requests for reversals of credit card charges and are often tied to customer complaints. *Id.* ¶ 51. Mastercard and Visa have established strict limits on the percentages of chargebacks they will tolerate from any one account. *Id.* ¶ 52. Merchants exceeding those limits are heavily fined and may lose their merchant processing accounts. *Id.*

Cybernet Ventures, Inc.

21. Cybernet Ventures, Inc. ("Cybernet") runs an AVS called "Adult Check." Lane Decl., 46. Cybernet, through its Adult Check brand, bills itself as the leading AVS on the Internet. *Id.* ¶ 48. Adult Check claims to have approximately 300,000 "regular" sites and 14,000 "Gold" sites using its service. Umbreit Decl., ¶ 24.

22. Based on Adult Check's image requirements, it estimates that there are over 20 million images available on participating web sites. *Id.* On an average day, Cybernet authenticates an average of 1.9 million Adult Check IDs. *Id.* ¶ 12.

Adult Check's Internal Organization

23. Individual "webmasters" run the websites that make up the Adult Check "network."[7] *See, e.g.*, Lane Decl., ¶ 58. These webmasters are not charged to use the Adult Check service. Umbreit Decl., ¶ 7.

24. Each webmaster is responsible for running the website, including creating the site's content, finding a server to host the site and other technical details, as well as promoting the site. Lane Decl., ¶¶ 34-36.

25. When a new user visits one of these sites, they are directed to Cybernet's site on adultcheck.com to register with Adult Check. Farmer Decl., ¶ 14; Umbreit Decl. ¶¶ 9, 10.

26. Cybernet has two tiers of membership available, a "regular" membership and an "Adult Check Gold" membership. *See, e.g.*, Umbreit ¶ 24. For $19.95 every three months, a regular member receives access to all sites using the AVS, except for the Gold sites. Zadeh Decl., Ex. 1 at 2. The Gold sites contain more images, more diversity, and generally meet more criteria aimed at ensuring these sites are higher-quality than those available to "regular" members. *See, e.g.*, Zadeh Decl., Ex. 1 at 19-20 (contrasting requirements); Umbreit Decl., ¶ 22. The Gold memberships are more expensive and provide access to all the websites classified as Adult Check Gold (approximately 14,000 sites) for a price of $19.95 per month. Zadeh Decl., Ex. 4.

27. All fees paid by these members go directly to Cybernet. On a semi-monthly basis Cybernet then pays each individual webmaster a commission attributed to the site where the member originally signed up for his or her Adult Check membership. Umbreit Decl., ¶ 13; Zadeh Decl., Ex. 1 at 8-10.

28. There are two main factors driving an AVS service's success, the quantity of images available on the participating websites and their quality. *See* Lane Decl., ¶ 54; Umbreit Decl. ¶ 22. There is also a need to prevent a redundancy of similar sites because this dilutes the experience of viewers, increasing dissatisfaction with a service and increasing the likelihood of users leaving the service or requesting

chargebacks. Lane Decl., ¶ 57; Zadeh Decl., Ex. 1 at 21.

29. Adult Check has a financial incentive to insure that the participating websites are numerous, somewhat distinctive and contain images that attract users. As a result Adult Check has adopted a variety of guidelines concerning the content provided by the websites using its name and services. Zadeh Decl, Ex. 1 at 15-24.

30. Adult Check has divided up its websites into six tiers. They are as follows:

Tier 1. Adult Check exclusive sites with only Adult Check ads or no ads at all;

Tier 2. Adult Check exclusive sites with both Adult Check ads and non-Adult Check ads;

Tier 3. Adult Check Exclusive sites with non-Adult Check ads.

Tier 4. Non-exclusive sites with only Adult Check ads or no adds ad all;

Tier 5. Non-exclusive sites with both Adult Check ads and non-Adult Check ads;

Tier 6. Non-exclusive sites with non-Adult Check ads.

Each tier involves greater value for users along a spectrum defined by greater commitment to the Adult Check brand.

See Zadeh Decl., Ex. 1 at 16.

31. Cybernet views sites and assigns keywords to further efficiency of an internal search engine that it provides as a service to consumers. Zadeh Decl., Ex. 12 at 63.

32. Part of Cybernet's Adult Check service is a linking service found on adultcheck.com. Cybernet provides links to various webpages organized by category, including categories devoted to celebrity sites. *See, e.g.*, Zadeh Decl., Exs. 72 & 81.

33. Adult Check also provides a search function that searches for content within the Adult Check affiliated websites and webpages. Umbreit Decl., ¶17.

Adult Check Policies

34. Adult Check has also endorsed a number of "General Policies," including:

1) Any unlawful activities or activities that, within the sole and absolute discretion of Adult Check may be or are harmful to its reputation, image, goodwill (including but not limited to inappropriate Usenet postings or spamming) will result in immediate termination;

2) Illegal content is strictly prohibited. Illegal content includes, but is not limited to: minors, rape and bestiality;

3) Fraud, illegal activities, unfair or deceptive trade practices or violation of the Adult Check Policies will result in immediate termination of your account; and

4) Violation of the Adult Check limited use license of trademarks and copyrighted materials is prohibited.

Zadeh Decl., Ex. 1 at 13.

35. Adult Check also has a policy related to its Links Page, which leads Adult Check users to various sites and webpages by providing a directory organized by category. In order to be listed on the Links Pages:

1) A site may not display, publish, link to or provide access to any images, pictures, stories, video clips or any other media portraying any content that is deemed illegal in the United States. Any site containing content deemed illegal in the United States will be removed from the Links Page and the account will be deactivated;

2)	Each Adult Check Site must contain unique, quality and adequate content. The quality, uniqueness and adequacy of the content is solely within the discretion of AC, but generally means at least 30 pictures of sufficient quality to provide value to the Adult Check customer. These guidelines are loose and subjective to insure that there is a definite benefit for the Adult Check customers without requiring them to pay extra fees;

3)	A participating site must be placed in the appropriate category of the Links Pages and the description of the site must be accurate. Any deceptive information is grounds for removing the site from the Links Page.

4)	Site names and site descriptions must not be false, misleading or deceptive.

5)	Multiple sites owned by the same person or entity must be designed as individual sites and may not be listed more than once.

6)	Feeder sites, must also comply with the minimal standards.

7)	Membership sites, requiring further membership fees must provide content before an Adult Check customer is required to pay any fees.

8)	The webmaster is responsible for providing all content. Cybernet disclaims any responsibility for content.

9)	All sites are reviewed and monitored for continued compliance.

10)	Each site submitted must be unique. Templated sites will not be accepted for placement on the links page. Templated sites are defined as two or more sites that are created or appear to the viewer as substantially identical, despite minor variations such as site title.

11)	The use of any registered trademark, trade name, copyright or exclusive publicity right without proper authority or written consent of the owner, will not be permitted on any Adult Check site. Violation of this policy will, among other things, result in the removal of the violating site from the Links pages and the termination of the website's affiliation with Adult Check.

Zadeh Decl., Ex. 1 at 15, 16.

36.	Adult Check also has a Child Pornography policy. Adult Check classifies its Child Pornography policy as "zero tolerance." This policy is enforced anywhere images, words or inferences relating to child pornography are used in conjunction with the Adult Check system. Adult Check explicitly states: "This is *not* limited to sites linked to from our links pages," thus implying it applies to all content accessed through the use of Adult Check passwords. When this policy is violated, the site will be closed, removed from the Adult Check system without warning, the limited use license for the Adult Check script will be revoked and the offender must remove all links and references to Adult Check from the offender's sites, presumably going beyond the single webpage or site where the offending material appears. Zadeh Decl., Ex. 1 at 14, 15 (emphasis added to quote).

37.	Prior to August 8, 2001, Cybernet's policy on copyright and trademark violations was self-characterized as "neutral." In an email, one employee put it this way:

	If Webmaster A contacts us and says that Webmaster B is violating his or her copyrights or trademarks we will do one thing and one thing only. Adult Check will forward an email from Webmaster A to Webmaster B. It is then Webmaster B's responsibility to reply to Webmaster A and solve the matter.

It would never be a good idea for Adult Check to take any other stance in these matters. Doing so would open a huge amount of legal liability due to the possibility of error. Webmaster A could be lying and Webmaster B could have designed the site first and it could have actually been Webmaster A who copied it! This is why we stay neutral.

Zadeh Decl., Ex. 20 at 240; see also Mausner Decl., Ex. C at 97.

38. Since August 8, 2001, Cybernet has promulgated a copyright policy labeled "Digital Millennium Copyright Act ("DMCA") policy". Under this policy, a notice of infringement sent to Cybernet must include:

1) A physical or electronic signature of the owner or a person authorized to act on behalf of the owner;

2) An identification of the copyrighted work and if it is located on a web page, the specific address of the web page should be provided;

3) ID of the material that is claimed to be infringing or the subject of infringing activity;

4) statement of good faith belief that use of the material is not authorized by the copyright owner, its agent or the law;

According to Cybernet's "DMCA Policy", upon receipt of a written notification meeting *all* of its criteria, Cybernet will:

1) Act expeditiously to remove links or disable access to the allegedly infringing material;

2) Take reasonable steps to promptly notify the accused subscriber; and

3) forward a copy of the written notification to the accused subscriber.

This policy then provides for a counter notification procedure to be used by webmasters accused of infringement. Finally, "in appropriate circumstances where [Cybernet] receives multiple notices, subscribers to [its] age verification services will be terminated."

Zadeh Decl., Ex. 1 at 21-24.

39. There is no credible evidence that Cybernet actively enforces its "DMCA policy." Rather there is evidence that four months after the policy became effective and well after this action had begun, clearly infringing pictures were on websites identified by Perfect 10 in its Second Amended Complaint, *see* Zadeh Decl., Ex. 76, as well as blatantly infringing pictures on sites listed in the Third Amended Complaint, see Zadeh Decl., Ex. 31.

Conduct by Adult Check Affiliated Websites

40. Sites affiliated with Adult Check have engaged in a range of conduct, of which a representative sample includes:

41. On August 6, 2001, a website affiliated with Adult Check, named FemCelebs and located at animald.com, contained identical copies of at least three Perfect 10 magazine covers. Zadeh Decl., Ex. 8. Perfect 10 was assigned rights of publicity by the pictured models. Zadeh Decl., Ex. 117

42. On December 19, 2001, another Adult Check affiliated website, Celebrities Online, located at *www.celebs-online.com*, displayed identical copies of several photographs containing pictures derived from the Perfect 10 magazine and Perfect 10's website. The pictured model had assigned her rights of publicity to Perfect 10. Several of the pictures contained the words Perfect 10 as well as a Perfect 10 copyright notice. Zadeh Decl., Ex. 31.

43. On December 20, 2001, another site affiliated with Adult Check, Before & After, located at joebosco.com, displayed identical pictures derived from Perfect 10's magazine and containing models who had assigned their rights of publicity to Perfect 10. Zadeh Decl., Ex. 38.

44. On December 22, 2001, fredd38.com, part of the websites owned by defendants FTV, ftv.net, Vic Toria, and AEI Productions (collectively, "the FTV defendants"), and affiliated with Adult Check, displayed a picture purporting to be Christina Aguilera posing topless, but actually contained a photograph of a Perfect 10 model found on its website, altered by adding Ms. Aguilera's head. Zadeh Decl., Ex. 46. This model had assigned her rights of publicity to Perfect 10.

45. On December 11, 2001, the website located at celeblust.com, also owned by the FTV defendants displayed a picture purporting to be a topless Faith Hill, but actually contained a digitally altered image of a Perfect 10 model. Zadeh Decl., Ex. 57.

46. These examples are not isolated and Perfect 10 has found more than 10,000 copies of Perfect 10 images on approximately 900 websites affiliated with Adult Check.[8] Zadeh Decl., 46.

Defaults Entered

47. Sean Devine has had a default entered against him based on Perfect 10 images and models displayed on the website BabesofBablyon.com. *See* Zadeh Decl., Ex. 115.

48. Default has been entered against defendants Funet, Inc. and AEI Productions, Inc., supported by Zadeh Decl., Ex. 116 & Ex. 114.

Extent of Problematic Images and Sites

49. A significant number of the images found on websites affiliated with Adult Check consist of images:

1) containing celebrities who have not consented to the use of such images;

2) contain the heads of celebrities superimposed on other models, including Perfect 10 models;

3) identical to those protected by Perfect 10's copyrights;

4) displaying Perfect 10's trademarks;

5) displaying copies of Perfect 10's images with another identifying mark placed on the image; and

6) containing images of models who have assigned their rights of publicity to Perfect 10.

50. Celebrity websites make up approximately 4,000 of the 314,000 websites affiliated with Adult Check. They may make up as many as 2,000,000 of the images found on the Adult Check affiliated sites. Umbreit Decl. ¶19.

51. Some of these websites identify themselves as "fake." Zadeh Decl., Ex. 107.

52. Some of these websites portray graphic scenes and create the impression that the celebrities mentioned are affiliated with the action presented.

53. Cybernet chooses which websites are placed in the celebrity category.

Notice to Cybernet of Problems on Affiliated Sites

54. Cybernet was provided with notice of 18 celebrities that objected to usage of their identities and/or images on Adult Check affiliated sites back in November 27, 2000. Zadeh Reply Decl. ("Zadeh Decl. II"), Ex. 19 at 267.[9]

55. On January 7, 2002, Perfect 10 provided a number of declarations to the Court from celebrities, generally providing:

I have not licensed any pornographic website or any affiliate of such website to sue or exploit my name, likeness or identity. In general, I do not want any entity to use or exploit my name, likeness or identity, without my express written permission, or the permission of my manager or someone with the authority to act on my behalf.

Aguilera Decl.

56. In order for a site to be accepted into the Adult Check system, Cybernet reviews the site. Zadeh Decl., Ex. 30 at 287a.

57. Among the considerations in reviewing these sites, Cybernet looks for potentially underage images and overuse of celebrity images. *Id.* at 287b.

58. On February 27, 2001, three months after a group of celebrities provided Adult Check with direct notice that use of their images was not allowed, an Adult Check employee refused to accept a site because, among other reasons:

> Please make sure that your site does not have any of the following models in its principal content [incl. models listed in request] . . . . This content cannot be allowed since it would continue to oversaturate our links page.

Zadeh Decl., Ex. 30 at 287b.

59. Generally, Cybernet considers an image to be oversaturated if it appears 7 to 10 times. *Id.*, Ex. 1 at 21; Ex. 30 at 287b.

60. Cybernet has a staff of twelve that reviews sites when they initially join Adult Check, with a goal of doing monthly reviews, and the staff also does

spot checking. Mausner Decl., Ex. C at 102, 114.

61. Cybernet actively reviews and directs affiliated webmasters on the appearance and content of their sites. Zadeh Decl., Ex. 30.

62. Cybernet provides Adult Check webmasters with a variety of tools to help them develop their websites. *See, e.g.*, Zadeh Decl., Exs. 1, 18.

63. Adult Check's Knowledge Base does not discuss protection of copyrights, trademarks or publicity rights. *See* Zadeh Decl., Ex. 18.

IV. CONCLUSIONS OF LAW

1. There is not a serious question on the merits concerning Cybernet's liability for direct copyright infringement of Perfect 10's copyrights.

2. There is a strong likelihood of success for Perfect 10's contributory copyright infringement claims against Cybernet.

3. There is a strong likelihood of success for Perfect 10's vicarious copyright infringement claims against Cybernet.

4. There is a substantial question whether or not Cybernet is a provider of online services under the Digital Millennium Copyright Act ("DMCA").

5. If Cybernet qualifies as an online service provider under the DMCA there is little likelihood that any DMCA "safe harbor" will apply.

6. There is not a strong likelihood of success on Perfect 10's direct liability claims against Cybernet for violating the models' publicity rights assigned to Perfect 10.

7. There is a strong likelihood of success on Perfect 10's claims of aiding and abetting liability for Cybernet's role in the violations of the publicity rights assigned to Perfect 10.

8. Perfect 10 has standing to assert as an unfair business practice the abuse of publicity rights for those persons who have provided Cybernet with actual

notice that use of their images is not authorized.

9. There is a strong likelihood of success on Perfect 10's claim that Cybernet has violated California's unfair business practices act by violating the rights of publicity for those persons who have provided Cybernet with actual notice that use of their images is not authorized.

10. There is not a strong likelihood of success on Perfect 10's claims that Cybernet is liable for contributory trademark infringement of Perfect 10's trademark rights.

11. Cybernet has not made a good faith effort to root out illegal conduct among its webmasters and gains direct financial gains as a result.

11. *[sic]* Cybernet is a competitor of Perfect 10's.

12. There is a strong likelihood that Perfect 10 will prevail on its claim that Cybernet's practices are "unfair" under the unfair business practices act.

13. The unclean hands and laches doctrines are not applicable to this motion.

14. Harm is presumed for unfair competition, violations of copyright, and for trademark infringement.

15. Perfect 10 has shown a strong likelihood that it will suffer irreparable harm if the unfair business practices, copyright violations, and trademark violations are not enjoined.

16. Enjoining these practices is consistent with the public interest.

17. Enjoining these practices will not result in an inequitable burden on Cybernet.

18. The balance of hardships tips in favor of Perfect 10.

V. PRELIMINARY INJUNCTION STANDARDS

In the Ninth Circuit, two interrelated tests exist for determining the propriety of the issuance of a preliminary injunction. Under the first test, the Court may not issue a preliminary injunction unless: (1) the moving party has established a strong likelihood of success on the merits; (2) the moving party will suffer irreparable injury and has no adequate remedy at law if injunctive relief is not granted; (3) the balance of hardships tips in favor of the movant; and (4) granting the injunction is in the public interest. *See Martin Int'l Olympic Comm.*, 740 F2d 670, 674-75 (1984); *Greene v. Bowen*, 639 F Supp 554, 558 (ED Cal 1986). Under the alternative test, a plaintiff must show either (1) a combination of probable success on the merits and the possibility of irreparable injury; or (2) that a serious question exists going to the merits and that the balance of hardships tip sharply in the plaintiff's favor. *See First Brands Corp. v. Fred Meyer, Inc.*, 809 F2d 1378, 1381 (9th Cir 1987).

The two tests represent "a continuum of equitable discretion whereby the greater the relative hardship to the moving party, the less probability of success must be shown." *Regents of Univ. of Calif. v. ABC, Inc.*, 747 F2d 511, 515 (9th Cir 1984). *See also Benda v. Grand Lodge of Int'l Ass'n of Machinists*, 584 F2d 308, 315 (9th Cir 1978).

VI. LIKELIHOOD OF SUCCESS

A. COPYRIGHT INFRINGEMENT

1. Direct Infringement

To prove copyright infringement, a plaintiff must prove two elements: (1) ownership of a valid copyright, and (2) copying of protectable expression by the defendant. *Baxter v. MCA, Inc.*, 812 F2d 421, 423 (9th Cir 1987). Infringement occurs when a defendant violates one of the exclusive rights of the copyright holder. 17 USC §501(a). Direct infringement does not require intent or any particular state of mind, although willfulness is relevant to the award of statutory damages. 17 USC §504(c).

a. Does Perfect 10's Registered Copyright In Its Magazines Cover The Individual Pictures Involved Here?

Cybernet's first line of defense is to challenge the adequacy of Perfect 10's showing of copyright protection for its claimed images. Opp'n at 18. Cybernet contends that the copyright registrations produced in this motion involve collective works, the Perfect 10 magazines and the Internet site, but the registrations do not establish copyrights in the individual pictures. Opp'n at 18. Cybernet's only authority is a quote to 15 USC §103(b) which provides:

> The copyright in a compilations or derivative work extends only to the material contributed by the author of such work and distinguished from the preexisting material employed in the work and does not imply an exclusive right in the preexisting material. The copyright in such work is independent of, and does not alter or enlarge the scope, duration, ownership, or subsistence of, any copyright protection in the preexisting material.

15 USC §103(b).

It is unclear exactly what Cybernet is challenging—Perfect 10's ability to bring suit under the Copyright Act, the scope of the registrations, the entitlement to the presumption of prima facie validity as to the copyright registration, or directly challenging Perfect 10's claimed copyright in these images.

As an initial matter, where the owner of a copyright for a collective work also owns the copyright for a constituent part of that work, registration of the collective work is sufficient to permit an infringement action under 15 USC §411(a). [10] Moreover, the Court finds that Perfect 10 is entitled to treat the copyright registrations as prima facie evidence that the individual pictures are copyrighted. *See Autoskill, Inc. v. National Educ. Support Sys., Inc.*, 994 F2d 1476, 1487-88 (10th Cir 1993), *disagreed with on other grounds, Parker v. Bain*, 68 F3d 1131, 1136 n. 8 (9th Cir 1995); *cf.* 17 USC §404 (similar principle with regard to reach of copyright notice in collective work). Perfect 10's copyright registrations for the magazine issues indicate that they are collective works where contributions to the work were works "made for hire." *See, e.g.*, Mausner Decl., Ex. A at 9. The website registration recognizes that the two-dimensional text and photographs on the site include contributions made for hire and incorporate photographs published in the Perfect 10 magazine. *Id.* at 7-8. The Court concludes this is sufficient to raise the presumption of validity, particularly where Cybernet has made no sustained argument to the contrary. [11] Perfect 10 has shown a strong likelihood that it owns a valid copyright in the asserted images.

b. Has Cybernet Violated Any of Perfect 10's Rights Under the Copyright Act?

Cybernet's other argument fares better. Cybernet contends that it cannot be held directly liable for any copyright infringement carried out by its affiliated websites because "no infringing files exist on any computer equipment owned by Cybernet." Opp'n at 19. Perfect 10 does not address this argument in its reply papers and the Court finds that there is little likelihood of success on this claim. Assuming that websites on the Adult Check system infringe Perfect 10's copyrights, there is no evidence that Cybernet owns any of these websites or otherwise engages in directly infringing activity in the classic sense.

There might exist another route to direct liability, however. Computer technology, and in particular the Internet, has created a challenge to copyright's strict liability scheme. Because of the architecture of the web and the workings of computer technology, almost any business that utilizes computer hardware to create access to the Internet or to store content may find its hardware creating or displaying infringing material as a result of decisions by third-parties (the system's users) without the business doing any truly volitional actions.

Religious Technology Center v. Netcom On-line Comm. Servs., Inc., 907 F Supp 1361 *[1 ILR (P&F) 778]* (ND Cal 1995), illustrates this point vividly. In *Religious Technology*, a disgruntled former Church of Scientology member was accused of posting copyrighted works on the Internet. *Id.* at 1365-66. This member used a bulletin board service (BBS) to gain access to the Internet, and the BBS in turn used the facilities of Netcom to provide this access. *Id.* at 1366. When the initial defendant sent his postings to the Internet, the information was automatically stored briefly on the BBS's computer and then automatically copied on Netcom's computer. *Id.* at 1367. Once on Netcom's computers, the messages were then available to Netcom's users and eventually to all users that participated in a service called Usenet. *Id.* at 1367-68.

The Ninth Circuit in a previous case, *MAI Systems Corp. v. Peak Computer, Inc.*, 991 F2d 511, 518 *[1 ILR (P&F) 71]* (9th Cir 1993) had upheld a finding of copyright infringement where a repair person who was not authorized to use a computer owner's licensed operating system software had merely turned on the computer.[12] The relevant copying in *MAI Systems* was the loading of the operating system into the computer's memory long enough to check an "error log." 991 F2d at 518. Similarly, in *Religious Technology*, the existence of the messages on the system were "sufficiently 'fixed' to constitute recognizable copies under the Copyright Act." 907 F Supp at 1368.

Nevertheless, the *Religious Technology* court found Netcom was not liable for direct copyright infringement. *Id.* at 1372-73. First the court noted that Netcom had not initiated the copying. *Id.* at 1368. The court then analogized Netcom's creation of a system that automatically and uniformly creates temporary copies of all data through it to a copying machine. *Id.* at 1369. The court rejected the possibility that such actions could violate the exclusive right to reproduce a work absent some further element of volition or causation, relying on the unreasonable liability such a regime would create. *Id.*

Similarly, the Netcom court rejected the argument that the storage of the works on Netcom's system for up to eleven days violated the plaintiffs' right to publicly distribute and display their works. *Id.* at 1371-72. The court found that there was the same causation and volition problems that infected the reproduction claim. *Id.* at 1372. The actions of the BBS provider were automatic and indiscriminate. *Id.* Moreover, the court pointed to the fact that Netcom did not maintain an archive of files for its users, thus it could not be said to be supplying a product to users. *Id.* This contrasted with some of its competitors that created or controlled content available to their subscribers. *Id.* The failure to establish violation of the plaintiffs' reproduction, distribution or display rights by Netcom thus defeated plaintiffs' direct infringement theory. *See id.* at 1370, 1373.

Following the *Religious Technology* decision, another district court found that a BBS operator that knew about copyright infringement on its service and encouraged others to upload infringing products onto his service could not be held liable on a direct infringement theory. *See Sega Enterprises, Ltd. v. MAPHIA*, 948 F Supp 923, 931 *[2 ILR (P&F) 168]* (ND Cal 1996). This was so because the activity charged had no bearing on whether the BBS operator "directly caused" the copying to occur. *Id.*

Finally, in *Playboy Enterprises, Inc. v. Russ Hardenburgh, Inc.*, 982 F Supp 503, 512 *[2 ILR (P&F) 13]* (ND Ohio 1997), a district court found direct infringement despite its agreement with the rationale of *Religious Technology*. The *Hardenburgh* court stressed that a direct infringer must "actually engage" in one of the activities reserved to copyright owners. *Id.* In *Hardenburgh*, the court found that the defendant BBS providers engaged in two of the activities exclusively reserved for copyright owners. *Id.* at 513.

First, the court found the defendants had distributed and displayed copies of Playboy photographs. *Id.* This finding hinged on the defendant's policy of encouraging subscribers to upload files onto its system, viewing the files in the upload file, and then moving the uploaded files into files generally available to subscribers. *Id.* This transformed the defendants from passive providers of a space to active participants in the process of copyright infringement. The moving of the files, accomplished by employees constituted the distribution, and the display of those copes *[sic]* after the BBS's employees placed the files there violated the right of display. *Id.*

The principle distilled from these cases is a requirement that defendants must *actively* engage in one of the activities recognized in the Copyright Act.[13] Based on the evidence before the Court it appears that Cybernet does not use its hardware to either store the infringing images or move them from one location to another for display. This technical separation between its facilities and those of its webmasters prevents Cybernet from engaging in reproduction or distribution, and makes it doubtful that Cybernet publicly displays the works. Further, there is currently no evidence that Cybernet has prepared works based upon Perfect 10's copyrighted material. The Court therefore concludes that there is little likelihood that Perfect 10 will succeed on its direct infringement theory.

2. Contributory Infringement

Liability for contributory copyright infringement attaches when "one who, with knowledge of the infringing activity, induces, causes or materially contributes to the infringing conduct of another." *A&M Records, Inc. v. Napster, Inc.*, 239 F3d 1004, 1019 *[7 ILR (P&F) 1]* (9th Cir 2001) ("*Napster II*"). Put differently, liability exists if the defendant engages in personal conduct that encourages or assists the infringement. *Id.* The standard for the knowledge requirement is objective, and is satisfied where the defendant knows or has reason to know of the infringing activity. *Gershwin Publishing Corp. v. Columbia Artists Mgmt., Inc.*, 443 F2d 1159, 1162 (2d Cir 1971).

a. Cybernet's Knowledge

Cybernet's only argument against Perfect 10's contributory infringement theory is that Cybernet lacks the requisite knowledge to be held liable. Opp'n at 20. Cybernet relies heavily on Perfect 10's failure to contact Cybernet with its claims before beginning the present litigation. *Id.* According to Cybernet, although it employs twelve site reviewers, even if they had seen Perfect 10 copyright notices on various sites, they would not necessarily know Perfect 10's copyrights were infringed because they might be licensed. *Id.* at 20-21.

In contrast, there is evidence that Steven Easton of the Association for the Protection of Internet Copyright contacted Cybernet with approximately 2,000 e-mails, beginning in 1996 or 1997, notifying Cybernet of alleged copyright infringement on its system.[14] Easton Decl. ¶ 2. Perfect 10 has also brought forward evidence that Cybernet was notified of generic potential copyright infringement by users in 2001. Zadeh Decl., Ex. 102. Additionally, Cybernet's site reviewers review every site before allowing the sites to utilize the Adult Check system, and attempt to review other sites monthly. Mausner Decl., Ex. C at 102, 114; Zadeh Decl., Ex. 30. Although they might not detect every copyright violation, there is evidence that many sites contain disclaimers to the effect, "we do not hold copyrights for these works." Farmer Depo. at 121:19-21. Finally, Perfect 10's Second Amended Complaint, filed on June 15, 2001, contained notice of Perfect 10's allegations concerning potential infringement on 77 different websites.

This evidence of notice compares favorably with the allegations of notice in *Fonovisa, Inc. v. Cherry Auction, Inc.*, 76 F3d 259 (9th Cir 1996). In *Fonovisa*, the Fresno County Sheriff's Department seized 38,000 counterfeit tapes (copyright holders unstated) from a swap meet approximately a year and a half before the plaintiff filed suit. *See Fonovisa, Inc. v. Cherry Auction, Inc.*, 847 F Supp 1492, 1494 (ED Cal 1994) *rev'd* 76 F3d 259 (9th

Cir 1996) ("*Fonovisa I*"). Additionally, the swap meet had received a letter six months before the suit from a police officer who "observed that several casual vendors of Latin audio music tapes had abandoned their booths upon his arrival." *Id.* at 1494. Finally, three months before the suit an investigator for the plaintiff witnessed infringing sales of counterfeit goods. *Id.* After the First Amended Complaint was served, investigators then revisited the swap meet where they found many vendors selling "counterfeits at tellingly low prices." *Id.* at 1495. On appeal from the district court's dismissal of the claim, the Ninth Circuit stated "There is no question that plaintiff adequately alleged the element of knowledge in this case." *Fonovisa*, 76 F3d at 264.

Perfect 10 has raised at least a serious question on the issue of knowledge. The Court finds that there is a strong likelihood of success in proving general knowledge of copyright infringement prior to Perfect 10's filing of the complaint. There are also serious questions as to Cybernet's constructive knowledge of infringement of Perfect 10's copyrights *prior* to the complaint raised by this general knowledge, Cybernet's review of sites containing Perfect 10 images and the likelihood of those sites containing copyright disclaimers. Further, there appears to be little question that Cybernet has been provided with actual notice of a large number of alleged infringements since June 2001.[15] The Court thus finds there is a strong likelihood of success that Perfect 10 will satisfy the knowledge requirement for contributory liability.

b. Cybernet's Material Contribution to Infringing Activity

The Court also finds that there is a strong likelihood that Perfect 10 will succeed in establishing Cybernet's material contributions to the infringing activity. Cybernet markets the Adult Check brand through advertising, it pays webmasters commissions directly based upon the number of Adult Check users that register through the site, it provides technical and content advice, it reviews sites, and it attempts to control the quality of the "product" it presents to consumers as a unified brand. Cybernet's entire business model is premised on harnessing the competitive pressures between individual webmasters into a cooperative system that benefits the webmasters by increasing the overall value to consumers. Cybernet's role in this system is crucial, and it profits accordingly, only paying out approximately 1/2 of each subscriber's payments to the participating websites for each of its users, who access the system close to 2 million times daily.

In *Fonovisa* the Ninth Circuit had "little difficulty" in holding the allegations directed at a swap meet, where the vendors were selling counterfeit goods, sufficient to show material contribution. 76 F3d at 263. As the court observed, "it would be difficult for the infringing activity to take place in the massive quantities alleged without the support services provided by the swap meet," including the provision of space, utilities, parking, advertising, plumbing and customers. *Id.* Similarly, Cybernet's hand in Adult Check, and in particular its steady payments to infringing sites along with its advertising, materially contribute to the growth and proliferation of any infringement. This conclusion comports with both *Napster* decisions and with *Religious Technology*.[16] The Court finds the evidence before it supports the conclusion that Perfect 10 has a strong likelihood of establishing material contribution by Cybernet to activity that infringes Perfect 10's copyrights.

c. Contributory Infringement—Conclusion

The Court therefore finds that there is at least a serious question on the merits of Perfect 10's contributory infringement claim against Cybernet prior to the filing of the present suit and a strong likelihood of success on its claims stemming from Cybernet's post-filing conduct.

3. Vicarious Copyright Infringement

Courts have extended vicarious liability in the copyright context to defendants that have (1) the right and ability to exercise control over a directly infringing party and its activities and (2) obtained a direct financial benefit from the infringing activities. *Fonovisa*, 76 F3d at 262.

a. Direct Financial Interest

Cybernet argues that it does not have a sufficiently direct financial interest to be held liable for vicarious copyright infringement. Opp'n at 22-23. The Court strongly disagrees. Cybernet markets the Adult Check brand based on both the number of images and their quality. Zadeh Decl., Ex. 4; Lane Decl. ¶¶ 54, 57. Perfect 10 has brought forward evidence that it has sunk significant resources into developing high-quality adult images. Taking

Perfect 10's allegations of 10,000 infringing images at face value, as Cybernet does for purposes of this test, *see* Opp'n at 22, Cybernet benefits from the draw posed by the existence of these works provided at a cost far below that provided by the copyright owner. *See Fonovisa*, 76 F3d at 263-64; Lane Decl. ¶81; *see also Napster II*, 239 F3d at 1023 ("Ample evidence supports the district court's finding that Napster's future revenue is directly dependent upon 'increases in user base.' More users register with the Napster system as the quality and quantity of available music increases.") Cybernet benefits directly from these infringing sites to the extent that they have brought in new users because the new customers pay Cybernet directly. In addition, there is the ancillary benefit brought in by the incremental additional value these sites pose to consumers, who gain access to all sites by paying the Adult Check membership fee. *Cf. Religious Technology*, 907 F Supp at 1377 (granting defendant summary judgment where no evidence "that Netcom's policy directly financially benefits Netcom, such as by attracting new subscribers.") Moreover, the Court finds that there is a strong likelihood that Perfect 10 will establish a "symbiotic interest" between Cybernet and the infringing websites based on the close interrelationship between Cybernet and its affiliated websites, a relationship that appears to outside consumers as if Adult Check constitutes a single brand. *See Adobe Systems, Inc. v. Canus Productions, Inc.*, 173 F Supp 2d 1044, 1051 (CD Cal 2001) (discussing "symbiotic interest"). It should be noted that *all* the money associated with these websites flows directly to Cybernet before some of it is returned to the individual site owners as "commissions." The Court concludes that this evidence creates a strong likelihood Perfect 10 will establish this direct financial interest.

Cybernet relies on *Adobe Systems*, 173 F Supp 2d at 1052, to argue otherwise. *Adobe Systems* involves a copyright action against the proprietor of weekly computer fairs where approximately one hundred pirated copies of Adobe Systems software were located at shows that averaged up to 15,000 attendees per weekend. *Id.* at 1047. On plaintiff's motion for summary judgment the court discussed *Fonovisa* and its requirement of direct financial benefit. *Id.* at 1050-53.

The *Adobe Systems* court read into *Fonovisa*'s discussion of vicarious liability a requirement to show "a direct financial benefit to the defendant from the 'draw' of the infringing products." *Id.* at 1050. At different points in the opinion this idea was expressed in language such as:

- "the sale of the counterfeit products must in fact be *the* 'draw' for customers to the venue." *Id.* at 1050 (emphasis added).

- "Plaintiffs must show that the vendor's infringement constitutes a draw to the venue to the extent that the economic interests of the direct infringer and those of the landlord become closely intertwined." *Id.* at 1051.

- "[P]laintiff bears the burden of demonstrating a direct financial benefit to the landlord from 'customers seeking to purchase infringing recordings' and profits which 'flow directly from customers who want to buy the counterfeit recordings.' " *Id.* at 1050.

- "Without the requirement that the counterfeit goods provide *the main* customer draw, *Fonovisa* would "provide essentially for the limitless expansion of vicarious liability into spheres wholly unintended by the court." *Id.* at 1051 (emphasis added).

- "*Fonovisa* found a symbiotic relationship existed between the infringing vendors and the landlord because 'the very success of the landlord's venture depends on the counterfeiting activity (and thus the landlord has every incentive to allow the activity to continue).' " *Id.* at 1051.

The *Adobe Systems* court then concluded that on the facts of the case, where both the number of infringements and the apparent impact of these infringements was small, there was not a symbiotic relationship and that there were triable issues of fact remaining as to whether the infringing products constituted a draw. *Id.* at 1052.

Similarly in *Religious Technology*, the court found no evidence of direct financial benefit for Netcom where it received a fixed fee. 907 F Supp at 1376-77. The court also found that there was no evidence that infringement by Netcom users enhanced the value of Netcom's services to subscribers or attracted new subscribers. *Id.* at 1377.

This case is unlike *Religious Technology* because Cybernet receives more than a fixed fee. The income derived from each website is directly based on the site's initial popularity. The more consumers appreciate the content of a page, the more money Cybernet receives. Cybernet's income stream pays no regard to a site's respect for copyright or lack thereof. Additionally, Cybernet (and Adult Check) depends on content to attract consumers. Cybernet has given no reason to believe that these pages do not attract consumers, thereby creating a financial benefit to Cybernet.[17]

In comparison to *Adobe Systems*, the present facts pose a closer question, however. Cybernet attempts to hide behind the sheer volume of images on its sites to argue that even 10,000 infringing images does not establish a sufficiently direct financial interest or relationship. Opp'n at 22. The Court disagrees. In *Adobe Systems*, the court implied that the small number of infringing articles was insufficient to support a conclusion that these items provided "a significant draw" bringing consumers to the fairs. 173 F Supp 2d at 1053. In contrast, the Court concludes that there is a strong likelihood Perfect 10 will establish a large number of infringing sites. *Cf. Playboy v. Webbworld*, 968 F Supp 1171, 1177 *[2 ILR (P&F) 58]* (finding sufficient financial interest where defendants received a percentage of fixed fee and there were sixty-seven infringing images on site). The Court also concludes that the fortunes of these sites and Cybernet are sufficiently tied to create the requisite direct financial benefit. *See Napster II*, 239 F3d at 1023. The Court therefore concludes that Perfect 10 has shown a strong likelihood of success as to the direct financial interest element of vicarious liability.

b. Right or Ability to Control

Cybernet argues that it lacks the right and ability to control the websites because it cannot "affirmatively work as some sort of Internet 'hall monitor,' policing an unruly class of webmasters and responding instantaneously when any copyright infringement occurs." Opp'n at 23. In making this argument, it invokes the protection of the Digital Millennium Copyright Act's "notice and taken-down" provision, which will be dealt with below rather than addressed in this section. Its argument attempts to distinguish the Adult Check system from Napster's system because the images used in the Adult Check system do not pass through Cybernet's hardware. Opp'n at 25. Further, Cybernet argues that it is constrained in its right and ability to control by requirements of actual notice. *Id.*

The notice argument is not relevant as it does not address Cybernet's control abilities. Rather it addresses when those abilities should be exercised. Focusing on the ability to control the sites found in its system, the Court concludes that Perfect 10 has established a strong likelihood of success. As mentioned earlier, Cybernet has a monitoring program in place. Under this program, participating sites receive detailed instructions regard *[sic]* issues of layout, appearance, and content. Cybernet has refused to allow sites to use its system until they comply with its dictates. Most importantly, it monitors images to make sure that celebrity images do not oversaturate the content found within the sites that make up Adult Check. Zadeh Decl., Ex. 30. It forbids certain types of images. This ability to control other types of images belies any attempt to argue that Cybernet does not exercise sufficient control over its webmasters to monitor and influence their conduct or to deny copyright offenders the benefits of its service. *See Religious Technology*, 907 F Supp at 1375 (right and ability to control where "police" powers exercised in past); *see also Napster I*, 114 F Supp 2d at 920-21 (online services improved methods of blocking users "tantamount to an admission that defendant can, and sometimes does, police its service").

Cybernet, like the swap meet in *Fonovisa*, not only has the right to terminate webmasters at will, it controls consumer access, and promotes its services. *See Fonovisa*, 76 F3d at 262; *Napster I*, 144 F Supp 2d at 920. Combined with its detailed policing of sites, these activities are sufficient to establish a strong likelihood of success for Perfect 10's argument that Cybernet has the right and ability to control the participating websites.

c. Vicarious Liability—Conclusion

Because Perfect 10 has shown a strong likelihood of establishing a direct financial benefit and the right and ability to control websites that engage in infringing activity, the Court finds there is a strong likelihood of success on Perfect 10's claims for vicarious copyright infringement liability.

4. DMCA

In 1998 Congress passed Title II of the Digital Millennium Copyright Act ("DMCA"), Pub L. 105-304, Title II, §202(a), 112 Stat 2877 (1998) (*codified at* 17 USC §512). The DMCA marked Congress' entry into the online copyright fray. The DMCA created a series of four "safe harbors" to protect "providers of online services" from liability, primarily monetary, based on claims of copyright infringement attributable to the actions of users. *See* 17 USC §§512(a)-(d),(j). In order to qualify for these safe harbors, a provider of online services must:

1) adopt a policy that provides for the termination in appropriate circumstances of subscribers and account holders of the service provider's system or network who are repeat infringers;

2) reasonably implement the policy; and

3) inform subscribers and account holders of the service provider's system or network about the policy.

See 17 USC §512(i). The service provider and its policy must also not interfere with "standard technical measures" used by copyright owners to protect copyrighted works.[18] *See* 17 USC §512(i)(1)(B).

These "safe harbors" do not affect the question of ultimate liability under the various doctrines of direct, vicarious, and contributory liability. *See* H.R. Rep. 105-551(II), at 50 (July 22, 1998); S. Rep. 105-190, at 19 (May 11, 1998). Rather they limit the relief available against service providers that fall within these safe harbors. *See* 17 USC §§512(a),(b)(1),(c)(1), (d), & (j).

Of these "safe harbors," Cybernet only invokes the harbors provided by section 512(c), governing information residing on the systems or networks at the direction of users, and section 512(d), governing information location tools ("web browsers"). Moreover, these "safe harbors" could not apply prior to August 8, 2001, the date Cybernet adopted its policy it claims is aimed at compliance with the DMCA. *See Costar Group, Inc. v. Loopnet, Inc.*, 164 F Supp 2d 688, 698 n. 4 *[9 ILR (P&F) 720]* (D Md 2001).

a. Is Cybernet A "Service Provider"?

Cybernet devotes a single sentence to arguing that it is a "service provider" as the term is defined in section 512(k)(1)(B). Opp'n at 25. This section defines a service provider as a "provider of online services or network access, or the operator of facilities therefor," and includes entities "offering the transmission, routing, or providing of connections for digital online communications, between or among points specified by a user, of material of the user's choosing, without modification to the content of the material as sent or received." 17 USC §512(k). Section 512(k)(1)(B)'s definition has been interpreted broadly. *See ALS Scan, Inc. v. RemarQ Communities, Inc.*, 239 F3d 619, 623 *[7 ILR (P&F) 69]* (4th Cir 2001); *Hendrickson v. eBay*, 165 F Supp 2d 1082, 1087 *[8 ILR (P&F) 573]* ("eBay clearly meets the DMCA's broad definition of online "service provider"). Although there appears to be uniform agreement that the definition is broad, or at least broader than the definition of 512(k)(1)(A) concerning conduit-type services, the Court has found no discussion of this definition's limits.

Perfect 10 argues that section 512(c) was drafted with the limited purpose of protecting Internet infrastructure services in mind. Reply at 18. It contends that the definition for a provider of online services or network access does not include services that "participate in the selection or screening of that data or take an interest in the content of that data." *Id.* at 18 n. 19. The inclusion of section 512(d) which creates a "safe harbor" for copyright infringement resulting from the use of information location tools by service providers, which include directories, indexes, references, pointers and hypertext links, strongly suggests that the definition of service provider is meant to include services that only provide location service tools, as well as services providing internet access and such tools. *See* H.R. Rep. 105-551 (II), at 58 (identifying Yahoo! as an example); *cf. also* 47 USC §231(b)(3) (reach of Child Online Protection Act defined by similar categories). The Court adopts that reading and will not use Perfect 10's proposed interpretation to evaluate Cybernet's ability to invoke the protection of section 512's safe harbors.

Nevertheless, Cybernet has made this a more complicated issue than it probably should be by its insistence that it does not host any infringing images and no image files pass through any of its computers. Opp'n at 21. This appears to be part of an overall strategy to deny that Cybernet is anything more than an age verification service, somehow beyond the reach of copyright law, with no responsibility for the actions taken on the sites of the individual webmasters. It may be a close question whether such a service qualifies as a "provider of online services."[19] For the moment, however, the Court will assume that Cybernet is a "provider of online services" as defined in section 512(k).

b. Does Cybernet Meet the Minimal Qualifications of Section 512(i)?

The initial hurdle Cybernet must meet in order to qualify for section 512(k)'s restrictions on injunctive relief is found in section 512(i). These provisions require an online service provider to develop, promulgate and reasonably implement a policy providing for termination in appropriate circumstances of repeat copyright infringers. 17 USC §512(i). In crafting these policies, Congress has given a vague indication of what constitutes "appropriate" circumstances.

In the House and Senate Reports considering this subsection, both used identical language. *See Ellison v. Robertson*, 189 F Supp 2d 1051, 2002 WL 407696 *1, *12 *[10 ILR (P&F) 386]* (CD Cal 2002). The Committees each "recognize[d] that there are different degrees of on-line copyright infringement, from the inadvertent and noncommercial, to the willful and commercial." H.R. Rep. 105-551 (II), at 61; S. Rep. 105-190, at 62. The Committees also stated that the provision was not intended to undermine principles governing knowledge of infringement and protection of privacy rights "by suggesting that a provider must investigate *possible* infringements, *monitor* its service, or make *difficult* judgments as to whether conduct is or is not infringing." H.R. Rep. 105-551 (II), at 61 (emphasis added); S. Rep. 105-190, at 62 (same). The Committees than *[sic]* appeared to immediately qualify these statements by stating: "However, those who repeatedly or flagrantly abuse their access to the Internet through disrespect for the intellectual property rights of others should know that there is a *realistic* threat of losing that access." H.R. Rep. 105-551 (II), at 61 (emphasis added); S. Rep. 105-190, at 62 (emphasis added).

Although the last sentence appears directed at the instigators of infringement, each Committee also noted that the DMCA preserves "strong incentives" for "qualifying" service providers to cooperate with copyright holders. H.R. Rep. 105-551 (II), at 49; S. Rep. 105-190, at 20. The Court shares concerns expressed by Nimmer and a sister court in this district in recognizing the language of the statute and the legislative history of this section are less than models of clarity. *See Ellison*, 189 F Supp 2d at ___, 2002 WL 406796 at *13 n. 15 (treating section 512(i) as a mere threat based on language and history); 3 *Nimmer on Copyright* §12B.02[B][2], at 12B-25 & 12B-26 (identifying questions left open by statute). Nevertheless, the Court reads section 512(i) to imply some substantive responsibilities for service providers, particularly if the statute is to be read with the apparently broad reach advocated by the other courts that have considered this section.

The legislative history does provide some guidelines as to what a section 512(i) policy might look like. The service provider might not need to provide for active investigation of possible infringement. [20] No court in construing these requirements should make the knowledge standards more demanding than those found in section 512(c). *See* H.R. Rep. 105-551 (II), at 61. The service provider might not need to take action for isolated infringing acts by single users. *See* 17 USC §512(i) (referring to repeat infringers). The service provider need not act or address difficult infringement issues. *See* H.R. Rep. 105-551 (II), at 61. It may not require the service provider to actively monitor for copyright infringement. *See id.*

When confronted with "appropriate circumstances," however, such service providers should reasonably implement termination. *See* 17 USC §512(i). These circumstances would appear to cover, at a minimum, instances where a service provider is given sufficient evidence to create actual knowledge of blatant, repeat infringement by particular users, particularly infringement of a willful and commercial nature. *See* H.R. Rep. 105-551 (II), at 61. An evaluation of any such policy would be informed by an awareness of the service provider's function, existing technology, and the expressed Congressional desire not to undermine the privacy and knowledge requirements of the statute, while leaving the law in its "evolving state." *See* S. Rep. 105-190, at 18.

This interpretation tracks that of the *Costar* court, which found that there were material issues of fact whether a provider of real estate services on the web implemented a "reasonable" termination policy, as well as whether it acted expeditiously in taking down access to infringing material under section 512(c). *See* 164 F Supp 2d at 704. Under this reading, section 512(i) is focused on infringing users, whereas 512(c) is focused primarily on the infringing material itself. This line of reasoning becomes particularly forceful when one considers the limitations on injunctive relief found in section 512(1). [21]

Making the entrance into the safe harbor too wide would allow service providers acting in complicity with infringers to approach copyright infringement on an image by image basis without ever targeting the source of these images. *See* 17 USC §512(c)(1)(C) (only requiring service providers to remove or disable access to the infringing material). It would encourage a risk-taking approach, whereby service providers could allow repeat infringers to flood the web with infringing images knowing the service providers' ignorance of new infringements and the limited relief under 512(1) would prevent anything more than token action and no financial exposure, while the service provider continues to profit on a "non-discriminatory" basis. The incentives for such action were eloquently phrased by Cybernet in support of its arguments why they should not be held accountable for copyright infringement under the Adult Check brand: "a webmaster will quickly switch from one [AVS] to another if he or she feels the AVS is attempting to exert too much control over the content of the participating sites." Lane Decl. ¶62.

The Court does not read section 512 to endorse business practices that would encourage content providers to turn a blind eye to the source of massive copyright infringement while continuing to knowingly profit, indirectly or not, from every single one of these same sources until a court orders the provider to terminate each individual account. [22] *Cf. Costar*, 164 F Supp 2d at 705 (restricting application of section 512's "financial benefit" test). The Court does recognize that section 512(1) allows for court orders terminating user accounts, but it also recognizes that online service providers are meant to have strong incentives to work with copyright holders. The possible loss of the safe harbor provides that incentive and furthers a regulatory scheme in which courts are meant to play a secondary role to self-regulation. *See, e.g.*, 17 USC §512(i)(2)(A). The Court thus views 512(i) as creating room for enforcement policies less stringent or formal than the "notice and take-down" provisions of section 512(c), but still subject to 512(i)'s "reasonably implemented" requirement. It therefore respectfully parts ways with the interpretation of 512(i) in *Ellison*, in order to maintain the "strong incentives" for service providers to prevent their services from becoming safe havens or conduits for known repeat copyright infringers, at the very least. [23]

The allegations against Cybernet and the evidence before the Court is consistent with just such a jaded view of Cybernet's activities. Even in opposition, right after pointing out that "some number of webmasters have switched to other AVS vendors and some have even encouraged Cybernet's customers to cancel their subscriptions," Cybernet disclaims any intent to impose "impossible affirmative duties upon itself." Opp'n at 24. In the context of this litigation, the Court sees this as an implicit argument that rooting out repeat infringers imposes such "impossible" duties and finds it runs against Cybernet's argument that it is actually trying to cope with repeat infringers.

In opposition to the present motion, Cybernet does assert that it has taken action against individual webmasters as well as against infringing sites. Umbreit Decl. ¶¶ 26-31. Cybernet has not, however, submitted any documentary evidence to support these assertions. Perfect 10's moving papers included examples of infringing conduct on sites that have been identified since the beginning of this litigation. Significantly, in its Opposition Cybernet maintains it does "what it has the power to do—namely, remove from the Cybernet search engine and links page any website about which it has received a notice of infringement," without addressing its power to stop providing its AVS service to known infringers. Opp'n at 12. The Court finds this lone declaration, unsupported by any documentary evidence, contradicted by evidence in the record, and flying in the face of Cybernet's consistent resistance to the proposition that it could,

would or should exercise any control over its webmasters, simply not credible. The record supports the conclusion that Cybernet has taken great pains to avoid shouldering the burdens of the copyright regime, all the while profiting from pirates. [24]

Because the Court finds that there is a strong likelihood that Cybernet cannot establish that it has "reasonably implemented" a policy directed at *terminating* repeat infringers, even in "appropriate circumstances," there is little likelihood that it can avail itself of section 512's safe harbors.

c. Could Cybernet qualify for the safe harbors if it is a "service provider" and has "reasonably implemented" a repeat infringer policy?

Even assuming Cybernet could somehow bring itself over the section 512(k) and (i) hurdles to have its conduct evaluated under sections 512(c) and (d), the Court finds that there is a strong likelihood Perfect 10 will prevail on its copyright claims. First the Court notes that Cybernet's assertion that these sections could "exempt" Cybernet from liability is without merit. Section 512 does not affect the elements of copyright liability. Instead, it affects the remedies available for any infringement which might be found. The Court will nevertheless address why it believes Cybernet does not comply with the explicit substantive requirements of the DMCA or qualify for either the section 512(c) ("information storage") or (d) ("information location tool") safe harbors.

1. Deficiencies In Notice Procedures

Both the section 512(c) and (d) safe harbors governing information storage and connecting activity, such as link and search engines, respectively, contain parallel notification and counter-notification requirements in an attempt to balance the duties of service providers, the rights of copyright owners and the rights of other users. In general outline, the notice and take-down provisions work as follows:

1) A copyright owner must contact the service provider and provide written notice meeting certain criteria, *see* 17 USC §512(c)(3);

2) If the notice fails to fully comply with the stated notice requirements, but

substantially complies with three requirements aimed at identifying infringing sites, works and users, the service provider must promptly attempt to contact the person complaining or takes other reasonable steps to assist in the receipt of notification that complies with the requirements, [25] *see* 17 USC §512(c)(3)(B);

3) Once notice is received, the service provider must expeditiously remove or disable access to the material and must notify the affected user promptly, *see* 17 USC §512(c)(1)(B);

4) The affected user may then submit a counter-notification consisting of a statement, under penalty of perjury, that the user had a good faith belief that the material was removed as a result of a mistake or misidentification of the material, *see* 17 USC §512(g)(3); and

5) Upon receiving a counter-notification, the service provider has 10-14 days to replace the material unless the provider's designated agent receives notice that the complaining party has filed a court action, *see* 17 USC §512(2)(C).

a. Deviations From Notice Requirements

Cybernet's procedures depart from this statutory scheme in several quite significant ways. First, Cybernet's policy states that it requires a complaint to meet all its stated notice requirements and there is no indication that Cybernet tries to work with parties whose notice falls within the statute's notice-saving clause, section 512(c)(3)(B)(ii). Second, and even more problematic, Cybernet has altered the notice requirements themselves. Whereas section 512 states "if multiple copyrighted works at a single online site are covered by a single notification, a representative list of such works at that site" must be provided, 17 USC §512(c)(3)(A), Cybernet does not appear to allow such a representative list, and it requests only the specific web page at which a given work is located, rather than the site. These apparently small differences might seem innocent enough, but in the framework of this litigation it appears to be an intent to upset the Congressionally apportioned burden between copyright holder and service provider by placing the entire burden on the copyright owner. These differences, combined with the failure to show any flexibility on its policy that a notification meet all of Cybernet's standards, leads the Court to conclude that Cybernet has failed to structure a notice system that complies with section 512.

b. Deviation From Counter-Notification Requirements

The conclusion above is reinforced by Cybernet's counter-notification requirements. The DMCA's counter-notification statement, with its good-faith requirement stated under penalty of perjury, separates good-faith infringers and innocent users from those who knowingly infringe copyrights. *See* 17 USC §512(g)(3). This requirement implicates the "reasonably implemented" policy of §512(i) because there is an implication that a party who cannot sign the required statement is a knowing infringer. Thus, the counter-notification procedures appear to serve the generally self-policing policy that section 512 reflects. Cybernet's counter-notification procedures allow knowing infringers to sidestep this requirement.

By stating under penalty of perjury that they removed the named infringing material, a knowing infringer will be reestablished on the Adult Check system. *See* Zadeh Decl., Ex. 1 at 23. On the one hand, this makes sense to the extent that Adult Check can only disable individual pages or sites because it cannot directly access the content. On the other hand, this also allows Cybernet to reinstate an infringer without the Congressionally-required statement and provides cover for Cybernet to water down its termination policy by treating these minimalist take-down statements as neither an admission nor a denial of the copyright infringement allegations, regardless of how blatant the infringement might be. Although there is no evidence on this issue, the record before the Court provides substantial evidence of resistance on Cybernet's part towards addressing copyright violations by its "unruly" webmasters. The DMCA is a carefully-balanced, although sometimes unclear, piece of legislation. *See Ellison*, 189 F Supp 2d 1051, 2002 WL 407696 at *15 n. 16. [26] Cybernet's DMCA "variant" appears to upset that balance.

2. Direct Financial Benefit and Right and Ability to Control

Both relevant sections exclude from the safe harbor service providers that "receive a benefit directly attributable to the infringing activity, in a case in which the service provider has the right and ability to control such activity." 17 USC §512(c)(1)(B),(d)(2). Here, there is significant evidence that Cybernet receives a direct financial benefit. *See supra.*

In *Costar Group*, 164 F Supp 2d at 704-05, the district court found that a real estate website, which charged the same price to infringing and non-infringing users and did not charge for the service where the infringement was found, did not receive a sufficiently direct benefit to fall within the statute. *Id.* In so concluding, the Court distinguished the *Fonovisa* line of cases discussed previously by looking to the slightly different language of the statute ("does not receive a financial benefit directly attributable to the infringing activity") and, once again, the legislative history of the DMCA. *See id.* at 705.

This legislative history states:

> In determining whether the financial benefit criterion is satisfied, courts should take a common-sense, fact-based approach, not a formalistic one. In general, a service provider conducting a legitimate business would not be considered to receive a "financial benefit directly attributable to the infringing activity" where the infringer makes the same kind of payment as non-infringing users of the provider's service. . . . It would however, include any such fees where the value of the service lies in providing access to infringing material.

H.R. Rep. 105-551 (II), at 54.

The *Costar* court looked at the fact that neither infringing nor non-infringing users paid anything for the service and concluded that the direct financial benefit was lacking. *Id.* at 705. The Court expresses no opinion on the question whether the "directly attributable" language is narrower or equivalent to the general vicarious infringement requirements. Rather, the direct flow of income to Cybernet based on the number of new Adult Check users that sign up to Adult Check from infringing sites establishes that direct relationship. *See supra.* The more new

visitors an infringing site attracts, the more money Cybernet makes. This is quite different from the situation in *Costar* where the site made money on other services it offered, which were not directly tied to the infringing activity. *See* 174 F Supp 2d at 704. Applying the common-sense, fact-based approach, the Court finds that the financial benefit is highly likely to be sufficiently direct to work against Cybernet's reliance on the safe harbor.

Similarly, with regard to the right and ability to control, the Court agrees with the *Hendrickson* and *Costar* courts that closing the safe harbor based on the mere ability to exclude users from the system is inconsistent with the statutory scheme. *See Hendrickson*, 165 F Supp 2d at 1093-94; *Costar*, 164 F Supp 2d at 704. As mentioned earlier, section 512 is meant to encourage some level of copyright enforcement activity by service providers, not to punish it. In the parlance of contributory patent infringement cases dealing with the intent requirement for contributory liability of trademark licensors, there must be "something more."[27] Here Cybernet prescreens sites, gives them extensive advice, prohibits the proliferation of identical sites, and in the variety of ways mentioned earlier exhibits precisely this slightly difficult to define "something more."

This combination of financial benefit and ability to control makes it highly unlikely that Cybernet may avail itself of the DMCA safe harbor provisions.

3. Failure to Provide Evidence of Expeditious Removal

Additionally, there is no credible evidence presented to the Court that Cybernet has ever *expeditiously* removed infringing material from its system, disabled links, or altered its search engine under its variant of the DMCA policy. Thus, this lack of evidence also defeats Cybernet's likelihood of success in trying to fit into the safe harbor.

4. Conclusions Relevant to Both Safe Harbors

The Court therefore finds that there is little likelihood that Cybernet will qualify for either the information location tool or information storage safe harbors.

5. Copyright Infringement Conclusion

Based on the previous discussion, the Court concludes that Perfect 10 has established a strong likelihood of success for its claims that Cybernet is liable for contributory and vicarious copyright infringement, and has a strong likelihood of showing Cybernet cannot avail itself of section 512's safe harbors. There is, however, a residual chance that Cybernet will qualify for 17 USC §512(d)'s safe harbor for search engines, but not links.

B. Likelihood of Success on Unfair Competition Claims

Perfect 10's unfair competition claims under California Business & Professions Code §17200 ("section 17200") primarily descend from allegations concerning various rights of publicity. Perfect 10 argues these claims implicate both the "unlawful" and "unfair" prongs of section 17200. [28] *See Cel-Tech Communications, Inc. v. Los Angeles Cellular Telephone Co.*, 20 Cal 4th 163, 181 (1999) (discussing various prongs of unfair competition statute). These rights of publicity claims are asserted on behalf of two groups, Perfect 10 models who have assigned their publicity rights to Perfect 10, and other unaffiliated persons, primarily celebrities.

1. Rights of Publicity—Perfect 10 Models

California recognizes two causes of action based on rights of publicity. The first is a common law right that has been recognized since 1931. *Gionfriddo v. Major League Baseball*, 94 Cal App 4th 400, 408 (Cal App 2001). The elements of this right are:

1) the defendant's use of the plaintiff's identity;

2) the appropriation of plaintiff's name or likeness to defendant's advantage, commercially or otherwise;

3) lack of consent; and

4) resulting injury.

Id. at 409. The common law right also requires that this right "be balanced against the public interest in the dissemination of news and information consistent with the democratic processes under the constitutional guaranties of freedom of speech and of the press." *Id.* (citations omitted).

In addition, California has a statutory right, codified at California Civil Code §3344 ("section 3344"). Section 3344 provides:

Any person who knowingly uses another's name . . . photograph, or likeness, in any manner, on or in products, merchandise, or

goods, . . . without such person's prior consent, . . . shall be liable for any damages sustained by the person or persons injured as a result thereof.

Cal. Civ. Code §3344. For purposes of the statute, a use of a name, image and likeness in connection with any news or public affairs broadcast does not constitute a use for which consent is required. Cal. Civ. Code §3344(d). Additionally, the section does not apply to the owners or employees of any medium used for advertising, unless the owners or employees have knowledge of an unauthorized use. Cal. Civ. Code §3344(f).

Neither party contests that third parties operating under the Adult Check name have infringed the rights of publicity assigned to Perfect 10 by a number of models. Nor does either party suggest that direct liability would not be appropriate against those third-parties under either theory. Similarly, Perfect 10 does not assert any direct liability theory against Cybernet. The likelihood of success thus boils down to a question of "aiding and abetting."

a. Could Aiding and Abetting Liability Exist?

California has adopted the joint liability principle laid out in the Restatement (Second) of Torts §876. [29] Under the Restatement,

For harm resulting to a third person from the tortious conduct of another, one is subject to liability if he:

a) does a tortious act in concert with the other in pursuit to a common design with him, or

b) knows that the other's conduct constitutes a breach of duty and gives substantial assistance or encouragement so to conduct himself, or

c) gives substantial assistance to the other in accomplishing a tortious result and his own conduct, separately considered, constitutes a breach of duty to the third person.

Restatement (Second) of Torts §876.

Cybernet argues that there is no case directly recognizing the applicability of this doctrine to the right of publicity torts. Opp'n at 28. The Court finds this argument unpersuasive, as the Restatement provides a background principle for all tort liability in the state of California. *See Saunders*, 27 Cal App 4th at 846.

Nor does the Court find convincing Cybernet's argument that the right of publicity itself contains an actual knowledge requirement. Opp'n at 28. Cybernet's citations refer to the requirement that broadcasters of advertisements must have actual knowledge before they can be held liable. *See* Cal. Civ. Code §3344(f). Cybernet does not claim to be a medium used for advertising, and the Court only focuses on rights of publicity infringements located on the websites, not infringements associated with webmaster banner ads. Rather, Cybernet argues that the knowledge requirement of section 3344(f) is a requirement for "aider and abettor" liability under the statute.

The Court concludes otherwise. Although section 3344(f) provides clear evidence that secondary liability can be imposed for violations of publicity rights, it also provides evidence that the California legislature created a heightened knowledge requirement limited to broadcasters of advertisements. *See, e.g., TRW, Inc. v. Andrews*, 534 US 19 (2001) (applying the "expressio unius est exclusio alterius" canon). The California legislature has not extended this requirement to defendants like Cybernet. *Cf. Newcombe v. Adolf Coors Co.*, 157 F3d 686, 694 (9th Cir 1998) (allowing claim to proceed against company and ad agency where another artist created work). The Court therefore defaults to the background assumption that secondary liability exists and it is found in conformance to the requirements established in the Restatement.

b. Is Secondary Liability Likely to Exist?

Perfect 10 has primarily focused its secondary theory of liability on the second branch of the Restatement, requiring actual knowledge of the tortious conduct and substantial participation. Mot. at 32-35. The Court agrees with Perfect 10 that there is a serious question on the merits of the substantial participation prong. As it stands, in the absence of argument to the contrary, the Court looks to the contributory infringement framework of copyright trademark law, where it has already found just such participation, thus leading the Court to conclude Perfect 10 has established a strong likelihood of success with regard to Cybernet's

substantial participation. *See supra*. The Court recognizes, however, that the substantial participation requirement has not been a particular subject of discussion among the California courts, and the parties have not done more than refer to the issue in passing.[30]

Perfect 10 also points to the notification it provided Cybernet covering rights of publicity being violated by websites in the Adult Check network. Mot. at 35. In response Cybernet argues perfunctorily that Perfect 10 has not shown that the owners of Cybernet had knowledge of the unauthorized use of Perfect 10 model images. Opp'n at 28. The Court fails to grasp the significance of the owners' knowledge absent an assertion that Cybernet is an advertising medium, an assertion that the present record would not support. As to Perfect 10 carrying its burden to show actual knowledge, the Court finds that the notification provided Cybernet by the Second Amended Complaint, especially when supplemented by the physical examples of alleged violations provided in a July 12, 2001 letter to Cybernet's counsel, *see* Mausner Decl., Ex. 47, filed In Support of Pl. Opp'n to Mot. to Dismiss, Aug. 9, 2001, is enough to create a strong likelihood that Perfect 10 will prevail in showing actual knowledge on Cybernet's part.

The Court finds the likelihood of success with regard to both elements of the Restatement test creates a strong likelihood that Perfect 10 will succeed on its unfair competition claim to the extent it predicates liability on an aiding and abetting theory for the violation's of Perfect 10's rights of publicity.

2. Secondary Liability for Violating the Rights of Publicity of Other Celebrities

Perfect 10 has also argued that Cybernet violates the publicity rights of third-party celebrities by tolerating the presence of fake nude pictures that either claim to be actual pictures of these celebrities or that advertise themselves as "fakes." Mot. at 31.

a. Standing

In an earlier order, the Court found that Perfect 10 had adequately plead *[sic]* constitutional standing to assert these rights under the unfair competition statute. *See Perfect 10, Inc. v. Cybernet Ventures, Inc.*, 167 F Supp 2d 1114, 1125 *[10 ILR (P&F) 415]* (CD Cal 2001). Then in a subsequent order, the Court addressed the prudential limitations on standing by reading Perfect 10's complaint as one directed primarily at protecting its own interests and not necessarily vindicating the rights of third-parties. *See* Motion Granting in Part and Denying in Part Second Motion to Dismiss at 21 ("2d MTD Order"). This running battle over standing continues in the present motion.

Cybernet argues that Perfect 10 lacks standing because it is not a competitor of Adult Check. Opp'n at 32. Cybernet makes this argument by mischaracterizing the plain language of Perfect 10's contentions in a state court action. *See* Jenal Decl., Ex. A at 7 (state court brief). This parallel case concerned Perfect 10's access to former Cybernet employees, presumably contacted for purposes of investigating the facts underlying this action. Cybernet does not quote the relevant language in full in its papers, but it does assert that "As a factual matter, Perfect 10 admits it is not Cybernet's competitor." Opp'n at 32. The Court finds that, as a factual matter, this is simply incorrect.

The unquoted portion of the brief states:

> The fact that Perfect 10 does not compete against Cybernet for the purpose of trade secret law *does not mean that Cybernet cannot be sued by Perfect 10 in the federal action for unfair competition* [.] Cybernet permits and assists its Adult Check Websites to steal photos and images from Perfect 10 magazine and <www.perfect10.com> and unlawfully display those photos and images. It also provides consumer access to that stolen property for a fee.

Jenal Decl., Ex. A at 7 (emphasis added).

The Court finds this mischaracterization to be fairly blatant and it plays into the Court's concerns over the credibility of Cybernet's declarants.[31] Moreover, the Court has concerns about Cybernet playing "fast and loose" with its assertions, and warns Cybernet that judicial estoppel is a doctrine that may not work to its benefit.

Turning to the merits, Cybernet and Perfect 10 both compete for consumers' adult entertainment viewing dollars. They both peddle images on the web in an industry where, by Cybernet's own admission, price counts. The Court finds this is a strong indication of competition, particularly where Adult Check webmasters attract consumers using Perfect 10's own material. *Cf. Brookfield*

Communications, Inc. v. West Coast Entertainment Corp., 174 F3d 1036, 1063-65 *[2 ILR (P&F) 492]* (9th Cir 1999) (discussing initial interest confusion). Because the record supports a finding of competition and Cybernet has raised no other arguments, the Court finds that Perfect 10 has met Cybernet's current standing challenge.

b. Likelihood of Success—Third Party Rights

As this again disposes of the standing issues raised by the parties, the Court then turns to the question of Perfect 10's likelihood of success when it comes to third-party rights of publicity. There are two relevant classes of celebrities—those that have complained to Cybernet and those that have not. Mindful of the prudential limitations on standing despite Perfect 10's status as Cybernet's competitor, *see Viceroy Gold Corp. v. Aubry*, 75 F3d 482, 488 (9th Cir 1995), the Court concludes that Perfect 10 only stands a likelihood of success on its claims of unfair competition for those celebrities who have already complained to Cybernet about unauthorized uses of their publicity rights.[32]

The Court finds that there are indeed celebrities who have complained to Cybernet about uses of their images. *See* Milano Decl. Cybernet has not made any argument that it has taken any actions to remove these offending images or sites from its service. This combination of actual knowledge, acceptance of the benefits from these sites, and lack of action, if proved at trial, which the Court finds likely, would expose Cybernet to aiding and abetting liability for these celebrity images as well. *See supra*. Limited to those celebrities who have complained about use of their images and identities, the Court therefore finds a strong likelihood that Perfect 10 will succeed on its claim against Cybernet based on the violations of third-party celebrities' publicity rights. This predicate act also provides a strong likelihood of success for Perfect 10's unfair competition claim.

3. Ultimate Likelihood of Success on Unfair Competition Claim

The Court concludes that the likelihood of success on these right of publicity claims creates a high likelihood of success on both the "unlawful" and "unfair" prongs of California's unfair competition statute, section 17200. *See Sun Microsystems, Inc. v. Microsoft, Inc.*, 87 F Supp 2d 992, 999 (ND Cal 2000) (discussing similar competitive injury sufficient to meet "unfair" prong as "incipient violation of antitrust laws"); *Cel-Tech*, 20 Cal 4th at 180 (discussing "unlawful" prong).

The Court recognizes that application of secondary liability principles is particularly applicable for claims of unfair competition, as the California Supreme Court recognized as far back as 1935: "When a scheme is evolved which on its face violates the fundamental rules of honesty and fair dealing, a court of equity is not impotent to frustrate the consummation because the scheme is an original one." *American Philatelic Soc'y v. Claibourne*, 3 Cal 2d 689, 698-99 (1935).

In *American Philatelic*, a purveyor of stamps altered his normal stamps to resemble rare perforated stamps. *Id.* at 692. He then sold these stamps to stamp dealers with clear notice that the stamps were not of the rare variety. *Id.* at 694. Nevertheless, his sales brochures and pricing established that he both anticipated and effectively encouraged these dealers to sell the stamps to the public as rare stamps. *Id.* The California Supreme Court had no problem finding these claims stated a claim under the unfair competition law. *Id.* at 697. *Saunders, American Philatelic*, and *Cel-Tech*'s quotation of *American Philatelic*'s equity language reinforce the Court's conclusion that Perfect 10's theory of aiding and abetting liability for Cybernet based on third-party violations of various rights of publicity has a strong likelihood of success.[33]

C. TRADEMARK INFRINGEMENT

1. Elements of Trademark Infringement

In order for Perfect to prevail on its trademark claim Perfect 10 must show:

1) that a mark is owned and associated with Perfect 10; and

2) the defendants' use of the mark is likely to cause confusion or mistake among the general public.

Sega Enterprises, Ltd. v. MAPHIA, 948 F Supp at 936.

2. Perfect 10's Trademark and Service Mark

Perfect 10 has brought forward its trademark and service mark registration certificates. Mausner Decl., Ex. B at 59, 62. This is prima facie evidence of the validity of the trademark, Perfect 10's ownership of the mark, and its exclusive right to use the mark. 15 USC §1057(b). At the same time,

Perfect 10 has asserted that it has trademark rights in the names of its models, but has not adequately established this fact.[34] *See* Mot. at 10. The Court therefore restricts its discussion to the "Perfect 10" trademark.

3. Direct Infringement—Standards

Perfect 10 advances two theories of trademark infringement that it claims are widespread on the Adult Check websites: unauthorized usage of its actual trademark and reverse palming off. Mot. at 39.

Section 1114 of the Lanham Act prohibits the use of "any reproduction, counterfeit, copy or colorable imitation of a registered mark in connection with the sale, offering for sale, distribution, or advertising of any good for services or in connection with such use [when such use] is likely to cause confusion." The statute is intended to protect consumers against deceptive designations of the origin of goods, as well as preventing the duplication of trademarks. *Westinghouse Elec. Corp. v. General Circuit Breaker & Elec. Supply, Inc.*, 106 F3d 894, 899 (9th Cir 1997). Direct usage of a mark by unauthorized users can lead to the public's belief that the mark's owner sponsors or otherwise approves of the use of the trademark. *Dallas Cowboy Cheerleaders, Inc. v. Pussycat Cinema, Ltd.*, 604 F2d 200, 204 (2d Cir 1979). This can satisfy the likelihood of confusion and can justify a court granting injunctive relief. *See id.* at 204-205.

Reverse passing off occurs when someone markets a product as their own, although the product was created by someone else. *See Summit Machine*, 7 F3d at 1437, 1441. This doctrine has been limited to situations of bodily appropriation. *Shaw v. Lindheim*, 919 F2d 1353, 1364 (9th Cir 1990).[35] Bodily appropriation is defined in the copyright context as "copying or unauthorized use of substantially the entire item." *See Cleary v. News Corp.*, 30 F3d 1255, 1261 (9th Cir 1994). In the context of reverse palming off, this definition is useful because it recognizes that slight modifications of a product might cause customer confusion, while products which are merely generally similar will not. *Id.*

4. Direct Infringement—Likelihood of Success

Perfect 10 has brought forward evidence that a number of Adult Check webmasters engage in both forms of trademark infringement. The Court therefore finds that there is a strong likelihood that Perfect 10 will establish direct infringement by individual Adult Check webmasters.

5. Contributory Infringement

Perfect 10 does not maintain that Cybernet has directly infringed its trademark. Rather, it relies on a theory of contributory liability. Contributory liability may be imposed where the defendant: (.1) intentionally induces another to infringe on a trademark or (2) continues to supply a product knowing that the recipient is using the product to engage in trademark infringement. *Fonovisa*, 76 F3d at 264. Perfect 10 does not argue that Cybernet intentionally induced the infringement and Cybernet correctly points out there is no evidence of such intentional inducement. Opp'n at 29. This brings the Court to the second method of establishing contributory infringement.

The Ninth Circuit has recognized that courts must consider the extent of control exercised by a defendant over a third-party's means of infringement when dealing with the second test and the fact pattern does not fit well into the "product" mold. *Lockheed Martin Corp. v. Network Solutions, Inc.*, 194 F3d 980, 984 *[4 ILR (P&F) 1]* (9th Cir 1999). Thus direct control and monitoring of the instrumentality used by a third-party to infringe the plaintiff's mark can lead to liability. *Id.* These considerations are similar, if not completely equivalent, to the principles applicable in the copyright context. *See Fonovisa*, 76 F3d at 265.

Although trademark liability is more narrowly circumscribed than copyright liability, similar principles underlie contributory trademark infringement. *See Fonovisa*, 76 F3d at 265. This second test can be met where one knows or has reason to know of the infringing activity, and it specifically covers those who are "willfully blind" to such activity. *Id.*

Cybernet maintains that there is no evidence that Cybernet had knowledge of the trademark infringement. Although the evidence is not as clear cut as Cybernet maintains, Perfect 10 does not contest the point. The Court therefore declines to express a view on the strength of Perfect 10's evidence with regard to contributory trademark infringement.

6. Trademark Conclusion

Because Perfect 10 has insufficiently asserted its argument against Cybernet for trademark infringement, the Court declines to find a strong likelihood of success at this point.

D. CONCLUSIONS—LIKELIHOOD OF SUCCESS

Perfect 10 has:

1) not established a strong likelihood of success on its direct copyright infringement claims against Cybernet;

2) established a strong likelihood of success on its contributory infringement claims against Cybernet;

3) established a strong likelihood of success on its vicarious infringement claims against Cybernet;

4) established a strong likelihood of success on its unfair competition claims against Cybernet based on rights of publicity assigned to Perfect 10;

5) established a strong likelihood of success on its unfair competition claims against Cybernet based on violations of third-party rights of publicity where those third-parties have complained to Cybernet about use of their images or identities by affiliated Adult Check webmasters;

6) has not established a likelihood of success on its trademark claims against Cybernet.

VII. UNCLEAN HANDS?

Cybernet contends that even if the Court could find that Perfect 10 has raised serious issues or a strong likelihood of success over its various claims, the Court should deny injunctive relief because of Perfect 10's "unclean hands." Opp'n at 38-39. The unclean hands doctrine may apply when the alleged misconduct occurs in a transaction directly related to the matter before the court and the conduct affects the equitable relationship between the litigants. *Newman v. Checkrite Cal., Inc.*, 912 F Supp 1354, 1376 (ED Cal 1995).

Cybernet points to two websites, *www.celebshop.com* and *www.celebrity pictures.com*, which contain Perfect 10 advertising banners. Opp'n at 38-39. Both websites, true to their names, contain the same type of pictures that Perfect 10 has fought against so vociferously in this action. Perfect 10, apparently realizing the awkward appearance, confesses that it entered into settlement agreements with several websites after complaining about infringements of Perfect 10 copyrights. Reply at 13; Zadeh Decl. II 13; Mausner Decl. II 8-14. According to these agreements, the sites would provide for banner advertising as part of the settlement terms. At the time, Perfect 10 claims it did not realize the unfair competitive advantage these types of sites had over its operation. Zadeh Depo. at 310-11.

The Court finds Perfect 10's basic explanation credible. Although these agreements do tarnish Perfect 10's crusading stance, they do not alter the strength of its arguments. Moreover, Cybernet's argument implies that the best solution to illicit behavior in an industry that appears to be rife with it, is to ignore it when the plaintiff appears sullied, too. The Court finds that there is a strong public interest in protecting intellectual property rights, and that the better solution is to bring parties into conformance with the law's dictates. The Court is also quite cognizant of the harms being inflicted on other third parties when policies that encourage pirating behavior of this kind are left unchecked. Although Perfect 10's hands are not "clean as snow," the Court finds the strength of their case and the public interest make this issue one better left to trial and finds it insufficient to justify denying injunctive relief. *See Goto.com v. Walt Disney Co.*, 202 F3d 1199, 1209-10 *[4 ILR (P&F) 393]* (9th Cir 2000); *EEOC v. Recruit U.S.A., Inc.*, 939 F2d 746, 753 (9th Cir 1991).

VIII. IRREPARABLE HARM

Cybernet makes three major arguments attacking Perfect 10's showing on the issue of irreparable harm. First, Cybernet invokes the doctrine of laches and argues that this defeats any inference of irreparable harm. Opp'n at 16-17. Additionally, Cybernet maintains that Perfect 10 has failed to establish a sufficient likelihood of success on its claims to entitle it to the presumption of irreparable harm granted to those who make a strong showing of copyright infringement or unfair business

practices. *Id.* at 16. Finally, Cybernet contends Perfect 10 has failed to show irreparable harm. *Id.* at 17. The Court will address each contention.

A. LACHES

Perfect 10 filed its complaint on March 20, 2001, served Cybernet in May, 2001 and filed the present motion on January 7, 2002. Cybernet argues that the nine month period from March until January defeats any inference of irreparable harm. Opp'n at 16-17. The Court does not agree. Perfect 10 points to the need for discovery and the stonewalling of Cybernet as reasons for the delay. Reply at 20-21. The Court find *[sic]* these explanations to be adequately supported by the record. They are strengthened by the constant stream of motions in the case, including three motions to dismiss and the multiplicity of theories in the case, which may have reasonably delayed the proceedings. *See Tough Traveler, Ltd. v. Outbound Prod.*, 60 F3d 964, 968 (2d Cir 1995). Further, there is no harm to plaintiff from the delay. *Cf. Ocean Garden Inc. v. Markettrade Co., Inc.*, 953 F2d 500, 508 (9th Cir 1991) (six months, no laches, no harm to plaintiff). If anything, the gap should have provided Cybernet with sufficient time to evaluate its systems, and put in place a program designed to adequately address its potential liability. The Court thus finds the nine month delay between the filing of the complaint and the filing of this motion is not sufficient to raise the laches bar. *Cf. Napster I*, 114 F Supp 2d at 900 (granting preliminary injunction nine months from the date complaint filed).

B. PERFECT 10'S FAILURE TO SHOW A SUFFICIENT LIKELIHOOD OF SUCCESS

In copyright and unfair competition cases, irreparable harm is presumed if once a sufficient likelihood of success is raised. *See Micro Star v. Formgen, Inc.*, 154 F3d 1107, 1109 (9th Cir 1998) (copyright); *Vision Sports, Inc. v. Melville Corp.*, 888 F2d 609, 612 n. 3 (9th Cir 1989) (unfair competition). Cybernet's contention that Perfect 10 has failed to show a sufficient likelihood of success to raise this presumption must fall as to the claims for which the Court has already concluded otherwise. Thus, irreparable harm may be presumed.

C. EVIDENCE OF PERFECT 10'S IRREPARABLE HARM

The Court need not rest on the presumption of irreparable harm, however. Cybernet argues that Perfect 10 has failed to provide any evidence of harm, *see* Opp'n at 17-18, but the Court finds the record justifies the conclusion that Perfect 10 will suffer irreparable harm. Perfect 10 and Adult Check are competitors. Adult Check is the largest AVS on the web and services approximately 2 million users each day. A significant number of the sites that attract these users and their funds utilize Perfect 10's copyrighted works, the images of celebrities who have complained about the use of their likenesses, or a combination of both, superimposing celebrities onto the bodies of Perfect 10's models. These sites charge less than Perfect 10, and Adult Check appears to contain more of Perfect 10's images than it owns itself. Cybernet's efforts to show the poor success of Perfect 10 reinforce this. Perfect 10 loses approximately $4 million to $5 million dollars per year. Just a small shift in the viewing habits of Adult Check's millions of users would have a significant effect on Perfect 10's bottom line. All told, the large losses being sustained by Perfect 10, suffered in this competitive context, justify a finding of irreparable harm.

D. BALANCE OF HARDSHIPS

The Court finds that the balance of hardships weighs significantly in favor of plaintiff, further justifying a grant of injunctive relief. Based on the evidence before the Court it appears that Cybernet profits from the infringing and unlawful activities of its webmasters without shouldering any of the undesired burdens associated with protection of intellectual property rights. The Court finds this willful blindness harms Perfect 10, defeats the rights of third-parties who find themselves displayed on these sites against their will, and skews the online adult market. Perfect 10 has already spent an inordinate amount of time researching these infringements, forced to pay a competitor in order to discover the infringing images on the Adult Check system. [36] Cybernet is not only in position to exercise its ability to control the content of the system—it already does when it suits its financial interests. Moreover, the tolerance of pirating behavior by the country's largest AVS system harms the public by rewarding illicit behavior. The balance of hardships favors Perfect 10 and favors injunctive relief.

The Court will therefore GRANT Perfect 10's motion for a Preliminary Injunction. The Court does not, however, agree with Perfect 10's proposed terms.

X. TERMS OF THE INJUNCTION

Although the Court has concluded that Perfect 10 is entitled to injunctive relief, there are goals that must be kept in mind in crafting the scope of relief:

1) preventing future infringement;

2) preventing continuing infringement;

3) encouraging the cooperative system envisioned by Congress;

4) consistency with the statutory framework discussed above; and

5) striking the right balance between protecting intellectual property rights and avoiding unduly burdensome requirements on Cybernet and its users.

Evaluated against these goals, Perfect 10's proposed order suffers from some shortcomings. The Court therefore has modified the proposed injunction. At the hearing, both parties had questions and concerns over the Court's proposed injunction. The Court addresses the most salient points now.

During the hearing, Cybernet requested clarification on the scope of the first paragraph. This first paragraph covers websites directly operated by the defendants.

Additionally, Cybernet raised several objections to the Court's imposition of affirmative duties to search through its system for infringing material. First, Cybernet argued that these duties require more than the bare minimums of the DMCA. The injunction does require more than the bare minimum of the DMCA, but these affirmative duties are justified by the Court's scepticism that Cybernet can ever qualify for the DMCA's safe harbor provisions because of the DMCA's vicarious liability provisions. [37] Moreover, assuming Cybernet may eventually be entitled to take advantage of the safe-harbor provisions, the affirmative requirements of the injunction ensure that its prior disregard of copyrights is cured.

Second, Cybernet also objected that the injunction overall is too burdensome. The Court disagrees. The injunction simply requires Cybernet to utilize its current site review function to a) remedy past tolerance of infringing activity and b) prevent infringers from joining the Adult Check family. The injunction orders Cybernet to treat copyright protection and respect for rights of publicity as elements of its business model that are equally as important to Cybernet as currently are the color, layout, prevention of certain content, and prevention of over-saturating use of celebrities. It is no more burdensome than the injunction granted in Napster, and falls significantly short of the shut-down order the Ninth Circuit recently upheld. *See Napster III*, 2001 WL 227081 at *1; *Napster IV*, 284 F3d at ___, 2002 WL 449550 at *4.

Cybernet's argument, however, does have validity in light of Perfect 10's apparent belief that the injunction's terms create a strict liability for any infringing images found on the Adult Check sites. Perfect 10's reading of the injunction is incorrect. Cybernet has an affirmative duty as set out in the injunction, but the Court recognizes that not every violation of copyright or rights of publicity will be caught.

Instead, the injunction requires Cybernet's reviewing staff to take action against sites containing images which a *well-trained* site reviewer should catch. The adoption of a DMCA-compliant plan is meant to ensure the removal of infringing images that make it through the reviewers' initial screening of websites. The knowledge requirement goes beyond the DMCA's "red flag" test, however, because previous enforcement efforts suggest a strong tendency on Cybernet's part to enforce no more than it perceives to be the minimal requirements imposed upon it. The Court may revisit this issue if substantial questions of compliance with the injunction or burden issues arise, but it must be stressed that the injunction, like the DMCA, create a framework where all but the most difficult issues should be resolvable without the Court's intervention.

Third, Cybernet requested a multi-million dollar bond, but the Court concludes that a $600,000 bond is sufficient. The only requirements of the injunction beyond the DMCA's requirements or Cybernet's current practice of reviewing sites are the imposition of a single, thorough review of the Adult Check Gold sites, periodic review of infringing sites, and the training costs for Cybernet's review staff. Assuming a doubling of Cybernet's twelve-employee site review staff coupled with proper training, the Court

concludes that such a bond will be sufficient to meet Cybernet's increased costs. The parties should keep in mind that the terms of this preliminary injunction may differ significantly from the terms of any permanent injunction, should Perfect 10 succeed on its claims. The scope of this order is meant to address the situation as it now stands, not as it might be after a trial of the issues.

Finally, the Court has applied uniform standards in addressing the copyright and right of publicity concerns, despite the differing sources of the rights, because the Court recognizes the similar natures of the two rights insofar as technological limits and notice difficulties inhere in policing their use on the internet.

XI. CONCLUSION

For the reasons above, Perfect 10's motion for a preliminary injunction is GRANTED.

It is hereby ordered that during the pendency of this action and until final judgment is entered, defendants Cybernet Ventures, Inc. ("Cybernet"), AEI Productions, Inc., Sean Devine, Funet, Inc., F-T-V Corp., F-T-V.net and Vic Toria and their agents, servants, directors, officers, principals, employees, representatives, subsidiary and affiliated companies, assigns, and those acting in concert with them or at their direction (collectively, "Defendants") are enjoined as follows:

1. Defendants shall not do any of the following on or in connection with any websites individually operated by them: (a) invoke or display the name, likeness or identity of any of the "Identified Celebrities and Models" (as defined in paragraph 9 below); or (b) display, copy or distribute any "Perfect 10 Works" as defined in paragraph 11 below) or images substantially similar thereto (collectively, the "Prohibited Content").

2. Cybernet shall not include in its search engine or any database any of the Prohibited Content and Cybernet shall not produce any search results of any kind in which the names or identities of the Identified Celebrities and Models are invoked in search requests or queries on its search engine.

3. Cybernet shall not permit access to any "Identified Website" (as hereafter defined) via links on Cybernet's website or through the use of an Adult Check ID, nor shall Cybernet otherwise permit an Identified Website to use any of Cybernet's computer

facilities unless the Identified Website's owner, operator, or agent registered with Cybernet has complied with counter-notification procedures no less stringent than those found in 17 USC §512(g) and the website owner is not an appropriately terminated user under a policy complying with 17 USC §512(i). Cybernet shall use an identical counter-notification standard for alleged copyright and right of publicity violations. "Identified Website" shall mean any of the following:

(a) Any Adult Check website that Cybernet knows or has reason to know contains any Prohibited Content (as defined in Paragraph 10 below), unless the website operator produces Rights Documentation for all Prohibited Content or a counter-notification meeting standards no less stringent than those found in 17 USC §512(g).

(b) Any Adult Check website identified in Exhibit B to the Third Amended Complaint, unless the website operator produces Rights Documentation for all Prohibited Content or a counter-notification meeting standards no less stringent than those found in 17 USC §512(g).

(c) Any Adult Check website that Cybernet is given or has been given adequate notice that it contains Prohibited Content, unless the website operator produces Rights Documentation for alleged Perfect 10 Works and any content concerning the Identified Celebrities and Models or a counter-notification meeting standards no less stringent than those found in 17 USC §512(g).

4. Prior to their addition to the Adult Check network, Cybernet shall review the content of websites to determine whether they contain any Prohibited Content; if the website contains such content and such content is reasonably apparent, or the website specifically disclaims copyright ownership or permission for those images protected by the right of publicity, then it shall not be added to the Adult Check network, unless the website operator produces Rights Documentation for such content.

5. Cybernet shall review on a monthly basis the content of any website that has, at any time, removed content based on right of publicity or copyright allegations without submitting a statement to Cybernet containing at least the information identified in 17 USC §512(g), or is operated by a webmaster Cybernet knows or has reason to know has operated a website as described immediately above, in order to determine whether there exists any reasonably identifiable Prohibited Content on that website.

6. Within 90 days of entry of this Order, Cybernet shall review the content of each Gold website in order to determine whether there exists on the website any reasonably identifiable Prohibited Content.

7. Within 90 days of the entry of this Order, Cybernet shall require that each Adult Check Website in Cybernet's celebrity category produce for Cybernet's inspection, a copy of which shall be served on Perfect 10, Rights Documentation establishing its right to display the images of any person who has lodged a complaint with Cybernet about the use of his or her image on Adult Check affiliated websites. Cybernet shall treat any website as an Identified Website if it fails to produce such documentation for all such content.

8. Cybernet shall not include on its website or in promotional materials any statements that the Adult Check websites include images or "fake" images of celebrities for which Cybernet has received notice that the celebrity objects to the use of his or her image unless the reference reasonably reflects content on the websites for which Cybernet can produce Rights Documentation.

9. As used here, "Identified Celebrities and Models" shall mean any person who has assigned to Perfect 10 their right of publicity or any person who has complained to Cybernet about use of their images on Adult Check affiliated websites, in so far as these persons are identified in the Third Amended Complaint in this action, or any content concerning such persons, unless Cybernet can produce Rights Documentation that the particular content is authorized. "Identified Celebrities and Models" also shall include any person identified by Perfect 10 in a written statement delivered to Cybernet's designated agent, such written statement for right of publicity allegations directly asserted by Perfect

10 meeting the substantive requirements of 17 USC §512. "Identified Celebrities and Models" shall also include any new person complaining to Cybernet about the use of his or her images on Adult Check affiliated websites. Cybernet shall make publicly accessible a list of all "Identified Celebrities and Models," identifying their objection to the use of their images on Adult Check affiliated websites.

10. As used herein, "Rights Documentation" shall consist of a written license agreement or consent statement, signed by the person or persons whose images or identity is invoked or the person or persons' authorized agent, authorizing the display of the image on Adult Check websites, or a statement, under penalty of perjury, declaring why the website operator believes the display is authorized.

11. As used herein, "Perfect 10 Works" shall mean any copyrighted image or work of Perfect 10, or any part thereof.

12. Within ten (10) business days of the date of this Order, each of the Defendants shall serve upon plaintiff and file with the Court a report of compliance identifying the steps each has taken to comply with this Order. One hundred days following the date of this Order, Cybernet shall serve upon the plaintiff and file with the Court a further report of compliance identifying the steps it has taken to comply with Paragraphs 6 & 7 of this Order.

This Order shall be effective upon the filing of a bond in the amount of Six Hundred Thousand Dollars ($600,000) by plaintiff.

IT IS SO ORDERED.

———————

[1] See, e.g., Asseo v. Pan-America Grain Co., Inc., 805 F2d 23, 26 (1st Cir 1986) ("affidavits and other hearsay materials are often received in preliminary injunction proceedings").

[2] Perfect 10 has attempted to further elaborate on the authentication issue in its Reply to Evidentiary Objections ("Evid. Reply") and in Norman Zadeh's Second Declaration ("Zadeh Decl. II") ¶¶ 3-7, but the Court did not consider this information. Despite the general admissibility of these exhibits, there are individual exhibits that are insufficiently authenticated, see, e.g., Zadeh Decl., Ex. 17, and the Court does not rely on them in its findings of fact. Because of the sheer volume of

evidentiary objections, the Court's discussion must be held at a certain level of generality. Where either party's arguments on admissibility are persuasive, the Court simply disregards the problematic piece of evidence. The findings of fact that follow rest on evidence the Court finds admissible or proper for consideration in the context of this motion.

[3] There are several exhibits attributable to employees other than Brad Estes. These are authenticated through the discovery process, but the Court also finds that they should be appropriately considered because there is no indication that any of these employees have been deposed as of yet.

[4] When used for this purpose, the Court assumes they are subject to the best evidence rule, Fed. R. Evid. 1001. The Court finds that these printouts meet the Rule, for present purposes.

[5] Perfect 10 has not objected to Cybernet's request for judicial notice of this newspaper article.

[6] For purposes of this motion, the Court finds that Zadeh's role as CEO and familiarity with all aspects of Perfect 10's business lays an adequate foundation for information related to Perfect 10's market position, particularly as the Court finds the majority of Zadeh's testimony and declaration credible.

[7] "Webmasters" are the operators of the individual websites that can be accessed using an Adult Check ID.

[8] The Court finds Mr. Zadeh's testimony on this count to be credible and Cybernet has advanced no information to dispute it.

[9] The Court utilizes this evidence because it is consistent with a declaration submitted by Lin Milano to the Court in August 22, 2001. That declaration provides evidence of notice and the e-mail meets Cybernet's previous objection that Ms. Milano's declaration does not meet the best evidence rule. See Evid. Obj. to Decl. of Lin Milano, filed Aug. 23, 2001.

[10] Morris v. Business Concepts, Inc., 259 F3d 65, 68 (2d Cir 2001); see also 37 CFR 202.3(b)(3)(2001) ("the following shall be considered a single work: ... all copyrightable elements that are otherwise recognizable as self-contained works, that are included in a single unit of publication and in which the copyright claimant is the same."); Hilliard v. Mac's Place, Inc., 1994 WL 323961 *1 (WD Wash 1994).

[11] The Court finds the case of Cooling Systems & Flexibles, Inc. v. Stuart Radiator, Inc., 777 F2d 485, 490 (9th Cir 1985) abrogated on other grounds by Fogerty v. Fantasy, Inc., 510 US 517 (1994), distinguishable. There the Ninth Circuit refused to allow the plaintiff to use the presumption of validity to defeat the district court's finding that preexisting works did not bear a copyright

notice. *Id.* This result was consistent with the discretion afforded a district court in considering the evidentiary weight to be accorded a certificate of registration, see 17 USC §410(c). Additionally, evidence was brought in contradicting the presumption of validity and it was conceded the copyright covered a derivative work. 777 F2d at 489-90. Cybernet has not made an argument to establish similar points, nor addressed the Court's discretion under §410(c). In this case, the Court will therefore favor the presumption of validity over Cybernet's attempt to reverse this presumption for collective works by assuming that they are merely derivative works. Although Perfect 10 refers to the registered works as a "compilation" in its Reply, *see* Reply at 15, the Court notes that the certificates claim to cover "collective works."

[12] *But see* 17 USC §117 (limiting reach of exclusive rights in precisely this situation).

[13] *See also Kelly v. Arriba Software Corp.*, 280 F3d 934, 946 *[9 ILR (P&F) 675]* (9th Cir 2002) (holding company that designed search engine, which trolled web, found images and then inline linked and framed those images on its sites, was liable for direct infringement).

[14] This declaration is being used for the limited purpose as evidence of notice. The Court finds the declaration credible and interprets Mr. Easton's claim that he began notifying Cybernet of "violations of copyright under the DMCA" in 1996 or 1997, to be a claim that he began notifying Cybernet of alleged copyright violations at that time. The Court pauses to reflect on Cybernet's earlier objection to this declaration because [it] "is simply making prejudicial and defamatory allegations against Cybernet, which can no longer be permitted, let alone as evidence for this Court to consider," Evid. Obj. to Portions of Decls., filed December 17, 2001, in light of Cybernet's current evidence that "many of the notices sent by Steven Easton were deficient and thus, Cybernet *could* not act on them." Umbreit Decl. ¶ 26 (emphasis added). This is just another instance where Cybernet's prior invective undercuts its claims to be honestly working to address potential problems with its affiliated sites.

[15] Neither party addressed the role of post-filing conduct, but the Court notes that in *Fonovisa I*, 847 F Supp at 1495, and *A&M Records, Inc. v. Napster, Inc.*, 114 F Supp 2d 896, 918 *[5 ILR (P&F) 418]* (ND Cal 2000), aff'd. in part, rev'd in part, 239 F3d 1004 *[7 ILR (P&F) 1]* (9th Cir 2001) ("*Napster I*"), the courts relied to some extent upon allegations in the complaint and post-filing conduct.

[16] *See Napster II*, 239 F3d at 1022 (agreeing Napster provides "the site and facilities" for direct infringement because without its services users could not find what they wanted with the "ease of which defendant boasts"); *Napster I*, 114 F Supp 2d at 919-20; *Religious Technology*,

907 F Supp at 1375 (denying defendant's motion for summary judgment on this issue).

[17] Additionally, the participating websites actually pay no fees to Cybernet. Instead they are paid by Cybernet.

[18] The definition of standard technical measures includes a requirement that they be "developed pursuant to a broad consensus of copyright owners and service providers in an open, fair, voluntary, multi-industry standards process." 17 USC §512(i)(2)(A). There is no indication that the "strong urging" of both the House and Senate committees reporting on this bill has led to "all of the affected parties expeditiously [commencing] voluntary, inter-industry discussions to agree upon and implement the best technological solutions available to achieve these goals." H.R. Rep. 105-551(II), at 61; S. Rep. at 52. It thus appears to be an open question if *any* conduct or policy could interfere with "standard technical measures." *See* 3 *Nimmer on Copyright* §12B.02[B][3], at 12B-29 ("Given the incentives of the various parties whose consensus is required before any such technical measures can win adoption, it seems unlikely . . . that the need for any such monitoring will eventuate.")

[19] Because Cybernet does run a web-page, adultcheck.com and maintains computers to govern access to the Adult Check family's websites there is good reason to believe that it is an "online service provider" under 512(k)(1)(B). *Cf.* 47 USC 231(e) (mentioning broad range of online services that an "Internet access service" could also provide); *ALS Scan*, 239 F3d at 623; *Hendrickson*, 165 F Supp 2d at 1087. At the same time the fact that no images pass through Cybernet's hardware makes Cybernet a poor fit for the categories established by the DMCA, *see* 17 USC §§512(a)-(d), and Cybernet's service appears to fall outside the parallel definitions of 47 USC 231(b).

[20] *See* H.R. Rep. 105-551 (II), at 61. The statement above is qualified by the "standard technical measures" language in section 512(i), which *may* require such action. *See* H.R. Rep. 105-551 (II), at 53 ("a service provider need not monitor its service or affirmatively seek facts indicating infringing activity (except to the extent consistent with a standard technical measure complying with new subsection [i])"). A failure to impose an affirmative duty on service providers to hunt out infringers does not mean, however, that *copyright holders* cannot investigate potentially infringing activities and notify providers under a "reasonably implemented" section 512(i) policy.

[21] Section 512(1) provides that a service provider under subsection (a) may only be restrained from providing access to an infringer by terminating the account or from providing access to a specific, identified online location outside the United States. *See* 17 USC 512(1)(B).

There is no ability to order such a provider to take down material, presumably because such material is no longer on the system. *See* 17 USC 512(a)(4) (limiting time copy may reside on system to that "reasonably necessary for the transmission, routing, or provision of connections"). In contrast, service providers, as the term is defined for the other three safe harbor provisions may be restrained from providing access to the material, providing system access to the infringer, or such other injunctive relief as may be considered necessary to restrain infringement at a particular location, if it is the least burdensome form of relief available to the service provider. *See* 17 USC §512(1)(A).

²² In response to the unstated premise of Cybernet's arguments that enforcement of the Copyright Act would hurt its business, but not address the ultimate source of the infringement, the Court finds itself sympathetic to the observation in *Playboy v. Webbworld*: "If a business cannot be operated within the bounds of the Copyright Act, then perhaps the question of its legitimate existence needs to be addressed." 968 F Supp at 1175. *See also Napster II*, 239 F3d at 926 ("Although even a narrow injunction may so fully eviscerate Napster, Inc. as to destroy its user base . . . the business interests of an infringer do not trump a rights holder's entitlement to copyright protection.")

²³ This case appears to offer an example of such behavior. In Perfect 10's Third Amended Complaint, it identified a site, *www.celebpics.com*, as one of the problematic Adult Check sites. In its preliminary injunction papers, Perfect 10 now complains about the website *www.newcelebpics.com*. *See* Zadeh Decl., Ex. 79. Although issues of ownership are unclear at this point, the inference of repeat activity is difficult to avoid.

²⁴ This conclusion, formed on the basis of Perfect 10's initial evidence and Cybernet's opposition, obviated any need to consider Perfect 10's reply exhibits.

²⁵ The Court is inclined to read this "or" in the non-exclusive sense.

²⁶ The differences between 512(a) and (c), particularly section 512(a)'s lack of any take-down requirement and its limitation of injunctive relief to banning users may be traceable to its language limiting the safe harbor to those situations where "no such copy is maintained on the system or network in a manner ordinarily accessible to such anticipated recipients for a longer period than is reasonably necessary for the transmission, routing or provision of connections." *Cf. Religious Technology*, 907 F Supp at 1370, 1375 (rejecting direct liability theory based on eleven day storage, but allowing contributory liability theory to go to jury); *cf. also* 17 USC §512(n) ("Subsections (a), (b), (c), and (d) describe separate and distinct functions" but failure to qualify for one safe harbor "shall not affect a determination of whether that service provider qualifies for the limitations" under other categories). Thus, (a) and (c) might be read as the difference between basic infrastructure transmission functions and storage functions, with some service providers engaging in both at the same time. *But see Ellison*, 189 F Supp 2d 1051, 2002 WL 407696 at *14 (CD Cal 2002) (adopting different interpretation).

²⁷ *See LA Gear, Inc. v. E.S. Originals, Inc.*, 859 F Supp 1294, 1301 (CD Cal 1994). Although the Court recognizes the contexts are very different—one dealing with intent, one with control—this indefinite language trying to identify when there is sufficient involvement to infer either, adequately captures the nature of the inquiry.

²⁸ In light of its conclusions below, the Court need not address the "fraudulent" arm of the statute.

²⁹ *See Pasadena Unified School Dist. v. Pasadena Fed. of Teachers*, 72 Cal App 3d 100, 113 (1977), *overruled on other grounds, City & County of San Francisco v. United Ass'n of Journeyman & Apprentices*, 42 Cal 3d 810, 812 (1986) (as general principle for intentional torts); *Saunders v. Superior Court*, 27 Cal App 4th 832, 846 (1994) (as principle for unfair competition claims).

³⁰ The Court thus reserves the right to revisit this issue at a later time.

³¹ In the interest of fairness, the Court notes that Perfect 10 has also on occasion been known to adopt strained readings in support of its position. *See* Mot. at 22 (reading Cybernet's instructions to webmasters to "sell sizzle, not steak" as advice to show improper pictures to prospective customers before they log onto Adult Check). Nevertheless, Cybernet has shown a much greater tendency to make assertions that simply cross the line of credulity. *Compare* First Mot. to Dismiss at 13 ("Quite frankly, given the nature of the entertainment business, it would seem that there is no such thing as bad publicity for these kinds of people [referring to celebrities.]") *with* Rudolph Decl., Ex. A, filed Dec. 3, 2001 at 9-10 (graphic depiction of pop star in digitally-altered "action shot").

³² The Court finds the differences in proof between those who have complained and those who have not will strongly effect [sic] the likelihood of success. Further, this ensures that there is a sufficient unity of interest and that the use of any image is truly "unfair" and/or "unlawful." *See Viceroy Gold*, 75 F3d at 488 (goal of third-party standing is to avoid adjudicating rights a third-party might not wish to assert and to ensure effective advocacy). To the extent third-party standing is implicated, both goals recognized in *Viceroy* are met once a person has complained about use of their image. Although the relationship between Perfect 10 and those who have complained is not close, based on the evidence

before the Court, their interests align and the ability of these third-parties to assert their rights is severely hindered by the architecture of Cybernet and the internet. This is evidenced by the large investment of time and resources devoted by Perfect 10 to identifying individual images and sites for this litigation.

[33] The Court finds *Emery v. Visa Int'l Serv. Assoc.*, 95 Cal App 4th 952 (2002), is not applicable to the present situation. In *Visa* the alleged unfair practice involved a duty to investigate the truth of statements made by others—a duty specifically defeated by California case law, Visa's lack of control, and an alleged unlawful act that involved a violation of California's Penal Code. Cybernet's power to police extends much farther than the policing of one's mark referred to in Visa and the predicate acts are based on civil doctrines of liability.

[34] Perfect 10 has produced assignments of "any" trademark rights owned by the models, but has failed to present any evidence that they had trademark rights to give.

[35] The considerations under California state law for reverse palming off are the same as they are for reverse palming off under the Lanham Act. *See Summit Machine*, 7 F3d at 1441-42.

[36] The Court observes that the operations of the Adult Check system, with Cybernet's service understandably preventing unfettered access, also works to prevent various intellectual property rights holders from effectively protecting their rights. This situation poses a difficult challenge to section 512's accommodation of "standard technical measures" where it is unclear that any such standard has been developed.

[37] *See supra; A&M Records, Inc. v. Napster, Inc.*, 2001 WL 227083 *1 *[7 ILR (P&F) 244]* (ND Cal 2001) (requiring Napster to use "reasonable measures" to identify variations in file names) ("*Napster III*"); *see also A&M Records, Inc. v. Napster, Inc.*, 284 F3d 1091, 2002 WL 449550 *1, *4 *[10 ILR (P&F) 1]* (9th Cir 2002) (affirming shut-down order where Napster "failed to prevent infringement of all of plaintiffs' noticed copyrighted works" because "more could be done to maximize the effectiveness of the new filtering mechanism") ("*Napster IV*").

Perry

v.

Sonic Graphic Systems, Inc.

United States District Court,
Eastern District of Pennsylvania

April 13, 2000

5 ILR (P&F) 529

Civil Action No. 98-2084

Liability of service provider for copyright infringement unclear.

Where a graphics company had posted on its web site plaintiff's copyrighted photographs—in violation of the terms of the parties' licensing agreement—it was unclear whether the operator of a "virtual mall" on which the company's web site was stored would also be liable for copyright infringement. Section 202 of the Digital Millennium Copyright Act, 17 USC §512(c)(1), may apply, which, with certain limitations, provides that "[a] service provider shall not be liable . . . for infringement of copyright by reason of the storage at the direction of a user of material that resides on a system or network controlled or operated by or for the service provider . . . ." Because the operator's role in the infringement is unclear, the court cannot rule on the claim at the summary judgment stage. — **Perry v. Sonic Graphic Systems, Inc., 5 ILR (P&F) 529 [ED Pa, 2000].**

MEMORANDUM AND ORDER

J. CURTIS JOYNER, J. Plaintiff, Wayne J. Perry has sued defendants Sonic Graphics Systems, Inc. ("Sonic"), Bradley Konia, and Network Analysis Group, Inc. ("NAG"), alleging four counts: (i) copyright infringement by Sonic and Mr. Konia; (ii) breach of contract by Sonic; (iii) copyright infringement by NAG; and (iv) contributory infringement by Sonic. This Court has original jurisdiction over Plaintiff's copyright claims under 28 USC 1331, and supplementary jurisdiction over Plaintiff's state claim claims under 28 USC 1367(a). Presently before the Court is Plaintiff's Motion for Summary Judgment On All Counts. For the following reasons, Plaintiff's Motion is granted in part and denied in part.

BACKGROUND

Plaintiff, Wayne J. Perry, is a professional photographer. On January 9, 1995, Mr. Perry and Defendant Bradley Konia, acting on behalf of Defendant Sonic, signed a Licensing Agreement, which granted Sonic the right to use a set of photographs taken by Mr. Perry as follows: "[o]ne time non-exclusive use of the images listed below for up to 2,000 copies of the 1995 Sonic Graphic

Systems' capability/pricing brochure in the original first edition's six (6) page layout within a 12 month period of this license/invoice date for local distribution only." *See* Plaintiff's Memorandum, Ex. 4. The Licensing Agreement further stated that "[n]o alterations may be made in these provisions without the express written consent of the Photographer." *Id.* The photographs in question have all been registered with the United States Copyright Office.

On February 17, 1995, the parties both signed another agreement stating that the parties had agreed to substitute another of Plaintiff's photographs for one listed in the original Agreement. This document concluded with "[n]o alterations may be made in these provisions without the express written consent of the Photographer. The TERMS and CONDITIONS on the reverse side of License/Invoice #1448; January 9, 1995 apply unless specifically stated otherwise above." Plaintiff's Memorandum, Ex. 5.

During the course of 1995, Plaintiff discovered that Sonic was distributing its brochure containing its photographs to areas such as Oregon and Kentucky. *See* Plaintiff's Memorandum, Ex. 10. Further, Plaintiff found his photographs posted on

Sonic's web site. *See Id.* at Ex. 11. Sonic also used at least one of Plaintiff's images for a large poster-sized print in its waiting room. *See Id.* at Ex. 13 (stating "[o]ther than the poster prints in our waiting room, there have been no additional uses of the images.").

Plaintiff complained to Defendants that these uses constituted copyright infringement, thus setting off an argument between Plaintiff and Defendant Bradley Konia, the President of Sonic. Mr. Konia protested to Plaintiff that although he signed the Licensing Agreement, he did not believe that Plaintiff intended to enforce it. In a letter to Plaintiff, Mr. Konia wrote on Sonic letterhead: "It never occurred to me that you would want to be compensated for the use of your images. Sure, that's the way you earn your living, but we did so much for you that I thought our relationship had transcended a strictly business relationship." Plaintiff's Memorandum Ex. 12.

Plaintiff subsequently filed suit against Defendants, alleging four counts: copyright infringement by Sonic and Mr. Konia (Count I), breach of contact by Sonic (Count II), Copyright Infringement by NAG (Count III), and contributory infringement by Sonic (Count IV). Defendant Sonic has also filed a Motion to Dismiss, which is concurrently denied by a separate order of this Court.

DISCUSSION

I. Summary Judgment Standard

Summary judgment is appropriate where the pleadings, depositions, answers to interrogatories, and admissions on file, together with the affidavits, reveal no genuine issue of material fact, and the moving party is entitled to judgment as a matter of law. Fed. R. Civ. P. 56(c). Our responsibility is not to resolve disputed issues of fact, but to determine whether any factual issues exist to be tried. *Anderson v. Liberty Lobby, Inc.*, 477 US 242, 247-49 (1986). The presence of "a mere scintilla of evidence" in the nonmovant's favor will not avoid summary judgment. *Williams v. Borough of West Chester*, 891 F2d 458, 460 (3d Cir 1989) (citing *Anderson*, 477 US at 249). Rather, we will grant summary judgment unless "the evidence is such that a reasonable jury could return a verdict for the nonmoving party." *Anderson*, 477 US at 248.

In making this determination, all of the facts must be viewed in the light most favorable to the non-moving party and all reasonable inferences must be drawn in favor of the non-moving party. *Id.* at 256. Once the moving party has met the initial burden of demonstrating the absence of a genuine issue of material fact, the non-moving party must establish the existence of each element of its case. *J.F. Feeser, Inc. v. Serv-A-Portion, Inc.*, 909 F2d 1524, 1531 (3d Cir 1990) (*citing Celotex Corp. v. Catrett*, 477 US 317, 323 (1986)).

II. Plaintiff's Copyright Infringement Claim Against Sonic (Count I)

A claim for copyright infringement has two elements: (1) that the Plaintiff owned the copyrighted material; and (2) that the Defendant infringed on at least one of the five exclusive rights set out in 17 USC 106. *See Ford Motor Co. v. Summit Motor Prods.*, 930 F2d 277, 290-91 (3d. Cir 1991). Plaintiff has submitted Certificates of Registration from the U.S. Copyright Office concerning the pictures at issue in this case. The Third Circuit has held that such Certificates "constitute *prima facie* evidence of the validity and ownership of the material." *Id.* at 291. Defendant's Response to Plaintiff's Motion for Summary Judgment does not address the validity of Plaintiff's Certificates of Registration, nor does it in any way address the issue of Plaintiff's ownership of the photographs at issue in this case. Accordingly there is no genuine issue of material fact as to whether Plaintiff owned the photographs at issue in this case, and the Court determines that Plaintiff did own the photographs at issue in this case.

The exclusive rights granted to a copyright holder are set out in 17 USC 106, which states in part:

106. Exclusive rights in copyrighted works

Subject to sections 106 through 120, the owner of a copyright under this title has the exclusive rights to do and to authorized [*sic*] any of the following:

1. to reproduce the copyrighted work in copies or phonorecords. . .

2. to prepare derivative works based upon the copyrighted work;

3. to distribute copies or phonorecords of the copyrighted work to the public by sale or other

transfer of ownership, or by rental, lease, or lending. . . .

17 USC 106. Plaintiff has presented evidence that Sonic used his photographs in its brochures, in a large-sized poster, and on its web site. Sonic's use of Plaintiff's photographs, if unauthorized, would thus infringe the exclusive rights listed in 17 USC 106(1) and (3). Plaintiff argues that the only authority granted to Sonic to use its photographs was contained in the Licensing Agreement of January 9, 1995. Sonic argues that Plaintiff gave "implied permission for the uses complained of." Defendants' Response at 6. In the alternative, Sonic argues that the determination of this case requires resolution of ambiguities in the licensing agreement, which are issues of fact that should be left to the jury, and that therefore summary judgment is inappropriate at this time.

1. The Licensing Agreement Does Not Contain Ambiguities that Justify the Admission of Parole Evidence or Preclude Summary Judgment.

Sonic argues that the Licensing Agreement must be considered in the context of Plaintiff's conduct and the nature of the relationship between the parties. This is parol evidence, and is only admissible here if the contract is ambiguous. *See Mellon Bank, N.A. v. Aetna Bus. Credit, Inc.*, 619 F2d 1001, 1010 n. 9 (3d Cir 1980). The best description of Pennsylvania's parol evidence rule comes from the Supreme Court of Pennsylvania, in a case that was cited approvingly by the Third Circuit in *Mellon Bank*:

> The rule enunciated in *Gianni v. Russell & Co., Inc.*, 281 Pa. 320 (1924), is firmly embedded in the law of Pennsylvania and from that rule we will not permit a deviation for it is essential that the integrity of written contracts be maintained. . . . Where parties, without any fraud or mistake, have deliberately put their engagements in writing, the law declares the writing to be not only the best, but the only, evidence of their agreement. . . [U]nless fraud, accident or mistake be averred, the writing constitutes the agreement between the parties, and its terms cannot be added to nor subtracted from by parol evidence.

United Ref. Co. v. Jenkins, 410 Pa. 126, 134 (1963) (emphasis and citations omitted). *See Mellon Bank* at 1010. "When a written contract is clear and unequivocal, its meaning must be determined by its contents alone." *Id.* (citation omitted).

Sonic argues that there are two ambiguities in the Licensing Agreement, that could allow parol evidence to be considered in this case. First, Sonic argues that the phrase "local distribution" is ambiguous. Plaintiff has submitted evidence that Sonic used his photographs in brochures that were distributed as far away as Oregon. *See* Plaintiff's Memorandum, Ex. 10. Sonic has not responded to this evidence nor has it denied Plaintiff's allegation. Although the word "local" is indeed undefined, it is unreasonable to suggest that the phrase "local distribution" was intended to refer to the entire United States, as it would have to if it were to encompass both Pennsylvania and Oregon.[1] Under Pennsylvania law, when a party argues that a contract contains an ambiguity, that party must be able to point to a reasonable alternative interpretation for the ambiguity. *See Mellon Bank, N.A. v. Aetna Bus. Credit, Inc.*, 619 F2d 1001, 1012 n. 13 (3d Cir 1980) (stating that "if no 'reasonable' alternative meanings are put forth, then the writing will be enforced as the judge reads it on its 'face' "); *Hutchison v. Sunbeam Coal Corp.*, 513 Pa. 192, 201 (1986) (stating that "[a] contract is ambiguous if it is reasonably susceptible of different constructions and capable of being understood in more than one sense.") (emphasis added). The Court is not required to entertain unreasonable interpretations of potentially ambiguous contract terms. *See, e.g., In re F.A. Potts & Co*, 115 B.R. 66, 69-70 (ED Pa 1990) (Giles, J.) (holding that "[a]n evidentiary hearing may be warranted where a 'reasonable alternative interpretation is suggested'. . . [n]o reasonable alternative interpretation exists in this case.") (emphasis in original). As the Court finds Sonic's proposed interpretation to be unreasonable, and as the Court cannot find any reasonable interpretation of the phrase "local distribution" that would embrace areas as far away from Pennsylvania as Oregon, the Court does not find that this phrase opens the door to the admission of parol evidence.

Sonic also argues that the phrase "original first edition six page layout" is ambiguous, because "[t]he brochure in question was a four page layout, and the terms 'original first edition' were not defined within the body of the agreement." Defendant's Response at 3. The Court finds the phrase "original first edition" to be clear, and Sonic does not elaborate on its confusion regarding this phrase.[2] Further, the Court does not find any reasonable ambiguity concerning the phrase "six page layout," which clearly referred to the brochure that Sonic distributed.[3] Sonic does not propose an alternative to the interpretation that this phrase refers to the brochure containing Plaintiff's photographs that Sonic distributed. Since "no reasonable alternative meanings [have been] put forth," the Court does not find the phrase in question to be an ambiguity that opens the door to the admission of parol evidence. *Mellon Bank, N.A., supra* at 1012 n. 13.

Thus, the Court does not find any ambiguities in the Licensing Agreement warranting the introduction of parol evidence, and so the Court cannot consider Sonic's arguments regarding Plaintiff's conduct and the nature of the relationship between the parties. Sonic's second argument is that summary judgment is inappropriate because ambiguities in the Licensing Agreement must be resolved by a jury. For the reasons discussed above, the Court does not agree with Sonic that such ambiguities exist in the Licensing Agreement.

1. Sonic's Use of Plaintiff's Images Exceeded the Scope of the Licensing Agreement.

The Licensing Agreement states, in part, that it grants to Sonic a "[o]ne time non-exclusive use of the images. . .for up to 2,000 copies of the 1995 Sonic Graphics Systems' layout within a 12 month period of this license/invoice date for local distribution only." Plaintiff's Memorandum, Ex. 4. Plaintiff has submitted evidence that Sonic printed more than 2,000 copies of its brochure containing Plaintiff's photographs. *See Id.* at Ex. 13 (Sonic admitting that "[w]e printed an additional 2,000 brochures in December of 1995."). Plaintiff has also submitted evidence that his images were used on Sonic's web site for approximately three months. *See Id.* (Sonic admitting that "[y]our images were available for a brief period of time (approx 3 months, from October to December) at http://www.fastcolor.com."). Plaintiff has submitted further evidence that one of his photographs was used by Sonic to create a large print displayed in Sonic's waiting room. *See Id.* (Sonic stating that "[o]ther than the poster prints in our waiting room, there have been no additional uses of the images."). All of

these uses exceed the limited license granted by the Licensing Agreement. Sonic's Response, in turn, does not deny any of these uses. Accordingly, the Court finds that Sonic use of Plaintiff's photographs exceeded the scope of the Licensing Agreement.

1. Sonic's Use of Plaintiff's Images Violated Plaintiff's Exclusive Rights under 17 USC 106.

Plaintiff's exclusive rights for his images are set out at 17 USC 106, which states in part:

106. Exclusive rights in copyrighted works

Subject to sections 106 through 120, the owner of a copyright under this title has the exclusive rights to do and to authorized [*sic*] any of the following:

1. to reproduce the copyrighted work in copies or phonorecords. . .

2. to prepare derivative works based upon the copyrighted work;

3. to distribute copies or phonorecords of the copyrighted work to the public by sale or other transfer of ownership, or by rental, lease, or lending. . . .

17 USC 106.

Plaintiff has shown that Sonic used his photographs in brochures that exceeded the authorization of the Licensing Agreement. This violates Plaintiff's exclusive rights under 17 USC 106(1)-(3). Plaintiff has also shown that Sonic used his photographs in a large-sized poster displayed in Sonic's waiting room, which was not authorized by the Licensing Agreement. This violates Plaintiff's exclusive rights under 17 USC 106(1) and (2). Plaintiff has additionally shown that Sonic used his photographs on its web site, which was not authorized by the Licensing Agreement. This violates Plaintiff's exclusive rights under 17 USC 106(1)-(3).

Conclusion

As the Licensing Agreement is not ambiguous, and as parol evidence should not be considered in interpreting the Licensing Agreement, the Licensing Agreement will be read on its face. Sonic's use of Plaintiff's images exceeded the scope of the Licensing Agreement, and thus was unauthorized. Sonic's use infringed on Plaintiff's exclusive rights set out under 17 USC 106, and therefore Plaintiff is entitled to summary judgment on his copyright infringement claim against Sonic.

III. Plaintiff's Copyright Infringement Claim Against Bradley Konia (Count I).

Plaintiff's Motion for Summary Judgment does not address his copyright infringement claim against Bradley Konia. He discusses no evidence supporting his claim. Further, there are important legal issues relating to Plaintiff's ability to recover on this claim that are not discussed in Plaintiff's Memorandum. Plaintiff's Complaint states that Mr. Konia is liable, in part, because he "benefitted financially [from the infringement] by virtue of his ownership of Sonic stock." Complaint at 36. This raises the issue of whether the corporate veil should be pierced in this case, which Plaintiff has not briefed at all. *See In re Blatsein*, 192 F3d 88, 100 (3d Cir 1999) (stating that "Pennsylvania law. . .recognizes a strong presumption against piercing the corporate veil."). Therefore summary judgment cannot be entered on this claim.

IV. Plaintiff's Breach of Contract Claim Against Sonic (Count II).

Under Pennsylvania law, a breach of contract claim requires Plaintiff to prove four elements: (1) the existence of the contract to which plaintiff and defendant were parties; (2) the essential terms of the contract; (3) a breach of the duty imposed by the contract; and (4) that damages resulted from the breach. *See Caplan v. Fellheimer*, 5 F Supp 2d. 299, 302-03 (ED Pa 1998). Plaintiff's Memorandum presents evidence that it has satisfied each element of a breach of contract claim, and Sonic's Response addresses only one issue: whether the Licensing Agreement contained ambiguities. The Court has rejected those arguments above. Sonic has presented no other arguments relating to the validity of the Licensing Agreement, the terms of that agreement as read on its face, and whether it breached the Licensing Agreement as read on its face. The Court determines that the Licensing Agreement was a valid contract, and that Sonic breached the clear terms of that contract. Provided that Plaintiff can prove the existence of damages, he will prevail on his breach of contract claim.

V. Plaintiff's Copyright Infringement Claim Against NAG (Count III).

As discussed above, a copyright infringement claim has two elements: (1) that the Plaintiff owned the copyrighted material; and (2) that the Defendant infringed on at least one of the five exclusive rights set out in 17 USC 106. *See Ford Motor Co.*, 930 F2d at 290-91 (3d. Cir 1991). Plaintiff has proven ownership of the images in question. *See supra* at II. Plaintiff appears to relate to the use of his images in designing Sonic's web site, which could constitute an infringement on several of the exclusive rights set out in 17 USC 106, including the right to prepare derivative works based on the copyrighted work, and the right to distribute copes [*sic*] of the copyrighted work. However, Plaintiff's Memorandum does not clearly brief this issue. NAG operates Webmart, which is a "virtual mall" on which Sonic's web site was stored. *See* Plaintiff's Memorandum at 7. Plaintiff seems to state that Kevin Justice of the Red Hot Media Stuff advertising agency actually designed the web site, and delivered the finished copy to NAG, but Plaintiff does not identify the relationship between Mr. Justice and NAG. Accordingly, it is unclear if NAG is in a position to be liable for copyright infringement, because NAG's role in the alleged infringement is unclear. For example, 17 USC 512(c)(1) may apply, which with certain limitations, provides that "[a] service provider shall not be liable. . .for infringement of copyright by reason of the storage at the direction of a user of material that resides on a system or network controlled or operated by or for the service provider. . . ." 17 USC 512(c)(1). The Court therefore cannot rule on this claim at the summary judgment stage.

VI. Plaintiff's Contributory Infringement Claim Against Sonic (Count IV).

Because the Court cannot determine at the summary judgment stage whether NAG is liable for copyright infringement, the Court similarly cannot determine whether Sonic is liable as a contributory infringer for NAG's infringement.

CONCLUSION

The Licensing Agreement does not contain ambiguities preventing summary judgment in this case. Further, the Licensing Agreement contains no ambiguities justifying the admission of parol evidence. There is no genuine issue of material fact as to whether Sonic violated the Licensing Agreement, as read on its face. Plaintiff has proven that he owned the images in question in this case, and that Sonic used those images in violation of Plaintiff's exclusive rights under 17 USC 106. Accordingly, Sonic is liable for copyright infringement. The amount of damages however, cannot be determined at the summary judgment stage. Plaintiff has not sufficiently briefed the issue of statutory damages, and actual damages are an issue of fact that must be decided by a jury. Accordingly, a trial will be held to determine the amount of damages.

Plaintiff has not at all briefed his copyright infringement claim against Bradley Konia. Summary judgment on this claim is denied.

Plaintiff has also proven all of the elements of his breach of contract claim against Sonic, except for damages. Plaintiff will therefore be granted summary judgment on the claim, with the issue of damages to be determined at the above-mentioned trial.

Finally, Plaintiff has not satisfied the standard for summary judgment on his copyright infringement claim against NAG, nor for his claim that Sonic contributed to NAG's infringement. Summary judgment is denied on those claims.

An appropriate Order follows.

ORDER

AND NOW, this 11th day of April, 2000, upon consideration of Plaintiff's Motion for Summary Judgment On All Counts (Document No. 22), and the responses of the parties thereto, and in accordance with the foregoing Memorandum, it is hereby ORDERED that the Motion is GRANTED in part and DENIED in part, as follows:

1. Summary Judgment is GRANTED in favor of Plaintiff against Defendant Sonic Graphics Systems, Inc. for copyright infringement (Count I), and for breach of contract (Count II). A trial will be held to determine the amount of damages for both claims.

2. Summary Judgment is DENIED on Count I against Defendant Bradley Konia.

3. Summary judgment is DENIED on Counts III and IV.

[1] Indeed, although it is not evidence that the Court will consider in making its determination, Mr. Konia appeared to have an understanding of the phrase "local distribution" that was significantly more narrow than the one put forward by Defendants in response to Plaintiff's Summary Judgment Motion. In a letter to Plaintiff written on Sonic's letterhead, Mr. Konia stated: "[d]istribution is generally local, unless an out-of-state customer specifically requests information." Plaintiff's Memorandum, Ex. 13.

[2] Sonic may note that its Response to Plaintiff's Motion for Summary Judgment is, in general, a bit light. The Court is all for brevity, but in this case Plaintiff's Motion for Summary Judgment makes out a prima facie case of copyright infringement. Sonic responded with a six page Memorandum in which the "Argument" section is less than one page. The problem is not the Response's brevity, but rather its failure to make arguments necessary to oppose Plaintiff's Motion.

[3] Although it is not evidence that the Court will consider because it has found the phrase in question to not be ambiguous, it is worth nothing that Mr. Konia, acting as Sonic's agent, clearly believed that the Licensing Agreement referred to the brochures it sent out, when he wrote in a letter to Plaintiff: "Unless we reach an agreement with you by January 9, we will cease distributing brochures using your images at that time. . . . You have a choice. You can totally screw us over and make a powerful and highly vocal enemy, or you can give us a break by extending the license agreement to at least give us time to get a new brochure together." Plaintiff's Memorandum Ex. 12.

RealNetworks, Inc.
v.
Streambox, Inc.

United States District Court,
Western District of Washington

January 18, 2000

5 ILR (P&F) 251

No. C99-2070P

Software that circumvents copyright protections likely violates DMCA.

Defendant's software (Streambox VCR), which enables end-users to access and download copies of files that are streamed over the Internet, likely violates §§1201(a)(2) and 1201(b) of the Digital Millennium Copyright Act (DMCA). Plaintiff's technology allows Internet users to obtain real-time delivery and instant playback of audio and video content over the Internet, while affording protection to copyright owners against the piracy of copyrighted works. Plaintiff's technology employs two security measures: (1) a "Secret Handshake," which ensures that files encoded in plaintiff's "RealMedia" format and stored on a server equipped with plaintiff's software (RealServer) will be sent only to a computer equipped with plaintiff's end-user software (RealPlayer); and (2) the "Copy Switch," which is a piece of data in all RealMedia files that contains the content owner's preference regarding whether the streamed files may be copied by end-users. Through the use of these security measures, owners of audio and video content can prevent the unauthorized copying of their content. Defendant's software, however, circumvents the Secret Handshake and ignores the Copy Switch, thus allowing end-users to download RealMedia files. The Secret Handshake constitutes a "technological measure" that "controls access" to copyrighted works within the meaning of 17 USC §1201(a)(3)(B), and the Copy Switch constitutes a "technological measure" that effectively protects the right of a copyright owner to control the unauthorized copying of its work within the meaning of 17 USC §1201(b)(2)(B). Given the circumvention capabilities of defendant's software, Streambox VCR meets the test for liability under the DMCA; it is not entitled to the same "fair use" protections afforded to video cassette recorders in *Sony Corp. v. Universal City Studios, Inc.*, 464 US 471 (1984). Moreover, §1201(c)(3) affords defendant no defense; that section provides no immunity for products that circumvent technological measures in violation of §§1201(a)(2) or (b)(1). — **RealNetworks, Inc. v. Streambox, Inc., 5 ILR (P&F) 251 [WD Wash, 2000].**

Plaintiff likely to suffer irreparable harm from software that violates DMCA.

It is not yet settled whether a plaintiff who shows a reasonable likelihood of success on a claim arising under §1201 of the Digital Millennium Copyright Act (DMCA) is entitled to a presumption of irreparable harm. Assuming that such a plaintiff is entitled to the presumption, the plaintiff in the present case would be so entitled, for plaintiff has shown that defendant's software (Streambox VCR), which enables end-users to access and download copies of files that are streamed over the Internet, likely violates §§ 1201(a)(2) and 1201(b) of the DMCA. In the event that such a presumption is not applicable, plaintiff has demonstrated that it would likely suffer irreparable harm if the Streambox VCR is distributed, for the software circumvents plaintiff's security measures, and will necessarily undermine the confidence that plaintiff's existing and potential customers have in those measures. An injunction against the VCR also would serve the public interest because the VCR's ability to circumvent plaintiff's security measures would likely reduce the willingness of copyright owners to make their audio and video works accessible to the public over the Internet. — **RealNetworks, Inc. v. Streambox, Inc., 5 ILR (P&F) 251 [WD Wash, 2000].**

File conversion software not likely to violate DMCA.

Defendant's software (Streambox Ripper), which enables the conversion of files from plaintiff's RealMedia format to other formats, does not likely violate §1201(b) of the Digital Millennium Copyright Act (DMCA). Although plaintiff maintains that the primary purpose and only commercially significant use for the Ripper would be to enable consumers to prepare unauthorized "derivatives" of copyrighted audio or video content in the RealMedia format in violation of 17 USC §106(2), the Ripper has legitimate purposes and commercially significant uses. The Ripper may be used by content owners, including copyright holders, to convert their content from the RealMedia format to other formats. The Ripper may also be used by consumers to convert audio and video files that they acquired with the content owner's permission from RealMedia to other formats. Thus, plaintiff has not demonstrated that it is likely to succeed on its claims that the Ripper violates §§1201(b)(1)(A) or (B) of the DMCA. Moreover, there is little evidence that content owners use the RealMedia format as a "technological measure" to prevent end-users from making derivative works. Plaintiff has not introduced evidence that a substantial number of content owners would object to having end-users convert RealMedia files that they legitimately obtain into other formats, nor has plaintiff submitted substantial evidence that the Ripper's alleged violations of §1201(b) will cause plaintiff injury. — **RealNetworks, Inc. v. Streambox, Inc., 5 ILR (P&F) 251 [WD Wash, 2000].**

Plug-in software arguably creates a derivative work.

Although plaintiff has not demonstrated that it is likely to succeed on its copyright infringement claim with regard to defendant's software (known as "Streambox Ferret"), plaintiff has raised serious questions going to the merits of the claim, thereby entitling plaintiff to a preliminary injunction. The Ferret, which consumers may install as a plug-in to plaintiff's RealPlayer software, alters the visual appearance and operation of RealPlayer. Specifically, it adds a button to RealPlayer's graphical user interface, which allows the user to switch between plaintiff's search engine and defendant's search engine. Use of the Ferret may also result in replacement of the logo of plaintiff's search engine with that of defendant's. Consumers who install the Ferret arguably create a derivative work under 17 USC §106(2) without the copyright owner's authorization. They also arguably violate their license agreement with plaintiff. The balance of hardships here clearly favors plaintiff. — **RealNetworks, Inc. v. Streambox, Inc., 5 ILR (P&F) 251 [WD Wash, 2000].**

For RealNetworks Inc., plaintiff: *James A. DiBoise, David H. Kramer,* Wilson, Sonsini, Goodrich & Rosati, Palo Alto, CA, *Robert D. Stewart,* McNaul, Ebel, Nawrot, Helgren & Vance, Seattle, WA.

For Streambox Inc., defendant: *Robert J. Carlson,* Christensen O'Connor, Johnson & Kindness, PLLC, Seattle, WA, *Chun M. Ng,* Blakely Sokoloff Taylor & Zafman, Kirkland, WA.

ORDER ON PLAINTIFF'S MOTION FOR PRELIMINARY INJUNCTION

INTRODUCTION

MARSHA J. PECHMAN, District Judge. Plaintiff RealNetworks, Inc. ("RealNetworks") filed this action on December 21, 1999 *[4 ILR (P&F) 2185]*. RealNetworks claims that Defendant Streambox has violated provisions of the Digital Millennium Copyright Act ("DMCA"), 17 USC §1201 *et seq.*, by distributing and marketing products known as the Streambox VCR and the Ripper. RealNetworks also contends that another Streambox product, known as the Ferret, is unlawfully designed to permit consumers to make unauthorized modifications to a software program on which RealNetworks holds the copyright.

On December 21, 1999, RealNetworks applied for a temporary restraining order to bar Streambox from manufacturing, distributing, selling, or marketing the VCR, the Ripper, and the Ferret. On December 23, 1999, Chief Judge Coughenour of this Court entered a Temporary Restraining Order *[4 ILR (P&F) 271]*, finding RealNetworks was likely to succeed on the merits of its claims and that it was suffering irreparable harm from Streambox's conduct. The Court also ordered Streambox to show cause as to why the restraints contained in the

Temporary Restraining Order should not be continued as a preliminary injunction.

After expedited briefing, a show cause hearing was held on January 7, 2000 before the Court. Both parties were permitted to submit overlength briefs in support of their arguments. The Court further requested that both parties submit the highlight portions of the legislative history of the DMCA that they believe to be relevant to interpreting the statute with respect to Plaintiff's claims under the statute.

The Court, having considered the papers and pleadings filed herein and having heard oral argument from the parties, concludes that a preliminary injunction should be entered to enjoin the manufacture, distribution, and sale of the Streambox VCR and the Ferret during the pendency of this action. The Court does not conclude that a preliminary injunction should be entered with respect to the Ripper. Pursuant to Fed. R. Civ. P. 52(a), the Court's findings of fact and conclusions of law are stated below.

FINDINGS OF FACT

RealNetworks

1. RealNetworks is a public company based in Seattle, Washington that develops and markets software products designed to enable owners of audio, video and other multimedia content to send their content to users of personal computers over the Internet.

2. RealNetworks offers products that enable consumers to access audio and video content over the Internet through a process known as "streaming." When an audio or video clip is "streamed" to a consumer, no trace of the clip is left on the consumer's computer, unless the content owner has permitted the consumer to download the file.

3. Streaming is to be contrasted with "downloading," a process by which a complete copy of an audio or video clip is delivered to and stored on a consumer's computer. Once a consumer has downloaded a file, he or she can access the file at will, and can generally redistribute copies of that file to others.

4. In the digital era, the difference between streaming and downloading is of critical importance. A downloaded copy of a digital audio or video file is essentially indistinguishable from the original, and such copies can often be created at the touch of a button. A user who obtains a digital copy may supplant the market for the original by distributing copies of his or her own. To guard against the unauthorized copying and redistributing of their content, many copyright owners do not make their content available for downloading, and instead distribute the content using streaming technology in a manner that does not permit downloading.

5. A large majority of all Internet Web pages that deliver streaming music or video use the RealNetworks' format.

RealNetworks' Products

6. The RealNetworks' products at issue in this action include the "RealProducer," the "RealServer" and the "RealPlayer." These products may be used together to form a system for distributing, retrieving and playing digital audio and video content via the Internet.

7. Owners of audio or video content may choose to use a RealNetworks product to encode their digital content into RealNetworks' format. Once encoded in that format, the media files are called RealAudio or RealVideo (collectively "RealMedia") files.

8. After a content owner has encoded its content into the RealMedia format, it may decide to use a "RealServer" to send that content to consumers. A RealServer is a software program that resides on a content owner's computer that holds RealMedia files and "serves" them to consumers through streaming.

9. The RealServer is not the only available means for distributing RealMedia files. RealMedia files may also be made available on an ordinary web server instead of a RealServer. An end-user can download content from an ordinary web server using nothing more than a freely available Internet browser such as Netscape's Navigator or Microsoft's Internet Explorer.

10. To download streaming content distributed by a RealServer, however, a consumer must employ a "RealPlayer." The RealPlayer is a software program that resides on an end-user's computer and must be used to access and play a streaming RealMedia file that is sent from a RealServer.

RealNetworks' Security Measures

11. RealNetworks' products can be used to enable owners of audio and video content to make their content available for consumers to listen to or

view, while at the same time securing the content against unauthorized access or copying.

12. The first of these measures, called the "Secret Handshake" by RealNetworks, ensures that files hosted on a RealServer will only be sent to a RealPlayer. The Secret Handshake is an authentication sequence which only RealServers and RealPlayers know. By design, unless this authentication sequence takes place, the RealServer does not stream the content it holds.

13. By ensuring that RealMedia files hosted on a RealServer are streamed only to RealPlayers, RealNetworks can ensure that a second security measure, which RealNetworks calls the "Copy Switch," is given effect. The Copy Switch is a piece of data in all RealMedia files that contains the content owner's preference regarding whether or not the stream may be copied by end-users. RealPlayers are designed to read this Copy Switch and obey the content owner's wishes. If a content owner turns on the Copy Switch in a particular RealMedia file, when that file is streamed, an end-user can use the RealPlayer to save a copy of that RealMedia file to the user's computer. If a content owner does not turn on the Copy Switch in a RealMedia file, the RealPlayer will not allow an end-user to make a copy of that file. The file will simply "evaporate" as the user listens to or watches it stream.

14. Through the use of the Secret Handshake and the Copy Switch, owner of audio and video content can prevent the unauthorized copying of their content if they so choose.

15. Content owners who choose to use the security measures described above are likely to be seeking to prevent their works from being copied without their authorization. RealNetworks has proffered declarations from copyright owners that they rely on RealNetworks security measures to protect their copyrighted works on the Internet. Many of these copyright owners further state that if users could circumvent the security measures and make unauthorized copies of the content, they likely would not put their contents up on the Internet for end-users.

16. Many copyright owners make content available on their Web site as a means to attract end-users to the Web site; that is, to drive "traffic" to the Web site. The more traffic a Web site generates, the more it can charge for advertisements placed on

the Web site. Without RealNetworks' security measures, a copyright owner could lose the traffic its content generates. An end-user could obtain a copy of the content after only one visit and listen to or view it repeatedly without ever returning to the Web site. That end-user could also redistribute the content to others who would then have no occasion to visit the site in the first instance.

17. Copyright owners also use RealNetworks' technology so that end-users can listen to, but not record, music that is on sale, either at a Web site or in retail stores. Other copyright owners enable users to listen to content on a "pay-per-play" basis that requires a payment for each time the end-user wants to hear the content. Without the security measures afforded by RealNetworks, these methods of distribution could not succeed. End-users could make and redistribute digital copies of any content available on the Internet, undermining the market for the copyrighted original.

18. RealNetworks' success as a company is due in significant part to the fact that it has offered copyright owners a successful means of protecting against unauthorized duplication and distribution of their digital works.

The RealPlayer Search Functionality

19. In addition to its content playing and content protection capabilities, the RealPlayer enables end-users to search the Internet for audio and video content. Currently, a company known as Snap! LLC supplies the search services available to end-users through the RealPlayer under a contract with RealNetworks.

20. Under RealNetworks' contract with Snap, the search bar on the bottom of the RealPlayer's graphical user interface (the screen end-users view and interact with) is emblazoned with Snap's logo. An end-user can input a search request by inserting "key words" into the search bar. The RealPlayer then uses Snap's search services to locate specific content corresponding to the search request from among the millions of media files available on the Internet. The RealPlayer then routes the end-user to a Web site maintained and co-branded by RealNetworks and Snap, where the names and locations of the files responsive to the search request are displayed.

21. Through this process, Snap garners visibility and visitors, enhancing Snap's ability to sell

advertising and products. Snap compensates RealNetworks for the promotional value it receives based on the number of searches performed by users who are directed to the Snap search engine. RealNetworks maintains that it has earned several million dollars from its contract with Snap.

Streambox

22. Defendant Streambox, Inc. is a Washington corporation which provides software products for processing and recording audio and video content, including but not limited to content which is streamed over the Internet. Streambox also maintains a searchable database of Internet web addresses of various audio and video offerings on the Internet. The Streambox products at issue in this case are known as the Streambox VCR, the Ripper, and the Ferret.

Streambox VCR

23. The Streambox VCR enables end-users to access and download copies of RealMedia files that are streamed over the Internet. While the Streambox VCR also allows users to copy RealMedia files that are made freely available for downloading from ordinary web servers, the only function relevant to this case is the portions of the VCR that allow it to access and copy RealMedia files located on RealServers.

24. In order to gain access to RealMedia content located on a RealServer, the VCR mimics a RealPlayer and circumvents the authentication procedure, or Secret Handshake, that a RealServer requires before it will stream content. In other words, the Streambox VCR is able to convince the RealServer into thinking that the VCR is, in fact, a RealPlayer.

25. Having convinced a RealServer to begin streaming content, the Streambox VCR, like the RealPlayer, acts as a receiver. However, unlike the RealPlayer, the VCR ignores the Copy Switch that tells a RealPlayer whether an end-user is allowed to make a copy of (*i.e.*, download) the RealMedia file as it is being streamed. The VCR thus allows the end-user to download RealMedia files even if the content owner has used the Copy Switch to prohibit end-users from downloading the files.

26. The only reason for the Streambox VCR to circumvent the Secret Handshake and interact with a RealServer is to allow an end-user to access and make copies of content that a copyright holder has placed on a RealServer in order to secure it against unauthorized copying. In this way, the Streambox VCR acts like a "black box" which descrambles cable or satellite broadcasts so that viewers can watch pay programming for free. Like the cable and satellite companies that scramble their video signals to control access to their programs, RealNetworks has employed technological measures to ensure that only users of the RealPlayer can access RealMedia content placed on a RealServer. RealNetworks has gone one step further than the cable and satellite companies, not only controlling access, but also showing copyright owners to specify whether or not their works can be copied by end-users, even if access is permitted. The Streambox VCR circumvents both the access control and copy protection measures.

27. The Streambox VCR can be distinguished from a third-party product sold by RealNetworks called GetRight. GetRight enables end-users to download RealAudio files that have been placed on a web server, but not RealAudio files placed on a RealServer.

28. A copyright owner that places a RealMedia file onto a web server instead of a RealServer does not make use of protections offered by the RealNetworks security system. Thus, when GetRight is used to obtain such a file, it need not and does not circumvent RealNetworks' access control and copyright protection measures. GetRight cannot access materials available from a RealServer because it cannot perform the requisite Secret Handshake. Unlike GetRight, the Streambox VCR circumvents the Secret Handshake and enables users to make digital copies of content that the copyright owner has indicated that it should not be copied.

29. Once an unauthorized, digital copy of a RealMedia file is created it can be redistributed to others at the touch of a button.

30. Streambox's marketing of the VCR notes that end-users can "download RealAudio and RealMedia files as easily as you would any other file, then reap the benefits of clean, unclogged streams straight from your hard drive" and that the product can be used by "savvy surfers who enjoy taking control of their favorite Internet music/video clips."

31. The Streambox VCR poses a threat to RealNetworks' relationships with existing and potential customers who wish to secure their content for transmission over the Internet and must decide whether to purchase and use RealNetworks' technology. If the Streambox VCR remains available, these customers may opt not to utilize RealNetworks' technology, believing that it would not protect their content against unauthorized copying.

Streambox Ripper

32. Streambox also manufactures and distributes a product called the Streambox Ripper. The Ripper is a file conversion application that allows conversion (adaptation) of files from RealMedia format to other formats such as .WAV, .RMA, and MP3. The Ripper also permits conversion of files between each of these formats, *i.e.*, .WAV to .WMA and .WAV to MP3.

33. The Ripper operates on files which are already resident on the hard disk of the user's computer. The Ripper permits users to convert files that they have already created or obtained (presumably through legitimate means) from one format to another.

34. Streambox has proffered evidence that one potential use of the Ripper would be to permit copyright owners to translate their content directly from the RealMedia format into other formats that they may wish to utilize for their own work. Streambox has provided examples of various content owners who need a way to convert their own RealMedia files into different formats, such as .WAV for editing, or .WMA to accommodate those users who wish to access the content with a Windows Media Player instead of a RealPlayer. In addition, content which is freely available, such as public domain material and material which users are invited and even encouraged to access and copy, may be converted by the Ripper into a different file format for listening at a location other than the user's computer.

Streambox Ferret

35. Streambox manufactures, markets, and distributes a third product called the Streambox Ferret. The Ferret may be installed as a "plug-in" application to the RealPlayer.

36. When a consumer installs the Ferret as a plug-in to the RealPlayer, the RealPlayer's graphical user interface is configured with an added button, which allows the user to switch between the Snap search engine and the Streambox search engine. The use of the Ferret may also result in replacement of the "Snap.Com" logo that appears on the RealPlayer's graphical user interface with a "Streambox" logo.

37. When consumers install the Ferret as a plug-in to the RealPlayer, the visual appearance and operation of the RealPlayer is altered.

CONCLUSIONS OF LAW

1. The Court has jurisdiction over this action under 28 USC §§1331 and 1338.

2. The Court finds that RealNetworks has standing to pursue DMCA claims under 17 USC §1203, which affords standing to "any person" allegedly injured by a violation of sections 1201 and 1202 of the DMCA.

Preliminary Injunction Standard

3. To obtain a preliminary injunction, a party must show either (1) a combination of probable success on the merits and the possibility of irreparable harm, or (2) that serious questions are raised and the balance of hardships tips in its favor. *Apple Computer v. Formula Int'l, Inc.*, 725 F2d 521, 523 (9th Cir 1984). These are not separate tests, but rather "opposition ends of a single 'continuum in which the required showing of harm varies inversely with the required showing of meritoriousness.'" *Rodeo Collection v. West Seventh*, 812 F2d 1215, 1217 (9th Cir 1987); *Cadence Design Sys., Inc. v. Avant! Corp.*, 125 F3d 824, 826 (9th Cir 1997), *cert, denied*, 118 S Ct 1795 (1998) (quotation omitted).

4. RealNetworks argues that a plaintiff who demonstrates a reasonable likelihood of success on claims under section 1201 of the DMCA is entitled to a presumption of irreparable harm. In support of this argument, RealNetworks cites cases in which such a presumption was afforded to plaintiffs who brought copyright infringement claims. *See Cadence Design Sys., Inc. v. Avant! Corp.*, 125 F3d 824, 827 (9th Cir 1997), *cert. denied*, 118 S Ct 1795, and *Triad Sys, Corp. v. Southeastern Express*, 64 F3d 1330, 1335 (9th Cir 1995).

5. RealNetworks' claims against the Streambox VCR and the Ripper, by contrast, arise under section 1201 of the DMCA, and thus do not constitute copyright "infringement" claims. *See* 1 Nimmer on Copyright (1999 Supp), §12.A17[B] (noting that section 1201 of the DMCA occupies "a niche distinct from copyright infringement" and that section 1201 is removed from the Act's definition of copyright infringement.) Because the DMCA is a recently-enacted statute, there appears to be no authority holding that a plaintiff seeking a preliminary injunction who shows a reasonable likelihood of success on a claim arising under section 1201 of the DMCA is entitled to a presumption of irreparable harm.

RealNetworks Has Demonstrated a Reasonable Likelihood of Success on its DMCA Claims With Respect to the Streambox VCR

6. The DMCA prohibits the manufacture, import, offer to the public, or trafficking in any technology, product, service, device, component, or part thereof that: (1) is primarily designed or produced for the purpose of circumventing a technological measure that effectively "controls access to" a copyrighted work or "protects a right of a copyright owner;" (2) has only limited commercially significant purpose or use other than to circumvent such technological protection measures; or (3) is marketed for use in circumventing such technological protection measures. 17 USC §§1201(a)(2), 1201(b).

Parts of the VCR Are Likely to Violate Sections 1201(a)(2), and 1201(b)

7. Under the DMCA, the Secret Handshake that must take place between a RealServer and a RealPlayer before the RealServer will begin streaming content to an end-user appears to constitute a "technological measure" that "effectively controls access" to copyrighted works. *See* 17 USC §1201(a)(3)(B) (measure "effectively controls access" if it "requires the application of information or a process or a treatment, with the authority of the copyright holder, to gain access to the work"). To gain access to a work protected by the Secret Handshake, a user must employ a RealPlayer, which will supply the requisite information to the RealServer in a proprietary authentication sequence.

8. In conjunction with the Secret Handshake, the Copy Switch is a "technological measure" that effectively protects the right of a copyright owner to control the unauthorized copying of its work. *See* 17 USC §1201(b)(2)(B) (measure "effectively protects" right of copyright holder if it "prevents, restricts or otherwise limits the exercise of a right of a copyright owner"); 17 USC §106(a) (granting copyright holder exclusive right to make copies of its work). To access a RealMedia file distributed by a RealServer, a user must use a RealPlayer. The RealPlayer reads the Copy Switch in the file. If the Copy Switch in the file is turned off, the RealPlayer will not permit the user to record a copy as the file is streamed. Thus, the Copy Switch may restrict others from exercising a copyright holder's exclusive right to copy its work.

9. Under the DMCA, a product or part thereof "circumvents" protections afforded a technological measure by "avoiding bypassing, removing, deactivating or otherwise impairing" the operation of that technological measure. 17 USC §§1201(b)(2)(A), 1201(a)(2)(A). Under that definition, at least a part of the Streambox VCR circumvents the technological measures RealNetwork affords to copyright owners. Where a RealMedia file is stored on a RealServer, the VCR "bypasses" the Secret Handshake to gain access to the file. The VCR then circumvents the Copy Switch, enabling a user to make a copy of a file that the copyright owner has sought to protect.

10. Given the circumvention capabilities of the Streambox VCR, Streambox violates the DMCA if the product or a part thereof: (i) is primarily designed to serve this function; (ii) has only limited commercially significant purposes beyond the circumvention; or (iii) is marketed as a means of circumvention. 17 USC §§1201(a)(2)(A-C), 1201(b)(b)(A-C). These three tests are disjunctive. *Id.* A product that meets only one of the three independent bases for liability is still prohibited. Here, the VCR meets at least the first two.

11. The Streambox VCR meets the first test for liability under the DMCA because at least a part of the Streambox VCR is primarily, if not exclusively, designed to circumvent the access control and copy protection measures that RealNetwork affords to copyright owners. 17 USC §§1201(a)(2)(A), 1201(b)(c)(A).

12. The second basis for liability is met because a portion of the VCR that circumvents the Secret Handshake so as to avoid the Copy Switch has no significant commercial purpose other than to enable users to access and record protected content. 17 USC §1201(a)(2)(B), 1201(b)(d)(B). There does not appear to be any other commercial value that this capability affords.

13. Streambox's primary defense to Plaintiff's DMCA claims is that the VCR has legitimate uses. In particular, Streambox claims that the VCR allows consumers to make "fair use" copies of RealMedia files, notwithstanding the access control and copy protection measures that a copyright owner may have placed on that file.

14. The portions of the VCR that circumvent the Secret Handshake and Copy Switch permit consumers to obtain and redistribute perfect digital copies of audio and video files that copyright owners have made clear they do not want copied. For this reason, Streambox's VCR is entitled to the same "fair use" protections the Supreme Court afforded to video cassette recorders used for "time-shifting" in *Sony Corp. v. Universal City Studios, Inc.*, 464 US 417, 78 L Ed 2d 574, 104 S Ct 774 (1984).

15. The *Sony* decision turned in large part on a finding that substantial numbers of copyright holders who broadcast their works either had authorized or would not object to having their works time-shifted by private viewers. *See Sony*, 464 US at 443, 446. Here, by contrast, copyright owners have specifically chosen to prevent the copying enabled by the Streambox VCR putting their content on RealServers and leaving the Copy Switch off.

16. Moreover, the *Sony* decision did not involve interpretation of the DMCA. Under the DMCA, product developers do not have the right to distribute products that circumvent technological measures that prevent consumers from gaining unauthorized access to or making unauthorized copies of works protected by the Copyright Act. Instead, Congress specifically prohibited the distribution of the tools by which such circumvention could be accomplished. The portion of the Streambox VCR that circumvents the technological measures that prevent unauthorized access to and duplication of audio and video content therefore runs afoul of the DMCA.

17. This point is underscored by the leading treatise on copyright, which observes that the enactment of the DMCA means that "those who manufacture equipment and products generally can no longer gauge their conduct as permitted or forbidden by reference to the *Sony* doctrine. For a given piece of machinery might qualify as a stable item of commerce, with a substantial noninfringing use, and hence be immune from attack under *Sony*'s construction of the Copyright Act—but nonetheless still be subject to suppression under Section 1201." 1 Nimmer on Copyright (1999 Supp), §12A.18[B]. As such, "equipment manufacturers in the twenty-first century will need to vet their products for compliance with Section 1201 in order to avoid a circumvention claim, rather than under *Sony* to negate a copyright claim." *Id.*

18. Streambox also argues that the VCR does not violate the DMCA because the Copy Switch that it avoids does not "effectively protect" against the unauthorized copying of copyrighted works as required by §1201(a)(3)(B). Streambox claims this "effective" protection is lacking because an enterprising end-user could potentially use other means to record streaming audio content as it is played by the end-user's computer speakers. This argument fails because the Copy Switch, in the ordinary course of its operation when it is on, restricts and limits the ability of people to make perfect digital copies of a copyrighted work. The Copy Switch therefore constitutes a technological measure that effectively protects a copyright owner's rights under section 1201(a)(3)(B).

19. In addition, the argument ignores the fact that before the Copy Switch is even implicated, the Streambox VCR has already circumvented the Secret Handshake to gain access to an unauthorized RealMedia file. That alone is sufficient for liability under the DMCA. *See* 17 USC §1201(i)(e).

20. Streambox's last defense to liability for the VCR rests on Section 1201(c)(3) of the DMCA which it cites for the proposition that the VCR is not required to respond to the Copy Switch. Again, this argument fails to address the VCR's circumvention of the Secret Handshake, which is enough, by itself, to create liability under Section 1201(a)(2).

21. Moreover, Section 1201(c)(3) states that "nothing in this section shall require . . . a response

to any particular technological measure, so long as . . . the product . . . does not otherwise fall within the prohibitions of subsections (a)(2) or (b)(1)." 17 USC §1201(c)(3). As the remainder of the statute and the leading copyright commentator make clear, Section 1201(c)(3) does not provide immunity for products that circumvent technological measures in violation of Sections 1201(a)(2) or (b)(1). *See* 17 USC §1201(c)(3) (a product need not respond to a particular measure "so long as such . . . product . . .does not otherwise fall within the prohibitions of subsections (a)(2) or (b)(1)." (emphasis added); 1 Nimmer on Copyright (1999 Supp), §12A.05[C]. If the statute meant what Streambox suggests, any manufacturer of circumvention tools could avoid DMCA liability simply by claiming it chose not to respond to the particular protection that its tool circumvents.

22. As set forth above, the Streambox VCR falls within the prohibitions of sections 1201(a)(2) and 1201(b)(1). Accordingly, Section 1201(c)(3) affords Streambox no defense.

RealNetworks is Likely to Suffer Irreparable Harm With Respect to the VCR

23. RealNetworks argues that because it has demonstrated a reasonable likelihood of success on its DMCA claims concerning the VCR, it is entitled to a presumption of irreparable harm. As noted above, however, this point is not settled.

24. Assuming that a plaintiff who demonstrates a reasonable likelihood of success with respect to claims arising under section 1201 of the DMCA is entitled to a presumption of irreparable harm, RealNetworks would be entitled to such a presumption.

25. In the event that such a presumption is not applicable, RealNetworks has demonstrated that it would likely suffer irreparable harm if the Streambox VCR is distributed. The VCR circumvents RealNetworks' security measures, and will necessarily undermine the confidence that RealNetworks' existing and potential customers have in those measures. It would not be possible to determine how many of RealNetworks' existing or potential customers declined to use the company's products because of the perceived security problems created by the VCR's ability to circumvent RealNetworks' security measures.

26. An injunction against the VCR also would serve the public interest because the VCR's ability to circumvent RealNetworks' security measures would likely reduce the willingness of copyright owners to make their audio and video works accessible to the public over the Internet.

RealNetworks Has Not Demonstrated that It Is Reasonably Likely to Succeed on its DMCA Claim With Respect to the Ripper

27. RealNetworks also alleges that Streambox's marketing and distribution of the Ripper violates section 1201(b) (but not section 1201(a)(2)) of the DMCA.

28. RealNetworks maintains that the primary purpose and only commercially significant use for the Ripper would be to enable consumers to prepare unauthorized "derivatives" of copyrighted audio or video content in the RealMedia format in violation of 17 USC §106(2).

29. The Ripper has legitimate purposes and commercially significant uses. For example, the Ripper may be used by content owners, including copyright holders, to convert their content from the RealMedia format to other formats. Streambox has submitted evidence that at least some content owners would use the Ripper for this legitimate purpose. The Ripper may also be used by consumers to convert audio and video files that they acquired with the content owner's permission from RealMedia to other formats. RealNetworks has not demonstrated that it is likely to succeed on its claims that the Ripper violates sections 1201(b)(1)(A) or (B) of the DMCA.

30. RealNetworks' DMCA claims with respect to the Ripper rely largely on its argument that the proprietary RealMedia format constitutes a technological measure that effectively protects a right of a copyright owner because it prevents end-users from making derivative works based on audio or video content that a consumer obtains in RealMedia format. RealNetworks did not offer this argument in any detail in its opening memorandum.

31. There is little evidence that content owners use the RealMedia format as a "technological measure" to prevent end-users from making derivative works. In any case, RealNetworks has not introduced evidence that a substantial number of content owners would object to having end-users

convert RealMedia files that they legitimately obtain into other formats.

32. Similarly, RealNetworks has not submitted substantial evidence that the Ripper's alleged violations of section 1201(b) will cause RealNetworks injury. None of the numerous declarations submitted by RealNetworks' customers or recording industry employees express concern that the Ripper will permit RealMedia files to be converted to other formats. Instead, persons who submitted these declarations indicate that they are concerned that unnamed Streambox products will permit consumers to acquire unauthorized copies of copyrighted works that are made available only in the streaming format. These concerns appear to relate to the functions of the Streambox VCR, not to the functions of the Ripper. The Ripper functions as a "converter," not as a copier. As such, these declarations do not suggest that the Ripper's alleged violations of section 1201(b) will result in any injury to RealNetworks in the form of lost customers or business.

33. RN further alleges that Streambox's marketing of the Ripper violates section 1201(b)(1)(C) of the DMCA. The brief quotes from Streambox's promotional materials that RealNetworks references do not appear to urge consumers to buy the Ripper in order to create derivative works in violation of the Copyright Act. The evidence submitted by RealNetworks is not sufficient to show a reasonable likelihood of success on its claims under section 1201(b)(1)(C).

34. In light of Streambox's demonstration that the Ripper has legitimate and commercially significant uses, RealNetworks has not shown that it is likely to succeed on its DMCA claims with respect to the product.

35. Even if RealNetworks had raised a "serious question" about the Ripper's alleged violation of the DMCA, RealNetworks has not demonstrated that the balance of hardships tips sharply in its favor. As noted above, RealNetworks has not submitted evidence that the sale of the Ripper would cause it to lose customers or goodwill. By contrast, enjoining the Ripper would deprive Streambox of the ability to market a potentially valuable product with legitimate uses.

RealNetworks Has Demonstrated that It Is Entitled to a Preliminary Injunction with Respect to the Ferret

36. Finally, RealNetworks claims that Streambox commits contributory and/or vicarious copyright infringement by distributing the Ferret product to the public. In order to prevail on such claims, RealNetworks must demonstrate that consumers who use the Ferret as a plug-in to the RealPlayer infringe RealNetworks' rights as a copyright owner. RealNetworks alleges that consumers who install the Ferret as a plug-in application to a RealPlayer create an unauthorized derivative of the RealPlayer, thus violating RealNetwork's rights under 17 USC §106(2).

37. RealNetworks holds a valid copyright registration for version 7 of the RealPlayer, which constitutes *prima facie* evidence that RealNetworks is the owner of the copyright to the program. *See Apple Computer, Inc. v. Formula Int'l, Inc.*, 725 F2d 521, 523 (9th Cir 1984).

38. Streambox does not dispute that consumers who use the Ferret as a plug-in to a RealPlayer create a change to the RealPlayer user interface by adding a clickable button that permits the user to access the Streambox search engine, rather than the Snap search engine.

39. Streambox claims that changes that the Ferret makes to the RealPlayer do not constitute the creation of a derivative work. To support this argument, Streambox cites generally the Ninth Circuit's decision in *Lewis Galoob Toys, Inc. v. Nintendo of America, Inc.*, 964 F2d 965 (9th Cir 1992). As RealNetwork notes, however, the court in *Galoob* held that the manufacturer of a product that altered the audiovisual displays of a Nintendo game did not commit contributory copyright infringement because the "the altered displays do not incorporate a portion of a copyrighted work in some concrete or permanent form." *Id.* at 968. Here, by contrast, the alterations to the RealPlayer assume a more concrete form than the altered displays at issue in *Galoob*.

40. However, the Court is not persuaded that RealNetworks has demonstrated that it is likely to succeed on its contributory/vicarious copyright infringement claims with respect to the Ferret. The facts and issues presented in the principal case that RealNetworks relies upon, *Micro Star v. Formgen*,

Inc., 154 F3d 1107 (9th Cir 1998), do not appear to be completely analogous to the situation here. In addition, RealNetworks' argument that consumers who install the Ferret breach a license agreement that they must agree to in order to obtain the RealPlayer was first raised in RealNetworks' reply brief.

41. Nonetheless, the Court concludes that RealNetworks has raised serious questions going to the merits of its claims. It is undisputed that consumers who install the Ferret as a plug-in application to the RealPlayer cause the graphical interface of the RealPlayer to be modified, arguably creating a derivative work under 17 USC §106(2) without the copyright owner's authorization. In addition, RealNetworks has proferred evidence that end-users who install the Ferret are violating a license agreement with RealNetworks.

42. A plaintiff seeking a preliminary injunction who raises serious questions going to the merits of its claim is entitled to an injunction if the balance of hardships tips sharply in its favor. *See Micro Star v. Formgen, Inc.*, 154 F3d 1107, 1109 (9th Cir 1998).

43. The balance of hardships here clearly favors RealNetworks. The Ferret's ability to permit consumers to modify the RealPlayer jeopardizes RealNetworks' exclusive relationship with Snap. In addition, each time a consumer opts to use the Streambox search engine that is present on a modified RealPlayer rather than the Snap search engine that is present on an unmodified RealPlayer costs RealNetworks royalty payments from Snap, and it would be difficult if not impossible to calculate the lost revenue to RealNetworks.

44. By contrast, the hardship that Streambox would experience if an injunction issued against the product would not be nearly as severe. The Ferret plug-in simply provides consumers with a way to access the Streambox search engine through the RealPlayer. The Streambox search engine is already accessible to consumers in other places. If the Ferret is not available for distribution as a plug-in to the RealPlayer, consumers will still have the ability to conveniently access and use the Streambox search engine.

CONCLUSION

Consistent with the findings of facts and conclusions of law above, the Court hereby ORDERS that:

During the pendency of this action, Defendant Streambox, Inc. and its officers, agents, servants, employees and attorneys, and those persons in active concert and participation with Streambox, Inc. who receive actual notice of this Preliminary Injunction, are restrained and enjoined from manufacturing, importing, licensing, offering to the public, or offering for sale:

a) versions of the Streambox VCR or similar products that circumvent or attempt to circumvent RealNetworks' technological security measures, and from participating or assisting in any such activity;

b) versions of the Streambox Ferret or similar products that modify RealNetworks' RealPlayer program, including its interface, its source code, or its object code, and from participating or assisting in any such activity.

Plaintiff's motion for a preliminary injunction with respect to the Streambox Ripper is DENIED.

This Order shall be effective immediately, on the condition that RealNetworks continues to maintain security with the Clerk in the amount of $1,000,000 for the payment of such costs and damages as may be incurred by Streambox if it is found that Streambox was wrongfully enjoined by this Order.

The TRO *[4 ILR (P&F) 271]* entered by Judge Coughenour on December 23, 1999, and extended by the Court until 5:00 p.m. on January 18, 2000, is hereby VACATED by this Order.

The clerk is directed to provide copies of this order to all counsel of record.

_____

Sony Computer Entertainment America, Inc.

v.

Gamemasters

**United States District Court,
Northern District of California**

November 4, 1999

**1999 ILRWeb (P&F) 3001, 87 F Supp 2d 976,
54 USPQ2d 1401**

No. C 99-02743 TEH

Product that circumvents PlayStation's geographical restrictions likely violates DMCA.

Plaintiff, a manufacturer of an electronic game system, is likely to succeed on its claim that defendants' sale of device that modifies plaintiff's system to allow users to play games sold in foreign countries violates the Digital Millennium Copyright Act (DMCA). Plaintiff specifically designed its system to access only those games with data codes that match the geographical location of the game console itself. The device sold by Defendants circumvents that mechanism and thus appears to be a device whose primary function is to circumvent "a technological measure (or a protection afforded by a technological measure) that effectively controls access to a system protected by a registered copyright. . . ." 17 USC §1201(a)(2)(A). Section 1203 authorizes the court to issue a preliminary injunction to prevent violations of the DMCA. — **Sony Computer Entertainment America, Inc. v. Gamemasters, 1999 ILRWeb (P&F) 3001 [ND Cal, 1999].**

Scott D. Baker, William R. Overend, Crosby Heafey Roach & May, San Francisco, CA, for Plaintiff.

Glen L. Moss, Ann Murphy, Moss & Murphy, Hayward, CA, *Albert J.C. Chang*, law Offices of Albert J.C. Chang, Rowland Heights, CA, *David R. Schwarz*, Law Offices of David R. Schwarcz, Los Angeles, CA, *Manny D. Pokotilow*, Caesar Rivise Bernstein & Cohen, Inc., Philadelphia, PA, *David Pressman*, San Francisco, CA, for Defendants.

ORDER GRANTING PLAINTIFF'S REQUEST FOR PRELIMINARY INJUNCTION

HENDERSON, *District Judge.*

1. This civil action is brought by Sony Computer Entertainment America Inc., against Michael and Carol Chaddon, d.b.a. GameMasters, Inc., for trademark and copyright infringement, contributory trademark and contributory copyright infringement, violation of the Digital Millennium Copyright Act, and state and federal unfair competition laws.

2. This matter is now before the Court on plaintiff's motion for a preliminary injunction. Based upon the evidentiary record, the parties' moving papers, and arguments of counsel, IT IS HEREBY ORDERED, ADJUDGED AND DECREED:

I. Procedural Posture

3. In January 1999, SCEA learned that Defendants were selling allegedly counterfeit accessories for SCEA's PlayStation video game. An SCEA employee, Jerry Jessop, purchased an allegedly counterfeit PlayStation memory card, video game controller, and a device known as the "Game Enhancer" from the GameMaster's store in San Leandro on January 17, 1999. After some analysis, SCEA concluded that the peripheral items were counterfeit. Plaintiff has attached copies of the packaging of both products as exhibits. (Jessop Decl. Ex. B).

4. On June 10, 1999, SCEA filed *ex parte* for a Temporary Restraining Order ("TRO"). On June 11,

1999, this Court granted SCEA's request for a TRO and Order for Seizure and Impoundment of Counterfeit Goods and directed that all motions and papers be filed under seal. We also directed the parties to appear and Show Cause why a Preliminary Injunction should not Issue and ordered an Expedited Discovery schedule.

5. On June 15, 1999, SCEA carried out the Seizure Order impounding numerous allegedly counterfeit accessories (including 41 memory cards, 2 CD-ROM mechanism boxes; a Japanese Dual Shock Controller, and 7 PlayStation cases) totaling approximately $4,000 in value. (M.Chaddon Decl. at 4:13). Upon closer scrutiny, Sony determined that about $3,000 of these products were not counterfeit and returned them (45 Dual Shock Controllers and 6 Digital Controllers). (M.Chaddon Decl. Ex. D, Pltf. M. at 8 n. 6). Defendants claim that the remaining goods were being sold legally and were not counterfeit. These goods consisted of such items as "replacement housing" repair parts and Sony products initially sold in Japan or foreign jurisdictions. Plaintiff SCEA claims that in addition to the allegedly counterfeit games and peripheral accessories SCEA originally targeted, the seizure uncovered counterfeit PlayStation memory cards and alternate versions of the "Game Enhancer" device.

6. On July 26, 1999, the parties stipulated to an extension of the TRO which the Court signed the same day.

7. On November 1, 1999, the Court heard arguments from the parties on Why a Preliminary Injunction Should Not Issue.

The Court adopts the following Findings of Fact and Conclusions of Law:

Findings of Fact

The Parties

1. Plaintiff, Sony Computer Entertainment America Inc. is a corporation organized and existing under the laws of Delaware, with its principal place of business in Foster City, California.

2. Defendants, Michael Chaddon and Carol Chaddon are the co-owners of GameMasters, Inc. Michael Chaddon works as the Manager, while Carol Chaddon works as a retail sales person. GameMasters, Inc., is a small retail shop in San Leandro, California which sells used games and

peripheral accessories for use with the Sony PlayStation, in addition to new games and accessories purchased from third party vendors other than Sony. The Chaddon's have operated this business since 1992.[1]

3. Defendants have impleaded several of their wholesalers and suppliers as third party defendants to this lawsuit: TOMMO, Inc.; S & I MARKETING Inc.; BRIAN BROWN IMPORTS; MAT ELECTRONICS, Inc.; and INNOVATION TECHNOLOGY, Inc. Of the Third Party defendants named in this lawsuit, only TOMMO, Inc. filed an answer within the 20 days allotted by Rule 12 of the Federal Rules of Civil Procedure. All other Third Party defendants are technically in default.

The Suit

4. This suit is for 1) trademark infringement, 2) trademark counterfeiting, 3) contributory trademark infringement, 4) contributory copyright infringement in violation of federal law (15 USC §1114, "Lanham Act"), 5) violation of the Digital Millennium Copyright Act, 17 USC §1201, 6) unfair competition in violation of state law, Cal. Bus. & Prof.Code §17500 and 7) unfair competition in violation of federal law pursuant to the Lanham Act.

5. Defendants assert counterclaims against SCEA for 1) copyright and trademark misuse, 2) declaratory relief and 3) antitrust violations.

6. Though not at issue in the pending motion, Defendants assert claims against the Third Party defendants for 1) breach of warranty of title in violation of Cal. Comm.Code §2312 et. seq., 2) equitable indemnity, 3) declaratory relief, and 4) implied indemnity.

Plaintiff SCEA's Trademarks and Copyrights

7. SCEA is a worldwide manufacturer of home entertainment products, including the PlayStation game console. The PlayStation is an electronic game system designed to allow users to play CD-Rom video games at home on a television. The device is popular; since 1994, approximately 50 million of these consoles have been sold worldwide. (Hopkins Decl. ¶4.) SCEA is the exclusive United States licensee of the federally registered trademarks that correspond to its PlayStation game console.

8. SCEA owns federally registered trademarks to the "PLAYSTATION" trademark (U.S. Registration Nos. 1,903,261), "PlayStation" stylized

trademark (U.S. Registration Nos. 2,053,625), and "PS" stylized letter and design trademark (U.S. Registration Nos. 1,975,267), along with trademarks for titles and logos of video games compatible with the PlayStation console (U.S. Registration Nos. 2,181,062 ("Jet Moto"); U.S. Registration Nos. 2,012,799 ("Twisted Metal"); and 2,088,405 ("Football Gamebreaker")). (Hopkins Decl. Ex. A,B,D).

9. The PlayStation stylized "PS" trademark is a four-color, three-dimensional graphic design in which a vertically-oriented "P" is connected to a horizontally-oriented "S" appearing in a black box. (Hopkins Decl. ¶6). The trade dress in which PlayStation products have been continuously packaged and marketed since 1995 by SCEA includes use of the trademarks and other features as follows:

I. Cover Panel

1. A picture of the peripheral device appears in a slightly diagonal position across the front of the cover.

2. The picture is presented on a black background with a nimbus of light behind and above the upper left portion of the device.

3. (a) The PS insignia appears on the upper right corner of the cover in a black box framed by a white border and a "TM" just outside the lower right corner of the box. (b) The "P" is red and vertically angled as if it represents the front side of a three dimensional cube. The "S" is yellow, green and blue, and is horizontally angled below the "P" in the position of the bottom face of a three dimensional cube. (c) The bottom of the "P" meets with the bottom of the "S." (d) Below the PS insignia, "PlayStation" appears in small white print.

4. The trademark "PlayStation" appears in the trademarked design font in large white letters across the bottom of the cover with a smaller "TM" at the end of the text. The "P" and "S" in PlayStation are capitalized and the other letters are lowercase.

5. "Sony" appears in large white letters below the lower left half of the peripheral device picture.

II. Side Panels

1. The side panels have a smaller picture of the device on a grey and white background and the "PS" insignia is reproduced in a black box similar to that on the cover.

2. "PlayStation" appears in the design font in large grey letters across the bottom of the panel much as it is presented on the cover.

III. Top Panel

The top panel is a black background with the "PS" logo reproduced in a black box in the upper right corner similar to that on the cover, and "PlayStation" appears in the design font in large white letters in the lower left corner much as it is presented on the cover.

(See Hopkins Decl. Ex. C).

10. All of said registrations are valid, subsisting, remain in full force and effect, and under 15 USC §1057(B), are "prima facie evidence of the validity of the registration, of registrants' ownership of the mark and of registrants' exclusive right to use the mark in commerce. . . ." 15 USC §1057(B).

11. SCEA distributes the PlayStation game console, authorized video games and other related products only to retailers, sales representatives and distributors, who then sell the authorized products bearing the protected marks to the public. SCEA's trademarks have been extensively used, advertised and promoted throughout the United States and worldwide. As a result, the marks have achieved broad national recognition as identifying SCEA as the exclusive source of its products and distinguishing such products from those of others.

12. SCEA has built up extensive goodwill in its PlayStation marks through the world-wide sale of PlayStation products, games and accessories. This goodwill represents a valuable asset to plaintiff.

Defendant's Use of the Marks

A. Video Game Controller

13. Among the items SCEA seized from defendants' store on June 15, 1999, were 52 game controllers (1 Japanese Dual Shock Controller; 45 Dual Shock controllers; 6 Digital controllers). Game controllers are hand held peripheral devices used to play and direct the video game. Plaintiff has

submitted color copies of the packaging for these controllers. (Jessop Decl. Ex. B).

14. The trade dress of the authorized SCEA game controller is the same as the detailed description provided above. Although the seized game controllers' trade dress is not identical to that of the authentic controllers, the seized items' packaging bears substantially similar, if not identical, replicas of SCEA's stylized "PS" PlayStation trademark and "PLAYSTATION" trademark. Moreover, the device is labeled the "SonyPad PS." (Jessop Decl. ¶16-18, Ex. B).

B. Memory Cards

15. On June 15, 1999, SCEA seized and analyzed 41 memory cards designed for use with the Sony PlayStation. A memory card is a small plastic cartridge which plugs into a port on the front of the PlayStation game console to allow users to save their game progress for later play. Plaintiff has included color copies of the packaging for the memory cards. (Jessop Decl. ¶¶9-14, Ex. B). While the packagings of the seized memory cards varies, each package in question bears a substantially similar, if not identical, replica of Sony's stylized "PS" PlayStation trademark. [2]

C. Game Console Moldings

16. SCEA seized seven game console moldings. Plaintiff submitted color photocopies of some of these moldings at the November 1, 1999 hearing. According to the declaration of SCEA's Hardware Engineering Manager for the PlayStation game console, Jerry Jessop, the moldings are identical to "SCEA's '5500 series' PlayStation console mold[s]" except made in various colors. (Jessop Decl. ¶8). Jessop declares that these console cases contain unauthorized reproductions of SCEA's stylized "PS" trademark. The seized moldings appear to be the same as the SCEA manufactured PlayStation casing except in various colors, however, there are no observable references to the PlayStation or SCEA trademarks on the items in question.

D. CD Mechanism Boxes

17. SCEA seized two "CD Mechanism Boxes." It is unclear from the parties' briefings exactly what the nature or function of these items are as no explanation has been provided and no exhibits. According to the declaration of Jerry Jessop, the boxes bear SCEA trademarks even though SCEA "does not sell these products separately." (Jessop Decl. ¶15).

E. Game Enhancer Device

18. SCEA seized a device known variously as the "Game Enhancer", the "GameKillers", "Game Blaster Pro", the "Wizard" or "Code Wizard." (hereafter "Game Enhancer") (Def. Opp. at 5). Plaintiff has included copies of the Game Enhancer packaging and user instructions, from one of the devices, as exhibits. (Jessop Decl. Ex C & D). All wording on the Game Enhancer packaging is in Japanese except the words "Action Replay" borne upon the four side panels of the box. The packaging bears no replicas of any SCEA trademarks. However, the front of the box bears two white stickers which state in English that the device "Plays Japanese Imports . . . works like a Gameshark." (Jessop Decl. Ex C). Another white sticker states "External Mod-Chip for all PlayStation models." (Jessop Decl. Ex C). The lower right hand corner of the back of the Game Enhancer box states in English, "[t]his is not an official Sony Product." (Jessop Decl. Ex C).

19. The Game Enhancer is an external device manufactured by numerous companies which, when plugged into the PlayStation game console, performs at least two functions. [3]

First, the Game Enhancer permits users to modify the rules of a specific game. The device makes temporary modifications to the video game's computer program allowing a user to "cheat" *i.e.*, to make the game harder or easier by giving themselves a handicap or an advantage. For example, a player might input a certain code to give his game character infinite "lives" or unlimited ammunition. (Chaddon Decl. at 6). The Game Enhancer makes no permanent modifications to the underlying video game data and the modifications exist only while a specific game is being played. *Id.*

20. The second function of the Game Enhancer is to permit players to play games sold in Japan or Europe and intended by SCEA for use exclusively on Japanese or European PlayStation consoles. (Chaddon Decl. ¶10, Jessop Decl. ¶¶17-24). The PlayStation console is designed to operate only when encrypted data is read from a CD-ROM that verifies that the CD is an authorized, legitimate SCEA product licensed for distribution in the same

geographical territory of the console's sale. (Pltf. Mo. at 20). Games not licensed for distribution in the same territory as that of the console's sale cannot be played on the PlayStation without a device such as the Game Enhancer. (*Id.*; Jessop Decl. ¶16).

21. The Game Enhancer comes with instructions explaining how a user may configure the PlayStation console to play "imports." After inserting an authorized CD game, the user is instructed to find a means of holding the disc cover switch in the closed position while keeping the lid or disc cover open. Under normal operation, the disc cover switch only stays down when the disc cover is closed. The switch can be improperly kept down while the disc is open in a variety of ways. The Game Enhancer is then turned on and its internal operating system is selected for execution, thereby replacing the PlayStation console's internal operating system. The validity and territorial codes are then read and the CD is considered valid and acceptable for operation. The instructions direct a user to hit the "select" button on the game controller which signals the console to stop the CD motor. Once the motor is stopped, the consumer is instructed to remove the "U.S." game CD and replace it with "the CD game you want to play." Once the game has been loaded, the Game Enhancer returns control to the PlayStation's operating system. However, since the console has already verified the previous U.S. CD and does not know that the CD has been replaced, the import or other CD may be played as if it was a U.S. CD. (Jessop Decl. TRO ¶¶19-24). Both parties submitted copies of Game Enhancer or Game Enhancer like user instructions which contains a section entitled "Play Imports." (Jessop Decl. Ex. D; Chaddon Decl. Ex. C). [4]

22. The Game Enhancer is similar to numerous other video game modification devices which allow the player to "cheat" such as the "Pro Action Replay" manufactured by Datel Ltd. of Great Britain, or the "Game Shark" manufactured by SCEA. However, the Game Enhancer, unlike the original Pro Action Replay or Game Shark device, enables users to play imported, *i.e.*, non- territory games as described above. (Jessop Decl. ¶19).

23. SCEA contends that the Game Enhancer performs a third function: allowing users to play "backups," i.e., counterfeit copies of original PlayStation software. (Jessop Decl. ¶19). Defendants contend that the Game Enhancer does not enable the console to play counterfeit games. (Chaddon Decl. ¶14). The user instructions for the Game Enhancer refer to "Play Imports" but do not in anyway refer to "backups" or "bootlegs" or "copies." [5] SCEA has submitted advertising from a website for the Game Doctor which suggests that the Game Enhancer 5.0 does in fact enable users to play counterfeit games, but no evidence suggests that GameMasters sold or possessed the Game Enhancer 5.0. (Overend Suppl. Decl. C).

24. SCEA contends that the Game Enhancer device poses a safety hazard to the consumer by instructing consumers to defeat the CD safety interlock switch, i.e., the disc cover switch, potentially exposing the consumer to "the laser beam emitted from the lens of" the PlayStation unit which "may be harmful to the eyes." (Jessop Decl. ¶24, quoting PlayStation Instruction Manual). The PlayStation Instruction Manual admonishes users: As the laser beam . . . may be harmful to the eyes, do not attempt to disassemble the casing. . . . *Id.*

Conclusions of Law

1. This Court has jurisdiction over this action pursuant to 15 USC section 1121, as it arises under the Lanham Act, pursuant to 28 USC section 1331 as it presents a federal question, pursuant to 28 USC section 1338(a), as this suit concerns an act of Congress relating to patents, copyrights and trademarks. We have supplemental jurisdiction over plaintiff and defendants' state law claims under 28 USC section 1367 and the doctrines of ancillary and pendent jurisdiction.

2. Venue is proper in this Federal District court pursuant to 28 USC Section 1391(b) and 1400(a) because defendants reside within this judicial district and a substantial part of the events giving rise to the alleged claims occurred in this district.

3. Congress has expressly vested the Federal Courts with ". . . power to grant injunctions, according to the principles of equity and upon such terms as the court may deem reasonable, to prevent the violation of any right of the registrant of a mark registered in the Patent and Trademark Office." 15 USC §1116; 17 USC 1203 (injunctive relief for violations of Digital Millennium Copyright Act).

4. A federal registration of a service mark constitutes *prima facie* evidence of the exclusive right to use the registered mark in the United States. 15 USC §1115(A).

Standard for Preliminary Injunctive Relief

5. The preliminary injunction is an equitable remedy. As such, it is an extraordinary remedy, and the burden is on the moving party to make a clear showing that the remedies at law are inadequate. CHARLES A. WRIGHT & ARTHUR R. MILLER, FEDERAL PRACTICE AND PROCEDURE §2948.

6. Generally, a court may issue a preliminary injunction if it determines:

(1) the moving party will suffer irreparable injury if the relief is denied;

(2) the moving party will probably prevail on the merits;

(3) the balance of potential harm favors the moving party; and, depending on the nature of the case,

(4) the public interest favors granting relief. *Johnson v. California State Board of Accountancy*, 72 F3d 1427, 1430 (9th Cir 1995).

7. The Ninth Circuit has adopted an alternative standard under which the moving party may meet its burden by demonstrating either:

(1) a combination of probable success on the merits *and* the possibility of irreparable injury if relief is not granted;

Or

(2) the existence of serious questions going to the merits *and* that the balance of hardships tips sharply in its favor. *Id.* (emphasis added)

8. Under this last part of the alternative test, even if the balance of hardships tips decidedly in favor of the moving party, it must be shown, as an irreducible minimum, that there is a fair chance of success on the merits. *Stanley v. University of Southern California*, 13 F3d 1313, 1319 (9th Cir 1994). The alternative standards are not separate tests but rather the opposite ends of a single continuum in which the required showing of harm varies inversely with the required showing of meritoriousness. *The Republic of the Phillippines v. Marcos*, 862 F2d 1355, 1362 (9th Cir 1988).

9. In the trademark context, the standard for issuing a preliminary injunction tracks the traditional standard with a few exceptions. First, likelihood of success on the merits is demonstrated by proving that a person's infringing use of the mark "is likely to cause confusion, or to cause mistake, or to deceive . . . as to the origin, sponsorship, or approval of his or her goods, services, or commercial activities by another person. . . ." 15 USC §1125(a)(1)(A); *New West Corp. v. NYM Co. of Cal., Inc.*, 595 F2d 1194, 1201 (9th Cir 1979) ("the ultimate test is whether the public is likely to be deceived or confused by the similarity of the marks"). [6]

Second, in the Ninth Circuit, eight factors are traditionally considered in determining the likelihood of confusion:

1. strength of the mark;

2. proximity of the goods;

3. similarity of the marks;

4. evidence of actual confusion;

5. marketing channels used;

6. types of goods and degree of care likely to be exercised by the purchaser;

7. defendant's intent in selecting the mark; and

8. likelihood of expansion of the product lines.

AMF Inc. v. Sleekcraft Boats, 599 F2d 341, 348-49 (9th Cir 1979); *see also Vision Sports, Inc. v. Melville Corp.*, 888 F2d 609, 616 (9th Cir 1989) (same factors used in trade dress analysis). However, the Ninth Circuit has emphasized that at the preliminary injunction stage, "the trial court is not required to consider all of those factors" since the record will not likely be sufficient to permit thorough consideration. *Apple Computer, Inc. v. Formula Intern. Inc.*, 725 F2d 521, 526 (9th Cir 1984) (affirming issuance of preliminary injunction on grounds that trade names were "confusingly similar" despite district court's failure to consider the eight *AMF* factors).

Third, once plaintiff establishes a likelihood of confusion, "it is ordinarily presumed that the plaintiff will suffer irreparable harm if injunctive relief does not issue." *Rodeo Collection, Ltd. v. West Seventh*, 812 F2d 1215, 1220 (9th Cir 1987) (citing *Apple Computer*, 725 F2d at 526), *cited and followed in*, *Vision Sports*, 888 F2d at 612 n. 3.

10. Loss of business is not the test of irreparable injury in motions for preliminary injunctions against

the use of a trademark. The fact that plaintiff has had the symbol of its reputation placed in the hands of another is irreparable injury. *Visa International Service Association v. Bankcard Holders of America*, 1981 WL 40539, 211 USPQ 28, 39 (ND Cal 1981)(the mere fact that the plaintiff has had the symbol of its reputation placed in the hands of another constitutes irreparable injury).

11. The district court has broad discretion in deciding whether or not to issue a preliminary injunction, *K-2 Ski Co. v. Head Ski Co.*, 467 F2d 1087 (9th Cir 1972), and will not be overturned on appeal unless the district court abused its discretion or based its decision on an erroneous legal standard or on clearly erroneous findings of fact. *Triad Systems Corp. v. Southeastern Express Co.*, 64 F3d 1330, 1334 (9th Cir 1995).

Probable Success on the Merits

12. Trademark infringement occurs when a person uses a mark in commerce, without the registrant's consent, in a manner that is likely to cause confusion, mistake or deception. 15 USC §1114. To prevail at trial, SCEA must prove that there is such a likelihood of confusion in defendant's use of the trademark.

13. SCEA may establish a *prima facie* case of trademark infringement by showing 1) rightful ownership of the marks in suit and 2) likelihood of confusion or mistake amongst the public from the defendants' use of the marks. *Jockey Club, Inc. v. Jockey Club of Las Vegas*, 595 F2d 1167 (9th Cir 1979).

14. Plaintiffs have provided the Court with trademark registration certificates for the titles and designs for the PlayStation trademarks discussed above; this creates a presumption of exclusive ownership. 15 USC §1115(A).

15. A simple comparison between the seized game controller and memory card packaging and the authentic game controller and memory card packaging confirms not merely a strong likelihood of confusion, but the inevitably of it. The packaging of these two types of items seized by Plaintiff from Defendants' store bears trademarks that are identical to, or substantially indistinguishable from, SCEA's registered trademarks.

16. Jerry Jessop, SCEA's Hardware Engineering Manager, attests that based upon his experience, a visual inspection of the memory cards and their packaging led him to conclude that they were counterfeit. (Overend Decl. Ex 4, ¶¶9-14). *Inter alia*, the pictures and writings on defendants' products are "poor quality, fuzzy and unclear," the registered trademark symbol is too large to be consistent with proper usage, and the "S" in the stylized "PS" trademark on the memory cards themselves is of irregular thickness. *Id.*

17. Jessop similarly concluded that the game controllers were counterfeit based upon his expertise and a visual inspection. (*Id.* at ¶¶16-18).

18. Defendant claims that neither the memory cards nor the game controllers are counterfeit but provides no evidence to support this claim.

19. The counterfeit memory card bears marks *identical* to the PlayStation stylized trademark. In fact, some of the cards are contained within identical packaging colors as authentic SCEA memory cards. Confusion over the origin and authenticity of the products is inescapable—the packaging is identical.

20. Although the allegedly counterfeit controller pad packagings are not identical to that of SCEA authorized controllers, there is a strong likelihood of confusion between these products as well. The seized game controller packagings bear trademarks that are identical to, or substantially indistinguishable from, SCEA's registered trademarks.

21. We are convinced that for the game pad controllers and the memory card, a high likelihood of confusion exists between Defendants' products and Plaintiff's and therefore, Plaintiff is likely to succeed upon its claims of trademark and copyright infringement. Consumers are likely to assume that defendants' product originated from plaintiff.

22. SCEA has also charged defendants with trademark counterfeiting. Trademark counterfeiting occurs by producing or selling a product that bears a "counterfeit" trademark. 3 J. Thomas McCarthy, MCCARTHY ON TRADEMARKS AND UNFAIR COMPETITION, §25.10, AT 25-14 (4TH ED. 1997); 15 USC §1116(D)(B)(I). Section 1114 of the Lanham Act, which establishes the trademark counterfeiting cause of action, prohibits the use of "any reproduction, counterfeit, copy, or colorable imitation of a registered mark in connection with the sale . . . of any goods . . . [where] such use is

likely to cause confusion . . . or to deceive." 15 USC §1114(1)(a).

23. As with the Trademark Infringement claim, a simple comparison of SCEA's trademarks with those on the game controllers, memory cards and CD Mechanism Boxes shows that the marks they use are either identical or substantially indistinguishable from SCEA's legitimate authorized marks. Thus, plaintiff has a good chance of succeeding on it's trademark counterfeiting claim.

24. Plaintiff has not demonstrated a strong likelihood of success on its claims relating to the game console moldings. While the seized moldings look similar in form to the PlayStation console, the seized moldings bear no trademarks at all. There is a cast relief of an image whose outline is similar to the PlayStation stylized trademark, but there is no mark.

25. Defendants claim that it is nearly impossible for them to know if a wholesaler has mistakenly provided an illegal game in a shipment because the manufacturers often use minor variations of its trademarks in packaging identical games. (Chaddon Decl. ¶21). However, "willful blindness" is no defense to a charge of knowing and intentional counterfeiting. It is enough that a retailer "failed to inquire further because he was afraid of what the inquiry would yield." *Louis Vuitton S.A. v. Lee*, 875 F2d 584, 590 (7th Cir 1989).

26. SCEA charges defendants with contributing to unnamed others' trademark infringement and copyright infringement of SCEA's intellectual property rights in the PlayStation marks and PlayStation video games through its sales of the Game Enhancer device discussed above.

27. Contributory infringement occurs when the defendant either intentionally induces a third party to infringe the plaintiff's mark or supplies a product to a third party with actual or constructive knowledge that the product is being used to infringe the service mark. *Inwood Laboratories, Inc. v. Ives Laboratories, Inc.*, 456 US 844, 853-54, 102 S Ct 2182, 72 L Ed 2d 606 (1982). The classic statement of the doctrine is in *Gershwin Publishing Corp. v. Columbia Artists Management*, 443 F2d 1159, 1162 (2nd Cir 1971) ("[O]ne who, with knowledge of the infringing activity, induces, causes or materially contributes to the infringing conduct of another, may be held liable as a 'contributory' infringer."); *see*

also Universal City Studios v. Sony Corp. of America, 659 F2d 963, 975 (9th Cir 1981), *rev'd on other grounds*, 464 US 417, 104 S Ct 774, 78 L Ed 2d 574 (1984) (adopting *Gershwin* in this circuit).

28. SCEA alleges only the latter basis for contributory infringement liability and therefore must prove that GameMasters supplied a product to third parties with actual or constructive knowledge that its product was being used to infringe SCEA's other marks. *Id.* at 854, 102 S Ct 2182.

29. This proof necessarily begs the question of whether or not the Game Enhancer is in fact being used to infringe upon SCEA's trademark or copyright rights. SCEA has submitted no evidence showing any likelihood that third parties are infringing SCEA's marks through use of the Game Enhancers sold by Defendants.

30. Moreover, the gravamen of a contributory infringement action is the defendant's knowledge. If the Chaddons continued to supply a product knowing that the consumer or third party was using the product to engage in trademark infringement, they would clearly be liable. *Inwood*, 456 US at 854-5, 102 S Ct 2182. However, the scant evidence and allegations by SCEA only state that Chaddon supplied a product that consumers *could have used* to engage in trademark infringement.

31. Secondly, it is not clear exactly how, if at all, the Game Enhancer itself enables trademark infringement since the games in question are Sony manufactured, Sony authorized, authentic PlayStation Games. It would seem that the games, legally, validly manufactured and sold in Japan, for example, do not become transformed into illegal, bootleg infringing games merely because they are transported across the ocean and sold by third parties who may choose to do so. A consumers choice to play the non-territorial game cannot be the infringing activity. *Los Angeles New Service v. Reuters Television International*, 149 F3d 987, 994 (9th Cir 1988).

32. SCEA's arguments that sales of the Game Enhancer constitute contributory trademark and copyright infringement appear to be based more so upon its claims that "the device was specifically designed to facilitate and enable the sale of the bootleg games that infringe SCEA's trademarks."

SCEA claims that sales of this device undermine SCEA's profits from authorized PlayStation video games and threatens its ability to control the quality of products bearing its registered marks.[7]

33. However, it is not clear that the Game Enhancer facilitates the use of games that are truly counterfeit. SCEA has provided no evidence suggesting that the Game Enhancer enables the PlayStation to play "back up" or "counterfeit" games. This Court has declarations from Plaintiff saying the Game Enhancer does allow play of "counterfeit" games and declarations from Defendants saying that it does not. There is no reference to "back up" or "bootleg" games anywhere in the Game Enhancer instructions. The games which the GameEnhancer enables consumers to play upon the PlayStation are not necessarily illegal games, rather they may be legitimate and authorized Sony products, but authorized only for sale in foreign territories such as Japan.

34. In addition to the questions raised above, the record is grossly lacking in evidence of defendants' actual knowledge of either type of infringement by third parties, or of facts sufficient to prove defendant's constructive knowledge. Defendants argue that they have no knowledge of how consumers may use the Game Enhancer beyond the "cheat" / play import functions nor could they control such additional use.

35. We cannot say as a matter of law that SCEA is likely to prevail upon the merits of its contributory copyright or contributory trademark infringement claims based upon defendant's sale of the Game Enhancer because 1) there is insufficient evidence of defendants' actual or constructive knowledge, and 2) there is insufficient evidence before this Court that the Game Enhancer enables the play of counterfeit, and not merely imported but authentic, SCEA video games.

36. From the above discussion however, it is clear that plaintiff has shown "the existence of serious questions on the merits" of its contributory claims. However, we need not address whether "the balance of the hardships tips" in SCEA's favor because we find that SCEA is likely to succeed upon its claim that defendants' sale of the Game Enhancer violates the Digital Millennium Copyright Act. 17 USC §1201.

37. The Digital Millennium Copyright Act, among other things, prohibits distribution of any product or device which:

1) is primarily designed or produced for the purpose of circumventing a technological measure (or a protection afforded by a technological measure) that effectively controls access to a system protected by a registered copyright or effectively protects a right of a copyright owner in a registered work or portion thereof;

2) has only limited commercially significant purpose or use other than to circumvent such a technological measure (or protection afforded it);

Or

3) is marketed for use in circumventing such a technological measure (or protection afforded by it). 17 USC §1201(a)(2)-(3) and (b)(1)-(2) (Public Law 105-304, October 28, 1998).

38. Section 1201 also prohibits manufacture or distribution of technologies, products and services used to circumvent technological measures which control access. The prohibition applies only if such circumventing technologies are primarily designed for this purpose, have only limited commercial purpose beyond such circumventing purpose, or are marketed for the prohibited purpose. This provision is immediately effective. *See generally* Katherine C. Spelman, Current Developments in Copyright Law 1999, 567 Practicing Law Institute / Patents, Copyrights, Trademarks, and Literary Property Course Handbook Series 31, 49.

39. Defendant concedes in its opposition papers that "[t]he Game Enhancer makes temporary modifications to the [PlayStation] computer program . . . [c]hanging these codes with the Game Enhancer does not alter the underlying software made by SONY." (Def. Opp. at 6). Based upon the declarations before this Court, the Game Enhancer's distinguishing feature appears to be its ability to allow consumers to play import or non-territorial SCEA video games. As discussed above, SCEA specifically designed the PlayStation console to access only those games with data codes that match the geographical location of the game console itself. The Game Enhancer circumvents the mechanism on the PlayStation console that ensures the console

operates only when encrypted data is read from an authorized CD-ROM. (Pltf's Reply at 7). Thus, at this stage, the Game Enhancer appears to be a device whose primary function is to circumvent "a technological measure (or a protection afforded by a technological measure) that effectively controls access to a system protected by a registered copyright. . . ." 17 USC §1201(a)(2)(A).

40. Plaintiff has demonstrated that it is likely to prevail upon the merits of its claim that defendant's sale of the Game Enhancer violates the Digital Millennium Copyright Act. Title 17 of the United States Code section 1203 authorizes this Court to issue a preliminary injunction to prevent violations of the Digital Millennium Copyright Act. 17 USC 1203.

Irreparable Injury

1. The law infers irreparable harm from a *prima facie* showing of likelihood of success on the merits of a trademark infringement claims. *International Jensen v. Metrosound U.S.A., Inc.*, 4 F3d 819, 827 (9th Cir 1993). SCEA has pled that the sales of these unauthorized products in deceptively similar if not identical trade dress constitutes an irreparable injury in, *inter alia*, the form of lost goodwill. Defendant claims that since each of the products in question is available from numerous other retail sources both in this geographical region and via the Internet, GameMasters continued sale of the products will result in no actual harm to SCEA.

2. This argument does not comport with Ninth Circuit standards for determining irreparable injury in this context. It is well settled in this Circuit that where the movant has demonstrated a likelihood of success upon the merits of its intellectual property claims, irreparable injury is to be presumed. *Metro Publishing Ltd. v. San Jose Mercury News*, 987 F2d 637, 640 (9th Cir 1993); *Apple*, 725 F2d at 525; *Triad Systems Corp. v. Southeastern Express Co.*, 64 F3d 1330, 1335 (9th Cir 1995). Moreover, GameMaster's argument suggests that plaintiff's must protect its intellectual property rights in an "all or nothing" fashion, suing every infringing retailer at once or suing none at all.

3. Absent injunctive relief, consumers may mistakenly purchase Defendants' products thinking SCEA is their true and original source. These purchases would cause SCEA not only to lose substantial sales of legitimate authorized products,

but also to jeopardize the good will it has accrued in the quality of its products.

4. Defendants are also incorrect in claiming that SCEA must prove that GameMasters will violate SCEA's intellectual property rights in the future. Injunctive relief is appropriate even where defendants have ceased their illegal conduct. *Polo Fashions, Inc. v. Dick Bruhn, Inc.*, 793 F2d 1132 (9th Cir 1986) (reversing district court's refusal of injunctive relief where defendant voluntarily ceased infringing activity shortly after suit was brought); *Sierra On-Line, Inc. v. Phoenix Software, Inc.*, 739 F2d 1415 (9th Cir 1984)(although defendant had stopped using disputed term, injunction was appropriate).

Contract Claim Defense

1. Defendants offer a rather ephemeral and misguided argument that SCEA's claims and the ensuing dispute are more properly viewed as "a commercial dispute under Article 2 of the California Commercial Code." (Def. Opp. at 13). Defendant apparently claims that since it is merely a retailer selling merchandise secured from third parties, its cross claims against these third parties should supplant plaintiff's claims under federal trademark law. The argument is non-sensical and unsupported by the case defendant provides, *Sun Microsystems v. Microsoft Corp.*, 188 F3d 1115, 1999 WL 635783 (9th Cir 1999). As plaintiff points out, *Sun* involved two companies which had contracted with one another for licensing rights. SCEA and GameMasters have no licensing agreements and no other Commercial or contractual relationship. (Pltf. Reply at 4). Defendant will have ample opportunity to press its contract or warranty claims upon those parties with whom it actually has such relationships.

Copyright Misuse Defense

1. Defendants argue that plaintiff should be denied injunctive relief because it is misusing its copyright and trademark rights, specifically by trying to extend or enlarge the privileges bestowed by these rights. GameMasters argues that plaintiff is actually seeking to enjoin sales of the Game Enhancer because it competes with a similar product manufactured by SCEA, the Game Shark. The GameShark and the GameEnhancer are not the same product as only the Game Enhancer allows users to play non-authorized, non-territory video games by circumventing the PlayStation's built in controls.

SCEA's targeting of the GameEnhancer is based upon a sound construction of the Digital Millennium Copyright Act as demonstrated by the above analysis. The injunction shall issue.

Modification of Relief Ordered Issues

1. A portion of plaintiff's proposed preliminary injunction prevents defendant from using color photo-copies of SCEA video-game covers to display the second hand games for sale from defendant's inventory. (See ¶4 of proposed Prel. Inj). Defendants essentially argue that their display of photocopied game covers is a "fair use" because it prevents shoplifting.

2. The Copyright Act of 1976 confers upon copyright holders the exclusive right to prepare and authorize others to prepare derivative works based on their copyrighted works. *See* §17 USC 106(2). A derivative work must incorporate a protected work in some concrete or permanent "form." The Copyright Act's defines a derivative work as follows:

> A "derivative work" is a work based upon one or more preexisting works, such as a translation, musical arrangement, dramatization, fictionalization, motion picture version, sound recording, *art reproduction*, abridgment, condensation, or any other form in which a work may be recast, transformed, or adapted.

17 USC §101 (emphasis added), *see Mirage Editions*, 856 F2d at 1342

3. Defendant's use of plaintiff's copyrighted images for commercial use is clearly prohibited by federal copyright laws. The photocopies are derivative works used to promote sales of defendant's product which supplant purchaser's demand for plaintiff's product. While a commercial use does not by itself preclude a defense of fair use, "every commercial use of copyrighted material is presumptively an unfair exploitation of the monopoly privilege that belongs to the owner of the copyright." *Sony Corp. of Am. v. Universal City Studios, Inc.*, 464 US 417, 451, 104 S Ct 774, 78 L Ed 2d 574 (1984). Plaintiff is well within it's rights in prohibiting such use. Moreover, we believe that a small bit of well channeled creative energy can discern a method of informing the customer of defendants' inventory without inviting theft.

4. Enjoining sale of imported games. Paragraph 5 of SCEA's proposed preliminary injunction would prohibit GameMasters from selling SCEA games made for the Japanese or Asian markets. This issue was discussed above in considering SCEA's likelihood of prevailing upon its contributory infringement claims. It is unclear whether under current Tariff and Customs laws, GameMasters is entitled to sell such games or whether SCEA is entitled to define them as "unauthorized" and enjoin their sale. Plaintiff cites no cases on the matter and defendant's citations are inapposite. The injunction here issued does not prevent the sale or rental of such valid SCEA non-territorial products in their original packaging.

Preliminary Injunction Order

IT IS THEREFORE ORDERED, ADJUDGED AND DECREED that the Defendants, their agents, servants, employees, representatives, successors and assigns, and all other persons, firms, or corporations acting in concert, privity or participation with them be, and hereby are, enjoined from:

1. Advertising, promoting, distributing, selling, transporting or purchasing the Game Enhancer, or any device that permits a consumer to play or use on the PlayStation unauthorized ("unauthorized" is defined, for the purpose of this Order only, to mean non-SCEA products, as well as SCEA products which are manufactured, sold or distributed without license or other authority from SCEA, its parents, affiliates, or subdivisions) copies, colorable imitations, or otherwise infringing versions of SCEA's copyrighted products;

2. Advertising, promoting, distributing, selling, transporting or purchasing the Game Enhancer, or any other device that permits a consumer to play or use foreign made SCEA games that could not otherwise be played on the PlayStation without the Game Enhancer device;

3. Advertising, promoting, distributing, selling, transporting or purchasing the Game Enhancer device, or any other device that directly or contributorily violates SCEA's rights under the Digital Millennium Copyright Act, 17 USC §1201, which provides that no person shall manufacture,

import, offer to the public, provide, or otherwise traffic in any technology, product, service, device, component, or part thereof, which (a) is primarily designed or produced for the purpose of circumventing a technological measure that effectively controls access to a work protected under Title 17 of the United States Code, b) has only limited commercially significant purpose or use other than to circumvent a technological measure that effectively controls access to a work protected under Title 17 of the United States Code, c) is marketed by that person or another in concert with that person with that person's knowledge for use in circumventing a technological measure that effectively controls access to a work protected under Title 17 of the United States Code, d) is primarily designed or produced for the purpose of circumventing protection afforded by a technological measure that effectively protects a right of a copyright owner under Title 17 of the United States Code in a work or a portion thereof, e) has only limited commercially significant purpose or use other than to circumvent protection afforded by a technological measure that effectively protects a right of a copyright owner under Title 17 of the United States Code in a work or a portion thereof, or f) is marketed by that person or another in concert with that person with that person's knowledge for use in circumventing protection afforded by a technological measure that effectively protects a right of a copyright owner under Title 17 of the United States Code in a work or portion thereof;

4. Using SCEA's trademarks, logos or trade dress, or any reproduction, counterfeit, copy or colorable imitation of said marks, logos or trade dress, in connection with the purchase, sale, transportation, manufacture or distribution of unauthorized peripheral products and accessories that are intended to be used in connection with the PlayStation game console, or in any manner likely to cause others to believe that Defendants' products are connected with, or authorized

by, SCEA or are SCEA's branded products, when they are not;

5. Passing off, distributing, selling or enabling others to pass off, sell or distribute any unauthorized copies or versions of SCEA's peripheral products or accessories;

6. Misrepresenting that unauthorized products advertised, promoted or sold by Defendants are SCEA products or are affiliated with SCEA, when they are not:

7. Engaging in any other activity constituting an infringement or contributory infringement of SCEA's intellectual property;

8. Using SCEA's trademarks, logos or trade dress, or any reproduction, counterfeit, copy or colorable imitation of said marks, logos or trade dress, in connection with the purchase, sale, transportation, manufacture or distribution of unauthorized peripheral products and accessories, not the products of SCEA, intended to be used in connection with the PlayStation game console, or in any manner likely to cause others to believe that Defendant's products are connected with SCEA or are SCEA's branded products;

9. Committing any other acts calculated to cause purchasers to believe that unauthorized products are SCEA products, including, but not limited to, the display, promotion, advertisement, manufacture, distribution, transfer or sale of any product which is not authorized by SCEA, but which displays an SCEA trademark;

10. Distributing, selling or promoting any unauthorized peripheral products or accessories intended to be used in connection wit the PlayStation game console, wherein the product is represented, either expressly or by implication, as being a SCEA product or as being authorized by SCEA;

11. Representing to any wholesaler, retailer, customer, potential customer or the public that a peripheral product or accessory supplied by Defendants that was intended to be used in connection with the PlayStation game console originates from SCEA or that said product has been licensed, sponsored or approved by SCEA or is in some way

connected or affiliated with SCEA, if such product represented is not authorized by SCEA;

12. Purchasing, leasing, borrowing or otherwise obtaining any unauthorized peripheral products or accessories intended to be used in connection with the PlayStation game console, or any other unauthorized SCEA products, where such products bear any SCEA trademark, label or packaging, or any colorable imitations thereof;

13. Moving, discarding, destroying, selling, transferring or otherwise disposing of:

a. Any peripheral products and accessories bearing or utilizing any SCEA Trademarks, or any colorable imitations thereof;

b. Any containers, labels, wrappers, stickers, signs or other material containing any SCEA Trademarks or markings, or any colorable imitations thereof;

c. Any sales, promotional or advertising materials bearing any SCEA Trademarks, or any colorable imitations thereof;

d. Any documents and records, including any electronically or computer stored records or data, relating in any way to the manufacture, distribution, sale or promotion of any peripheral products and accessories that have been or are intended to be sold as an authentic SCEA product;

e. Any documents and records, including any electronically or computer stored records or data, relating in any way to the purchase, acquisition, manufacture, distribution, sale, promotion or disposition of peripheral products and accessories that bear any of SCEA's Trademarks;

f. Any goods, labels, signs, prints, packages, wrappers, brochures, promotional materials, printing devices, and documents relating in any way to the promotion,

manufacture, distribution, purchase, acquisition or sale of the Game Enhancer, or any other device that directly or contributorily violates SCEA's rights under the Digital Millennium Copyright Act, 17 USC §1201.

IT IS FURTHER ORDERED, ADJUDGED AND DECREED:

That the Preliminary Injunction shall remain in effect throughout the pendency of this suit and until further Court Order.

IT IS FURTHER ORDERED, ADJUDGED AND DECREED:

That SCEA has posted a bond in the amount of $25,000.00 as security determined adequate for the payment of such damages as any person may be entitled to recover as a result of the preliminary injunction set forth herein, and that such bond shall remain in effect pending further Court Order.

IT IS FURTHER ORDERED, ADJUDGED AND DECREED:

That the Order for Seizure and Impoundment of Counterfeit Goods entered on June 11, 1999, was properly issued and is hereby confirmed. See 15 USC 1116(d)(10)(A).

IT IS FURTHER ORDERED, ADJUDGED AND DECREED:

That the Seal imposed on this case is hereby dissolved.

IT IS FURTHER ORDERED, ADJUDGED AND DECREED:

That SCEA shall immediately return to GameMasters the replacement housings seized and discussed above.

IT IS SO ORDERED.

---

[1] Michael Chaddon has been charged in a separate proceeding with criminal copyright infringement in violation of Title 17 USC section 506(a), and Title 18 USC section 2319(b)(3). Chaddon was arraigned on October 22, 1999, and plead Not Guilty. *U.S.A. v. Chaddon*, No. CR 99-40212 WDB, Oakland Venue (ND Cal 1999).

2   For example, one package bears the PlayStation trademark vertically ascending the left edge of the front of the package. Just above this writing is a substantially similar, if not identical, replica of Sony's stylized "PS" PlayStation trademark. The memory card itself is housed under clear plastic molding in the center of the cardboard swatch. The back of the package bears a substantially similar, if not identical, replica of Sony's stylized "PS" PlayStation trademark in the upper left hand corner.

3   The Game Enhancer is manufactured by third party defendant Innovation Technology, distributed through S & I Marketing, TOMMO, Inc., Brian Brown and other companies. (Third Party Compl ¶13).

4   The Court draws its discussion entirely from the GameEnhancer instructions submitted by both parties as exhibits and the accompanying declarations. At the Nov. 1, 1999, hearing, plaintiff's counsel demonstrated how a consumer would attach a Game Enhancer type device to the PlayStation Console. However, plaintiff made no showing that the Game Enhancer type device he demonstrated at trial was the same type as that sold by the Defendants. Defense counsel rightly objected and the Court disregards the presentation.

5   At the Nov. 1, 1999, hearing, plaintiff's counsel suggested that "imports" was a term of art encompassing counterfeit or bootleg games as well as actual imports. The Court finds no basis or evidence supporting plaintiff's definition of the term "imports."

6   The same principles apply to trade dress infringement. *Two Pesos, Inc. v. Taco Cabana Inc.*, 505 US 763, 112 S Ct 2753, 120 L Ed 2d 615 (1992).

7   SCEA also claims that use of the Game Enhancer poses a safety hazard to the public by circumventing PlayStation safety devices designed to protect users from exposure to "potentially harmful laser energy." Each PlayStation instruction manual sold with each game console warns: "As the laser beam emitted from the lens of this unit may be harmful to the eyes, do not attempt to disassemble the casing. Refer for technical assistance. Call [Sony ph. number]."

United States

v.

Sklyarov
(Criminal Complaint)

**United States District Court,
Northern District of California**

July 10, 2001

8 ILR (P&F) 2106

No. 5-01-257P

Russian national indicted for eBook cracking software.

A criminal complaint filed by the Federal Bureau of Investigation alleges that defendant, a Russian national, violated 17 USC §1201(b)(1)(A) by manufacturing and offering to the public a software program designed to circumvent software copyright protection measures. Defendant is allegedly employed by a Russian company that distributes a software key over the Internet that unlocks copyright protections in Adobe's eBook reader program and allows eBook reader users to read electronic books without paying any fee to the bookseller. Further, defendant's software allows users to duplicate electronic books freely and make them available for usage on any computer. — **United States v. Sklyarov (Criminal Complaint), 8 ILR (P&F) 2106 [ND Cal, 2001].**

NORTHERN DISTRICT OF CALIFORNIA
COUNTY OF SANTA CLARA

SS: AFFIDAVIT FOR COMPLAINT

Daniel J. O'Connell, being duly sworn, deposes and states;

Introduction

1. I submit this affidavit in support of a criminal complaint and an arrest warrant for Dmitry Sklyarov, for violation of Title 17, US Code, Section 1201(b)(1)(A)—circumvention of copyright protections, and Title 18, United States Code, Section 2—aiding and abetting.

2. Title 17, United States Code, Section 1201(b) states in relevant part:

(1) No person shall manufacture, import, offer to the public, provide, or otherwise traffic in any technology, product, service, device, component, or part thereof, that—

(A) is primarily designed or produced for the purpose of circumventing protection afforded by a technological measure that effectively protects a right of a copyright owner under this title in a work or a portion thereof;

. . .

(2) As used in this subsection—

(A) to "circumvent protection afforded by a technological measure" means avoiding, bypassing, removing, deactivating, or otherwise impairing a technological measure.

3. Title 17, United States Code, Section 1204, states in relevant part:

(a) In general.—Any person who violates section 1201 or 1202 willfully and for purposes of commercial advantage or private financial gain,

(1) shall be fined not more than $500,000 or imprisoned for not more than 5 years or both, for the first offense; and

(2) shall be fined not more than $1,000,000 or imprisoned for not more than 10 years, or both, for any subsequent offense.

Background of Affiant

4. I have been employed as a Special Agent for the Federal Bureau of Investigation for over twenty-five years. I am currently assigned to the High Tech Squad at San Jose, California, which has responsibility for the theft of intellectual property, theft of trade secrets, and violations of U.S. copyright laws. I have participated in such intellectual property related investigations since passage of the Economic Espionage Act of 1996.

Basis for Charges

5. On June 26, 2001, I met with representatives of Adobe Systems, Incorporated (Adobe), located in San Jose, California. Kevin Nathanson, Group Products Manager, eBooks, Adobe, told me the following:

a. Adobe produces computer software, including a software product named Adobe eBook Reader.

b. eBook Reader works as follows: after users upload the program onto their personal computer systems, the users can contact a *[sic]* Internet Web based electronic bookseller such as Amazon.com or Barnes and Noble.com and purchase a book titles *[sic]* in an electronic format known as an eBook. As a result of a series of seamless transactions taking place between the electronic bookseller, an Adobe Server, and the customer's computer, users may only open and view the encrypted eBook on the specific computer that the user utilized to engage in the transaction. Because the process is taking place outside the view or control of the user, the user never sees the verification/decryption process taking place between the eBook file and the Adobe eBook Reader. Nevertheless, because the book sold in encrypted form and only accessible through the eBook Reader and is not duplicatable, the copyright holder's interest in the book is protected.

c. Adobe is being victimized by a Russian company named Elcomsoft. Elcomsoft is distributing a key over the Internet in the form of a software program that illegally unlocks copyright protections on the eBook files. This unlocking key is available for purchase on the Internet at http://www.elcomsoft.com/aebpr.html. The commercial name given by Elcomsoft to this unlocking key program is Advanced eBook Processor (AEBPR).

6. Nathanson and Daryl Spano, technical Investigator, Investigations/Anti-Piracy, Adobe, showed me Elcomsoft literature they observed on the Internet which describes a program to decrypt eBook in Adobe Acrobat eBook Reader format (PDF files with EBX security handler) as well as Adobe Acrobat PDF files protected using a standard security method, WebBuy Technology, or any other Acrobat security plug-in (like FileOpen, SoftLock etc.). The decrypted file can be opened in any PDF viewer (*e.g.*, Adobe Acrobat Reader) without any restrictions—*i.e.*, with edit, copy print, annotate functions enabled. All versions of Adobe Acrobat are supported. It also can decrypt eBook Pro (*.EBK) files, extracting all html pages and images from them.

7. Nathanson told me that the real damage done by the AEBPR program is that it creates a "naked file" that enables anyone to read the eBook on any computer without paying the fee to the bookseller. Only one legitimate copy of the encrypted eBook needs be purchased originally and after the protections are stripped through usage of the Elcomsoft program, there are no restrictions and the eBook can be duplicated freely and made available for usage on any computer.

8. Daryl Spano told me the following:

a. Adobe purchased a copy of the Elcomsoft unlocking software over the Internet, and an Adobe engineer told Spano that the unlocking key worked as Elcomsoft claimed.

b. Adobe purchased the program from Elcomsoft through a U.S. based company that Elcomsoft was using as a means of collecting a $99 fee for purchase and usage of the unlocking key. Nathanson and Spano told me that this company was Register Now! (www.regnow.com) Dept #1170-75, P.O. Box 1816 Issaquah, Washington 98027, 1-877-353-7297. Register Now! collected the $99 fee that pays for the unlocking key. Thereafter, Elcomsoft, after receiving verification from Register Now!, electronically sent the unlocking key registration code from Elcomsoft to the purchaser (Adobe) in San Jose, California, in the Northern District of California. Spano provided documents to me reflecting the transaction and showing that the unlocking key was purchased by Adobe on June 26, 2001.

c. The Elcomsoft unlocking software was downloaded for free directly from the Elcomsoft site without purchasing the key. However, the software obtained without the unlocking key allowed one to view only approximately ten percent of an eBook in the Adobe format. In order to get the complete book, the person downloading the Elcomsoft software was required by pay Elcomsoft the $99 fee through the RegNow website to obtain the unlocking key.

d. A review of the opening screen on the Elcomsoft software purchased showed that a person named Dmitry Sklyarov is identified as being the copyright holder of the Elcomsoft program. Spano exhibited this opening screen to me and provided me with a copy of the screen. Spano also provided me a copy of the E-mail from Elcomsoft managing director Vladimir Katalov furnishing the unlocking key after the fee had been paid to Elcomsoft through the RegNow website.

e. Adobe has learned that Dmitry Sklyarov is slated to speak on July 15, 2001 at a conference entitled Defcon-9 at Las Vegas Nevada. Spano told me that he learned that Sklyarov is scheduled to make a presentation related to the AEBPR software program.

9. Nathanson told me that thus far, Elcomsoft has defeated Adobe's Version 2.1 eBook Reader and has threatened in literature on its website to issue a "crack" for Acrobat eBook Reader Version 2.2 that has just been released.

10. Nathanson and Spano stated that Adobe has attempted to prevent Elcomsoft from providing the unlocking key to the public and has been resisted in this effort by Elcomsoft. Adobe has sent "cease and desist" letters to Elcomsoft, RegNow and the Internet Service Provider for Elcomsoft, Verio Inc.

Independent Investigation

11. On July 2, 2001, I viewed the Internet home page of RegNow, www.regnow.com". The following products were listed for purchase through the website:

- Advanced PDF Password Recovery (Pro)

- Recover passwords to Adobe Acrobat PDF files

- Elcomsoft Co. Ltd.

- Advanced PDF Password Recovery

- Decrypt protected Adobe Acrobat PDF files.

- Elcomsoft Co. Ltd.

- Advanced eBook Processor (Discount)

- Decrypt protected Adobe Acrobat PDF files and eBooks

- Elcomsoft Co. Ltd.

When I used a computer mouse to select the above listed programs for purchase through the RegNow website, I was directed to the home page of Elcomsoft.com.

12. On July 2 and 3, 2001, I observed the following information on the ELCOMSOFT website in which Elcomsoft describes its business activity.

"Elcomsoft Co.Ltd. is a privately owned software development company headquartered in Moscow, Russia. Established in 1990, Elcom specializes in producing Windows productivity and utility applications for businesses and individuals. . ." "Elcomsoft Co.Ltd. is a member of the Russian Cryptology Association (RCA) and a lifetime member of the Association of Shareware Professionals (ASP). Elcomsoft is also a Microsoft Independent Software Vendor (ISV) partner. . ."

13. I observed that the Elcomsoft website "home page" showed the following information among a listing of new products and their release dates:

"June 26, 2001 New versions of Advanced eBook Processor and Advanced NT Security Explorer now available" and "June 20, 2001 New product has been released: Advanced eBook Processor. Decrypt eBooks for Adobe Acrobat eBook Reader and PDFs protected with all security plug-ins, including WebBuy!"

14. I observed that Elcomsoft described its product and made certain comments about its legality as follows:

Advanced eBook Processor . . . .

06/20/2001 We have released our new program and called it AEBPR (Advanced eBook Processor). The only thing the program does is: converting documents from Acrobat eBook format (compiled for Adobe Acrobat eBook Reader) to the plain Acrobat format (PDF). Again, that's all: from one Adobe format to another. But PDF is much wider used, because there are (free) PDF viewers for a lot of hardware platforms (from workstations to PDAs) and operating systems (Windows, Mac, Linux etc), while Acrobat eBook Reader is available for Windows and Mac only.

This program works only with eBooks you legally own, *i.e.,* purchased from one of online stores like Amazon or Barnes & Noble. So we were absolutely sure that the owner of eBook has all rights to read the book he purchased where he wants and how he wants.

The demo version of AEBPR allows to convert only first 10% of the book content. To protect unauthorized distribution of eBooks on the piracy market, we have set the "border" price for this program—$99, which is much more than an average eBook cost (most eBooks are being sold from $10 to $30, and there are a lot free ones).

You can download a demo version of AEBPR here, here or here (please note that current release of our program does not support the latest version of Adobe eBook Reader, 2.2; that is the result of unpredicted Adobe reaction to our release of this program—see below).

06/25/2001 We have received a notification from Adobe Anti-Piracy Enforcement team in which they claimed that our program is illegal and we need to remove it immediately from our site. They said they give us 5 days otherwise they will "pursue us aggressively". . . .

06/26/2001 We have received an E-mail from our ISP, Verio Inc. They wrote that Adobe has contacted them to shut down our Web site (again, immediately). As Adobe wrote to Verio, the reason was: the site "offers downloads to their copyrighted software published by Adobe Systems." Obviously—this is not true, we never distributed any software copyrighted by Adobe Systems. But as you can see, Adobe is not even going to collect the correct information (what laws, copyrights and terms-of-use have been violated), but just started their aggressive actions before 5-day period (they set themselves) has expired. Really, they did not want to give us a time to consult with our attorneys! Verio gave us 6 hours to remove this page (the one you are reading now). So we moved the site to another ISP. . . .

06/27/2001 (2:19:30 PM) Verio has contacted us again, this time not asking for something, but just with a notification: "Host blocked: www.elcomsoft.com/aebpr.html—198.63.210.56 port 80 (www)" You can see, that since they were not able to close our web site completely, they simply disabled access to it on their routers. Moreover, they have blocked the whole IP address of our server, so not only this site, but also lots of other (not only ours) web sites became completely out of reach! But we already had a few mirrors ready, and after this unfriendly action from Verio, we have updated appropriate DNS records. In 6 hours, our web site was accessible again!

06/28/2001 (10:57 AM) Adobe has sent a complaint to RegNow, our billing service (5 days are still not expired!). This time they called it "unauthorized distribution of software". . . .

RegNow asked us for advice what they should do in this situation. We didn't want them to be involved in our problems, and so asked to stop sales of AEBPR. . . .

07/03/2001 Now it's time for the brutal truth on Adobe eBook protection. We claim that ANY eBook protection, based on Acrobat PDF format (as Adobe eBook Reader is), is ABSOLUTELY insecure just due to the nature of this format and encryption system developed by Adobe. The general rule is: if one can open particular PDF file or eBook on his computer (does not matter with what kind of permissions/restrictions), he can remove that protection (by converting that file into "plain", unprotected PDF. Not very much experience needed. In brief: ANY security plugin (actually, eBooks are protected with security plug-in as well: EBX) does nothing but returns a decryption key to Adobe Acrobat Reader or Adobe Acrobat eBook Reader. Plug-in can make various hardware verifications, use parallel port dongles, connect to the publisher's web site and use asymmetric encryption, etc, but all ends up with a decryption key, because the Reader needs it to open the files. And when the key is there, we can use it to decrypt the document removing all permissions.

Below is the list (not complete) of Acrobat-based protections supported by Advanced eBook Processor:

? "standard" PDF encryption,

? BPTE_Rot13 (used by New Paradigm Resources Group, Inc.),

? FileOpen (by FileOpen Systems),

? SoftLock (by SoftLock Services, Inc.).

? Internet Standards Australia

? Adobe's Web Buy

? Adobe's eBook Reader (GlassBook Reader)

We claim that by aggressively pushing of standards, unapproved by professional cryptologists, to the fast growing electronic books market and with pursuing of independent researchers who tries to highlight the problems, Adobe Systems violates the rights of books authors and publishers, which may result the unauthorized distribution of their books in the Internet. . . ."

15. On July 2, 2001, I reviewed the web site for the "Defcon-9" convention scheduled for July 13-15, 2001, in Las Vegas Nevada. I observed that an individual identified as Dmitry Sklyarov and an individual identified as Andy Malyshev are listed as speakers who are to discuss the Acrobat eBook reader.

16. The web site of the Defcon-9 conference described it as follows:

an annual computer underground party for hackers held in Las Vegas, Nevada. It has been held every summer for the past eight years. Over those years it has grown in size, and attracted people from all over the planet. People attend to meet others into hacking, hang out with old friends, listen to new speeches or just hack on the network. That's what it is all about in a nutshell. Meeting other people and learning something new. Last year over 4,200 people showed up. That makes us (Currently) the largest hacking convention on the planet.

17. The Defcon-9 website described Dmitry Sklyarov's speech topic as follows:

Dmitry Sklyarov

Andy Malyshev

eBooks security—theory and practice

Security aspects of electronic books and documents, and a demonstration of how weak they are: "standard" PDF encryption, Rot13 (used by New Paradigm Resources Group, Inc.), FileOpen (by FileOpen Systems), SoftLock (by SoftLock Services, Inc.), Adobe's Web Buy, Adobe's eBook Reader (GlassBook Reader) InterTrust DocBox plug-in.

Documents publishing in electronic form have a lot of advantages against traditional on-paper publishing. You could easily find list of such advantages on web server of any company, which provides eBook solutions. But nobody perfects, and there is one big problem that related with eBooks. Information in electronic form could be duplicated and transmitted, and there is no reliable way to take control over that processes. There are several solutions from different companies that were developed to prevent unauthorized distribution of the electronic documents.

18. The Defcon 9 website also included the following statement from "Dmitry Sklyarov":

My name is Dmitry Sklyarov. I'm employee of the Elcomsoft Company. As we have demonstrated in our speech on Black Hat

Win2K Security (February 2001), encryption in Microsoft Office documents is very weak and password protection may be removed without any problems in most cases. In this speech I'll try to cover password protection aspects of electronic books and documents. The most attention will be paid to documents in PDF format. . . .

19. On July 5, 2001, I spoke via telephone with Tom Diaz, Senior Engineering Manager for the eBook Development Group of Adobe. In response to my question, Diaz affirmed that he believes the Elcomsoft software program, coupled with the Elcomsoft unlocking key, circumvents protection afforded by a technological measure developed by Adobe for its Acrobat eBook Reader either by avoiding, bypassing, removing, deactivating, or otherwise impairing the technological measure.

Conclusion

20. Based on the foregoing, I believe Dmitry Sklyarov, employee of Elcomsoft and the individual listed on the Elcomsoft software products as the copyright holder to the program sold and produced by Elcomsoft, known as the Advanced eBook Processor, has willfully and for financial gain imported, offered to the public, provided, and otherwise trafficked in a technology, product, service, and device that is primarily designed or produced for the purpose of circumvention a technological measure that effectively controls access to a work protected under Title 17, namely books distributed in a form readable by the Adobe eBook Reader, in violation of Title 17, United States Code, Section 1201(b)(1)(A) and Title 18, United States Code, Section 2.

> Daniel J. O'Connell
> Special Agent
> Federal Bureau of Investigation

Sworn and subscribed before me this 10 day of July, 2001

PATRICIA V. TRUMBULL

United States Magistrate Judge

United States

v.

Elcom Ltd. a/k/a Elcomsoft Co. Ltd. (Indictment)

United States District Court,
Northern District of California

August 28, 2001

8 ILR (P&F) 2157

No. 5-01-257P

[The criminal complaint in this case can be found at 8 ILR (P&F) 2106. — Ed.]

Russian software firm, programmer indicted for allegedly conspiring to bypass software protections.

Defendants, a Russian software company and programmer, are indicted, pursuant to 18 USC §371, for allegedly conspiring to traffic in software designed to circumvent copyright protections in violation of 17 USC §§1201(b)(1)(A) and 1201(b)(1)(C). Defendants allegedly produced and sold a software program, known as AEBPR, designed to allow users of the Adobe eBook reader to override copyright protection functions that allow publishers and distributors of electronic books to restrict users' ability to copy and print the material. The government alleges that the method and means of the conspiracy involves the creation and distribution of AEBPR and that defendants committed the overt acts of offering AEBPR for sale on their web site and selling a copy to a purchaser in California in furtherance of the conspiracy. — **United States v. Elcom Ltd. a/k/a Elcomsoft Co. Ltd. (Indictment), 8 ILR (P&F) 2157 [ND Cal, 2001].**

Russian software firm, programmer indicted for allegedly trafficking in software designed to bypass copyright protections.

Defendants, a Russian software company and programmer, are indicted on two counts of allegedly trafficking in software designed to circumvent copyright protections in violation of 17 USC §§1201(b)(1)(A). Defendants allegedly produced and sold a software program, known as AEBPR, designed to allow users of the Adobe eBook reader to override copyright protection functions that allow publishers and distributors of electronic books to restrict users' ability to copy and print the material. The government alleges that defendants offered AEBPR for sale in the United States on their web site and sold a copy to a purchaser in California. — **United States v. Elcom Ltd. a/k/a Elcomsoft Co. Ltd. (Indictment), 8 ILR (P&F) 2157 [ND Cal, 2001].**

Russian software firm, programmer indicted for allegedly trafficking in software marketed to bypass copyright protections.

Defendants, a Russian software company and programmer, are indicted on two counts of allegedly trafficking in software marketed for the purpose of circumventing copyright protections in violation of 17 USC §§1201(b)(1)(C). Defendants allegedly produced and sold a software program, known as AEBPR, designed to allow users of the Adobe eBook reader to override copyright protection functions that allow publishers and distributors of electronic books to restrict users' ability to copy and print the material. The government alleges that defendants knowingly marketed AEBPR in the United States for use in circumventing eBook copyright protection measures and that defendants sold a copy of AEBPR to a purchaser in California. — **United States v. Elcom Ltd. a/k/a Elcomsoft Co. Ltd. (Indictment), 8 ILR (P&F) 2157 [ND Cal, 2001].**

INDICTMENT

The Grand Jury charges:

BACKGROUND

1. At all times relevant to the indictment:

a. Defendant Elcom Ltd., a/k/a Elcomsoft Co. Ltd. ("Elcomsoft"), was a software company headquartered in Moscow, Russia.

b. Adobe Systems, Inc., ("Adobe") was a software company headquartered in San Jose, California, that produced publishing software for various media including the world wide web, print, and video.

c. Defendant Dmitry Sklyarov was employed by Elcomsoft as a computer programmer and cryptanalyst.

d. RegNow was an online software delivery and payment service based in Issaquah, Washington.

e. Adobe distributed a product titled "Adobe Acrobat eBook Reader" that provided technology for the reading of books in digital form ("ebooks") on personal computers.

f. Consumers who wished to purchase ebooks formatted for the Adobe Acrobat eBook Reader ("eBook Reader") could download a free copy of the eBook Reader to their personal computer and then purchase the ebook from an online retailer. Upon purchasing the ebook from the online retailer, a series of electronic communications between and among the computers of the online retailers—including, typically, an Adobe-supplied server—and the consumer's computer authorized the ebook to be read on the computer from which the purchase was made.

g. When an ebook purchased for viewing in the Adobe eBook Reader format was sold by the publisher or distributor, the publisher or distributor of the ebook could authorize or limit the purchaser's ability to copy, distribute, print, or have the text read audibly by the computer. Adobe designed the eBook Reader to permit the management of such digital rights so that in the ordinary course of its operation, the eBook Reader effectively permitted the publisher or distributor of the ebook to restrict or limit the exercise of certain copyright rights of an owner of the copyright for an ebook distributed in the eBook Reader format.

2. On a date prior to June 20, 2001, defendant Dmitry Sklyarov and others wrote a program called the Advanced eBook Processor ("AEBPR") the primary purpose of which was to remove any and all limitations on an ebook purchaser's ability to copy, distribute, print, have the text read audibly by the computer, or any other limitation imposed by the publisher or distributor of an ebook in the eBook Reader format, as well as certain other ebook formats.

3. On or about June 20, 2001, defendant Elcomsoft and others made the AEBPR program available for purchase on the elcomsoft.com website. Individuals wishing to purchase the AEBPR program were permitted to download a partially-functional copy of the program from elcomsoft.com and then were directed to pay approximately $99 to an online payment service RegNow, based in Issaquah, Washington. Upon making a payment via the RegNow website, Elcomsoft and other persons provided purchasers a registration number permitting full-use of the AEBPR program.

THE CONSPIRACY

COUNT ONE: (18 USC §371)—Conspiracy to Traffic in Technology Primarily Designed to Circumvent, and Marketed for use in Circumventing, Technology that Protects a Right of a Copyright Owner)

4. Paragraphs One through Three are realleged and incorporated in Count One.

5. On or about dates unknown, but beginning no later than June 20, 2001 and continuing until July 15, 2001, both dates being approximate and inclusive, in Santa Clara County, in the Northern District of California, and elsewhere, the defendants

ELCOM LTD.

a/k/a ELCOMSOFT CO. LTD.

and

DMITRY SKLYAROV,

and other persons, did knowingly and intentionally conspire, for purposes of commercial advantage and private financial gain, to willfully offer to the public, provide, and traffic in a technology, product, device, component, and part thereof, that was primarily designed and produced for the purpose of circumventing, and was marketed by the defendants, and others acting in concert with the defendants with the defendants' knowledge, for use in circumventing protection afforded by a technological measure that effectively protected a right of a copyright owner under Title 17 of the United States Code, in a work and portion thereof, in violation of Title 17, United States Code, Sections 1201(b)(1)(A) and 1201(b)(1)(C).

METHODS AND MEANS OF THE CONSPIRACY

6. It was part of the conspiracy that the defendants and others did create the AEBPR program primarily to permit users of the program to circumvent copyright protections from ebook files.

7. It was further part of the conspiracy that the defendants did market, offer to the public, and traffic in the AEBPR program by making it available for purchase on the elcomsoft.com website and soliciting purchasers of the program by email.

8. It was further part of the conspiracy that the defendants and others did make the AEBPR program available on a computer server in Chicago, Illinois, from which any individual with access to the Internet could download a free copy of the program that permitted the individual to circumvent the copyright protections on approximately ten percent of an ebook.

9. It was further part of the conspiracy that the defendants did charge a fee of approximately $99 for a fully operational version of the AEBPR program that would circumvent copyright protections on a complete ebook, and contracted with an online payment service, RegNow, to collect payments for the fully functional AEBPR program.

10. It was further part of the conspiracy that the defendants did provide a registration number permitting full use of the AEBPR program after a purchaser had paid for the program via the online payment service, RegNow.

OVERT ACTS

11. As part of the conspiracy, and to further the objects thereof, the defendants committed the following overt acts in the Northern District of California:

a. Beginning on or about June 20, 2001, the defendants offered the Advanced eBook Processor for sale in San Jose, California, and elsewhere, on the elcomsoft.com website;

b. On or about June 26, 2001, the defendants caused a purchaser in San Jose, California to send a payment of approximately $99 to RegNow; and

c. On or about June 26, 2001, the defendants sent a registration key for a copy of the AEBPR program to an individual purchaser in San Jose, California, who had made a payment of approximately $99 to RegNow.

All in violation of Title 18, United States Code, Section 371.

COUNT TWO: (17 USC §1201(b)(1)(A) and 18 USC §2—Trafficking in Technology Primarily Designed to Circumvent Technology that Protects a Right of a Copyright Owner)

12. Paragraphs One through Three are realleged and incorporated in Count Two.

13. On or about and between June 20, 2001 and July 15, 2001, both dates being approximately and inclusive, in Santa Clara County, in the Northern District of California, and elsewhere, the defendants

ELCOM LTD.

a/k/a ELCOMSOFT CO. LTD.

and

DMITRY SKLYAROV

did willfully, and for purposes of commercial advantage and private financial gain, offer to the public and traffic in a technology, product, device, component, and part thereof, that was primarily designed and produced for the purpose of circumventing protection afforded by a technological measure that effectively protected a right of a copyright owner under Title 17 of the United States Code, in a work and portion thereof, in that the defendants offered the AEBPR program to the public for sale in the Northern District of California.

All in violation of Title 17, United States Code, Section 1201(b)(1)(A) and Title 18, United States Code, Section 2.

COUNT THREE:(17 USC §1201(b)(1)(A) and 18 USC §2—Trafficking in Technology Primarily Designed to Circumvent Technology that Protects a Right of a Copyright Owner)

14. Paragraphs One through Three are realleged and incorporated in Count Three.

15. On or about June 26, 2001, in Santa Clara County, in the Northern District of California, and elsewhere, the defendants

ELCOM LTD.

a/k/a ELCOMSOFT CO. LTD.

and

DMITRY SKLYAROV

did willfully, and for the purposes of commercial advantage and private financial gain, provide and traffic in a technology, product, device, component, and part thereof, that was primarily designed and produced for the purpose of circumventing protection afforded by a technological measure that effectively protected a right of a copyright owner under Title 17 of the United States Code, in a work or portion thereof, in that the defendants sold a copy of the AEBPR program to an individual in the Northern District of California.

All in violation of Title 17, United States Code, Section 1201(b)(1)(A) and Title 18, United States Code, Section 2.

COUNT FOUR: (17 USC §1201(b)(1)(C) and 18 USC §2—Trafficking in Technology Marketed For Use for Circumventing Technology that Protects a Right of a Copyright Owner)

16. Paragraphs One through Three are realleged and incorporated in Count Four.

17. On or about and between June 20, 2001 and July 15, 2001, both dates being approximate and inclusive, in Santa Clara County, in the Northern District of California, and elsewhere, the defendants

ELCOM LTD.

a/k/a ELCOMSOFT CO. LTD.

and

DMITRY SKLYAROV

did willfully, and for the purposes of commercial advantage and private financial gain, offer to the public and traffic in a technology, product, device, component, and part thereof, that was marketed by the defendants and others acting in concert with the defendants with the defendants' knowledge, for use in circumventing protection afforded by a technological measure that effectively protected a right of a copyright owner under Title 17 of the United States Code, in a work or portion thereof, in that the defendants marketed the AEBPR program in the Northern District of California.

All in violation of Title 17, United States Code, Section 1201(b)(1)(C) and Title 18, United States Code, Section 2.

COUNT FIVE: (17 USC §1201(b)(1)(C) and 18 USC §2—Trafficking in Technology Marketed for Use in Circumventing Technology that Protects a Right of a Copyright Owner)

18. Paragraphs One through Three are realleged and incorporated in Count Five.

19. On or about June 26, 2001, in Santa Clara County, in the Northern District of California, and elsewhere, the defendants

ELCOM LTD.

a/k/a ELCOMSOFT CO. LTD.

and

DMITRY SKLYAROV

did willfully, and for purposes of commercial advantage and private financial gain, provide and traffic in a technology, product, device, component, and part thereof, that was marketed by the defendants and others acting in concert with the defendants with the defendants' knowledge, for use in circumventing protection afforded by a technological measure that effectively protected a right of a copyright owner under Title 17 of the United States Code, in a work and portion thereof, in that the defendants sold a copy of the AEBPR program in the Northern District of California.

All in violation of Title 17, United States Code, Section 1201(b)(1)(C) and Title 18, United States Code, Section 2.

Robert S. Mueller III
United States Attorney

/s/ Elizabeth de la Vega
Chief, San Jose Division

United States
v.
Elcom Ltd.
a/k/a Elcomsoft Co. Ltd.
(Order Denying Motion to Dismiss Indictment for Lack of Subject Matter Jurisdiction)

**United States District Court,
Northern District of California**

March 27, 2002

10 ILR (P&F) 610

No. CR 01-20138 RMW

[Defendant's motion to dismiss the indictment for lack of jurisdiction is reported at 10 ILR (P&F) 2068. The indictment in this case may be found at 8 ILR (P&F) 2157. — Ed.]

U.S. court has jurisdiction over Russian software company in DMCA prosecution.

U.S. courts have subject matter jurisdiction over the prosecution of a Russian software company for violating the Digital Millennium Copyright Act, 17 USC §1201. The conduct for which defendants have been charged occurred in the United States, including offering software for sale on the Internet from a server located in the U.S., selling software to purchasers located in the U.S., and using an online payment service located in the U.S. As a result, there is sufficient conduct occurring within the United States to provide jurisdiction on a territorial basis. — **United States v. Elcom Ltd. a/k/a Elcomsoft Co. Ltd. (Order Denying Motion to Dismiss Indictment for Lack of Subject Matter Jurisdiction), 10 ILR (P&F) 610 [ND Cal, 2002].**

ORDER DENYING DEFENDANTS' MOTION TO DISMISS INDICTMENT FOR LACK OF SUBJECT MATTER JURISDICTION

RONALD M. WHYTE, *District Judge.* On March 4, 2002, the court heard defendant Elcom Ltd.'s motion to dismiss the indictment for lack of subject matter jurisdiction. Having considered the papers submitted by the parties and the arguments made at the hearing on the motion, defendant's motion is denied.

The court need not reach the issue of whether the Digital Millennium Copyright Act has extraterritorial application because the trafficking conduct for which defendants have been charged occurred in the United States. The conduct which underlies the indictment includes Elcomsoft's offering its AEBPR program for sale over the internet, from a computer server physically located in the United States. Purchasers obtained copies of the program in the United States. A copy of the program was sold to a purchaser in California. Payments were directed to, and received by, an entity in the United States.

There is sufficient conduct occurring within the United States for there to be subject matter jurisdiction over this matter on a territorial basis.

Defendant's motion to dismiss the indictment for lack of subject matter jurisdiction is therefore denied.

United States
v.
Elcom Ltd.
a/k/a Elcomsoft Co. Ltd.
(Order Denying Motions to Dismiss Indictment on Constitutional Grounds)

**United States District Court,
Northern District of California**

May 8, 2002

**10 ILR (P&F) 611, 2002 ILRWeb (P&F) 1449,
203 F Supp 2d 1111**

No. CR 01-20138 RMW

[The criminal complaint in this case is located at 8 ILR (P&F) 2106. The indictment may be found at 8 ILR (P&F) 2157. The motion to dismiss indictment for violation of due process is located at 10 ILR (P&F) 2081. The brief amicus curiae of the Electronic Frontier Foundation may be found at 10 ILR (P&F) 2095. The order denying dismissal for lack of subject matter jurisdiction is located at 10 ILR (P&F) 610. — Ed.]

DMCA anti-circumvention provision does not violate due process.

A provision of the Digital Millennium Copyright Act, 17 USC §1201(b), banning the manufacture and trafficking in technology designed to circumvent software usage restrictions satisfies due process requirements by providing defendants with adequate notice of proscribed conduct. Defendants contend that §1201(b) is inherently vague because it does not ban the distribution and manufacture of circumvention tools primarily designed to enable fair uses but makes it impossible to determine which tools are banned. Although Congress attempted to strike a balance between the rights of copyright owners and the public's fair use rights by not prohibiting the *use* of tools designed to circumvent use restrictions in copyrighted works, §1201(b) clearly prohibits the manufacture and distribution of all such tools, regardless of whether the resulting circumvention constitutes fair use or infringement. Accordingly, §1201(b) allows a person to conform his or her conduct to a comprehensible standard and is not unconstitutionally vague. — **United States v. Elcom Ltd. a/k/a Elcomsoft Co. Ltd. (Order Denying Motions to Dismiss Indictment on Constitutional Grounds), 10 ILR (P&F) 611 [ND Cal, 2002].**

DMCA anti-circumvention provision implicates First Amendment rights.

A provision of the Digital Millennium Copyright Act, 17 USC §1201(b), banning the manufacture and trafficking in technology designed to circumvent software usage restrictions implicates the First Amendment because the prohibited software tools contain protected speech. Although the government contends that banning the sale of technology does not constitute a restriction on speech, a ban on the sale of an item that contains protected speech triggers First Amendment protection. The object code in circumvention software is protected speech because it is merely one additional translation of speech into a new, and different, language. — **United States v. Elcom Ltd. a/k/a Elcomsoft Co. Ltd. (Order Denying Motions to Dismiss Indictment on Constitutional Grounds), 10 ILR (P&F) 611 [ND Cal, 2002].**

DMCA anti-circumvention provision does not infringe on defendants' free speech rights.

A provision of the Digital Millennium Copyright Act, 17 USC §1201(b), banning the manufacture and trafficking in technology designed to circumvent software usage restrictions does not infringe on defendants' free speech rights by prohibiting them from selling a program designed to circumvent use restrictions on Adobe's e-Book reader. Although §1201(b) restricts the right to distribute software that contains protected speech, the statute's prohibition is a content-neutral regulation based on the software's function, rather than its expressive content, warranting only an intermediate level of scrutiny. As such, §1201(b) need only further an important or substantial government interest with incidental restrictions on First Amendment freedoms no greater than are essential to the furtherance of that interest. Congress, in passing §1201(b), expressed the legitimate and substantial interests of preventing the unauthorized copying of copyrighted works and promoting electronic commerce. Section 1201(b) is sufficiently tailored to meet the government's interests because they would be promoted less effectively in the absence of §1201(b) and because the statute does not burden substantially more speech than necessary. Although a restriction on the distribution of circumvention technology may make it more difficult for the public to exercise fair uses in individual electronic copies of protected works, the fair use rights themselves have not been eliminated or prohibited. Similarly, the mere fact that an electronic copy of a public domain work might have use restrictions does not remove the work from the public domain. — **United States v. Elcom Ltd. a/k/a Elcomsoft Co. Ltd. (Order Denying Motions to Dismiss Indictment on Constitutional Grounds), 10 ILR (P&F) 611 [ND Cal, 2002].**

DMCA anti-circumvention provision is not unconstitutionally overbroad.

The Digital Millennium Copyright Act (DMCA), 17 USC §1201, which bans the manufacture and trafficking in technology designed to circumvent software access and usage restrictions, does not facially violate the First Amendment for overbreadth. Facial attacks on overbreadth grounds are limited to situations in which a statute, by its terms, seeks to regulate patently expressive or communicative conduct. The DMCA, on the other hand, is directed to the marketing of technology, including both software and hardware, and is not directly aimed at expressive conduct. Even if the DMCA directly regulated expression, however, it does not restrict or alter the public's rights in public domain or copyrighted works; the statute merely impacts the public's ability to access and use individual copies of those works. The mere fact that the DMCA may restrict the public's ability to make back-up copies of digital media for personal use does not significantly compromise or impair any First Amendment rights, even if such a use constitutes a fair use under the Copyright Act. — **United States v. Elcom Ltd. a/k/a Elcomsoft Co. Ltd. (Order Denying Motions to Dismiss Indictment on Constitutional Grounds), 10 ILR (P&F) 611 [ND Cal, 2002].**

DMCA anti-circumvention provision is not void for vagueness.

The Digital Millennium Copyright Act (DMCA), 17 USC §1201, which bans the manufacture and trafficking in technology designed to circumvent software access and usage restrictions, does not facially violate the First Amendment for vagueness. Defendants contend that the language of the DMCA, in criminalizing the manufacture and sale of a device with a limited commercially significant purpose that is primarily designed for the purpose of circumventing copyright control measures, regulates expression based on the motive of the speaker and provokes uncertainty about what expressive conduct is prohibited. The DMCA, however, is not a content-based restriction on speech that can be attacked on vagueness grounds. Even if the DMCA constituted a content-based restriction, however, the statute's provisions, read together with other provisions of federal copyright law, are sufficiently clear to withstand a vagueness attack. — **United States v. Elcom Ltd. a/k/a Elcomsoft Co. Ltd. (Order Denying Motions to Dismiss Indictment on Constitutional Grounds), 10 ILR (P&F) 611 [ND Cal, 2002].**

Congress did not exceed its authority in enacting the DMCA.

Congress had sufficient authority under the Commerce Clause of the U.S. Constitution to enact the Digital Millennium Copyright Act (DMCA), 17 USC §1201, and did not exceed its authority under the Intellectual Property Clause in so doing. The DMCA prohibits trafficking in copyright circumvention technology and is designed to prohibit wrongdoers from engaging in online piracy by unlawfully copying and distributing copyrighted works. As such, it is reasonable to conclude that the DMCA regulates activity affecting interstate commerce and is authorized by the Commerce Clause. The DMCA is also fundamentally consistent with the goals of the Intellectual Property Clause because it seeks to further the rights of intellectual property owners. Additionally, the DMCA is not irreconcilably inconsistent with any constitutional limitation on the power of Congress to create intellectual property rights because the statute does not affect the existing rights of the public to access and use public domain and copyrighted works. — **United States v. Elcom Ltd. a/k/a Elcomsoft Co. Ltd. (Order Denying Motions to Dismiss Indictment on Constitutional Grounds), 10 ILR (P&F) 611 [ND Cal, 2002].**

Scott Frewing, Assistant United States Attorney, San Jose, CA, Counsel for Plaintiff

Joseph M. Burton, Stephen H. Sutro, Duane Morris LLP, San Francisco, CA, Counsel for Defendant Elcomsoft.

John Keker, Daralyn J. Durie, Michael D. Celio, Keker & Van Nest, San Francisco, CA, Specially Appearing as Of Counsel for Defendant.

ORDER DENYING DEFENDANT'S MOTIONS TO DISMISS THE INDICTMENT ON CONSTITUTIONAL GROUNDS

RONALD M. WHYTE, *District Judge.* On April 1, 2002, the court heard defendant Elcom Ltd.'s motions to dismiss the indictment for violation of due process and on First Amendment grounds. The government opposed the motions. The court has considered the papers submitted by the parties and amici curiae and had the benefit of oral argument on the motions, and for the reasons set forth below, defendant's motions to dismiss the indictment are denied.

BACKGROUND

1. The Technology: eBooks and the AEBPR

Adobe Systems is a software company headquartered in San Jose, California. Adobe's Acrobat eBook Reader product provides the technology for the reading of books in digital form (*i.e.*, electronic books, or "ebooks") on personal computers. Use of the Adobe eBook format allows publishers or distributors of electronic books to control the subsequent distribution of the ebook, typically by limiting the distribution to those who pay for a copy. Diaz Decl. ¶5. These restrictions are imposed by the publisher's use of the Adobe Content Server, which allows the publisher to grant or withhold a range of privileges from the consumer. For example, the ebook publisher may choose whether the consumer will be able to copy the ebook, whether the ebook can be printed to paper (in whole, in part, or not at all), whether the "lending function" is enabled to allow the user to lend the ebook to another computer on the same network of computers, and whether to permit the ebook to be read audibly by a speech synthesizer program. *Id.* ¶8. When a consumer purchases an ebook formatted for Adobe Acrobat eBook Reader from an Internet website, the ebook is downloaded directly to the consumer's computer from the ebook distributor's Adobe Content Server.[1] The ebook is accompanied by an electronic "voucher" which is recognized and read by the Adobe Acrobat eBook Reader,[2] which then "knows" that the copy of the ebook can only be read on the computer onto which it has been downloaded. *Id.* ¶9. Thus, typically, the purchaser of an ebook may only read the ebook on the computer onto which the ebook was downloaded but may not e-mail or copy the ebook to another computer. The user may or may not be able to print the ebook in paper form or have it audibly read by the computer. *Id.* ¶¶5-9.

The indictment alleges that "[w]hen an ebook purchased for viewing in the Adobe eBook Reader format was sold by the publisher or distributor, the publisher or distributor of the ebook could authorize or limit the purchaser's ability to copy, distribute, print, or have the text read audibly by the computer. Adobe designed the eBook Reader to permit the management of such digital rights so that in the ordinary course of its operation, the eBook Reader effectively permitted the publisher or distributor of the ebook to restrict or limit the exercise of certain copyright rights of an owner of the copyright for an ebook distributed in the eBook Reader format." Indictment ¶1(g).

Defendant Elcomsoft Company Ltd. ("Elcomsoft") developed and sold a product known as the Advanced eBook Processor ("AEBPR"). AEBPR is a Windows-based software program that allows a user to remove use restrictions from Adobe Acrobat PDF files and files formatted for the Adobe eBook Reader. The program allows a purchaser of an eBook Reader formatted electronic book to convert the format to one that is readable in any PDF viewer without the use restrictions imposed by the publisher. Katalov Decl. ¶6. Thus, the restrictions imposed by the publisher are stripped away, leaving the ebook in a "naked PDF" format that is readily copyable, printable, and easily distributed electronically. The conversion accomplished by the AEBPR program enables a purchaser of an ebook to engage in "fair use" of an ebook without infringing the copyright laws, for example, by allowing the lawful owner of an ebook to read it on another computer, to make a back-up copy, or to print the ebook in paper form. The same technology, however, also allows a user to engage in copyright infringement by making and distributing unlawful copies of the ebook. Defendant was indicted for alleged violations of Section 1201(b)(1)(A) and (C) of the Digital Millennium Copyright Act ("DMCA"), 17 USC §§1201(b)(1)(A) and (C), for allegedly trafficking in and marketing of the AEBPR.

2. The DMCA

Congress enacted the DMCA following the adoption of the World Intellectual Property Organization Copyright Treaty as an expansion of traditional copyright law in recognition of the fact that in the digital age, authors must employ protective technologies in order to prevent their works from being unlawfully copied or exploited. As described by one court:

> In December 1996, the World Intellectual Property Organization ("WIPO"), held a diplomatic conference in Geneva that led to the adoption of two treaties. Article 11 of the relevant treaty, the WIPO Copyright Treaty, provides in relevant part that contracting states "shall provide adequate legal protection and effective legal remedies against the circumvention of effective technological measures that are used by authors in connection with the exercise of their rights under this Treaty or the Berne Convention and that restrict acts, in respect of their works, which are not authorized by the authors concerned or permitted by law."

The adoption of the WIPO Copyright Treaty spurred continued Congressional attention to the adaptation of the law of copyright to the digital age. Lengthy hearings involving a broad range of interested parties both preceded and succeeded the Copyright Treaty. . . . [A] critical focus of Congressional consideration of the legislation was the conflict between those who opposed anti-circumvention measures as inappropriate extensions of copyright impediments to fair use and those who supported them as essential to proper protection of copyrighted materials in the digital age. The DMCA was enacted in October 1998 as the culmination of this process.

Universal City Studios, Inc. v. Reimerdes, 111 F Supp 2d 294, 315-16 *[6 ILR (P&F) 1]* (SD NY 2000) (citations omitted), *aff'd* 273 F3d 429 *[9 ILR (P&F) 330]* (2d Cir 2001).

Through the DMCA, Congress sought to prohibit certain efforts to unlawfully circumvent protective technologies, while at the same time preserving users' rights of fair use. Some understanding of the interplay between copyright and fair use is essential to understanding the issues confronting Congress and the issues presented here. Fair use and copyright are discussed in more detail below, but in brief, copyright grants authors the exclusive right to make and distribute copies of their original works of authorship but the doctrine of fair use permits a certain amount of copying for limited purposes without infringing the copyright, notwithstanding the exclusive rights of the copyright owner.

As part of the balance Congress sought to strike in protecting the rights of copyright owners while preserving fair use, Congress enacted three new anti-circumvention prohibitions, Section 1201(a)(1), Section 1201(a)(2) and Section 1201(b). The first two provisions target circumvention of technological measures that effectively control *access* to a copyrighted work; the third targets circumvention of technological measures that impose limitations on the *use* of protected works.

With regard to the first category, Congress banned both the act of circumventing access control restrictions as well as trafficking in and marketing of devices that are primarily designed for such circumvention. Specifically, Section 1201(a)(1)(A) provides that "[n]o person shall circumvent a technological measure that effectively controls access to a work protected under this title." Thereafter, Section 1201(a)(2) provides that:

[n]o person shall manufacture, import, offer to the public, provide or otherwise traffic in any technology, product, service, device, component, or part thereof, that—

(A) is primarily designed or produced for the purpose of circumventing a technological measure that effectively controls access to a work protected under this title;

(B) has only limited commercially significant purpose or use other than to circumvent a technological measure that effectively controls access to a work protected under this title [17 USC §1 *et seq.*]; or

(C) is marketed by that person or another acting in concert with that person with that person's knowledge for use in circumventing a technological measure that effectively controls access to a work protected under this title.

17 USC §1201(a)(2).

The third prohibition, however, addresses a different circumvention, specifically, circumventing a technological measure that imposes limitations on the use of a copyrighted work, or in the words of the statute, that "effectively protects the right of a copyright owner." Using language quite similar to Section 1201(a)(2), the Act provides that:

[n]o person shall manufacture, import, offer to the public, provide or otherwise traffic in any technology, product, service, device, component, or part thereof, that—

(A) is primarily designed or produced for the purpose of circumventing protection afforded by a technological measure that effectively protects a right of a copyright owner under this title [17 USCA §1 *et seq.*] in a work or a portion thereof;

(B) has only limited commercially significant purpose or use other than to circumvent protection afforded by a technological measure that effectively protects a right of a copyright owner under this title in a work or a portion thereof; or

(C) is marketed by that person or another acting in concert with that person with that person's knowledge for use in circumventing protection afforded by a technological measure that effectively protects a right of a copyright owner under this title in a work or a portion thereof.

17 USC §1201(b). Unlike Section 1201(a), however, Congress did not ban the act of circumventing the use restrictions. Instead, Congress banned only the trafficking in and marketing of devices primarily designed to circumvent the use restriction protective technologies. Congress did not prohibit the act of circumvention because it sought to preserve the fair use rights of persons who had lawfully acquired a work. *See* H.R. Rep. 105-551, pt. 1, at 18 (1998); Burton Decl. Ex. N.; Exemption to Prohibition on Circumvention of Copyright Protection Systems for Access Control Technologies, 65 FR 64557 (2000) (codified at 37 CFR §201) ("The prohibition in section 1201(b) extends only to devices that circumvent copy control measures. The decision not to prohibit the conduct of circumventing copy controls was made, in part, because it would penalize some noninfringing conduct such as fair use."). In fact, Congress expressly disclaimed any intent to impair any person's rights of fair use: "Nothing in this section shall affect rights, remedies, or defenses to copyright infringement, including fair use, under this title [17 USCA §1 *et seq.*]." 17 USC §1201(c)(1).[3] Thus, circumventing use restrictions is not unlawful, but in order to protect the rights of copyright owners while maintaining fair use, Congress banned trafficking in devices that are primarily designed for the purpose of circumventing any technological measure that "effectively protects a right of a copyright owner," or that have limited commercially significant purposes other than circumventing use restrictions, or that are marketed for use in circumventing the use restrictions.

The difficulty is created by Section 1201(b)'s use of the phrase "effectively protects a right of a copyright owner" to define the prohibited device because the rights of a copyright owner are intertwined with the rights of others. The rights of a copyright owner include the exclusive rights to reproduce the copyrighted work, to prepare derivative works based upon the copyrighted work, to distribute copies by sale or otherwise, to perform the copyrighted work publicly, and to display the copyrighted work publicly. *See* 17 USC §106. Exceptions to the copyright owner's exclusive rights are set forth in 17 USC §§107-120. One of those exceptions is that the copyright owner loses control over the disposition of a copy of a work upon the sale or transfer of the copy. 17 USC §109. Thus, once a published copy is sold, the copyright owner has no right to restrict the further sale or transfer of that copy. *Id.* In addition, one of the most significant exceptions to the rights of a copyright owner is the doctrine of fair use. 17 USC §107.

Fair use is a defense to copyright infringement, allowing a certain amount of direct copying for certain uses, without the permission of the copyright owner and notwithstanding the copyright owner's exclusive rights. Section 107 provides that the fair use of a copyrighted work for purposes such as criticism, comment, news reporting, teaching, scholarship or research is not an infringement of a copyright. 17 USC §107. Section 107 also sets forth a series of factors for determining whether any particular use is a "fair use," including: "(1) the purpose and character of the use, including whether such use is of a commercial nature or is for nonprofit educational purposes; (2) the nature of the copyrighted work; (3) the amount and substantiality of the portion used in relation to the copyrighted work as a whole; and (4) the effect of the use upon the potential market for or value of the copyrighted work." *Id.* There is no bright line test for determining whether any particular use is a "fair use" or is instead an act of copyright infringement, and each use requires a case-by-case determination. *See Harper & Row, Publishers, Inc. v. Nation Enters.*, 471 US 539, 549 (1985).

The interplay between fair use and copyright weaves throughout defendant's motions to dismiss. The parties dispute whether Congress banned, or intended to ban, all circumvention tools or instead banned only those circumvention devices that would facilitate copyright infringement, and if, as a result, the DMCA is unconstitutionally vague. The parties also dispute whether, because of its effect on the fair use doctrine, the DMCA is an unconstitutional infringement upon the First Amendment and whether Congress had the power to enact the legislation. It is to these issues the court will next turn.

DISCUSSION

Defendant's two motions to dismiss the indictment challenge the constitutionality of the DMCA on a number of grounds. Defendant

contends that Section 1201(b) is unconstitutionally vague as applied to Elcomsoft and therefore violates the Due Process Clause of the Fifth Amendment. Defendant also contends that Section 1201(b) violates the First Amendment on several grounds: because it constitutes a content-based restriction on speech that is not sufficiently tailored to serve a compelling government interest, because it impermissibly infringes upon the First Amendment rights of third parties to engage in fair use, and because it is too vague in describing what speech it prohibits, thereby impermissibly chilling free expression. Finally, defendant contends that Congress exceeded its constitutional power in enacting the DMCA, and that the Act is therefore unconstitutional. Each argument will be addressed.

1. Fifth Amendment Due Process Challenge

Defendant first contends that Section 1201(b) is unconstitutionally vague as applied to Elcomsoft because it does not clearly delineate the conduct which it prohibits. Due Process Motion at 13. A statute violates the Due Process Clause of the Fifth Amendment if its prohibitions are not clearly defined. *Grayned v. City of Rockford*, 408 US 104, 108 (1972). Vagueness may invalidate a statute for either of two reasons: first, the statute may fail to provide the kind of notice that will enable ordinary people to understand what conduct it prohibits, and second, the statute may authorize or encourage arbitrary and discriminatory enforcement. *City of Chicago v. Morales*, 527 US 41, 56 (1999) (citing *Kolender v. Lawson*, 461 US 352, 357 (1983)). " 'It is established that a law fails to meet the requirements of the Due Process Clause if it is so vague and standardless that it leaves the public uncertain as to the conduct it prohibits. . . .' " 527 US at 56 (plurality) (quoting *Giaccio v. Pennsylvania*, 382 US 399, 402-03 (1966)). A criminal statute is not vague if it provides adequate notice of the prohibited conduct in terms that a reasonable person of ordinary intelligence would understand. *United States v. Martinez*, 49 F3d 1398, 1403 (9th Cir 1995), *cert. denied*, 516 US 1065 (1996) (superseded by statute on other grounds).

Defendant argues that the DMCA bans only those tools that are primarily designed to circumvent usage control technologies in order to enable copyright infringement. Defendant reaches this conclusion because Congress did not ban the act of circumventing use control technologies and expressly refused to do so in order to avoid treading on legitimate fair use. Defendant thus argues that:

> [t]he legislative history and the language of the DMCA establish that Congress did not prohibit the act of circumventing usage control technologies. For reasons directly related to that decision, it also did not ban *all* tools which might be used to circumvent usage control technologies. Congress sought to prohibit only those tools which are intended to be used to circumvent usage control technologies for the purpose of copyright infringement. Section 1201(b) does not provide a constitutionally adequate notice of this prohibition.

Due Process Motion at 14. From the premise that Congress has banned only those tools that are intended to circumvent usage control technologies for the purpose of copyright infringement, defendant then argues that the statute is unconstitutionally vague. "Section 1201(b) is doomed to inherent vagueness because not all tools are banned, and the language of the statute renders it impossible to determine which tools it in fact bans." *Id.* at 15. Defendant argues that because of the nature of the interplay between copyright owners' rights and fair use, any circumvention of a usage control technology for a legitimate purpose—such as for a fair use—must invariably involve circumvention of a technology that "protects the right of a copyright owner." Accordingly, there is no way for a manufacturer to know whether its tool is lawful. Moreover, this statutory vagueness leads to arbitrary enforcement.

The government's opposition brief does not directly address defendant's argument that some circumvention tools are prohibited while other circumvention tools are allowed. At the hearing, however, the government contended that the DMCA imposes a blanket ban on all circumvention tools. According to the government, Section 1201(b) does not prohibit only those tools that circumvent usage controls for the purpose of facilitating copyright infringement; the statute also prohibits tools that circumvent usage controls for the purpose of enabling fair use. Thus, if all tools that are primarily designed or produced for the purpose of circumventing protections afforded by technological measures are banned, the statute is not impermissibly vague.

Thus, the court's initial task is to determine whether the DMCA bans trafficking in all circumvention tools, regardless of whether they are designed to enable fair use or to facilitate infringement, or whether instead the statute bans only those tools that circumvent use restrictions for the purpose of facilitating copyright infringement. If all circumvention tools are banned, defendant's void-for-vagueness challenge necessarily fails.

The court must first consider the statutory language enacted by Congress. Despite defendant's repeated citations to the legislative history, if the language of the statute is clear, there is no need to resort to the legislative history in order to determine the statute's meaning. *Recording Indus. Ass'n of Am. v. Diamond Multimedia Sys., Inc.*, 180 F3d 1072, 1076 *[3 ILR (P&F) 66]* (9th Cir 1999). Section 1201(b) provides that:

> [n]o person shall manufacture, import, offer to the public, provide or otherwise traffic in any technology, product, service, device, component, or part thereof, that—
>
> > (A) is primarily designed or produced for the purpose of circumventing protection afforded by a technological measure that effectively protects a right of a copyright owner under this title [17 USCA §1 *et seq.*] in a work or a portion thereof . . . .

17 USC §1201(b). The section is comprised of three parts: 1) trafficking in "any technology," "product," "service," "device," "component" or "part thereof"; 2) that is "primarily designed or produced for the purpose of circumventing protection afforded by a technological measure"; and 3) a technological measure that "effectively protects a right of a copyright owner" under the copyright statute.

The first element targets "any technology, product, service, device, component, or part thereof." This language is not difficult to decipher and is all-encompassing: it includes any tool, no matter its form, that is primarily designed or produced to circumvent technological protection.

Next, the phrase "circumvent protection afforded by a technological measure" is expressly defined in the statute to mean: "avoiding, bypassing, removing, deactivating, or otherwise impairing a technological measure." 17 USC §1201(b)(2)(A).

Finally, the statute provides that "a technological measure 'effectively protects a right of a copyright owner under this title' if the measure, in the ordinary course of its operation, prevents, restricts, or otherwise limits the exercise of a right of a copyright owner under this title." *Id.* §1201(b)(2)(B). The rights of a copyright owner are specified in 17 USC §106. These include the exclusive rights:

(1) to reproduce the copyrighted work in copies or phonorecords;

(2) to prepare derivative works based upon the copyrighted work;

(3) to distribute copies or phonorecords of the copyrighted work to the public by sale or other transfer of ownership, or by rental, lease, or lending;

(4) in the case of literary, musical, dramatic, and choreographic works, pantomimes, and motion pictures and other audiovisual works, to perform the copyrighted work publicly;

(5) in the case of literary, musical, dramatic, and choreographic works, pantomimes, and pictorial, graphic, or sculptural works, including the individual images of a motion picture or other audiovisual work, to display the copyrighted work publicly;

and

(6) in the case of sound recordings, to perform the copyrighted work publicly by means of a digital audio transmission.

17 USC §106. Putting Section 1201(b)(2)(B) together with Section 106, a technological measure "effectively protects the right of a copyright owner" if, in the ordinary course of its operation, it prevents, restricts or otherwise limits the exercise of any of the rights set forth in Section 106, such as the rights to reproduce the work, prepare derivative works, distribute copies of the work, perform the work publicly or by digital audio transmission, or display the work publicly.

Taken in combination, Section 1201(b) thus prohibits trafficking in any tool that avoids, bypasses, removes, deactivates, or otherwise impairs any technological measure that prevents, restricts or otherwise limits the exercise of the right to reproduce the work, prepare derivative works, distribute copies of the work, perform the work publicly or by digital audio transmission, or display

the work publicly. In short, the statute bans trafficking in any device that bypasses or circumvents a restriction on copying or performing a work. Nothing within the express language would permit trafficking in devices designed to bypass use restrictions in order to enable a fair use, as opposed to an infringing use. The statute does not distinguish between devices based on the uses to which the device will be put. Instead, all tools that enable circumvention of use restrictions are banned, not merely those use restrictions that prohibit infringement. Thus, as the government contended at oral argument, Section 1201(b) imposes a blanket ban on trafficking in or the marketing of any device that circumvents use restrictions.

Because the statutory language is clear, it is unnecessary to consider the legislative history to determine congressional intent or the scope of the statute. Nevertheless, statements within the legislative history support the interpretation reached above. Congress was concerned with promoting electronic commerce while protecting the rights of copyright owners, particularly in the digital age where near exact copies of protected works can be made at virtually no cost and distributed instantaneously on a worldwide basis. S. Rep. No. 105-190, at 8 (1998), Burton Decl. Exh. P. Congress recognized that "most acts of circumventing a technological copyright protection measure will occur in the course of conduct which itself implicates the copyright owners rights," *i.e.*, acts of infringement. *Id.* at 29. Accordingly,

[p]aragraph (b)(1) prohibits manufacturing, importing, offering to the public, providing, or otherwise trafficking in certain technologies, products, services, device, components, or parts thereof *that can be used to circumvent a technological protection measure* that effectively protects a right of a copyright owner under title 17 in a work or portion thereof. . . . Like paragraph (a)(2), this provision is designed to protect copyright owners . . . .

Id. at 29-30 (emphasis added). Congress thus recognized that most uses of tools to circumvent copy restrictions would be for unlawful infringement purposes rather than for fair use purposes and sought to ban all circumvention tools that "can be used" to bypass or avoid copy restrictions.

Defendant relies heavily on congressional intent to preserve fair use but that congressional intent does not change the analysis. The Act expressly disclaims any intent to affect the rights, remedies, limitations, or defenses to copyright infringement, including the right of fair use. 17 USC §1201(c). Congress' expressed intent to preserve the right of fair use is not inconsistent with a ban on trafficking in circumvention technologies, even those that could be used for fair use purposes rather than infringement. Fair use of a copyrighted work continues to be permitted, as does circumventing use restrictions for the purpose of engaging in a fair use, even though engaging in certain fair uses of digital works may be made more difficult if tools to circumvent use restrictions cannot be readily obtained.

The inescapable conclusion from the statutory language adopted by Congress and the legislative history discussed above is that Congress sought to ban all circumvention tools because most of the time those tools would be used to infringe a copyright. Thus, while it is not unlawful to circumvent for the purpose of engaging in fair use, it is unlawful to traffic in tools that allow fair use circumvention. That is part of the sacrifice Congress was willing to make in order to protect against unlawful piracy and promote the development of electronic commerce and the availability of copyrighted material on the Internet.

Accordingly, there is no ambiguity in what tools are allowed and what tools are prohibited because the statute bans trafficking in or the marketing of *all* circumvention devices. Moreover, because all circumvention tools are banned, it was not necessary for Congress to expressly tie the use of the tool to an unlawful purpose in order to distinguish lawful tools from unlawful ones. Thus, the multi-use device authorities cited by defendant, such as the statutes and case law addressing burglary tools and drug paraphernalia, offer defendant no refuge. The law, as written, allows a person to conform his or her conduct to a comprehensible standard and is thus not unconstitutionally vague. *Coates v. City of Cincinnati*, 402 US 611, 614 (1971). Therefore, defendant's motion to dismiss the indictment on due process grounds is denied.

2. First Amendment Challenges

Defendant asserts several First Amendment challenges, arguing that the DMCA violates the First Amendment as applied to the sale of the AEBPR, that the DMCA violates the First Amendment because it infringes the First Amendment rights of third parties, and that the DMCA violates the First Amendment because it is impermissibly vague, thus chilling otherwise protected speech. As an initial matter, however, the government contends that review under the First Amendment is unnecessary. The government offers two arguments: 1) the statute bans the sale of technology and the sale of technology is not "speech"; and 2) the AEBPR, in object code form, is not speech protected by the First Amendment. Neither argument is persuasive.

First, the government erroneously contends that the DMCA does not implicate the First Amendment because defendant's sale of circumvention technology is not speech. While selling is the act giving rise to potential criminal liability under Section 1201(b), the DMCA bans trafficking in the AEBPR, software which at some level contains expression, thus implicating the First Amendment. As noted by defendant in reply, the government could not ban the sale of newspapers without implicating the First Amendment, even if newspapers themselves were not banned. First Amendment Reply at 4. First Amendment scrutiny is triggered because the statute bans the sale of something that at some level contains protected expression. *See Arkansas Writers' Project, Inc. v. Ragland*, 481 US 221, 227-28 (1987) (invalidating tax on magazines, with exceptions based on content, as inconsistent with First Amendment); *Simon & Schuster, Inc. v. Members of N.Y. State Crime Victims Bd.*, 502 US 105, 116 (1991) (invalidating as inconsistent with the First Amendment New York's "Son of Sam" law, which required a criminal's income from works describing his crime be deposited into an escrow account for the benefit of victims of crime).

Second, the government contends that computer code is not speech and hence is not subject to First Amendment protections. The court disagrees. Computer software is expression that is protected by the copyright laws and is therefore "speech" at some level, speech that is protected at some level by the First Amendment. *See Sony Computer Entm't v. Connectix Corp.*, 203 F3d 596, 602 (9th Cir) (recognizing that object code may be copyrighted as expression under 17 USC §102(b)), *cert. denied*, 531 US 871 (2000). While there is some disagreement over whether object code, as opposed to source code, is deserving of First Amendment protection, the better reasoned approach is that it is protected. Object code is merely one additional translation of speech into a new, and different, language. *See Universal City Studios, Inc. v. Corley*, 273 F3d 429, 445-49 *[9 ILR (P&F) 330]* (2d Cir 2001) (recognizing that code is speech); *Reimerdes*, 111 F Supp 2d at 326-27; *Bernstein v. U.S. Dep't of State*, 922 F Supp 1426, 1436 *[1 ILR (P&F) 762]* (ND Cal 1996) (recognizing that source code is speech but not reaching the object code issue). As the *Reimerdes* court explained:

> It cannot be seriously argued that any form of computer code may be regulated without reference to First Amendment doctrine. The path from idea to human language to source code to object code is a continuum. As one moves from one side to the other, the levels of precision and, arguably, abstraction increase, as does the level of training necessary to discern the idea from the expression. Not everyone can understand each of these forms. Only English speakers will understand English formulations. Principally those familiar with the particular programming language will understand the source code expression. And only a relatively small number of skilled programmers and computer scientists will understand the machine readable object code. But each form expresses the same idea, albeit in different ways.

> All modes by which ideas may be expressed or, perhaps, emotions evoked—including speech, books, movies, art, and music—are within the area of First Amendment concern. As computer code—whether source or object—is a means of expressing ideas, the First Amendment must be considered before dissemination may be prohibited or regulated. In that sense, computer code is covered, or as sometimes said, "protected" by the First Amendment. But that conclusion still leaves for determination the level of scrutiny to be applied in determining the

constitutionality of regulation of computer code.

111 F Supp 2d at 326-27 (footnotes omitted).

Accordingly, it is appropriate to consider defendant's First Amendment challenges.

A. Whether the DMCA Violates the First Amendment as Applied to the Sale of AEBPR

Defendant first argues that the DMCA, as applied to the sale of defendant's AEBPR, violates the First Amendment. Defendant's argument is structured as follows: computer code is speech protected by the First Amendment; the DMCA regulates that speech based upon its content because it bans the code that conveys a certain message (*i.e.*, circumventing use restrictions); content-based regulations must be narrowly tailored; the DMCA is not narrowly tailored; ergo, the DMCA is unconstitutional. *See* First Amendment Reply at 1.

In opposition, the government argues that under the appropriate level of scrutiny, the DMCA does not violate the First Amendment as applied to the sale of the AEBPR. The government argues that strict scrutiny is not appropriate because the statute does not target speech and is content-neutral with respect to speech. Under intermediate scrutiny, the government has legitimate interests in promoting electronic commerce and in protecting the rights of copyright owners, and the statute is sufficiently tailored to achieve those objectives without unduly burdening free speech.

In order to determine whether the DMCA violates the First Amendment as applied to the sale of the AEBPR, the court must first determine the appropriate level of scrutiny to apply to the statute. As a general matter, content-based restrictions on speech are permissible only if they serve a compelling state interest and do so by the least restrictive means. *Turner Broadcasting Sys., Inc. v. FCC*, 512 US 622, 680 (1994) (citing *Boos v. Barry*, 485 US 312, 321 (1988)); *Corley*, 273 F3d at 449 (quoting *Sable Communications of Cal. v. FCC*, 492 US 115, 126 (1989)). On the other hand, if a statute or regulation is content-neutral, it

> will be sustained if "it furthers an important or substantial governmental interest; if the governmental interest is unrelated to the suppression of free expression; and if the incidental restriction on alleged First

Amendment freedoms is no greater than is essential to the furtherance of that interest." To satisfy this standard, a regulation need not be the least speech-restrictive means of advancing the Government's interests. "Rather, the requirement of narrow tailoring is satisfied 'so long as the . . . regulation promotes a substantial government interest that would be achieved less effectively absent the regulation.' " Narrow tailoring in this context requires, in other words, that the means chosen do not "burden substantially more speech than is necessary to further the government's legitimate interests."

Turner Broadcasting, 512 US at 662 (citations omitted).

When speech and non-speech elements are combined in a single course of conduct, a sufficiently important government interest in regulating the non-speech element can justify incidental intrusions on First Amendment freedoms. *United States v. O'Brien*, 391 US 367 (1968); *Junger v. Daley*, 209 F3d 481, 485 *[5 ILR (P&F) 122]* (6th Cir 2000) (applying intermediate scrutiny to regulations banning exportation of encryption software).

The principal inquiry in determining whether a statute is content-neutral is whether the government has adopted a regulation of speech because of agreement or disagreement with the message it conveys. *Ward v. Rock Against Racism*, 491 US 781, 791 (1989). The government's purpose is the controlling consideration. *Id.* Here, the parties have pointed to no portion of the legislative history that demonstrates a congressional intent to target speech because of its expressive content. Rather, Congress sought ways to further electronic commerce and protect intellectual property rights, while at the same time protecting fair use. In order to balance these priorities, Congress sought to ban trafficking in any technology or device that could be used to circumvent technological restrictions that served to protect the rights of copyright owners.

Defendant contends that because this occurs in a digital arena, the technological measures necessarily involve computer code and, thus, necessarily implicate speech protected by the First Amendment. Defendant further argues that the regulation is not content-neutral because it only bans a certain type of speech—speech that allows the circumvention of protection measures—and therefore that strict scrutiny must be applied. "Indeed, it is precisely the content of the code that causes the government to regulate it." First Amendment Reply at 5.

Defendant's argument, however, stretches too far. In the digital age, more and more conduct occurs through the use of computers and over the Internet. Accordingly, more and more conduct occurs through "speech" by way of messages typed onto a keyboard or implemented through the use of computer code when the object code commands computers to perform certain functions. The mere fact that this conduct occurs at some level through expression does not elevate all such conduct to the highest levels of First Amendment protection. Doing so would turn centuries of our law and legal tradition on its head, eviscerating the carefully crafted balance between protecting free speech and permissible governmental regulation.

On its face, the statute does not target speech. Section 1201(b) bans trafficking in devices, whether software, hardware, or other. Thus, strict scrutiny is not appropriate in the absence of any suggestion that Congress sought to ban particular speech, qua speech. Courts that have considered the issue in the context of the DMCA have determined that Congress was not concerned with suppressing ideas but instead enacted the anti-trafficking measures because of the function performed by the code. *Reimerdes*, 111 F Supp 2d at 329 ("The reason that Congress enacted the anti-trafficking provision of the DMCA had nothing to do with suppressing particular ideas of computer programmers and everything to do with functionality."); *Corley*, 273 F3d at 454. Thus, to the extent that the DMCA targets computer code, Congress sought to ban the code not because of what the code says, but rather because of what the code does.

Defendant contends that these authorities are wrongly decided and that it is impossible to regulate the "functional" aspects of computer code without necessarily regulating the content of the expressive aspects of the code. Divorcing the function from the message, however, is precisely what the courts have done in other contexts, for example, in determining what portions of code are protectable by copyright and what uses of that same code are permitted as fair uses. *See Connectix*, 203 F3d at

602-03 (recognizing that computer programs pose unique problems in copyright context because they are both expressive and functional utilitarian articles; copyright protects only the expression, and fair use allows incidental copying for the purpose of reverse engineering code to determine its unprotected functional aspects).

Accordingly, the court concludes that intermediate scrutiny, rather than strict scrutiny, is the appropriate standard to apply. Under this test, the regulation will be upheld if it furthers an important or substantial government interest unrelated to the suppression of free expression, and if the incidental restrictions on First Amendment freedoms are no greater than essential to the furtherance of that interest. *Turner Broadcasting*, 512 US at 662. By this standard, a statute is constitutional as long as it "promotes a substantial governmental interest that would be achieved less effectively absent the regulation" and the means chosen do not burden substantially more speech than is necessary to further the government's legitimate interests. *Id.*

1) The Governmental Interests

In this case, there are two asserted governmental interests: preventing the unauthorized copying of copyrighted works and promoting electronic commerce. As noted in the House Report:

> The debate on this legislation highlighted two important priorities: promoting the continued growth and development of electronic commerce; and protecting intellectual property rights. These goals are mutually supportive. A thriving electronic marketplace provides new and powerful ways for the creators of intellectual property to make their works available to legitimate consumers in the digital environment. And a plentiful supply of intellectual property— whether in the form of software, music, movies, literature, or other works—drives the demand for a more flexible and efficient electronic marketplace.

H.R. Rep. No. 105-551, pt. 2, at 23 (1998), Burton Decl. Exh. O.

Congress recognized that a primary threat to electronic commerce and to the rights of copyright holders was the plague of digital piracy. The Senate Report notes:

> Due to the ease with which digital works can be copied and distributed worldwide virtually instantaneously, copyright owners will hesitate to make their works readily available on the Internet without reasonable assurance that they will be protected against massive piracy. Legislation implementing the treaties provides this protection and creates the legal platform for launching the global digital on-line marketplace for copyrighted works. It will facilitate making available quickly and conveniently via the Internet the movies, music, software, and literary works that are the fruit of American creative genius. It will also encourage the continued growth of the existing off-line global marketplace for copyrighted works in digital format by setting strong international copyright standards.

S. Rep. No. 105-190, at 8 (1998), Burton Decl. Exh. P. Congress has elsewhere expressed its concern over the state of intellectual property piracy:

> Notwithstanding [penalties for copyright infringement] copyright piracy of intellectual property flourishes, assisted in large part by today's world of advanced technologies. For example, industry groups estimate that counterfeiting and piracy of computer software cost the affected copyright holders more than $11 billion last year (others believe the figure is closer to $20 billion). In some countries, software piracy rates are as high as 97% of all sales. The U.S. rate is far lower (25%) but the dollar losses ($2.9 billion) are the highest worldwide. The effect of this volume of theft is substantial: lost U.S. jobs, lost wages, lower tax revenue, and higher prices for honest purchasers of copyrighted software. Unfortunately, the potential for this problem to worsen is great.

Reimerdes, 111 F Supp 2d at 335 n. 230 (citing H.R. Rep. No. 106-216 (1999)).

These governmental interests are both legitimate and substantial.

2) Whether Section 1201(b) is Sufficiently Tailored

The next step is to determine whether these governmental interests would be promoted less effectively absent the regulation and whether the means chosen burden substantially more speech than is necessary to further the government's interests. *Turner Broadcasting*, 512 US at 662.

Without the ban on trafficking in circumvention tools, the government's interest in promoting electronic commerce, preserving the rights of copyright holders, and preventing piracy would be undermined. The absence of effective technological restrictions to prevent copyright infringement would inevitably result in even more rampant piracy, with a corresponding likely decrease in the willingness of authors and owners of copyrighted works to produce them in digital form or make the works available on-line. Thus, there is little question that the governmental interests would be promoted less effectively in the absence of the regulation. Nevertheless, there is substantial disagreement between the parties with regard to whether or not the regulation "substantially burdens more speech than is necessary" to achieve the government's interests.

Defendant contends that the DMCA burdens substantially more speech than is necessary to protect copyright holders from digital copyright pirates. First, defendant contends that it was not necessary to ban all circumvention tools, because those tools can serve legitimate purposes. Congress had other options more narrowly tailored to prevent the harm sought: it could have made the penalties for infringement more severe or it could have criminalized the use of the Internet to distribute infringing copies. Second, defendant argues that the DMCA fails to pass constitutional review because

> the government's approach to the DMCA effectively eliminates fair use, limits noninfringing uses and prevents access to material in the public domain and uncopyrightable material protected by "technological measures." Many of these uses are themselves protected expression and none of them constitute copyright infringement. The anti-trafficking provisions of the DMCA do not "respon[d] precisely to the substantive problem which legitimately concern[ed]" [Congress] and that it therefore do [sic, does] not comport with the First Amendment.

First Amendment Motion at 12 (citing *Members of the City Council of L.A. v. Taxpayers for Vincent*, 466 US 789, 810 (1984)).

The government responds that there are numerous exceptions to the DMCA that demonstrate that the DMCA is sufficiently tailored to withstand intermediate scrutiny:

> Congress carefully balanced, *inter alia*, the needs of law enforcement and other government agencies, computer programmers, encryption researchers, and computer security specialists against the serious problems created by circumvention technology. *See* 17 USC §§1201(e)-1201(g), 1201(j). That defendant Elcomsoft's conduct did not fall within the exceptions does not suggest, let alone prove, the DMCA sweeps to broadly.

Opposition Brief at 24 (citing *Fed. Election Comm'n v. National Right to Work Comm.*, 459 US 197, 208 (1982) ("statutory prohibitions and exceptions" regarding political contributions by corporations and unions held "sufficiently tailored . . . to avoid undue restriction on the associational interests asserted" by political organization)).

Defendant's arguments are not persuasive. First, the DMCA does not "eliminate" fair use. Although certain fair uses may become more difficult, no fair use has been prohibited. Lawful possessors of copyrighted works may continue to engage in each and every fair use authorized by law. It may, however, have become more difficult for such uses to occur with regard to technologically protected digital works, but the fair uses themselves have not been eliminated or prohibited.

For example, nothing in the DMCA prevents anyone from quoting from a work or comparing texts for the purpose of study or criticism. It may be that from a technological perspective, the fair user my find it more difficult to do so—quoting may have to occur the old fashioned way, by hand or by re-typing, rather than by "cutting and pasting" from existing digital media. Nevertheless, the fair use is still available. Defendant has cited no authority which guarantees a fair user the right to the most technologically convenient way to engage in fair use. The existing authorities have rejected that argument. *See Corley*, 273 F3d at 459 ("We know of no authority for the proposition that fair use, as protected by the Copyright Act, much less the Constitution, guarantees copying by the optimum method or in the identical format of the original. . . . Fair use has never been held to be a guarantee of access to copyrighted material in order to copy it by the fair user's preferred technique or in the format of the original.")

In the same vein, the DMCA does not "prevent access to matters in the public domain" or allow any publisher to remove from the public domain and acquire rights in any public domain work. Nothing within the DMCA grants any rights to anyone in any public domain work. A public domain work remains in the public domain and no party has any intellectual property right in the expression of that work. A flaw in defendant's argument is that it presumes that the only available version of a public domain work is an electronic, technology-protected, version. If a work is in the public domain, any person may make use of that expression, for whatever purposes desired. To the extent that a publisher has taken a public domain work and made it available in electronic form, and in the course of doing so has also imposed use restrictions on the electronic version, the publisher has not gained any lawfully protected intellectual property interest in the work. The publisher has only gained a technological protection against copying that particular electronic version of the work.

The situation is little different than if a publisher printed a new edition of Shakespeare's plays, but chose to publish the book on paper that was difficult to photocopy. Copy protection measures could be employed, similar to what is now commonly done on bank checks, so that the photocopy revealed printing that is otherwise unnoticeable on the original, perhaps rendering the text difficult to read on the photocopy. Would the publisher have thus recaptured Shakespeare's plays from the public domain? No, the publisher has gained no enforceable rights in the works of Shakespeare; all that has happened is that the purchaser of the copy-protected book would be unable to easily make a photocopy of that particular book.

Publishing a public domain work in a restricted format does not thereby remove the work from the public domain, even if it does allow the publisher to control that particular electronic copy. If this is an evil in the law, the remedy is for Congress to prohibit use or access restrictions from being imposed upon public domain works. Or perhaps, if left to the market, the consuming public could decline to purchase public domain works packaged with use restrictions.

In addition, the alternatives proposed by defendant—enacting more severe penalties for copyright infringement—may not be as effective at preventing widespread copyright infringement and electronic piracy as is banning the trafficking in or the marketing of the tools that allow piracy to thrive. Congress certainly could have approached the problem by targeting the infringers, rather than those who traffic in the tools that enable the infringement to occur. However, it is already unlawful to infringe, yet piracy of intellectual property has reached epidemic proportions. Pirates are world-wide, and locating and prosecuting each could be both impossible and ineffective, as new pirates arrive on the scene. But, pirates and other infringers require tools in order to bypass the technological measures that protect against unlawful copying. Thus, targeting the tool sellers is a reasoned, and reasonably tailored, approach to "remedying the evil" targeted by Congress. In addition, because tools that circumvent copyright protection measures for the purpose of allowing fair use can also be used to enable infringement, it is reasonably necessary to ban the sale of all circumvention tools in order to achieve the objectives of preventing widespread copyright infringement and electronic piracy in digital media. Banning the sale of all circumvention tools thus does not substantially burden more speech than is necessary.

Under intermediate scrutiny, it is not necessary that the government select the least restrictive means of achieving its legitimate governmental interest. By its very nature, the intermediate scrutiny test allows some impingement on protected speech in order to achieve the legitimate governmental objective. A sufficiently important government interest in regulating the targeted conduct can justify incidental limitations on First Amendment freedoms. *O'Brien*, 391 US 367. Having considered the arguments asserted by the parties, the court finds that the DMCA does not burden substantially more speech than is necessary to achieve the government's asserted goals of promoting electronic commerce, protecting copyrights, and preventing electronic piracy.

B. Overbreadth Challenge: Does the DMCA Substantially Burden the First Amendment Rights of Others?

Defendant next asserts a facial challenge to the DMCA, contending that the statute is overbroad because it infringes upon the First Amendment rights of third parties. In a facial challenge on overbreadth grounds, the challenger contends that the statute at issue is invalid because it is so broadly written that it infringes unacceptably on the First Amendment rights of third parties. *Anderson v. Nidorf*, 26 F3d 100, 103 (9th Cir 1994), *cert. denied*, 514 US 1035 (1995); *Taxpayers for Vincent*, 466 US at 798-99. "A statute will be declared unconstitutional only if the court finds 'a "realistic danger that the statute itself will significantly compromise recognized First Amendment protections of parties not before the Court.' " The overbreadth must be not only 'real, but substantial as well, judged in relation to the statute's plainly legitimate sweep.' " *Nidorf*, 26 F3d at 104 (citing *New York State Club Ass'n v. City of New York*, 487 US 1, 11 (1988) and *Broadrick v. Oklahoma*, 413 US 601, 615 (1973)). Defendant contends that the DMCA is unconstitutionally overbroad on two grounds: first, the statute impairs the First Amendment right to access non-copyrighted works; and second, the statute precludes third parties from exercising their rights of fair use.

The fatal flaw in defendant's argument, however, is that facial attacks on overbreadth grounds are limited to situations in which the statute or regulation by its terms regulates spoken words or expressive conduct. In *Roulette v. City of Seattle*, 97 F3d 300 (9th Cir 1996), the Ninth Circuit noted that "the Supreme Court has entertained facial freedom-of-expression challenges only against statutes that, 'by their terms,' sought to regulate 'spoken words,' or patently 'expressive or communicative conduct' such as picketing or handbilling." *Id.* at 303. Reviewing Supreme Court precedent, the Ninth Circuit concluded that "[t]he lesson we take from *Broadrick* and its progeny is that a facial freedom of speech attack must fail unless, at a minimum, the challenged statute 'is directed narrowly and specifically at expression or conduct commonly associated with expression.' " *Id.* at 305 (citations omitted). Because the statute at issue in *Roulette* was addressed to conduct that was not commonly associated with expression—sitting or lying on sidewalks—the Ninth Circuit rejected the facial attack on the ordinance.

Under *Roulette*, defendant's facial attack on the DMCA necessarily fails. By its terms, the statute is directed to trafficking in or the marketing of "any technology, product, service, device, component, or part thereof," that circumvents usage control restrictions. The statute is not directed "narrowly and specifically at expression or conduct commonly associated with expression." Software as well as hardware falls within the scope of the Act, as does any other technology or device. Accordingly, an overbreadth facial challenge is not available.

Even if the DMCA were to be considered a statute directed at conduct commonly associated with expression and the court were to consider the merits of the facial challenge, however, defendant's argument is ultimately unsuccessful. In order to prevail on a facial overbreadth challenge, defendant must establish that there is a realistic danger that the First Amendment rights of third parties will be significantly compromised. Defendant bases its argument on the assertion that the DMCA "significantly compromises" the First Amendment rights of third parties in two ways: 1) it impacts third parties' rights to access public domain and non-copyrighted works; and 2) it impacts the fair use rights of third parties, which it contends are protected by the First Amendment. Assuming for the sake of discussion that these asserted rights are protected by the First Amendment, an issue which is not clear,[4] defendant's challenge nevertheless fails because the DMCA does not substantially impair those rights.

Defendant first argues that the DMCA "runs afoul of the First Amendment because it places almost unlimited power in the hands of copyright holders to control information, including information that is not even protected by copyright. Society has a strong interest in the free flow of such information." First Amendment Motion at 13 (citing *First Nat'l Bank of Boston v. Bellotti*, 435 US 765, 783 (1978)). Thus, according to defendant, because society has a strong interest in the free flow of such information which is based in the First Amendment, the DMCA violates the First Amendment by allowing others to impair that interest.

The argument is not compelling. *Bellotti* recognized that the First Amendment extends beyond protection of the press and the self-expression of individuals and includes prohibiting the government from limiting the stock of information from which members of the public may draw. 435 US at 783. Assuming for the sake of argument that it would violate the First Amendment for the government to grant exclusive copyright-like rights in works that have already entered the public domain, that situation is not presented here. The hole in defendant's argument is that the DMCA does not grant anyone exclusive rights in public domain works or otherwise non-copyrighted expression. A public domain work remains in the public domain. Any person may use the public domain work for any purpose—quoting, republishing, critiquing, comparing, or even making and selling copies. Publishing the public domain work in an electronic format with technologically imposed restrictions on how that particular copy of the work may be used does not give the publisher any legally enforceable right to the expressive work, even if it allows the publisher to control that particular copy.

Similarly, with regard to the argument that fair use rights are impaired, as discussed above, the DMCA does not eliminate fair use or substantially impair the fair use rights of anyone. Congress has not banned or eliminated fair use and nothing in the DMCA prevents anyone from quoting from a work or comparing texts for the purpose of study or criticism. The fair user may find it more difficult to engage in certain fair uses with regard to electronic books, but nevertheless, fair use is still available.

Defendant makes much of the right to make a back-up copy of digital media for personal use, holding this right up as an example of how the DMCA eliminates fair use. Defendant relies heavily on *Recording Industry Association of America v. Diamond Multimedia Systems*, 180 F3d 1072 *[3 ILR (P&F) 66]* (9th Cir 1999), for the assertion that the right to make a copy of electronic media for personal, noncommercial use, is a paradigmatic fair use consistent with the Copyright Act. First Amendment Motion at 16. But, defendant overstates the significance and holding of that decision. The Ninth Circuit was not presented with, and did not hold, that the right to make a copy for personal use is protected as a fair use right or protected as a right guaranteed by the Constitution. Rather, the Ninth Circuit was discussing the Audio Home Recording Act of 1992, 17 USC §1001, and the statutory

exemption for home taping which protects all noncommercial copying by consumers of digital and analog musical recordings. The court held that copying for personal, noncommercial use was consistent with the Audio Home Recording Act's main purpose of facilitating personal use. *Id.* at 1079.

Courts have been receptive to the making of an archival copy of electronic media in order to safeguard against mechanical or electronic failure. *See Vault Corp. v. Quaid Software Ltd.*, 847 F2d 255, 267 (5th Cir 1988). Making a back-up copy of an ebook, for personal noncommercial use would likely be upheld as a non-infringing fair use. But the right to make a back-up copy of "computer programs" is a statutory right, expressly enacted by Congress in Section 117(a), and there is as yet no generally recognized right to make a copy of a protected work, regardless of its format, for personal noncommercial use. There has certainly been no generally recognized First Amendment right to make back-up copies of electronic works. Thus, to the extent the DMCA impacts a lawful purchaser's "right" to make a back-up copy, or to space-shift that copy to another computer, the limited impairment of that one right does not significantly compromise or impair of the First Amendment rights of users so as to render the DMCA unconstitutionally overbroad.

C. Whether the DMCA Is Unconstitutionally Vague Under the First Amendment

Defendant's final First Amendment challenge is that the DMCA is unconstitutionally vague under the First Amendment because it "provokes uncertainty among speakers" about precisely what speech is prohibited. *Reno v. ACLU*, 521 US 844, 871 *[1 ILR (P&F) 1]* (1997). Defendant argues that "[t]he DMCA criminalizes the manufacture and sale of a device that 'is *primarily designed* or produced for the purpose of circumventing a technological measure that effectively controls access[5] to a work protected under this title' if the device has 'only *limited commercially significant purpose* or use other than to circumvent a technological measure.' " First Amendment Motion at 17. Defendant's premise is that the DMCA regulates expression based at least in part upon the motive of the speaker, specifically, the purpose for which the program was primarily designed and the extent to which there was a commercially significant purpose in doing so other than the circumvention of copyrighted works. In order to determine if the code violates the DMCA, the seller must assess all possible uses of the technology and determine which are the *"significant purpose[s]"* and what it is "primarily" designed to do. First Amendment Reply at 13.

In opposition, the government argues that the statutory language "primarily designed or produced for" is substantially similar to language that has been upheld in other cases, citing the Supreme Court's decisions in *Village of Hoffman Estates v. The Flipside, Hoffman Estates, Inc.*, 455 US 489 (1982) ("designed for" and "marketed primarily for use" drug law not unconstitutionally vague), and *Posters 'N' Things, Ltd. v. United States*, 511 US 513 (1994) ("primarily intended . . . for use" drug law not unconstitutionally vague), as well as the Second Circuit's decision in *Richmond Boro Gun Club, Inc. v. City of New York*, 97 F3d 681, 685-86 (2d Cir 1996) ("designed for" gun law not unconstitutionally vague). The government does not address defendant's argument that the "limited commercially significant purpose" phrase renders the statute impermissibly vague, nor does it address the vagueness argument in the context of the alleged impermissible chilling effect on First Amendment rights.

In reply, defendant argues that this statute is distinguishable from the drug paraphernalia statute at issue in *Flipside*, 455 US 489, because

> it should be obvious that it is considerably easier to determine if an item was "designed or marketed for use with illegal drugs" than if it was "primarily designed or produced for the purpose of circumventing a technological measure that effectively controls access to a work protected under" Title 17 of the United States Code. The challenged provision in *Flipside* requires only a rudimentary knowledge of illegal drug use. The DMCA, by contrast, requires knowledge of (a) the primary and secondary uses of immensely sophisticated technology, (b) whether the technology "effectively" controls access *vis a vis* other controls, and (c) knowledge of the provisions of Title 17 of the United States Code, which regulates copyrights including its provision as they relate to fair use. The DMCA, to put it mildly, is significantly more difficult to understand, and thus more vague.

First Amendment Reply at 12-13.

Once again, defendant's arguments are not persuasive. The primary flaw in defendant's argument is that the court rejects the contention that the DMCA is a content-based restriction on speech and thus *Reno v. ACLU* is inapplicable. *Reno v. ACLU* involved a challenge to the Communications Decency Act's provisions that sought to protect minors from harmful material on the Internet. The CDA sought to protect children from the primary harmful effects of "indecent" and "patently offensive" speech and was thus a content-based blanket restriction on speech. 521 US at 868. Among the challenged provisions was the knowing transmission of "obscene or indecent" messages to any recipient under 18 years of age and the knowing sending or displaying to a person under 18 years of age any message "that, in context, depicts or describes, in terms patently offensive as measured by contemporary community standards, sexual or excretory activities or organs." *Id.* at 859-60. The Court held that the statutory language—"indecent" and "in context, depicts or describes, in terms patently offensive as measured by contemporary community standards, sexual or excretory activities or organs"—was unconstitutionally vague in the absence of statutory definitions, and as a result would "provoke uncertainty among speakers about how the two standards relate to each other and just what they mean" thereby causing a chilling effect on free speech. *Id.* at 871-72, 874. Here, by contrast, the DMCA is not a content-based restriction on speech and its restrictions do not "provoke uncertainty among speakers" about what speech is permitted and what speech is prohibited. The statute is not unconstitutionally vague in violation of the First Amendment.

In addition, defendant's attempt to distinguish *Flipside* and the other authorities is not persuasive, and ultimately, *Flipside* and *Posters 'N' Things* are controlling. The "primarily designed for" and "marketed for use" language is not unconstitutionally vague. Similarly, the "has only limited commercially significant purpose other than to circumvent protection afforded by a technological measure that effectively protects the right of a copyright owner under this title" is also not unconstitutionally vague. [6] Section 106 sets forth the rights of a copyright owner; Section 107 sets forth the criteria for the fair use exception. Together with the definitions contained in Section 1201(b)(2), the DMCA's prohibition on trafficking in technologies that circumvent use and copy restrictions is sufficiently clear to withstand a vagueness attack.

3. Congressional Authority to Enact the DMCA

Defendant's final challenge is that Congress exceeded its authority in enacting the DMCA and that, as a result, the statute is unconstitutional. The federal government is one of enumerated powers and Congress may exercise only those powers granted to it. *McCulloch v. Maryland*, 4 Wheat. 316, 4 L Ed 579 (1819); *United States v. Lopez*, 514 US 549, 566 (1995). The Constitution contains several express grants of power to Congress, among them the Intellectual Property Clause and the Commerce Clause.

Under the Intellectual Property Clause, Congress is empowered "to promote the Progress of Science and the useful Arts, by securing for limited Times to Authors and Inventors the exclusive Right to their respective Writings and Discoveries." U.S. Const., art. I, §8 cl. 8. This power, while broad, is not unlimited. More than a century ago, the Supreme Court held that Congress could not exercise its Intellectual Property power to grant exclusive rights in matters other than "writings" or "discoveries" such that the Trademark Act of 1876 was not a proper exercise of Congress' Intellectual Property power.[7] *The Trade-Mark Cases*, 100 US 82, 93-94 (1879). Congress may not, for example, grant exclusive rights to writings that do not constitute original works of authorship. *Feist Publ'ns v. Rural Tel. Serv. Co.*, 499 US 340 *[1 ILR (P&F) 180]* (1991). Similarly, the Intellectual Property Clause limits Congress' powers so that patents may only be granted in new inventions that are not obvious in view of the existing art and Congress may not authorize the issuance of a patent whose effects are to remove existing knowledge from the public domain. *Graham v. John Deere Co. of Kan. City*, 383 US 1, 6 (1966).

Under the Commerce Clause, Congress' power is quite broad. Congress may regulate the use of the channels of interstate commerce; may regulate and protect the instrumentalities of interstate commerce, including persons or things in interstate commerce; and may regulate those activities having a substantial relation to, or which substantially affect, interstate commerce. *Lopez*, 514 US at 558-59. Once again, however, the power is not unlimited and Congress does not have the authority to legislate matters that are of such a local character that there is too remote a connection to interstate commerce. *Id.* at 559. Both parties also agree that, as broad as Congress' Commerce Power is, Congress may not use that power in such a way as to override or circumvent another constitutional restraint. *Ry. Labor Executives' Ass'n v. Gibbons*, 455 US 457 (1982) (striking down an act by Congress under the Commerce Clause that violated the Bankruptcy Clause's uniformity requirement). First Amendment Reply at 13; Opposition at 14.

Defendant argues that Congress exceeded its powers under the Intellectual Property Clause in enacting the DMCA. The government responds that Congress used its Commerce Power to regulate trafficking in devices for gain. Thus, the issue presented is whether the DMCA was within Congress' Commerce Power, generally, and if so, whether Congress was nevertheless prohibited from enacting the DMCA because of other restraints on Congress' power imposed by the Intellectual Property Clause.

With regard to the first issue, Congress plainly has the power to enact the DMCA under the Commerce Clause. "The commerce power 'is the power to regulate; that is, to prescribe the rule by which commerce is to be governed. This power, like all others vested in Congress, is complete in itself, may be exercised to its utmost extend, and acknowledges no limitations, other than are prescribed by the Constitution.'" *Lopez*, 514 US at 553 (citing *Gibbons v. Ogden*, 9 Wheat. 1, 196, 6 L Ed 23 (1824)). The DMCA prohibits conduct that has a substantial effect on commerce between the states and commerce with foreign nations. Trafficking in or the marketing of circumvention devices "for gain," as proscribed by Sections 1201(b) and 1204, has a direct effect on interstate commerce. To the extent that circumvention devices enable wrongdoers to engage in on-line piracy by unlawfully copying and distributing copyrighted works of authorship, the sale of such devices has a direct effect on suppressing the market for legitimate copies of the works. Accordingly, there is a rational basis for concluding that the regulated activity sufficiently affects interstate commerce to establish that Congress had authority under the Commerce Clause to enact the legislation. *Lopez*, 514 US at 557; *United States v. Moghadam*, 175 F3d 1269, 1276-77 (11th Cir 1999) (finding the anti-bootlegging statute to have a sufficient connection to interstate and foreign commerce to meet the *Lopez* test).

The more difficult question, however, is whether Congress was nevertheless precluded from enacting the DMCA by restraints imposed by the Intellectual Property Clause. The Eleventh Circuit was presented with this same issue in the context of the anti-bootlegging statute in *Moghadam*, 175 F3d 1269. The statute in that case prohibited persons from making unauthorized recordings of live performances, in effect, granting copyright-like protection to live performances. The defendant challenged the constitutionality of the statute, contending that the Intellectual Property power extended only to "writings" and "inventions," and that a live performance was not a "writing." The government argued that the statute was a valid exercise of Congress' Commerce Power. In a well-reasoned opinion, the Eleventh Circuit first analyzed Supreme Court precedents that could be read to conflict with each other—*The Trade-Mark Cases*, 100 US 82 (1879), *Heart of Atlanta Motel, Inc. v. United States*, 379 US 241 (1964), and *Railway Labor Executives' Association v. Gibbons*, 455 US 457 (1982)—and then resolved the tension in those cases to decide the case before it.

> We note that there is some tension between the former line of cases (*Heart of Atlanta Motel*, the *Trade-Mark Cases* and *Authors League* [*of America, Inc. v. Oman*, 790 F2d 220 (2d Cir 1986)]) and the *Railway Labor Executives* case. The former cases suggest that in some circumstances the Commerce Clause can be used by Congress to accomplish something that the [Intellectual Property] Clause might not allow. But the *Railway Labor Executives* case suggests that in some circumstances the Commerce Clause cannot be used to eradicate a limitation placed upon Congressional power in another grant of power.

Moghadam, 175 F3d at 1279-80. The court then resolved the tension as follows:

> [W]e take as a given that there are some circumstances, as illustrated by *Railway Labor Executives*, in which the Commerce Clause cannot be used by Congress to eradicate a limitation placed upon Congress in another grant of power. For the reasons that follow, we hold that the instant case is not one such circumstance. We hold that the [Intellectual Property] Clause does not envision that Congress is positively forbidden from extending copyright-like protection under other constitutional clauses, such as the Commerce Clause, to works of authorship that may not meet the fixation requirement inherent in the term "Writings." The grant itself is stated in positive terms, and does not imply any negative pregnant that suggests that the term "Writings" operates as a ceiling on Congress' ability to legislate pursuant to other grants. Extending quasi-copyright protection to unfixed live musical performances is in no way inconsistent with the [Intellectual Property] Clause, even if that Clause itself does not expressly authorize such protection. Quite the contrary, extending such protection actually complements and is in harmony with the existing scheme that Congress has set up under the [Intellectual Property] Clause. A live musical performance clearly satisfies the originality requirement. Extending quasi-copyright protection also furthers the purpose of the [Intellectual Property] Clause to promote the progress of the useful arts by securing some exclusive rights to the creative author. . . .
>
> For the foregoing reasons, we conclude that extending copyright-like protection in the instant case is not fundamentally inconsistent with the fixation requirement of the [Intellectual Property] Clause. By contrast, the nonuniform bankruptcy statute at issue in *Railway Labor Executives* was irreconcilably inconsistent with the uniformity requirement of the Bankruptcy Clause of the Constitution.

Id., 175 F3d at 1280-81.

Accordingly, *Moghadam* provides an instructive guide and analytical framework for resolving the constitutional question posed. If the statute passed by Congress "is not fundamentally inconsistent with" the Intellectual Property clause and is otherwise within Congress' Commerce Power to enact, then the statute is not an unconstitutional exercise of congressional power. On the other hand, if the statute is "irreconcilably inconsistent" with a requirement of another constitutional provision, then the enactment exceeds congressional authority even if otherwise authorized by the Commerce Clause. With this teaching in mind, the court turns to the DMCA and the Intellectual Property Clause.

The first issue is to determine whether the DMCA is "not fundamentally inconsistent" with the purpose of the Intellectual Property Clause. The purpose of the Intellectual Property Clause is to promote the useful arts and sciences. Thus, the government is empowered to grant exclusive rights to inventors and authors in their respective inventions and original works of authorship, for limited times. This allows the inventor/author a reasonable time in which to reap the economic fruits of his or her inventive or creative labor. As a result of this economic incentive, people are encouraged to engage in inventive and originally expressive endeavors, thereby promoting the arts and sciences. In addition, because the grant of property rights is to be of limited duration, the public will generally benefit, once the exclusive rights expire and the invention or expression becomes dedicated to the public.

According to the government's brief, the DMCA and its legislative history demonstrate that Congress' intent was to protect intellectual property rights and thus promote the same purposes served by the Intellectual Property Clause. The government specifically argues that

[a]s reflected in the legislative history of the DMCA, Congress recognized that while the purpose of the DMCA was to protect intellectual property rights, the means of doing so involved a dramatic shift from the regulation of the use of information to the regulation of the devices by which information is delivered. 144 Cong. Rec. E2136-2. For this reason, the legislators viewed the legislation as "paracopyright" legislation that could be enacted under the Commerce Clause. *Id.* at 2137. Such a step by Congress to protect the market for digital content as an action under the Commerce

Clause cannot be said to override Constitutional restraints of the Intellectual Property Clause, because Congress' fundamental motivation was to protect rights granted under the Intellectual Property Clause in the digital world. Congress recognized that traditional intellectual property laws regulating the use of information border on unenforceable in the digital world; only regulation of the devices by which information is delivered will successfully save constitutionally guaranteed intellectual property rights. *See* S. Rep. 105-190, at 8 ("Due to the ease with which digital works can be copied and distributed worldwide virtually instantaneously, copyright owners will hesitate to make their works readily available on the Internet without reasonable assurance that they will be protected against massive piracy.")

Opposition at 15.

The argument carries some weight. Protecting the exclusive rights granted to copyright owners against unlawful piracy by preventing trafficking in tools that would enable widespread piracy and unlawful infringement is consistent with the purpose of the Intellectual Property Clause's grant to Congress of the power to "promote the useful arts and sciences" by granting exclusive rights to authors in their writings. [8] In addition, Congress did not ban the use of circumvention tools out of a concern that enacting such a ban would unduly restrict the fair use doctrine and expressly sought to preserve fair use. *See* 17 USC §1201(c). Therefore, on the whole, the DMCA's anti-device provisions are not fundamentally inconsistent with the Intellectual Property Clause.

The second half of the analysis is to determine whether the DMCA is nevertheless "irreconcilably inconsistent" with a limitation contained within the Intellectual Property Clause. Here, defendant and the amici curiae make several arguments, some of which have already been addressed. Defendant and the amici curiae contend that the DMCA is irreconcilably inconsistent with the Intellectual Property Clause because: 1) the Act eliminates fair use; 2) the Act allows publishers to recapture works from the public domain and obtain copyright-like protection in those works; and 3) the Act violates the "limited times" clause by effectively granting copyright owners perpetual rights to protect their works.

The first two contentions have been addressed, and rejected, above. While the DMCA may make certain fair uses more difficult for digital works of authorship published with use restrictions, fair use has not been eliminated. Similarly, the argument that Congress' ban on the sale of circumvention tools has the effect of allowing publishers to claim copyright-like protection in public domain works is tenuous and unpersuasive. Nothing within the DMCA grants any rights to anyone in any public domain work. A public domain work remains in the public domain and any person may make use of the public domain work for any purpose.

Finally, the DMCA does not allow a copyright owner to effectively prevent an ebook from ever entering the public domain, despite the expiration of the copyright. *See* Amici EFF Brief at 16. Upon the expiration of the copyright, there is no longer any protectable intellectual property right in the work's expression. The expression may be copied, quoted, republished in new format and sold, without any legally enforceable restriction on the use of the expression. The publisher/copyright owner has no right to prevent any user from using the work any way the user prefers. At best, the publisher has a technological measure embedded within the digital product precluding certain uses of that particular copy of the work and, in many cases, the user/ purchaser has acquiesced in this restriction when purchasing/licensing the work. *See* End User License Agreements, O'Connell Decl. Exhs. A-D. The essence of a copyright is the legally enforceable exclusive rights to reproduce and distribute copies of an original work of authorship, to make derivative works, and to perform the work publicly, for a limited period of time. 17 USC §§106, 302-303. None of those rights is extended beyond the statutory term merely by prohibiting the trafficking in or marketing of devices primarily designed to circumvent use restrictions on works in electronic form.

Accordingly, the DMCA does not run afoul of any restraint on Congress' power imposed by the Intellectual Property Clause. Section 1201(b) of the DMCA was within Congress' Commerce Power to enact, and because it is not irreconcilably inconsistent with any provision of the Intellectual Property Clause, Congress did not exceed its constitutional authority in enacting the law.

CONCLUSION

For the foregoing reasons, defendant's motions to dismiss the indictment on constitutional grounds are DENIED.

---

[1] The purchases are frequently accompanied by an End User License Agreement which may contain contractual language limiting the user's rights to use the ebook, including the rights to sell or transfer the ebook or to copy or distribute the content of the ebook without the publisher's permission. *See* Declaration of O'Connell, Exh. A (EBIA Agreement, ¶4), Exh. B. (Sybex Agreement, ¶2), Exh. C (Forth Inc. Agreement, Part III).

[2] Adobe distributes the eBook Reader program free of charge and users download the software directly from the Internet onto their computers.

[3] Congress also enacted specific provisions to protect certain uses, including exceptions for law enforcement, reverse engineering, encryption research and security testing. 17 USC §1201(e)-(g) and 1201(f).

[4] The [sic] is no direct authority for the proposition that the doctrine of fair use is coextensive with the First Amendment, such that "fair use" is a First Amendment right. As noted by the Second Circuit, "the Supreme Court has never held that fair use is constitutionally required, although some isolated statements in its opinions might arguably be enlisted for such a requirement." *Corley*, 273 F2d at 458. There is plainly a tension between the First Amendment's command that "Congress shall make no law . . . abridging the freedom of speech" and the copyright laws which grant limited monopolies to authors to publish and profit from their original works of authorship. 1 M.B. Nimmer & D. Nimmer, *Nimmer on Copyright*, §1.10[A] at 1-61.55 to 1-61.56. Several courts have recognized that the limitations on copyright, such as the idea-expression dichotomy and to some extent fair use, are what serve to protect First Amendment interests. *See Harper & Row*, 471 US at 560; *Campbell v. Acuff-Rose Music, Inc.*, 510 US 569 (1994) (noting that some opportunity for fair use has been thought necessary to fulfill copyright's purpose of promoting the progress of science and the useful arts). The Supreme Court has also described the doctrine as an "equitable rule of reason." *Sony Corp. of Am. v. Universal City Studios, Inc.*, 464 US 417, 448 (1984). So too, the Ninth Circuit has never held that fair use is a right guaranteed by the First Amendment. *L. A. News Serv. v. Tullo*, 973 F2d 791 (9th Cir 1992), relied on by defendant, did not hold that "fair use" is a constitutional right under the First Amendment, although it did recognize that First Amendment concerns

are addressed in the copyright field through the idea/ expression dichotomy and the fair use doctrine. *Id.* at 795. *See also Connectix*, 203 F3d at 602-03 (discussing fair use with no mention of First Amendment underpinnings); *Dr. Seuss Enters., L.P. v. Penguin Books USA, Inc.*, 109 F3d 1394, 1399 (9th Cir) (fair use is an equitable rule of reason requiring the careful balancing of multiple factors in light of the purposes of copyright), *cert. dismissed*, 521 US 1146 (1997).

[5]   Defendant's vagueness challenge thus appears to erroneously challenge Section 1201(a)(2)'s prohibition on trafficking in technology that is primarily designed to circumvent access restrictions, rather than Section 1201(b)'s ban on trafficking in devices that circumvent use restrictions. The language of the two statutes is similar, however, and the court will treat the argument as if asserted against Section 1201(b).

[6]   Defendant appears to contend that the legal complexity of a statute may render it unconstitutionally vague, but cites no authority in support of that assertion. If legal complexity is sufficient to support a vagueness challenge, the Internal Revenue Code would almost certainly have been struck down long ago.

[7]   The Court also held that the Trademark Act could not have been enacted pursuant to Congress' Commerce Powers, but that aspect of the Court's holding was superseded by the development of the Court's Commerce Clause jurisprudence over the next 100 years.

[8]   Nevertheless, the argument also stretches too far. Under that same reasoning, Congress would be authorized to extend perpetual copyrights, a result plainly prohibited by the "Limited Times" clause. *See Moghadam* 175 F3d at 1281 (noting that the "Limited Times" requirement of the Intellectual Property clause forbids Congress from conferring intellectual property rights of perpetual duration, citing *Pennock v. Dialogue*, 27 US (2 Pet.) 1, 16-17, 7 L Ed 327, 333 (1829)).

Universal City Studios, Inc.
v.
Reimerdes

**United States District Court,
Southern District of New York**

February 2, 2000

4 ILR (P&F) 399, 82 F Supp 2d 211

00 Civ. 0277 (LAK)

Motion picture copyright; enjoining distribution of DVD-encryption-cracking software.

Defendants are enjoined pursuant to the anti-circumvention provisions of the Digital Millennium Copyright Act from distributing via their Internet web sites a computer program that permits users to decrypt and copy plaintiffs' copyrighted motion pictures from digital versatile disks (DVD). The likelihood that continued distribution of defendants' cracking program (DeCSS) would result in infringement of plaintiffs' copyrights established irreparable injury; plaintiffs had an extremely high likelihood of success on the merits; and, were the court required to conduct such a balancing, the hardship likely to befall defendants (mere delay) were the injunction improperly granted was greatly outweighed by the likely economic loss to plaintiffs were the injunction improperly withheld. That the injunction constituted a prior restraint on speech did not render it objectionable in light of the minimal free speech interests involved and the all but incalculable damage that could be suffered were it withheld. — **Universal City Studios, Inc. v. Reimerdes, 4 ILR (P&F) 399 [SD NY, 2000].**

Digital Millennium Copyright Act exceptions; distribution of DVD-encryption-cracking software.

Defendants, individuals who desired to distribute via their Internet web sites a computer program (DeCSS) that permits users to decrypt and copy plaintiffs' copyrighted motion pictures from digital versatile disks (DVD), were not exempted from the coverage of the anti-circumvention provisions of the Digital Millennium Copyright Act by that statute's own exceptions. Defendants were not covered by the "service providers" exception, since it did not appear that they were providers of Internet services and since that exception provides protection only from liability for copyright infringement, not from the anti-circumvention provisions. Defendants did not qualify for the Reverse Engineering exception, since their contention that DeCSS was necessary to achieve interoperability between computers running on the LINUX system and DVDs was unsupported, misdirected (in that the program ran also under Windows, a much more common operating system, and therefore could not be said to have been developed "solely" as a LINUX interoperability application), and immaterial (since the legislative history of the DMCA makes it clear that it authorizes reverse engineering but not circumvention of security systems). Further, there was no evidence to suggest that defendants' activities were undertaken as part of a program of good faith encryption research or security testing. — **Universal City Studios, Inc. v. Reimerdes, 4 ILR (P&F) 399 [SD NY, 2000].**

Distribution of DVD-encryption-cracking software; fair use.

Defendants in an action seeking to enjoin distribution via defendants' Internet web sites of a computer program (DeCSS) that permits users to decrypt and copy plaintiffs' copyrighted motion pictures from digital versatile disks (DVD) could not claim protection under the "fair use" doctrine since they were sued not for copyright infringement but for offering to the public technology primarily designed to circumvent technological measures that control access to copyrighted works. — **Universal City Studios, Inc. v. Reimerdes, 4 ILR (P&F) 399 [SD NY, 2000].**

DVD encryption cracking; Constitutional considerations.

The anti-circumvention provisions of the Digital Millennium Copyright Act are not unconstitutional as applied to prevent the distribution by web site operators of a computer program (DeCSS) that permits users to decrypt and copy copyrighted motion pictures from digital versatile disks (DVD). Even if the program constituted speech protected by the First Amendment (which was far from clear), restriction of the dissemination of cracking programs was within Congress's authority under the Copyright and Necessary and Proper Clauses; Congress's conclusion in enacting the DMCA that the restriction of technologies for the circumvention of technological copyright protections would facilitate the robust development and worldwide expansion of electronic commerce, communications, research, development, and education could not be dismissed as unreasonable. Moreover, the computer code at issue did little to advance the goals of free speech, achievement of a democratic society and discouragement of social violence. — **Universal City Studios, Inc. v. Reimerdes, 4 ILR (P&F) 399 [SD NY, 2000].**

MEMORANDUM OPINION

Appearances:

Leon P. Gold, Jon Baumgarten, William M. Hart, Kenneth Rubenstein, PROSAKUER ROSE LLP, Attorneys for Plaintiffs.

Peter L. Katz, Robin D. Gross, Allonn E. Levy, HUBER & SAMUELSON PC, Attorneys for Defendants.

LEWIS A. KAPLAN, District Judge. This case is another step in the evolution of the law of copyright occasioned by advances in technology. Plaintiff motion picture studios brought this action to enjoin defendants from providing a computer program on their Internet Web sites that permits users to decrypt and copy plaintiffs' copyrighted motion pictures from digital versatile disks ("DVDs"). They rely on the recently enacted Digital Millennium Copyright Act ("DMCA"). [1]

On January 20, 2000, the Court granted plaintiffs' motion for a preliminary injunction and indicated that this opinion would follow.

Facts

Plaintiffs in this case are eight major motion picture studios which are engaged in the business of producing, manufacturing and/or distributing copyrighted and copyrightable material, including motion pictures. Motion pictures usually are first released for theatrical distribution and later to consumers in "home video" formats such as videotape, laserdisc and, most recently, DVD.

DVDs

DVDs are five-inch wide discs that, in this application, hold full-length motion pictures. They are the latest technology for private home viewing of recorded motion pictures. This technology drastically improves the clarity and overall quality of a motion picture shown on a television or computer screen.

CSS

DVDs contain motion pictures in digital form, which presents an enhanced risk of unauthorized reproduction and distribution because digital copies made from DVDs do not degrade from generation to generation. Concerned about this risk, motion picture companies, including plaintiffs, insisted upon the development of an access control and copy prevention system to inhibit the unauthorized reproduction and distribution of motion pictures before they released films in the DVD format. The means now in use, Content Scramble System or CSS, is an encryption-based security and authentication system that requires the use of appropriately configured hardware such as a DVD player or a computer DVD drive to decrypt, unscramble and play back, but not copy, motion pictures on DVDs. CSS has been licensed to hundreds of DVD player manufacturers and DVD content distributors in the United States and around the world.

CSS has facilitated enormous growth in the use of DVDs for the distribution of copyrighted movies to consumers. DVD movies first were introduced in the United States in 1996. Over 4,000 motion pictures now have been released in that format in the United States, and movies are being issued on DVDs at the rate of over 40 new titles per month in addition to rereleases of classic films. More than 5 million DVD players have been sold, and DVD disc sales now exceed one million units per week.

DeCSS

In October 1999, an individual or group, believed to be in Europe, managed to "hack" CSS[2] and began offering, via the Internet, a software utility called DeCSS that enables users to break the CSS copy protection system and hence to make and distribute digital copies of DVD movies.

The Motion Picture Association of America ("MPAA") almost immediately acted under the provisions of the DMCA by demanding that Internet service providers remove DeCSS from their servers and, where the identities of the individuals responsible were known, that those individuals stop posting DeCSS. These efforts succeeded in removing a considerable share of the known postings of DeCSS.

On December 29, 1999, the licensor of CSS, DVD CCA, commenced a state court action in California for the misappropriation of its trade secrets as embodied in the DeCSS software. On the same day, the state court judge without explanation denied the plaintiff's motion for a temporary restraining order.[3] Members of the hacker community then stepped up efforts to distribute DeCSS to the widest possible audience in an apparent attempt to preclude effective judicial relief. One individual even announced a contest with prizes (copies of DVDs) for the greatest number of copies of DeCSS distributed, for the most elegant distribution method, and for the "lowest tech" method.

Defendants

Defendants each are associated with Web sites that were distributing DeCSS at the time plaintiffs moved for injunctive relief. Internet registry information indicates that defendant Shawn Reimerdes owns and is the administrative, technical and billing contact for a Web site bearing the domain name dvd-copy.com. Defendant Roman Kazan is listed as the technical contact for krackdown.com and the technical, administrative and zone contact for escape.com, which are registered to Krackdown and Kazan Corporation, respectively. Defendant Eric Corley, a/k/a Emmanuel Goldstein, is similarly

listed for a Web site with the domain name 2600.com, registered to 2600 Magazine. None of the defendants submitted any evidence in opposition to the motion, and the Court in all the circumstances infers that each personally has been involved in providing and distributing DeCSS over the Internet via these Web sites.

Discussion

In order to obtain a preliminary injunction, the movant must show "(a) irreparable harm, and (b) either (1) a likelihood of success on the merits, or (2) sufficiently serious questions going to the merits to make them fair grounds for litigation and a balance of hardships tipping decidedly in its favor."[4]

A. Irreparable Injury

The requirement of immediate and irreparable injury is satisfied in this case. Copyright infringement is presumed to give rise to such harm.[5] In this case, plaintiffs do not allege that defendants have infringed their copyrights, but rather that defendants offer technology that circumvents their copyright protection system and thus facilitates infringement. For purposes of the irreparable injury inquiry, this is a distinction without a difference. If plaintiffs are correct on the merits, they face substantially the same immediate and irreparable injury from defendants' posting of DeCSS as they would if defendants were infringing directly. Moreover, just as in the case of direct copyright infringement, the extent of the harm plaintiffs will suffer as a result of defendants' alleged activities cannot readily be measured, suggesting that the injury truly would be irreparable.[6]

B. Likelihood of Success

Plaintiffs' sole claim is for violation of the anti-circumvention provisions of the DMCA. They contend that plaintiffs' posting of DeCSS violates Section 1201(a)(2) of the statute, which prohibits unauthorized offering of products that circumvent technological measures that effectively control access to copyrighted works. Defendants respond that (1) they have been named improperly as defendants, (2) the posting of DeCSS falls within one of the DMCA exceptions and is not illegal under the statute, (3) application of the DMCA to prohibit posting of DeCSS violates defendants' First Amendment rights, and (4) a preliminary injunction would constitute an unlawful prior restraint on protected speech.

1. Defendants Are Properly Named

Defendants contend that plaintiffs' claim against all three defendants must be dismissed because defendants are not the owners of the Web sites containing the offending material and therefore are not the "real parties in interest." They rely on Rule 17 of the Federal Rules of Civil Procedure. [7]

In relevant part, Federal Rule 17 states that "[e]very action shall be *prosecuted* in the name of the real party in interest." [8] This rule does not apply to defendants, as they are not prosecuting this action. Further, whether defendants own the Web sites at issue is not dispositive of anything. Plaintiffs claim that defendants' conduct violates the DMCA. If plaintiffs make such a showing, they will win on the merits. If they fail, defendants will be absolved of liability. As defendants have failed to submit affidavits or other materials indicating that they had nothing to do with the offending Web sites, the Court infers from the evidence before it, for the purpose of this motion, that they are responsible for the content of the sites. Of course, plaintiffs will bear the burden of proof on this issue at trial. [9]

2. DMCA Violation

Section 1201(a)(2) of the Copyright Act, part of the DMCA, provides that:

"No person shall . . . offer to the public, provide or otherwise traffic in any technology . . . that—

"(A) is primarily designed or produced for the purpose of circumventing a technological measure that effectively controls access to a work protected under [the Copyright Act];

"(B) has only limited commercially significant purpose or use other than to circumvent a technological measure that effectively controls access to a work protected under [the Copyright Act]; or

"(C) is marketed by that person or another acting in concert with that person with that person's knowledge for use in circumventing a technological measure that effectively controls access to a work protected under [the Copyright Act]." [10]

"[C]ircumvent a technological measure" is defined to mean descrambling a scrambled work, decrypting an encrypted work, or "otherwise to avoid, bypass, remove, deactivate, or impair a technological measure, without the authority of the copyright owner." [11] The statute explains further that "a technological measure 'effectively controls access to a work' if the measure, in the ordinary course of its operation, requires the application of information or a process or a treatment, with the authority of the copyright owner, to gain access to a work." [12]

Here, it is perfectly clear that CSS is a technological measure that effectively controls access to plaintiffs' copyrighted movies because it requires the application of information or a process, with the authority of the copyright owner, to gain access to those works. Indeed, defendants conceded in their memorandum that one cannot in the ordinary course gain access to the copyrighted works on plaintiffs' DVDs without a "player key" issued by the DVD CCA that permits unscrambling the contents of the disks. [13] It is undisputed also that DeCSS defeats CSS and decrypts copyrighted works without the authority of the copyright owners. As there is no evidence of any commercially significant purpose of DeCSS other than circumvention of CSS, defendants' actions likely violated Section 1201(a)(2)(B). Moreover, although defendants contended at oral argument that DeCSS was not designed primarily to circumvent CSS, that argument is exceptionally unpersuasive. [14] In consequence, plaintiffs have an extremely high likelihood of prevailing on the merits unless defendants' activities come within one of the exceptions in the DMCA or unless there is a constitutional impediment to this conclusion.

Defendants contend that their activities come within several exceptions contained in the DMCA and the Copyright Act and constitute fair use under the Copyright Act. They are unlikely to prevail on any of these contentions.

a. Service Provider Exception

Defendant Roman Kazan alone argues that his conduct falls under Section 512(c) of the Copyright Act, [15] which provides limited protection from liability for copyright infringement by certain service providers for information resident on a system or network owned or controlled by them. [16] This argument fails for several reasons.

First, Mr. Kazan offered no proof that he is a service provider within the meaning of Section 512(c). [17] But that point ultimately is unnecessary to the result.

Section 512(c) provides protection only from liability for copyright infringement.[18] Plaintiffs seek to hold defendants liable not for copyright infringement, but for a violation of Section 1201(a)(2), which applies only to circumvention products and technologies. Section 512(c) thus does not apply here.

b. Reverse Engineering Exception

Defendants claim also to fall under Section 1201(f) of the statute, which provides that, notwithstanding Section 1201(a)(2)—

"a person who has lawfully obtained the right to use a copy of a computer program may circumvent a technological measure that effectively controls access to a particular portion of that program for the sole purpose of identifying and analyzing those elements of the program that are necessary to achieve interoperability of an independently created computer program with other programs . . . to the extent that any such acts of identification and analysis do not constitute infringement under this title."[19]

They contend that DeCSS is necessary to achieve interoperability between computers running on the Linux system and DVDs and that this exception therefore is satisfied.[20] This contention fails for three reasons.

First, defendants have offered no evidence to support this assertion.

Second, even assuming that DeCSS runs under Linux, it concededly runs under Windows—a far more widely used operating system—as well. It therefore cannot reasonably be said that DeCSS was developed "for the sole purpose" of achieving interoperability between Linux and DVDs.

Finally, and most important, the legislative history makes it abundantly clear that Section 1201(f) permits reverse engineering of copyrighted computer programs only and does not authorize circumvention of technological systems that control access to other copyrighted works, such as movies.[21] In consequence, the reverse engineering exception does not apply.

c. Encryption Research

Section 1201(g) provides in relevant part that:

"Notwithstanding the provisions of subsection (a)(2), it is not a violation of that subsection for a person to—

"(A) develop and employ technological means to circumvent a technological measure for the sole purpose of that person performing the acts of good faith encryption research described in paragraph (2); and

"(B) provide the technological means to another person with whom he or she is working collaboratively for the purpose of conducting the acts of good faith encryption research described in paragraph (2) or for the purpose of having that other person verify his or her acts of good faith encryption research described in paragraph (2)."[22]

Paragraph (2) in relevant part permits circumvention of technological measures in the course of good faith encryption research if:

"(A) the person lawfully obtained the encrypted copy, phonorecord, performance, or display of the published work;

"(B) such act is necessary to conduct such encryption research;

"(C) the person made a good faith effort to obtain authorization before the circumvention; and

"(D) such act does not constitute infringement under this title . . . ."[23]

In determining whether one is engaged in good faith encryption research, the Court is instructed to consider factors including whether the results of the putative encryption research are disseminated in a manner designed to advance the state of knowledge of encryption technology versus facilitation of copyright infringement, whether the person in question is engaged in legitimate study of or work in encryption, and whether the results of the research are communicated in a timely fashion to the copyright owner.[24]

There has been a complete failure of proof by defendants on all of these factors. There is no evidence that any of them is engaged in encryption research, let alone good faith encryption research. It appears that DeCSS is being distributed in a manner specifically intended to facilitate copyright infringement. There is no evidence that defendants have made any effort to provide the results of the DeCSS effort to the copyright owners. Surely there is no suggestion that any of them made a good faith effort to obtain authorization from the copyright owners. Accordingly, plaintiffs are likely to prevail in their contention that defendants' activities are not protected by Section 1201(g).

d. Security testing

Defendants contend also that their actions should be considered exempt security testing under Section 1201(j) of the statute.[25] This exception, however, is limited to "assessing a computer, computer system, or computer network, solely for the purpose of good faith testing, investigating, or correcting [of a] security flaw or vulnerability, with the authorization of the owner or operator of such computer system or computer network."[26]

The record does not indicate that DeCSS has anything to do with testing computers, computer systems, or computer networks. Certainly defendants sought, and plaintiffs' granted, no authorization for defendants' activities. This exception therefore has no bearing in this case.

e. Fair use

Finally, defendants claim that they are engaged in a fair use under Section 107 of the Copyright Act.[27] They are mistaken. Section 107 of the Act provides in critical part that certain uses of copyrighted works that otherwise would be wrongful are "not . . . infringement[s] of copyright."[28] Defendants, however, are not here sued for copyright infringement. They are sued for offering to the public and providing technology primarily designed to circumvent technological measures that control access to copyrighted works and otherwise violating Section 1201(a)(2) of the Act. If Congress had meant the fair use defense to apply to such actions, it would have said so.

3. Constitutionality of DMCA

Defendants contend that the DeCSS computer program is protected speech and that the DMCA, at least insofar as it purports to prohibit the dissemination of DeCSS to the public, violates the First Amendment.

As a preliminary matter, it is far from clear that DeCSS is speech protected by the First Amendment.

In material respects, it is merely a set of instructions that controls computers.[29] Courts that have considered the question whether program code is constitutionally protected expression have divided on the point.[30] Nevertheless, this Court assumes for purposes of this motion, although it does not decide, that even the executable code is sufficiently expressive to merit some constitutional protection. That, however, is only the beginning of the analysis.

a. Constitutionality of the DMCA

As some commentators have said, "Copyright law restricts speech: it restricts you from writing, painting, publicly performing, or otherwise communicating what you please."[31] And though it might conceivably be argued that the First Amendment, which was adopted after the ratification of the Constitution itself, trumped the Copyright Clause and forbids all restraint or punishment of copyright infringement,[32] this argument has been rejected by the Supreme Court, which views the Bill of Rights and the original Constitution as a single instrument and has made it unmistakably clear that the First Amendment does not shield copyright infringement.[33] Indeed, copyright is an "engine of free expression" because it "supplies the economic incentive to create and disseminate ideas."[34] To the extent there is any tension between free speech and protection of copyright, the Court has found it to be accommodated fully by traditional fair use doctrine,[35] with expression prohibited by the Copyright Act and not within the fair use exception considered unprotected by the First Amendment.[36]

The conclusion that copyright infringement may be proscribed consistently with the First Amendment does not end the inquiry, however. This case concerns the DMCA rather than the older aspects of the Copyright Act. The DMCA sweeps more broadly by prohibiting production and dissemination of technology that can circumvent measures taken to protect copyright, not merely infringement of copyright itself. It is a prophylactic measure. In consequence, further First Amendment analysis of the DMCA is warranted. Nevertheless, the DMCA appears to be a legitimate exercise of Congress' power.

The Copyright Clause empowers Congress "[t]o promote the Progress of Science and useful Arts, by securing for limited Times to Authors . . . the

exclusive Right to their respective Writings . . . ." [37]
The Necessary and Proper Clause further provides
that Congress may "make all Laws which shall be
necessary and proper for carrying into Execution
the foregoing Powers . . . ." [38] Hence, the Necessary
and Proper Clause grants Congress the power to do
that which is necessary and proper to prevent others
from publishing protected writings for the duration
of the copyright.

The scope of Congress' power under the
Necessary and Proper Clause is broad. As Chief
Justice Marshall wrote in *McCulloch v. Maryland*, [39]
"Let the end be legitimate, let it be within the scope
of the Constitution, and all means which are
appropriate, which are plainly adapted to that end,
which are not prohibited but consistent with the letter
and spirit of the constitution, are constitutional." [40]
Moreover, the Supreme Court has made clear that
Congress should be accorded substantial deference
in determining how best to protect copyright in an
age of rapid technological change. [41]

In enacting the DMCA, Congress found that the
restriction of technologies for the circumvention of
technological means of protecting copyrighted
works "facilitate[s] the robust development and
world-wide expansion of electronic commerce,
communications, research, development, and
education" by "mak[ing] digital networks safe places
to disseminate and exploit copyrighted materials." [42]
That view can not be dismissed as unreasonable.
Section 1201(a)(2) of the DMCA therefore is a
proper exercise of Congress' power under the
Necessary and Proper Clause.

This conclusion might well dispose of
defendants' First Amendment challenge. Given
Congress' justifiable view that the DMCA is
instrumental in carrying out the objective of the
Copyright Clause, there arguably is no First
Amendment objection to prohibiting the
dissemination of means for circumventing
technological methods for controlling access to
copyrighted works. But the Court need not rest on
this alone.

In determining the constitutionality of
governmental restriction on speech, courts
traditionally have balanced the public interest in the
restriction against the public interest in the kind of
speech at issue. [43] This approach seeks to determine,
in light of the goals of the First Amendment, how

much protection the speech at issue merits. It then
examines the underlying rationale for the challenged
regulation and assesses how best to accommodate
the relative weights of the interests in free speech
interest and the regulation. [44]

As Justice Brandeis wrote, freedom of speech
is important both as a means to achieve a democratic
society and as an end in itself. [45] Further, it
discourages social violence by permitting people to
seek redress of their grievances through meaningful,
non-violent expression. [46] These goals have been
articulated often and consistently in the case law.

The computer code at issue in this case does
little to serve these goals. Although this Court has
assumed that DeCSS has at least some expressive
content, the expressive aspect appears to be minimal
when compared to its functional component. [47]
Computer code primarily is a set of instructions
which, when read by the computer, cause it to
function in a particular way, in this case, to render
intelligible a data file on a DVD. It arguably "is
best treated as a virtual machine . . . ." [48]

On the other side of this balance lie the interests
served by the DMCA. Copyright protection exists
to "encourage individual effort by personal gain" [49]
and thereby "advance public welfare" [50] through the
"promot[ion of] the Progress of Science and useful
Arts." [51] The DMCA plainly was designed with these
goals in mind. It is a tool to protect copyright in the
digital age. It responds to the risks of technological
circumvention of access controlling mechanisms
designed to protect copyrighted works distributed
in digital form. It is designed to further precisely
the goals articulated above, goals of unquestionably
high social value.

This is quite clear in the specific context of this
case. Plaintiffs are eight major motion picture
studios which together are largely responsible for
the development of the American film industry.
Their products reach hundreds of millions of viewers
internationally and doubtless are responsible for a
substantial portion of the revenue in the international
film industry each year. To doubt the contribution
of plaintiffs to the progress of the arts would be
absurd. DVDs are the newest way to distribute
motion pictures to the home market, and their
popularity is growing rapidly. The security of DVD
technology is central to the continued distribution
of motion pictures in this format. The dissemination

and use of circumvention technologies such as DeCSS would permit anyone to make flawless copies of DVDs at little expense.[52] Without effective limits on these technologies, copyright protection in the contents of DVDs would become meaningless and the continued marketing of DVDs impractical. This obviously would discourage artistic progress and undermine the goals of copyright.

The balance between these two interests is clear. Executable computer code of the type at issue in this case does little to further traditional First Amendment interests. The DMCA, in contrast, fits squarely within the goals of copyright, both generally and as applied to DeCSS. In consequence, the balance of interests in this case falls decidedly on the side of plaintiffs and the DMCA.

b. Distribution of DeCSS as Part of a Course of Conduct in Violation of Law

Application of the DMCA to prohibit posting of DeCSS appears constitutional also because that posting is part of a course of conduct the clear purpose of which is the violation of law.

This line of reasoning first was articulated by the Supreme Court in *Giboney v. Empire Storage & Ice Co*,[53] where the Court upheld an injunction against peaceful picketing by union members despite the contention that the picketers were attempting only to publicize truthful facts about a labor dispute. Although labor picketing traditionally enjoys First Amendment protection, the Court declined to extend such protection in *Giboney* on the ground that the picketing was integral to a course of conduct in violation of a valid criminal statute prohibiting restraint of trade.[54] The Court warned that, as a general matter, the government "cannot consistently with our Constitution abridge [First Amendment] freedoms to obviate slight inconveniences or annoyances,"[55] but found that where the allegedly protected speech is "used as an essential and inseparable part of a grave offense against an important public law," it shall not be "immunize[d] ... from state control."[56] The Court held further that "it has never been deemed an abridgment of freedom of speech or press to make a course of conduct illegal merely because the conduct was in part initiated, evidenced, or carried out by means of language, either spoken, written or printed."[57] This principle has been applied in both criminal and non-

criminal contexts as long as the offense in question is defined by a valid statutory scheme promoting an important public interest.[58]

As has been discussed already, it no longer is open to doubt that the First Amendment does not shield copyright infringement. The fundamental purpose of DeCSS is to circumvent the technological means, CSS, that ensures that the exclusive rights of the holders of copyright in DVD movies—including importantly the exclusive right to make copies—are protected against infringement. Even assuming that some would use DeCSS only to view copyrighted motion pictures which they lawfully possessed, and thus arguably not infringe plaintiffs' copyrights, the record clearly demonstrates that the chief focus of those promoting the dissemination of DeCSS is to permit widespread copying and dissemination of unauthorized copies of copyrighted works. The dissemination of DeCSS therefore is the critical component of a course of conduct, the principal object of which is copyright infringement. That DeCSS arguably is expressive to some degree does not alter that reality. In light of *Giboney* and its progeny, defendants cannot latch onto the expressive aspect in order to shield a key aspect of a chain of events, the main purpose of which is unlawful. Application of the DMCA to prohibit production and dissemination of DeCSS therefore does not violate the First Amendment.

c. Vagueness

Defendants contend summarily that the DMCA is "vague on its face and as applied."[59] It is settled in this circuit that a party who "engages in some conduct that is clearly proscribed [by the challenged statute] cannot complain of the vagueness of the law as applied to the conduct of others."[60] The record in this case strongly supports the contention that defendants' conduct fits comfortably within the statute. In consequence, defendants' claim of vagueness is frivolous.

d. Overbreadth

Defendants allege that the DMCA is overbroad in that it "unquestionably attaches sanctions to protected conduct" and exerts clear "chilling effects" by restricting dissemination of protected computer code, limiting the rights of users to receive this code, and curtailing the rights of all Linux users to decrypt DVDs.[61]

In order to challenge a statute on overbreadth grounds, a party first must show that the enactment reaches a "substantial amount of constitutionally protected conduct." [62] Defendants have not done so here. The claim of overbreadth therefore fails.

4. Prior Restraint

Few phrases are as firmly rooted in our constitutional jurisprudence as the maxim that "[a]ny system of prior restraints of expression comes to [a] Court bearing a heavy presumption against its constitutional validity." [63] Yet there is a significant gap between the rhetoric and the reality. Courts often have upheld restrictions on expression that many would describe as prior restraints, [64] sometimes by characterizing the expression as unprotected [65] and on other occasions finding the restraint justified despite its presumed invalidity. [66] Moreover, the prior restraint doctrine, which has expanded far beyond the Blackstonian model [67] that doubtless informed the understanding of the Framers of the First Amendment, [68] has been criticized as filled with "doctrinal ambiguities and inconsistencies result[ing] from the absence of any detailed judicial analysis of [its] true rationale" [69] and, in one case, even as "fundamentally unintelligible." [70] Nevertheless, the doctrine has a well established core: administrative preclearance requirements for and preliminary injunctions against speech as conventionally understood are presumptively unconstitutional. Yet that proposition does not dispose of this case.

The classic prior restraint cases were dramatically different from this one. *Near v. Minnesota* [71] involved a state procedure for abating scandalous and defamatory newspapers as public nuisances. *New York Times Co. v. United States* [72] dealt with an attempt to enjoin a newspaper from publishing an internal government history of the Vietnam War. *Nebraska Press Association v. Stuart* [73] concerned a court order barring the reporting of certain details about a forthcoming murder case. In each case, therefore, the government sought to suppress speech at the very heart of First Amendment concern—expression about public issues of the sort that is indispensable to self government. And while the prior restraint doctrine has been applied well beyond the sphere of political expression, we deal here with something new altogether—computer code, a fundamentally utilitarian construct even assuming it embodies some expressive element. Hence, it would be a mistake simply to permit its assumed expressive element to drive a characterization of the code as speech no different from the Pentagon Papers, the publication of a newspaper, or the exhibition of a motion picture and then to apply prior restraint rhetoric without a more nuanced consideration of the competing concerns.

In this case, the considerations supporting an injunction barring the posting of DeCSS pending a trial on the merits are very substantial indeed. Copyright and, more broadly, intellectual property piracy are endemic, as Congress repeatedly has found. [74] The interest served by prohibiting means that facilitate such piracy—the protection of the monopoly granted to copyright owners by the Copyright Act—is of constitutional dimension. There is little room for doubting that broad dissemination of DeCSS would seriously injure or destroy plaintiffs' ability to distribute their copyrighted products on DVDs and, for that matter, undermine their ability to sell their products to the "home video" market in other forms. The potential damages probably are incalculable, and these defendants surely would be in no position to compensate plaintiffs for them if plaintiffs were remitted only to *post hoc* damage suits.

On the other side of the coin, the First Amendment interests served by the dissemination of DeCSS prior to a trial on the merits are minimal. The fact that there may be some expressive content in the code should not obscure the fact that its predominant character is no more expressive than an automobile ignition key—it is simply a means, electronic in one case and mechanical in the other, of causing the machine with which it is used to function in a particular way. Hence, those of the traditional rationales for the prior restraint doctrine that relate to inhibiting the transmission and receipt of ideas are of attenuated relevance here, even assuming that skilled programmers might learn something about encryption from studying the DeCSS code. Indeed, even academic commentators who take the extreme position that most preliminary injunctions in intellectual property cases are unconstitutional prior restraints concede that there is no First Amendment obstacle to preliminary injunctions barring distribution of copyrighted computer object code or restraining the construction of a new building based on copyrighted architectural drawings because the functional aspects of these types of information are "sufficiently nonexpressive." [75]

To be sure, there is much to be said in most circumstances for the usual procedural rationale for the prior restraint doctrine: prior restraints carry with them the risk of erroneously suppressing expression that could not constitutionally be punished after publication. [76] In this context, however, that concern is not fully persuasive, both because the enjoined expressive element is minimal and because of the procedural context of the case. This injunction was issued only on a finding, after an adversarial proceeding, that plaintiffs have a very strong likelihood of ultimate success on the merits. [77] The Court offered (and defendants thus far have declined) a virtually immediate trial on the merits, thus ensuring that the duration of the restraint prior to a final determination will be as brief as defendants wish. [78] Hence, even assuming that preliminary injunctions that affect expression even incidentally to the regulation of other action should be granted only on the clearest showing after an adversary hearing and where the party enjoined may promptly obtain a final determination on the merits, those requirements have been satisfied here.

Accordingly, the Court holds that the prior restraint doctrine does not require denial of the preliminary injunction in this case. [79]

Conclusion

For the foregoing reasons, the Court granted plaintiffs' motion for a preliminary injunction and entered such an order on January 20, 2000. The foregoing, together with those made on the record on that date, constitute the Court's findings of fact and conclusions of law.

SO ORDERED.

---

[1] 17 USC §1201 *et seq.*

[2] Recent reports indicate that Norwegian police have arrested an individual said first to have hacked CSS. *See* Mike Godwin, *Teen Co-Creator of DVD Decryption Program Arrested at Norwegian Home*, E-COMMERCE LAW WEEKLY, Feb. 2, 2000.

[3] The same court reportedly granted the plaintiff's motion for a preliminary injunction following the decision in this case.

[4] *Richard Feiner & Co. v. Turner Ent. Co., MGM/UA*, 98 F3d 33, 34 (2d Cir 1996) (citing *inter alia Jackson Dairy, Inc. v. H.P. Hood & Sons, Inc.*, 596 F2d 70, 72 (2d Cir 1979) (per curiam)).

[5] *See Fisher-Price, Inc. v. Well-Made Toy Mfg. Corp.*, 25 F3d 119, 124 (2d Cir 1994).

[6] Defendants suggest that plaintiffs delayed bringing this action, thereby undermining their claim of irreparable injury. Although undue delay in some circumstances can defeat a presumption of irreparable injury, *see Markowitz Jewelry Co., Inc. v. Chapal/Zenray, Inc.*, 988 F Supp 404, 406 (SD NY 1994), that is so only where the delay is unexplained and unjustified. If a party is unaware at the outset of the scope of the threat or pursues with reasonable dispatch other means to remedy the problem without coming to court, there is no undue delay. *See Gilliam v. American Broadcasting Companies, Inc.*, 538 F2d 14, 25 (2d Cir 1976). In this case, plaintiffs first learned of the appearance of DeCSS on the Internet in late October 1999. Schumann Decl. ¶10; Attaway Decl. ¶7. Plaintiffs immediately sought to address the problem by approaching Internet service providers and met with some success. Attaway Decl. ¶8. After a state court in California declined to issue a temporary restraining order in a case involving misappropriation of trade secrets on December 29, 1999, the dissemination of DeCSS became more widespread. Attaway Decl. ¶9. As this motion was brought by order to show cause on January 14, 2000, the Court finds that plaintiffs acted with reasonable speed and that any delay was not undue.

[7] FED. R. CIV. P. 17.

[8] Emphasis added.

[9] Defendant Roman Kazan argues also that, since this action was filed, DeCSS has been removed from the Web site that he allegedly controls. This does not moot the claim against him. *See United States v. W. T. Grant*, 345 US 629 (1953).

[10] 17 USC §1201(a)(2). *See also* 1 MELVILLE B. NIMMER & DAVID NIMMER, NIMMER ON COPYRIGHT ("NIMMER") §12A.03[1][a], at 12A-16 (1999).

[11] 17 USC §1201(a)(3)(A).

[12] *Id.* §1201(a)(3)(B).

[13] Def. Mem. at 3.

[14] Defendants contended that DeCSS was intended only to permit persons in lawful possession of copyrighted disks to play them for their own use on computers running under the Linux operating system rather than Windows. Tr. at 28. Indeed, they suggested that this is the only

possible use of DeCSS and that DeCSS does not permit the user to copy DVDs. *Id.* at 28-30. But the arguments are unpersuasive for two reasons.

First, defendants have submitted no evidence—as distinguished from unsubstantiated assertions at oral argument—to support these contentions. Second, even if DeCSS were intended and usable solely to permit the playing, and not the copying, of DVDs on Linux machines, the playing without a licensed CSS "player key" would "circumvent a technological measure" that effectively controls access to a copyrighted work and violate the statute in any case.

[15] 17 USC §512(c).

[16] Def. Mem. at 6-7.

[17] 17 USC §512(k) ("[T]he term 'service provider' means a provider of online services or network access, or the operator of facilities therefore, and includes an entity" "offering the transmission, routing, or providing of connections for digital online communications, between or among points specified by a users, of material of the user's choosing, without modification to the content of the material as sent or received.").

[18] *Id.* §512(c)(1).

[19] 17 USC §1201(f)(1).

[20] Def. Mem. at 8-9.

[21] S. Rep. No. 105-190 (1998); H.R. Rep. 105-551(II) (1998).

[22] 17 USC §1201(g)(4).

[23] *Id.* §1201(g)(2).

[24] *Id.* §1201(g)(3).

[25] Def. Mem. at 11-12.

[26] *Id.* §1201(j)(1).

[27] Def. Mem. at 12. *See* 17 USC §107.

[28] 17 USC §107.

[29] Defendants asserted at oral argument that DeCSS, or some versions of it, contain programmer's comments, "which are non-executable appendages to lines of executable code." *Tradescape.com v. Shivaram*, No. 99 Civ. 8990 (LAK), 1999 WL 1102767, *8 (SD NY Dec. 7, 1999). Such comments are protected by the First Amendment. Plaintiffs, however, have disclaimed any effort to restrain dissemination of programmer comments as distinguished from executable code.

[30] *Compare Bernstein v. United States Dept. of Justice*, 176 F3d 1132, 1141 *[2 ILR (P&F) 602]* (holding that encryption software in source code form is constitutionally protected expression but expressing no opinion with respect to object code), *rehearing in banc granted, opinion withdrawn*, 192 F3d 1308 *[3 ILR (P&F) 500]* (9th Cir 1999); *with Junger v. Daley*, 8 F Supp 2d 708, 715-18 *[2 ILR (P&F) 573]* (ND Ohio 1998) (holding that encryption software in source code form is functional rather than expressive and therefore not protected speech); *Karn v. United States Dept. of State*, 925 F Supp 1, 9 n.19 (D DC 1996) (assuming that source code is protected speech when joined with commentary, but stating that source code alone is "merely a means of commanding a computer to perform a function"); R. Polk Wagner, *The Medium Is the Mistake: The Law of Software for the First Amendment*, 51 STAN. L. REV. 387 (1999) (arguing that focus of analysis in software cases should be on whether government interests supporting regulation are related to suppression of expression, not on whether code itself is intended to be or understood as expressive); Mark A. Lemley & Eugene Volokh, *Freedom of Speech and Injunctions in Intellectual Property Cases*, 48 DUKE L.J. 147, 236-37 (1998) ("most executable software is best treated as a virtual machine rather than as protected expression").

[31] Lemley & Volokh, *supra*, 48 DUKE L.J. at 165-66.

[32] This argument is posited by the Nimmers, who nevertheless do not embrace it. *See* 1 NIMMER §1.10[A], at 1-66.44 to 1-66.45 (1999).

[33] *See generally Harper & Row Publishers Inc. v. Nation Enterprises*, 471 US 539, 555-60 (1985).

[34] *Id.* at 558.

[35] *See id.* at 560. *See also Wainwright Securities, Inc. v. Wall Street Transcript Corp.*, 558 F2d 91, 95 (2d Cir 1977), *cert. denied*, 434 US 1014 (1978) ("Conflicts between interests protected by the first amendment and the copyright laws thus far have been resolved by application of the fair use doctrine."); *Nihon Keizai Shimbun Inc. v. Comline Business Data, Inc.*, 166 F3d 65, 74 (2d Cir 1999).

[36] *See, e.g., Nihon Keizai Shimbum*, 166 F3d at 74.

[37] U.S. CONST., art. I, §8.

[38] *Id.*

[39] 4 Wheat. (17 U.S.) 316 (1819).

[40] *Id.* at 421.

[41] *See Sony Corp. of America v. Universal City Studios*, 464 US 417, 434 (1984) ("Sound policy, as well as history, supports or consistent deference to Congress when major technological innovations alter the market for copyrighted materials. Congress has the constitutional authority and the institutional ability to accommodate fully the varied permutations of competing interests that are inevitably implicated by such new technology.").

[42] S. REP. No. 105-190, 105th Cong., 2d Sess. (1998).

[43] 1 NIMMER §§1.10[A]-1.10[B][1], at 1-66.45 to 1-74. This "definitional balancing" is to be distinguished from "ad hoc balancing," which seeks to balance only the particular interests of the parties before the court, rather than the more general public interests in the kind of speech and the governmental regulation at issue. According to the Nimmers, ad hoc balancing has proven unsatisfactory and generally has been replaced by the definitional balancing method. *Id.* §1.10[A], at 1-67. *See also Konigsberg v. State Bar of Calif.*, 366 US 36 (1961).

[44] This kind of balancing has been utilized in cases involving *inter alia* obscenity, privacy, and libel. 1 NIMMER §1.10[A], at 1-68 (citing *Roth v. United States*, 354 US 476 (1957) (obscenity); *Time, Inc. v. Hill*, 385 US 374 (1967) (privacy); *New York Times v. Sullivan*, 376 US 254 (1964) (libel)).

[45] *Whitney v. California*, 274 US 357, 375 (1927) (Brandeis, J. concurring) (cited in 1 NIMMER §1.10[B], at 1-72 to 1-73). *See also Nixon v. Shrink Missouri Gov't PAC*, No. 98-963, 2000 WL 48424, *14 (U.S. Jan. 24, 2000) (Breyer, J., concurring); *Wallace v. Jaffree*, 472 US 38, 48 (1985); *Mills v. Alabama*, 384 US 214, 218-19 (1966).

[46] *Id.*

[47] *Junger*, 8 F Supp 2d at 715-18; *Karn*, 925 F Supp at 9 n. 19; Lemley & Volakh, 48 DUKE L. J. at 236-37.

[48] Lemley & Volakh, 48 DUKE L.J. at 236-37.

[49] *Mazer v. Stein*, 347 US 201, 219 (1953).

[50] *Id.*

[51] U.S. CONST. art. II, §8.

[52] Schumann Decl. ¶¶4-5.

[53] 336 US 490, 498 (1949).

[54] *Id.* at 498.

[55] *Id.* at 501-02.

[56] *Id.* at 502.

[57] *Id.*

[58] *See, e.g., Hughes v. Superior Court*, 339 US 460 (1950) (injunction against picketing to secure compliance with demand that store adopt race-based hiring policy on ground that it contravenes state policy against involuntary employment on racial lines); *Pittsburgh Press Co. v. Pittsburgh Comm'n on Human Relations*, 413 US 376 (1973) (injunction against newspaper's furtherance of illegal sex discrimination by placing of job advertisements in gender-designated columns); *National Society of Professional Engineers v. United States*, 435 US 679

(1978) (injunction under Sherman Act against professional association's adoption of official opinions, policy statements or guidelines implying that competitive bidding was unethical); *NLRB v. Local No. 3*, 828 F2d 936 (2d Cir 1987) (injunction against union's threat to strike as violation of National Labor Relations Act's prohibition on unfair labor practices).

[59] Def. Mem. at 13.

[60] *Village of Hoffman Estates v. Flipside, Hoffman Estates, Inc.*, 455 US 489, 495 (1982).

[61] Def. Mem. at 13.

[62] *Village of Hoffman Estates*, 455 US at 494.

[63] *New York Times Co. v. United States*, 403 US 713, 714 (1971) (per curiam) (quoting *Bantam Books, Inc. v. Sullivan*, 372 US 58, 70 (1963)).

[64] *See, e.g., Posadas de Puerto Rico Assoc. v. Tourism Co. of Puerto Rico*, 478 US 328 (1986) (upholding restrictions on casino gambling advertising); *Times Film Corp. v. Chicago*, 365 US 43 (1961) (upholding local ordinance requiring review of films by municipal officials as prerequisite to issuance of permits for public screening); *Salinger v. Random House, Inc.*, 811 F2d 90 (2d Cir) (enjoining biographer's use of subject's unpublished letters as copyright infringement), *cert. denied*, 484 US 890 (1987); *Dallas Cowboy Cheerleaders v. Pussycat Cinema, Ltd.*, 604 F2d 200 (2d Cir 1979) (enjoining distribution of film on ground that actresses' uniforms infringed plaintiff's trademark). *See generally* LAURENCE H. TRIBE, AMERICANCONSTITUTIONAL LAW §12-36, at 1045-46 (1988) (hereinafter TRIBE).

[65] *See, e.g., Charles of the Ritz Group, Ltd. v. Quality King Distributors, Inc.*, 832 F2d 1317 (2d Cir 1987) (upholding injunction against commercial slogan on ground that slogan created a likelihood of confusion and is therefore "beyond the protective reach of the First Amendment"); *Vondran v. McLinn*, No. 95-20296, 1995 WL 415153, *6 (ND Cal. July 5, 1995) (enjoining defendant's false and disparaging remarks regarding plaintiff's patented process for making fiber reinforced concrete on the ground that the remarks are not protected by the First Amendment).

[66] *See, e.g., Times Film Corp. v. Chicago*, 365 US 43 (1961) (upholding local ordinance requiring review by city officials of all films as a prerequisite to grant of permit for public screening despite concerns of First Amendment violations); *Posadas de Puerto Rico Assoc.*, 478 US 328 (upholding restrictions on advertising despite finding that the advertising fell within ambit of First Amendment); *Dallas Cowboys Cheerleaders, Inc.*, 604 F2d 200 (enjoining distribution of film for trademark infringement despite claim that injunction violated distributor's First Amendment rights).

[67] 4 WILLIAM BLACKSTONE, COMMENTARIES ON THE LAWS OF ENGLAND 151-52 (1769).

[68] *See Pittsburgh Press Co.*, 413 US at 390.

[69] Martin H. Redish, *The Proper Role of the Prior Restraint Doctrine in First Amendment Theory*, 70 VA. L. REV. 53, 54 (1983) (hereinafter "Redish"). *See also* TRIBE §12-34, at 1040-41 (2d ed. 1988).

[70] John Calvin Jeffries, Jr., *Rethinking Prior Restraint*, 92 YALE L.J. 409, 419 (1983).

[71] 283 US 697 (1931).

[72] 403 US 713.

[73] 427 US 539 (1976).

[74] *See* H.R. REP. 106-216, 106th Cong., 1st Sess. (1999) ("Notwithstanding [penalties for copyright infringement] copyright piracy of intellectual property flourishes, assisted in large part by today's world of advanced technologies. For example, industry groups estimate that counterfeiting and piracy of computer software cost the affected copyright holders more than $11 billion last year (others believe the figure is closer to $20 billion). In some countries, software piracy rates are as high as 97% of all sales. The U.S. rate is far lower (25%), but the dollar losses ($2.9 billion) are the highest worldwide. The effect of this volume of theft is substantial: lost U.S. jobs, lost wages, lower tax revenue, and higher prices for honest purchasers of copyrighted software. Unfortunately, the potential for this problem to worsen is great."); S. REP. 106-140, 106th Cong., 1st Sess. (1999) ("Trademark owners are facing a new form of piracy on the Internet caused by acts of 'cybersquatting.'"); S. REP. 105-190, 105th Cong., 2d Sess. (1998) ("Due to the ease with which digital works can be copied and distributed worldwide virtually instantaneously, copyright owners will hesitate to make their works readily available on the Internet without reasonable assurance that they will be protected against massive piracy."); H.R. REP. 105-339, 105th Cong., 1st Sess. (1997) ("[C]opyright piracy flourishes in the software world.").

[75] Lemley & Volokh, 48 DUKE L.J. at 210 & n.275.

[76] *See, e.g., Pittsburgh Press Co.*, 413 US at 390 ("The special vice of a prior restraint is that communication will be suppressed . . . before an adequate determination that it is unprotected by the First Amendment."); Lemley & Volokh, 48 DUKE L.J. at 200-02, 211; *see* Redish, 70 VA. L. REV. at 75-83.

[77] *See* Lemley & Volokh, 48 DUKE L.J. at 211-12, 215 (acknowledging that high likelihood of success diminishes risk of erroneous suppression of protected speech).

[78] *See Freedman v. Maryland*, 380 US 51, 59 (1965).

[79] As the Court has found a strong likelihood of success on the merits, it is not necessary to analyze the balance of hardships. Nonetheless, were such analysis appropriate, the Court would find the balance to tip decidedly in plaintiffs' favor. Were the injunction erroneously granted, defendants would risk a delay in their ability to make DeCSS available on their Web sites. As they have made no claim that dissemination of DeCSS is particularly time sensitive, the Court finds this risk to be relatively benign. In contrast, were the injunction wrongly denied, plaintiffs would face a choice between continued infringement of their copyrights as a result of illegal DVD decryption or voluntary deferral of release of DVDs until the matter is fully litigated as well as the cannibalization of the market for their products via other media. Either option likely would result in substantial economic losses for plaintiffs.

Universal City Studios, Inc.
v.
Reimerdes

**United States District Court,
Southern District of New York**

**August 17, 2000
as amended September 6, 2000**

6 ILR (P&F) 1, 111 F Supp 2d 294

00 Civ. 0277 (LAK)

[The court's Amended Final Judgment appears at 6 ILR (P&F) 794; the Second Circuit affirmed this decision in an opinion reported at 9 ILR (P&F) 330.—Ed.]

Posting of DVD decryption code violates anti-trafficking provision of DMCA.

Defendants violated the anti-trafficking provision of the Digital Millennium Copyright Act (DMCA), 17 USC §1201(a)(2), by posting on their own web site a computer program that permits users to decrypt and copy plaintiffs' copyrighted motion pictures from digital versatile disks (DVDs). Plaintiffs' encryption system, called Content Scramble System or CSS, permits movies in DVD format to be viewed only on players and computer drives equipped with licensed technology that permits the devices to decrypt and play—but not copy—the films. Computer hackers devised a program called DeCSS that circumvents CSS and allows CSS-protected DVDs to be copied and played on devices that lack the licensed decryption technology. DeCSS is unquestionably a "technology" designed to "circumvent a technological measure" within the meaning of §1201(a)(2). The court rejects defendants' contention that CSS is not protected under §1201(a)(2)(A) because it does not "effectively control" access to plaintiffs' works if DeCSS or some other decryption program is employed. Such a construction is indefensible because it would limit the statute's application to access control measures that thwart circumvention, but withhold those measures that can be circumvented. The court also rejects the suggestion that DeCSS was not "designed" for the purpose of circumventing CSS; the motivation of those who wrote DeCSS is immaterial to whether defendants violated §1201(a)(2)'s anti-trafficking provision. — **Universal City Studios, Inc. v. Reimerdes, 6 ILR (P&F) 1 [SD NY, 2000].**

Posting of DVD decryption code; DMCA reverse engineering exemption inapplicable.

Defendants, who posted a computer program (DeCSS) that permits users to decrypt and copy plaintiffs' copyrighted motion pictures from digital versatile disks (DVDs), are not exempted from the coverage of the anti-circumvention provisions of the Digital Millennium Copyright Act (DMCA) under the reverse engineering exception, 17 USC §1201(f). Section 1201(f) permits circumvention of access control measures in order to achieve interoperability with another computer program and to make information acquired through such efforts available to others for the purpose of achieving interoperability by that statute's own exceptions. Defendants' contention that DeCSS is necessary to achieve interoperability between DVD and computers running the Linux system fails. First, defendants themselves did not do any reverse engineering, but simply took DeCSS off someone else's web site. Moreover, DeCSS was neither developed nor disseminated "solely for the purpose" of achieving interoperability, as required under §1201(f). DeCSS runs on the far more widely used Windows operating system as well as on Linux, and its developers knew that it could be used to decrypt and play DVD movies on Windows. — **Universal City Studios, Inc. v. Reimerdes, 6 ILR (P&F) 1 [SD NY, 2000].**

Posting of DVD decryption code; DMCA security testing exemption inapplicable.

Defendants, who posted a computer program (DeCSS) that permits users to decrypt and copy plaintiffs' copyrighted motion pictures from digital versatile disks (DVDs), are not exempted from the coverage of the anti-circumvention provisions of the Digital Millennium Copyright Act (DMCA) under the security testing exemption at 17 USC §1201(j). That exception is limited to assessing a computer system for security flaws with the authorization of the system operator. The record does not indicate that DeCSS has anything to do with such testing or that defendants had been granted any such authorization. — **Universal City Studios, Inc. v. Reimerdes, 6 ILR (P&F) 1 [SD NY, 2000].**

Posting of DVD decryption code; fair use doctrine inapplicable.

Defendants, who posted a computer program (DeCSS) that permits users to decrypt and copy plaintiffs' copyrighted motion pictures from digital versatile disks (DVDs), may not rely on the fair use doctrine to escape liability for violating the anti-trafficking provision of the Digital Millennium Copyright Act (DMCA), 17 USC §1201(a)(2). First, the fair use doctrine is a defense to copyright infringement; defendants here are being sued not for copyright infringement but for violating §1201(a)(2) of the DMCA. If Congress had meant for the fair use defense to apply to such actions it would have said so. Indeed, as the legislative history demonstrates, the decision not to make a fair use defense to a claim under §1201(a) was quite deliberate. Congress struck a balance in the DMCA by carefully limiting the statute's §1201(a)(1) prohibition to the act of circumvention itself, leaving the traditional fair use defenses fully applicable once a person has obtained authorized access to a work. Further, Congress delayed the effective date of the §1201(a)(1) prohibitions pending further investigation of how best to reconcile it with fair use concerns. Moreover, Congress created a series of exceptions to aspects of §1201(a) that it thought "fair," including reverse engineering, security testing, good faith encryption, and certain uses by libraries, archives, and educational institutions. Defendants' reliance on *Sony Corp. v. Universal City Studios*, 464 US 417 (1984), is misplaced for *Sony* does not apply to the activities with which defendants are charged. Even if it did, it would not govern here; Sony involved a construction of the Copyright Act that has been overruled by the later enactment of the DMCA. — **Universal City Studios, Inc. v. Reimerdes, 6 ILR (P&F) 1 [SD NY, 2000].**

Linking to sites that post DVD decryption code violates anti-trafficking provision of DMCA.

The anti-trafficking provision of the Digital Millennium Copyright Act (DMCA), 17 USC §1201(a)(2), prohibits defendants' practice of "linking" to other sites that make available a computer program that permits users to decrypt and copy plaintiffs' copyrighted motion pictures from digital versatile disks (DVDs). Plaintiffs' encryption system, called Content Scramble System or CSS, permits movies in DVD format to be viewed only on players and computer drives equipped with licensed technology that permits the devices to decrypt and play—but not copy—the films. Computer hackers devised a program called DeCSS that circumvents CSS and allows CSS-protected DVDs to be copied and played on devices that lack the licensed decryption technology. When defendants were enjoined from posting DeCSS on their own site, they electronically linked users to other sites still offering DeCSS and encouraged other sites that had not been enjoined to offer the program. The anti-trafficking provision of the DMCA is implicated where one presents, holds out, or makes a circumvention technology or device available, knowing its nature, for the purpose of allowing others to acquire it. To the extent that defendants link to sites that automatically commence the process of downloading DeCSS upon a user being transferred by the hyperlinks, defendants are engaged in the functional equivalent of transferring the DeCSS code to the user. While links to pages that offer content other than DeCSS might be potentially more troubling, that is not this case, for defendants made sure that the "mirror" sites were in fact posting DeCSS. — **Universal City Studios, Inc. v. Reimerdes, 6 ILR (P&F) 1 [SD NY, 2000].**

Constitutionality of anti-trafficking provision of DMCA.

The anti-trafficking provision of the Digital Millennium Copyright Act, 17 USC §1201(a)(2), is not unconstitutional as applied to the posting of computer code (DeCSS) that permits users to decrypt and copy copyrighted motion pictures from digital versatile disks (DVD). While computer code is a means of expressing ideas and therefore subject to some First Amendment protection, the DMCA is a constitutionally permissible "content-neutral" restriction on speech that is not motivated by a desire to limit the message. Rather, it is focused squarely upon the effect of the distribution of the functionality that the code provides.

Section 1201(a)(2) furthers an important governmental interest: the protection of copyrighted works stored on digital media from the vastly expanded risk of piracy in the electronic age. Furthermore, the prior restraint doctrine does not require denial of an injunction in this case. The challenged provision is not unconstitutionally overbroad, nor is it void for vagueness. — **Universal City Studios, Inc. v. Reimerdes, 6 ILR (P&F) 1 [SD NY, 2000].**

Constitutionality of anti-trafficking provision of DMCA.

The anti-trafficking provision of the Digital Millennium Copyright Act, 17 USC §1201(a)(2), does not violate the First Amendment as applied to the practice of "linking" to other sites that make available a computer program that permits users to decrypt and copy plaintiffs' copyrighted motion pictures from digital versatile disks (DVDs), provided that clear and convincing evidence shows that those responsible for the link (1) know at the relevant time that the offending material is on the linked-to site; (2) know that it is circumvention technology that may not lawfully be offered; and (3) create or maintain the link for the purpose of disseminating that technology. As those conditions are met in this case, an anti-linking injunction does no violence to the First Amendment. — **Universal City Studios, Inc. v. Reimerdes, 6 ILR (P&F) 1 [SD NY, 2000].**

Award of attorney's fees inappropriate in DMCA test case.

Although the Digital Millennium Copyright Act (DMCA) permits awards of costs and attorney's fees to the prevailing party in the discretion of the court, an award of attorney's fees would be inappropriate here, since this was a test case raising important issues. There is no comparable reason, however, for failing to award costs, particularly as taxable costs are related to the excessive discovery demands in the case. — **Universal City Studios, Inc. v. Reimerdes, 6 ILR (P&F) 1 [SD NY, 2000].**

OPINION

Appearances:

Leon P. Gold, Jon A. Baumgarten, Charles S. Sims, Scott P. Cooper, William M. Hart, Michael M. Mervis, Carla M. Miller, PROSKAUER ROSE LLP, Attorneys for Plaintiffs

Martin Garbus, George E. Singleton, David Y. Atlas, Edward Hernstadt, FRANKFURT, GARBUS, KLEIN & SELZ, P.C., Attorneys for Defendants

Contents

LEWIS A. KAPLAN, District Judge. Plaintiffs, eight major United States motion picture studios, distribute many of their copyrighted motion pictures for home use on digital versatile disks ("DVDs"), which contain copies of the motion pictures in digital form. They protect those motion pictures from copying by using an encryption system called CSS. CSS-protected motion pictures on DVDs may be viewed only on players and computer drives equipped with licensed technology that permits the devices to decrypt and play—but not to copy—the films.

Late last year, computer hackers devised a computer program called DeCSS that circumvents the CSS protection system and allows CSS-protected motion pictures to be copied and played on devices that lack the licensed decryption technology. Defendants quickly posted DeCSS on their Internet web site, thus making it readily available to much of the world. Plaintiffs promptly brought this action under the Digital Millennium Copyright Act (the "DMCA")[1] to enjoin defendants from posting DeCSS and to prevent them from electronically "linking" their site to others that post DeCSS.

Defendants responded with what they termed "electronic civil disobedience"—increasing their efforts to link their web site to a large number of others that continue to make DeCSS available.

Defendants contend that their actions do not violate the DMCA and, in any case, that the DMCA, as applied to computer programs, or code, violates the First Amendment.[2] This is the Court's decision after trial, and the decision may be summarized in a nutshell.

Defendants argue first that the DMCA should not be construed to reach their conduct, principally because the DMCA, so applied, could prevent those who wish to gain access to technologically protected copyrighted works in order to make fair—that is, non-infringing—use of them from doing so. They argue that those who would make fair use of technologically protected copyrighted works need means, such as DeCSS, of circumventing access control measures not for piracy, but to make lawful use of those works.

Technological access control measures have the capacity to prevent fair uses of copyrighted works as well as foul. Hence, there is a potential tension between the use of such access control measures and fair use. Defendants are not the first to recognize that possibility. As the DMCA made its way through the legislative process, Congress was preoccupied with precisely this issue. Proponents of strong restrictions on circumvention of access control measures argued that they were essential if copyright holders were to make their works available in digital form because digital works otherwise could be pirated too easily. Opponents contended that strong anti-circumvention measures would extend the copyright monopoly inappropriately and prevent many fair uses of copyrighted material.

Congress struck a balance. The compromise it reached, depending upon future technological and commercial developments, may or may not prove ideal.[3] But the solution it enacted is clear. The potential tension to which defendants point does not absolve them of liability under the statute. There is no serious question that defendants' posting of DeCSS violates the DMCA.

Defendants' constitutional argument ultimately rests on two propositions—that computer code, regardless of its function, is "speech" entitled to maximum constitutional protection and that computer code therefore essentially is exempt from regulation by government. But their argument is baseless.

Computer code is expressive. To that extent, it is a matter of First Amendment concern. But computer code is not purely expressive any more than the assassination of a political figure is purely a political statement. Code causes computers to perform desired functions. Its expressive element no more immunizes its functional aspects from regulation than the expressive motives of an assassin immunize the assassin's action.

In an era in which the transmission of computer viruses—which, like DeCSS, are simply computer code and thus to some degree expressive—can disable systems upon which the nation depends and in which other computer code also is capable of inflicting other harm, society must be able to regulate the use and dissemination of code in appropriate circumstances. The Constitution, after all, is a framework for building a just and democratic society. It is not a suicide pact.

I. The Genesis of the Controversy

As this case involves computers and technology with which many are unfamiliar, it is useful to begin by defining some of the vocabulary.

A. The Vocabulary of this Case

1. Computers and Operating Systems

A computer is "a digital information processing device . . . consist[ing] of central processing components . . . and mass data storage . . . certain peripheral input/output devices . . . , and an operating system." Personal computers ("PCs") are computers designed for use by one person at a time. "[M]ore powerful, more expensive computer systems known as 'servers' . . . are designed to provide data, services, and functionality through a digital network to multiple users." [4]

An operating system is "a software program that controls the allocation and use of computer resources (such as central processing unit time, main memory space, disk space, and input/output channels). The operating system also supports the functions of software programs, called 'applications,' that perform specific user-oriented tasks . . . . Because it supports applications while interacting more closely with the PC system's hardware, the operating system is said to serve as a 'platform.' " [5]

Microsoft Windows ("Windows") is an operating system released by Microsoft Corp. It is the most widely used operating system for PCs in the United States, and its versions include Windows 95, Windows 98, Windows NT and Windows 2000.

Linux, which was and continues to be developed through the open source model of software development, [6] also is an operating system. [7] It can be run on a PC as an alternative to Windows, although the extent to which it is so used is limited. [8] Linux is more widely used on servers. [9]

2. Computer Code

"[C]omputers come down to one basic premise: They operate with a series of on and off switches, using two digits in the binary (base 2) number system—0 (for off) and 1 (for on)." [10] All data and instructions input to or contained in computers therefore must be reduced [to] the numerals 1 and 0. [11]

"The smallest unit of memory in a computer," a bit, "is a switch with a value of 0 (off) or 1 (on)." [12] A group of eight bits is called a byte and represents a character—a letter or an integer. [13] A kilobyte ("K") is 1024 bytes, a megabyte ("MB") 1024 kilobytes, and a gigabyte ("GB") 1024 kilobytes. [14]

Some highly skilled human beings can reduce data and instructions to strings of 1's and 0's and thus program computers to perform complex tasks by inputting commands and data in that form. [15] But it would be inconvenient, inefficient and, for most people, probably impossible to do so. In consequence, computer science has developed programming languages. These languages, like other written languages, employ symbols and syntax to convey meaning. The text of programs written in these languages is referred to as source code. [16] And whether directly or through the medium of another program, [17] the sets of instructions written in programming languages—the source code—ultimately are translated into machine "readable" strings of 1's and 0's, known in the computer world as object code, which typically are executable by the computer. [18]

The distinction between source and object code is not as crystal clear as first appears. Depending upon the programming language, source code may contain many 1's and 0's and look a lot like object code or may contain many instructions derived from spoken human language. Programming languages the source code for which approaches object code are referred to as low level source code while those that are more similar to spoken language are referred to as high level source code.

All code is human readable. As source code is closer to human language than is object code, it tends to be comprehended more easily by humans than object code.

3. *The Internet and the World Wide Web*

The Internet is "a global electronic network, consisting of smaller, interconnected networks, which allows millions of computers to exchange information over telephone wires, dedicated data cables, and wireless links. The Internet links PCs by means of servers, which run specialized operating systems and applications designed for servicing a network environment." [19]

Internet Relay Chat ("IRC") is a system that enables individuals connected to the Internet to participate in live typed discussions. [20] Participation in an IRC discussion requires an IRC software program, which sends messages via the Internet to the IRC server, which in turn broadcasts the messages to all participants. The IRC system is capable of supporting many separate discussions at once.

The World Wide Web (the "Web") is "a massive collection of digital information resources stored on servers throughout the Internet. These resources are typically provided in the form of hypertext documents, commonly referred to as 'Web pages,' that may incorporate any combination of text, graphics, audio and video content, software programs, and other data. A user of a computer connected to the Internet can publish a page on the Web simply by copying it into a specially designated, publicly accessible directory on a Web server. Some Web resources are in the form of applications that provide functionality through a user's PC system but actually execute on a server." [21]

A web site is "a collection of Web pages [published on the Web by an individual or organization] . . . . Most Web pages are in the form of 'hypertext'; that is, they contain annotated references, or 'hyperlinks,' to other Web pages. Hyperlinks can be used as cross-references within a single document, between documents on the same site, or between documents on different sites." [22]

A home page is "one page on each Web site . . . [that typically serves as] the first access point to the site. The home page is usually a hypertext document that presents an overview of the site and hyperlinks to the other pages comprising the site." [23]

A Web client is "software that, when running on a computer connected to the Internet, sends information to and receives information from Web servers throughout the Internet. Web clients and servers transfer data using a standard known as the Hypertext Transfer Protocol ('HTTP'). A 'Web browser' is a type of Web client that enables a user to select, retrieve, and perceive resources on the Web. In particular, Web browsers provide a way for a user to view hypertext documents and follow the hyperlinks that connect them, typically by moving the cursor over a link and depressing the mouse button." [24]

4. *Portable Storage Media*

Digital files may be stored on several different kinds of storage media, some of which are readily transportable. Perhaps the most familiar of these are so called floppy disks or "floppies," which now are 3 ½ inch magnetic disks upon which digital files may be recorded. [25] For present purposes, however, we are concerned principally with two more recent developments, CD-ROMs and digital versatile disks, or DVDs.

A CD-ROM is a five-inch wide optical disk capable of storing approximately 650 MB of data. To read the data on a CD-ROM, a computer must have a CD-ROM drive.

DVDs are five-inch wide disks capable of storing more than 4.7 GB of data. In the application relevant here, they are used to hold full-length motion pictures in digital form. They are the latest technology for private home viewing of recorded motion pictures and result in drastically improved audio and visual clarity and quality of motion pictures shown on televisions or computer screens. [26]

5. *The Technology Here at Issue*

CSS, or Content Scramble System, is an access control and copy prevention system for DVDs developed by the motion picture companies, including plaintiffs. [27] It is an encryption-based system that requires the use of appropriately configured hardware such as a DVD player or a computer DVD drive to decrypt, unscramble and play back, but not copy, motion pictures on DVDs.[28] The technology necessary to configure DVD players and drives to play CSS-protected DVDs[29] has been licensed to hundreds of manufacturers in the United States and around the world.

DeCSS is a software utility, or computer program, that enables users to break the CSS copy protection system and hence to view DVDs on unlicenced players and make digital copies of DVD movies.[30] The quality of motion pictures decrypted by DeCSS is virtually identical to that of encrypted movies on DVD.[31]

DivX is a compression program available for download over the Internet.[32] It compresses video files in order to minimize required storage space, often to facilitate transfer over the Internet or other networks.[33]

B. Parties

Plaintiffs are eight major motion picture studios. Each is in the business of producing and distributing copyrighted material including motion pictures. Each distributes, either directly or through affiliates, copyrighted motion pictures on DVDs.[34] Plaintiffs produce and distribute a large majority of the motion pictures on DVDs on the market today.[35]

Defendant Eric Corley is viewed as a leader of the computer hacker community and goes by the name Emmanuel Goldstein, after the leader of the underground in George Orwell's classic, *1984*.[36] He and his company, defendant 2600 Enterprises, Inc., together publish a magazine called *2600: The Hacker Quarterly,* which Corley founded in 1984,[37] and which is something of a bible to the hacker community.[38] The name "2600" was derived from the fact that hackers in the 1960's found that the transmission of a 2600 hertz tone over a long distance trunk connection gained access to "operator mode" and allowed the user to explore aspects of the telephone system that were not otherwise accessible.[39] Mr. Corley chose the name because he regarded it as a "mystical thing,"[40] commemorating something that he evidently admired. Not surprisingly, *2600: The Hacker Quarterly* has included articles on such topics as how to steal an Internet domain name,[41] access other people's e-mail,[42] intercept cellular phone calls,[43] and break into the computer systems at Costco stores[44] and Federal Express.[45] One issue contains a guide to the federal criminal justice system for readers charged with computer hacking.[46] In addition, defendants operate a web site located at <http://www.2600.com> ("2600. com"), which is managed primarily by Mr. Corley and has been in existence since 1995.[47]

Prior to January 2000, when this action was commenced, defendants posted the source and object code for DeCSS on the 2600.com web site, from which they could be downloaded easily.[48] At that time, 2600.com contained also a list of links to other web sites purporting to post DeCSS.[49]

C. The Development of DVD and CSS

The major motion picture studios typically distribute films in a sequence of so-called windows, each window referring to a separate channel of distribution and thus to a separate source of revenue. The first window generally is theatrical release, distribution, and exhibition. Subsequently, films are distributed to airlines and hotels, then to the home market, then to pay television, cable and, eventually, free television broadcast. The home market is important to plaintiffs, as it represents a significant source of revenue.[50]

Motion pictures first were, and still are, distributed to the home market in the form of video cassette tapes. In the early 1990's, however, the major movie studios began to explore distribution to the home market in digital format, which offered substantially higher audio and visual quality and greater longevity than video cassette tapes.[51] This technology, which in 1995 became what is known today as DVD,[52] brought with it a new problem—increased risk of piracy by virtue of the fact that digital files, unlike the material on video cassettes, can be copied without degradation from generation to generation.[53] In consequence, the movie studios became concerned as the product neared market with the threat of DVD piracy.[54]

Discussions among the studios with the goal of organizing a unified response to the piracy threat began in earnest in late 1995 or early 1996.[55] They eventually came to include representatives of the consumer electronics and computer industries, as well as interested members of the public,[56] and focused on both legislative proposals and technological solutions.[57] In 1996, Matsushita Electric Industrial Co. ("MEI") and Toshiba Corp., presented—and the studios adopted—CSS.[58]

CSS involves encrypting, according to an encryption algorithm,[59] the digital sound and graphics files on a DVD that together constitute a motion picture. A CSS-protected DVD can be decrypted by an appropriate decryption algorithm that employs a series of keys stored on the DVD and the DVD player. In consequence, only players and drives containing the appropriate keys are able to decrypt DVD files and thereby play movies stored on DVDs.

As the motion picture companies did not themselves develop CSS and, in any case, are not in the business of making DVD players and drives, the technology for making compliant devices, *i.e.*, devices with CSS keys, had to be licensed to consumer electronics manufacturers.[60] In order to ensure that the decryption technology did not become generally available and that compliant devices could not be used to copy as well as merely to play CSS-protected movies, the technology is licensed subject to strict security requirements.[61] Moreover, manufacturers may not, consistent with their licenses, make equipment that would supply digital output that could be used in copying protected DVDs.[62] Licenses to manufacture compliant devices are granted on a royalty-free basis subject only to an administrative fee.[63] At the time of trial, licenses had been issued to numerous hardware and software manufacturers, including two companies that plan to release DVD players for computers running the Linux operating system.[64]

With CSS in place, the studios introduced DVDs on the consumer market in early 1997.[65] All or most of the motion pictures released on DVD were, and continue to be, encrypted with CSS technology.[66] Over 4,000 motion pictures now have been released in DVD format in the United States, and movies are being issued on DVD at the rate of over 40 new titles per month in addition to rereleases of classic films. Currently, more than five million households in the United States own DVD players,[67] and players are projected to be in ten percent of United States homes by the end of 2000.[68]

DVDs have proven not only popular, but lucrative for the studios. Revenue from their sale and rental currently accounts for a substantial percentage of the movie studios' revenue from the home video market.[69] Revenue from the home market, in turn, makes up a large percentage of the studios' total distribution revenue.[70]

D. The Appearance of DeCSS

In late September 1999, Jon Johansen, a Norwegian subject then fifteen years of age, and two individuals he "met" under pseudonyms over the Internet, reverse engineered a licensed DVD player and discovered the CSS encryption algorithm and keys.[71] They used this information to create DeCSS, a program capable of decrypting or "ripping" encrypted DVDs, thereby allowing playback on non-compliant computers as well as the copying of decrypted files to computer hard drives.[72] Mr. Johansen then posted the executable code on his personal Internet web site and informed members of an Internet mailing list that he had done so.[73] Neither Mr. Johansen nor his collaborators obtained a license from the DVD CCA.[74]

Although Mr. Johansen testified at trial that he created DeCSS in order to make a DVD player that would operate on a computer running the Linux operating system,[75] DeCSS is a Windows executable file; that is, it can be executed only on computers running the Windows operating system.[76] Mr. Johansen explained the fact that he created a Windows rather than a Linux program by asserting that Linux, at the time he created DeCSS, did not support the file system used on DVDs.[77] Hence, it was necessary, he said, to decrypt the DVD on a Windows computer in order subsequently to play the decrypted files on a Linux machine.[78] Assuming that to be true,[79] however, the fact remains that Mr. Johansen created DeCSS in the full knowledge that it could be used on computers running Windows rather than Linux. Moreover, he was well aware that the files, once decrypted, could be copied like any other computer files.

In January 1999, Norwegian prosecutors filed charges against Mr. Johansen stemming from the development of DeCSS.[80] The disposition of the Norwegian case does not appear of record.

E. The Distribution of DeCSS

In the months following its initial appearance on Mr. Johansen's web site, DeCSS has become widely available on the Internet, where hundreds of sites now purport to offer the software for download.[81] A few other applications said to decrypt CSS-encrypted DVDs also have appeared on the Internet.[82]

In November 1999, defendants' web site began to offer DeCSS for download.[83] It established also a list of links to several web sites that purportedly "mirrored" or offered DeCSS for download.[84] The links on defendants' mirror list fall into one of three categories. By clicking the mouse on one of these links, the user may be brought to a page on the linked-to site on which there appears a further link to the DeCSS software.[85] If the user then clicks on the DeCSS link, download of the software begins. This page may or may not contain content other than the DeCSS link.[86] Alternatively, the user may be brought to a page on the linked-to site that does not itself purport to link to DeCSS, but that links, either directly or via a series of other pages on the site, to another page on the site on which there appears a link to the DeCSS software.[87] Finally, the user may be brought directly to the DeCSS link on the linked-to site such that download of DeCSS begins immediately without further user intervention.[88]

F. The Preliminary Injunction and Defendants' Response

The movie studios, through the Internet investigations division of the Motion Picture Association of America ("MPAA"), became aware of the availability of DeCSS on the Internet in October 1999.[89] The industry responded by sending out a number of cease and desist letters to web site operators who posted the software, some of which removed it from their sites.[90] In January 2000, the studios filed this lawsuit against defendant Eric Corley and two others.[91]

After a hearing at which defendants presented no affidavits or evidentiary material, the Court granted plaintiffs' motion for a preliminary injunction barring defendants from posting DeCSS.[92] At the conclusion of the hearing, plaintiffs sought also to enjoin defendants from linking to other sites that posted DeCSS, but the Court declined to entertain the application at that time in view of plaintiffs' failure to raise the issue in their motion papers.[93]

Following the issuance of the preliminary injunction, defendants removed DeCSS from the 2600.com web site.[94] In what they termed an act of "electronic civil disobedience,"[95] however, they continued to support links to other web sites purporting to offer DeCSS for download, a list which had grown to nearly five hundred by July 2000.[96] Indeed, they carried a banner saying "Stop the

MPAA" and, in a reference to this lawsuit, proclaimed:

> "We have to face the possibility that we could be forced into submission. For that reason it's especially important that as many of you as possible, all throughout the world, take a stand and mirror these files."[97]

Thus, defendants obviously hoped to frustrate plaintiffs' recourse to the judicial system by making effective relief difficult or impossible.

At least some of the links currently on defendants' mirror list lead the user to copies of DeCSS that, when downloaded and executed, successfully decrypt a motion picture on a CSS-encrypted DVD.[98]

G. Effects on Plaintiffs

The effect on plaintiffs of defendants' posting of DeCSS depends upon the ease with which DeCSS decrypts plaintiffs' copyrighted motion pictures, the quality of the resulting product, and the convenience with which decrypted copies may be transferred or transmitted.

As noted, DeCSS was available for download from defendants' web site and remains available from web sites on defendants' mirror list.[99] Downloading is simple and quick—plaintiffs' expert did it in seconds.[100] The program in fact decrypts at least some DVDs.[101] Although the process is computationally intensive, plaintiffs' expert decrypted a store-bought copy of *Sleepless in Seattle* in 20 to 45 minutes.[102] The copy is stored on the hard drive of the computer. The quality of the decrypted film is virtually identical to that of encrypted films on DVD.[103] The decrypted file can be copied like any other.[104]

The decryption of a CSS-protected DVD is only the beginning of the tale, as the decrypted file is very large—approximately 4.3 to 6 GB or more depending on the length of the film[105]—and thus extremely cumbersome to transfer or to store on portable storage media. One solution to this problem, however, is DivX, a compression utility available on the Internet that is promoted as a means of compressing decrypted motion picture files to manageable size.[106]

DivX is capable of compressing decrypted files constituting a feature length motion picture to approximately 650 MB at a compression ratio that involves little loss of quality. [107] While the compressed sound and graphic files then must be synchronized, a tedious process that took plaintiffs' expert between 10 and 20 hours, [108] the task is entirely feasible. Indeed, having compared a store-bought DVD with portions of a copy compressed and synchronized with DivX (which often are referred to as "DivX'd" motion pictures), the Court finds that the loss of quality, at least in some cases, is imperceptible or so nearly imperceptible as to be of no importance to ordinary consumers. [109]

The fact that DeCSS-decrypted DVDs can be compressed satisfactorily to 650 MB is very important. A writeable CD-ROM can hold 650 MB. [110] Hence, it is entirely feasible to decrypt a DVD with DeCSS, compress and synchronize it with DivX, and then make as many copies as one wishes by burning the resulting files onto writeable CD-ROMs, which are sold blank for about one dollar apiece. [111] Indeed, even if one wished to use a lower compression ratio to improve quality, a film easily could be compressed to about 1.3 GB and burned onto two CD-ROMs. But the creation of pirated copies of copyrighted movies on writeable CD-ROMs, although significant, is not the principal focus of plaintiffs' concern, which is transmission of pirated copies over the Internet or other networks.

Network transmission of decrypted motion pictures raises somewhat more difficult issues because even 650 MB is a very large file that, depending upon the circumstances, may take a good deal of time to transmit. But there is tremendous variation in transmission times. Many home computers today have modems with a rated capacity of 56 kilobits per second. DSL lines, which increasingly are available to home and business users, offer transfer rates of 7 megabits per second. [112] Cable modems also offer increased bandwidth. Student rooms in many universities are equipped with network connections rated at 10 megabits per second. [113] Large institutions such as universities and major companies often have networks with backbones rated at 100 megabits per second. [114] While effective transmission times generally are much lower than rated maximum capacities in consequence of traffic volume and other considerations, there are many environments in which very high transmission rates may be achieved. [115] Hence, transmission times ranging from three [116] to twenty minutes [117] to six hours [118] or

more for a feature length film are readily achievable, depending upon the users' precise circumstances. [119]

At trial, defendants repeated, as if it were a mantra, the refrain that plaintiffs, as they stipulated, [120] have no direct evidence of a specific occasion on which any person decrypted a copyrighted motion picture with DeCSS and transmitted it over the Internet. But that is unpersuasive. Plaintiffs' expert expended very little effort to find someone in an IRC chat room who exchanged a compressed, decrypted copy of *The Matrix*, one of plaintiffs' copyrighted motion pictures, for a copy of *Sleepless in Seattle*. [121] While the simultaneous electronic exchange of the two movies took approximately six hours, [122] the computers required little operator attention during the interim. An MPAA investigator downloaded between five and ten DVD-sourced movies over the Internet after December 1999. [123] At least one web site contains a list of 650 motion pictures, said to have been decrypted and compressed with DivX, that purportedly are available for sale, trade or free download. [124] And although the Court does not accept the list, which is hearsay, as proof of the truth of the matters asserted therein, it does note that advertisements for decrypted versions of copyrighted movies first appeared on the Internet in substantial numbers in late 1999, following the posting of DeCSS. [125]

The net of all this is reasonably plain. DeCSS is a free, effective and fast means of decrypting plaintiffs' DVDs and copying them to computer hard drives. DivX, which is available over the Internet for nothing, with the investment of some time and effort, permits compression of the decrypted files to sizes that readily fit on a writeable CD-ROM. Copies of such CD-ROMs can be produced very cheaply and distributed as easily as other pirated intellectual property. While not everyone with Internet access now will find it convenient to send or receive DivX'd copies of pirated motion pictures over the Internet, the availability of high speed network connections in many businesses and institutions, and their growing availability in homes, make Internet and other network traffic in pirated copies a growing threat.

These circumstances have two major implications for plaintiffs. First, the availability of DeCSS on the Internet effectively has compromised plaintiffs' system of copyright protection for DVDs, requiring them either to tolerate increased piracy or to expend resources to develop and implement a replacement system unless the availability of DeCSS is terminated. [126] It is analogous to the publication of a bank vault combination in a national newspaper. Even if no one uses the combination to open the vault, its mere publication has the effect of defeating the bank's security system, forcing the bank to reprogram the lock. Development and implementation of a new DVD copy protection system, however, is far more difficult and costly than reprogramming a combination lock and may carry with it the added problem of rendering the existing installed base of compliant DVD players obsolete.

Second, the application of DeCSS to copy and distribute motion pictures on DVD, both on CD-ROMs and via the Internet, threatens to reduce the studios' revenue from the sale and rental of DVDs. It threatens also to impede new, potentially lucrative initiatives for the distribution of motion pictures in digital form, such as video-on-demand via the Internet. [127]

In consequence, plaintiffs already have been gravely injured. As the pressure for and competition to supply more and more users with faster and faster network connections grows, the injury will multiply.

II. The Digital Millennium Copyright Act

A. Background and Structure of the Statute

In December 1996, the World Intellectual Property Organization ("WIPO"), held a diplomatic conference in Geneva that led to the adoption of two treaties. Article 11 of the relevant treaty, the WIPO Copyright Treaty, provides in relevant part that contracting states "shall provide adequate legal protection and effective legal remedies against the circumvention of effective technological measures that are used by authors in connection with the exercise of their rights under this Treaty or the Berne Convention and that restrict acts, in respect of their works, which are not authorized by the authors concerned or permitted by law." [128]

The adoption of the WIPO Copyright Treaty spurred continued Congressional attention to the adaptation of the law of copyright to the digital age. Lengthy hearings involving a broad range of interested parties both preceded and succeeded the Copyright Treaty. As noted above, a critical focus of Congressional consideration of the legislation was the conflict between those who opposed anti-circumvention measures as inappropriate extensions of copyright and impediments to fair use and those who supported them as essential to proper protection of copyrighted materials in the digital age. [129] The DMCA was enacted in October 1998 as the culmination of this process. [130]

The DMCA contains two principal anticircumvention provisions. The first, Section 1201(a)(1), governs "[t]he act of circumventing a technological protection measure put in place by a copyright owner to control access to a copyrighted work," an act described by Congress as "the electronic equivalent of breaking into a locked room in order to obtain a copy of a book." [131] The second, Section 1201(a)(2), which is the focus of this case, "supplements the prohibition against the act of circumvention in paragraph (a)(1) with prohibitions on creating and making available certain technologies . . . developed or advertised to defeat technological protections against unauthorized access to a work." [132] As defendants are accused here only of posting and linking to other sites posting DeCSS, and not of using it themselves to bypass plaintiffs' access controls, it is principally the second of the anticircumvention provisions that is at issue in this case. [133]

B. Posting of DeCSS

1. Violation of Anti-Trafficking Provision

Section 1201(a)(2) of the Copyright Act, part of the DMCA, provides that: "No person shall . . . offer to the public, provide or otherwise traffic in any technology . . . that—

"(A) is primarily designed or produced for the purpose of circumventing a technological measure that effectively controls access to a work protected under [the Copyright Act];

"(B) has only limited commercially significant purpose or use other than to circumvent a technological measure that effectively controls access to a work protected under [the Copyright Act]; or

"(C) is marketed by that person or another acting in concert with that person with that person's knowledge for use in circumventing a technological measure that effectively controls access to a work protected under [the Copyright Act]." [134]

In this case, defendants concededly offered and provided and, absent a court order, would continue to offer and provide DeCSS to the public by making it available for download on the 2600.com web site. DeCSS, a computer program, unquestionably is "technology" within the meaning of the statute. [135] "[C]ircumvent a technological measure" is defined to mean descrambling a scrambled work, decrypting an encrypted work, or "otherwise to avoid, bypass, remove, deactivate, or impair a technological measure, without the authority of the copyright owner," [136] so DeCSS clearly is a means of circumventing a technological access control measure. [137] In consequence, if CSS otherwise falls within paragraphs (A), (B) or (C) of Section 1201(a)(2), and if none of the statutory exceptions applies to their actions, defendants have violated and, unless enjoined, will continue to violate the DMCA by posting DeCSS.

a. Section 1201(a)(2)(A)

(1) CSS Effectively Controls Access to Copyrighted Works

During pretrial proceedings and at trial, defendants attacked plaintiffs' Section 1201(a)(2)(A) claim, arguing that CSS, which is based on a 40-bit encryption key, is a weak cipher that does not "effectively control" access to plaintiffs' copyrighted works. They reasoned from this premise that CSS is not protected under this branch of the statute at all. Their post-trial memorandum appears to have abandoned this argument. In any case, however, the contention is indefensible as a matter of law.

First, the statute expressly provides that "a technological measure 'effectively controls access to a work' if the measure, in the ordinary course of its operation, requires the application of information or a process or a treatment, with the authority of the copyright owner, to gain access to a work." [138] One cannot gain access to a CSS-protected work on a DVD without application of the three keys that are required by the software. One cannot lawfully gain access to the keys except by entering into a license with the DVD CCA under authority granted by the copyright owners or by purchasing a DVD player or drive containing the keys pursuant to such a license. In consequence, under the express terms of the statute, CSS "effectively controls access" to copyrighted DVD movies. It does so, within the

meaning of the statute, whether or not it is a strong means of protection. [139]

This view is confirmed by the legislative history, which deals with precisely this point. The House Judiciary Committee section-by-section analysis of the House bill, which in this respect was enacted into law, makes clear that a technological measure "effectively controls access" to a copyrighted work if its *function* is to control access:

> "The bill does define the *functions* of the technological measures that are covered— that is, what it means for a technological measure to 'effectively control access to a work' . . . and to 'effectively protect a right of a copyright owner under this title' . . . . The practical, common-sense approach taken by H.R. 2281 is that if, in the ordinary course of its operation, a technology actually works in the defined ways to control access to a work . . . then the 'effectiveness' test is met, and the prohibitions of the statute are applicable. This test, which focuses on the function performed by the technology, provides a sufficient basis for clear interpretation." [140]

Further, the House Commerce Committee made clear that measures based on encryption or scrambling "effectively control" access to copyrighted works, [141] although it is well known that what may be encrypted or scrambled often may be decrypted or unscrambled. As CSS, in the ordinary course of its operation—that is, when DeCSS or some other decryption program is not employed— "actually works" to prevent access to the protected work, it "effectively controls access" within the contemplation of the statute.

Finally, the interpretation of the phrase "effectively controls access" offered by defendants at trial—viz., that the use of the word "effectively" means that the statute protects only successful or efficacious technological means of controlling access—would gut the statute if it were adopted. If a technological means of access control is circumvented, it is, in common parlance, ineffective. Yet defendants' construction, if adopted, would limit the application of the statute to access control measures that thwart circumvention, but withhold protection for those measures that can be circumvented. In other words, defendants would have the Court construe the statute to offer protection where none is needed but to withhold protection precisely where protection is essential. The Court declines to do so. Accordingly, the Court holds that CSS effectively controls access to plaintiffs' copyrighted works.[142]

(2) DeCSS Was Designed Primarily to Circumvent CSS

As CSS effectively controls access to plaintiffs' copyrighted works, the only remaining question under Section 1201(a)(2)(A) is whether DeCSS was designed primarily to circumvent CSS. The answer is perfectly obvious. By the admission of both Jon Johansen, the programmer who principally wrote DeCSS, and defendant Corley, DeCSS was created solely for the purpose of decrypting CSS—that is all it does.[143] Hence, absent satisfaction of a statutory exception, defendants clearly violated Section 1201(a)(2)(A) by posting DeCSS to their web site.

b. Section 1201(a)(2)(B)

As the only purpose or use of DeCSS is to circumvent CSS, the foregoing is sufficient to establish a *prima facie* violation of Section 1201(a)(2)(B) as well.

c. The Linux Argument

Perhaps the centerpiece of defendants' statutory position is the contention that DeCSS was not created for the purpose of pirating copyrighted motion pictures. Rather, they argue, it was written to further the development of a DVD player that would run under the Linux operating system, as there allegedly were no Linux compatible players on the market at the time.[144] The argument plays itself out in various ways as different elements of the DMCA come into focus. But it perhaps is useful to address the point at its most general level in order to place the preceding discussion in its fullest context.

As noted, Section 1201(a) of the DMCA contains two distinct prohibitions. Section 1201(a)(1), the so-called basic provision, "aims against those who engage in unauthorized circumvention of technological measures . . . . [It] focuses directly on wrongful conduct, rather than on those who facilitate wrongful conduct . . . ."[145] Section 1201(a)(2), the anti-trafficking provision at issue in this case, on the other hand, separately bans offering or providing technology that may be used to circumvent technological means of controlling access to copyrighted works.[146] If the means in question meets any of the three prongs of the standard set out in Section 1201(a)(2)(A), (B), or (C), it may not be offered or disseminated.

As the earlier discussion demonstrates, the question whether the development of a Linux DVD player motivated those who wrote DeCSS is immaterial to the question whether the defendants now before the Court violated the anti-trafficking provision of the DMCA. The inescapable facts are that (1) CSS is a technological means that effectively controls access to plaintiffs' copyrighted works, (2) the one and only function of DeCSS is to circumvent CSS, and (3) defendants offered and provided DeCSS by posting it on their web site. Whether defendants did so in order to infringe, or to permit or encourage others to infringe, copyrighted works in violation of other provisions of the Copyright Act simply does not matter for purposes of Section 1201(a)(2). The offering or provision of the program is the prohibited conduct—and it is prohibited irrespective of why the program was written, except to whatever extent motive may be germane to determining whether their conduct falls within one of the statutory exceptions.

2. Statutory Exceptions

Earlier in the litigation, defendants contended that their activities came within several exceptions contained in the DMCA and the Copyright Act and constitute fair use under the Copyright Act. Their post-trial memorandum appears to confine their argument to the reverse engineering exception.[147] In any case, all of their assertions are entirely without merit.

a. Reverse engineering

Defendants claim to fall under Section 1201(f) of the statute, which provides in substance that one may circumvent, or develop and employ technological means to circumvent, access control measures in order to achieve interoperability with another computer program provided that doing so does not infringe another's copyright[148] and, in addition, that one may make information acquired through such efforts "available to others, if the person [in question] . . . provides such information solely for the purpose of enabling interoperability of an independently created computer program with other programs, and to the extent that doing so does not constitute infringement . . . ." [149] They contend that DeCSS is necessary to achieve interoperability between computers running the Linux operating system and DVDs and that this exception therefore is satisfied. [150] This contention fails.

First, Section 1201(f)(3) permits information acquired through reverse engineering to be made available to others only by the person who acquired the information. But these defendants did not do any reverse engineering. They simply took DeCSS off someone else's web site and posted it on their own.

Defendants would be in no stronger position even if they had authored DeCSS. The right to make the information available extends only to dissemination "solely for the purpose" of achieving interoperability as defined in the statute. It does not apply to public dissemination of means of circumvention, as the legislative history confirms. [151] These defendants, however, did not post DeCSS "solely" to achieve interoperability with Linux or anything else.

Finally, it is important to recognize that even the creators of DeCSS cannot credibly maintain that the "sole" purpose of DeCSS was to create a Linux DVD player. DeCSS concededly was developed on and runs under Windows—a far more widely used operating system. The developers of DeCSS therefore knew that DeCSS could be used to decrypt and play DVD movies on Windows as well as Linux machines. They knew also that the decrypted files could be copied like any other unprotected computer file. Moreover, the Court does not credit Mr. Johansen's testimony that he created DeCSS solely for the purpose of building a Linux player. Mr. Johansen is a very talented young man and a member of a well known hacker group who viewed "cracking" CSS as an end it [sic] itself and a means of demonstrating his talent and who fully expected that the use of DeCSS would not be confined to Linux machines. Hence, the Court finds that Mr. Johansen and the others who actually did develop DeCSS did not do so solely for the purpose of making a Linux DVD player if, indeed, developing a Linux-based DVD player was among their purposes.

Accordingly, the reverse engineering exception to the DMCA has no application here.

b. Encryption research

Section 1201(g)(4) provides in relevant part that:

"Notwithstanding the provisions of subsection (a)(2), it is not a violation of that subsection for a person to—

"(A) develop and employ technological means to circumvent a technological measure for the sole purpose of that person performing the acts of good faith encryption research described in paragraph (2); and

"(B) provide the technological means to another person with whom he or she is working collaboratively for the purpose of conducting the acts of good faith encryption research described in paragraph (2) or for the purpose of having that other person verify his or her acts of good faith encryption research described in paragraph (2)." [152]

Paragraph (2) in relevant part permits circumvention of technological measures in the course of good faith encryption research if:

"(A) the person lawfully obtained the encrypted copy, phonorecord, performance, or display of the published work;

"(B) such act is necessary to conduct such encryption research;

"(C) the person made a good faith effort to obtain authorization before the circumvention; and

"(D) such act does not constitute infringement under this title . . . ." [151]

In determining whether one is engaged in good faith encryption research, the Court is instructed to consider factors including whether the results of the putative encryption research are disseminated in a manner designed to advance the state of knowledge of encryption technology versus facilitation of copyright infringement, whether the person in question is engaged in legitimate study of or work in encryption, and whether the results of the research are communicated in a timely fashion to the copyright owner. [152]

Neither of the defendants remaining in this case was or is involved in good faith encryption research. [153] They posted DeCSS for all the world to see. There is no evidence that they made any effort to provide the results of the DeCSS effort to the copyright owners. Surely there is no suggestion that either of them made a good faith effort to obtain authorization from the copyright owners. Accordingly, defendants are not protected by Section 1201(g). [154]

c. Security testing

Defendants contended earlier that their actions should be considered exempt security testing under Section 1201(j) of the statute. [155] This exception, however, is limited to "assessing a computer, computer system, or computer network, solely for the purpose of good faith testing, investigating, or correcting [of a] security flaw or vulnerability, with the authorization of the owner or operator of such computer system or computer network." [156]

The record does not indicate that DeCSS has anything to do with testing computers, computer systems, or computer networks. Certainly defendants sought, and plaintiffs' granted, no authorization for defendants' activities. This exception therefore has no bearing in this case. [157]

d. Fair use

Finally, defendants rely on the doctrine of fair use. Stated in its most general terms, the doctrine, now codified in Section 107 of the Copyright Act, [158] limits the exclusive rights of a copyright holder by permitting others to make limited use of portions of the copyrighted work, for appropriate purposes, free of liability for copyright infringement. For example, it is permissible for one other than the copyright owner to reprint or quote a suitable part of a copyrighted book or article in certain circumstances. The doctrine traditionally has facilitated literary and artistic criticism, teaching and scholarship, and other socially useful forms of expression. It has been viewed by courts as a safety valve that accommodates the exclusive rights conferred by copyright with the freedom of expression guaranteed by the First Amendment.

The use of technological means of controlling access to a copyrighted work may affect the ability to make fair uses of the work. [159] Focusing specifically on the facts of this case, the application of CSS to encrypt a copyrighted motion picture requires the use of a compliant DVD player to view or listen to the movie. Perhaps more significantly, it prevents exact copying of either the video or the audio portion of all or any part of the film. [160] This latter point means that certain uses that might qualify

as "fair" for purposes of copyright infringement— for example, the preparation by a film studies professor of a single CD-ROM or tape containing two scenes from different movies in order to illustrate a point in a lecture on cinematography, as opposed to showing relevant parts of two different DVDs—would be difficult or impossible absent circumvention of the CSS encryption. Defendants therefore argue that the DMCA cannot properly be construed to make it difficult or impossible to make any fair use of plaintiffs' copyrighted works and that the statute therefore does not reach their activities, which are simply a means to enable users of DeCSS to make such fair uses.

Defendants have focused on a significant point. Access control measures such as CSS do involve some risk of preventing lawful as well as unlawful uses of copyrighted material. Congress, however, clearly faced up to and dealt with this question in enacting the DMCA.

The Court begins its statutory analysis, as it must, with the language of the statute. Section 107 of the Copyright Act provides in critical part that certain uses of copyrighted works that otherwise would be wrongful are "not . . . infringement[s] of copyright." [161] Defendants, however, are not here sued for copyright infringement. They are sued for offering and providing technology designed to circumvent technological measures that control access to copyrighted works and otherwise violating Section 1201(a)(2) of the Act. If Congress had meant the fair use defense to apply to such actions, it would have said so. Indeed, as the legislative history demonstrates, the decision not to make fair use a defense to a claim under Section 1201(a) was quite deliberate.

Congress was well aware during the consideration of the DMCA of the traditional role of the fair use defense in accommodating the exclusive rights of copyright owners with the legitimate interests of noninfringing users of portions of copyrighted works. It recognized the contention, voiced by a range of constituencies concerned with the legislation, that technological controls on access to copyrighted works might erode fair use by preventing access even for uses that would be deemed "fair" if only access might be gained. [162] And it struck a balance among the competing interests.

The first element of the balance was the careful limitation of Section 1201(a)(1)'s prohibition of the act of circumvention to the act itself so as not to "apply to subsequent actions of a person once he or she has obtained authorized access to a copy of a [copyrighted] work . . . ."[163] By doing so, it left "the traditional defenses to copyright infringement, including fair use, . . . fully applicable" provided "the access is authorized."[164]

Second, Congress delayed the effective date of Section 1201(a)(1)'s prohibition of the act of circumvention for two years pending further investigation about how best to reconcile Section 1201(a)(1) with fair use concerns. Following that investigation, which is being carried out in the form of a rule-making by the Register of Copyright, the prohibition will not apply to users of particular classes of copyrighted works who demonstrate that their ability to make noninfringing uses of those classes of works would be affected adversely by Section 1201(a)(1).[165]

Third, it created a series of exceptions to aspects of Section 1201(a) for certain uses that Congress thought "fair," including reverse engineering, security testing, good faith encryption research, and certain uses by nonprofit libraries, archives and educational institutions.[166]

Defendants claim also that the possibility that DeCSS might be used for the purpose of gaining access to copyrighted works in order to make fair use of those works saves them under *Sony Corp. v. Universal City Studios, Inc.*[167] But they are mistaken. *Sony* does not apply to the activities with which defendants here are charged. Even if it did, it would not govern here. *Sony* involved a construction of the Copyright Act that has been overruled by the later enactment of the DMCA to the extent of any inconsistency between *Sony* and the new statute.

Sony was a suit for contributory infringement brought against manufacturers of video cassette recorders on the theory that the manufacturers were contributing to infringing home taping of copyrighted television broadcasts. The Supreme Court held that the manufacturers were not liable in view of the substantial numbers of copyright holders who either had authorized or did not object to such taping by viewers.[168] But *Sony* has no application here.

When *Sony* was decided, the only question was whether the manufacturers could be held liable for infringement by those who purchased equipment from them in circumstances in which there were many noninfringing uses for their equipment. But that is not the question now before this Court. The question here is whether the possibility of noninfringing fair use by someone who gains access to a protected copyrighted work through a circumvention technology distributed by the defendants saves the defendants from liability under Section 1201. But nothing in Section 1201 so suggests. By prohibiting the provision of circumvention technology, the DMCA fundamentally altered the landscape. A given device or piece of technology might have "a substantial noninfringing use, and hence be immune from attack under *Sony*'s construction of the Copyright Act— but nonetheless still be subject to suppression under Section 1201."[169] Indeed, Congress explicitly noted that Section 1201 does not incorporate *Sony*.[170]

The policy concerns raised by defendants were considered by Congress. Having considered them, Congress crafted a statute that, so far as the applicability of the fair use defense to Section 1201(a) claims is concerned, is crystal clear. In such circumstances, courts may not undo what Congress so plainly has done by "construing" the words of a statute to accomplish a result that Congress rejected. The fact that Congress elected to leave technologically unsophisticated persons who wish to make fair use of encrypted copyrighted works without the technical means of doing so is a matter for Congress unless Congress' decision contravenes the Constitution, a matter to which the Court turns below. Defendants' statutory fair use argument therefore is entirely without merit.

C. Linking to Sites Offering DeCSS

Plaintiffs seek also to enjoin defendants from "linking" their 2600.com web site to other sites that make DeCSS available to users. Their request obviously stems in no small part from what defendants themselves have termed their act of "electronic civil disobedience"—their attempt to defeat the purpose of the preliminary injunction by (a) offering the practical equivalent of making DeCSS available on their own web site by electronically linking users to other sites still offering DeCSS, and (b) encouraging other sites that had not been enjoined to offer the program. The dispositive question is whether linking to another web site containing DeCSS constitutes "offer[ing DeCSS] to the public" or "provid[ing] or otherwise traffic[king]" in it within the meaning of the DMCA. [171] Answering this question requires careful consideration of the nature and types of linking.

Most web pages are written in computer languages, chiefly HTML, which allow the programmer to prescribe the appearance of the web page on the computer screen and, in addition, to instruct the computer to perform an operation if the cursor is placed over a particular point on the screen and the mouse then clicked. [172] Programming a particular point on a screen to transfer the user to another web page when the point, referred to as a hyperlink, is clicked is called linking. [173] Web pages can be designed to link to other web pages on the same site or to web pages maintained by different sites. [174]

As noted earlier, the links that defendants established on their web site are of several types. Some transfer the user to a web page on an outside site that contains a good deal of information of various types, does not itself contain a link to DeCSS, but that links, either directly or via a series of other pages, to another page on the same site that posts the software. It then is up to the user to follow the link or series of links on the linked-to web site in order to arrive at the page with the DeCSS link and commence the download of the software. Others take the user to a page on an outside web site on which there appears a direct link to the DeCSS software and which may or may not contain text or links other than the DeCSS link. The user has only to click on the DeCSS link to commence the download. Still others may directly transfer the user to a file on the linked-to web site such that the download of DeCSS to the user's computer automatically commences without further user intervention.

The statute makes it unlawful to offer, provide or otherwise traffic in described technology. [175] To "traffic" in something is to engage in dealings in it, [176] conduct that necessarily involves awareness of the nature of the subject of the trafficking. To "provide" something, in the sense used in the statute, is to make it available or furnish it. [177] To "offer" is to present or hold it out for consideration. [178] The phrase "or otherwise traffic in" modifies and gives meaning to the words "offer" and "provide." [179] In

consequence, the anti-trafficking provision of the DMCA is implicated where one presents, holds out or makes a circumvention technology or device available, knowing its nature, for the purpose of allowing others to acquire it.

To the extent that defendants have linked to sites that automatically commence the process of downloading DeCSS upon a user being transferred by defendants' hyperlinks, there can be no serious question. Defendants are engaged in the functional equivalent of transferring the DeCSS code to the user themselves.

Substantially the same is true of defendants' hyperlinks to web pages that display nothing more than the DeCSS code or present the user only with the choice of commencing a download of DeCSS and no other content. The only distinction is that the entity extending to the user the option of downloading the program is the transferee site rather than defendants, a distinction without a difference.

Potentially more troublesome might be links to pages that offer a good deal of content other than DeCSS but that offer a hyperlink for downloading, or transferring to a page for downloading, DeCSS. If one assumed, for the purposes of argument, that the *Los Angeles Times* web site somewhere contained the DeCSS code, it would be wrong to say that anyone who linked to the *Los Angeles Times* web site, regardless of purpose or the manner in which the link was described, thereby offered, provided or otherwise trafficked in DeCSS merely because DeCSS happened to be available on a site to which one linked. [180] But that is not this case. Defendants urged others to post DeCSS in an effort to disseminate DeCSS and to inform defendants that they were doing so. Defendants then linked their site to those "mirror" sites, after first checking to ensure that the mirror sites in fact were posting DeCSS or something that looked like it, and proclaimed on their own site that DeCSS could be had by clicking on the hyperlinks on defendants' site. By doing so, they offered, provided or otherwise trafficked in DeCSS, and they continue to do so to this day.

III. *The First Amendment*

Defendants argue that the DMCA, at least as applied to prevent the public dissemination of DeCSS, violates the First Amendment to the Constitution. They claim that it does so in two ways.

First, they argue that computer code is protected speech and that the DMCA's prohibition of dissemination of DeCSS therefore violates defendants' First Amendment rights. Second, they contend that the DMCA is unconstitutionally overbroad, chiefly because its prohibition of the dissemination of decryption technology prevents third parties from making fair use of plaintiffs' encrypted works, and vague. They argue also that a prohibition on their linking to sites that make DeCSS available is unconstitutional for much the same reasons.

A. Computer Code and the First Amendment

The premise of defendants' first position is that computer code, the form in which DeCSS exists, is speech protected by the First Amendment. Examination of that premise is the logical starting point for analysis. And it is important in examining that premise first to define terms.

Defendants' assertion that computer code is "protected" by the First Amendment is quite understandable. Courts often have spoken of certain categories of expression as "not within the area of constitutionally protected speech,"[181] so defendants naturally wish to avoid exclusion by an unfavorable categorization of computer code. But such judicial statements in fact are not literally true. All modes of expression are covered by the First Amendment in the sense that the constitutionality of their "regulation must be determined by reference to First Amendment doctrine and analysis."[182] Regulation of different categories of expression, however, is subject to varying levels of judicial scrutiny. Thus, to say that a particular form of expression is "protected" by the First Amendment means that the constitutionality of any regulation of it must be measured by reference to the First Amendment. In some circumstances, however, the phrase connotes also that the standard for measurement is the most exacting level available.

It cannot seriously be argued that any form of computer code may be regulated without reference to First Amendment doctrine. The path from idea to human language to source code to object code is a continuum. As one moves from one to the other, the levels of precision and, arguably, abstraction increase, as does the level of training necessary to discern the idea from the expression. Not everyone can understand each of these forms. Only English speakers will understand English formulations. Principally those familiar with the particular programming language will understand the source code expression. And only a relatively small number of skilled programmers and computer scientists will understand the machine readable object code. But each form expresses the same idea, albeit in different ways.[183]

There perhaps was a time when the First Amendment was viewed only as a limitation on the ability of government to censor speech in advance.[184] But we have moved far beyond that. All modes by which ideas may be expressed or, perhaps, emotions evoked—including speech, books, movies, art, and music—are within the area of First Amendment concern.[185] As computer code—whether source or object—is a means of expressing ideas, the First Amendment must be considered before its dissemination may be prohibited or regulated. In that sense, computer code is covered or, as sometimes is said, "protected" by the First Amendment.[186] But that conclusion still leaves for determination the level of scrutiny to be applied in determining the constitutionality of regulation of computer code.

B. The Constitutionality of the DMCA's Anti-Trafficking Provision

1. Defendants' Alleged Right to Disseminate DeCSS

Defendants first attack Section 1201(a)(2), the anti-trafficking provision, as applied to them on the theory that DeCSS is constitutionally protected expression and that the statute improperly prevents them from communicating it. Their attack presupposes that a characterization of code as constitutionally protected subjects any regulation of code to the highest level of First Amendment scrutiny. As we have seen, however, this does not necessarily follow.

Just as computer code cannot be excluded from the area of First Amendment concern because it is abstract and, in many cases, arcane, the long history of First Amendment jurisprudence makes equally clear that the fact that words, symbols and even actions convey ideas and evoke emotions does not inevitably place them beyond the power of government. The Supreme Court has evolved an analytical framework by which the permissibility of particular restrictions on the expression of ideas must [be] determined.

Broadly speaking, restrictions on expression fall into two categories. Some are restrictions on the voicing of particular ideas, which typically are referred to as content based restrictions. Others have nothing to do with the content of the expression— *i.e.*, they are content neutral—but they have the incidental effect of limiting expression.

In general, "government has no power to restrict expression because of its message, its ideas, its subject matter, or its content . . . ." [187] "[S]ubject only to narrow and well-understood exceptions, [the First Amendment] does not countenance governmental control over the content of messages expressed by private individuals." [188] In consequence, content based restrictions on speech are permissible only if they serve compelling state interests by the least restrictive means available. [189]

Content neutral restrictions, in contrast, are measured against a less exacting standard. Because restrictions of this type are not motivated by a desire to limit the message, they will be upheld if they serve a substantial governmental interest and restrict First Amendment freedoms no more than necessary. [190]

Restrictions on the nonspeech elements of expressive conduct fall into the content-neutral category. The Supreme Court long has distinguished for First Amendment purposes between pure speech, which ordinarily receives the highest level of protection, and expressive conduct. [191] Even if conduct contains an expressive element, its nonspeech aspect need not be ignored. [192] "[W]hen 'speech' and 'nonspeech' elements are combined in the same course of conduct, a sufficiently important governmental interest in regulating the nonspeech element can justify incidental limitations on First Amendment freedoms." [193] The critical point is that nonspeech elements may create hazards for society above and beyond the speech elements. They are subject to regulation in appropriate circumstances because the government has an interest in dealing with the potential hazards of the nonspeech elements despite the fact that they are joined with expressive elements.

Thus, the starting point for analysis is whether the DMCA, as applied to restrict dissemination of DeCSS and other computer code used to circumvent access control measures, is a content based restriction on speech or a content neutral regulation. Put another way, the question is the level of review that governs the DMCA's anti-trafficking provision as applied to DeCSS—the strict scrutiny standard applicable to content based regulations or the intermediate level applicable to content neutral regulations, including regulations of the nonspeech elements of expressive conduct.

Given the fact that DeCSS code is expressive, defendants would have the Court leap immediately to the conclusion that Section 1201(a)(2)'s prohibition on providing DeCSS necessarily is content based regulation of speech because it suppresses dissemination of a particular kind of expression. [194] But this would be a unidimensional approach to a more textured reality and entirely too facile.

The "principal inquiry in determining content neutrality . . . is whether the government has adopted a regulation of speech because of [agreement or] disagreement with the message it conveys." [195] The computer code at issue in this case, however, does more than express the programmers' concepts. It does more, in other words, than convey a message. DeCSS, like any other computer program, is a series of instructions that causes a computer to perform a particular sequence of tasks which, in the aggregate, decrypt CSS-protected files. Thus, it has a distinctly functional, non-speech aspect in addition to reflecting the thoughts of the programmers. It enables anyone who receives it and who has a modicum of computer skills to circumvent plaintiffs' access control system.

The reason that Congress enacted the anti-trafficking provision of the DMCA had nothing to do with suppressing particular ideas of computer programmers and everything to do with functionality—with preventing people from circumventing technological access control measures—just as laws prohibiting the possession of burglar tools have nothing to do with preventing people from expressing themselves by accumulating what to them may be attractive assortments of implements and everything to do with preventing burglaries. Rather, it is focused squarely upon the effect of the distribution of the functional capability that the code provides. Any impact on the dissemination of programmers' ideas is purely incidental to the overriding concerns of promoting the distribution of copyrighted works in digital form while at the same time protecting those works from piracy and other violations of the exclusive rights of copyright holders. [196]

These considerations suggest that the DMCA as applied here is content neutral, a view that draws support also from *City of Renton v. Playtime Theatres, Inc.* [197] The Supreme Court there upheld against a First Amendment challenge a zoning ordinance that prohibited adult movie theaters within 1,000 feet of a residential, church or park zone or within one mile of a school. Recognizing that the ordinance did "not appear to fit neatly into either the 'content based' or the 'content-neutral' category," it found dispositive the fact that the ordinance was justified without reference to the content of the regulated speech in that the concern of the municipality had been with the secondary effects of the presence of adult theaters, not with the particular content of the speech that takes place in them. [198] As Congress' concerns in enacting the anti-trafficking provision of the DMCA were to suppress copyright piracy and infringement and to promote the availability of copyrighted works in digital form, and not to regulate the expression of ideas that might be inherent in particular anti-circumvention devices or technology, this provision of the statute properly is viewed as content neutral. [199]

Congress is not powerless to regulate content neutral regulations that incidentally affect expression, including the dissemination of the functional capabilities of computer code. A sufficiently important governmental interest in seeing to it that computers are not instructed to perform particular functions may justify incidental restrictions on the dissemination of the expressive elements of a program. Such a regulation will be upheld if:

> "it furthers an important or substantial governmental interest; if the governmental interest is unrelated to the suppression of free expression; and if the incidental restriction on alleged First Amendment freedoms is no greater than is essential to the furtherance of that interest." [200]

Moreover, "[t]o satisfy this standard, a regulation need not be the least speech-restrictive means of advancing the Government's interests." [201] "Rather, the requirement of narrow tailoring is satisfied 'so long as the ... regulation promotes a substantial

government interest that would be achieved less effectively absent the regulation.' " [202]

The anti-trafficking provision of the DMCA furthers an important governmental interest—the protection of copyrighted works stored on digital media from the vastly expanded risk of piracy in this electronic age. The substantiality of that interest is evident both from the fact that the Constitution specifically empowers Congress to provide for copyright protection [203] and from the significance to our economy of trade in copyrighted materials. [204] Indeed, the Supreme Court has made clear that copyright protection itself is "the engine of free expression." [205] That substantial interest, more-over, is unrelated to the suppression of particular views expressed in means of gaining access to protected copyrighted works. Nor is the incidental restraint on protected expression—the prohibition of trafficking in means that would circumvent controls limiting access to unprotected materials or to copyrighted materials for noninfringing purposes—broader than is necessary to accomplish Congress' goals of preventing infringement and promoting the availability of content in digital form. [206]

This analysis finds substantial support in the principal case relied upon by defendants, *Junger v. Daley.* [207] The plaintiff in that case challenged on First Amendment grounds an Export Administration regulation that barred the export of computer encryption software, arguing that the software was expressive and that the regulation therefore was unconstitutional. The Sixth Circuit acknowledged the expressive nature of computer code, holding that it therefore was within the scope of the First Amendment. But it recognized also that computer code is functional as well and said that "[t]he functional capabilities of source code, particularly those of encryption source code, should be considered when analyzing the governmental interest in regulating the exchange of this form of speech." [208] Indeed, it went on to indicate that the pertinent standard of review was that established in *United States v. O'Brien,* [209] the seminal speech-versus-conduct decision. Thus, rather than holding the challenged regulation unconstitutional on the theory that the expressive aspect of source code immunized it from regulation, the court remanded the case to the district court to determine whether the *O'Brien* standard was met in view of the functional aspect of code. [210]

Notwithstanding its adoption by the Sixth Circuit, the focus on functionality in order to determine the level of scrutiny is not an inevitable consequence of the speech-conduct distinction. Conduct has immediate effects on the environment. Computer code, on the other hand, no matter how functional, causes a computer to perform the intended operations only if someone uses the code to do so. Hence, one commentator, in a thoughtful article, has maintained that functionality is really "a proxy for effects or harm" and that its adoption as a determinant of the level of scrutiny slides over questions of causation that intervene between the dissemination of a computer program and any harm caused by its use. [211]

The characterization of functionality as a proxy for the consequences of use is accurate. But the assumption that the chain of causation is too attenuated to justify the use of functionality to determine the level of scrutiny, at least in this context, is not.

Society increasingly depends upon technological means of controlling access to digital files and systems, whether they are military computers, bank records, academic records, copyrighted works or something else entirely. There are far too many who, given any opportunity, will bypass those security measures, some for the sheer joy of doing it, some for innocuous reasons, and others for more malevolent purposes. Given the virtually instantaneous and worldwide dissemination widely available via the Internet, the only rational assumption is that once a computer program capable of bypassing such an access control system is disseminated, it will be used. And that is not all.

There was a time when copyright infringement could be dealt with quite adequately by focusing on the infringing act. If someone wished to make and sell high quality but unauthorized copies of a copyrighted book, for example, the infringer needed a printing press. The copyright holder, once aware of the appearance of infringing copies, usually was able to trace the copies up the chain of distribution, find and prosecute the infringer, and shut off the infringement at the source.

In principle, the digital world is very different. Once a decryption program like DeCSS is written, it quickly can be sent all over the world. Every recipient is capable not only of decrypting and perfectly copying plaintiffs' copyrighted DVDs, but also of retransmitting perfect copies of DeCSS and thus enabling every recipient to do the same. They likewise are capable of transmitting perfect copies of the decrypted DVD. The process potentially is exponential rather than linear. Indeed, the difference is illustrated by comparison of two epidemiological models describing the spread of different kinds of disease. [212] In a common source epidemic, as where members of a population contract a non-contagious disease from a poisoned well, the disease spreads only by exposure to the common source. If one eliminates the source, or closes the contaminated well, the epidemic is stopped. In a propagated outbreak epidemic, on the other hand, the disease spreads from person to person. Hence, finding the initial source of infection accomplishes little, as the disease continues to spread even if the initial source is eliminated. [213] For obvious reasons, then, a propagated outbreak epidemic, all other things being equal, can be far more difficult to control.

This disease metaphor is helpful here. The book infringement hypothetical is analogous to a common source outbreak epidemic. Shut down the printing press (the poisoned well) and one ends the infringement (the disease outbreak). The spread of means of circumventing access to copyrighted works in digital form, however, is analogous to a propagated outbreak epidemic. Finding the original source of infection (e.g., the author of DeCSS or the first person to misuse it) accomplishes nothing, as the disease (infringement made possible by DeCSS and the resulting availability of decrypted DVDs) may continue to spread from one person who gains access to the circumvention program or decrypted DVD to another. And each is "infected," i.e., each is as capable of making perfect copies of the digital file containing the copyrighted work as the author of the program or the first person to use it for improper purposes. The disease metaphor breaks down principally at the final point. Individuals infected with a real disease become sick, usually are driven by obvious self-interest to seek medical attention, and are cured of the disease if medical science is capable of doing so. Individuals infected with the "disease" of capability of circumventing measures controlling access to copyrighted works in digital form, however, do not suffer from having that ability. They cannot be relied upon to identify themselves to those seeking to control the "disease." And their self-interest will motivate some to misuse the capability, a misuse that, in practical terms, often will be untraceable. [214]

These considerations drastically alter consideration of the causal link between dissemination of computer programs such as this and their illicit use. Causation in the law ultimately involves practical policy judgments. [215] Here, dissemination itself carries very substantial risk of imminent harm because the mechanism is so unusual by which dissemination of means of circumventing access controls to copyrighted works threatens to produce virtually unstoppable infringement of copyright. In consequence, the causal link between the dissemination of circumvention computer programs and their improper use is more than sufficiently close to warrant selection of a level of constitutional scrutiny based on the programs' functionality.

Accordingly, this Court holds that the anti-trafficking provision of the DMCA as applied to the posting of computer code that circumvents measures that control access to copyrighted works in digital form is a valid exercise of Congress' authority. It is a content neutral regulation in furtherance of important governmental interests that does not unduly restrict expressive activities. In any case, its particular functional characteristics are such that the Court would apply the same level of scrutiny even if it were viewed as content based. [216] Yet it is important to emphasize that this is a very narrow holding. The restriction the Court here upholds, notwithstanding that computer code is within the area of First Amendment concern, is limited (1) to programs that circumvent access controls to copyrighted works in digital form in circumstances in which (2) there is no other practical means of preventing infringement through use of the programs, and (3) the regulation is motivated by a desire to prevent performance of the function for which the programs exist rather than any message they might convey. One readily might imagine other circumstances in which a governmental attempt to regulate the dissemination of computer code would not similarly be justified. [217]

2. Prior Restraint

Defendants argue also that injunctive relief against dissemination of DeCSS is barred by the prior restraint doctrine. The Court disagrees.

Few phrases are as firmly rooted in our constitutional jurisprudence as the maxim that "[a]ny system of prior restraints of expression comes to [a] Court bearing a heavy presumption against its constitutional validity." [218] Yet there is a significant gap between the rhetoric and the reality. Courts often have upheld restrictions on expression that many would describe as prior restraints, [219] sometimes by characterizing the expression as unprotected [220] and on other occasions finding the restraint justified despite its presumed invalidity. [221] Moreover, the prior restraint doctrine, which has expanded far beyond the Blackstonian model [222] that doubtless informed the understanding of the Framers of the First Amendment, [223] has been criticized as filled with "doctrinal ambiguities and inconsistencies result[ing] from the absence of any detailed judicial analysis of [its] true rationale" [224] and, in one case, even as "fundamentally unintelligible." [225] Nevertheless, the doctrine has a well established core: administrative preclearance requirements for and at least preliminary injunctions against speech as conventionally understood are presumptively unconstitutional. Yet that proposition does not dispose of this case. [226]

The classic prior restraint cases were dramatically different from this one. *Near v. Minnesota* [227] involved a state procedure for abating scandalous and defamatory newspapers as public nuisances. *New York Times Co. v. United States* [228] dealt with an attempt to enjoin a newspaper from publishing an internal government history of the Vietnam War. *Nebraska Press Association v. Stuart* [229] concerned a court order barring the reporting of certain details about a forthcoming murder case. In each case, therefore, the government sought to suppress speech at the very heart of First Amendment concern—expression about public issues of the sort that is indispensable to self government. And while the prior restraint doctrine has been applied well beyond the sphere of political expression, we deal here with something new altogether—computer code, a fundamentally utilitarian construct, albeit one that embodies an expressive element. Hence, it would be a mistake simply to permit its expressive element to drive a characterization of the code as speech no different from the Pentagon Papers, the publication of a newspaper, or the exhibition of a motion picture and then to apply prior restraint rhetoric without a more nuanced consideration of the competing concerns.

In this case, the considerations supporting an injunction are very substantial indeed. Copyright and, more broadly, intellectual property piracy are endemic, as Congress repeatedly has found.[230] The interest served by prohibiting means that facilitate such piracy—the protection of the monopoly granted to copyright owners by the Copyright Act—is of constitutional dimension. There is little room for doubting that broad dissemination of DeCSS threatens ultimately to injure or destroy plaintiffs' ability to distribute their copyrighted products on DVDs and, for that matter, undermine their ability to sell their products to the home video market in other forms. The potential damages probably are incalculable, and these defendants surely would be in no position to compensate plaintiffs for them if plaintiffs were remitted only to *post hoc* damage suits.

On the other side of the coin, the First Amendment interests served by the dissemination of DeCSS on the merits are minimal. The presence of some expressive content in the code should not obscure the fact of its predominant functional character—it is first and foremost a means of causing a machine with which it is used to perform particular tasks. Hence, those of the traditional rationales for the prior restraint doctrine that relate to inhibiting the transmission and receipt of ideas are of attenuated relevance here. Indeed, even academic commentators who take the extreme position that most injunctions in intellectual property cases are unconstitutional prior restraints concede that there is no First Amendment obstacle to injunctions barring distribution of copyrighted computer object code or restraining the construction of a new building based on copyrighted architectural drawings because the functional aspects of these types of information are "sufficiently nonexpressive."[231]

To be sure, there is much to be said in most circumstances for the usual procedural rationale for the prior restraint doctrine: prior restraints carry with them the risk of erroneously suppressing expression that could not constitutionally be punished after publication.[232] In this context, however, that concern is not persuasive, both because the enjoined expressive element is minimal and because a full trial on the merits has been held.[233] Accordingly,

the Court holds that the prior restraint doctrine does not require denial of an injunction in this case.

3. Overbreadth

Defendants' second focus is the contention that Section 1201(a)(2) is unconstitutional because it prevents others from making fair use of copyrighted works by depriving them of the means of circumventing plaintiffs' access control system.[234] In substance, they contend that the anti-trafficking provision leaves those who lack sufficient technical expertise to circumvent CSS themselves without the means of acquiring circumvention technology that they need to make fair use of the content of plaintiffs' copyrighted DVDs.[235]

As a general proposition, "a person to whom a statute constitutionally may be applied may not challenge that statute on the ground that it conceivably may be applied unconstitutionally to others in situations not before the Court."[236] When statutes regulate speech, however, "the transcendent value to all society of constitutionally protected expression is deemed to justify 'attacks on overly broad statutes with no requirement that the person making the attack demonstrate that his own conduct could not be regulated by a statute drawn with the requisite narrow specificity.' "[237] This is so because the absent third parties may not exercise their rights for fear of triggering "sanctions provided by a statute susceptible of application to protected expression."[238] But the overbreadth doctrine " 'is 'strong medicine' .... employed ... with hesitation, and then 'only as a last resort' "because it conflicts with "the personal nature of constitutional rights and the prudential limitations on constitutional adjudication," including the importance of focusing carefully on the facts in deciding constitutional questions.[239] Moreover, the limited function of the overbreadth doctrine " 'attenuates as the otherwise unprotected behavior that it forbids the State to sanction moves from 'pure speech' toward conduct and that conduct—even if expressive—falls within the scope of otherwise valid criminal laws . . . .' "[240] As defendants concede, "where conduct and not merely speech is involved, . . . the overbreadth of a statute must not only be real, but substantial as well, judged in relation to the statute's plainly legitimate sweep."[241]

Factors arguing against use of the overbreadth doctrine are present here. To begin with, we do not here have a complete view of whether the interests of the absent third parties upon whom defendants rely really are substantial and, in consequence, whether the DMCA as applied here would materially affect their ability to make fair use of plaintiffs' copyrighted works.

The copyrighted works at issue, of course, are motion pictures. People use copies of them in DVD and other formats for various purposes, and we confine our consideration to the lawful purposes, which by definition are noninfringing or fair uses. The principal noninfringing use is to play the DVD for the purpose of watching the movie—viewing the images and hearing the sounds that are synchronized with them. Fair uses are much more varied. A movie reviewer might wish to quote a portion of the verbal script in an article or broadcast review. A television station might want to broadcast part of a particular scene to illustrate a review, a news story about a performer, or a story about particular trends in motion pictures. A musicologist perhaps would wish to play a portion of a musical sound track. A film scholar might desire to create and exhibit to students small segments of several different films to make some comparative point about the cinematography or some other characteristic. Numerous other examples doubtless could be imagined. But each necessarily involves one or more of three types of use: (1) quotation of the words of the script, (2) listening to the recorded sound track, including both verbal and non-verbal elements, and (3) viewing of the graphic images.

All three of these types of use now are affected by the anti-trafficking provision of the DMCA, but probably only to a trivial degree. To begin with, all or substantially all motion pictures available on DVD are available also on videotape.[242] In consequence, anyone wishing to make lawful use of a particular movie may buy or rent a videotape, play it, and even copy all or part of it with readily available equipment. But even if movies were available only on DVD, as someday may be the case, the impact on lawful use would be limited. Compliant DVD players permit one to view or listen to a DVD movie without circumventing CSS in any prohibited sense. The technology permitting manufacture of compliant DVD players is available to anyone on a royalty-free basis and at modest cost, so CSS raises no technological barrier to their manufacture. Hence, those wishing to make lawful

use of copyrighted movies by viewing or listening to them are not hindered in doing so in any material way by the anti-trafficking provision of the DMCA.[243]

Nor does the DMCA materially affect quotation of language from CSS-protected movies. Anyone with access to a compliant DVD player may play the movie and write down or otherwise record the sound for the purpose of quoting it in another medium.

The DMCA does have a notable potential impact on uses that copy portions of a DVD movie because compliant DVD players are designed so as to prevent copying. In consequence, even though the fair use doctrine permits limited copying of copyrighted works in appropriate circumstances, the CSS encryption of DVD movies, coupled with the characteristics of licensed DVD players, limits such uses absent circumvention of CSS.[244] Moreover, the anti-trafficking provision of the DMCA may prevent technologically unsophisticated persons who wish to copy portions of DVD movies for fair use from obtaining the means of doing so. It is the interests of these individuals upon which defendants rely most heavily in contending that the DMCA violates the First Amendment because it deprives such persons of an asserted constitutional right to make fair use of copyrighted materials.[245]

As the foregoing suggests, the interests of persons wishing to circumvent CSS in order to make lawful use of the copyrighted movies it protects are remarkably varied. Some presumably are technologically sophisticated and therefore capable of circumventing CSS without access to defendants' or other purveyors' decryption programs; many presumably are not. Many of the possible fair uses may be made without circumventing CSS while others, i.e., those requiring copying, may not. Hence, the question whether Section 1201(a)(2) as applied here substantially affects rights, much less constitutionally protected rights, of members of the "fair use community" cannot be decided in bloc, without consideration of the circumstances of each member or similarly situated groups of members. Thus, the prudential concern with ensuring that constitutional questions be decided only when the facts before the Court so require counsels against permitting defendants to mount an overbreadth challenge here.[246]

Second, there is no reason to suppose here that prospective fair users will be deterred from asserting their alleged rights by fear of sanctions imposed by the DMCA or the Copyright Act.

Third, we do not deal here with "pure speech." Rather, the issue concerns dissemination of technology that is principally functional in nature. The same consideration that warrants restraint in applying the overbreadth doctrine to statutes regulating expressive conduct applies here. For reasons previously expressed, government's interest in regulating the functional capabilities of computer code is no less weighty than its interest in regulating the nonspeech aspects of expressive conduct.

Finally, there has been no persuasive evidence that the interests of persons who wish access to the CSS algorithm in order to study its encryption methodology or to evaluate theories regarding decryption raise serious problems. The statute contains an exception for good faith encryption research. [247]

Accordingly, defendants will not be heard to mount an overbreadth challenge to the DMCA in this context.

4. Vagueness

Defendants argue also that the DMCA is unconstitutionally vague because the terms it employs are not understandable to persons of ordinary intelligence and because they are subject to discriminatory enforcement. [248]

As the Supreme Court has made clear, one who "engages in some conduct that is clearly proscribed [by the challenged statute] cannot complain of the vagueness of the law as applied to the conduct of others." [249] There can be no serious doubt that posting a computer program the sole purpose of which is to defeat an encryption system controlling access to plaintiff's copyrighted movies constituted an "offer to the public" of "technology [or a] product" that was "primarily designed for the purpose of circumventing" plaintiffs' access control system. [250] Defendants thus engaged in conduct clearly proscribed by the DMCA and will not be heard to complain of any vagueness as applied to others.

C. Linking

As indicated above, the DMCA reaches links deliberately created by a web site operator for the purpose of disseminating technology that enables the user to circumvent access controls on copyrighted works. The question is whether it may do so consistent with the First Amendment.

Links bear a relationship to the information superhighway comparable to the relationship that roadway signs bear to roads but they are more functional. Like roadway signs, they point out the direction. Unlike roadway signs, they take one almost instantaneously to the desired destination with the mere click of an electronic mouse. Thus, like computer code in general, they have both expressive and functional elements. Also like computer code, they are within the area of First Amendment concern. Hence, the constitutionality of the DMCA as applied to defendants' linking is determined by the same *O'Brien* standard that governs trafficking in the circumvention technology generally.

There is little question that the application of the DMCA to the linking at issue in this case would serve, at least to some extent, the same substantial governmental interest as its application to defendants' posting of the DeCSS code. Defendants' posting and their linking amount to very much the same thing. Similarly, the regulation of the linking at issue here is "unrelated to the suppression of free expression" for the same reason as the regulation of the posting. The third prong of the *O'Brien* test as subsequently interpreted—whether the "regulation promotes a substantial government interest that would be achieved less effectively absent the regulation" [251] —is a somewhat closer call.

Defendants and, by logical extension, others may be enjoined from posting DeCSS. Plaintiffs may seek legal redress against anyone who persists in posting notwithstanding this decision. Hence, barring defendants from linking to sites against which plaintiffs readily may take legal action would advance the statutory purpose of preventing dissemination of circumvention technology, but it would do so less effectively than would actions by plaintiffs directly against the sites that post. For precisely this reason, however, the real significance of an anti-linking injunction would not be with U.S. web sites subject to the DMCA, but with foreign sites that arguably are not subject to it and not subject to suit here. An anti-linking injunction to that extent would have a significant impact and thus materially advance a substantial governmental purpose. In consequence, the Court concludes that an injunction against linking to other sites posting DeCSS satisfies the *O'Brien* standard. There remains, however, one further important point.

Links are "what unify the [World Wide] Web into a single body of knowledge, and what makes the Web unique." [252] They "are the mainstay of the Internet and indispensable to its convenient access to the vast world of information." [253] They often are used in ways that do a great deal to promote the free exchange of ideas and information that is a central value of our nation. Anything that would impose strict liability on a web site operator for the entire contents of any web site to which the operator linked therefore would raise grave constitutional concerns, as web site operators would be inhibited from linking for fear of exposure to liability. [254] And it is equally clear that exposing those who use links to liability under the DMCA might chill their use, as some web site operators confronted with claims that they have posted circumvention technology falling within the statute may be more inclined to remove the allegedly offending link rather than test the issue in court. Moreover, web sites often contain a great variety of things, and a ban on linking to a site that contains DeCSS amidst other content threatens to restrict communication of this information to an excessive degree.

The possible chilling effect of a rule permitting liability for or injunctions against Internet hyperlinks is a genuine concern. But it is not unique to the issue of linking. The constitutional law of defamation provides a highly relevant analogy. The threat of defamation suits creates the same risk of self-censorship, the same chilling effect, for the traditional press as a prohibition of linking to sites containing circumvention technology poses for web site operators. Just as the potential chilling effect of defamation suits has not utterly immunized the press from all actions for defamation, however, the potential chilling effect of DMCA liability cannot utterly immunize web site operators from all actions for disseminating circumvention technology. And the solution to the problem is the same: the adoption of a standard of culpability sufficiently high to immunize the activity, whether it is publishing a

newspaper or linking, except in cases in which the conduct in question has little or no redeeming constitutional value.

In the defamation area, this has been accomplished by a two-tiered constitutional standard. There may be no liability under the First Amendment for defamation of a public official or a public figure unless the plaintiff proves, by clear and convincing evidence, that the defendant published the offending statement with knowledge of its falsity or with serious doubt as to its truth. [255] Liability in private figure cases, on the other hand, may not be imposed absent proof at least of negligence under *Gertz v. Robert Welch, Inc.* [256] A similar approach would minimize any chilling effect here.

The other concern—that a liability based on a link to another site simply because the other site happened to contain DeCSS or some other circumvention technology in the midst of other perfectly appropriate content could be overkill— also is readily dealt with. The offense under the DMCA is offering, providing or otherwise trafficking in circumvention technology. An essential ingredient, as explained above, is a desire to bring about the dissemination. Hence, a strong requirement of that forbidden purpose is an essential prerequisite to any liability for linking.

Accordingly, there may be no injunction against, nor liability for, linking to a site containing circumvention technology, the offering of which is unlawful under the DMCA, absent clear and convincing evidence that those responsible for the link (a) know at the relevant time that the offending material is on the linked-to site, (b) know that it is circumvention technology that may not lawfully be offered, and (c) create or maintain the link for the purpose of disseminating that technology. [257] Such a standard will limit the fear of liability on the part of web site operators just as the *New York Times* standard gives the press great comfort in publishing all sorts of material that would have been actionable at common law, even in the face of flat denials by the subjects of their stories. And it will not subject web site operators to liability for linking to a site containing proscribed technology where the link exists for purposes other than dissemination of that technology.

In this case, plaintiffs have established by clear and convincing evidence that these defendants linked to sites posting DeCSS, knowing that it was a circumvention device. Indeed, they initially touted it as a way to get free movies,[258] and they later maintained the links to promote the dissemination of the program in an effort to defeat effective judicial relief. They now know that dissemination of DeCSS violates the DMCA. An anti-linking injunction on these facts does no violence to the First Amendment. Nor should it chill the activities of web site operators dealing with different materials, as they may be held liable only on a compelling showing of deliberate evasion of the statute.

IV. Relief

A. Injury to Plaintiffs

The DMCA provides that "[a]ny person injured by a violation of section 1201 or 1202 may bring a civil action in an appropriate United States court for such violation."[259] For the reasons set forth above, plaintiffs obviously have suffered and, absent effective relief, will continue to suffer injury by virtue of the ready availability of means of circumventing the CSS access control system on their DVDs. Defendants nevertheless argue that they have not met the injury requirement of the statute. Their contentions are a farrago of distortions.

They begin with the assertion that plaintiffs have failed to prove that decrypted motion pictures actually are available.[260] To be sure, plaintiffs might have done a better job of proving what appears to be reasonably obvious. They certainly could have followed up on more of the 650 movie titles listed on the web site described above to establish that the titles in fact were available. But the evidence they did adduce is not nearly as meager as defendants would have it. Dr. Shamos did pursue and obtain a pirated copy of a copyrighted, DivX'd motion picture from someone he met in an Internet chat room. An MPAA investigator downloaded between five and ten such copies. And the sudden appearance of listings of available motion pictures on the Internet promptly after DeCSS became available is far from lacking in evidentiary significance. In any case, in order to obtain the relief sought here, plaintiffs need show only a threat of injury by reason of a violation of the statute.[261] The Court finds that plaintiffs overwhelmingly have established a clear threat of injury by reason of defendants' violation of the statute.

Defendants next maintain that plaintiffs exaggerate the extent of the threatened injury. They claim that the studios in fact believe that DeCSS is not a threat.[262] But the only basis for that contention is a couple of quotations from statements that the MPAA or one or another studio made (or considered making but did not in fact issue) to the effect that it was not concerned about DeCSS or that it was inconvenient to use.[263] These statements, however, were attempts to "spin" public opinion.[264] They do not now reflect the actual state of affairs or the studios' actual views, if they ever did.

Third, defendants contend that there is no evidence that any decrypted movies that may be available, if any there are, were decrypted with DeCSS. They maintain that "[m]any utilities and devices . . . can decrypt DVDs equally well and often faster and with greater ease than by using DeCSS."[265] This is a substantial exaggeration. There appear to be a few other so-called rippers, but the Court finds that DeCSS is usable on a broader range of DVDs than any of the others. Further, there is no credible evidence that any other utility is faster or easier to use than DeCSS. Indeed, the Court concludes that DeCSS is the superior product, as evidenced by the fact that the web site promoting DivX as a tool for obtaining usable copies of copyrighted movies recommends the use of DeCSS, rather than anything else, for the decryption step[266] and that the apparent availability of pirated motion pictures shot up so dramatically upon the introduction of DeCSS.[267]

B. Permanent Injunction and Declaratory Relief

Plaintiffs seek a permanent injunction barring defendants from posting DeCSS on their web site and from linking their site to others that make DeCSS available.

The starting point, as always, is the statute. The DMCA provides in relevant part that the court in an action brought pursuant to its terms "may grant temporary and permanent injunctions on such terms as it deems reasonable to prevent or restrain a violation. . . ."[268] Where statutes in substance so provide, injunctive relief is appropriate if there is a reasonable likelihood of future violations absent such relief[269] and, in cases brought by private plaintiffs, if the plaintiff lacks an adequate remedy at law.[270]

In this case, it is quite likely that defendants, unless enjoined, will continue to violate the Act. Defendants are in the business of disseminating information to assist hackers in "cracking" various types of technological security systems. And while defendants argue that they promptly stopped posting DeCSS when enjoined preliminarily from doing so, thus allegedly demonstrating their willingness to comply with the law, their reaction to the preliminary injunction in fact cuts the other way. Upon being enjoined from posting DeCSS themselves, defendants encouraged others to "mirror" the information—that is, to post DeCSS—and linked their own web site to mirror sites in order to assist users of defendants' web site in obtaining DeCSS despite the injunction barring defendants from providing it directly. While there is no claim that this activity violated the letter of the preliminary injunction, and it therefore presumably was not contumacious, and while its status under the DMCA was somewhat uncertain, it was a studied effort to defeat the purpose of the preliminary injunction. In consequence, the Court finds that there is a substantial likelihood of future violations absent injunctive relief.

There also is little doubt that plaintiffs have no adequate remedy at law. The only potential legal remedy would be an action for damages under Section 1203(c), which provides for recovery of actual damages or, upon the election of the plaintiff, statutory damages of up to $2,500 per offer of DeCSS. Proof of actual damages in a case of this nature would be difficult if not virtually impossible, as it would involve proof of the extent to which motion picture attendance, sales of broadcast and other motion picture rights, and sales and rentals of DVDs and video tapes of movies were and will be impacted by the availability of DVD decryption technology. Difficulties in determining what constitutes an "offer" of DeCSS in a world in which the code is available to much of the world via Internet postings, among other problems, render statutory damages an inadequate means of redressing plaintiffs' claimed injuries. Indeed, difficulties such as this have led to the presumption that copyright and trademark infringement cause irreparable injury, [271] i.e., injury for which damages are not an adequate remedy.[272] The Court therefore holds that the

traditional requirements for issuance of a permanent injunction have been satisfied. Yet there remains another point for consideration.

Defendants argue that an injunction in this case would be futile because DeCSS already is all over the Internet. They say an injunction would be comparable to locking the barn door after the horse is gone. And the Court has been troubled by that possibility. But the countervailing arguments overcome that concern.

To begin with, any such conclusion effectively would create all the wrong incentives by allowing defendants to continue violating the DMCA simply because others, many doubtless at defendants' urging, are doing so as well. Were that the law, defendants confronted with the possibility of injunctive relief would be well advised to ensure that others engage in the same unlawful conduct in order to set up the argument that an injunction against the defendants would be futile because everyone else is doing the same thing.

Second, and closely related, is the fact that this Court is sorely "troubled by the notion that any Internet user . . . can destroy valuable intellectual property rights by posting them over the Internet."[273] While equity surely should not act where the controversy has become moot, it ought to look very skeptically at claims that the defendant or others already have done all the harm that might be done before the injunction issues.

The key to reconciling these views is that the focus of injunctive relief is on the defendants before the Court. If a plaintiff seeks to enjoin a defendant from burning a pasture, it is no answer that there is a wild fire burning in its direction. If the defendant itself threatens the plaintiff with irreparable harm, then equity will enjoin the defendant from carrying out the threat even if other threats abound and even if part of the pasture already is burned.

These defendants would harm plaintiffs every day on which they post DeCSS on their heavily trafficked web site and link to other sites that post it because someone who does not have DeCSS thereby might obtain it. They thus threaten plaintiffs with immediate and irreparable injury. They will not be allowed to continue to do so simply because others may do so as well. In short, this Court, like others than have faced the issued [sic], is "not persuaded that modern technology has withered the strong right arm of equity." [274] Indeed, the likelihood is that this decision will serve notice on others that "the strong right arm of equity" may be brought to bear against them absent a change in their conduct and thus contribute to a climate of appropriate respect for intellectual property rights in an age in which the excitement of ready access to untold quantities of information has blurred in some minds the fact that taking what is not yours and not freely offered to you is stealing. Appropriate injunctive [275] and declaratory relief will issue simultaneously with this opinion.

V. Miscellaneous Contentions

There remain for consideration two other matters, plaintiffs' application for costs and attorney's fees and defendants' pretrial complaints concerning discovery.

The DMCA permits awards of costs and attorney's fees to the prevailing party in the discretion of the Court. [276] Insofar as attorney's fees are concerned, this is an exception to the so-called "American rule" pursuant to which each side in a litigation customarily bears its own attorney's fees. As this was a test case raising important issues, it would be inappropriate to award attorney's fees pursuant to the DMCA. [277] There is no comparable reason, however, for failing to award costs, particularly as taxable costs are related to the excessive discovery demands that the Court already has commented upon. [278]

A final word is in order in view of defendants' repeated pretrial claims that their discovery efforts were being thwarted. During the course of the trial, they applied for leave to take one deposition, which was granted. At no point did they make any showing that they were hampered in presenting their case or meeting the plaintiffs' case by virtue of any failure to obtain discovery. They applied for no continuance. They have not sought a new trial. And though they estimated that their case would take several weeks to present, the entire trial was completed in six days. Indeed, in the Court's view, the trial fully vindicated its pretrial assessment that there were, in actuality, very few genuinely disputed questions of material fact, and most of those involved expert testimony that was readily available to both sides. [279] Examination of the trial record will reveal that virtually the entire case could have been stipulated, although the legal conclusions to be

drawn from the stipulated facts of course would have remained a matter of controversy.

VI. Conclusion

In the final analysis, the dispute between these parties is simply put if not necessarily simply resolved.

Plaintiffs have invested huge sums over the years in producing motion pictures in reliance upon a legal framework that, through the law of copyright, has ensured that they will have the exclusive right to copy and distribute those motion pictures for economic gain. They contend that the advent of new technology should not alter this long established structure.

Defendants, on the other hand, are adherents of a movement that believes that information should be available without charge to anyone clever enough to break into the computer systems or data storage media in which it is located. Less radically, they have raised a legitimate concern about the possible impact on traditional fair use of access control measures in the digital era.

Each side is entitled to its views. In our society, however, clashes of competing interests like this are resolved by Congress. For now, at least, Congress has resolved this clash in the DMCA and in plaintiffs' favor. Given the peculiar characteristics of computer programs for circumventing encryption and other access control measures, the DMCA as applied to posting and linking here does not contravene the First Amendment. Accordingly, plaintiffs are entitled to appropriate injunctive and declaratory relief.

SO ORDERED.

---

[1]   17 USC §1201 *et seq.*

[2]   Shortly after the commencement of the action, the Court granted plaintiffs' motion for a preliminary injunction barring defendants from posting DeCSS. *Universal City Studios, Inc. v. Reimerdes,* 82 F Supp 2d 211 *[4 ILR (P&F) 399]* (SD NY 2000). Subsequent motions to expand the preliminary injunction to linking and to vacate it were consolidated with the trial on the merits. This opinion reflects the Court's findings of fact, conclusions of law and decision on the merits.

The Court notes the receipt of a number of *amicus* submissions. Although many were filed by defendants' counsel on behalf of certain *amici,* and therefore were of debatable objectivity, the *amicus* submissions considered as a group were helpful.

[3] David Nimmer, *A Riff on Fair Use in the Digital Millennium Copyright Act*, 148 U. PA. L. REV. 673, 739-41 (2000) (hereinafter *A Riff on Fair Use*).

[4] *United States v. Microsoft Corp.*, 84 F Supp 2d 9, 13 (D DC 1999). The quotations are from a finding of fact in the *Microsoft* case of which the Court, after notice to and without objection by the parties, takes judicial notice. Tr. at 1121. Subsequent references to *Microsoft* findings reflect similar instances of judicial notice without objection.

[5] *United States v. Microsoft Corp.*, 84 F Supp 2d at 13.

[6] Open source is a software development model by which the source code to a computer program is made available publicly under a license that gives users the right to modify and redistribute the program. The program develops through this process of modification and redistribution and through a process by which users download sections of code from a web site, modify that code, upload it to the same web site, and merge the modified sections into the original code. Trial transcript ("Tr.") (Craig) at 1008.

[7] Tr. (Pavlovich) at 936.

[8] Tr. (DiBona) at 994-95.

[9] *Id.*

[10] THE NEW YORK PUBLIC LIBRARY, SCIENCE DESK REFERENCE 496 (1995) (hereinafter SCIENCE DESK REFERENCE); *see also* Tr. (Felten) at 758-59; Hon. Shira A. Scheindlin & Jeffrey Rabkin, *Electronic Discovery in Federal Civil Litigation: Is Rule 34 Up to the Task?* 34 B. C. L. REV. 327, 333-35 (2000).

[11] Tr. (Felten) at 759; Scheindlin & Rabkin, 34 B. C. L. REV. at 333-35.

[12] SCIENCE DESK REFERENCE, at 501.

[13] *Id.*

[14] *Id.*

[15] *See* Tr. (Felten) at 759-60.

[16] The Court's findings with respect to the definitions of source code and object code are taken from the trial testimony of Robert Schumann, Tr. at 258, and Drs. Edward Felten, Tr. at 738-39, 757-63, David S. Touretzky, Tr. at 1065-91, and Andrew Appel, Tr. at 1096, and the deposition testimony of Dr. Harold Abelson, Ex. AZO at 34-37, 45-49. *See also* Ex. BBE.

[17] Frequently, programs written in such languages must be transformed or translated into machine readable form by other programs known as compilers.

[18] This to some degree is an oversimplification. Object code often is directly executable by the computer into which it is entered. It sometimes contains instructions, however, that are readable only by computers containing a particular processor, such as a Pentium processor, or a specific operating system such as Microsoft Windows. In such instances, a computer lacking the specific processor or operating system can execute the object code only if it has an emulator program that simulates the necessary processor or operating system or if the code first is run through a translator program that converts it into object code readable by that computer. Ex. BBE.

[19] *United States v. Microsoft Corp.*, 84 F Supp 2d at 13.

[20] Tr. (Shamos) at 67-68.

[21] *United States v. Microsoft Corp.*, 84 F Supp 2d at 13.

[22] *Id.* at 14.

[23] *Id.*

[24] *Id.*

[25] Not too many years ago, the most common transportable storage media were 5 ¼ inch flexible magnetic disks. Their flexibility led to their being referred to as "floppies." They have been replaced almost entirely with today's 3 ½ inch disks, which are enclosed in hard plastic housings and which therefore are not flexible or "floppy." The earlier name, however, has stuck.

[26] Tr. (King) at 403-04.

[27] Tr. (Shamos) at 24.

[28] *Id.* at 24-25.

[29] Such devices are referred to subsequently as compliant.

[30] Tr. (Shamos) at 25.

[31] Tr. (Schumann) at 273

[32] Tr. (Ramadge) at 911.

[33] *Id.* at 911-12.

[34] Ex. 2.1-2.34; 3.1-3.34.

[35] Tr. (King) at 404.

[36] Tr. (Corley) at 787, 827.

[37] Tr. (Corley) at 777, 790, 795; Ex. 1.1, 1.2, 1.3, 1.4, 1.5, 1.6, 1.7, 1.8, 1.11, 1.12, 1.13, 1.14, 1.15, 1.16; 79 (Corley Dec.) ¶ 1.

[38] *See* Tr. (Corley) at 781.

[39] Tr. (Corley) 786-87.

[40] *Id.* at 787.

[41] Ex. 1.2 (Redomega Crim, *How Domains Are Stolen*, 2600: THE HACKER QUARTERLY, Summer 2000, at 43).

[42] Ex. 1.16 (Schlork, *Snooping via MS-Mail*, 2600: THE HACKER QUARTERLY, Winter 1996-97, at 28).

[43] Ex. 1.14 (Thomas Icom, *Cellular Interception Techniques*, 2600: THE HACKER QUARTERLY, Spring 1995, at 23).

[44] Ex. 1.12 (nux, *Fun at Costco*, 2600: THE HACKER QUARTERLY, Summer 1999, at 12).

[45] Ex. 1.19 (PhranSys Drak3, *Hacking FedEx*, 2600: THE HACKER QUARTERLY, Autumn 1997, at 14).

[46] Ex. 1.19 (Agent Steal, *Busted! A Complete Guide to Getting Caught*, 2600: THE HACKER QUARTERLY, Autumn 1997, at 6).

[47] Tr. (Corley) at 790; Ex. 52-54, 64, 79 (Corley Dec.) ¶ 20; 97.

Interestingly, defendants' copyright both their magazine and the material on their web site to prevent others from copying their works. Tr. (Corley) at 832; Ex. 96 (Corley Dep.) at 23-24.

[48] Tr. (Corley) at 791; Ex. 28.

[49] Tr. (Corley) at 791, 829, 848; Ex. 28.

[50] Tr. (King) at 402.

[51] *Id.* at 404, 468.

[52] *Id.* at 408, 468, 470.

[53] *Id.* at 404-05.

[54] *Id.* at 404-05, 468-70.

[55] *Id.* at 406.

[56] *Id.* at 405-06, 471, 476-78.

[57] *Id.* at 405, 470-71, 479.

[58] *Id.* at 406-07, 502-04.

[59] An algorithm is a recipe that contains instructions for completing a task. It can be expressed in any language, from natural spoken language to computer programming language. Ex. AZO (Abelson Dep.) at 9-10.

[60] The licensing function initially was performed by MEI and Toshiba. Subsequently, MEI and Toshiba granted a royalty free license to the DVD Copy Control Association ("DVD CCA"), which now handles the licensing function. Tr. (King) at 485-86, 510; Ex. XXY (Attaway Dep.) at 31. The motion picture companies themselves license CSS from the DVD CCA. Ex. XYY (Attaway Dep.) at 31-32.

[61] *See, e.g.,* Ex. AHV §§5, 6.2.

[62] Tr. (King) at 450-51, 492-93; Ex. XXY (Attaway Dep.) at 61-62; Ex. AHV.

[63] The administrative fee is one million yen, now about $9,200, for each "membership category" selected by the licensee. Twelve membership categories are available, and one or more are selected by a licensee depending on the use which the licensee intends to make of the licensed technology. The membership categories are: content provider, authoring studio, DVD disc replicator, DVD player manufacturer, DVD-ROM drive manufacturer, DVD decoder manufacturer, descramble module manufacturer, authentication chip manufacturer for DVD-ROM drive, authenticator manufacturer for DVD decoder, integrated product manufacturer, and reseller. Ex. AJB, AIZ, AOV, AOU, AOQ.

[64] Tr. (King) at 437-38; *see also* Tr. (Pavlovich) at 961; Ex. BD.

[65] Tr. (King) at 408-09.

[66] *Id.* at 409.

[67] *Id.* at 417-18.

[68] *Id.* at 442.

[69] Revenue from the distribution of DVDs makes up approximately 35 percent of Warner Brothers' total worldwide revenue from movie distribution in the home video market. *Id.* at 403.

[70] Distribution in the home video market accounts for approximately 40 percent of Warner Brothers' total income from movie distribution. *Id.*

[71] Tr. (Johansen) at 619-22, 633, 639.

[72] *Id.* at 619-21, 634; (Schumann) at 246-48. Mr. Johansen testified that the "De" in DeCSS stands for "decrypt." Tr. (Johansen) at 628.

[73] Tr. (Johansen) at 622-23, 638; Ex. 9 at SCH-000846. Mr. Johansen did not post the source code on his Web site. Tr. (Johansen) at 635.

[74] Tr. (Johansen) at 620.

[75] *Id.* at 620.

[76] *Id.* at 621-22.

[77] *Id.* at 621-22, 624; (Stevenson) at 214.

[78] Tr. (Johansen) at 623.

[79] Substantial questions have been raised both at trial and elsewhere as to the veracity of Mr. Johansen's claim. *See* Ex. CS, at S10006 ("Our analysis indicates that the primary technical breakthroughs were developed outside of the Linux development groups.").

[80] Tr. (Johansen) at 626-27.

[81] Ex. 97, 107, 126.

[82] Tr. (Stevenson) at 217-18, 226-29; (Schumann) at 290, 338-41; (Johansen) at 641; (Reider) at 681-85. One, DOD (Drink or Die) Speed Ripper, does not work with all DVDs that DeCSS will decrypt. *Id.*; Ex. CS, at S10011; Ex. 9. Some of these programs perform only a portion of what DeCSS does and must be used in conjunction with others in order to decrypt the contents of a DVD. Tr. (Schuman) at 290, 338-39. Some of defendants' claims about these other means proved baseless at trial. *See* Tr. (Pavlovich) at 965-68.

[83] Tr. (Corley) at 791; Ex. 28.

[84] Tr. (Corley) at 791, 829, 848; Ex. 28.

[85] Tr. (Corley) at 829-30, 845.

[86] *Id.* at 831, 845.

[87] *Id.* at 829-30, 845.

[88] *Id.* at 830; (Shamos) at 38. As Mr. Corley testified, the download process generally begins with the appearance of a dialog box, or small window, prompting the user to confirm the location on the user's computer hard drive where the downloaded software will be stored. The actual download does not begin until the user provides the computer with this information. Tr. (Corley) at 830. It is possible also to create a link that commences the download immediately upon being clicked. *See* Tr. (Touretzky) at 1082-83.

[89] Tr. (Reider) at 652.

[90] Tr. (King) at 435, 548; (Reider) at 653; Ex. 55.

[91] The other two defendants entered into consent decrees with plaintiffs. Plaintiffs subsequently amended the complaint to add 2600 Enterprises, Inc. as a defendant.

[92] Preliminary Injunction, Jan. 20, 2000 (DI 6); *Universal City Studios, Inc.*, 82 F Supp 2d 211.

[93] Tr., Jan. 20, 2000 (DI 17) at 85.

[94] Tr. (Corley) at 791; Ex. 51.

[95] Tr. (Corley) at 834; Ex. 96 (Corley Dep.) at 151-53.

[96] Tr. (Corley) at 791; Ex. 79 (Corley Dec.) ¶ 21; 126.

[97] Ex. 106.

[98] Tr. (Shamos) at 36-42; (Schumann) at 272-73; 265-66 (defendants' stipulation that their web site links to other sites containing executable copies of DeCSS).

[99] Tr. (Shamos) at 36-42; (Schumann) at 272-73.

[100] Tr. (Shamos) at 39-40; *see also* Ex. AYZ (Hunt Dep.) at 18.

[101] Tr. (Shamos) at 41-42; (Schumann) at 272-73.

[102] Tr. (Shamos) at 41-42, 156.

[103] Tr. (Schumann) at 273; Ex. AYZ (Hunt Dep.) at 26.

[104] Tr. (Johansen) at 628; *see also* Ex. AZN (Simons Dep.) at 48.

[105] Tr. (Shamos) at 42; (Ramadge) at 900.

[106] *See* Tr. (Shamos) at 54-56; Ex. 112-13.

[107] DivX effects what is known as "lossy" compression—it achieves its reduction in file size by eliminating some of the data in the file being compressed. The trick, however, is that it seeks to do so by eliminating data that is imperceptible, or nearly so, to the human observer. Tr. (Shamos) at 43-44; (Ramadge) at 882-98.

[108] Tr. (Shamos) at 51.

[109] Defendants produced an expert whose DivX of a DeCSS decrypted file was of noticeably lower quality than that of plaintiffs' expert's DivX'd film. The reasons for the difference are not clear. The Court is satisfied, however, that it is possible to make high quality 650 MB DivX'd copies of many films.

[110] Tr. (Ramadge) at 930.

[111] Tr. (Shamos) at 56-57. The copies do not require resynchronization of the sound and graphics.

[112] Tr. (Shamos) at 95.

[113] Tr. (Shamos) at 89-90, 98; (Peterson) at 865; (Pavlovich) at 943.

[114] Tr. (Shamos) at 90; (Felten) at 772; (Peterson) at 879.

[115] *See, e.g.,* Tr. (Peterson) at 861, 875-76.

[116] *Id.* (Shamos) at 87-88.

[117] *Id.*

[118] *Id.* at 77.

[119] It should be noted here that the transmission time achieved by plaintiff's expert, Dr. Shamos, almost certainly was somewhat skewed because the work was done late at night on a university system after the close of the regular school year, conditions favorable to high effective transmission rates due to low traffic on the system.

[120] Tr. (Schumann) at 334-36.

[121] Tr. (Shamos) at 68-76.

[122] *Id.* at 76-77.

[123] Ex. AYY (Reider Dep.) at 98-101; *see also id.* at 121-23.

[124] Ex. 116B.

[125] Tr. (Reider) at 661.

[126] Tr. (King) at 418.

[127] *Id.* at 420.

[128] WIPO Copyright Treaty, Apr. 12, 1997, Art. 11, S. Treaty Doc. No. 105-17 (1997), available at 1997 WL 447232.

[129] There is an excellent account of the legislative history of the statute. Nimmer, *A Riff on Fair Use,* 148 U. PA. L. REV. at 702-38.

[130] *See generally* S. REP. NO. 105-190, 105th Cong., 2d Sess. ("SENATE REP."), at 2-8 (1998).

[131] H.R. REP. No. 105-551(I), 105th Cong., 2d Sess. ("JUDICIARY COMM. REP."), at 17 (1998).

[132] *Id.* at 18.

[133] Plaintiffs rely also on Section 1201(b), which is very similar to Section 1201(a)(2) except that the former applies to trafficking in means of circumventing protection offered by a technological measure that effectively protects "a right of a copyright owner in a work or a portion thereof" whereas the latter applies to trafficking in means of circumventing measures controlling access to a work. *See generally* 1 MELVILLE B. NIMMER & DAVID NIMMER, NIMMER ON COPYRIGHT ("NIMMER") § 12A.03[C] (1999). In addition, as noted below, certain of the statutory exceptions upon which defendants have relied apply only to Section 1201(a)(2).

[134] 17 USC § 1201(a)(2). *See also* 1 NIMMER § 12A.03[1][*a*], at 12A-16.

[135] In their Post-Trial Brief, defendants argue that "at least some of the members of Congress" understood § 1201 to be limited to conventional devices, specifically 'black boxes,' as opposed to computer code." Def. Post-Trial Mem. at 21. However, the statute is clear that it prohibits "*any technology,*" not simply black boxes. 17 USC § 1201(a)(2) (emphasis added).

[136] 17 USC § 1201(a)(3)(A).

[137] Decryption or avoidance of an access control measure is not "circumvention" within the meaning of the statute unless it occurs "without the authority of the copyright owner." 17 USC § 1201(a)(3)(A). Defendants posit that purchasers of a DVD acquire the right "to perform all acts with it that are not exclusively granted to the copyright holder." Based on this premise, they argue that DeCSS does not circumvent CSS within the meaning of the statute because the Copyright Act does not grant the copyright holder the right to prohibit purchasers from

decrypting. As the copyright holder has no statutory right to prohibit decryption, the argument goes, decryption cannot be understood as unlawful circumvention. Def. Post-Trial Mem. 10-13. The argument is pure sophistry. The DMCA proscribes trafficking in technology that decrypts or avoids an access control measure without the copyright holder consenting to the decryption or avoidance. *See* JUDICIARY COMM. REP. at 17-18 (fair use applies "where the access is authorized"). Defendants' argument seems to be a corruption of the first sale doctrine, which holds that the copyright holder, notwithstanding the exclusive distribution right conferred by Section 106(3) of the Copyright Act, 17 USC § 106(3), is deemed by its "first sale" of a copy of the copyrighted work to have consented to subsequent sale of the copy. *See generally* 2 NIMMER §§ 8.11-8.12.

[138] *Id.* § 1201(a)(3)(B).

[139] *RealNetworks, Inc. v. Streambox, Inc.,* No. 2:99CV02070, 2000 WL 127311, *9 [5 ILR (P&F) 251]* (WD Wash. Jan. 18, 2000).

[140] HOUSE COMM. ON JUDICIARY, SECTION-BY-SECTION ANALYSIS OF H.R. 2281 AS PASSED BY THE UNITED STATES HOUSE OF REPRESENTATIVES ON AUGUST 4, 1998 ("SECTION-BY-SECTION ANALYSIS"), at 10 (Comm. Print 1998) (emphasis in original).

[141] H.R. REP. No. 105-551(II), 105th Cong., 2d Sess. ("COMMERCE COMM. REP."), at 39 (1998).

[142] Defendants, in a reprise of their argument that DeCSS is not a circumvention device, argue also that CSS does not effectively control access to copyrighted works within the meaning of the statute because plaintiffs authorize avoidance of CSS by selling their DVDs. Def. Post-Trial Mem. 10-13. The argument is specious in this context as well. *See supra* note 137.

[143] Tr. (Johansen) at 619; (Corley) 833-34.

[144] Def. Post-Trial Mem. at 2.

[145] 1 NIMMER § 12A.03[A], at 12A-15 (1999 Supp.).

[146] *See id.* § 12A.03[B], at 12A-25 to 12A-26.

[147] *See* Def. Post-Trial Mem. at 13.

[149] *Id.* § 1201(f)(3).

[150] Def. Post-Trial Mem. at 13-15.

[151] COMMERCE COMM. REP. at 43.

[152] 17 USC § 1201(g)(4).

[151] *Id.* § 1201(g)(2).

[152] *Id.* § 1201(g)(3).

[153] Ex. 96 (Corley Dep.) at 33.

[154] In any case, Section 1201(g), where its requirements are met, is a defense only to claims under Section 1201(a)(2), not those under Section 1201(b).

[155] Def. Mem. in Opp. to Prelim. Inj. (DI 11) at 11-12.

[156] Id. §1201(j)(1).

[157] Like Section 1201(g), moreover, Section 1201(j) provides no defense to a Section 1201(b) claim.

[158] 17 USC §107.

[159] Indeed, as many have pointed out, technological means of controlling access to works create a risk, depending upon future technological and commercial developments, of limiting access to works that are not protected by copyright such as works upon which copyright has expired. See, e.g., Nimmer, A Riff on Fair Use, 148 U. PA. L. REV. at 738-40; Hannibal Travis, Comment, Pirates of the Information Infrastrcuture: Blackstonian Copyright and the First Amendment, 15 BERKELEY TECH. L. J. 777, 861 (2000) (hereinafter Pirates of the Information Infrastructure); Yochai Benkler, Free as the Air to Common Use: First Amendment Constraints on Enclosure of the Public Domain, 74 NYU L. REV. 354, 421 (1999);

[160] Of course, one might quote the verbal portion of the sound track, rerecord both verbal and nonverbal portions of the sound track, and video tape or otherwise record images produced on a monitor when the DVD is played on a compliant DVD player.

[161] 17 USC §107.

[162] See, e.g., COMMERCE COMM. REP. 25-26.

[163] JUDICIARY COMM. REP. 18.

[164] Id.

[165] 17 USC §§1201(a)(1)(B)-(E).

The rule-making is under way. 65 F.R. 14505-06 (Mar. 17, 2000); see also <http://www.loc.gov/copyright/1201/anticirc.html> (visited July 28, 2000).

[166] 17 USC §§1201(d), (f), (g), (j).

[167] 464 US 417 (1984).

[168] Id. at 443, 446.

[169] RealNetworks, Inc., 2000 WL 127311, at *8 (quoting 1 NIMMER §12A.18[B], at 12A-130) (internal quotation marks omitted).

[170] SECTION-BY-SECTION ANALYSIS 9 ("The Sony test of 'capab[ility] of substantial noninfringing uses,' while still operative in cases claiming contributory infringement of copyright, is not part of this legislation . . . .").

[171] 17 USC §1201(a)(2).

[172] Tr. (Schumann) at 275-76.

[173] Id. at 261-62.

[174] For example, a web page maintained by a radio station might provide a hyperlink to a weather report by programming its page to transfer the user to a National Weather Service site if the user clicks on the "weather" hyperlink.

[175] 17 USC §1201(a)(2).

[176] See 2 THE COMPACT EDITION OF THE OXFORD ENGLISH DICTIONARY 3372 (1971).

[177] See 2 id. 2340.

[178] See 1 id. 1979.

[179] See, e.g., Strom v. Goldman, Sachs & Co., 202 F3d 138, 146-47 (2d Cir 1999).

[180] See DVD Copy Control Ass'n, Inc. v. McLaughlin, No. CV 786804, 2000 WL 48512, *4 [5 ILR (P&F) 54] (Cal. Super. Jan. 21, 2000) ("website owner cannot be held responsible for all of the content of the sites to which it provides links"); Richard Raysman & Peter Brown, Recent Linking Issues, N.Y.L.J., Feb. 8, 2000, p. 3, col. 1 (same).

[181] Roth v. United States, 354 U.S. 476, 483 (1957) (obscenity). See also, e.g., Sable Comm. of Cal., Inc. v. FCC, 492 U.S. 115, 124 (1989) (obscenity); Bose Corp. v. Consumers Union of United States, 466 U.S. 485, 504 (1984) (libel, obscenity, fighting words, child pornography); Beauharnais v. Illinois, 343 U.S. 250, 266 (1952) (defamation); Chaplinsky v. New Hampshire, 315 U.S. 568, 571-72 (1942) (fighting words).

[182] Robert Post, Encryption Source Code and the First Amendment, 15 BERKELEY TECH. L. J. 713, 714 (2000); see R.A.V. v. City of St. Paul, Minnesota, 505 US 373, 382 (1992) (statements that categories of speech are "unprotected" are not literally true; characterization indicates only that they are subject to content based regulation).

[183] The Court is indebted to Professor David Touretzky of Carnegie-Mellon University, who testified on behalf of defendants, for his lucid explication of this point. See Tr. (Touretzky) at 1066-84 & Ex. BBE, CCO, CCP, CCQ. As will appear, however, the point does not lead the Court to the same conclusion as Dr. Touretzky.

[184] LEONARD LEVY, FREEDOM OF SPEECH IN EARLY AMERICAN HISTORY: LEGACY OF SUPPRESSION passim (1960); see also 4 RONALD D. ROTUNDA & JOHN E. NOWAK, TREATISE ON CONSTITUTIONAL LAW §20.5 (1999); 4 WILLIAM BLACKSTONE, COMMENTARIES ON THE LAWS OF ENGLAND 151-52 (1769).

[185] See, e.g., Hurley v. Irish-American Gay, Lesbian and Bisexual Group, 515 US 557, 569 (1995).

186 *Junger v. Daley,* 209 F3d 481, 485 *[5 ILR (P&F) 122]* (6th Cir 2000); *Bernstein v. U.S. Dept. of State,* 176 F3d 1132, 1141 *[2 ILR (P&F) 602], reh'g granted and opinion withdrawn,* 192 F3d 1308 *[3 ILR (P&F) 500]* (9th Cir 1999); *Bernstein v. U.S. Dept. of State,* 922 F. Supp. 1426, 1436 *[1 ILR (P&F) 762]* (N.D. Cal. 1996) (First Amendment extends to source code); *see Karn v. U.S. Dept. of State,* 925 F Supp 1, 10 *[1 ILR (P&F) 512]* (D DC 1996) (assuming First Amendment extends to source code).

187 *Police Department of the City of Chicago v. Mosely,* 408 U.S. 92, 95-96 (1972).

188 *Turner Broadcasting System, Inc. v. FCC,* 512 US 622, 641 (1994); *accord, R.A.V.,* 505 US at 382-83.

189 *Sable Comm. of Cal., Inc. v. FCC,* 492 US at 126.

190 *Turner Broadcasting System, Inc.,* 512 US at 662 (citing *United States v. O'Brien,* 391 US 367, 377 (1968)).

191 *See, e.g., United States v. O'Brien,* 391 US at 376.

192 During the Vietnam era, many who opposed the war, the draft, or both burned draft cards as acts of protest. Lower federal courts typically concluded or assumed that the expression inherent in this act of protest brought the behavior entirely within the scope of the First Amendment. THOMAS I. EMERSON, THE SYSTEM OF FREEDOM OF EXPRESSION 82 (1970). In *United States v. O'Brien,* 391 US at 376, however, the Supreme Court rejected "the view that an apparently limitless variety of conduct can be labeled 'speech' whenever the person engaged in the conduct intends thereby to express an idea" and adopted a new approach, discussed below, to the regulation of expressive conduct as opposed to pure speech. *Accord, Spence v. State of Washington,* 418 US 405, 410 (1974). The point for present purposes is that the presence of expression in some broader mosaic does not result in the entire mosaic being treated as "speech."

193 *Id.* at 376.

194 Def. Post-Trial Mem. at 15-16.

195 *Ward v. Rock Against Racism,* 491 US 781, 791 (1989); *accord, Hill v. Colorado,* 120 S Ct 2480, 2491 (2000); *Turner Broadcasting System, Inc.,* 512 US at 642; *Madsen v. Women's Health Center, Inc.,* 512 US 753, 763 (1994).

196 *See generally Turner Broadcasting System, Inc.,* 512 US at 646-49 (holding that "must-carry" provisions of the Cable Television Consumer Protection and Competition Act of 1992 are content neutral in view of "overriding congressional purpose . . . unrelated to the content of expression" manifest in detailed legislative history).

197 475 US 41 (1986).

198 *Id.* at 46-49; *see also Young v. American Mini Theatres, Inc.,* 427 US 50, 71 n. 34 (1976).

199 *See Karn,* 925 F Supp at 10 (regulations controlling export of computer code content neutral); Benkler, 74 NYU L. REV. at 413 (DMCA "content and viewpoint neutral").

200 *Turner Broadcasting System, Inc.,* 512 US at 662 (quoting *O'Brien,* 391 US at 377 (internal quotation marks omitted)); *see also, e.g., United States v. Weslin,* 156 F3d 292, 297 (2d Cir 1998).

201 *Turner Broadcasting System, Inc.,* 512 US at 662; *see also Hill,* 120 S Ct at 2494.

202 *Ward,* 491 US at 799 (quoting *United States v. Albertini,* 472 US 675, 689 (1985)).

203 U.S. CONST., art. I, §8 (Copyright Clause).

204 COMMERCE COMM. REP. 94-95; SENATE REP. 21-22, 143.

205 *Harper & Row, Publishers, Inc. v. Nation Enterprises,* 471 US 539, 558 (1985).

206 It is conceivable that technology eventually will provide means of limiting access only to copyrighted materials and only for uses that would infringe the rights of the copyright holder. *See, e.g.,* Travis, 15 BERKELEY TECH. L.J. at 835-36; Mark Gimbel, Note, Some Thoughts on the Implications of Trusted Systems for Intellectual Property Law, 50 Stan. L. Rev. 1671, 1875-78 (1998); Mark Stefik, *Shifting the Possible: How Trusted Systems and Digital Property Rights Challenge Us to Rethink Digital Publishing,* 12 BERKELEY TECH. L.J. 137, 138- 40 (1997). We have not yet come so far.

207 209 F3d 481 *[5 ILR (P&F) 122]* (6th Cir. 2000).

208 *Id.* at 485.

209 391 US at 377.

210 209 F3d at 485.

211 *See* Lee Tien, *Publishing Software as a Speech Act,* 15 BERKELEY TECH. L. J. 629, 694-701 (2000). Professor Tien's analysis itself has been criticized. Robert Post, *Encryption Source Code and the First Amendment,* 15 BERKELEY TECH. L. J. 715 (2000).

212 This perhaps is not as surprising as first might appear. Computer "viruses" are other programs, an understanding of which is aided by the biological analogy evident in their name. *See, e.g.,* Jeffrey O. Kephart, Gregory B. Sorkin, David M. Chess and Steve R. White, *Fighting Computer Viruses,* SCIENTIFIC AMERICAN, (visited Aug. 16, 2000) <http://www.sciam.com/1197issue/1197kephart.html>.

[213] DAVID E. LILIENFELD & PAUL D. STOLLEY, FOUNDATIONS OF EPIDEMIOLOGY 38-41 & Fig. 3-1 (3d ed. 1994); JOHN P. FOX, CARRIE E. HALL & LILA R. ELVEBACK, EPIDEMIOLOGY—MAN AND DISEASE 246-47 (1970).

[214] Of course, not everyone who obtains DeCSS or some other decryption program necessarily will use it to engage in copyright infringement, just as not everyone who is exposed to a contagious disease contracts it. But that is immaterial. The critical point is that the combination of (a) the manner in which the ability to infringe is spread and (b) the lack of any practical means of controlling infringement at the point at which it occurs once the capability is broadly disseminated render control of infringement by controlling availability of the means of infringement far more critical in this context.

[215] See, e.g., Guido Calabresi & Jeffrey O. Cooper, New Directions in Tort Law, 30 VAL. U. L. REV. 859, 870-72 (1996).

[216] As has been noted above, some categories of speech, which often have been referred to inaccurately as "unprotected," may be regulated on the basis of their content. R.A.V., 505 US at 382-83. These have included obscenity and "fighting words," to name two such categories. The determination of the types of speech which may be so regulated has been made through a process termed by one leading commentator as "definitional" balancing—a weighing of the value of free expression in these areas against its likely consequences and the legitimate interests of government. Melville B. Nimmer, The Right to Speak from Time to Time: First Amendment Theory Applied to Libel and Misapplied to Privacy, 56 CAL. L. REV. 935, 942 (1968); see R.A.V., 505 US at 382-83. Thus, even if one accepted defendants' argument that the anti-trafficking prohibition of the DMCA is content based because it regulates only code that "expresses" the programmer's "ideas" for circumventing access control measures, the question would remain whether such code—code designed to circumvent measures controlling access to private or legally protected data—nevertheless could be regulated on the basis of that content. For the reasons set forth in the text, the Court concludes that it may. Alternatively, even if such a categorical or definitional approach were eschewed, the Court would uphold the application of the DMCA now before it on the ground that this record establishes an imminent threat of danger flowing from dissemination of DeCSS that far outweighs the need for unfettered communication of that program. See Landmark Communications, Inc. v. Virginia, 435 US 829, 842-43 (1978).

[217] For example, one might imagine a computer program the object of which was to teach the user a particular view of a subject, e.g., evolution or creationism.

Such a program, like this one, would be within the area of First Amendment concern and functional. Yet a regulation barring its use would be subject to a quite different analysis. Such a ban, for example, might be based on the content of the message the program caused the computer to deliver to the student-user and thus quite clearly be content based. Similarly, the function—teaching—would not involve the same likelihood that the dissemination would bring about a harm that the government has a legitimate right to prevent.

[218] New York Times Co. v. United States, 403 US 713, 714 (1971) (per curiam) (quoting Bantam Books, Inc. v. Sullivan, 372 US 58, 70 (1963)).

[219] See, e.g., Posadas de Puerto Rico Assoc. v. Tourism Co. of Puerto Rico, 478 US 328 (1986) (upholding restrictions on casino gambling advertising); Times Film Corp. v. Chicago, 365 US 43 (1961) (upholding local ordinance requiring review of films by municipal officials as prerequisite to issuance of permits for public screening); Salinger v. Random House, Inc., 811 F2d 90 (2d Cir) (enjoining biographer's use of subject's unpublished letters as copyright infringement), cert. denied, 484 US 890 (1987); Dallas Cowboys Cheerleaders v. Pussycat Cinema, Ltd., 604 F2d 200 (2d Cir 1979) (enjoining distribution of film on ground that actresses' uniforms infringed plaintiff's trademark). See generally LAURENCE H. TRIBE, AMERICAN CONSTITUTIONAL LAW §12-36, at 1045-46 (1988) (hereinafter TRIBE).

[220] See, e.g., Charles of the Ritz Group, Ltd. v. Quality King Distributors, Inc., 832 F2d 1317 (2d Cir 1987) (upholding injunction against commercial slogan on ground that slogan created a likelihood of confusion and is therefore "beyond the protective reach of the First Amendment"); Vondran v. McLinn, No. 95-20296, 1995 WL 415153, *6 (N.D. Cal. July 5, 1995) (enjoining defendant's false and disparaging remarks regarding plaintiff's patented process for making fiber reinforced concrete on the ground that the remarks are not protected by the First Amendment).

[221] See, e.g., Times Film Corp., 365 US 43 (upholding local ordinance requiring review by city officials of all films as a prerequisite to grant of permit for public screening despite concerns of First Amendment violations); Posadas de Puerto Rico Assoc., 478 US 328 (upholding restrictions on advertising despite finding that the advertising fell within ambit of First Amendment); Dallas Cowboys Cheerleaders, Inc., 604 F2d 200 (enjoining distribution of film for trademark infringement despite claim that injunction violated distributor's First Amendment rights).

[222] 4 WILLIAM BLACKSTONE, COMMENTARIES ON THE LAWS OF ENGLAND 151-52 (1769).

[223] *See Pittsburgh Press Co. v. Pittsburgh Comm. on Human Rel.*, 413 US 376, 390 (1973).

[224] Martin H. Redish, *The Proper Role of the Prior Restraint Doctrine in First Amendment Theory*, 70 VA. L. REV. 53, 54 (1983) (hereinafter "Redish"). *See also* LAURENCE H. TRIBE, AMERICAN CONSTITUTIONAL LAW §12-34, at 1040-41 (2d ed. 1988).

[225] John Calvin Jeffries, Jr., *Rethinking Prior Restraint*, 92 YALE L.J. 409, 419 (1983).

[226] Despite the conventional wisdom, it is far from clear that an injunction necessarily is a prior restraint. Our circuit, for example, has suggested that the prior restraint doctrine does not apply to content neutral injunctions. *See e.g., Dallas Cowboys Cheerleaders, Inc.*, 604 F2d at 206. At least one commentator persuasively has argued that there is little justification for placing injunctions, at least permanent injunctions issued after trial, in a disfavored constitutional position. Jeffries, 92 YALE L.J. at 426-34. Nevertheless, there is no reason to decide that question in this case. The following discussion therefore assumes that the permanent injunction plaintiff seeks would be a "prior restraint," although it concludes that it would not be unconstitutional.

[227] 283 US 697 (1931).

[228] 403 US 713 (1971).

[229] 427 US 539 (1976).

[230] *See* H.R. REP. 106-216, 106th Cong., 1st Sess. (1999) ("Notwithstanding [penalties for copyright infringement] copyright piracy of intellectual property flourishes, assisted in large part by today's world of advanced technologies. For example, industry groups estimate that counterfeiting and piracy of computer software cost the affected copyright holders more than $11 billion last year (others believe the figure is closer to $20 billion). In some countries, software piracy rates are as high as 97% of all sales. The U.S. rate is far lower (25%), but the dollar losses ($2.9 billion) are the highest worldwide. The effect of this volume of theft is substantial: lost U.S. jobs, lost wages, lower tax revenue, and higher prices for honest purchasers of copyrighted software. Unfortunately, the potential for this problem to worsen is great."); S. REP. 106-140, 106th Cong., 1st Sess. (1999) ("Trademark owners are facing a new form of piracy on the Internet caused by acts of 'cybersquatting.'"); S. REP. 105-190, 105th Cong., 2d Sess. (1998) ("Due to the ease with which digital works can be copied and distributed worldwide virtually instantaneously, copyright owners will hesitate to make their works readily available on the Internet without reasonable assurance that they will be protected against massive piracy."); H.R. REP. 105-339, 105th Cong., 1st

Sess. (1997) ("[C]opyright piracy flourishes in the software world.").

[231] Mark A. Lemley & Eugene Volokh, *Freedom of Speech and Injunctions in Intellectual Property Cases*, 48 DUKE L.J. 147, 210 & n. 275 (1998).

[232] *See, e.g., Pittsburgh Press Co.*, 413 US at 390 ("The special vice of a prior restraint is that communication will be suppressed . . . before an adequate determination that it is unprotected by the First Amendment."); Lemley & Volokh, 48 DUKE L.J. at 200-02, 211; *see* Redish, 70 VA. L. REV. at 75-83.

[233] *See* Lemley & Volokh, 48 DUKE L.J. at 211-12, 215 (acknowledging that high likelihood of success diminishes risk of erroneous suppression of protected speech).

[234] Def. Post-Trial Mem. at 22-24.

[235] *Id.* at 22.

Defendants argue also that the DMCA as applied is overbroad in that "it would prohibit defendants from posting and making programs such as DeCSS available in any form, from English to any level of computer code." *Id.* The overbreadth doctrine, however, enables litigants to challenge a statute not merely because their own First Amendment rights are violated, but because the statute may cause others to abstain from constitutionally protected expression. *Broadrick v. Oklahoma*, 413 U.S. 601, 612 (1973). This aspect of defendants' argument, which in any case is an overstatement, therefore does not refer to overbreadth in the sense relevant here.

[236] *Broadrick*, 413 US at 610.

[237] *Gooding v. Wilson*, 405 US 518, 520-21 (1972) (quoting *Dombrowski v. Pfister*, 380 US 479, 486 (1965)).

[238] *Gooding*, 405 US at 521.

[239] *Los Angeles Police Department v. United Reporting Pub. Corp.*, 120 S Ct 483, 489 (1999) (quoting *New York v. Ferber*, 458 US 747, 769 (1982) (quoting *Broadrick*, 413 US at 613)).

[240] *Id.* at 489 (quoting *Ferber*, 458 US at 770 (quoting *Broadrick*, 413 US at 615)).

[241] *Broadrick*, 413 US at 612.

[242] Tr. (King) at 441.

[243] Defendants argue that the right of third parties to view DVD movies on computers running the Linux operating system will be materially impaired if DeCSS is not available to them. However, the technology to build a Linux-based DVD player has been licensed by the DVD CCA to at least two companies, and there is no reason to think that others wishing to develop Linux players could not obtain licenses if they so chose. Tr. (King) at 437-38. Therefore, enforcement of the DMCA to prohibit the

posting of DeCSS would not materially impair the ability of Linux users to view DVDs on Linux machines. Further, it is not evident that constitutional protection of free expression extends to the type of device on which one plays copyrighted material. Therefore, even assuming *arguendo* that the ability of third parties to view DVD movies on Linux systems were materially impaired by enforcement of the DMCA in this case, this impairment would not necessarily implicate the First Amendment rights of these third parties.

[244] CSS encryption coupled with the characteristics of compliant DVD players also forecloses copying of digital sound files. It is not clear, however, that this is a substantial impediment to copying sound from motion picture DVDs. A DVD can be played on a compliant player and the sound re-recorded. Whether the sound quality thus obtained would be satisfactory might well depend upon the particular use to which the copy was put.

[245] The same point might be made with respect to copying of works upon which copyright has expired. Once the statutory protection lapses, the works pass into the public domain. The encryption on a DVD copy of such a work, however, will persist. Moreover, the combination of such a work with a new preface or introduction might result in a claim to copyright in the entire combination. If the combination then were released on DVD and encrypted, the encryption would preclude access not only to the copyrighted new material, but to the public domain work. As the DMCA is not yet two years old, this does not yet appear to be a problem, although it may emerge as one in the future.

[246] Defendants argue that "there is now a full evidentiary record" and that the overbreadth issue therefore should be decided. Def. Post-Trial Mem. at 22 n. 11. With respect, the evidence as to the impact of the anti-trafficking provision of the DMCA on prospective fair users is scanty and fails adequately to address the issues.

This is not to minimize the interests of the *amici* who have submitted briefs in this case. The Court simply does not have a sufficient evidentiary record on which to evaluate their claims.

[247] 17 USC §1201(g).

[248] Def. Post-Trial Mem. at 24.

[249] *Village of Hoffman Estates v. Flipside,* 455 US 489, 495 (1982).

[250] *See* 17 USC §1201(a)(2)(A).

[251] *Ward,* 491 US at 799 (quoting *United States v. Albertini,* 472 US 675, 689 (1985)).

[252] *ACLU v. Reno,* 929 F Supp 824, 837 *[1 ILR (P&F) 651]* (ED Pa. 1996), *aff'd,* 521 US 844 *[1 ILR (P&F) 1]* (1997).

[253] Richard Raysman & Peter Brown, *Recent Linking Issues,* N.Y.L.J., Feb. 8, 2000, p. 3, col. 1.

[254] *Cf. New York Times Co. v. Sullivan,* 376 US 254, 271-73, 283-88 (1964).

[255] *Id.* at 283; *Curtis Pub. Co. v. Butts,* 388 U.S. 130, 155 (1967); *St. Amant v. Thompson,* 390 US 727, 731 (1968); ROBERT D. SACK, SACK ON DEFAMATION §1.2.4 (3d ed. 1999).

[256] 418 US 323, 347-38 (1974).

[257] In evaluating purpose, courts will look at all relevant circumstances. Sites that advertise their links as means of getting DeCSS presumably will be found to have created the links for the purpose of disseminating the program. Similarly, a site that deep links to a page containing only DeCSS located on a site that contains a broad range of other content, all other things being equal, would more likely be found to have linked for the purpose of disseminating DeCSS than if it merely links to the home page of the linked-to site.

[258] Tr. (Corley) at 820.

[259] 17 USC §1203(a).

[260] Def. Post-Trial Mem. at 27-28.

[261] The statute expressly authorizes injunctions to prevent or restrain violations, 17 USC §1203(b)(1), thus demonstrating that the requisite injury need only be threatened.

[262] Def. Post-Trial Mem. at 28.

[263] *Id.* at 28-29.

[264] *See, e.g.,* Ex. AYZ (Hunt Dep.) at 94-104.

[265] *Id.* 30.

[266] Ex. 113.

[267] Defendants' argument would lack merit even if there were credible proof that other circumvention devices actually exist and produce results comparable to DeCSS. The available movies must have been decrypted with DeCSS or something else. As far as this record discloses, any such device or technology would violate the DMCA for the same reasons as does DeCSS. In consequence, this case comes within the principle of *Summers v. Tice,* 33 Cal. 2d 80, 199 P2d 1 (1948). Where, as here, two or more persons take substantially identical wrongful actions, one and only one of which had to be the source of the plaintiffs' injury, and it is equally likely that one inflicted the injury as the other, the burden of proof on causation shifts to the defendants, each of which is liable absent proof that its action did not cause the injury. *See*

4 Fowler V. Harper & Fleming James, Jr., THE LAW OF TORTS §§101-04 (2d ed. 1996).

Defendants' efforts to avoid the consequences of this common sense principle are unpersuasive. They argue, for example, that plaintiffs may not invoke the theory unless they join as defendants everyone who may have contributed to the injury. Def. Post-Trial Mem. at 32 n. 18 (citing Ex. UZ). It would be difficult to imagine a more nonsensical requirement in the context of this case. Where, as here, harm is done by dissemination of information over the Internet, probably by a substantial number of people all over the world, defendants' proposed rule would foreclose judicial relief anywhere because joinder of all plainly would be impossible in any one place, and technology does not permit identification of which wrongdoer's posting or product led to which pirated copy of a copyrighted work.

[268]   17 USC §1203(b)(1).

[269]   *See, e.g., SEC v. Unique Financial Concepts, Inc.*, 196 F3d 1195, 1199 n. 2 (2d Cir 1999) (injunction under Section 20(b) of the Securities Act of 1933, 15 USC §77t(b), which permits an injunction "upon a proper showing," requires "a reasonable likelihood that the wrong will be repeated"); *CFTC v. Hunt*, 591 F2d 1211, 1220 (7th Cir. 1979) (same under Commodity Exchange Act, 7 USC §13a-1(b)); *SEC v. Bausch & Lomb Inc.*, 577 F2d 8, 18 (2d Cir 1977) (reasonable likelihood of future violations required under §21(d) of Securities Exchange Act of 1934, 15 USC §78u(d), which permits an injunction "upon a proper showing" where person "engaged or . . . about to engage in" violation of statute).

[270]   *See, e.g., Rondeau v. Mosinee Paper Corp.*, 422 US 49, 57 (1975) (injunctive relief in private action under §13(d) of the Securities Exchange Act of 1934, 15 USC §78m(d), as added by the Williams Act, requires a showing of irreparable harm and inadequacy of legal remedies).

[271]   *Tough Traveler, Ltd. v. Outbound Prods.*, 60 F3d 964, 967-68 (2d Cir 1995) (trademark); *Fisher-Price, Inc. v. Well-Made Toy Mfg. Corp.*, 25 F3d 119, 124 (2d Cir 1994) (copyright).

[272]   *See, e.g., Northwestern Nat'l Ins. Co. v. Alberts*, 937 F2d 77, 80 (2d Cir 1991) ("The irreparable injury requisite . . . overlaps with the absent lack of adequate remedy at law necessary to establish the equitable rights."); *Buffalo Forge Co. v. Ampco-Pittsburgh Corp.*, 638 F2d 568, 569 (2d Cir 1981) ("There must also be a showing of irreparable harm, the absence of an adequate remedy at law, which is the *sine qua non* for the grant of such equitable relief.")

[273]   *Religious Tech. Ctr. v. Netcom On-Line Comm. Servs., Inc.*, 923 F Supp 1231, 1256 (ND Cal. 1995).

[274]   *Com-Share, Inc. v. Computer Complex, Inc.*, 338 F Supp 1229, 1239 (ED Mich. 1971).

[275]   During the trial, Professor Touretzky of Carnegie Mellon University, as noted above, convincingly demonstrated that computer source and object code convey the same ideas as various other modes of expression, including spoken language descriptions of the algorithm embodied in the code. Tr. (Touretzky) at 1068-69; Ex. BBE, CCO, CCP, CCQ. He drew from this the conclusion that the preliminary injunction irrationally distinguished between the code, which was enjoined, and other modes of expression that convey the same idea, which were not, *id.*, although of course he had no reason to be aware that the injunction drew that line only because that was the limit of the relief plaintiffs sought. With commendable candor, he readily admitted that the implication of his view that the spoken language and computer code versions were substantially similar was not necessarily that the preliminary injunction was too broad; rather, the logic of his position was that it was either too broad *or* too narrow. *Id.* at 1070-71. Once again, the question of a substantially broader injunction need not be addressed here, as plaintiffs have not sought broader relief.

[276]   17 USC §1203(b)(4)-(b)(5).

[277]   *See Fogerty v. Fantasy, Inc.*, 510 US 517, 534 (1994) (articulating factors relevant to fee awards under the Copyright Act).

[278]   *Universal City Studios, Inc. v. Reimerdes*, 00 Civ. 0277 (LAK), 2000 WL 987285 (SD NY July 17, 2000).

[279]   The chief factual issue actually litigated at trial was the speed with which decrypted files could be transmitted over the Internet and other networks.

Universal City Studios, Inc.
v.
Corley

**United States Court of Appeals,
Second Circuit**

November 28, 2001

9 ILR (P&F) 330, 273 F3d 429

No. 00-9185

DMCA not susceptible to narrow interpretation so as to avoid alleged constitutional defects.

The anti-trafficking and anti-circumvention provisions of the Digital Millennium Copyright Act (DMCA), 17 USC §1201(a)(1), (a)(2), and (b)(1), are not susceptible to a narrow interpretation, notwithstanding alleged ambiguities raised by appellants in their constitutional challenge. First, §1201(c)(1)—which provides that "[n]othing in this section shall affect rights, remedies, limitations or defenses to copyright infringement, including fair use, under this title"—cannot be read to allow the circumvention of encryption technology protecting copyrighted material when the material is put to "fair uses" exempt from copyright liability. Subsection (c)(1) clearly and simply clarifies that the DMCA targets the circumvention of digital walls guarding copyrighted material (and trafficking in circumvention tools), but does not concern itself with the use of those materials after circumvention has occurred. Second, §1201(c)(4)—which provides that "[n]othing in this section shall enlarge or diminish any rights of free speech or the press for activities using consumer electronics, telecommunications, or computing products"—is clearly precatory: Congress could not "diminish" constitutional rights of free speech even if it wished to, and the fact that Congress also expressed a reluctance to "enlarge" those rights cuts against appellants' effort to infer a narrowing construction of the Act from this provision. Third, §1201(a)(3)(A)—which exempts from liability those who would "decrypt" an encrypted DVD with the authority of a copyright owner—does not include those who would "view" a DVD with the authority of a copyright owner. In any event, appellants offered no evidence that motion picture studios have either explicitly or implicitly authorized DVD buyers to circumvent encryption technology to support use on multiple platforms. — **Universal City Studios, Inc. v. Corley, 9 ILR (P&F) 330 [2d Cir, 2001].**

Constitutional challenge to DMCA based on Copyright Clause ignored.

The court declines to address a constitutional challenge to the Digital Millennium Copyright Act (DMCA) based on the Copyright Clause, where appellants had raised the issue only in a footnote to their brief [7 ILR (P&F) 2005]. The appeal seeks reversal of a district court order [6 ILR (P&F) 1] enjoining appellants from posting and hyperlinking to a computer program (called DeCSS) that permits third parties to decrypt and copy copyrighted motion pictures from digital versatile disks. In a footnote to their brief, appellants contended that the DMCA, as construed by the district court, exceeds the constitutional authority of Congress to grant authors copyrights for a "limited time," U.S. Const. art. I, §8, cl. 8, because it "empower[s] copyright owners to effectively secure perpetual protection by mixing public domain works with copyrighted materials, then locking both up with technological protection measures." Arguments presented only in a footnote are not entitled to appellate consideration. Although the argument was elaborated in an *amici curiae* brief [7 ILR (P&F) 2087], such a brief is not normally the method for injecting new issues into an appeal, at least where the parties are competently represented by counsel. Moreover, to whatever extent the argument might have merit at some future time in a case with a properly developed record, the argument is entirely premature and speculative at this time. There is not even a claim, much less evidence, that any party has sought to prevent copying of public domain works or that the injunction prevents appellants from copying such works. — **Universal City Studios, Inc. v. Corley, 9 ILR (P&F) 330 [2d Cir, 2001].**

Computer code, programs constitute "speech" for First Amendment purposes.

Computer code and computer programs constructed from code can merit First Amendment protection. Communication does not lose constitutional protection as "speech" simply because it is expressed in the language of computer code, and computer programs, which are essentially instructions to a computer, are "speech" as well. The fact that a program has the capacity to direct the functioning of a computer does not mean that it lacks the additional capacity to convey information, and it is the conveying of information that renders instructions "speech" for purposes of the First Amendment. It is not pure speech, however, since it can yield a functional result without human comprehension of its content. Thus, it requires a First Amendment analysis that treats code as combining speech and non-speech elements, *i.e.*, expressive and functional elements. The functionality of computer code properly affects the scope of its First Amendment protection. — **Universal City Studios, Inc. v. Corley, 9 ILR (P&F) 330 [2d Cir, 2001].**

Injunction against posting of decryption code does not violate First Amendment.

An injunction [6 ILR (P&F) 794] prohibiting appellants from posting on their web site a computer program (called DeCSS) that allows users to decrypt and copy movies on digital versatile disks does not violate the First Amendment. DeCSS has both a non-speech and a speech component. The Digital Millennium Copyright Act (DMCA), as applied to appellants, and the injunction target only the non-speech component, *i.e.*, DeCSS's functional capability to instruct a computer to decrypt DVD movies. That functional capability is not speech within the meaning of the First Amendment. The government's interest in preventing unauthorized access to encrypted copyrighted material is unquestionably substantial, and the regulation of DeCSS by prohibiting its posting plainly serves that interest, which is unrelated to the suppression of free expression. [Affirming 6 ILR (P&F) 1.] — **Universal City Studios, Inc. v. Corley, 9 ILR (P&F) 330 [2d Cir, 2001].**

Injunction against linking to decryption code does not violate First Amendment

An injunction [6 ILR (P&F) 794] prohibiting appellants from providing hyperlinks to other sites containing a computer program (called DeCSS) that allows users to decrypt and copy movies on digital versatile disks does not violate the First Amendment. A hyperlink has both a non-speech and a speech component. The Digital Millennium Copyright Act (DMCA), as applied to appellants, targets only the non-speech component, *i.e.*, the hyperlink's functional capability to bring the content of the linked web page to the user's screen. The injunction's linking prohibition validly regulates appellants' opportunity to enable anyone anywhere to gain unauthorized access to copyrighted movies on DVD. So as not to burden more speech than is necessary, the terms of the prohibition were properly limited by requiring clear and convincing evidence that those responsible for the link (a) know at the relevant time that the offending material is on the linked-to site, (b) know that it is circumvention technology that may not lawfully be offered, and (c) create or maintain the link for the purpose of disseminating that technology. Notwithstanding appellants' arguments to the contrary, an intent to cause harm is not required. [Affirming 6 ILR (P&F) 1.] — **Universal City Studios, Inc. v. Corley, 9 ILR (P&F) 330 [2d Cir, 2001].**

Application of DMCA to prohibit posting of decryption code does not eliminate fair use.

The Digital Millennium Copyright Act (DMCA), as the basis for enjoining appellants from posting and hyperlinking to a computer program that allows users to decrypt and copy movies on digital versatile disks, does not unconstitutionally eliminate the fair use doctrine. Without deciding whether fair use may in fact have constitutional protection, the appellate court holds that the argument is beyond the scope of the lawsuit because: (1) appellants do not claim to be making fair use of any copyrighted materials, and nothing in the injunction prevents them from making such fair use; (2) to whatever extent the anti-trafficking provisions of the DMCA might prevent others from copying portions of DVD movies in order to make fair use of them, the evidence as to the impact of the anti-trafficking provisions on prospective fair users is scanty and fails adequately to address the issues; and (3) appellants have provided no support for their premise that fair use of DVD movies is constitutionally required to be made by copying the original work in its original format. [Affirming 6 ILR (P&F) 1.] — **Universal City Studios, Inc. v. Corley, 9 ILR (P&F) 330 [2d Cir, 2001].**

Before: NEWMAN and CABRANES, Circuit Judges, and THOMPSON,* District Judge.

Kathleen Sullivan, Stanford, Cal. (*Martin Garbus, Edward Hernstadt*, Frankfurt Garbus Kurnit Klein & Selz, New York, N.Y.; *Cindy A. Cohn, Lee Tien, Robin Gross*, Elec. Frontier Found., San Francisco, Cal., on the brief), for Defendants-Appellants.

Charles S. Sims, New York, NY (*Leon P. Gold, Jon A. Baumgarten, Carla M. Miller, Matthew J. Morris*, Proskauer Rose, New York, N.Y., on the brief), for Plaintiffs-Appellees.

Daniel S. Alter, Asst. U.S. Atty., New York, NY (*Mary Jo White*, U.S. Atty., *Marla Alhadeff*, Asst. U.S. Atty., New York, NY, on the brief), for Intervenor United States of America.

(*Prof. Peter Jazsi*, Wash. College of Law, American Univ., Wash., D.C.; *Prof. Jessica Litman*, Wayne State Univ., Detroit, Mich.; *Prof. Pamela Samuelson*, Univ. of Cal. at Berkeley, Berkeley, Cal.; *Ann Beeson, Christopher Hansen*, American Civil Liberties Union Foundation, New York, NY, submitted a brief in support of Defendants-Appellants, for *amici curiae* American Civil Liberties Union *et al.*).

(*Andrew Grosso*, Wash., DC, submitted a brief in support of Defendants-Appellants for *amicus curiae* ACM Committee on Law and Computing Technology).

(*James S. Tyre*, Culver City, Cal., submitted a brief in support of Defendants-Appellants, for *amici curiae* Dr. Harold Abelson *et al.*).

(*Edward A. Cavazos, Gavino Morin*, Cavazos, Morin, Langenkamp & Ferraro, Austin, Tex., submitted a brief in support of Defendants-Appellants, for *amici curiae* Ernest Miller *et al.*).

(*Arnold G. Rheinhold*, Cambridge, Mass., submitted a brief *amicus curiae* in support of Defendant-Appellant 2600 Enterprises, Inc.).

(*Prof. Julie E. Cohen*, Georgetown Univ. Law Center, Wash., DC, submitted a brief in support of Defendants-Appellants, for *amici curiae* intellectual property law professors).

(*Jennifer S. Granick*, Stanford, Cal., submitted a brief in support of Defendants-Appellants, for *amici curiae* Dr. Steven Bellovin *et al.*).

(*Prof. Yochai Benkler*, NY Univ. School of Law, New York, NY; *Prof. Lawrence Lessig*, Stanford Law School, Stanford, Cal., submitted a brief *amici curiae* in support of Defendants-Appellants).

(*David A. Greene*, First Amendment Project, Oakland, Cal.; *Jane E. Kirtley, Erik F. Ugland*, Silha Center for the Study of Media Ethics and Law, Univ. of Minn., Minneapolis, Minn.; *Milton Thurm*, Thurm & Heller, New York, NY, submitted a brief in support of Defendants-Appellants, for *amici curiae* Online News Ass'n *et al.*).

(*Prof. Rodney A. Smolla*, Univ. of Richmond School of Law, Richmond, Va., submitted a brief in support of Plaintiffs-Appellees, for *amici curiae* Prof. Erwin Chemerinsky *et al.*).

(*David E. Kendall, Paul B. Gaffney*, Williams & Connolly, Wash., DC; *David M. Proper*, National Football League and NFL Properties, New York, NY; *Thomas J. Ostertag*, Office of the Commissioner of Baseball, New York, NY, submitted a brief in support of Plaintiff-Appellees, for *amici curiae* Recording Ind. Ass'n of Am. *et al.*).

(*Jeffrey L. Kessler, Robert G. Sugarman, Geoffrey D. Berman*, Weil, Gotshal & Manges LLP, New York, NY, submitted a brief in support of Plaintiffs-Appellees, for *amicus curiae* DVD Copy Control Ass'n, Inc.).

JON O. NEWMAN, Circuit Judge. When the Framers of the First Amendment prohibited Congress from making any law "abridging the freedom of speech," they were not thinking about computers, computer programs, or the Internet. But neither were they thinking about radio, television, or movies. Just as the inventions at the beginning and middle of the 20th century presented new First Amendment issues, so does the cyber revolution at the end of that century. This appeal raises significant First Amendment issues concerning one aspect of computer technology—encryption to protect materials in digital form from unauthorized access. The appeal challenges the constitutionality of the Digital Millennium Copyright Act ("DMCA"), 17 USC §1201 *et seq.* (Supp V 1999) and the validity of an injunction entered to enforce the DMCA.

Defendant-Appellant Eric C. Corley and his company, 2600 Enterprises, Inc., (collectively "Corley," "the Defendants," or "the Appellants") appeal from the amended final judgment of the

United States District Court for the Southern District of New York (Lewis A. Kaplan, District Judge), entered August 23, 2000, enjoining them from various actions concerning a decryption program known as "DeCSS." *Universal City Studios, Inc. v. Reimerdes*, 111 F Supp 2d 346 *[6 ILR (P&F) 794]* (SD NY 2000) ("*Universal II*"). The injunction primarily bars the Appellants from posting DeCSS on their web site and from knowingly linking their web site to any other web site on which DeCSS is posted. *Id.* at 346-47. We affirm.

Introduction

Understanding the pending appeal and the issues it raises requires some familiarity with technical aspects of computers and computer software, especially software called "digital versatile disks" or "DVDs," which are optical media storage devices currently designed to contain movies.[1] Those lacking such familiarity will be greatly aided by reading Judge Kaplan's extremely lucid opinion, *Universal City Studios, Inc. v. Reimerdes*, 111 F Supp 2d 294 *[6 ILR (P&F) 1]* (SD NY 2000) ("*Universal I*"), beginning with his helpful section "The Vocabulary of this Case," *id.* at 305-09.

This appeal concerns the anti-trafficking provisions of the DMCA, which Congress enacted in 1998 to strengthen copyright protection in the digital age. Fearful that the ease with which pirates could copy and distribute a copyrightable work in digital form was overwhelming the capacity of conventional copyright enforcement to find and enjoin unlawfully copied material, Congress sought to combat copyright piracy in its earlier stages, before the work was even copied. The DMCA therefore backed with legal sanctions the efforts of copyright owners to protect their works from piracy behind digital walls such as encryption codes or password protections. In so doing, Congress targeted not only those pirates who would *circumvent* these digital walls (the "anti-circumvention provisions," contained in 17 USC §1201(a)(1)), but also anyone who would *traffic* in a technology primarily designed to circumvent a digital wall (the "anti-trafficking provisions," contained in 17 USC §1201(a)(2), (b)(1)).

Corley publishes a print magazine and maintains an affiliated web site geared towards "hackers," a digital-era term often applied to those interested in techniques for circumventing protections of computers and computer data from unauthorized access. The so-called hacker community includes serious computer-science scholars conducting research on protection techniques, computer buffs intrigued by the challenge of trying to circumvent access-limiting devices or perhaps hoping to promote security by exposing flaws in protection techniques, mischief-makers interested in disrupting computer operations, and thieves, including copyright infringers who want to acquire copyrighted material (for personal use or resale) without paying for it.

In November 1999, Corley posted a copy of the decryption computer program "DeCSS" on his web site, http://www.2600.com ("2600.com").[2] DeCSS is designed to circumvent "CSS," the encryption technology that motion picture studios place on DVDs to prevent the unauthorized viewing and copying of motion pictures. Corley also posted on his web site links to other web sites where DeCSS could be found.

Plaintiffs-Appellees are eight motion picture studios that brought an action in the Southern District of New York seeking injunctive relief against Corley under the DMCA. Following a full non-jury trial, the District Court entered a permanent injunction barring Corley from posting DeCSS on his web site or from knowingly linking via a hyperlink to any other web site containing DeCSS. *Universal II*, 111 F Supp 2d at 346-47. The District Court rejected Corley's constitutional attacks on the statute and the injunction. *Universal I*, 111 F Supp 2d at 325-45.

Corley renews his constitutional challenges on appeal. Specifically, he argues primarily that: (1) the DMCA oversteps limits in the Copyright Clause on the duration of copyright protection; (2) the DMCA as applied to his dissemination of DeCSS violates the First Amendment because computer code is "speech" entitled to full First Amendment protection and the DMCA fails to survive the exacting scrutiny accorded statutes that regulate "speech"; and (3) the DMCA violates the First Amendment and the Copyright Clause by unduly obstructing the "fair use" of copyrighted materials. Corley also argues that the statute is susceptible to, and should therefore be given, a narrow interpretation that avoids alleged constitutional objections.

Background

For decades, motion picture studios have made movies available for viewing at home in what is called "analog" format. Movies in this format are placed on videotapes, which can be played on a video cassette recorder ("VCR"). In the early 1990s, the studios began to consider the possibility of distributing movies in digital form as well. Movies in digital form are placed on disks, known as DVDs, which can be played on a DVD player (either a stand-alone device or a component of a computer). DVDs offer advantages over analog tapes, such as improved visual and audio quality, larger data capacity, and greater durability. However, the improved quality of a movie in a digital format brings with it the risk that a virtually perfect copy, *i.e.*, one that will not lose perceptible quality in the copying process, can be readily made at the click of a computer control and instantly distributed to countless recipients throughout the world over the Internet. This case arises out of the movie industry's efforts to respond to this risk by invoking the anti-trafficking provisions of the DMCA.

I. CSS

The movie studios were reluctant to release movies in digital form until they were confident they had in place adequate safeguards against piracy of their copyrighted movies. The studios took several steps to minimize the piracy threat. First, they settled on the DVD as the standard digital medium for home distribution of movies. The studios then sought an encryption scheme to protect movies on DVDs. They enlisted the help of members of the consumer electronics and computer industries, who in mid-1996 developed the Content Scramble System ("CSS"). CSS is an encryption scheme that employs an algorithm configured by a set of "keys" to encrypt a DVD's contents. The algorithm is a type of mathematical formula for transforming the contents of the movie file into gibberish; the "keys" are in actuality strings of 0's and 1's that serve as values for the mathematical formula. Decryption in the case of CSS requires a set of "player keys" contained in compliant DVD players, as well as an understanding of the CSS encryption algorithm. Without the player keys and the algorithm, a DVD player cannot access the contents of a DVD. With the player keys and the algorithm, a DVD player can display the movie on a television or a computer screen, but does not give a viewer the ability to use the copy function of the computer to copy the movie or to manipulate the digital content of the DVD.

The studios developed a licensing scheme for distributing the technology to manufacturers of DVD players. Player keys and other information necessary to the CSS scheme were given to manufacturers of DVD players for an administrative fee. In exchange for the licenses, manufacturers were obliged to keep the player keys confidential. Manufacturers were also required in the licensing agreement to prevent the transmission of "CSS data" (a term undefined in the licensing agreement) from a DVD drive to any "internal recording device," including, presumably, a computer hard drive.

With encryption technology and licensing agreements in hand, the studios began releasing movies on DVDs in 1997, and DVDs quickly gained in popularity, becoming a significant source of studio revenue.[3] In 1998, the studios secured added protection against DVD piracy when Congress passed the DMCA, which prohibits the development or use of technology designed to circumvent a technological protection measure, such as CSS. The pertinent provisions of the DMCA are examined in greater detail below.

II. DeCSS

In September 1999, Jon Johansen, a Norwegian teenager, collaborating with two unidentified individuals he met on the Internet, reverse engineered a licensed DVD player designed to operate on the Microsoft operating system, and culled from it the player keys and other information necessary to decrypt CSS. The record suggests that Johansen was trying to develop a DVD player operable on Linux, an alternative operating system that did not support any licensed DVD players at that time. In order to accomplish this task, Johansen wrote a decryption program executable on Microsoft's operating system.[4] That program was called, appropriately enough, "DeCSS."

If a user runs the DeCSS program (for example, by clicking on the DeCSS icon on a Microsoft operating system platform) with a DVD in the computer's disk drive, DeCSS will decrypt the DVD's CSS protection, allowing the user to copy the DVD's files and place the copy on the user's hard drive. The result is a very large computer file that can be played on a non-CSS-compliant player and copied, manipulated, and transferred just like any other computer file. [5] DeCSS comes complete with a fairly user-friendly interface that helps the user select from among the DVD's files and assign the decrypted file a location on the user's hard drive. The quality of the resulting decrypted movie is "virtually identical" to that of the encrypted movie on the DVD. *Universal I*, 111 F Supp 2d at 308, 313. And the file produced by DeCSS, while large, can be compressed to a manageable size by a compression software called "DivX," available at no cost on the Internet. This compressed file can be copied onto a DVD, or transferred over the Internet (with some patience). [6]

Johansen posted the executable object code, but not the source code, for DeCSS on his web site. The distinction between source code and object code is relevant to this case, so a brief explanation is warranted. A computer responds to electrical charges, the presence or absence of which is represented by strings of 1's and 0's. Strictly speaking, "object code" consists of those 1's and 0's. Trial Tr. at 759 (Testimony of Professor Edward Felten). While some people can read and program in object code, "it would be inconvenient, inefficient and, for most people, probably impossible to do so." *Universal I*, 111 F Supp 2d at 306. Computer languages have been written to facilitate program writing and reading. A program in such a computer language—BASIC, C, and Java are examples—is said to be written in "source code." Source code has the benefit of being much easier to read (by people) than object code, but as a general matter, it must be translated back to object code before it can be read by a computer. This task is usually performed by a program called a compiler. Since computer languages range in complexity, object code can be placed on one end of a spectrum, and different kinds of source code can be arrayed across the spectrum according to the ease with which they are read and understood by humans. *See* Trial Exhibits BBC (Declaration of David S. Touretzky), BBE (Touretzky Article: *Source v. Object Code: A False Dichotomy*). Within months of its appearance in executable form on Johansen's web site, DeCSS was widely available on the Internet, in both object code and various forms of source code. *See* Trial Exhibit CCN (Touretzky Article: *Gallery of CSS Descramblers*).

In November 1999, Corley wrote and placed on his web site, 2600.com, an article about the DeCSS phenomenon. His web site is an auxiliary to the print magazine, *2600: The Hacker Quarterly*, which Corley has been publishing since 1984. [7] As the name suggests, the magazine is designed for "hackers," as is the web site. While the magazine and the web site cover some issues of general interest to computer users—such as threats to online privacy—the focus of the publications is on the vulnerability of computer security systems, and more specifically, how to exploit that vulnerability in order to circumvent the security systems. Representative articles explain how to steal an Internet domain name and how to break into the computer systems at Federal Express. *Universal I*, 111 F Supp 2d at 308-09.

Corley's article about DeCSS detailed how CSS was cracked, and described the movie industry's efforts to shut down web sites posting DeCSS. It also explained that DeCSS could be used to copy DVDs. At the end of the article, the Defendants posted copies of the object and source code of DeCSS. In Corley's words, he added the code to the story because "in a journalistic world, . . . [y]ou have to show your evidence . . . and particularly in the magazine that I work for, people want to see specifically what it is that we are referring to," including "what evidence . . . we have" that there is in fact technology that circumvents CSS. Trial Tr. at 823. Writing about DeCSS without including the DeCSS code would have been, to Corley, "analogous to printing a story about a picture and not printing the picture." *Id.* at 825. Corley also added to the article links that he explained would take the reader to other web sites where DeCSS could be found. *Id.* at 791, 826, 827, 848.

2600.com was only one of hundreds of web sites that began posting DeCSS near the end of 1999. The movie industry tried to stem the tide by sending cease-and-desist letters to many of these sites. These efforts met with only partial success; a number of sites refused to remove DeCSS. In January 2000, the studios filed this lawsuit. [8]

III. The DMCA

The DMCA was enacted in 1998 to implement the World Intellectual Property Organization Copyright Treaty ("WIPO Treaty"), which requires contracting parties to "provide adequate legal protection and effective legal remedies against the circumvention of effective technological measures that are used by authors in connection with the exercise of their rights under this Treaty or the Berne Convention and that restrict acts, in respect of their works, which are not authorized by the authors concerned or permitted by law." WIPO Treaty, Apr. 12, 1997, art. 11, S. Treaty Doc. No. 105-17 (1997), available at 1997 WL 447232. Even before the treaty, Congress had been devoting attention to the problems faced by copyright enforcement in the digital age. Hearings on the topic have spanned several years. *See, e.g.*, WIPO Copyright Treaties Implementation Act and Online Copyright Liability Limitation Act: Hearing on H.R. 2281 and H.R. 2280 Before the Subcomm. on Courts and Intellectual Property of the House Comm. on the Judiciary, 105th Cong. (1997); NII Copyright Protection Act of 1995: Hearings on H.R. 2441 Before the Subcomm. on Courts and Intellectual Property of the House Comm. on the Judiciary, 104th Cong. (1996); NII Copyright Protection Act of 1995: Joint Hearing on H.R. 2441 and S. 1284 Before the Subcomm. on Courts and Intellectual Property of the House Comm. on the Judiciary and the Senate Comm. on the Judiciary, 104th Cong. (1995); H.R. Rep. No. 105-551 (1998); S. Rep. No. 105-190 (1998). This legislative effort resulted in the DMCA.

The Act contains three provisions targeted at the circumvention of technological protections. The first is subsection 1201(a)(1)(A), the anti-circumvention provision. [9] This provision prohibits a person from "circumvent[ing] a technological measure that effectively controls access to a work protected under [Title 17, governing copyright]." The Librarian of Congress is required to promulgate regulations every three years exempting from this subsection individuals who would otherwise be "adversely affected" in "their ability to make noninfringing uses." 17 USC §1201(a)(1)(B)-(E).

The second and third provisions are subsections 1201(a)(2) and 1201(b)(1), the "anti-trafficking provisions." Subsection 1201(a)(2), the provision at issue in this case, provides:

> No person shall manufacture, import, offer to the public, provide, or otherwise traffic in any technology, product, service, device, component, or part thereof, that
>
> (A) is primarily designed or produced for the purpose of circumventing a technological measure that effectively controls access to a work protected under this title;
>
> (B) has only limited commercially significant purpose or use other than to circumvent a technological measure that effectively controls access to a work protected under this title; or
>
> (C) is marketed by that person or another acting in concert with that person with that person's knowledge for use in circumventing a technological measure that effectively controls access to a work protected under this title.

Id. §1201(a)(2). To "circumvent a technological measure" is defined, in pertinent part, as "to descramble a scrambled work . . . or otherwise to . . . bypass . . . a technological measure, without the authority of the copyright owner." *Id.* 1201(a)(3)(A).

Subsection 1201(b)(1) is similar to subsection 1201(a)(2), except that subsection 1201(a)(2) covers those who traffic in technology that can circumvent "a technological measure that *effectively controls access* to a work protected under" Title 17, whereas subsection 1201(b)(1) covers those who traffic in technology that can circumvent "protection afforded by a technological measure *that effectively protects a right of a copyright owner* under" Title 17. *Id.* §1201(a)(2), (b)(1) (emphases added). In other words, although both subsections prohibit trafficking in a circumvention technology, the focus of subsection 1201(a)(2) is circumvention of technologies designed to *prevent access* to a work, and the focus of subsection 1201(b)(1) is circumvention of technologies designed to *permit access* to a work but *prevent copying* of the work or some other act that infringes a copyright. *See* S. Rep. No. 105-190, at 11-12 (1998). Subsection 1201(a)(1) differs from both of these anti-trafficking subsections in that it targets the use of a circumvention technology, not the trafficking in such a technology.

The DMCA contains exceptions for schools and libraries that want to use circumvention technologies to determine whether to purchase a copyrighted product, 17 USC 1201(d); individuals using circumvention technology "for the sole purpose" of trying to achieve "interoperability" of computer programs through reverse-engineering, *id.* 1201(f);

encryption research aimed at identifying flaws in encryption technology, if the research is conducted to advance the state of knowledge in the field, *id.* 1201(g); and several other exceptions not relevant here.

The DMCA creates civil remedies, *id.* §1203, and criminal sanctions, *id.* §1204. It specifically authorizes a court to "grant temporary and permanent injunctions on such terms as it deems reasonable to prevent or restrain a violation." *Id.* §1203(b)(1).

IV. Procedural History

Invoking subsection 1203(b)(1), the Plaintiffs sought an injunction against the Defendants, alleging that the Defendants violated the anti-trafficking provisions of the statute. On January 20, 2000, after a hearing, the District Court issued a preliminary injunction barring the Defendants from posting DeCSS. *Universal City Studios, Inc. v. Reimerdes*, 82 F Supp 3d 211 *[4 ILR (P&F) 399]* (SD NY 2000).

The Defendants complied with the preliminary injunction, but continued to post links to other web sites carrying DeCSS, an action they termed "electronic civil disobedience." *Universal I*, 111 F Supp 2d at 303, 312. Under the heading "Stop the MPAA [(Motion Picture Association of America)]," Corley urged other web sites to post DeCSS lest "we . . . be forced into submission." *Id.* at 313.

The Plaintiffs then sought a permanent injunction barring the Defendants from both posting DeCSS and linking to sites containing DeCSS. After a trial on the merits, the Court issued a comprehensive opinion, *Universal I*, and granted a permanent injunction, *Universal II*.

The Court explained that the Defendants' posting of DeCSS on their web site clearly falls within section 1201(a)(2)(A) of the DMCA, rejecting as spurious their claim that CSS is not a technological measure that "effectively controls access to a work" because it was so easily penetrated by Johansen, *Universal I*, 111 F Supp 2d at 318, and as irrelevant their contention that DeCSS was designed to create a Linux-platform DVD player, *id.* at 319. The Court also held that the Defendants cannot avail themselves of any of the DMCA's exceptions, *id.* at 319-22, and that the alleged importance of DeCSS to certain fair uses of encrypted copyrighted material was immaterial to their statutory liability, *id.* at 322-

24. The Court went on to hold that when the Defendants "proclaimed on their own site that DeCSS could be had by clicking on the hyperlinks" on their site, they were trafficking in DeCSS, and therefore liable for their linking as well as their posting. *Id.* at 325.

Turning to the Defendants' numerous constitutional arguments, the Court first held that computer code like DeCSS is "speech" that is "protected" (in the sense of "covered") by the First Amendment, *id.* at 327, but that because the DMCA is targeting the "functional" aspect of that speech, *id.* at 328-29, it is "content neutral," *id.* at 329,[10] and the intermediate scrutiny of *United States v. O'Brien*, 391 US 367, 377 (1968), applies, *Universal I*, 111 F Supp 2d at 329-30. The Court concluded that the DMCA survives this scrutiny, *id.* at 330-33, and also rejected prior restraint, overbreadth, and vagueness challenges, *id.* at 333-39.

The Court upheld the constitutionality of the DMCA's application to linking on similar grounds: linking, the Court concluded, is "speech," but the DMCA is content-neutral, targeting only the functional components of that speech. Therefore, its application to linking is also evaluated under *O'Brien*, and, thus evaluated, survives intermediate scrutiny. However, the Court concluded that a blanket proscription on linking would create a risk of chilling legitimate linking on the web. The Court therefore crafted a restrictive test for linking liability (discussed below) that it believed sufficiently mitigated that risk. The Court then found its test satisfied in this case. *Id.* at 339 41.

Finally, the Court concluded that an injunction was highly appropriate in this case. The Court observed that DeCSS was harming the Plaintiffs, not only because they were now exposed to the possibility of piracy and therefore were obliged to develop costly new safeguards for DVDs, but also because, even if there was only indirect evidence that DeCSS availability actually facilitated DVD piracy,[11] the threat of piracy was very real, particularly as Internet transmission speeds continue to increase. *Id.* at 314 15, 342. Acknowledging that DeCSS was (and still is) widely available on the Internet, the Court expressed confidence in

the likelihood . . . that this decision will serve notice on others that "the strong right arm of equity" may be brought to bear against them absent a change in their conduct and thus contribute to a climate of appropriate respect for intellectual property rights in an age in which the excitement of ready access to untold quantities of information has blurred in some minds the fact that taking what is not yours and not freely offered to you is stealing.

Id. at 345.

The Court's injunction barred the Defendants from: "posting on any Internet web site" DeCSS; "in any other way . . . offering to the public, providing, or otherwise trafficking in DeCSS"; violating the anti trafficking provisions of the DMCA in any other manner, and finally "knowingly linking any Internet web site operated by them to any other web site containing DeCSS, or knowingly maintaining any such link, for the purpose of disseminating DeCSS." *Universal II*, 111 F Supp 2d at 346-47.

The Appellants have appealed from the permanent injunction. The United States has intervened in support of the constitutionality of the DMCA. We have also had the benefit of a number of *amicus curiae* briefs, supporting and opposing the District Court's judgment. After oral argument, we invited the parties to submit responses to a series of specific questions, and we have received helpful responses.

Discussion

I. Narrow Construction to Avoid Constitutional Doubt

The Appellants first argue that, because their constitutional arguments are at least substantial, we should interpret the statute narrowly so as to avoid constitutional problems. They identify three different instances of alleged ambiguity in the statute that they claim provide an opportunity for such a narrow interpretation.

First, they contend that subsection 1201(c)(1), which provides that "[n]othing in this section shall affect rights, remedies, limitations or defenses to copyright infringement, including fair use, under this title," can be read to allow the circumvention of encryption technology protecting copyrighted material when the material will be put to "fair uses" exempt from copyright liability.[12] We disagree that

subsection 1201(c)(1) permits such a reading. Instead, it clearly and simply clarifies that the DMCA targets the circumvention of digital walls guarding copyrighted material (and trafficking in circumvention tools), but does not concern itself with the use of those materials after circumvention has occurred. Subsection 1201(c)(1) ensures that the DMCA is not read to prohibit the "fair use" of information just because that information was obtained in a manner made illegal by the DMCA. The Appellants' much more expansive interpretation of subsection 1201(c)(1) is not only outside the range of plausible readings of the provision, but is also clearly refuted by the statute's legislative history.[13] *See Commodity Futures Trading Commission v. Schor*, 478 US 833, 841 (1986) (constitutional doubt canon "does not give a court the prerogative to ignore the legislative will").

Second, the Appellants urge a narrow construction of the DMCA because of subsection 1201(c)(4), which provides that "[n]othing in this section shall enlarge or diminish any rights of free speech or the press for activities using consumer electronics, telecommunications, or computing products." This language is clearly precatory: Congress could not "diminish" constitutional rights of free speech even if it wished to, and the fact that Congress also expressed a reluctance to "enlarge" those rights cuts against the Appellants' effort to infer a narrowing construction of the Act from this provision.

Third, the Appellants argue that an individual who buys a DVD has the "authority of the copyright owner" to view the DVD, and therefore is exempted from the DMCA pursuant to subsection 1201(a)(3)(A) when the buyer circumvents an encryption technology in order to view the DVD on a competing platform (such as Linux). The basic flaw in this argument is that it misreads subsection 1201(a)(3)(A). That provision exempts from liability those who would "decrypt" an encrypted DVD with the authority of a copyright owner, not those who would "view" a DVD with the authority of a copyright owner.[14] In any event, the Defendants offered no evidence that the Plaintiffs have either explicitly or implicitly authorized DVD buyers to circumvent encryption technology to support use on multiple platforms.[15]

We conclude that the anti-trafficking and anti-circumvention provisions of the DMCA are not susceptible to the narrow interpretations urged by the Appellants. We therefore proceed to consider the Appellants' constitutional claims.

II. Constitutional Challenge Based on the Copyright Clause

In a footnote to their brief *[7 ILR (P&F) 2005]*, the Appellants appear to contend that the DMCA, as construed by the District Court, exceeds the constitutional authority of Congress to grant authors copyrights for a "limited time," U.S. Const. art. I, §8, cl. 8, because it "empower[s] copyright owners to effectively secure perpetual protection by mixing public domain works with copyrighted materials, then locking both up with technological protection measures." Brief for Appellants at 42 n. 30. This argument is elaborated in the *amici curiae* brief *[7 ILR (P&F) 2087]* filed by Prof. Julie E. Cohen on behalf of herself and 45 other intellectual property law professors. *See also* David Nimmer, *A Riff on Fair Use in the Digital Millennium Copyright Act*, 148 U Pa L Rev 673, 712 (2000). For two reasons, the argument provides no basis for disturbing the judgment of the District Court.

First, we have repeatedly ruled that arguments presented to us only in a footnote are not entitled to appellate consideration. *Concourse Rehabilitation & Nursing Center Inc. v. DeBuono*, 179 F3d 38, 47 (2d Cir 1999); *United States v. Mapp*, 170 F3d 328, 333 n. 8 (2d Cir 1999); *United States v. Restrepo*, 986 F2d 1462, 1463 (2d Cir 1993). Although an *amicus* brief can be helpful in elaborating issues properly presented by the parties, it is normally not a method for injecting new issues into an appeal, at least in cases where the parties are competently represented by counsel. *See, e.g., Concourse Center*, 179 F3d at 47.

Second, to whatever extent the argument might have merit at some future time in a case with a properly developed record, the argument is entirely premature and speculative at this time on this record. There is not even a claim, much less evidence, that any Plaintiff has sought to prevent copying of public domain works, or that the injunction prevents the Defendants from copying such works. As Judge Kaplan noted, the possibility that encryption would preclude access to public domain works "does not yet appear to be a problem, although it may emerge as one in the future." *Universal I*, 111 F Supp 2d at 338 n. 245.

III. Constitutional Challenges Based on the First Amendment

A. Applicable Principles

Last year, in one of our Court's first forays into First Amendment law in the digital age, we took an "evolutionary" approach to the task of tailoring familiar constitutional rules to novel technological circumstances, favoring "narrow" holdings that would permit the law to mature on a "case-by-case" basis. *See Name.Space, Inc. v. Network Solutions, Inc.*, 202 F3d 573, 584 n. 11 *[4 ILR (P&F) 356]* (2d Cir 2000). In that spirit, we proceed, with appropriate caution, to consider the Appellants' First Amendment challenges by analyzing a series of preliminary issues the resolution of which provides a basis for adjudicating the specific objections to the DMCA and its application to DeCSS. These issues, which we consider only to the extent necessary to resolve the pending appeal, are whether computer code is speech, whether computer programs are speech, the scope of First Amendment protection for computer code, and the scope of First Amendment protection for decryption code. Based on our analysis of these issues, we then consider the Appellants' challenge to the injunction's provisions concerning posting and linking.

1. Code as Speech

Communication does not lose constitutional protection as "speech" simply because it is expressed in the language of computer code. Mathematical formulae and musical scores are written in "code," *i.e.*, symbolic notations not comprehensible to the uninitiated, and yet both are covered by the First Amendment. If someone chose to write a novel entirely in computer object code by using strings of 1's and 0's for each letter of each word, the resulting work would be no different for constitutional purposes than if it had been written in English. The "object code" version would be incomprehensible to readers outside the programming community (and tedious to read even for most within the community), but it would be no more incomprehensible than a work written in Sanskrit for those unversed in that language. The undisputed evidence reveals that even pure object code can be, and often is, read and understood by experienced programmers. And source code (in any of its various levels of complexity) can be read by many more. *See Universal I*, 111 F Supp 2d at 326. Ultimately, however, the ease with which a work is comprehended is irrelevant to the constitutional inquiry. If computer code is distinguishable from conventional speech for First Amendment purposes, it is not because it is written in an obscure language. *See Junger v. Daley*, 209 F3d 481, 484 *[5 ILR (P&F) 122]* (6th Cir 2000).

2. Computer Programs as Speech

Of course, computer code is not likely to be the language in which a work of literature is written. Instead, it is primarily the language for programs executable by a computer. These programs are essentially instructions to a computer. In general, programs may give instructions either to perform a task or series of tasks when initiated by a single (or double) click of a mouse or, once a program is operational ("launched"), to manipulate data that the user enters into the computer.[16] Whether computer code that gives a computer instructions is "speech" within the meaning of the First Amendment requires consideration of the scope of the Constitution's protection of speech.

The First Amendment provides that "Congress shall make no law ... abridging the freedom of speech ...." U.S. Const. amend. I. "Speech" is an elusive term, and judges and scholars have debated its bounds for two centuries. Some would confine First Amendment protection to political speech. *E.g.*, Robert Bork, *Neutral Principles and Some First Amendment Problems*, 47 Ind. L.J. 1 (1971). Others would extend it further to artistic expression. *E.g.*, Marci A. Hamilton, *Art Speech*, 49 Vand. L. Rev. 73 (1996).

Whatever might be the merits of these and other approaches, the law has not been so limited. Even dry information, devoid of advocacy, political relevance, or artistic expression, has been accorded First Amendment protection. *See Miller v. California*, 413 US 15, 34 (1973) ("The First Amendment protects works which, taken as a whole, have serious literary, artistic, political, or scientific value ...." (emphasis added)); *Roth v. United States*, 354 US 476, 484 (1957) (First Amendment embraces "[a]ll ideas having even the slightest redeeming social importance," including the " 'advancement of truth, science, morality, and arts in general.' " (quoting 1 Journals of the Continental Congress 108 (1774))); *Board of Trustees of Stanford University v. Sullivan*, 773 F Supp 472,

474 (D DC 1991) ("It is ... settled ... that the First Amendment protects scientific expression and debate just as it protects political and artistic expression."); *see also* Kent Greenawalt, *Speech, Crime and the Uses of Language* 85 (1989) ("[A]ssertions of fact generally fall within a principle of freedom of speech ...."); *cf. Virginia State Board of Pharmacy v. Virginia Citizens Consumer Council, Inc.*, 425 US 748, 763 (1976) ("prescription drug price information" is "speech" because a consumer's interest in "the free flow of commercial information" may be "keener by far" than "his interest in the day's most urgent political debate").

Thus, for example, courts have subjected to First Amendment scrutiny restrictions on the dissemination of technical scientific information, *United States v. Progressive, Inc.*, 467 F Supp 990 (WD Wis 1979), and scientific research, *Stanford University*, 773 F Supp at 473, and attempts to regulate the publication of instructions,[17] *see, e.g., United States v. Raymond*, 228 F3d 804, 815 (7th Cir 2000) (First Amendment does not protect instructions for violating the tax laws); *United States v. Dahlstrom*, 713 F2d 1423, 1428 (9th Cir 1983) (same); *Herceg v. Hustler Magazine, Inc.*, 814 F2d 1017, 1020-25 (5th Cir 1987) (First Amendment protects instructions for engaging in a dangerous sex act); *United States v. Featherston*, 461 F2d 1119, 1122-23 (5th Cir 1972) (First Amendment does not protect instructions for building an explosive device); *see also Bernstein v. United States Department of State*, 922 F Supp 1426, 1435 *[1 ILR (P&F) 762]* (ND Cal 1996) ("Instructions, do-it-yourself manuals, [and] recipes" are all "speech").[18]

Computer programs are not exempted from the category of First Amendment speech simply because their instructions require use of a computer. A recipe is no less "speech" because it calls for the use of an oven, and a musical score is no less "speech" because it specifies performance on an electric guitar. Arguably distinguishing computer programs from conventional language instructions is the fact that programs are executable on a computer. But the fact that a program has the capacity to direct the functioning of a computer does not mean that it lacks the additional capacity to convey information, and it is the conveying of information that renders instructions "speech" for purposes of the First Amendment.[19] The information conveyed by most "instructions" is how to perform a task.

Instructions such as computer code, which are intended to be executable by a computer, will often convey information capable of comprehension and assessment by a human being. [20] A programmer reading a program learns information about instructing a computer, and might use this information to improve personal programming skills and perhaps the craft of programming. Moreover, programmers communicating ideas to one another almost inevitably communicate in code, much as musicians use notes. [21] Limiting First Amendment protection of programmers to descriptions of computer code (but not the code itself) would impede discourse among computer scholars, [22] just as limiting protection for musicians to descriptions of musical scores (but not sequences of notes) would impede their exchange of ideas and expression. Instructions that communicate information comprehensible to a human qualify as speech whether the instructions are designed for execution by a computer or a human (or both).

Vartuli is not to the contrary. The defendants in *Vartuli* marketed a software program called "Recurrence," which would tell computer users when to buy or sell currency futures contracts if their computers were fed currency market rates. The Commodity Futures Trading Commission charged the defendants with violating federal law for, among other things, failing to register as commodity trading advisors for their distribution of the Recurrence software. The defendants maintained that Recurrence's cues to users to buy or sell were protected speech, and that the registration requirement as applied to Recurrence was a constitutionally suspect prior restraint. We rejected the defendants' constitutional claim, holding that Recurrence "in the form it was sold and marketed by the defendants" did not generate speech protected by the First Amendment. *Vartuli*, 228 F3d at 111.

Essential to our ruling in *Vartuli* was the *manner* in which the defendants marketed the software and intended that it be used: the defendants told users of the software to follow the software's cues "with no second-guessing," *id.*, and intended that users follow Recurrence's commands "mechanically" and "without the intercession of the mind or the will of the recipient," *id.* We held that the values served by the First Amendment were not advanced by these instructions, even though the instructions were expressed in words. *Id.* We acknowledged that some

users would, despite the defendants' marketing, refuse to follow Recurrence's cues mechanically but instead would use the commands as a source of information and advice, and that, as to these users, Recurrence's cues might very "well have been 'speech.'" *Id.* at 111-12. Nevertheless, we concluded that the Government could require registration for Recurrence's intended use because such use was devoid of any constitutionally protected speech. *Id.* at 112.

Vartuli considered two ways in which a programmer might be said to communicate through code: to the user of the program (not necessarily protected) and to the computer (never protected). [23] However, this does not mean that *Vartuli* denied First Amendment protection to all computer programs. Since *Vartuli* limited its constitutional scrutiny to the code "as marketed," *i.e.*, as an automatic trading system, it did not have occasion to consider a third manner in which a programmer might communicate through code: to another programmer.

For all of these reasons, we join the other courts that have concluded that computer code, and computer programs constructed from code can merit First Amendment protection, *see Junger*, 209 F3d at 484; [24] *Bernstein*, 922 F Supp at 1434-36; *see also Bernstein*, 176 F3d at 1140-41; *Karn v. United States Department of State*, 925 F Supp 1, 9-10 *[1 ILR (P&F) 512]* (D DC 1996) (assuming, without deciding, that source code with English comments interspersed throughout is "speech"), although the scope of such protection remains to be determined.

3. The Scope of First Amendment Protection for Computer Code

Having concluded that computer code conveying information is "speech" within the meaning of the First Amendment, we next consider, to a limited extent, the scope of the protection that code enjoys. As the District Court recognized, *Universal I*, 111 F Supp 2d at 327, the scope of protection for speech generally depends on whether the restriction is imposed because of the content of the speech. Content-based restrictions are permissible only if they serve compelling state interests and do so by the least restrictive means available. *See Sable Communications of California, Inc. v. FCC*, 492 US 115, 126 (1989). A content-neutral restriction is permissible if it serves a substantial governmental interest, the interest is unrelated to the suppression of free expression, and the regulation is narrowly tailored, which "in this context requires . . . that the means chosen do not 'burden substantially more speech than is necessary to further the government's legitimate interests.' " *Turner Broadcasting System, Inc. v. FCC*, 512 US 622, 662 (1994) (quoting *Ward v. Rock Against Racism*, 491 US 781, 799 (1989)). [25]

"[G]overnment regulation of expressive activity is 'content neutral' if it is justified without reference to the content of regulated speech." *Hill v. Colorado*, 530 US 703, 720 (2000). "The government's purpose is the controlling consideration. A regulation that serves purposes unrelated to the content of expression is deemed neutral, even if it has an incidental effect on some speakers or messages but not others." *Ward*, 491 US at 791. The Supreme Court's approach to determining content-neutrality appears to be applicable whether what is regulated is expression, *see id.* at 791-93 (regulation of volume of music), conduct, *see O'Brien*, 391 US at 377, or any "activity" that can be said to combine speech and non-speech elements, *see Spence v. Washington*, 418 US 405, 410-11 (1974) (applying *O'Brien* to "activity" of displaying American flag hung upside down and decorated with a peace symbol).

To determine whether regulation of computer code is content-neutral, the initial inquiry must be whether the regulated activity is "sufficiently imbued with elements of communication to fall within the scope of the First . . . Amendment[ ]." *Id.* at 409; *see also Name.Space*, 202 F3d at 585. Computer code, as we have noted, often conveys information comprehensible to human beings, even as it also directs a computer to perform various functions. Once a speech component is identified, the inquiry then proceeds to whether the regulation is "justified without reference to the content of regulated speech." *Hill*, 530 US at 720.

The Appellants vigorously reject the idea that computer code can be regulated according to any different standard than that applicable to pure speech, *i.e.*, speech that lacks a nonspeech component. Although recognizing that code is a series of instructions to a computer, they argue that code is no different, for First Amendment purposes, than blueprints that instruct an engineer or recipes that instruct a cook. *See* Supplemental Brief for Appellants at 2, 3. [26] We disagree. Unlike a blueprint or a recipe, which cannot yield any functional result

without human comprehension of its content, human decision-making, and human action, computer code can instantly cause a computer to accomplish tasks and instantly render the results of those tasks available throughout the world via the Internet. The only human action required to achieve these results can be as limited and instantaneous as a single click of a mouse. These realities of what code is and what its normal functions are require a First Amendment analysis that treats code as combining nonspeech and speech elements, *i.e.*, functional and expressive elements. *See Red Lion Broadcasting Co. v. FCC*, 395 US 367, 386 (1969) ("[D]ifferences in the characteristics of new media justify differences in the First Amendment standards applied to them." (footnote omitted)).

We recognize, as did Judge Kaplan, that the functional capability of computer code cannot yield a result until a human being decides to insert the disk containing the code into a computer and causes it to perform its function (or programs a computer to cause the code to perform its function). Nevertheless, this momentary intercession of human action does not diminish the nonspeech component of code, nor render code entirely speech, like a blueprint or a recipe. Judge Kaplan, in a passage that merits extensive quotation, cogently explained why this is especially so with respect to decryption code:

> [T]he focus on functionality in order to determine the level of scrutiny is not an inevitable consequence of the speech-conduct distinction. Conduct has immediate effects on the environment. Computer code, on the other hand, no matter how functional, causes a computer to perform the intended operations only if someone uses the code to do so. Hence, one commentator, in a thoughtful article, has maintained that functionality is really "a proxy for effects or harm" and that its adoption as a determinant of the level of scrutiny slides over questions of causation that intervene between the dissemination of a computer program and any harm caused by its use.
>
> The characterization of functionality as a proxy for the consequences of use is accurate. But the assumption that the chain of causation is too attenuated to justify the

use of functionality to determine the level of scrutiny, at least in this context, is not.

Society increasingly depends upon technological means of controlling access to digital files and systems, whether they are military computers, bank records, academic records, copyrighted works or something else entirely. There are far too many who, given any opportunity, will bypass security measures, some for the sheer joy of doing it, some for innocuous reasons, and others for more malevolent purposes. Given the virtually instantaneous and worldwide dissemination widely available via the Internet, the only rational assumption is that once a computer program capable of bypassing such an access control system is disseminated, it will be used. And that is not all.

There was a time when copyright infringement could be dealt with quite adequately by focusing on the infringing act. If someone wished to make and sell high quality but unauthorized copies of a copyrighted book, for example, the infringer needed a printing press. The copyright holder, once aware of the appearance of infringing copies, usually was able to trace the copies up the chain of distribution, find and prosecute the infringer, and shut off the infringement at the source.

In principle, the digital world is very different. Once a decryption program like DeCSS is written, it quickly can be sent all over the world. Every recipient is capable not only of decrypting and perfectly copying plaintiffs' copyrighted DVDs, but also of retransmitting perfect copies of DeCSS and thus enabling every recipient to do the same. They likewise are capable of transmitting perfect copies of the decrypted DVD. The process potentially is exponential rather than linear.

. . .

These considerations drastically alter consideration of the causal link between dissemination of computer programs such as this and their illicit use. Causation in the law ultimately involves practical policy judgments. Here, dissemination itself carries very substantial risk of imminent harm because the mechanism is so unusual by which dissemination of means of circumventing access controls to copyrighted works threatens to produce virtually unstoppable infringement of copyright. In consequence, the causal link between the dissemination of circumvention computer programs and their improper use is more than sufficiently close to warrant selection of a level of constitutional scrutiny based on the programs' functionality.

Universal I, 111 F Supp 2d at 331-32 (footnotes omitted). The functionality of computer code properly affects the scope of its First Amendment protection.

4. The Scope of First Amendment Protection for Decryption Code

In considering the scope of First Amendment protection for a decryption program like DeCSS, we must recognize that the essential purpose of encryption code is to prevent unauthorized access. Owners of all property rights are entitled to prohibit access to their property by unauthorized persons. Homeowners can install locks on the doors of their houses. Custodians of valuables can place them in safes. Stores can attach to products security devices that will activate alarms if the products are taken away without purchase. These and similar security devices can be circumvented. Burglars can use skeleton keys to open door locks. Thieves can obtain the combinations to safes. Product security devices can be neutralized.

Our case concerns a security device, CSS computer code, that prevents access by unauthorized persons to DVD movies. The CSS code is embedded in the DVD movie. Access to the movie cannot be obtained unless a person has a device, a licensed DVD player, equipped with computer code capable of decrypting the CSS encryption code. In its basic function, CSS is like a lock on a homeowner's door, a combination of a safe, or a security device attached to a store's products.

DeCSS is computer code that can decrypt CSS. In its basic function, it is like a skeleton key that can open a locked door, a combination that can open a safe, or a device that can neutralize the security device attached to a store's products.[27] DeCSS enables anyone to gain access to a DVD movie without using a DVD player.

The initial use of DeCSS to gain access to a DVD movie creates no loss to movie producers because the initial user must purchase the DVD. However, once the DVD is purchased, DeCSS enables the initial user to copy the movie in digital form and transmit it instantly in virtually limitless quantity, thereby depriving the movie producer of sales. The advent of the Internet creates the potential for instantaneous worldwide distribution of the copied material.

At first glance, one might think that Congress has as much authority to regulate the distribution of computer code to decrypt DVD movies as it has to regulate distribution of skeleton keys, combinations to safes, or devices to neutralize store product security devices. However, despite the evident legitimacy of protection against unauthorized access to DVD movies, just like any other property, regulation of decryption code like DeCSS is challenged in this case because DeCSS differs from a skeleton key in one important respect: it not only is capable of performing the function of unlocking the encrypted DVD movie, it also is a form of communication, albeit written in a language not understood by the general public. As a communication, the DeCSS code has a claim to being "speech," and as "speech," it has a claim to being protected by the First Amendment. But just as the realities of what any computer code can accomplish must inform the scope of its constitutional protection, so the capacity of a decryption program like DeCSS to accomplish unauthorized—indeed, unlawful—access to materials in which the Plaintiffs have intellectual property rights must inform and limit the scope of its First Amendment protection. *Cf. Red Lion*, 395 US at 386 ("[D]ifferences in the characteristics of new media justify differences in the First Amendment standards applied to them.").

With all of the foregoing considerations in mind, we next consider the Appellants' First Amendment challenge to the DMCA as applied in the specific prohibitions that have been imposed by the District Court's injunction.

B. First Amendment Challenge

The District Court's injunction applies the DMCA to the Defendants by imposing two types of prohibition, both grounded on the anti-trafficking provisions of the DMCA. The first prohibits posting DeCSS or any other technology for circumventing CSS on any Internet web site. *Universal II*, 111 F Supp 2d at 346-47, ¶1(a), (b). The second prohibits knowingly linking any Internet web site to any other web site containing DeCSS. *Id.* at 347, ¶1(c). The validity of the posting and linking prohibitions must be considered separately.

1. Posting

The initial issue is whether the posting prohibition is content-neutral, since, as we have explained, this classification determines the applicable constitutional standard. The Appellants contend that the anti-trafficking provisions of the DMCA and their application by means of the posting prohibition of the injunction are content-based. They argue that the provisions "specifically target . . . scientific expression based on the particular topic addressed by that expression—namely, techniques for circumventing CSS." Supplemental Brief for Appellants at 1. We disagree. The Appellants' argument fails to recognize that the target of the posting provisions of the injunction—DeCSS—has both a nonspeech and a speech component, and that the DMCA, as applied to the Appellants, and the posting prohibition of the injunction target only the nonspeech component. Neither the DMCA nor the posting prohibition is concerned with whatever capacity DeCSS might have for conveying information to a human being, and that capacity, as previously explained, is what arguably creates a speech component of the decryption code. The DMCA and the posting prohibition are applied to DeCSS solely because of its capacity to instruct a computer to decrypt CSS. That functional capability is not speech within the meaning of the First Amendment. The Government seeks to "justif[y]," *Hill*, 530 US at 720, both the application of the DMCA and the posting prohibition to the Appellants solely on the basis of the functional capability of DeCSS to instruct a computer to decrypt CSS, *i.e.*, "without reference to the content of the regulated speech," *id*. This type of regulation is therefore content-neutral, just as would be a restriction on trafficking in skeleton keys identified because of their capacity to unlock jail cells, even though some of the keys happened to bear a slogan or other legend that qualified as a speech component.

As a content-neutral regulation with an incidental effect on a speech component, the regulation must serve a substantial governmental interest, the interest must be unrelated to the suppression of free expression, and the incidental restriction on speech must not burden substantially more speech than is necessary to further that interest. *Turner Broadcasting*, 512 US at 662. The Government's interest in preventing unauthorized access to encrypted copyrighted material is unquestionably substantial, and the regulation of DeCSS by the posting prohibition plainly serves that interest. Moreover, that interest is unrelated to the suppression of free expression. The injunction regulates the posting of DeCSS, regardless of whether DeCSS code contains any information comprehensible by human beings that would qualify as speech. Whether the incidental regulation on speech burdens substantially more speech than is necessary to further the interest in preventing unauthorized access to copyrighted materials requires some elaboration.

Posting DeCSS on the Appellants' web site makes it instantly available at the click of a mouse to any person in the world with access to the Internet, and such person can then instantly transmit DeCSS to anyone else with Internet access. Although the prohibition on posting prevents the Appellants from conveying to others the speech component of DeCSS, the Appellants have not suggested, much less shown, any technique for barring them from making this instantaneous worldwide distribution of a decryption code that makes a lesser restriction on the code's speech component.[28] It is true that the Government has alternative means of prohibiting unauthorized access to copyrighted materials. For example, it can create criminal and civil liability for those who gain unauthorized access, and thus it can be argued that the restriction on posting DeCSS is not absolutely necessary to preventing unauthorized access to copyrighted materials. But a content-neutral regulation need not employ the least restrictive means of accomplishing the governmental objective. *Id.* It need only avoid burdening "substantially more speech than is necessary to further the government's legitimate interests." *Id.* (internal quotation marks and citation

omitted). The prohibition on the Defendants' posting of DeCSS satisfies that standard.[29]

2. Linking

In considering linking, we need to clarify the sense in which the injunction prohibits such activity. Although the injunction defines several terms, it does not define "linking." Nevertheless, it is evident from the District Court's opinion that it is concerned with "hyperlinks," *Universal I*, 111 F Supp 2d at 307; *see id.* at 339.[30] A hyperlink is a cross-reference (in a distinctive font or color) appearing on one web page that, when activated by the point-and-click of a mouse, brings onto the computer screen another web page. The hyperlink can appear on a screen (window) as text, such as the Internet address ("URL") of the web page being called up or a word or phrase that identifies the web page to be called up, for example, "DeCSS web site." Or the hyperlink can appear as an image, for example, an icon depicting a person sitting at a computer watching a DVD movie and text stating "click here to access DeCSS and see DVD movies for free!" The code for the web page containing the hyperlink contains a computer instruction that associates the link with the URL of the web page to be accessed, such that clicking on the hyperlink instructs the computer to enter the URL of the desired web page and thereby access that page. With a hyperlink on a web page, the linked web site is just one click away.[31]

In applying the DMCA to linking (via hyperlinks), Judge Kaplan recognized, as he had with DeCSS code, that a hyperlink has both a speech and a nonspeech component. It conveys information, the Internet address of the linked web page, and has the functional capacity to bring the content of the linked web page to the user's computer screen (or, as Judge Kaplan put it, to "take one almost instantaneously to the desired destination." *Id.*). As he had ruled with respect to DeCSS code, he ruled that application of the DMCA to the Defendants' linking to web sites containing DeCSS is content-neutral because it is justified without regard to the speech component of the hyperlink. *Id.* The linking prohibition applies whether or not the hyperlink contains any information, comprehensible to a human being, as to the Internet address of the web page being accessed. The linking prohibition is justified solely by the functional capability of the hyperlink.

Applying the *O'Brien/Ward/Turner Broadcasting* requirements for content-neutral regulation, Judge Kaplan then ruled that the DMCA, as applied to the Defendants' linking, served substantial governmental interests and was unrelated to the suppression of free expression. *Id.* We agree. He then carefully considered the "closer call," *id.*, as to whether a linking prohibition would satisfy the narrow tailoring requirement. In an especially carefully considered portion of his opinion, he observed that strict liability for linking to web sites containing DeCSS would risk two impairments of free expression. Web site operators would be inhibited from displaying links to various web pages for fear that a linked page might contain DeCSS, and a prohibition on linking to a web site containing DeCSS would curtail access to whatever other information was contained at the accessed site. *Id.* at 340.

To avoid applying the DMCA in a manner that would "burden substantially more speech than is necessary to further the government's legitimate interests," *Turner Broadcasting*, 512 US at 662 (internal quotation marks and citation omitted), Judge Kaplan adapted the standards of *New York Times Co. v. Sullivan*, 376 US 254, 283 (1964), to fashion a limited prohibition against linking to web sites containing DeCSS. He required clear and convincing evidence

> that those responsible for the link (a) know at the relevant time that the offending material is on the linked-to site, (b) know that it is circumvention technology that may not lawfully be offered, and (c) create or maintain the link for the purpose of disseminating that technology.

Universal I, 111 F Supp 2d at 341. He then found that the evidence satisfied his three-part test by his required standard of proof. *Id.*

In response to our post-argument request for the parties' views on various issues, including specifically Judge Kaplan's test for a linking prohibition, the Appellants replied that his test was deficient for not requiring proof of intent to cause, or aid or abet, harm, and that the only valid test for a linking prohibition would be one that could validly apply to the publication in a print medium of an address for obtaining prohibited material. Supplemental Brief for Appellants at 14. The Appellees and the Government accepted Judge Kaplan's criteria for purposes of asserting the validity of the injunction as applied to the Appellants, with the Government expressing reservations as to the standard of clear and convincing evidence. Supplemental Brief for Appellees at 22-23; Supplemental Brief for Government at 19-21.

Mindful of the cautious approach to First Amendment claims involving computer technology expressed in *Name.Space*, 202 F3d at 584 n. 11, we see no need on this appeal to determine whether a test as rigorous as Judge Kaplan's is required to respond to First Amendment objections to the linking provision of the injunction that he issued. It suffices to reject the Appellants' contention that an intent to cause harm is required and that linking can be enjoined only under circumstances applicable to a print medium. As they have throughout their arguments, the Appellants ignore the reality of the functional capacity of decryption computer code and hyperlinks to facilitate instantaneous unauthorized access to copyrighted materials by anyone anywhere in the world. Under the circumstances amply shown by the record, the injunction's linking prohibition validly regulates the Appellants' opportunity instantly to enable anyone anywhere to gain unauthorized access to copyrighted movies on DVDs.[32]

At oral argument, we asked the Government whether its undoubted power to punish the distribution of obscene materials would permit an injunction prohibiting a newspaper from printing addresses of bookstore locations carrying such materials. In a properly cautious response, the Government stated that the answer would depend on the circumstances of the publication. The Appellants' supplemental papers enthusiastically embraced the arguable analogy between printing bookstore addresses and displaying on a web page links to web sites at which DeCSS may be accessed. Supplemental Brief for Appellants at 14. They confidently asserted that publication of bookstore locations carrying obscene material cannot be enjoined consistent with the First Amendment, and that a prohibition against linking to web sites containing DeCSS is similarly invalid. *Id.*

Like many analogies posited to illuminate legal issues, the bookstore analogy is helpful primarily in identifying characteristics that *distinguish* it from the context of the pending dispute. If a bookstore proprietor is knowingly selling obscene materials, the evil of distributing such materials can be prevented by injunctive relief against the unlawful distribution (and similar distribution by others can be deterred by punishment of the distributor). And if others publish the location of the bookstore, preventive relief against a distributor can be effective before any significant distribution of the prohibited materials has occurred. The digital world, however, creates a very different problem. If obscene materials are posted on one web site and other sites post hyperlinks to the first site, the materials are available for instantaneous worldwide distribution before any preventive measures can be effectively taken.

This reality obliges courts considering First Amendment claims in the context of the pending case to choose between two unattractive alternatives: either tolerate some impairment of communication in order to permit Congress to prohibit decryption that may lawfully be prevented, or tolerate some decryption in order to avoid some impairment of communication. Although the parties dispute the extent of impairment of communication if the injunction is upheld and the extent of decryption if it is vacated, and differ on the availability and effectiveness of techniques for minimizing both consequences, the fundamental choice between impairing some communication and tolerating decryption cannot be entirely avoided.

In facing this choice, we are mindful that it is not for us to resolve the issues of public policy implicated by the choice we have identified. Those issues are for Congress. Our task is to determine whether the legislative solution adopted by Congress, as applied to the Appellants by the District Court's injunction, is consistent with the limitations of the First Amendment, and we are satisfied that it is.

IV. Constitutional Challenge Based on Claimed Restriction of Fair Use

Asserting that fair use "is rooted in and required by both the Copyright Clause and the First Amendment," Brief for Appellants at 42, the Appellants contend that the DMCA, as applied by the District Court, unconstitutionally *"eliminates* fair use" of copyrighted materials, *id.* at 41 (emphasis added). We reject this extravagant claim.

Preliminarily, we note that the Supreme Court has never held that fair use is constitutionally required, although some isolated statements in its opinions might arguably be enlisted for such a requirement. In *Stewart v. Abend*, 495 US 207 (1990), cited by the Appellants, the Court merely noted that fair use " 'permits courts to avoid rigid application of the copyright statute when, on occasion, it would stifle the very creativity which that law is designed to foster,' " *id.* (quoting *Iowa State University Research Foundation, Inc. v. American Broadcasting Cos.*, 621 F2d 57, 60 (2d Cir 1980)); *see also Harper & Row, Publishers, Inc. v. Nation Enterprises*, 471 US 539, 560 (1985) (noting "the First Amendment protections already embodied in the Copyright Act's distinction between copyrightable expression and uncopyrightable facts and ideas, and the latitude for scholarship and comment traditionally afforded by fair use"). In *Campbell v. Acuff-Rose Music, Inc.*, 510 US 569 (1994), the Court observed, "From the infancy of copyright protection, some opportunity for fair use of copyrighted materials has been thought necessary to fulfill copyright's very purpose, '[t]o promote the Progress of Science and useful Arts . . . .' "[33] *Id.* at 575 (citation omitted); *see generally* William F. Patry, *The Fair Use Privilege in Copyright Law* 573-82 (2d ed. 1995) (questioning First Amendment protection for fair use).

We need not explore the extent to which fair use might have constitutional protection, grounded on either the First Amendment or the Copyright Clause, because whatever validity a constitutional claim might have as to an application of the DMCA that impairs fair use of copyrighted materials, such matters are far beyond the scope of this lawsuit for several reasons. In the first place, the Appellants do not claim to be making fair use of any copyrighted materials, and nothing in the injunction prohibits them from making such fair use. They are barred from trafficking in a decryption code that enables unauthorized access to copyrighted materials.

Second, as the District Court properly noted, to whatever extent the anti-trafficking provisions of the DMCA might prevent others from copying portions of DVD movies in order to make fair use of them, "the evidence as to the impact of the anti-trafficking provision[s] of the DMCA on prospective fair users is scanty and fails adequately to address the issues." *Universal I*, 111 F Supp 2d at 338 n. 246.

Third, the Appellants have provided no support for their premise that fair use of DVD movies is constitutionally required to be made by copying the original work in its original format.[34] Their examples of the fair uses that they believe others will be prevented from making all involve copying in a digital format those portions of a DVD movie amenable to fair use, a copying that would enable the fair user to manipulate the digitally copied portions. One example is that of a school child who wishes to copy images from a DVD movie to insert into the student's documentary film. We know of no authority for the proposition that fair use, as protected by the Copyright Act, much less the Constitution, guarantees copying by the optimum method or in the identical format of the original. Although the Appellants insisted at oral argument that they should not be relegated to a "horse and buggy" technique in making fair use of DVD movies,[35] the DMCA does not impose even an arguable limitation on the opportunity to make a variety of traditional fair uses of DVD movies, such as commenting on their content, quoting excerpts from their screenplays, and even recording portions of the video images and sounds on film or tape by pointing a camera, a camcorder, or a microphone at a monitor as it displays the DVD movie. The fact that the resulting copy will not be as perfect or as manipulable as a digital copy obtained by having direct access to the DVD movie in its digital form, provides no basis for a claim of unconstitutional limitation of fair use. A film critic making fair use of a movie by quoting selected lines of dialogue has no constitutionally valid claim that the review (in print or on television) would be technologically superior if the reviewer had not been prevented from using a movie camera in the theater, nor has an art student a valid constitutional claim to fair use of a painting by photographing it in a museum. Fair use has never been held to be a guarantee of access to copyrighted material in order to copy it by the fair user's preferred technique or in the format of the original.

Conclusion

We have considered all the other arguments of the Appellants and conclude that they provide no basis for disturbing the District Court's judgment. Accordingly, the judgment is affirmed.

———

* Honorable Alvin W. Thompson, United States District Court for the District of Connecticut, sitting by designation.

[1] DVDs are similar to compact disks (CDs), but differ, among other things, in that they hold far more data. For detailed information concerning DVDs and CDs, *see* "Fast Guide to CD/DVD" at http://searchWindowsManageability.techtarget.com/sDefinition/0,,sid_gci514667,00.html (last updated Aug. 3, 2001).

[2] "2600" has special significance to the hacker community. It is the hertz frequency ("a unit of frequency of a periodic process equal to one cycle per second," Webster's Third New International Dictionary 1061 (1993)) of a signal that some hackers formerly used to explore the entire telephone system from "operator mode," which was triggered by the transmission of a 2600 hertz tone across a telephone line, Trial Tr. at 786-87, or to place telephone calls without incurring long-distance toll charges, *United States v. Brady*, 820 F Supp 1346, 1355 & n. 18 (D Utah 1993). One such user reportedly discovered that the sound of a toy whistle from a box of Cap'n Crunch cereal matched the telephone company's 2600 hertz tone perfectly. *Id.* at 1355 n. 18.

[3] By the end of 1997, most if not all DVDs that were released were encrypted with CSS. Trial Tr. at 409; *Universal I*, 111 F Supp 2d at 310. Moreover, DVD players were projected to be in ten percent of United States homes by the end of 2000. Trial Tr. at 442; *Universal I*, 111 F Supp 2d at 310. In fact, as of 2000, about thirty-five percent of one studio's worldwide revenue from movie distribution was attributable to DVD sales and rentals. Trial Tr. at 403; *Universal I*, 111 F Supp 2d at 310 n. 69.

[4] An operating system works with the computer to perform the application's instructions. Generally, an executable application can be played only on the operating system for which it is designed, although interoperability has been improving. At the time of the trial, DeCSS could be run only on the Microsoft Windows operating system. Trial Tr. at 245 (Testimony of Robert W. Schumann).

[5] An item of some controversy, both in this litigation and elsewhere, is the extent to which CSS-encrypted DVDS can be copied even without DeCSS. The record leaves largely unclear how CSS protects against the *copying of a DVD*, as contrasted with the *playing of a DVD on an unlicensed player*. The Defendants' experts insisted that there is nothing about the way CSS operates that prevents the copying of a DVD. Declaration of Frank Stevenson ¶23 ("Bit-for-bit copying, which precisely duplicates the content of one DVD to another, results in a fully-playable product."); Trial Tr. at 751 (Testimony of Professor Edward Felten) (CSS "could [not] have prevented the encrypted content from being

copied to somewhere else"); Deposition of Barbara Simons at 48-49, 77. Some of the Plaintiffs' experts countered simply that "copying to a hard drive is something that compliant DVD players are not allowed to do," without explaining why. Trial Tr. at 37 (Testimony of Dr. Michael I. Shamos); *see also* Deposition of John J. Hoy at 347-8; Deposition of Fritz Attaway at 83. Another expert indicated that while a DVD movie can be copied to a computer's hard drive in encrypted form, the movie cannot be played without a DVD actually present in the DVD drive. Deposition of Robert W. Schumann at 153; Second Supplemental Declaration of Robert W. Schumann ¶15. This expert did not identify the mechanism that prevents someone from copying encrypted DVDs to a hard drive in the absence of a DVD in the disk drive.

However, none of this detracts from these undisputed findings: some feature of either CSS itself, or another (unidentified) safeguard implemented by DVD manufacturers pursuant to their obligations under the CSS licensing scheme, makes it difficult to copy a CSS-encrypted DVD to a hard drive and then compress that DVD to the point where transmission over the Internet is practical. *See Universal I*, 111 F Supp 2d at 338. Conversely, a DVD movie file without CSS encryption is easily copied, manipulated, and transferred. *See id.* at 313. In other words, it might very well be that copying is not blocked by CSS itself, but by some other protection implemented by the DVD player manufacturers. Nonetheless, in decrypting CSS, the DeCSS program (perhaps incidentally) sidesteps whatever it is that blocks copying of the files.

While there may be alternative means of extracting a non-encrypted, copyable movie from a DVD—for example, by copying the movie along with its encryption "bit-by-bit," or "ripping" a DVD by siphoning movie file data after CSS has already been decrypted by a licensed player—DeCSS is the superior means of acquiring easily copyable movies, *see id.* at 342, and in fact, is recommended by a DVD compression web site as the preferred tool for obtaining a decrypted DVD suitable for compression and transmission over the Internet, *see id.* We acknowledge the complexity and the rapidly changing nature of the technology involved in this case, but it is clear that the Defendants have presented no evidence to refute any of these carefully considered findings by the District Court.

⁶ The District Court determined that even at high speeds, typical of university networks, transmission times ranged from three minutes to six hours. The Court noted, however, that "the availability of high speed network connections in many businesses and institutions, and their growing availability in homes, make internet and other network traffic in pirated copies a growing threat." *Universal I*, 111 F Supp 2d at 315.

⁷ Defendant 2600 Enterprises, Inc., is the company Corley incorporated to run the magazine, maintain the web site, and manage related endeavors like merchandising.

⁸ The lawsuit was filed against Corley, Shawn C. Reimerdes, and Roman Kazan. 2600 Enterprises, Inc., was later added as a defendant. At an earlier stage of the litigation, the action was settled as to Reimerdes and Kazan. *See Universal II*, 111 F Supp 2d at 346.

⁹ For convenience, all references to the DMCA are to the United States Code sections.

¹⁰ In a supplemental Order, the Court corrected a typographical error in its opinion in *Universal I* by changing the first sentence of the first full paragraph at 111 F Supp 2d 328 to read "Restrictions on the nonspeech elements of expressive conduct fall into the content-neutral category." *Universal City Studios Inc. v. Reimerdes*, No. 00 Civ. 0277 (LAK) (SD NY Aug. 17, 2001).

¹¹ For example, advertisements for pirated DVDs rose dramatically in number after the release of DeCSS on the web, and DVD file compression web sites recommend the use of DeCSS. *Universal I*, 111 F Supp 2d at 342.

¹² In Part IV, *infra*, we consider the Appellants' claim that the DMCA is unconstitutional because of its effect on opportunities for fair use of copyrighted materials.

¹³ The legislative history of the enacted bill makes quite clear that Congress intended to adopt a "balanced" approach to accommodating both piracy and fair use concerns, eschewing the quick fix of simply exempting from the statute all circumventions for fair use. H.R. Rep. No. 105-551, pt. 2, at 25 (1998). It sought to achieve this goal principally through the use of what it called a "fail-safe" provision in the statute, authorizing the Librarian of Congress to exempt certain users from the anti-circumvention provision when it becomes evident that in practice, the statute is adversely affecting certain kinds of fair use. See 17 USC §1201(a)(1)(C); H.R. Rep. No. 105-551, pt. 2, at 36 ("Given the threat of a diminution of otherwise lawful access to works and information, the Committee on Commerce believes that a 'fail-safe' mechanism is required. This mechanism would . . . allow the . . . [waiver of the anti-circumvention provisions], for limited time periods, if necessary to prevent a diminution in the availability to individual users of a particular category of copyrighted materials.").

Congress also sought to implement a balanced approach through statutory provisions that leave limited areas of breathing space for fair use. A good example is subsection 1201(d), which allows a library or educational institution to circumvent a digital wall in order to determine whether it wishes legitimately to obtain the material behind the wall. *See* H.R. Rep. No. 105-551, pt. 2, at 41. It would be strange for Congress to open small, carefully limited windows for circumvention to permit fair use in subsection 1201(d) if it then meant to exempt in subsection 1201(c)(1) *any* circumvention necessary for fair use.

[14] This is actually what subsection 1201(a)(3)(A) means when read in conjunction with the *anti-circumvention* provision. When read together with the *anti-trafficking* provisions, subsection 1201(a)(3)(A) frees an individual to traffic in encryption technology designed or marketed to circumvent an encryption measure if the owner of the material protected by the encryption measure authorizes that circumvention.

[15] Even if the Defendants had been able to offer such evidence, and even if they could have demonstrated that DeCSS was "primarily designed . . . for the purpose of" playing DVDs on multiple platforms (and therefore not for the purpose of "circumventing a technological measure"), a proposition questioned by Judge Kaplan, *see Universal I*, 111 F Supp 2d at 311 n. 79, the Defendants would defeat liability only under subsection 1201(a)(2)(A). They would still be vulnerable to liability under subsection 1201(a)(2)(C), because they "marketed" DeCSS for the copying of DVDs, not just for the playing of DVDs on multiple platforms. *See, e.g.*, Trial Tr. at 820.

[16] For example, a program (or part of a program) will give a computer the direction to "launch" a word-processing program like WordPerfect when the icon for WordPerfect is clicked; a program like WordPerfect will give the computer directions to display letters on a screen and manipulate them according to the computer user's preferences whenever the appropriate keys are struck.

[17] We note that instructions are of varied types. *See Vartuli*, 228 F3d at 111. "Orders" from one member of a conspiracy to another member, or from a superior to a subordinate, might resemble instructions but nonetheless warrant less or even no constitutional protection because their capacity to inform is meager, and because it is unlikely that the recipient of the order will engage in the "intercession of . . . mind or . . . will" characteristic of the sort of communication between two parties protected by the Constitution, *see id.* at 111-12 (noting that statements in the form of orders, instructions, or commands cannot claim "talismanic immunity from constitutional limitations" but "should be subjected to careful and particularized analysis to ensure that no speech entitled to First Amendment protection fails to receive it"); Kent Greenawalt, *Speech and Crime*, Am. B. Found. Res. J. 645, 743-44 (1980).

[18] These cases almost always concern instruction on how to commit illegal acts. Several courts have concluded that such instructions fall outside the First Amendment. However, these conclusions never rest on the fact that the speech took the form of instructions, but rather on the fact that the instructions counseled the listener how to commit illegal acts. *See, e.g., Rice v. Paladin Enterprises, Inc.*, 128 F3d 233, 247-49 (4th Cir 1997); *United States v. Barnett*, 667 F2d 835, 842 (9th Cir 1982). None of these opinions even hints that instructions are a form of speech categorically outside the First Amendment.

[19] Of course, we do not mean to suggest that the communication of "information" is a prerequisite of protected "speech." Protected speech may communicate, among other things, ideas, emotions, or thoughts. We identify "information" only because this is what computer programs most often communicate, in addition to giving directions to a computer.

[20] However, in the rare case where a human's mental faculties do not intercede in executing the instructions, we have withheld protection. *See Vartuli*, 228 F3d at 111.

[21] Programmers use snippets of code to convey their ideas for new programs; economists and other creators of computer models publish the code of their models in order to demonstrate the models' vigor. Brief of *Amici Curiae* Dr. Harold Abelson *et al.* at 17; Brief of *Amici Curiae* Steven Bellovin *et al.* at 12-13; *see also Bernstein v. United States Department of Justice*, 176 F3d 1132, 1141 *[2 ILR (P&F) 602]* (9th Cir) (concluding that computer source code is speech because it is "the preferred means" of communication among computer programmers and cryptographers), *reh'g en banc granted and opinion withdrawn*, 192 F3d 1308 *[3 ILR (P&F) 500]* (9th Cir 1999).

[22] Reinforcing the conclusion that software programs qualify as "speech" for First Amendment purposes—even though they instruct computers—is the accelerated blurring of the line between "source code" and conventional "speech." There already exist programs capable of translating English descriptions of a program into source code. Trial Tr. at 1101-02 (Testimony of Professor Andrew Appel). These programs are functionally indistinguishable from the compilers that routinely translate source code into object code. These new programs (still apparently rudimentary) hold the potential for turning "prose" instructions on how to write a computer program into the program itself. Even if there were an argument for exempting the latter from First Amendment protection, the former are clearly protected for the reasons set forth in the text. As technology becomes more sophisticated, instructions to other humans will increasingly be executable by computers as well.

[23] *Vartuli* reasoned that the interaction between "programming commands as triggers and semiconductors

as a conduit," even though communication, is not "speech" within the meaning of the First Amendment and that the communication between Recurrence and a customer using it as intended was similarly not "speech." *Vartuli* , 228 F2d at 111.

[24] The reasoning of *Junger* has recently been criticized. *See* Orin S. Kerr, *Are We Over Protecting Code? Thoughts on First-Generation Internet Law*, 57 Wash. & Lee L. Rev. 1287 (2000). Prof. Kerr apprehends that if encryption code is First Amendment speech because it conveys "ideas about cryptography," *Junger*, 209 F3d at 484, all code will be protected "because code will always convey information about itself." *Kerr, supra*, at 1291. That should not suffice, he argues, because handing someone an object, or example, a padlock, is a good way of communicating how that object works, yet a padlock is not speech. *Id*. at 1291-92. However, code does not cease to be speech just because some objects that convey information are not speech. Both code and a padlock can convey information, but only code, because it uses a notational system comprehensible by humans, is communication that qualifies as speech. Prof. Kerr might be right that making the communication of ideas for information the test of whether code is speech provides First Amendment coverage to many, perhaps most, computer programs, but that is a consequence of the information-conveying capacity of the programs, not a reason for denying them First Amendment coverage.

[25] The Supreme Court has used slightly different formulations to express the narrow tailoring requirement of a content-neutral regulation. In *O'Brien*, the formulation was "if the incidental restriction on alleged First Amendment freedoms is no greater than is essential to the furtherance of that interest." 391 US at 377. In *Ward*, the formulation was " 'so long as the . . . regulation promotes a substantial government interest that would be achieved less effectively absent the regulation.' " 491 US at 799 (quoting *United States v. Albertini*, 472 US 675, 689 (1985)). *Ward* added, however, that the regulation may not "burden *substantially more* speech than is necessary to further the government's legitimate interests." *Id*. (emphasis added). *Turner Broadcasting* quoted both the "no greater than is essential" formulation from *O'Brien*, *see Turner Broadcasting*, 512 US at 662, and the "would be achieved less effectively" formulation from *Ward*, *see id*. *Turner Broadcasting* made clear that the narrow tailoring requirement is less demanding than the least restrictive means requirement of a content-specific regulation, *id*., and appears to have settled on the "substantially more" phrasing from *Ward* as the formulation that best expresses the requirement, *id*. That is the formulation we will apply.

[26] This argument is elaborated by some of the *amici curiae*. "In the absence of human intervention, code does not function, it engages in no conduct. It is as passive as

a cake recipe." Brief of *Amici Curiae* Dr. Harold Abelson *et al*. at 26.

[27] More dramatically, the Government calls DeCSS "a digital crowbar." Brief for Intervenor United States at 19.

[28] Briefs of some of the *amici curiae* discuss the possibility of adequate protection against copying of copyrighted materials by adopting the approach of the Audio Home Recording Act of 1992, 17 USC §1002(a), which requires digital audio tape recorders to include a technology that prevents serial copying, but permits making a single copy. *See, e.g.*, Brief of *Amici Curiae* Benkler and Lessig at 15. However, the Defendants did not present evidence of the current feasibility of a similar solution to prevent serial copying of DVDs over the Internet. Even if the Government, in defending the DMCA, must sustain a burden of proof in order to satisfy the standards for content-neutral regulation, the Defendant must adduce enough evidence to create fact issues concerning the current availability of less intrusive technological solutions. They did not do so in the District Court. Moreover, we note that when Congress opted for the solution to serial copying of digital audio tapes, it imposed a special royalty on manufacturers of digital audio recording devices to be distributed to appropriate copyright holders. *See* 17 USC §§1003-1007. We doubt if the First Amendment required Congress to adopt a similar technology/royalty scheme for regulating the copying of DVDs, but in any event the record in this case provides no basis for invalidating the anti-trafficking provisions of the DMCA or the injunction for lack of such an alternative approach.

[29] We have considered the opinion of a California intermediate appellate court in *DVD Copy Control Ass'n v. Bunner*, No. H021153, 2001 WL 1340619 *[9 ILR (P&F) 114]* (Cal Ct App, 6th Dist Nov. 1, 2001), declining, on First Amendment grounds, to issue a preliminary injunction under state trade secrets law prohibiting a web site operator from posting DeCSS. To the extent that *DVD Copy Control* disagrees with our First Amendment analysis, we decline to follow it.

[30] "Hyperlinks" are also called "hypertext links" or "active links."

[31] "Linking" not accomplished by a hyperlink would simply involve the posting of the Internet address ("URL") of another web page. A "link" of this sort is sometimes called an "inactive link." With an inactive link, the linked web page would be only four clicks away, one click to select the URL address for copying, one click to copy the address, one click to "paste" the address into the text box for URL addresses, and one click (or striking the "enter" key) to instruct the computer to call up the linked web site.

[32] We acknowledge that the prohibition on linking restricts more than Corley's ability to facilitate instant access to DeCSS on linked web sites; it also restricts his ability to facilitate access to whatever protected speech is available on those sites. However, those who maintain the linked sites can instantly make their protected material available for linking by Corley by the simple expedient of deleting DeCSS from their web sites.

[33] Although we have recognized that the First Amendment provides no entitlement to use copyrighted materials beyond that accorded by the privilege of fair use, except in "an extraordinary case," *Twin Peaks Productions Inc. v. Publications International Ltd.*, 996 F2d 1366, 1378 (2d Cir 1993), we have not ruled that the constitution guarantees any particular formulation or minimum availability of the fair use defense.

[34] As expressed in their supplemental papers, the position of the Appellants is that "fair use extends to works in whatever form they are offered to the public," Supplemental Brief for Appellants at 20, by which we understand the Appellants to contend not merely that fair use may be made of DVD movies but that the fair user must be permitted access to the digital version of the DVD in order to directly copy excerpts for fair use in a digital format.

[35] In their supplemental papers, the Appellants contend, rather hyperbolically, that a prohibition on using copying machines to assist in making fair use of texts could not validly be upheld by the availability of "monks to scribe the relevant passages." Supplemental Brief for Appellants at 20.

In re Verizon Internet Services, Inc. Subpoena Enforcement Matter

United States District Court, District of Columbia

January 21, 2003

12 ILR (P&F) 640, 2003 ILRWeb (P&F) 1023

Civil Action 02-MS-0323 (JDB)

ISP subject to DMCA subpoena power; must reveal identity of alleged infringer.

An Internet service provider must comply with a subpoena issued under the Digital Millennium Copyright Act (DMCA), requiring it to reveal the identity of a subscriber alleged to have unlawfully traded copyrighted music online. 17 USC §512(h) permits a copyright owner to obtain and serve a subpoena on a "service provider" provided the copyright owner, *inter alia*, complies with the copyright infringement notification requirement found in §512(c), which pertains to copyrighted material *stored* on a service provider's network or system. Because of the reference to subsection (c), the ISP argued that the subpoena power set forth in §512(h) does not apply where, as here, the service provider acts merely as a passive conduit. The court disagrees. Based on the language and structure of the DMCA, the subpoena power in §512(h) applies to all Internet service providers within the scope of the DMCA, not just to those service providers storing information on a system or network at the direction of a user. The textual definition of "service provider" found in §512(k) leaves no doubt that the subpoena power in subsection (h) applies to all service providers, regardless of the functions a service provider may perform under the four categories set out in subsections (a) through (d). The purpose and legislative history of the DMCA support this construction. Furthermore, the ISP's suggestion that John Doe actions are an adequate alternative remedy is not convincing. John Doe actions would be at odds with the design of Congress under the DMCA, which commands "expeditious" issuance of and response to subpoenas under subsection (h). Although the court declines to rule on certain constitutional issues raised by *amici curiae*, those issues nevertheless do not reveal an obviously fatal constitutional flaw in the DMCA subpoena process. — **In re Verizon Internet Services, Inc. Subpoena Enforcement Matter, 12 ILR (P&F) 640 [D DC, 2003].**

MEMORANDUM OPINION

JOHN D. BATES, *District Judge.* The Recording Industry Association of America ("RIAA")[1] has moved *[11 ILR (P&F) 2063]* to enforce a subpoena served on Verizon Internet Services ("Verizon") under the Digital Millennium Copyright Act of 1998 ("DMCA" or "Act"), 17 USC §512. On behalf of copyright owners, RIAA seeks the identity of an anonymous user of Verizon's service who is alleged to have infringed copyrights with respect to more than 600 songs downloaded from the Internet in a single day. The copyright owners (and thus RIAA) can discern the Internet Protocol address, but not the identity, of the alleged infringer—only the service provider can identify the user. Verizon argues *[11 ILR (P&F) 2069]* that the subpoena relates to material transmitted over Verizon's network, not stored on it, and thus falls outside the scope of the subpoena power authorized in the DMCA. RIAA counters that the subpoena power under section 512(h) of the DMCA applies to all Internet service providers, including Verizon, whether the infringing material is stored on or simply transmitted over the service provider's network.

The case thus presents a core issue of statutory interpretation relating to the scope of the subpoena authority under the DMCA. The parties, and several *amici curiae*, agree that this is an issue of first impression of great importance to the application of copyright law to the Internet. Indeed, they concede that this case is presented as a test case on the DMCA subpoena power. Based on the language and structure of the statute, as confirmed by the purpose and history of the legislation, the Court concludes that the subpoena power in 17 USC §512(h) applies to all Internet service providers within the scope of the DMCA, not just to those service providers storing information on a system or network at the direction of a user. Therefore, the Court grants RIAA's motion to enforce, and orders Verizon to comply with the properly issued and supported subpoena from RIAA seeking the identity of the alleged infringer.

BACKGROUND

An assessment of this issue requires some understanding of both the DMCA and the subpoena served by RIAA on Verizon. Although the subpoena power is specifically delineated in section 512(h), that language cannot be isolated from the structure and purpose of the DMCA, and RIAA's subpoena to Verizon must be assessed in that context.

1. The Digital Millennium Copyright Act

The DMCA amended chapter 5 of the Copyright Act, 17 USC §501 *et seq.*, and created a new section 512 entitled "Limitations on liability relating to material online." As the title indicates, the DMCA is designed primarily to limit the liability of Internet service providers for acts of copyright infringement by customers who are using the providers' systems or networks. Section 512 contains limitations on the liability of service providers for four general categories of activity set forth in subsections (a) through (d). The statute thereby creates a series of "safe harbors" that allow service providers to limit their liability for copyright infringement by users if certain conditions under the Act are satisfied. "The limitations in subsections (a) through (d) protect qualifying service providers from liability for all monetary relief for direct, vicarious and contributory [copyright] infringement." S. Rep. No. 105-190, at 20 (1998).

Under the DMCA, an Internet service provider falls within one of these four subsections based on how the allegedly infringing material has interacted with the service provider's system or network. To qualify for a "safe harbor," the service provider must fulfill the conditions under the applicable subsection and the conditions of subsection (*i*), which includes the requirement that a service provider implement and inform its users of its policy to terminate a subscriber's account in cases of repeat copyright

infringement. *See* 17 USC §512(i)(1)(A). Under subsection (a), which Verizon contends is applicable here, if the service provider meets certain conditions it will not be liable for the user's copyright infringement when the service provider **transmits** the copyrighted material over its system or network:

> (a) Transitory digital network communications. A service provider shall not be liable . . . for infringement of copyright by reason of the provider's transmitting, routing, or providing [Internet] connections for, material through a system or network controlled or operated by or for the service provider, or by reason of the intermediate and transient storage of that material in the course of such transmitting, routing, or providing connections . . . .

Id. §512(a). On the other hand, subsection (c), the other subsection most relevant here, pertains to copyrighted material that is **stored** on the service provider's network or system:

> (c) Information residing on systems or networks at direction of users. . . . A service provider shall not be liable . . . for infringement of copyright by reason of the storage at the direction of a user of material that resides on a system or network controlled or operated by or for the service provider . . . .

Id. §512(c)(1).[2] Under subsection (c), a service provider must also designate an agent to receive notifications of claimed infringement from copyright owners. *Id.* §512(c)(2).

Of particular importance here, subsection (c)(3)(A) spells out requirements to be met by copyright owners for effective notification of copyright infringement under subsection (c). The notification of claimed infringement must be in a writing provided to the designated agent, and must include the following—a "signature of a person authorized to act on behalf of the [copyright] owner"; identification of the copyrighted work allegedly infringed (or a list of multiple copyrighted works covered by a single notification); identification of the allegedly infringing material "that is to be removed or access to which is to be disabled," and information to enable the provider to locate the material; information to permit the provider to contact the complaining party; a statement of good faith belief that the use complained of is not authorized; and a "statement that the information in the notification is accurate, and under penalty of perjury, that the complaining party is authorized to act on behalf of the owner." *Id.* §512(c)(3)(A)(i)-(vi). This notification requirement is located within subsection (c), and there is no similar notification requirement within subsection (a) or elsewhere in section 512. The subsection (c)(3) notification requirement is referenced, however, in the conditions under both subsection (b) and subsection (d). *See id.* §§512(b)(2)(E) & (d)(3).

The DMCA also contains a novel provision in subsection (h)—which lies at the heart of the dispute before the Court—permitting a copyright owner to obtain and serve a subpoena on a service provider seeking the identity of a customer alleged to be infringing the owner's copyright. The subpoena is issued by the clerk of any United States District Court upon a request by the copyright owner (or one authorized to act on the owner's behalf) containing the proposed subpoena, "a copy of a notification described in subsection (c)(3)(A)," and a sworn declaration ensuring that the subpoena is solely to obtain the identity of the alleged infringer, which information will be used only to protect rights to the copyright. *Id.* §512(h)(2). The subpoena, in turn, authorizes and orders the recipient service provider "to expeditiously disclose" information sufficient to identify the alleged infringer. *Id.* §512(h)(3). The clerk "shall expeditiously issue" the subpoena if it is in proper form, the declaration is properly executed, and "the notification filed satisfies the provisions of subsection (c)(3)(A)." *Id.* §512(h)(4). The service provider, upon receipt of the subpoena, "shall expeditiously disclose" the information required by the subpoena to the copyright owner (or authorized person). *Id.* §512(h)(5). The issuance, delivery and enforcement of subpoenas is to be governed (to the extent practicable) by the provisions of the Federal Rules of Civil Procedure dealing with subpoenas duces tecum. *Id.* §512(h)(6).

2. RIAA's Subpoena to Verizon

On July 24, 2002, RIAA served a subpoena on Verizon seeking identifying information about an anonymous copyright infringer allegedly using Verizon's network to download copyrighted songs through peer-to-peer software provided by KaZaA,

without the copyright holders' authorization. *See* Motion to Enforce, Ex. A. Along with the subpoena, RIAA provided Verizon with a list of more than 600 files (predominantly individual songs, most by well-known artists) allegedly downloaded by the user on one day. *Id.*, Ex. B. The subpoena included the user's specified Internet Protocol (IP) address, to enable Verizon to locate the computer where the infringement occurred. In addition to the IP address, RIAA provided the time and date when the songs were downloaded and furnished a declaration, under penalty of perjury, that the information was sought in good faith and would only be used in connection with "protecting the rights" of RIAA members. *Id.*, Ex. B (letter from Whitehead to Crowder dated July 24, 2002). RIAA also requested that Verizon "remove or disable access to the infringing sound files." *Id.*

Verizon responded by letter refusing to comply with RIAA's subpoena. *Id.*, Ex. D (letter from Daily to Whitehead dated Aug. 6, 2002). Verizon emphasized its view that the DMCA subpoena power applies only if the infringed material is stored or controlled on the service provider's system or network under subsection (c). *Id.* at pp. 2-3. Verizon stated: "The allegedly infringing contents of the [downloaded files] do not reside on any system or network controlled or operated by or for [Verizon], but . . . are stored on the hardware of the Customer. Thus, neither §512(c)(3)(A) nor §512(h) is applicable for this reason alone." *Id.* According to Verizon, a subpoena under the DMCA is "conditioned" on notification under section 512(c)(3)(A), "and that provision is addressed to 'material that resides on a system or network *controlled or operated by or for [a] service provider.*' " *Id.* (emphasis in original). In contrast, Verizon stressed, it only provided the customer with Internet connectivity service. *Id.* Verizon also refused RIAA's request to terminate the user's Internet connection. *Id.* at 3. Verizon's position, therefore, is that because it only provided the alleged infringer with an Internet connection, it falls under subsection (a) of section 512, not under subsection (c), and it is thus outside the subpoena authority of subsection (h), which Verizon contends is limited to service providers storing material under subsection (c).

RIAA, on the other hand, is of the view that the DMCA subpoena power under section 512(h) applies to all service providers within the provisions of subsections (a) through (d), including Verizon in the instant case. [3] Given Verizon's refusal to comply with the subpoena, RIAA moved pursuant to 17 USC §512(h)(6) and Fed. R. Civ. P. 45(c)(2)(B) to enforce the subpoena. Substantial briefing (including submissions by *amici curiae* on both sides *[11 ILR (P&F) 2081, 11 ILR (P&F) 2091]*) and a hearing followed.

ANALYSIS

This case turns on the meaning and scope of the provisions of the DMCA. "As in all statutory construction cases, we begin with the language of the statute." *Barnhart v. Sigmon Coal Co.*, 534 US 438, 450 (2002); *see also United States v. Braxtonbrown-Smith*, 278 F3d 1348, 1352 (DC Cir 2002). The first step "is to determine whether the language at issue has a plain and unambiguous meaning with regard to the particular dispute in the case." *Robinson v. Shell Oil Co.*, 519 US 337, 340 (1997) (citing *United States v. Ron Pair Enters., Inc.*, 489 US 235, 240 (1989)). If so, and if the statutory scheme is "coherent and consistent," then the inquiry ceases. *Barnhart*, 534 US at 450 (quoting *Robinson*, 519 US at 340). Nonetheless, "[s]tatutory construction 'is a holistic endeavor,' and, at a minimum, must account for a statute's full text, language as well as punctuation, structure, and subject matter." *Connecticut Nat'l Bank v. Germain*, 503 US 249, 254 (1992) (quoting *United Savings Ass'n of Texas v. Timbers of Inwood Forest Assocs., Ltd.*, 484 US 365, 371 (1988)). Hence, "courts should disfavor interpretations of statutes that render language superfluous." *Connecticut Nat'l Bank*, 503 US at 253. But as the Supreme Court has explained:

> [C]anons of construction are no more than rules of thumb that help courts determine the meaning of legislation, and in interpreting a statute a court should always turn first to one, cardinal canon before all others. We have stated time and again that courts must presume that a legislature says in a statute what it means and means in a statute what it says there.

Id. at 254; *accord Ron Pair Enters., Inc.*, 489 US at 241-42; *United States v. Goldenberg*, 168 US 95, 102-103 (1897). "When the words of a statute are unambiguous, then, this first canon is also the last: 'judicial inquiry is complete.'" *Connecticut Nat'l*

Bank, 503 US at 254 (quoting *Rubin v. United States*, 449 US 424, 430 (1981)); *see also Ratzlaf v. United States*, 510 US 135, 147-48 (1994) ("There are, we recognize, contrary indications in the statute's legislative history. But we do not resort to legislative history to cloud a statutory text that is clear."); *Barnhill v. Johnson*, 503 US 393, 401 (1992).

Here, the statutory language and structure lead to a single result—the section 512(h) subpoena authority applies to service providers within not only subsection (c) but also subsections (a), (b), and (d) of section 512. Moreover, the purpose and history of the DMCA are consistent with that conclusion.

1. Statutory Definition of "Service Provider"

The statutory text of the DMCA provides clear guidance for construing the subpoena authority of subsection (h) to apply to all service providers under the Act. The term "service provider" is employed repeatedly in subsection (h). The request to the clerk is "to issue a subpoena to a service provider for identification of an alleged infringer" (§512(h)(1)); the subpoena "shall authorize and order the service provider receiving the notification and the subpoena" to disclose the identifying information to the extent it is available to the service provider (§512(h)(3)); a proper subpoena shall be executed by the clerk, who shall return it to the requester "for delivery to the service provider" (§512(h)(4)); and upon receipt "the service provider shall expeditiously disclose" the information required by the subpoena "regardless of whether the service provider responds to the notification" (§512(h)(5)).

The question, then, is whether the "service provider" repeatedly referenced in subsection (h) is limited to one described by subsection (c) or instead includes those described in subsections (a), (b) and (d) of section 512 as well. The DMCA answers that question unequivocally.

The Act provides two distinct definitions of "service provider"—a narrow definition as the term is used solely within subsection (a), and a broader definition governing all other subsections, which specifically includes a "service provider" under subsection (a) as well:

> (k) Definitions.—
>
> > (1) Service provider.—
> >
> > > (A) As used in subsection (a), the term "service provider" means an entity

offering the transmission, routing, or providing of connections for digital online communications, between or among points specified by a user, of material of the user's choosing, without modification to the content of the material as sent or received.

(B) As used in this section, other than subsection (a), the term "service provider" means a provider of online services or network access, or the operator of facilities therefor, and includes an entity described in subparagraph (A).

17 USC §512(k); *see also ALS Scan, Inc. v. RemarQ Communities, Inc.*, 239 F3d 619, 623 *[7 ILR (P&F) 69]* (4th Cir 2001) (the DMCA "defines a service provider broadly").

The textual definition of "service provider" in subsection (k) leaves no doubt, therefore, that the subpoena power in subsection (h) applies to all service providers, regardless of the functions a service provider may perform under the four categories set out in subsections (a) through (d). The broad definition in subsection (k)(1)(B)—"a provider of online services or network access"—expressly applies to the term "service provider" as used in subsection (h), since the narrow definition found in subsection (k)(1)(A) is applicable only to the term as used in subsection (a). By the plain text of the statute, moreover, the term "service provider" as employed in subsection (h) encompasses those entities defined in subsection (k)(1)(A), which explicitly includes "service providers" under subsection (a) such as Verizon (an "entity offering the transmission, routing, or providing of connections for digital online communications"). In short, Verizon contends that it has only provided an Internet connection, and thus is within subsection (a) of the DMCA; but the definition of "service provider" in subsection (k) applicable to the subpoena authority under subsection (h) squarely includes subsection (a) entities such as Verizon that are "providing . . . connections for digital online communications." Given the broad definition of "service provider" in subsection (k)(1)(B), and the use of that defined term throughout subsection (h), the Court must, under well-established statutory construction tools, read these provisions together, as a whole. *See United States v. Wilson*, 290 F3d

347, 355 (DC Cir 2002) ("It is the 'classic judicial task' of construing related statutory provisions 'to make sense in combination.'") (quoting *United States v. Fausto*, 484 US 439, 453 (1988)). Applying the statutory definition of "service provider" leaves no doubt whatsoever, then, that the DMCA subpoena authority reaches a subsection (a) service provider such as Verizon contends it is here.[4]

Verizon's response is to downplay the subsection (k) definition, dismissing it as "beside the point." But the language is clear, and the Court cannot overlook the governing definition of service provider in subsection (k)(1)(B), which plainly sets the scope of the subsection (h) subpoena power. Rather, the Court must take into account all relevant parts of the statute. *See United States Telecom Ass'n v. FCC*, 227 F3d 450, 463 *[6 ILR (P&F) 79]* (DC Cir 2000) (noting "the well-accepted principle of statutory construction that requires every provision of a statute to be given effect"); *Qi-Zhuo v. Meissner*, 70 F3d 136, 139 (DC Cir 1995) (courts have "endlessly reiterated [the] principle of statutory construction . . . that all words in a statute are to be assigned meaning, and that nothing therein is to be construed as surplusage"). "If a statute defines a term in its definitional section, then that definition controls the meaning of the term wherever it appears in the statute." *Lilly v. Internal Revenue Service*, 76 F3d 568, 571 (4th Cir 1996); *see also Colautti v. Franklin*, 439 US 379, 392 n. 10 (1979) ("[A] definition which declares what a term 'means' . . . excludes any meaning that is not stated."); *Florida Dep't of Banking & Fin. v. Board of Governors of Fed. Reserve Sys.*, 800 F2d 1534, 1536 (11th Cir 1986) ("It is an elementary precept of statutory construction that the definition of a term in the definitional section of a statute controls the construction of that term wherever it appears throughout the statute."). It would simply make no sense here to dismiss the statutory definition of "service provider" as irrelevant.

As Verizon explained in its letter to RIAA refusing to comply with the subpoena, "the only service [Verizon] provides to the Customer is Internet connectivity." Motion to Enforce, Ex. D, at p. 2 (letter from Dailey to Whitehead dated Aug. 6, 2002). But the broad definition of "service provider" under subsection (k)(1)(B) that is expressly applicable to subsection (h), together with the fact that Verizon indisputably provided network access to the alleged infringer, lead ineluctably to the conclusion that the subpoena authority of the DMCA applies to all service providers within the scope of the Act, including those like Verizon falling under subsection (a).

2. The Statutory Structure

Verizon's assertions to the contrary are refuted by the structure and language of the DMCA. An essential condition for a valid subpoena under subsection 512(h), Verizon claims, "is a notification to the service provider that complies with subsection (c)(3)(A)." Verizon Opp. at pp. 2-3. Therefore, Verizon argues, it is implicit that a subpoena may only be issued to service providers described in subsection (c)—in other words, "to [those] service providers who have stored offending material on their own system or network." Id. at p. 3. Verizon notes that, in contrast, "subsection (a)—the provision of section 512 for service providers acting simply as passive transmitters, as Verizon was here—contains no provision for any notification of claimed infringers, much less notification that 'satisfies the requirements of (c)(3)(A).' " Id. Thus, Verizon reasons, RIAA's subpoena to it is invalid because Verizon is not storing the infringing material on its system or network, but is simply providing "Internet connectivity" or acting as a "passive conduit" under subsection (a), and hence need not comply with the notification requirement in subsection (c)(3)(A).

The Court disagrees with Verizon's strained reading of the Act, which disregards entirely the clear definitional language of subsection (k). The holistic character of statutory construction requires an examination of all relevant text, and of language as well as structure. See Connecticut Nat'l Bank, 503 US at 254. Not only the language but also the structure of the DMCA dispenses with the contentions advanced by Verizon.

Verizon contends that the Court should infer that the subpoena authority under subsection (h) only applies to subsection (c) in light of the reference in subsection (h)(2)(A) to the notification requirement of subsection (c)(3)(A). But that reference does not mean that subsection (h) only applies to service providers described in subsection (c). In fact, the notification provision in subsection (c) is also referenced elsewhere in the DMCA, including in subsections (b)(2)(E) and (d)(3). The latter

references confirm the expectation that notifications like that described in subsection (c)(3) will at times be needed in settings under subsections (b) and (d), and hence are not confined to subsection (c) settings. Subsection (h), moreover, is written without limitation or restriction as to its application. It is entitled "Subpoena to identify infringer"—not "Subpoena to identify infringer storing copyrighted material on a service provider's network" or "Subpoena to identify infringer relating to subsection (c)." If Congress intended to restrict or limit the subsection (h) subpoena authority based on where the infringing material resides, one would expect to see that limitation spelled out in subsection (h). And if Congress intended to limit subsection (h) subpoenas strictly to service providers under subsection (c), it certainly could have made such a limitation explicit.

There is simply nothing in the text of the statute that states, or even suggests, that the subpoena authority in subsection (h) applies only to those service providers described in subsection (c). Indeed, subsection (h) does not require, as Verizon contends, a copyright owner to comply fully with subsection (c)(3)(A). The references in subsection (h) to "a notification described in" (see §§512(h)(2)(A) & (h)(5)) or that "satisfies the provisions of" (see §512(h)(4)) subsection (c)(3)(A) do not by their language limit the subpoena authority. Rather, these references are consistent with the construction that when a subpoena under subsection (h) is sought against a service provider falling within subsections (a), (b) or (d), the copyright owner or authorized person must then provide a notification like the one always required under subsection (c) but not otherwise required under (a), (b) or (d). Thus, as part of the process to obtain a subpoena, subsection (h)(2)(A) simply requires a copyright owner to file with the clerk the type of "notification described in subsection (c)(3)(A)."

Significantly, then, if Congress had intended subsection (h) subpoenas to apply solely to subsection (c) service providers, it could have stated such a limitation in subsection (h), or stated that subsection (h) does not apply to subsections (a), (b) or (d), or even have placed the subpoena authority itself within subsection (c). But Congress did not do so. Instead, the subpoena authority in the DMCA is contained in a stand-alone subsection, just as separate from subsection (c) as it is from subsections (a), (b), and (d).[5] It is a "fundamental canon of statutory construction that the words of a statute must be read in their context and with a view to their place in the overall statutory scheme." *FDA v. Brown & Williamson Tobacco Corp.*, 529 US 120, 133 (2000).

Verizon's proposed construction does not comport with other aspects of the Act either. A court must consider "the particular statutory language at issue, as well as the language and design of the statute as a whole." *KMart v. Cartier, Inc.*, 486 US 281, 291 (1988). There is no discernable reason why Congress would limit the subpoena authority under subsection (h) to subsection (c) service providers alone. To begin with, the burden on a service provider in identifying an apparent infringer is no different depending on which subsection of 512 is implicated.[6] Indeed, considering the four-part structure of the liability limitations under the DMCA, subsections (a) through (d) together with the subpoena authority under subsection (h) only "make sense in combination" if construed so that the subpoena authority extends to service providers in all four categories. *See Fausto*, 484 US at 453; *Wilson*, 290 F3d at 355. Otherwise, the statute would fail significantly to address many contexts in which a copyright owner needs to utilize the subpoena process in order to discern the identity of an apparent copyright infringer. And although Verizon has attempted to justify an exclusion of just subsection (a) service providers from the reach of the subpoena authority, the position advanced by Verizon logically supports confining the subpoena authority to subsection (c) service providers alone, whereas the statutory language and structure certainly provide no basis for differentiating service providers within subsection (a) from those within subsections (b) and (d) as to the scope of the subpoena power. Moreover, whatever rationale warrants distinguishing among subsections (a) through (d) for purposes of the safe harbor liability protections, there is no corresponding rationale for such distinctions regarding a subpoena power that entails merely identifying infringers.

Importantly, Verizon's construction does not square with Congress's express and repeated direction to make the subpoena process "expeditious." *See, e.g.*, 17 USC §§512(h)(3), (h)(4) & (h)(5) (subpoena shall require service provider to expeditiously disclose identity of infringer; clerk

shall expeditiously issue subpoena; and service provider shall expeditiously disclose identity of infringer upon receipt of subpoena). The statute contemplates a rapid subpoena process designed quickly to identify apparent infringers and then curtail the infringement. The copyright holder, however, cannot readily determine whether its infringed material was stored on or merely transmitted across the service provider's system, and hence whether it faces a subsection (c) or subsection (a) situation. As a result, if the copyright owner could only utilize the subpoena process for subsection (c) service providers, it would have to establish at the outset that the service provider fell within subsection (c) in the particular case at hand. Hence, in many instances an initial contested factual issue would ensue in court with respect to where the material is stored, resulting in potentially lengthy delays in obtaining identifying information about the infringer. Such complication and delay hardly comports with the language peppered throughout subsection (h) indicating that the subpoena process should be "expeditious." In fact, there is an important reason why Congress required service providers to act promptly upon receipt of a subpoena to prevent further infringement—"the ease with which digital works can be copied and distributed worldwide virtually instantaneously." S. Rep. No. 105-190, at 8.[7]

Verizon's construction thus makes little sense from a policy standpoint. Verizon has provided no sound reason why Congress would enable a copyright owner to obtain identifying information from a service provider storing the infringing material on its system, but would not enable a copyright owner to obtain identifying information from a service provider transmitting the material over its system (or, indeed, from a service provider engaged in system caching under subsection (b) or providing information location tools under subsection (d)). After all, the information obtained simply permits the copyright owner to take steps directly with the infringer to prevent further infringement. It is unlikely, the Court concludes, that Congress would seek to protect copyright owners in only some of the settings addressed in the DMCA, but not in others.

In short, Verizon's position that the subpoena power in subsection (h) only applies to subsection (c) service providers, and not to subsection (a) (or for that matter to subsections (b) and (d)) service providers, would create a huge loophole in Congress's effort to prevent copyright infringement on the Internet. There is little doubt that the largest opportunity for copyright theft is through peer-to-peer ("P2P") software, as used by the alleged infringer here. One *amici* characterizes such P2P software as "the biggest revolution to happen on the Internet since the advent of email or the World Wide Web—millions of individuals use P2P now, and the number is growing exponentially." Br. of *Amicus Curiae* U.S. Internet Service Provider Assoc. at p. 6. Even Verizon states that "more than 100 million copies of [KaZaA's] peer-to-peer file sharing software have been download-ed, and more than two million of its users are commonly online at any given time." Verizon Opp. at p. 8. Because peer-to-peer users most often swap materials over the Internet that are stored on their own computers—not on the service providers' networks—such activity is within subsection (a), not subsection (c). Thus, under Verizon's reading of the Act, a significant amount of potential copyright infringement would be shielded from the subpoena authority of the DMCA.[8] That would, in effect, give Internet copyright infringers shelter from the long arm of the DMCA subpoena power, and allow infringement to flourish. The Court can find nothing in the language or structure of the statute that suggests Congress intended the DMCA to protect only a very limited portion of copyrighted material on the Internet.

3. The Purpose and History of the DMCA

"The traditional tools [of statutory construction] include examination of the statute's text, legislative history, and structure, as well as its purpose." *Natural Resources Defense Council, Inc., v. Daley*, 209 F3d 747, 752 (DC Cir 2000). Here, the text and structure of the DMCA are clear, as explained above, and "we do not resort to legislative history to cloud a statutory text that is clear." *Ratzlaf v. United States*, 510 US at 147-48. Nonetheless, common sense suggests that an assessment of the subpoena authority under the DMCA may benefit from an understanding of the purpose and history of the legislation. *See Wisconsin Public Intervenor v. Mortier*, 501 US 597, 611 n. 4 (1991).

Congress not only sought to limit the liability of service providers under the DMCA, but also intended to assist copyright owners in protecting their copyrights. The legislative history makes clear that in enacting the DMCA, Congress attempted to balance the liability protections for service providers with the need for broad protection of copyrights on the Internet.[9] The clear purpose of the DMCA, evident in its legislative history, confirms that the scope of the subsection (h) subpoena power extends to service providers within subsection (a) as well as subsection (c).

The dual purpose and balance of the DMCA has been recognized by the courts. The Fourth Circuit has explained that "[t]he DMCA was enacted both to preserve copyright enforcement on the Internet and to provide immunity to service providers from copyright infringement liability for 'passive,' 'automatic' actions in which a service provider's system engages through a technological process initiated by another without the knowledge of the service provider." *ALS Scan, Inc. v. RemarQ Communities, Inc.*, 239 F3d 619, 625 *[7 ILR (P&F) 69]* (4th Cir 2001). Other courts note this balancing as well. "Congress was concerned with promoting electronic commerce while protecting the rights of copyright owners, particularly in the digital age where near exact copies of protected works can be made at virtually no cost and distributed instantaneously on a worldwide basis." *United States v. Elcom Ltd.*, 203 F Supp 2d 1111, 1124 *[10 ILR (P&F) 611]* (ND Cal 2002) (citing S. Rep. No. 105-190, at 8). In short, Congress sought "to protect against unlawful piracy and promote the development of electronic commerce and the availability of copyrighted material on the Internet." *Id.* at 1125.

Congress thus created tradeoffs within the DMCA: service providers would receive liability protections in exchange for assisting copyright owners in identifying and dealing with infringers who misuse the service providers' systems. At the same time, copyright owners would forgo pursuing service providers for the copyright infringement of their users, in exchange for assistance in identifying and acting against those infringers.

> Title II [of the DMCA] preserves strong incentives for service providers and copyright owners to cooperate to detect and deal with copyright infringements that take place in the digital networked environment. At the same time, it provides greater certainty to service providers concerning their legal

exposure for infringements that may occur in the course of their activities.

S. Rep. No. 105-190, at 20. "[T]he Committee believes it has appropriately balanced the interests of content owners, on-line and other service providers, and information users in a way that will foster the continued development of electronic commerce and the growth of the Internet." H.R. Rep. No. 105-551 (II), at 21; *see also* H.R. Rep. No. 105-551(I), at 11 (noting that remedies "ensur[e] that it is possible for copyright owners to secure the cooperation of those with the capacity to prevent ongoing infringement").[10] In striking this balance, Congress was driven by the observation that unless copyright owners have the ability to protect their copyrights on the Internet, they will be less likely to make their works available online:

> Due to the ease with which digital works can be copied and distributed worldwide virtually instantaneously, copyright owners will hesitate to make their works readily available on the Internet without reasonable assurance that they will be protected against massive piracy. . . . [This legislation] will facilitate making available quickly and conveniently via the Internet the movies, music, software, and literary works that are the fruit of the American creative genius.

S. Rep. No. 105-190, at 8.

Congress also recognized that the Internet created unprecedented opportunities for copyright infringement, and sought to provide assistance to copyright owners in light of the technological developments surrounding the Internet:

> Copyright laws have struggled through the years to keep pace with emerging technology from the struggle over music played on a player piano roll in the 1900's to the introduction of the VCR in the 1980's. With this constant evolution in technology, the law must adapt in order to make digital networks safe places to disseminate and exploit copyrighted materials. . . . Title II [of the DMCA] clarifies the liability faced by service providers who transmit potentially infringing material over their networks. In short, Title II ensures that the efficiency of the Internet will continue to improve and that

the variety and quality of services on the Internet will expand.

S. Rep. No. 105-190, at 1-2. As Senator Leahy explained, "[t]he DMCA is a product of the Senate Judiciary Committee's recognition that ours is a time of unprecedented challenge to copyright protection. . . . This bill is a well-balanced package of proposals that address the needs of creators, consumers and commerce in the digital age and well into the next century." *Id.* at 68.

Congress was concerned about the ability of copyright owners to protect their creative investments in light of rapid technological innovations on the Internet that make copyright theft easy, virtually instantaneous, and undetectable. Therefore, in exchange for the liability protections afforded to service providers in subsections (a) through (d) of the DMCA, Congress sought through subsection (h) to require service providers to assist copyright owners in identifying infringers using the service providers' systems. If, as Verizon contends, service providers only have such obligations when the infringing material is stored on their systems, then service providers falling within subsection (a)—a large portion of those addressed by the DMCA—would receive the liability protections of the Act without the corresponding obligation to assist copyright owners in identifying infringers. There is no logical connection between the line Verizon seeks to draw and the objectives Congress sought to achieve through the DMCA. Verizon's reading would thus undermine the balance Congress established in the DMCA, and does not comport with the Act's purpose and history.[11] It is not for this Court to second-guess the compromises, negotiations, or even brokered deals that produced the DMCA; rather, the Court's role is to interpret the statute as enacted by Congress, and the clear language and structure of the DMCA must therefore control. *See Barnhart*, 534 US at 460-61.

Complicating this assessment somewhat is the fact that two new technology developments underlying the issues in this case—peer-to-peer (P2P) software and "bots," a software tool used by copyright owners to monitor the Internet and detect unauthorized distribution of copyrighted material— were "not even a glimmer in anyone's eye when the DMCA was enacted" by Congress in 1998.[12] RIAA contends that P2P software makes Internet copyright piracy easy and immediate, while Verizon counters that "bots" will inundate service providers with thousands of computer-generated subpoenas seeking to identify infringers. Whether or not Congress was able to anticipate these technologies in enacting the DMCA, however, the courts cannot read new provisions or exceptions into a statute in order to accommodate future technological developments. Particularly in the field of copyright, federal courts must defer to Congress' expertise and constitutional authority.

The Constitution assigns to Congress the authority to "promote the Progress of Science and useful Arts, by securing for limited Times to Authors and Inventors the exclusive Right to their respective Writings and Discoveries." U.S. Const., art. I, §8, cl. 8. The Supreme Court has long deferred to Congress on the scope and nuances of copyright law, especially regarding new technologies:

> Sound policy, as well as history, supports our consistent deference to Congress when major technological innovations alter the market for copyrighted materials. Congress has the constitutional authority and the institutional ability to accommodate fully the varied permutations of competing interests that are inevitably complicated by such new technology.

Sony Corp. v. Universal City Studios, Inc., 464 US 417, 431 (1984); *see also Teleprompter Corp. v. CBS, Inc.*, 415 US 394, 414 (1974) ("Detailed regulation of these relationships, and any ultimate resolution of the many sensitive and important problems in [the copyright] field, must be left to Congress."); *Fortnightly Corp. v. United States Television, Inc.*, 392 US 390, 401 (1968) (Court refused "to render a compromise decision . . . [to] accommodate various competing considerations of copyright, communications, and antitrust policy. We decline that invitation. That job is for Congress."). As recently as last week, the Supreme Court reiterated that "we defer substantially to Congress" on copyright law, that "we are not at liberty to second-guess congressional determinations and policy judgments" regarding copyright issues, and that "it is generally for Congress, not the courts, to decide how best to pursue the Copyright Clause's objectives." *Eldred v. Ashcroft*, No. 01-618, slip op. at 14, 17, 22 *[2003 ILRWeb (P&F) 1013]* (S Ct Jan 15, 2003) (citing *Sony Corp.*, 464 US at 429, and *Stewart v. Abend*, 495 US 207, 230 (1990)).

Notwithstanding these technological advancements, then, this Court will not attempt to re-balance the competing interests among service providers and copyright holders to address P2P software or "bots" that can roam the Internet detecting infringing material. As the Supreme Court stated in *Fortnightly*, "[t]hat job is for Congress." 392 US at 401. To date, Congress has spoken through the text, structure and purpose of the DMCA, under which, the Court concludes, RIAA's subpoena to Verizon meets the requirements spelled out in subsection (h) and therefore is valid. [13]

4. "John Doe" Actions As an Alternative

Verizon maintains that under its construction of the DMCA, with the subsection (h) subpoena power limited to service providers under subsection (c), owners would still have an adequate means to protect their copyrights. Verizon suggests that as an alternative RIAA may bring a "John Doe" action in federal court to obtain information identifying copyright infringers who, under subsection (a) of the DMCA, transmit infringing material over a service provider's network. As Verizon sees it, the copyright owner would file a complaint against John Doe, the unnamed infringer, and a third-party subpoena would then be issued and served on the service provider pursuant to Fed. R. Civ. P. 45. The service provider would then inform John Doe (its customer) of the lawsuit. Under this process, Verizon asserts, there would be protections, both procedural and substantive, for the user's rights, and service providers would have the opportunity to seek to quash the subpoena.

The short answer to Verizon's suggestion is that there is absolutely nothing in the DMCA or its history to indicate that Congress contemplated copyright owners utilizing John Doe actions in federal court to obtain the identity of apparent infringers, rather than employing the subsection (h) process specifically designed by Congress to address that need. Moreover, as Verizon concedes, the burden on service providers is certainly no greater with a DMCA subpoena than with a Rule 45 third-party subpoena.

The additional burden on copyright owners, however, would be considerable, given the effort and expense associated with pursuing such John Doe suits in court. Congress has noted the vast extent of copyright piracy over the Internet, and growing numbers of suits involving disputes over the sufficiency of allegations of infringement and other issues would, in turn, likely undermine the determination of copyright owners to prosecute such actions. Importantly, the time and delay associated with filing complaints and pursuing third-party subpoenas in court would undermine the ability of copyright owners to act quickly to prevent further infringement of their copyrights. That is at odds with the design of Congress through the DMCA, which commands "expeditious" issuance of and response to subpoenas under subsection (h). Moreover, Verizon overlooks altogether the burden on the federal courts from large numbers of such actions. Federal courts have exclusive jurisdiction over copyright actions, and considering the extent of Internet copyright piracy could become inundated with John Doe actions seeking the identity of copyright infringers. *See NBC, Inc. v. Copyright Royalty Tribunal*, 848 F2d 1289, 1295 (DC Cir 1988) ("the federal courts . . . have exclusive jurisdiction over actions 'arising under' the Copyright Act, such as infringement actions"). Undoubtedly, the John Doe actions contemplated by Verizon would be more complex (involving three-party litigation) and time consuming than occasional enforcement actions for DMCA subpoenas.

Not only are John Doe actions more burdensome and less timely, but in several important ways they are less protective of the rights of service providers and Internet users than is the section 512(h) process. The DMCA mandates that a copyright holder fulfill several requirements under subsection (h) before the holder can obtain information from the service provider identifying the infringer. These protections ensure that a service provider will not be forced to disclose its customer's identifying information without a reasonable showing that there has been copyright infringement. Thus, to obtain a subsection (h) subpoena a copyright owner must have a "good faith belief that the use of the material in the manner complained of is not authorized by the copyright owner, its agent, or the law," §512(c)(3)(A)(v), and must provide a "statement that the information in the notification is accurate, and under penalty of perjury, that the complaining party is authorized to act on behalf of the owner of an exclusive right that is allegedly infringed," §512(c)(3)(A)(vi). Moreover, Congress required a copyright owner to submit

a sworn declaration to the effect that the purpose for which the subpoena is sought is to obtain the identity of an alleged infringer and that such information will only be used for the purpose of protecting rights under this title.

17 USC §512(h)(2)(c). These requirements provide substantial protection to service providers and their customers against overly aggressive copyright owners and unwarranted subpoenas. Indeed, they provide greater threshold protection against issuance of an unsupported subpoena than is available in the context of a John Doe action. And, of course, nothing in the DMCA precludes a service provider from raising non-compliance or other objections to a subsection (h) subpoena. *See, e.g., ALS Scan, Inc. v. RemarQ Communities, Inc.*, 239 F3d 619 *[7 ILR (P&F) 69]* (4th Cir 2001) (action addressing service provider's resistance to subpoena for non-compliance with the DMCA). [14]

Given these various protections incorporated into the DMCA subpoena process, [15] the Court concludes that Verizon's suggestion that John Doe actions are an adequate alternative remedy is not convincing. There is nothing in the DMCA to indicate that Congress intended that result. Such actions would be unworkable, far too slow, and uneconomical for copyright holders, and much too burdensome for the federal courts. Congress did not, in the Court's view, contemplate some service providers subject to the DMCA facing expeditious subsection (h) subpoenas, while others would only have to provide information identifying infringers through the slower, more cumbersome process of a John Doe action. Indeed, Verizon's suggestion would mean subpoenas under subsection (h)—if limited to subsection (c) service providers—would be delayed by complex factual issues involving whether a subsection (c) setting was actually presented, while subpoenas to all other service providers would be pursuant to even more burdensome, and slower, John Doe actions. Such a cumbersome, dual structure is flatly inconsistent with the "expeditious" subsection (h) subpoena process, and would run a serious risk of dissuading copyright owners from seeking the identity of apparent infringers and protecting their copyrights. [16] That result would be contrary to Congressional intent as evidenced in the text, structure and history of the DMCA.

5. The DMCA and the Constitution

A number of possible constitutional challenges to the subsection (h) subpoena power have been identified by *amici curiae*. Verizon, however, does not assert that the subpoena power in subsection (h), as applied to service providers (like Verizon) under subsection (a), is unconstitutional; instead, Verizon merely states that it "raises substantial questions." [17] RIAA accordingly has not fully briefed the various constitutional issues raised by the *amici curiae* supporting Verizon. Hence, the Court is without the benefit of full development of these issues by the parties.

Unless raised by the parties, a court normally should not entertain statutory or constitutional challenges asserted solely by *amici*. *See, e.g., A.D. Bedell Wholesale Co. v. Phillip Morris, Inc.*, 263 F3d 239, 266 (3rd Cir 2001) ("Although the Cato Institute, *amicus curiae* for plaintiffs, argues constitutional claims, new issues raised by an *amicus* are not properly before the court in the absence of exceptional circumstances.") (quoting *General Eng'g Corp. v. Virgin Islands Water and Power Auth.*, 805 F2d 88, 92 (3rd Cir 1986)). Indeed, in construing the DMCA, the Second Circuit refused to consider a constitutional challenge briefly addressed by the defendant in a footnote, although fully examined by an *amicus*. *See Universal City Studios, Inc. v. Corley*, 273 F3d 429 *[9 ILR (P&F) 330]* (2d Cir 2001). Without a "properly developed record," the court found that the defendant effectively waived the constitutional challenge: "Although an *amicus* brief can be helpful in elaborating issues properly presented by the parties, it is normally not a method for injecting new issues . . . , at least in cases where the parties are competently represented by counsel." *Id.* at 445. Here, because Verizon is not raising any explicit constitutional challenge to the DMCA, the Court is wary of considering such issues. [18]

Even if the Court were to consider a constitutional challenge here, it must be noted that any constitutional problems faced by service providers or their customers would exist under Verizon's construction of the DMCA as well. The Court's authority and users' anonymity are equally at issue with subsection (c) as with subsection (a), and the First Amendment interest—the identity of the user—is identical no matter which subsection is invoked.

It is also clear that the First Amendment does not protect copyright infringement. *See Harper & Row, Publs., Inc. v. Nation Enters.*, 471 US 539, 555-60 (1985); *Zacchini v. Scripps-Howard*, 433 US 562, 574-78 (1977). Moreover, the Supreme Court recently confirmed in *Eldred v. Ashcroft* that the proximity of the Copyright Clause and the First Amendment demonstrates "the Framers' view [that] copyright's limited monopolies are compatible with free speech principles," and that copyright serves to promote First Amendment ideals as " 'the engine of free expression.' " Slip op. at 28-29 (quoting *Harper & Row*, 471 US at 558). The Court noted "built-in First Amendment accommodations" in copyright law, including the distinction between ideas and expression and the "fair use" doctrine, which it found "are generally adequate to address" First Amendment concerns relating to asserted rights to use the speech of others. *Id.* at 29, 31; *see Nihon Keizai Shimbun, Inc. v. Comline Bus. Data, Inc.*, 166 F3d 65, 74 (2d Cir 1999) ("We have repeatedly rejected First Amendment challenges to injunctions from copyright infringement on the ground that First Amendment concerns are protected by and coextensive with the fair use doctrine."). Here, of course, the various protections incorporated into subsection (h), and discussed supra, further guard against First Amendment concerns.

Nor is this an instance where the anonymity of an Internet user merits free speech and privacy protections. Certainly, the Supreme Court has recognized that, in some situations, the First Amendment protects a speaker's anonymity. *See, e.g., Watchtower Bible & Tract Society of New York, Inc. v. Village of Stratton*, 122 S Ct 2080, 2090 (2002) (municipal ordinance requiring pamphleteers to disclose names implicates "anonymity interests" rooted in the First Amendment); *Buckley v. Am. Constitutional Law Foun., Inc.*, 525 US 182 (1999) (state requirement forcing petitioners to wear identification badge violated First Amendment because it infringed on petitioners' anonymity); *McIntyre v. Ohio Elections Comm.*, 514 US 334 (1995) (the right to speak anonymously "exemplifies the purpose behind the Bill of Rights, and the First Amendment in particular"). Lower federal courts have specifically recognized that the First Amendment may protect an individual's anonymity on the Internet. *See, e.g., Doe v. 2TheMart.com, Inc.*, 140 F Supp 2d at 1097 ("the constitutional rights of Internet users, including the right to speak anonymously, must be carefully safeguarded"); *ACLU v. Johnson*, 4 F Supp 2d 1029, 1033 (D NM 1998), *aff'd*, 194 F3d 1149 *[4 ILR (P&F) 145]* (10th Cir 1999) (upholding First Amendment right to communicate anonymously over the Internet); *ACLU of Georgia v. Miller*, 977 F Supp 1228, 1230 *[1 ILR (P&F) 256]* (ND Ga 1997) (recognizing constitutional right to communicate anonymously and pseudonymously on the Internet). The Internet and Worldwide Web provide an unprecedented electronic megaphone for the expression of ideas and an unparalleled opportunity for a national—even international—town square for expression. *See, e.g., Reno v. ACLU*, 521 US 844, 853 *[1 ILR (P&F) 1]* (1997) ("Through the use of chat rooms, any person with a phone line can become a town crier with a voice that resonates farther than it could from any soapbox.").

But neither Verizon nor any *amici* has suggested that anonymously downloading more than 600 songs from the Internet without authorization is protected expression under the First Amendment.[19] To be sure, this is not a case where Verizon's customer is anonymously using the Internet to distribute speeches of Lenin, Biblical passages, educational materials, or criticisms of the government—situations in which assertions of First Amendment rights more plausibly could be made. As the Supreme Court explained in *Watchtower Bible & Tract Society*, the purpose of protecting anonymous expression is to safeguard those "who support causes anonymously" and those who "fear economic or official retaliation," "social ostracism," or an unwanted intrusion into "privacy." 122 S Ct at 2089. The materials RIAA alleges are being infringed include more than 600 copyrighted recordings by well-known artists. RIAA has shown that the copyright owners have not authorized such use; moreover, the fact that these copyrighted materials were shared over the peer-to-peer software of KaZaA only reinforces the belief that copyrights are being infringed. There is no evidence, or even suggestion, in the record to indicate that downloading or transmitting these recordings is somehow protected expression.[20]

Interestingly, Verizon's argument that a copyright owner seeking to obtain information about an alleged infringer should use a John Doe action undercuts the contention that the DMCA subpoena process violates the Internet user's right to anonymity. The First Amendment problems, if any, would be the same in either litigation setting, and the user could assert its rights and objections to either subpoena.[21] Hence, if the John Doe action alternative poses no First Amendment issue, the subsection (h) subpoena process does not either.

The Court does not, however, resolve the constitutional issues identified by Verizon and several *amici*. Absent a clear challenge by Verizon, and full briefing and development by the parties, it is not appropriate to do so. But certainly the issues raised do not reveal an obviously fatal constitutional flaw in the subpoena process available under the DMCA.[22]

CONCLUSION

Based on the text and structure of the Digital Millennium Copyright Act, as confirmed by the purpose and history of the Act, the Court concludes that the subpoena authority of section 512(h) applies to all service providers within the coverage of the Act, including Verizon and other service providers falling within subsection (a). With copyright legislation such as the DMCA, "[t]he wisdom of Congress' action . . . is not within [the Court's] province to second guess." *Eldred v. Ashcroft*, slip op. at 32. Therefore, the Court grants RIAA's motion to enforce its subpoena, and orders Verizon to comply with the subpoena. A separate order has been issued on this date.

————————

[1] RIAA is the industry trade association for sound and music recordings, whose members create and distribute the overwhelming majority of all music sold in the United States. RIAA is authorized to enforce the copyrights of its members.

[2] Subsection (b) covers "system caching," which is the temporary storage of allegedly infringing material on the provider's system or network, while subsection (d) relates to "information location tools," which refer or link users to an online location having infringing material through the use of "a directory, index, reference, pointer, [ ] hypertext link" or other information location tool. *Id.* §§512(b) & (d).

[3] Hence, RIAA submits that it does not matter for purposes of enforcement of the subpoena whether Verizon comes within subsection (a) or subsection (c) in this case; in either event, RIAA contends, the subpoena is valid.

[4] The legislative history of the DMCA comports with this reading of the definitional language of subsection

(k). The Senate Report explains that "[t]he second definition of 'service provider,' set forth in subsection (j)(1)(b), applies to the term as used in any other subsection of section 512." S. Rep. No. 105-190, at 54 (subsection (j)(1)(b) ultimately became subsection (k)(1)(B)). "This definition includes, for example, services such as providing Internet access, e-mail, chat room and web page hosting services," and "[t]he definition also specifically includes any entity that falls within the first definition of service provider." *Id.* at 54-55. *See also* H.R. Rep. No. 105-551 (II), at 64 (1998) (definition of 'service provider' "includes, for example, services such as providing Internet access, email," etc.).

[5] Verizon also points out that under subsection (c)(3)(A)(iii) a copyright owner must identify the infringing material "that is to be removed or access to which is to be disabled." In order to remove or disable access to the material, Verizon argues, the material must be stored on its system—an indication that Congress intended subsection (h) to apply only to those service providers who store infringing material on their systems. The Court is not persuaded. To begin with, a subpoena issued pursuant to subsection (h) is used to identify the infringer, not to force the service provider to remove material or disable access to it. The requirement for the notification is simply that it identify the infringing material to be removed, not that removal be effectuated. In addition, a copyright owner can meet the requirement under subsection (c)(3)(A)(iii) if it can disable access to material. Here, Verizon certainly can disable access to the material by terminating the account altogether. Verizon makes clear to customers in its terms of service that the use of its network for copyright infringement is strictly forbidden, and can result in a variety of sanctions, including termination. In fact, the DMCA *requires* service providers, in order to obtain the various safe harbor protections, to implement "a policy that provides for termination in appropriate circumstances of subscribers and account holders of the service provider's system or network who are repeat infringers." 17 USC §512(i)(1)(A). Verizon counters that terminating service is too harsh, and may prevent other family members from having Internet service. But again, the requirement is only identification of infringing material, not actual removal or access denial. There is nothing, moreover, to prevent a family member from opening another account. In any event, it is irrelevant whether the service provider is able, or intends, to disable access to the material. *See id.* §512(h)(5) ("service provider shall expeditiously disclose to the copyright owner . . . the information required by the subpoena, . . . regardless of whether the service provider responds to the notification").

[6] Arguably, the total burden on service providers may be heavier from subpoenas relating to subsection (a), as there may be more infringement occurring with

subsection (a) service providers than with subsection (c) service providers. But in exchange for complying with subpoenas under subsection (h), service providers receive liability protection from any copyright infringement—direct or vicarious—by their users. Hence, any additional burden is offset by that protection, which, of course, is exactly the contemplation reflected in the structure of the DMCA.

[7] The consequence of delaying the receipt of information identifying an infringer was highlighted by *amicus curiae* Motion Picture Association of America. If Warner Brothers sought to obtain by subpoena information identifying an alleged infringer disseminating the latest Warner Brothers' movie release over the Internet, but needed first to establish that the movie was stored on the service provider's system, the movie could be distributed all over the world in the meantime, dramatically diminishing the value of the copyright.

[8] Verizon recognizes the extent of this resulting loophole. In addressing the burden on service providers if subsection (h) applied to subsection (a), Verizon conceded at oral argument that far more infringement occurs with subsection (a) service providers: "There are, under subsection (a), far greater number of uses, e-mail, for instance, is part of subsection (a). The whole Internet is potentially drawn into subsection (a)." Tr. of Hearing (Oct. 4, 2002) at p. 61. Indeed, as one District Court observed in construing an unrelated provision of the DMCA, "piracy of intellectual property has reached epidemic proportions." *United States v. Elcom Ltd.*, 203 F Supp 2d 1111, 1132 *[10 ILR (P&F) 611]* (ND Cal 2002).

[9] To the extent the statutory language in the DMCA is unclear, "the legislative history of the DMCA can be useful in fleshing out its meaning given the paucity of precedent interpreting the statute." *Costar Group, Inc. v. Loopnet, Inc.*, 164 F Supp 2d 688, 700 *[9 ILR (P&F) 720]* (D Md 2001).

[10] "The DMCA affects [service providers'] liability by insulating [providers] from liability as long as they comply with certain statutory requirements designed to facilitate content providers' efforts to protect their copyrighted material." A. Yen, *Internet Service Provider Liability for Subscriber Copyright Infringement, Enterprise Liability, and the First Amendment*, 99 Geo. L. J. 1833, 1881 (2000).

[11] This balance was adopted with substantial input from the service providers. In fact, the large service providers, including AOL and others, were heavily involved in negotiating these tradeoffs in the legislation. "Title II, for example, reflects 3 months of negotiations supervised by Chairman Hatch and assisted by Senator Ashcroft among the major copyright owners and the major

OSP's and [Internet Service Providers]." S. Rep. No. 105-190, at 9.

[12] Br. of *Amicus Curiae* Alliance for Public Technology, *et al.*, at p. 6.

[13] Verizon has not challenged RIAA's subpoena to Verizon on the ground that it does not meet the notification requirements under subsections (c)(3)(A) or (h)(2). RIAA provided a notification described in (c)(3)(A), including the identity of the copyright works infringed, a statement in good faith that the use of the works is not authorized, and a sworn declaration that the purpose of the subpoena is to obtain the identity of the infringer and that the information will only be used to protect rights to the copyright. *See* Motion to Enforce, Ex. B.

[14] The DMCA also provides disincentives for false representations under the Act, making it costly for anyone to seek a subpoena on the basis of intentional misrepresentations, and thereby further ensuring that subpoenas will only be used in circumstances of good faith allegations of copyright infringement. Subsection (f) of the Act provides:

> Misrepresentations—Any person who knowingly materially misrepresents under this section (1) that material or activity is infringing, or (2) that material or activity was removed or disabled by mistake or misidentification, shall be liable for any damages, including costs and attorneys' fees, incurred by the alleged infringer . . . or by a service provider, who is injured by such misrepresentations, as the result of the service provider relying upon such misrepresentation in removing or disabling access to the material or activity claimed to be infringing . . . .

17 USC §512(f).

[15] Indeed, the requirements for obtaining a section 512(h) subpoena are precisely the type of procedural requirements that other courts have imposed for subpoenas on service providers to identify anonymous posters of messages on the Internet. *See Doe v. 2TheMart.com. Inc.*, 140 F Supp 2d 1088, 1095 *[7 ILR (P&F) 386]* (WD Wash 2001) (party seeking subpoena to service provider to identify anonymous non-party must show subpoena sought in "good faith" and that identifying information sought is directly and materially relevant to core claim and unavailable from any other source); *see also Columbia Ins. Co. v. Seescandy.com*, 185 FRD 573, 578-79 *[2 ILR (P&F) 631]* (ND Cal 1999).

[16] When the Court asked Verizon's counsel whether John Doe actions might be so expensive that they would "scare off" copyright owners, he responded that "[t]here is that possibility" given the protections and "hoops that have to be gone through under the John Doe suits." Tr. of Hearing (Oct. 4, 2002) at p. 62.

[17] Verizon devotes only two sentences and a footnote to the constitutional issues, contending that the subsection (h) subpoena authority, if broadly construed, raises substantial Article III (judicial power) and First Amendment (freedom to engage in anonymous speech) questions. *See* Verizon Opp. at p. 4.

[18] RIAA and Verizon have acknowledged that Verizon may not have standing to raise a challenge to the subpoena based on the user's alleged First Amendment or other constitutional interests. The Court need not address that issue here.

[19] RIAA notes, moreover, that the alleged infringer is not truly anonymous—Verizon knows the identity.

[20] The Ninth Circuit has twice upheld injunctions ordering a defendant to disable its file transferring service and shut down the service, without finding any First Amendment violation. *See A&M Records, Inc. v. Napster, Inc.*, 284 F3d 1091 *[10 ILR (P&F) 1]* (9th Cir 2001); *A&M Records, Inc. v. Napster, Inc.*, 239 F3d 1004, 1028 *[7 ILR (P&F) 1]* (9th Cir 2001) ("First Amendment concerns in copyright are allayed by the presence of the fair use doctrine" and "[u]ses of copyrighted material that are not fair uses are rightfully enjoined"). This Court, however, is not being asked to enjoin the peer-to-peer software used here; litigation against KaZaA is proceeding in other courts across the country. All that is at issue here is the identity of the apparent infringer using Verizon's system, and whether the DMCA requires Verizon to produce that limited information.

[21] The *amici* also challenge the subsection (h) subpoena power on the ground that under Article III of the Constitution there must be a "case or controversy" before the Court to provide jurisdiction to issue a subpoena. Again, Verizon has made it clear that it is not raising an Article III challenge to the DMCA, but only noting a "policy consideration" relevant in interpreting the DMCA, and there has been no briefing on this issue by the parties. *See* Tr. of Hearing (Oct. 4, 2002) at p. 61. Of course, the DMCA includes a provision in subsection (h)(6) requiring that the issuance and enforcement of subpoenas "shall be governed to the greatest extent practicable by those provisions of the Federal Rules of Civil Procedure governing the issuance, service, and enforcement of a subpoena duces tecum." That protection ensures that service providers served with subpoenas can resort to the Federal Rules, including Fed. R. Civ. P. 45, which specifically addresses subpoena enforcement and the rules for quashing a subpoena.

[22] Arguably, a First Amendment challenge by Verizon would be facial rather than as applied, and thus it would have to be shown that in virtually every application the DMCA offends the First Amendment by requiring the production of the identity of an anonymous user. *See United States v. Salerno*, 481 US 739, 745 (1987). That is a heavy burden for Verizon to satisfy.